R 346.7301 Am35h 1998
The Americans with
Disabilities Act : access

Y0-EFE-885

THE AMERICANS WITH DISABILITIES ACT:
ACCESS AND ACCOMMODATIONS

Guidelines for WITHDRAWN
Human Resources,
Rehabilitation, and
Legal Professionals

STAFFORD LIBRARY
COLUMBIA COLLEGE
1001 ROGERS STREET
COLUMBIA, MO 65216

THE AMERICANS WITH DISABILITIES ACT:
ACCESS AND ACCOMMODATIONS

*Guidelines for
Human Resources,
Rehabilitation, and
Legal Professionals*

THE AMERICANS WITH DISABILITIES ACT:
ACCESS AND ACCOMMODATIONS

Guidelines for
Human Resources,
Rehabilition, and
Legal Professionals

EDITORS

Nancy Hablutzel, J.D., Ph.D.   **Brian T. McMahon, Ph.D., C.R.C.**

S^t_L

St. Lucie Press
Boca Raton   Boston   London   New York   Washington, D.C.

v R
346.7301
Am 35h
1998

Library of Congress Cataloging-in-Publication Data

Catalog information is available from the Library of Congress.

This book contains information obtained from authentic and highly regarded sources. Reprinted material is quoted with permission, and sources are indicated. A wide variety of references are listed. Reasonable efforts have been made to publish reliable data and information, but the author and the publisher cannot assume responsibility for the validity of all materials or for the consequences of their use.

Neither this book nor any part may be reproduced or transmitted in any form or by any means, electronic or mechanical, including photocopying, microfilming, and recording, or by any information storage or retrieval system, without prior permission in writing from the publisher.

The consent of CRC Press LLC does not extend to copying for general distribution, for promotion, for creating new works, or for resale. Specific permission must be obtained from CRC Press LLC for such copying.

Direct all inquiries to CRC Press LLC, 2000 Corporate Blvd., N.W., Boca Raton, Florida 33431.

Trademark Notice: Product or corporate names may be trademarks or registered trademarks, and are used only for identification and explanation, without intent to infringe.

© 1992 by Paul M. Deutsch Press, Inc.
© 1998 by CRC Press LLC
St. Lucie Press is an imprint of CRC Press LLC

No claim to original U.S. Government works
International Standard Book Number 1-878205-41-2
Library of Congress Card Number 92-72144
Printed in the United States of America   2 3 4 5 6 7 8 9 0
Printed on acid-free paper

Dedications

This book, or at least my part of it, is dedicated to the several
people responsible for its conception and production: first, to
my co-editor, Brian McMahon, who thought this would be a
great idea; second, to Ann Groom, our competent and professional editor, a true delight to work with; third, to my husband
Phil, undoubtedly the kindest, most thoughtful and supportive,
as well as intelligent, man on Earth; next, to my daughter/
partner Margo Lynn, the most gifted writer I know, and
without whom much of this simply would not have been done;
finally, to our son Bob, a chip off the old block, and without
whom most of this book would still be in the wrong computer
format and not printable.

Nancy Hablutzel, J.D., Ph.D.

To Madeline M. McMahon, world-class editor, business
partner, listener, and mother.

Brian T. McMahon, Ph.D., C.R.C.

Contents

DEDICATIONS .... *v*

FOREWORD .... *ix*
    Al Condeluci, Ph.D.

ABOUT THE EDITORS .... *xvii*

CONTRIBUTING AUTHORS.. *xviii*

SECTION I: RELEVANT BACKGROUND

1. **Development of the ADA** **3**
    Frank G. Bowe, Ph.D., LL.D.
2. **Disabling Attitudes: When Image Begets Impairment** **11**
    Charlene DeLoach, Ph.D.
3. **Legal Overview** .... **·35**
    Nancy Hablutzel, J.D., Ph.D.
    Margo Lynn Hablutzel, J.D.
    Vickie A. Gillio, J.D.

SECTION II: EMPLOYMENT ISSUES AND ANSWERS

4. **Issues in Recruitment and Selection** **63**
    David Vandergoot, Ph.D.
    Brian T. McMahon, Ph.D., C.R.C.
5. **Employment Testing and Evaluation** **79**
    Mark LoVerde, M.S.
    Brian T. McMahon, Ph.D., C.R.C.
    Gary W. Morris, Ph.D.
6. **Human Resources Support for Current Employees** **89**
    Paul L. Scher, C.R.C.
7. **Reinforcing the Need for Progressive Human Resources Practices** **101**
    Thomas M. Ziemba, Ph.D.
    Brian T. McMahon, Ph.D., C.R.C.
8. **The Changing Nature and Role of Job Analysis** **129**
    Roger O. Weed, Ph.D.
    Brian T. McMahon, Ph.D., C.R.C.
9. **Employer-based Disability Management Strategies and Work Return Transition Programs** **139**
    Donald E. Shrey, Ph.D., C.R.C.
    Robert E. Breslin, M.S., C.R.C.

10. **Alcohol and Drug Testing in the Workplace** 155
   Peter R. Bulmer, J.D.
11. **AIDS/HIV Disease and Employment** 169
   Leslie McAllan, Ph.D., C.R.C., N.C.C.
   Gary Hollander, Ph.D.
12. **Considerations for the Rehabilitation Consultant** 199
   Brian T. McMahon, Ph.D., C.R.C.
   Linda R. Shaw, Ph.D., C.R.C.

**SECTION III: IMPROVING PUBLIC ACCESS AND
            REVENUE ENHANCEMENT**

13. **Barrier Removal by Private Entities** 215
   Lei Ann Marshall-Cohen, J.D.
14. **Environmental Barriers: Questions and Answers** 225
   Heidi Gerstman, J.D.
15. **Access to Public Transportation** 237
   Margo Lynn Hablutzel, J.D.
16. **Access to Telecommunication** 243
   Pamela Ransom, J.D., M.S.W.
17. **Tax Incentives** 253
   John B. Palmer III, J.D.
   Heidi Gerstman, J.D.
18. **Issues in Customer Satisfaction** 259
   Carolyn B. Thompson, C.R.C.
19. **Resources for Job Accommodation** 273
   Linda R. Shaw, Ph.D., C.R.C.
   Ginny C. Linder, M.H.S., C.R.C.

APPENDICES

Appendix 1: Choosing the Words You Use About and With People With
             Disabilities 293
             Carolyn B. Thompson, C.R.C.
Appendix 2: President Bush's Remarks at Signing Ceremony 297
Appendix 3: Complete Text of ADA (P.L. #101) 303
Appendix 4: Complete Text of ADA Regulations 335
Appendix 5: Compendium of Legal Resources 657
Appendix 6: Compendium of Technical Assistance Resources 669
Appendix 7: Technical Assistance Manual on the Employment
             Provisions (Title I) of the ADA 761
Appendix 8: EEAC ADA Implementation Planning Checklist 939
             Lorence L. Kessler

INDEX 955

Foreword

Justice delayed, is justice.

Martin Luther King
Letters from the Birmingham Jail,
1963

Equality, I spoke the word, as if a wedding vow, ah, but I was so much older then, I'm younger than that now.

Bob Dylan
My Back Pages,
1964

Justice. It seems like such a simple concept; so right; so natural. Yet, this notion of justice is an elusive thing. At times, we feel that we are treated in a just way, and then at other times, we may experience what we perceive as an injustice.

Academically, we know that justice is about rights. Indeed, Webster's Dictionary (1975) defines justice as:

> 1. being righteous 2. fairness 3. being correct 4. sound reason 5. reward or penalty as deserved 6. the use of authority to uphold what is right, just or lawful 7. the administration of law.

All these aspects of the definition of justice make sense. We know that justice is about fairness and sound reason. It implies that rights will be upheld and that a common decency to people shall prevail.

Yet, in a more visceral interpretation, we know that this definition is incredibly subjective. For most of us, justice is a concept that applies differently. When we use terms like *rights*, *fairness*, and *common sense*, the immediate next thought then revolves around the person making the judgement. We all have a different sense of the finer points of what is right and wrong, and although our heritage as Americans suggests some common aspect to these themes, for the most part they are variable.

All of us reading these words can recall a time when we have felt injustice. It might have been a feeling of misinterpretation or exclusion, or times when we were not chosen for a job or promotion and felt we were best qualified, or when we were offended by something we read or heard. Deep or not, all of these, and hundreds (if not thousands) of other times, injustice occurs in or around our lives. Forget formal rules of laws, if we feel or perceive injustice, it is then a reality to us.

This whole issue of injustice is further complicated when one party perceives injustice and the other party sees themselves as "just doing their job." All through the civil rights movement in the United States in the 50s and 60s, African-Americans pushed the system and were often beaten back, literally and figuratively, by people who were just doing their jobs.

Even today, there is example after example of these differing perspectives of justice. Just two weeks before I started writing these words I had this same type of experience. I was on my way home from a speaking engagement at Lake Tahoe, Nevada. Arriving early in Reno for my flight, I decided to stop on my way to the airport at a neighboring shopping plaza. I was after a Valentine's Day gift for my wife and daughter. With plenty of time to spare, I was sauntering around the plaza stopping here and there, looking for that perfect gift. Now, to really understand this story, you must know that I was dressed very casually. I had just come from the mountains, hadn't shaved that morning, and was sporting my trusty apple cap (a large droopy hat that conjures up thoughts of Ellis Island at the turn of the century). Needless to say, I had a distinct look. After failing in my quest for a gift, I headed to the plaza restaurant with a couple books. Once in the eatery, I decided to call home, and headed for the phone. I had just picked up the receiver when two large men approached me, one on either side. In a breath one said, "Reno police. Would you step outside please."

In this day of "America's Funniest Home Videos" and "Candid Camera," you can imagine my reaction. With a wry smile I said, "Yeah, O.K., where's the camera?" The big guy to my right, with his piercing look, was the first tip-off that, just maybe, the camera guys were not there.

As I was ushered outside, my other escort asked if I had any weapons on me. Before I could answer, two Reno squad cars, complete with flashing lights, screeched to where we stood. Four uniformed police joined our little party, and before I knew it, I was surrounded by six, big cops. Now this video camera thing again flashed through my mind. This time it was the ominous footage of L.A. Police beating Rodney King senseless. After a harrowing 10 minutes, I was finally cleared and allowed to get back to my business. This was only after my car and luggage were searched, I was intimidated and embarrassed.

Now, in light of this story, was an injustice levied? Were these police just doing their job? Indeed, there was a robbery in the area, and I was spotted "loitering" in the plaza. Were my rights infringed by the interrogation I experienced?

So, what do we do about this matter of justice? Do we work in detail to interpret a more refined letter of the law to solidify when and how injustice might occur? Do we attempt, as a society, to clearly define right and wrong? The answers to these questions is *yes*. Indeed, as a society, we Americans are obsessed with attempting to clarify, through laws, the boundaries of society. We continue to etch deeper lines to guide us in our execution of justice through laws and the basic interpretation of justice.

Perhaps the greatest breakthrough in this effort, at least since the Declaration of Independence, was the Civil Rights Act of 1964. If ever there was a law to interpret the parameters of rights and justice it was this landmark measure. Still, in the years that followed the Civil Rights Act of 1964, injustices occurred. As society became more sensitive to peoples' civil rights, the abuses shifted from overt to subtle. There was, and still is, a deep lingering feeling in America that some people have, or should have more rights than others. Old ways die hard.

All around us today, inspite of the '64 Act and others since, are examples of injustice, exclusion, or just plain hate. The charge of racism, sexism, anti-semitism, and yes, handicappism are a part of the reality fabric of society. Indeed, in one bizarre week in October 1991, most Americans sat glued to the televised U.S. Senate Judicial Committee hearings on now Supreme Court Justice Clarence Thomas where charges of sexism, racism, and high-tech lynching sailed into the living rooms of our nation.

Added to this debate on justice is another duly complex notion—that of equality. Our passion for justice is clearly rivaled by the quest for equality in America. Yet this concept, too, needs to be examined. The Webster's Dictionary (1975) states that *equality* is a derivative of the word *equal*, which means:

> 1. of the same size, quality, intensity, value, etc. 2. having the same rank, rights, importance, etc. 3. fair, impartial, just, equal laws 4. having the strength, ability, requirements that are needed 5. balanced, level, even.

Just as with justice, the idea of equality is one that is evasive. Are people equal, with the same rank? Do we have a balanced and impartial system or society? In fact, how do we even attempt to measure these things? These too, are not easy questions. Even the most basic of reviews show time and again that equality, like justice, is one of those elusive butterflies.

Although the ideal of equality sounds good, so many qualifying elements to this concept make it difficult to discern. Our dream is that we are all equal, yet social stratification pushed by age difference, sex difference, cultural difference, and the like obstruct this notion. Added to this are the economic advantages brought by wealth, status, and position. The net effect is that equality is not much more than a myth. As George Orwell (1945) contended in his haunting book, *Animal Farm*, "some animals are more equal than others."

This review of justice and equality though cursory, is not meant to be negative. Justice and equality are critical and need to be studied, examined, and defined. It's just that these concepts are taxing to human understanding. People differ in their perspectives on what they mean and how they should be implemented.

And so now we have an Americans with Disabilities Act, the ADA. For the first time ever, people with disabilities have a law that speaks to justice and equality. Justice and equality in public accommodation, in transportation, in communication, in municipal government affairs, and in the workplace.

Yet, as we have learned from the Civil Rights Act of 1964, there is more to justice and equality than a law, or even the court's interpretation of the law. In fact, as I reflect on the issues of justice and equality, especially when framed in laws that are designed to protect rights, we must incorporate a whole new dimension; that of the "spirit" of law.

It is amazing to me, that try as we may to control society through laws and dictums and orders, people really don't embrace a social notion until their spirit is ready. There is something about us that just doesn't want to be forced. Maybe it's our pioneer heritage, or our resolve as a collection of people, or maybe it's just plain stubbornness. Still we hold back.

This "digging in" is all around us. It is especially true when we face a new law that we might feel is not relevant to us, or not needed at all. In fact, almost any action that impacts our routine or pushes the status quo seems to be abrasive to most people. Consider your feelings when necessary work on your main route to work forces you on a long and jammed detour. You know it is an important repair to the road, something that will result in a permanent improvement, yet you're annoyed or put out because your routine is changed.

As I think about this kind of digging in, I am convinced that change is really not accepted or embraced until we see the reasons for the change on a deeper level. It's as if we need to see with our hearts rather than react from our heads. This type of consciousness is clearly a spiritual thing.

If we pause to look more deeply at this aspect of spirituality there is an interesting history. Probably the first person to examine American culture and identify this notion of spirit was Alexis deTocqueville (1848) in his penetrating book, *Democracy in America*. As a student of societies, deTocqueville spent a few years travelling and analyzing America. He was looking for nuances that set our society apart from Europe. One of his observations was the propensity in America for the development of community associations designed to solve problems or meet goals. These associations were informally structured and driven by the common goodwill. This more spiritual sense of organizing for the common good, to a certain extent, was born from our rural roots and pioneer notions. They fused together to create what deTocqueville called "habits of the heart." These "habits" were both practical and spiritual.

In an interesting sociological follow-up, Robert Bellah and associates (1985) examine how America has changed since deTocqueville's visit and writing. Their review and speculation on changes were reported in their book, aptly titled, *Habits of the Heart*. Among other reasons, Bellah et al. suggest that our spiritual notions have slowly eroded since the mid-1800s. They report that the mechanization and isolation created during the industrial revolution led to a tired and vulnerable population. Although most of those influenced by these industrial changes were people who lived in urban areas, these people began to shift their perspectives. Rather than be responsible to each other, these workers turned inward and expected government and services to watch out for society.

In the years that followed other influences occurred, but the march toward introversion and homogeneity was well on its way. To a certain extent, as industrialization brought isolation in the workplace, it also brought more money to the worker. With more money in hand there was more ability to buy what one needed rather than to rely on associations. These trends led to people looking inward, rather than outward, toward others.

As I think about deTocqueville's work and Bellah's analysis, I am drawn to explore this notion of homogeneity and heterogeneity. Although we consider ourselves as a heterogeneic society, most of our patterns are homogeneic. We tend to spend time with and relate to people who are often very much like us. This propensity, I believe, affects our habits of the heart, and in turn, our spirituality. We become less interested in others and begin to reject or even fear diversity.

It seems to me, however, that spirituality is about understanding and respecting diversity. If most of our societal patterns are to remain homogeneic, then the result will be less and less opportunity to see difference. This growing isolation can lead to suspicion, and retreat from those we perceive as different. This fear and retreat then, can clearly dampen or stunt our spirituality.

Another point in this review of spirituality revolves around dependence and independence. We all have this drive to be independent, to control our environment, and be autonomous. Yet, the ultimate aspect of independence is to be totally autonomous. This means virtual isolation. We have this picture of the strong independent person who can do it all by him- or herself.

Surely today we know two key things in this debate around independence. One is that none of us are totally capable of independence. All of us, to a greater or lesser degree, need other people. We have dependencies that can only be solved through other people. The other point is that through relationships and diversity we find richness in our own lives. In fact, if we are successful in our lives it is because of other people around us. The key is not independence, but interdependence.

In my book, *Interdependence: The Route to Community* (Condeluci, 1991), I explored this concept of interdependence. If we are to really achieve the goals embellished in the ADA, we must recognize that the spirit of acceptance is critical. Interdependence is about that healthy balance between our need for autonomy and for others.

So what will it take to get people to embrace the spirit of the ADA? Some tell me that it will take court hearings and a forcing of the ADA on the public. They contend that people will not include people with disabilities until they are forced. They want action, and they want it now.

Others say that we must be patient; that people will come around to warm up when they are given the time and space. These folks are from the camp that "Rome wasn't built in a day"; that society must be allowed to adjust at its own pace; that things will happen when society is ready.

To me, I think the answer to this spirit thing is somewhere in the middle of these two perspectives. We need to realize that aggressive action, now that the ADA is law, may have a polarizing effect. Some people will react in a bitter way to being forced, even when the forced change is protected by the law. Indeed, lessons from civil rights confirm this fear.

On the other side, waiting for evolved change is also not the answer to spiritual acceptance. The depth of the roots of handicappism has run too long to expect that people on the streets will change their perspective. Society will just not open up to this type of difference until the change is pushed.

This idea of approach can be simplified in looking at some of Saul Alinsky's writings on the matter of change. In *Rules for Radicals*, Alinsky (1971) suggests that there are basically two veins to change. One is within the system, a type of evolutionary approach. The other is outside the system, that of revolution. To Alinsky, there are pros and cons to both approaches, and in his works, suggest a balanced passage to change.

The evolutionary approach works through the system for change. It is slower, more tedious, and often has serious compromise in the final results. For the change agent, the results, though somewhat diluted, are often much more stable and permanent because the change comes from within. At risk, however, is that the change agent can be coerced in the process and accept far less than is just or within the scope of the law.

On the revolutionary side, Alinsky (1971) tells us that change happens much more rapidly. One solid court ruling can be sweeping. Additionally, the change agent will win more. The risks, however, are that the change is not embraced or owned by society. It is a bitter pill, and often it takes a long, long time before people forget. Often, too, when resistance can happen, it will.

So what should we do? We have before us an excellent book that does an impeccable job in outlining the ADA and providing detail in what it offers. This book should be read and re-read. We must know our rights and the boundaries to injustice. This is clearly the starting point to change.

We must also recognize that change is a multifaceted phenomena. It has a tangible and intangible face. For us the tangible aspects of making the ADA real are found on the pages of this book. The intangible notions are found in our hearts. As much as we learn about the ADA, we must do an equally good job at understanding spirituality. We must be able to rekindle the habits of the heart. We must reculture people to want to change, not merely be forced.

As we begin to implement the ADA, we should think about the concept of interdependence. We must show clearly that the ADA is not just about giving access to people with disabilities. Sure this is a part of the ADA, but only one part. The other equally important part is to display conclusively what the ADA offers the community. For as much as the ADA opens doors to community life for people who have been denied, it opens the community to the gifts, capacities, and contributions of a forgotten group. This new influx of Americans, I believe, can breathe a new life into a homogeneous, and somewhat stale community. They will help communities to adapt and adjust; and in turn will help frame a whole new definition of the word *community*.

It is this notion of interdependence, this empowering relationship between community and people with disabilities that will be the ADA's greatest contribution. Both community and people with disabilities will be liberated to learn, grow, discover, and adjust together. And as this happens a whole new spirit will be lit. We will all confront our own realities and discover, that our similarities are far greater than any differences we might have.

Al Condeluci, Ph.D.
McKees Rocks, PA
March 1, 1992

References

Alinsky, S. (1971). *Rules for radicals*. New York: Random House.

Bellah, R., Madsen, R., Sullivan, W., Swidler, A., & Tipton, S. (1985). *Habits of the heart*. Berkeley, CA: University of California Press.

Condeluci, A. (1991). *Interdependence: The route to community*. Orlando, FL: Paul M. Deutsch Press, Inc.

Orwell, G. (1945). *Animal farm*. London, England: Secker & Warburg.

deTocqueville, A. (1848). *Democracy in America*. Edited by J. P. Mager. New York: Harper & Row, 1966.

Webster's new world dictionary. (1975) (Second concise ed.). New York: Simon and Schuster.

About the Editors ——————

BRIAN T. MCMAHON, PH.D., C.R.C.

Dr. McMahon is Associate Professor and Director of the Rehabilitation Counselor Training Program at the University of Wisconsin–Milwaukee. He is also a Certified Rehabilitation Counselor and Consulting Psychologist with offices in Milwaukee and Chicago. Dr. McMahon has authored over 50 publications regarding the vocational rehabilitation of severely disabled persons.

In the 1980s, he developed or supervised nine head injury rehabilitation programs at five levels of care across five states. Dr. McMahon is a former Board Member of the American Psychological Association Division of Rehabilitation Psychology and the National Council on Rehabilitation Education. He is also past-President of the American Rehabilitation Counseling Association. He is currently a national speaker on the Americans with Disabilities Act and its implications.

NANCY HABLUTZEL, J.D., PH.D.

Dr. Hablutzel received her Ph.D. in Educational Psychology from Loyola University of Chicago and her J.D. (with honors) from IIT Chicago-Kent College of Law. She was, for many years, the Executive Director of the Legal Clinic for the Disabled in Chicago. She is a member of the adjunct faculties of Lewis University, Loyola University of Chicago, and IIT Chicago-Kent College of Law, and served for many years on the Juvenile Justice Committee of the Illinois State Bar Association, including occupying all the offices, and is currently the secretary of the Chicago Bar Association's Corporation Law Committee.

Dr. Hablutzel has been a frequent speaker at national meetings of the American Bar Association as well as many meetings of local bar associations. Topics include special education and disability law issues, especially implementation of the Americans with Disabilities Act. She received the Marion Goldman Award for Outstanding Service to the Hearing Impaired Community from the Chicago Hearing Society, and is listed in *Who's Who Among American Women*, *Who's Who in the Midwest*, and *Who's Who in American Law*.

Contributing Authors

Chapter 1
FRANK G. BOWE, PH.D.

Professor, Department of Counseling, Research, Special Education and Rehabilitation, Hofstra University, Hempstead, NY; Member, U.S. House of Representatives Task Force on the Rights and Empowerment of Americans with Disabilities; Recipient, 1992 "Distinguished Service Award of the President of the United States" for work on disability policy over the past 20 years.

Chapter 9
ROBERT E. BRESLIN, M.S., C.R.C.

Vocational Rehabilitation and Disability Management Consultant, University of Cincinnati Center for Occupational Health, Cincinnati, OH; Former Program Case Manager, NeuroCare, Concord, CA; Former Program Case Manager, Timber Ridge Ranch, Benton, AR; Former Vocational Rehabilitation Consultant, Rehabilitation Management, Chicago, IL; Certified Rehabilitation Counselor and Licensed Professional Counselor (Ohio); Member, National Association of Rehabilitation Professionals in the Private Sector, American Rehabilitation Counseling Association.

Chapter 10
PETER R. BULMER, J.D.

Attorney, Labor and Employment Practice Area, Hopkins & Sutter, Chicago, IL; J.D. cum laude, Creighton University School of Law; Vice Chair, American Bar Association/Young Lawyers' Division Labor and Employment Law Committee.

Foreword
AL CONDELUCI, PH.D.

Executive Director, UCP (United Cerebral Palsy) of Pittsburgh; Adjunct Instructor, Community College of Allegheny County; Field Instructor, University of Pittsburgh; Member, National Head Injury Foundation, National Rehabilitation Association, PA Rehabilitation Association.

Chapter 2
CHARLENE DELOACH, PH.D.

Associate Professor, Department of Counseling and Personnel Services, Memphis State University, Memphis, TN.

Chapters 14 and 17
HEIDI GERSTMAN, J.D.

Senior Associate, Hopkins & Sutter, Chicago, IL; Litigator with an employment discrimination specialty; J.D. cum laude, Georgetown University Law Center, 1986; Associate Editor of *The Tax Lawyer,* an American Bar Association-sponsored law journal. Member, American Bar Association (Litigation Section, Labor and Employment Law Section).

Chapter 3
VICKIE A. GILLIO, J.D.

Principal, Kusper & Raucci Chartered, Chicago, IL; J.D., University of Illinois, College of Law, Champaign, 1972; Former General Counsel, Waubonsee Community College, Sugar Grove, IL; Adjunct Professor, Negotiations, Chicago-Kent IIT, College of Law; Professor, Public Law, Masters Public Administration program, Illinois Institute of Technology; Member, Chicago Bar Association, International Law Committee Member, Member, sub-committee on Twinning American Bar Association, Employment Rights Section; International Employment and Labor Section.

Chapters 3 and 15
MARGO LYNN HABLUTZEL, J.D.

Private Practice, Chicago, IL; Former Judicial Clerk and Law School Instructor; Former Chair, Chicago Bar Association and American Bar Association Committees on Delivery of Legal Services to Persons with Disabilities.

Chapter 11
GARY HOLLANDER, Ph.D.

Psychologist, Sinai Samaritan Medical Center, Milwaukee, WI; Clinical Assistant Professor, University of Wisconsin School of Medicine, Department of Psychiatry, Milwaukee.

Appendices 7 and 8
LORENCE L. KESSLER

Partner, McGuiness & Williams, Washington, DC, specializing in labor and employment law; Counsel, Affirmative Action Practices Committee of the Equal Employment Advisory Council (EEAC); Former Law Clerk to Chief Judge Rabe F. Marsh, U.S. District Court, Western District of Pennsylvania.

Chapter 19, Appendices 5 and 6
GINNY C. LINDER, M.H.S., C.R.C.

Lecturer, University of Florida, Department of Rehabilitation Counseling; Vocational Evaluator and Counselor, Spinal Treatment and Rehabilitation Program for Chronic Pain; Certified Rehabilitation Counselor; Chair, Alachua County ADA Employers Advisory Committee; President, North Central Florida Rehabilitation Association.

Chapter 5
MARK A. LOVERDE, M.S.

Manager of Human Resource Process Development, Ameritech Services Inc., Hoffman Estates, IL; Member, Academy of Management, Personnel & Human Resources Division, Research Methods Division; Member, Greater Chicago Association of Industrial/Organizational Psychologists.

Chapter 13
LEI ANN MARSHALL-COHEN, J.D.

Of Counsel, Monahan & Cohen, Chicago, IL; Legal Consultant, National Center for Access Unlimited, Chicago, IL; Former Chief, Disabled Persons Advocacy Division—Office of the Illinois Attorney General.

Chapter 11
LESLIE C. MCALLAN, Ph.D., N.C.C., C.R.C.

Assistant Professor, Department of Special Education and Rehabilitation, University of Arizona, Tucson.

Chapter 5
GARY W. MORRIS, PH.D.

Director, Human Resource Process Development, Ameritech Services Inc., Hoffman Estates, IL; Former Assistant Professor of Psychology, Illinois Institute of Technology, Chicago, IL; Member, American Statistical Association, American Psychological Association, Society of Industrial/Organizational Psychology; President, Greater Chicago Association of Industrial/Organizational Psychologists.

Chapter 17
JOHN B. PALMER III, J.D.

Partner, Hopkins & Sutter, Chicago, IL; Adjunct Professor, IIT Chicago-Kent College of Law; J.D. magna cum laude, University of Michigan, 1977 (Order of the Coif); Member, American Bar Association (Section of Taxation).

Chapter 16
PAMELA RANSOM, J.D., M.S.W.

Staff Counsel and Senior Consultant, Issue Dynamics, Inc., Washington, DC; J.D., IIT Chicago-Kent College of Law; Past Deputy Director of the City of Chicago Mayor's Office for People with Disabilities; Past Executive Director of the Chicago Hearing Society.

Chapter 6
PAUL L. SCHER, C.R.C.

Rehabilitation Services Consultant, Department of Human Resource Administration, Sears Roebuck and Company, Chicago, IL; Director, Chicago Lighthouse for Blind and Visually Impaired Persons; Director, Midwest Association of Business, Rehabilitation and Industry; Member, Policy Advisory Committee, Institute on Rehabilitation and Disability Management, Washington, DC; Member, Advisory Committee, Department of Applied Life Studies, Rehabilitation Education Center, University of Illinois-Urbana; Member, National Rehabilitation Association and National Rehabilitation Counseling Association.

Chapters 12, 19, Appendices 5 and 6
LINDA R. SHAW, PH.D., C.R.C.

Assistant Professor, University of Florida Department of Rehabilitation Counseling; Executive Council Member-at-Large and Program Committee Chair, American Rehabilitation Counseling Association; Member, Board of Directors, Florida Rehabilitation Counseling Association; Member, Faculty Advisory Council to Florida Licensure Board for Mental Health Counseling, Marriage and Family Therapy and Clinical Social Work; Member, Florida Head Injury Advisory Council Education/Research Committee.

Chapter 9
DONALD E. SHREY, PH.D., C.R.C.

Director of Disability Management, University of Cincinnati Center for Occupational Health; Associate Professor, Department of Physical Medicine & Rehabilitation, Cincinnati, OH.

Chapter 18 and Appendix 1
CAROLYN B. THOMPSON, C.R.C.

President, CBT Training Systems, Inc., Frankfort, IL; Former Director of Human Resources, JVS, Chicago, IL; Board Member, The National Rehabilitation Association, The National Association of Service Providers in Private Rehabilitation; Member, The Society of Human Resource Managers, The American Society of Association Executives, The Illinois Chamber of Commerce, The National Rehabilitation Association Job Placement Division.

Chapter 4
DAVID VANDERGOOT, PH.D.

Vice President of Research, National Center for Disability Services (formerly Human Resources Center), Albertson, NY; Former Director, Research and Training Institute, Albertson, NY; Adjunct Associate Professor, Hofstra University, Hempstead, NY and Hunter College.

Chapter 8
ROGER O. WEED, PH.D., C.R.C., C.I.R.S., F.N.R.C.A

Associate Professor/Coordinator of graduate rehabilitation counseling, Georgia State University; Adjunct Faculty, Center for Rehabilitation Technology, Georgia Institute of Technology; national catastrophic injury consultant and trainer of rehabilitation professionals; Board of Directors, National Association of Rehabilitation Professionals in the Private Sector; Named 1991 "Outstanding Educator" by the National Association of Rehabilitation Professionals; Member, National Rehabilitation Association, National Head Injury Foundation, National Spinal Cord Injury Association, Georgia Rehabilitation Association, National Rehabilitation Counseling Association, National Association of Rehabilitation Professionals in the Private Sector, Private Rehabilitation Suppliers of Georgia, RESNA (Association for Advancement of Rehabilitation and Assistive Technologies), Individual Case Management Association, American Amputee Foundation.

Chapter 7
THOMAS M. ZIEMBA, PH.D.

Manager, Human Resources Consulting Practice, KPMG Peat Marwick, Chicago, IL; Former Vice President of Human Resources at a large Midwestern financial institution; Former Executive Director of the Midwest's largest facility devoted to the vocational rehabilitation of people with brain injuries.

Section I

Relevant Background

1

Development of the ADA

Frank G. Bowe, Ph.D., LL.D.

The Americans with Disabilities Act (PL 101-336), signed into law on July 26, 1990, was almost seven years in the making. That surprises many people who do not realize that it took so long for the law to become reality. The Act, popularly called "ADA," became the law of the land at a time of political conservatism in America, at a time of retrenchment in the federal role in governance, and at a time of deregulation in many sectors of the economy. Seen in this context, seven years is a short timeframe.

The ADA is federal law today due to one person, above and beyond the many thousands of others who worked for its enactment. Justin W. Dart, Jr., son of the Reagan "kitchen cabinet" member and a lifelong Republican, had the vision to conceive the ADA and the perseverance to see his vision become reality. For three years, Dart chaired a private-sector body created by Rep. Major R. Owens (D-NY), chairman of the Select Education Subcommittee in the House. Dart's U.S. House of Representatives' Task Force on the Rights and Empowerment of Americans with Disabilities brought several hundred thousand adults and children with disabilities from all 50 states into the ADA "movement." The Task Force was an entirely voluntary effort: no one was paid, nor were any expenses covered by Congress. Dart himself traveled to every one of the states, at his own expense, holding hearings to solicit the input of people with disabilities, parents, employers, educators, and state and local government officials.

The ADA's beginnings may be traced to discussions held in Washington, DC, in 1983 between Dart, then a member of the National Council on the Handicapped (later renamed National Council on Disability, or NCD), Lex Frieden, then Executive Director of the Council, and others, including occasionally myself, then a consultant to the Council. Dart, a long-time disability advocate from Texas, observed that federal civil rights for people with disabilities applied only to "the public sector" (i.e., government agencies, federal contractors, federal grantees). These provisions, codified in federal law as sections 501, 503, and 504, respectively, of the Rehabilitation Act of 1973 (PL 93-112) were useful, Dart said, but they did not go far enough. It was important that similar civil rights be extended fully to the "private sector," that is, to corporations that do not do business with the federal government.

Into the Private Sector

Rules interpreting sections 501, 503, and 504 appeared between 1975 and 1978 after spirited debates over the meaning of such terms as *reasonable accommodation*. Section 501 requires federal agencies to practice nondiscrimination in the employment of persons with disabilities. The idea was that federal agencies would become "model employers," showing the nation how to advance employment among Americans with disabilities. The federal civilian workforce numbered about 2.8 million when section 501 was enacted. It did not grow in size over the next decade. Today, it remains constrained at just under three million due to pressures related to the federal deficit. Thus, section 501's impact has been more limited than was envisioned by Congress when the Rehabilitation Act was enacted in 1973.

Section 503, although it used the term *affirmative action*, takes a similar nondiscrimination approach. It applies to private companies holding contracts with federal agencies. Grumman, for example, makes airplanes; ARA Services provides food and vending services; and Bic makes pens—all under contracts with federal agencies. Some 75,000 companies are federal contractors, most of them large firms. Many of these companies, including most of the Fortune 500, actually lost workers during the 1980s, shedding several million jobs. Thus, section 503's impact on the private employment of persons with disabilities has been more modest than anyone could have predicted in 1973.

Regulations implementing section 504 began appearing in April 1977, after nationwide demonstrations in which Dart, Frieden, and many others participated. As Executive Director of the American Coalition of Citizens with Disabilities (ACCD) at the time, I helped plan these protests because I believed section 504 was by far the most important of the three civil rights sections of the Rehabilitation Act's Title V. That was because section 504 applies to any entity, public or private, receiving federal grants. Thus, its impact was far-reaching: transportation, housing, schools, colleges, libraries, social services, and even prisons. The Reagan "New Federalism" movement, however, limited the expected growth of federal grants. Throughout the nation, private nonprofit organizations, libraries and other grant-assisted entities found their federal grants cut or at least not increased, constraining new employment.

As section 504 was implemented, other restrictions became evident. In housing, for example, only federally constructed or directly assisted public housing was covered by section 504. The effect was to limit the expansion of accessible housing to a very small segment of the housing market. In transportation, federal court decisions and U.S. Department of Transportation regulations restricted section 504's impact by setting a low "special efforts" standard that was widely ignored by mass transit agencies coast to coast.

This is not to understate the importance of Title V of the Rehabilitation Act. Sections 501, 503, and 504 established a framework in which employers could extend to people with disabilities fair employment opportunities. In particular, case histories developed in implementing these statutes created case law providing that access need not be unduly burdensome on employers. Thanks to sections 503 and 504, we learned that making new buildings accessible adds only about 1%

to the cost of construction, while retrofitting existing structures could be, and frequently was, far more expensive. Many thousands of adults with disabilities found employment because of sections 501, 503, and 504. Again, case history revealed that the large majority of "reasonable accommodations" needed to effect employment for these workers cost $500 or less. These findings were to be tremendously important in convincing Congress that the ADA mandates were not likely to unduly burden smaller companies. Still, Dart, Frieden, Burgdorf, and other advocates had expected more, especially from section 504. Particularly revealing were Census Bureau data showing that the employment rate of adults with disabilities actually declined in the 1980s (Bowe, 1991).

Justin Dart knew all this. He was convinced that only by extending section 504-like access requirements to small- and mid-sized businesses—which accounted for the bulk of new jobs in the 1980s—would people with disabilities find the employment they needed to build lives of independence and self-sufficiency. Senator Tom Harkin (D-IA), chairman of the Senate Subcommittee on the Handicapped (later renamed Subcommittee on Disability Policy), which has jurisdiction over major disability programs and his chief counsel Robert Silverstein knew it, too. They helped pave the way for the ADA by working to extend access requirements to private housing in the 1988 Fair Housing Amendments Act, PL 100-430. That Act requires accessible and adaptable design in all housing complexes with four or more apartments, regardless of whether any federal funds are involved (Bowe, 1990).

Drafting and Re-drafting the Act

Lex Frieden assigned the job of developing Dart's idea to Robert Burgdorf, a staff attorney for the National Council on Disability. Burgdorf was a former staff member of the U.S. Commission on Civil Rights and before that had worked for many years on developmental disability issues in Maryland. He was senior editor of the landmark *Legal Rights of Handicapped Persons: Cases, Materials, and Texts* (Burgdorf, 1980). After a great deal of discussion and debate by Council members, Burgdorf's draft bill appeared in the Council's February 1986 publication, *Toward Independence: An Assessment of Federal Laws and Programs Affecting Persons with Disabilities.*

During the second session of the 100th Congress, the draft bill was introduced into Congress. The May 1988 introductions were largely pro forma: Dart and his supporters knew that insufficient time remained in the 100th Congress for the bill to be enacted. Nonetheless, 124 Representatives and 26 Senators signed on as co-sponsors. Still, since 1988 was a presidential election year, not much else happened with the bill. However, in August, both George Bush, the Republican candidate, and Michael Dukakis, the Democratic candidate, endorsed the Act "in principle." These endorsements were to be crucial. When George Bush won the election that November 8th, he was already on record as supporting the ADA.

The May 1988 bill used a broad-brush approach. It forbade discrimination against people with disabilities and spelled out new privileges of complaint, appeal, and private right of action paralleling those enjoyed by women and members of ethnic and racial minority groups. It also required that television broadcasters caption their programs. It did not cover housing, because that was being dealt with separately in what became the Fair Housing Amendments Act of

1988. It also did not cover air transportation, because PL 99-435, the Air Carrier Access Act of 1986, already had forbidden discrimination in air travel on the basis of disability.

When the 101st Congress convened in January 1989, it quickly became evident that the Burgdorf draft would have to be changed significantly. Senator Harkin and Subcommittee counsel Robert Silverstein wanted a bill that more specifically explicated both the rights of individuals with disabilities and the obligations of private entities, including employers. The work of rewriting the draft was performed largely by Silverstein, who was in constant contact with Dart and others at the National Council on Disability. Silverstein, an attorney, had formerly been chief counsel of the House Select Education Subcommittee, the House counterpart to Harkin's Senate Subcommittee. Prior to that, he had worked as an attorney for the federal Department of Health, Education, and Welfare (bifurcated in 1980 into the Department of Health and Human Services and the Department of Education). He knew from experience in human services and civil rights that the most effective statutory language is specific and clear, giving courts relatively little leeway in watering them down.

In May 1989, the revised bill, now with five main titles, was again introduced. This version of the bill dropped the television captioning requirement, because Senator Harkin had decided to pursue that separately (PL 101-431, the Television Decoder Circuitry Act of 1990, requires that virtually all new TV sets made or sold in the U.S. be equipped with built-in caption chips.). Sponsors in the Senate, in addition to Harkin, were Ted Kennedy (D-MA) and David Durenberger (R-MN). Kennedy, the five-term Senator, chaired the influential Labor and Human Resources Committee. He played a critical role, particularly in negotiations with the White House, in the passage of the ADA. Durenberger, the second-term Senator, was important as the only Senate Republican co-sponsor at introduction. His sponsorship helped demonstrate bipartisan support for the bill.

On the same day, an identical version was introduced in the House by Representatives Tony Coelho (D-CA), Hamilton Fish (R-NY), and Steny Hoyer (D-MD). Coelho was Majority Whip at the time; he later resigned in response to ethical questions about personal loans. The forced resignation of a key sponsor might have derailed the bill. However, thanks to Hoyer's leadership, that did not happen. The five-term Congressman from Landover, Maryland steered the bill steadily forward. He later served as floor manager during the House debate. Also crucial, but unfortunately often overlooked, was the support of New York's Fish. The 11-term Congressman from Newburgh/Wappinger Falls, NY, was the lone House Republican sponsor at introduction. Mr. Fish was critical not only in demonstrating bipartisan support for the bill but also in negotiations with the White House. Throughout the long, often acrimonious debate about the allegedly "antibusiness" provisions in Titles I and III, Mr. Fish's calm reassurances that the ADA was consistent with Republican beliefs was helpful in keeping the bill moving forward. He was, Dart later said, "a hero" in passing the ADA.

The bill as introduced in the House and Senate in May 1989 had five titles. The first explained what was considered to be "discrimination" and outlined the duties of covered entities. Title II dealt with employment in any private business employing 15 or more workers and dealing in interstate commerce. Title III required state and local governments to obey section 504-like requirements, explicitly rejecting any excuses based on the Tenth Amendment. It also mandated access to local public transportation. Title IV covered private businesses that serve the public, such as hotels, restaurants, and recreation facilities, to make them accessible to and usable by people with disabilities. Title V required access to telecommunications for persons who use Telecommunications Devices for the Deaf (TDDs) by creating a network of dual-party relay services in which operators translate text to voice and voice to text thus enabling all deaf and hearing persons to have unrestricted telephone conversations.

By any measure, the ADA was a complex bill. What few Americans understood was that its very complexity could unravel its chances of passage. Senator Kennedy used his seniority and stature to claim jurisdiction over the entire bill for his Labor and Human Resources Committee and its Subcommittee on Disability Policy. Throughout 1989 and 1990, Kennedy and Harkin negotiated with committee chairmen with jurisdiction over different themes reflected in the bill, such as Senator Hollings (D-SC), chairman of the Commerce, Science and Transportation Committee; Senator Biden (D-DE), chairman of the Judiciary Committee; and others. Thus, in the Senate, Kennedy and Harkin maintained tight control and amassed broad support for this far-reaching bill.

During the summer of 1989, a great deal of negotiation took place between Senator Kennedy and White House Chief of Staff John Sununu. As a result, the bill was once again substantially reworked. Compensatory and punitive damages were dropped as penalties for discrimination; remaining were back-pay and reinstatement remedies. However, the bill stated that the remedies would be those of the Civil Rights Act of 1964; thus, if that Act were to be amended, as, in fact, occurred in November 1991, any remedies included in the amendments would also apply to the ADA. The bill was also restructured and tightened, with the original Title I moved to Title V, Title II moving up to become Title I, and so on.

Separate negotiations took place between disability advocates and business lobbyists over provisions in specific titles. Title IV, for example, telecommunication relay centers, was reworked several times. At one point, a new quasi-governmental entity was to be created which would oversee relay calls. That was dropped in favor of a simpler approach that drew upon the 1934 Communications Act's "universal service" language and amended that Act by adding a new section, section 225. The 1934 Act said, in relevant part, that telecommunications services were to be "available, so far as possible, to all the people of the United States." It was a fairly simple matter to redefine "all the people" to include people who need TDDs. The FCC was given authority to enforce the new section of the 1934 Act. By the end of summer, the White House and the Congress were in agreement. The Senate passed the ADA, 76-8, on September 7, 1989.

To the House and Back Again

In the House, no one committee chairperson took control as Kennedy had in the Senate. Instead, four full committees and seven subcommittees retained jurisdiction over the bill. From September 1989 to May 1990 extensive negotiations took place as the bill worked its way through the various committees of jurisdiction. Silverstein remained active. Anxious to avoid any unraveling of the Senate-White House compromise, he was in constant touch with Dart and other advocates lobbying the bill through the House, and with House committee staff members. Silverstein had a goal: to avoid, if at all possible, the need for a House-Senate conference on the ADA. Thus, as each change in the ADA was debated in the four House Committees, Silverstein in turn discussed those with key Senate committee chairmen and staff directors. The bill as finally passed by the House on May 22, 1990, by a vote of 403-20, was thus something the Senate felt it could accept.

There were some exceptions. Most notable among them was one provision, added on both the House and Senate floors during debate, that allowed entities with food operations to exclude persons with AIDS from employment. This had been added by Members fearing the transmission of the HIV virus through food handling. The House and Senate committee chairmen knew that U.S. Department of Health and Human Services Secretary Louis Sullivan was on record as saying that such transmission was impossible. The conference committee, accordingly, removed the exclusion from the bill, substituting a requirement that Sullivan study the matter and issue a report that would "review all infectious and communicable diseases which may be transmitted through handling the food supply." Sullivan's conclusion, of course, already was known; thus the "report" was a face-saving concession to Members sponsoring the floor amendments. This was one of the rare instances in which a House-Senate conference committee deleted from pending legislation a provision adopted by both houses.

The conference bill was passed by the House on July 12, 1990, and by the Senate the following day. It was signed into law by President Bush in a large ceremony on the South Lawn of the White House on Thursday, July 26, 1990. More than 3,000 advocates, parents, and government officials witnessed the signing.

The ADA in Reflection

Writing this now, and reflecting back, I am struck again by the magnitude of the effort Justin Dart exerted to give us the Americans with Disabilities Act. The nationwide movement we at the American Coalition of Citizens with Disabilities had mounted in 1977 reached just a few thousand people with disabilities. Dart and his Task Force empowered hundreds of thousands to write, call, telegraph, and visit their Senators and Representatives on behalf of the ADA.

I am also impressed anew by the remarkable breadth of the ADA. Some provisions already are being implemented. Title II's requirement that all new commuter buses be wheelchair lift-equipped, for example, took effect in August 1990. In time, as cities and counties replace aging bus fleets, there will be a nearly 100% accessible public transit bus system. Title IV's mandate that all telephone companies support dual-party relay services for TDD users already has spurred such relays in more than half the states, well before Title IV's effective date.

Harder to foresee is Title I's effect on employment. Today, most American adults with disabilities do not work. That simple statement still stuns me, although it is based on analyses I have done myself of Census Bureau data (Bowe, 1991). Will the ADA change that? I don't know. True, the ADA will cover some seven million employers. However, for many persons with disabilities, significant and often-troubling questions surround the decision to forego federal disability benefits in favor of a paycheck. The ADA did nothing to address the confusing web of rules and regulations governing Supplemental Security Income (SSI) or Social Security Disability Insurance (SSDI). For adults with disabilities who try to get jobs but find only discrimination, lawyers trained in disability employment law remain few and far between. Thirteen years ago in *Handicapping America* (Bowe, 1978), I described the "inaccessible counsel" dilemma posed by the shortage of attorneys knowledgeable about how to prosecute disability rights infringements.

Hopefully, the ADA as a landmark piece of legislation will stimulate lawyers nationwide to learn.

Justin Dart, Lex Frieden, Robert Burgdorf, myself, and many others share a vision of a truly independent life for Americans with disabilities. The ADA is a giant leap toward that vision. I hope it fulfills its very considerable promise.

References

Bowe, F. (1991). *Adults with disabilities: A portrait*. Washington, DC: President's Committee on Employment of People with Disabilities. Limited supply of desktop-published copies available. Many of the same data are available in McNeil, J., & Bennefield, R., *Labor force status and other characteristics of persons with a work disability: 1981 to 1988*. Washington, DC: U.S. Bureau of the Census, Current Population Reports, Special Studies, Series P-23, No. 160, July 1989. Available from the U.S. Government Printing Office, Washington, DC 20402, it is a statistical report requiring the reader to re-calculate many values in order to acquire the information reported in the Bowe reference. Unfortunately, budget cuts at the President's Committee forced desktop publishing of the latter document. Questions should be directed to the Committee on (202) 376-6200, or by writing: PCEPD, 1331 F Street NW, Washington, DC 20004-1107.

Bowe, F. (1978). *Handicapping America*. New York: Harper & Row.

Bowe, F. (1990). Into the private sector: Rights and people with disabilities. *Journal of Disability Policy Studies, 1*(1), 87-99.

Burgdorf, R. (Ed.) (1980). *Legal rights of handicapped persons: Cases, materials, and texts*. Baltimore: Brookes.

National Council on Disability (1986). *Toward independence: An assessment of Federal laws and programs affecting persons with disabilities*. Washington, DC: U.S. Government Printing Office.

2

Disabling Attitudes:
When Image Begets Impairment

Charlene DeLoach, Ph.D.

Without the willingness of the deputy director at my first job, I probably wouldn't have been hired. He was willing to take a chance on an inexperienced woman in a wheelchair at a time (1970) when few people would. After that first job, it was easier because I had proven I could work from a wheelchair and with 14-18 year-old delinquents at that! That made it harder for others to turn me down at other jobs.

J. P.: Rehabilitation social worker with juvenile rheumatoid arthritis and bilateral lower limb amputations.

At graduation time I had 22 interviews with companies and only one job offer–State Farm Insurance in Bloomington and this offer was due to the influence of John Lars Johnson, University of Illinois' Placement Director for the College of Commerce. With that offer in hand, I came back to Louisville (keep in mind this was 1967) and went to an employment agency. While I appreciated State Farm's offer, the job was in computer programming and I frankly felt it was not the field for me. When I went to the local employment agency, they referred me to the Continental Insurance Company and I went for an interview. I was nervous to say the least. Continental's manager was a guy named "Bud H." The first thing Bud said to me was, "You're on four wheels and I'm on two feet and we'll start from there." I called Bud this summer when I heard he was retiring. I told Bud how much I had appreciated the chance to prove myself. He was glad to hear from me but I don't think Bud realizes to this day what an essential role he played in my life. The world needs more "Buds." It also probably needs more (any) affirmative action programs to encourage employers to take more chances in hiring disabled people.

W. B.: Insurance underwriter and wheelchair user due to poliomyelitis.

I encountered reservations about my ability to perform at every level but have found individuals who were willing to give me a chance to prove myself. I am starting at Kaiser Permanente in July. They told me at the second interview that they had contacted offices in California to see if individuals in wheelchairs could perform appropriately. When I was applying for positions within the National Health Service Corporation I encountered direct discrimination and feel that I was not offered positions because of my disability. I documented this discrimination and was then offered my position in Baltimore where I worked for three years.

L. F.: Physician who, as a teenager, sustained a
spinal cord injury, resulting in paraplegia.

Your attitude is more important than employers'. You must always be positive about your health and never use it as an excuse, even if you're dying!

M. C.: Associate Judge and wheelchair user with quadriplegia
due to a spinal cord injury she acquired in 1944.
She was appointed to the bench in 1986.

The above quotes are representative of the comments made by respondents to a recent survey of college alumni with a variety of physical and sensory disabilities. Two hundred alumni, who were well established in their chosen occupational fields, rated the importance of factors that they identified as having an impact on their career development. These respondents indicated attitudes were as essential to their ability to attain and maintain employment as barrier-free environments, and were second in importance only to the acquisition of a college education itself.

While these quotes are representative of the opinions of the college alumni who were surveyed, the occupational and financial successes of these college graduates are not representative of Americans with disabilities in general. As a whole, persons with disabilities remain the most disadvantaged minority group in America. Their unemployment rate is estimated to range between 64% (Harris, 1986) and 79%. They have lower average incomes and fewer years of education than African-Americans, Hispanics, women, or any large ethnic or religious group. If any other minority group had 43 million members and an equally dismal history of poverty, lack of education, and unemployment, remedial social policies would have been implemented long ago, or at least as early as the Civil Rights Act of 1964 which did not extend its protective provisions to persons with disabilities. Nonetheless, changes have occurred which should ultimately benefit both individuals with disabilities and society-at-large. A wealth of factors has contributed to those changes, including medical and technological advances which give individuals with severely disabling conditions the potential to lead healthy, productive lives; the increased number individuals who are elderly—one-third of whom over the age of 65 have substantial functional limitations—(Blake, 1981; Dunn, 1981), and who have a great deal of political clout through organizations for the older American, such as the American Association for Retired Persons (AARP); and the decline in number of younger persons entering the labor market, with the subsequent need to utilize all persons who can contribute their talents to the production of needed goods and services. But perhaps most potent of all the factors contributing to change is the impact of increasingly favorable media coverage on public attitudes toward people with disabilities. Since the late 1970s, there has been a subtle shift in media portrayals of persons with disabilities, both in selection of stories deemed newsworthy and of the language used to convey those stories. Stephen Hawkins, the physicist with amyeotrophic lateral sclerosis, has been granted a public forum for the expression of his personal feelings about his disability, as well as for discussing his theories concerning the nature of the universe. Fewer demeaning newspaper headlines are seen, (e.g., "Crippled Orphan Finds Home"), and more television programs include persons with disabilities as part of the general social milieu (e.g., the person using a wheelchair in the Lou Grant newsroom, in advertisements for blue jeans or vans).

Societal changes cannot result without some pre-existing alteration in societal attitudes which, in turn, have the greatest impact when they are expressed, not only through the public media but through legislation at every level of government. But for that expression to take place in either media or legislation, there must be strong grass roots support for altering the image of any minority group. Attitudes are the feelings and emotions that both reflect and shape the underlying values of a society and of the individuals who are members of that society. Attitudes, therefore, are powerful determinants not only of government policy which affects groups such as the disabled, but also of the tone and tenor of the daily interactions of minority groups members with nonmembers.

To be sure there has been some improvement in attitudes toward persons with disabilities. If this were not true, the Americans with Disabilities Act of 1990 would never have been drafted, much less been passed by both Houses of Congress and signed into law. Still the true tests of attitude change are the actions that result from that change. A law remains nothing but words on paper until regulations are issued which transform those words into concrete changes in behavior, monies are appropriated which finance those changes, and sanctions are enforced when mandated changes do not occur.

Unfortunately, earlier legislation which promised needed improvements in the treatment of persons with disabilities has a long history of weak implementation. For example, the Architectural Barriers Act of 1968 was a toothless tiger, resulting in little significant barrier removal, until the Rehabilitation Act of 1973 created the Architectural and Transportation Barriers Compliance Board (ATBCB) to enforce compliance with 1968 Act. But from the outset, until it was reconstituted in 1978, the Board consisted largely of representatives from the very governmental agencies it was intended to oversee, and did not enforce compliance with existing accessibility standards (Gorski, 1981; DeLoach, Wilkins, & Walker, 1983).

Sources of Disabling Attitudes

One of the more intriguing aspects of attitudes toward persons with disabilities is that, despite the fact that they share the negative consequences of minority-group membership in this society, there has been an entrenched reluctance to recognize them as members of a distinct minority group. With high unemployment and low educational levels, the majority of adults with disabilities live, and continue to live, in poverty. Moreover, persons with disabilities have encountered, and continue to encounter, rigid patterns of segregation in housing, employment, and transportation, and exclusion from polling places and juries. Like women and members of racial, religious, and ethnic groups, persons with disabilities have experienced the full range of discriminatory behaviors—harassment, imputations of biological inferiority, prejudice, and stigmatization. In fact, there are only two major ways in which persons with disabilities, as a group, differ from other minorities: not having the minority characteristic in common with significant others and having a functional limitation as the basis for group membership (Hahn, 1985).

Not having the minority characteristic in common with one's family has two major consequences. First, the individual with a disability lacks access to a shared survival lore that has been refined and passed down through generations of those who share the stigmatizing characteristic. Second, he or she lacks an essential kinship bond that can be forged only by a mutual, tacit understanding of the day-to-day significance of living with a disabling condition. For the child with a disability, or for the adult who has just acquired a disability, this means having to rely on strangers—such as rehabilitation and medical professionals—to identify the full range of available treatments or rehabilitation options, and to provide reliable and trustworthy advice as to the most appropriate option. Moreover, this early dependence on persons with no familial ties or no shared cultural similarity may have prolonged negative effects on their levels of self-esteem and self-acceptance (DeLoach & Greer, 1981).

However, it is the existence of a functional limitation that creates the greatest impediment to the evolution of more positive attitudes toward persons with disabling conditions and to their subsequent social advancement. Research on attitudes toward persons with disabilities consistently indicates that overt attitudes are mildly positive or neutral but that covert attitudes are negative, even hostile (Stahly, 1988; Tyler, 1989; Jackman, 1983; Yuker & Block, 1979). According to Hahn (1985), when citizens with disabilities attempt to apply the minority group model to the analysis of the social problems facing them, they are at worst harshly criticized or at best listened to patiently. However, there is no intention on the part of others to alter their preconception that persons with disabling conditions are vastly different from any other identifiable group of human beings because of their functional limitations. The widely held assumption, which is most resistant to change and which persists despite factually based confrontation, is that other minority groups have experienced discrimination which is unfair but avoidable, but when it comes to persons with disabilities, prejudice is tolerable and even expected. Ironically, it is nondisabled helping professionals who tend to be most reluctant to accept the fact that the social limitations faced by persons with disabilities are equally unjust and remediable (Harris, 1984). To professionals, especially in the allied health fields, psychology, counseling, and special education, "...bias and discrimination usually appeared to be regarded simply as another unfortunate burden that has been imposed upon people with disabilities" (Hahn, 1985, p. 301).

The lack of comprehension and empathy which the grievances of persons with mobility impairments encountered during the civil rights movement of the 1960s continues even today. For example, at the time of the bus boycotts, activists with disabilities pointed out that whereas black Americans felt discriminated against because they had to sit in the back of the bus, persons with disabilities couldn't even get on the bus. Thirty years later, the situation, at least for those who are disabled, remains unchanged. Then as now, too many in positions of power and influence refuse to give credence to the fact that for someone with a mobility impairment, an inaccessible environment *creates* a functional limitation that an accessible environment can *eliminate*.

J. L., a participant in another research study of alumni with disabilities from the University of Illinois (DeLoach, 1989), worked fulltime for 10 years in a company that produced durable medical equipment. During that entire 10-year period, she was unable to utilize the company's bathroom facilities. Moreover, when, as a middle manager, she had meetings scheduled one after the other in each of the company's two conference rooms, she had to exit one entrance and wheel around the block to get to the second conference room, which was on a different level and accessible only from outside the building. The final indignity, she wrote, was that she was sometimes reprimanded for arriving late to these meetings. At the time of the study, after 10 years of continuous employment during which she received frequent promotions and despite an unremitting but unsuccessful crusade for accessibility, she submitted her resignation and accepted a better paying but less personally satisfying job.

The negative impact of a functional limitation on the attitudes of other persons is far out of proportion to the consequences of that limitation on an individual's potential to prosper and lead a satisfying, productive life (as the quotes from the four college alumni at this chapter's beginning attest). There are two major theories which attempt to explain individual and societal reactions to persons with a functional limitation. The first deals with the social values that are placed on health and illness in American society.

Social Roles and the American Value System

A historian who has researched the roles played by persons with disabilities in American history, Lenihan (1977) points out that independence is an intrinsic American value. This concept includes both freedom from the need to rely on others and freedom to make choices affecting one's own life without interference from others. The perceived desirability of autonomous and self-reliant behaviors was reinforced by the rigors which immigrants to the colonies faced. To protect established colonists from responsibilities which would have been a hardship for them to assume, measures were taken to insure that new arrivals would not be a drain on the resources and energies of those who were already here. Laws required that bond be posted by each ship's captain or owner, so that any would-be colonists who were transported to the New World and who were unable to take care of their own survival needs could be supported by the forfeited monies until they could be returned to the Old World. Similarly, each settlement had its own residency law which established the length of time necessary before new arrivals could become legal residents. During these probationary periods, individuals and their families had to prove they were self-sustaining, and if they could not they were forced to return to their previous place of residence, be that another settlement or their former home in the Old World. The purpose of the colonial legislation, according to Lenihan (1977), was to prevent the New World from being inundated by the ills of the Old, where large cities like Paris and London teemed with unemployment and poverty.

The equating of disability with dependence, of functional limitation with vocational and personal insufficiency stems from the belief that disability is synonymous with illness, a condition which is deemed to lead to total, if only temporary incapacity. In his 1958 treatise, *Health and Illness in the Light of*

American Values and Social Structure, Parsons explains the status in American society of someone with a chronic illness or disability. According to Parsons, in the American value system "health," the desirable state, is equated with productivity, with the ability to competently fulfill one's social roles: spouse, parent, worker, and so on. "Illness," the undesirable state, is equated with incapacity, with the inability to assume one's social responsibilities.

When an individual becomes ill, society demands a ritualistic response from that individual: an admission that one's illness is an undesirable state, and the faithful execution of whatever regimen is prescribed to restore the desirable state (i.e., health). Similarly, when an individual is ill, a ritualistic response is expected on the part of others: exoneration of the person who is ill from all social responsibilities, a moratorium on expectations, and overt demonstration of solicitude and support.

While illness, within limits, relieves people from the demands of their usual social roles, the state of being ill is only conditionally sanctioned in a society that recognizes health as the only natural—that is, "good"—state. Within this culture, sympathy and exoneration from work, familial, and community responsibilities are granted only if a person recognizes and openly admits that the illness is "bad" and willingly and eagerly undertakes whatever treatment is deemed necessary for restoration to health, the "desirable" state. What is more, illness is considered to be an invariably temporary condition *IF* the person who is ill upholds the correct cultural values and carries out the appropriate remedial measures. Any individual, therefore, will receive special consideration (i.e., sympathy and exoneration from responsibilities) only for a limited time, during which he or she must both continue to admit that being ill is totally undesirable and strive to regain the capacity for "independent achievement and economic productivity" (DeLoach, Wilkins, & Walker, 1983, p. 58).

What happens, then, when an illness is chronic or when an accident, illness, or congenital condition results in a permanent functional impairment? Because society has no clear cut social mechanism for incorporating that person's situation into existing, acceptable social roles and rituals, a person with a disability is labeled and treated as a deviant member of society. The ritualistic response which works well in cases of acute illness or temporarily disabling conditions proves ineffectual. Sympathy may alternate with increasingly frequent periods of irritation, followed by subsequent feelings of guilt. Exoneration from responsibilities may transmute into externally imposed rigid patterns of segregation which prevent the resumption of former social roles which is possible through compensatory techniques and home or job modifications. As happened so often in the past and still occurs now, the "shut-in" becomes the "shut-out," due to lack of social accommodations which would restore the capacity to contribute and to partake of the best that life has to offer.

The expectation that disability, like illness, prevents one from being an effective employee, marital partner, parent, or neighbor results from the phenomenon of "spread." "Spread" is a concept which Wright (1960) uses to describe the process of generalization when, in reference to persons with a disability, knowledge of a specific cognitive or physical limitation leads to the assumption that there must exist a similar limitation in every other area of functioning. The concept of spread explains why people often shout at persons with a visual impairment, as though any visual loss must also result in diminished auditory acuity. Even medical personnel who are cognitively aware that a diagnosis of expressive aphasia means that a person has an impaired ability to respond verbally and no associated impairment in the executive functions of comprehension, sequencing, and analytic problem-solving are not immune to spread. Nonetheless, they often treat competent adults with expressive aphasia as though they were uncomprehending, incompetent children. Spread also explains attitudes like those expressed by a faculty member at a northeastern university who verbally equates physical disability with lack of academic ability, and who works to ensure that no students with disabilities, because of their alleged incompetence, enroll or remain enrolled in his classes.

Rather than labeling persons–with or without disabilities–as either competent or incompetent, it would be more accurate to think of and to treat all human beings as partially competent, as having their own unique patterns of strengths and weaknesses. In discussing the issues underlying the ethical principle of autonomy (i.e., the duty to allow others to make decisions affecting their own lives), Beauchamp and Childress (1989) discuss the fact that competence is a necessary precondition to the full exercise of the human right of autonomy. They contend that, ethically, the obligation to respect the autonomy of others cannot be negated, even following a court judgement that a person is legally incompetent. As Beaucamp and Childress point out, whereas the core meaning of the concept of competence is the ability to perform a task, "the criteria of different competencies vary from context to context because the criteria are relative to specific tasks. For example, the criteria for someone's competence to stand trial, to raise dachshunds, to write checks, or to lecture to law students are starkly different (p. 80)."

The label "disability," however, through the phenomenon of spread, carries with it the connotation of incompetence, regardless of the reality that whatever functional limitation exists will be specific and limited in its effect. Perhaps the most potent evidence of the negative feelings and emotions engendered by the term *disability* stems from the abortion issue. The single area of agreement between the pro-choicers, who ascribe to autonomy as the pre-eminent ethical principle, and the pro-lifers, who ascribe to that of nonmaleficence (the duty to do no harm), is the ethical acceptability of aborting a fetus with a discernable mental or physical disability. Even for those who consider themselves pro-lifers, when a disability exists, its presence alone is judged sufficient to abrogate a human being's right to justice (the duty to give human beings what is their due, in this instance the right to live with, as well as without, a functional limitation).

Derogation of Those Perceived as Victims

The second of the two major theories which attempt to explain individual and social reactions to persons with disabling conditions is the social-psychological theory of victimization (Lerner, 1971). In the model of victimization, persons who experience a traumatic event in their lives are seen as personally culpable, as being morally responsible for the situation in which they find themselves. They are, therefore, stigmatized. Moreover, the disabling condition for which they are victimized is perceived as their predominant characteristic. It alone can obviate any claim which other characteristics give them to be treated with respect and courtesy. The social covenant which tacitly exists among other unrelated human beings is nullified. They are treated as though they do not exist, are actively ostracized, or are stereotyped and assigned denigrating labels. Just as those who are homeless are sometimes described as deliberately choosing to live on the streets or just as those who are abused are often blamed for precipitating violent acts toward themselves by their own inappropriate behaviors, persons—particularly with nonvisible disabilities or a history of disability—are believed to have gotten what they deserved (Stahly, 1988). According to social psychologists, most people believe, indeed have a profound need to believe, in a just world. This "just world" hypothesis allows people to believe they can prevent tragic events from occurring in their lives, and to believe that those who do experience such events do so because of faulty behavior or character. If people even entertain the thought that they cannot entirely control what happens to them, or to those for whom they care, they will lose all assurance they have had that they can escape the fate of those they perceive to be victims (Lerner & Simmons, 1966).

The need to derogate those who are perceived as victims seems to be strongest when the perceiver and the perceived are most similar. To those who have no disability, a person with a visibly disabling condition is so noticeably different that it is not difficult to believe that the person with the disability is vastly dissimilar. It is when someone seems to be very similar that the need to assign blame intensifies, in order to create a self-protective difference where none exists.

Moreover, Lerner (1971) discovered that derogation of a perceived victim is greatest when a victim's behavior cannot be faulted. If the perceived victim was not at fault, then one must assume the situation is beyond human control—a frightening assumption which can be tempered only by psychologically distancing oneself from the person who is perceived as helpless (Lerner & Simmons, 1966). Although heart disease has a higher occurrence rate and a higher mortality rate than cancer, persons with disabilities resulting from cancer experience greater stigma and derogation than persons with a cardiac disability (Maguire, 1985; Stahly, 1988). Since the cause of cancer is generally unknown, persons who acquire cancer are deemed incapable of preventing the onset of the disease, while persons with cardiac disabilities are seen as contributing to the disability process through smoking, an unhealthy diet, and refusing to exercise appropriately. Since those with cardiac disabilities are perceived to have had more control over factors that could have prevented their heart disease, they are felt to be less threatening and, consequently, experience less derogation and stigmatization than persons with cancer or other seemingly unpreventable conditions.

Although perceived similarity can be threatening if the similarity is with persons who have experienced unpreventable traumatic events, perceived similarity has been found to be closely related to positive attitudes. In a study by Fichten and Amsel (1986), college students with no disabilities were asked to describe the traits of their fellow students, those who used wheelchairs and those who were not disabled. The researchers found there were clear differences in the perceived traits of the two groups. While both desirable and undesirable traits were assigned by the subjects to both groups, fewer socially desirable traits and more socially undesirable traits were assigned to students with disabilities than to those without. Moreover, while a few socially desirable traits were common to both groups, none of the undesirable traits were the same. In fact, when the traits themselves were assessed for "similarity" or "dissimilarity," it was clear the traits assigned to those who were not disabled were clearly the opposite of those assigned to college students with disabilities.

Fichten and Amsel's (1986) study supports Goffman's (1963) contention that those who stigmatize others justify their attitudes on the basis that members of the stigmatized group are "different." Those who are regarded as stigmatized may be seen as having subhuman qualities or superhuman qualities, but they are never viewed as similarly and equally human. And since people tend to like and to seek out the company of those whom they perceive as being like themselves, allowed to pursue the most comfortable course they are unlikely to initiate contact that might result in more positive attitudes over time.

Initiating Attitude Change

The Americans with Disabilities Act (ADA) of 1990 is no more designed, primarily, to initiate a positive attitude change toward citizens with disabilities than the Civil Rights Act of 1964 was designed, primarily, to initiate a positive attitude change toward the groups which were protected under that Act. Indeed, it can be argued that legislative protection is mandated only when the natural inclination of the general populace is to engage in discriminatory behaviors toward particular groups in our society.

Rather, the goal of the ADA is to enforce behavioral change, that is to mandate access to education, housing, transportation, and employment to a degree that was heretofore partially or fully denied, depending on the attitudes of any one would-be employer, landlord, college administrator, or proprietor of restaurants, grocery stores, and so on. Previous legislation had opened the doors to colleges, universities, businesses, and agencies that received funds from federal grants or monies which were appropriated to implement federal legislation. While sections 503 and 504 of the Rehabilitation Act of 1973 mandated access and affirmative action in businesses in which the workforce exceeded a certain size and which received federal funding above a certain amount, compliance at best was minimal and limited in scope.

But as the preamble to the ADA infers, attitudes toward persons with disabilities have become somewhat more positive. The ADA itself is proof of that, not only in the provisions mandated by the Act but in the very wording of the title of the law–*Americans with Disabilities*. For the first time major federal legislation granted recognition that citizens with disabilities were primarily that–Americans who, among their numerous other traits, also happened to have a disability.

Language Usage and Attitude Awareness

Language is no less powerful a factor in raising the consciousness of and promoting attitudinal change toward persons with disabilities than it has proven to be in regard to issues of gender, racial, ethnic, and religious bias. How much underlying attitudes toward members of these minority groups have changed is difficult to assess, but few who are not black are comfortable today using terms in public other than *black* or *African-American* when referring to Americans of African descent.

Since language both expresses and influences ideation, social psychologists believe careful use of language can result in less stereotypic thought patterns and diminish the tendency to stigmatize others. Today the style manuals of many professional organizations advise authors to "avoid writing in a manner that reinforces questionable attitudes and assumptions about people" (American Psychological Association, 1983, p. 43).

The style guidelines from other professional organizations, such as the National Rehabilitation Association (NRA), are very detailed and address nearly all the issues raised under the heading *Sources of Disabling Attitudes* in this chapter. According to the NRA guidelines (1985), the appropriate manner of referring to or portraying individuals with disabilities in speech or in writing is as follows:

Reference to Disability

The fact that an individual has a disability should be mentioned only when the disability is important to a story or portrayal. For example, if a business person receives a reward for contributions to the community, identifying that person as disabled confounds the issue of outstanding community service. Some readers may think the award was given because the person was disabled. Other readers may interpret the story not as an objective account of the honoring of an outstanding individual, but rather to point out how extraordinary it is when a person with a disability is either a business person or an active participant in the community.

Similarly, as in the title of the 1990 Act, when it is deemed necessary to refer to a disability, it is important to emphasize the person, rather than the person's disabling condition. By having the descriptor follow (i.e., "person with arthritis" rather than preceding as in "arthritic person"), and by not using an adjective as a noun (i.e., "an arthritic"), the misconception that a disability is an individual's predominant characteristic may be avoided, thereby limiting spread.

Inappropriate and Appropriate Descriptors

Value-laden or subjective descriptors (e.g., "victim of ...," "afflicted with ...," "suffering from..."), which imply an individual is helpless or in severe distress should be avoided, as should descriptors which diminish an individual's capabilities (e.g., "confined to a wheelchair"). Instead, it is important to describe the individual's situation as objectively as possible by saying or writing that the individual "has..." or "has experienced..." and "uses a wheelchair or "is a wheelchair user."

The term *confined to a wheelchair* is singularly inappropriate for two reasons. First, many people who use wheelchairs use them intermittently (e.g., the person who is receiving kidney dialysis treatments and who experiences wide fluctuations in energy level between dialysis sessions, the person with paresis or ataxia who can walk and who chooses to use a wheelchair when traveling long distances or in environments where the surface underfoot may be rough or unstable). The misconception that everyone who uses a wheelchair must be unable to function without one can result in unnecessary problems for those whose use depends on the circumstances in which they find themselves. Acquaintances who see them walking one day and wheeling another may suspect them of malingering or of being hypochondriacs. Strangers may accost them when they utilize parking spaces which are reserved for persons with disabilities but which are not only for the convenience of persons who have visible mobility impairments.

The second reason is the need to understand that a wheelchair is a mobility aid that grants freedom of movement for both those who use them intermittently and as well as those who, with no wheelchair available, would be confined, but confined to bed. The harm created by the misconception that a wheelchair is imprisoning goes far beyond reinforcing negative attitudes toward those who use them. Far too many persons who are elderly and are unsteady to the point where they are in danger of falling, or persons who have cardiac conditions and cannot stand for long periods or walk long distances, lead unnecessarily restricted lives because they themselves have negative stereotypes about wheelchairs and wheelchair users and, consequently, refuse adamantly to accept the freedom of movement that a wheelchair provides.

Prejorative Implications

One should avoid using qualifying statements which are demeaning because they imply a particular individual would not be expected to have a certain attribute simply because of a disabling condition. In short, one should beware of any qualifying statement that begins with a "but" (e.g., "She was blind but was exceedingly bright," "He used a wheelchair for most of his life but he towered over others in his profession") when writing or speaking about such individuals.

One of the most prevalent myths concerning disability, as Parsons (1958) indicated, is the misconception that disability is synonymous with illness, and that consequently persons with disabilities experience ill health. When discussing the onset of a disability, one should avoid describing the period of time that a person has been disabled as "since he or she became sick." A disability is not a disease, which has connotations of being both debilitating and contagious. There are many different disabling conditions and, as Trieschmann's (1986) research indicates, the majority of individuals who have disabilities such as cerebral palsy, spinal cord injury, hearing impairments, most visual impairments, mental retardation, and so on, are not chronically ill. According to Trieschmann, individuals with disabilities may experience better health, either because of their ongoing contact with health specialists or because having a disability has made them aware of the dangers of an unhealthy lifestyle as few other things can.

The most damaging impact of the "disability-equals-illness myth" is upon the attitudes of potential employers. Despite decades of corroborative studies by major companies–Rand, Dow, and IBM to name a few–the fact that workers with disabilities have had lower overall absenteeism and accident rates than other workers has done little to eliminate fears that a workforce comprised of many persons with disabilities is a workforce in danger of being decimated by illness and injury (Journal of American Insurance, 1986; Tyler, 1989). Therefore, behaviors that counter the myth that "disability-equals-ill health" were and continue to be regarded as essential in the fight against prejudice in the world of work.

Anecdotal evidence abounds that workers with disabilities who become ill or who have become increasingly incapacitated due to a progressive condition, such as Friedreich's ataxia or multiple sclerosis, often go to great lengths to see that their job responsibilities are fulfilled, even at great cost or inconvenience to themselves. S.S., a plant manager in a large city in the Mid-South, had experienced few problems with his multiple sclerosis for the first 25 years he worked for his company. Then, in the late 1970s he experienced an exacerbation of his condition which resulted in daily periods of extreme fatigue. Combined with muscle weakness in his lower limbs, this made it difficult for him to climb up and down the stairways within the plant as often as his job required. In addition, he became more susceptible to high temperatures, so that on very hot days he was unable to walk from his car in the parking lot, and so had to crawl into the building where, after a short time in the air-conditioned environment, he was able to stand and walk.

Not wanting his off-site supervisor to know about his situation and not feeling that he could afford to retire, S.S., with the cooperation of a co-worker and with the loyal support of those whom he supervised, worked out a procedure which allowed him to continue fulfilling his job responsibilities. The two major changes he made were: (1) he began to drive his car directly into the plant where he could go from the air-conditioned environment of his vehicle to the air-conditioned environment of his work site and (2) he had his co-worker assume some of his more physically demanding job tasks in exchange for which he assumed some of his co-worker's more routine and boring job duties. This ad hoc job restructuring meant that instead of having Saturday and Sunday off, S.S. had to spend his Saturdays at the plant catching up on the extra clerical tasks he had assumed as part of his restructured job. For two and one-half years, this system worked well until one hot summer day, his supervisor paid an unannounced visit to the plant, saw S.S.'s car inside the building and asked what it was doing there. S.S. ended up being forced to retire earlier than he had intended, but he had added two and one-half years of credit toward that retirement.

Opprobrious and Preferred Word Usage

For every minority group there is undoubtedly one stigmatizing word, one verbal weapon, which has more power than any other to hurt, to humiliate, to shrivel the soul of the individual against whom it is used. For those who are black it is *nigger*, for those who are women it is *bitch*, for those who are disabled it is *cripple*. Unlike most dictionary definitions of *nigger* which clearly identify it as an offensive term, the words *bitch* and *cripple* tend to be objectively defined, with no value judgements appended. But although persons who are disabled do not, as a whole, agree on what are the most acceptable terms to describe themselves, there is a nearly unanimous agreement that the word *cripple*, with its connotations of something that is twisted, ugly, and perverted, should be exorcised from written, if not spoken language.

While *cripple* is an opprobrious term which has been, and to some degree continues to be, used to refer to persons with various types of disabling conditions, the following terms have been identified as being unacceptable, or inappropriate, when used in reference to members of disability groups:

> **birth defect:** Considered to be inappropriate when used to refer to a condition of human beings. The preferred term to describe a disability which has been present from birth is *congenital disability*.

> **blind:** Considered to be appropriate only when used in reference to persons with a total loss of vision. For persons with partial vision, the preferred terms are *person who is partially sighted* or *person with partial vision*.

> **deaf:** Considered to be appropriate only when used in reference to persons with a total loss of hearing. For persons with partial hearing, the preferred terms are *partial (or severe) hearing loss* or *hearing impairment*.

deformed, victim, sufferer, invalid (and cripple): Considered to be demeaning and derogatory when used in reference to an individual with any functional limitation. To refer to persons with a permanent condition that interferes with their ability to do something independently—walk, see, hear, talk, dress, learn, lift, work, and so on, the preferred terms (even over handicapped—see below) are *person with a disability* or *person who is disabled.*

deviant, mentally deranged, maniac, crazy, lunatic, and mad: Considered to be demeaning and derogatory when used to refer to persons who have lost the social and/or vocational skills to function independently. To refer to persons with functional behavioral limitations, the preferred terms are *persons who are mentally ill* or *person with a mental disorder.*

fit: Considered inappropriate when used to describe the involuntary muscular contraction that is symptomatic of epilepsy. "Fit" connotes mental derangement, willful emotional outbursts, or loss of emotional control. The correct term to describe the involuntary muscular contractions associated with epilepsy is *seizure.*

idiot, moron, mentally deficient/defective, imbecile, retardate, and feeble-minded: Considered to be derogatory when used to describe persons who, from birth, have developed mentally at a rate significantly below average. To refer to such individuals, the preferred term is *person with mental retardation.*

Mongoloid(ism): Considered to be inappropriate when used to describe a form of mental retardation involving improper chromosomal division at conception. The preferred term is *Down Syndrome.*

mute, deaf-mute, deaf and dumb: Considered to be inappropriate or derogatory, depending on whether these terms are used to refer to someone with a severe, prelingual hearing impairment and who is unable to engage in effective verbal communication or someone who is unable to speak at all, but who is not deaf. The appropriate term for describing a person who cannot speak at all is *person who cannot speak.* The appropriate term to describe persons with a limited ability to speak or with different speech patterns is *person with a speech impairment.*

normal: Considered inappropriate when used to refer to persons without disabilities, because it implies that persons with disabilities are abnormal. The generally preferred, through somewhat controversial term for describing persons without disabilities is *person who is able-bodied.*

spastic: Considered inappropriate to describe a person with a movement disorder the onset of which occurs anytime from the first trimester of pregnancy through the early developmental years, and in which primitive reflex patterns persist. The appropriate term to use to refer to such individuals is *person with cerebral palsy*.

special: Considered incorrect when used to describe that which is different or uncommon about any person and condescending when used to describe persons with disabilities, in general. For example, a preferred term for "special education" would be *habilitation education* or *rehabilitation education* (National Rehabilitation Association, 1985).

With full awareness of how the unconscious use of language affects both an individual's perception of the world and one person's perception of another, a debate has raged among persons with disabilities and their advocates as to what should be their overall preferred descriptor–*disabled, handicapped, impaired, physically (mentally) challenged, differently abled*–the list goes on. In an attempt to correct what Hahn (1985) would describe as the distortion in sociological perspectives concerning persons with disabilities, due to the confounding but irrefutable fact that disability invariably entails some functional limitation, a choice has been made to use and to clearly differentiate between the terms *disabled* and *handicapped*.

As a potential precursor to positive attitude change in reference to persons with permanent functional limitations, the word *disability* is now being used to indicate that an individual has some functional limitation due to an alteration in anatomy (internal or external physical configuration, such as short stature or missing limbs) or physiology (organic processes, such as paralysis, decreased cardiac function, or ineffectiveness of the immune system). According to this definition, a disability is considered to be a relatively stable limitation in the ability to walk, to coordinate fine motor movements, to see, to hear, to comprehend, to respond appropriately to what is seen and heard, and so on. A disability, then, is considered to be a relatively stable condition, because even progressive disabling conditions remain notably unaltered during the space of a day or several hours.

The term *handicap*, however, has been designated to indicate a functional limitation that fluctuates according to the circumstances in which individuals find themselves. It follows, then, that the severity of an individual's handicap depends on the social policies and resulting accommodations of the society in which that person lives, as well as on immediate environmental conditions, such as stairs or the attitudes of those that an individual encounters.

For example, someone who needs to use a wheelchair is disabled. Whether or not this person is also handicapped depends entirely upon if, at any moment, he or she finds steps or a ramp when approaching a building or a city bus. A person who is blind is disabled, but whether or not that person is handicapped when handed a menu in a restaurant depends on several factors. Is the menu in Braille and can the individual read Braille? Or does the individual use and carry an Opticon–a reading aid that uses a hand-held camera to translate printed words into electromagnetic impulses which can be interpreted through touch?

The logic behind the deliberate selection and the clear differentiation of the terms *disability* and *handicap* is quite clear. It is to make the point that functional limitations that stem from handicaps are secondary to pre-existing disabling conditions. These limitations can totally or largely be eliminated through environmental modifications and social accommodations.

Fine, Flunk, and Fire "The Disabled" ━━━━━━

In the survey from which the quotes at the beginning of this chapter were abstracted, almost all of the respondents indicated they believed attitudes were extremely important in contributing to their ability to obtain and maintain employment. But as the quote from the federal judge indicates, nearly one-fourth of those who clarified their ratings with comments addressed the attitudes of persons with disabilities themselves, rather than the attitudes of others–of employers and of co-workers.

As members of the wider society, persons with disabilities cannot avoid being influenced by the covert and overt messages that bombard them every day of their lives, and that tell them that they are unemployable, undesirable, unwanted. During a Muscular Dystrophy Telethon, Jerry Lewis once pushed an empty wheelchair out from behind a curtain and mournfully stated, "The man who sits in this wheelchair will never work again...." Newspaper and magazine articles decry the lack of infants for couples who are anxiously waiting to adopt a child, while children who have disabilities are left wanting for a permanent home.

One of the most deleterious effects of being a stigmatized person is, as Stahly (1988) points out, assuming blame for a situation in which one is blameless. But equally deleterious can be the denial of responsibility for those situations for which one is responsible. It is difficult for those who receive continual feedback that they are different or contradictory feedback because they are viewed as different (e.g., minor achievements overvalued because so little is expected of them, or minor faults magnified because incompetence and ineptitude is exactly what is expected), to maintain a clear perspective. It is difficult for them to attain an accurate estimation of their own individual strengths and weaknesses, of their virtues and foibles, and of when they are blameless and when they are indeed responsible.

Some individuals eventually give up and internalize the negative evaluations of others, settling for what secondary gains they can garner–sympathy instead of acceptance, perhaps not realizing that "sympathy is but the other side of the coin of aversion" (Fichten & Amsel, 1986, p. 419). The choice of disability benefit payments instead of renumerative employment is another example of secondary gain. These individuals may be convinced they could never be hired for or successfully hold a job. Others struggle on in their quest for an education, for a job, for a family of their own, and for acceptance in the communities in which they live. Some succeed.

What the framers and supporters of the ADA intended was legislative support which would help to ensure that persons with disabilities would succeed or fail on the basis of their abilities and motivation, not on the basis of having or not having a disability or of having one type of disability instead of another. What the framers and supporters of the ADA did not intend was that the disadvantages which citizens with disabilities had previously experienced would be supplanted by unfair advantages. Just as the factor of disability was not to play a role in whether someone was hired when that person was able to carry out a job's responsibilities, neither was the factor of disability to enhance employment opportunities for those who were not qualified job applicants. If persons with disabilities are to attain social equity, then the cost of that equity needs to be clearly comprehended by everyone, but especially by those who are disabled. And for a segment of our society which has been treated erratically, at times overestimated, and at times underestimated, it is and will continue to be difficult to acquire the stable and unbiased self-evaluation necessary to choose wisely and succeed in this highly competitive society.

To to call attention to the problems of the erroneous feedback that his students had been experiencing, Richard Harris, the coordinator of services for students with disabilities at Ball State University, posted a sign in his office which admonishes the reader to "fine, flunk, and fire the handicapped." Although the sign has shocked and angered many who have encountered it for the first time–parents, students, faculty members, and fellow administrators–the sign remains in place and the policy it embodies remains in force (Harris, 1984).

Fine "The Disabled"

Under the policy of "fine, flunk and fire," it is made clear from the outset to new students with disabilities that the same rules, regulations, and sanctions that apply to other students, apply to them as well. If they violate traffic or parking regulations they will be ticketed and expected to pay the resulting fines. If they violate the college's code of student conduct, they will receive a sanction ranging from a written reprimand to expulsion, depending on the severity of the violation involved.

To enforce a different set of standards for one group of students versus another is not only unjust, it serves as a wedge which enhances diversification and promotes dissension. Not to "fine" when a fine is called for sends one of two equally undesirable messages to members of an already socially devalued group. Lowered standards of acceptable conduct imply the individuals in question are incapable of adhering to expected levels of socially responsible behavior. In addition, lowered standards discount the value of such individuals' contributions to an optimally coordinated, cooperative social system based on mutual respect and trust.

Moreover, when a minority group is involved, what may appear to be a special privilege or consideration in the short run may prove to be exceedingly disadvantageous in the long run. For example, an earlier Tennessee code which governed the parking regulations on the campuses of that state's colleges and universities stipulated a yearly, uniform parking fee of $21 for students, faculty, and staff, including persons with disabilities. Following a revision in the code, on-campus parking fees were both raised and stratified: $150 per year for faculty and staff, $50 per year for students, and $30 per year for "persons with disabilities."

Reactions to the revised code were predictable. Literally hundreds of faculty and staff, who had never before had the need nor the desire to utilize parking reserved for persons with disabilities, had the fact that they were disabled certified by a physician and began using the limited number of conveniently situated spaces. Students with mobility impairments, who previously only had to compete with faculty with mobility impairments for parking, now found they had to arrive on campus early in the morning if they were to find a place to park for their mid-morning and early afternoon classes. Moreover, many able-bodied faculty and staff began to express open resentment toward their colleagues who earned equivalent salaries but who, because they were disabled, were assessed greatly reduced parking fees.

Legislation such as the Tennessee code both reflects stereotypic attitudes toward persons with disabilities and enhances already existing negative attitudes. Disability alone should not result in standards, be they expressed in fines or fees, which differ from the standards (or expectations) for the rest of society. To do so justifies the evaluation of individuals on the basis of their functional limitations instead of their capabilities, which in the example above is the ability of faculty and staff with disabilities to pay the same fees as their colleagues.

Flunk "The Disabled"

The major premise behind the policy of "flunk the disabled" is that favorable but inaccurate evaluations are destructive, not supportive. As anyone who counsels or advises students with disabilities can testify, many college faculty members think it is a kindness to assess the work of students who are disabled less stringently than they assess the work of other students. Far too many professors believe students with disabilities are not pursuing their college degrees to enhance their career potential, but rather to "enrich their existence" or merely to "have something to do with their time." Others avoid giving honest feedback to students who have problems with comprehension or with performing at a satisfactory level, because they want to avoid the need to offer students who are experiencing difficulties extra time and help.

As happens all too frequently in college as in elementary or secondary schools, persons with disabilities are given higher evaluations than they deserve—known as the "B for blind" phenomenon. The result is that individuals who receive inaccurate feedback develop an erroneous confidence in the level of their knowledge, skills, and aptitudes. Sometimes they go through an entire undergraduate program secure in the belief that they are adequate or more than adequate students. Then they may enter graduate school where the grades they did not really earn help them to gain acceptance, sometimes even in the light of borderline GRE or MAT scores. Ultimately, they apply for a job and are hired, often with the aid of equally inflated job references.

The consequences of not flunking those who do not deserve to pass can be manifold: destruction of a sense of self-esteem which was based on false assumptions, unanticipated failures in an advanced degree program, or traumatizing job loss. Any pre-existing doubts of college administrators or prospective employers concerning acceptance of graduate school or employment applications from persons who are disabled will be reinforced. Moreover, the credentials of subsequent applicants will be tarnished, due to unacceptable performance on the part of those who were passed when they should have been flunked.

Fire "The Disabled"

Unlike "fine" and "flunk," the admonition to "fire the disabled" is designed to assist graduates with their transition into the working world. Employers have expressed many reservations concerning the addition of unfamiliar persons with disabilities to their workforce. Placement experts have discovered that the placement strategy with the highest success rate occurs when individuals who became disabled while they were already employed return to their former job or accept a different job with the same employer (Geist & Calzaretta, 1982). A disability may affect specific job skills, but is less likely to affect what is termed the "work personality." The work personality includes all the necessary preconditions to job productivity: motivation, basic attitude toward work, energy level, responsibility, reliability, work habits (e.g., promptness, attention to detail, loyalty), and so on.

Not only does a prospective employer have no personal experience with a stranger who applies for a position but many college graduates with disabilities have had little or no job experience from which the employer may conclude that an applicant does or does not have the requisite attitudes, work habits, and personality factors for the job under consideration. Therefore, one of the major concerns employers have expressed when considering the possibility of hiring an applicant with a disability is, "What if this person proves to be unsuitable for this position? How can I fire someone who is disabled?"

To help overcome the obstacle of employers' fears of having to terminate their employment, students are coached to, at some point during a job interview, interject the comment, "If you do decide to hire me and you find my work is unsatisfactory, I want your promise that you will fire me!" Not only does this statement serve to allay an employer's fears that an individual who is disabled may be too fragile emotionally to handle the prospect, much less the fact of having their employment terminated, it is a public declaration on the part of the job applicant that he or she ascribes to the idea that continuation of employment should be based on satisfactory job performance.

Attitudes And Employment

To work and to love effectively, according to Freud, is the true measure of one's mental health and successful social adjustment. In comparison to most research subjects' reluctance to give written responses, the lengthy comments which were quoted at the beginning of this chapter, and which were volunteered by survey respondents, underscore the importance they attach to attitudes in influencing their ability to be effective workers.

Attitudes of employers which affect the employment potential of individuals with disabilities include the reluctance to hire based upon the reluctance to fire, as pointed out earlier. In addition, however, in reference to employees with disabilities, employers have concerns about their basic job skills and competencies; their ability to perform tasks safely; the perceived increase in the cost of workers' compensation insurance, the feasibility and cost of any required environmental or job modifications (especially in light of the number of equally qualified applicants without disabilities); and the willingness of co-workers to work cooperatively and effectively alongside them.

In regard to job qualifications, the law is quite specific. Employers are not expected to hire persons from any minority group who do not have the qualifications required to perform job tasks competently. What is clarified by the law is that the presence of a disability alone is not an acceptable reason for denying employment. In fact, there is abundant research evidence that the job performance of persons with disabilities, as evaluated by managers and supervisors, is consistently rated as equal to or superior to that of able-bodied co-workers (Harris, 1987).

The danger in citing research evidence which portrays workers with disabilities as average or above average is that such research will only contribute to the tendency to stereotype—albeit positively stereotype—persons who are disabled. One might suspect that the prevailing prejudice against hiring persons who are disabled has resulted in such a stringent preselection of those who have been allowed to enter the workforce that the majority of those who are employed represent the best, the brightest, and certainly the most determined and persistent of those who were seeking employment. Truly desirable (i.e., realistic) attitudes toward persons who are disabled will be attained only if such persons are seen as representing the entire gamut of human traits, ranging from responsible to irresponsible, from achievement-oriented to disinterested, from energetic to grudgingly responsive, with most falling somewhere in between. Employers should no more anticipate that a job applicant with a disability will be an outstanding employee than they should presume that such an applicant will be an unsatisfactory worker. As should be done with all other job applicants, the skills, knowledge and aptitudes of each applicant who has a disability should be assessed and evaluated objectively, and in terms of the specific requirements of the job under consideration. Then and only then should the decision be made to hire or not to hire. In its simplest terms this is what ADA requires.

In terms of increased insurance costs, according to the Journal of American Insurance (JAI), employers who hire disabled workers do not see an increase in their workers' compensation insurance premiums. A study cited by the JAI found that "90 percent of 279 companies surveyed reported no effect on insurance costs as a result of hiring disabled employees (1986, p. 17)." Should a second injury occur to a previously disabled worker, each state has legislation which covers second injuries and which ensures that an employer cannot be held liable for a greater disability than that which ensued from an injury which occurred while the worker was currently employed. Moreover, evidence exists that persons who are already disabled often have better safety records than those who are not. In a 1981 Du Pont survey, supervisors rated 96% of employees with disabilities as average or above average in the safe performance of duties, compared to 92% for other workers (JAI, 1986). The possibility of becoming more functionally limited than one already is may create a heightened awareness of the dangers of unsafe working conditions and a greater respect for prescribed safety procedures.

In an attempt to allay employer concerns about the feasibility of providing accommodations for employees with functional limitations, a national data bank of information on environmental and job modifications has been established. Not only does the Job Accommodation Network (JAN) provide information about the wide range of existing accommodations that are already provided by the nation's employers, it enables one employer to talk to another employer about what would be the best solution to solve the work-related functional problems of an individual with a particular functional limitation, and how to do so at the lowest possible cost. Only 35% of persons with disabilities who are working now have required any type of job accommodation by their employer and most of these were well under $100 (Harris, 1987; JAI, 1986).

Moreover, once an accommodation has been made, such as installing a ramp at a business's entrance for someone who uses a wheelchair, employers have made an investment which benefits more than one individual. An accessible entrance paves the way for expansion of services to customers and fellow business persons who also use wheelchairs, eliminates the cost of modifications for the next person hired who uses a wheelchair, and simplifies the work duties of any employee who must move heavy cartons or equipment in and out of the business facility. Like ramps on public buildings or curb cuts on street corners, accommodations which are a necessity for persons with mobility impairments are also convenient for and tend to be utilized often by persons who are not disabled.

Many employers, in light of the periodic swings in the economy, tend to lose sight of the fact that the next few decades will bring a marked reduction in the number of younger workers. The current rise in unemployment rates masks the fact that, according to some estimates, by 1995 there will be 26% fewer persons between the ages of 16 and 19, when most begin their entry into the workforce (Tyler, 1989). According to the Dole Foundation (JAI, 1986), as many as five million individuals who are disabled and who are between the ages of 16 and 64 are presently capable of working. According to Harris (1986), 65% of unemployed adults with disabilities want to work. The increase in numbers of persons who are of retirement age and above, coupled with the decreasing numbers of younger workers, especially in an era where education and technical skills are increasingly valued over bodily strength and agility, enhances the employment potential of persons whose functional limitations affect their ability to perform certain job tasks but not to perform others. Moreover, as Tyler (1989) points out, coping with a disability "frequently leads to the development of strength of character and ingenuity in finding new and imaginative ways of handing complex problems" (p. 6). Such traits as these are essential in many areas of employment today.

Finally, a major concern of employers is the issue of collegiality, which is essential to the morale and optimum functioning of any group of individuals who on a long-term basis must work together to attain mutual goals. The question of acceptance of co-workers is a special concern to employers who have individuals with AIDS in their workforce. According to Schachter, Geidt, and von Seeburg, lawyers who specialize in employment and labor law, managers have legal obligations toward employees with AIDS, since "the syndrome of suppressed immune function is clearly a disability or infirmity caused by an illness (1987, p. 48)." When co-workers refuse to work with a fellow employee with AIDS, Schachter et al. (1987) suggest that the employer first ensure that the co-workers have an accurate understanding of AIDS and are given appropriate precautionary guidelines. Then, although there is no legal responsibility to do so, the employer might agree to accommodate the co-worker with a transfer. If a transfer is not feasible and the co-worker continues to refuse to return to the worksite or to work with the employee with AIDS, according to Schachter et al. (1987), the employer has the right to replace the co-worker.

In their study of attitudes toward persons with both apparent (e.g., cerebral palsy) and nonapparent disabilities (e.g., epilepsy), Grand, Bernier, and Strohmer (1982) discovered that people are more accepting of persons with disabilities in work situations than in other social situations. Research in general suggests that the basis for reducing the tendency to stereotype and to stigmatize persons with disabilities is allowing them to share authority and responsibility within the context of externally structured, extended contact with nondisabled peers (Anthony, 1972; Bender, 1981; Fichten & Amsel, 1986). When people anticipate that their interactions with another person will continue, they are more likely to view that person positively than those who anticipate their interactions will be attenuated (Knight & Vallacher, 1981). Any initial negative reactions on the part of co-workers can be expected to diminish when a person with a disability actually becomes part of the workforce.

Therefore, persons with disabilities have a great hope that when fully implemented, the American With Disabilities Act of 1990 will provide them with an impetus to participate in remunerative employment that has long been lacking. At worst, entry into the job market will mean greater financial security and more of a chance to share in the material rewards which are so abundant in this society. At best, the forced reciprocity with those who have had no previous personal experience with disability may result in a widespread, positive change in attitudes. Then the employment of applicants with disabilities will no longer depend upon a chance encounter with someone like "Bud," or upon the need to prove themselves by continuing to work "even if you're dying."

References

American Psychological Association. (1983). *Publication manual.* Washington, DC: American Psychological Association.

Anthony, W. (1972). Societal rehabilitation: Changing society's attitudes toward the physically and mentally disabled. *Rehabilitation Psychology, 19,* 117-126.

Beauchamp, T., & Childress, J. (1989). *Principles of biomedical ethics* (3rd ed.). New York: Oxford University Press.

Bender, L. (1981). 1980 Presidential Address to the American Academy for Cerebral Palsy and Developmental Medicine. *Developmental Medicine and Child Neurology, 23,* 103-108.

Blake, R. (1981). Disabled older Americans: A demographic analysis. *Journal of Rehabilitation, 47,* 19-27.

DeLoach, C. (1989). Gender, career choice and occupational outcomes among college alumni with disabilities *Journal of Applied Rehabilitation Counseling, 47,* 19-27.

DeLoach, C., & Greer, B. (1981). *Adjustment to severe physical disability: A metamorphosis.* New York: McGraw-Hill.

DeLoach, C., Wilkins, R., & Walker, G. (1983). *Independent living: Philosophy process and services.* Baltimore: University Park Press.

Dunn, D. (1981). Vocational rehabilitation of the older worker. *Journal of Rehabilitation, 47,* 76-81.

Fichten, C., & Amsel, R. (1986). Trait attributions about college students with a physical disability: Circumplex analyses and methodological issues. *Journal of Applied Social Psychology, 16,* 410-427.

Geist, C., & Calzaretta, W. (1982). *Placement handbook for counseling disabled persons.* Springfield, IL: Charles Thomas.

Goffman, E. (1963). *Stigma: Notes on the management of a spoiled identity.* Englewood Cliffs, NJ: Prentice-Hall.

Gorski, R. (1981). Is the Barriers Board heading for a last hurrah? *Disabled USA. 4,* 7-9.

Grand, S., Bernier, J., & Strohmer, D. (1982). Attitudes toward disabled persons as a function of social context and specific disability. *Rehabilitation Psychology, 27,* 165-174.

Hahn, H. (1985). Disability policy and the problem of discrimination. *American Behavioral Scientist, 28,* 293-318.

Harris, L. (1986). *Disabled Americans' self-perception: Bringing disabled Americans into the mainstream.* (Study 845009). New York: Louis Harris and Associates, Inc.

Harris, L. (1987). *The CID survey II: Employing disabled Americans.* (Study 864009). New York: Louis Harris and Associates, Inc.

Harris, R. (1984). *Reflections through the looking glass.* Columbus, OH: Association on Handicapped Student Service Programs in Post-Secondary Education.

Jackman, M. (1983). Enabling the disabled. *Perspectives: The Civil Rights Quarterly, 15,* 23-26.

Journal of American Insurance. (1986). Hiring the handicapped: Overcoming physical and psychological barriers in the job market. *Journal of American Insurance, 65,* 13-19.

Knight, J., & Vallacher, R. (1981). Interpersonal engagement in social perception: The consequences of getting into the action. *Journal of Personality and Social Psychology, 44,* 990-999.

Lenihan, J. (1977). Disabled Americans: A history. *Performance.* Washington, DC: President's Commission on Employment of the Handicapped.

Lerner, M. (1971). Observer's evaluation of the victim, justice, guilt, and veridical perceptions. *Journal of Personality & Social Psychology, 20,* 127-135.

Lerner, M. (1974). Social psychology of justice and interpersonal attraction. In T. Huston (Ed.), *Foundations of interpersonal attraction.* New York: Academic Press.

Lerner, M., & Simmons, C. (1966). Observer's reactions to the "innocent victim": Compassion or rejection? *Journal of Personality & Social Psychology, 4,* 202-210.

Maguire, P. (1985). The psychological impact of cancer. *British Journal of Hospital Medicine, 2,* 100-103.

National Rehabilitation Association. (March, 1985). *Newsletter, 41,* 6-7.

Parsons, T. (1958). Health and illness in the light of American values and social structure. In E. G. Jace (Ed.), *Patients, physicians, and illness.* Glencoe, IL: Free Press.

Schachter, V., Geidt, T., & von Seeburg, S. (1987). *AIDS: A manager's guide.* New York: Executive Enterprises.

Stahly, G. (1988). Psychosocial aspects of the stigma of cancer: An overview. *Journal of Psychosocial Oncology, 6,* 3-27.

Trieschmann, R. (1986). *Aging with a disability.* New York: Demos Press.

Tyler, G. (1989). Disabled people—One solution to the youth shortage? *Management Services, 33,* 6-8.

Wright, B. (1960). *Physical disability: A psychological approach.* New York: Harper & Row.

Yuker, H., & Block, J. (1979). *Challenging barriers to change: Attitudes toward the disabled.* New York: Human Resources Center.

3

Legal Overview

Nancy Hablutzel, J.D., Ph.D.
Margo Lynn Hablutzel, J.D.
Vickie A. Gillio, J.D.

Although other types of discrimination have been prohibited by federal law for over 20 years, until 1990 there was no similar single law protecting the rights of persons with disabilities. This finally changed with the passage of the Americans with Disabilities Act (ADA). The scope of the ADA is far broader than any other federal law which prohibits discrimination. The goal of the ADA is to eliminate discrimination against persons with disabilities in employment, education, and recreation, and to require equal access to a broad range of facilities and services.

Defining Disability

Definitions of Disability under the Americans with Disabilities Act of 1990

The ADA uses the term *individuals with disabilities* to focus attention on the person, not the disability. Unlike previous federal laws, the ADA does not list specific disabilities. Instead, the ADA generally defines *disability* as:

1. A physical or mental impairment that substantially limits one or more of the major life activities of such individual;
2. A record of such an impairment; or
3. Being regarded as having such an impairment.

The legislative history of the ADA indicates that *a physical or mental impairment* under the ADA includes the following:

1. Any physiological disorder or condition, cosmetic disfigurement, or anatomical loss affecting one or more systems of the body including the following: the neurological system; the musculoskeletal system; the special sense organs and respiratory organs, including speech organs; the cardiovascular system; the reproductive system; the digestive system; the geni-

tourinary system; the hemic and lymphatic systems; the skin; and the endocrine systems.
2. Any mental or psychological disorder, such as mental retardation, organic brain syndrome, emotional or mental illness, and specific learning disabilities.

Certain populations are specifically excluded from protection under the ADA. The following are not considered to be, in and of themselves, a "disability" under the ADA:

1. Transvestism (§508);
2. Homosexuality and bisexuality (§511);
3. Transvestism and transsexualism (§511[b][1]);
4. Pedophilia, exhibitionism, and voyeurism (§511[b][1]);
5. Gender identity disorders (unless there is a physical cause) (§511[b][1]);
6. Compulsive gambling (§511[b][2]);
7. Pyromania (§511[b][2]);
8. Kleptomania (§511[b][2]);
9. A person with a communicable disease which can be transmitted through food handling (a list of which is to be published annually by the Secretary of Health and Human Services) may be denied employment in a job involving food handling if there is no reasonable accommodation which would eliminate that risk (§103[d]); and
10. Current abusers of alcohol or drugs.

Under the ADA, current abuse[1] of alcohol[2] or illegal drugs[3] is not considered a disability, and therefore is not a protected condition.[4] However, a person may not be denied health services or drug rehabilitation services based solely upon current drug or alcohol abuse.[5]

Once a person has become rehabilitated and is not currently abusing illegal drugs, he or she may not be discriminated on because of the past abuse.[6] Persons who are not substance abusers, but are erroneously believed to be substance abusers, are protected under the ADA.[7]

The ADA specifically provides that drug testing and related procedures are not prohibited.[8] There is a fine distinction, because the Act only permits drug testing to determine whether a person remains rehabilitated, "however, nothing in this section shall be construed to encourage, prohibit, restrict, or authorize the conducting of testing for the illegal use of drugs."[9]

Employers who are covered by the ADA have the authority to:[10]

1. Prohibit the illegal use of drugs and the use [of] alcohol at the workplace by all employees;
2. Require that employees shall not be under the influence of alcohol or be engaging in the illegal use of drugs at the workplace;
3. Require that employees behave in conformance with the requirements established under the Drug-Free Workplace Act of 1988 (41 U.S.C. §§701 *et seq.*);

4. Hold an employee who engages in the illegal use of drugs or who is an alcoholic to the same qualification standards for employment or job performance and behavior that such entity holds other employee, even if any unsatisfactory performance or behavior is related to the drug use or alcoholism of such employee; and

5. May, with respect to Federal regulations regarding alcohol and the illegal use of drugs, require that:

   a. Employees comply with the standards established in such regulations of the Department of Defense, if the employees of the covered entity are employed in an industry subject to such regulations, including complying with regulations (if any) that apply to employment in sensitive positions in such an industry, in the case of employees of the covered entity who are employed in such positions (as defined in the regulations of the Department of Defense);

   b. Employees comply with the standards established in such regulations of the Nuclear Regulatory Commission, if employees of the covered entity are employed in an industry·subject to such regulations, including complying with regulations (if any) that apply to employment in sensitive positions in such an industry, in the case of employees of the covered entity who are employed in such positions (as defined in the regulations of the Nuclear Regulatory Commission); and

   c. Employees comply with the standards established in such regulations of the Department of Transportation, if the employees of the covered entity are employed in a transportation industry subject to such regulations, including complying with such regulations (if any) that apply to employment in sensitive positions in such an industry, in the case of employees of the covered entity who are employed in such positions (as defined in the regulations of the Department of Transportation).

Graph of Determination

The graph entitled "Determining Disability Under the Americans with Disabilities Act of 1990" has been designed as a quick way to determine whether a person qualifies for protection under the ADA.

Definitions of Disability Under Other Federal Laws

1. Section 504 of the Rehabilitation Act of 1973

a. Section 504 of the Rehabilitation Act of 1973 defines *handicapped individual* as:

> [A]ny person who (i) has a physical or mental impairment which substantially limits one or more of such person's major life activities,[11] (ii) has a record of such an impairment, or (iii) is regarded as having such an impairment.[12]

Determining Disability Under the
Americans with Disabilities Act of 1990

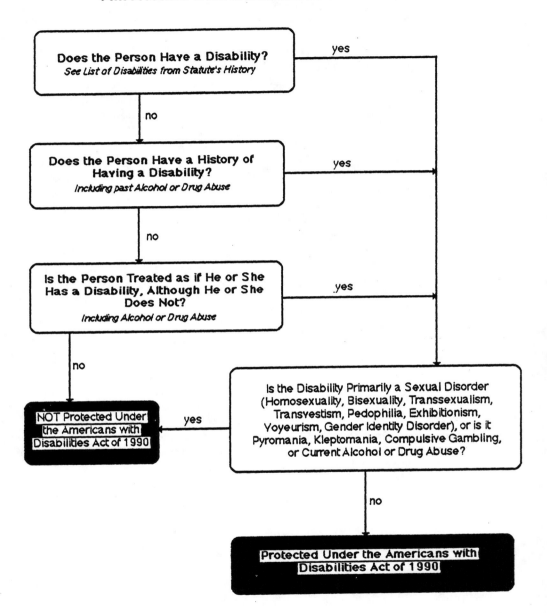

The term *severe handicap* means the disability which requires multiple services over an extended period of time and results from amputation, blindness, cancer, cerebral palsy, cystic fibrosis, deafness, heart disease, hemiplegia, mental retardation, mental illness, multiple sclerosis, muscular dystrophy, neurological disorders (including stroke and epilepsy), paraplegia, quadriplegia and other spinal cord conditions, renal failure, respiratory or pulmonary dysfunction, and any other disability specified by the Secretary in regulations he shall prescribe.[13]

b.   The following conditions have been found to be a handicap under section 504: *Transsexualism* (maybe) [Doe v. U.S. Postal Services, Civ. 84-3296 (slip op. available on Lexis©) (D.C. D.C. 1985)]; *obesity* [S.D.H.R. v. Xerox Corp., 478 N.Y.S.2d 982, 102 A.D.2d 543, *aff'd* 491 N.Y.S. 2d 106, 65 N.Y.2d 213, 480 N.E.2d 695 (1985)]; *susceptibility to tuberculosis,* even though tuberculosis is a chronic contagious disease; [Arline v. School Board of Nassau County, 772 F.2d 759 (11th Cir. 1985)]; *back abnormality or limp* which has no affect on person's life is a protected disability *if it is perceived as a disability* [OFCCP v. E.E. Black, Ltd., 19 FEP Cases 1625 (1979)]; *diabetes mellitus* [Bentivegna v. U.S. Department of Labor, 694 F.2d 619 (9th Cr. 1982)]; *unusual sensitivity to cigarette smoke,* necessitating a totally smoke-free environment [Vickers v. VA, 29 FEP Cases 1197(1982)].

c.   The following conditions have been found *not* to be a handicap under section 504: *Varicose veins* [Osterlong v. Walters, 595 F.Supp. 27 (1985)]; *left handedness* [de la Torres v. Bolger, 610 F.Supp. 593 (D.C. Tex. 1985), *aff'd* 781 F.2d 1134 (5th Cir. 1986)]; *non-smoking* [GASP v. Mecklenburg co., 356 S.E.2d 477 (1979)], although a person unusually sensitive to cigarette smoke, who needed to work in a totally smoke-free environment, was found to be "handicapped" under the definition [Vickers v. VA, 29 FEP Cases 1197 (1982)]; *temporary disability* (fractured and dislocated ankle) [Grimard v. Carlston, 567 F.2d 1171 (1978)].

d.   In the past, *alcoholism and drug addiction* were protected unless they interfered with the safety of others or are a threat to property [Squires v. Wisconsin Labor and Industry Review Commission, 284 N.W.48 (1980); Blitz v. Northwest Airlines, Inc., 37 F.E.P. Cases 171 (Minn. App. Ct. 1985); Simpson v. Reynolds Metals Co., Inc., 629 F.2d 1226 (7th Cir. 1980); Davis v. Bucher, 451 F.Supp. 791 (E.D. Pa. 1978); and Beazer v. New York City Transit Authority, 399 F.Supp. 1032 (S.D.N.Y. 1975) *aff'd* 588 F.2d 91 (2d Cir. 1977)]. However, the ADA changed the Rehabilitation Act so that the two laws would harmonize, and substance abuse is no longer a protected category under the Rehabilitation Act of 1973.[14]

2. *Individuals with Disabilities Education Act (Formerly: Education for All Handicapped Children Act, P.L. 94-142, as amended)*

a.   The Individuals with Disabilities Education Act, which provides for a free, appropriate public education for all children with disabilities between the ages of 3 and 21 years, defines *disability* as mentally retarded, hard of hearing, deaf, speech or language impaired, visually handicapped, seriously emotionally disturbed, orthopedically impaired, or other health impaired children, or children with specific learning disabilities, who by reason thereof require special education and related services.[15]

b. *Related services* are defined as developmental, corrective, or supportive services which are required to enable a child with a disability to benefit from the special education services offered. They include transportation, speech pathology and audiology, psychological services, physical and occupational therapy, recreation, early identification and assessment of disabilities, counseling services, medical services for diagnostic or evaluation services, school health services (e.g., dispensing medication, testing lung capacity, and other services needed by the child to remain in school and obtain the full benefit from the special education), social work services in school, parent counseling and training, and rehabilitation counseling.

3. Social Security Act and Regulations

a. The current definition of *disability* for Social Security purposes is:

[I]nability to engage in any substantial gainful activity by reason of any medically determinable physical or mental impairment which can be expected to result in death or which has lasted or can be expected to last for a continuous period of not less than 12 months;

[A]n individual...shall be determined to be under a disability only if his physical or mental impairment or impairments are of such severity that he is not only unable to do his previous work but cannot, considering his age, education, and work experience, engage in another kind of substantial gainful work which exists in the national economy, regardless of whether such work exists in the immediate area in which he lives, or whether a specific job vacancy exists for him, or whether he would be hired if he applied for work. For purposes of the preceding sentence (with respect to any individual), "work which exists in the national economy" means work which exists in significant numbers either in the region where such individual lives or in several regions of the country.[16]

b. The simplest way to determine whether a claimant qualifies for Social Security Disability is to follow the Social Security Disability Evaluation flow chart:[17]

Social Security Disability Evaluation

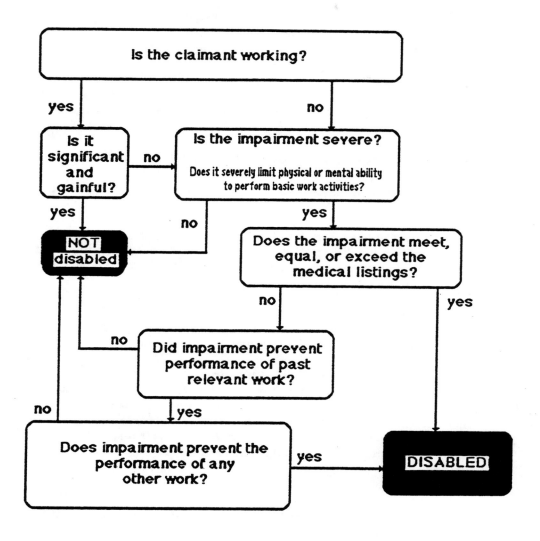

4. Fair Housing Act

a. The Fair Housing Act prohibits discrimination against any person on the basis of "race, color, religion, sex, handicap, familial status, or national origin." The Act defines *handicap* as:[18]

> (1) A physical or mental impairment which substantially limits one or more of a person's major life activities.
> (2) A record of having such an impairment.
> (3) Being regarded as having such an impairment.

b. AIDS is generally recognized as a handicap under the Fair Housing Act.[19] However, current, illegal use of or addiction to a controlled substance (e.g., marijuana, heroin, cocaine, and many others) is specifically not considered a handicap under the Fair Housing Act.[20]

5. Air Carrier Access Act and Federal Aviation Authority Regulations

a. General Provisions and Definition of *Otherwise Qualified Handicapped Person*

The Air Carrier Access Act (ACAA) prohibits discrimination against "otherwise qualified handicapped" persons by any airline in providing them with transportation. The Act defines a *handicapped individual* as a person with:

> (1) A physical or mental impairment which substantially limits one or more of a person's major life activities.
> (2) A record of having such an impairment.
> (3) Being regarded as having such an impairment.

To be an "otherwise qualified handicapped individual," the person with disabilities must pay the fare, have the ability and be willing to comply with reasonable requests of airline personnel,[21] and whose transportation would not violate FAA regulations; requests are *not* considered reasonable if they are neither safety-related nor necessary to provide the transportation, or if they are not consistent with the applicable regulations.

b. Presumption of Qualification and Specific Exceptions

All persons are presumed to be qualified to travel by air unless the carrier has a reasonable and specific reason for doubting this. The carrier may require a person with disabilities to travel with a companion if the person would require extraordinary care during the flight, such as assistance with eating (which does not include simply unwrapping the flatware or describing the type and location of foods on the tray), lavatory assistance, or nursing services. If the person cannot feed him- or herself and elects not to eat during the flight, or if the person is incontinent or unable to use the lavatory without assistance but makes other provision for waste disposal, the air carrier cannot either deny the person transportation or require that she or he be accompanied by an attendant.

5

Employment Testing and Evaluation

Mark LoVerde, M.S.
Brian T. McMahon, Ph.D., C.R.C.
Gary W. Morris, Ph.D.

Introduction

Those critical portions of the employment provisions (Title I) of the Americans with Disabilities Act which pertain to this chapter are the following:

Qualification Standards, Tests, and Other Selection Criteria

It is unlawful for a covered entity to use qualification standards, employment tests, or other selection criteria that screen out or tend to screen out an individual with a disability or a class of individuals with disabilities, on the basis of disability, unless the standard, test, or other selection criteria, as used by the covered entity, is shown to be job-related for the position in question and is consistent with business necessity (CFR 1630.10).

Administration of Tests

It is unlawful for a covered entity to fail to select and administer tests concerning employment in the most effective manner to ensure that, when a test is administered to a job applicant or employee who has a disability that impairs sensory, manual, or speaking skills, the test results accurately reflect the skills, aptitude, or whatever other factor the test purports to measure, rather than reflecting the particular disability of such employee or applicant (except where such skills are the factors that the test purports to measure) (CFR 1630.11). (The reader is strongly encouraged to read the Appendix to Part 1630–Interpretive Guidance on Title I of the ADA–pertinent to 1630.10 and 1630.11 before proceeding.)

The intent of this chapter is to describe the proposed approach of one employer, Ameritech Corporation, in response to these specific Title I regulations. Ameritech is a premier provider of telecommunications and information services, with headquarters in the Midwest. Taking a lead in dealing with the new ADA regulations, Ameritech formed an ADA Task Force in 1990 similar to that described in Chapter 12. The Subcommittee on Testing and Accommodations, of which these authors are members, is concerned with a myriad of human resources issues including maximizing the accessibility of the employment testing process. Accordingly, it recently drafted these *proposed* guidelines to recommend modifications to the existing employment testing process.

It is important to note that these are proposed recommendations which have not been approved as policy by Ameritech at the time of this writing. The document is described here only to stimulate similar planning among other employers which will hopefully include dialogue with local consumer groups. Ultimately, it is hoped that some revised version of these guidelines will soon be used as reference material for those who design and supervise employee selection programs at Ameritech companies.

Guidelines for Testing and Evaluating Individuals with Disabilities

Pertinent Background

The ADA is a federal statute designed to eliminate discrimination against individuals with disabilities. Title I of this act prohibits discrimination in employment against qualified individuals with disabilities who, with or without reasonable accommodation, can perform the essential functions of a given job (hereafter, ADA will refer to Title I of the Act). The ADA also places an obligation on employers to make reasonable accommodations to the known physical or mental limitations of individuals with disabilities.

This document is intended to provide guidelines for administering tests, interviews, evaluations, or other qualification standards to individuals with disabilities covered under the ADA. For the purposes of this document, the term *test* will be used for all of these standards. (Note: Prerequisites such as work experience and educational requirements will also fall under the provisions of the ADA.)

Before proceeding with the guidelines, relevant terms will be clarified:

Disability

Job candidates are considered to have a disability if they:

1) have a physical or mental impairment that substantially limits one or more major life activities;
2) have a record of such an impairment; or
3) are regarded as having such an impairment.

A *known disability* is a disability, as defined above, about which the candidate has voluntarily provided information or which, after a job offer has been extended, has been identified by the company's medical department during the physical examination.

For testing purposes, identification of disability should generally be made only by the candidate. Unless a candidate has requested accommodation, there is no known disability and the candidate should be treated accordingly. Even where there is an apparent disability, there should be no notation unless the candidate volunteers the information. Additionally, identification of a current employee's disability by the employee's supervisor is not acceptable since the employee may not wish to be identified as a person with a disability.

Qualified

Individuals with disabilities are considered qualified if they satisfy the skill, experience, education, and other job-related requirements of the job they desire or hold *and* are capable of performing the essential functions of the job, with or without reasonable accommodation, at the time of the job action in question. Possible future incapacitation is not grounds for considering a person unqualified.

Essential Functions

These are job tasks that are fundamental and not marginal. Current job descriptions will be important in determining what are essential and what are marginal job functions. Essential functions may be broadly defined as activities every incumbent must perform to satisfactorily perform a given job. Other indicators of essentialness are: 1) the function is the reason the position exists; 2) the function is so specialized that incumbents are hired on the basis of their expertise or ability to perform it; or 3) there are a limited number of employees available to perform the function.

Marginal functions are those activities which are not essential. It may be important that someone in the title or position perform the function, but it is marginal if it is not essential that all incumbents do so. Take, for example, a position in a benefits office. If the office were staffed by only one or two incumbents at a time, using the telephone (hearing and speaking) to answer employee questions would be an essential function of the job. If, in comparison, a number of incumbents were available to answer questions over the phone, it might be considered a marginal function of the position since not every incumbent would need to perform that function.

Reasonable Accommodation

This term refers to any action on the part of the employer that would enable the qualified candidate with a disability to perform (or qualify for) the job but would not impose an undue hardship on the employer. From a testing perspective, reasonable accommodation means making adjustments to the testing process to ensure that the test accurately measures the abilities of the candidate rather than reflecting the disability (unless the disability relates directly to the skill the test measures).

Reasonable accommodations may include, but are not limited to, such things as making testing facilities readily accessible (or administering testing in accessible locations); modifying the presentation of testing, training materials, or information (e.g., timed vs. untimed, written vs. Braille, oral vs. signed language); or utilizing alternative measures of a skill, knowledge, or ability.

Undue Hardship

This is normally conceived of as an action requiring significant difficulty or expense on the part of the employer. This determination is made, however, with respect to the size and resources of the employer. For the purposes of testing, undue hardship would also include any action which would fundamentally alter the nature and purpose, violate the security, or negate the utility of a test.

Situations Which Call for the Use of These Guidelines

This document is intended as a guide or aid for addressing testing, interviewing, assessment, or other evaluation situations where there is an individual with a known physical, mental, or other disability. These guidelines pertain specifically to the above situations and are not intended for use in any other aspect of employment. *Most of the disabling conditions which will require application of these guidelines will involve sensory, manual, or speaking impairments.*

Initial Contacts with Candidates

During initial contact (both internal and external), candidates should be instructed that, if they have a disability which may require accommodation on our tests, they should inform the employment office prior to testing. The opportunity to request accommodation should be included with application forms, in any pretest telephone conversations, as part of any automated test scheduling process, and on any pretest information, notices, or forms sent to candidates. Candidates who request accommodation should be scheduled for an individual accommodation discussion.

At Testing Sessions

At the start of a test session, the test administrator should explain the general nature of the tests to be administered and ask, for a final time, whether any candidate requires accommodation. A candidate requesting accommodation at this time should be scheduled for an Individual Accommodation Discussion (IAD) and excused from that particular testing session.

If candidates do not realize the need for an accommodation until after starting the test, they should notify the administrator immediately. They should then be scheduled for an IAD, excused from that particular testing session and rescheduled for testing at a later date using the accommodations agreed upon in the IAD. As a general rule, this procedure should not apply to candidates who have attempted more than half of the test or passed half of the allotted time before requesting accommodation.

In interpreting the above guideline, each distinct component of a test battery should be considered a separate test. Candidates should not receive accommodated retesting for those tests which they have already completed. If, for example, candidates do not notify the test administrator of the need for accommodation until they have begun the fourth and final component of a four-part test battery, they would only be accommodated and retested on that test. The scores from the first test session would be used for the first three tests of the battery. Candidates with

However, a carrier may refuse transportation to a person who requires "extensive" special assistance by the carrier without advance notice from the person.[22] These services include on-board oxygen for medical use, assistance with boarding and deplaning, and assistance in moving through the terminal. The carrier may charge "reasonable, nondiscriminatory" amounts for these services, *if and only if* it makes the same charges to all passengers. The carrier may *not* charge for services which are required because its aircraft is not readily accessible.

Persons who use guide dogs, canes, or crutches must be allowed to keep them on the plane. If space does not allow this the carrier shall check the wheelchair and provide it promptly at the door of the aircraft. Battery-operated wheelchairs and personal oxygen supplies shall be accepted as baggage, and shall not be subjected to restrictions placed upon fragile items.

c.   Separate Facilities and Accessibility of Facilities

Discrimination includes denying air transportation to a qualified person, even if separate or different service is available, and providing the person with disabilities with separate or different services unless they are reasonably necessary or are requested by the person.

Further, the air carrier's facilities, services, and reservation system must be readily accessible to and useable by persons with disabilities. All aircraft must be reasonably accessible to persons with mobility impairments. However, not every facility or every part of the facility used for a given flight must be accessible.

Air carriers must ensure that hearing-impaired and visually-impaired passengers have timely access to important information (e.g., safety or emergency information and information about flight delays, schedule changes, gate changes). Air carriers must allow visually or hearing-impaired persons with guide dogs to be accompanied on the aircraft with their dogs.

d.   FAA Regulations about Seating

In 1990, the FAA established regulations which specify that air carriers should seat in the "exit rows" (those rows by an exit) only those persons who are physically capable of opening the emergency exits if needed. Persons who may be removed from the exit row include those who cannot understand English, who are physically frail or disabled and unable to open the exit, who are blind, who are under the age of 15 or accompanied by small children, or who are considered obese. A person may also be removed from the exit row if she or he does not wish to assist in opening the exit door.

Several lawsuits have been filed on behalf of various classes of persons, primarily persons with disabilities and those who may be considered obese, challenging the constitutionality of these regulations, but as of this writing no decisions have been made. In the past, persons with disabilities (particularly visual impairments) have filed lawsuits, primarily under the Rehabilitation Act of 1973, challenging practices which deny them any seat on an airplane except one immediately adjacent to an exit door. The airlines have defended this practice on grounds of passenger safety, and so far these arguments have been upheld in court.[23]

The Americans with Disabilities Act and Other Federal and State Laws

It is important to realize that, significant though the ADA is for persons with disabilities, it does not exist in a vacuum. It must be examined in context with a patchwork of preexisting federal and state laws. Certain laws and regulations have greater effect in some areas, and it should be noted that, for state laws, where the state law is more comprehensive than the ADA, the state law will control.

The ADA defines *disability* as a physical or mental impairment that substantially limits one or more of the major life activities of such individuals; a record of such an impairment; or being regarded as having such an impairment.[24] This definition is echoed in many federal laws, such as section 504 of the Rehabilitation Act of 1973;[25] the Fair Housing Act;[26] and the Air Carrier Access Act of 1986.[27]

With respect to each of these laws, the ADA will control unless the other law is stronger or more specific. For example, while the ADA and ACAA both provide for accessible facilities and equal access to services, the ACAA and related regulations are more specific as to what services must be offered and why differences in services are permitted or forbidden. The Fair Housing Act is unequalled by any portion of the ADA except in a very general way, and so for questions of accessibility to housing, the Fair Housing Act would be the primary authority.

Given the very specific focus of the Social Security Act and the Individuals with Disabilities Education Act, it is not surprising that their definitions differ significantly from that in the ADA, and that their areas are not addressed by the ADA. For questions of whether a person qualifies for Social Security Disability benefits, the Social Security Act and related regulations will control. The ADA makes no attempt to supersede the Individuals with Disabilities Education Act in any way, although, of course, schools and related facilities must be accessible under the ADA's provisions addressed to accessibility of public accommodations.

Equal Rights to Employment

The provisions outlawing discrimination in employment will take effect in stages. Employers with 25 or more employees are (as of July 1992) prohibited from discriminating against persons with disabilities in hiring, firing, promotion, training, compensation, or any other term or condition of employment. Employers with 15 or more employees will be covered as of July 1994.

Employers covered by Title I of the ADA include:

1. All governmental bodies;
2. Private sector: employers, employment agencies, labor organizations, joint labor-management committees;

3. Employers who have "15 or more employees for each working day in each of 20 or more calendar weeks in the current or preceding calendar year" (there are a few exceptions); and
4. Public accommodations and services which are owned, leased, or operated by private entities.

Under the ADA, a person with a disability has the right to expect his or her employer to "reasonably accommodate" the disability, unless this would be an "undue hardship" on the employer's operations. The "reasonable accommodation" requires employers to make their workplaces readily accessible to and useable by persons with disabilities and, if necessary, to restructure work schedules or re-assign the employee to another position. Examples of reasonable accommodation include removing the center drawer of a desk so that a wheelchair could fit under it or placing a paper cup dispenser by a water fountain. Auxiliary aids and devices which will assist a worker with disabilities in performing her or his job must be provided by the employer. These include special computer software and hardware which would enable a visually impaired person to use a computer, or a TDD (telecommunication device for the deaf) onsite to speak to a hearing-impaired worker at home. Examples of reasonable accommodations are given in Table 1.

What will be considered an "undue hardship" is unclear and attempts to define it will undoubtedly be the source of much litigation. Expense alone will not absolve an employer from its responsibilities, but the effect on the employer's business can be considered. And while violations of other employees' seniority rights have been found to be an undue hardship under state laws, the ADA expressly states that it controls over rights under a collective bargaining agreement.

Congressional tax credits for compliance with the ADA may be available to some businesses. The conditions for receipt of these tax credits are:

1. Small businesses—which are defined as having *either*:
   a. $1,000,000 or less in gross receipts, *or*
   b. 29 or fewer employees.
2. Small businesses which incur expenditures of $250 to $10,250 receive 50% tax credit.
3. Eligible expenditures include: removing architectural, communication, physical, or transportation barriers; providing qualified interpreters or readers; acquiring or modifying equipment or devices.

Key Definitions: Title I (Employment)

Employee: Any individual employed by an employer.[28] A person is considered qualified for the position if she or he can, with or without reasonable accommodation,[29] perform the essential functions of the job as determined by the employer.[30]

Employer: A person engaged in an industry affecting commerce, who has 25/15[31] or more employees for each working day in 20 or more calendar weeks per year.[32] Exceptions include the United States of America (federal government), any corporation wholly owned by the federal government, Indian tribes, or a bona fide private membership club (not a labor organization) which is exempt from taxation under §501(c) of the Internal Revenue Code of 1986.[33]

Table 1. Reasonable Accommodation in Employment–Definition and Examples

The Americans with Disabilities Act, section 101(9), states that "reasonable accommodation" may include (A) making existing facilities readily accessible to and useable by an individual with disabilities; and (B) job restructuring, part-time or modified work schedules, reassignment to a vacant position, acquisition or modification of equipment or devices, appropriate adjustment or modifications of examinations, training materials or policies, the provision of qualified readers or interpreters, and other similar accommodations for individuals with disabilities.

Impairment	Reasonable Accommodation	Rights
Hearing	Special equipment (e.g., telephone amplifier, flashing alarms) Assistance (interpreter) Modified work schedule Bring hearing dog	Employment can be denied only if it is a legitimate job requirement Promotion must be on the same terms as if not impaired
Visual	Special equipment (e.g., talking computer) Assistance (reader, note-taker) Modified work schedule Bring guide dog	Cannot be denied employment due to insurance costs, workers' compensation liability, preference of co-workers or clients Can deny employment only if it is a demonstrable safety hazard
Mobility	Special equipment Assistance Modified work schedule Accessibility to workplace (unless prohibitively expensive)	Cannot be denied employment due to insurance costs, workers' compensation liability, or the preferences of co-workers or clients All employee areas (restrooms, cafeterias) must be made accessible
Developmental Disability	Special equipment Assistance (special instruction)	Can be refused employment only if she or he cannot perform the job safely and efficiently

(Continued)

Impairment	Reasonable Accommodation	Rights
Learning Disability	Special equipment Assistance Modified work schedule Modified employment testing	Can be denied job if unable to perform safely and efficiently Same benefits as other employees Consider for promotion on an equal basis with others unless disability affects job performance
Mental Illness	Leave of absence for treatment	Can be denied job or promotion if she or he cannot perform job safely and efficiently Can be required to provide the results of a required psychological evaluation Not required to provide information about illness unless job related
Kidney Disorder	Special equipment Assistance Modified work schedule	Cannot be denied employment due to insurance costs May be required to provide results of a physical examination Cannot be fired unless problem affects ability to do job safely and efficiently Health risk associated with job must be demonstrable
Diabetes	Special assistance Special equipment Modified work schedule	Cannot to denied employment due to insurance costs, needs for leave of absence Can lose job if condition develops which affects ability to perform job safely and efficiently

(Continued)

Impairment	Reasonable Accommodation	Rights
Epilepsy	Equipment (safety switch) Informational training for co-workers	Cannot be denied employment unless safety risk is demonstrable in that job
		Cannot be denied employment due to insurance costs, workers' compensation liability, preferences of co-workers or clients
		May be required to provide results of physical examination
		Not required to provide information about illness unless it is job related

Commission: The Equal Employment Opportunity Commission.[34]

Auxiliary Aids and Services: By definition,[35] these include:

1. Qualified interpreters or other effective methods of making aurally delivered materials available to individuals with hearing impairments;
2. Qualified readers, taped texts, or other effective methods of making visually delivered materials available to individuals with visual impairments;
3. Acquisition or modification of equipment or devices; and
4. Other similar services and actions.

State: The ADA affects all states of the United States of America, as well as the District of Columbia, the Commonwealth of Puerto Rico, Guam, American Samoa, the Virgin Islands, the Trust Territory of the Pacific Islands, and the Commonwealth of the Northern Mariana Islands.[36]

Entity: Any employer, employment agency, labor organization, or joint labor-management committee.[37]

Direct Threat: A significant risk to the health or safety of others which cannot be eliminated by reasonable accommodation(s).[38]

Drugs: Any controlled substance defined in schedules I through V of section 202 of the Controlled Substances Act.[39]

Public Accommodations and Transportation ━━━

Outside the employment setting, privately owned and operated businesses and facilities designated as "places of public accommodation" also fall under the ADA. Hotels, restaurants, theaters, stadiums, convention centers, museums and libraries, schools, recreational facilities, and all sales and service establishments of any size (e.g., grocery and clothing stores, banks, hospitals, law offices), must follow the requirements of the ADA. These facilities are required to make their premises accessible to persons with disabilities by removing all architectural and communications barriers unless those changes cannot be done "without much difficulty or expense."

Ways by which the owners of these establishments must now make their premises more accessible include widening doors, installing ramps and elevators, installing Braille signs in elevators and other places, and connecting amplifying devices to telephones. Just how extensive the requirements will be is unclear because the business' available defense (of "undue hardship") is also not defined in detail. By way of example, however, it is possible that financial institutions will be required to lower their automated teller machines to make them more accessible to those confined in wheelchairs and possibly to equip them with electronic "voices" for visually impaired persons. Businesses sponsoring events may risk penalties if sign language interpreters are not provided.

Title III says that: *No individual shall be discriminated against on the basis of disability in the full and equal enjoyment of the goods, services, facilities, privileges, advantages, or accommodations of any place of public accommodation by any person who owns, leases (or leases to), or operates a place of public accommodation.*

Title III prohibits:

1. Denial of participation;
2. Unequal benefits; and
3. Separate benefits (except where necessary and equivalent).

Settings must be integrated wherever possible to provide equal benefits.

Key Definitions: Title III (Public Accommodations)

Private Entity: Any entity other than a public entity, as defined above.[40]

Public Accommodation: Private entities may be considered public accommodations if their operations affect commerce. These would include an inn, hotel, motel, or other place of lodging (except one of five or fewer rooms for rent which is occupied by the proprietor as his or her residence, such as a bed-and-breakfast); a restaurant, bar, or other establishment for serving food or drink; a cinema, theater, concert hall, stadium, or other place of exhibition or entertainment; an auditorium, convention center, lecture hall, or other place of public gathering; a bakery, grocery store, clothing store, hardware store, shopping center, or other sales or retail establishment; a laundromat, dry cleaner, bank, barbershop, beauty shop, travel service, shoe repair service, funeral parlor, gas station, office of an accountant or lawyer, pharmacy, insurance office, professional office of a health care provider, or other service establishment; a terminal, depot, or other station used for specified public transportation; a museum, library, gallery, or other place of public display or collection; a park, zoo, amusement park, or other place of recreation; a nursery, elementary, secondary, undergraduate, or postgraduate private school, or other place of education; a day care center, senior citizen center, homeless shelter, food bank, adoption agency, or other social service center establishment; or a gymnasium, health spa, bowling alley, golf course, or other place of exercise or recreation.[41]

Commercial Facilities: Any facility which is intended for nonresidential use and whose operation will affect commerce.[42]

Commerce: Travel, trade, traffic, commerce, transportation, or communication between or among any of these: the several states, any foreign country or territory or possession and any state, or between points in the same state if the journey passes through another state or a foreign country.[43]

Demand Responsive System: Any system providing transportation of individuals by vehicle, which is not a fixed-route system.[44] A "fixed-route system" is defined as one on which a vehicle is operated along a prescribed route according to a fixed schedule.[45]

Readily Achievable: Easily accomplished without undue difficulty or expense. Factors to be considered in determining whether the accommodation is readily achievable include the nature and cost of the accommodation; the overall financial resources of the facility (of both that specific outlet and the whole employer if it is a nationwide chain or has multiple offices); the number of persons employed both in that outlet and by the employer as a whole; the effect of the accommodation on the resources or operation of the outlet or employer; the geographic separation between the affected outlet and the employer as a whole; and the nature of the operation performed at the affected outlet.[46]

Companies providing public transportation also come within the ADA's coverage. Buses, subways, trains, and airplanes must modify their services to make them available to persons with disabilities. This includes not only the vehicles themselves, but also the stations or terminals where passengers wait. The only exception is for currently-in-force regulations created by the Federal Aviation Administration (see the separate section on the Air Carrier Access Act), which allows airline personnel to seat persons with disabilities in non-exit rows to ensure the safety of all passengers in the event of an emergency.

Title II states that: *No qualified individual with a disability shall, by reason of such disability, be excluded from participation in or be denied the benefits of the services, programs, or activities of a public entity, or be subjected to discrimination by any such entity.*

Title II covers all public air, rail, and bus transportation. *It includes all related facilities, such as terminals and stations.*

Title II - Part I

Intracity Bus and Rail

1. Paratransit is allowed *but only* if no alternative is available or
    if the alternative would be financially unreasonable;
2. New facilities must be accessible; existing facilities must be
    modified;
3. Public entities operating fixed-route systems *must* purchase
    only accessible vehicles (unless on National Register); and
4. One car per train *must* be accessible.

Title II - Part II

Intercity and Commuter Rail

1. One car per train *must* be accessible;
2. New cars *must* be accessible;
3. Rules apply to *single-level* cars, but not to *bi-level* cars; however,
    bi-level dining cars should be accessible; and
4. New facilities must be accessible; existing facilities must be
    modified.

Key Definitions: Title II (Public Services)

Public Entity: Any state or local government, including any department, agency,
special purpose district, or other instrumentality; or the National Railroad
Passenger Corporation and any commuter authority as defined in section 103(8)
of the Rail Passenger Service Act.[47]

Qualified Person with a Disability: Any individual with a disability who, with or
without reasonable modifications to rules, policies or practices of the public entity,
or by the removal of architectural, communication, or transportation barriers, or
by the provision of auxiliary aids and services, meets the essential requirements
for eligibility to receive the services offered by the public entity, or to participate
in programs or activities provided by the public entity.[48]

Telecommunications

Even the telephone companies face new obligations, because the ADA requires
them to provide services for the hearing and speech impaired so that persons who
use a telecommunications device for the deaf (TDD) will be able to communicate
with persons and entities who are not equipped with TDDs by way of a relay
service. Using these systems, one party calls an operator, who will speak to the
hearing party and will use a TDD to speak to the nonhearing or nonspeaking party.

Title IV provides for: *A rapid, nationwide communication service which*
includes *interstate and intrastate telecommunications relay services...to hearing-*
impaired and speech-impaired individuals.

Title IV requires that: *Each common carrier providing telephone voice transmission shall, not later than 3 years after the date of enactment..., provide...throughout the area in which it offers service, telecommunications relay services, individually,...*

Key definitions: Title IV (Telecommunications)

Common Carrier: Any common carrier engaged in interstate or intrastate communication by wire or radio.[49]

TDD: A *T*elecommunications *D*evice for the *D*eaf; a machine that uses graphic communication to transmit signals through a wire or radio communication system.[50]

Relay Service: Telephone transmission services that enable a hearing- or speech-impaired person to communicate with a person without an impairment, in a manner which is functionally equivalent to the way two persons who have no such impairment would communicate by telephone; a service which enables two-way communication between a person using a TDD and a person who does not use a TDD.[51]

Enforcement and Remedies

As with any law, the ADA would be of little use if it did not provide for penalties against those who do not comply. Each Title of the ADA lists not only the effective date of the provisions in that title (see the chart at the end of Appendix 3), but also provides information as to which entity is responsible for enforcement of the title, and what remedies are available.

Title I: Employment

The Equal Employment Opportunity Commission is responsible for enforcing the provision of Title I. The ADA states that it has the same "powers, remedies, and procedures set forth in sections 705, 706, 707, 709, and 710 of the Civil Rights Act of 1964."[52] These include working with regional, state, local, and other agencies; paying witness fees for witnesses summoned by the Commission; furnishing technical assistance to those who request it; assisting in conciliation or mediation attempts; making technical studies where necessary; intervening in a civil action where appropriate;[53] and conducting investigations.[54] A suit may be brought in the appropriate federal district court.[55]

Title II: Public Entities

If a public entity violates the rights of a qualified person with a disability, the ADA provides that "[t]he remedies, procedures, and rights set forth in section 505 of the Rehabilitation Act of 1973" shall apply.[56] This section references section 717 of the Civil Rights Act of 1964, and says that "a court may take into account the reasonableness of the cost of any necessary workplace accommodation, and the availability of alternatives therefore or other appropriate relief in order to achieve an equitable and appropriate remedy."[57] The court may also grant the prevailing party the right to collect attorney's fees from the other party.[58]

Title III: Public Accommodations by Private Entities

The Attorney General of the United States has the intermeshed duties of investigating allegations of violations of Title III of the ADA, and periodically reviewing how entities covered by Title III are complying with its requirements.[59] The Attorney General may, after notice and a public hearing, certify that state or local laws, regulations, building codes, or other ordinances establish accessibility requirements that meet or exceed the minimums established by the ADA.[60]

If the Attorney General finds there is either a pattern or practice of discrimination by a given entity or group of entities, or that the discrimination raises an issue of public importance, the Attorney General may file a civil suit in federal district court.[61] The court may take several actions, including:

1. a. Granting temporary, preliminary, or permanent relief;
    b. Providing an auxiliary aid or service, or modification of policy, practice, or procedure, or alternative method; and
    c. Making facilities readily accessible to and useable by individuals with disabilities;
2. May award such other relief as the court considers to be appropriate, including monetary damages to persons aggrieved when requested by the Attorney General; and
3. May, to vindicate the public interest, assess a civil penalty against the entity in an amount:
    a. Not exceeding $50,000 for a first violation; and
    b. Not exceeding $100,000 for any subsequent violation.[62]

The court will consider evidence of good faith compliance with Title III of the ADA, including whether the entity could have reasonably anticipated the need to provide the particular auxiliary aid being requested.[63]

The ADA also provides that no civil action can be brought for any act or omission which results in inaccessibility of a place of public accommodation, if it occurs within six months after the effective date of Title III for businesses employing 25 employees or fewer and having gross receipts of $1,000,000 or less; or if it occurs within one year after the effective date of Title III for businesses employing 10 employees or fewer and having gross receipts of $500,000 or less.[64]

Title IV: Telecommunications

The ADA changes the Communications Act of 1934 to provide for telecommunications relay services, and states that the Federal Communications Commission shall receive complaints alleging violations of Title IV, and that it shall resolve the complaint within 180 days.[65] The ADA also provides that the Federal Communications Commission has "the same authority, functions, and power with respect to common carriers engaging in intrastate communication as the Commission has...with respect to any common carrier engaging in interstate communication."[66]

Posting and Notice Requirements Under the ADA ━━━

This section describes the posting and notice requirements required under the ADA, 42 U.S.C.S. §§12101 *et. seq.* The posting and notice provision references both who is covered and the effective date provisions of the Act.

The posting notices provision is set forth near the beginning of the Act. The provision is set forth in 42 U.S.C.S. §12115 as follows:

> Every employer, employment agency, labor organization, or joint labor-management committee covered under this title shall post notices in an accessible format to applicants, employees, and members describing the applicable provisions of this Act, in the manner prescribed by §711 of the Civil Rights Act of 1964. (42 U.S.C. §2000e-10)[67]

(July 26, 1990, P.L. 1010336, Title I, §105, 104 Stat. 336).[68] The applicable provision of the Civil Rights Act of 1964 is as follows:

"Posting of notices; penalties

> A. Every employer, employment agency, and labor organization, as the case may be, shall post and keep posted in conspicuous places upon its premises where notices to employees, applicants for employment, and members are customarily posted a notice to be prepared or approved by the Commission setting forth excerpts from or summaries of, the pertinent provisions of this subchapter and information pertinent to the filing of a complaint.
> B. A willful violation of this section shall be punishable by a fine of not more than $100 for each separate offense.

Pub. L. 88-352, Title VII, §711, July 2, 1964, 78 Stat. 265

Section 1601.30 Chapter of the Code of Federal Regulations states:

> "A. Every employer, employment agency, labor organization, and joint labor-management committee controlling an apprenticeship or other training program, as the case may be, shall post and keep posted in conspicuous places upon its premises where notices to employees, applicants, for employment, members, and trainees, are customarily posted, the following notice:

EQUAL EMPLOYMENT OPPORTUNITY IS THE LAW
DISCRIMINATION IS PROHIBITED

> By the Civil Rights Act of 1964, as amended, and by Executive Order Numbers 11246 and 11375.

Americans with Disabilities Act
Effective Dates

Title	Who Will Be Affected	Date
Title I	Employers with 25 or more employees	July 26, 1992
	Employers with 15 or more employees	July 26, 1994
Title II	Local & State Governments	January 26, 1992
	Public transportation–accessible stations & paratransit	January 26, 1992
	one-car-per-train	July 26, 1995
	Amtrak: Must have half of cars accessible	July 26, 1995
	All cars must be accessible	July 26, 2000
	Key commuter stations must be accessible	July 26, 1993
	All stations must be accessible	July 26, 2010
Title III	Public Accommodations	
	Up to 25 employees and $1,000,000 revenues	July 26, 1992
	Up to 10 employees and $500,000 revenues	July 26, 1993
	Public Transportation by Private Entities	July 26, 1992
Title IV	24-hour Nationwide Relay Service	July 26, 1993

Title VII of the Civil Rights Act of 1964, as amended, administered by the Equal Employment Opportunity Commission prohibits discrimination because of Race, Color, Religion, Sex, or National Origin by employers with 15 or more employees, by Labor Organizations having a hiring hall of 15 or more members, by Employment Agencies, and by Joint Labor-Management Committees for Apprenticeship or Training.

Any person who believes he or she has been discriminated against should contact:

The Equal Employment Opportunity Commission, 2401 E Street, N.W., Washington, DC 20506 or any of its district offices.

Executive Order Numbers 11246 and 11375 administered by the Office of Federal Contract Compliance Programs prohibits discrimination because of Race, Color, Religion, Sex or National Origin, and requires affirmative action to ensure equality of opportunity in all aspects of employment by all Federal Governmental Contractors and Subcontractors, and by contractors and subcontractors performing work under a federally assisted construction contract regardless of the number of employees in either case.

Any person who believes he or she has been discriminated against should contact:

> The Office of Federal Contract Compliance Programs, U.S. Department of Labor, Washington, DC 21210.

B. Copies of such notice may be obtained on request from the Commission.

C. Section 711(b) of Title VII makes failure to comply with this section punishable by a fine of not more than $100 for each separate offense.

Case law that has arisen under this section of the statute has indicated that a labor organization's affirmative duty is limited to posting of notices. It is not required to seek out individuals for referral.[69] The courts have indicated, however, that failure to post notices describing employee's rights does result in an equitable tolling of the statute of limitations until the employee learns of his or her statutory right to nondiscrimination.[70] Additionally, the courts have held that an employer is equitably estopped from raising a defense that the discrimination action was time barred, because of its own failure to post notices as required.[71]

The posting notices provision applies to the same entities who are defined under *covered entity* in the act:

> The term *covered entity* means an employer, employment agency, labor organization, or joint labor-management committee.

Employer is defined as follows:

> The term *employer* means a person engaged in an industry affecting commerce who has 15 or more employees for each working day in each of 20 or more calendar weeks in the current or preceding calendar year, and any agent of such person, except that, for two years following the effective date of this title, an employer means a person engaged in an industry affecting commerce who has 25 or more employees for each working day in each of 20 or more calendar weeks in the current or preceding year, and any agent of such person (42 U.S.C.S. §12111 [4]).[72]

The exceptions to employer include the United States, a corporation wholly owned by the government of the United States, an Indian tribe; or a bona fide private posting on an elevated bulletin board. A visually impaired individual may not be able to read a posting with provisions in small print. In fact, another communication, in another form may have to be distributed to inform the blind (e.g., a tape recording of a message of rights of employees may have to be distributed or mode available to blind employees). However, it is not clear that the Justice Department and EEOC will interpret the effective dates in the same manner.

Notice posting requirements are certainly required by the act. However, at this point, the EEOC has not developed regulations for guidance, nor have there been developed a sample posting notice. It is reasonable to speculate that notice posting may be more extensive than the Title VII notice on which it is based in order to truly provide information to the disabled of their rights.

Conclusion

Passage of the ADA indicates a recognition, however belated, that persons with disabilities are entitled to the same opportunities as those without disabilities. We must hope that the enforcement policies and practices will support this.

Notes

[1] "The term *illegal use of drugs* means the use of drugs, the possession or distribution of which is unlawful under the Controlled Substances Act (21 U.S.C. §812). Such use does not include the use of a drug taken under supervision by a licensed health care professional or other uses authorized by the Controlled Substances Act or other provisions of Federal Law." Americans with Disabilities Act, P. L. 101-336, §101(6)A, §510(d)(1).

[2] Americans with Disabilities Act, P. L. 101-336, §104.

[3] Defined as "a controlled substance, as defined in schedules I through V of section 202 of the Controlled Substance Act." Americans with Disabilities Act, P. L. 101-336, §101(6)(B), §510(d)(2).

[4] Americans with Disabilities Act, P. L. 101-336, §104(a), §510(a).

[5] Americans with Disabilities Act, P. L. 101-336, §510(c).

[6] Americans with Disabilities Act, P. L. 101-336, §104(b)(1),(2), §510(b)(1),(2).

[7] Americans with Disabilities Act, P. L. 101-336, §104(b)(3), §510(b)(3).

[8] Americans with Disabilities Act, P. L. 101-336, §510(b).

[9] Americans with Disabilities Act, P. L. 101-336, §104(d)(2), §510(b). There is a specific exception for transportation employees, who may be randomly tested if they have safety-sensitive duties which an on-duty impairment would jeopardize. Americans with Disabilities Act, P. L. 101-336, §104(e).

[10] Americans with Disabilities Act, P. L. 101-336, §104(c).

[11] *Major life activities* include "caring for oneself, performing manual tasks, walking, seeing, hearing, speaking, breathing, learning and working." 45 CFR Subtitle A, §84.3(j)(2)(ii).

[12] 29 U.S.C. §706(7)(B) (1982). *See* 45 C.F.R. Subtitle A. §§84.3(j)(2)(iii),(iv).

[13] 29 U.S.C. §706(13)(1982).

[14] Americans with Disabilities Act, P. L. 101-336, §512(b), (c).

[15] 20 U.S.C. §140(a)(1) (1982).

[16] 20 CFR 404.1505(a), 404.1508; *see also* 42 U.S.C. §1382c (1982).

[17] Based upon the regulations at 20 CFR 404.1505 (1990); *see generally* 20 CFR Part 404.

[18] 42 U.S.C. §3602(h) (1982).

[19] Baxter V. City of Belleville, Illinois, 720 F.Supp. 720 (S.D. Ill. 1989); Association of Relatives and Friends of AIDS Patients (A.F.A.P.S.) v. Regulations and Permits Administration/Administracion de Reglamentos y Permisos, 740 F.Supp. 95 (D. Puerto Rico, 1990).

[20] 42 U.S.C. §3602(h) (1982).

[21] The person with disabilities may be accompanied by "a responsible adult passenger" who can assist with the understanding and compliance.

[22] However, the airlines may not require the passenger to sign a medical waiver or release form. Jacobson v. Delta Airlines, Inc., 742 F.2d 1202 (9th Cir. 1984), *cert. dismissed*, 471 U.S. 1062, 105 S.Ct. 2129, 85 L.Ed.2d 493.

[23] Anderson v. USAir, Inc., 619 F.Supp. 1191 (D.C.D.C.), *aff'd* 818 F.2d 49, 260 U.S.App. D.C. 183 (1985).

[24] Americans with Disabilities Act of 1990, P.L. 101-336, §3(2).

[25] 29 U.S.C. §§701 *et seq.* (1982).

[26] 42 U.S.C. §§3601-3619 (1982).

[27] 42 U.S.C. §§1301 & 1374 (1982).

[28] Americans with Disabilities Act of 1990, P. L. 101-336, §101(4).

[29] Americans with Disabilities Act of 1990, P. L. 101-336, §101(9) defines "reasonable accommodation" as:

> (A) making existing facilities used by employees readily accessible to and useable by individuals with disabilities; and
>
> (B) Job restructuring, part-time or modified work schedules, reassignment to a vacant position, acquisition or modification of equipment or devices, appropriate adjustment or modifications of examinations,

training manuals or policies, the provision of qualified readers or interpreters, and other similar accommodations for individuals with disabilities.

Note, however, if the accommodation causes "undue hardship," as defined in section 101(10), the employer may be released from the requirement of making that accommodation. Factors to be considered in determining whether the accommodation would impose an undue hardship include the nature and cost of the accommodation; the overall financial resources of the facility or employer, both that specific outlet and the whole employer if it is a nationwide chain or has multiple offices; the number of persons employed both in that office and by the employer as a whole; the effect of the accommodation on the resources or operation of the facility or employer; the geographic separation between the affected office and the employer as a whole; and the nature of the operation performed at the affected office.

[30] Americans with Disabilities Act of 1990, P. L. §101-336, 101(8). A written job description created before the employer began to advertise for or interview applicants will be considered evidence of the essential functions of the job.

[31] See the chart of Effective Dates to determine when the Americans with Disabilities Act begins to apply; employers with 25 or more employees must comply two years earlier than those with 15 or more employees. Also, these numbers *are total employees for the whole company*; an employer cannot avoid complying with the ADA by having fewer than 15 persons employed at any one office, facility, store, restaurant, etc.

[32] Americans with Disabilities Act of 1990, P. L. 101-336, §101(5)(A).

[33] Americans with Disabilities Act of 1990, P. L. 101-336, §101(5)(B).

[34] Americans with Disabilities Act of 1990, P. L. 101-336, §101(1).

[35] Americans with Disabilities Act of 1990, P. L. 101-336, §3(2).

[36] Americans with Disabilities Act of 1990, P. L. 101-336, §3(1).

[37] Americans with Disabilities Act of 1990, P. L. 101-336, §101(2); *see also* §101(7).

[38] Americans with Disabilities Act of 1990, P. L. 101-336, §101(3).

[39] Americans with Disabilities Act of 1990, P. L. 101-336, §101(6)(B); *see* 21 U.S.C. §§321 *et seq.*

[40] Americans with Disabilities Act of 1990, P. L. 101-336, §301(6).

[41] Americans with Disabilities Act of 1990, P. L. 101-336, §301(7).

[42] Americans with Disabilities Act of 1990, P. L. 101-336, §301(2). Railroad locomotives, freight cars, and cabooses; railroad cars described in §242 (regarding public transportation by intercity and commuter rail), railroad rights-of-way, or facilities covered or expressly exempted from coverage under the Fair Housing Act of 1968 (42 U.S.C. §§3601 *et seq.*)

[43] Americans with Disabilities Act of 1990, P. L. 101-336, §301(1).

[44] Americans with Disabilities Act of 1990, P. L. 101-336, §301(3); *vehicle* is defined in §301(11).

[45] Americans with Disabilities Act of 1990, P. L. 101-336, §301(4).

[46] 45 C.F.R., Subtitle A, §84.12.

[47] Americans with Disabilities Act of 1990, P. L. 101-336, 201(1); for the definition of "commuter authority," *see* 45 U.S.C. §§501 *et seq.*

[48] Americans with Disabilities Act of 1990, P. L. 101-336, §201(2).

[49] Americans with Disabilities Act of 1990, P. L. 101-336, §401(a)(1).

[50] Americans with Disabilities Act of 1990, P. L. 101-336, §401(a)(2).

[51] Americans with Disabilities Act of 1990, P. L. 101-336, §401(a)(3).

[52] Americans with Disabilities Act of 1990, P. L. 101-336, §107.

[53] 42 U.S.C. §2000e-4(g).

[54] 42 U.S.C. §2000e-8.

[55] 42 U.S.C. §2000e-5(h)(3). Section 2000e-5 as a whole delineates the Commission's ability to bring suit, (*see also* 42 U.S.C. §2000e-6) and includes commentary regarding the Commission's ability to use court action to compel compliance with court decisions, where necessary. 42 U.S.C. §2000e-5(i).

[56] Americans with Disabilities Act of 1990, P. L. 101-336, §203.

[57] 29 U.S.C. §794a(a)(1).

[58] 29 U.S.C. §794a(b).

[59] Americans with Disabilities Act of 1990, P. L. 101-336, §308(b)(1)(A)(i).

[60] Americans with Disabilities Act of 1990, P. L. 101-336, §308(b)(1)(A)(ii). The certification provides rebuttable evidence that the law, regulation, building code, or other ordinance meets or exceeds the minimums in the ADA, but this presumption may be countered by competent evidence.

[61] Americans with Disabilities Act of 1990, P. L. 101-336, §308(b)(1)(B).

[62] Americans with Disabilities Act of 1990, P. L. 101-336, §308(b)(2). The amount in part (B) does not include punitive damages. Americans with Disabilities Act of 1990, P. L. 101-336, §308(b)(4).

[63] Americans with Disabilities Act of 1990, P. L. 101-336, §308(b)(5).

[64] Americans with Disabilities Act of 1990, P. L. 101-336, §310(b). The exception applies only with regard to section 302 of the Americans with Disabilities Act of 1990, and specifically does not apply if the premises are new construction covered by section 303 of the Americans with Disabilities Act of 1990.

[65] Americans with Disabilities Act of 1990, P. L. 101-336, §401(e)(2).

[66] Americans with Disabilities Act of 1990, P. L. 101-336, §401(b)(2).

[67] 42 U.S.C. §2000e-10.

[68] July 26, 1990 P. L. 101-336, Title I, Section 105, 104 Stat. 336.

[69] Dobbins v. Int'l. Brotherhood of Elect. Workers, AFL-CIO, 292 F.Supp. 413 (D.C. Ohio 1968).

[70] Robinson v. Caulkins Indiantown Citrus Co., 701 F.Supp. 208 (S.D. Fla. 1988).

[71] Earnhardt v. Com. of Puerto Rico, 582 F.Supp. 25 (D.C. Puerto Rico), aff'd 744 F. 2d 1 (1983).

[72] 42 U.S.C.S. §1221(4)

Section II

Employment Issues and Answers

4

Issues in Recruitment and Selection

David Vandergoot, Ph.D.
Brian T. McMahon, Ph.D., C.R.C.

Considerations in Employee Recruitment ━━━━━━

One of the important values underlying the ADA is that persons with disabilities should have access to the same opportunities others have. This includes participating in the labor market. Employers use a variety of recruiting resources to generate job applicants needed for job openings and should continue to use those that have worked best for them. However, it is doubtful these resources will recruit many people with disabilities, who tend to look for jobs primarily through vocational rehabilitation agencies or friends and families. Many employers accept applications from acquaintances of their current employees, but probably have little background in working with rehabilitation programs. This chapter explores how these recruiting resources can be used more effectively. Other resources which could significantly improve the size and the quality of the applicant pool are described as well.

In keeping with the spirit of the ADA, employers might request that all their recruiting resources provide an ample supply of applicants with disabilities. It is likely that these recruiters are covered by the ADA also, and if they are in the business of providing job referral services, these must be accessible to people with disabilities. Employees should expect and demand quality referrals of applicants with disabilities from every recruiting resource used. Each one should be expected to ensure a good flow of qualified applicants with disabilities. Actively reaching out to qualified people with disabilities through recruiting resources will ultimately result in a high-quality work force.

Recruiting Internally

There are over 43 million people in the United States with disabilities. Twenty-three million are of working age. This is a sizable market. However, if one includes family members as part of this group, then it is likely that between 75 and 100 million persons are directly affected by disability. Many current employees know someone with a disability. Employers should make it known through newsletters, special announcements and postings, and policy statements, that current employees are encouraged to recruit their friends, family members, and acquaintances who have disabilities.

Some employers provide a bonus to employees who recommend a person to be hired. This would be a good motivator to stimulate referrals of persons with disabilities. These referrals provide excellent job candidates who typically share the same values as current employees. A current employee is not likely to risk his or her reputation by referring unqualified candidates. Since the employee knows the types of workers an employer wants, these referrals are usually well screened. This strategy also sends a message to employees that disability does not have to be a negative factor. Many people acquire disabilities over the course of their working lives. An employer that actively recruits applicants with disabilities using current employees sends a message to them that even if they acquire a disability, they are employed by an employer which values such workers.

There is one internal source available to many employers that is rarely considered. This source is the pool of persons who are employees but who are receiving workers' compensation or long-term disability benefits. Many of these persons have the potential to return to work. Their capabilities are known to employers, which have invested in them, both when they were actively working and while they have been unable to work. Many insurance carriers have begun rehabilitation programs and are willing to support the cost of rehabilitation if a return to work is possible. These are resources companies can use and/or recover. These formerly active employees are likely to welcome an inquiry about their capacity to come back to work.

Vocational Rehabilitation Agencies

State Rehabilitation Programs

Almost all communities have organizations that provide employment assistance to people with disabilities. Each state has a vocational rehabilitation agency which uses a combination of federal and state tax dollars to provide services including evaluation, training, and job placement. The federal government has encouraged state programs to reach out through active marketing campaigns to let employers know of the labor pool available to them through these agencies. Although states have responded well to this leadership, these agencies are quite small with limited funds and too few professionals to contact even a small percentage of employers. However, these agencies are easy to locate under state programs listed in telephone directories. Establishing contact with them will give an employer access to a diverse and large labor supply.

State rehabilitation agencies are the single largest recruiting resource of persons with disabilities. Agencies operate under a philosophy of providing a person with the support to reach their full potential and will frequently invest a great deal in an individual. This includes providing college education as well as other types of education and skill training. Thus, it is possible to gain access to highly skilled people through the state agencies. However, these agencies are required to serve all people with disabilities, including those who compete for lower level or unskilled positions that are characteristic of the "secondary labor market" (i.e., associated with low wages, high turnover, inferior benefits, and undesirable working conditions). Special supported employment programs have been set up to equip persons with the capabilities to fill these positions very successfully.

Probably the best way to work with state agencies is to request that one or two rehabilitation professionals serve as liaisons with the employer's human resources representatives. These individuals should be given a thorough orientation to the human resources needs of the employer. Tours of employers' facilities would be very useful, and would enable liaisons to match appropriate candidates to the types of jobs available. The rehabilitation professionals could also help a company identify possible areas needing accommodations under the ADA. As job openings occur, employer representatives could inform the liaisons who would review rosters to see if qualified candidates with disabilities were available. This service is free to employers. Other benefits are available through state agencies, including possible tax advantages for hiring persons with disabilities and making reasonable accommodations. State agencies also, on occasion, can provide additional assistance to a new employee (e.g., training support, purchase of tools, counseling) to ensure that the job goes well.

Nonprofit Rehabilitation Programs

Many communities have other programs serving persons with disabilities, such as those affiliated with Goodwill Industries, Easter Seals, or United Cerebral Palsy, although a majority of them are independent. Often these programs are closely tied with the state agency, which subsidizes them to provide many of the employment services previously described. Therefore, a relationship with the state agency will also provide access to applicants from these nonprofit programs. However, an employer should develop relationships with both. The nonprofit programs can usually provide more direct assistance on behalf of a person since they do not serve as many persons as the state agency. They tend to know the individuals better and can assess which candidates are likely to be the best matches. Staff of these programs typically have more time to give personal attention to the candidate and the employer during the recruiting process.

Employers are advised to establish the same type of liaison with representatives of these programs as they do with the state agency. Even in large metropolitan areas, it is unlikely that more than three or four of these programs exist. After initial contacts are made and liaisons become familiar with company needs, simple phone contacts are usually all that is needed for them to review their candidates to see if any meet job requirements. An employer can gain access to additional resources and expertise by maintaining liaisons with the state agency and the nonprofit programs since they both work together to build a person's employment potential.

Programs Representing Persons with Disabilities

Independent Living Centers

There are an increasing number of organizations which promote equal access and community opportunities for people with disabilities. Patterning their efforts after the civil rights movement of the sixties, persons with disabilities banded together and actively challenged society to institute changes that would give them the same cultural, social, and economic opportunities enjoyed by others. This led to the independent living movement of the seventies, which is still growing in popularity today. Many communities have independent living centers, which are nonprofit programs run by people with disabilities to promote the interests of all those with disabilities. These are self-help organizations, and as such, they usually do not provide the same type of employment services as rehabilitation programs. For example, they rarely provide the same type of prescreening and job-matching services. Their main value as recruiting resources is that they have communitywide contacts with many people with disabilities. Independent living centers are communication hubs for the disability community. A great number of persons can be reached through their newsletters, events, and networks.

These centers inform many potential candidates of job openings. Employers should initiate contacts with the independent living centers. The centers usually can be identified through local rehabilitation programs. Placing position announcements with them will tap into a large supply of potential applicants and there will probably be no fee for this service. It might also be wise to consider placing paid advertisements of employer goods and/or services in publications of these centers, if this option exists. This will accomplish several things. It will demonstrate that an employer is indeed aware of the disability community and willing to invest in it. As stated earlier, this is a large consumer group with considerable purchasing power. As people with disabilities become aware of an employer's goods and services, they are more likely to consider purchasing them and also working for the company. Having a relationship with an independent living program is likely to foster good will for an employer in the community and make it easier to attract applicants with disabilities.

Local Chapters of National Organizations

There are many organizations which have a mission to meet the needs of people who have a particular disability. The American Federation for the Blind and the National Multiple Sclerosis Society are examples. Many communities have local chapters. Since membership is usually limited to those with the disability of concern, the potential applicant pool is not as large as might be tapped through independent living centers. However, these organizations have newsletters, events, and networks through which position announcements can be made. Perhaps the most efficient way to work with these groups is to send them announcements of job openings which can be circulated to their members. They are typically not in a position to provide recruiting services beyond this. Although few applicants can be expected through these resources, some might develop. However, using these organizations in even the small way suggested here is likely to lead to good will for a company in the local community.

Governors' and Mayors' Committees for the Employment of Persons with Disabilities

Each state has followed the lead of the President's Committee on Employment for Persons with Disabilities by creating Governors' Committees that seek to promote the employment of people with disabilities. The major focus of these programs is to create greater awareness of how these people can fill the labor market requirements of businesses. In some larger cities, Mayors' Committees have been set up as well. These programs use a variety of public relations efforts to acquaint the business community with the potential of persons with disabilities and the recruiting services available through local vocational rehabilitation programs. The committees rarely provide services on their own. Rather, they tend to look for ways to link organizations that support persons with disabilities to those businesses that have a current demand for qualified workers. Committees have sponsored task forces of employers to define work force needs. Committees then work with rehabilitation programs to define ways they can provide better recruiting services to employers. As a result, rehabilitation programs have established job referral networks which pool their applicants to improve the chances a worker will be found to match an employer's job order. An employer then has a single point of contact to tap into all the community rehabilitation recruiting resources. This greatly reduces the time spent in advertising position openings. State and local committees have also encouraged Job Fairs that bring together many eligible applicants and employers who can mutually evaluate each other to see if good matches exist. These fairs represent convenient and inexpensive ways for an employer to quickly review many potential candidates for job openings. Committees can help employers gain access to many other community resources. Employers can locate committees in telephone directories or through the state vocational rehabilitation agency.

State Employment Agencies

These state agencies maintain rosters of persons who are looking for work and accept job orders from employers. The main service, which is free, is to match persons on the roster to the job openings. This is an inexpensive system to use but the actual number of jobs filled is usually quite small. However, these employment agencies have agreements with the state vocational rehabilitation agencies and can specifically target persons with disabilities upon request. They also make special efforts to find employment for veterans, including those with disabilities. Since these agencies are so easy to use, they should be part of any employer's regular recruiting strategies.

For-Profit Employment Agencies

The expense associated with these agencies is usually the greatest to employers, but often leads to hiring persons who are the most desirable. Private employment agencies are not the best resources to use to recruit persons with disabilities since they rarely use these agencies as part of their job search strategies. However, many of these for-profit agencies are also covered by the ADA and must provide the same services to persons with disabilities as they do to others. Employers should expect to get an adequate number of persons with disabilities referred to them through these for-profit agencies and should make this expectation clear. Requests for these referrals should be made and, if not forthcoming, additional pressure added with the possibility of going to other sources which might do a better job of recruiting persons with disabilities. In this way, employers can fulfill the expectations of the ADA by creating a demand for people with disabilities among these for-profit agencies which typically do not make active efforts to recruit them. With these expectations placed upon them, for-profit agencies will be more inclined to seek out and serve persons with disabilities.

School-based Placement Services

Local Schools

During the last 10 years, national and state governments have emphasized reducing the high dropout rate of students from high schools. One group with a particularly high dropout rate has been students with disabilities. To reverse this trend, schools have developed programs to keep youth in school and to transition them into desirable postsecondary outcomes, including competitive employment. Vocational education has been one approach that has the potential of keeping these at-risk students involved in completing their education. These programs are more reality-based and permit students to demonstrate talents that traditional academic coursework would not require.

Schools have worked to broaden their vocational offerings and to include more students with disabilities in these courses. Many schools have turned to local employers to provide information about the types of skills in demand for which students should receive training. In this way, schools have attempted to provide programs that enable graduates to be competitive in local labor markets. Frequently, schools look for opportunities to provide some of this training "on-the-job" through work experience programs in cooperation with local employers. This enables students to receive a wider diversity of training, including the valuable experience of learning the interpersonal skills necessary to retain a job.

Employers also benefit from providing this work experience since it gives them an opportunity to train prospective employees in skills specific to their needs at very little cost. The schools also provide additional support to the students to help them adjust from a school to a work environment. There are no requirements to hire a student after training is completed. However, if an employer has an opening and has valued the student's work, a job offer is frequently made. It is not necessary to participate in the training programs to hire a graduate. The schools typically provide job placement assistance and have the personnel to work with employers who are interested in hiring. Students with disabilities often are also served by the state rehabilitation agency so the benefits of working through these agencies can be added to those to be obtained from the schools. Simply contacting the local high school can lead to youth and young adults who are anxious to begin their careers and who would value entry level positions.

College Placement Services

Most colleges and universities have been required to accommodate students with disabilities for almost 20 years, according to section 504 of the Rehabilitation Act of 1973. All programs offered by these schools must be accessible to these students with disabilities, including placement services. Many employers, particularly larger ones, are traditional users of these placement programs. Students with disabilities should be of the same quality as any of the other recruits obtained through the placement service. As with other recruiting services, companies should clearly state their expectations that students with disabilities be available through any of the services offered, particularly for interviewing when employer's representatives visit. If these students do not appear to be available through these means, employers should contact the many campus offices that have been created to serve the needs of students with disabilities. These are often called Disabled

Student Services Offices and they can work with the placement services program to ensure that students with disabilities are all adequately served.

Considerations in Employee Selection

Pre-employment screening is a valuable process which reveals capabilities persons are likely to use in the successful performance of available jobs. If done well, screening for the best people is worth the required investment of time and money. The ADA expects companies to give people with disabilities an equal chance at competing for jobs. It does not require companies to hire people with disabilities who are not qualified for openings. Companies should continue to screen applicants as they usually do, but use some precaution to ensure that these processes do not in some way discriminate on the basis of disability.

Reasonable Accommodation

The ADA requires companies to consider the impact of reasonable accommodations when determining the qualifications of a person with a disability. Reasonable accommodations refer to job modifications, environmental changes, equipment, special tools and devices, and other approaches that enable a person with a disability to perform job tasks that he or she could not do otherwise, but which he or she is qualified to do with the accommodation. For example, many jobs require or expect the worker to communicate using the telephone. Persons with certain hearing impairments may not be able to do this particular job function, but can do all other aspects of the job. There are technological devices and systems, and other options, which permit a person with a hearing impairment to communicate over the telephone and, therefore, with reasonable accommodation could perform the job.

Employees are expected to evaluate a person's qualifications with potential *reasonable* accommodations in mind. A qualified person is one who has the necessary education, experience, and skills in his or her background to compete for a job. The ADA expects companies to provide accommodations if the person with a disability is judged to be qualified. If these are not provided to an otherwise qualified person, a company is open to a charge of discrimination. However, a company may defend against such a charge if it can show that providing accommodations would be an "undue hardship." The ADA provides general guidelines for determining what is an undue hardship. Basically, the costs of accommodating a person would be weighed against the resources and capacity of the company to afford it. Congress has legislated some relief for companies through tax credits and incentives, and state vocational rehabilitation agencies might also provide assistance.

The concept of reasonable accommodations has been in practice for Federal government agencies, grantees, and contractors since 1973. Research on the costs of accommodations made by these employers shows that over 50% cost nothing and that 80% of accommodations cost less than $500. The average cost per accommodation is about $260. Typically, the amount spent on these accommodations is far outweighed by the productive capacity an individual will be able to give a company over his or her tenure on the job (Berkley Planning Associates, 1982).

This chapter outlines a process for screening individuals with disabilities and illustrates how reasonable accommodations can be applied at every step. Screening typically begins with a review of documents, such as a resumé or application form, and proceeds to a personal contact with those applicants possessing the apparent job qualifications. Formal or informal criteria are usually in place for evaluation and comparison of applicants. The ADA requires that every person be given equal opportunity to access all the screening steps, that the criteria are unrelated to disability, and that all criteria be applied equally to all candidates. Since the ADA uses the phrase "essential functions of the job" in relation to these hiring criteria, the next section will take an in-depth look at the concept of essential functions.

Essential Functions of the Job

Knowing the essential functions of the job are important for at least two reasons under the ADA. First, these functions are assumed to reflect the fundamental (not marginal) performance requirements of the job. These must be known to determine if a person with a disability is qualified with or without reasonable accommodations. Second, all criteria, or standards, used by a company to select employees must be valid predictors of successful performance on the job.

Employers are obligated to screen individuals with disabilities giving consideration to how reasonable accommodations can improve their performance expectations. Accommodations can take many different forms depending on the tasks of the job. Unless these tasks are clearly specified, including the tools, materials, knowledge, and other relevant factors needed on the job, it will not be possible to thoroughly review those accommodations which have a potential impact.

Companies frequently use a variety of employment tests to help provide information about the capacities of applicants. These can be paper-and-pencil tests, task simulations, or structured exercises. The ADA requires that there is a demonstrated relationship between these tests and the job. One clear way of providing evidence of the validity of criteria based on such tests is to show that performance on the tests has a relationship to performance on essential job functions.

The ADA recognizes that company personnel are likely to be the best judges of the essential functions of jobs within companies. The best way for an employer to establish and document essential functions is within job descriptions. Accurate descriptions should be in place for all jobs currently available at the time the ADA is enforced. This will provide evidence that an employer did not prepare any job description to avoid hiring any particular individual with a disability. These descriptions should clearly specify all tasks, knowledge, standards, tools, machines, processes, and materials that are part of the job. These descriptions should be made available to all applicants. Those with disabilities may be able to suggest reasonable accommodations with which they are familiar and, perhaps, have a rehabilitation professional review it for other possibilities. The ADA states that technical assistance will be available to employers and that ignorance of reasonable accommodation options is not a defense against discrimination charges. If employment tests are used, the applicants should be informed of their purpose and their relevance to the selection process. This assumes the company can document objective evidence of the validity of these tests. Again, companies should obtain evidence of job-relatedness of tests before they are used to evaluate candidates with disabilities. If such evidence is not available for certain tests, their use should be discontinued. Regardless of relevance of the ADA, eliminating the use of invalid tests will be of value since it will make the selection process more efficient and effective.

The EEOC regulations to implement the equal employment provisions of the ADA provide the following additional information regarding essential functions:

> (1) In general. The term 'essential functions' means the fundamental job duties of the employment position the individual with a disability holds or desires. The term 'essential functions' does not include the marginal functions of the position.

> (2) A job function may be considered essential for any of several reasons, including but not limited to the following:

>> (a) The function may not be essential because of the limited number of employees available among whom the performance of that job function can be distributed; and/or
>> (b) The function may be highly specialized so that the incumbent in the position is hired for his or her expertise or ability to perform the particular function.

> (3) Evidence of whether a particular function is essential includes, but is not limited to:

>> (a) The employer's judgment as to which functions are essential;
>> (b) Written job descriptions prepared before advertising or interviewing applicants for the job;
>> (c) The amount of time spent on the job performing the function;
>> (d) The consequences of not requiring the incumbent to perform the function;
>> (e) The terms of a collective bargaining agreement;
>> (f) The work experience of past incumbents in the job; and/or
>> (g) The current work experience of incumbents in similar jobs.

The Interpretive Guidance on Title I of the ADA provide even further clarification of essential functions (Appendix to Part 1630.2 (n); see Appendix 3).

Applications

Completing application forms is a standard practice that almost all companies use. The ADA mandates that companies do not discriminate against people with disabilities in the application process or in the use of information obtained from that process.

The application process must be accessible to people with disabilities. If individuals cannot apply for jobs, they cannot work. First, they must have access to the personnel or managerial staff who conduct the hiring process. Several issues must be considered here. Obviously, the physical environment must be accessible. For people with mobility impairments and those who use wheelchairs, this may require reserved parking places marked expressly for drivers with disabilities. It may also require entry and exit points that are free from steps and have easy-to-open doors. Public areas (e.g., reception, waiting, and rest rooms) should be spacious enough to permit use by these applicants. In any case, since the personnel offices are frequently visited by current employees who may have disabilities, the need for providing access to personnel functions is apparent.

The second concern is to ensure that the application forms do not pose barriers to persons with disabilities. For individuals who cannot see the forms well enough or who cannot read them, accommodations will have to be made. For persons with low vision, large print forms may be sufficient. For those with no vision, Braille instructions would be desirable to permit the applicant to read independently. Another alternative would be to provide a person to serve as a reader who could also complete the form under direction from the applicant. Local community agencies serving persons with visual impairments can provide guidance on how to provide accommodations.

Care must be taken to encourage persons with little or no reading ability to be forthright in revealing this and that assistance is available without fear of penalty. Many persons have learning disabilities which hinder their ability to read well enough to complete the application forms. Due to discrimination experienced in the past, many do not want to acknowledge this limitation and find the application process to be embarrassing. Simply posting signs encouraging persons to request reading assistance is not sufficient for obvious reasons. Staff persons administering the application process should openly request of applicants if any assistance might be needed and to provide it in a sensitive way. Any company operating in this fashion will send a clear signal that it is a good company to work for and further the process of establishing loyalty and dedication among employees.

A final concern must be given to what information is requested on the application form itself. A company may not ask if a person has a disability since the label itself has no bearing on what a person can or cannot do. Experience and research have shown that persons with the same disability may have widely divergent abilities, knowledge, and interests. A company may ask if a person can do the essential functions of a job being sought. For this to be done, however, the job and its essential functions should be described to applicants. Since this may be difficult to do, it may be best to limit the information collected on application forms to biographical data that are relevant to qualifications (e.g., education, work history factors). In some instances, it may be obvious that persons completing the forms have disabilities. If their education and work histories are comparable to other applicants they must be given equal consideration. Simply having knowledge that a person has a disability has no bearing on whether he or she can do the jobs under question. If an applicant's education and work background is comparable to those of others who are invited to continue the screening process, then they should continue also to ensure that discrimination on the basis of disability is avoided.

Tests and Other Formal Screening Practices

Many companies use performance tests of one kind or another to help predict candidates with the best potential of being successful on the job. Paper-and-pencil tests, task simulations, job samples, and other criterion reference tests have been developed as selection tools. The ADA speaks to two issues regarding these tools. First, as already stated, these tests must be valid predictors of how persons actually perform the essential functions of the job. A company must be able to show that the tests measure job-related performance and that the performances measured actually reflect essential job functions. Although not directly stated, these tests would have to be routinely given to all candidates. Tests cannot be used only for applicants with disabilities since this would amount to discriminating on the basis of disability.

Secondly, the ADA is quite clear that these tests must not adversely impact on people with disability because of the nature of their disabilities. For example, many tests require reading to complete the test, but reading itself may not be an essential function of the job. Someone being tested to operate a motor vehicle may be asked to complete a written test regarding traffic laws. This test may relate to an essential function of the job, operating a vehicle within the law, and it may be a good predictor of job performance. However, someone with a learning disability may have a difficult time responding to the test and fail to pass it, not because of ignorance of the law but because of poor reading ability.

If a situation exists in which a person's disability interferes with performance on a screening test, the ADA requires that reasonable accommodations be provided to remove the barrier created by disability. For someone with a learning disability who does not read well, written tests might be administered orally or by audiotape recordings. Persons with hearing impairments may need to have interpreters present during test situations so that they have an opportunity to learn instructions and clarify them. Adaptive equipment would be essential to providing fair competition for individuals with little use of their hands and arms who wish to work at occupations requiring use of the telephone and who are tested using telephone equipment during the screening process.

One final note regarding formal screening procedures: the environment in which the screening is to take place must be accessible to persons with disabilities. Not only must they be able to get to the testing site, they should have access to other facilities such as rest rooms, drinking fountains, and parking. Dealing with the physical environment should not be stressful or physically taxing to the extent that it would hinder performance on the screening tests.

The EEOC regulations to implement the equal employment provisions of the ADA provide the following additional information regarding qualification standards, test, and other selection criteria:

> It is unlawful for a covered entity to use qualification standards, employment tests or other selection criteria that screen out or tend to screen out an individual with a disability or a class of individuals with disabilities, on the basis of disability, unless the standard, test or other selection criteria, as used by the covered entity, is shown to be job-related for the position in question and is consistent with business necessity.

It is unlawful for a covered entity to fail to select and administer tests concerning employment in the most effective manner to ensure that, when a test is administered to a job applicant or employee who has a disability that impairs sensory, manual, or speaking skills, the test results accurately reflect the skills, aptitude, or whatever other factor of the applicant or employee that the test purports to measure, rather than reflecting the impaired sensory, manual, or speaking skills of such employee or applicant (except where such skills are the factors that the test purports to measure).

The Interpretive Guidance on Title I of the ADA provide even further clarification regarding these issues (Appendix to Part 1630.10, 1630.11; see Appendix 3).

Interviewing and Medical Examinations

The interview is a critical event for the company as well as the applicant. Two decisions need to be made correctly if the interview process is to be successful. The company must decide which applicant is best. The applicant who is offered the job also must decide if the company is a good one to work for. The quality of the information exchanged is key to making the right decisions. Research suggests that an honest exchange of information that helps each party set appropriate expectations leads to the most satisfactory employment decisions. This requires that the positives and the negatives of the job and the applicant be examined. Both parties should be forthright in exploring all the pros and cons. If this approach is part of the typical interviewing process, then people with disabilities will have a good climate in which to apply for jobs.

Before good communication can occur, the interviewer must be sure that a person can participate in the interview so that his or her qualifications can be fairly represented. For example, someone with a hearing impairment who knows sign language will need to have an interpreter present. As with any personnel process, the ADA requires that the interview also be reasonably accommodated.

In spite of the care given to the hiring process, interviewers should be trained to assess applicants with disabilities fairly. Attitudes about disability, particularly those that attribute too much to the impact of disability, or not enough, are common in our society. Research has found that there are even those who blame persons for having a disability. Interviewers must be clear about their attitudes and be sure that inappropriate ones do not interfere with their decision making. They must realize that the impact of disability cannot be stereotyped. The experience of disability impacts on each person in a unique way.

To comply with the ADA, interviewers should not ask applicants if they have a disability. Again, under the law and in fact, the presence of a disability is irrelevant to the issue of selecting a qualified candidate for a job. However, the interviewer may inquire about the capabilities of a person to perform the essential functions of the job. It is at this point that the interviewer should also invite the applicant to suggest any reasonable accommodations that enhance ability to perform these essential functions. The applicant is likely to be the best informed person about possible accommodations for the job being considered.

It is good personnel practice to ensure that each candidate interviewed be thoroughly knowledgeable about the job under consideration. This is especially true for people with disabilities. The more awareness of the job an applicant has the more he or she can suggest reasonable accommodations. The individual may already have the accommodation needed and would be willing to bring it to the job at no cost to the company. However, whether a person offers this or not should have no bearing on the hiring decision unless the accommodation needed would meet the "undue hardship" provision under which a company could be released from the obligation to provide a reasonable accommodation.

To screen someone fairly these steps should be taken:

1) A thorough explanation of all job requirements is provided.
2) Relevant information about an applicant's qualifications, including the availability of reasonable accommodations is obtained.
3) The qualifications to be used in judging candidates are openly reviewed and feedback given about how the applicant measures up.
4) The interviewer does a self-assessment after the interview to ensure that personal attitudes about disability are not affecting the judgements made about the candidate.
5) Consideration is given to reasonable accommodations. Local rehabilitation professionals are good consultants about the types of accommodations that are available and how they might be provided, including sharing of costs.

These steps should lead to appropriate decisions being made, ones that are fair to the company as well as to the person with a disability. Regardless of decision made, a careful record should be maintained outlining the information obtained from the steps listed above. This record should note the decision made and the reasons. This last step should ensure that no reason based solely on disability was used in the selection process.

Medical examinations are occasionally used to screen a person's ability to work at a specific job. The ADA is quite clear about how these examinations must be administered to ensure that they are not used unfairly with persons who have disabilities. The ADA does not permit any medical examination or procedure to be done as part of pre-employment screening. However, pre-employment inquiries are allowed as long as the questions relate to how well someone can do the essential functions of the job. Medical examinations and procedures are permitted after a job offer is made and results can be used to condition an offer only if certain requirements are met. These are:

1) All employees being considered for the job are examined in the same way.
2) If examination results are used as screening criteria, they must relate to essential functions of the job.

The ADA also requires that information gathered from these examinations be kept in medical files separate from regular personnel files and that they be confidential. Supervisors should only know what is necessary for providing reasonable accommodations and for implementing restrictions of tasks on duties, if these are necessary. The information can also be made available to first aid or safety personnel in case emergency medical treatment is required. Persons, including medical personnel, who will use the information from the medical examination to make decisions about a person's employment must know essential functions of the jobs for which the individual is being considered. This again reinforces the need for job descriptions which define specifically what a job requires.

Finally, the ADA specifically permits testing for illegal use of drugs. Drug tests are not regarded as medical examinations for employment purposes. Companies may elect to apply these tests to applicants or employees. The ADA specifically acknowledges that certain occupations, such as those in the transportation industry, may require such testing to ensure the welfare of the public. The ADA in no way restricts the use of such tests in these instances. The ADA does not recognize that a person actively abusing illegal substances has a disability. Applicants or employees abusing illegal drugs are not protected by the ADA. A company may elect to impose penalties on these workers and not be exposed to charges of discrimination.

The EEOC regulation to implement the equal employment provisions of the ADA provide the following additional information regarding pre-employment inquiries and medical examinations:

> 1630.13(a) Pre-employment examination or inquiry. Except as permitted by section 1630.14, it is unlawful for a covered entity to conduct a medical examination of an applicant or to make inquiries as to whether an applicant is an individual with a disability or as to the nature of severity of such disability.

> 1630.14(a) Acceptable pre-employment inquiry. A covered entity may make pre-employment inquiries into the ability of an applicant to perform job-related functions, and/or may ask an applicant to describe or to demonstrate how, with or without reasonable accommodation, the applicant will be able to perform job-related functions.

> 1630.14(b) Employment entrance examination. A covered entity may require a medical examination (and/or inquiry) after making an offer of employment to a job applicant and before the applicant begins his or her employment duties, and may condition an offer of employment on the results of such examination (and/or inquiry), if all entering employees in the same job category are subjected to such an examination (and/or inquiry) regardless of disability.

> (1) Information obtained under paragraph (b) of this section regarding the medical condition or history of the applicant shall be collected and maintained on separate forms and in separate medical files and be treated as a confidential medical record, except that: (i) Supervisors and managers may be informed regarding necessary restrictions on the work or duties of the employee and necessary accommodations; (ii) First aid and safety personnel may be informed, when appropriate, if the disability

might require emergency treatment; and (iii) Government officials investigating compliance with this part shall be provided relevant information on request.

(2) The results of such examination shall not be used for any purpose inconsistent with this part.

(3) Medical examinations conducted in accordance with this section do not have to be job-related and consistent with business necessity. However, if certain criteria are used to screen out an employee or employees with disabilities as a result of such an examination or inquiry, the exclusionary criteria must be job-related and consistent with business necessity, and performance of the essential job functions cannot be accomplished with reasonable accommodation as required in this part. (See section 1630.15 [b] Defenses to charges of discriminatory application of selection criteria.)

The Interpretive Guidance on Title I of the ADA provide even further clarification regarding pre-employment inquiries and medical examinations (Appendix to Part 1630.13(a); 1630.14 (a)(b)(d); see Appendix 3).

Summary

Employers are encouraged to actively recruit persons with disabilities through whatever means they currently use to attract good candidates. People with disabilities should have access to all these job lead resources. Even when using the want ads and other advertising media, employers should mention their willingness to consider persons with disabilities. Employers that recruit at professional conferences and trade organization meetings should solicit the participation of people with disabilities. These actions do not have to be viewed as good will gestures, although it may be favorably seen as such by many. Rather, such activities should be a part of an employer's strategy to attract the best available employees. After all, the ADA only requires that an employer hire persons with disabilities who are qualified to perform the essential functions of jobs. The more candidates an employer recruits the greater chance it will have to select qualified people. Many persons with disabilities are both available and qualified.

The ADA expects that persons with disabilities will be given an equal opportunity to compete with other persons for available jobs. The ADA does not require affirmative action. It does require, and suggests procedures to guarantee, that the qualifications of applicants to perform essential job tasks be given the greatest weight in making personnel decisions. Complying with the ADA will ensure that companies offer positions to applicants with the best qualifications, regardless of whether they have disabilities.

Reference

Berkley Planning Associates. (1982). A study of accommodations provided to handicapped employers by federal contractors: A final report. (Contract No. J-9-E-1-009). Washington, DC: U.S. Department of Labor, Employment Standards Administration.

disabilities who notify the company of a need for accommodation after failing to meet company standards (or after exceeding the above guidelines), may be accommodated upon retesting. The normal retest period, however, would apply.

Verification of Need for Accommodation

Unless the need for accommodation is readily apparent (e.g., candidate has lost both arms and is required to take a paper-and-pencil test), candidates requesting accommodation may be asked to provide written documentation of their need for accommodation at or before the (IAD). This documentation should be provided by a doctor, counselor, psychologist, speech therapist, or other relevant licensed professional. The documentation should be on original office letterhead and should include:

1) The qualifications of the professional;
2) The date of the candidate's most recent visit (should be within the last three years);
3) A brief description of how the candidate's disability would affect the ability to pass the test in its current format (e.g., unable to process visual information); and
4) The documentation may also include suggestions regarding possible accommodations (optional).

For this documentation to be most useful, the professional may be supplied with information about the test, focusing on the nature and modality of the test items. Pretest information pamphlets would be useful but may not be sufficient in all circumstances. Should interviewers doubt the qualifications of the professional or the authenticity of the documentation, or have any other concerns about the documentation, they should consult with their supervisor.

Individual Accommodation Discussion (IAD)

The IAD should be conducted by an experienced interviewer who is familiar with the objectives and requirements of the ADA. The interviewer should also become familiar with the requirements of the targeted job and the circumstances of the candidate's situation in advance of the IAD.

While it is preferable to hold the IAD in person, it may be held over the telephone if circumstances warrant. Accommodations may be required to hold the discussion (e.g., scheduling the discussion in an accessible location, providing a sign language interpreter). At the start of the discussion, the candidate should be informed of the purpose of the meeting. The interviewer should emphasize that the meeting is strictly informational and that suggestions or recommendations regarding accommodations which are discussed in the meeting will not necessarily imply a commitment on the part of the organization or the candidate. The interviewer should document the entire IAD in detail.

The IAD should address the following areas at a minimum:

The Nature of the Job

First, the interviewer should read along with the candidate the essential job functions from the job description or position request. The interviewer may objectively elaborate on the functions described, especially with regard to performance and attendance standards, but should neither add nor exaggerate performance requirements. After each essential function is read, the interviewer may ask candidates if they are able to perform that function.

Next, the interviewer should review with the candidate those essential functions and performance standards most likely to be affected by the candidate's circumstances. If candidates reply that they would be able to perform the essential functions of the job, the interviewer should ask if they would require accommodations to do so. If candidates state that they are unable to perform any essential function of the job because of their disability, the interviewer should ask if there are any accommodations that would enable the candidate to effectively perform the essential function.

Candidates who state that they would be able to perform the essential functions of the job but would require accommodations may be asked to describe the accommodations they would require. Candidates should be probed for any additional information they can provide about the accommodations (e.g., the manufacturer of a particular piece of equipment). Candidates are not required, however, to know all the necessary specifics about the accommodations they request.

If, at any time, an interviewer is unconvinced about a candidate's stated ability to perform the essential functions of the job or is unfamiliar with how an accommodation would enable the candidate to perform the job, he or she may ask the candidate to explain or demonstrate how they would be able to perform those functions. In such instances, it may be necessary to provide an accommodation for the demonstration itself.

The Nature of the Testing

If candidates maintain that they are capable of performing the job, with or without accommodation, the IAD should then focus on the testing required for the job. The interviewer should inform the candidate that there are tests required for the job. The interviewer should next tell the candidate the name of the test(s) and ask if they have received any information or brochures regarding the tests. If so, the interviewer should determine what information the candidate has received.

The interviewer should describe each test, focusing on what the test requires the candidate to do (e.g., solve mathematical equations, play the role of a service representative, check columns of information for errors), how the materials and instructions are presented (e.g., visually, orally), the type of response format the candidate will use (e.g., oral, written, machine scannable, multiple choice, short answer), and the time in which the candidate must complete the test. Much, but not all, of this information is contained in the pretest information pamphlets currently provided to candidates.

The interviewer should next ask candidates if they would require any accommodations to the testing process to enable them to perform their best on the test. Although the initial suggestions should generally be the candidate's, this should be an interactive discussion. The interviewer should seek to clarify the candidate's suggestions and should offer additional suggestions as warranted.

The atmosphere of the discussion should be one of honesty and candor, but consensus is not always required. For example, the interviewer may directly deny certain requests. Examples might include requests to use calculators or computers (except where currently allowed), previews of the actual test, and dropping testing or replacing it with "probationary hiring."

It is further recommended that, where possible, the interviewer bring representative materials from the test to the discussion, with the stipulation that these materials do not compromise the security or utility of the test. These materials may include such things as pretest information packages, blank answer sheets, or examples of the type font, size, and spacing used in the test (taken from sample items at the beginning of the test). If the interviewer is sufficiently familiar with the candidate's disability beforehand, samples of appropriately accommodated test materials may also be made available, provided that these materials do not compromise the test.

Closing the IAD meeting

At the end of the IAD, the interviewer should thank candidates for their input, emphasize that the organization is an equal opportunity employer which complies with the terms of the ADA, and reemphasize that the discussion does not imply a commitment on the part of either party to implement any particular accommodation. The interviewer should also provide candidates with a telephone number to call if they have additional questions or suggestions.

If the candidate and the interviewer are in agreement about straightforward accommodations, the interviewer should write up a Testing Accommodation Plan (TAP) and explain the plan to the candidate (see below). If the interviewer is uncertain that the accommodations are practical, consistent with company policy, or in the company's best interest; if the interviewer is not authorized to make commitments regarding the accommodation; or if the accommodation plan would be complex or time-consuming to document, candidates should be informed that they will be contacted and receive a written TAP from the interviewer in the near future.

If the candidate and the interviewer are not in general agreement about the accommodations, they should schedule a second discussion at a later date. Where appropriate, additional technical assistance (e.g., the resources given in the Compendium of Technical Assistance Resource Appendix at the end of this book) may be sought. In circumstances where several discussions have failed to bring about agreement, candidates should be informed that they will soon receive a written TAP from the interviewer, which they may accept or reject.

The Testing Accommodation Plan (TAP)

Once a testing accommodation strategy has been decided upon, the candidate should be notified, in writing, or via the appropriate medium, about the accommodations. This notification, the TAP, will be a written description of the specific accommodations which the company agrees to make to the testing procedures or conditions. The accommodation plan will constitute a formal commitment on the part of the organization with regard to testing processes only, and only as these apply to this particular candidate and position.

Candidates should then respond, in writing, as to whether or not they agree with the TAP, and if not, why not. They should be made aware that this will constitute a formal commitment on their part to accept or refuse the accommodations offered. Should a candidate refuse the TAP, the reasons for doing so may or may not change the plan. If they do, the candidate should be sent a revised TAP.

Testing the Candidate

First and foremost, testing sites should be accessible or should be made accessible to all candidates. In cases where this is not possible, the administrator may need to schedule the candidate for a new testing site or go to a location accessible to the candidate. Special care must be taken in off-site circumstances to guarantee the security of the test content.

Once the company and candidate have agreed upon a TAP, arrangements should be made to schedule testing. At the time of the scheduled testing, all accommodations should be in place. Prior to the start of the test, the test administrator should verify that the candidate concurs that the accommodations in place are those which were agreed upon. Minor environmental adjustments (e.g., lighting, noise levels, volume) may be necessary at this time.

If, after beginning the test, the candidate notifies the administrator that they are still having difficulties with the test as a result of their disability, the administrator may stop the test session and discuss the situation with the candidate. If reasonable accommodations can be made at that time, the administrator may make the accommodations and restart testing from the beginning. If accommodations cannot be made at that time, the candidate should be rescheduled.

Post-Test Interviews

After testing or other evaluation steps, external applicants for nonmanagement jobs generally go through a nonmanagement intake interview. At this stage, all applicants who have not previously self-identified may be given or read the job description and attendance requirements for the job(s) for which they are applying. The interviewer may then ask candidates whether or not they are able to perform essential functions of the job in question with or without accommodations. The interviewer may also ask whether or not candidates are able to meet the attendance requirements for the job (as occurs for all candidates). If candidates respond that they are unable to perform the essential job functions or meet attendance requirements due to limitations caused by a disability, or that they would need accommodations to do so, this would constitute voluntary identification of a disability. At this point, or upon completing the standard interview, the interviewer should initiate a discussion similar to the first part of the IAD described earlier.

After Successful Completion of Testing

As suggested in the ADA definition, passing the test and satisfying other job-related requirements are only the initial steps in determining whether or not a

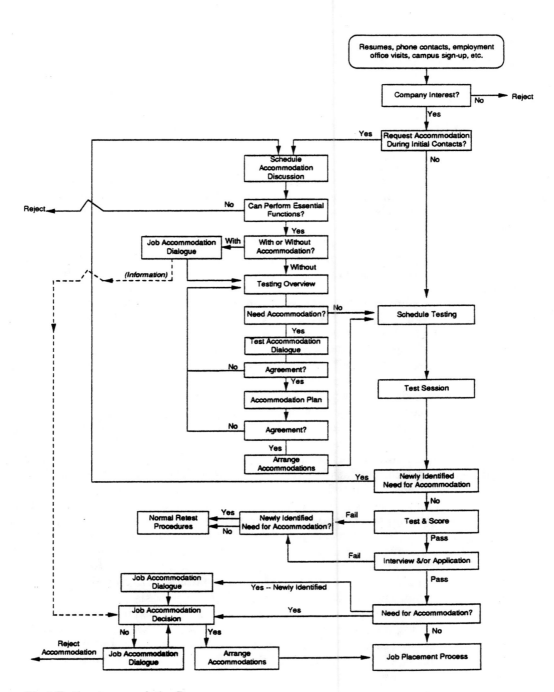

Fig. 1 Testing Accommodation Process

candidate is a "qualified individual with a disability." The second determination is whether or not the individual can, with or without reasonable accommodation, perform the essential functions of the job. Much of the information needed to make this determination will have been obtained from the candidate during the IAD. This information should be reviewed at this time by the interviewer or someone else authorized to make employment and accommodation decisions. The details of this step are beyond the scope of this chapter but will include both the determination of whether or not the candidate can perform the essential functions and whether or not the identified accommodations are reasonable. It is recommended that candidates again be consulted at this stage.

Summary and Conclusions

The schemata represented in Figure 1 is intended to summarize the proposed testing process as it applies to all candidates (internal and external). These may or may not become binding procedures, depending upon whether or not these recommendations (or some revised version thereof) should ultimately become approved as policy.

The larger internal technical report from Ameritech, from which this chapter was excerpted, contains additional useful reference information. For example, one appendix lists several types of general disabling conditions and some specific tests which would most likely have an adverse effect upon performance without modification. Accompanying these are some possible accommodations for each disabling condition, however the appendix does not presume to contain a comprehensive list of disabilities, tests affected by disabilities, or accommodations. It is further acknowledged that accommodation examples which are listed are not necessarily appropriate for all tests or for all candidates. As emphasized repeatedly in the ADA, in the appendices of the technical report, and throughout this book, candidates with disabilities should be dealt with only on a case-by-case basis, acknowledging their significant individual differences and needs.

A second appendix in the larger technical report contains case studies of actual attempts (successful and unsuccessful) to accommodate individuals with disabilities. Included are summaries of specific questions and situations which have arisen regarding accommodated testing, pertinent background on each situation, the accommodations suggested by each party, the accommodation agreed upon, how the accommodation worked in actual practice, and the outcome of testing. Future case examples will be added and each situation is followed and updated as time goes on. These instances may prove useful in helping to identify options and alternatives to discuss with candidates in the IAD. They should, however, be used only as a starting point and a source of ideas, and not become institutionalized as rules or firmly established precedents. Again, candidates with disabilities requesting accommodation must be dealt with on a case-by-case basis.

It is intended that the proposed recommendations described in this chapter be regarded as a living document of flexible guidelines as well as a compendium of Ameritech experiences which (with each subsequent revision) will ultimately improve the degree of access by all qualified individuals with disabilities to the testing and employment options at Ameritech.

6

Human Resources Support for Current Employees

Paul L. Scher, C.R.C.

Introduction

It is the year 2010. "Excellent Incorporated" employs 3,500 persons. The firm is showing a small profit on the domestic and international market through the manufacture and service of a practical electronics product. The CEO, "Conscious Caring," believes her company's success is due to the fact that the workforce is motivated to do its best. Morale surveys indicate high levels of satisfaction. Workers' compensation costs are the lowest for Excellent Incorporated's industry. Little time is consumed settling discrimination complaints because of specific Affirmative Action practices which are exercised daily. Direct efforts are applied to keep channels of communication open between workers and management at all levels. Industrial engineers on the staff have seen to it that workstations are ergonomically constructed so workers' compensation costs are low. Good safety and efficient methods in procedure abound.

15% of the workforce voluntarily reports a physical, mental, or learning disability on the voluntary Selective Placement survey maintained daily by the personnel office in compliance with section 503 of the Rehabilitation Act (Under the ADA employers cannot inquire about a person's disability. As long as confidentiality is maintained perhaps data can be accumulated for statistical purposes.). While a special fund is available to assist department managers to cover the cost of reasonable accommodations, little was expended since most of the arrangements cost nothing, or impact only slightly on the managers' budgets.

Mentoring is the explicit responsibility of everyone, especially supervisors and managers. At Excellent Incorporated, one's performance rating, in part, is based on the supervisor's or manager's ability to develop those for whom he or she is responsible so as to qualify for promotion. The practice of asking experienced workers to serve as sponsor or mentor to one who is having more difficulty than others is recognized and is a common practice.

A surprising number of supervisors and managers, and even two representatives on the 12-member board of directors are people with disabilities. When interviewed by a reporter from the President's Committee on Employment of People with Disabilities, Conscious Caring said that performance evaluations are objective, and training opportunities are open to all who, by performance and interests, merit consideration. Interpreters for deaf employees and readers for blind employees are provided when they are scheduled for training or companywide meetings.

In this environment, a physical, mental, or learning disability is regarded simply as a characteristic of the individual. The problems that may result from this characteristic, if any, can usually be neutralized on the job through awareness training and/or reasonable accommodation.

Nonexempt employees are credited for one hour's pay weekly upon documentation that they've attended the company's health club or contracted facility at locations away from headquarters. Employee assistance program services are available to all and periodic health education on pertinent topics is offered at reasonable intervals. Within this setting, employees with disabilities, their co-workers, their supervisors, and their managers are aware of individual needs while meeting the requirements of production, service, and management. The management of a disability is everyone's responsibility and all have common interests in assisting one another to return to work should illness, injury, or chronic disability strike. The company culture at Excellent Incorporated requires minimal effort to assure that employees with disabilities receive the same opportunities for promotion and privileges as all other workers.

The basic principles underlying sports medicine are applied to workers who become injured. It is important to the company to return the injured worker to a modified duty job, their original job, or a change of assignment as quickly as possible so as to retain their skill and experience, and to reduce potential workers' compensation liability.

In this atmosphere, the uniqueness of the individual is taken for granted. Recognition of the fact that some persons with disabilities have to do their job in an unconventional manner is beside the point. The point is that the individual is permitted and encouraged to do so. Different viewpoints are accepted, but management realizes its objective is to get everyone to focus on the company's and work unit's goals. It doesn't matter who is disabled or who is a member of a minority as long as all understand and do their part so that Excellent Incorporated succeeds.

Discussion

Compensation

It goes without saying that hourly employees need to be paid the same wage for the same quantity of work that is performed. Pay ranges are acceptable, based on years of service, varying environmental settings, and excellence above the norm. Most salaried employees who perform similar types of work are compensated based upon performance, but may be financially rewarded for documented output beyond normal expectations, successful innovation, or a proven track record of preparing those they supervise for promotion.

Promoting Disabled Employees

Performance evaluation systems which are fair, the availability of a career ladder, and the profitability of the business all have a bearing on opportunities for advancement. The surest way to obtain the best person for a given job and to avoid employment discrimination litigation is to administer an equal pay program with statistically validated criteria for making judgements about one's performance in relation to a standard. This system should apply to disabled employees as well as nondisabled and to anyone who works for a given employer. But what about the individual who, because of a disability, is not able to perform up to expectations? From the standpoint of promotability, the question is moot.

What about an employee who cannot perform the essential functions of the job because of a disability? Perhaps this situation arose as the aftermath of a downsizing when jobs were combined. An alternative assignment that will capitalize on the employee's abilities and experience should be identified, or the employee may be dismissed like any nondisabled worker unable to perform at an acceptable level. Documentation of both performance and efforts to overcome the handicapping effects of the disability are the only criteria that apply in a retention, transfer, promotion, or termination.

For example, if one's physical limitations are so severe that it is so difficult to travel, and if the next step up the promotional ladder requires frequent travel, then a greater effort has to be made to see if the disabled person can be slotted in an area where acquired skills and knowledge would apply without travel. But if there is not and this fact is documented, the employee has the option to perform the present job while waiting for a more manageable opportunity or to seek employment elsewhere. The disabled employee should be given the option to accept the available assignment or wait for a more practical opportunity. If the disabled employee is qualified, don't decide for them that their disability prevents them from doing the job.

Keep a log of the efforts made to reward the disabled employee with a higher level position. Such a record will have a double effect. First, it will document to the satisfaction of the worker with a disability that a genuine effort to accommodate was made. Second, it will illustrate for the manager a way by which the handicapping effects of a disability can be circumvented in order to perform on a new job. Faith in the believability of an employee's history will flush out whether or not the capable disabled associate is held back because of their disability and the issues related thereto can be confronted directly. Always, without exception, evaluate the disabled worker on the basis of the criteria set for measuring the performance of all persons holding that assignment. Do not rate a disabled worker differently because they "do so well for their condition." To do so is demeaning and will work to keep the disabled employee from ever catching up to expected levels of performance.

Lotito, Jones, Pimental, & Baker (1990) have defined some of the important issues regarding upward mobility. They point out that disabled workers often receive a poorer quality of supervision than nondisabled individuals. An unpromotable worker can be created by lack of appropriate supervision. The supervisor may lack confidence in managing the disabled worker as he or she would anyone else. Additional problems include hesitating to talk to disabled workers regarding problems, a false belief that the worker was hired because of a disability rather than capability, and unfamiliarity with the best means for communicating with some workers with specific disabilities. But they point out that a survey revealed that the differences in promotion patterns were often related to the personality of the supervisor. Where the supervisor and employee worked together to achieve promotability, the greatest successes were found.

Lotito et al. (1990) point out that besides the capability of the worker, accommodations might have to be provided to enable the employee to do the essential elements of the job. It is only on the essential elements that individuals may be considered for promotion.

If conference rooms are inaccessible, disabled workers may be excluded from the meetings and the information they pick up is second hand. The ADA requires that employees be able to attend such meetings. These problems can be minimized. Appropriate awareness training can sensitize supervisors and managers to disability issues so that disabled workers are supervised and measured against the same criteria of performance of all other workers. Establishing a comfortable communications link with the employee facilitates flexibility.

Mentoring is important because work decisions are made through the informal network across the lunch table, and at social parties where one's colleagues are invited. If disabled workers are excluded from these gatherings, they are at a disadvantage. Lunchrooms and recreation areas need to be accessible. Time spent engaged in training to facilitate work diversity and in cultivating an appropriate company culture where everyone feels comfortable is definitely worth it both from a production standpoint and to reduce the waste or legal expense that can inadvertently occur when discrimination charges are filed. This is why a supervisor's performance evaluation should include an element of mentoring.

Retention of Workers

To minimize the number of work injuries, disability policy might specify that it is the responsibility of all personnel to assist each other to return to work should illness, injury, or chronic disabilities strike. If the purpose of early return to work is clearly understood, this will remove much of the prejudice that accompanies disability will be removed. An awareness that a person who becomes disabled would like to live as near a normal life as possible and that anyone can "join the club" is not hard to instill. This spirit will facilitate workers assuming the responsibilities required of an early return-to-work program. When management shows that modified duty jobs can be developed, and everyone can see that recovering workers are being retained, workers will do what they can to assist each other and management regarding the identification of appropriate jobs. Making safety everyone's responsibility will also lower the number of potential work injuries. A way to develop capable disabled managers is to retain those persons who develop a disability. An alert company mindful of cultural diversity will solve a lot of its people problems, including the retention and upward movement of disabled workers.

At Sears, it has been this author's experience that associates with disabilities performing at the average or superior level blend into the background of their work unit, so that their disability disappears. They fit into a team and are often included as members of the informal network.

At Hewlett-Packard, emphasis has been on outreach rather than upward mobility. The fact that disabled persons in middle- and upper-level management are few is a concern to the company. Technical jobs are going overseas. Disabled persons who are qualified are concerned because they feel they will be passed over for supervisory and management positions. Philosophically, the company believes that career development and upward mobility are not the same. Lateral moves are encouraged, since they give each worker, disabled or not, broader experience so as to qualify when promotions are available. The company asked its disabled associates about their goals and then followed up on the results of their aims three years hence, in a study. A number of issues appeared to be important in determining whether or not career moves for these workers were successful. For example, personal characteristics of the employee or the employee's supervisor; the most successful promotions occurred when the employee and the employee's manager worked together to achieve the employee's goals. The manager's description of the characteristics of those who succeeded most were: (1) a positive attitude; (2) a sense of humor; (3) self-motivation; (4) determination; (5) people skills; (6) risk-taking; and (7) a strong ego. The follow-up also concluded that those disabled employees who had been segregated in school did not have the appropriate experiences to help move them along.

Informal means by which company culture is transmitted meant that the disabled employee had to work extra hard to be included. Managers at Hewlett-Packard said that they relied on the employees with disabilities to educate them about their needs and the available resources to help overcome their limitations. They expected disabled employees to tell them what they can and cannot do and what accommodations are necessary. Managers seem to expect to spend more time mentoring these employees and to use more patience in correcting problems as they arise. The disabled employees are also expected to assume the responsibility for educating co-workers about their disabilities and for putting their colleagues at ease. Finally, the Hewlett-Packard study found that accommodations were not an issue, but that the experience that some disabled lack, causes management to be more reluctant to give them an opportunity, than is the case with the nondisabled (Ingram, 1988).

Undoubtedly, employees with disabilities are promoted. It is likely that those who are promoted based on their performance, have no record of linkage between their disability and their promotion since it was simply done on the basis of merit. In comparison, anecdotal evidence and statistical evidence indicate that people with disabilities do not hold a proportionate number of management positions given the size of the population.

Dupont and IBM both produce publications that discuss their Affirmative Action programs for disabled employees. *Equal To The Task* (Drach, 1990) refers to a doctor with a severe visual limitation who directs laboratory research in the photographic sciences which is critical to new product development for the imaging systems department. Dupont has accommodated this employee by procuring a closed circuit television enlarger and other visual aids. Another example cites a mail agent with supervisory responsibilities who routes the mail efficiently in spite of his cerebral palsy and epilepsy. Elsewhere, an assistant store manager who lost his leg during military service functions effectively.

IBM: An Ongoing Commitment discusses a wide variety of products and services developed by IBM to meet the needs of disabled customers (Dietel, 1990). It points out that accommodations have been made by modifying buildings as well as software for its customers and its own employees. *About Your Company* (the IBM employee's handbook) is tape-recorded for reading-impaired employees. A variety of telecommunication devices and the use of a sign language interpreter are available for deaf employees. Their booklet shows few people with disabilities actually working. A very small person is shown performing her job as a secretary. Custom-designed furniture was purchased for her comfort. The company's policy is correct, and this writer knows from personal experience with IBM employees that disabled individuals are represented in managerial ranks (Ingram, 1989).

Since 1986, Days Inn has pursued qualified persons with disabilities as a means of procuring competent employees. A reservations sales agent who uses a wheelchair was rapidly promoted to the position of network controller. A second reservations agent who uses a wheelchair because of spina bifida was promoted to sales supervisor. Disabled persons work in public relations, accounting, reservations and sales, and management information systems. Since 1986, 25 individuals who are disabled work at headquarters and others are represented at over 1,000 locations at Days Inn (Miller, 1990).

Eastman Kodak's chief executive officer actively serves on the board of directors of the National Organization of Disability. Equipment specifically designed to assist disabled persons has been installed in their facilities. Elevators with control panels in Braille assist employees who are blind while wide aisles make it easier for those using wheelchairs to get about. A variety of equipment is available to facilitate the communication of hearing-impaired employees. The computer messaging system is particularly helpful to employees who are totally deaf. Sign language interpreters are made available when necessary. Eastman Kodak, based in Rochester, New York, is in close proximity to the National Technical Institute for the Deaf. "D2" is a program designed to train disabled persons in computer programming. A computer software engineer lives with multiple sclerosis and was retained as his condition deteriorated by making appropriate accommodations. A maintenance planner is a veteran who uses a wheelchair. Several disabled individuals are holding middle management positions (Eastman Kodak, 1989).

This information is excerpted from a variety of public information pamphlets that discuss Affirmative Action activities designed to attract employees with disabilities. The examples found indicate upward mobility, though the positions cited seemed fairly close to the bottom of the promotional ladder. Over time, and with the presence of the ADA, those employees who have begun to move up will likely climb higher, and those entering the labor market may find it easier to move from the first, to the second, to the third rung. It appears, however, that specific actions will have to be taken to see to it that the personnel system behaves equally toward everyone where promotability is concerned.

Equal Pay for Equal Work

We mentioned that equal pay for equal work with sufficient elasticity to recognize exceptional performance is appropriate in the management of one's employees. Now let us suppose that an employee with a disability can do almost all of the essential functions of the job, but not quite all of them. The employee has exceeded expectation in the current assignment and is being considered for a promotion. At this point, the new assignment can be restructured so that those functions which the disabled person cannot perform can be assigned to other colleagues.

Let us assume that these tasks can be quantified in respect to the amount of responsibilities and time which these duties require. It should be arguable that when the disabled employee is assigned to the restructured assignment, if the quantity of work to be completed is not as great as those doing the unrestructured job, then the pay rate may be reduced for the job.

A good rule to follow is to always pay the job, not the person doing it. This will require that your job descriptions remain accurate so that when several are compared in a common group, similarities and differences will be truly evident. In restructuring a job, if it is concluded that the disabled employee performing the restructured job is able to do equivalent work to that of others, then equal pay should be given. When the quantity of work is the same for both jobs, even though a few tasks may differ, then both jobs should pay the same rate.

Try to avoid creating a dead-end job since this will lock in an employee who might otherwise have greater potential. Also, remember that if the restructured assignment pays less than an otherwise comparable assignment, you should demonstrate that other individuals may be placed on the same job. Case law holds that you may have to pay the same wage or salary to the restructured position that you do for the unaltered assignment.

Promotability

Let us assume that when the restructured job description is completed, it becomes clear that the person being promoted will not do a couple of the tasks required to gain experience for promotability. What happens?

Experience is a bit of a problem. If, for example, the otherwise qualified employee with a disability seeks to do a job which requires travel, but is handicapped in this respect, it is very difficult to provide an equivalent work experience. In this case, the ADA would seem to imply only truly qualified individuals should be considered for the position. Management and the disabled employee would then have to agree that the disabled person remain in the current position until an assignment opens up which would provide an equivalent range of experience, or a different kind of experience that qualifies one for promotion where travel is not required.

A detailed discussion regarding the eligibility of the disabled employee should be held. In this way, disabled employees will find it difficult to argue that they were placed in jobs that they cannot perform since they were forewarned of the absolute necessity for travel. If the disabled employee is promoted to an assignment where they cannot perform the essential tasks then the only alternatives are to terminate the employee for poor performance, or allow them to return to a position that they are able to perform in spite of their disability. We cannot overemphasize the importance of knowing what tasks each job requires, how those tasks are performed, and under what conditions they are performed. Appropriate job descriptions make it possible to determine what accommodations are practical. Accurate, honest, and current job descriptions will be your best defense against possible charges alleging discrimination on the basis of physical or mental disability under the ADA.

Both for equal pay and promotability, job descriptions are your resource for placing qualifiable people into the jobs your business requires. Accurate job descriptions will also make it possible to properly place workers who are recovering from injury into modified assignments, or into other jobs which they can perform if they are permanently handicapped by an acquired disability. But remember, good job descriptions are only one tool for charting a flexible course for placement advancement.

An additional plus is that by making early return to work and selective placement a culturally acceptable practice, the cost of workers' compensation will be reduced and the experience of many competent workers will be preserved to your advantage. The continuing accuracy of job descriptions make return to work, promotion, and placement easier when disability is a characteristic to be considered, since they allow you to begin charting a course toward suitable placement.

Transfer, Layoff, Downsizing, and Termination

If a company is involved in a collective bargaining arrangement, most likely the labor-management contract contains specific clauses dealing with these matters. Hopefully, when developing a labor-management contract, consideration will be given to disabled persons in respect to seniority. Often, the jobs that require minimal physical ability are held as rewards for long-term employees thereby reducing possible placement of younger disabled persons. For those companies which are not union organized, local, state, and federal employment laws pertain to disabled persons as well as everyone else.

When in doubt, be sure that the same procedures are applied to disabled workers as to everyone else. The same issues that pertain to upward mobility also apply to transfers. During times of downsizing, disabled persons are as subject to layoff as anyone else. Recognizing that a person with a disability is likely to find it more difficult to obtain a job elsewhere, management may take a second look at whether or not there really is not an alternative assignment left for disabled employees.

When a permanent downsizing is in progress and a consulting outplacement firm is utilized, care should be taken to ensure that the disabled employees receive the same opportunity for counseling and outplacement as do other workers. At Sears, the outplacement firm was more than willing to work with disabled associates whose jobs were eliminated. The placement agency requested that they work on an individual basis with the impacted disabled employees. But Sears encouraged the firm to include disabled workers in the same group meetings and group counseling sessions as nondisabled associates. The reason for this is that the experienced disabled worker facing unemployment needs to understand that their frustrations, anxieties, and concerns for the future are no different than the concerns of the nondisabled colleagues.

Additional assistance for the disabled employee being terminated may be warranted because of the difficultly the individual will have in finding another position compared to their able-bodied surplus colleagues. A disabled employee should be put in contact with the local Project with Industry, the local state office of the Department of Rehabilitation Services, or the special placement unit of the public employment service. Since there is much paperwork when qualifying for help from a public agency, the employer may wish to lend assistance by helping the disabled employee process these forms.

Documentation of these additional efforts will also serve to provide a sound and honest defense against any possible charge of discrimination that the disabled worker may file. This advice is equally applicable to all those being terminated, but especially to minorities who have specific antidiscrimination laws available to them.

Termination should be based on business necessity or poor work performance. If all workers' performances are appropriately documented and ratings are objectively based on statistically established criteria, disabled workers who are not performing effectively can and should be dismissed on the same basis as any other "square peg in a round hole." If a disabled worker files a discrimination charge, the company will be able to show both to the complainant and to the investigating agency that the decision to terminate was based on performance and that the measure of performance applied was that used in evaluating all other workers at the same level.

Benefits Eligibility, Entitlements, Early Retirement, and Pension Liability

The best way to minimize the cost of all the plans listed above is to coordinate all of them in a systematic manner so as to prevent overlapping. The health plan and workers' compensation coverage should be compatible so that a common method of medical management can apply to both programs. Long-term disability and workers' compensation coverage should provide for appropriate linkage, but specific requirements must be met under workers' compensation laws. While many of the benefits under a health or long-term disability plan are voluntary, the impact of federal, state, and local laws require that all of these coverages apply equally to all workers. Some of the latitudes available for election differ between exempt and nonexempt employees. The particularities of any one coverage will have to be detailed by the appropriate specialist within the employment organization or a representative of the insurance carrier. Your responsibility should be to instruct plan administrators that the same provisions must apply to disabled workers on the same basis that they apply to nondisabled workers. Information about these plans should be offered in Braille, large type, or recorded form where appropriate. Interpreters should be provided for deaf employees at benefits meetings. Availability of these services or an equivalent is required under the ADA.

Health Insurance

It is common that pre-existing conditions are excluded from health insurance coverages at least for a specified time. The ADA requires that employees with disabilities be insured on the same basis as are all nondisabled employees at the same premium cost. But insurance carriers are given the latitude to set different rates for statistically provable high-risk groups. It is quite correct that certain illnesses and degenerative conditions statistically demonstrate a need for a greater amount of medical and hospital care when compared to the general public.

We recommend that any pre-existing disability exclusions extend no longer than a new employee's probation. One's previous employer is required to permit the individual to remain on their former hospital plan at their own expense under COBRA for a limited period.

Most group insurance, particularly workers' compensation insurance, is based on the average injury experience of companies that are similar within a given industry. It does not really matter who you employ. The expensive medical cases that contribute to rising costs tend to develop as the workforce ages, so that the employer is basically obligated to meet the needs of the worker and the worker's family anyway. Health plans and long-term disability are affected by strict government regulation under COBRA. Conditions under which one may have access to their pension is covered under ERISA. Both laws make it difficult to write exceptions for specific individuals.

Long-Term Disability

Guidelines for the administration of long-term disability insurance fall under COBRA and a variety of state laws. It may be that to help a particular worker who has developed a disability due to either injury or illness, there is a desire to qualify him or her for benefits earlier, or in a different amount than is specified in the policy. But an exception cannot be made for an individual unless it is made for all of those covered. Classes of exceptions have to be spelled out in the insurance contract.

Early Retirement and Pensions

Early retirement is often available upon demonstration that the individual can no longer perform an occupation and, in fact, would have extreme difficulty obtaining another job. Such happenstance should be coordinated with the long-term disability policy because the accrued pension may not be paid out until the claimant reaches age 65. It is to the employer's advantage to be sure that medical retirement is not used as a substitute for poor performance dismissal. In comparison, it is equally advantageous for the employer to accommodate an experienced employee who becomes disabled. The disabled worker might be eligible for social security benefits which can serve to supplement his or her income while absorbing some of the employer's costs. New amendments to the social security act permit extended work trial experience before losing SSDI eligibility if one tries to return to work once eligible.

While there may be times when it is financially prudent to minimize the number of individuals with specific disability types on one's payroll, if these individuals are qualified to perform available jobs, discriminating against them for insurance purposes is definitely not legal under the ADA and under the conditions stated in many state laws.

Summary Recommendations

- Establish a requirement that the performance of all workers be evaluated on the basis of objective criteria with an awareness that, as far as the job is concerned, race, sex, national origin, age, and disability have no bearing.
- Provide for the availability of sponsors and mentors who are willing to help new employees, especially those representing minorities and disabled persons, to become integrated with the company's social structure and culture.
- Endeavor to achieve a workforce in which workers with disabilities are represented at every level of the organization.
- Establish a safety program that will minimize the number of work-related injuries.
- Create an early return-to-work program which makes all associates responsible for assisting those recovering from illness or injury to return to work by developing an awareness that disability is a fact-of-life, and that anyone so affected would want to live as nearly as normal as possible.
- When reducing workforce or terminating employees, apply the same criteria to disabled individuals that apply to everyone else.

- During downsizing, assist the disabled worker to make contact with those agencies that have experience in placing persons with disabilities.
- Document all efforts to counsel or assist the worker about to be displaced so that the worker and the company will know that the company has made a reasonable effort to assist the terminated disabled individual.
- Establish a broad cafeteria-type health plan with minimal exclusions which will promote the employee's security.
- When a worker who has qualified for SSDI returns to work, take advantage of the work trial period to minimize the company's exposure and the entitlement of the employee.

References ━━━━━━━━━━━━━━━━━━━━━━━

Dietel, D. (1990). IBM: An ongoing commitment. IBM's national support center for people with disabilities. *WorkLife(1)*2, 25-28. Washington, DC: President's Committee on Employment of People with Disabilities.

Drach, R. L. (1990). Extraordinary people. In Equal to the task #2: 1990 Dupont survey (pp. 2-23). Wilmington, DE: Dupont.

Eastman Kodak. (1989). Strength in diversity. In The possible dream (p. 8). Rochester, NY: Author.

Ingram, R. (1988). Investing in America's future: Career development and upward mobility. The Hewlett-Packard Experience. *WorkLife, (3)*1, 1-2. Washington, DC: President's Committee on Employment of People with Disabilities.

Ingram, R. (1989). Diversity in the workplace. *WorkLife(2)*4, 10-11. Washington, DC: President's Committee on Employment of People with Disabilities.

Lotito, M. J., Jones, C., Pimental, R., & Baker, L. (1990). Section II. Attitudes and reactions. In *The Americans with Disabilities Act: Making the ADA work for you* (pp. 21-24). Northridge, CA: Milt Wright & Associates, Inc./ Jackson, Lewis, Schnitzler, & Krupman.

Miller, S. L. (1990). Upward mobility at Days Inns of America. *WorkLife (3)*1, 9-10. Washington, DC: President's Committee on Employment of People with Disabilities.

7

Reinforcing the Need for Progressive Human Resources Practices

Thomas M. Ziemba, Ph.D.
Brian T. McMahon, Ph.D. C.R.C.

Introduction

The Americans With Disabilities Act (ADA) has numerous implications for employers, as well as public and private employees, in every industry. The implications for employers are qualitatively different than those of prior legislation which were intended to regulate, monitor, and remedy employment practices considered to be unfair to protected classes. For example, Executive Order 11246 requires that covered employers must prepare an annual report on minority and female representation within their organization, and compare this to the labor market estimates of available workers with appropriate qualifications. The ADA requirements contain no similar provisions. Rather, the ADA is proactive, and in some cases definitive, in outlining the circumstances which result in discrimination against qualified individuals with disabilities. Once identified, the ADA prescribes appropriate behavior to remove these barriers. One only needs to read the ADA Title I Regulations and Interpretive Guidelines (supplied as an Appendix) to obtain a sense of the level of detail provided.

The primary thesis of this chapter is that with respect to the employment provisions of the ADA, compliance can best be accomplished by adopting or following progressive human resources programs, policies, and practices which have been advocated by numerous researchers, students of organizational behavior and rehabilitation, and human resources practitioners during the last decade. This is not to imply that new programs and policies are not needed, but simply to suggest that employers who have adopted fieldtested human resources (HR) programs will more readily comply with the intent as well as the letter of the ADA. To ensure compliance, as well as to ensure that HR programs are structured for maximum effectiveness, every organization should conduct a careful review of its HR programs and supporting policies. Broad guidelines are available for conducting this review. Biles and Schuler (1986), for example, provide a comprehensive approach to conducting a HR function review. The following section is intended to provide organizations with an orientation to the review as it pertains to the ADA.

Reviewing Human Resource Policies

In this section, the critical areas of HR policies which merit review are highlighted to ensure that they facilitate the employment of individuals with disabilities. Recommendations grounded in fundamentally sound HR practices are advanced to guide compliance with the ADA and to ensure that the organization benefits from progressive and fair HR programs and policies for all employees and employment candidates. Virtually all organizations maintain a set of HR policies which guide managerial and employee behavior. The HR policies establish the official standards of behavior for the organization, and as such should be the initial focus of review. Unfortunately, organizations differ greatly in the scope of behavior covered in their policies, and in the detailed guidance found in policy language. As a starting point, it is important the HR policies are documented in a precise and comprehensive manner to ensure that supervisors and managers understand and apply them in a fair and uniform manner. A lack of clear guidance opens the door for bias against individuals with disabilities.

To be more specific, the following HR policies, practices, and program areas should be carefully reviewed to maximize compliance with the ADA:

- Employee Selection and Classification
- Discipline
- Time Off
- Salary Administration

Initially, the review should take the form of a desk audit of written policies contained in manuals or employee handbooks. Ideally, this will be followed by a review of actual practices as well.

In some cases, the HR policies may be supported by a full-scale program complete with supporting administrative guidelines. In other cases, policies are essentially statements of the organization's position (e.g., maintaining an "employment-at-will" relationship with employees, providing employees with time off under certain conditions). It is important that these supporting programs and administrative guidelines become part of the review process. If an organization does not have written policies in the areas identified in this review, then it is strongly recommended that they be developed.

The key policy topic areas suggested for review are outlined below. Each policy topic is highlighted by issues which represent potential challenges to the organization. A recommendation is then offered to develop or revise a policy to meet the pertinent requirements. Consistent with the theme of this chapter, recommendations were developed to meet two compatible goals: 1) to foster compliance with the ADA, and 2) to promote a progressive HR management posture within the organization.

Employee Selection and Classification

This portion of the review addresses employee recruitment, selection, classification, and orientation policies and programs. The selection practices outlined in the organization's HR policies are a window to its basic approach to human resources management. In general, HR policies and practices which facilitate the selection of the most qualified candidate, in an objective and unbiased manner, are applicable to persons with disabilities. A fundamental starting point in promoting a fair and unbiased selection process for all candidates is to establish a clear linkage between the skills, job knowledge, and abilities needed to perform the essential functions of the job and the criteria used to assess the candidate's qualifications. Seven relevant policy topics and recommendations are provided in Table 1.

Discipline

An organization's disciplinary policy influences how willing that organization is to retain and develop an employee when performance standards are not met or company policies are not adhered to. Disciplinary policies and practices will need to be carefully reviewed in the context of the ADA, because qualified employees with disabilities may not fully meet performance standards *without an accommodation*. Redekel (1989) highlighted the typical employer's perspective regarding termination of employees with disabilities prior to the ADA:

> The existence of a medical disability cannot be a cause for discipline, except in cases of fraud, because the necessary element of employee volition of fault is missing. Employees can be terminated, however, where their medical disabilities prevent them from performing their jobs, or attending work regularly; where the disability places the employees themselves or their coworkers in danger; where reasonable accommodation for the disabilities is not possible; and where there is little, or uncertain, hope for improvement of the medical conditions within a reasonable period of time. (p. 292)

It is clear that this perspective requires rethinking in the post-ADA era.

Generally speaking, disciplinary activities related to attendance or the inability to meet performance standards represent the preponderance of all disciplinary actions. There is no evidence to suggest that individuals with disabilities are more likely to fail to meet performance standards or have poor attendance records in comparison to other workers. In fact, a 1989 Harris poll of approximately 900 employers indicated that employees with disabilities have a good or excellent rating on their overall job performance (Gerber, 1990).

The onset of a disability during employment or an accommodation for a disability may involve time off during the workday for professional assistance. Or, in some instances, a reasonable accommodation may be made by providing additional time to meet specific performance standards. Because of a failure to meet specific guidelines of attendance and job performance, an individual with a disability may technically violate the organization's attendance or job performance policies. If the employer allows exceptions to the stated company policy on discipline, then the opportunity for unfair and biased treatment of all employees increases. An employer's best preparation is to make sure that the disciplinary policy is unambiguous regarding both appropriate performance standards and unauthorized time off. A progressive disciplinary process which incorporates flexibility and a focus on improvement is likely to meet the needs of most employees. It is emphasized that the ADA explicitly does *not* require that performance standards themselves be lowered or modified. However, a difficult

Table 1. Employee Selection and Classification

Policy Topic / Issue	Recommendation
Employee Recruitment, Selection, and Promotion *Issue:* Existing selection standards and promotion criteria are reviewed and modified, if necessary, to make the selection process accessible to all applicants and employees.	• Modify recruitment, selection, and promotion policies only to explicitly recognize the application of reasonable accommodations when necessary. • Ensure qualifications, job requirements, and promotion criteria stated in both external advertisements and internal postings, are linked to essential job functions. • Provide examples of alternative job qualifications related to performing essential job functions. • Provide examples of modifications to selection procedures (e.g., aptitude tests) to illustrate the desire to provide access to the hiring process.
Employment-at-Will *Issue:* The development of special "probationary" periods may be provided to individuals with specific disabilities as an accommodation to promote learning and adjustment to certain work situations.	• Ensure application blanks, handbooks, written policies, and offer letters do not contain language suggesting guaranteed or permanent employment after completing the probationary period.
Employee Classifications (part-time versus full-time) *Issue:* A reduced work week may be utilized as an accommodation, which changes the employee's status from full-time to part-time.	• Explain clearly that eligibility in benefit programs may be negatively impacted by reasonable accommodations which reduces the work week below specific hour requirements.

Hours of Work
 	
Issue: A qualified applicant or employee can perform the essential job requirements with modifications to the work context (change location), work pace (prevent fatigue through rest breaks), or work schedule.
	• Develop policies which foster the utilization of alternative work schedules and work locations which may provide reasonable accommodations for a variety of disabilities (e.g.,
	    flexible schedules,
	    extended breaks,
	    job sharing,
	    work-at-home options).

(Continued)

Table 1. Employee Selection and Classification (con't)

Policy Topic / Issue	Recommendation
• **Orientation** *Issue:* Individuals with certain disabilities may require special accommodations to facilitate their orientation to the workplace, such as information about the company, their job, or integration into a work group.	• Be prepared to convert orientation materials (e.g., large-print handbooks) which describe job requirements, company policies, and other critical procedural information. • Provide supervisory training and awareness training to facilitate work group integration.
• **Access to Personnel Files** *Issue:* Employers need to maintain confidential records describing the medical profile of employees while communicating specific restrictions to appropriate personnel (e.g., supervisors) in order to implement reasonable accommodations.	• Maintain separate files (paper or computer records) for medical records to assure that information regarding an employee's disability does not "bias" the supervisor's view of the employee's capabilities. • Utilize customized information sheets, separate from the medical file, to inform supervisors regarding the necessary restrictions related to the work or duties of the employee and any reasonable accommodations.

situation may arise when an employee with a disability is subjected to the disciplinary process when an accommodation could have been provided to enable that employee to meet the performance standard. Three representative disciplinary policy topics and recommendations are provided in Table 2.

Time Off

Virtually all organizations maintain formal or informal policies which stipulate the nature and amount of time off available to an employee. Typically, time off policies fall into two categories: discretionary and involuntary. The discretionary category includes vacation, and both excused paid absences (e.g., jury duty) and excused unpaid absences (e.g., time off for dependent care). The involuntary category includes sick days, and short- and long-term disability programs.

The concept of reasonable accommodation may expand the employer's frame of reference in discovering ways to bring injured employees back to work (see Chapter 9). That is, employees who otherwise might be absent due to a disability may be able to return to work by modifying the work environment or work schedule. A broad and flexible excused paid or excused unpaid time off policy (which is available to *all* employees to deal with medical, family, or professional development needs) fits the definition of a progressive policy. An individual with

Table 2. Discipline

Policy Topic / Issue	Recommendation
• **Absenteeism / Tardiness** *Issue:* Unplanned time off for medical appointments or rest may be a reasonable accommodation.	• Ensure that attendance requirements are explicit and communicated to all employees, but are subjected to modification in the case of reasonable accommodations.
• **Failure to Meet Performance Standards** *Issue:* An employee fails to meet performance expectations with or without a reasonable accommodation.	• Objective performance standards should be documented in a job description which specifies the essential job functions, then communicated clearly to each employee. • The disciplinary process should specify a time frame for performance improvement and state the type of improvement required.
• **Progressive Discipline** *Issue:* An employee with a disability fails to meet performance standards or demonstrates excessive absenteeism or tardiness.	• The disciplinary policy should be embedded in a progressive disciplinary framework and should include a review of the circumstances surrounding the behavior at issue. Technical assistance may be required to advise management on ways to remove barriers to employee performance improvement.

a disability can take advantage of a progressive time off policy without requiring a reasonable accommodation because of the flexibility inherent in that policy. This is an excellent example of how a proactive policy can meet the needs of all employees. Two representative policy topics and recommendations are provided in Table 3.

Salary Administration

Employers will need to be vigilant regarding the design and administration of their compensation programs. As noted in section 1630.4 of the ADA, discrimination against a qualified individual with a disability is prohibited in the "...rates of pay or any other form of compensation and changes in compensation." Discrimination is also unlawful in "...job assignments, job classifications, organizational structures, position descriptions, lines of progression, and seniority lists." All of these factors are controlled by HR policies related to the salary administration program.

Almost all large organizations maintain policies which outline salary administration procedures. These include the maintenance of job descriptions; utilization

| Table 3. Time Off ||
Policy Topic / Issue	**Recommendation**
• **Excused Paid and Excused Unpaid Time Off** *Issue:* Reasonable accommodations in the form of time off may make an otherwise qualified individual with a disability able to perform a job.	• Establish definitive guidelines to govern the excused paid time off allowed for events such as jury duty or professional development. A flexible excused unpaid time off policy represents an excellent opportunity to provide a uniform benefit which can be utilized by an employee with a disability who requires this type of accommodation without formally requesting an accommodation. This will promote fair treatment of all employees.
• **Sick Days and Vacation Time** *Issue:* New hires are likely to have fewer sick days accrued or available under most policies. This may impact the retention of a few individuals with disabilities who require time off to receive professional services.	• Consider the adoption of "no fault" time off programs which combine vacation and sick time to maximize the number of days available. Immediate eligibility for a full year of "no fault" time off may also be considered. Under this program, a greater number of days are immediately available.

of job evaluation programs; and methods of establishing hiring rates and salary increases. In larger organizations, the policy review should focus on assuring that policies are not out-of-date (e.g., using job evaluation factors which are no longer relevant). In smaller organizations, the typical problem is that policies do not exist to guide salary administration practices. Alternately, where formal salary administration programs do exist, management and supervisors sometimes utilize too much discretion in interpreting and applying the policy. A review of the various components of the salary administration program is presented in greater detail later in this chapter.

To ensure that salaries are administered in a fair and unbiased manner for all employees, four representative policy topics and recommendations are provided in Table 4.

Human Resources Policy Review Process

While the checklists of policy topics presented in Tables 1 through 4 are not exhaustive, they do provide a basis for a review of key HR policies and procedures related to compliance with the ADA. In addition, the recommendations for each policy issue will promote a proactive approach to HR management. A simple desk audit of policies is only one component of the policy review process. The following

Table 4. Compensation-Related Policies

Policy Topic / Issue	Recommendation
• **Job Value** *Issue:* The organization's value of a job category occupied by individuals with disabilities is inadvertently set lower than other job categories which are comparable in terms of size, effort, responsibility and working conditions.	• Ensure that job evaluation factors are relevant to essential job functions. • Define or review procedures to establish the "value" of a job using a job description which contains an explicit listing of essential job functions as the basis for review.
• **Job Descriptions** *Issue:* The value of a job is negatively impacted because nonessential aspects of the job (e.g., physical requirements) are overrepresented in the job description or the job evaluation plan.	• Ensure that essential job requirements are documented in both written job descriptions and job evaluation plans.
• **Salary Administration** *Issue:* An individual who is able to perform a job with a reasonable accommodation receives a lower salary than others in the same or similar job to "compensate" for the accommodation.	• Establish salary ranges for each job and use the minimum, midpoint, and maximum of each salary range as a guideline for setting starting salaries, taking into consideration the qualifications of the candidate and current labor market conditions. Costs of accommodations must be excluded from the salary-setting equation. • The authorization to establish actual salaries for individuals should include a review by the HR function to ensure uniform administration across the organization.
• **Performance Evaluation** *Issue:* An individual with a disability receives an unsatisfactory performance review because of the inability to perform a marginal aspect of the job.	• Ensure that performance criteria are linked to essential job functions. • Maintain a formal review process which regularly addresses the job relevance of performance criteria.

additional steps are recommended in conducting a comprehensive HR policy review:

- Assign to a single, senior level manager or HR executive the responsibility for reviewing and maintaining progressive policies in the key areas identified in this section;
- Encourage the development of additional HR policies or policy modifications to promote compliances with the ADA;
- Obtain endorsement and approval by senior management for all HR policies or policy revisions;
- Evaluate a policy communication strategy for managers, supervisors, and employees which addresses the availability of HR policy manuals and other communication vehicles;
- Review the appropriateness and level of documentation of key HR policies and practices;
- Determine the level of uniform and fair administration of HR policies by conducting a supervisory or user practices survey; and
- Design and implement HR policy training on an ongoing basis.

Assessment and Selection of Individuals with Disabilities

Virtually any decision to hire, promote, terminate, or compensate an employee is based upon the qualifications or abilities of the individual, the past performance of the individual, the potential contribution an individual can make to an organization, and a host of personal characteristics (e.g., physical features, personal likeability) which may not be relevant to job performance. Those characteristics not relevant to the job may promote untested assumptions about what a person can do based on stereotypes associated with the characteristic. To the extent that personal characteristics of individuals (unrelated to the job) are allowed to influence the hiring or utilization of individuals with disabilities, the likelihood that the organization will underutilize all employees is increased.

The development of objective criteria to guide selection decisions which eliminate the ADA-related barriers is consistent with: 1) accepted practices advocated in other compliance guidelines (e.g., *Uniform Guidelines on Employee Selection Procedures* [U.S. Equal Employment Opportunity Commission et al., 1978]); 2) the validation of selection procedures advocated by the American Psychological Association (1989) (e.g., *Principles for the Validation and Use of Personnel Selection Resources, 2nd Edition)*; and the writings of numerous organizational researchers and practitioners (e.g., Manese, 1986).

The ADA does not require employers to hire unqualified individuals, nor does it require employers to give preference to persons with disabilities. Section 1630.10 of the ADA contains a specific provision to ensure that individuals with disabilities are not excluded from job opportunities unless they are actually unable to do the job (i.e., "...to ensure that there is a fit between job criteria and an applicant's [or employee's] actual ability to do the job). The ADA further states that the existence or consequence of a disability must not be a factor in employment decisions.

The questions arise in addressing the requirements of the ADA Title I. What are the employment "decisions" which must be considered? How does an organization eliminate the potential for adverse impact in the application of criteria to hire, promote, terminate, or modify employment conditions for an individual with a disability?

Types of Selection Decisions

Table 5 highlights some of the key decisions that, in effect, are selection decisions. Table 5 clearly illustrates that many of the decisions are post-employment actions. For example, terminating an employee due to an economic downturn represents a selection decision. It is important that the organization view selection in the broadest sense to include its various forms in all aspects of employment.

The typical ways information is gathered about an individual when making these decisions are also presented in Table 5 to highlight that a selection criterion

Table 5. Types of Selection Decisions

Key Decisions	Information Gathering Mechanism
• Selection	• Interviews
	• Paper and Pencil Tests
	• Pre-employment Performance and Accomplishment Records
• Promotion	• Performance Evaluation and Accomplishment Records
• Employee Evaluation	• Performance Appraisal
• Layoff / Termination	• Performance Record / Measure of Potential

or "test" is more than a "paper-and-pencil measure" of aptitude or achievement. Clearly, an important consideration is that employee assessment and selection goes beyond the hiring gate in the forms of promotion, performance evaluation, and involuntary termination decisions. It is recommended that all selection criteria and information-gathering mechanisms involved in the change of an employee's status, be reviewed. Those reviews which promote valid selection decisions and compliance with the ADA are highlighted in the remainder of this section.

Employment Tests

The language in the ADA contains specific guidance regarding the application of selection criteria and the measurement of candidate qualifications. section 1630.10 of the ADA is applicable to all types of selection criteria including safety requirements, vision or auditory requirements, walking requirements, lifting requirements, and employment tests.

Should the mention of employment tests in the ADA discourage the use of such instruments in the selection of job candidates? Those organizations which rely upon valid, structured "paper-and-pencil measures" to assess candidate qualifications are likely not to be discouraged by the requirements of the ADA. As Manese (1986, p. 12) notes, "...there is a realization that there are probably no real alternatives to conventional tests when such factors as validity, adverse impact, fairness, operational feasibility, and cost effectiveness are considered." Research which compares the performance of tests with unstructured selection methods (e.g., interviews) has shown repeatedly that reliable and valid tests provide the most accurate and unbiased method of employee selection and performance prediction.

Two selection methods or "tests" which must be carefully reviewed are pre-employment interviews and "paper-and-pencil measures" of skills, aptitudes, abilities, job knowledge, or achievement. Given the emphasis in the ADA upon essential job functions it is critical that selection methods utilize criteria that are highly job-related and predictive of job-performance. Job-relatedness can be demonstrated, in part, by linking the essential job functions with criteria utilized in the selection process.

A review of "paper-and-pencil tests" should take place at two levels. First, the test should be a reliable and valid measure of the ability to perform the essential functions of the job. Professionals trained in industrial/organizational psychology or selection test development have the relevant background to determine if a test is a valid measure of essential job functions. The second level of review addresses the administration of tests. A rather extensive explanation addressing the administration of tests is outlined in section 1630.11 of the ADA. Important issues to guide the review of test administration are listed in Table 6.

As noted in Table 6, the ADA provides very specific guidelines to ensure that individuals with disabilities can access the hiring process. Organizations which rely on standardized tests to screen candidates should undertake a careful review of the test administration process (see Chapter 5). Part of the standardization of many tests (e.g., measures of intelligence) includes a strictly timed administration and uniform application of "paper-and-pencil formats." Deviations from standardized administration protocols make the use of normative data very difficult for purposes of test interpretation. Professionals, such as rehabilitation psychologists, industrial/organizational psychologists, or test developers, should be consulted to interpret test results obtained from nonstandardized test administrations. Individuals with disabilities may need accommodations which go beyond the obvious requirements for visual or auditory impairments. For example, individuals who have experienced head injury may fatigue quickly (which would negatively impact their performance in completing a timed test).

Table 6. Guidelines for Reviewing Test Administration

Test Administration Issue	Recommended Action
• An applicant seeks to inform the organization that he or she requires a reasonable accommodation for purposes of taking a selection test.	• Organizations may invite applicants on application forms and/or test announcements to identify their needs for reasonable accommodation.
• The acknowledgement, just prior to testing, that a disability will negatively impact test performance.	• Candidate may be rescheduled for the accommodated test at the next testing date. A test-taking accommodation is only required if the organization knows in advance of the need for accommodation.
• A developing awareness that a disability will negatively impact test-taking behavior after a test administration has begun.	• The individual with a disability must inform the employer that he or she has become aware of the need for an accommodation.
• Individual exhibits a disability that impairs sensory, manual, or speaking skills.	• Identify a test format which does not require the use of the impaired skill. This represents a "reasonable accommodation."
• The lack of alternative testing formats (e.g., giving a test orally instead of in written format) to provide a reasonable accommodation.	• The skill, aptitude, ability may be assessed in another manner (e.g., measuring deductive reasoning by verbally responding to specific case examples rather than answering multiple choice questions presented in a "paper and pencil format").
• An individual with a specific disability may require more time to take the test due to cognitive or perceptual processing limitations.	• Extended time frames may be utilized as a reasonable accommodation except when speed is linked to the essential job functions.

Specific standards already exist to guide the administration of tests to individuals with disabilities. Three relevant guidelines from the *Standards for Educational and Psychological Testing* (APA, 1985) are highlighted below:

> Empirical procedures should be used whenever possible to establish time limits for modified forms of timed test rather than simply allowing "handicapped test takers" a multiple of the standard time. Fatigue should be investigated as a potentially important factor when time limits are extended. (p. 79)

> In assessing characteristics of individuals with "handicapping" conditions, the test used should use either regular or special norms for calculating derived scores, depending on the purpose of the testing....(p. 80)

> People who modify tests for "handicapped" people should have available to them psychometric expertise for so doing. (p. 79)

Some tests have alternative forms which can be utilized for testing individuals with specific disabilities. For example, the Wechsler scales, which measure different facets of adult intelligence, have been adapted for individuals with severe visual impairments (Wechsler, 1955). Reading comprehension may be a barrier for individuals with specific disabilities. Some "paper-and-pencil tests" (e.g., the SRA Nonverbal Form) measure general learning ability relatively independent of language and reading skills (McMurry & King, 1976). Resources available to the test development professional to identify tests with forms for specific disabilities include the manuals of test publishers, *The Mental Measurements Yearbook* (Mitchell, 1985) and *Tests in Print* (Anastasi, 1985).

Unfortunately, the availability of alternative formats for standardized employment tests is still rather limited. Evidence from educational testing programs has yielded mixed results regarding the impact of modified test administration upon the scores of individuals with disabilities (Rock, Bennett, & Jirele, 1988). In addition, the effects of modifying their administration in terms of extended time, extra rest, presentation in Braille or cassette, and the like have not been areas of extensive research for tests typically used in the employment setting. It is best for the organization to solicit the assistance of industrial/organizational psychologists who are well versed in selection test development and test validation. The financial investment in improving the selection program is money well spent to hire or promote the most qualified individuals.

The Selection Interview

The selection interview is the most popular method of obtaining and combining information about an applicant's qualifications. Numerous researchers have noted that the employment interview is open to many biases and plagued with various pitfalls. Unlike the "paper-and-pencil test," the interview process makes irrelevant impairments more pronounced, or in some cases may even cause an interviewer to erroneously regard the individual as having a disability. Interviewer rating errors are likely to introduce significant bias into the selection decision (Schneider & Schmidt, 1986). Many of these biases are related to the physical characteristics of interviewee (e.g., the interviewee's attractiveness and age). Three other common sources of rating errors are:

- *Halo Effects*, in which either good or poor performance on one selection criterion biases the evaluation of other criteria resulting in an artificially inflated or depressed evaluation;
- *Contrast Effects*, in which the individual with a disability receives a lower evaluation because individuals without disabilities present a more favorable impression in areas not related to job performance; and

- *Confirmation Bias*, in which the interviewer looks for information to confirm pre-existing stereotypes of a person with a particular disability.

One method to combat bias in the interview is to provide a more structured framework for observing and recording behavior. Many organizations have developed interview guides which utilize general traits as selection criteria. A typical guide is displayed below:

Traits	Characteristic Displayed		
	High	**Medium**	**Low**
Decision-making Ability	_____	_____	_____
Judgement	_____	_____	_____
Oral Communication	_____	_____	_____
Written Communication	_____	_____	_____
Interpersonal Skills	_____	_____	_____
Comments			

While this guide is an improvement over recording general impressions, it may result in using criteria which have little relevance to the performance of essential job functions. The use of generic traits (e.g., decision-making ability) are likely to increase the opportunity for bias to creep into the selection interview. Generic trait assessments should be replaced with job-specific assessment criteria. For example, the type of written communication might be specified as "ability to express ideas in a written format." Note that the emphasis is not on "writing" but rather on the generation of ideas. Consistent with the theme of this chapter, linking selection criteria to essential job functions will result in the improved identification of successful employees.

The selection interview also can be improved through interviewer training. The effectiveness of the interviewer in obtaining validated, reliable information is largely dependent on the skill of the individual. Areas of interviewer training found to be particularly effective are listed below:

- Question/Topic development
- Understanding worker diversity
- Emphasis on job-relevant criteria
- Reduction of rater errors (e.g., halo effects)
- Inappropriate questions related to race, gender, or disability

In addition to interviewer training, structured interview techniques can improve the identification of successful employees. The structured interview technique is characterized by a structured format for recording evaluations; focusing questions upon skills associated with essential job functions documented in an accurate job description; and applying a common set of selection criteria to all applicants for a similar job (Maurer & Fay, 1988). Types of structured interviews include:

- *Behavior description interviews*, which focus upon past behavior and measure typical (rather than maximum) performance;
- *Situation interviews*, which focus upon what the applicant would do in a particular situation; and
- *Comprehensive structured interviews*, which contain situational, job knowledge, job simulation, and worker requirement components. All three methods involve the recording of results utilizing a structured scoring guide.

In summary, the ADA will create an opportunity for organizations to review and improve all of the selection methods utilized to hire, promote, or terminate employees. The following steps should be taken to improve the selection program and to ensure that selection decisions are fair and job-related:

- Link selection criteria to essential job functions;
- Expand awareness among management in the organization that selection decisions go beyond the hiring gate;
- Adapt and improve administration of "paper-and-pencil assessments" of applicant qualifications for individuals with disabilities;
- Reduce selection biases by structuring the interview process and training interviewers; and
- Identify modifications in the selection process which are needed to promote accessibility to the candidate evaluation process.

Salary Administration and Compensation

The ADA requires that organizations review every aspect of their salary administration program. The salary administration program provides guidelines for the fair and equitable determination of salaries and promotes internal equity in terms of salaries for similar job responsibilities. The salary administration program also provides specifications for the "official record" of the requirements of each job in the form of job descriptions. Job descriptions are likely to be the primary source of documentation (and evidence) regarding essential job functions (see Chapter 8).

A fundamental assumption underlying effective HR management is that job values and compensation decisions are grounded in job-relevant criteria. In effect, the emphasis placed on "essential" job functions by the ADA is perfectly consistent with demonstrating job relevance of personnel decisions. Three components of the salary administration program in every organization should be reviewed to ensure that they promote fair treatment for employees with disabilities, as well as provide a foundation for solid compensation decisions. These components are:

- *Job descriptions.* Do job descriptions explicitly list the essential functions of the job and provide a basis for validating these as essential? Organizations should develop and maintain job descriptions which validate and document essential job functions. It is imperative that the organization identify the essential job functions to ensure disabled individuals (or other individuals for that matter) are not denied fair compensation because they did not effectively perform marginal functions of the position. The job analysis approach used to identify essential job functions will determine the nature and format of the job description.

- *Job evaluation factors.* Is there a relationship between the essential functions of jobs in the organization and the types of factors used to determine the internal equity of jobs? As noted in section 1630.4 of the ADA, it is unlawful to discriminate in "...rates of pay or any other form of compensation or changes in compensation." The job evaluation approach, and factors used to determine the internal value and internal equity of jobs in the job evaluation program should be based in part on essential job functions.

- *Performance evaluation criteria.* Is there a close link between performance criteria used to evaluate individual performance and the essential job functions? Performance evaluation criteria provide the basis to measure employee performance and therefore impact changes in compensation. As such, they should be job-related *and weighted* to reflect the more important aspects (essential functions) of the job.

These three salary administration program components are important because they impact conditions of employment (e.g., the hiring, promotion, and compensation of employees). For example, job requirements in job descriptions are often used as a source of information for developing selection criteria to screen candidates. If the job description is not based on essential job functions, then both pre- and post-employment decisions may be based on trivial or marginal aspects of the job.

The ADA explicitly acknowledges the organization's latitude in establishing performance standards. As noted in section 1630.2(M) of the ADA, "...[essential functions inquiry] is not intended to second guess an employer's business judgment with regard to production standards." Also, the ADA does not require the lowering of performance standards to accommodate an individual with a disability. However, performance evaluation ratings are typically based on the degree to which performance standards are met. Therefore, it is critical that performance standards be linked to essential job functions. Again, establishing standards based on the marginal rather than the essential aspects of the job in conducting a performance review may be unfair to individuals with disabilities who effectively perform essential job functions.

Job Analysis Approaches

The language in the ADA provides broad guidelines which do not outline in detail the ways an organization goes about defining the essential functions for each job. However, developing a job analysis approach and a job description format to facilitate compliance with the ADA should be one of the first activities an organization undertakes to ensure that all HR programs do not present artificial barriers for individuals with disabilities.

Defining and documenting essential job functions requires careful development and validation of the written job description and a corresponding job analysis approach to collect job information. Validation in this context means that important and frequently performed activities are listed in the job description, and are derived from the analysis of actual activities performed by job incumbents. Job descriptions should assist in the identification of reasonable accommodations as well. A number of features should be incorporated into the job analysis approach to ensure that the resulting job description contains an accurate summary of essential job functions:

- Work observation by trained job analysts;
- A breakdown of the job into its component parts;
- Use of job analysis questionnaires resulting in estimates of importance, criticality, time spent on activities or frequency, for each component of the job;
- Input into and agreement upon the job requirements by both incumbents and supervisors; and
- Utilization of an Update/Maintenance schedule to keep job descriptions current.

These guidelines imply that defining essential job functions will require a quantitative rather than a qualitative approach. That is, estimates will need to be made regarding which component parts are more important or "essential" relative to others. Quantitative approaches for making these estimates include: ratings by content experts, incumbents, or supervisors; time/motion specifications; written production records; or computer monitoring.

Beyond describing the components of a job, it is important to obtain an estimate of the importance or criticality of each component of the job. The following are traditional parameters used to estimate criticality:

- Importance;
- Frequency;
- Percent of time spent on the activity relative to total time available;
- Criticality of the activity to successful performance;
- Combination measures (importance times frequency); and
- Consequences of failure to perform the task properly.

Typical sources of input to identify the essential functions of the job include persons such as job incumbents, job analysts, supervisors, and third parties (e.g., an independent consultant), and documents including policy manuals, production records, and strategic planning documents. These sources are more relevant for existing jobs. Newly created jobs are typically defined by managers or the hiring staff who must prepare hiring criteria for the job. Ideally, multiple sources can also be utilized to describe the components of the target jobs. To the degree that sources agree on the presence of key activities, the reliability of the resulting description is enhanced.

Two key principles of job analysis are nearly universally accepted:

- Different job analysis techniques lead to qualitatively different kinds of job information, and
- Different types of job information have applicability to different HR management procedures (Mitchell, 1991). Selection of an appropriate format for both job analysis and the resulting job description will impact the degree to which essential job functions are clearly defined.

A number of job analysis approaches and job description formats have been described in the organizational management literature and are used by job analysts and compensation consultants (Page & Van de Voot, 1989) (e.g., task-oriented, worker-oriented, job dimension-oriented formats). Therefore, the job analysis/job description program provides the foundation to define the essential job functions; provides information for a host of other HR management programs; and offers insights into the types of accommodations which may be explored for specific disabilities (Campion, 1989). The development or revision of a job analysis approach can be a very costly and time-consuming process for any organization. Each of the above approaches to job analysis are reviewed in this section for their applicability to the ADA and their overall utility for other HR programs in the organization.

Task-oriented Approach

A task-oriented job analysis approach defines task activities which outline detailed job requirements. Each task statement represents a single activity. Often, 50 or more task statements can be identified for a job. Examples of task statements for a "911" call taker job follow:

Task 1: Utilize precise questioning techniques to obtain emergency information quickly from caller.

Task 2: Use specific protocols to interview caller regarding the location and nature of problem.

Task 3: Use voice tone and repetitive questioning to calm excited or anxious callers.

Task 4: Obtain critical information from callers such as a description of events to code and forward to the appropriate police or fire agency.

Task statements can readily be utilized to identify essential job functions since each task activity can be rated on a host of quantifiable parameters. Furthermore, the key skills associated with each task can be identified and used to identify reasonable accommodations if necessary. Most organizations, however, find that identifying tasks for each job and maintaining task-oriented job descriptions are too costly and time-consuming. This approach presents an information management challenge, particularly in organizations that have large numbers of single-incumbent jobs.

Worker-oriented Approach

Worker-oriented job analysis techniques focus on worker requirements rather than job responsibilities. Emphasis is upon processes engaged in by the worker to accomplish a task. Worker-oriented processes are placed in a questionnaire format which is typically used by a trained job analyst to describe the job. One popular instrument is the *PAQ* or *Position Analysis Questionnaire* (McCormick, Jeanneret, & Mecham, 1972) which contains 187 items organized according to the following six worker-oriented dimensions:

- *Information input*: Where and how does the worker get the information he or she uses in performing his or her job?
- *Mental processes*: What reasoning, decision-making, planning, and information-processing activities are involved in performing the job?
- *Work output*: What physical activities does the worker perform and what tools or devices does he or she use?
- *Relationship with other persons*: What relationships with other people are required in performing the job?
- *Job context*: In what physical or social contexts is the work performed?
- *Other job characteristics*: What activities, conditions, or characteristics other than those described above are relevant to the job?

The worker-oriented approach is well suited to the identification of physical, perceptual, or cognitive requirements of jobs which may have a relationship to various types of disabilities. Worker-oriented descriptions of jobs also foster the development of selection criteria which are typically skill-, aptitude-, or ability-oriented. Due to the emphasis on the job incumbent, rather than the job itself, a job description listing essential functions may be difficult to produce without adding task statements to the job descriptions. This limits the overall utility for other HR management programs and increases the cost of developing the job description.

Job Dimension-oriented Approach

The job dimension-oriented approach provides descriptive, broad categories of activities which represent a balance between detailed task statements and a summary description of the job. Typically, a menu of job dimensions is developed (based upon job analysis interviews) which is customized for a job function (e.g., accounting, sales). This menu is utilized to guide the job analysis. Examples of job dimensions for an accounting job are presented below:

- *Develop accounting controls, policies, and procedures*: Develop and implement accounting controls, policies, and procedures to ensure that the assets, liabilities, and earnings of the corporation are properly stated;
- *Devise accounting policies*: Work with various areas to devise new accounting principles, policies, and reports and work with computer systems personnel in the development of new automated programs;
- *Evaluate accounting packages*: Evaluate accounting packages and recommend the most appropriate; and
- *Provide advice on financial accounting issues*: Assist in structuring transactions to provide the optimum return for the company considering the risk and reward of all alternatives.

Essential job functions can be readily identified using job-oriented dimensions. Job analysis questionnaires are constructed for categories of dimensions representing broad job functions. These dimensions can be placed into "menus" for job incumbents, supervisors, or job analysts to select the relevant dimensions for their individual jobs. Typically, a job can be described using 15 or fewer job dimensions, which can then be rated on parameters such as importance and frequency by incumbents, supervisors, or job analysts to identify essential functions. Because jobs described using job dimensions are easily defined and rated by job "experts" (e.g., supervisors, job incumbents), they can readily be utilized for other HR programs. These include:

- Hiring criteria for the selection program;
- Evaluation criteria for the performance appraisal program; or
- Job evaluation factors to assess the internal equity and external competitiveness of jobs.

Furthermore, entry level qualifications in the form of skills and aptitudes, historical examples of accommodations, and potential new accommodations can be linked to job-oriented dimensions. Because the identification of essential job functions is critical to compliance with the ADA, and due to the high costs associated with job analysis and the preparation of job descriptions, it is critical that the utility of the job analysis/job description program be maximized. As noted before, the utility of the job information differs depending on the job analysis approach and job description format adopted by the organization. Table 7 summarizes the utility of each job analysis method based on four criteria: definition of essential requirements, cost of data collection and maintenance, utility for HR programs, and utility for identifying accommodations.

As Table 7 indicates, the job dimension-oriented approach provides the overall greatest utility to the organization. However, depending on the desired use of the job analysis information, other approaches may be a more reasonable choice for a particular organization.

Table 7. Summary of Three Approaches to Job Analysis

Job Analysis Approach	Defines Essential Job Requirements	Cost in Terms of Time and Expense to Prepare Job Descriptions	Application to Human Resource Programs	Utility for Identifying Accommodations
Task-oriented	Moderate	High	Moderate	Moderate
Job Dimension-oriented	High	Low	Numerous	Moderate
Worker-oriented	Moderate	Moderate	Moderate	High

Job Evaluation Factors

As noted previously, the ADA prohibits discrimination against individuals with a disability in terms of compensation and changes in compensation. The organization's job evaluation program typically provides a foundation for base salary compensation. Many organizations utilize job evaluation plans which contain multiple factors, and weight each factor to reflect its importance in determining internal pay values. These are labeled *point factor* plans. In applying the point factor approach, jobs are evaluated on a set number of factors and a total "score" is calculated. Total scores are then converted to compensation ranges for individual jobs.

A key concern brought about by the ADA is that job evaluation factors and weights for the factors (if weights are used) may result in lower job values for positions held by individuals with disabilities. Their is a greater likelihood for this to occur when the job evaluation factors are only relevant to a portion of the organization's jobs, or are heavily weighted by specific factors which overemphasize the physical or perceptual requirements of jobs. Job evaluation factors should be reviewed and modified, if necessary, to ensure they reflect the essential functions for all jobs within the organization. Making job evaluation factor definitions consistent with essential job functions can reduce the opportunity for bias and, in effect, upgrade the job evaluation program by improving its job-relatedness.

As an example, a job evaluation plan may contain a factor such as *visual effort* to measure the degree to which a job requires concentrated attention to detail. Jobs which require considerable visual effort would receive a higher value on this factor. Since it is likely that individuals with visual impairments may not be performing jobs requiring visual effort, a bias is built into the program by assigning a higher value to jobs likely to be held by those without visual impairments. Defining the same factor as *attention to detail* rather than visual effort opens up other avenues to satisfactory job performance which are not dependent on a single sensory modality. Individuals with visual impairment may be able to attend to detail by using auditory receivers or other job aids.

Another aspect of the job evaluation program which should be reviewed is the weight assigned to each job evaluation factor. For example, a job evaluation factor, such as decision-making, may reflect 20% of the job evaluation point total; a factor measuring physical requirements may also reflect 20% of the evaluation point total. Employees not able to perform certain physical activities would receive lower values since they may not be in jobs requiring these activities. A more careful review may reveal, however, that physical requirements represent only a small fraction of the essential job functions across all jobs in the organization. Thus, adjusting the weight for physical requirements to 10% and raising the weight for decision-making to 30% may be justified, and may make the evaluation plan more consistent with the structure of jobs in the organization. Also, in this example, it is recognized that decision-making requirements are likely to make a greater contribution to organizational performance than physical activities.

It will be very important to review job evaluation plans to ensure that jobs held by individuals with disabilities are not assigned lower job values than other jobs which require similar levels of skill, effort, and responsibility. There are precedents for this concern. Much discussion has been devoted to defining job evaluation factors which are gender neutral in order to make job evaluation programs fair to all groups, even though some jobs have been traditionally held by men or women (Risher, 1989). It is likely that a similar effort will be needed to eliminate trivial or poorly constructed factors which penalize job incumbents with specific disabilities by devaluing the job evaluation plan and consequently assigning lower wages to jobs held by individuals with disabilities.

How does an organization efficiently design or modify an evaluation plan, to reflect their values, or construct a hierarchy of jobs to maintain internal equity within the organization? An automated job evaluation program can be utilized to quickly update the existing job evaluation program or install a new program. Features to be considered in selecting an automated program include:

- Building upon the present job evaluation system;
- Utilizing organization job evaluation factors;
- Producing reports to compare job values from the current job evaluation plans with job values based on the new job evaluation plans;
- Compatibility of installation with the organization's PC; and
- Providing user-friendly reports.

Performance Appraisal Criteria

The performance appraisal program provides the foundation for a host of employee transactions (e.g., compensation adjustments, promotions, terminations). Unlike job evaluation plans and job descriptions, which are applied in a uniform manner throughout the organization, the performance appraisal process is personal and employee-specific. As such, it is critical that the criteria used to assess individual performance are securely linked to essential job functions.

Job dimensions which are weighted can easily be converted to job-relevant performance criteria. Because job dimensions are focused on the job rather than the employee, effective performance can result from different approaches to the job. Individuals with disabilities, with or without a reasonable accommodation, may attain the same level of proficiency as other employees by using different behavior to achieve effective job performance.

Because job dimensions are job-related and reduce the likelihood that personal traits are used as a basis for performance evaluations, their use: 1) provides managers with the opportunity to pinpoint specific performance strengths and weaknesses; 2) facilitates the identification of accommodations; and 3) reduces the opportunity for bias against individuals with disabilities. Features of such a performance appraisal program are presented in Table 8. Such a program will not only reduce the opportunity for adverse impact against individuals with disabilities, but will also ensure that performance appraisals are job-related and effective for all employees.

Table 8. Performance Appraisal Program Features

- **Job-relevant**   Job dimensions are linked to essential functions of the job.

- **Comprehensive**   Multiple job dimensions are evaluated (up to nine) allowing for variability in performances.

- **Targeted**   Job dimensions are weighted to reflect important activities.

- **Flexible**   Managers select job dimensions and modify weights based on changing requirements of the job.

- **Consistent**   The same jobs use similar job dimensions to ensure evaluation criteria are used in a uniform manner.

- **Promote Feedback**   Job dimensions are evaluated individually which promotes an assessment of strengths, weaknesses, and the development of improvement suggestions.

In summary, the major components of the salary administration program are reviewed to eliminate opportunities for bias to creep into decision-making processes which may negatively impact upon individuals with disabilities. Furthermore, given the rapidly changing nature of jobs and the dynamic criteria available to assess employee performance, it makes good business sense to update the organization's salary administration program regularly. Basing compensation and appraisal decisions on essential job functions reflects a principle which should be at the heart of every HR program decision.

Suggested steps for reviewing the salary administration program and defining essential job functions for all job groups in the organization include:

- Review current uses (implicit or explicit) of job information;
- Implement a job dimension-oriented job analysis/job description program which has multiple uses for the organization *and* defines essential job functions;
- Review the current job evaluation program and recalibrate it against essential job functions using job evaluation factors customized for the organization; and
- Develop a performance appraisal program which utilizes job dimensions based upon essential job functions as performance criteria.

Human Resources Training for Managers Under the ADA

The ADA opens up numerous opportunities for management training. Key training topics and the likely target groups for each type are provided below:

- *Understanding worker diversity in the workplace.* Targeted toward first line supervisors, the focus involves creating an awareness of the cultural underpinnings of workplace behavior. This training can readily be expanded to include disability awareness issues.
- *Conducting a structured interview.* Targeted toward managers with recruitment and hiring responsibilities, the focus is upon using job-relevant criteria in the screening of job candidates. Methods to reduce potential interviewer biases, such as the use of scoring guides, are another focal point of the training.
- *Integrating staff into the work group.* Targeted toward supervisors and members of intact work teams, this training addresses how to orient new staff into a work team. The more cohesive the work team, the more this training is needed to properly assimilate individuals with disabilities. Improving awareness of the needs, roles, and responsibilities of all team members is the key ingredient of this program.
- *Identifying reasonable accommodations.* Targeted at HR staff and supervisors, the focus is upon identifying job accommodations including job redesign techniques, adaptable equipment, or possible modifications to work rules. The primary focus should be on how to carefully review job information to generate ideas leading to reasonable accommodations.
- *Linking human resources decisions to essential job functions.* Targeted at HR staff and supervisors, this training focuses upon skill development in analyzing jobs and identifying job dimensions to use as criteria in various HR decisions.

- *Performance appraisal training.* Targeted at all supervisors and managers, recommended topics include:

    -Identifying job dimensions to reflect essential job functions;
    -Measuring performance against the job dimension;
    -Analyzing performance and gaps;
    -Documenting reasons for the evaluation;
    -Communicating expectations to the employee in terms of goals or standards;
    -Coaching to motivate and learn;
    -Listening to suggestions and criticism; and
    -Linking rewards to performance.

This list will not be unfamiliar to organizations which have an active, "nuts and bolts training program" for supervisors and managers. For example, worker diversity is currently of considerable importance to all employers. Perhaps the key training topic brought about by the ADA is identifying reasonable accommodations for individuals with disabilities. The content of this training program will serve to increase awareness of how to identify potential accommodations. For example, Gerber (1990) points out specific examples of the type of accommodations that can be made in the workplace and the programs sponsored by various companies.

Conclusion

The authors maintain that among the many positive effects of the ADA is the strong reinforcement of the need to review and improve overall HR policies and practices. Careful and *consistent* attention to the development of progressive HR policies, assessment and selection methods, salary administration and compensation programs, and management training is the single best way to achieve full compliance with the letter and spirit of the ADA. As with additional business development, the benefits beyond basic compliance are as obvious as they are abundant.

References

American Psychological Association. (1989). *Principles for the validation and use of personnel selection resources* (2nd ed.). Washington, DC: Author.

American Psychological Association. (1985). *Standards for educational and psychological testing*. Committee to Develop Standards for Educational and Psychological Testing of the American Educational Research Association, the American Psychological Association, and the National Council on Measurement in Education. Washington, DC: Author.

Anastasi, A. (1985). Psychological testing (4th ed.). New York: McMillan Publishing Co., Inc.

Biles, G., & Schuler, R. S. (1986). *Audit handbook of human resource practices: Auditing the effectiveness of the human resources functions*. Alexandria, VA: The American Society for Personnel Administration.

Campion, M. A. (1989). Ability requirement implications of job design and interdisciplinary perspectives. *Personnel Psychology, 42*, 1-24.

Gerber, B. (1990). The disabled: Ready, willing, and able. *Training*, December, 29-36.

Manese, W. R. (1986). *Fair and effective employment testing: Administrative, psychometric, and legal issues for the human resources professional*. New York: Quorum Books.

Maurer, S. D., & Fay, C. (1988). Effect of situational interviews, conventional structured interviews, and training with Interview Rating Agreement: An experimental analysis. *Personnel Psychology, 41*(2), 329-344.

McCormick, E. J., Jeanneret, P. A., & Mecham, R. C. (1972). A study of job characteristics and job dimensions as based on the Position Analysis Questionnaire. *Journal of Applied Psychology, 56*, 347-367.

McMurry, R. N., & King, J. E. (1976). *SRA Nonverbal Form*. Chicago, IL.: Science Research Associates.

Mitchell, J. V. (Ed.). (1985). *9th mental measurements yearbook*. Lincoln, NE: Buros Institute of Mental Measurements.

Mitchell, T. W. (1991). Comprehensive job analysis: Multipurpose or any purpose. *The Industrial-Organizational Psychologist, 29*(2), 69-74.

Page, R. C., & Van de Voot, D. M. (1989). Job analysis and human resources planning. In W. F. Cascio (Ed.), *Human resources planning, employment, and placement*. Washington, DC: Bureau of National Affairs, Inc.

Redekel, J. R. (1989). *Employee discipline: Policies and practices*. Washington, DC: The Bureau of National Affairs, Inc.

Risher, H. W. (1989). Job evaluation: Validity and reliability. *Compensation and Benefits Review*, (January-February) 22-36.

Rock, D. A., Bennett, R. E., & Jirele, T. (1988). Facility structure of the Graduate Record Examinations General Test in handicaps *vs.* nonhandicap groups. *Journal of Applied Psychology, 73*,(3), 383-392.

Schneider, B., & Schmidt, J. (1986). *Staffing organizations*. Glenview, IL: Scott Foresman and Company.

U.S. Equal Employment Opportunity Commission, U.S. Civil Service Commission, U.S. Department of Labor, & U.S. Department of Justice. (1978). Uniform guidelines on employee selection procedures. *Federal Register, 43*, 166, 38295-38309.

Wechsler, D. (1955). *Manual for the Wechsler Adult Intelligence Scale*. New York: The Psychological Corporation.

8

The Changing Nature and Role of Job Analysis

Roger O. Weed, Ph.D.
* Brian T. McMahon, Ph.D., C.R.C.

Job Analysis in an ADA Context

The employment provisions (Title I) of the Americans with Disabilities Act (ADA) do not pertain to all individuals of working age who meet the legal definition of disability. They apply only to "qualified" individuals, that is, persons who: satisfy the requisite skill, experience, education, and other job-related requirements of the position; and can perform the essential functions of the position, with or without accommodation.

In determining essential functions, which are the fundamental (not marginal) job duties of the employment position, there are a variety of forms of evidence which will apply. The most important of these is likely to be the following:

> Written job descriptions prepared before advertising or interviewing applicants for a job. (Federal Register, Part 1630.2[n][3][ii])

These job descriptions will be more compelling if they are derived from a job analysis conducted regularly by trained professionals.

The accurate determination of essential job functions through job analysis is also important because essential functions may be subjected to a variety of forms of reasonable accommodation, save one–job restructuring. The ADA does *not* require the job restructuring of *essential job functions* as a form of reasonable accommodation.

Job analysis is also mentioned in the Appendix to Part 1630, Interpretive Guidance, on Title I of the Americans with Disabilities Act. This section outlines a recommended Process of Determining Appropriate Reasonable Accommodation–a "problem solving approach" (CFR 1630.09[a]). The first step in that process is to..."analyze the particular job involved and determine its purpose and essential functions." Thus, job analysis is explicitly recommended as the basis for most effective reasonable accommodations, which must be considered in determining

---

* Appreciation is extended to Celeste Taylor and Terry Blackwell for their contributions to an earlier article which provided significant background for this chapter.

who is qualified, in providing access to employment testing and selection procedures, in actual performance of job duties, and in the question of removing or minimizing direct threat. Job analysis procedures may take on a slightly different character when the information derived is used to address different employment considerations (e.g., Chapter 11 provides more specific recommendations on the uses of job analysis to achieve essentialness).

The ADA further stipulates that the primary purpose of a medical examination (conducted after an offer of employment but prior to the onset of employment activity) is to determine the individual's ability to perform the essential functions of the job. Accordingly, the physician will have to be equipped with a written job description, photographs, or other job preview information which contributes to his or her understanding of essential job functions. In the future, job analysis findings will routinely be used by physicians, especially as they may relate to:

1) agility tests or fitness-for-duty examinations which are job-related and consistent with business necessity; or

2) the physician's own contribution to the search for appropriate accommodations.

Historical Relevance of Job Analysis

Since the 1930s, job analysis has been the primary scientific means by which an understanding of essential job functions has been achieved. It has traditionally been used for additional applications such as identifying worker traits and avoiding unnecessary risks in employee selection. Job analysis can also enhance the value of labor market surveys which are used to determine the employability (ability to do a job) and placability (ability to get a job) of individuals with disabilities. Once an appropriate job and employer have been identified, a job analysis can determine the compatibility of the worker traits with the factors of that job, and also reveal the willingness of an employer to modify the job or otherwise accommodate the worker (Weed, Taylor, & Blackwell, 1991).

The importance of job analysis cannot be overstated, because research has clearly demonstrated that when individuals with disabilities are properly placed, they have greater probabilities of long-term career satisfaction and success (Du Pont, 1981; Field & Weed, 1988; Weed & Field, 1990; Wright, 1980). One study revealed that 78% of successfully rehabilitated clients had some job analysis performed, compared to 58% in the sample as a whole (Seyler & Chauvin, 1989). Some states, such as California, actually require that a job analysis be conducted for workers' compensation clients prior to job placement.

Relevant publications , many of which are published by the United States Department of Labor (USDOL), which have direct relevance to job analysis procedures and are familiar to experienced job analysts include the following:

> *Dictionary of Occupational Titles, (4th ed.)* (USDOL, 1986);
> *Guide for Occupational Exploration* (USDOL, 1979);
> *Occupational Outlook Handbook* (USDOL, 1990-91);
> *Characteristics of Occupations Defined in the Dictionary of*
>   *Occupational Titles* (USDOL, 1981);
> *Job Analysis for the Private Sector* (Blackwell & Conrad, 1990);
> *On-site Job Analysis Training Manual* (Donham, 1990);

Classification of Jobs (Field & Field, 1988);
Handbook for Analyzing Jobs (USDOL, 1972); and
A Guide to Job Analysis (Materials Development Center, 1982).

In recent times, however, it has become evident that job analysis standards need to be upgraded especially for use in insurance rehabilitation wherein certain procedural deficiencies appear most evident. Toward this end, Weed et al. (1991) have recommended expansion of the traditional ingredients of a job analysis to include the important dimensions contained in Table 1.

* Table 1. Summary of Suggested Worker Traits for Job Analysis

Physical Demands	Comments
Lifting/Strength	Include frequency and duration
Sit	Include frequency and duration
Stand	Include frequency and duration
Walk	Include distance and duration
Climb	Include type and frequency
Balance	Include examples
Stoop	Include examples
Bend	Include examples
Reach	Include unilateral/bilateral and feeling
Handle	Include unilateral/bilateral and feeling
Finger	Include unilateral/bilateral and feeling
Feel	Include sensation requirements
Talk	Include examples
Hear	Include examples
Vision	Include near, far, and depth
Eye/hand/foot	Include examples

Working Conditions	
Inside, outside	Both or unusual details
Cold/changes	Include protective gear
Heat/changes	Include protective gear
Wet	Include hazards
Humid	Include examples
Noise	Include decibels and frequency
Vibrations	Include examples
Hazards	Include examples of risk of injury
Fumes/odors/dust	Include hazardous materials

(continued)

* Reproduced with permission from Weed, Taylor, and Blackwell © (1991).

Table 1. Summary of Suggested Worker Traits for Job Analysis (con't)

General Educational Development Levels	Comments
Reasoning	Vocational relevant information
Math	Include practical examples
Language	Include practical examples
Reading	Include practical examples
Job Training Time	Education and training requirements
Aptitudes	
Intelligence	General learning ability
Verbal	Vocabulary needs
Numerical	Concrete examples
Spatial	Vocationally relevant
Form perception	Vocationally relevant
Clerical perception	Vocationally relevant
Motor coordination	Give examples
Finger dexterity	Bilateral/unilateral
Manual dexterity	Bilateral/unilateral
Eye/hand/foot coordination	Give examples
Color discrimination	Give examples
Interests	Relate to *Guide for Occupational Exploration*
Personality Factors	Include reward values and personal characteristics
	Varied duty
	Short cycle
	Control over task
	Dealing with people
	Influencing others
	Stress and risk taking
	Subjective or objective evaluation of information
	Interpret feelings
	Meet precise standards
Job Description	Include special clothing and tool requirements
DOT Definition	Compare to job description and to worker traits and *Classification of Jobs*
Work Hours/Overtime	Also note seasonal employment

Additional Job Analysis Considerations

Weed et al. (1991) emphasized the importance of deriving job analysis information from multiple sources (see Chapter 11). They illustrated how both incumbents and supervisors will tend to remember only certain tasks which stand out in their minds, or how some injured workers may only remember those tasks which they feel they can no longer perform. The authors of this chapter also reviewed hundreds of job descriptions for a variety of large Midwestern employers to assess their viability in an ADA context. The following problems were observed with regularity:

1) Frequently there was no statement of the purpose for each job (i.e., why does this position exist with respect to the overall mission of the organization?).

2) The "general duties" provided for most jobs were good behavioral descriptors which delineated specific activities performed. They were measurable and objective. However, they sometimes contained statements which more accurately represented qualifications, working conditions, or tools/equipment used. Such statements do not belong under a category of "general duties."

3) Estimates of time spent on each task (either frequency or duration) were often lacking.

4) For many job descriptions, information was not available as to how and when the task statements were derived or revised.

5) For some job descriptions, job description questionnaires were used to obtain data. The format was generally good but it was suspected that the designer of the questionnaire did the following:

    a. A section termed *Essential Functions / Responsibilities* was simply renamed from *Responsibilities*. There was no attempt to identify for the user what was meant by *Essential Functions* and no evidence that this section was intended to get at ADA-relevant information.

    b. When time spent in performing each function was requested, the number of "essential" functions reported was between five and eight (maximum space available) and the percentages always added to 100%. These percentages were not validated by observation. It appeared to be assumed that the essential functions were exhaustive and that there were no marginal tasks.

    c. There was no effort by respondents to relate allegedly essential functions to the purpose statement. The ranking of functions by importance did not correspond logically to the relationship of each function to purpose.

    d. Information about the past work experience of current or former incumbents was not available.

    e. Supervisors were asked to write out "important aspects of this position." This question was clearly confusing to respondents, some of whom answered variably with qualifications, activities, desirable personal characteristics, rationale/purpose for the job, etc.

Additional serious concerns related to this particular job description questionnaire exercise included:

    f. The respondent's understanding of the information requirements and directions in each section;

    g. The respondent's compliance with directions;

    h. The limited sources of information obtained (i.e., no direct observation);

    i. The lack of consistency between incumbent and supervisory responses and their prospective reconciliation;

    j. The uses of or further refinement of these data; and

    k. The repeated attempts by many respondents to use this instrument to justify their positions, perhaps reflective of the climate during the current reorganization.

To address these problems in one organization, all managers whose responsibilities included the development and periodic revision of job descriptions were invited to participate in a training session to determine in a collaborative fashion the specific components of an appropriate job description, as well as the methods by which job content might most accurately be derived. The training content for this session is given in Table 2.

The intention of this training exercise was to build consensus regarding a mechanism by which responsible managers would build appropriate ADA considerations into the routine development and revision processes for their job descriptions. Every effort was made to lead the training group toward the more widespread use of job analysis conducted on a regular basis by trained professionals.

Weed et al. (1991) offer the following additional considerations for the improvement of job analysis:

1) Ensure that the job is specifically observed by a trained rater so that the information derived will be objective and accurate. The observation period should be long enough to equip the rater to answer detailed questions about the job.

2) Photographs or videotapes of representative job duties are strongly encouraged.

3) Go beyond physical demands in identifying those areas which state law and good rehabilitation practice suggest are relevant to suitable job placement (see Table 1).

4) Inquire as to what specific duties the employer is willing to modify, restructure, or otherwise accommodate.

5) Identify architectural barriers which might compromise access to the specified work area, as well as alternatives to the traditional locus of employment.

6) The job analysis is not complete until it is reviewed and approved by the incumbent, supervisor, and employer for thoroughness and accuracy.
7) Ethical considerations relating to accuracy and objectivity are the same for job analysis as for any professional rehabilitation activity.

Table 2. Identifying Essential Job Functions: A Training Outline

I. 45 minutes
Rationale for Revising Job Descriptions
    A. Overview of ADA Title I
    B. Motivation to Derive *Essential Functions*
        1. Determinant of *Qualified*
        2. Impact Upon Reasonable Accommodation Inquiry
        3. Impact Upon Medical Examinations
        4. Impact Upon All Personnel Actions
        5. Impact Upon Job Restructuring
    C. Probabilities and Nature of EEOC Enforcement

II. 15 minutes
Overview of Activities of the Corporate ADA Task Force

III. 15 minutes
Review of All Documents in Which Current Job Content is Described

IV. 75 minutes
Understanding the Legalities of *Essential Functions*
    A. Definition
    B. Three Legal Determinants of *Essentialness*
    C. Seven Forms of Legal Evidence for *Essentialness*

V. 30 minutes
Review of Current Status and Problems with
    Job Descriptions

VI. 30 minutes
Recommended Job Descriptions: Experiences of Other Employers

VII. 120 minutes
Working Group Action Plan Development
    A. Desirable Job Description Components
    B. Job Description Revision Process
    C. Job Description Revision Schedule

VIII. 30 minutes
Expected Outcomes, Accountability, Follow-up

These and other selected topics which might be included in a job analysis are included in Table 3.

* Table 3. Job Analysis Checklist

✓	Have you included all physical demands of the job? (Strength, sit, stand, walk, climb, balance, stoop, bend, reach, handle, finger, feel, talk, hear, vision, and eye/hand/foot requirements.)
✓	Have you included the working conditions? (Inside, outside, cold, heat, wet, humid, noise, vibration, hazards, fumes, odors, and dust.)
✓	What are the general education requirements? (Reasoning, math, language, and reading.)
✓	What are the entry level training requirements? (High school, vocational school, on-the-job, college, etc.)
✓	What aptitudes are required? (Intelligence, verbal, numerical, spatial, form perception, clerical perception, motor coordination, finger dexterity, manual dexterity, eye/hand/foot coordination, and color discrimination.)
✓	What interests are appropriate? (Refer to the *Guide for Occupational Exploration*)
✓	What personality factors (temperaments) are important? (Varied duty, short cycle, control over task, dealing with people, influencing others, stress and risk taking, subjective or objective evaluation of information, interpret feelings, meet precise standards.)
✓	Have you obtained the employer's job description?
✓	Have you compared the description with the *Dictionary of Occupational Titles* definition?
✓	What are the normal work hours?
✓	Is overtime likely?
✓	Did you observe the job long enough to fully understand all of the details and requirements?
✓	Would pictures or a video of the job be appropriate to describe the job?
✓	Will the employer modify the job? (Flex time, restructure, job share, etc.)
✓	Are special clothing or tools required?
✓	Will rehabilitation technology make the job more accessible to the client?
✓	What architectural barriers exist? Can they be eliminated?
✓	Did the employer approve the job as analyzed?
✓	Did the client approve the job as analyzed?
✓	Did the client's physician approve the job as analyzed?
✓	Is the employer likely to hire this person?

* Reproduced with permission from Weed, Taylor, and Blackwell © 1991.

Conclusion

Job analysis has always been an important part of the vocational rehabilitation process. Its importance is enhanced by the new requirements of the ADA. With proper modifications and enhancements, job analysis may be the single most important tool in facilitating smooth and successful job placements. As stated by Weed et al. (1990):

> Through communication, cooperation, and coordination of efforts, clients can be properly placed, enhancing the potential for long-term employment success and promoting the image of rehabilitation as a valuable profession.

References

Blackwell, T., & Conrad, A. (1990). *Job analysis for the private sector*. Athens, GA: E & F Vocational Services.

Donham, D. (1990). *On-site job analysis training manual*. Seattle, WA: WKRS.

Du Pont. (1981). *Equal to the task*. Wilmington, DE: Author.

Field, T., & Field, J. (1988). *Classification of jobs*. Athens, GA: E & F Vocational Services.

Field, T., & Weed, R. (1988). *Transferable work skills*. Athens, GA: E & F Vocational Services.

Materials Development Center. (1982). *A guide to job analysis*. Stout, WI: Author.

Seyler, C., & Chauvin, J. (1989). Placement technique variables and subject variables associated with successful rehabilitation outcome. *Journal of Private Sector Rehabilitation, 4*(1), 3-7.

USDOL. (1972). *Handbook for analyzing jobs*. Washington, DC: Author.

USDOL. (1979). *Guide to occupational exploration*. Washington, DC: Author.

USDOL. (1981). *Characteristics of occupations defined in the Dictionary of Occupational Titles*. Washington, DC: Author.

USDOL. (1986). *Dictionary of occupational titles (4th ed.)*. Washington, DC: Author.

USDOL. (1990-91). *Occupational outlook handbook*. Washington, DC: Author.

Weed, R., Taylor, C., & Blackwell, T. (1991). Job analysis and the private sector. *Journal of Private Sector Rehabilitation, 6*(4), 153-158.

Weed, R., & Field, T. (1990). *Rehabilitation consultants handbook*. Athens, GA: E & F Vocational Services.

Wright, G. (1980). *Total rehabilitation*. Boston: Little, Brown and Company.

9

Employer-based Disability Management Strategies and Work Return Transition Programs

Donald E. Shrey, Ph.D., C.R.C.
Robert E. Breslin, M.S., C.R.C.

Introduction

Throughout the past decade, industry-based disability management interventions and work return transition programs have become increasing prevalent among business and industry. Rapidly escalating workers' compensation costs have been mirrored by increased collaboration among employers and rehabilitation providers within the disability management arena. The Americans with Disabilities Act (ADA) offers protection to all individuals considered disabled, as defined in the Act. Workers with job-related injuries, illnesses, and disabilities are among those protected by the ADA. As a protected class under the ADA, requirements to accommodate workers with disabilities have profound implications for both the worker with a disability and the employer. The purpose of this chapter is to examine the implications of Title I of the ADA for workers with disabilities, their employers, and rehabilitation professionals.

This chapter also examines disability management interventions as an effective mechanism for facilitating employer compliance with Title I of the ADA. Effective disability management programs and interventions are reviewed in this chapter, too. Model on-site disability management programs are examined, with respect to targeted objectives, program features, intervention outcomes, and implications for compliance with the ADA.

The ADA and Injured Workers

In July 1990, President Bush signed the ADA into law. This law is intended to extend civil rights protection similar to that found in other civil rights legislation related to race, sex, age, and ethnicity to individuals with disabilities (Morrissey, 1990). The law is effective on the second anniversary of its signing in July 1992.

The employment-related provisions of the ADA will be enforced by the Equal Employment Opportunities Commission, which is also responsible for disseminating information to employers regarding their responsibilities under the ADA (Tysse, 1990).

The ADA specifically addresses issues of equal access in the areas of employment, public accommodations, public transportation, and telecommunications. The Act also extends to the private sector the concept of *reasonable accommodation*, which has been the standard required among recipients of federal funds since 1973. It is anticipated that the ADA will have a significant impact upon the recruitment, screening, hiring, supervision, and firing of employees in the United States, particularly when issues of disability are involved (Morrissey, 1991). The employment-related provisions in Title I of the Act cover all employers with 25 or more employees in 1992 and all employers with 15 or more employees by 1994.

The initial focus regarding the ADA among legal experts, employers, and the disability community has been centered on issues related to new applications for employment from individuals with disabilities. Much of the early ADA literature addresses the process of recruiting, evaluating, interviewing, and accommodating the job applicant with a disability under the provisions of the ADA (Lotito & Pimentel, 1990; Morrissey, 1991). Human resource professionals, attorneys, rehabilitation professionals, and medical practitioners provided training and technical assistance in these areas months before the Equal Employment Opportunity Commission had released the final Title I regulations.

Paradoxically, the most immediate and profound implications of the ADA for employers may be related to currently employed workers with impairments that compromise their work performance (Lotito & Pimentel, 1990). There is no specific mention of workers' compensation in the Act. However, there is no language in the ADA which excludes protection among individuals with acquired industrial injuries and occupational illnesses. The ADA definition of an "individual with a disability" is based, in part, on the individual being limited in a "major life activity" because of physical or mental impairment. The law specifically identifies work activity as an example of a "major life activity." Consequently, any individual with permanent physical, psychological, or intellectual limitations which prohibit a return to work will certainly fall under the protection of the Act.

The history of case law which developed since the signing of the Rehabilitation Act of 1973 further supports the view that workers with injuries and disabilities will be protected. Several cases (Hutchins v. Erie City and County, 1981; Johnson v. Sullivan, 1991) have addressed arguments regarding the application of civil rights protections to the area of workers' compensation. Employers who have relied on the argument that workers' compensation was intended to serve as an exclusive remedy for individuals sustaining industrial injuries have not been successful in avoiding antidiscrimination actions.

The Equal Employment Opportunities Commission (EEOC) addressed several workers' compensation-related issues in the preamble to the proposed ADA employment regulations which it circulated for comment in August 1990. Workers' compensation issues and the potential impact of the Title I regulations on the management of industrial injury were the focus of a significant number of the comments received by the EEOC. Such was the strength of the response that, when final regulations were published in July 1991 (Federal Register, Vol. 56, No. 144), workers' compensation was identified as a significant source of continuing controversy by the EEOC.

Comments received by the EEOC were reportedly "split decisively and divisively along service provider and employer lines" (Siska, 1991). Comments from the business and industry interest groups (e.g., U.S. Chamber of Commerce) reflected employers' needs to utilize medical and claims information in the administration and defense of workers' compensation claims. Advocates for persons with disabilities from the rehabilitation community insisted that confidentiality be maintained, with respect to a protected individual's medical information and prior workers' compensation history. The intent, of course, was to avoid potential discriminatory employment practices associated with access to this information.

In response to comments and concerns expressed regarding these issues, the regulations were amended to include specific language allowing employers to utilize medical information in the defense and administration of workers' compensation claims. Other difficult issues were acknowledged, such as the employer's need for information regarding prior workers' compensation injuries and claims in order to access second injury funds. However, these issues were not specifically addressed in the body of the regulations. According to the report of the *EEOC Final ADA Regulations*, the EEOC intended to continue examination of workers' compensation issues, and address them more specifically in the technical assistance manuals to be available to employers in January 1992 (Equal Employment Opportunity Commission, 1991).

The ultimate impact of the ADA on the employment of individuals with disabilities will be difficult to assess until dispute resolution processes and litigation have resulted in legal precedents and case law. This seems especially true when considering those injured workers covered under the nation's various workers' compensation laws, who also meet the ADA's definition of "qualified individual with a disability." However, the following facts seem irrefutable, based upon review of the Act, the rules developed by the EEOC, and the opinions of legal and other experts.

1. Injured workers and other employees who develop disabilities during the course of employment do fall under the protection of the ADA.

Although no specific language exists in the ADA regulations specifically related to persons with work-related injuries, there is no indication that these individuals are unprotected by the law, provided they meet the definition of "qualified individual with a disability" and are employed by "covered entities" (e.g., employers not specifically excluded from coverage by the ADA).

2. Employers ("covered entities") will be bound by the provisions of Title I, section 102 of the ADA, as well as the Final Rule as published by the EEOC, when evaluating an injured worker's readiness to return to work, when making decisions regarding the reintegration of an individual with a disability into the workplace, and in performing all of the other claims and personnel administration functions related to the employment relationship with an employee having an acquired disability.

This point is significant, in that it requires employers to consider the accommodation of a qualified individual's physical or mental impairments prior to a denial of employment that is based upon the individual's inability to perform the "essential functions of the job." According to the law, reasonable accommodations may include, but are not limited to, "making existing facilities used by employees readily accessible and useable by individuals with disabilities; and job restructuring, part-time or modified work schedules, reassignment to a vacant position, acquisition or modification of equipment or devices, appropriate adjustment or modifications of examinations, training materials, or policies, the provision of qualified readers or interpreters, and other similar accommodations for individuals with disabilities."

> 3. Failure to receive technical assistance will not be a defense under the ADA.

The primary responsibility for the ADA compliance falls upon the "covered entity" or employer. Although the EEOC acknowledges that insufficient attention has been paid to issues of workers' compensation, employers must comply with the law. According to section 506 of the ADA, which outlines the Federal government's plan for the dissemination of information and the provision of technical assistance, any failure to develop or disseminate technical assistance on the part of the government is no excuse for the employer to fail to comply with the regulations. Given the broad mandate for equal employment rights contained in Title I of the ADA, the Act presents significant challenge to American business, industry, and government, even if the country's various workers' compensation insurance systems were operating efficiently and cost-effectively.

The Challenges of ADA Compliance Considered in the Context of the Current Workers' Compensation Crisis

The terms *workers' compensation* and *crisis* have become synonymous to business and industry, insurance underwriters, and government leaders. The cost of workers' compensation premiums escalated to an estimated total of $45 billion in 1989 (Thompson, 1990). It is projected that the cost of disability in the United States will reach $200 billion by the year 2000 (Farrell, Knowlton, & Taylor, 1989). In some states, employers have been confronted with a 300% increase in injured worker medical costs during the past decade (Galvin, 1989). When increased health insurance costs are factored in, there has been a 400% increase in injury and illness costs to U.S. employers in the past 15 years (Victor, 1989).

Additionally, the changing demographics of America's workforce provoke additional concerns related to disability and health care costs. According to the projections of the U.S. Department of Labor (1988), the median age of U.S. workers will increase from 34.6 in 1980 to 38.9 by the turn of the century. Researchers have identified a positive correlation between increasing age and incidence of disability (Nagi, 1976; McNeil, 1982; Lewis, 1989). Longer courses of rehabilitation and associated costs accompany the increased incidence of disability among older workers (Myers, 1983).

Given this bleak scenario, employers may view the ADA as an additional obstacle to the difficult task of managing hemorrhaging disability costs. Employers may also be tempted to view the financial and human costs of disability as an unavoidable and expected expense of conducting business. Employers having such perceptions are likely to perceive the ADA as a direct threat to their profitability, and a burden to be circumvented, if at all possible. Even a cursory examination of technical assistance programs being promoted by human resource and legal experts would reveal ample anecdotal evidence to support such views. For example, the focus among corporate legal counsel has been the development of defensible legal positions when dealing with disability-related personnel decisions, as opposed to the implementation of innovative compliance strategies. If employers view the Act as merely another intrusive and expensive government regulation, they will likely manage their compliance strategies in a manner which will promote the economic self-interests of labor and trial attorneys and other high-paid consultants.

The central theme of this chapter is that compliance with the ADA and controlling injury and disability costs are not mutually exclusive concepts. There exists a growing body of evidence that disability management strategies and interventions are effective in controlling the personal and economic costs of injury and disability. The next section of this chapter examines disability management concepts, in light of the spirit of the ADA.

Disability Management: Employer Response to a Rapidly Changing Business Environment

In an era characterized by intensified global economic competition and an impending shortage of skilled workers, the human and financial costs of disability to industry and society have become more apparent. Foresighted employers are reevaluating traditional methods of preventing and managing disability in an attempt to lessen its adverse impact. The impetus behind this reexamination is multifaceted. The rising cost of disability to employers, manifested in terms of increased insurance costs and decreased productivity has been well-documented.

As previously noted, workers' compensation costs have increased dramatically in the past 15 years. It has been estimated that the total cost of health care in the U.S. will soon constitute 12% of the gross national product (Habeck, 1991). Given the current system of private health insurance, much of this cost will be borne directly by employers. The remainder will be paid indirectly by employers and employees in the form of taxes. These costs, in terms of an impact on business climate, are a significant issue in interstate competition for business development. Similarly, expenditures related to workplace disability have a direct impact on the overall cost of doing business in the United States. This, of course, has important implications for competitiveness of American goods and services in the world marketplace.

In addition to direct costs of medical care and wage replacement associated with workplace disability, there are "hidden" costs associated with an employer's passive response to worker disability. These costs are related to employee suffering, labor relations problems, litigation, and the reduction of a skilled labor pool. Many of these problems are the manifestation of an irresponsible or misguided management.

Although labor-management dissention arising from work-related disability is not a new phenomenon, such conflicts are particularly troubling when considered in the context of current management theory. For example, consider the projected impact of an aging generation of baby boomers on the incidence and severity of disability. As described by Brandt (1990), the baby boomer has benefitted from living in a time of unprecedented economic prosperity. The result of this shared generational experience is a large demographic cohort which is more highly educated and mobile, geographically and vocationally, than its predecessors. This has led management theorists such as Peters, Drucker, and Ouchi to advocate approaches to personnel and operations management which rely less on techniques of planning and control, and more on the development of consensus and the cultivation of shared corporate values, goals, and culture. This style of management, termed *management by consent* (Brandt, 1990) stresses the importance of employee involvement in the decision-making process. It places a premium on the development of mutual commitments between employer and employee. It implicitly places primary value upon the people who work in an organization and makes the attraction and retention of skilled employees a central function of management.

Disability disrupts the employment relationship and often results in the permanent separation of a trained worker from his or her accustomed work. The employment relationship is typically strained by a disabling accident or illness because of a lack of communication between employer and worker, inappropriate claims investigation and administration procedures, financial pressures resulting from administrative delays in the processing of medical bills and wage replacement payments, and unnecessary litigation (Shrey, 1989). The factors associated with disability in the workplace are complex. They may include medical, psychosocial, vocational, economic, labor relations, and environmental issues. The resolution of workplace disability requires a multidisciplinary approach that addresses these factors in a coordinated fashion. This approach is typically identified as *disability management*.

The Disability Management Concept ━━━━━━━━

Employer-based disability management programs have been implemented in a variety of companies with varying degrees of success. Disability management has been defined as an active, planful process of coordinating the activities of labor, management, insurance carriers, health care providers, and vocational rehabilitation professionals for the purpose of minimizing the impact of injury, disability, or disease on a worker's capacity to successfully perform his or her job (Shrey, 1990). Disability management involves the use of services, people, and materials to minimize the impact and cost of disability to employers and employees and encourages return to work for employees with disabilities (Schwartz, Watson, Galvin, & Lippoff, 1989). Operationally defined, disability management is a proactive process which jointly empowers labor and management to exercise both control and responsibility as decision-makers, planners, and coordinators of interventions and services. Disability management includes prevention programs, rehabilitation, and safe work return programs designed to control the personal and economic costs of workplace injury and disability (Shrey & Breslin, in press).

ADA Compliance and Disability Management

The purpose of this section is to discuss the implications of disability management services and interventions, with respect to employer compliance with the ADA. Typically, disability management programs in industry are designed to: 1) *prevent lengthy work disruptions* among employees with medical impairments that effect work performance; 2) promote a safe and timely *return to work* among employees receiving workers' compensation or sickness and accident benefits; and 3) *accommodate* workers with disabilities who are less than fully capable of performing full-duty work (Shrey, 1990). Generally, these programs are designed to protect the employability of workers, whether they have job-related or non-job-related disabilities. The ADA regulations, in effect, enforce the employer's obligations toward this protected class of individuals. However, disability management interventions and programs established for workers with disabilities also have important implications for persons with disabilities who are pursuing employment.

Both injured workers and nonworking persons with disabilities require reasonable accommodations. Injured workers need an opportunity to transition *back to work*; nonworking persons with disabilities often require an initial transition *into work*. The development of a successful worker-job "fit" is a function of both the capabilities of the worker and the requirements of the job. According to the ADA, job accommodations are required to enable the person with a disability to perform the essential job tasks. The rehabilitation and business literature describes model disability management programs, all of which have relevance to the spirit and letter of the ADA. Taulbee (1991) described several disability management programs in business and industry, including important outcomes having relevance to ADA compliance. Consumer Power Company's program resulted in a 48% decrease in the number of work days lost due to recordable lost-time injuries. Safeway Stores saved $8 for each dollar spent, and reduced back injuries and related costs by 50%. Marriott, with 20,000 employees in 50 states, reduced the number of workers' compensation cases by 30 to 50%, saved $4 for every dollar spent, and reduced litigated workers' compensation cases by 50%. Avers (1989) reported on the General Motors Buick-Oldsmobile-Cadillac Metal Fabrication and Assembly Plants in Lordstown, Ohio, with its estimated annual savings of $3 million, including $50,000 saved by creating a nontraditional, light-duty recycling job. Patenaude (1989) described the disability management program of Lockheed Missile and Space Company, which reduced worker visits for physical therapy and associated costs by 50% during the first year of its operation. Habeck (1991) reported on the features and outcomes of several on-site disability management programs. Both public and private employers were cited, including the City of Lansing, Steelcase Corporation, Walbro Corporation, Walt Disney World, Herman Miller Corporation, and Federal Express. The following elements, which relate closely to the achievement of ADA compliance, are common among most successful disability management programs (Habeck, 1991):

1. Joint labor-management commitment and involvement
2. Employee education and involvement
3. Multidisciplinary interventions (e.g., medical, vocational, psychological, ergonomics, engineering)
4. Case management/case coordination
5. Effective disability prevention strategies
6. Utilization of employer-based and community resources
7. Early intervention and early return to work philosophy
8. Supportive policies and procedures to facilitate accommodations and jobsite modifications
9. A system that ensures accountability of all parties
10. A management information system for program evaluation

Specific disability management interventions having direct relevance to ADA compliance include: 1) evaluating the physical capacity of the individual; 2) developing functional descriptions of essential job duties; and 3) making reasonable accommodations. According to Owen (1990), employers become aware of disabilities among their workers through the benefit program evaluation and entitlement process (e.g., workers' compensation, short-term and long-term disability). Entitlement to these programs can bring a worker under the protection of the ADA. In such cases, it is essential to functionally evaluate both the worker and the job, and to coordinate a reasonable accommodation analysis in the absence of the worker's complete recovery.

Interventions related to ADA compliance should be integrated with an employer's existing disability management or work return transition program. Wellness, prevention, employee assistance, and related programs are designed to protect the employability of the worker. Mandatory reasonable accommodation requirements under the ADA can become a major objective within an employer's existing disability management program.

One major development reflected in the disability management literature is the recent growth of joint labor-management supported disability management programs. Bruyere and Shrey (1991) reviewed several model programs, many of which were guided by labor-management steering committees. For example, Hinds (1988) described a variety of successful "Ability Management Programs" designed to retain injured and disabled employees. Habeck, Williams, Dugan, and Ewing (1989) and Tate and associates (1987) analyzed disability management practices in Buick-Oldsmobile-Cadillac and Herman Miller, Inc. Davidson (1985) described rehabilitation in the 3M corporation. Galvin (1983) cited disability management research conducted at Kimberly-Clark Corporation, Control Data Corporation, and Volvo Corporation. Gates, Taler, and Akabas (1989) described the benefits of an Early Intervention Program implemented with union assistance. Hester and Decelles (1990) reported on a study of the effect of employer size on disability benefits and cost containment practices. The success of these programs promotes the importance of joint commitment, support, and active participation of labor and management.

The ADA and the Employer-based Work Return Transition Model

There is a growing trend among business and industry to reduce lost time and associated workers' compensation costs by developing on-site work return transition (WRT) programs (Bruyere & Shrey, 1991). *Transitional work* is any job or combination of tasks and functions that may be performed safely and with remuneration by an employee whose physical capacity to perform functional job demands has been compromised (Shrey & Olsheski, in press).

Work return transition program concepts are relevant to ADA compliance, in that they encourage and support an injured employee's safe and timely return to work. They also provide accommodations to workers with disabilities, affording them an opportunity to gradually "transition" into performing an expanded range of essential job tasks through conditioning, safe work practices education, and work re-adjustment (Frieden, 1989).

WRT programs are designed to: 1) *reduce lengthy periods of work disruption* among employees with disabilities; 2) promote safe and timely *work return* activities among employees receiving workers' compensation or other insurance benefits; and 3) *accommodate* workers with disabilities having compromised capacities to perform the full range of essential job functions (Shrey, 1990).

The Principle of Occupational Bonding

Occupational bonding is the central principle to creating an effective WRT program (Bruyere & Shrey, 1991). This principle refers to establishing a mutually beneficial relationship between the worker and the employer. To resolve potentially adversarial relationships between workers and employers, it is important to clarify the employer's intentions as well as the worker's expectations. When both worker and employer value strategies that protect the employability of the worker, the occupational bond becomes strengthened. Work return transition programs serve as concrete evidence of the employer's intentions. Through proper education and orientation, the worker's expectations become less suspicious and employer attitudes become less cynical.

Structure and Organization of WRT Programs

Corporate policy, labor relations issues, and other organizational factors are important when developing WRT programs. In keeping with the spirit of the ADA, employer creativity and flexibility are critical. Employer-based WRT programs require: 1) objective worker evaluations; 2) an analysis of job tasks and physical functions; 3) on-site clinical supervision; and 4) a gradual work return plan that increases the worker's capacity to return to full-duty. Thus, the concepts of *functional job analysis* and *reasonable accommodation* are implicit to WRT program operations.

Meaningful Productive Work

Functional job analyses allow for categorizing jobs by degree of physical and vocational demands to allow direct comparison with the worker's physical and vocational capabilities. All workers should be offered meaningful work for fair pay. Anything less is degrading to the worker with a disability and will likely promote conflict, litigation, and labor relations problems.

Job Accommodations and Ergonomics

Work return transition programs in industry promote the development of a successful worker-job "fit," which is a function of both the capabilities of the worker and the requirements of the job. Job accommodations, such as tool redesign, ergonomically sound workstations, adaptive devices, or work schedule modifications are all effective methods that enable the worker to perform essential job tasks (Gross, 1988). These same interventions can be utilized in a preventive manner to identify and redesign jobs which are likely to cause future injuries.

Formalized Policy and Procedure

Compliance with the ADA requires more than access to resources and services. It requires a strong corporate commitment, a skilled and supportive labor-management team, and pro-active policies and procedures. "Protecting the employability of the worker" is the common ground upon which joint labor-management supported disability management programs are built. For example, formalized WRT programs delineate eligibility, entrance and exit criteria, thus resolving collective bargaining issues. The roles of key personnel, accommodation methods, dispute resolution procedures, and program evaluation issues are fully addressed in formalized programs (Randolph & Dalton, 1989).

Employers that provide transitional work opportunities for individuals with disabilities demonstrate a real commitment to the ADA. Work return transition programs promote the continued labor force participation of persons with disabilities, while simultaneously reducing financial liabilities associated with work-related injuries. Persons with disabilities who participate in transitional work are able to minimize the economic, physical, psychological, social, and domestic losses related to discriminatory employment practices and accommodation barriers.

The Role of the Joint Labor-Management Committee

Typically, joint labor-management committees on disability management are designed to ensure checks and balances related to the fair treatment of workers with injuries and disabilities. They often establish the policies, procedures, and protocols for operating on-site work return transition programs. Frequently, these programs are an outgrowth of previously established safety and health commit-tees. Committee members conduct a variety of decision-making activities regard-ing the development of light-duty options, ergonomic job modifications, and worker accommodations. They may also function as an objective grievance mechanism, when resolving disputes over wage replacement and benefit issues. Overall, the joint labor-management committee functions in the areas of educa-tion, program development, disability management service implementation, and program evaluation. These functional areas within the committee structure are central, in the context of ADA compliance integration. An important consider-ation, with respect to the ADA, is the expansion of the committee's function to incorporate a dispute resolution system related to Title I compliance. The follow-ing section reviews several dispute resolution mechanisms, and suggests a dispute resolution model for ADA compliance.

A Suggested Dispute Resolution Model for the ADA

In recent years, courts have become overloaded with a wide variety of claims, resulting in a complex, expensive, slow, and sometimes unresponsive system for resolving disputes. The range of solutions available to the highly structured court system places limits on the design of appropriate remedies to disputes. Courts can be utilized to delay dispute settlement. By their nature, court proceedings promote an adversarial climate which may further antagonize involved parties and decrease the likelihood of the utilization of technical assistance or expertise to resolve disputes. As individuals with disabilities become increasingly aware of their rights under the ADA, this situation will certainly be exacerbated, unless alternative methods are utilized to avoid unnecessary litigation.

Alternative Dispute Resolution (ADR) programs are an alternative to the courts and federal agencies which often prove to be faster, more flexible, and more cost-effective. There are several forms of ADRs, which include arbitration, mediation, fact-finding, med-arb, court-ordered arbitration, voluntary/ad hoc arbitration, negotiation, conciliation, mini-trials, and rent-a-judge. Arbitration may be binding or nonbinding, generally involves less formal procedures, and has more flexible rules. Mediation uses an impartial party to facilitate discussion between the disputants, suggests possible solutions, and may assist parties in reaching a voluntary agreement. Participation in negotiation is voluntary. Dispu-tants represent themselves and determine the procedures to be utilized as well as the criteria used in arriving at resolution. The U.S. Arbitration Act, the Federal Rules of Civil Procedure (Rule 16 a), and the Federal Rules of Evidence all provide a basis and support for the use of ADRs. The Uniform Arbitration Act has been accepted by approximately half of the states and the American Arbitration Association has established a series of rules for its arbitration proceedings in the various industrial settings (Marks, Johnson, & Szanton, 1984).

The suggested model for resolving ADA-related disputes represents a func-tional expansion of the joint labor-management committee on disability manage-ment. Committee members serve an investigative function, and delineate specific recommendations for resolving complaints related to discrimination, reasonable accommodation, and other protected rights. This committee's functions may become further expanded to facilitate the provision of technical assistance to individuals and covered entities that have rights and duties under Title II and III of the ADA. The following steps outline the suggested procedures for receiving and responding to ADA-related complaints:

Step 1: Filing a Complaint

A complaint may be initiated by the individual directly contacting a committee member, or through referral by a party representing the complainant including covered entity, employer, public relations services, ombudsman, personnel officers, labor union representatives, or advocacy representatives.

Step 2: Intake of Case Record Information

A record of the complaint will be established, based on an oral statement or a written statement from the complainant. The record will include name and title of the complainant and respondent (i.e., covered entity charged in the complaint) the nature, date, and alleged facts of the complaint, the requested action to resolve the complaint, and a summary of the investigation steps. The joint labor-management committee will function as a neutral third party to facilitate resolution of the dispute.

Step 3: Investigation

The employer-based committee will be empowered to act promptly in the investigation and resolution of the complaint. Specific time limitations for the investigation of a complaint will be determined at the time of intake. Meetings may be initiated with the complainant or the respondent, separately or jointly, and with others involved in or with knowledge of the dispute. The purpose of these interviews will be to review the facts and details of the complaint, define the issues, and to identify solutions or remedies to resolve the complaint.

Step 4: Provide Information Regarding External Resources

An alternative dispute resolution function of the committee will be to inform the complainant about the availability of external agencies, such as the Civil Rights Commission, Equal Employment Opportunity Commission, Department of Education, Office of Civil Rights, Department of Health and Human Services, Department of Labor, Department of Justice, American Arbitration Association, Institute for Human Awareness, and the Office of Federal Contract Compliance Programs, for filing allegations of unlawful discrimination.

Step 5: Complaint Is Not Substantiated

A detailed report will be provided to the complainant if the committee's investigative actions cannot substantiate supportive facts to the discriminatory allegations. The respondent will also be provided with the details of the perceived problems and encouraged to address these problems in a show of good faith.

Step 6: Complaint is Substantiated

After careful review of the facts and needs, the joint labor-management committee will make specific recommendations and propose steps for resolving the dispute. This may include providing technical assistance to respondents or assisting respondents to link with external resources. Dispute resolution techniques may range from the development of formal written work return plans to informal job modifications. A continuum of procedures primarily involving arbitration, mediation, and negotiation may be used to facilitate resolution of disputes. Other variations or combinations of procedures include med-arb, conciliation, ombudsman, and mini-trials.

Step 7: Case Resolution

If the respondent elects not to take the recommended action, or an agreeable solution is not achieved, a written summary of resolution efforts will be completed and provided to the complainant and respondent. If the complainant is dissatisfied with the outcome of these steps, he or she will be advised of the availability of external agency resources and procedures. The joint labor-management committee's involvement in the dispute will cease at this step.

Conclusion

Protecting the rights of injured workers is an important component of the ADA. Every year thousands of workers become disabled through industrial accidents and occupational disease. Without the accommodations required by the ADA, workers with disabilities risk similar discrimination as other individuals with disabilities. This chapter discussed disability management interventions and services, as an important mechanism in ADA compliance.

The workers' compensation crisis was also discussed in this chapter. The profound impact of rapidly escalating workers' compensation costs will be experienced by American business and industry throughout the next decade. Just as this crisis offers a challenge to industry, the ADA creates an opportunity. With a decreasing labor pool, an aging workforce, and increased worldwide competition, employers must focus on protecting the employability of the American worker. This chapter reviewed exemplary disability management programs, with a particular emphasis on on-site work return transition programs. Such programs offer a range of promising models that can be easily replicated, provided they have the joint support of labor and management. The essential conditions common to successful disability management programs were outlined, and the importance of the joint labor-management committee was reviewed. Finally, a model dispute resolution process was discussed as a mechanism for achieving and sustaining a positive bond between the worker and the employer.

References

Americans with Disabilities Act of 1990. (1990). Report of the 101st Congress 101-596. Washington, DC: U.S. Government Printing Office.

Avers, L. (1989). Hard at work. *Ohio Monitor*, 5-10.

Brandt, S. (1990). *Entrepreneuring in established companies*. New York: New American Library.

Bruyere, S., & Shrey, D. (1991). Disability management in industry: A joint labor-management process. *Rehabilitation Counseling Bulletin, 34*(3), 227-242.

Davidson, G. (1985). *Private sector efforts to control disability-related health costs*. Paper presented at the meeting on Economics of Disability, U.S. Department of Education, National Institute of Handicapped Research, Washington, DC.

Equal Employment Opportunity Commission. (1991).Equal employment opportunity for individuals with disabilities. Final Rule. *Federal Register, 56*, 144.

Farrell, G., Knowlton, S., & Taylor, M. (1989). Second chance: Rehabilitating the American worker: A case management approach to long-term disability can result in savings. *Journal of Private Sector Rehabilitation, 4*, 3-4.

Frieden, J. (1989). Cost containment strategies for workers' compensation. *Business and Health*, Oct., 48-53.

Galvin, D. (1983). Health promotion, disability management, and rehabilitation at the workplace. *The Interconnector, 6*(2), 1-6.

Galvin, D. (1989). Disability management: An overview of a cost-effective, human investment strategy. In E. Welch (Ed.), *Workers' compensation: Strategies for lowering costs and reducing workers' suffering* (pp. 39-54). Fort Washington, PA: LRP Publications.

Gates, L., Taler, Y., & Akabas, S. (1989). Optimizing return to work among disabled workers: A new approach towards cost containment. *Benefits Quarterly 5*(2), 19-27.

Gross, C. (1988). Ergonomic workplace assessments are the first step in injury treatment. *Occupational Safety and Health*, May 16-19, 84.

Habeck, R. (1991). Managing disability in industry. *NARPPS Journal and News, 6*(4), 141-146.

Habeck, R., Williams, C., Dugan, K., & Ewing, M. (1989). Balancing human and economic costs in disability management. *Journal of Rehabilitation, 55*(4), 16-19.

Hester, E. J., & Decelles, P. G. (1990). *The effect of employer size on disability benefits and cost-containment practices*. Topeka, KS: Menninger Foundation.

Hinds, K. F. (1988). *Workers' compensation cost control: A maverick approach*. Pensacola, FL: Ability Management Associates Publications.

Hutchins v. Erie City and County, etc. 516 F. Supp. 1265 (1981).

Johnson v. Sullivan. 764 F. Supp. 1053 (1991).

Lewis, K. (1989). Persons with disabilities and the aging factor. *Journal of Rehabilitation, 55*(4), 12-13.

Lotito, M., & Pimentel, R. (1990). *Making the ADA work for you*. Northridge, CA: Milt Wright and Associates, Inc.

Marks, J., Johnson, E., & Szanton, P. (1984). *Dispute resolution in America: Process in evolution, (1984)*. Washington, DC: The National Institute for Dispute Resolution.

McNeil, J. (1982). *Labor force status and other characteristics of persons with a work disability*. Washington, DC: U.S. Government Printing Office.

Morrissey, P. (1990). *The Americans with Disabilities Act*. Washington, DC: Report to the United States House of Representatives, Committee on Education and Labor.

Morrissey, P. (1991). *Civil rights for the disabled: A primer for corporate America*. Fort Washington, PA: LRP Publications.

Myers, J. (1983). Rehabilitation of older workers. *Rehab Briefs, 4*(8).

Nagi, S. (1976). An epidemiology of disability among adults in the United States. *Millbank Memorial Fund Quarterly, 51*, 439-468.

Owen, P. (1990). *The Americans with Disabilities Act: An employer's perspective: Obstacle or opportunity?* Riverside, NJ: McMillan.

Patenaude, S. (1989). Promoting functional ability in industry. *Industrial Rehabilitation Quarterly, 2*(1), 34, 40-41.

Randolph, S., & Dalton, P. (1989). Limited duty work: An innovative approach to early return to work. *American Association of Occupational Health Nurses Journal, 37*(11), 446-452.

Schwartz, G., Watson, S., Galvin, D., & Lippoff, E. (1989). *The disability management sourcebook*. Washington, DC: Washington Business Group on Health.

Shrey, D. (1989). The impact of labor relations on disability in industry. *The Disability Manager, 2*(3), 1-3.

Shrey, D. (1990). Disability management: An employer-based rehabilitation concept. In S. J. Scheer (Ed.), *Assessing the vocational capacity of the impaired worker* (pp. 89-106). Aspen, CO: Aspen Publishers.

Shrey, D., & Breslin, R. (in press). Disability management in industry: A multidisciplinary model for the accommodation of workers with disabilities. *The International Journal of Industrial Ergonomics*. (Amsterdam).

Shrey, D., & Olsheski, J. (in press). Disability management and industry-based work return transition programs. In Caplan (Ed.), *A state of the art review in physical medicine and rehabilitation for industrial medicine*. Philadelphia, PA: Hanley & Belfus Publishers.

Siska, D. (1991). Workers' compensation concerns: ADA's most derisive issue? *Mainstream, 16*(4), 13-14. Washington, DC: Mainstream, Inc.

Tate, D., Munrowd, D., Habeck, R., Kasim, R., Adams, L., & Shepard, D. (1987). *Disability management and rehabilitation outcomes: The Buick-Oldsmobile-Cadillac Lansing product team report*. East Lansing: Michigan State University, School of Health Education, Counseling, Psychology, and Human Performance, Disability Management Project.

Taulbee, P. (1991). Corralling runaway workers' comp costs. *Business & Health, 9*(4), 46-55.

Thompson, R. (1990). Fighting the high cost of workers' comp. *Nation's Business*, (March), 20-26.

Tysse, J. (1990). *Analysis of the employment-related provisions of the Americans with Disabilities Act*. Washington, DC: McGuiness and Williams.

U.S. Department of Labor, Bureau of Labor Statistics. (1988). *Projections 2,000*. Washington, DC: U.S. Government Printing Office.

Victor, R. B. (1989). *Medical cost containment in workers' compensation: Innovative approaches*. Boston: Workers' Compensation Research Institute.

10

Alcohol and Drug Testing in the Workplace

Peter R. Bulmer, J.D.

The Americans With Disabilities Act and its regulations (collectively referred to as the ADA) should not be viewed as an obstacle to alcohol and drug testing programs, but only as one of many considerations to be taken into account when determining whether and how to implement such a program in the workplace. This chapter will review the impact of the ADA upon an employer's formulation and implementation of an alcohol and drug policy that includes testing of applicants and employees.

First, this chapter places the ADA in the context of the other statutes and decisional laws affecting testing of applicants and employees. Second, the ADA's treatment of alcohol and drug testing is reviewed. Third, this chapter closes with a discussion of common components to a legal and practical alcohol and drug testing policy.

Restrictions Outside of the ADA

Federal Government

During the Reagan Administration, the federal government took the lead in active efforts to eliminate drugs from the workplace. Executive Order (E.O.) 12564 mandates that federal workplaces be drug-free;[1] and the Drug-Free Workplace Act of 1988 (the Act) requires direct federal contractors and direct recipients of federal grants to institute limited measures to promote a drug-free work environment.[2]

Neither E.O. 12564 nor the Act requires testing for drugs or alcohol. Testing by defense contractors, however, is required by the Department of Defense Interim Drug-Free Work Force Rule (DOD Rule),[3] and testing by certain transportation industry employers is required by statute and by Department of Transportation regulations (DOT Regulations).[4] As far as drug *testing* is concerned, the government's focus–as narrowed by court decisions–primarily is on safety-sensitive jobs in safety-sensitive industries.

E.O. 12564

Signed by President Reagan on September 15, 1986, E.O. 12564 prohibits the use of illegal drugs by employees of any agency of the Executive Branch, whether on or off duty. It further directs each agency to develop and implement a drug-free workplace plan that must include drug testing of employees in sensitive positions as well as on a voluntary basis. The order also permits testing based on reasonable suspicion of drug use, attendant to accidents or unsafe practices, and as part of or a follow-up to counseling or rehabilitation.

The Drug-Free Workplace Act

The guts of the Act is the seven-point drug-free workplace program required of covered employers. The Act stipulates that:

1) the employer must publish a statement (a) notifying employees that the unlawful manufacture, distribution, dispensation, possession, or use of a controlled substance is prohibited at work, and (b) specifying the actions to be taken against violators of the policy;

2) in the statement the employer must notify each employee that, as a condition of employment under the contract/grant, the employee will (a) abide by the terms of the statement, and (b) notify the employer of any criminal drug statute conviction for a violation occurring in the workplace within five days of the conviction;

3) the employer must give a copy of the statement to each employee engaged in the performance of the federal contract or grant;

4) the employer must establish a drug-free awareness program to inform employees about (a) the dangers of drug abuse in the workplace, (b) the employer's policy of maintaining a drug-free workplace, (c) any available drug counseling, rehabilitation, and employee assistance programs, and (d) the penalties that may be imposed upon employees for drug abuse violations;

5) the employer must notify the contracting/granting agency within 10 days after receiving actual notice of a workplace drug conviction either from an employee or otherwise;

6) within 30 days of receiving notice of a workplace drug conviction, the employer must either (a) discipline the convicted employee, or (b) require him or her to participate satisfactorily in a drug abuse assistance or rehabilitation program; and

7) the employer must make a good faith effort to continue to maintain a drug-free workplace by complying with the requirements of the Act.[5]

These prescribed elements of a drug-free workplace program actually are fairly innocuous. The Act is perhaps more notable for what it does *not* require. It does not require drug testing, it does not prohibit alcohol at work, it does not require searches of employees or objects suspected of violating the principle of a drug-free workplace, and it does not require the establishment of an employee assistance program (EAP). Indeed, the Act does not require any sanction unless an employee is *convicted* of violating a criminal drug statute and the violation occurred *in the workplace*. And, although the Act prohibits drug "use" in the workplace, the absence of an express prohibition on reporting to work "under the influence" of drugs has provoked one commentator to question whether such omission allows an employee to "beat the system" by using drugs on nonworking time away from the workplace (e.g., just before work, during lunch, other breaks).[6]

Department of Defense Interim Rule

The DOD Rule applies to defense contracts involving access to classified information and any other defense contract under which the contracting officer determines that inclusion of a drug-free workforce clause is necessary for reasons of national security or for specified health or safety reasons.[7] Under a covered defense contract, the DOD Rule requires the contractor to implement a program containing the following components:

1) employee assistance emphasizing high-level direction, education, counseling, rehabilitation, and coordination with available community resources;
2) supervisory training to assist in identifying and addressing illegal drug use by contractor employees;
3) self-referrals and supervisory referrals to treatment for substance abuse; and
4) the means (including testing) for identifying illegal drug users.[8]

Covered defense contractors must institute drug testing for employees in "sensitive" positions.[9] The DOD Rule itself does not mention random testing, but the Department of Defense has taken the position that employees in such positions must be tested on a random basis (the extent of and criteria for random testing are left up to the contractor).[10] Further, the DOD Rule authorizes, but does not require, drug testing in the following circumstances: (a) where there is reasonable suspicion of employee drug use; (b) where the employee has been involved in an accident or unsafe practice; (c) as a follow-up to counseling or rehabilitation programs; and (d) on a voluntary basis.[11]

The DOD Rule requires contractors to adopt "appropriate personnel procedures" for handling employees who test positive.[12] If an employee is discovered to be using drugs illegally on the job, he or she may not be kept on duty or allowed to perform in a sensitive position until the contractor has determined that he or she is fit for duty.[13]

Transportation Industry Employers

Employees in safety-sensitive positions in the transportation industry are subject to random drug and alcohol testing under the Omnibus Transportation Employee Testing Act of 1991 (OTETA),[13a] which was signed by President Bush on October 28, 1991 as part of the Department of Transportation and Related Agencies Appropriations Act, 1992 (HR 2942). OTETA applies to the air, rail, trucking, and mass transit industries. OTETA does not affect the previously issued DOT Regs to the extent those regulations are not inconsistent with the provisions of the OTETA.

The DOT Regulations are the most comprehensive and thorough drug testing rules yet in place in the private sector. They apply to employees regulated by the Federal Aviation Administration, the Federal Highway Administration, the Federal Railroad Administration, the U.S. Coast Guard, the Urban Mass Transportation Administration, and the Research and Special Programs Administration.[14] In addition to the DOT Regulations, each agency has issued its own set of regulations covering employees in the industry.

The DOT Regulations require employers in the transportation industry to test applicants and employees in safety-sensitive positions for the presence of marijuana, cocaine, opiates, amphetamines, and PCP. Covered employees are subject to random tests, tests as part of routine physicals, tests upon reasonable suspicion of drug use, and post-accident tests. In addition, some agencies require follow-up tests and/or rehabilitation following the return to work of an employee who tested positive for drugs. Employees who test positive must be taken off the job and may only be reinstated after testing negative and receiving the approval of a medical officer.

As important as the testing requirements are, arguably even more important are the testing procedures detailed by the DOT Regulations.[15] These procedures liberally adopt and add to the procedures contained in guidelines issued by the Department of Health and Human Services (DHHS).[16] The DHHS guidelines contain "how-to" procedures for collection of urine samples, transmission of the samples to the testing laboratory and evaluation of test results, quality control measures required of the laboratories, recordkeeping and reporting requirements, and standards and procedures for the certification of laboratories.

In addition to the above requirements, the DOT Regulations impose specific notification and recordkeeping requirements upon covered employers and require employers to establish EAPs that include education and training components.[17]

State Governments

Following the lead of the federal government, at least 14 states have passed legislation or issued executive orders designed to eliminate drug use from public employment;[18] and at least four states have enacted laws similar to the federal Drug-Free Workplace Act and which apply to recipients of state contracts and/or financial assistance.[19] Moreover, at least 16 states have enacted laws directly regulating the use of alcohol and/or drug tests by private employers.[20] Several municipalities also have local ordinances regulating such testing.[21]

In states without comprehensive private-sector drug-testing legislation, employers still must be mindful of protections afforded employees under state fair employment laws, court decisions, or indirectly under other laws. In short, a multistate employer contemplating the development of a uniform drug-testing program first must examine the statutes and court decisions of each jurisdiction in which it is located or does business.

Drug Testing Litigation

Public Sector

In 1989, the U.S. Supreme Court decided two cases in which the Court for the first time addressed questions of drug testing in the workplace. Although both cases arose from the public sector, the Court's reasoning in these cases sets a legal benchmark of sorts against which state courts can be expected to measure the legality of drug testing by private employers.

One of the cases involved the U.S. Customs Service rule requiring drug testing of employees applying for "sensitive" jobs (i.e., jobs either involving the intercept of illegal drugs or requiring that the employee carry a firearm).[22] The Court approved of such testing, finding that it was reasonable in light of the government's interest in preventing employment of drug users in such positions. In the opinion of the Court, the government's interest outweighed the privacy interests of the employees.

The second case brought the DOT Regulations before the Court.[23] Specifically, the Court considered the regulations' rule requiring testing of railroad employees who had been involved directly in an accident. The Court ruled that the employees' privacy interests were outweighed by the government's interest in ensuring public safety. The Court also noted that the railroad employees had a diminished expectation of privacy given that railroads are so highly regulated by the government.

These two cases each involved direct constitutional challenges to the authority of the government's rules requiring drug testing, and each challenge was based on the Fourth Amendment right to be free from unreasonable governmental invasions of privacy. The government's authority was upheld by the Court because of the importance of the objectives promoted by the drug testing rules–keeping drug users out of positions in which their drug use raised an inherent question of trustworthiness (e.g., drug enforcement agents) or safety (e.g., carrying a gun and ensuring the safe operation of trains).

Employers in the public sector can take heart from the Court's approval of drug testing in principle. The precise boundaries of permissible testing in the public sector, however, remain to be delineated incrementally through judges' decisions. Thus far, public employers can safely assume that only testing closely related to the protection of public or employee safety is legally permissible. Also, because they did not provoke a challenge in the case decided by the Court, the testing procedures set forth in the DOT Regulations should serve as the model for alcohol and drug-testing programs.

Private Sector

Whereas public sector drug-testing litigation is rooted in constitutional principles, such litigation involving private, nonregulated employers rarely raises constitutional issues.[24] Instead, challenges to drug testing by private employers–which are comparatively few–are more likely to rely on statutory and common law "tort" theories.

The statutes representing potential swords for use in attacking drug testing at work generally are of two types. The first and obvious type are state statutes directly regulating drug testing in the workplace.[25] The second type are statutes which expressly provide that individuals enjoy a right to privacy.[26]

However, the typical legal challenges asserted against or emanating from drug-testing programs are based on "tort" theories such as invasion of privacy,[27] intentional or negligent infliction of emotional distress,[28] retaliatory discharge in violation of public policy,[29] wrongful discharge in violation of an implied contractual promise of good faith and fair dealing,[30] and defamation.[31] Suffice it to say that an employee disciplined under an alcohol or drug policy has several arrows in his legal quiver. The employer's greatest protection—or its greatest vulnerability—is the alcohol and drug policy itself, in conjunction with the actual procedures used to enforce the policy. In other words, a properly drafted policy that also is implemented properly affords an employer the greatest protection from liability; conversely, a lax policy *or* a failure to follow proper procedures invites disaster in court.

Alcohol and Drug Testing Under the ADA

The ADA contains a section devoted solely to drugs and alcohol in the workplace.[32] This section essentially covers illegal drug use in three topic areas: the definition of a protected individual under the ADA; permissible personnel policies; and drug testing.

"Qualified Individuals With A Disability"

Current users of illegal drugs are expressly excluded from the definition of "qualified individual with a disability" and thus are not protected by the ADA.[33] The interpretive Appendix to the EEOC Regulations expressly states that an employer may reject an applicant or discharge an employee because of his or her current drug use free from liability under the ADA.[34]

Although the EEOC Regulations do not define "current" drug use, the Appendix explains that the reference to "current" drug use "is not intended to be limited to the use of drugs on the day of, or within a matter of days or weeks before, the employment action in question. Rather, the provision is intended to apply to the illegal use of drugs that has occurred recently enough to indicate that the individual is actively engaged in such conduct."[35]

The ADA does *not* exclude alcoholics from the definition of "qualified individual with a disability," but, instead, the Appendix interprets the ADA as *including* alcoholics within the definition.[36] Also, the ADA explicitly protects rehabilitated drug users and those undergoing rehabilitation, as well as those who are erroneously perceived as being current drug users.[37]

Workplace Policies

The ADA permits employers to impose at least the following conditions of employment:

1) to prohibit the illegal use of drugs and the use of alcohol at the workplace by all employees;

2) to require that employees shall not be under the influence of alcohol or be engaging in the illegal use of drugs at the workplace;

3) to require that employees behave in conformance with the requirements established under the federal Drug-Free Workplace Act;

4) to hold an employee who engages in the illegal use of drugs or who is an alcoholic to the same qualification standards for employment or job performance and behavior that such entity holds other employees, even if any unsatisfactory performance or behavior is related to the drug use or alcoholism of such employee; and

5) to require that covered employees comply with applicable regulations issued by the Department of Defense, the Nuclear Regulatory Commission, and the Department of Transportation.[38]

Alcohol and Drug Testing

The ADA assumes a "neutral" posture on drug testing in the workplace; the ADA neither authorizes nor prohibits such testing.[39] However, the ADA does exclude drug tests from the definition of "medical examination,"[40] thus removing what, as a practical matter, would have been a significant obstacle to the efficient use of drug testing. Curiously, the ADA makes no mention of testing for alcohol, and it is likely that this omission will invite the argument that Congress intended to include alcohol testing within the ADA's definition of prohibited medical examinations.

In addition, the EEOC Regulations specifically require that "any information" about the medical condition or history of an individual tested for drugs be maintained in confidence (as with the results of a permitted medical examination), subject only to the disclosure of information regarding the illegal use of drugs.[41]

Common Testing Requirements and Procedures ▬▬

Three Steps Prior to Implementation of an Alcohol and Drug Policy

Step 1: Should You Have One?

Assuming your company is not subject to the Drug-Free Workplace Act, the DOD Rule, the DOT Regulations, the OTETA, or any other government drug-free workplace requirements—that is, assuming you do not *have* to have one—the first decision to be made is whether you even want or should have an alcohol and drug policy (with or without a testing component). What would be the purpose of the program? Is it safety to the employees or the public? Or is it to increase production? Are you implementing the program in response to a real or perceived workplace drug problem? Or are you doing it because everyone else seems to be doing it? Are you doing it to punish drug users, or as a means to help them deal with the problem? Do your reasons for wanting a policy make sense to you and other members of management? What effect will the implementation of the policy have on employee morale?

Remember, just because you do not test employees for drug use or do not have a formal, written work rule against drug use, does not mean you are helpless to eliminate actual drug users or alcohol abusers from your workforce. After all, if someone is not performing the job up to your standards, you normally may discharge them on that basis alone, and the ADA does not alter this fundamental workplace maxim.[42]

While contemplating the desirability of an alcohol and drug policy, do not forget your bargaining obligations to the union (if any) that represents the *employees* who would be subject to the policy. You have an obligation to bargain with the union over the decision to institute a policy as well as over the content of the policy.[43] However, you need not bargain with any union over the decision or content of a policy with respect to job applicants.[44]

Step 2: Listing the Policy Goals or Objectives

Once you have decided why you want an alcohol and drug policy, list the goals or objectives you hope to attain through the policy. This list will prove very useful to whomever actually ends up drafting the policy.

Avoid "canned" or generic alcohol and drug policies. To be effective, the policy should be one that is tailored to your company's particular concerns.

Step 3: Drafting the Policy

Having decided to implement an alcohol and drug policy that aims to achieve the desired objectives, the policy must be drafted. The content of such a policy is beyond the scope of this chapter. However, discussed below are four broad areas that must be addressed in drafting an alcohol and drug policy.

1. **"When" to Test**

   Testing most commonly is required in two situations: first, as part of the job application process; and, second, when the employer has objective reasons to believe the employee is under the influence of drugs or has violated the employer's alcohol and drug policy. Post-accident testing and unannounced testing following an employee's return from a drug rehabilitation program are also common components in many policies.

   Less common is random testing. Unquestionably the most controversial manner of testing, random testing generally can best be defended where it is required by government regulations or where it is applied only to employees in safety-sensitive or hazardous jobs.

2. **"How" to Test**

   The most prevalent means of conducting drug tests is urinalysis, although others are available.[45] The employee provides a urine sample at a "collection site," which may be a doctor's office, a clinic, or even a washroom on the employer's premises. Strict chain-of-custody procedures begin at the collection site and follow the sample to the laboratory. Normally, and at a minimum, these procedures include sealing the sample, labeling the sample with the employee's name and/or other identifying information (e.g., social security number), and then scrupulously completing a chain-of-custody form that accounts for the transfer of the sample from the collection site by identifying the person who handled the sample, the time during which such person was in control of the sample, and the locations from and to which the person transferred the sample. The chain-of-custody form thereafter is updated at the laboratory each time a technician handles the sample.

The initial "drug screen" test performed on the sample is the "EMIT" (Enzyme Multiple Immunoassay Technique). The EMIT is reported to be 95% accurate.[46] If the drug screen is positive, the sample should be tested a second time to confirm the result. The confirmatory test reputed to be as close to 100% accurate as technology allows is the "GC/MS" (Gas Chromatography/Mass Spectrometry) (it also is three to four times more expensive than the EMIT). Due to its accuracy, the GC/MS is the confirmatory test required by most government regulations, state statutes, and courts.

3. What the Test Results Mean

A test is "positive" when it reveals the presence of drugs quantified at or above the threshold level set by government regulation or the laboratory. Generally, the threshold levels are those contained in the DHHS guidelines.[47] The threshold levels contained in the DHHS guidelines are intended to eliminate reliance on relatively insignificant levels of drugs that could result from inconsequential drug intake or passive inhalance (e.g., being in a room where marijuana is being or has been smoked). The presence of drugs below the threshold levels registers as a negative result.

What a drug test does not—and with current technology cannot—determine is impairment. That is, a confirmed positive for cocaine tells us that the employee has a certain concentration of cocaine in his or her system, but it does not reflect whether he or she was, is, or will be impaired or somehow less able to function. The distinction between the tests' reliability in detecting drug *use* and their inability to detect *impairment* on the job is often raised by employees in challenging disciplinary action taken in reliance on positive drug tests. By and large, however, courts have not been sympathetic to this argument.[48] Employers nonetheless are well advised to avoid references to "impairment" in any drug policy. Instead, the policy should state that the *presence* of drugs in the system is considered a violation of the policy.

4. How Employers Should Use the Results

Even where drug testing is conducted within the law, employers are cautioned against assuming that it also is lawful to terminate an employee solely on the basis of a positive drug test. The accuracy of such an assumption varies from state to state.

For example, under a California statute, employers with 25 or more employees must reasonably accommodate any employee who wants to enter a rehabilitation program (unless the accommodation imposes an undue hardship on the employer).[49] Laws in Iowa, Minnesota, and Vermont require employers to offer "first-time offenders" the chance to enroll in an EAP.[50]

Further, handicap protection laws may require that certain drug users be reasonably accommodated by their employer. As with so many other areas of employment law, the answer to the employer's question, "Can we discipline the employee?" depends on the particular state's law and the circumstances surrounding the violation.

Notes ▄▄▄▄▄▄▄▄▄▄▄▄▄▄▄▄▄▄

1. E.O. 12564 (1988), *reprinted in* Lab. Rels. Expediter (BNA), at LRX 4411.
2. The Act is codified at 41 U.S.C.A. 701 *et seq*. (1989).
3. The DOD Rule is found at 48 C.F.R. 223.75 and 252.223-7500 (1988).
4. Omnibus Transportation Employee Testing Act of 1991, Pub. L. 102-143. The DOT Regs are found at 53 Fed. Reg. 47002 (1988). In addition, the Nuclear Regulatory Commission has issued regulations requiring certain private employers licensed to construct or operate nuclear reactors to implement alcohol and drug testing as part of a required fitness-for-duty program. *See* 10 C.F.R. 26.2 *et seq*. (1990).
5. 41 U.S.C.A. 702(a)(1) (contractors) and 703(a)(1) (grant recipients).
6. Olsen, "Legal and Practical Considerations in Developing a Substance Abuse Program," 6 *The Labor Lawyer* 859, 862 (1990).
7. 48 C.F.R. 223.7504.
8. 48 C.F.R. 252.223-7500(c).
9. 48 C.F.R. 252.223-7500(c)(4)(i).
10. In February 1989, and in response to numerous inquiries from federal contractors regarding testing and other issues, the Department of Defense issued a series of "Questions and Answers" on the DOD Rule which are available upon request. In it the Department states that "While the word 'random' does not appear in [the DOD Rule], that is what is contemplated."
11. 48 C.F.R. 252.223-7500(c)(4)(ii). However, the testing provisions of the DOD Rule do not apply "to the extent they are inconsistent with state or local law" or with certain collective bargaining agreements. *Id*. 252.223-7500(e).
12. 48 C.F.R. 252.223-7500(d).
13. 48 C.F.R. 252.223-7500(d).
13a. Pub. L. 102-143 (1991).
14. *See* 53 Fed. Reg. 47002 (1988).
15. The DOT drug-testing procedures are found at 54 Fed. Reg. 49854 (1989).
16. The DHHS "Mandatory Guidelines for Federal Workplace Drug Testing Programs" are found at 53 Fed. Reg. 11970 (1988).
17. *See, e.g.,* 49 C.F.R. 391.87 (notification and recordkeeping) and 391.121 (EAP).
18. Ariz. Rev. Stat. Ann. 15-513 (school district transportation employees), 28-414.01 (applicants to drive school buses), and 44-770(A)(8-9) (state employees); Ark. E.O.-89-2; Fla. Stat. Ann. 112.0455; Ga. Code Ann. 21-2-140, 45-20-90 *et seq*. (held unconstitutional in *Georgia Ass'n of Educators v. Harris*, 794 F. Supp. 1110 [N. D. Ga. 1990]) and 45-23-1 *et seq*.; Ill. Rev. Stat. Ch. 111-2/3, 347, 702.24 (public mass transit employees); Kan. Stat. Ann 75-4362 (certain state employees) and S.B. 270, 1, L. 1990 (mental health employees); La. Rev. Stat. Ann. 49:1015; 1991 Miss. Laws 610; Nev. Rev. Stat. 193.105; N.J. E.O. 204; N.M. State Personnel Board Rule 14; S.D. Codified Laws Ann. 23-3-64 *et seq*. and S.D. E.O. 89-17; Tenn. Code Ann. 41-1-122 (Department of Corrections employees); Utah Code Ann. 67-19-33, 67-19-36. *See also* Washington, D.C. Mayor's Order No. 90-27.
19. Cal. Gov't Code 8350 *et seq*.; Ga. Code Ann. 50-24-1 *et seq*.; Ill. Rev. Stat. Ann ch. 127, 132.11 *et seq*.; S.C. Code Ann. 44-107-10 *et seq*.
20. Conn. Gen. Stat. Ann. 31-51t to 31-51aa; Fla. Stat. Ann. 440.09(3); Haw. Rev. Stat. tit. 19, 329B-1 *et seq*.; Iowa Code Ann. 730.5; La. Rev. Stat. Ann. 49:1001 *et seq*.; Me. Rev. Stat. Ann. tit. 26, 681 *et seq*.; Md. Health Gen. Code Ann. 17-214.1; Minn. Stat. Ann. 181.950 *et seq*.; 1991 Miss. Laws 610; Mo. Rev. Stat. 287.120(1, 3-7); Mont. Code Ann. 39-2-304; Neb. Rev. Stat. 48-1901 *et seq*.; Or. Rev. Stat. Ann. 659.225 and Or. Admin. R. 471-30-130, 471-30-140; R.I. Gen. Laws 28-6.5-1; Utah Code Ann. 34-38-1 *et seq*.; Vt. Stat. Ann. tit. 21, 511 *et seq*.
21. *See, e.g.,* Art. 33A San Francisco Code; Ord. No. 5195, Boulder Rev. Code.
22. *National Treasury Employees Union v. Von Raab*, 109 S. Ct. 1384 (1989).
23. *Skinner v. Railway Labor Executives Association*, 109 S. Ct. 1402. (1989).

24. Although it does not happen often, employees have challenged private employer drug testing policies under state constitutional guarantees of an individual's "right to privacy." *See, e.g., Wilkinson v. Times Mirror Corp.*, 215 Cal. App. 3d 1034, 264 Cal. Rptr. 194 (1989) (holding that the California constitution's guarantee of individual privacy applied as against a private employer, but that a private employer nonetheless could lawfully test job *applicants* for drugs); *Luedtke v. Nabors Alaska Drilling, Inc.*, 768 P.2d 1123 (Alaska 1989) (rejecting an employee's state constitutional challenge to his employer's drug testing program, the court held that the Alaska constitution's guarantee of individual privacy did not apply to the private employment relationship).

25. See the statutes cited in note 20 above.

26. *See, e.g.,* Mass. Gen. Laws Ann. ch. 214, 1B; Wis. Stat. Ann. 895.50.

27. Plaintiffs have met with mixed success under this theory. *See, e.g., Neal v. Corning Glass Works Corp.*, 5 IER Cases (BNA) 1636 (S.D. Ohio 1989) (employee was permitted to proceed to trial on his invasion of privacy claim arising out of his employer's failure to obtain his consent to the employer's receipt of drug test results); *DiTomaso v. Electronic Data Systems*, 3 IER Cases (BNA) 1700 (E.D. Mich. 1988) (dismissing employee's invasion of privacy claim arising out of employer's drug testing program).

28. *See, e.g., Kelley v. Schlumberger Technology Corp.*, 849 F.2d 41 (1st Cir. 1988) (upholding a jury verdict of $125,000 in damages for negligent infliction of emotional distress arising out of drug testing procedures–specifically, the visual observation of the plaintiff while he provided his urine sample); *Luck v. Southern Pacific Transportation Co.*, 218 Cal. App. 3d 1, 267 Cal. Rptr. 618 (1990) (upholding on other grounds a jury verdict of $485,042 in damages based in part on intentional infliction of emotional distress), *cert. denied*, 111 S. Ct. 344 (U.S. 1990).

29. Plaintiffs have enjoyed mixed success under this theory. *Compare Greco v. Halliburton Co.*, 674 F. Supp. 1447 (D. Wyo. 1987), *Hennessey v. Coastal Eagle Point Oil Co.*, 247 N.J. Super. Ct. App. Div. 297, 589 A.2d 170 (1991), and *Hershberger v. Jersey Shore Steel Co.*, 394 Pa. Super. 363, 575 A.2d 944 (1990) (no public policy implicated by drug testing) *with Semore v. Pool*, 217 Cal. App. 3d 1087, 266 Cal. Rptr. 280 (1990) (random drug testing violates public policy).

30. *See Luck v. Southern Pacific Transportation Co.* cited in note 28 above.

31. *See Houston Belt & Terminal Railway Co. v. Wherry*, 548 S.W. 2d 743 (Tex. Ct. App. 1976), *cert. denied and appeal dismissed*, 434 U.S. 962 (1977).

32. Title I, 104. *See also* 29 C.F.R. 1630.3.

33. *Id.*, 104(a).

34. *See* 56 Fed. Reg. 35745-46 (7/26/91). Note, however, that until the employment of provisions of the ADA take effect in July 1992, some *current* drug users *are* protected from discrimination under the Rehabilitation Act of 1973. Specifically, that Act presently (*i.e.,* until the effective date of the ADA) excludes from its definition of handicapped individuals "any individual who is an alcoholic or drug abuser whose current use . . . prevents such individual from performing the duties of the job . . . or whose employment . . . would constitute a direct threat to property or the safety of others." 29 U.S.C. 706(8)(B).

35. 56 Fed. Reg. 35745-46 (7/26/91). The Appendix adds that "current" drug use includes the use of illegal drugs that "has occurred recently enough so that continuing use is a real and ongoing problem." *Id.* at 35746.

36. *See* 56 Fed. Reg. 35752 (7/26/91) (comments on Section 1630.16(b)).

37. Title I, 104(b).

38. *Id.*, 104(c). *See also* 29 C.F.R. 1630.16(b).

39. Title I, 104(d). *See also* 29 C.F.R. 1630.16(c).

40. Title I, 104(d)(1). *See also* 29 C.F.R. 1630.16(c).

41. 29 C.F.R. 1630.16(c)(3).

42. This maxim presumes, of course, that the individual is not otherwise a qualified individual with a disability. In addition, employers should consult their respective states' antidiscrimination laws to ensure that state law does not afford greater protection than the ADA.

It should be noted as well that there may be risks involved in *not* testing employees for alcohol abuse and drug use. *See, e.g., Chesterman v. Barmon*, 82 Or. App. 1, 727 P.2d 130 (1986), *aff'd*, 305 Or. 439, 753 P.2d 404 (1988) (holding that an employer's liability to a third party for injuries caused by its employee while on drugs is to be decided by the jury); *Otis Engineering Corp. v. Clark*, 688 S.W.2d 307 (Tex. 1983) (holding the employer liable for injuries inflicted by its intoxicated employee after he was sent home for being drunk on the job).

43. *See Johnson-Bateman Co.*, 295 NLRB No. 26 (1989).

44. *See Star Tribune*, 295 NLRB No. 63 (1989).

45. Samples of blood and even hair can be analyzed for the presence of alcohol or drugs.

46. *See Wykoff v. Resig*, 613 F. Supp. 1504 (N.D. Ind. 1985); *Peranzo v. Coughlin*, 608 F. Supp. 1504 (S.D.N.Y. 1985).

47. The guidelines set the following minimum concentration levels necessary to register a "positive" *initial* test result (expressed in nanograms per milliliter): cocaine: 300; marijuana: 100: opiates: 300; PCP: 25; and amphetamines: 1000. The minimum concentration levels necessary to register a "positive" *confirmatory* (GC/MS) test result are: cocaine: 150; marijuana: 15; opiates: 300; PCP: 25; and amphetamines: 500. 53 Fed. Reg. at 11983.

48. *See Jones v. McKenzie*, 833 F.2d 335 (D.C. Cir. 1987), *vacated*, 490 U.S. 1001 (1989) (mem.), *modified*, 878 F.2d 1476 (D.C. Cir. 1989) (per curiam). In *Jones*, the trial court upheld a public employee's challenge to the drug test administered by her employer, a school district. The trial court appeared to rely in part on the inability of the drug screen to verify impairment. On appeal, the appellate court reversed the trial court without expressly deciding the use-vs.-impairment issue.

It is likely that the use-vs.-impairment distinction will receive increasing attention by plaintiffs (or, more accurately, plaintiffs' lawyers) in those states that recognize an implied covenant of good faith and fair dealing, particularly where the plaintiff claims he uses drugs "casually," and only on nonwork time away from the employer's premises. The expected argument is that drug use on personal time and off company property does not constitute good cause for termination *unless* such use affects the employee's ability to do his job.

49. *See Cal. Lab. Code* 1025 *et seq*.

50. *See* Iowa Code Ann. 730.5(3)(f); Minn. Stat. Ann. 181.953(10)(b); Vt. Stat. Ann. tit. 21, 513(c)(3).

11

AIDS/HIV Disease and Employment

Leslie McAllan, Ph.D., C.R.C., N.C.C.
Gary Hollander, Ph.D.

Introduction

The Americans with Disabilities Act (ADA) is an important piece of legislation designed to protect the rights of persons with disabilities who previously have been discriminated against in our society. In a speech at Gallaudet University, Senator Tom Harkin (D-IA), Chairperson of the Senate Subcommittee on Disability Policy, stated, "Together we will not rest until every vestige of discrimination against Americans with disabilities is removed from our society and every citizen with a disability is accorded the respect and dignity he or she deserves" (McCrone, 1990, p. 8). Later, during debate on the Senate floor, Harkin emphasized, "Today, Congress opens the doors to all Americans with disabilities. Today we say *no* to ignorance, *no* to fear, *no* to prejudice" (Wolfe, 1990, p. 2). Very few other modern illnesses or disabilities carry with them the extreme potential for ignorance, fear, and prejudice as AIDS/HIV disease. This chapter explores the relationship between the ADA, these three factors of ignorance, fear, and prejudice, and the experience of people with HIV disease.

Acquired Immune Deficiency Syndrome (AIDS), or HIV disease, has been referred to as an epidemic, a challenge (Kubler-Ross, 1987), a plague, a punishment, a scourge, a demonic disease (Sontag, 1990), and, according to former Surgeon General Koop, the number one health issue of the 80s and 90s. Government statistics record 157,525 reported cases of AIDS in the United States (Wisconsin Department of Health and Social Services, 1991). This number reflects only those persons diagnosed as having AIDS and who were reported to the Centers for Disease Control. An estimated 100 times the above number of persons could be infected with the Human Immunodeficiency Virus (HIV).

The magnitude of the problems associated with HIV disease prevents its comprehensive treatment in this chapter. However, since the disease is a relatively newly designated disabling condition, a closer examination of its effects on those with the virus and on the general working public is warranted. Following this discussion of the experiences of those with HIV disease, this chapter briefly examines the sociological impact of HIV disease. Upon this experiential framework, the chapter relates the disease to the Americans with Disabilities Act and provides a legal context in which the ADA was developed. Finally, examples and practical applications are provided to assist the reader in examining current employment policies and developing modifications as necessary.

The Experience of People with HIV Disease

Human immunodeficiency virus (HIV) is a retrovirus that, through a relatively complex process, infects various cells associated with the human immune system (Groopman & Gurley, 1987; Gorman & Kertzner, 1990; Hall, 1990; McCutchan, 1990; Perdew, 1990). There are numerous consequences of HIV infection, and the range of clinical consequences of HIV infection includes a further designation of Acquired Immune Deficiency Syndrome (AIDS).

A diagnosis of AIDS is a diagnosis *by definition*; that is, it is a combination of symptoms and signs called a *syndrome*. Although AIDS may present through a variety of combinations of symptoms, common to all presentations is the presence of HIV. Though the usefulness of the term *AIDS* has been brought into question (Ostrow, Solomon, Mayer, & Haverkos, 1987), it remains the acronym of choice among the general public to describe what is actually a constellation of diseases that are associated with the advanced presentation of HIV. Throughout this chapter the term *HIV* will be used to denote the human immunodeficiency virus, while HIV disease will refer to the full range of diseases that can be attributed to the virus. AIDS also will be used in two ways, first in reference to the set of diseases that constitute diagnosis of the syndrome. Further, the term *AIDS* will be used when referring to research findings that specifically refer to AIDS, even if the present authors do not concur with the appellation.

The difficulty with which the layperson can understand the essential nature of HIV disease, let alone distinguish between HIV disease and AIDS, reflects not only. the complexity the virus, but also our general ignorance about health, sexuality, and drug use. Fear of infection and prejudice against those who are infected (or those viewed as most likely to be infected) sustains this general ignorance, making information about transmission seemingly unattainable to broad sections of the population.

This constellation of diseases which result in an AIDS diagnosis brings with it a set of social stressors (Blendon & Donelan, 1988; Christ, Siegel, & Moynihan, 1988) and psychological problems (Cohen, 1990; Dilley, Ochitill, Perl, & Volberding, 1985). The complexity and overlay of the biological, social, and psychological consequences of HIV can make appropriate management of qualified employees with HIV disease a highly challenging process for those who do not remain informed.

People with AIDS identify uncertainty, isolation, work, finances, and loss of status, self-esteem, and relationships as stressful during their illness (Dilley et al., 1985; Fawzy, Namir, Wolcott, Mitsuyasyu, & Gottlieb, 1989). They also identify other stressors, including dealing with a life-threatening disease, negative prognosis, need for hospitalizations, and concerns about infecting others (Feldmann, 1989). Many of these problems will only be addressed by improved treatments and prognosis for people with HIV disease, but the effects of others can be significantly ameliorated by reducing the ignorance, fear, and prejudice that has surrounded HIV disease.

To better understand the impact of HIV disease on persons infected with the virus, the remainder of this section explores some of the physiological features of

the disease, the social impact of the disease on infected persons, and the psychological consequences of these features.

Physiological Aspects of HIV Disease

HIV disease is an acquired illness which reduces the body's capacity to resist
specific types of infections and cancers. Usually the virus is transmitted through
intimate sexual contact, in particular anal and vaginal intercourse, or through
exposure to HIV-infected blood, in particular through the sharing of needles in
intravenous drug use or the use of contaminated blood products prior to their
routine testing (see Table 1). HIV disease can also be transmitted from a mother
with the virus to her fetus before birth or the infant at birth. Even before a person
with HIV disease has symptoms, the infection can be detected by a blood antibody
test, known as an *HIV antibody test*.

Fear has fueled myths about transmission of the HIV virus. HIV is not a
contagious disease like tuberculosis, but is rather an infectious disease (see Table 1).
HIV is not spread through casual contact with the infected person. HIV is not
spread through the use of toilet facilities, mosquito stings, or shaking hands.
Therefore, HIV cannot be transmitted by sharing office objects like phones,
pencils, typewriters, or eating utensils. Fluids released in sneezing, coughing,
saliva, or tears do not contain high enough concentrations of HIV to cause
infection. However, fear of HIV is spread by ignorance and the failure to learn
about its transmission.

Table 1. Transmission of HIV

HIV is transmitted by:	Vaginal or anal sex Contaminated needles Exposure to infected blood Mothers to fetuses
HIV is NOT transmitted by:	Casual contact Donating blood Sneezing, coughing, saliva, tears Use of toilets, mosquito stings, shaking hands, sharing office objects (e.g., telephones, pencils, typewriters) or eating utensils

People actually diagnosed with AIDS test positive on the HIV antibody test and
have developed some unusual viral, fungal, or bacterial infections or rare cancers.
Somewhere in the course of the disease, the person with AIDS is likely to
experience alterations in blood counts, enlarged lymph nodes, loss of weight, and
diarrhea. Shortness of breath, dermatological complaints, fatigue, loss of memory,
and loss of appetite also may indicate that some specific opportunistic infection is

present or that a direct destruction of cells by HIV itself is occurring. Each of these symptoms can affect HIV-infected workers. Some effects, like memory loss, may even impair the capacity of some workers to effectively comply with current job requirements. However, for other workers, symptoms may not be present, be minimal, or be episodic.

The length of survival after diagnosis varies according to the specific infections which a person with AIDS contracts. Sex, age, ethnic background, and access to health care also significantly impact the survival of people with AIDS. A decade ago, diagnosis was quickly followed by serious complications and death. Today, many people with HIV disease, even after diagnosis with AIDS, contribute significantly in the workplace for many years with either no workplace accommodation, or with minor accommodations.

In fact, the vast majority of people with HIV disease have no symptoms and actually may be unaware of their infectious status. Ignorance, fear, and prejudice again contribute to this situation. Uninformed people are likely to dismiss early signs or symptoms, preferring to see them as flu symptoms or something less malignant than HIV.

People who have been specifically diagnosed with AIDS, in comparison, have likely been very sick, at least at some time (see Table 2). Indeed, the diagnosis of HIV often stems from the presence of some opportunist infection or cancer, not merely from the presence of HIV. People with AIDS may, therefore, also require evaluation and consistent help from a physician and health care team. This help likely will take the form of medical management of their infections, monitoring of blood counts, application of pharmacological treatments, nutritional counseling, and mental health care.

Table 2. Diseases Associated with AIDS

The Centers for Disease Control (CDC) has listed several diseases that are indicative of AIDS. These are briefly described here:

- *Candidiasis*–a yeast-like fungal infection, usually of the esophagus, that contributes to painful swallowing and to white patches in the mouth.
- *Cytomegalovirus*–a common herpes virus that may cause blindness, pneumonia, and inflammations in the immune-compromised person.
- *Mycobacterioses*–these are the classic and atypical tuberculoses that are found unusually frequently among people with HIV disease.
- *Kaposi's Sarcoma (KS)*–a once rare malignant tumor that attacks vital organs. On the walls of blood vessels, KS causes dark blotches and bumps to appear on the skin which are generally painless until they block circulation.
- *Pneumocystis carinii Pneumonia (PCP)*–though symptoms are like those of other types of pneumonia, this disease has had high fatality rates among people with AIDS.
- *Toxoplasmosis*–a disease caused by a single cell animal (protazoan) that affects the central nervous system.
- *Cryptococcosis*–a disease cause by a fungus that most frequently causes meningitis, but may also involve the lungs or other organs.
- *Cryptosporidiosis*–cause by a protazoan, this disease produces severe diarrhea, dehydration, and malnutrition.

Like cancer, HIV disease is life-threatening, involves younger adults, is biologically malignant, stresses the social network, is complicated by organic mental disorders, and has associated phases of deterioration (Wolcott, Fawzy, & Pasnau, 1985). One person with HIV disease may feel energetic, fit, and stable for long periods of time, even years. Another may experience numerous infections, an overall malaise, or rapid decline in capacity to perform activities of daily living. Even this latter person is likely to experience episodes of generally good health.

Further, like many of those with cancer, people with HIV disease are likely to experience symptoms secondary to medications and treatments. The medications associated with AIDS care may have considerable physical and psychological side effects. Busch (1990) notes that the primary HIV battery of drugs, including AZT, Pentamedine, and Bactrim can have a side effect of depression. Adding these to the standard medications with depressive side effects also used by HIV-positive patients—antibiotics, antiviral agents, antineoplastic drugs (Swenson, Erman, LaBelle, & Dimsdale, 1989)—may result in a further predisposition to depressed mood and thinking. Side effects of standard HIV disease medications may also include headaches, weakness in extremities, altered blood counts, nausea, vomiting, and seizures.

Men and women with HIV disease likely experience periods of generally good health during which their physical functioning may approach baseline levels. Though the term *remission* is normally not used in reference to HIV disease, there still can be an extended episode of improvement. During these times, the employee may again gain a sense of power over the daily work routine that had been a major challenge only days earlier. Earlier accommodations in the workplace, or decisions to leave work, may be reexamined by the person with HIV disease and the employer. This experience is similar to that of many cancer patients.

Also like cancer patients, people with HIV disease experience loss of social affiliation, lengthy periods of tactile isolation (Wolcott et al., 1985), and the witnessing of others who have died from the same disease (Martin, 1988). People with HIV disease more often may experience these deaths among friends who have become physically debilitated and cognitively impaired while they have known them. These experiences constitute part of the social implications for those with HIV disease.

Social Impact of HIV Disease on Those Infected

Kelly (1989) has argued that 90% of people with HIV disease would be stigmatized because of sexual preference, drug use, or other social factors, even if AIDS did not exist. Nationally, 66% of AIDS patients have been identified as homosexual or bisexual males and another 21% have been identified as intravenous (IV) drug users (WDHSS, 1991). The stigmatization of association with these groups may account for depressive symptomatology among people with HIV disease such as discouragement, disappointment, and self-criticism. However, even within these groups of gay and bisexual males and IV drug users, there exists a wide range of social experiences and psychological adjustments. Primary in the consideration of social aspects of HIV disease is the general attitude toward those with HIV which is notable for its high degree of prejudice.

An analysis of 53 national and international opinion surveys (Blendon & Donelan, 1988) points to some of the social stresses that people with HIV experience. For example, most Americans would support laws that would require some loss of individual privacy or civil rights to control the spread of AIDS. While still in the minority, 20% of Americans describe people with AIDS as "offenders" who are getting what they deserve and a greater percentage still would tattoo those who are HIV positive. Although only about one in 10 say they would refuse to work with someone with AIDS, 25% still believe they could be infected by being sneezed or coughed upon. Fear of drinking from the same fountain, using the same toilet, or sharing a telephone still abounds. In short, people with HIV disease may face discriminatory attitudes and even hostility from a substantial number of Americans. They are fully aware of the potential for ostracism and isolation.

Not surprisingly, people with AIDS report discrimination in housing, jobs, health care, insurance, and public assistance. Even temporary income loss due to illness may necessitate that they find alternative housing arrangements and reduce their own living expenses. The cost of standard medications used to treat opportunistic infections and slow the progress of HIV likely amount to $1,000 per month and more. The cash flow necessary to cover these treatment expenses, even if high quality insurance coverage will eventually reimburse the individual, represents a financial situation for which most people are ill-prepared.

Fear of disclosure about their health status, sexual preference, or history of drug use may make even the most otherwise pleasant job stressful. For example, some former intravenous drug users may have been abstinent long enough to put their lives back together and to create a social network unaware of their drug histories. But this abstinence might not be long enough to have protected them from HIV infection. Thus, old self-judgement, recrimination, and guilt are interjected into their perception of the workplace which had previously been a sign of success and recovery. Similar processes can occur for gay and bisexual men who have worked to keep their sexual preference secret. Hemophiliacs with HIV may also experience work stress when fearing judgements about their health status or about mistaken identification as IV drug users, bisexuals, or gays.

See Table 3 for a list of Social Stressors of People with HIV Disease.

Table 3. Social Stressors of People with HIV Disease

Loss of social affiliation
Periods of isolation
Witnessing others die of AIDS, especially friends and partners
Judgements of others about sexual behavior or drug use
Stigmatization of having HIV disease
Fear of contaminating others
Fear of others becoming contaminated
Discrimination in housing, health care, insurance, public assistance
  and employment
Income loss
Reduction in standard of living
Financial crises related to medical bills
Progressive need to be independent

The culture and framework for experience among people with HIV disease can be shaken by the requirement to disclose personal information to health care professionals and others who are likely to be quite different from them. Racial and ethnic minorities and gay men have been disproportionately overrepresented among people with HIV disease. At a time when they may want understanding of their unique experience, they are likely to be required to give highly personal information about their sexual experiences to medical and social service providers who are likely from the majority culture. Social differences, fear, and prejudice can make these same professionals disinclined to engage even in casual conversation with someone with AIDS (Kelly, St. Lawrence, Smith, Hood, & Cook, 1987).

People with HIV disease are also likely to notice friends, family members, and acquaintances becoming fearful, avoidant, or rejecting. Further, these significant traditional emotional supports may be slow to adapt to the reality that the person with HIV disease—most often someone under the age of 40—may become progressively dependent, impaired, or fatigued.

Hundreds of AIDS Service Organizations (ASOs) have sprung up nationally to address many of the social problems encountered by the person with HIV disease. These community-based organizations often provide an array of services from advocacy and legal counsel to housing and food delivery. Emotional and practical support are delivered by professional and paraprofessional employees and volunteers through ASOs. Services often include buyers' clubs for drugs, case management, financial counseling, home care, medical referrals, support groups, and religious, counseling, and social services referrals (see Table 4).

Table 4. Services Provided by AIDS Service Organizations

Advocacy
Legal Counsel
Housing and Housing Assistance
Food Delivery
Emotional Support
Support Groups
Practical Support
Buyers' Clubs for Drugs
Case Management
Financial Counseling
Home Care
Medical Referrals
Religious Counseling
Social Service Referrals

With significant personal effort and the assistance of ASOs and other support systems, many people with HIV disease attain a level of accommodation with the social consequences of AIDS. Their renewed determination to make the best of a bad situation contributes to healthy attitudes towards work, friendship, family, medical care, and church. Some people with HIV disease, forced to leave the workplace early due to medical problems or social constraint, find in ASOs an opportunity to redirect their frustration into useful volunteer service that satisfies their needs to both contribute and belong.

But services of ASOs only work for those who utilize them, and many, particularly those without significant symptoms, do not seek services because that act in itself constitutes an admission that they have a serious medical problem and are members of a stigmatized group. This complex labyrinth of ignorance, fear, and prejudice results in social stress and stigmatization. These features in turn contribute to an increased likelihood that the person with HIV disease will experience psychological distress (Hollander, 1990).

Psychological Impact of HIV Disease

The depressive reaction of many HIV-infected patients has been well-documented (Christ et al., 1988; Cohen, 1990; Dilley et al., 1985; Fawzy et al., 1989; Fernandez, Holmes, Levy, & Ruiz, 1989; Kessler et al., 1988; Krener & Miller, 1989; Marzuk et al., 1988; O'Dowd & McKegney, 1990; Viney, Henry, Walker, & Crooks, 1989; Vomvouras, 1989; Wolcott et al., 1985). HIV disease also has been associated with organic brain syndrome, delirium, dementia, substance abuse disorder, adjustment disorder with depressed or anxious mood, and bereavement (Cohen, 1990).

All people with AIDS have experienced at least one of the biological diseases associated with depression (Kupfer, 1983), namely endocrinopathies, metabolic disorders, viral infections, cancers, and central nervous system disorders. They also have likely been influenced by prescribed drugs that have been associated with the onset of depression (Busch, 1990; Zelnik, 1987). People with HIV disease, like patients with cancer (Derogatis et al., 1983), further experience a high degree of depression simply related to their medical problems, their illness, and their poor prognosis. Probably due to high levels of social stress and stigmatization, prevalence rates of depression among people with AIDS are even higher than those with end stage cancer (Hollander, 1991).

Gay and bisexual males and IV drug users with HIV disease recognize that their health condition traces directly to past sexual and drug use behaviors. Knowing that their health is no longer stable nor likely to improve, they are especially susceptible to a string of thoughts that may include negative attributions, guilt, and self-deprecation that is consistent with depression. Unable to either change their HIV status or reduce its ultimate effects through bargaining, changing contingencies, or ignoring their disease, these people ascribe increasing negative power to the virus as the general source of their problems. The prevalent stigma associated with HIV disease and IV drug use or homosexual identification reinforces the perceived accuracy of their negative thoughts.

In the presence of all the social stress to which those with HIV disease are exposed and the personal loss of health, stamina, and ability, it is small wonder that people with AIDS may periodically feel extreme anxiety. Dealing with impending death can also trigger these anxious reactions, sometimes lasting for days and weeks at a time, during which they may feel unusually jumpy, shaky, or tense. They also may note dizziness, abdominal distress, palpitations, and shortness of breath that is associated both with their disease and their psychological status.

People who are referred to as the "worried well" are individuals who are not infected, but are concerned about their potential risks. These persons may report laboratory evidence that they are not infected yet still believe they have symptoms (Cochran & Mays, 1989). Clinical manifestations can include:

- acute and chronic anxiety with panic attacks;
- agitated depression;
- obsessional thoughts involving morbid preoccupation with AIDS symptoms;
- hypochondriacal reactions to autonomic anxiety symptoms that can appear like AIDS symptoms (e.g., loss of appetite and weight, sweats, rashes, lethargy); and
- guilt over fear of having infected another person (Cochran & Mays, 1989).

Such psychological and physiological responses can have a major impact on the ability of some persons to function in their daily social and work life (Fullilove, 1989).

Other major themes experienced by the worried well are those of loss and fear. HIV disease has been referred to as "a tragic disease of losses" (Lehman, 1990, p. 4). Loss most commonly is associated with the person with HIV disease; however, loss can be a major factor at a community and societal level as well. The presence of this mysterious, usually sexually transmitted disease has forced a change in social perceptions of intimacy and resulting behaviors.

The worried well can contribute to the psychological distress experienced by others in the workplace. Their absence from work due to anxiety and preoccupation with hypochondriacal reactions certainly affects productivity and efficiency. But the worried well may also displace their anxiety and depression directly and indirectly on those with HIV disease. For example, their highly value-laden responses to HIV disease may draw attention to those with the virus or make the person with HIV even more fearful of disclosure.

In sum, people with HIV disease experience high rates of depression and anxiety. Their HIV status contributes significantly to their depression as does their experience of health problems. Their depression is associated with a tendency toward negative thoughts including self-blame, self-deprecation, and faulty attribution for their problems. This discomfort is expressed through sad, irritable, and anxious moods. The presence of substantial social reinforcement for these negative thoughts, including stigma related to HIV status, sexual preference, and drug use, likely contributes to the increased prevalence of depression relative to other medically ill people in the workplace.

It would be inaccurate to assume, however, that all who have tested positive for the HIV antibody are seriously psychologically impaired. More often, after a period of adjustment, people with HIV disease learn to cope with the ambiguities and episodes associated with HIV. They learn to reach out to old support systems or to create new ones. And even though serious illness may eventually contribute to depression, they reestablish means to address their problems and exact from life the best it has to offer as they deal with the challenges of medical care and social constraint.

Sociological Impact of HIV Disease

HIV Disease in the Workplace

Discrimination in the workplace can result from societal perceptions of HIV disease. In this society it is perceived as a disease of stigmatized groups, a sexually transmitted disease, and a terminal illness (Palmer, 1989). When a stigmatizing disease strikes already stigmatized groups of people, responses are rationalized and hostility is tolerated which might otherwise be considered inhumane. In the workplace, for example, workers might endorse limiting privacy rights by insisting that they know the health status of clients or co-workers. Retired Admiral James D. Watkins (cited in Blendon & Donelan, 1988), chairman of the President's Commission on AIDS, stated that the threat of discrimination is "the most significant obstacle to progress" against the epidemic (p. 1022). According to the U.S. Supreme Court, the myths and fears people have about disability and persons with disabilities can be as much of a handicap as the disability itself (Bayer & Gostin, 1989). The Supreme Court acknowledged that contagiousness can lead to the highest level of public fear and misapprehension.

After examining 53 national and international public opinion surveys regarding AIDS, Blendon and Donelan (1988) agreed that, "studies have shown that on issues such as this, when Americans and their families may be threatened, public opinion is likely to reflect trends in intolerance and discrimination" (p. 1022). Their review of surveys resulted in the following observations:

- Most Americans see the AIDS epidemic as leading to increased discrimination against those with the virus or active disease.
- Most Americans see the control of AIDS as requiring some loss of individual privacy and possible restrictions on civil rights.
- A substantial minority of Americans see AIDS as a deserved punishment for offensive or immoral behavior and show signs of intolerance and outright hostility to those with the disease.
- Many say they would refuse to work alongside someone who had AIDS and would support the rights of employers to fire such workers.
- Many parents say they would take their child out of school to avoid contact with a classmate with AIDS.
- A substantial minority believe that those with AIDS should not be allowed to live in their neighborhood or community, and they favor landlords' having the right to evict those with the disease.
- The public overwhelmingly opposes discrimination in access to hospital care for patients with AIDS.
- Public opinion about AIDS exists today in a context of little personal, experience with the epidemic (pp. 1023-1025).

The authors concluded that the more personally threatened people feel by the disease, the more hostility and discrimination likely will occur.

HIV disease is the first epidemic to strike modern industrial nations in over a decade, and it has destroyed the illusion that the world has become invulnerable to such global medical tragedies (Bayer & Gostin, 1989). In discussing cultural metaphors regarding tuberculosis, cancer, and HIV disease, Sontag (1990) concluded that the perception of HIV disease as contagious, its association with sex and death, and the inability of medical technology to find a cure combine to enhance fear, moral judgements, stigmatization, and discrimination. Bayer and Gostin (1989) suggested that times of epidemics also are times of social tension, and that fears related to this tension exacerbate other social divisions. They reported:

> Irrational fears of AIDS are typically at the root of HIV-related discrimination. Public opinion surveys reveal that a consistent minority harbor anxieties about and antipathies toward those with HIV infection. In the United States some one-quarter of the public believe people with HIV should be excluded from schools, workplace and other public settings. Twenty-five percent also assert that individuals suffering [sic] from HIV-related disorders should not be treated with compassion. (p. 265)

Attitudes and beliefs which contribute to discrimination at work, in the community, and even in the home, are founded in ignorance and fear. The challenges faced by employers who are a part of this society are addressed in the following section.

Roots of Prejudicial Behavior

HIV disease has had a tremendous impact on society as a whole. According to Ergas (1987), "Culturally, AIDS has called renewed attention to sex and sexuality, awakened fears of contagion and epidemic disasters, and inspired a new literature of disease" (p. 35). It has affected this culture "in the social, psychosocial, moral and ethical arena" and has affected persons "whose lives have been oppressed [by] racism, sexism, poverty, and violence..." (Enlow, 1984). According to Bennett (1987), "Society reacts to any new disease with incredulity, fascination and speculation" (p. 529). Bennett (1987) added that HIV disease is particularly fascinating because of its relationship to "sexual activity and especially unusual sexual activity." For employers to effectively manage HIV disease in the workplace, a basic understanding of the nature of HIV-related ignorance and fear is essential.

Ignorance regarding disability, and HIV disease specifically, is still a major problem in society. After over 10 years of public educational campaigns targeted at society—especially so-called "risk groups," medical personnel, and employers—myths about the transmission, cause, and nature of HIV disease abound. Periodically, information surfaces which implies that HIV disease can be transmitted readily by casual contact. On the other extreme, campaigns have been launched to convince people that they are not susceptible to the virus because they do not belong to groups commonly associated with the disease. Such campaigns perpetuate myths and increase ambiguous messages in that they concentrate on "risk-groups" rather than on risk behaviors.

In the early years of HIV disease, information presented by scientists, politicians, media representatives, and others charged with the responsibility of responding to HIV disease, used language which was cautious and terminology which directly and indirectly supported unsubstantiated beliefs and enhanced fears. Government response was slow and quiet (Shilts, 1988). Medical representatives qualified their statements with words and phrases like "probably," "to the best of our knowledge," and "it is highly unlikely, but possible." And all concerned referred to HIV disease as "deadly," "lethal," "hopeless," and "mysterious." In addition, persons with HIV disease were referred to as "victims" and "survivors" resulting in implications which assigned blame and created the perception of fatalness. Language, policies or lack of policies, and beliefs about HIV disease fostered ignorance and confusion. American culture has a need for certainty and a belief that science can provide the answers–HIV disease brought probability and possibility into the common language of science (Silin, 1987).

Unfortunately, HIV disease became the focus of ignorance which existed long before awareness of the disease itself. Misperceptions about epidemics in general have contributed to the belief that HIV disease is a punishment for living in an unhealthy way (Sontag, 1990). The circumstances surrounding HIV disease have been compared to other epidemics in recent history, including tuberculosis and syphilis (Brandt, 1988). The connections between HIV disease, sexually transmitted diseases, and social morality is emphasized in the following statement (Palmer, 1989):

> Previously, venereal diseases and now AIDS became a symbol for social disorder and moral decay, a metaphor of evil. (p. 45)

HIV disease also is seen as a "plague" with all of the fears, mystery, uncontrollability, and uncertainty that accompanies that term (Silin, 1987). In the presence of ignorance of this magnitude accompanied by intense fear, people may attempt to gain some sense of control by clinging to a rigid moral code.

The intense fear associated with HIV disease and its routes of transmission has interfered with efforts to respond to the disease (Friedland, 1987). In a comparison study of health care professional's perceptions of persons with cancer, HIV disease, diabetes, and heart disease (Katz, Hass, Parisi, & Astone, 1987), persons with HIV disease were the most negatively evaluated and most rejected group. HIV disease also was seen as the most deadly and least understood of the four conditions. Fears of contagion and possible death on the job have resulted in behaviors by health care workers which include avoidance, taking extreme precautions, and verbal expression of fears (Meisenhelder & LaCharite, 1989).

In comparing social attitudes toward cancer and HIV disease, Sontag (1990) noted that cancer is perceived as a disease which strikes individuals, and HIV disease is seen as a disease which strikes individuals who are members of "risk groups." Asch (1984) concluded that categorization and separation of persons into groups results in the perpetuation of stereotyped myths about these groups. Asch observed that "...the mere placement of people into groups enhances notions of between-group differences and minimizes within-group differences" (p. 532). This "risk group" thinking, which has been present from the start, has unleashed hidden and not so hidden prejudices. References to the "general public" also have enhanced this type of thinking by implying that members of risk groups are not part of society (Silin, 1987).

Societal perceptions regarding the persons perceived to be affected most by HIV disease also enhance fear. The spread of HIV infection is linked with volitional acts that can involve sex between men, prostitution, and IV drug use, all of which are regarded by some people and institutions as both immoral and illegal (Bayer &

Gostin, 1989). These groups can appear to represent a threat to society (Hughey, 1986). As a result of this perceived threat, HIV disease has been described as, "a disease of the 'Other'–that is, a disease of people we do not know and in whose lives we are not implicated" (Silin, 1987, p. 9). This association of HIV disease with previously stigmatized groups has contributed to the belief on the part of some that HIV is a punishment or moral judgement on society.

Throughout this section reactions to HIV disease which enhance the potential for discrimination have been discussed. Individual rights to preventive information, to adequate health care, and to privacy all have been threatened for persons with HIV infection (Silin, 1987). People with HIV disease "...have been fired from their jobs, evicted from their homes, denied hospital care, and even refused mortician services" (Melton & Gray, 1988, p. 61). A national opinion poll found that 66% of workers surveyed would be concerned about sharing a bathroom with someone who had HIV disease and 37% would refuse to share tools or equipment (Melton & Gray, 1988).

Although the prevalence of discriminatory attitudes and beliefs in the general public and in the workplace has prompted the development of legislation to protect the rights of those with HIV disease, existing laws have not been adequate (Blendon & Donelan, 1988). A brief history of controversy and legislation in relation to the ADA is explored in the following section.

The ADA, the Law, and HIV Disease

Legislation to protect persons with disabilities which includes persons with HIV disease is not new. As has been shown elsewhere in this book, the ADA has roots in the Civil Rights Act of 1964 and the Rehabilitation Act of 1973 and its amendments. Since the implementation of these acts, case law has documented an impressive history of controversy, discussion, and decisions with regard to HIV disease.

Pre-ADA Controversy and Opinions

The history of legislation and case law surrounding HIV disease is very complex. Federal legislation represents only one small aspect of that history. State and local laws vary throughout the country and the ADA is relatively weak in comparison to some of these laws in relation to HIV disease. Some cities and states had created legislation which covered all employers within their jurisdiction and included regulations on HIV testing, discrimination against persons with HIV disease or persons perceived as having HIV disease, and discrimination on the basis of sexual orientation. A thorough discussion of local laws is beyond the scope of this chapter, however, it is important that employers be aware of local laws when designing internal policies. Some examples of controversy regarding definition of handicap, fear of contagion, and fear of persons perceived to be most at risk for HIV disease, which have had an influence on the ADA, follow directly.

The lack of clarity surrounding the diagnosis of HIV disease and its implications in relation to legal protection was reflected in early discussions at all levels of government. The Justice Department presented an *opinion* on the application of section 504 of the definitions of disability and handicap in the Rehabilitation Act to persons with AIDS, AIDS-Related Complex, or Infection with the AIDS virus

(Cooper, 1986). Their analysis, which was not considered to be law, attempted to determine if each of the diagnoses related to HIV disease qualified as a handicap. The Justices concluded that a diagnosis of AIDS qualified as a handicap under the law by virtue of the fact that AIDS "substantially limits the major life activity of resisting disabling and ultimately fatal diseases and may directly cause brain damage and disorders" (Cooper, 1986, pp. 22-23). However, the Justices argued that "immune carriers" were not considered handicapped and that no uniform policy could be stated for persons with AIDS-Related Complex.

The opinion offered by the Justice Department (Cooper, 1986) also attempted to address issues related to fear of contagion. Throughout their statement, the Justices erroneously referred to HIV disease as a contagious disease and concluded that section 504 of the Rehabilitation Act did not apply to persons discriminated against because of fear that they would spread the disease to others. The Justices wrote "...if the defendant's discriminatory decision is based on concern about contagion rather than on the adverse effects of the disease on its host, section 504 is not violated" (Cooper, 1986, p. 32). They also concluded that the 1974 amendments to the Rehabilitation Act, which expanded the definition of handicap, did not include discrimination on the basis of contagion. At the time of their *initial* opinion, the Justices allowed that persons could be fired over concern of spread of the disease, even if that concern was not justified.

Much of the early controversy surrounding HIV disease involved perceptions about the nature of homosexuality and persons who abuse drugs. The fear that strong, protective legislation for persons with HIV disease could be construed as promoting homosexuality and drug use prompted much political debate. It appeared to be impossible for politicians to discuss HIV disease-related discrimination without becoming concerned about appearing to endorse homosexuality as a healthy option. For example, Senator Helms (R-NC) introduced legislation in 1988 which prevented the use of federal funds to "provide AIDS education, information, or prevention materials and activities that promote or encourage, directly, homosexual sexual activities" (Department of Labor, Health and Human Relations, and Education, and Related Agencies Appropriations Act, section 514, 1988). The original proposal included the phrase, "promote or encourage, directly or indirectly," but last-minute debate resulted in the removal of the word *indirectly*. In addition, the amendment required all material to emphasize sexual abstinence outside a monogamous marriage and abstinence from the use of illegal intravenous drugs.

Case law surrounding drug use and abuse has centered primarily on confidentiality. Federal laws existed which protected the confidentiality of records of any persons treated for drug abuse prior to the ADA (Pascal, 1987). These laws protected oral as well as written records and applied to any institution conducted, regulated, or directly or indirectly assisted by the federal government. At the time, these laws did not protect disclosure with regard to HIV disease. State and local laws were more strict in some states and included protection of HIV disease-related information as well as drug abuse and general medical records. Discussions related to definition of handicap, fear of contagion, and protection of persons perceived to be at risk continued during early work on the ADA. The final bill represents some clear decisions and some compromises.

The ADA

In an attempt to create strong and clear legislation, the authors of the ADA indirectly supported awareness and understanding about HIV disease through the language they used, their emphasis on changing attitudes towards persons with all types of disabilities, and their willingness to directly address "infection with HIV" as a disability. The wording of the ADA supports education as a means of prevention and as a "reasonable accommodation." Employers are encouraged to provide accurate information to employees for their own health information and better understanding of their risks in the workplace. It is recommended that employees who refuse to work next to someone who does not pose a threat simply be educated, transferred to another area, or fired.

The final ADA reflects careful attention to information from the scientific community's growing body of knowledge regarding the diagnosis of HIV disease, fear of contagion, and discrimination against persons perceived to be at risk. In reference to definition of disability and protection under the law, "Infection with the Human Immunodeficiency Virus" is listed in the Senate Report which accompanied the bill as an example of one of the "conditions, diseases and infections" covered (Harkin, 1990, p. 3). Persons who are HIV infected, perceived to be HIV infected, or who are living with someone who is HIV infected are covered under the law if they are qualified to perform the essential functions of a job. In addition, an employer may not require HIV testing of persons who are already employed unless the employer can show that such testing is necessary for the person to be able to do the job. An employer may require a medical exam, including an HIV test, after an offer of employment but prior to the onset of work activity provided it is required of all persons hired for similar positions. Employers may conduct voluntary medical examinations as long as the results of those examinations are kept confidential.

When a fear of contagion issue was raised during early debate on the ADA in the House, Representative Jim Chapman (D-TX) proposed an amendment that would have allowed employers to place workers with contagious diseases in alternative forms of employment (Wolfe, 1990). The Chapman Amendment failed and the conclusion was reached that fear of contagion was not a basis for discrimination. The decision regarding fear of contagion may reflect a previous change in thinking on the part of the Justice Department. In 1988 the Justices reversed their previous decision on fear of contagion in a *Memorandum of Counsel to the President* (Kmiec, 1988). They concluded that firing over the concern of the spread of the disease *was not* allowable under the Rehabilitation Act. Perrit (1990) noted that:

> Legislative history of the ADA makes it clear that discriminating against persons with contagious diseases based on unsubstantiated perceptions of the threat of contagion violates the ADA...but mere fear of contagion by other employees does not weaken the victim's [sic] status as otherwise qualified, because the fear is not supported by objective evidence of risk. (p. 29)

It is interesting to note that in early case discussions, HIV disease consistently was referred to as a *contagious disease*. The ADA and its recent interpretations have softened the language by intermittently referring to HIV disease as an *infectious disease.* Such a change gradually can have an impact on perceptions of the nature of the disease and the resulting fear.

The ADA has given employers certain specified rights in relation to contagious diseases. It allows employers to deny a position or benefit to a person shown to have a contagious or infectious disease which poses a significant risk of transmission to others provided reasonable accommodation cannot be made. In addition, with respect to the food handling industry, the Secretary of Health and Human Services is mandated to publish a list of contagious diseases within six months of implementation of the bill and on a yearly basis thereafter. This mandate removes the burden from the employer to make decisions about the contagious nature of diseases.

Before the ADA existed, the Centers for Disease Control had offered guidelines to employers to help address fears related to contagion. The Centers recommended that there be no restrictions on persons with HIV disease unless there was evidence of other infections or illnesses which might be contagious (Wing, 1986). Simple recommendations were provided as a guide to employers (see Table 5). Basic precautions relevant to the transmission of all infectious diseases, with specific guidelines about blood spills, open wounds, and cleaning of equipment, were reemphasized.

Table 5. Ten Principles for the Workplace

1. People with AIDS or HIV infection are entitled to the same rights and opportunities as people with other serious or life-threatening illnesses.
2. Employment policies must, at a minimum, comply with federal, state, and local laws and regulations.
3. Employment policies should be based on the scientific and epidemiological evidence that people with AIDS or HIV infection do not pose a risk of transmission of the virus to co-workers through ordinary workplace contact.
4. The highest levels of management and union leadership should unequivocally endorse nondiscriminatory employment policies and educational programs about AIDS.
5. Employers and unions should communicate their support of these policies to workers in simple, clear, and unambiguous terms.
6. Employers should provide employees with sensitive, accurate, and up-to-date education about risk reduction in their personal lives.
7. Employers have a duty to protect the confidentiality of employees' medical information.
8. To prevent work disruption and rejection by co-workers of an employee with AIDS or HIV infection, employers and unions should undertake education for all employees before such an incident occurs and as needed thereafter.
9. Employers should not require HIV screening as part of pre-employment or general workplace physical examinations.
10. In those special occupation settings where there may be a potential risk of exposure to HIV (for example, in health care, where workers may be exposed to blood or blood products), employers should provide specific, ongoing education and training, as well as the necessary equipment, to reinforce appropriate infection control procedures and ensure that they are implemented (Citizens Commission on AIDS, 1990).

Finally, although Senator Harkin (1990) assured people that the ADA is not considered by most persons to be a "gay rights" bill, the fact that the ADA specifically *excludes* homosexuality and bisexuality from qualification as handicaps, disabilities, or behavior disorders suggests a major legislative change in perceptions with regard to homosexuality. Unfortunately, some recent summaries of the bill have erroneously suggested that the ADA refers to homosexuality and bisexuality as behavior disorders. The relationship between discrimination based on HIV disease and discrimination based on sexual orientation still is very strong. As employers develop uniform internal policies and attempt to strengthen their commitment to persons with HIV disease, it also would be beneficial to publicly express antidiscrimination policies regarding sexual orientation.

Persons who abuse illegal drugs also have experienced prejudice in our culture. To prevent discrimination against persons using, or perceived to be using, illegal drugs, *and* to protect the employer, the ADA very carefully discusses the difference between current active use and past use. Under the law, employers are given the right to prohibit active use of alcohol and illegal drugs in the workplace, to require sobriety on the job, to permit adverse treatment of unsatisfactory performance related to drug use or alcoholism, and to require compliance with the Drug-free Workplace Act (41 U.S.C. 701 *et seq.*).

Compliance with the ADA in relation to HIV disease will not be difficult for some employers. Experience with HIV disease, informed discussions, progressive thinking, commitment to social change, and/or previous legislation have resulted in the creation of exemplary programs and policies. Other employers may find compliance more difficult and challenging. Examples and practical applications which may be of assistance to those employers are considered next.

Examples and Practical Applications ━━━━━━━

Employers can comply with the letter of the ADA law in relation to HIV disease with very little difficulty. Many employers may be able to modify current Affirmative Action policies only slightly. Senator Harkin (1990) attempted to assuage potential employer concerns about the complexity and cost of implementation of the ADA by stating:

> All a business needs to know is that it is unlawful to discriminate against a person because of his or her medical condition...if the person is otherwise qualified for the job or has paid for the service. As far as *accommodations* and *auxiliary aids* are concerned, it is the responsibility of the person with the *disability* to identify *for* the business the particular disability at issue and the type of accommodation or aid needed. (pp. 3-4)

Although Harkin's suggestions are valid with regard to persons with most disabilities, it is important to recognize that persons who are stigmatized, or perceive themselves to be stigmatized, may be unwilling or unable to identify their condition or offer potential solutions. Fears of breaches of confidentiality, retribution, discrimination, and judgement can prevent persons from making their situation known to an employer (Bayer & Gostin, 1989).

Compliance with the full intent of the law may be more difficult than compliance with the letter of the law. Prejudice is not easy to eradicate. The judgements people hold about others are very personal and deeply rooted in beliefs about each other and the world. According to the ADA, fear and prejudice do not constitute legitimate employer defenses with regard to discrimination. An employer's best defenses are clear and consistent policies, clear job descriptions based on actual essential functions, a track record of fair treatment of all employees, documented sincere efforts at reasonable accommodation, and a history of employment of qualified personnel regardless of disability or other potentially discriminating characteristics. But employers must be informed about their options and willing to comply. In the next two sections, motivation for compliance and suggestions about providing education are discussed.

Motivation

HIV disease was listed by employers as one of their top three concerns in a survey by *Fortune* magazine (Backer, 1988). In the same survey, one in five employers said they had at least one person with HIV disease in their workplace. The real cost to employers "in young, productive, and often brilliant careers cut short–most deaths are between 20 and 49 years" can be staggering (Bennett, 1987, p. 535). According to the San Francisco AIDS Foundation (1987) and its pre-ADA *AIDS in the Workplace* materials, employers can:

1. Prevent disruption of the workplace.
2. Avoid costly litigation.
3. Comply with changing legal requirements.
4. Establish consistent and standard company policies.
5. Reduce health care costs.
6. Enhance employer/employee relations.
7. Provide management and employees with up-to-date AIDS information.
8. Promote a responsible public image.

To these examples the following are added:

9. Reinforce sound public relations for employers through public involvement in preventing and solving social problems. For example, Du Pont (1990) committed itself to hiring persons with disabilities, "to fill the business need for qualified employees; to satisfy the human need for meaningful employment; and to better the welfare of a community, a nation and the world" (p. 17).
10. Prepare for the presence of persons with HIV disease in the workplace. The likelihood of their presence increases daily.
11. Limit the influence of ignorance, fear, and prejudice through creative workplace policies.

After the signing of the ADA, Senator Harkin (D-IA) stated that one of the purposes of the legislation is "...to provide clear, strong, consistent, enforceable standards addressing all forms of discrimination against individuals on the basis of disability" (Harkin, 1990, p. 1). The elimination of discriminatory practices depends in part on the employer's willingness to reduce ignorance and fear. Ignorance can be addressed through the provision of educational opportunities for employees through direct training, consultation services, seminars, and/or referral resources, but the process of education is somewhat more involved in relation to HIV disease. Specific issues related to education about HIV disease are addressed next.

Education about HIV Disease

The motto of the San Francisco AIDS Foundation is, "The best defense against AIDS is information." There are many ways that employers can become more educated about HIV disease and its impact on the work environment. Workshops on HIV disease in the workplace have become relatively common in recent years. These workshops are designed to help employers learn the facts about HIV disease, develop universal or specific policies, learn to educate their employees, and respond to changing legislative and political demands. More recently, government agencies, private companies, and publishers have offered written and audiovisual materials to make information more accessible to smaller companies and those in rural areas. Most efforts are aimed at educating the employer with the assumption that the employer will educate their employees.

Education about the facts regarding HIV disease in a clear, direct, and concise manner which is free of judgements is a key component of all training. Programs can address irrational fears, help people make realistic risk estimates for themselves, and help people learn new ways to cope with living in a culture in which HIV disease is a constant presence (Backer, 1988). Human Resources Departments, Employee Assistance Programs, and community ASOs all are appropriate employer and employee resources.

Unfortunately, inaccurate beliefs tend to persist even in the presence of a growing body of knowledge about and history with HIV disease. Besides the confusing public messages described above, Slusher (1989) argued that "belief perseverance" is a significant factor in individual responses to HIV disease. Belief perseverance results from people's beliefs about the causal nature of disease and makes it more difficult for them to change their belief systems. Slusher maintained that people have many inaccurate explanations for HIV disease which are substantiated by experiences they have had with other viruses (e.g., colds, flu) which are not necessarily similar to HIV disease. Associations with general beliefs about epidemics, sexually transmitted diseases, plagues, and other life-threatening illnesses make the provision of accurate information about HIV disease more difficult and complex.

Responding to concerns about misperceptions and inaccurate information based on belief perseverance, Slusher (1989) argued that AIDS education programs must include scientifically based, alternative explanations about HIV disease which can be understood by the participants. Slusher cautioned that epidemiological data alone was insufficient and could lead to further confusion. Information programs focused toward employers should also address practical issues related to productivity and cost, especially with regard to barriers, insurance rates, attendance, and schedule flexibility (Matkin, 1983).

The provision of accurate information may not be enough when the goal becomes one of addressing social attitudes toward persons with disabilities. Some social scientists have observed that information must be *combined with* contact with persons with disabilities to be most effective in changing attitudes (Perry & Apostal, 1986; Anthony, 1972; Silin, 1987). Closeness to or previous relationships with persons with HIV disease or persons who are gay have been found to be the most significant variables with regard to attitudes (Grieger & Ponterotto, 1988; Ross, 1988). However, results of a recent survey suggested that 90% of persons who responded believed they did not know anyone personally affected by HIV disease (Blendon & Donelan, 1988).

Attitudes people hold regarding HIV disease which reflect shame, irrationality, morality, risk, fright, threat, and ambivalence complicate education about the disease (Hughey, 1986). Hughey agreed that information alone tended to reinforce the stigma and negative evaluations which are held about people with HIV disease and argued that all information must be presented in a manner which is not only sensitive to *what* is being said, but also to *how* it is being said. Perry and Apostal (1986) reinforced the importance of addressing affective, cognitive, and behavioral issues in educational programs.

Employers who choose to provide education can help address the problem of negative attitudes in part by including persons with HIV disease, significant others to persons with HIV disease, and employers of persons with HIV disease in their educational programs. However, attempts at providing effective education in a context of fear can be frustrating. Educators and employers may find themselves caught in a vicious circle: ignorance leading to fear and prejudice, and fear and prejudice maintaining ignorance. Employers have an opportunity to break this vicious cycle by acknowledging the fear associated with HIV disease. Educational efforts and responses to persons with HIV disease, and persons fearful of being near someone with HIV disease, can be enhanced by understanding and compassion. But this fear cannot be allowed to be immobilizing. Acknowledgement is only the first step. People may need opportunities to express their fears and ask questions. Part of an employer's responsiveness can include the creation of such opportunities within the agency or the development of resources within the community which can be made available to employees. It is suggested that training programs include group process and video techniques which can help address these underlying fears (Stevens & Muskin, 1987).

Response to HIV disease on the part of society must include a recognition of the political, social, personal, and economic impact of the disease. Employers have the potential to modify the attitudes of workers toward persons with HIV disease in a profound way. The workplace is a safe and familiar environment which allows for the opportunity to disseminate information in a nonthreatening manner. According to Silin (1987):

> AIDS invites the educator to create...public spaces out of which shared understandings of the social good, public virtue, and civic responsibility can emerge. This would be a world in which overt or covert acts of violence against the Other—racial, religious, economic, sexual—would be replaced by new forms of hospitality. In the Judaeo-Christian tradition, inhospitality to the stranger is a transgression of the community code that bonds host and guest in mutual respect. To claim this pedagogical authority would bring to the fore the political and moral concerns that ground educational practice. (p. 27)

Hospitality to strangers, respect for individuals, the willingness to learn, and the provision of opportunities have been a tradition in our society. The workplace has been a dominant force in the creation and maintenance of these aspects of our culture. HIV disease is a challenge and an opportunity for employers to carry on these traditions. The development and dissemination of fair and comprehensive policies can be an important initial step in this process.

Policies

Many agencies and companies have offered suggestions to employers with regard to developing policies. Several major corporations and unions already have developed their own policies and offered them as models to employers. Policies range from general catastrophic illness guidelines to specific recommendations and benefits related to job-sharing, flex-time, and benefits counseling (Backer, 1988). A list of resources for employers which address some of these concerns is provided at the end of the chapter. The remainder of this chapter is devoted to the presentation of general and specific planning guidelines in relation to life-threatening illnesses and HIV disease.

Planning and Life-threatening Illness

A particularly useful planning framework for employers who are just beginning to put their policies into writing was suggested by Backer (1988). Backer's Strategic Planning Model can be particularly effective for companies that wish to face the challenge of HIV disease since it is based on sound management principles which include employee participation. The following guidelines were offered:

1. Top management must be committed to provide leadership and financial and personnel resources to the AIDS policy or program.
2. An Employee Advisory Committee or task force must be created to plan and implement the program.
3. External resources must be mobilized, including those from the local community, employer organizations, health care systems, educators, and consultants.
4. An analysis must be made of the internal (workers' attitudes, risk factors) and external (community attitudes and supports) contexts in which the AIDS policy and program will be placed.
5. Organizational policy must be in writing, including the interface with existing benefits and human resources policies.
6. Education and prevention activities must be provided for top management, supervisors, workers, and families.
7. Benefits review and modifications are important in order to support needed service for workers or family members with AIDS or AIDS-related complex (ARC).
8. Worksite modifications are needed to protect the safety of all workers, including those with AIDS or ARC.
9. Needed supports and services must be developed for workers with AIDS or ARC, including a case management approach.

10. Activities for community involvement must be planned, including employer donations. Employers who are active in developing AIDS programs can also serve as role models for volunteer activities by workers. (pp. 985-986)

These suggestions provide a guide to employers who wish to address any issue in the workplace and stress involvement of all persons in the planning process.

An example of a specific policy which addresses HIV disease and other life-threatening illnesses in the workplace was offered by Bank of America in 1985 (Halcrow, 1986). It is repeated here because it is an excellent example of pre-ADA progressive thinking which essentially can be implemented by other employers with few changes.

Bank of America recognizes that employees with life-threatening illnesses including, but not limited to, cancer, heart disease, and AIDS, may wish to continue to engage in as many of their normal pursuits as their condition allows, including work.

As long as these employees are able to meet acceptable performance standards, and medical evidence indicates that their conditions are not a threat to themselves or others, managers should be sensitive to their conditions and ensure that they are treated consistently with other employees.

At the same time, Bank of America seeks to provide a safe work environment for all employees and customers. Therefore, precautions should be taken to ensure that an employee's condition does not present a health and/or safety threat to other employees or customers.

Consistent with this concern for employees with life-threatening illnesses, Bank of America offers the following range of resources available through Personnel Relations:

- Management and employee education and information on terminal illness and specific life-threatening illnesses.
- Referral to other agencies and organizations which offer supportive services for life-threatening illnesses.
- Benefit consultation to assist employees in effectively managing health, leave, and other benefits.

Guidelines

When dealing with situations involving employees with life-threatening illnesses, managers should:

1. Remember that an employee's health condition is personal and confidential, and reasonable precautions should be taken to protect information regarding an employee's health condition.
2. Contact Personnel Relations if you believe that you or other employees need information about terminal illness, or a specific life-threatening illness, or if you need further guidance in managing a situation that involves an employee with a life-threatening illness.
3. Contact Personnel Relations if you have any concern about the possible contagious nature of an employee's illness.

4. Contact Personnel Relations to determine if a statement should be obtained from the employee's attending physician that continued presence at work will pose no threat to the employee, co-workers, or customers. Bank of America reserves the right to require an examination by a medical doctor appointed by the Company.
5. If warranted, make reasonable accommodation for employees with life-threatening illnesses consistent with the business needs of the division/unit.
6. Make a reasonable attempt to transfer employees with life-threatening illnesses who request a transfer and are experiencing undue emotional stress.
7. Be sensitive and responsive to co-worker's concerns, and emphasize employee education available through Personnel Relations.
8. Not give special consideration beyond normal transfer requests for employees who feel threatened by a co-worker's life-threatening illness.
9. Be sensitive to the fact that continued employment for an employee with a life-threatening illness may sometimes be therapeutically important in the remission or recovery process, or may help to prolong that employee's life.
10. Encourage employees to seek assistance from established community support groups for medical treatment and counseling services. Information on these can be requested through Personnel Relations or Corporate Health. (pp. 126-127)

Bank of America chose to incorporate HIV disease into a broad policy on life-threatening illnesses. The policy is very direct about the company's overall position, specific resources available to employees, and the role of managers. In the next section, the need for policies which specifically address HIV disease, as well as a sample of such a policy, is discussed.

HIV Disease-specific Policies

There is no consistent agreement about the need for written policies with regard to HIV disease. Aberth (1986) observed that there was a difference on this point between employers on the East Coast and employers on the West Coast. West Coast employers tended to believe in written policies covering HIV disease, East Coast employers did not. Aberth (1986) also noted that employers in the East tended to be plagued with discrimination suits, but it was uncertain if the lack of written policies led to the suits or if the number of suits led to caution about putting policies in writing.

Employers easily can create an atmosphere which openly acknowledges compassionate concern for persons with HIV disease. Highly visible written policies which address HIV disease specifically can send a message to employees that the company is willing to be receptive to their concerns. These policies also can indicate assurance of protection from discrimination based on sexual orientation, drug use, or relationship to persons with HIV disease. Such direct and specific policies can be justified on the basis of the intensely personal responses to people with HIV disease presented earlier in this chapter, as well as on the basis of sound employment practices which justify other policies within organizations. Visible policies backed by fair practices encourage persons to be open with employers about a variety of work-related health concerns which can be dealt with openly and in a proactive manner.

A few key areas are crucial to the development of HIV disease-specific policies. These areas, not likely to be emphasized in policies for other life-threatening illnesses, address confidentiality, testing, and co-worker fears. Because of the stigma associated with HIV disease and the legal constraints of many state laws, confidentiality of information regarding HIV status is essential. Confidentiality of test results is also, therefore, necessary. However, the discussion of testing also raises the debate over requiring HIV testing to take place as a condition of new or continued employment.

Perrit (1990) noted that it would be difficult to sustain an argument for HIV testing because of the invasion of privacy, the cost of inadvertent disclosure, the fact that the disease is not contagious, and the current lack of a cure for the disease. Furthermore, the ADA prohibits employers from requiring a medical examination unless such examination or inquiry is shown to be job-related and consistent with business necessity (Harkin, 1990). Finally, HIV-specific policies will benefit all involved if they clearly define how co-workers incapacitated by fear of HIV disease will be managed.

It also may be helpful for employers to have guidelines which address the process of decision making in relation to reasonable accommodation. The following strategies were suggested by Aberth (1986):

- Providing communication and educational resources to dissipate any fears about contagion.
- Referring patients to community services that provide emotional support and medical treatment.
- Reminding managers an employee's health condition is personal and confidential.
- Reminding managers to be sensitive to co-workers' concerns as well as to those of the patient. (p. 122)

General guidelines for helping employers make decisions involving persons with HIV disease include:

- Stay current with the latest information from the CDC, the American Hospital Association, and other recognized authorities on AIDS and infectious diseases. Keep company policies concerning AIDS as close to the recommendations of these groups as possible.
- Identify the specific duties of the position that will be inconsistent with company policies concerning AIDS.
- Evaluate the current state of the employee's health with respect to his [sic] ability to carry out duties consistent with company policies concerning AIDS.
- Attempt a reasonable accommodation of the employee that is consistent with company policies concerning AIDS. (Wing, 1986, p. 117)

Other suggestions include publication of articles in the company newspaper, dissemination of information to all levels of employees, and presentation of public forums (Aberth, 1986). Managers can be provided with videotapes, brochures, and other materials to help educate their employees.

Obviously the sample policies and suggestions included in this section were tailored to the organizations for which they were developed. Therefore, considerable adaptation is required to make them fit the diverse needs of companies of different sizes. The following resources can assist in the development of company policies:

1. AIDS in the Workplace Materials (Publication I029)
    AIDS and the Workplace: Resources for Workers, Managers, and Employers (Publication B461)
    National AIDS Information Clearinghouse
    P. O. Box 6003
    Rockville, MD 20850
    1-800-458-5231
2. Local AIDS Service Organization
    1-800-342-2437
3. Local Red Cross
4. State and Local Health Departments
5. National Leadership Coalition on AIDS
    1150 17th St., N. W., Suite 202
    Washington, DC 20036
    (202) 429-0930

Conclusion

HIV disease presents a challenge to employers seeking to comply with the provisions of the ADA in a humane and comprehensive fashion that acknowledges the needs of all employees, yet recognizes the employer's need to remain profitable and productive. The common experiences of those with HIV disease and the sociological impact of HIV disease were discussed in this chapter as an experiential framework that supports the provisions of the ADA. The examples and practical applications provided are intended to assist the reader in the construction of workplace policies that are in compliance with ADA specifications and sensitive to the special needs of those with HIV infection. Employers will need to become familiar with federal regulations interpreting the ADA as they are made available.

References

Aberth, J. (1986). AIDS: The human element. *Personnel Journal, 65*(8), 119-123.

Anthony, W. A. (1972). Societal rehabilitation: Changing society's attitudes toward the physically and mentally disabled. *Rehabilitation Psychology, 17*(3), 117-126.

Asch, A. (1984). The experience of disability. *American Psychologist, 39,* 529-536.

Backer, T. E. (1988). Managing AIDS at work: Psychology's role. *American Psychologist, 43,* 983-987.

Bayer, R., & Gostin, L. (1989). Legal and ethical issues in AIDS. In M. S. Gottlieb (Ed.), *Current topics in AIDS: Volume 2.* New York: John Wiley & Sons.

Bennett, F. J. (1987). AIDS as a social phenomenon. Tenth International Conference of the Social Sciences and Medicine (1987, Sitges, Spain). *Social Science and Medicine, 25*(6), 529-539.

Blendon, R. J., & Donelan, K. D. (1988). Occasional notes. Discrimination against persons with AIDS: The public's perspective. *The New England Journal of Medicine, 319,* 1022-1026.

Brandt, A. M. (1988). The syphilis epidemic and its relation to AIDS. *Science, 239*(4838), 375-380.

Busch, K. (1990). *Psychiatric aspects of AIDS.* Sioux Falls, SD: University of South Dakota School of Medicine.

Christ, G. H., Siegel, K., & Moynihan, R. T. (1988). Psychosocial issues: Prevention and treatment. In V. T. DeVita, S. Hellman, & S. A. Rosenberg (Eds.), *AIDS: Etiology, diagnosis, treatment, and prevention* (2nd ed.) (pp. 321-337). Philadelphia, PA: Lippincott.

Citizens Commission on AIDS. (1990). *Responding to AIDS: Ten principles for the workplace.* New York: Author.

Cochran, S. D., & Mays, V. M. (1989). Women and AIDS-related concerns: Roles for psychologists in helping the worried well. *American Psychologist, 44,* 529-535.

Cohen, M. A. (1990). Biopsychosocial approach to the human immunodeficiency virus epidemic: A clinician's primer. *General Hospital Psychiatry, 12,* 98-123.

Cooper, C. J. (1986, June 20). *Memorandum for Ronald E. Robertson, General Council: Application of Section 504 of the Rehabilitation Act to persons with AIDS, AIDS-Related Complex, or infection with the AIDS virus.* US Department of Justice, Washington, DC.

Department of Labor, Health and Human Relations, and Education, and Related Agencies Appropriations Act (1988). *Public Law 100-202,* Title 5.

Derogatis, L. R., Morrow, G. R., Fetting, J., Penman, D., Piasetsky, S., Schmale, A. M., Henrichs, M., & Carnicke, C. L. (1983). The prevalence of psychiatric disorders among cancer patients. *Journal of the American Medical Association, 249,* 751-757.

Dilley, J. W., Ochitill, H. N., Perl, M., & Volberding, P. A. (1985). Findings in psychiatric consultations with patients with acquired immune deficiency syndrome. *American Journal of Psychiatry, 142,* 82-86.

Du Pont (1990). *Equal to the task: 1990 Du Pont survey of employment of people with disabilities.* Du Pont, Attn: G51932, P. O. Box 80029, Wilmington, DE 19880-0029.

Enlow, R. W. (1984). Special session. *Annals of the New York Academy of Sciences, 437,* 290-311.

Ergas, Y. (1987, Dec.). The social consequences of the AIDS epidemic: A challenge for the social sciences. *Social Science Research Council, 41*(3/4), 33-39.

Fawzy, F. I., Namir, S., Wolcott, D. L., Mitsuyasyu, R. T., & Gottlieb, M. S. (1989). The relationship between medical and psychological status in newly diagnosed gay men with AIDS. *Psychiatric Medicine, 7*(2), 23-33.

Feldmann, T. B. (1989, May). Role of the consultation-liaison psychiatrist in the treatment of AIDS patients. *Journal of the Kentucky Medical Association, 85,* 249-252.

Fernandez, F., Holmes, V. F., Levy, J. K, & Ruiz, P. (1989). Consultation-liaison psychiatry and HIV-related disorders. *Hospital and Community Psychiatry, 40,* 146-153.

Friedland, G. (1987). Fear of AIDS. Special issue: Acquired immunodeficiency syndrome. *New York State Journal of Medicine, 87*(5), 260-261.

Fullilove, M. T. (1989). Anxiety and stigmatizing aspects of HIV infection. *Journal of Clinical Psychiatry, 50*(11), 5-8.

Gorman, J. M., & Kertzner, R. (1990). Psychoneuroimmunology and HIV infection. *Journal of Neuropsychiatry, 2,* 241-252.

Grieger, I., & Ponterotto, J. G. (1988). Students' knowledge of AIDS and their attitudes toward gay men and lesbian women. *Journal of College Student Development, 29,* 415-422.

Groopman, J. E., & Gurley, J. (1987). Biology of HIV infection. In *Information on AIDS for the practicing physician* (Vol. 2) (pp. 17-23). Chicago, IL: American Medical Association.

Halcrow, A. (1986). AIDS: The corporate response. *Personnel Journal, 65*(8), 123-127.

Hall, T. (1990, June 17). After AIDS diagnosis, some embrace life. *The New York Times,* pp. 1, 14.

Harkin, T. (1990, July 26). *Responses to issues raised about the Americans with Disabilities Act of 1990.* Chair, Senate Subcommittee on Disability Policy: Washington, DC (202) 224-6265.

Hollander, G. W. (1991). Psychometric indications of depression among homosexual males infected with human immunodeficiency virus. (Doctoral dissertation, University of Wisconsin-Milwaukee, 1990). *Dissertation Abstracts International, 52*(2), 1062B.

Hughey, J. D. (1986). *A communication configuration of AIDS.* Chicago, IL: International Communication Association, Information Systems Division. (ERIC Document Reproduction Service No. ED 277061).

Katz, I., Hass, R. G., Parisi, N., & Astone, J. (1987). Laypeople's and health care personnel's perceptions of cancer, AIDS, cardiac, and diabetic patients. *Psychological Reports, 60*, 615-629.

Kelly, J. A. (1989). Helping patients cope with AIDS and other HIV conditions. *Comprehensive Therapy, 15*(7), 56-62.

Kelly, J. A., St. Lawrence, J. S., Smith, S., Hood, H. B., & Cook, D. J. (1987). Stigmatization of AIDS patients by physicians. *American Journal of Public Health, 77*, 789-791.

Kessler, R. C., O'Brien, K., Joseph, J. G., Ostrow, D. G., Phair, J. P., Chmiel, J. S., Wortman, C. B., & Emmons, C. A. (1988). Effects of HIV infection, perceived health and clinical status on a cohort at risk for AIDS. *Social Science Medicine, 27*, 569-578.

Kmiec, D. W. (1988, Sept. 27). *Memorandum for Council to the President: Application of Section 504 of the Rehabilitation Act to HIV infected individuals.* Washington, DC: U.S. Department of Justice.

Krener, P., & Miller, F. B. (1989). Psychiatric response to HIV spectrum disease in children and adolescents. *Journal of the American Academy of Child and Adolescent Psychiatry, 28*, 596-605.

Kubler-Ross, E. (1987). *AIDS: The ultimate challenge.* New York: MacMillan Publishing Co.

Kupfer, D. J. (1983). Toward a unified view of affective disorders. In M. R. Zales (Ed.), *Affective and schizophrenic disorders: New approaches to diagnosis and treatment* (pp. 225-265). New York: Brunner/Mazel.

Lehman, M. K. (1990, Nov./Dec.). ADAMHA fights AIDS: Research, education, and prevention programs. ADAMHA news supplement. *ADAMHA News, 16*(6), 1-4; (Rockville, MD: U.S. Dept. of Health and Human Services).

Martin, J. L. (1988). Psychological consequences of AIDS-related bereavement among gay men. *Journal of Consulting and Clinical Psychology, 56*, 856-862.

Marzuk, P. M., Tierney, H., Tardiff, K., Gross, E. M., Morgan, E. B., Hsu, M., & Mann, J. J. (1988). Increased risk of suicide in persons with AIDS. *Journal of the American Medical Association, 259*, 1333-1337.

Matkin, R. E. (1983, July/Aug./Sept.). Educating employers to hire disabled workers. *Journal of Rehabilitation*, 60-63.

McCrone, W. P. (1990). Senator Tom Harkin: Reflections on disability policy. *Journal of Rehabilitation, 56*(2), 8.

McCutchan, J. A. (1990). Virology, immunology, and clinical course of HIV infection. *Journal of Consulting and Clinical Psychology, 58*, 5-12.

Meisenhelder, J. B., & LaCharite, C. L. (1989). Fear of contagion: A stress response to acquired immune deficiency syndrome. *Advances in Nursing Science, 11*(2), 29-38.

Melton, G. B., & Gray, J. N. (1988). Dilemmas in AIDS research: Individual privacy and public health. *American Psychologist, 41*, 60-64.

O'Dowd, M. A., & McKegney, F. P. (1990). AIDS patients compared with others seen in psychiatric consultation. *General Hospital Psychiatry, 12*, 50-55.

Ostrow, D. G., Solomon, S. L., Mayer, K. H., & Haverkos, H. (1987). Classification of the clinical spectrum of HIV infection in adults. In *Information on AIDS for the practicing physician* (Vol. 1) (pp. 7-16). Chicago, IL: American Medical Association.

Palmer, S. J. (1989). Religious revival in American life: AIDS as metaphor. *Society, 26*(2), 44-50.

Pascal, C. B. (1987). Selected legal issues about AIDS for drug abuse treatment programs. *Journal of Psychoactive Drugs, 19*(1), 1-12.

Perdew, S. (1990). *Facts about AIDS: A guide for health care providers.* Philadelphia, PA: Lippincott.

Perrit (1990). *ADA Handbook.* Baltimore, MD: Wiley Press.

Perry, D. C., & Apostal, R. A. (1986, Oct./Nov./Dec.). Modifying attitudes of business leaders toward disabled persons. *Journal of Rehabilitation, 52*(4), 35-38.

Ross, M. W. (1988). Components and structure of attitudes toward AIDS. *Hospital and Community Psychiatry, 39*, 1306-1308.

San Francisco AIDS Foundation. (1987). *AIDS in the workplace* (Brochure). San Francisco, CA: Author.

Shilts, R. (1988). *And the band played on.* New York: Penguin.

Silin, J. G. (1987). The language of AIDS: Public fears, pedagogical responsibilities. *Teachers College Record, 89*, 3-19.

Slusher, M. P. (1989). *Effective AIDS education: Superior effects of biological information over epidemiological information.* Saratoga, Springs, NY: Author.

Sontag, S. (1990). *Illness as metaphor and AIDS and its metaphors.* New York: Doubleday.

Stevens, L. A., & Muskin, P. R. (1987). Techniques for reversing the failure of empathy towards AIDS patients. *Journal of the American Academy of Psychoanalysis, 15*, 539-551.

Swenson, J. R., Erman, M., Labelle, J., & Dimsdale, J. E. (1989). Extrapyramidal reactions: Neuropsychiatric mimics in patients with AIDS. *General Hospital Psychiatry, 11*, 248-253.

Viney, L. L., Henry, R., Walker, B. M., & Crooks, L. (1989). The emotional reactions of HIV antibody positive men. *British Journal of Medical Psychology, 62*, 153-161.

Vomvouras, S. (1989). Psychiatric manifestations of AIDS spectrum disorders. *Southern Medical Journal, 82*, 352-357.

Wing, D. L. (1986). AIDS: The legal debate. *Personnel Journal, 65*(8), 114-119.

Wisconsin Department of Health and Social Services. (1991, January). AIDS surveillance summary: Wisconsin and U.S. *Wisconsin AIDS/HIV Update.* Madison, WI: Author.

Wolcott, D. L., Fawzy, F. I., & Pasnau, R. O. (1985). Acquired immune deficiency syndrome (AIDS) and consultation liaison psychiatry. *General Hospital Psychiatry, 7*, 280-292.

Wolfe, R. (Ed.). (1990, July/August). ADA becomes law of the land. *Professional report of the National Rehabilitation Counseling Association, 31*, 1-2.

Zelnik, T. (1987). Depressive effects of drugs. In O. G. Cameron (Ed.), *Presentations of depression: Depressive symptoms in medical and other psychiatric disorders* (pp. 355-399). New York: John Wiley & Sons.

12

Considerations for the Rehabilitation Consultant

Brian T. McMahon, Ph.D., C.R.C.
Linda R. Shaw, Ph.D.

Introduction

The ADA has resulted in an unprecedented opportunity for rehabilitation professionals to form partnerships with employers through the provision of consultation. The law provides an impetus for employers to seek out consultation among the rehabilitation community. Many enterprising rehabilitation professionals have anticipated a sudden interest among employers for accessing their expertise by hanging out the "consultant" shingle. The consulting relationship has many advantages for both parties. The employer possesses the opportunity to ensure persons with disabilities equal rights within the workplace and the rehabilitation consultant possesses the knowledge and skills needed by the employer to accomplish this end.

Unfortunately, many rehabilitation professionals launched themselves into the consulting business armed with only a superficial awareness of the needs and concerns of employers, and of the ADA itself. In the rush to attend to the obvious high-impact provisions of Title I of the ADA, it is easy to overlook some of the more subtle issues regarding the employer's agenda and some of the subtle, yet crucially important portions of the law itself.

This chapter represents an effort to expand on areas of concern for rehabilitation consultants and to examine some of the subtleties of employer attitudinal and compliance issues. The role of the consultant in developing and/or participating on an ADA task force is discussed as an example of an exemplary consultant-employer endeavor.

Employer Reaction and Response

Is the ADA to be Taken Seriously?

The rehabilitation consultant marketing his or her services is sure to be asked this question and to confront some skepticism on the part of employers. A partial answer to this important question is suggested in the "Findings and Purposes" (Section 2) of the ADA itself. It speaks of the current inferior status of a discrete and insular minority of 43,000,000 Americans who are seriously and pervasively isolated and segregated, and severely disadvantaged. It speaks of documented discrimination and outright exclusion, and purposeful and unequal treatment, which are rooted in stereotypes and which have no redress in federal law. One would expect such language from the disability rights community, but because these are the words of the United States Congress, they comprise one of the single most eloquent and direct statements of societal culpability ever observed in print. The known facts are that unemployment for working-age adults with disabilities continues to hover at the 65% level; it has increased gradually over the past 20 years; it is higher still within each "affected class," (e.g., 73% for women with disabilities, 77% for Hispanics with disabilities, 78% for blacks with disabilities) (Bowe, 1990).

Although most employers are concerned about their employees and regard them as valuable assets, others, who are less sympathetic to the social inequities, are sometimes compelled by the financial motivations behind the ADA. Employers are heavily invested in combating the effects of disability on productivity through such means as employee assistance programs, referral to rehabilitation, selective job placement, and disability management programs (Habeck, Leaky, Hunt, Chan, & Welch, 1991; Schwartz, Watson, Galvin, & Lipoff, 1989). The rising costs of health insurance, disability maintenance payments, social security, and workers' compensation are regarded in some circles as uncontrollable. Finally, the aging of the workforce, the trend toward earlier retirement, and the reality that older workers experience more illness, injury, or physical impairments which require a longer time for recuperation and more extensive medical care before returning to work are well documented (Hester, 1991). The question of whether or not the ADA will be enforced is often raised in the context of the nondiscrimination provisions of Title V of the 1973 Rehabilitation Act. The answer is unknown as the enforcement mechanisms are heavily influenced by the politics, priorities, and consequent resource allocation of the executive branch of federal government. There is reason to believe, however, that the ADA may be enforced more rigorously than the 1973 Rehabilitation Act. For example, the scope and coverage of the ADA are far greater than in the Rehabilitation Act. There was strong legislative support for the ADA, which passed 377-28-27 in the House of Representatives, and 91-6-3 in the Senate. There was also significantly greater involvement by persons with disabilities in the legislative and regulatory processes, and markedly more awareness by consumers and the general public. There is a proliferation of research and training at all levels (e.g., workshops, seminars, institutes, books, monographs, journal articles and special issues, print and electronic media presentations), and most disability and rehabilitation issues of the day are presented in an ADA context. There is a reasonable government financial commitment to the rapid development of technical assistance. Perhaps most telling, the regulations supportive of the ADA were delivered on time by the respective enforcement agencies. Finally, the passage of the 1991 Civil Rights Act increases the financial risks of noncompliance. People will be more likely to file grievances and seek redress with monetary damages of up to $300,000 per incident at stake.

The Range of Employer Responses

Employers have not been silent in voicing their opinions about the ADA. Lobbyists for employer groups were active in the process of establishing the legal and regulatory documents that were promulgated, although the level of their activity has varied at different stages in the process. It is sometimes helpful to put the topic of employer response in context. For discussion purposes only, let us conceive of the development and implementation of the ADA in terms of a contest between employer groups and disability rights activists. It is important to note that the development and implementation of the ADA was not and is not intended to be an adversarial process. Should this occur, the intent of the law will clearly suffer. For discussion purposes only, however, let us consider the employment provisions of the ADA (Title I only) in terms of an adversarial process, a football game which has 4 quarters. If we were to conceive of the First Quarter as the enactment of the law, it is safe to say that the disability rights community scored a touchdown (7 points) while the employer community observed and studied the law and its impact. On balance, the disability rights movement won a major victory in the passage of the ADA, the single most important civil rights law since 1964 and one which will, in these authors' opinions, change the way we live and conduct business in America forever. The breadth and scope of the ADA are enormous, and it is possible that even the most deliberative lawmaker did not appreciate its full consequences.

Employers asserted themselves far more aggressively during the Second Quarter when regulations and interpretive guidelines were developed. The employer community scored two field goals (6 points), prevailing on such issues as direct threat, verification of need for accommodation, agility tests, job restructuring, collective bargaining, and other issues. The disability rights community prevailed on the issues of personal assistants, cost-sharing to minimize undue hardship, and prohibitions against workers' compensation history inquiries, and other issues–thus scoring three points. The playing field was leveled, and the score at halftime is much closer: 10-6. Much remains to be determined in a long second half as the EEOC Compliance Manual is developed, and future court decisions further clarify the specifics of the law.

Employer responses to the ADA have been varied. It appears that they may be classified into three broad groups. The first group is comprised of those organizations, typically larger employers with well-developed human resource functions, who are heavily involved in providing comment on the regulatory process, purchasing educational materials, attending training seminars, and establishing or re-establishing liaison with disability rights organizations and providers of rehabilitation services. These employers are termed *on board* as they are aware of the opportunity in the ADA as well as the legal requirements. Their overall "good faith" responses take many creative forms and these will position them well in terms of both legal compliance and the new markets which will be accessed through such proactive activities. In some instances there are long-standing model practices in these organizations, and their current policies and practices far exceed the requirements of the ADA. Those who frequently provide ADA-related training often observe that employers in this group are self-motivated and are the least in need of the training which they seek.

A second group of employers may be termed *reluctant and reserved*. Some in their ranks seek training, others do not. Their questions and concerns appear to be around establishing the minimum levels of compliance. They often inquire defensively about penalties and remedies for breach. In more candid moments, they may reveal that they are closely comparing the costs of litigation vs. the costs of compliance, and will ultimately respond in the least expensive manner. Many small businesses fall into this category. While employers within small companies may not object in principle, they are often resistant due to concerns about cost and a lack of resources with which to access advice and expertise (Drury, 1991). Employers within the *reluctant and reserved* category lack experience with the disability rights and rehabilitation communities, but on balance tend to be eager to learn and are open to the possibilities which the ADA might bring about.

The third group of employers is the focus of greatest concern. They are the *employers of choice* who are not about to be told by government at any level whom they can hire, fire, promote, or accommodate. Their posture at training programs is not observable, because they rarely, if ever, attend. They regard disability rights and rehabilitation professionals as naive, social parasites who never had to meet a payroll. Regrettably, these same employers attend and even organize training functions designed around the circumvention of ADA requirements. They underestimate the disability rights movement, the benefits of compliance, and the consequences of noncompliance while overestimating the costs of compliance, even at a minimal level.

Attitudinal Barriers

In Chapter 2, Charlene DeLoach provides an exceptional treatise regarding the relationship between attitudes and various ADA issues. It is worth reinforcing here that the lawmakers clearly demonstrated their own awareness that attitudinal barriers are a primary impediment to the full integration of individuals with disabilities in American society. This is reflected in the broad definition of disability, the repeated checks against employer presumptions of incapacity, the protection of associates of individuals with disability, the requirements regarding accommodation, and other provisions.

There is no presumption in the ADA that the current attitudes of employers are more positive or negative than those of the general public. Extensive research into this question reveals that they are not. Data reflecting measures of public attitudes typically reveal a normal curve with a large segment of seemingly neutral attitudes (McDaniel, 1976). Further scrutiny has demonstrated conclusively that the majority holds attitudes which are not neutral, but indifferent (i.e., most of us would just rather not deal with or even think about disability). This is statistically normal and psychologically understandable in that focusing upon disability tends to remind us of the fragility of good health, and ultimately of our own mortality. This "existential anxiety" may be the most potent explanation for the massive societal indifference which exists regarding disability and individuals with disability (Livneh, 1982; Hahn, 1988).

The ADA maintains, however, that regardless of how statistically normal such indifference is, regardless of how uncomfortable it may be to interact with individuals with disability, integration can and must occur, because "...the continuing existence of unfair and unnecessary discrimination and prejudice denies people with disabilities the opportunity to compete on an equal basis and to pursue those opportunities for which our free society is justifiably famous...(ADA, Section 2[a]9)." Rehabilitation professionals have long held an awareness of the handicapping effects of employer attitudes on the employability of their clients and have focused considerable effort on effecting attitude change. Interestingly, however, when persons with disabilities are asked about the factors which pose the greatest employment handicaps, they do not overwhelmingly stress attitudinal issues, instead emphasizing such factors as lack of available jobs, lack of accessible and affordable transportation, limited education and experience, and the handicapping consequences of their disability (Louis Harris Associates, 1986; McCarthy, 1988). McCarthy (1988) maintains that the negative attitudes of employers continue to be stressed by rehabilitation consultants as a major placement barrier as a sort of "scapegoating mechanism" for their continued difficulty in effecting successful placements. McCarthy (1988) notes that:

> The point is not that negative attitudes toward persons with disabilities in the workplace are negligible, but that there are numerous other issues and agendas that also need to be addressed to improve the employment and opportunity structure...[e.g.,] architectural. (pp. 250-251)

The ADA flows from such a perspective and seeks to expand occupational opportunity not by focusing primarily on attitudinal issues, but rather by mandating the removal of the "other agendas and issues" cited by McCarthy above. Nevertheless, history has proven that legislated approaches to obliterating discrimination have been accompanied by much resistance when prejudicial attitudes are involved. Such legal changes tend to result in "reactivity," a tendency to resist when one perceives that one's freedom of choice has been restricted. It is the opinion of the authors that while attitude change programs alone have been insufficient in ensuring nondiscriminatory job practices, the implementation of the ADA may be facilitated by providing meaningful practical assistance to employers within the context of effective disability awareness training. Such training may serve to diminish employer anxiety, dispel misconception, and facilitate the development of a proactive stance toward compliance. It would be impossible to conceive of any meaningful assistance provided to employers which was not built upon a foundation of disability awareness training.

Portrayal Issues

An EEOC investigator arrives at a place of business with a positive and progressive reputation to begin an initial investigation pursuant to a potential class action discrimination complaint involving an issue of race. A number of personnel records of Black and Hispanic employees are selected, and upon cursory review the investigator notes immediately that each is replete with written statements which constitute racial slurs and defamatory language.

As inconceivable as this might appear now, most rehabilitation consultants can attest that many personnel records of employees with disabilities contain terminology which is stereotypical and offensive. The general problem involves terms which tend to either equate the individual with the disability, or at a minimum emphasize the disability which by extension creates an image of inferiority. Such defamatory terms are matters of long-standing usage, and most people, including employers, probably do not understand that their language is offensive.

The ADA itself is a model of the use of nondisabling language. It is logical to conclude that those who enforce it will regard the use of such terms, verbal or written, as supportive of a mentality and long-standing pattern of discrimination. Even the most aggressive, good faith compliance activity will be readily diminished by the prevalence of disabling language. Managers should be encouraged to conduct a random audit of representative personnel records, and to provide disability awareness training to those in need at a level of immediacy and intensity consistent with the scope of the problem.

Appendix 1 (*Choosing the Words You Use About and with People with Disabilities*) provides some general guidelines which should help employees to choose and use words that will create positive images and attitudes when talking with and about people with disabilities.

Financial Concerns

In the provision of ADA-related training to employers, it becomes clear that there are disproportionate concerns about the topics of reasonable accommodation and undue hardship. Many of these are centered around the presumption of high tech, expensive, permanent modifications to equipment. Such concerns are clearly unwarranted.

To be sure, far greater expenses are likely to be incurred in compliance with Title II and Title III. Little comfort is taken from descriptions of tax deductions and credits as these are described. What is rarely presented is a discussion of the potential new markets and revenues which can result from improved access. Employers continually underestimate the numbers of disabled Americans and their associated purchasing power.

One of the authors was retained in a gender-related class action discrimination matter in a large Midwestern bank in 1979. Subsequent to consultation regarding the litigation, the author was asked to assist in the development of an affirmative action plan and program relating to persons with disabilities pursuant to compliance with section 503 of the 1973 Rehabilitation Act. It was casually observed that the bank had a rather large number of employees with deafness and hearing impairments. After conducting a brief assessment of their needs, it was arranged that sign language classes be offered by the local Hearing Society for all employees after working hours. Literally hundreds of employees completed a basic course, over 25 an intermediate course, and several an advanced course over the next two years resulting in a dramatic improvement in the integration and job satisfaction of these employees. Other qualified applicants with hearing impairment came forward and were hired. Awareness of their needs extended to the community of persons with deafness and teller and loan officers with sign language abilities were designated. TTYs were put in strategic locations. Word spread quickly and it was discovered (with delight) that the number of customers with hearing impairments was increasing at a dramatic rate.

As momentum built, additional markets were identified. This bank became the first in the area to provide Braille versions of bank statements upon request. Raised letters and Braille markings were put on automatic teller machines. Again, it was observed that the demand for these services was remarkably high. Associates of persons with disabilities and other customers without disabilities commended the bank on its sensitivity and awareness.

Eventually most competing banks replicated these services. That this particular bank was the very first to do so, however, is a fact that has not been forgotten and even today tens of millions of dollars in new revenues are attributed to these modifications which were once regarded as "too costly." In a survey of over 2,000 federal contractors, Berkeley Planning Associates (1982) found that over 70% of respondents agreed that job accommodation was beneficial in public relations. Less than 10% disagreed.

A Closer Look at the Employment Provisions

Reasonable Accommodation

Most rehabilitation professionals are likely to conceive of the provision of technical assistance as centered around the subject of reasonable accommodation. With respect to this subject, responsible consultants should act consistently with the intent of the lawmakers by encouraging employers to consult first with each individual with disability regarding accommodations. This is important for two reasons. First, individuals with disabilities have often been overlooked in the determination of their rehabilitation, attendant, employment, and independent living needs. If this were not the case, Congress would not have legislatively mandated the documentation of client participation in the planning of both rehabilitation and special education services. Second, individuals with disabilities are unequivocally the best single source (although not the only reliable source) of information regarding accommodations as they relate to their unique circumstances.

The EEOC's recognition of this is reflected in 1030.2(o)(3) which reads:

> To determine the appropriate reasonable accommodation it may be necessary for the covered entity to initiate informal, interactive process with the qualified individual with a disability in need of accommodation. This process should identify the precise limitations resulting from the disability and potential reasonable accommodations that could overcome those limitations.

It is noted with some amusement that even the EEOC seems to approach this subject gingerly. Their carefully phrased suggestion may be paraphrased as follows:

> If you want to know what someone needs to compete, you might begin by asking him or her.

Every rehabilitation consultant has a favorite story about a frustrating consultive visit in which they were retained at great expense to answer questions which were never even put to the employee or applicant in question. The fact that this could occur is somewhat indicative of the aforementioned attitudinal issues, and somewhat indicative of imperfect human resources practices.

It has also been clarified in the Title I regulations that although individuals with disability must be consulted regarding accommodations, and consideration given to their preferences, the final decision regarding the selection and imple-mentation of the most appropriate accommodation rests with the employer. If this accommodation does indeed enable the individual to perform essential job func-tions and the individual refuses it, then he or she is no longer qualified and as such forfeits the protection of Title I.

Beyond Accommodation

Experienced rehabilitationists are somewhat concerned that there exists a lack of balance in the emphasis given to one form of employment discrimination (i.e., failure to make reasonable accommodation) vs. the other five forms mentioned in the ADA. These and the causes for concern follow:

Association with an Individual with a Disability

This is intended to protect relatives, friends, or associates of individuals with disability from employment discrimination. Excellent illustrations of precisely how this might occur are provided in the *Interpretive Guidelines to the ADA*. Two points are worth noting. First, employers are NOT required to reasonably accommodate associates, although other forms of discrimination are unlawful. Second, the inclusion of protections for associates makes the scope of the ADA virtually incalculable.

Qualification Standards, Testing, and Other Selection Criteria

The significant specifics of this prohibition are described in Chapters 5 and 7. The points worth noting are that all employment activities pursuant to actually procuring employment must themselves be accessible, and thus rehabilitationists might expect significant interface with industrial/organizational psychologists and others who develop standards, tests, and other selection criteria.

Contractual Relationship

Discrimination may not occur directly or indirectly, as through a contract which has a discriminatory effect. Collective bargaining agreements, contracts with hotels for training activity, and arrangements with an outside employment agency (including a rehabilitation placement specialist) are noteworthy examples.

Limiting, Classifying, and Segregating

This provision requires employment decisions based upon individual qualifica-tions and not upon presumptions about what individuals with a given impairment can or cannot do. It is unlawful to require separate work areas, separate lines of advancement, limited job duties, or unevenly applied benefits to individuals with disabilities. This area is important enough for further consideration. For example, many well-known, large employers which have for years received considerable recognition in vocational rehabilitation for their substantial levels of hiring individuals with disabilities may be highly vulnerable to complaints of "limiting, classifying, and segregating." This is true because such employers frequently hire large numbers of individuals with "disability type X," with which they are experienced and comfortable, and place them into "occupation Y." The obvious implication is that such placements are stereotypical and show little regard for the individuality or multipotentiality of the persons involved. Remember that the ADA is deliberately vague with respect to certain definitions and requirements so as to encourage a highly individualized, case-by-case analysis of the proper fit between an individual's education, abilities, and experience, and the essential functions and requirements of the job. Additionally, "occupation Y" is frequently a secondary labor market position, characterized by low wages, high turnover, lack of advancement opportunity, limited or unconventional hours, poor working conditions, and/or inferior benefits.

Such practices are often the result of good intentions coupled with "authoritarian virtuousness" by employers with the full complicity of rehabilitation job placement specialists. They result from attempts to answer the question, "What types of jobs do we have that handicapped people can do?" This is a false question replete with presumptions of inferior performance. Both employers and job placement specialists are encouraged to review their "model programs" in the context of this important ADA requirement.

Impact Upon Supported Employment Arrangements

Supported employment is paid work in a variety of settings, particularly regular work sites, specially designed for individuals with disabilities (1) for whom competitive employment has not traditionally occurred, and (2) who, because of their disabilities, need intensive, ongoing support to perform in a work setting (*Federal Register*, 5/27/87). Supported employment initiatives have resulted in the employment of many severely disabled individuals for whom any gainful activity was once regarded as infeasible, and has had a positive impact upon supplanting the largely ineffective sheltered workshop system in America. Supported employment has innumerable advantages over sheltered work including its immediate application, face validity, and normalizing effects (Mahaffey & Ridgely, 1991).

ADA lawmakers, employers, vocational rehabilitation professionals, and disability rights advocates have been careful to distinguish supported from competitive employment at every opportunity, so as not to adversely affect current and prospective supported employment arrangements. For example, care has been taken to emphasize that supported employment is not an example of "reasonable accommodations." Employers are not required to accommodate unqualified applicants or employees (1) who are not qualified (i.e., who cannot satisfy the requisite skill, experience, education, and other job-related requirements) and (2) who cannot perform, with or without accommodation, the essential functions of the job. This notwithstanding, the examples of reasonable accommodation given in the ADA and its interpretive guidelines include: job restructuring, alternative schedules of work, reassignment to a vacant position, adaptive equipment or devices, modified examinations, training materials, or policies; qualified readers or interpreters; use of leave time for treatments, accessible transportation, reserved parking spaces, personal assistants for required job duties, and the like. Any experienced rehabilitationist recognizes that these examples are identical to any standard list of supports as the term is defined in supported employment (i.e., "any activity which sustains job productivity to acceptable levels"). While supported employment is not required as an accommodation, the accommodations required are traditional supports with which many employers and rehabilitationists have significant experience.

Another point of interest is that if the distinction between competitive and supported employment is not continually reinforced, employers may become increasingly reluctant to engage in certain models of supported employment (e.g., benchwork, mobile work crew, enclave) (Wehman, 1990) for fear of being accused of "limiting, classifying, and segregating" employees with disabilities *or* of effectively supporting discrimination through a contract. Even in the less segregated "supported jobs" or "job coaching" model of supported employment, the distinction between a job coach performing his or her responsibilities and the provision of a "personal assistant to perform required job duties" will require clarification and documentation on a case-by-case basis which outlines the specific nature of the employment arrangement.

Finally, it may be the grandest of coincidences that supported employment in the 1990s is moving beyond job coaching in the direction of "natural supports," that is, interventions other than job coaching which build upon the formal (e.g., human resources policies and procedures) and informal (e.g., "surplus interactions" among employees) supports which are characteristic of the natural work environment (Nisbet & Hagner, 1988). This trend was already well underway when the ADA employment provisions came along. Together these provide further support for the concept that perhaps it is true that primary responsibility for the vocational rehabilitation of severely disabled Americans is shifting from the vocational rehabilitation profession to the employer community.

Beyond Employee Selection

A common misconception among many persons in the employer, rehabilitation, and disability rights community is that the ADA is some sort of "hire the handicapped" law. Putting aside the regrettable disabling language observed in this expression, it must be emphasized that only the first of five titles of the ADA even pertain to employment, and within the employment provisions it is clear that ALL PERSONNEL ACTIONS MUST BE UNRELATED TO EITHER THE EXISTENCE OR CONSEQUENCE OF THE DISABILITY. This means that job application, interviewing, employee selection, hiring procedures, and other "front-end" human resources activities are effected. The regulations are clear that all qualification standards, tests, and other selection criteria must be related to the essential functions of the job, consistent with business necessity, and themselves addressed by reasonable accommodations. Thus, matters of accessibility and reasonable accommodation are not strictly restricted to the execution of essential job functions, but they apply to accessible test formats, test conditions, and test sites (examples only).

"All personnel actions" also applies to "during employment" activities including performance appraisal, compensation, benefits administration, training and career development, promotion and advancement, relocation, transfer, retention and discharge, disciplinary practices, and all other terms, conditions, and privileges of employment. It is reinforced repeatedly that the enhancement of accessibility and the provision of accommodations do not extend to the lowering of production standards, as long as such standards are evenly applied in actual practice.

Impact Upon Medical Examinations

This issue is well-delineated in the regulations and requires little elaboration here. It will be required that employment medical examinations may be required subsequent to an offer of employment and prior to the assumption of employment if, and only if, certain conditions are met. These include:

1) All entrants into the same specific job category must also be required to have a medical examination.
2) Areas of inquiry during the medical examination are not restricted in the same way that employment interviewing is restricted (i.e., the examination is regarded as a confidential doctor-patient relationship). Information obtained in the medical examination, however, must be kept confidential in accordance with the requirements of the law.
3) The medical examination is intended to ascertain the individual's capacity to perform essential job functions with accommodation.

All three of these stipulations have profound implications and are likely to significantly alter conduct during the employment medical examination. Although speculative at this juncture, it is predicted that ultimately:

1) Physicians must be equipped with an understanding of precisely what the essential job functions are with respect to the position in question.
2) Physicians must become involved in the quest for the proper placement and most appropriate reasonable accommodation to perform the essential job functions.
3) Eventually, traditional medical examinations are likely to give way to physical capacity or even functional capacity examinations.
4) Should the physician recommend against hiring, an immediate human resources and legal review will likely follow, and the applicant will likely be allowed to submit a written challenge to the findings involving his or her own physician and other objective evidence, especially in matters of "direct threat."
5) Only relevant medical specialties will be involved in the conduct of employment medical examinations (e.g., specialists in physiatry or occupational medicine).

The ADA Opportunity Task Force

Perhaps one of the more gratifying experiences for any rehabilitation consultant is the opportunity to assist in the development of and to participate on an ADA Opportunity Task Force. Originally conceived as a "compliance" task force, some committees eventually adopt the term *opportunity* because they come to realize the promise of the ADA and choose to portray their activities in a positive light.

This is a working committee typically formed by a progressive employer the objectives of which may include:

1) development of an informational package for each strategic business unit; and
2) development of policy, implementation plans, and compliance objectives.

Task force members typically include representatives from the following entities or departments:

Affirmative Action/Equal Employment Opportunity
Legal
Benefits
Human Resources
Labor
Medical
Marketing and Communications
Real Estate
Vocational Rehabilitation
Disability Community or Current Employees with Disabilities

Subcommittees may be organized around such issues as Selection and Recruitment, Communications, Training, Testing, and Accommodations. Typical activities include (examples only):

- a thorough training on the ADA and implementing regulations as they are released;
- procurement of all necessary training, newsletters, and educational materials to keep abreast of all pertinent information;
- development of inhouse training resources;
- survey of all disability-related policies, programs, and practices in the organization and its facilities;
- revision of all human resources policies and practices in the context of ADA requirements;
- periodic input from "focus groups" involving current employees with disabilities;
- an initial review of all public accommodations in light of ADA Title III requirements;
- an initial revision of all job descriptions to discriminate essential from marginal job functions;
- communication of Task Force activities to all employees;
- review of all job applications and bringing them in line with ADA requirements;
- development of guidelines for testing and evaluating applicants with disabilities; and
- eliciting support of organized labor for all activities above.

The effective rehabilitation consultant may work on a project basis with the entire Task Force as well as with each subcommittee. The consultant assumes a posture which is largely educational, facilitative, and advisory. The intent is to build support and enthusiasm for compliance activities, focus upon the positive image and business development which accrues from Task Force projects, and encourage initiatives and problem solving among those who must ultimately live with the new law and its impact.

References

Berkeley Planning Associates. (1982). *A study of accommodation provided to handicapped employees by federal contractors: Final report.* Prepared under U.S. Department of Labor, Employment Standards Administration Contract No. J-9-E-0009, Vols. I & II.

Bowe, F. (1990). Employment and people with disabilities: Challenges for the nineties. *OSERS News in Print, 3*(3), 2-6.

Drury, D. (1991). Disability management in small firms. *Rehabilitation Counseling Bulletin, 34*(3), 243-256.

Habeck, R. V., Leaky, M. J., Hunt, H. A., Chan, F., & Welch, E. M. (1991). Employer factors related to workers' compensation claims and disability management. *Rehabilitation Counseling Bulletin, 34*(3), 210-226.

Hahn, H. (1988). The politics of physical differences: Disability and discrimination. *Journal of Social Issues, 44*(1), 39-47.

Hester, E. (1991). Workers who become disabled. In S. Scher (Ed.), *Multidisciplinary perspectives in the vocational assessment of impaired workers* (pp. 1-25). Rockville, MD: Aspen Publishers.

Livneh, H. (1982). On the origins of negative attitudes toward people with disabilities. *Rehabilitation Literature, 43*, 338-347.

Louis Harris Associates. (1986). *The ICD survey of disabled Americans: Bringing disabled Americans into the mainstream.* New York: Author.

Mahaffey, D., & Ridgely, M. (1991). Supported employment and the vocational rehabilitation process. In B. T. McMahon & L. R. Shaw (Eds.), *Work worth doing: Advances in brain injury rehabilitation* (pp. 169-200). Orlando: Paul M. Deutsch Press, Inc.

McCarthy, H. (1988). Attitudes that affect employment opportunities for persons with disabilities. In H. E. Yuker (Ed.), *Attitudes toward persons with disabilities* (pp. 246-261). New York: Springer Publishing Co., Inc.

McDaniel, J. (1976). *Physical disability and human behavior (2nd ed.).* New York: Pergamon.

Nisbet, J., & Hagner, D. (1988). Natural supports in the workplace: A reexamination of supported employment. *Journal of the Association for Persons with Severe Handicaps, 13*, 260-267.

Schwartz, E. G., Watson, D. S., Galvin, E. D., & Lipoff, E. (1989). *The disability management sourcebook.* Washington, DC: Washington Business Group on Health/Institute for Rehabilitation and Disability Management.

U.S. Department of Labor, Bureau of Labor Statistics (March, 1988). *Projections 2000.* Washington, DC: U.S. Government Printing Office.

Wehman, P. (1990). Supported employment: Model implementation and evaluation. In J. S. Kreutzer & P. Wehman (Eds.), *Community integration following traumatic brain injury* (pp. 185-204). Baltimore: Paul H. Brookes.

Section III

Improving Public Access and Revenue Enhancement

13

Barrier Removal by Private Entities

Lei Ann Marshall-Cohen, J.D.

Introduction

The Americans with Disabilities Act of 1990 (P. L. 101-336) provides a clear and comprehensive federal mandate prohibiting discrimination against people with disabilities in such key areas as employment, state and local government services, transportation, public accommodations, and communications. Its purpose is to assure that the more than 43 million Americans with physical or mental disabilities will be fully integrated into the mainstream of society.

Title III of the Americans with Disabilities Act of 1990 (hereafter ADA) is the most technical and dramatic section of this sweeping new law. It imposes new responsibilities on private entities that own, lease, or operate a place of public accommodation to insure that people with disabilities can function freely in society by being provided equal access to all public services and facilities. The impact of these requirements cannot be overstated. The ADA will affect access to the workplace, public transportation, leisure activities (e.g., theaters, health clubs, restaurants), and program accessibility. This chapter presents a roadmap of the technical requirements of Title III, including the implementing regulations that were issued by the U.S. Department of Justice on July 26, 1991 (28 C.F.R. Part 36).

General Requirements of Title III

The Title revolves around the key prohibition of discrimination on the basis of disability in the full and equal enjoyment of goods, services, facilities, privileges, advantages, and accommodations in any place of public accommodation. A place of public accommodation is defined to be a private entity whose operations affect commerce. The term *affecting commerce* is very broad and applies to virtually all businesses and service providers. Examples of places of public accommodation include restaurants, theaters, libraries, dry cleaners, barbershops, offices, grocery stores, zoos, and schools.

This broad prohibition contains five key components. First, denial of participation in activities or provision of a separate or unequal benefit is prohibited. Note, however, that separate benefits are not prohibited where necessary to provide a service, good, or other opportunity as effectively as those provided to others. This provision permits the practice under many state laws of designating parking closest to an accessible path of travel for drivers or passengers with disabilities. Second, individuals with disabilities shall be afforded the most integrated setting appropriate for the receipt of goods, services, facilities, privileges, advantages, and accommodations. Theater seating in the back rows only for persons using wheelchairs is an example of unlawful segregation. Third, individuals with disabilities shall not be denied the opportunity to participate in integrated programs and activities. Thus, although a special recreation program for people with disabilities sponsored by a health club (e.g., a basketball team for wheelchair users) is a permissible separate benefit, an individual who uses a wheelchair could not be prohibited from participating in other nonspecialized club activities. Fourth, individuals and entities cannot use standards, criteria, or administrative methods that have the effect of or perpetuate discrimination against people with disabilities. Finally, discrimination against individuals who associate with or otherwise have a relationship with a person with a disability is also prohibited. This protection includes family relationships, friends, co-workers, and others.

To promote the goal of integration, four specific categories of prohibited activities are identified. First, eligibility criteria for participation in an activity must be neutral and cannot screen out people with disabilities. For example, a car rental company can require that all drivers who rent vehicles be licensed. However, the company could not refuse to rent a vehicle to a licensed driver who was deaf if that individual otherwise met the company's rental criteria. An exception may be granted if the entity can show such criteria are necessary for safety reasons. The legislative history uses the example of height requirements for certain amusement park rides that may have the effect of discriminating against people of short stature.

Second, the ADA requires reasonable modification of policies that may have a discriminatory impact. A restaurant may have a policy of refusing to admit animals. This policy would be discriminatory if applied to a patron who is visually impaired and accompanied by a guide dog. An airport limousine company may have a policy of charging riders double for extra baggage and has historically considered wheelchairs and guide dogs in that category, thus charging customers with disabilities a double fare. Such a practice is impermissible under the ADA.

The ADA offers an exception to this requirement if to modify the policy would fundamentally alter the nature of the service offered. To illustrate, a botanical garden may have a rule prohibiting people from touching plants. Arguably, such a rule may limit the enjoyment of a patron who is visually impaired and wants to feel the plants. However, the garden has a legitimate interest in protecting the plants from possible harm. Thus, the policy would probably survive scrutiny under the ADA.

Third, public accommodations must provide auxiliary aids and services if necessary to assure that a person with a disability is not excluded, denied services, segregated, or otherwise treated differently than others. Examples of auxiliary aids and services include the availability of print materials in Braille, provision of interpreters or readers, and the provision of assistive devices. Again, an exception is provided if the requirement is unduly burdensome or would fundamentally alter the nature of the service provided. A restaurant would not be required to provide a copy of its menu in Braille as long as its staff was willing to read the menu to a visually impaired patron who requested such assistance.

Finally, the ADA requires places of public accommodation to ensure the removal of barriers that prohibit the full and equal enjoyment of their premises by people with disabilities. This mandate introduces one of the new and key concepts in the ADA: that barriers be removed where "readily achievable." The standard of readily achievable is new. It is defined as "easily accomplishable and able to be carried out without much difficulty or expense." Factors to be considered in determining whether an action is readily achievable include: 1) the size of the public accommodation including the number of employees, size and location of the physical plant, and budget; 2) the overall financial resources of the facility including the impact of the change required; 3) the type of operation including the composition of the workforce and geographic separateness or other relationship of the particular facility to the covered entity; and 4) the nature and the cost of the action needed. Although the term is new, the legislative history and regulations provide some indication of its scope. It is intended to be a significantly lesser standard than the undue burden standard utilized elsewhere in the ADA. Thus, while the readily achievable standard does not require major structural renovations, removal of barriers through such actions as the installation of grab bars, adding Braille markings to an elevator control panel, or constructing ramps over several steps are examples of its application. The regulations also establish four priorities for barrier removal: entering a facility, access to service areas, access to restrooms and, finally, other areas. Note that this standard applies to barrier removal in existing facilities. New construction and alterations of facilities are discussed below.

If the removal of a barrier is not readily achievable the entity is still responsible for providing reasonable alternatives. For example, a community group holds its monthly meetings at a bank where the second floor conference room is accessible only by stairs. Installation of a chair lift or elevator may not be structurally possible or affordable. However, the group would be required to move its meeting location to the ground floor or some other accessible location to comply with the ADA.

There is a general exception to the specific requirements for integration under Title III where the individual with a disability poses a direct threat to the health and safety of others that cannot be eliminated through policy modification or provision of appropriate auxiliary aids and services. The regulations are clear that objective evidence must support any such conclusion. The exception is intended to be narrow.

Responsibility for implementation of the ADA falls on owners, operators, landlords, and tenants. For example, if a retail store is operating as a tenant in a multistory office building, an action alleging discrimination under Title III could be filed against the store, the building management group, and the owners of the structure. Assignment of responsibility for providing accessibility features is determined by the lease for parties in a landlord-tenant relationship. In short, Congress made clear its intention to require that structural and programmatic access extend throughout the private sector. The unwavering message is that the integration of people with disabilities into all aspects of society is no longer limited to government entities or companies that do business with the government, but now extends throughout the private sector as well.

Specific Requirements for Structural Access ━━━━

Structural access is best approached by differentiating between new construction and alterations. In addition, there are some requirements in the ADA that are applicable to both new construction and alterations. These will be discussed as a separate section below.

New Construction

The ADA requires that new construction of public accommodations and commercial facilities completed for first occupancy by January 26, 1993 be "readily accessible to and useable by" persons with disabilities. The dual descriptive terms of *public accommodation* and *commercial facilities* are intended to cast a wide net encompassing virtually all types of facilities in the private sector. Commercial facilities are defined as nonresidential facilities that are not public accommodations and whose activities will affect commerce. For example, factories or warehouses may not be considered public accommodations, but would nonetheless be covered by the ADA as commercial facilities.

Newly constructed facilities must meet the design standards issued as part of the Title III regulations: the *ADA Accessibility Guidelines for Buildings and Facilities*. These standards provide technical design information to assure accessibility. The ADA creates a very narrow exception to this new standard for instances where it is structurally impracticable to provide access. However, if any portion of such a facility can be made even partially accessible, it will be required to do so.

Alterations

The scope of the alterations requirement under the ADA is the same as for new construction: both public accommodations and commercial facilities are covered. The ADA is triggered when alterations are undertaken that affect the usability of a facility or a part thereof; then the altered portion is to be made accessible in compliance with the *ADA Accessibility Guidelines*. If alterations affect the usability of or access to a primary function in the facility, then the requirements for accessibility are greater: the altered portion, a path of travel, bathrooms, telephones, and drinking fountains must all meet the access requirements. This scheme looks at the evolution of a building over time. As different parts of a facility are remodeled, altered or added to, accessibility is gradually improved. Eventually, the building will be fully accessible. The alterations section of the ADA went into effect on January 26, 1992, one year earlier than the new construction requirement.

In the remodeling context, an exception is made to the path of travel requirement where the changes required to achieve accessibility are disproportionate to the overall alteration project in terms of cost and scope. If the ratio exceeds 20%, a requirement that changes be made to the "maximum extent feasible" is substituted.

Sections of the ADA Applicable to Both New Construction and Alterations

There are two significant exemptions in the ADA that exclude categories of facilities. First, private clubs, as that term is defined in the Civil Rights Act of 1964, are exempt from coverage. Second, and certainly more significant in terms of the number of facilities covered, is an exemption for all entities controlled by religious organizations. The regulations emphasize that control by the religious entity is the key. Churches, temples, educational facilities, and hospitals that are church-operated, for example, are excluded from coverage. Places of public accommodation that lease space from a religiously controlled entity are not exempt. Note also that in many instances, religiously controlled facilities may need to meet the requirements of state laws that may require access. State and local laws that offer comparable or stricter coverage are not preempted by the ADA.

The ADA also sets forth an elevator exception for certain structures. Elevators are not required if a building is less than three stories or less than 3,000 square feet per floor unless the facility is a shopping center, mall, or contains the office of a health care provider. In addition, provision is made for the U.S. Attorney General to require additional categories of buildings to provide elevator access even if otherwise exempt based on a showing of need in community usage. For example, the legislative history indicates that unique facilities, such as a municipal airport or the only banquet facility available for public functions in a small town, should be accessible. In such instances, the Attorney General has the authority to limit the exemption.

Transportation Access

The other major thrust of Title III is the requirement that private providers of public transportation become accessible. In Title II, the ADA establishes specific requirements and timetables for public providers of public transportation, such as most city bus and subway services. Private providers are covered by Title III.

The transportation requirements include the same specific categories of prohibited activities discussed in the General Requirements of Title III section above. Private providers primarily engaged in the business of transportation must examine their business practices to assure that eligibility criteria are nondiscriminatory, to provide auxiliary aids and services where appropriate, to make reasonable modifications in policies that may have a discriminatory impact, and to remove barriers. For example, if a cab driver refuses to pick up a passenger who uses a wheelchair and possibly needs assistance into the cab because he or she does not want to help the person, that conduct is a violation of the ADA. The ADA differentiates between providers who are not primarily in the transportation business (e.g., a hotel chain that operates complimentary van service between the local airport and the hotel facilities, the shuttle service at a ski resort) and providers such as private bus companies that are primarily in the business of providing public transportation.

Nonprimary Providers

The ADA requires that providers who operate a fixed route system, such as a private bus service that maintains a fixed schedule, and who purchase or lease a vehicle with a capacity of more than 16 passengers, make that vehicle "readily accessible to and usable by" persons with disabilities. Lifts, spaces for securement of wheelchairs, and other such features are required by this section. This requirement became effective for solicitations entered 30 days after the effective date of the ADA, beginning August 26, 1990. Where the solicitation is for the purchase or lease of vehicles with a capacity of less than 16, the entity, when viewed in its entirety, must offer equivalent service (e.g., paratransit, the use of a portable boarding device, the use of an alternative vehicle).

The requirement for a demand responsive system, such as a hotel white phone courtesy van, is that equivalent service be provided. This requirement applies generally and is not triggered by the purchase or lease of vehicles. However, for purchases or leases of vehicles with a seating capacity of more than 16 for which solicitations are made after August 26, 1990, the vehicles must be accessible unless the system provides equivalent service.

Finally, there is a separate set of requirements for over-the-road buses. That term is defined as a bus with an elevated passenger deck located over a baggage compartment (e.g., a Greyhound bus). Those providers must comply with the same requirements as are applicable to primary providers of transportation services (see below).

Private Providers Primarily in the Transportation Business

For those private providers that are primarily in the transportation business, the requirements concerning the purchase or lease of a new vehicle, not including a car, small van, or over-the-road bus, became effective 30 days after enactment, August 26, 1990. The standard requires vehicles to be readily accessible to and useable by people with disabilities. An exception is created when the entity operates a system that is solely demand responsive where equivalent service is provided.

Over-the-road buses are treated separately as a result of fierce legislative wrangling that resulted in compromise provisions. Entities that purchase or lease over-the-road buses must comply with a specific set of regulations to be issued after the completion of a three-year feasibility study. The study is to be completed by July 1993 and is to be conducted by the Office of Technology Assessment and an advisory board comprised of industry representatives, individuals with disabilities who are potential bus riders, and technical experts. Specific issues to be considered in the study are outlined in the ADA including anticipated demand, cost and effectiveness of making buses accessible, design adaptations, and the impact of such requirements on over-the-road bus service generally, particularly in rural areas. Based on the findings of this study, the President has the authority to extend deadlines for compliance by one year.

Final regulations for the over-the-road industry are to be issued one year after completion of the study, no later than July 26, 1994. Those regulations will then go into effect seven years after enactment of the law for small providers and six years after enactment for other providers. It is this seven- and six-year scheme that can be extended one year based upon the conclusions of the study discussed above. In the interim, the regulations that require general accessibility will apply, except no structural changes (e.g., the installation of lifts, the purchase of boarding devices) will be mandated until the final regulations are issued.

Entities that purchase or lease small vans seating less than eight are required to make the vehicles readily accessible to and useable by people with disabilities unless an equivalent service that is accessible is available. These requirements became effective August 26, 1990.

The requirements for the purchase or lease of a passenger rail car also utilize the standard of readily accessible to and useable by people with disabilities, effective August 26, 1990. Where rail cars are remanufactured to extend their life more than 10 years, they must be readily accessible to and useable by people with disabilities to the maximum extent feasible. There is an exception for historic rail cars where provision of accessibility features would significantly alter the character of such cars. A historic rail car is defined as a rail passenger car that is at least 30 years old, is no longer being manufactured, and which has a consequential association with events or persons significant to the past or reflects distinctive types of cars or past time periods.

Other than the specific requirements governing over-the-road buses, the final regulations to implement this section were issued by the U.S. Department of Transportation on September 6, 1991 (49 C.F.R. Parts 27, 37, and 38).

Programmatic Access

The prohibitions of discrimination that are applicable to this Title III as a whole have an obvious impact on programmatic access. In addition, there is a specific section in the ADA that requires entities that offer examinations or courses relating to applications, licensing, or certification for secondary, postsecondary, professional, or trade purposes make them available in a place and manner accessible to people with disabilities. In the alternative, other accessible arrangements can be offered if the alternatives are comparable to the services provided to others. For example, a candidate for the beautician licensing exam may require an accommodation in the length of time to complete the exam based on a learning disability. Similarly, a high school student who uses a wheelchair cannot be denied the opportunity to take the S.A.T. because the test is offered in an inaccessible location. Either temporary access must be provided or an alternative comparable site that is accessible must be offered.

Effective Date

The majority of the provisions of the Title III became effective 18 months after enactment, on January 26, 1992. The exceptions in the areas concerning public transportation are specifically the purchase or lease of new vehicles on fixed route and demand responsive systems, the purchase or lease of new vehicles, small vans, new or remanufactured rail cars by primary providers, and the significantly longer timetables for compliance applicable to over-the-road buses. In the area of structural access, new construction requirements take effect 30 months after enactment, in January 26, 1993.

There is a phase-in period for the broad prohibitions of discrimination in programmatic access as they apply to small businesses but not the more specific requirements of structural access. Those businesses that have 25 or fewer employees and gross receipts of $1 million or less have an extra six months to comply, until July 26, 1992. Very small businesses, those with 10 or fewer employees and gross receipts of $500,000 or less are granted an extra year, until January 26, 1993. These provisions are intended to provide small employers ample opportunity to study the regulations that are issued under this section and bring themselves into compliance.

Enforcement

A two-pronged enforcement scheme is provided under this Title. First, individuals are provided a private right of action as under the Civil Rights Act of 1964. This provides that preventive relief is available (e.g., permanent and temporary injunctions or orders to make facilities accessible, provide auxiliary aids, or modify policies). Monetary damages are not available as a remedy. Attorneys' fees are also available to the prevailing party. In structural access cases, remedies are available for what can be called *anticipatory discrimination*: complainants do not have to wait for the concrete to be poured if the construction or alteration to a facility is going to be in violation of the ADA.

Second, the U.S. Attorney General has the authority to enforce the ADA where a pattern and practice of discrimination is evident or where there is an issue of general public importance. The remedies available in those suits include equitable relief and specified monetary penalties. No punitive damages are available. Finally, there is an express requirement that the good faith efforts of the entity being sued to comply with the ADA must be considered.

The ADA and Existing Laws

One measure of the significance of the ADA is to view it in the context of existing federal law. Prior to passage of the ADA, three key laws existed at the federal level that addressed the rights of people with disabilities. The Rehabilitation Act of 1973, more typically known as section 504, prohibits discrimination against persons with disabilities by federal agencies, entities that contract or subcontract with the federal government, and entities or programs that receive federal financial assistance. The prohibition against discrimination is expressly tied to receipt of federal monies. However, the Rehabilitation Act contains only a broad prohibition of discrimination against persons with disabilities. Thus the delineation of specific violations of the Act was left to the regulations issued by various federal agencies and court interpretations.

The recent amendments to the federal Fair Housing Act expressly include people with disabilities as a protected category. In fact, early versions of the ADA legislation contained a section related to housing. That language was excised from the draft of the ADA and utilized instead as amendatory language in what is now called the Fair Housing Amendments Act. Basically, that act prohibits discrimination against persons with disabilities in all aspects of real estate transactions including purchase or rental of facilities. It also contains specific requirements regarding structural accessibility in new construction and alterations of certain multistory housing.

Finally, the Architectural Barriers Act requires specific structural access to all buildings or facilities owned, leased, or used by agencies of the federal government. That law contains the federal requirements for accessibility to facilities such as post offices, federal courthouses, and social security administration offices.

Viewing the Rehabilitation Act, the Fair Housing Amendments Act, and the Architectural Barriers Act, together as the major laws that existed in the pre-ADA landscape illustrates clearly that discriminatory conduct in the private sector was not reached by any federal law. This void is filled by Title III of the ADA.

The ADA must also be viewed in the context of state law. Most states have enacted civil rights laws that include discrimination against people with disabilities as prohibited conduct. Many states also have enacted laws that regulate structural accessibility to insure access for people with disabilities. However, these laws vary by state as to their scope, enforcement, and remedies. The ADA specifically provides that where state laws are stricter, they are not preempted. Thus, the ADA provides a uniform and comprehensive minimum standard for accessibility nationwide that has not previously existed.

Financial Incentives for Access

The ADA itself contains no appropriation of funds to assist in meeting the costs of compliance with the requirements of the Act. However, recent changes to the Tax Code offer private businesses two vehicles to offset the cost of making structural accommodations and providing auxiliary aids. First, there has been a long-standing provision in the Code that permitted businesses to take a tax deduction of up to $35,000 annually for changes to the premises that improved accessibility (§190). This section has now been amended to offer a deduction of up to $15,000 for such changes. However, a corollary provision has been added that offers a tax credit, not to exceed $5,125 (50% of an amount exceeding $250, but less than $10,250 annually) to certain small business taxpayers for the costs of accessibility improvements or the costs of providing auxiliary aids to employees (e.g., the costs of interpreter or reader services or assistive devices) (§44). To be eligible, a business must have gross receipts of $1 million or less or not more than 30 full-time employees. This new credit, referred to as the Disabled Access Credit, became available in tax year 1991.

Conclusion

As this description of the requirements of Title III makes clear, implementation of this section of the ADA will have far-reaching consequences in both the private and public sectors. Some of the concepts of the Title are familiar; some are created in the ADA for the first time. The landscape of disability rights law is forever altered by this Act in a manner that will change the opportunities for people with disabilities in all aspects of their lives.

14

Environmental Barriers:
Questions and Answers

Heidi Gerstman, J.D.

The Americans with Disabilities Act (ADA) has largely been treated by the media as employment legislation. While it will clearly have a significant impact on employers, it stands to have an even greater impact on the overall infrastructure of American business. Title III of the ADA, which regulates the manner in which goods and services are provided to individuals with disabilities, has not yet received much publicity–but when businesses begin to realize how pervasive its requirements are, and how costly it can be to ignore those requirements, Title III's goal of integrating individuals with disabilities into mainstream society will come to be regarded by the business community as the social milestone that it is.

Background Information

Q: When did the ADA become law?
   A: On July 26, 1990.

Q: What is the ADA?
   A: It is sweeping civil rights legislation which prohibits discrimination on the basis of a disability.

Q: What is a disability?
   A: The ADA defines disability to mean: (a) a physical or mental impairment that substantially limits one or more of the major life activities of an individual; (b) a record of such an impairment; or (c) being regarded as having such an impairment.

Q: What percentage of the population is estimated to have disabilities?
   A: There are roughly 250 million people in the country and approximately 43 million of them have disabilities.

Q: *Approximately how many individuals with disabilities will benefit from improved access to goods and services?*

A: There are an estimated 1,341,000 individuals who are reported to use a wheelchair and/or a walker. There are an estimated 5,191,000 individuals who are unable to walk up a flight of stairs. There are an estimated 1,741,000 individuals who are deaf in both ears. There are an estimated 7,694,000 individuals who have difficulty hearing what is said in a normal conversation with another person.

Q: *What is the goal of the ADA?*

A: One of the primary goals is to achieve full integration of individuals with disabilities into society.

Overview of the ADA

Q: *How is the ADA organized?*

A: The ADA is broken down into five titles. Title I pertains to employment; Title II pertains to public services, including public transportation; Title III pertains to public accommodations and services provided by private entities; Title IV pertains to telecommunications; and Title V contains miscellaneous provisions.

Q: *What is Title I?*

A: In Title I, the ADA prohibits employers from discriminating against qualified individuals with a disability, and requires employers to make reasonable accommodations which will permit individuals with disabilities to work and advance in their careers.

Q: *What is the effective date for Title I?*

A: July 26, 1992 is the effective date for employers of 25 employees or more, but employers with 15 to 24 employees have an additional two years before the ADA becomes effective. Employers with fewer than 15 employees do not fall within the purview of Title I, but must comply with other state and federal laws prohibiting handicap discrimination.

Q: *What is Title II?*

A: In Title II, the ADA prohibits discrimination against individuals with disabilities who use programs or services provided by a department, agency, special purpose district, or other instrumentality of a state or local government, or by commuter authorities of the Rail Passenger Service Act.

Q: *What is the effective date for Title II?*

A: January 26, 1992.

Q: *What is Title III?*

A: In Title III, the ADA prohibits private entities from discriminating against individuals with disabilities in the provision of goods, services, and facilities.

Q: *What is the effective date for Title III?*

A: January 26, 1992. However, except for new construction, no civil action can be brought against businesses with 25 employees or less and gross receipts of $1 million or less for an extra six months and there is an extra year of compliance for businesses with 10 or fewer employees and gross receipts of $500,000 or less.

Q: *What is Title IV?*

A: In Title IV, the ADA provides that any common carrier engaged in interstate or intrastate communications by wire or radio must provide hearing-impaired and speech-impaired individuals with the functional equivalent of telephone service.

Q: *What is the effective date for Title IV?*

A: July 26, 1993.

Scope of Title III Coverage

Q: *Are there any size limitations for Title III?*

A: Title III has no such limitations, other than the minimal requirement that the operation of the entity must affect commerce.

Q: *Who is covered by Title III?*

A: Title III prohibits discrimination on the basis of disability in places of public accommodation by any person who owns, leases, leases to, or operates a place of public accommodation.

Q: *What businesses are covered?*

A: Virtually every business is covered by Title III. The categories of facilities represented in the definition of public accommodation for purposes of the ADA include: (1) places of lodging; (2) establishments serving food or drink; (3) places of exhibition or entertainment; (4) places of public gathering; (5) sales or rental establishments; (6) service establishments; (7) stations used for specified public transportation; (8) places of public display or collection; (9) places of recreation; (10) places of education; (11) social service center establishments; and (12) places of exercise.

Q: *What if a facility does not qualify as a place of public accommodation?*

A: It still may be a commercial facility and, as such, would be subject to the new construction and alterations requirements of the ADA.

Q: *What is a commercial facility?*

A: Commercial facilities are defined as facilities that are intended for non-residential use and the operations of which will affect commerce. This term is to be interpreted broadly so that it will cover those commercial establishments that are not included within the definition of public accommodation—such as office buildings, factories, and other places in which employment will occur.

Q: Are there any exclusions?

A: The only exclusions from Title III coverage are private clubs, religious entities, and public entities.

Legal Obligations Imposed by Title III

Q: How will the ADA impact on existing accessibility laws?

A: Any rules promulgated under the ADA will not set lower accessibility standards than those included in existing accessibility laws, such as the Uniform Federal Accessibility Standards (UFAS) and the Minimum Guidelines and Requirements for Accessible Design (MGRAD).

Q: In one word, what is the objective of Title III?

A: Access.

Q: Do facilities have an obligation to provide access regardless of cost?

A: Under the ADA, facilities have a clear obligation to remove barriers to individuals with disabilities–but there is a limit on that obligation. When evaluating what a facility can and should do to improve access for an individual with disabilities, the test is whether the improvement is readily achievable.

Q: What does "readily achievable" mean?

A: Readily achievable is a key term with respect to existing facilities. Readily achievable under the ADA means "easily accomplishable and able to be carried out without much difficulty or expense." This standard only requires facilities to provide physical access that can be achieved without extensive restructuring or burdensome expense.

Q: How can you determine whether the improvement is readily achievable?

A: The ADA lists various factors, which include: (1) the nature and cost of the action needed; (2) the overall financial resources of the facility or facilities involved in the action; the number of persons employed at such facility; the effect on expenses and resources, or the impact otherwise of such action upon the operation of the facility; (3) the overall financial resources of the covered entity; the overall size of the business of a covered entity with respect to number of its employees; the number, type, and location of its facilities; and (4) the type of operation or operations of the covered entity, including the composition, structure, and functions of the workforce of such entity; the geographic separateness, administrative or fiscal relationship of the facility or facilities in question to the covered entity.

Q: What are examples?

A: The readily achievable standard would be applied to the installation of an elevator, installation of a ramp, lowering of drinking fountains, lowering of sinks, rearranging of furniture, and installation of automatic doors.

Q: *What if the proposed barrier removal is not readily achievable?*

A: Alternative measures must be taken to make goods and services accessible. Such measures could include retrieving merchandise, relocating activities, and providing home delivery.

Q: *What is the standard for evaluating nonstructural changes?*

A: Undue burden is the key term for evaluating the obligation of a facility to provide auxiliary aids and services. The term *undue burden* means "significant difficulty or expense," and serves as a limitation on any obligations arising under the ADA in the same way that readily achievable does. The primary difference, however, is that readily achievable is a lower standard than the undue burden standard for auxiliary aids.

Q: *What are examples?*

A: The undue burden standard would be applied to the provision of qualified readers, interpreters, Brailled documents, and other auxiliary aids.

Allocating Responsibility for Barrier Removal

Q: *What if a barrier to access must be removed in a leased building? Who has the responsibility for removing it, the landlord or the tenant?*

A: The ADA covers sublessees, management companies, and any other entity that owns, leases, leases to, or operates the place of public accommodation. Thus, the responsibility has to be allocated between the landlord that owns the building that houses the place of public accommodation, and the tenant that owns or operates the place of public accommodation.

Q: *How will the responsibility be allocated?*

A: The allocation of responsibility between the parties, both in common areas and within places of public accommodation, may be determined by contract.

Q: *Should the lease be considered?*

A: Yes. The lease agreement is controlling in any analysis. The ADA was not intended to change existing landlord/tenant responsibilities as set forth in the lease.

The Importance of Integration

Q: *What constitutes discrimination under Title III of the ADA?*

A: Title III prohibits two main types of discrimination. The first is to deny an individual with a disability the right to participate in or benefit from the goods, services, privileges, advantages, or accommodations of the place of public accommodation. The second is to provide a good, a service, or a privilege which is different, separate, or unequal to those provided to nondisabled persons. Different or separate benefits are only permitted when necessary in order to provide an effective opportunity to individuals with disabilities.

Q: *How should the operator of a facility make decisions about participation by individuals with disabilities?*

A: The goal of the ADA is to provide individuals with disabilities with goods and services in the most integrated setting possible. Thus, these prohibitions are intended to end the exclusion and segregation of individuals with disabilities based on presumptions, patronizing attitudes, fears, and stereotypes. As a result of these new standards, entities that provide public accommodations are required to make decisions about participation based on facts applicable to that particular individual and not based on presumptions as to what classes of individuals with certain disabilities can or cannot do.

Q: *When can eligibility criteria be applied?*

A: Eligibility criteria can only be applied if they can be shown to be necessary for the provision of the goods and services being offered. For example, a public accommodation may not require that an individual with a disability be accompanied by an attendant, or that a drivers license be required for check cashing privileges.

Q: *May the operator of a facility offer modified participation to individuals with disabilities?*

A: Yes. It is still acceptable to offer modified participation for persons with disabilities, but modified participation is only acceptable if it is presented as a choice rather than a requirement.

Q: *Is safety a legitimate concern?*

A: Yes. An entity that provides a public accommodation does not have to permit an individual to participate if that individual with a disability poses a direct threat to the health or safety of others.

Q: *What is a direct threat?*

A: A direct threat is defined as a significant risk to the health or safety of others that cannot be eliminated by the modification of policies, practices, or procedures or by the provision of auxiliary aids or services. It is important to note, however, that the determination that a person poses a direct threat to the health or safety of others may not be based on generalizations or stereotypes.

Q: *How would the operator of a facility properly make that determination?*

A: It must be based on an individualized assessment that relies on current medical evidence or on the best available objective evidence that determines the nature, duration, and severity of the risk, the probability that the potential injury will actually occur, and whether reasonable modifications of policies, practices, or procedures will mitigate the risk.

Q: *Will this determination require the services of a physician?*

A: Not necessarily, although it may be difficult to make such an assessment without the services of a physician. Moreover, the business may be negligent if it does not identify a safety risk to its patrons and an injury occurs.

Q: *What about safety rules based on actual risks?*

A: An entity that provides a public accommodation may impose neutral rules that would tend to screen out individuals with disabilities, if that would be necessary for the safe operation of the public accommodation. For example, an entity may have height requirements for amusement park rides, as safety requirements of that nature are based on actual risks and not on speculation, stereotypes, or generalizations about disabilities.

Q: *Will the installation of adequate accessibility features satisfy the ADA?*

A: Not necessarily. Another important component of providing ready access to persons with disabilities is maintaining accessibility features in a manner that enables individuals with disabilities to use them. For example, an inoperable elevator, a locked automated door, or access paths that are obstructed by potted plants are not usable by individuals with disabilities. This is not to say that an isolated instance of mechanical failure would be a violation of the ADA. However, repeated mechanical failures due to improper or inadequate maintenance could violate the ADA.

Q: *Can entities that provide public accommodations place a surcharge on an individual with a disability or a group of individuals with disabilities to cover the costs of modifications?*

A: No. Because these modifications are required to provide individuals with disabilities with nondiscriminatory treatment, they cannot be required to pay for the provision of such a service.

Eliminating Communication Barriers

Q: *What are the facility's obligations with respect to communication barriers?*

A: Facilities have an obligation to communicate effectively with their customers, clients, patients or participants who have disabilities affecting hearing, vision, or speech. However, the auxiliary aid requirement is a flexible one; a public accommodation can choose among various alternatives, as long as the result is effective communication.

Q: *Could you please give an example?*

A: A restaurant need not provide menus in Braille for patrons who are vision impaired so long as the waiters are available to read the menu. If the auxiliary aid or service is effective, it should pass muster.

Q: *Is there a numerical formula for determining whether an action is readily achievable or an undue burden?*

A: No. The ADA takes a flexible case-by-case approach.

New Construction and Alterations

Q: *Is new construction treated differently from an existing facility under the ADA?*
A: Yes. The ADA requires that newly constructed or altered places of public accommodation or commercial facilities be readily accessible to and usable by individuals with disabilities. Thus, while the ADA only requires modest expenditures to provide access to existing facilities that are not otherwise being altered, it does require that all new construction be accessible to individuals with disabilities. In addition, altered portions of a facility must be readily accessible to and usable by individuals with disabilities, to the maximum extent feasible.

Q: *What is the effective date for the new construction requirements?*
A: The ADA provides generally that all facilities designed and constructed for first occupancy later than January 26, 1993, or for which the last application for a building permit or permit extension is certified as complete after January 26, 1992, must be readily accessible to and usable by individuals with disabilities, provided that such accessibility is not structurally impracticable.

Q: *Are elevators required?*
A: The ADA requires the installation of an elevator in facilities that are three stories or more and have more than 3,000 square feet per story. Elevators are also required in shopping centers and the professional offices of a health care provider.

Q: *What is the relevant date for alterations to facilities?*
A: An alteration will be deemed to be undertaken after January 26, 1992 if the physical alteration of the property commences after that date. This is significant because any altered features of the facility or portion of the facility that can be made accessible shall be made accessible.

Q: *What if the alteration reduces access while in progress?*
A: While alterations are being made, it is necessary to keep a path of travel open to any area of a facility that contains a primary function, such as the customer services lobby of a bank. However, such a path of travel may not be readily achievable (and thus may not be required) if the costs of keeping it accessible are disproportionate in cost and scope to the cost of the overall alteration.

Q: *When is a cost considered disproportionate?*
A: The cost of providing an accessible path of travel to a primary function area will be deemed disproportionate when the cost exceeds 20% of the cost of the overall alteration. However, even when deemed disproportionate, the path of travel must still be made accessible to the extent that it can be made accessible without incurring disproportionate costs.

Q: *When are elevators required in altered facilities?*

A: The ADA does not require the installation of an elevator in an altered facility that is less than three stories or has less than 3,000 square feet per story unless it is a facility which houses a shopping center or mall, the professional office of a health care provider, a terminal, depot, or other station used for specified public transportation, or an airport passenger terminal. For such facilities, an elevator must be installed unless structurally impracticable.

Q: *What if the building is a historic property?*

A: If a building is a historic property, then access will be assessed in terms of whether it will threaten or destroy the historic features of the facility. If it would, then alternate methods of accessibility must be provided.

Penalties for Noncompliance

Q: *Do individuals with disabilities have standing to sue?*

A: Yes. Moreover, with respect to new construction, the ADA permits a private suit by an individual who has reasonable grounds for believing that he or she is about to be subjected to discrimination in violation of the ADA. Thus, the ADA authorizes suits to prevent the construction of facilities with architectural barriers.

Q: *Why?*

A: The purpose of this is to avoid the costly retrofitting that would be required if suits were not permitted until after the facilities had been completed.

Q: *Are there any limitations on that right to sue?*

A: The only precondition is that the individual bringing the suit have reasonable grounds for believing that a violation is about to occur.

Q: *What kind of relief is available?*

A: Injunctive relief can be issued if a facility has failed to remove architectural barriers in existing facilities or has failed to make new construction and alterations accessible to individuals with disabilities. Injunctive relief would include an order to alter these facilities to make them readily accessible to and usable by persons with disabilities to the extent required by Title III. Injunctive relief can also include the provision of auxiliary aids or services, modification of a policy, or the provision of alternative methods.

Q: *Who is responsible for enforcement?*

A: The Attorney General is responsible for enforcing Title III. The Department of Justice will investigate any complaints, issue findings related to any violations found, and attempt to obtain voluntary compliance.

Q: *Can the Department of Justice use the information it obtains as a basis for litigation?*

A: Yes. If the Department has reasonable cause to believe that any person or group of persons is engaged in a pattern or practice of resistance to the full enjoyment of any of the rights granted by Title III, and this raises an issue of general public importance, the Attorney General may commence a civil action in the appropriate United States District Court.

Q: *Are monetary damages available?*

A: Yes. The courts may also vindicate the public interest by assessing a civil penalty in an amount not exceeding $50,000 for a first violation and not exceeding $100,000 for any subsequent violation.

Q: *What constitutes a first violation?*

A: Any determinations of multiple violations in one trial on liability would be counted as a single violation. A second violation would not accrue until another suit were brought and the accommodation were again held in violation.

Q: *Are punitive damages available?*

A: No. Monetary damages do not include punitive damages. They do, however, include all forms of compensatory damages, including out of pocket expenses and damages for pain and suffering. The courts are also authorized to award attorneys' fees.

Q: *What if the facility attempted to comply with the ADA?*

A: The courts will give consideration to any good faith effort by a business to attempt to comply with the ADA, but the good faith standard does not imply that an entity can demonstrate good faith simply by showing that it did not willfully, intentionally, or recklessly disregard the law.

Q: *Does compliance with state laws and local building codes demonstrate compliance with the ADA?*

A: Not necessarily. However, on the application of a State or local government, the Assistant Attorney General may certify that a code meets or exceeds the minimum requirements of Title III of the ADA by issuing a certification of equivalency. Such certification would be rebuttable evidence that the facility complied with the ADA by complying with the state law or local ordinance.

Tax Incentives for Compliance

Q: *Are there any tax credits available for compliance?*

A: Yes. The Internal Revenue Code does provide certain tax credits for attempts to comply with the ADA. For example, it allows a deduction of up to $15,000 per year for expenses associated with the removal of qualified architectural and transportation barriers. It also permits eligible small businesses to receive a tax credit for certain costs of compliance with the ADA.

Q: Which small businesses are eligible?

A: An eligible small business is one whose gross receipts do not exceed $1 million or whose workforce consists of fewer than 30 full-time employees. Qualifying businesses may claim a credit of up to 50% of eligible access expenditures that exceed $250 but do not exceed $10,250.

Q: What steps should businesses take to comply with Title III?

A: Businesses must review their operations generally for ways to improve access. They should remove architectural barriers, communication barriers, and transportation barriers in vehicles used for transporting individuals. They should evaluate eligibility criteria and policies, practices, and procedures.

Q: What other steps should businesses consider?

A: If a business is committed to improving access, meeting with groups or associations of individuals with disabilities can provide tremendous insights and assistance. These groups have the experience and perspective to provide valuable advice on expanding the accessibility of facilities in ways that will benefit both business and individuals with disabilities.

15

Access to Public Transportation

Margo Lynn Hablutzel, J.D.

Who is Covered?

The Americans with Disabilities Act of 1990 is applicable to any public entity that provides general or special transportation service by bus, rail, or any other conveyance for the general public on a regular and continuing basis. This includes intercity and commuter rail; light rail; private entities under contract with a public entity; and shuttle services provided by public universities and special purpose districts. The ADA does *not* include public school transportation, which is usually covered under the Individuals with Disabilities Education Act (20 U.S.C. secs. 1400 *et seq.*).

The ADA also covers private entities engaged primarily in the business of transporting people and whose operations affect commerce, or which are not primarily in the business of transporting people but which provide fixed route or demand responsive service, or otherwise transport people. These include corporate shuttle bus services; hotel and rental car shuttles; aerial tramways; and over-the-road buses, such as Greyhound.

How are Public Entities Affected?

New vehicles acquired by public entities operating fixed route systems (e.g., bus systems, trains) must be readily accessible if acquired after August 25, 1990, whether leased or purchased. Used vehicles acquired after August 25, 1990, also must be accessible, but there is an exception if the entity made a good faith effort to acquire a readily accessible vehicle in accordance with Department of Transportation regulations.

Remanufactured vehicles are those which existed before the ADA and are updated or reconstructed for use. The best example is San Francisco's trolley car system. The ADA contains an exception for historic vehicles where alteration

---

* This chapter is based upon a speech given by Jeffrey T. Gilbert, Esq., Sachnoff & Weaver, Ltd., Chicago, at the American Bar Association Annual Meeting, August 11, 1991.

would materially affect the historic correctness or value of the vehicle, and where an alternative method of transportation is available.

Public entities operating demand responsive services must insure that all new vehicles are readily accessible, unless the system, when viewed in its entirety, provides a level of service to persons with disabilities that is equivalent to the level of service provided to individuals without disabilities. This means that the system must offer equivalent service to persons with and without disabilities, but all vehicles need not be accessible. The standards will be prescribed by the Department of Transportation, and the entity will have to file statements in support of the system.

There will be temporary relief for public entities where bus lifts are unavailable, by allowing the entity to obtain a limited duration waiver of the requirement for new buses under certain circumstances. The entity must notify Congress that it is seeking the waiver, and there are stiff penalties for fraudulent applications.

Paratransit may be offered as a complement to fixed route (bus) service operated by a public entity. The service must be comparable to that offered to persons without disabilities, and must meet certain eligibility criteria. The entity will not be required to offer paratransit service if to do so would subject the entity to an undue financial burden.

Planning for paratransit must be done with public participation, and a plan must be filed with the Department of Transportation. Paratransit service provided by others within the filing entity's service area will be taken into consideration.

With regard to paratransit service, the ADA is to be construed as establishing minimum standards for paratransit service.

How are Private Entities Affected?

If a private entity is providing service under contract to a public entity, then it must comply with the rules applicable to public entities (above). Otherwise, the private entity must comply with the rules outlined below.

The ADA does not require private entities to purchase or lease accessible vehicles if the entity did not plan to make any new purchases or leases, but the ADA does require that any vehicles purchased or leased will have to comply with accessibility requirements under the ADA. However, by no later than 1996, private entities *must* obtain accessible vehicles or provide equivalent services to all riders.

If the private entity is primarily engaged in the business of transporting people, all new vehicles (other than automobiles and over-the-road buses) must be readily accessible, except for vehicles acquired for use solely in a demand responsive system, and vans which carry fewer than eight people (including the driver). However, the exception applies only if the entity can demonstrate that its system, viewed in its entirety, provides equivalent service for persons with disabilities.

If the private entity is not primarily in the business of transporting people, then its vehicles that carry 16 or fewer persons, which are used in fixed route service, must be readily accessible, unless the entity can demonstrate equivalent service for persons with disabilities. One example would be a van or other vehicle provided by an employer to transport employees from and to a commuter train station. If the entity offers a demand responsive service, such as transportation from one area of a campus to another, these vehicles need not be readily accessible if the entity can demonstrate that it offers equivalent service to employees with and without disabilities.

Private entities operating over-the-road bus service (e.g., Greyhound), must comply with interim requirements until a currently ongoing study concerning over-the-road bus service is completed and final regulations are issued. The study continues through July 26, 1993, and the final regulations are due July 26, 1996, for large entities, and July 26, 1997, for small entities. The interim regulations focus on provision of services, not the acquisition of hardware. Passengers will have to give 48 hours' notice to the entity of any special needs before a trip, and under the interim regulations accessible bathrooms on the vehicles are not required.

Are Transportation Facilities Covered by the ADA?

Under the ADA, transportation facilities used in the provision of designated public transportation services must also be accessible. New facilities must be accessible from their construction.

Existing facilities must be altered to be accessible. The altered portion of a facility, to the maximum extent feasible, shall be readily accessible to and useable by persons with disabilities, including persons who use wheelchairs. Key alterations are those that affect or could affect usability of or access to an area containing a primary function of the facility (e.g., waiting rooms, washrooms, ticket counters). There is a limitation where the cost of additional work is disproportionate to the cost and scope of overall alterations to the facility, which is deemed to be over 20% of the work done.

Certain existing facilities may remain unaltered, if the program or activity conducted in the facility, when viewed in its entirety, is already readily accessible to and useable by persons with disabilities. Also, facilities which are not considered a "Key Station" need not be made accessible to wheelchairs in the absence of other structural alterations.

There is also no requirement to make services available to persons who use wheelchairs if they cannot utilize or benefit from such services.

Key stations for rapid and light rail transit systems, such as stations where routes connect or transfers occur, must be designated by July 1993, but this deadline can be extended for up to 30 years under certain circumstances, as when the designation would require that "extraordinarily expensive structural changes" be made to the station. Department of Transportation criteria will be used to determine what stations should be regarded as key stations.

Transportation facilities operated by private entities are also covered under the ADA as are those operated by public entities, and new construction must be accessible. It should be noted that most commercial facilities will be treated as places of public accommodation under Title III of the ADA, according to Department of Justice regulations.

How are Intercity And Commuter Rail Covered by the ADA?

Intercity (e.g., Amtrak) and commuter rail transit systems must comply with a "one-car-per-train" rule. This means that by July 26, 1995, all intercity and commuter trains must have at least one car per train that is readily accessible to persons with disabilities, including persons who use wheelchairs. There is no provision in the ADA for temporary relief from this requirement where lifts are unavailable.

Special rules apply to single level passenger coaches in intercity use. By July 26, 1995, these coaches must contain a number of spaces for persons who use wheelchairs to park and secure their chairs, and to fold and store their chairs and transfer to a seat, equal to one-half the number of single level coaches on the train. Thus, a train with 10 single-level coaches must offer five of each kind of these seats. This requirement doubles by July 26, 2000, to one of each type of seat per coach. Also, no more than two of each of such spaces may be located in any one coach car. Special rules apply to dining cars in intercity use.

The rules applying to the acquisition of intercity and commuter rail cars requires that new cars purchased or leased after August 25, 1990, must be accessible. Used cars purchased or leased after August 25, 1990, must also be accessible, unless the entity can demonstrate in good faith that it tried to obtain an accessible car and could not. Remanufactured intercity or commuter rail cars must also be accessible, with no exception offered for historic vehicles (unlike the examples given in the section on public entities above).

New stations, of course, must be accessible. However, the cost of accessibility (either changes to new construction or alterations to existing facilities) must be divided on the basis of responsibility. One "responsible person or entity" must be designated in the context of existing stations, and the "costs to the cost causer" will be distributed among entities on the basis of equitable apportionment; public entities will be included in the apportionment where appropriate. If the entities which share a given station cannot cooperate, this constitutes discrimination. Key stations will have a project manager designated to oversee the alterations.

For key stations, accessibility must be achieved "as soon as practicable." All stations in intercity rail transportation systems, must be accessible by July 2010. Key stations in commuter rail transportation system must be accessible by July 1993, although this time period can be extended for up to 20 years under certain circumstances. Existing stations may remain unaltered if any program or activity of the facility, when viewed in its entirety, is readily accessible to and useable by persons with disabilities, and the facility need not be altered to accommodate wheelchairs if persons using wheelchairs would not be able to partake of the services offered at that facility.

Are Entities Required to Train Personnel to Provide Services?

Public and private entities are required to provide training for its staff to give them the proficiency, as appropriate, to ensure safe and proper operation of equipment and treatment of individuals with disabilities. This includes testing of and training in the use of all vehicles, lifts, etc., as well as proper maintenance of them. Both wheelchairs and three-wheeled mobility aids must be accommodated at the facility. All operators must be trained to provide assistance as necessary or upon request.

What are the Accessibility Standards?

The Department of Transportation issued regulations on September 6, 1991.These comply with the ADA's specifications that the standards shall comply with the minimum guidelines and requirements issued by the Architectural and Transportation Barriers Compliance Board.

Until final regulations are issued, interim accessibility requirements under the ADA specify that new construction or newly acquired vehicles shall comply with the Uniform Federal Accessibility Standards, unless it is more than one year after the Architectural and Transportation Barriers Compliance Board issues its standards, in which case those are the ones which shall apply.

Who Can Enforce the Requirements?

The ADA provides that the remedies, procedures, and rights delineated in section 505 of the Rehabilitation Act of 1973 (29 U.S.C. sec. 794a) shall be available to any person alleging discrimination on the basis of disability by exclusion from participation in or denial of the benefits of the services, programs, or activities of any entity, as described above.

Section 505 of the Rehabilitation Act of 1973 refers to the remedies and procedures in section 717 of the Civil Rights Act of 1964 (42 U.S.C. sec. 2000e-16), and further specifies that title VI of the Civil Rights Act of 1964 (42 U.S.C. secs. 2000d et seq.) would apply to recipients of Federal assistance. Also, the law specifically includes reasonable attorneys fees as part of the costs which may be awarded to the prevailing party.

Section 717 of the Civil Rights Act of 1964 states that remedies may include annual review and approval of plans of action and related progress reports; consultation with and soliciting recommendations from interested individuals, groups, and organizations; establishing training and education programs; and gives deadlines for action on complaints and enforcement of the law.

16

Access To Telecommunication

Pamela Ransom, J.D., M.S.W.

> [Alexander Graham] Bell had invented the device that more than
> any other would prove their undoing, closing hosts of jobs to them,
> and depriving them of all the services and comforts that would be
> carried thereafter by an undulating current and no longer by a
> person. (Lane, 1984)

Text Telephones

The telephone has significantly changed the way in which we communicate. Much of what used to be face-to-face communication is now accomplished over the telephone wires. However, for people with severe hearing or speech disabilities, the telephone has been an insurmountable barrier to communication for more than a century. It seems ironic that Alexander Graham Bell, a teacher of the deaf, and whose wife was deaf from birth, would be the person to create such a device.

For decades, the telephone has been inaccessible for hundreds of thousands of hearing- and speech-disabled Americans. In the 1960s, Robert Weitbrecht, deaf person himself, invented a modem which enabled Western Union teletypewriters (TTYs) to communicate with each other over the telephone lines. It was this invention that broke through the telecommunication barrier.

In 1968 there were a mere 25 TTY users reported in the United States (Potomac Telecom, Inc., 1985). Then, as technology improved in the 1970s and 1980s, TTY usage became more widespread. These new devices became known as *telecommunications devices for the deaf* (TDDs).

Today, these devices are known as *text telephones* (TTs). A text telephone is plugged directly into the telephone jack, or the telephone handset is placed into the modem's acoustic couplers. It has a keyboard similar to that of a typewriter or computer, on which to type a message. The conversation is typed back and forth via the telephone lines, and the visual readouts of the conversation are generated on the TT's LED display screen or a paper print-out.

Digital signals from the text telephones are transmitted at two different speeds: Baudot and ASCII. The Baudot code was first used for telegraph communication. During the late 1960s, as new technology advanced, well-meaning businesses donated their old teletypewriters to people who were deaf. This created a broad base of devices using the Baudot code. By today's standards, Baudot is a very slow mode of transmission (at 45.5. baud). ASCII (American Standard Code for Information Interchange) provides for faster transmissions at 300 baud, and is capable of communicating with computers. Switching over to an all ASCII text telephone system and utilizing computers would greatly enhance telecommunication capabilities for people who have hearing or speech disabilities.

Numerous benefits would be realized by "phasing in" an ASCII-based text telephone system: standard computer parts could be utilized, which would lower costs and increase availability; ASCII text telephones would be able to incorporate other computer functions with only minimal increases in costs; an ASCII-based text telephone system could be more easily integrated into the increasingly computerized general telephone system; and communication access would be significantly broadened, as text telephone users would also be able to communicate with computers (Jensema, 1990).

In the future, ASCII-capable text telephones must be able to transmit at not only 300 baud, but also 1200, 2400, and 3600 baud. If transmission speeds do not keep pace with present technology we will be once again limiting telecommunications access.

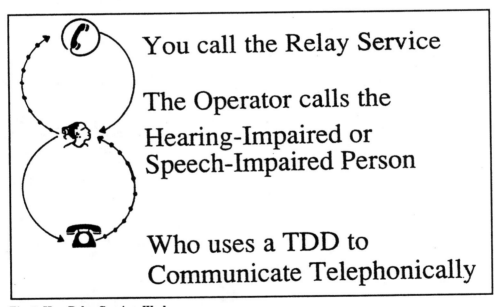

You call the Relay Service

The Operator calls the

Hearing-Impaired or Speech-Impaired Person

Who uses a TDD to Communicate Telephonically

Fig. 1. How Relay Services Work

Telecommunication Relay Services

The first telecommunication relay service was established in 1967, when 20 families in St. Louis, Missouri, paid $2.00 per month for relay services operated out of a "hearing" person's home (Peltz-Strauss, 1991).

Then in the mid-1970s, not-for-profit organizations began to offer telecommunication relay services. As a result of scarce resources, often not-for-profits provided these services on a limited basis, with volunteers.

In 1987, the first state-wide telecommunication relay service was implemented in California. It was the first service available on a 24-hour basis, 7 days a week, providing professional telephone operators.

The following years found numerous other states establishing intrastate relay services. By way of example, telecommunication relay service became operational in Illinois in July 1990. During the first full month of service, 31,000 calls were placed through the relay center. One year later, call volume had increased to more than 67,000 calls monthly.

Now, with the enactment of the Americans with Disabilities Act, common carriers will be required to provide both intrastate and interstate telecommunications relay services to people living within the 50 states.

Telecommunications

Title IV of the Americans with Disabilities Act

The ADA mandates that common carriers provide functionally equivalent access to the telecommunications network for people with hearing and speech disabilities. This access is to be provided through the establishment of intrastate and interstate relay services.

The ADA, with very broad brush strokes, set forth guidelines from which the Federal Communications Commission (FCC) was to promulgate the regulations for telecommunications relay services. The ADA guidelines (see Appendix at back of text) require that: "(1) telecommunications relay services operate everyday for 24 hours per day; (2) users of telecommunications relay services pay rates no greater than the rates paid for functionally equivalent voice communication services with respect to such factors as the duration of the call, the time of day and the distance from point of origin to point of termination; (3) prohibit relay operators from failing to fulfill the obligations of common carriers by refusing calls or limiting the length of calls that use telecommunications relay services; (4) prohibit relay operators from disclosing the content of any relayed conversation and from keeping records of the content of any such conversation beyond the duration of the call; and (5) prohibit relay operators from intentionally altering a relayed conversation (Americans with Disabilities Act, 1990)."

Federal Communications Commission

Report and Order

The FCC released its Report and Order on July 26, 1991. These regulations further define the broad statutory outline set forth in the ADA. The regulations provide some clarification, however, the FCC leaves much of Title IV to the interpretation of the states.

The FCC regulations can be organized into four general topic areas:

- Provision of Telecommunication Relay Services,
- Mandatory Minimum Standards for Provision of Interstate and Intrastate Telecommunication Relay Services,
- State Certification Process for Intrastate Telecommunication Relay Services, and
- FCC-Suggested Options to the States.

Provision of Telecommunication Relay Services

The FCC regulations require that, by July 26, 1992, each common carrier (both intrastate and interstate) providing telephone transmission services, shall provide telecommunications relay service (TRS) within the area in which it provides services.

There are several ways in which this may be accomplished. The common carrier can provide the telecommunication relay service itself, it may designate a provider through a competitive bidding process, or a common carrier can work in conjunction with other common carriers in other states to provide regional telecommunication relay services.

Mandatory Minimum Standards

The FCC in its Report and Order, addresses three areas of minimum standards: operational, technical, and functional.

Operational Standards

The FCC requires that both the intrastate and interstate telecommunication relay services must meet the following minimum operational standards:

(1) Communication assistants (CAs) must be "sufficiently trained to effectively meet the specialized communications needs of individuals with hearing and speech disabilities; and that CAs have competent skills in typing, grammar, spelling, interpretation of typewritten American Sign Language (ASL), and familiarity with hearing and speech disability cultures, languages and etiquette (Federal Communications Commission, 1991e)."

The FCC delegates the responsibility of ensuring "sufficiently trained CAs" to the telecommunication relay service (TRS) provider. Each TRS provider determining CA operational standards, rather than national CA standards of service, will promote an inconsistency in the quality of service across the nation.

(2) "CAs are prohibited from disclosing the content of any relayed conversation regardless of content and from keeping records of the content of any conversation beyond the duration of a call. CAs are prohibited from intentionally altering a relayed conversation and must relay all conversation verbatim unless the relay user specifi-

cally requests summarization (Federal Communications Commission, 1991f)."

This confidentiality standard presents two general legal issues: a liability issue and a conflict-of-law issue.

CAs providing interstate TRS will be subject to the same standards of conduct as that of telephone operators under the Communications Act of 1934. Section 705(a) of the Communications Act of 1934 "prohibits the disclosure of any telephone conversation except under limited circumstances related to law enforcement (Federal Communications Commission, 1991a)." It appears that this prohibition will be applicable only to interstate TRS thus ensuring the confidentiality of the vast majority of relayed conversations.

What happens, however, if the CA relays a conversation which is an illegal act (e.g., drug sales, solicitation)? To what extent will there be legal liability? Common carriers do not enjoy absolute immunity if the telephone lines are used for illegal purposes. There must be "knowing involvement in the unlawful transmissions" before the common carrier will be held liable.

In regards to the conflict-of-laws issue, this question arises in the area of intrastate TRS. What happens if a state statute conflicts with the ADA's requirement of confidentiality? There are presently a number of states that require their CAs to report relayed conversations involving child abuse. If there is a conflict between a state statute and the ADA confidentiality provisions, the state statute will "be preempted by the ADA to the extent they effect relay communications (Federal Communications Commission, 1991b)."

(3) The FCC regulations require that CAs provide services consistent with the obligations of common carriers. "CAs are prohibited from refusing single or sequential calls or limiting the length of calls utilizing relay services (Federal Communications Commission, 1991g)."

(4) "TRS shall be capable of handling any type of call normally provided by common carriers (Federal Communications Commission, 1991g)." To achieve access, which is "functionally equivalent" to the general telephone network, TRS users must have the same access to pay telephones, collect calls, credit card calling, and the like. Common carriers will be required to handle any type of call unless they can prove that it is not feasible to do so.

(5) "CAs shall handle emergency calls in same manner as they handle any other TRS calls (Telecommunication Relay Services)." Although CAs will handle these emergency calls, TRS will not satisfy Title II requirements that call for all emergency service centers, including "911," to be accessible to text telephone and computer modem users. Title II specifically requires that there be direct access to these emergency centers and not through a third party.

Technical Standards

The FCC requires that TRS providers conform with the following standards:

(1) TRS providers shall be capable of communicating in Baudot and ASCII formats.

(2) The blockage rate for TRS users should be comparable to that of voice telephone users, and therefore 85% of all calls will be answered within 10 seconds, and no more than 30 seconds shall elapse between the CAs obtaining the dialing information and the actual dialing of the number.

(3) TRS users will have access to their chosen interexchange carrier.

(4) TRS facilities shall provide services 24 hours a day, seven days a week, and back-up electrical power features will be comparable to equipment in normal central offices.

(5) Voice carry-over (VCO) and hearing carry-over (HCO) will be standard features of TRS. Voice carry-over is "a reduced form of TRS where the person with the hearing disability is able to speak directly to the other end user. The CA types the response back to the person with the hearing disability. The CA does not voice the conversation (Federal Communications Commission, 1991c)." Hearing carry-over is "a reduced form of TRS where the person with the speech disability is able to listen to the other end user and, in reply, the CA speaks the text as typed by the person with the speech disability. The CA does not type any conversation (Federal Communications Commission, 1991c)."

Functional Standards

Within this section, the FCC discusses complaint procedures, cost recovery, and TRS rates.

The FCC is the administrative agency responsible for the resolution of complaints within 180 days of filing. The regulations then proceed to explain the complaint procedure as it relates to intrastate TRS.

In regards to cost recovery, the costs of providing interstate TRS will be recovered from all subscribers for every interstate service and the cost of intrastate TRS will be recovered from the intrastate jurisdiction. The FCC has requested additional proposals from interested parties regarding the actual cost recovery mechanisms which would be implemented.

Also related to the cost recovery issue, is whether the intrastate TRS cost should be separately listed on subscribers' telephone bills. This has become a contested issue in a number of states.

The ADA mandates the provision of universal telephone service to all TRS users. In regards to interstate TRS, the FCC determined that "in order to provide universal telephone service to all TRS users as mandated by the ADA, carriers are required to recover interstate TRS costs as part of the cost of interstate telephone services and not as a specifically identified charge on subscribers' lines (Federal Communications Commission, 1991d)."

It appears, however, that the FCC regulations have differentially applied this mandate of universal service to interstate and intrastate TRS, thus contradicting the intent of the ADA. The FCC does not prohibit the labeling of intrastate TRS costs, as it does for interstate TRS. The FCC, instead, has said that if intrastate TRS costs are labeled on subscribers' telephone bills, it must not be done in a manner which offends the public.

Separately itemizing intrastate TRS costs on phone bills will give the incorrect impression to the subscriber that he or she is paying for something "extra," whereas TRS is an integral part of universal telephone service. This "labeling" will only irritate subscribers thus generating consumer calls to local exchange carriers.

Interstate TRS is a cost of telephone service, and therefore it would follow that intrastate TRS is also a cost of telephone service. It is the routine practice of common carriers, not to separately identify cost of service items on subscribers' telephone bills. Therefore, it would be argued that the singling out of intrastate TRS costs, regardless of the language used, and identifying those costs on subscribers' bills would be discriminatory and offensive to the public. Labeling of intrastate TRS costs would contradict the ADA's mandate to eliminate discrimination against people with disabilities.

It is hoped that the FCC will amend its regulations, and that state public utility commissions will prohibit the labeling of both interstate and intrastate TRS costs on telephone bills.

State Certification

Although it is the common carrier that is legally responsible for providing "functional equivalency" to the telecommunications network through TRS, it is the state that is responsible for FCC certification of the TRS. To be in compliance with the ADA, all states must have their TRS certified by July 26, 1992. The intrastate TRS must meet or exceed all the operational, technical, and functional standards contained in Section 64.604 of the FCC regulations. State certification will remain in effect for five years, at which time it must be renewed.

FCC-Suggested Options to the States

The FCC has identified a number of issues that were presented by interested parties during the development of the Title IV regulations. The FCC presented the following as suggestions to the states regarding intrastate TRS:

- to staff TRS with a number of CAs who have fluency in the dominant foreign language of their particular state;
- to allow hearing- and speech-disabled TRS users to designate whether they want the voice of a male or female CA;
- common carriers may provide call discounts for hearing- and speech-disabled TRS users (because it takes a longer amount of time to complete a conversation with a text telephone as compared to a voice conversation); and
- to develop consumer advisory councils to obtain valuable feedback from TRS users.

The Impact of New Technology on TRS

The ADA requires that the FCC develop regulations which will not discourage the application of new technology to the TRS. It is this development of new technology which will improve the cost-effectiveness of TRS and also reduce future TRS call volumes through improved direct communication technology.

New technologies to include VCO, HCO, and ASCII have already been integrated into the TRS system. These technologies will increase the transmission speed of TRS communications, resulting in a more cost-efficient service.

In addition, the application of voice synthesis and voice recognition has exciting implications. TRS is a very labor-intensive service. It may be possible, in some situations, to totally eliminate the CA, processing the conversation using speech synthesis and recognition technologies.

New technology will also decrease the reliance on TRS by providing a new mode of visual telecommunication. Interactive video telephones, transmitted through fiber optic cables will enable people who use sign language, and hard-of-hearing people who rely on speech reading cues, to communicate directly over the telephone. It is hoped that interactive video telephones, which are presently being marketed to corporations, will soon be within the financial grasp of everyone.

> The telephone is an integral part of our everyday lives, a critical link to the mainstream of society. However, for more 100 years since the telephone was invented, people with severe hearing and speech disabilities have been literally 'locked out' of the telecommunications network....Telecommunications access is no longer a luxury, it is a right. (Ransom, 1990)

It is Title IV of the ADA which extends this right to people with hearing and speech disabilities. Through the establishment of telecommunication relay services, additional people will be given access to the telephone network. This will benefit us all.

References

Americans with Disabilities Act, P.L. 101-336. July 26, 1990, Title IV, Section 225, (d) (1) (c)-(g).

Federal Communications Commission. (1991a). Report and Order. July 26, 1991. P. 7.

Federal Communications Commission. (1991b). Report and Order. July 26, 1991. P. 8.

Federal Communications Commission. (1991c). Report and Order. July 26, 1991, Section 64.601.

Federal Communications Commission. (1991d). Report and Order. July 26, 1991, Section 64.601, p. 16-17.

Federal Communications Commission. (1991e). Report and Order. July 26, 1991, Section 64.604 (a) (1).

Federal Communications Commission. (1991f). Report and Order. July 26, 1991, Section 64.604 (a) (2).

Federal Communications Commission. (1991g). Report and Order. July 26, 1991, Section 64.604 (a) (3).

Jensema, C. (1990). *Telecommunications for the hearing impaired: An era of technological change* (p. 70). Washington, DC: Gallaudet University.

Lane, H. (1984). *When the mind hears: A history of the deaf.* New York: Random House.

Potomac Telecom, Inc. (1985). *A short history of the telecommunications device for the deaf.* Potomac, MD: Potomac Telecom, Inc.

Peltz-Strauss, K. (1991). *Extending telecommunications service to Americans with disabilities* (seminar transcript). Washington, DC: The Annenberg Washington Program.

Ransom, P. (1991). How does the Americans with Disabilities Act of 1990 promote universal phone service? (p. 22). In *Telecommunications services to Americans with disabilities* (seminar transcript). Washington, DC: Annenberg Washington Program.

17

Tax Incentives

* John B. Palmer III, J.D.
Heidi Gerstman, J.D.

On July 26, 1990, President Bush signed into law the Americans with Disabilities Act (ADA), the most sweeping civil rights legislation in more than 25 years. Effective in phases that began in January 1992, the ADA prohibits discrimination against individuals with disabilities in four general areas–employment, public accommodations and services, goods and services provided by businesses, and telecommunications. The cost of compliance with certain provisions of the ADA (particularly Titles I and III) could be substantial for many businesses, especially small businesses; however, tax incentives are available to mitigate the impact of these costs. This chapter summarizes the obligations imposed on private businesses by the ADA and describes the tax benefits available to businesses seeking to comply with its requirements.

Brief Overview of the ADA

Title I of the ADA prohibits employers from discriminating against individuals with disabilities and requires employers to make reasonable accommodations which will permit individuals with disabilities to work and advance in their careers. Title I becomes effective on July 26, 1992 for employers of 25 employees or more. Employers with 15 to 24 employees have until July 26, 1994 to comply with the ADA. Employers with fewer than 15 employees do not fall within the purview of Title I of the ADA, but must comply with other state and federal laws prohibiting handicap discrimination.

Although Title I has received the most media attention to date, Title III will probably have a greater financial impact on businesses. Title III of the ADA prohibits private entities from discriminating against individuals with disabilities in the provision of goods, services, and facilities. Unlike Title I, it applies to all businesses, regardless of size, and therefore will have a substantial impact on small businesses not otherwise covered by the ADA. Title I, which is limited to employers of 15 or more employees, imitates the breadth and scope of Title VII of

* The authors would like to thank Jim Salvey for his assistance in preparing this chapter.

the Civil Rights Act of 1964. Title III has no such limitations, other than the minimal requirement that the operation of the entity must affect commerce.

Under Title III, a business will be considered to be engaging in discriminatory conduct if it denies an individual or class of individuals the opportunity to participate in or benefit from the goods, services, facilities, privileges, or advantages offered by the entity on the basis of their disability. It is also discriminatory conduct for a business to provide a good, service, facility, privilege, or advantage to an individual with a disability that is different, separate, or unequal to that afforded to nondisabled persons, unless it is necessary to do so in order to provide an opportunity that is as effective as that provided to nondisabled persons. The goal of Title III is for businesses to provide individuals with disabilities with goods, services, facilities, privileges, and advantages in the most integrated setting appropriate to the needs of the individual.

The effect of Title III is that businesses will be required to remove architectural barriers and provide auxiliary aids to ensure access to facilities. Title III became effective on January 26, 1992; however, with the exception of new construction, no civil action can be brought against businesses with 25 employees or less and gross receipts of $1 million or less until July 26, 1992, and businesses with 10 or fewer employees and gross receipts of $500,000 or less have until January 26, 1993 to comply (Department of Justice, Nondiscrimination on the Basis of Disability by Public Accommodations and in Commercial Facilities, 56 Fed. Reg. 36, §36 .508 at 7480).

Tax Incentives for Compliance with the ADA

Businesses which seek to comply with the ADA can mitigate the costs of compliance by taking advantage of two separate tax incentives provided by the Internal Revenue Code (I.R.C.). One of these incentives is in the form of a tax credit under I.R.C. §44 (hereinafter referred to as the *disabled access credit*) for certain expenditures incurred by small businesses in connection with complying with the ADA. The other is a deduction provided under I.R.C. §190 for the costs of removing architectural and transportation barriers to the handicapped and elderly.

The Disabled Access Credit

I.R.C. §44 was enacted on November 5, 1990 as part of the 1990 Omnibus Budget and Reconciliation Act. It provides eligible small businesses with a tax credit of up to $5,000 for "eligible access expenditures" incurred in complying with any part of the ADA. Businesses will generally incur expenses under Titles I and III, the employment and public accommodations portions of the ADA.

The disabled access credit provided by I.R.C. §44 is available only to an "eligible small business." This term is defined to include any person who *either* had gross receipts in the preceding taxable year of $1,000,000 or less, or employed fewer than 30 full-time employees (i.e., employees who were employed at least 30 hours per week for 20 or more calendar weeks) during the preceding tax year (I.R.C. §44[b]). Taxpayers who cannot satisfy either of these requirements are not entitled to claim the disabled access credit, but may be eligible for the deduction afforded by I.R.C. §190 (which is discussed below).

A broad range of expenditures required by Titles I and III of the ADA qualify as eligible access expenditures for purposes of the disabled access credit, including:

1) The costs of removing architectural, communication, physical, or transportation barriers which prevent a business from being accessible to, or usable by, individuals with disabilities;
2) The costs of providing qualified interpreters or other effective methods of making orally delivered materials available to individuals with hearing impairments;
3) Expenditures incurred in connection with the provision of qualified readers, taped texts, and other effective methods of making visually delivered materials available to individuals with visual impairments;
4) The costs of acquiring or modifying equipment or devices for individuals with disabilities; or
5) Expenditures incurred in providing other similar services, modifications, materials, or equipment (I.R.C. §44[c][2]).

However, to qualify for the credit, the expenditures must be "reasonable" *and* necessary to accomplish the purposes described above (I.R.C. §44[c][3]). In addition, the taxpayer is required to demonstrate that the barrier removal or service, material, equipment, or modification provided meets standards to be promulgated by the United States Department of the Treasury with the concurrence of the Architectural and Transportation Barriers Compliance Board. (As of the date of this writing, regulations under I.R.C. §44 have not been published.)

It should also be noted that the disabled access credit is not available with respect to expenditures incurred in connection with the construction of access facilities for properties "first placed in service" after the date of enactment of the Omnibus Reconciliation Act of 1990. This means that the credit is available only for improvements made to facilities that were placed in service before November 5, 1990, and is not available for new construction (I.R.C. §44[c][4]).

The amount of the credit allowed by I.R.C. §44 in any year is 50% of the eligible access expenditures above $250 and below $10,250 (I.R.C. §44[a]). Thus, the maximum credit is $5,000. In the case of a partnership, this $5,000 limitation is applied at both the partnership and the partner level. Thus, the partnership can allocate a maximum of $5,000 of credit among its partners, and each partner can claim a maximum of $5,000 of disabled access credit from all sources.

The disabled access credit is included in the taxpayer's general business credits, which are subject to the aggregate limitations on general business tax credits set forth in I.R.C. §38. To the extent these general business credits are rendered unusable by these limitations, the excess credit can be "carried forward" 15 years or "carried back" up to three years pursuant to I.R.C. §39. However, any excess credit attributable to the disabled access credit cannot be carried back to a taxable year ending before November 5, 1990 (the date of enactment of I.R.C. §44).

To claim the disabled access credit, the taxpayer must file I.R.S. Form 8826 (Disabled Access Credit). There is a trade-off for claiming the disabled access credit, and that is that the taxpayer cannot treat any expenditure for which a credit is claimed under I.R.C. §44 as a deduction or credit under any other provision of the I.R.C., or as an increase in the adjusted basis of any property (I.R.C. §44[d][7]).

Deduction for Removal of Barriers

Ordinarily, expenditures incurred in connection with the improvement of property—including the costs of improvements that benefit individuals with disabilities, to the extent they are not claimed as credits under I.R.C. §44—are required to be capitalized for tax purposes and recovered through depreciation deductions over the recovery period assigned to the property. I.R.C. §190, which was originally enacted as part of the Tax Reform Act of 1976, creates an exception to this requirement under which certain expenditures incurred in connection with the removal of architectural and transportational impediments to the mobility of handicapped and elderly individuals are permitted to be deducted in the year incurred. A handicapped individual is defined in I.R.C. §190 as "any individual who has a physical or mental disability (including but not limited to, blindness or deafness) which for such individual constitutes or results in a functional limitation to employment, or who has any physical or mental impairment (including, but not limited to, a sight or hearing impairment) which substantially limits one or more major life activities of such individual."

The deduction allowed by I.R.C. §190 is limited to expenditures incurred for the purpose of making any facility or public transportation vehicle "more accessible to, and usable by, handicapped and elderly individuals"; thus, in contrast to the disabled access credit, the deduction allowed under I.R.C. §190 is not available for the full range of expenditures mandated by the ADA.

Moreover, the deduction is further limited by Treas. Reg. §1.190-2, which provides that in order to qualify for the deduction, the removal of a barrier must bring the facility or vehicle into conformity with standards established by the Secretary of the Treasury on the advice of the Architectural and Transportational Barriers Compliance Board. Over 22 separate barrier removal standards have been adopted in Treas. Reg. §1.190-2. For example, a deduction is not allowed under I.R.C. §190 for the costs of retrofitting a door or doorway, unless the door or doorway meets the following specifications:

1) It must have a clear opening at least 32 inches wide and must be operable by a single effort.
2) The floor on the inside and outside of a doorway must be level for at least 5 feet from the door in the direction the door swings and must extend at least 1 foot past the opening side of the doorway.
3) There must not be any sharp slopes or sudden changes in level at a doorway. The threshold must be flush with the floor. If the door has an automatic closer, it must be selected, placed, and set so as not to impair the use of the door by persons with handicaps.

Similarly, the costs of retrofitting a stairway on the premises cannot be deducted under I.R.C. §190 unless the stairway meets the following specifications:

1) It must have round nosing of between 1 and 1.5 inch radius.
2) It must have a handrail 32 inches high as measured from the tread at the face of the riser.

3) It must have at least one handrail that extends at least 18 inches past the top step and the bottom step, unless the handrail extension would itself pose a hazard.

See I.R.S. Publication 907, "Tax Information for Persons with Handicaps or Disabilities" (1990) for a more detailed statement of standards.

Unlike the disabled access credit, the deduction provided under I.R.C. §190 is available to both large and small businesses. However, the amount allowed to be deducted each year under I.R.C. §190 was reduced from $35,000 to $15,000 in the 1990 Omnibus Budget and Reconciliation Act of 1990, which also enacted the disabled access credit. This decision reflected a desire to shift the tax incentives from large businesses to small operators, who can less afford the expenditures required by the ADA, as well as a desire to mitigate the projected revenue loss resulting from the disabled access credit. For a more detailed discussion, *see* CONG. REC. S10736-10747 (daily ed. September 7, 1989); 136 CONG. REC. H2439-2440 (daily ed. May 17, 1990); "Dear Colleague" letter from Representatives Upton (R-MI) and Mfume (D-MD) to all Members of Congress (Oct. 23, 1989) (discussing H.R. 3500).

As noted earlier, taxpayers cannot claim both the disabled access credit under I.R.C. §44 and the barrier removal deduction under I.R.C. §190. However, if the expenditures incurred in any year for the removal of barriers for individuals with disabilities exceed the amount eligible for the disabled access credit, the excess expenditures can qualify for a deduction under I.R.C. §190.

It is essential that the taxpayer keep any and all records and documentation of expenses to be deducted under I.R.C. §190, such as architectural plans and blueprints, contracts, and any building permits. These records will help determine the taxpayer's deduction under I.R.C. §190, as well as document any adjustment to basis made for expenditures in excess of the amount deductible under this provision.

Conclusion

When reviewing their operations for ways to improve access, some businesses may find that significant expenditures would be required to achieve full compliance with the ADA. Under those circumstances, businesses may face difficult decisions about which improvements to make—particularly if faced with a forced allocation of already scarce resources. These tax incentives were designed to make the implementation of such improvements more palatable to businesses. Thus, to the extent that businesses incur costs in effectuating compliance with the ADA, these tax incentives are available and should be utilized.

18

Issues in Customer Satisfaction

Carolyn B. Thompson, C.R.R.

There are more than 43 million people with disabilities in the United States, all of whom are potential customers for your company's services and products. With the implementation of the Americans With Disabilities Act, you will be able to attract this customer market as never before. Improved, accessible transportation, public streets and services, and the improvements you make to your own physical facilities will give you access to these customers.

As with all your customers, you have to learn to look at your company and its services and products through the customers' eyes. That's the only way to know what customers actually want and to assure yourself of a piece of this huge market. Then you can provide service that exceeds their expectations.

Know Your Customers

Today's customers, including individuals with disabilities, are aware and demanding. If they don't get what they want, they'll go elsewhere. But if you know what motivates them and deliver services and products that meet their needs, you'll have obtained a distinct advantage over your competitors. This is particularly true of your current and potential customers with disabilities. The marketplace has ignored their needs for so long that fierce customer loyalty is easy to come by if you address and meet those needs. Customers with disabilities don't have vastly different needs than other customers. The needs are basic HUMAN NEEDS. They need to feel welcome and comfortable; receive timely and orderly service; be understood; receive help or assistance; feel important; be appreciated; be recognized or remembered; and be respected.

To provide all this to any of your customers you have to have a company policy and a well-trained staff. Your staff may not be familiar and comfortable with customers who have disabilities. This will cause them anxiety and a guarantee that the customer service experience will be far less than the one that meets HUMAN NEEDS.

Using Focus Groups To Learn What Customers With Disabilities Need

To really know what customers with disabilities think and want you have to ask them. A little internal marketing and research is a good place to start. Your company may have employees with disabilities and you may already know them and feel more comfortable asking them what they need as customers than you would unknown individuals. You can also contact people in your community through your employees. Many of them have friends and family who have disabilities and would be glad to tell you what they need as customers.

Any company or organization can make good use of focus groups to capture the general perceptions, expectations, and feelings of customers. This is true if your customers are internal or external, retail or wholesale, reseller or end-user. You can explore in-depth topics and observe the interaction between participants to get their reaction to current and planned services and products as well as the services that accompany those services/products.

The focus group should look at your company's current abilities to meet customers' HUMAN NEEDS. First, you must decide on the structure you will use to explore each of these subjects, ask for the reactions of the group members, and allow for interaction. To elicit response, you can: design written and/or verbal questions; use visuals (e.g., movies, videos, flipcharts, overheads, slides); use audiotapes; have product/service demonstrations; or ask group members to use products/services.

A skilled moderator is absolutely necessary in order to elicit information from all group members, control the usual group dynamics, and allow you to really listen to members (see Fig. 1). You will need to determine if the moderator or other consultants need to be hired from outside the organization or if you have someone in-house competent in research design and group leadership.

It is wise to use a minimum of two groups to eliminate the possibility that group members can't work together, group members have to drop out, or any other situation that causes the group to be dysfunctional. Also consider providing incentives to group members to convince them to participate. The greater the distance you ask people to come to meet, the busier the individuals lives are, and the longer you will occupy them, the greater the incentive. An incentive is anything that causes people to want to help you (e.g., money, free products/ services, the ability to help your company).

Most focus groups function best with 8 to 10 participants who are relatively similar in lifestyles and interests. Group members whose interests and lives vary dramatically may have so much difficulty relating to each other that your moderator will spend more time on group dynamics than helping you get information. The time commitment required of each member should be stated before the group begins its work. The number of in-person meetings, length of each meeting, amount of thought/work to be done outside of meetings, and the structure of the meetings all factor into the time commitment necessary to accomplish the task.

The structure of the meetings should be designed to make the group members most comfortable and able to work. You will need to learn something about each person in order to do this. Consider the location of group meetings, time of day, day of the week, frequency of meetings, seating, and need/desire for providing food and beverages. You also need to know and make any accommodations that individuals might require to fully participate. The best method to learn about each potential group member is to ask them their preferences and any accommodations they will need.

Make a commitment to use the information you obtain to write a customer service policy that includes customers with disabilities. This information and some of the individuals from the focus groups will also be beneficial when you train your employees to provide customer service to people with disabilities.

STOP TALKING	• you can't listen effectively and talk • use active silence (concentrate)
HEAR TOTALLY	• be alert • make eye contact • watch body language (55% of message) • listen to tone of voice (38% of message) • actual words used are only 7% of message
LISTEN FOR IDEAS	• don't listen for facts only
WITHHOLD EVALUATION	• use self-control • express neither pro nor con • create an open environment
DON'T JUDGE DELIVERY	• listen to content, skip over delivery errors
BE PATIENT	• allow periods of silence
EMPATHIZE	• show understanding • ask reflective/probing questions • enter the other's frame of reference • seek areas of common interest/agreement • stay objective, put own feelings aside
KEEP AN OPEN MIND	• don't react to emotional words • interpret emotional words
BE FLEXIBLE	• use 4 or 5 listening systems depending on speaker
GIVE FEEDBACK	• ask questions to clarify • make comments that encourage talking • use body language to acknowledge
RESIST DISTRACTIONS	• concentrate • know what distracts you and eliminate it
THOUGHT IS FASTER THAN SPEECH	• summarize mentally • anticipate where speaker is going

Fig. 1. Twelve Keys to Effective Listening

Setting Your Company's Direction Through Your Customer Service Policy

Your customer service policy is the rule by which your organization lives in order to ensure that it meets all customer expectations. The policy gives your company direction and standards by which to measure itself. The policy must be clearly defined, effective, continuously communicated, and consistently applied to all customers. It is not necessary nor advisable to have a separate customer service policy for each of your different customers (i.e., you shouldn't write and distribute a separate policy for customer service to customers with disabilities any more than you would for customers who are minorities).

Your policies set the tone for your company in terms of who really runs the show. Do you want your company "controlled" by management (done by the book), by servers (employees make all their own decisions), or by customers? Successful organizations maintain a balance among these three and write policies with this balance in mind. If you're a new organization you will be guided primarily by server or customer control. Your employees can have very personal relationships with customers and have the ability to handle their needs on an individual basis. As your company grows there will be the tendency to move toward "by the book" control. Your customers who have been dealing with your company since its early days often perceive this change and you may lose them. Customers tend to feel more comfortable with the personal, individualized service that occurs in organizations that allow some flexibility based on the customers' unique situations. They feel less comfortable with companies in which the employees and customers are bound by rigid, rote policy and where employees respond to each situation with, "I'll have to look up the policy on this matter."

For your company and employees to meet the HUMAN NEEDS of all your customers you need to give employees the flexibility necessary to create satisfaction. A well-trained staff will be able to do this without "giving away the store," the frequent concern of management and owners in giving this level of flexibility to employees. (Staff training will be discussed later in this chapter.)

Armed with the basic HUMAN NEEDS and the information from your focus groups you are ready to create a policy to meet these needs and expectations. Bring together a group of key people in your company to analyze the information you have and carefully create a policy utilizing these findings. This group must ask and answer several questions while writing the policy:

What are the goals of this policy?
What is the appropriate structure?
What words will best convey the meaning?
What are the implications for customers?
What are the implications for employees?
What are the implications for our company?

The structure of your policy will be reflective of your company's culture. Your customer service policy may be a one-sentence statement like "We try harder" or "Illinois Widgets will be a customer-focused organization." You may choose a set of operating principles like the ones below (see Fig. 2). Still another structure is one which emulates another well-known document like the Bill of Rights or the

Declaration of Independence (see Fig. 3). This type of customer service policy not only lists a wide array of things that the customer can expect from the company but does so in a visually recognizable way.

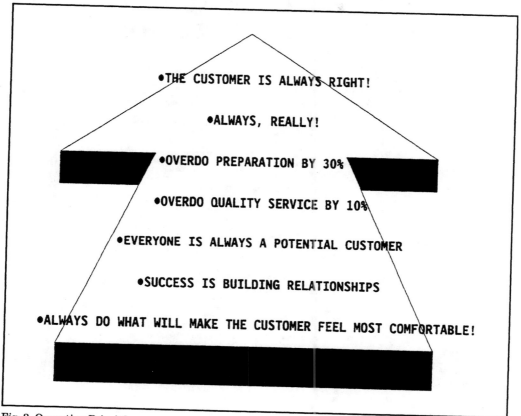

• THE CUSTOMER IS ALWAYS RIGHT!

• ALWAYS, REALLY!

• OVERDO PREPARATION BY 30%

• OVERDO QUALITY SERVICE BY 10%

• EVERYONE IS ALWAYS A POTENTIAL CUSTOMER

• SUCCESS IS BUILDING RELATIONSHIPS

• ALWAYS DO WHAT WILL MAKE THE CUSTOMER FEEL MOST COMFORTABLE!

Fig. 2. Operating Principles

The words you choose for your policy statement will also be reflective of your company's culture and must describe exactly what the customer should expect. Use words and phrases that define the policy in terms of goal-oriented standards as opposed to general statements.

Once you've agreed on your policy, print and distribute it to everyone in your organization and your focus groups for comment. Explain why the policies are necessary, how the policies were formulated, and what the implications are for everyone. Encourage feedback and re-write any parts of the policy that need revision based on the feedback. Print the policy in the final format you've chosen. This may include employee handbook, training manuals, customer invoices/ billing statements, signs in prominent places in your facility, signs on all employees' desks, and many other formats depending on the type of business you have. Have employees make a personal commitment to great customer service by signing their names to the policy. You may want to hold a special in-house event to kick off your new or improved customer service policy.

Publicize your policy in any place that customers and potential customers may read it (e.g., newspapers, special mailings to target customers, radio/television advertising, special events designed to announce your new or revised policy).

THE QUILL CUSTOMERS'
BILL OF RIGHTS

Restated and approved at Lincolnshire, Illinois, on Monday the First of May, One Thousand Nine Hundred and Eighty-nine.

The undersigned officers and the more than 1100 employees of Quill Corporation express a desire to clearly state the principles and ideals which guide all of us at Quill in our relationship with our customers.

We feel this unusual step is necessary at this time because we find ourselves, when we are customers...both as individuals and as a company...frequently dissatisfied with the way we are treated. Lack of interest, discourteousness, bad service, late deliveries and just plain bad manners are too common.

We can't tell others how to run their businesses (except by not buying from them). But we can and will run Quill as we feel a business should be run. Therefore, the following is a list of what we consider to be the inalienable rights of our customers. *We expect to be held to account whenever we deny any of these rights to any customer:*

1. As a customer, you are entitled to be treated like a real, individual, feeling human being...with friendliness, honesty and respect.

2. As a customer, you are entitled to full value for your money. When you buy a product, you should feel assured that it was a good buy and that the product is exactly as it was represented to be.

3. As a customer, you are entitled to a *complete* guarantee of satisfaction. This is especially true when you buy the product sight unseen through the mail or over the phone.

4. As a customer, you are entitled to fast delivery. Unless otherwise indicated, the product should be shipped within 8-32 hours. In the event of a delay, you are entitled to immediate notification, along with an honest estimate of the expected shipping date.

5. As a customer, you are entitled to speedy, courteous, knowledgeable answers on inquiries. You are entitled to all the help we can give in finding exactly the product or information you need.

6. As a customer, you are entitled to the privilege of being an individual and dealing with individuals. If there is a question on your account, you are entitled to talk with or correspond with another individual so the question can be resolved immediately on the most mutually satisfactory basis possible.

7. AS A CUSTOMER, YOU ARE ENTITLED TO BE TREATED EXACTLY AS WE WANT TO BE TREATED WHEN WE ARE SOMEONE ELSE'S CUSTOMER.

Jack Miller
Jack Miller
President

Harvey L. Miller
Harvey L. Miller
Secretary

Arnold Miller
Arnold Miller
Treasurer

COPYRIGHT 1979,
QUILL CORPORATION

Fig. 3. The Quill Customers' Bill of Rights

Publicity alone won't bring you scores of new customers, disabled or nondisabled. You must devise methods or procedures to ensure that everyone in your organization will provide great customer service on a day-to-day basis. Remember that a policy should be subject to constant, evolutionary improvement as needed. Establish a system for review of the policy itself as well as review of customer complaints that relate to your policy. Referring to, promoting, and acting on your customer service policy often will ensure you an up-to-date and invaluable document.

You should also set up a system to audit your company's and employees' performance in customer service. Your original focus groups of customers with disabilities, as well as a cross-section of all your customers is very useful. Be sure that your policies and practices meet the needs of your ever-changing customers. Your focus group members can be test customers in every phase of your customer service operation. They can then report their independent findings to your company. They may also make invaluable suggestions for improvement.

A Marketing Plan For Customers With Disabilities

At this point you've learned about the general HUMAN NEEDS and other needs of your customers with disabilities from your focus group and discovered that their needs aren't very different from those of nondisabled customers. Then you wrote or re-wrote your customer service policy to include anything that might improve service to this group of customers. You've already planned or are planning on training your staff to provide great customer service based on your policy to all customers, including those with disabilities. You know that the ADA will improve public accessibility, including transportation to your facility and you've made physical modifications to your property. Having done all these things, you are now expecting the portion of the 43 million people with disabilities who have interest in your service or product to descend on your company any day. This won't happen without some planning. You have to know where to find customers with disabilities so you can use your customer service policy and procedures to attract them and keep them as customers.

The same marketing research you use to determine where to find other special market groups can be used to find potential customers with disabilities. Again, your focus groups can be very useful. Don't make the mistake of assuming excess homogeneity across the group. If you use television advertising exclusively because you believe that all people with disabilities stay home a lot, aren't mobile, and that television is accessible to all people regardless of their disability and therefore they are able and desire to watch or listen to a lot of TV, you'll be missing all those people who don't watch TV. There are as many individual differences among people with disabilities and those who don't have disabilities. If you currently target your advertising to a certain income group, geographical location, age group, or interest group you will find potential customers with disabilities in each. This is also true of products and services that seem designed exclusively for people with disabilities (e.g., hearing aids, wheelchairs, special computer programs). These products may have a high concentration of customers with disabilities, but many nondisabled customers purchase them for someone who is disabled or, by knowing about them and where to get them, will buy them in the future for themselves if they become disabled.

People buy products and services because they need/like them, feel comfortable with the company, and see themselves as a user of the product or service. When people see others who are like them using a product or service they are more inclined to use it themselves. Companies now try to include a wide variety of people in their print, radio, and TV advertising. You see various cultures, ages, both sexes, single, married, and divorced people, and a growing number of people with disabilities represented. When including people with disabilities in your marketing and advertising don't make the mistake of using only one group of disabling conditions or placing them in one activity. All people who are disabled and potential customers of yours don't use a wheelchair and they don't all play wheelchair sports. You need to include a cross-section of people with disabilities and they need to be in roles that anyone could participate in. Identify the segment of the market you're after and include people with disabilities as opposed to featuring their disability. Figure 4 presents a Customer Marketing Plan.

Customer Marketing Plan

1. What are the services/products we'll provide?

2. Who are all our potential customers?

3. What do these identified customers value?

4. What do they need?

5. What will attract them to buy our services/products?

6. Where are our markets?

7. Who are our competitors?

8. What are the short-/long-term objectives of our company?

9. What is our marketing strategy?

10. What are our timelines?

11. What are our costs?

12. Who is responsible for carrying out each strategy?

13. Action plan--how will each of those responsible carry out the strategy?

14. How often will we review the plan (date)?

Fig. 4. Customer Marketing Plan

Train Your Staff and You'll Be Successful

People will forgive a lot if service is helpful and friendly. Sound easy? All you have to do is hire employees who can be helpful and friendly, right? People who are helpful and friendly in one situation are not always so in other, more stressful or unknown situations. To serve all customers well, your employees need:

Knowledge

- to perform the functions of their jobs
- to organize/prioritize their work activities
- about the needs of all their customers
- about what builds customer loyalty/confidence
- about the product/services
- about your company's organizational structure
- about policies and procedures
- about expectations
- about how their performance will be measured

Practice

- serving all types of customers
- solving customer problems autonomously
- handling stress
- listening actively
- talking with customers effectively
- empathizing with customers
- working as a team to meet customer needs

Your nondisabled staff will perceive customers with disabilities as "different" from themselves and will have difficulty meeting their HUMAN NEEDS effectively without some specific knowledge and practice. The best place to start is by showing your nondisabled staff the similarities between themselves and their customers with disabilities. Your focus group members, your staff who have disabilities, and/or outside consultants can be useful here. Review everyday activities such as getting up in the morning, eating meals/snacks, shopping, relationships, hobbies, entertainment, and jobs. A discussion of these activities between people who are disabled and nondisabled people will do more for your staff's comfort than any other single disability awareness exercise. During this discussion, your staff will learn that people with disabilities are not all that different, and they'll get information on what is different. Issues such as how someone treated them because of their disability, obstacles to wheelchairs, and ways to communicate comfortably with someone who is hearing-impaired will surely come up. The perceived differences between people who are disabled and nondisabled is what causes the most discomfort.

The other area of major discomfort is in dealing with the special needs of a person's particular disability (e.g., communication for someone who is hearing-impaired, effective mobility in an unknown place for someone who is blind, understanding someone with a speech impediment). If we don't know what the person's exact needs are and how to ask them, we feel uncomfortable and make the customer with a disability uncomfortable, too. Customers won't buy your services and products if they're uncomfortable! Provide your staff with knowledge about the general needs of people with various disabilities and always stress that these are general and that everyone is different. Have your staff practice asking people with disabilities what they need and how to provide it. PEOPLE WILL FORGIVE A LOT IF SERVICE IS HELPFUL AND FRIENDLY. Your customers with disabilities don't expect you to know their every need anymore than any of your other customers.

PEOPLE WHO ARE VISUALLY IMPAIRED

- don't raise your voice (unless they're also hard of hearing and have indicated that this is the best way to communicate
- speak directly to the person, not to a third party
- announce your presence and identify yourself
- describe any written information/signs needed
- if you have braille available, ask the person if they'd like to use it (not all people who are visually impaired use braille - some can use large type, magnifying glasses,etc. - ask!)
- use the words you normally use (don't avoid "look" and "see")
- if guiding the person somewhere, have person take your arm just above elbow and walk a half step ahead (they will continue to use their cane or guide dog)
- if person uses a guide dog, its ok to comment on the dog, pet it, etc.
- if you need to seat someone with a guide dog, make sure there is space out of the traffic path for the dog to lie down/sit
- offer to assist the person if they need descriptions of products (grocery, clothes, salad bar)
- hand the bill to the person indicating amount
- indicate denominations of bills when giving change (rarely necessary to indicate with coins)

PEOPLE WHO ARE HEARING IMPAIRED

- use your voice but don't shout (shouting distorts the sound of the word and the lip movements)
- use facial expressions and body language
- use pencil and paper
- be aware that even a small hearing loss hampers a person's ability to understand what you say - make sure the person understands what you've said
- get the person's attention before speaking (tap on shoulder, wave)
- face the person constantly when you speak and speak directly to them, even if using an interpreter
- don't cover your mouth, eat, smoke or chew gum while talking
- talk in a well lighted place
- try to talk in a quiet place (many people have some or residual hearing and noise is very distracting)
- be comfortable repeating or rephrasing what you say
- remember that not all people use sign language or read lips - ask them how they like to communicate and be flexible
- many people can use the telephone with an amplifier which requires nothing different of the speaker
- some people use Telecommunication Devices for the Deaf (TDDs) - you can purchase them to call your customers or for their use in your facility - you can also use your state phone company's Relay System if you don't have a TDD

Fig. 5. Providing Excellent Service to Customers with Disabilities
(Continued on next page)

PEOPLE WITH SPEECH IMPAIRMENTS	PEOPLE WITH AN ARM OR HAND AMPUTATION
• listen attentively • your manner should be encouraging, not correcting • be patient, don't try to help the person speak • never pretend to understand if you don't - ask short questions that require short answers in order to clarify	• it's ok to shake a left hand if right one is amputated • shake hands with prostheses (hooks, artificial hands) the same as you would regularly • ask if the person needs any assistance
PEOPLE WHO USE A WHEELCHAIRS	PEOPLE WITH OTHER DISABLING CONDITIONS
• ask them if they need assistance and tell them to let you know when they need it • always speak directly to the person, not to a third party • remember that people use wheelchairs for different reasons - don't assume that they can or can't walk and move or not move any parts of their body • if the person is going to a table, move a chair away to make room (occasionally a person who is able may want to transfer to the chair at the table, don't worry, they'll tell you) • a person trying on clothes may need assistance in the dressing room • in a restaurant the wait staff should drop by the table more often at first to make sure all needs are taken care of (possibly turning menu pages, positioning glass/utensils/plates, cutting food) • if person is paying by check, offer a hard writing surface if counter is too high • a person with limited use of upper extremities may need your assistance in order to pay • offer assistance with packages, baggage, etc.	• don't equate Cerebral Palsy or other disabilities which cause spasticity, awkwardness or speech difficulties with Mental Retardation - always ask if they need assistance and be patient for answer • people who are mentally retarded may need assistance in a variety of customer tasks - mental retardation affects everyone differently - ask if they need assistance and then be available to help but don't treat an adult like a child • there are numerous disabilities that won't be apparent to you in most customer service situations - be available to help all customers all the time! • learn all you can about a wide variety of disabilities

Fig. 5. Providing Excellent Service to Customers with Disabilities

Customers Are Partners In Your Success

There is now a body of empirical data (Sherlock, 1989) that exhibits the power of customer "stories" on future sales. Think about a recent example of poor customer service you received somewhere. You probably shared your unhappy story with others. On average, unhappy customers tell nine others about the unpleasant experience, while happy customers tell four or five others. What this means for your company is that you need to satisfy two customers for every dissatisfied customer—just to stay even! While unhappy customers are telling their friends and colleagues about the poor service they received, they rarely tell your company. They simply take their business elsewhere. Poor or even average customer service is extremely expensive. It can, and usually does, cause you to lose customers. On average, studies show that it's five times more expensive to get a new customer than to keep an existing customer.

To be competitive today you must provide extra special customer service to all your customers, including those with disabilities. You may want to designate an employee or team of employees to provide special services to your customers with disabilities. You may, instead, want to use them to guide the rest of your employees in providing the special services. The services include anything that meets peoples' HUMAN NEEDS: toll-free TDDs, wheelchairs/Amigos,® rest areas for shoppers to relax, arrangements for interpreters, and arrangements for staff to assist them throughout their time in your facility. These services don't diminish the need to provide whatever service an individual needs to buy and use your services and products, they only add to it. Publicizing the existence of these services will help attract customers with disabilities who need them and haven't been successful finding them. Most people with disabilities have had poor customer service experiences in the past. When they learn of your policies and hear from others about their positive experiences you'll gain many more potential customers.

In today's marketplace it's not sufficient to reach out and touch customers. It's necessary to develop as close to a personal relationship as possible. There are two keys to reaching and developing relationships with this vast group of mainly underserved and dissatisfied customers. First, satisfy current customers with disabilities and convert them into advocates for your products and services. Remember, they'll tell four or five others (some of whom may be disabled and some not) about your great customer service. Second, find customers (yours and your competitors') who have been lost through inadequate service, or never found or received adequate service. The first companies that meet their needs will get the lion's share of the business. Make it possible, comfortable, and enjoyable for customers with disabilities to buy and use your products and services.

Great customer service for any of your markets can't be copied because it is based on the attitudes of your management and employees much more than on policies. Delivering great customer service is largely a reactionary process more than a programmed set of actions. Customer service is evaluated 100% subjectively by the customer based on a certain expectation level. A level which varies greatly from customer to customer. What is acceptable to one customer is not acceptable to another and this is no less true of your customers with disabilities. Great customer service comes from your employees using their judgement to exceed customer expectations. Properly trained employees will make good judgements that will help you attract and keep your customers with disabilities. You've given them your support, training with an emphasis on knowledge and practice, the information received from your focus groups, and your company's customer service policy. Now give your employees the flexibility and autonomy to provide for the customer needs. Wouldn't you rather spend the company's money enhancing services and products for your customers than seeking new customers to replace those you lost?

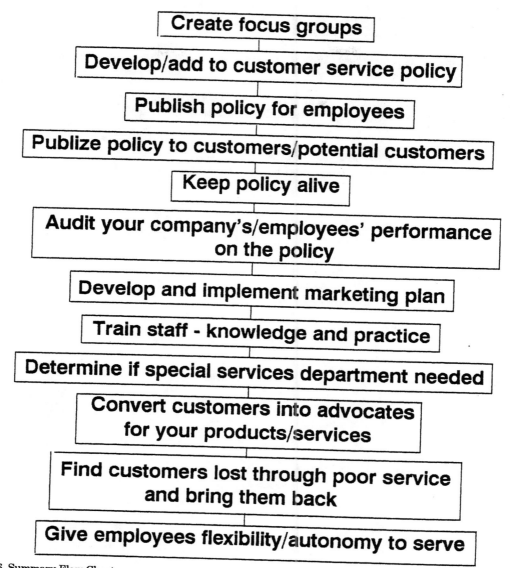

Fig. 6. Summary Flow Chart

Resources for Further Information

Blanchard, K. (1980). *Legendary service (video, slide program, audio, training workbook)*. Escondido, CA: Blanchard Training & Development, Inc.

California Governor's Committee for Employment of Disabled Persons. (1981). *Tilting at windmills*. Sacramento: California Governor's Committee for Employment of Disabled Persons.

Maloff, C., & Wood, S. M. (1988). *Business and social etiquette with disabled people: A guide to getting along with persons who have impairments in mobility, vision, hearing or speech.* Springfield, IL: Charles C. Thomas.

Quill Business Library (Ed.). (1989). *How to win through great customer service.* Lincolnshire, IL: Quill Corporation.

Schmidt, S. A. (1980). *Courtesy needs of the disabled customer.* Menomonie, WI: Materials Development Center, Stout Vocational Rehabilitation Institute, University of Wisconsin-Stout.

Sherlock, J. J. (1989). *Customer service: Is your association's for real?* Paper presented at the American Society of Association Executives Management Conference.

19

Resources for Job Accommodation

Linda R. Shaw, Ph.D., C.R.C.
Ginny C. Linder, M.H.S., C.R.C.

The Americans with Disabilities Act (ADA) is widely viewed as the most important piece of civil rights legislation for persons with disabilities in history. President Bush declared it to be "the world's first comprehensive declaration of equality for people with disabilities. Legally, it will provide our disabled community with a powerful expansion of protections and basic civil rights" (Verville, 1990). Unfortunately, there remains a large gap between legal protection and achieving the goals envisioned by supporters of the ADA. "The shortage—in many instances, non-existence—of accommodations for impaired individuals will be a thing of the past; the painstaking efforts of hundreds of thousands of our fellow citizens to use and enjoy the vast resources of this nation will at last be rewarded" (Gonzalez & Gordon, 1990, p. 951).

Problem of Implementation

The implementation of the Act will be neither automatic nor smooth, in the opinion of many. Earlier civil rights legislation with a much narrower scope has taken years to implement, often with compliance being achieved only after the filing of formal discrimination charges (Kaufman, 1987). The National Council on Disability (NCD) has developed an initiative entitled "ADA Watch" designed to "monitor and evaluate implementation of the law" (Parrino, 1990, p. 2). The initiative was deemed necessary due to the organization's observation that many businesses, industries, and public agencies responsible for complying with the law are unaware of their legal responsibilities and are unprepared to implement it.

Lack of Information and Awareness

Concerns about implementation of the law are rooted in several distinct but interrelated issues. First, many businesses, particularly small businesses, may be unaware of the law and their need to comply. Title V of the Rehabilitation Act of 1973 required those businesses and organizations receiving federal assistance to ensure physical and vocational access for persons with disabilities (Rubin &

Roessler, 1987). The law did not, however, apply to nonfederally funded businesses. The private sector has, consequently, been historically exempt from concerns about accessibility issues (Larson, 1986).

Even among those businesses which are aware that the law applies to them, there remains considerable confusion about its specific requirements. Many businesses delayed planning for compliance pending the release of the final regulatory guidelines. Those businesses that began their preparations experienced difficulty interpreting the law, prompting the publication of a spate of publications and presentations by attorneys and legal firms (Tysse, 1990; Perritt, 1990). Unfortunately, much of the information disseminated to the private sector of business and industry prior to the finalization of the regulations necessarily remained somewhat speculative. Furthermore, as with Title V of the 1973 Rehabilitation Act, much of the final interpretation will probably be defined in the courts in response to complaints, a process that is complex and lengthy. In the absence of current, precise guidelines, many businesses, particularly those without the resources to hire consultants and/or pay attorney's fees have taken a "wait and see" attitude.

Even those businesses who are prepared to take immediate steps to comply may find themselves stymied, however, by a lack of information about how to proceed. McCray (1987) notes that:

> Employers are....uninformed about job accommodation and most particularly, how the process of planning and installing accommodations takes place. They also lack insight into the many benefits of job accommodation. Both problems are especially common among small employers which often lack sufficient human resources to pay adequate attention to the issue. (p. 7)

Batavia, DeJong, Eckenhoff & Materson (1990) note that those businesses covered under the ADA will need technical assistance and specific advice on required modifications and workplace accommodations. They further suggest that businesses need information and recommend the development of "regional support networks to help businesses comply with the ADA" (p. 1014). McCray (1987) notes that even rehabilitation professionals are often ill-informed and poorly trained regarding job accommodations and suggests that we should not be surprised at employers' reluctance to take on the challenge alone.

Attitudinal Barriers

A second roadblock to implementation is the continuing prevalence of misconceptions about persons with disabilities and biases and prejudicial attitudes which develop as a result. Employers may fear that hiring persons with disabilities will result in increased absenteeism, high turnover, increases in insurance rates, morale problems with other employees, and a need to lower production standards or disrupt the normal flow of work activity (Granovetter, 1979). Businesses may prefer to maintain conditions that discourage patronage by customers with disabilities, if they are uncomfortable and/or feel other customers might also be uncomfortable in their presence. Furthermore, persons with disabilities may not be seen as desirable customers due to a general perception of them as "victims" with few resources (i.e., money to spend) at their disposal.

Cost

Perhaps the most problematic roadblock to implementation, however, is fear about the cost of implementation. Watson (1990) notes that "from the outset, businesses, especially small ones, have complained that compliance with the legislation would place an unfair financial burden on them" (p. 325). As McCray (1987) notes, "With an ample supply of qualified workers available, why go to the additional expense of hiring a worker who will need special attention or may even impose out of the ordinary expenses or risks to the company?" (pp. 6-7).

The ADA does not require employers to accommodate the needs of persons with disabilities when such accommodations would pose "an undue hardship." It defines *undue hardship* as "an action requiring significant difficulty or expense" (section 109 [9.10]). The law does not, however, specifically define how much difficulty or expense is "significant." An exact dollar figure was not specified in order to allow for consideration of such factors as business size, resources, and structure. However, such imprecise language has caused worry among employers that they will be forced to expend large amounts of money. These concerns are especially worrisome to small businesses which often operate on very small profit margins.

Such concerns among the business community are perfectly understandable. Entities which operate for profit can afford to accommodate the needs of disabled persons only to the extent that they are able to do so without placing their ability to maintain a profit margin in jeopardy. Unless they are convinced that this is possible and are assisted in this process by those prepared with the necessary information and expertise, implementation will be achieved slowly and with much resistance. The remainder of this chapter will attempt to provide useful information to businesses and to those persons attempting to assist businesses in accommodating the needs of persons with disabilities.

Employer Perceptions of Job Accommodation

In 1982, Berkeley Planning Associates was commissioned by the U.S. Department of Labor to conduct a study of federal contractors to determine their practices and attitudes regarding the provision of job accommodations to persons with disabilities. This study is particularly interesting at this juncture in the implementation of the ADA since it reflects the actual experiences of employers faced with the necessity of complying with section 503 of the Rehabilitation Act of 1973. A review of the experiences of other employers facing requirements similar to those of businesses affected by the ADA may help to allay some of the concerns of employers complying with the ADA today. The results of the employer survey are presented in Table 1.

A quick review of this table reveals that the great majority of employers agree that job accommodation attracts dependable workers and improves safety and productivity. More than half agree that persons with handicaps have less turnover. Employers felt that they had benefited greatly from a public relations perspective and tended to agree that the benefits had exceeded the costs. Problems with unions, co-workers, and customers were virtually nonexistent. Of particular interest, however, is the information related to cost. Less than 13% felt the costs

Table 1. Attitudes by Firm Size

Agrees that Accommodation:	Firm Size				Significance
	Small Firms (less than 100)	Firms 100-499	Intermediate Firms (500-2000)	Large Firms (over 2000)	
Attracts Dependable Workers	61.8% (34)	61.0% (100)	67.0% (85)	65.2% (66)	ns
Attracts Scarce Skills	30.8 (26)	31.9 (91)	36.3 (80)	34.4 (64)	ns
Handicapped-Less Turnover	45.7 (35)	61.1 (108)	49.5 (95)	41.4 (70)	.11
Handicapped-Good Attendance/Punctuality	34.2 (38)	58.2 (110)	44.2 (95)	28.6 (70)	.00
Improved Safety	65.8 (38)	56.3 (103)	52.8 (91)	71.0 (62)	ns
Improved Promotability	48.4 (31)	36.4 (99)	41.6 (89)	36.4 (66)	ns
Improved Productivity	62.9 (35)	59.8 (102)	62.0 (92)	64.7 (68)	ns
Benefits Exceeded Costs	54.8 (31)	47.9 (98)	47.3 (91)	51.6 (66)	.12
Beneficial in Public Relations	66.7 (39)	80.4 (107)	74.7 (95)	75.0 (68)	ns
Done to Comply with Law	29.7 (37)	30.8 (107)	34.0 (94)	41.2 (68)	ns
Uncertain with High Turnover Occupations	15.6 (31)	21.6 (88)	13.9 (79)	15.3 (59)	ns
Uncertain for Applicants Lacking Strong Skills	34.3 (32)	30.6 (98)	29.2 (89)	27.2 (66)	.13
Discouraged by Unions	0.0 (20)	6.9 (72)	3.6 (57)	9.5 (42)	ns
Discouraged by Co-Workers	2.8 (36)	6.0 (99)	3.3 (90)	3.0 (66)	ns
Discouraged by Customers	3.2 (31)	5.8 (86)	5.3 (75)	1.7 (59)	ns
Infeasible in Some Worksites	45.9 (37)	47.4 (93)	44.4 (81)	58.3 (60)	ns
Estimated Costs Exceeded Estimated Benefits	28.6 (28)	18.7 (91)	22.3 (85)	25.0 (64)	ns
Costs Exceeded Projections	19.2 (26)	7.4 (81)	14.1 (85)	19.7 (66)	ns
Costs Are Prohibitive	11.5 (26)	13.0 (77)	11.7 (77)	15.1 (66)	ns

Reprinted with permission from Berkeley Planning Associates: A study of accommodations provided to handicapped employees by federal contractors: Final Report prepared under U.S. Department of Labor, Employment Standards Administration Contract, June 1982, Volume I.

were prohibitive and, generally, costs were consistent with or below projections. Interestingly, over 50% of the accommodations were accomplished at no cost to the employer and over 80% cost less than $1,000. Taken together, this information suggests that employers who accommodated their disabled employees did not consider the costs to be unacceptable and felt the benefits more than justified the costs. Interestingly, this is true even for small businesses who may be presumed to have fewer resources at their disposal. McCray (1987) points out that the financial benefits of accommodating the needs of disabled employers must also be considered in light of the additional costs of *not* providing accommodations. The field of disability management has developed in response to the recognition that the cost of returning disabled employees to work are lower than the costs associated with disability payments, medical management, increased insurance premiums, lost productivity, and/or recruitment and training of replacement employees (Habeck, Shrey, & Growick, 1991; Schwartz, Watson, Galvin, & Lipoff, 1989). It is worth noting that the use of job accommodations has been shown to improve the probability of a successful placement with workers' compensation claimants, thereby reducing costs to the employer (Hester & DeCeles, 1991).

The types of accommodations most often undertaken are listed in Table 2.

Table 2. Types of Accommodations Provided

Accommodation Types	Frequency of Response	
	Number	Percent
Removing architectural barrier for individual	114	5.7
Adjusting the work environment (heat, light, ventilation)	56	2.8
Adjusting table, desk, bench, etc.	128	6.4
Other rearrangement of worksite	93	4.6
Relocating worksite	31	1.5
Modifying telephone, typewriter, etc.	57	2.8
Providing microfilm, dictaphone, audio-visual aids	23	1.1
Providing other special equipment, tools, or devices	95	4.7
Providing transportation or other mobility assistance while on job	65	3.2
Assigning tasks to other workers	177	8.8
Modifying work hours or schedules	104	5.2
Other modification of work procedures	179	8.9
Assigning aides, readers, etc.	64	3.2
Providing additional training	104	5.2
Orienting supervisors and co-workers to provide necessary assistance	362	18.0
Transferring employee to another job	175	8.7
Other	179	8.9

Reprinted with permission from Berkeley Planning Associates: A study of accommodations provided to handicapped employees by federal contractors: Final Report prepared under U.S. Department of Labor, Employment Standards Administration Contract, June 1982, Volume I.

The largest proportion of accommodations involved such activities as orienting supervisors and co-workers, modifying work procedures, and assigning tasks to other workers. Only 5.7% involved removal of architectural barriers, an accommodation often assumed to involve considerable expense.

The Berkeley study (1982) also attempted to determine what additional factors might motivate businesses to encourage the hiring of persons with disabilities and provide job accommodation, as necessary. Results of their survey regarding incentives is included in Table 3.

Table 3. Incentives by Firm Size (a)

Citing Strong or Some Incentive from Policy Option:	Number of Employees				Significance
	Small Firms (Under 100)	Firms 100-499	Intermediate Firms (500-2000)	Large Firms (over 2000)	
Tax credit for a portion of the cost of accommodation	83.3% (49)	80.9% (115)	64.9% (97)	61.8% (68)	.01 .17
Provision of free technical assistance for accommodation	69.8 (43)	63.4 (112)	63.5 (96)	65.2 (69)	ns .08
Increased enforcement of affirmative action regulations	62.5 (40)	55.4 (112)	57.0 (86)	65.2 (66)	ns .09
Placement efforts on behalf of specific applicants by vocational rehabilitation or other service-providing agencies	82.5 (40)	61.2 (104)	80.6 (93)	80.6 (67)	ns .12
Direct wage subsidy for severely handicapped workers whose productivity is below standard	48.8 (43)	47.1 (102)	40.7 (86)	32.2 (59)	.03 .17
Funding for more technical occupational training or work experience for handicapped persons	64.9 (37)	63.8 (107)	65.2 (89)	57.1 (63)	.17 .14
Provisions of information by the government documenting the advantages and profitability of hiring handicapped persons	43.6 (39)	44.4 (99)	54.0 (87)	39.3 (61)	ns .10
Other					

Reprinted with permission from Berkeley Planning Associates: A study of accommodations provided to handicapped employees by federal contractors: Final Report prepared under U.S. Department of Labor, Employment Standards Administration Contract, June 1982, Volume I.

Tax credits are considered to be a strong incentive for employers to hire and/or maintain employees with disabilities (see Chapter 17). Unfortunately, many businesses, especially small firms, are unaware of the existence of the Tax Credit Program. Almost as important as this financial incentive, however, is the availability of assistance regarding job placement. It may be that businesses who might otherwise wish to hire persons with disabilities have difficulty with recruitment and/or "fitting" a candidate's abilities to an appropriate job. Outside assistance in referring and placing appropriately skilled disabled persons would provide a strong incentive. The majority of the respondents also felt that the provision of free technical assistance for accommodation, the increased enforcement of affirmative action regulations, and funding for more technical occupational training or work experience for persons with handicaps would also serve as incentives.

As mentioned earlier, it is probable that some of the employers responded in the affirmative to the question about tax credits without even realizing that such a program exists. Special programs providing incentives to employers include:

Targeted Jobs Tax Credits (TJTC)–For hiring and training employees with disabilities; available through the Department of Labor, Private Industry Councils, and the State Vocational Rehabilitation Agency.

Architectural and Transportation Barriers Compliance Board (ATBCB) Tax Credits–For improving accessibility for employers and customers; available through the IRS, State Vocational Rehabilitation Agency or ATBCB.

Job Training and Partnership Act (JTPA)–For providing job training for disabled and other workers; available through the Department of Labor or Private Industry Council (PIC).

Special Minimum Wage Certificates–For employment at subminimum wages; available from the Department of Labor.

Resources

Although the ADA was signed into law on July 26th, 1990, resourceful employers, workers, consumers, and professionals in rehabilitation have been opening doors to successful job accommodation and access for much longer. Fortunately, an immense network of resources is already in place across the nation to help meet the needs of all persons concerned with meeting the ADA mandate.

The Compendium of Technical Assistance Resources Appendix at the end of this book consists of an annotated listing of organizations and resources available to assist persons needing ADA-related information and technical assistance. The resources include disability and advocacy organizations, technical assistance and publication-oriented organizations, and computerized databases.

Additionally, several federal agencies have recently funded projects intended to facilitate compliance with the ADA. These agencies include the National

Institute for Disability and Rehabilitation Research (NIDRR), the Department of Justice (DOJ), and the Rehabilitation Services Administration (RSA).

These projects will become major resources for information, materials, and technical assistance as they develop. Most maintain mailing lists and many will include toll-free information lines.

The ILRU Research and Training Center on Independent Living (1991) has summarized each of the projects as follows:

NIDRR: REGIONAL DISABILITY & BUSINESS ACCOMMODATION CENTERS (RDBACs)

RDBACs are big projects with major responsibilities: to disseminate information, including resource materials developed by the other ADA projects; to provide technical assistance directly and through referrals, which will involve developing and maintaining a regionwide pool of resource persons with expertise in needed areas; and to conduct training on disability issues as well as ADA provisions. RDBACs will be required to conduct assessments of ADA informational needs and preferred information conduits of its target audiences—which include businesses, disability organizations, state and local governments, educational institutions, news media, labor organizations, and other public and private service organizations.

RDBAC for Region I (Includes Connecticut, Maine, Massachusetts, New Hampshire, Rhode Island, and Vermont):
University of Southern Maine; Muskie Institute of Public Affairs
Jennifer Eckel
96 Falmouth Street; Portland, ME 04103
(207) 780-4430   (207) 780-4417 (FAX)

RDBAC for Region II (Includes New Jersey, New York, Puerto Rico, and the Virgin Islands):
United Cerebral Palsy Association of New Jersey
Richard Dodds
354 South Broad Street; Trenton, NJ 08608
(609) 392-4004   (609) 392-3505 (FAX)

RDBAC for Region III (Includes Delaware, Maryland, Pennsylvania, Virginia, Washington, DC, and West Virginia):
Independence Center of Northern Virginia
Sharon Mistler
2111 Wilson Boulevard; Arlington, VA 22201
(703) 525-3268   (703) 525-6835 (FAX)

RDBAC for Region IV (Includes Alabama, Florida, Georgia, Kentucky, Mississippi, North Carolina, South Carolina, Tennessee):
United Cerebral Palsy Association; The SMART Exchange
Shelley Kaplan
1776 Peachtree Street, Suite 310 North; Atlanta, GA 30309
(404) 888-0022   (404) 888-9006 (TDD)   (404) 888-9091 (FAX)

RDBAC for Region V (Includes Illinois, Indiana, Michigan, Minnesota, Ohio, Wisconsin):
University of Illinois at Chicago; Affiliated Program in Developmental Disabilities
David Braddock
1640 West Roosevelt Road; Chicago, IL 60608
(312) 413-1647 (V/TDD)   (312) 413-1326 (FAX)

RDBAC for Region VI (Includes Arkansas, Louisiana, New Mexico, Oklahoma, Texas):
ILRU Program; The Institute for Rehabilitation & Research
Lex Frieden
2323 S. Shepherd, Suite 1000; Houston, TX 77019
(713) 520-0232   (713) 520-5136 (TDD)   (713) 520-5785 (FAX)

RDBAC for Region VII (Includes Iowa, Kansas, Missouri, and Nebraska):
University of Missouri at Columbia
Jim deJong
401 East Locust Street; Columbia, MO 65201
(314) 882-3807   (314) 882-1727 (FAX)

RDBAC for Region VIII (Includes Colorado, Montana, North Dakota, South Dakota, Utah, Wyoming):
Meeting the Challenge, Inc.
Randy Dipner
3630 Sinton Road, Suite 103; Colorado Springs, CO 80907-5072
(719) 444-0252   (719) 444-0269 (FAX)

RDBAC for Region IX (Includes Arizona, California, Hawaii, Nevada, and the Pacific Basin):
Berkeley Planning Associates
Erica Jones
440 Grand Avenue, Suite 500; Oakland, CA 94610
(415) 465-7884   (415) 465-7885 (FAX)

RDBAC for Region X (Includes Alaska, Idaho, Oregon, Washington):
Washington State Governor's Committee
Toby Olson
212 Maple Park KG-11; Olympia, WA 98504
(206) 438-3168   (206) 438-3167 (TDD)   (206) 438-4014 (FAX)

NIDRR: MATERIALS DEVELOPMENT PROJECTS

NIDRR is funding four two-year projects to produce a core set of training and resource materials, including self-assessment survey guides, checklists, manuals, and reference lists, that can be used in the provision of training and technical assistance on ADA. The primary target audience includes people with disabilities and their family members, employers, public and private entities that operate public accommodations, and public and private service providers. NIDRR is requiring that the materials be available in a variety of accessible formats, understandable to a range of audiences with cognitive or linguistic differences, and have had people with disabilities involved in their development. Each project will focus on a specific area, as follows:

Employment
Cornell University
Susanne Bruyere
120 Day Hall; Ithaca, NY 14853-2801
(607) 255-9536   (607) 255-2763 (FAX)

Employment
International Association of Machinists; Center for Administration, Rehabilitation, and Employment Services
Angela Traiforos
1300 Connecticut Avenue, NW, Suite 912; Washington, DC 20036
(202) 857-5173   (202) 728-2969 (FAX)

Public Accommodation/Accessibility
Barrier Free Environments, Incorporated
Ronald Mace
Water Garden, Highway 70 West; Raleigh, NC 27622
(919) 782-7823 (V/TDD)   (919) 787-1984 (FAX)

Communications/Accessibility–a re-competition for this grant is now being conducted.

NIDRR: NATIONAL TRAINING PROJECTS

The two national training projects which NIDRR is funding are aimed at enhancing the capacity of organizations of persons with disabilities to facilitate ADA implementation. One is directed to building capacity in independent living center personnel to promote effective implementation of ADA in their communities. The other focuses developing a peer and family training network in which people with disabilities and their family members provide training in ADA to their peers nationwide. Both projects are required to develop training materials which are cross-disability in nature. The two projects are:

Local Capacity-Building for Independent Living
National Council on Independent Living
Anne-Marie Hughey
3607 Chapel Road; Newtown Square, PA 19073
(215) 353-6066   (215) 353-6083 (TDD)   (215) 353-6753 (FAX)

Peer and Family Training Network
Parent Information Center
Judith Raskin
151A Manchester Street; Concord, NH 03301
(603) 224-7005 (V/TDD)   (603) 224-4365 (FAX)

DEPARTMENT OF JUSTICE PROJECTS

The DOJ projects are intended to inform both people with disabilities and covered entities about their rights and responsibilities under Titles II (state and local government) and III (public accommodations) and to facilitate voluntary compliance with the regulation. Because the projects each focus on a different subject and target audience, they are described individually, as follows:

Council of Better Business Bureaus' Foundation
Barbara Bode
4200 Wilson Boulevard, Suite 800; Arlington, VA 22203-1804
(703) 276-0100   (703) 276-0634 (FAX)

> *Objectives:* 1) Assist businesses and people with disabilities to develop understanding of Title III of the Act; 2) clarify points of confusion about public accommodations and publish information for general distribution; 3) design replicable technical assistance seminar models for use by Bureaus in helping businesses understand Title III responsibilities and options; and 4) provide managers of dispute resolution processes with options for resolving public accommodations disputes.

Association for Retarded Citizens (ARC) of the United States
Sharon Davis
500 East Border, S-300; Arlington, TX 76010
(817) 261-6003   (817) 277-3491 (FAX)

> *Objectives:* 1) Serve as a national information center of Title III as it affects people with mental retardation and related disabilities; 2) inform the ARC's 1200 chapters in the U.S. about Title III and build their capacities to provide covered entities with information and other assistance about the law; and 3) inform and provide assistance to child care centers to comply with Title III and serve children with mental retardation and other disabilities.

National Association of Protection and Advocacy Systems
Bill Mitchell
900 Second Street, NW, Suite 211; Washington, DC 20002
(202) 408-9514   (202) 408-9520 (FAX)

> *Objective:* Build a nationwide network of advocacy agencies and Protection and Advocacy service providers who have working knowledge of the rights and responsibilities under Titles II and III of the ADA and provide them with the materials and skills

necessary to disseminate information and training to both individuals with disabilities and covered entities.

National Federation of the Blind
Duane Gerstenberger
1800 Johnson Street; Baltimore, MD 21230
(301) 659-9314   (301) 685-5653 (FAX)

> *Objectives:* 1) Encourage collaboration among blind individuals and covered entities for provision of nonvisually accessible information; and 2) assist such individuals and entities in efforts to prepare and distribute printed material in nonvisually accessible media.

National Restaurant Association
Robert Harrington
1200 Seventeenth Street, NW; Washington, DC 20036-3097
(202) 331-5985   (202) 331-2429 (FAX)

> *Objectives:* 1) Work with National Center for Access Unlimited to produce a 40-page booklet explaining ADA and its application in a restaurant setting; and 2) produce a short videotape to illustrate the importance of meeting accessibility standards and setting positive attitudes among staff.

Association on Handicapped Students Service Programs in Postsecondary Education
Jane E. Jarrow
Post Office Box 21192; Columbus, OH 43221-0192
(614) 488-4972   (614) 488-1174 (FAX)

> *Objectives:* 1) Develop jointly with the National Clearinghouse on Licensure Enforcement and Regulation a technical assistance manual regarding testing accommodation that addresses a broad-based testing market; and 2) maintain a toll-free hotline through which technical assistance on ADA will be provided.

Institute for Law & Policy Planning
Alan Kalmanoff
Post Office Box 5137; Berkeley, CA 94705
(415) 486-8121

Objective: Produce, in short and long versions, a film for use in educating representatives of businesses, especially smaller entities, in understanding their obligations to make existing facilities accessible and in interpreting the "readily achievable: requirements of the Act.

California Foundation on Employment & Disability
Tina Kerrigan
3820 Del Amo Boulevard, #201; Torrence, CA 90503
(213) 214-3420   (213) 214-4153 (FAX)

Objective: Provide information on ADA to people with disabilities, small business owners, service providers who do not speak English and those for whom English is a second language. The primary target groups are members of minority Asian and Hispanic communities who are isolated from mainstream sources by language, poverty, and culturally based attitudinal barriers.

Food Marketing Institute
Barbara A. Sisson
1750 K Street, NW, Suite 700; Washington, DC 20006
(202) 429-4523   (202) 429-4529 (FAX)

Objective: Acquaint members of the food marketing industry with the ADA and its accessibility standards through development of a Title III compliance manual and training seminars and promote voluntary compliance with the standards in a rapid, thorough, persuasive, and cost-effective manner.

American Foundation for the Blind
Scott Marshall
1615 M Street, NW, Suite 250; Washington, DC 20036
(202) 457-1498   (202) 457-1492 (FAX)

Objective: Provide legal and other technical assistance with respect to Titles II and III of the ADA relating to communications barriers of hearing and vision loss. Because most businesses have little experience accommodating the needs of deaf, hard-of-hearing, blind, low-vision, and deaf-blind individuals, technical assistance will be directed toward provision of auxiliary aids for individuals with communication impairments.

National Conference of States on Building Codes and Standards
Thomas R. McLane
505 Huntman Park Drive, Suite 210, Herndon, VA 22070
(703) 437-0100   (703) 481-3596 (FAX)

> *Objectives:* 1) Work with the Paralyzed Veterans of America to review state and local governmental accessibility codes, relevant DOJ regulations, and develop informational materials on procedures and model certification processes for states to follow; and 2) hold a national conference on these procedures and models for state and local regulatory officials and organizations representing people with disabilities.

Office of Grant and Research Development
Karen L. Michaelson
MS-10, Hargreaves 217; Eastern Washington University; Cheney, WA 99004-2415
(509) 359-6567   (509) 359-6693 (FAX)

> *Objectives:* Encourage voluntary compliance among daycare centers as covered entities under the ADA through: 1) assistance to local and regional organizations throughout the United States in the form of materials for use in workshops and classes; and 2) preparing compliance with the ADA in their local communities.

Disability Rights Education and Defense Fund
Liz Savage
2212 Sixth Street; Berkeley, CA 94710
(415) 644-2555

Washington, DC, office:
1633 Q Street, NW, Suite 220; Washington, DC 20009
(202) 986-0375   (202) 462-5624 (FAX)

> *Objective:* Provide high-quality, accurate, and reliable information about the ADA to businesses covered by Title III, state and local government entities, persons with disabilities, parents, advocates, and service providers through: 1) establishment of a toll-free telephone service and 2) training of five regional ADA technical assistance resource persons.

National Center for State Courts
Arl Williams
300 Newport Avenue; Williamsburg, VA 23185
(508) 470-1881   (508) 474-8088 (FAX)

Objectives: 1) Develop a national clearinghouse and resource center for local and state courts to focus on requirements and methods of compliance with ADA; 2) compile and disseminate a set of materials on compliance; 3) develop a model curriculum for training court personnel on ADA; and 4) provide technical assistance on compliance strategies in the courts.

American Hotel & Motel Association
Thomas F. Youngblood
1201 New York Avenue, NW; Washington, DC 20005-3931
(202) 289-3100   (202) 289-3106 (FAX)

Objectives: Develop and/or disseminate written information about the ADA, including a compliance handbook, throughout the lodging industry; and 2) conduct an extensive series of seminars nationwide.

The following are also recipients of DOJ grant awards. However, details on their projects were not available.

Government and Industry Affairs; Building Owners and Managers Assoc., International
James C. Dinegar
1201 New York Avenue, NW, Suite 300; Washington, DC 20005
(202) 408-2684   (202) 371-0181 (FAX)

Police Executive Research Forum
Sheldon Greenburg
2300 M Street, NW, Suite 910; Washington, DC 20037
(202) 466-7800   (202) 466-7826 (FAX)

National Rehabilitation Hospital
Don Ross
102 Irving Street, NW; Washington, DC 20010-2949
(202) 877-1000   (202) 829-5180 (FAX)

American Speech-Language-Hearing Association
Jo Ellen Williams
10801 Rockville Pike; Rockville, MD 20852
(301) 897-5700   (301) 571-0457 (FAX)

RSA: SHORT-TERM TRAINING PROJECT

The purpose of RSA's one-year project is to provide an ADA training course for pre-service educators and post-employment trainers of personnel working in state vocational rehabilitation agencies, independent living centers, client assistance programs, rehabilitation facilities, and other community-based programs for people with disabilities.

Region V Rehabilitation Continuing Education Program
Julie O'Brien
300 East Main Street, Suite 16; Carbondale, Illinois 62901
(618) 536-2461   (618) 453-6957 (FAX)

The ADA has profoundly affected the outlook for millions of persons with disabilities. By accessing the tremendous amount of expertise already available and through the ongoing development and utilization of new information, the promise of equal opportunity for *all* Americans, regardless of disability, may be realized.

REFERENCES

Architectural and Transportation Barriers Compliance Board. (1991). *Federal Register: Americans with Disabilities Act (ADA) Accessibility Guidelines for Buildings and Facilities; Proposed Rule. 36 CFR Part 1191, January 22, 1991.*

Batavia, A., DeJong, C., Eckenhoff, E. A., & Materson, R. S. (1990). After the Americans with Disabilities Act: The role of the rehabilitation community. *Archives of Physical Medicine and Rehabilitation, 71* (Nov.). 1014-1015.

Berkeley Planning Associates. (1982). *A study of accommodations provided to handicapped employees by federal contractors: Final report.* Prepared under U.S. Department of Labor, Employment Standards Administration, Contract No. J-9-E-1-0009, Volumes I & II.

Gonzalez, E. G., & Gordon, D. M. (1990). Americans with Disabilities Act: The crumbling of another wall. *Archives of Physical Medicine and Rehabilitation, 71* (Nov.), 951.

Granovetter, M. (1979). Placement as brokerage: Information problems in the labor market for rehabilitated workers. In D. Vandergoot & J. D. Worrall (Eds.), *Placement in rehabilitation* (pp. 83-101). Baltimore: University Park Press.

Habeck, R. V., Shrey, D. E., & Growick, B. S. (1991). *Rehabilitation Counseling Bulletin Special Issue: Disability Management and Industrial Rehabilitation, 34* (3).

Hester, E. J., & DeCeles, P. G. (1991). A comprehensive analysis of private sector rehabilitation services and outcomes for workers' compensation claimants. *Journal of Job Placement, 7*(2), 5-10.

ILRU Research & Training Center on Independent Living at the Institute for Rehabilitation and Research. (1991). *ILRU Insights, 9*(5-6). Special Fall Issue.

Kaufman, M. J. (1987). Federal and state handicapped discrimination laws: Toward an accommodating legal framework. *Loyola University Law Journal, 18,* 1119-1147.

Larson, D. A. (1986). What disabilities are protected under the rehabilitation act of 1973? *Memphis State University Law Review, 16,* 229-254.

McCray, P. M. (1987). *The job accommodation handbook.* Verndale, MN: RPM Press, Inc.

Parrino, S. S. (1990). ADA watch: An initiative to monitor and evaluate the implementation of the Americans with Disabilities Act. *Focus,* Fall, 1990, 2.

Perritt, H. H. (1990). *The Americans with Disabilities Act handbook.* Somerset, NJ: John Wiley & Sons.

Public Law 101-336. (1990). *Americans with Disabilities Act of 1990.* July 26, 1990.

Rubin, S. E., & Roessler, R. T. (1987). *Foundations of the vocational rehabilitation process* (3rd ed.). Austin, TX: Pro Ed.

Schwartz, E. G., Watson, D. S., Galvin, E. D., & Lipoff, E. (1989). *The disability management sourcebook.* Washington, DC: Washington Business Group on Health/ Institute for Rehabilitation and Disability Management.

Tysse, G. J. (1990). *Analysis of the employment-related provisions of the Americans with Disabilities Act (ADA).* Washington, DC: McGuiness & Williams.

Verville, R. E. (1990). The Americans with Disabilities Act: An analysis. *Archives of Physical Medicine and Rehabilitation, 71* (Nov), 1010-1013.

Watson, P. G. (1990). The Americans with Disabilities Act: More rights for people with disabilities. *Rehabilitation Nursing, 15*(6), 325-328.

Appendix 1

CHOOSING THE WORDS YOU USE ABOUT AND WITH PEOPLE WITH DISABILITIES

Prepared by Carolyn B. Thompson, C.R.R.

In the past, words have been used to describe or label people with disabilities that carried a negative connotation and thus created and perpetuated negative attitudes. Begin choosing and using words that will create positive images and attitudes when talking with and about people with disabilities.

Disability
A loss or reduction of functional ability or activity resulting from an impairment that interferes with a person's ability, for example, to walk, hear, learn, lift and/or any other ability.

Handicap
A condition or barrier caused by society or the environment resulting from the disability or even perceived disability. Examples: can't feed yourself because both arms were amputated; can't work because you have a speech impediment and employers think you don't have the mental ability for the job. (Derived from "cap in hand" which is associated with beggars and begging.)

Modification
Any change made necessary to decrease or eliminate the handicap. Examples: prosthesis so that the person can feed self; education/attitudinal change so that the speech impediment is no longer viewed as lack of mental ability.

Creates Negative Attitudes	Creates Positive Attitudes
the disabled, is disabled, a disabled person, is blind, the deaf, a retarded person	people with a disability, people who are blind, mentally retarded, etc. (use disability as an adjective/a descriptor, not a noun and not as the primary adjective)
stricken with, afflicted with, suffers from	person who has Cerebral Palsy, Epilepsy, etc.
a cripple, crippled, victim of, defective, deformed, invalid	person with a disability
physically challenged, special, differently able (these terms are cute and patronizing)	person with a disability
birth defect	born with, has a congenital disability
confined to/restricted to a wheelchair, wheelchair-bound	uses a wheelchair (most people view their wheelchair as liberating)
normal, able-bodied, healthy, whole	nondisabled
lame, maimed, withered, poor unfortunate	walks with a limp, had an arm amputated
retard, retarded, vegetable, idiot, imbecile, moron, dummy	person who is mentally retarded, person with a cognitive disability
Mongoloid	person with Down's Syndrome
former mental patient, insane, crazy, deviant, deranged	person with a mental illness
deaf and dumb, deaf mute	person who is hearing and speech impaired
deaf	hearing impaired (range of hearing loss: total-deaf; mild to moderate – hard-of-hearing)
blind	visually impaired (range of visual loss: total-blind; mild to moderate – low vision)
cerebral palsied, spastic, spaz	person with Cerebral Palsy
spinal cord-injured, paraplegic, para, quad-riplegic, quad, paralytic	person with paraplegia or quadriplegia
hunchback	person with a spinal curvature
Elephant Man's Disease	person with Neurofibromatosis
hare lip	person with a cleft palate
brain-damaged	person with a head injury
dwarf, midget	person of small stature

Appendix 2

PRESIDENT BUSH'S REMARKS AT SIGNING CEREMONY

Let the Shameful Wall of Exclusion Finally Come Tumbling Down

Welcome to every one of you, out there in this splendid scene of hope, spread across the South Lawn of the White House. I want to salute the members of the United States Congress, the House and the Senate who are with us today—active participants in making this day come true. (Applause.)

This is, indeed, an incredible day. Especially for the thousands of people across the nation who have given so much of their time, their vision, and their courage to see this Act become a reality.

You know, I started trying to put together a list of all the people who should be mentioned today. But when the list started looking a little longer than the Senate testimony for the bill, I decided I better give up, or we'd never get out of here before sunset. So, even though so many deserve credit, I will single out but a tiny handful. And I take those who have guided me personally over the years.

Of course, my friends, Evan Kemp and Justin Dart up here on the platform with me. (Applause.) And of course, I hope you'll forgive me for also saying a special word of thanks to two who—from the White House—Boyden Gray and Bill Roper, labored long and hard. (Applause.)

And I want to thank Sandy Parrino, of course, for her leadership and I again-- (applause)—it is very risky with all these members of Congress here who worked so hard. But I can say on a very personal basis, Bob Dole has inspired me. (Applause.)

And then, the organizations. So many dedicated organizations for people with disabilities who gave their time and their strength and, perhaps most of all, everyone out there across the breadth of this nation, the 43 million Americans with disabilities. You have made this happen. All of you have made this happen. (Applause.)

To all of you, I just want to say your triumph is that your bill will now be law, and that this day belongs to you. On behalf of our nation, thank you very, very much. (Applause.)

Three weeks ago we celebrated our nation's "Independence Day." Today, we're here to rejoice in and celebrate another 'Independence Day,' one that is long overdue. With today's signing of the landmark Americans with Disabilities Act, every man, woman and child with a disability can now pass through once-closed doors into a bright new era of equality, independence and freedom.

As I look around at all these joyous faces, I remember clearly how many years of dedicated commitment have gone into making this historic new civil rights Act a reality. It's been the work of a true coalition. A strong and inspiring coalition of people who have shared both a dream and a passionate determination to make that dream come true. It's been a coalition in the finest spirit. A joining of Democrats and Republicans. Of the Legislative and Executive Branches. Of federal and state agencies. Of public officials and private citizens. Of people with disabilities and without.

This historic Act is the world's first comprehensive declaration of equality for people with disabilities. The first. (Applause.) Its passage has made the United States the international leader on this human rights issue. Already, leaders of several other countries, including Sweden, Japan, the Soviet Union and all 12 members of the EEC, have announced that they hope to enact now similar legislation. (Applause.)

Our success with this Act proves that we are keeping faith with the spirit of our courageous forefathers who wrote in the Declaration of Independence: "We hold these truths to be self-evident, that all men are created equal, that they are endowed by their Creator with certain unalienable rights." These words have been our guide for more than two centuries as we've labored to form our more perfect union. But tragically, for too many Americans, the blessings of liberty have been limited or even denied.

The Civil Rights Act of '64 took a bold step towards righting that wrong. But the stark fact remained that people with disabilities were still victims of segregation and discrimination, and this was intolerable. Today's legislation brings us closer to that day when no Americans will ever again be deprived of their basic guarantee of life, liberty, and the pursuit of happiness. (Applause.)

This Act is powerful in its simplicity. It will ensure that people with disabilities are given the basic guarantees for which they have worked for so long and so hard. Independence, freedom of choice, control of their lives, the opportunity to blend fully and equally into the right mosaic of the American mainstream.

Legally, it will provide our disabled community with a powerful expansion of protections and then basic civil rights. It will guarantee fair and just access to the fruits of American life which we all must be able to enjoy. And then, specifically, first the ADA ensures that employers covered by the Act cannot discriminate against qualified individuals with disabilities. (Applause.) Second, the ADA ensures access to public accommodations such as restaurants, hotels, shopping centers and offices. And third, the ADA ensures expanded access to transportation services. (Applause.)

And fourth, the ADA ensures equivalent telephone services for people with speech or hearing impediments. (Applause.) These provisions mean so much to so many. To one brave girl in particular, they will mean the world. Lisa Carl, a young Washington State woman with cerebral palsy, who I'm told is with us today, now will always be admitted to her hometown theater.

Lisa, you might not have been welcome at your theater, but I'll tell you—welcome to the White House. We're glad you're here. (Applause.) The ADA is a dramatic renewal, not only for those with disabilities, but for all of us. Because along with the precious privilege of being an American comes a sacred duty—to ensure that every other American's rights are also guaranteed.

Together, we must remove the physical barriers we have created and the social barriers that we have accepted. For ours will never be a truly prosperous nation until all within it prosper. For inspiration, we need look no further than our own neighbors. With us in that wonderful crowd out there are people representing 18 of the daily points of light that I've named for their extraordinary involvement with the disabled community. We applaud you and your shining example. Thank you for your leadership for all that are here today. (Applause.)

Now, let me just tell you a wonderful story—a story about children already working in the spirit of the ADA. A story that really touched me. Across the nation, some 10,000 youngsters with disabilities are part of Little League's Challenger Division. Their teams play just like others, but—and this is the most remarkable part—as they play at their sides are volunteer buddies from conventional Little League teams. All of these players work together. They team up to wheel around the bases and to field grounders together and most of all, just to play and become friends. We must let these children be our guides and inspiration.

I also want to say a special word to our friends in the business community. You have in your hands the key to the success of this Act. For you can unlock a splendid resource of untapped human potential that, when freed, will enrich us all.

I know there have been concerns that the ADA may be vague or costly, or may lead endlessly to litigation. But I want to reassure you right now that my administration and the United States Congress have carefully crafted this Act. We've all been determined to ensure that it gives flexibility, particularly in terms of the timetable of implementation; and we've been committed to containing the costs that may be incurred.

This Act does something important for American business though, and remember this—you've called for new sources of workers. Well, many of our fellow citizens with disabilities are unemployed, they want to work and they can work. And this is a tremendous pool of people. (Applause.) And remember this is a tremendous pool of people who will bring to jobs diversity, loyalty, proven low turnover rate, and only one request, the chance to prove themselves.

And when you add together federal, state, local and private funds, it costs almost $200 billion annually to support Americans with disabilities, in effect, to keep them dependent. Well, when given the opportunity to be independent, they will move proudly into the economic mainstream of American life, and that's what this legislation is all about. (Applause.)

Our problems are large, but our unified heart is larger. Our challenges are great, but our will is greater. And in our America, the most generous, optimistic nation on the face of the earth, we must not and will not rest until every man and woman with a dream has the means to achieve it.

And today, America welcomes into the mainstream of life all of our fellow citizens with disabilities. We embrace you for your abilities and for your disabilities, for our similarities and indeed for our differences, for your past courage and your future dreams.

Last year, we celebrated a victory of international freedom. Even the strongest person couldn't scale the Berlin Wall to gain the elusive promise of independence that lay just beyond. And so together we rejoiced when that barrier fell.

And now I sign legislation which takes a sledgehammer to another wall, one which has—(applause)—one which has, for too many generations, separated Americans with disabilities from the freedom they could glimpse, but not grasp. Once again, we rejoice as this barrier falls, proclaiming together we will not accept, we will not excuse, we will not tolerate discrimination in America. (Applause.)

With, again, great thanks to the members of the United States Senate, many of whom are here today, and those who worked so tirelessly for this legislation on both sides of the aisles. And to those members of the House of Representatives with us here today, Democrats and Republicans as well, I salute you.

And on your behalf, as well as the behalf of this entire country, I now lift my pen to sign this Americans with Disabilities Act and say, let the shameful wall of exclusion finally come tumbling down. (Applause.)

God bless you all.

(The Act is signed.)
END 10:26 am EDT 7/26/90

Appendix 3

AMERICANS WITH DISABILITIES ACT OF 1990
P. L. 101-336

SECTION 1. SHORT TITLE; TABLE OF CONTENTS.

(a) SHORT TITLE. -- This Act may be cited as the "Americans with Disabilities Act of 1990".
(b) TABLE OF CONTENTS. -- The table of contents is as follows:
Sec. 1. Short title; table of contents.
Sec. 2. Findings and purposes.
Sec. 3. Definitions.

TITLE I -- EMPLOYMENT

Sec. 101. Definitions.
Sec. 102. Discrimination.
Sec. 103. Defenses.
Sec. 104. Illegal use of drugs and alcohol.
Sec. 105. Posting notices.
Sec. 106. Regulations.
Sec. 107. Enforcement
Sec. 108. Effective date.

TITLE II -- PUBLIC SERVICES

Subtitle A -- Prohibition Against Discrimination and Other Generally Applicable Provisions

Sec. 201. Definition.
Sec. 202. Discrimination.
Sec. 203. Enforcement.
Sec. 204. Regulations.
Sec. 205. Effective date.

Subtitle B -- Actions Applicable to Public Transportation Provided by public Entities Considered Discriminatory

Part I -- Public Transportation Other Than by Aircraft or Certain Rail Operations

Sec. 221. Definitions.
Sec. 222. Public entities operating fixed route systems.
Sec. 223. Paratransit as a complement to fixed route service.
Sec. 224. Public entity operating a demand responsive system.
Sec. 225. Temporary relief where lifts are unavailable.
Sec. 226. New facilities.
Sec. 227. Alterations of existing facilities.
Sec. 228. Public transportation programs and activities in existing facilities and one car per train rule.
Sec. 229. Regulations.
Sec. 230. Interim accessibility requirements.
Sec. 231. Effective date.

Part II -- Public Transportation by Intercity and Commuter Rail

Sec. 241. Definitions.
Sec. 242. Intercity and commuter rail actions considered discriminatory.
Sec. 243. Conformance of accessibility standards.
Sec. 244. Regulations.
Sec. 245. Interim accessibility requirements.
Sec. 246. Effective date.

TITLE III -- PUBLIC ACCOMMODATIONS AND SERVICES OPERATED BY PRIVATE ENTITIES

Sec. 301. Definitions.
Sec. 302. Prohibition of discrimination by public accommodations.
Sec. 303. New construction and alterations in public accommodations and commercial facilities.
Sec. 304. Prohibition of discrimination in specified public transportation services provided by private entities.
Sec. 305. Study.
Sec. 306. Regulations.
Sec. 307. Exemptions for private clubs and religious organizations.
Sec. 308. Enforcement.
Sec. 309. Examinations and courses.
Sec. 310. Effective dates.

TITLE IV -- TELECOMMUNICATIONS

Sec. 401. Telecommunications relay services for hearing-impaired and speech-impaired individuals.
Sec. 402. Closed-captioning of public service announcements.

TITLE V -- MISCELLANEOUS PROVISIONS

Sec. 501. Construction.
Sec. 502. State immunity.

Sec. 503. Prohibition against retaliation and coercion.
Sec. 504. Regulations by the Architectural and Transportation Barriers Compliance Board.
Sec. 505. Attorney's fee's.
Sec. 506. Technical assistance.
Sec. 507. Federal wilderness areas.
Sec. 508. Transvestites.
Sec. 509. Coverage of Congress and the agencies of the legislative branch.
Sec. 510. Illegal use of drugs.
Sec. 511. Definitions.
Sec. 512. Amendments to the Rehabilitation Act.
Sec. 513. Alternative means of dispute resolution.
Sec. 514. Severability.

SEC. 2. FINDINGS AND PURPOSES.

(a) FINDINGS. -- The Congress finds that --

(1) some 43,000,000 Americans have one or more physical or mental disabilities, and this number is increasing as the population as a whole is growing older;

(2) historically, society has tended to isolate and segregate individuals with disabilities, and, despite some improvements, such forms of discrimination against individuals with disabilities continue to be a serious and pervasive social problem;

(3) discrimination against individuals with disabilities persists in such critical areas as employment, housing, public accommodations, education, transportation, communication, recreation, institutionalization, health services, voting, and access to public services;

(4) unlike individuals who have experienced discrimination on the basis of race, color, sex, national origin, religion, or age, individuals who have experienced discrimination on the basis of disability have often had no legal recourse to redress such discrimination;

(5) individuals with disabilities continually encounter various forms of discrimination, including outright intentional exclusion, the discriminatory effects of architectural, transportation, and communication barriers, overprotective rules and policies, failure to make modifications to existing facilities and practices, exclusionary qualification standards and criteria, segregation, and relegation to lesser services, programs, activities, benefits, jobs, or other opportunities;

(6) census data, national polls, and other studies have documented that people with disabilities, as a group, occupy an inferior status in our society, and are severely disadvantaged socially, vocationally, economically, and educationally;

(7) individuals with disabilities are a discrete and insular minority who have been faced with restrictions and limitations, subjected to a history of purposeful unequal treatment, and relegated to a position of political powerlessness in our society, based on characteristics that are beyond the control of such individuals and resulting from stereotypic assumptions not truly indicative of the individual ability of such individuals to participate in, and contribute to, society;

(8) the Nation's proper goals regarding individuals with disabilities are to assure equality of opportunity, full participation, independent living, and economic self-sufficiency for such individuals; and

(9) the continuing existence of unfair and unnecessary discrimination and prejudice denies people with disabilities the opportunity to compete on an equal basis and to pursue those opportunities for which our free society is justifiably famous, and costs the United States billions of dollars in unnecessary expenses resulting from dependency and nonproductivity.

(b) PURPOSE -- It is the purpose of this Act --

(1) to provide a clear and comprehensive national mandate for the elimination of discrimination against individuals with disabilities;

(2) to provide clear, strong, consistent, enforceable standards addressing discrimination against individuals with disabilities;

(3) to ensure that the Federal Government plays a central role in enforcing the standards established in this Act on behalf of individuals with disabilities; and

(4) to invoke the sweep of congressional authority, including the power to enforce the fourteenth amendment and to regulate commerce, in order to address the major areas of discrimination faced day-to-day by people with disabilities.

SEC. 3. DEFINITIONS.

As used in this Act:

(1) AUXILIARY AIDS AND SERVICES. -- The term "auxiliary aids and services" includes --

(A) qualified interpreters or other effective methods of making aurally delivered materials available to individuals with hearing impairments;

(B) qualified readers, taped texts, or other effective methods of making visually delivered materials available to individuals with visual impairments;

(C) acquisition or modification of equipment or devices; and

(D) other similar services and actions.

(2) DISABILITY. -- The term "disability" means, with respect to an individual --

(A) a physical or mental impairment that substantially limits one or more of the major life activities of such individual;

(B) a record of such an impairment; or

(C) being regarded as having such an impairment.

(3) STATE. -- The term "State" means each of the several States, the District of Columbia, the Commonwealth of Puerto Rico, Guam, American Samoa, the Virgin Islands, the Trust Territory of the Pacific Islands, and the Commonwealth of the Northern Mariana Islands.

TITLE I -- EMPLOYMENT

SEC. 101. DEFINITIONS.

As used in this title:

(1) COMMISSION. -- The term "Commission" means the Equal Employment Opportunity Commission established by section 705 of the Civil Rights Act of 1964 (42 U.S.C. 2000e-4).

(2) COVERED ENTITY. -- The term "covered entity" means an employer, employment agency, labor organization, or joint labor-management committee.

(3) DIRECT THREAT. -- The term "direct threat" means a significant risk to the health or safety of others that cannot be eliminated by reasonable accommodation.

(4) EMPLOYEE. -- The term "employee" means an individual employed by an employer.

(5) EMPLOYER. --

(A) IN GENERAL. -- The term "employer" means a person engaged in an industry affecting commerce who has 15 or more employees for each working day in each of 20 or more calendar weeks in the current or preceding calendar year, and any agent of such person, except that, for two years following the effective date of this title, an employer means a person engaged in an industry affecting commerce who has 25 or more employees for each working day in each of 20 or more calendar weeks in the current or preceding year, and any agent of such person.

(B) EXCEPTIONS. -- The term "employer" does not include --

(i) the United States, a corporation wholly owned by the government of the United States, or an Indian tribe; or

(ii) a bona fide private membership club (other than a labor organization) that is exempt from taxation under section 501(c) of the Internal Revenue Code of 1986.

(6) ILLEGAL USE OF DRUGS. --

(A) IN GENERAL. -- The term "illegal use of drugs" means the use of drugs, the possession or distribution of which is unlawful under the Controlled Substances Act (21 U.S.C. 812). Such term does not include the use of a drug taken under supervision by a licensed health care professional, or other uses authorized by the Controlled Substances Act or other provisions of Federal law.

(B) DRUGS. -- The term "drug" means a controlled substance, as defined in schedules I through V of section 202 of the Controlled Substances Act.

(7) PERSON, ETC. -- The terms "person", "labor organization", "employment agency", "commerce", and "industry affecting commerce", shall have the same meaning given such terms in section 701 of the Civil Rights Act of 1964 (42 U.S.C. 2000e).

(8) QUALIFIED INDIVIDUAL WITH A DISABILITY. -- The term "qualified individual with a disability" means an individual with a disability who, with or without reasonable accommodation, can perform the essential functions of the employment position that such individual holds or desires. For the purposes of this title, consideration shall be given to the employer's judgment as to what functions of a job are essential, and if an employer has prepared a written description before advertising or interviewing applicants for the job, this description shall be considered evidence of the essential functions of the job.

(9) REASONABLE ACCOMMODATION. -- The term "reasonable accommodation" may include --

(A) making existing facilities used by employees readily accessible to and usable by individuals with disabilities; and

(B) job restructuring, part-time or modified work schedules, reassignment to a vacant position, acquisition or modification of equipment or devices, appropriate adjustment or modifications of examinations, training materials or policies, the provision of qualified readers or interpreters, and with other similar accommodations for individuals with disabilities.

(10) UNDUE HARDSHIP. --

(A) IN GENERAL. -- The term "undue hardship" means an action requiring significant difficulty or expense, when considered in light of the factors set forth in subparagraph (B).

(B) FACTORS TO BE CONSIDERED. -- In determining whether an accommodation would impose an undue hardship on a covered entity, factors to be considered include --

(i) the nature and cost of the accommodation needed under this Act;

(ii) the overall financial resources of the facility or facilities involved in the provision of the reasonable accommodation; the number of persons employed at such facility; the effect on expenses and resources, or the impact otherwise of such accommodation upon the operation of the facility;

(iii) the overall financial resources of the covered entity; the overall size of the business of a covered entity with respect to the number of its employees; the number, type, and location of its facilities; and

(iv) the type of operation or operations of the covered entity, including the composition, structure, and functions of the workforce of such entity; the geographic separateness, administrative, or fiscal relationship of the facility or facilities in question to the covered entity.

SEC. 102. DISCRIMINATION.

(a) GENERAL RULE. -- No covered entity shall discriminate against a qualified individual with a disability because of the disability of such individual in regard to job application procedures, the hiring, advancement, or discharge of employees, employee compensation, job training, and other terms, conditions, and privileges of employment.

(b) CONSTRUCTION. -- As used in subsection (a), the term "discriminate" includes --

(1) limiting, segregating, or classifying a job applicant or employee in a way that adversely affects the opportunities or status of such applicant or employee because of the disability of such applicant or employee;

(2) participating in a contractual or other arrangement or relationship that has the effect of subjecting a covered entity's qualified applicant or employee with a disability to the discrimination prohibited by this title (such relationship includes a relationship with an employ-

ment or referral agency, labor union, an organization providing fringe benefits to an employee of the covered entity, or an organization providing training and apprenticeship programs);

(3) utilizing standards, criteria, or methods of administration —

(A) that have the effect of discrimination on the basis of disability; or

(B) that perpetuate the discrimination of others who are subject to common administrative control;

(4) excluding or otherwise denying equal jobs or benefits to a qualified individual because of the known disability of an individual with whom the qualified individual is known to have a relationship or association;

(5)(A) not making reasonable accommodations to the known physical or mental limitations of an otherwise qualified individual with a disability who is an applicant or employee, unless such covered entity can demonstrate that the accommodation would impose an undue hardship on the operation of the business of such covered entity; or

(B) denying employment opportunities to a job applicant or employee who is an otherwise qualified individual with a disability, if such denial is based on the need of such covered entity to make reasonable accommodation to the physical or mental impairments of the employee or a applicant;

(6) using qualification standards, employment tests or other selection criteria that screen out or tend to screen out an individual with a disability or a class of individuals with disabilities unless the standard, test or other selection criteria, as used by the covered entity, is shown to be job-related for the position in question and is consistent with business necessity; and

(7) failing to select and administer tests concerning employment in the most effective manner to ensure that, when such test is administered to a job applicant or employee who has a disability that impairs sensory, manual, or

speaking skills, such test results accurately reflect the skills, aptitude, or whatever other factor of such applicant or employee that such test purports to measure, rather than reflecting the impaired sensory, manual, or speaking skills of such employee or applicant (except where such skills are the factors that the test purports to measure).

(c) MEDICAL EXAMINATIONS AND INQUIRIES. —

(1) IN GENERAL. — The prohibition against discrimination as referred to in subsection (a) shall include medical examinations and inquiries.

(2) PREEMPLOYMENT. —

(A) PROHIBITED EXAMINATION OR INQUIRY. — Except as provided in paragraph (3), a covered entity shall not conduct a medical examination or make inquiries of a job applicant as to whether such applicant is an individual with a disability or as to the nature or severity of such disability.

(B) ACCEPTABLE INQUIRY. — A covered entity may make preemployment inquiries into the ability of an applicant to perform job-related functions.

(3) EMPLOYMENT ENTRANCE EXAMINATION. — A covered entity may require a medical examination after an offer of employment has been made to a job applicant and prior to the commencement of the employment duties of such applicant, and may condition an offer of employment on the results of such examination, if —

(A) all entering employees are subjected to such an examination regardless of disability;

(B) information obtained regarding the medical condition or history of the applicant is collected and maintained on separate forms and in separate medical files and is treated as a confidential medical record, except that —

(i) supervisors and managers may be informed regarding necessary restrictions on the work or duties of the employee and necessary accommodations;

(ii) first aid and safety personnel may be informed,

when appropriate, if the disability might require emergency treatment; and

(iii) government officials investigating compliance with this Act shall be provided relevant information on request; and

(C) the results of such examination are used only in accordance with this title.

(4) EXAMINATION AND INQUIRY. —

(A) PROHIBITED EXAMINATIONS AND INQUIRIES. — A covered entity shall not require a medical examination and shall not make inquiries of an employee as to whether such employee is an individual with a disability or as to the nature or severity of the disability, unless such examination or inquiry is shown to be job-related and consistent with business necessity.

(B) ACCEPTABLE EXAMINATIONS AND INQUIRIES. — A covered entity may conduct voluntary medical examinations, including voluntary medical histories, which are part of an employee health program available to employees at that work site. A covered entity may make inquiries into the ability of an employee to perform job-related functions.

(C) REQUIREMENT. — Information obtained under subparagraph (B) regarding the medical condition or history of any employee are subject to the requirements of subparagraphs (B) and (C) of paragraph (3).

SEC. 103. DEFENSES.

(a) IN GENERAL. — It may be a defense to a charge of discrimination under this Act that an alleged application of qualification standards, tests, or selection criteria that screen out or tend to screen out or otherwise deny a job or benefit to an individual with a disability has been shown to be job-related and consistent with business necessity, and such performance cannot be accomplished by reasonable accommodation, as required under this title.

(b) QUALIFICATION STANDARDS. — The term "qualification standards" may include a requirement that an individual shall not pose a direct threat to the health or safety of other individuals in the workplace.

(c) RELIGIOUS ENTITIES. --

(1) IN GENERAL. -- This title shall not prohibit a religious corporation, association, educational institution, or society from giving preference in employment to individuals of a particular religion to perform work connected with the carrying on by such corporation, association, educational institution, or society of its activities.

(2) RELIGIOUS TENETS REQUIREMENT. -- Under this title, a religious organization may require that all applicants and employees conform to the religious tenets of such organization.

(d) LIST OF INFECTIOUS AND COMMUNICABLE DISEASES. --

(1) IN GENERAL. -- The Secretary of Health and Human Services, not later than 6 months after the date of enactment of this Act, shall --

(A) review all infectious and communicable diseases which may be transmitted through handling the food supply;

(B) publish a list of infectious and communicable diseases which are transmitted through handling the food supply;

(C) publish the methods by which such diseases are transmitted; and

(D) widely disseminate such information regarding the list of diseases and their modes of transmissibility to the general public.

Such list shall be updated annually.

(2) APPLICATIONS. -- In any case in which an individual has an infectious or communicable disease that is transmitted to others through the handling of food, that is included on the list developed by the Secretary of Health and Human Services under paragraph (1), and which cannot be eliminated by reasonable accommodation, a covered entity may refuse to assign or continue to assign such individual to a job involving food handling.

(3) CONSTRUCTION. -- Nothing in this Act shall be construed to preempt, modify, or amend any State, county, or local law, ordinance, or regulation applicable to food handling which is designed to protect the public health from individuals who pose a significant risk to the health or safety of others, which cannot be eliminated by reasonable accommodation, pursuant to the list of infectious or communicable diseases and the modes of transmissibility published by the Secretary of Health and Human Services.

SEC. 104. ILLEGAL USE OF DRUGS AND ALCOHOL.

(a) QUALIFIED INDIVIDUAL WITH A DISABILITY. -- For purposes of this title, the term "qualified individual with a disability" shall not include any employee or applicant who is currently engaging in the illegal use of drugs, when the covered entity acts on the basis of such use.

(b) RULES OF CONSTRUCTION. -- Nothing in subsection (a) shall be construed to exclude as a qualified individual with a disability an individual who --

(1) has successfully completed a supervised drug rehabilitation program and is no longer engaging in the illegal use of drugs, or has otherwise been rehabilitated successfully and is no longer engaging in such use;

(2) is participating in a supervised rehabilitation program and is no longer engaging in such use; or

(3) is erroneously regarded as engaging in such use, but is not engaging in such use; except that it shall not be a violation of this Act for a covered entity to adopt or administer reasonable policies or procedures, including but not limited to drug testing, designed to ensure that an individual described in paragraph (1) or (2) is no longer engaging in the illegal use of drugs.

(c) AUTHORITY OF COVERED ENTITY. -- A covered entity --

(1) may prohibit the illegal use of drugs and the use of alcohol at the workplace by all employees;

(2) may require that employees shall not be under the influence of alcohol or be engaging in the illegal use of drugs at the workplace;

(3) may require that employees behave in conformance with the requirements established under the Drug-Free Workplace Act of 1988 (41 U.S.C. 701 et seq.);

(4) may hold an employee who engages in the illegal use of drugs or who is an alcoholic to the same qualification standards for employment or job performance and behavior that such entity holds other employees, even if any unsatisfactory performance or behavior is related to the drug use or alcoholism of such employee; and

(5) may, with respect to Federal regulations regarding alcohol and the illegal use of drugs, require that --

(A) employees comply with the standards established in such regulations of the Department of Defense, if the employees of the covered entity are employed in an industry subject to such regulations, including complying with regulations (if any) that apply to employment in sensitive positions in such an industry, in the case of employees of the covered entity who are employed in such positions (as defined in the regulations of the Department of Defense);

(B) employees comply with the standards established in such regulations of the Nuclear Regulatory Commission, if the employees of the covered entity are employed in an industry subject to such regulations, including complying with regulations (if any) that apply to employment in sensitive positions in such an industry, in the case of employees of the covered entity who are employed in such positions (as defined in the regulations of the Nuclear Regulatory Commission); and

(C) employees comply with the standards established in such regulations of the Department of Transportation, if the employees of the covered entity are employed in a transportation industry subject to such regulations, including complying with such regulations (if any) that apply to employment in sensitive positions in such an industry, in the case of employees of the covered entity who are employed in such positions (as defined in the regulations of the Department of Transportation).

(d) DRUG TESTING. --

(1) IN GENERAL. -- For purposes of this title, a test to determine the illegal use of drugs shall not be considered a medical examination.

(2) CONSTRUCTION. -- Nothing in this title shall be construed to encourage, prohibit, or authorize the conducting of drug testing for the illegal use of drugs by job applicants or employees or making employment decisions based on such test results.

(e) TRANSPORTATION EMPLOYEES. -- Nothing in this title shall be construed to encourage, prohibit, restrict, or authorize the otherwise lawful exercise by entities subject to the jurisdiction of the Department of Transportation of authority to --

(1) test employees of such entities in, and applicants for, positions involving safety-sensitive duties for the illegal use of drugs and for on-duty impairment by alcohol; and

(2) remove such persons who test positive for illegal use of drugs and on-duty impairment by alcohol pursuant to paragraph (1) from safety-sensitive duties in implementing subsection(c).

SEC. 105. POSTING NOTICES.

Every employer, employment agency, labor organization, or joint labor-management committee covered under this title shall post notices in an accessible format to applicants, employees, and members describing the applicable provisions of this Act, in the manner prescribed by section 711 of the Civil Rights Act of 1964 (42 U.S.C. 2000e-10).

SEC. 106. REGULATIONS.

Not later than 1 year after the date of enactment of this Act, the Commission shall issue regulations in an accessible format to carry out this title in accordance with subchapter II

of chapter 5 of title 5, United States Code.

SEC. 107. ENFORCEMENT.

(a) POWERS, REMEDIES, AND PROCEDURES. -- The powers, remedies, and procedures set forth in sections 705, 706, 707, 709, and 710 of the Civil Rights Act of 1964 (42 U.S.C. 2000e-4, 2000e-5, 2000e-6, 2000e-8, and 2000e-9) shall be the powers, remedies, and procedures this title provides to the Commission, to the Attorney General, or to any person alleging discrimination on the basis of disability in violation of any provision of this Act, or regulations promulgated under section 106, concerning employment.

(b) COORDINATION. -- The agencies with enforcement authority for actions which allege employment discrimination under this title and under the Rehabilitation Act of 1973 shall develop procedures to ensure that administrative complaints filed under this title and under the Rehabilitation Act of 1973 are dealt with in a manner that avoids duplication of effort and prevents imposition of inconsistent or conflicting standards for the same requirements under this title and the Rehabilitation Act of 1973. The Commission, the Attorney General, and the Office of Federal Contract Compliance Programs shall establish such coordinating mechanisms (similar to provisions contained in the joint regulations promulgated by the Commission and the Attorney General at part 42 of title 28 and part 1691 of title 29, Code of Federal Regulations, and the Memorandum of Understanding between the Commission and the Office of Federal Contract Compliance Programs dated January 16, 1981 (46 Fed. Reg. 7435, January 23, 1981)) in regulations implementing this title and Rehabilitation Act of 1973 not later than 18 months after the date of enactment of this Act.

SEC. 108. EFFECTIVE DATE.

This title shall become effective 24 months after the date of enactment.

TITLE II -- PUBLIC SERVICES

Subtitle A -- Prohibition Against Discrimination and Other Generally Applicable Provisions

SEC. 201. DEFINITION.

As used in this title:

(1) PUBLIC ENTITY. -- The term "public entity" means --

(A) any State or local government;

(B) any department, agency, special purpose district, or other instrumentality of a State or States or local government; and

(C) the National Railroad Passenger Corporation, and any commuter authority (as defined in section 103(8) of the Rail Passenger Service Act).

(2) QUALIFIED INDIVIDUAL WITH A DISABILITY. -- The term "qualified individual with a disability" means an individual with a disability who, with or without reasonable modifications to rules, policies, or practices, the removal of architectural, communication, or transportation barriers, or the provision of auxiliary aids and services, meets the essential eligibility requirements for the receipt of services or the participation in programs or activities provided by a public entity.

SEC. 202. DISCRIMINATION.

Subject to the provisions of this title, no qualified individual with a disability shall, by reason of such disability, be excluded from participation in or be denied the benefits of the services, programs, or activities of a public entity, or be subjected to discrimination by any such entity.

SEC. 203. ENFORCEMENT.

The remedies, procedures, and rights set forth in section 505 of the Rehabilitation Act of 1973 (29 U.S.C. 794a) shall be the remedies, procedures, and rights this title provides to any person alleging discrimination on the basis of disability in violation of section 202.

SEC. 204. REGULATIONS.

(a) IN GENERAL. -- Not later than 1 year after the date of enactment of this Act, the Attorney General shall promulgate regulations in an accessible format that implement this subtitle. Such regulations shall not include any matter within the scope of the authority of the Secretary of Transportation under section 223, 229, or 224.

(b) RELATIONSHIP TO OTHER REGULATIONS. -- Except for "program accessibility, existing facilities", and "communications", regulations under subsection (a) shall be consistent with this Act and with the coordination regulations under part 41 of title 28, Code of Federal Regulations (as promulgated by the Department of Health, Education, and Welfare on January 13, 1978), applicable to recipients of Federal financial assistance under section 504 of the Rehabilitation Act of 1973 (29 U.S.C. 794). With respect to "program accessibility, existing facilities", and "communications", such regulations shall be consistent with regulations and analysis as in part 39 of title 28 of the Code of Federal Regulations, applicable to federally conducted activities under such section 504.

(c) STANDARDS. -- Regulations under subsection (a) shall include standards applicable to facilities and vehicles covered by this subtitle, other than facilities, stations, rail passenger cars, and vehicles covered by subtitle B.

Such standards shall be consistent with the minimum guidelines and requirements issued by the Architectural and Transportation Barriers Compliance Board in accordance with section 504(a) of this Act.

SEC. 205. EFFECTIVE DATE.

(a) GENERAL RULE. -- Except as provided in subsection (b), this subtitle shall become effective 18 months after the date of enactment of this Act.

(b) EXCEPTION. -- Section 204 shall become effective on the date of enactment of this Act.

Subtitle B -- Actions Applicable to Public Transportation Provided by Entities Considered discriminatory

Part I -- Public Transportation Other Than by Aircraft or Certain Rail Operations

SEC. 221. DEFINITIONS.

As used in this part:

(1) DEMAND RESPONSIVE SYSTEM. -- The term "demand responsive system" means any system of providing designated public transportation which is not a fixed route system.

(2) DESIGNATED PUBLIC TRANSPORTATION. -- The term "designated public transportation" means transportation (other than public school transportation) by bus, rail, or any other conveyance (other than transportation by aircraft or intercity or commuter rail transportation (as defined in section 241)) that provides the general public with general or special service (including charter service) on a regular and continuing basis.

(3) FIXED ROUTE SYSTEM. -- The term "fixed route system" means a system of providing designated public transportation on which a vehicle is operated along a prescribed route according to a fixed schedule.

(4) OPERATES. -- The term "operates", as used with respect to a fixed route system or demand responsive system, includes operation of such system by a person under a contractual or other arrangement or relationship with a public entity.

(5) PUBLIC SCHOOL TRANSPORTATION. -- The term "public school transportation" means transportation by schoolbus vehicles of schoolchildren, personnel, and equipment to and from a public elementary or secondary school and school-related activities.

(6) SECRETARY. -- The term "Secretary" means the Secretary of Transportation.

SEC. 222. PUBLIC ENTITIES OPERATING FIXED ROUTE SYSTEMS.

(a) PURCHASE AND LEASE OF NEW VEHICLES. -- It shall be considered discrimination for purposes of section 202 of this Act and section 504 of the Rehabilitation Act of 1973 (29 U.S.C. 794) for a public entity which operates a fixed route system to purchase or lease a new bus, a new rapid rail vehicle, a new light rail vehicle, or any other new vehicle to be used on such system, if the solicitation for such purchase or lease is made after the 30th day following the effective date of this subsection and if such bus, rail vehicle, or other vehicle is not readily accessible to and usable by individuals with disabilities, including individuals who use wheelchairs.

(b) PURCHASE AND LEASE OF USED VEHICLES. -- Subject to subsection (c)(1), it shall be considered discrimination for purposes of section 202 of this Act and section 504 of the Rehabilitation Act of 1973 (29 U.S.C. 794) for a public entity which operates a fixed route system to purchase or lease, after the 30th day following the effective date of this subsection, a used vehicle for use on such system unless such entity makes demonstrated good faith efforts to purchase or lease a used vehicle for use on such system that is readily accessible to and usable by individuals with disabilities, including individuals who use wheelchairs.

(c) REMANUFACTURED VEHICLES. --

(1) GENERAL RULE. -- Except as provided in paragraph (2), it shall be considered discrimination for purposes of section 202 of this Act and section 504 of the Rehabilitation Act of 1973 (29 U.S.C. 794) for a public entity which operates a fixed route system --

(A) to remanufacture a vehicle for use on such system so as to extend its usable life for 5 years or more, which remanufacture begins (or for which the solicitation is made) after the 30th day following the effective date of this subsection; or

(B) to purchase or lease for use on such system a remanufactured vehicle which has been remanufactured so as to extend its usable life for 5 years or more, which purchase or lease occurs after such 30th day and during the period in which the usable life is extended; unless, after remanufacture, the vehicle is, to the maximum extent feasible, readily accessible to and usable by individuals with disabilities, including individuals who use wheelchairs.

(2) EXCEPTION FOR HISTORIC VEHICLES. --

(A) GENERAL RULE. -- If a public entity operates a fixed route system any segment of which is included on the National Register of Historic Places and if making a vehicle of historic character to be used solely on such segment readily accessible to and usable by individuals with disabilities would significantly alter the historic character of such vehicle, the public entity only has to make (or to purchase or lease a remanufactured vehicle with) those modifications which are necessary to meet the requirements of paragraph (1) and which do not significantly alter the historic character of such vehicles.

(B) VEHICLES OF HISTORIC CHARACTER DEFINED BY REGULATIONS. -- For purposes of this paragraph and section 228(b), a vehicle of historic character shall be defined by the regulations issued by the Secretary to carry out this subsection.

SEC. 223. PARATRANSIT AS A COMPLEMENT TO FIXED ROUTE SERVICE.

(a) GENERAL RULE. -- It shall be considered discrimination for purposes of section 202 of this Act and section 504 of the Rehabilitation Act of 1973 (29 U.S.C. 794) for a public entity which operates a fixed route system (other than a system which provides solely commuter bus service) to fail to provide with respect to the operations of its fixed route system, in accordance with this section, paratransit and other special transportation services to individuals with disabilities, including individuals who use wheelchairs, that are sufficient to provide to such individuals a level of service (1) which is comparable to the level of designated public transportation services provided to

individuals without disabilities using such system; or (2) in the case of response time, which is comparable, to the extent practicable, to the level of designated public transportation services provided to individuals without disabilities using such systems.

(b) ISSUANCE OF REGULATIONS. -- Not later than 1 year after the effective date of this subsection, the Secretary shall issue final regulations to carry out this section.

(c) REQUIRED CONTENTS OF REGULATIONS. --

(1) ELIGIBLE RECIPIENTS OF SERVICE. -- The regulations issued under this section shall require each public entity which operates a fixed route system to provide the paratransit and other special transportation services required under this section --

(A)(i) to any individual with a disability who is unable, as a result of a physical or mental impairment (including a vision impairment) and without the assistance of another individual (except an operator of a wheelchair lift or other boarding assistance device), to board, ride, or disembark from any vehicle on the system which is readily accessible to and usable by individuals with disabilities;

(ii) to any individual with a disability who needs the assistance of a wheelchair lift or other boarding assistance device (and is able with such assistance) to board, ride, and disembark from any vehicle which is readily accessible to and usable by individuals with disabilities if the individual wants to travel on a route on the system during the hours of operation of the system at a time (or within a reasonable period of such time) when such a vehicle is not being used to provide designated public transportation on the route; and

(iii) to any individual with a disability who has a specific impairment-related condition which prevents such individual from traveling to a boarding location or from a disembarking location on such system;

(B) to one other individual accompanying the

individual with the disability; and

(C) to other individuals, in addition to the one individual described in subparagraph (B), accompanying the individual with a disability provided that space for these additional individuals is available on the paratransit vehicle carrying the individual with a disability and that the transportation of such additional individuals will not result in a denial of service to individuals with disabilities.

For purposes of clauses (i) and (ii) of subparagraph (A), boarding or disembarking from a vehicle does not include travel to the boarding location or from the disembarking location.

(2) SERVICE AREA. -- The regulations issued under this section shall require the provision of paratransit and special transportation services required under this section in the service area of each public entity which operates a fixed route system, other than any portion of the service area in which the public entity solely provides commuter bus service.

(3) SERVICE CRITERIA. -- Subject to paragraphs (1) and (2), the regulations issued under this section shall establish minimum service criteria for determining the level of services to be required under this section.

(4) UNDUE FINANCIAL BURDEN LIMITATION. -- The regulations issued under this section shall provide that, if the public entity is able to demonstrate to the satisfaction of the Secretary that the provision of paratransit and other special transportation services otherwise required under this section would impose an undue financial burden on the public entity, the public entity, notwithstanding any other provision of this section (other than paragraph (5)), shall only be required to provide such services to the extent that providing such services would not impose such a burden.

(5) ADDITIONAL SERVICES. -- The regulations issued under this section shall establish circumstances under which the Secretary may require a public entity to provide,

notwithstanding paragraph (4), paratransit and other special transportation services under this section beyond the level of paratransit and other special transportation services which would otherwise be required under paragraph (4).

(6) PUBLIC PARTICIPA-TION. -- The regulations issued under this section shall require that each public entity which operates a fixed route system hold a public hearing, provide an opportunity for public comment, and consult with individuals with disabilities in preparing its plan under paragraph (7).

(7) PLANS. -- The regulations issued under this section shall require that each public entity which operates a fixed route system --

(A) within 18 months after the effective date of this subsection, submit to the Secretary, and commence implementation of, a plan for providing paratransit and other special transportation services the requirements of this section; and

(B) on an annual basis thereafter, submit to the Secretary, and commence implementation of, a plan for providing such services.

(8) PROVISION OF SERVICES BY OTHERS. -- The regulations issued under this section shall --

(A) require that a public entity submitting a plan to the Secretary under this section identify in the plan any person or other public entity which is providing a paratransit or other special transportation service for individuals with disabilities in the service area to which the plan applies; and

(B) provide that the public entity submitting the plan does not have to provide under the plan such service for individuals with disabilities.

(9) OTHER PROVISIONS. -- The regulations issued under this section shall include such other provisions and require-ments as the Secretary determines are necessary to carry out the objectives of this sections.

(d) REVIEW OF PLAN. --

(1) GENERAL RULE. -- The Secretary shall review a plan submitted under this section for the purpose of determining whether or not such plan meets the requirements of this section, including the regulations issued under this section.

(2) DISAPPROVAL. -- If the Secretary determines that a plan reviewed under this subsection fails to meet the requirements of this section, the Secretary shall disapprove the plan and notify the public entity which submitted the plan of such disapproval and the reasons therefor.

(3) MODIFICATION OF DISAPPROVED PLAN. -- Not later than 90 days after the date of disapproval of a plan under this subsection, the public entity which submitted the plan shall modify the plan to meet the requirements of this section and shall submit to the Secretary, and commence implementation of, such modified plan.

(e) DISCRIMINATION DEFINED. -- As used in subsection (a), the term "discrimination" includes --

(1) a failure of a public entity to which the regulations issued under this section apply to submit, or commence implementation of, a plan in accordance with subsections (c)(6) and (c)(7);

(2) a failure of such entity to submit, or commence imple-mentation of, a modified plan in accordance with subsection (d)(3);

(3) submission to the Secretary of a modified plan under subsection (d)(3) which does not meet the requirements of this section; or

(4) a failure of such entity to provide paratransit or other special transportation services in accordance with the plan or modified plan the public entity submitted to the Secretary under this section.

(f) STATUTORY CONSTRUC-TION. -- Nothing in this section shall be construed as preventing a public entity --

(1) from providing paratransit or other special transportation services at a level which is greater than the level of such services which are required by this section,

(2) from providing paratransit or other special transportation services in addition to those paratransit and special transportation services required by this section, or

(3) from providing such services to individuals in addition to those individuals to whom such services are required to be provided by this section.

SEC. 224. PUBLIC ENTITY OPERATING A DEMAND RESPONSIVE SYSTEM.

If a public entity operates a demand responsive system, it shall be considered discrimina-tion, for purposes of section 202 of this Act and section 504 of the Rehabilitation Act of 1973 (29 U.S.C. 794), for such entity to purchase or lease a new vehicle for use on such system, for which a solicitation is made after the 30th day following the effective date of this section, that is not readily accessible to and usable by individuals with disabilities, including individu-als who use wheelchairs, unless such system, when viewed in its entirety, provides a level of service to such individuals equivalent to the level of service such system provides to individuals without disabilities.

SEC. 225. TEMPORARY RELIEF WHERE LIFTS ARE UNAVAILABLE.

(a) GRANTING. -- With respect to the purchase of new buses, a public entity may apply for, and the Secretary may temporarily relieve such public entity from the obligation under section 222(a) or 224 to purchase new buses that are readily accessible to and usable by individuals with disabilities if such public entity demon-strates to the satisfaction of the Secretary --

(1) that the initial solicita-tion for new buses made by the public entity specified that all new buses were to be lift-equipped and were to be otherwise accessible to and usable by individuals with disabilities;

(2) the unavailability from any qualified manufacturer of hydraulic, electromechanical, or other lifts for such new buses;

(3) that the public entity seeking temporary relief has made good faith efforts to locate

a qualified manufacturer to supply the lifts to the manufacturer of such buses in sufficient time to comply with such solicitation; and

(4) that any further delay in purchasing new buses necessary to obtain such lifts would significantly impair transportation services in the community served by the public entity.

(b) DURATION AND NOTICE TO CONGRESS. – Any relief granted under subsection (a) shall be limited in duration by a specified date, and the appropriate committees of Congress shall be notified of any such relief granted.

(c) FRAUDULENT APPLICATION. – If, at any time, the Secretary has reasonable cause to believe that any relief granted under subsection (a) was fraudulently applied for, the Secretary shall –

(1) cancel such relief if such relief is still in effect; and

(2) take such other action as the Secretary considers appropriate.

SEC. 226. NEW FACILITIES.

For purposes of section 202 of this Act and section 504 of the Rehabilitation Act of 1973 (29 U.S.C. 794), it shall be considered discrimination for a public entity to construct a new facility to be used in the provision of designated public transportation services unless such facility is readily accessible to and usable by individuals with disabilities, including individuals who use wheelchairs.

SEC. 227. ALTERATIONS OF EXISTING FACILITIES.

(a) GENERAL RULE. – With respect to alterations of an existing facility or part thereof used in the provision of designated public transportation services that affect or could affect the usability of the facility or part thereof, it shall be considered discrimination, for purposes of section 202 of this Act and section 504 of the Rehabilitation Act of 1973 (29 U.S.C. 794), for a public entity to fail to make such alterations (or to ensure that the alterations are made) in such a manner that, to the maximum extent feasible, the altered portions of the

facility are readily accessible to and usable by individuals with disabilities, including individuals who use wheelchairs, upon the completion of such alterations. Where the public entity is undertaking an alteration that affects or could affect usability of or access to an area of the facility containing a primary function, the entity shall also make the alterations in such a manner that, to the maximum extent feasible, the path of travel to the altered area and the bathrooms, telephones, and drinking fountains serving the altered area, are readily accessible to and usable by individuals with disabilities, including individuals who use wheelchairs, upon completion of such alterations, where such alterations to the path of travel or the bathrooms, telephones, and drinking fountains serving the altered area are not disproportionate to the overall alterations in terms of cost and scope (as determined under criteria established by the Attorney General).

(b) SPECIAL RULE FOR STATIONS. –

(1) GENERAL RULE. – For purposes of section 202 of this Act and section 504 of the Rehabilitation Act of 1973 (29 U.S.C. 794), it shall be considered discrimination for a public entity that provides designated public transportation to fail, in accordance with the provisions of this subsection, to make key stations (as determined under criteria established by the Secretary by regulation) in rapid rail and light rail systems readily accessible to and usable by individuals with disabilities, including individuals who use wheelchairs.

(2) RAPID RAIL AND LIGHT RAIL KEY STATIONS. –

(A) ACCESSIBILITY. – Except as otherwise provided in this paragraph, all key stations (as determined under criteria established by the Secretary by regulation) in rapid rail and light rail systems shall be made readily accessible to and usable by individuals with disabilities, including individuals who use wheelchairs, as soon as practicable but in no event later than the last day of the 3-year

period beginning on the effective date of this paragraph.

(B) EXTENSION FOR EXTRAORDINARILY EXPENSIVE STRUCTURAL CHANGES. – The Secretary may extend the 3-year period under subparagraph (A) up to a 30-year period for key stations in a rapid rail or light rail system which stations need extraordinarily expensive structural changes to, or replacement of, existing facilities; except that by the last day of the 20th year following the date of the enactment of this Act at least 2/3 of such key stations must be readily accessible to and usable by individuals with disabilities.

(3) PLANS AND MILESTONES. – The Secretary shall require the appropriate public entity to develop and submit to the Secretary a plan for compliance with this subsection –

(A) that reflects consultation with individuals with disabilities affected by such plan and the results of a public hearing and public comments on such plan, and

(B) that establishes milestones for achievement of the requirements of this subsection.

SEC. 228. PUBLIC TRANSPORTATION PROGRAMS AND ACTIVITIES IN EXISTING FACILITIES AND ONE CAR PER TRAIN RULE.

(a) PUBLIC TRANSPORTATION PROGRAMS AND ACTIVITIES IN EXISTING FACILITIES. –

(1) IN GENERAL. – With respect to existing facilities used in the provision of designated public transportation services, it shall be considered discrimination, for purposes of section 202 of this Act and section 504 of Rehabilitation Act of 1973 (29 U.S.C. 794), for a public entity to fail to operate a designated public transportation program or activity conducted in such facilities so that, when viewed in the entirety, the program or activity is readily accessible to and usable by individuals with disabilities.

(2) EXCEPTION. – Paragraph (1) shall not require a public entity to make structural

changes to existing facilities in order to make such facilities accessible to individuals who use wheelchairs, unless and to the extent required by section 227(a) (relating to alterations) or section 227(b) (relating to key stations).

(3) UTILIZATION. — Paragraph (1) shall not require a public entity to which paragraph (2) applies, to provide to individuals who use wheelchairs services made available to the general public at such facilities when such individuals could not utilize or benefit from such services provided at such facilities.

(b) ONE CAR PER TRAIN RULE. —

(1) GENERAL RULE. — Subject to paragraph (2), with respect to 2 or more vehicles operated as a train by a light or rapid rail system, for purposes of section 202 of this Act and section 504 of the Rehabilitation Act of 1973 (29 U.S.C. 794), it shall be considered discrimination for a public entity to fail to have at least 1 vehicle per train that is accessible to individuals with disabilities, including individuals who use wheelchairs, as soon as practicable but in no event later than the last day of the 5-year period beginning on the effective date of this section.

(2) HISTORIC TRAINS. — In order to comply with paragraph (1) with respect to the remanufacture of a vehicle of historic character which is to be used on a segment of a light or rapid rail system which is included on the National Register of Historic Places, if making such vehicle readily accessible to and usable by individuals with disabilities would significantly alter the historic character of such vehicle, the public entity which operates such system only has to make (or to purchase or lease a remanufactured vehicle with) those modifications which are necessary to meet the requirements of section 222(c)(1) and which do not significantly alter the historic character of such vehicle.

SEC. 229. REGULATIONS.

(a) IN GENERAL. — Not later than 1 year after the date of enactment of this Act, the Secretary of Transportation shall issue regulations, in an accessible format, necessary for carrying out this part (other than section 223).

(b) STANDARDS. — The regulations issued under this section and section 223 shall include standards applicable to facilities and vehicles covered by this subtitle. The standards shall be consistent with the minimum guidelines and requirements issued by the Architectural and Transportation Barriers Compliance Board in accordance with section 504 of this Act.

SEC. 230. INTERIM ACCESSIBILITY REQUIREMENTS.

If final regulations have not been issued pursuant to section 229, for new construction or alterations for which a valid and appropriate State or local building permit is obtained prior to the issuance of final regulations under such section, and for which the construction or alteration authorized by such permit begins within one year of the receipt of such permit and is completed under the terms of such permit, compliance with the Uniform Federal Accessibility Standards in effect at the time the building permit is issued shall suffice to satisfy the requirement that facilities be readily accessible to and usable by persons with disabilities as required under sections 226 and 227, except that, if such final regulations have not been issued one year after the Architectural and Transportation Barriers Compliance Board has issued the supplemental minimum guidelines required under section 504(a) of this Act, compliance with such supplemental minimum guidelines shall be necessary to satisfy the requirement that facilities be readily accessible to and usable by persons with disabilities prior to issuance of the final regulations.

SEC. 231. EFFECTIVE DATE.

(a) GENERAL RULE. — Except as provided in subsection (b), this part shall become effective 18 months after the date of enactment of this Act.

(b) EXCEPTION. — Sections 222, 223 (other than subsection (a)), 224, 225, 227(b), 228(b), and 229 shall become effective on the date of enactment of this Act.

PART II — PUBLIC TRANSPORTATION BY INTERCITY AND COMMUTER RAIL

SEC. 241. DEFINITIONS.

As used in this part:

(1) COMMUTER AUTHORITY. — The term "commuter authority" has the meaning given such term in section 103(8) of the Rail Passenger Service Act (45 U.S.C. 502(8)).

(2) COMMUTER RAIL TRANSPORTATION. — The term "commuter rail transportation" has the meaning given the term "commuter service" in section 103(9) of the Rail Passenger Service Act (45 U.S.C. 502(9)).

(3) INTERCITY RAIL TRANSPORTATION. — The term "intercity rail transportation" means transportation provided by the National Railroad Passenger Corporation.

(4) RAIL PASSENGER CAR. — The term "rail passenger car" means, with respect to intercity rail transportation, single-level and bi-level coach cars, single-level and bi-level dining cars, single-level and bi-level sleeping cars, single-level and bi-level lounge cars, and food service cars.

(5) RESPONSIBLE PERSON. — The term "responsible person" means —

(A) in the case of a station more than 50 percent of which is owned by a public entity, such public entity;

(B) in the case of a station more than 50 percent of which is owned by a private party, the persons providing intercity or commuter rail transportation to such station, as allocated on an equitable basis by regulation by the Secretary of Transportation; and

(C) in a case where no part owns more than 50 percent of a station, the persons providing intercity or commuter rail transportation to such station and the owners of the station, other than private party owners, as allocated on an equitable basis by regulation by the Secretary of Transportation.

(6) STATION. -- The term "station" means the portion of a property located appurtenant to a right-of-way on which intercity or commuter rail transportation is operated, where such portion is used by the general public and is related to the provision of such transportation, including passenger platforms, designated waiting areas, ticketing areas, restrooms, and, where a public entity providing rail transportation owns the property, concession areas, to the extent that such public entity exercises control over the selection, design, construction, or alteration of the property, but such term does not include flag stops.

SEC. 242. INTERCITY AND COMMUTER RAIL ACTIONS CONSIDERED DISCRIMINATORY.

(a) INTERCITY RAIL TRANSPORTATION. --

(1) ONE CAR PER TRAIN RULE. -- It shall be considered discrimination for purposes of section 202 of this Act and section 504 of the Rehabilitation Act of 1973 (29 U.S.C. 794) for a person who provides intercity rail transportation to fail to have at least one passenger car per train that is readily accessible to and usable by individuals with disabilities, including individuals who use wheelchairs, in accordance with regulations issued under section 244, as soon as practicable, but in no event later than 5 years after the date of enactment of this Act.

(2) NEW INTERCITY CARS.

(A) GENERAL RULE. -- Except as otherwise provided in this subsection with respect to individuals who use wheelchairs, it shall be considered discrimination for purposes of section 202 of this Act and section 504 of the Rehabilitation Act of 1973 (29 U.S.C. 794) for a person to purchase or lease any new rail passenger cars for use in intercity rail transportation, and for which a solicitation is made later than 30 days after the effective date of this section, unless all such rail cars are readily accessible to and usable by individuals with disabilities, including individuals who use wheelchairs, as prescribed by the Secretary of Transportation in regulations issued under section 244.

(B) SPECIAL RULE FOR SINGLE-LEVEL PASSENGER COACHES FOR INDIVIDUALS WHO USE WHEELCHAIRS. -- Single-level passenger coaches shall be required to --

(i) be able to be entered by an individual who uses a wheelchair;

(ii) have space to park and secure a wheelchair;

(iii) have a seat to which a passenger in a wheelchair can transfer, and a space to fold and store such passenger's wheelchair; and

(iv) have a restroom usable by an individual who uses a wheelchair, only to the extent provided in paragraph (3).

(C) SPECIAL RULE FOR SINGLE-LEVEL DINING CARS FOR INDIVIDUALS WHO USE WHEELCHAIRS. -- Single-level dining cars shall not be required to --

(i) be able to be entered from the station platform by an individual who uses a wheelchair; or

(ii) have a restroom usable by an individual who uses a wheelchair if no restroom is provided in such car for any passenger.

(D) SPECIAL RULE FOR BI-LEVEL DINING CARS FOR INDIVIDUALS WHO USE WHEELCHAIRS. -- Bi-level dining cars shall not be required to --

(i) be able to be entered by an individual who uses a wheelchair;

(ii) have space to park and secure a wheelchair;

(iii) have a seat to which a passenger in a wheelchair can transfer, or a space to fold and store such passenger's wheelchair; or

(iv) have a restroom usable by an individual who uses a wheelchair.

(3) ACCESSIBILITY OF SINGLE-LEVEL COACHES. --

(A) GENERAL RULE -- It shall be considered discrimina-tion for purposes of section 202 of this Act and section 504 of the Rehabilitation Act of 1973 (29 U.S.C. 794) for a person who provides intercity rail transportation to fail to have on each train which includes one or more single-level rail passenger coaches --

(i) a number of spaces --

(I) to park and secure wheelchairs (to accommodate individuals who wish to remain in their wheelchairs) equal to not less than one-half of the number of single-level rail passenger coaches in such train; and

(II) to fold and store wheelchairs (to accommodate individuals who wish to transfer to coach seats) equal to not less than one-half of the number of single-level rail passenger coaches in such train, as soon as practicable, but in no event later than 5 years after the date of enactment of this Act; and

(ii) a number of spaces

(I) to park and secure wheelchairs (to accommodate individuals who wish to remain in their wheelchairs) equal to not less than the total number of single-level rail passenger coaches in such train; and

(II) to fold and store wheelchairs (to accommodate individuals who wish to transfer to coach seats) equal to not less than the total number of single-level rail passenger coaches in such train, as soon as practicable, but in no event later than 10 years after the date of enactment of this Act.

(B) LOCATION. -- Spaces required by subparagraph (A) shall be located in single-level rail passenger coaches or food service cars.

(C) LIMITATION. -- Of the number of spaces required on a train by subparagraph (A), not more than two spaces to park and secure wheelchairs nor more than two spaces to fold and store wheelchairs shall be located in any one coach or food service car.

(D) OTHER ACCESSIBILITY FEATURES. -- Single-level rail passenger coaches and food service cars on which the spaces required by subparagraph (A) are located shall have a

restroom usable by an individual who uses a wheelchair
and shall be able to be entered
from the station platform by an
individual who uses a
wheelchair.

(4) FOOD SERVICE. --
(A) SINGLE-LEVEL
DINING CARS. -- On any train
in which a single-level dining
car is used to provide food
service --

(i) if such single-level
dining car was purchased after
the date of enactment of this
Act, table service in such car
shall be provided to a passenger
who uses a wheelchair if --

(I) the car adjacent to
the end of the dining car
through which a wheelchair
may enter is itself accessible to a
wheelchair;

(II) such passenger
can exit to the platform from the
car such passenger occupies,
move down the platform, and
enter the adjacent accessible car
described in subclause (I)
without the necessity of the
train being moved within the
station; and

(III) space to park
and secure a wheelchair is
available in the dining car at the
time such passenger wishes to
eat (if such passenger wishes to
remain in a wheelchair), or
space to store and fold a
wheelchair is available in the
dining car at the time such
passenger wishes to eat (if such
passenger wishes to transfer to
a dining car seat); and

(ii) appropriate
auxiliary aids and services,
including a hard surface on
which to eat, shall be provided
to ensure that other equivalent
food service is available to
individuals with disabilities,
including individuals who use
wheelchairs, and to passengers
traveling with such individuals.
Unless not practicable, a
person providing intercity rail
transportation shall place an
accessible car adjacent to the
end of a dining car described in
clause (i) through which an
individual who uses a
wheelchair may enter.

(B) BI-LEVEL DINING
CARS. -- On any train in which
a bi-level dining car is used to
provide food service --

(i) if such train includes
a bi-level lounge car purchased

after the date of enactment of
this Act, table service in such
lounge car shall be provided to
individuals who use wheelchairs and to other passengers;
and

(ii) appropriate
auxiliary aids and services,
including a hard surface on
which to eat, shall be provided
to ensure that other equivalent
food service is available to
individuals with disabilities,
including individuals who use
wheelchairs, and to passengers
traveling with such individuals.

(b) COMMUTER RAIL
TRANSPORTATION. --

(1) ONE CAR PER TRAIN
RULE. -- It shall be considered
discrimination for purposes of
section 202 of this Act and
section 504 of the Rehabilitation
Act of 1973 (29 U.S.C. 794) for a
person who provides commuter
rail transportation to fail to
have at least one passenger car
per train that is readily
accessible to and usable by
individuals with disabilities,
including individuals who use
wheelchairs, in accordance with
regulations issued under section
244, as soon as practicable, but
in no event later than 5 years
after the date of enactment of
this Act.

(2) NEW COMMUTER
RAIL CARS. --

(A) GENERAL RULE. -- It
shall be considered discrimination for purposes of section 202
of this Act and section 504 of
the Rehabilitation Act of 1973
(29 U.S.C. 794) for a person to
purchase or lease any new rail
passenger cars for use in
commuter rail transportation,
and for which a solicitation is
made later than 30 days after
the effective date of this section,
unless all such rail cars are
readily accessible to and usable
by individuals with disabilities,
including individuals who use
wheelchairs, as prescribed by
the Secretary of Transportation
in regulations issued under
section 244.

(B) ACCESSIBILITY. --
For purposes of section 202 of
this Act and section 504 of the
Rehabilitation Act of 1973 (29
U.S.C. 794), a requirement that a
rail passenger car used in
commuter rail transportation be
accessible to or readily
accessible to and usable by

individuals with disabilities,
including individuals who use
wheelchairs, shall not be
construed to require --

(i) a restroom usable by
an individual who uses a
wheelchair if no restroom is
provided in such car for any
passenger;

(ii) space to fold and
store a wheelchair; or

(iii) a seat to which a
passenger who uses a wheelchair can transfer.

(c) USED RAIL CARS. -- It
shall be considered discrimination for purposes of section 202
of this Act and section 504 of
the Rehabilitation Act of 1973
(29 U.S.C. 794) for a person to
purchase or lease a used rail
passenger car for use in
intercity or commuter rail
transportation, unless such
person makes demonstrated
good faith efforts to purchase or
lease a used rail car that is
readily accessible to and usable
by individuals with disabilities,
including individuals who use
wheelchairs, as prescribed by
the Secretary of Transportation
in regulations issued under
section 244.

(d) REMANUFACTURED
RAIL CARS. --

(1) REMANUFACTURING.
-- It shall be considered
discrimination for purposes of
section 202 of this Act and
section 504 of the Rehabilitation
Act of 1973 (29 U.S.C. 794) for a
person to remanufacture a rail
passenger car for use in
intercity or commuter rail
transportation so as to extend
its usable life for 10 years or
more, unless the rail car, to the
maximum extent feasible, is
made readily accessible to and
usable by individuals with
disabilities, including individuals who use wheelchairs, as
prescribed by the Secretary of
Transportation in regulations
issued under section 244.

(2) PURCHASE OR LEASE.
-- It shall be considered
discrimination for purposes of
section 202 of this Act and
section 504 of the Rehabilitation
Act of 1973 (29 U.S.C. 794) for a
person to purchase or lease a
remanufactured rail passenger
car for use in intercity or
commuter rail transportation
unless such car was

remanufactured in accordance with paragraph (1).

(e) STATIONS. --

(1) NEW STATIONS. -- It shall be considered discrimination for purposes of section 202 of this Act and section 504 of the Rehabilitation Act of 1973 (29 U.S.C. 794) for a person to build a new station for use in intercity or commuter rail transportation that is not readily accessible to and usable by individuals with disabilities, including individuals who use wheelchairs, as prescribed by the Secretary of Transportation in regulations issued under section 244.

(2) EXISTING STATIONS. --

(A) FAILURE TO MAKE READILY ACCESSIBLE. --

(i) GENERAL RULE. -- It shall be considered discrimination for purposes of section 202 of this Act and section 504 of the Rehabilitation Act of 1973 (29 U.S.C. 794) for a responsible person to fail to make existing stations in the intercity rail transportation system, and existing key stations in commuter rail transportation systems, readily accessible to and usable by individuals with disabilities, including individuals who use wheelchairs, as prescribed by the Secretary of Transportation in regulations issued under section 244.

(ii) PERIOD FOR COMPLIANCE. --

(I) INTERCITY RAIL. -- All stations in the intercity rail transportation system shall be made readily accessible to and usable by individuals with disabilities, including individuals who use wheelchairs, as soon as practicable, but in no event later than 20 years after the date of enactment of this Act.

(II) COMMUTER RAIL. -- Key stations in commuter rail transportation systems shall be made readily accessible to and usable by individuals with disabilities, including individuals who use wheelchairs, as soon as practicable but in no event later than 3 years after the date of enactment of this Act, except that the time limit may be extended by the Secretary of Transportation up to 20 years after the date of enactment of

this Act in a case where the raising of the entire passenger platform is the only means available of attaining accessibility or where other extraordinarily expensive structural changes are necessary to attain accessibility.

(iii) DESIGNATION OF KEY STATIONS. -- Each commuter authority shall designate the key stations in its commuter rail transportation system, in consultation with individuals with disabilities and organizations representing such individuals, taking into consideration such factors as high ridership and whether such station serves as a transfer or feeder station. Before the final designation of key stations under this clause, a commuter authority shall hold a public hearing.

(iv) PLANS AND MILESTONES. -- The Secretary of Transportation shall require the appropriate person to develop a plan for carrying out this subparagraph that reflects consultation with individuals with disabilities affected by such plan and that establishes milestones for achievement of the requirements of this subparagraph.

(B) REQUIREMENT WHEN MAKING ALTERATIONS. --

(i) GENERAL RULE. -- It shall be considered discrimination, for purposes of section 202 of this Act and section 504 of the Rehabilitation Act of 1973 (29 U.S.C. 794), with respect to alterations of an existing station or part thereof in the intercity or commuter rail transportation systems that affect or could affect the usability of the station or part thereof, for the responsible person, owner, or person in control of the station to fail to make the alterations in such a manner that, to the maximum extent feasible, the altered portions of the station are readily accessible to and usable by individuals with disabilities, including individuals who use wheelchairs, upon completion of such alterations.

(ii) ALTERATIONS TO A PRIMARY FUNCTION AREA. -- It shall be considered discrimination, for purposes of section 202 of this Act and

section 504 of the Rehabilitation Act of 1973 (29 U.S.C. 794), with respect to alterations that affect or could affect the usability of or access to an area of the station containing a primary function, for the responsible person, owner, or person in control of the station to fail to make the alterations in such a manner that, to the maximum extent feasible, the path of travel to the altered area, and the bathrooms, telephones, and drinking fountains serving the altered area, are readily accessible to and usable by individuals with disabilities, including individuals who use wheelchairs, upon completion of such alterations, where such alterations to the path of travel or the bathrooms, telephones, and drinking fountains serving the altered area are not disproportionate to the overall alterations in terms of cost and scope (as determined under criteria established by the Attorney General).

(C) REQUIRED COOPERATION. -- It shall be considered discrimination for purposes of section 202 of this Act and section 504 of the Rehabilitation Act of 1973 (29 U.S.C. 794) for an owner, or person in control, of a station governed by subparagraph (A) or (B) to fail to provide reasonable cooperation to a responsible person with respect to such station in that responsible person's efforts to comply with such subparagraph. An owner, or person in control, of a station shall be liable to a responsible person for any failure to provide reasonable cooperation as required by this subparagraph. Failure to receive reasonable cooperation required by this subparagraph shall not be a defense to a claim of discrimination under this Act.

SEC. 243. CONFORMANCE OF ACCESSIBILITY STANDARDS.

Accessibility standards included in regulations issued under this part shall be consistent with the minimum guidelines issued by the Architectural and Transportation Barriers Compliance Board under section 504(a) of this Act.

SEC. 244. REGULATIONS.

Not later than 1 year after the date of enactment of this Act, the Secretary of Transportation shall issue regulations, in an accessible format, necessary for carrying out this part.

SEC. 245. INTERIM ACCESSIBILITY REQUIREMENTS.

(a) STATIONS. -- If final regulations have not been issued pursuant to section 244, for new construction or alterations for which a valid and appropriate State or local building permit is obtained prior to the issuance of final regulations under such section, and for which the construction or alteration authorized by such permit begins within one year of the receipt of such permit and is completed under the terms of such permit, compliance with the Uniform Federal Accessibility Standards in effect at the time the building permit is issued shall suffice to satisfy the requirement that stations be readily accessible to and usable by persons with disabilities as required under section 242(e), except that, if such final regulations have not been issued one year after the Architectural and Transportation Barriers Compliance Board has issued the supplemental minimum guidelines required under section 504(a) of this Act, compliance with such supplemental minimum guidelines shall be necessary to satisfy the requirement that stations be readily accessible to and usable by persons with disabilities prior to issuance of the final regulations.

(b) RAIL PASSENGER CARS. -- If final regulations have not been issued pursuant to section 244, a person shall be considered to have complied with the requirements of section 242(a) through (d) that a rail passenger car be readily accessible to and usable by individuals with disabilities, if the design for such car complies with the laws and regulations (including the Minimum Guidelines and Requirements for Accessible Design and such supplemental minimum guidelines as are issued under section 504(a) of this Act) governing accessibility of such cars, to the extent that such laws and regulations are not inconsistent with this part and are in effect at the time such design is substantially completed.

SEC. 246. EFFECTIVE DATE.

(a) GENERAL RULE. -- Except as provided in subsection (b), this part shall become effective 18 months after the date of enactment of this Act.

(b) EXCEPTION. -- Sections 242 and 244 shall become effective on the date of enactment of this Act.

TITLE III -- PUBLIC ACCOMMODATIONS AND SERVICES OPERATED BY PRIVATE ENTITIES

SEC. 301. DEFINITIONS.

As used in this title:

(1) COMMERCE. -- The term "commerce" means travel, trade, traffic, commerce, transportation, or communication --

(A) among the several States;

(B) between any foreign country or any territory or possession and any State; or

(C) between points in the same State but through another State or foreign country.

(2) COMMERCIAL FACILITIES. -- The term "commercial facilities" means facilities --

(A) that are intended for nonresidential use; and

(B) whose operations will affect commerce.

Such term shall not include railroad locomotives, railroad freight cars, railroad cabooses, railroad cars described in section 242 or covered under this title, railroad rights-of-way, or facilities that are covered or expressly exempted from coverage under the Fair Housing Act of 1968 (42 U.S.C. 3601 et seq.).

(3) DEMAND RESPONSIVE SYSTEM. -- The term "demand responsive system" means any system of providing transportation of individuals by a vehicle, other than a system which is a fixed route system.

(4) FIXED ROUTE SYSTEM. -- The term "fixed route system" means a system of providing transportation of individuals (other than by aircraft) on which a vehicle is operated along a prescribed route according to a fixed schedule.

(5) OVER-THE-ROAD BUS. -- The term "over-the-road bus" means a bus characterized by an elevated passenger deck located over a baggage compartment.

(6) PRIVATE ENTITY. -- The term "private entity" means any entity other than a public entity (as defined in section 201(1)).

(7) PUBLIC ACCOMMODATION. -- The following private entities are considered public accommodations for purposes of this title, if the operations of such entities affect commerce --

(A) an inn, hotel, motel, or other place of lodging, except for an establishment located within a building that contains not more than five rooms for rent or hire and that is actually occupied by the proprietor of such establishment as the residence of such proprietor;

(B) a restaurant, bar, or other establishment serving food or drink;

(C) a motion picture house, theater, concert hall, stadium, or other place of exhibition or entertainment;

(D) an auditorium, convention center, lecture hall, or other place of public gathering;

(E) a bakery, grocery store, clothing store, hardware store, shopping center, or other sales or rental establishment;

(F) a laundromat, dry-cleaner, bank, barber shop, beauty shop, travel service, shoe repair service, funeral parlor, gas station, office of an accountant or lawyer, pharmacy, insurance office, professional office of a health care provider, hospital, or other service establishment;

(G) a terminal, depot, or other station used for specified public transportation;

(H) a museum, library, gallery, or other place of public display or collection;

(I) a park, zoo, amusement park, or other place of recreation;

(J) a nursery, elementary, secondary, undergraduate, or postgraduate private school, or other place of education;

(K) a day care center, senior citizen center, homeless shelter, food bank, adoption agency, or other social service center establishment; and

(L) a gymnasium, health spa, bowling alley, golf course, or other place of exercise or recreation.

(8) RAIL AND RAILROAD. -- The terms "rail" and "railroad" have the meaning given the term "railroad" in section 202(e) of the Federal Railroad Safety Act of 1970 (45 U.S.C. 431(e)).

(9) READILY ACHIEV-ABLE. -- The term "readily achievable" means easily accomplishable and able to be carried out without much difficulty or expense. In determining whether an action is readily achievable, factors to be considered include --

(A) the nature and cost of the action needed under this Act;

(B) the overall financial resources of the facility or facilities involved in the action; the number of persons employed at such facility; the effect on expenses and resources, or the impact otherwise of such action upon the operation of the facility;

(C) the overall financial resources of the covered entity; the overall size of the business of a covered entity with respect to the number of its employees; the number, type, and location of its facilities; and

(D) the type of operation or operations of the covered entity, including the composition, structure, and functions of the workforce of such entity; the geographic separateness, administrative or fiscal relationship of the facility or facilities in question to the covered entity.

(10) SPECIFIED PUBLIC TRANSPORTATION. -- The term "specified public transportation" means transportation by bus, rail, or any other conveyance (other than by aircraft) that provides the general public with general or special service (including

charter service) on a regular and continuing basis.

(11) VEHICLE. -- The term "vehicle" does not include a rail passenger car, railroad locomotive, railroad freight car, railroad caboose, or a railroad car described in section 242 or covered under this title.

SEC. 302. PROHIBITION OF DISCRIMINATION BY PUBLIC ACCOMMODA-TIONS.

(a) GENERAL RULE. -- No individual shall be discriminated against on the basis of disability in the full and equal enjoyment of the goods, services, facilities, privileges, advantages, or accommodations of any place of public accommodation by any person who owns, leases (or leases to), or operates a place of public accommodation.

(b) CONSTRUCTION. --
(1) GENERAL PROHIBI-TION. --
(A) ACTIVITIES. --
(i) DENIAL OF PARTICIPATION. -- It shall be discriminatory to subject an individual or class of individuals on the basis of a disability or disabilities of such individual or class, directly, or through contractual, licensing, or other arrangements, to a denial of the opportunity of the individual or class to participate in or benefit from the goods, services, facilities, privileges, advantages, or accommodations of an entity.

(ii) PARTICIPATION IN UNEQUAL BENEFIT. -- It shall be discriminatory to afford an individual or class of individuals, on the basis of a disability or disabilities of such individual or class, directly, or through contractual, licensing, or other arrangements with the opportunity to participate in or benefit from a good, service, facility, privilege, advantage, or accommodation that is not equal to that afforded to other individuals.

(iii) SEPARATE BENEFIT. -- It shall be discriminatory to provide an individual or class of individuals, on the basis of a disability or disabilities of such individual or class, directly, or through contractual, licensing, or other arrangements

with a good, service, facility, privilege, advantage, or accommodation that is different or separate from that provided to other individuals, unless such action is necessary to provide the individual or class of individuals with a good, service, facility, privilege, advantage, or accommodation, or other opportunity that is as effective as that provided to others.

(iv) INDIVIDUAL OR CLASS OF INDIVIDUALS. -- For purposes of clauses (i) through (iii) of this subparagraph, the term "individual or class of individuals" refers to the clients or customers of the covered public accommodation that enters into the contractual, licensing or other arrangement.

(B) INTEGRATED SETTINGS. -- Goods, services, facilities, privileges, advantages, and accommodations shall be afforded to an individual with a disability in the most integrated setting appropriate to the needs of the individual.

(C) OPPORTUNITY TO PARTICIPATE. -- Notwithstanding the existence of separate or different programs or activities provided in accordance with this section, an individual with a disability shall not be denied the opportunity to participate in such programs or activities that are not separate or different.

(D) ADMINISTRATIVE METHODS. -- An individual or entity shall not, directly or through contractual or other arrangements, utilize standards or criteria or methods of administration --

(i) that have the effect of discriminating on the basis of disability; or

(ii) that perpetuate the discrimination of others who are subject to common administrative control.

(E) ASSOCIATION. -- It shall be discriminatory to exclude or otherwise deny equal goods, services, facilities, privileges, advantages, accommodations, or other opportunities to an individual or entity because of the known disability of an individual with whom the individual or entity is known to have a relationship or association.

(2) SPECIFIC PROHIBITIONS. —

(A) DISCRIMINATION. — For purposes of subsection (a), discrimination includes —

(i) the imposition or application of eligibility criteria that screen out or tend to screen out an individual with a disability or any class of individuals with disabilities from fully and equally enjoying any goods, services, facilities, privileges, advantages, or accommodations, unless such criteria can be shown to be necessary for the provision of the goods, services, facilities, privileges, advantages, or accommodations being offered;

(ii) a failure to make reasonable modifications in policies, practices, or procedures, when such modifications are necessary to afford such goods, services, facilities, privileges, advantages, or accommodations to individuals with disabilities, unless the entity can demonstrate that making such modifications would fundamentally alter the nature of such goods, services, facilities, privileges, advantages, or accommodations;

(iii) a failure to take such steps as may be necessary to ensure that no individual with a disability is excluded, denied services, segregated or otherwise treated differently than other individuals because of the absence of auxiliary aids and services, unless the entity can demonstrate that taking such steps would fundamentally alter the nature of the good, service, facility, privilege, advantage, or accommodation being offered or would result in an undue burden;

(iv) a failure to remove architectural barriers, and communication barriers that are structural in nature, in existing facilities, and transportation barriers in existing vehicles and rail passenger cars used by an establishment for transporting individuals (not including barriers that can only be removed through the retrofitting of vehicles or rail passenger cars by the installation of a hydraulic or other lift), where

such removal is readily achievable; and

(v) where an entity can demonstrate that the removal of a barrier under clause (iv) is not readily achievable, a failure to make such goods, services, facilities, privileges, advantages, or accommodations available through alternative methods if such methods are readily achievable.

(B) FIXED ROUTE SYSTEM. —

(i) ACCESSIBILITY. — It shall be considered discrimination for a private entity which operates a fixed route system and which is not subject to section 304 to purchase or lease a vehicle with a seating capacity in excess of 16 passengers (including the driver) for use on such system, for which a solicitation is made after the 30th day following the effective date of this subparagraph, that is not readily accessible to and usable by individuals with disabilities, including individuals who use wheelchairs.

(ii) EQUIVALENT SERVICE. — If a private entity which operates a fixed route system and which is not subject to section 304 purchases or leases a vehicle with a seating capacity of 16 passengers or less (including the driver) for use on such system after the effective date of this subparagraph that is not readily accessible to or usable individuals with disabilities, it shall be considered discrimination for such entity to fail to operate such system so that, when viewed in its entirety, such system ensures a level of service to individuals with disabilities, including individuals who use wheelchairs, equivalent to the level of service provided to individuals without disabilities.

(C) DEMAND RESPONSIVE SYSTEM. — For purposes of subsection (a), discrimination includes —

(i) a failure of a private entity which operates a demand responsive system and which is not subject to section 304 to operate such system so that, when viewed in its entirety, such system ensures a level of service to individuals with disabilities, including individuals who use wheelchairs,

equivalent to the level of service provided to individuals without disabilities; and

(ii) the purchase or lease by such entity for use on such system of a vehicle with a seating capacity in excess of 16 passengers (including the driver), for which solicitations are made after the 30th day following the effective date of this subparagraph, that is not readily accessible to and usable by individuals with disabilities (including individuals who use wheelchairs) unless such entity can demonstrate that such system, when viewed in its entirety, provides a level of service to individuals with disabilities equivalent to that provided to individuals without disabilities.

(D) OVER-THE-ROAD BUSES. —

(i) LIMITATION ON APPLICABILITY. — Subparagraphs (B) and (C) do not apply to over-the-road buses.

(ii) ACCESSIBILITY REQUIREMENTS. — For purposes of subsection (a), discrimination includes (I) the purchase or lease of an over-the-road bus which does not comply with the regulations issued under section 306(a)(2) by a private entity which provides transportation of individuals and which is not primarily engaged in the business of transporting people, and (II) any other failure of such entity to comply with such regulations.

(3) SPECIFIC CONSTRUCTION. — Nothing in this title shall require an entity to permit an individual to participate in or benefit from the goods, services, facilities, privileges, advantages and accommodations of such entity where such individual poses a direct threat to the health or safety of others. The term "direct threat" means a significant risk to the health or safety of others that cannot be eliminated by a modification of policies, practices, or procedures or by the provision of auxiliary aids or services.

SEC. 303. NEW CONSTRUCTION AND ALTERATIONS IN PUBLIC ACCOMMODATIONS AND COMMERCIAL FACILITIES.

(a) APPLICATION OF TERM. -- Except as provided in subsection (b), as applied to public accommodations and commercial facilities, discrimination for purposes of section 302(a) includes --

(1) a failure to design and construct facilities for first occupancy later than 30 months after the date of enactment of this Act that are readily accessible to and usable by individuals with disabilities, except where an entity can demonstrate that it is structurally impracticable to meet the requirements of such subsection in accordance with standards set forth or incorporated by reference in regulations issued under this title; and

(2) with respect to a facility or part thereof that is altered by, on behalf of, or for the use of an establishment in a manner that affects or could affect the usability of the facility or part thereof, a failure to make alterations in such a manner that, to the maximum extent feasible, the altered portions of the facility are readily accessible to and usable by individuals with disabilities, including individuals who use wheelchairs. Where the entity is undertaking an alteration that affects or could affect usability of or access to an area of the facility containing a primary function, the entity shall also make the alterations in such a manner that, to the maximum extent feasible, the path of travel to the altered area and the bathrooms, telephones, and drinking fountains serving the altered area, are readily accessible to and usable by individuals with disabilities where such alterations to the path of travel or the bathrooms, telephones, and drinking fountains serving the altered area are not disproportionate to the overall alterations in terms of cost and scope (as determined under criteria established by the Attorney General).

(b) ELEVATOR. -- Subsection (a) shall not be construed to require the installation of an elevator for facilities that are less than three stories or have less than 3,000 square feet per story unless the building is a center, a shopping mall, or the professional office of a health care provider or unless the Attorney General determines that a particular category of such facilities requires the installation of elevators based on the usage of such facilities.

SEC. 304. PROHIBITION OF DISCRIMINATION IN SPECIFIED PUBLIC TRANSPORTATION SERVICES PROVIDED BY PRIVATE ENTITIES.

(a) GENERAL RULE. -- No individual shall be discriminated against on the basis of disability in the full and equal enjoyment of specified public transportation services provided by a private entity that is primarily engaged in the business of transporting people and whose operations affect commerce.

(b) CONSTRUCTION. -- For purposes of subsection (a), discrimination includes --

(1) the imposition or application by a entity described in subsection (a) of eligibility criteria that screen out or tend to screen out an individual with a disability or any class of individuals with disabilities from fully enjoying the specified public transportation services provided by the entity, unless such criteria can be shown to be necessary for the provision of the services being offered;

(2) the failure of such entity to --

(A) make reasonable modifications consistent with those required under section 302(b)(2)(A)(ii);

(B) provide auxiliary aids and services consistent with the requirements of section 302(b)(2)(A)(iii); and

(C) remove barriers consistent with the requirements of section 302(b)(2)(A) and with the requirements of section 303(a)(2);

(3) the purchase or lease by such entity of a new vehicle (other than an automobile, a van with a seating capacity of less than 8 passengers, including the driver, or an over-the-road bus) which is to be used to provide specified public transportation and for which a solicitation is made after the 30th day following the effective date of this section, that is not readily accessible to and usable by individuals with disabilities, including individuals who use wheelchairs; except that the new vehicle need not be readily accessible to and usable by such individuals if the new vehicle is to be used solely in a demand responsive system and if the entity can demonstrate that such system, when viewed in its entirety, provides a level of service to such individuals equivalent to the level of service provided to the general public;

(4)(A) the purchase or lease by such entity of an over-the-road bus which does not comply with the regulations issued under section 306(a)(2); and

(B) any other failure of such entity to comply with such regulations; and

(5) the purchase or lease by such entity of a new van with a seating capacity of less than 8 passengers, including the driver, which is to be used to provide specified public transportation and for which a solicitation is made after the 30th day following the effective date of this section that is not readily accessible to or usable by individuals with disabilities, including individuals who use wheelchairs; except that the new van need not be readily accessible to and usable by such individuals if the entity can demonstrate that the system for which the van is being purchased or leased, when viewed in its entirety, provides a level of service to such individuals equivalent to the level of service provided to the general public;

(6) the purchase or base by such entity of a new rail passenger car that is to be used to provide specified public transportation, and for which a solicitation is made later than 30 days after the effective date of this paragraph, that is not readily accessible to and usable by individuals with disabilities, including individuals who use wheelchairs; and

(7) the remanufacture by such entity of a rail passenger car that is to be used to provide specified public transportation so as to extend its usable life for 10 years or more, or the purchase or lease by such entity of such a rail car, unless the rail car, to the maximum extent feasible, is made readily accessible to and usable by individuals with disabilities, including individuals who use wheelchairs.

(c) HISTORICAL OR ANTIQUATED CARS. --

(1) EXCEPTION. -- To the extent that compliance with subsection (b)(2)(C) or (b)(7) would significantly alter the historic or antiquated character of a historical or antiquated rail passenger car, or a rail station served exclusively by such cars, or would result in violation of any rule, regulation, standard, or order issued by the Secretary of Transportation under the Federal Railroad Safety Act of 1970, such compliance shall not be required.

(2) DEFINITION. -- As used in this subsection, the term "historical or antiquated rail passenger car" means a rail passenger car --

(A) which is not less than 30 years old at the time of its use for transporting individuals;

(B) the manufacturer of which is no longer in the business of manufacturing rail passenger cars; and

(C) which --

(i) has a consequential association with events or persons significant to the past; or

(ii) embodies, or is being restored to embody, the distinctive characteristics of a type of rail passenger car used in the past, or to represent a time period which has passed.

SEC. 305. STUDY.

(a) PURPOSES. -- The Office of Technology Assessment shall undertake a study to determine

(1) the access needs of individuals with disabilities to over-the-road buses and over-the-road bus service; and

(2) the most cost-effective methods for providing access to over-the-road buses and over-the-road bus service to individuals with disabilities, particularly individuals who use wheelchairs, through all forms of boarding options.

(b) CONTENTS. -- The study shall include, at a minimum, an analysis of the following:

(1) The anticipated demand by individuals with disabilities for accessible over-the-road buses and over-the-road bus service.

(2) The degree to which such buses and service, including any service required under sections 304(b)(4) and 306(a)(2), are readily accessible to and usable by individuals with disabilities.

(3) The effectiveness of various methods of providing accessibility to such buses and service to individuals with disabilities.

(4) The cost of providing accessible over-the-road buses and bus service to individuals with disabilities, including consideration of recent technological and cost saving developments in equipment and devices.

(5) Possible design changes in over-the-road buses that could enhance accessibility, including the installation of accessible restrooms which do not result in a loss of seating capacity.

(6) The impact of accessibility requirements on the continuation of over-the-road bus service, with particular consideration of the impact of such requirements on such service to rural communities.

(c) ADVISORY COMMITTEE. -- In conducting the study required by subsection (a), the Office of Technology Assessment shall establish an advisory committee, which shall consist of --

(1) members selected from among private operators and manufacturers of over-the-road buses;

(2) members selected from among individuals with disabilities, particularly individuals who use wheelchairs, who are potential riders of such buses; and

(3) members selected for their technical expertise on issues included in the study, including manufacturers of boarding assistance equipment and devices.

The number of members selected under each of paragraphs (1) and (2) shall be equal, and the total number of members selected under paragraphs (1) and (2) shall exceed the number of members selected under paragraph (3).

(d) DEADLINE. -- The study required by subsection (a), along with recommendations by the Office of Technology Assessment, including any policy options for legislative action, shall be submitted to the President and Congress within 36 months after the date of the enactment of this Act. If the President determines that compliance with the regulations issued pursuant to section 306(a)(2)(B) on or before the applicable deadlines specified in section 306(a)(2)(B) will result in a significant reduction in intercity over-the-road bus service, the President shall extend each such deadline by 1 year.

(e) REVIEW. -- In developing the study required by subsection (a), the Office of Technology Assessment shall provide a preliminary draft of such study to the Architectural and Transportation Barriers Compliance Board established under section 502 of the Rehabilitation Act of 1973 (29 U.S.C. 792). The Board shall have an opportunity to comment on such draft study, and any such comments by the Board made in writing within 120 days after the Board's receipt of the draft study shall be incorporated as part of the final study required to be submitted under subsection (d).

SEC. 306. REGULATIONS.

(a) TRANSPORTATION PROVISIONS. --

(1) GENERAL RULE. -- Not later than 1 year after the date of the enactment of this Act, the Secretary of Transportation shall issue regulations in an accessible format to carry out sections 302(b)(2) (B) and (C) and to carry out section 304 (other than subsection (b)(4)).

(2) SPECIAL RULES FOR PROVIDING ACCESS TO OVER-THE-ROAD BUSES. --

(A) INTERIM REQUIRE-MENTS. --

(i) ISSUANCE. -- Not later than 1 year after the date of the enactment of this Act, the Secretary of Transportation shall issue regulations in an accessible format to carry out sections 304(b)(4) and 302(b)(2)(D)(ii) that require each Private entity which uses an over-the-road bus to provide transportation of individuals to provide accessibility to such bus; except that such regulations shall not require any structural changes in over-the-road buses in order to provide access to individuals who use wheelchairs during the effective period of such regulations and shall not require the purchase of boarding assistance devices to provide access to such individuals.

(ii) EFFECTIVE PERIOD. -- The regulations issued pursuant to this subparagraph shall be effective until the effective date of the regulations issued under subparagraph (B).

(B) FINAL REQUIRE-MENT. --

(i) REVIEW OF STUDY AND INTERIM REQUIRE-MENTS. -- The Secretary shall review the study submitted under section 305 and the regulations issued pursuant to subparagraph (A).

(ii) ISSUANCE. -- Not later than 1 year after the date of the submission of the study under section 305, the Secretary shall issue in an accessible format new regulations to carry out sections 304(b)(4) and 302(b)(2)(D)(ii) that require, taking into account the purposes of the study under section 305 and any recommendations resulting from such study, each private entity which uses an over-the-road bus to provide transportation to individuals to provide accessibility to such bus to individuals with disabilities, including individuals who use wheelchairs.

(iii) EFFECTIVE PERIOD. -- Subject to section 305(d), the regulations issued pursuant to this subparagraph shall take effect --

(I) with respect to small providers of transporta-tion (as defined by the Secretary), 7 years after the date of the enactment of this Act; and

(II) with respect to other providers of transporta-tion, 6 years after such date of enactment.

(C) LIMITATION ON REQUIRING INSTALLATION OF ACCESSIBLE RESTROOMS. -- The regulations issued pursuant to this paragraph shall not require the installation of accessible restrooms in over-the-road buses if such installa-tion would result in a loss of seating capacity.

(3) STANDARDS. -- The regulations issued pursuant to this subsection shall include standards applicable to facilities and vehicles covered by sections 302(b)(2) and 304.

(b) OTHER PROVISIONS. -- Not later than 1 year after the date of the enactment of this Act, the Attorney General shall issue regulations in an accessible format to carry out the provisions of this title not referred to in subsection (a) that include standards applicable to facilities and vehicles covered under section 302.

(c) CONSISTENCY WITH ATBCB GUIDELINES. -- Standards included in regula-tions issued under subsections (a) and (b) shall be consistent with the minimum guidelines and requirements issued by the Architectural and Transporta-tion Barriers Compliance Board in accordance with section 504 of this Act.

(d) INTERIM ACCESSIBILITY STANDARDS. --

(1) FACILITIES. -- If final regulations have not been issued pursuant to this section, for new construction or alterations for which a valid and appropriate State or local building permit is obtained prior to the issuance of final regulations under this section, and for which the construction or alteration authorized by such permit begins within one year of the receipt of such permit and is completed under the terms of such permit, compli-ance with the Uniform Federal Accessibility Standards in effect at the time the building permit is issued shall suffice to satisfy the requirement that facilities be readily accessible and usable by persons with disabilities as required under section 303, except that, if such final regulations have not been issued one year after the Architectural and Transporta-tion Barriers Compliance Board has issued the supplemental minimum guidelines required under section 504(a) of this Act, compliance with such supple-mental minimum guidelines shall be necessary to satisfy the requirement that facilities be readily accessible to and usable by persons with disabilities prior to issuance of the final regulations.

(2) VEHICLES AND RAIL PASSENGER CARS. -- If final regulations have not been issued pursuant to this section, a private entity shall be considered to have complied with the requirements of this title, if any, that a vehicle or rail passenger car be readily accessible to and usable by individuals with disabilities, if the design for such vehicle or car complies with the laws and regulations (including the Minimum Guidelines and Requirements for Accessible Design and such supplemental minimum guidelines as are issued under section 504(a) of this Act) governing accessibility of such vehicles or cars, to the extent that such laws and regulations are not inconsistent with this title and are in effect at the time such design is substantially completed.

SEC. 307. EXEMPTIONS FOR PRIVATE CLUBS AND RELIGIOUS ORGANIZA-TIONS.

The provisions of this title shall not apply to private clubs or establishments exempted from coverage under title II of the Civil Rights Act of 1964 (42 U.S.C. 2000-a(e)) or to religious organizations or entities controlled by religious organizations, including places of worship.

SEC. 308. ENFORCEMENT.

(a) IN GENERAL. --

(1) AVAILABILITY OF REMEDIES AND PROCE-DURES. -- The remedies and procedures set forth in section

204(a) of the Civil Rights Act of 1964 (42 U.S.C. 2000a-3(a)) are the remedies and procedures this title provides to any person who is being subjected to discrimination on the basis of disability in violation of this title or who has reasonable grounds for believing that such person is about to be subjected to discrimination in violation of section 303. Nothing in this section shall require a person with a disability to engage in a futile gesture if such person has actual notice that a person or organization covered by this title does not intend to comply with its provisions.

(2) INJUNCTIVE RELIEF. – In the case of violations of sections 302(b)(2)(A)(iv) and section 303(a), injunctive relief shall include an order to alter facilities to make such facilities readily accessible to and usable by individuals with disabilities to the extent required by this title. Where appropriate, injunctive relief shall also include requiring the provision of an auxiliary aid or service, modification of a policy, or provision of alternative methods, to the extent required by this title.

(b) ENFORCEMENT BY THE ATTORNEY GENERAL. –

(1) DENIAL OF RIGHTS. –

(A) DUTY TO INVESTIGATE. –

(i) IN GENERAL. – The Attorney General shall investigate alleged violations of this title, and shall undertake periodic reviews of compliance of covered entities under this title.

(ii) ATTORNEY GENERAL CERTIFICATION. – On the application of a State or local government, the Attorney General may, in consultation with the Architectural and Transportation Barriers Compliance Board, and after prior notice and a public hearing at which persons, including individuals with disabilities, are provided an opportunity to testify against such certification, certify that a State law or local building code or similar ordinance that establishes accessibility requirements meets or exceeds the minimum requirements of this Act for the accessibility and usability of covered facilities under this title. At any enforcement proceeding under this section, such certification by the Attorney General shall be rebuttable evidence that such State law or local ordinance does meet or exceed the minimum requirements of this Act.

(B) POTENTIAL VIOLATION. – If the Attorney General has reasonable cause to believe that –

(i) any person or group of persons is engaged in a pattern or practice of discrimination under this title; or

(ii) any person or group of persons has been discriminated against under this title and such discrimination raises an issue of general public importance,

the Attorney General may commence a civil action in any appropriate United States district court.

(2) AUTHORITY OF COURT. – In a civil action under paragraph (1)(B), the court –

(A) may grant any equitable relief that such court considers to be appropriate, including, to the extent required by this title –

(i) granting temporary, preliminary, or permanent relief;

(ii) providing an auxiliary aid or service, modification of policy, practice, or procedure, or alternative method; and

(iii) making facilities readily accessible to and usable by individuals with disabilities;

(B) may award such other relief as the court considers to be appropriate, including monetary damages to persons aggrieved when requested by the Attorney General; and

(C) may, to vindicate the public interest, assess a civil penalty against the entity in an amount –

(i) not exceeding $ 50,000 for a first violation; and

(ii) not exceeding $ 100,000 for any subsequent violation.

(3) SINGLE VIOLATION. – For purposes of paragraph (2)(C), in determining whether a first or subsequent violation has occurred, a determination in a single action, by judgment or settlement, that the covered entity has engaged in more than one discriminatory act shall be counted as a single violation.

(4) PUNITIVE DAMAGES. – For purposes of subsection (b)(2)(B), the term "monetary damages" and "such other relief" does not include punitive damages.

(5) JUDICIAL CONSIDERATION. – In a civil action under paragraph (1)(B), the court, when considering what amount of civil penalty, if any, is appropriate, shall give consideration to any good faith effort or attempt to comply with this Act by the entity. In evaluating good faith, the court shall consider, among other factors it deems relevant, whether the entity could have reasonably anticipated the need for an appropriate type of auxiliary aid needed to accommodate the unique needs of a particular individual with a disability.

SEC. 309. EXAMINATIONS AND COURSES.
Any person that offers examinations or courses related to applications, licensing, certification, or credentialing for secondary or post-secondary education, professional, or trade purposes shall offer such examinations or courses in a place and manner accessible to persons with disabilities or offer alternative accessible arrangements for such individuals.

SEC. 310. EFFECTIVE DATE.
(a) GENERAL RULE. – Except as provided in subsections (b) and (c), this title shall become effective 18 months after the date of the enactment of this Act.

(b) CIVIL ACTIONS. – Except for any civil action brought for a violation of section 303, no civil action shall be brought for any act or omission described in section 302 which occurs –

(1) during the first 6 months after the effective date, against businesses that employ 25 or fewer employees and have gross receipts of $ 1,000,000 or less; and

(2) during the first year after the effective date, against

businesses that employ 10 or fewer employees and have gross receipts of $ 500,000 or less.

(c) EXCEPTION. -- Sections 302(a) for purposes of section 302(b)(2)(B) and (C) only, 304(a) for purposes of section 304(b)(3) only, 304(b)(3), 305, and 306 shall take effect on the date of the enactment of this Act.

TITLE IV --
TELECOMMUNICATIONS

SEC. 401. TELECOMMUNICATIONS RELAY SERVICES FOR HEARING-IMPAIRED AND SPEECH-IMPAIRED INDIVIDUALS.

(a) TELECOMMUNICATIONS. -- Title II of the Communications Act of 1934 (47 U.S.C. 201 et seq.) is amended by adding at the end thereof the following new section:

"SEC. 225. TELECOMMUNICATIONS SERVICES FOR HEARING-IMPAIRED AND SPEECH-IMPAIRED INDIVIDUALS.

"(a) DEFINITIONS. -- As used in this section --

"(1) COMMON CARRIER OR CARRIER. -- The term 'common carrier' or 'carrier' includes any common carrier engaged in interstate communication by wire or radio as defined in section 3(h) and any common carrier engaged in intrastate communication by wire or radio, notwithstanding sections 2(b) and 221(b).

"(2) TDD. -- The term 'TDD' means a Telecommunications Device for the Deaf, which is a machine that employs graphic communication in the transmission of coded signals through a wire or radio communication system.

"(3) TELECOMMUNICATIONS RELAY SERVICES. -- The term 'telecommunications relay services' means telephone transmission services that provide the ability for an individual who has a hearing impairment or speech impairment to engage in communication by wire or radio with a hearing individual in a manner that is functionally equivalent to the ability of an individual who does not have a hearing

impairment or speech impairment to communicate using voice communication services by wire or radio. Such term includes services that enable two-way communication between an individual who uses a TDD or other nonvoice terminal device and an individual who does not use such a device.

"(b) AVAILABILITY OF TELECOMMUNICATIONS RELAY SERVICES. --

"(1) IN GENERAL. -- In order to carry out the purposes established under section 1, to make available to all individuals in the United States a rapid, efficient nationwide communication service, and to increase the utility of the telephone system of the Nation, the Commission shall ensure that interstate and intrastate telecommunications relay services are available, to the extent possible and in the most efficient manner, to hearing-impaired and speech-impaired individuals in the United States.

"(2) USE OF GENERAL AUTHORITY AND REMEDIES. -- For the purposes of administering and enforcing the provisions of this section and the regulations prescribed thereunder, the Commission shall have the same authority, power, and functions with respect to common carriers engaged in intrastate communication as the Commission has in administering and enforcing the provisions of this title with respect to any common carrier engaged in interstate communication. Any violation of this section by any common carrier engaged in intrastate communication shall be subject to the same remedies, penalties, and procedures as are applicable to a violation of this Act by a common carrier engaged in interstate communication.

"(c) PROVISION OF SERVICES. -- Each common carrier providing telephone voice transmission services shall, not later than 3 years after the date of enactment of this section, provide in compliance with the regulations prescribed under this section, throughout the area in which it offers service, telecommunications relay services, individually,

through designees, through a competitively selected vendor, or in concert with other carriers. A common carrier shall be considered to be in compliance with such regulations --

"(1) with respect to intrastate telecommunications relay services in any State that does not have a certified program under subsection (f) and with respect to interstate telecommunications relay services, if such common carrier (or other entity through which the carrier is providing such relay services) is in compliance with the Commission's regulations under subsection (d); or

"(2) with respect to intrastate telecommunications relay services in any State that has a certified program under subsection (f) for such State, if such common carrier (or other entity through which the carrier is providing such relay services) is in compliance with the program certified under subsection (f) for such State.

"(d) REGULATIONS. --

"(1) IN GENERAL. -- The Commission shall, not later than 1 year after the date of enactment of this section, prescribe regulations to implement this section, including regulations that --

"(A) establish functional requirements, guidelines, and operations procedures for telecommunications relay services;

"(B) establish minimum standards that shall be met in carrying out subsection (c);

"(C) require that telecommunications relay services operate every day for 24 hours per day;

"(D) require that users of telecommunications relay services pay rates no greater than the rates paid for functionally equivalent voice communication services with respect to such factors as the duration of the call, the time of day, and the distance from point of origination to point of termination;

"(E) prohibit relay operators from failing to fulfill the obligations of common carriers by refusing calls or limiting the length of calls that use telecommunications relay services;

"(F) prohibit relay operators from disclosing the content of any relayed conversation and from keeping records of the content of any such conversation beyond the duration of the call; and

"(G) prohibit relay operators from intentionally altering a relayed conversation.

"(2) TECHNOLOGY. – The Commission shall ensure that regulations prescribed to implement this section encourage, consistent with section 7(a) of this Act, the use of existing technology and do not discourage or impair the development of improved technology.

"(3) JURISDICTIONAL SEPARATION OF COSTS. –

"(A) IN GENERAL. – Consistent with the provisions of section 410 of this Act, the Commission shall prescribe regulations governing the jurisdictional separation of costs for the services provided pursuant to this section.

"(B) RECOVERING COSTS. – Such regulations shall generally provide that costs caused by interstate telecommunications relay services shall be recovered from all subscribers for every interstate service and costs caused by intrastate telecommunications relay services shall be recovered from the intrastate jurisdiction. In a State that has a certified program under subsection (f), a State commission shall permit a common carrier to recover the costs incurred in providing intrastate telecommunications relay services by a method consistent with the requirements of this section.

"(e) ENFORCEMENT. –

"(1) IN GENERAL. – Subject to subsections (f) and (g), the Commission shall enforce this section.

"(2) COMPLAINT. – The Commission shall resolve, by final order, a complaint alleging a violation of this section within 180 days after the date such complaint is filed.

"(f) CERTIFICATION. –

"(1) STATE DOCUMENTA-TION. – Any State desiring to establish a State program under this section shall submit documentation to the Commission that describes the program of such State for implementing intrastate telecommunications relay services and the procedures and remedies available for enforcing any requirements imposed by the State program.

"(2) REQUIREMENTS FOR CERTIFICATION. – After review of such documentation, the Commission shall certify the State program if the Commission determines that –

"(A) the program makes available to hearing-impaired and speech-impaired individuals, either directly, through designees, through a competitively selected vendor, or through regulation of intrastate common carriers, intrastate telecommunications relay services in such State in a manner that meets or exceeds the requirements of regulations prescribed by the Commission under subsection (d); and

"(B) the program makes available adequate procedures and remedies for enforcing the requirements of the State program.

"(3) METHOD OF FUNDING. – Except as provided in subsection (d), the Commission shall not refuse to certify a State program based solely on the   method such State will implement for funding intrastate telecommunication relay services.

"(4) SUSPENSION OR REVOCATION OF CERTIFICA-TION. – The Commission may suspend or revoke such certification if, after notice and opportunity for hearing, the Commission determines that such certification is no longer warranted. In a State whose program has been suspended or revoked, the Commission shall take such steps as may be necessary, consistent with this section, to ensure continuity of telecommunications relay services.

"(g) COMPLAINT. –

"(1) REFERRAL OF COMPLAINT. – If a complaint to the Commission alleges a violation of this section with respect to intrastate telecommunications relay services within a State and certification of the program of such State under subsection (f) is in effect, the Commission shall refer such complaint to such State.

"(2) JURISDICTION OF COMMISSION. – After referring a complaint to a State under paragraph (1), the Commission shall exercise jurisdiction over such complaint only if –

"(A) final action under such State program has not been taken on such complaint by such State –

"(i) within 180 days after the complaint is filed with such State; or

"(ii) within a shorter period as prescribed by the regulations of such State; or

"(B) the Commission determines that such State program is no longer qualified for certification under subsection (f).".

(b) CONFORMING AMEND-MENTS. – The Communications Act of 1934 (47 U.S.C. 151 et seq.) is amended –

(1) in section 2(b) (47 U.S.C. 152(b)), by striking "section 224" and inserting "sections 224 and 225"; and

(2) in section 221(b) (47 U.S.C. 221(b)), by striking "section 301" and inserting "sections 225 and 301".

SEC. 402. CLOSED-CAPTIONING OF PUBLIC SERVICE ANNOUNCE-MENTS.

Section 711 of the Communications Act of 1934 is amended to read as follows:

"SEC. 711. CLOSED-CAPTIONING OF PUBLIC SERVICE ANNOUNCEMENTS.

"Any television public service announcement that is produced or funded in whole or in part by any agency or instrumentality of Federal Government shall include closed captioning of the verbal content of such announcement. A television broadcast station licensee –

"(1) shall not be required to supply closed captioning for any such announcement that fails to include it; and

"(2) shall not be liable for broadcasting any such announcement without transmitting a closed caption unless the licensee intentionally fails to transmit the closed caption that was included with the announcement.".

TITLE V – MISCELLANEOUS PROVISIONS

SEC. 501. CONSTRUCTION.

(a) IN GENERAL. – Except as otherwise provided in this Act, nothing in this Act shall be construed to apply a lesser standard than the standards applied under title V of the Rehabilitation Act of 1973 (29 U.S.C. 790 et seq.) or the regulations issued by Federal agencies pursuant to such title.

(b) RELATIONSHIP TO OTHER LAWS. – Nothing in this Act shall be construed to invalidate or limit the remedies, rights, and procedures of any Federal law or law of an State or political subdivision of any State or jurisdiction that provides greater or equal protection for the rights of individuals with disabilities than are afforded by this Act. Nothing in this Act shall be construed to preclude the prohibition of, or the imposition of restrictions on, smoking in places of employment covered by title I, in transportation covered by title II or III, or in places of public accommodation covered by title III.

(c) INSURANCE. – Titles I through IV of this Act shall not be construed to prohibit or restrict –

(1) an insurer, hospital or medical service company, health maintenance organization, or any agent, or entity that administers benefit plans, or similar organizations from underwriting risks, classifying risks, or administering such risks that are based on or not inconsistent with State law; or

(2) a person or organization covered by this Act from establishing, sponsoring, observing or administering the terms of a bona fide benefit plan that are based on underwriting risks, classifying risks, or administering such risks that are based on or not inconsistent with State law; or

(3) a person or organization covered by this Act from establishing, sponsoring, observing or administering the terms of a bona fide benefit plan that is not subject to State laws that regulate insurance. Paragraphs (1), (2), and (3) shall not be used as a subterfuge to evade the purposes of title I and III.

(d) ACCOMMODATIONS AND SERVICES. – Nothing in this Act shall be construed to require an individual with a disability to accept an accommodation, aid, service, opportunity, or benefit which such individual chooses not to accept.

SEC. 502. STATE IMMUNITY.

A State shall not be immune under the eleventh amendment to the Constitution of the United States from an action in Federal or State court of competent jurisdiction for a violation of this Act. In any action against a State for a violation of the requirements of this Act, remedies (including remedies both at law and in equity) are available for such a violation to the same extent as such remedies are available for such a violation in an action against any public or private entity other than a State.

SEC. 503. PROHIBITION AGAINST RETALIATION AND COERCION.

(a) RETALIATION. – No person shall discriminate against any individual because such individual has opposed any act or practice made unlawful by this Act or because such individual made a charge, testified, assisted, or participated in any manner in an investigation, proceeding, or hearing under this Act.

(b) INTERFERENCE, COERCION, OR INTIMIDATION. – It shall be unlawful to coerce, intimidate, threaten, or interfere with any individual in the exercise or enjoyment of, or on account of his or her having exercised or enjoyed, or on account of his or her having aided or encouraged any other individual in the exercise or enjoyment of, any right granted or protected by this Act.

(c) REMEDIES AND PROCEDURES. – The remedies and procedures available under sections 107, 203, and 308 of this Act shall be available to aggrieved persons for violations of subsections (a) and (b), with respect to title I, title II and title III, respectively.

SEC. 504. REGULATIONS BY THE ARCHITECTURAL AND TRANSPORTATION BARRIERS COMPLIANCE BOARD.

(a) ISSUANCE OF GUIDELINES. – Not later than 9 months after the date of enactment of this Act, the Architectural and Transportation Barriers Compliance Board shall issue minimum guidelines that shall supplement the existing Minimum Guidelines and Requirements for Accessible Design for purposes of titles II and III of this Act.

(b) CONTENTS OF GUIDELINES. – The supplemental guidelines issued under subsection (a) shall establish additional requirements, consistent with this Act, to ensure that buildings, facilities, rail passenger cars, and vehicles are accessible, in terms of architecture and design, transportation, and communication, to individuals with disabilities.

(c) QUALIFIED HISTORIC PROPERTIES. –

(1) IN GENERAL. – The supplemental guidelines issued under subsection (a) shall include procedures and requirements for alterations that will threaten or destroy the historic significance of qualified historic buildings and facilities as defined in 4.1.7(1)(a) of the Uniform Federal Accessibility Standards.

(2) SITES ELIGIBLE FOR LISTING IN NATIONAL REGISTERS. – With respect to alterations of buildings or facilities that are eligible for listing in the National Register of Historic Places under the National Historic Preservation Act (16 U.S.C. 470 et seq.), the guidelines described in paragraph (1) shall, at a minimum, maintain the procedures and requirements established in 4.1.7 (1) and (2) of the Uniform Federal Accessibility Standards.

(3) Other sites. -- With respect to alterations of buildings or facilities designated as historic under State or local law, the guidelines described in paragraph (1) shall establish procedures equivalent to those established by 4.1.7(1) (b) and (c) of the Uniform

Federal Accessibility Standards, and shall require, at a minimum, compliance with the requirements established in 4.1.7(2) of such standards.

SEC. 505. ATTORNEY'S FEES.

In any action or administrative proceeding commenced pursuant to this Act, the court or agency, in its discretion, may allow the prevailing party, other than the United States, a reasonable attorney's fee, including litigation expenses, and costs, and the United States shall be liable for the foregoing the same as a private individual.

SEC. 506. TECHNICAL ASSISTANCE.

(a) PLAN FOR ASSISTANCE. --

(1) IN GENERAL. -- Not later than 180 days after the date of enactment of this Act, the Attorney General, in consultation with the Chair of the Equal Employment Opportunity Commission, the Secretary of Transportation, the Chair of the Architectural and Transportation Barriers Compliance Board, and the Chairman of the Federal Communications Commission, shall develop a plan to assist entities covered under this Act, and other Federal agencies, in understanding the responsibility of such entities and agencies under this Act.

(2) PUBLICATION OF PLAN. -- The Attorney General shall publish the plan referred to in paragraph (1) for public comment in accordance with subchapter II of chapter 5 of title 5, United States Code (commonly known as the Administrative Procedure Act).

(b) AGENCY AND PUBLIC ASSISTANCE. -- The Attorney General may obtain the assistance of other Federal agencies in carrying out subsection (a), including the National Council on Disability, the President's Committee on Employment of People with Disabilities, the Small Business Administration, and the Department of Commerce.

(c) IMPLEMENTATION. --

(1) RENDERING ASSISTANCE. -- Each Federal agency that has responsibility under

paragraph (2) for implementing this Act may render technical assistance to individuals and institutions that have rights or duties under the respective title or titles for which such agency has responsibility.

(2) IMPLEMENTATION OF TITLES. --

(A) TITLE I. -- The Equal Employment Opportunity Commission and the Attorney General shall implement the plan for assistance developed under subsection (a), for title I.

(B) TITLE II -- .

(i) SUBTITLE A. -- The Attorney General shall implement such plan for assistance for subtitle A of title II.

(ii) SUBTITLE B. -- The Secretary of Transportation shall implement such plan for assistance for subtitle B of title II.

(C) TITLE III. -- The Attorney General, in coordination with the Secretary of Transportation and the Chair of the Architectural Transportation Barriers Compliance Board, shall implement such plan for assistance for title III, except for section 304, the plan for assistance for which shall be implemented by the Secretary of Transportation.

(D) TITLE IV. -- The Chairman of the Federal Communications Commission, in coordination with the Attorney General, shall implement such plan for assistance for title IV.

(3) TECHNICAL ASSISTANCE MANUALS. -- Each Federal agency that has responsibility under paragraph (2) for implementing this Act shall, as part, of its implementation responsibilities, ensure the availability and provision of appropriate technical assistance manuals to individuals or entities with rights or duties under this Act no later than six months after applicable final regulations are published under titles I, II, III, and IV.

(d) GRANTS AND CONTRACTS. --

(1) IN GENERAL. -- Each Federal agency that has responsibility under subsection (c)(2) for implementing this Act may make grants or award contracts to effectuate the

purposes of this section, subject to the availability of appropriations. Such grants and contracts may be awarded to individuals, institutions not organized for profit and no part of the net earnings of which inures to the benefit of any private shareholder or individual (including educational institutions), and associations representing individuals who have rights or duties under this Act. Contracts may be awarded to entities organized for profit, but such entities may not be the recipients or grants described in this paragraph.

(2) DISSEMINATION OF INFORMATION. -- Such grants and contracts, among other uses, may be designed to ensure wide dissemination of information about the rights and duties established by this Act and to provide information and technical assistance about techniques for effective compliance with this Act.

(e) FAILURE TO RECEIVE ASSISTANCE. -- An employer, public accommodation, or other entity covered under this Act shall not be excused from compliance with the requirements of this Act because of any failure to receive technical assistance under this section, including any failure in the development or dissemination of any technical assistance manual authorized by this section.

SEC. 507. FEDERAL WILDERNESS AREAS.

(a) STUDY. -- The National Council on Disability shall conduct a study and report on the effect that wilderness designations and wilderness land management practices have on the ability of individuals with disabilities to use and enjoy the National Wilderness Preservation System as established under the Wilderness Act (16 U.S.C. 1131 et seq.).

(b) SUBMISSION OF REPORT. -- Not later than 1 year after the enactment of this Act, the National Council on Disability shall submit the report required under subsection (a) to Congress.

(c) SPECIFIC WILDERNESS ACCESS. --

(1) IN GENERAL. -- Congress reaffirms that nothing in the Wilderness Act is to be construed as prohibiting the use of a wheelchair in a wilderness area by an individual whose disability requires use of a wheelchair, and consistent with the Wilderness Act no agency is required to provide any form of special treatment or accommodation, or to construct any facilities or modify any conditions of lands within a wilderness area in order to facilitate such use.

(2) DEFINITION. -- For purposes of paragraph (1), the term "wheelchair" means a device designed solely for use by a mobility-impaired person for locomotion, that is suitable for use in an indoor pedestrian area.

SEC. 508. TRANSVESTITES.

For the purposes of this Act, the term "disabled" or "disability" shall not apply to an individual solely because that individual is a transvestite.

SEC. 509. COVERAGE OF CONGRESS AND THE AGENCIES OF THE LEGISLATIVE BRANCH.

(a) COVERAGE OF THE SENATE. --

(1) COMMITMENT TO RULE XLII. -- The Senate reaffirms its commitment to Rule XLII of the Standing Rules of the Senate which provides as follows:

"No member, officer, or employee of the Senate shall, with respects to employment by the Senate or any office thereof

"(a) fail or refuse to hire an individual;

"(b) discharge an individual; or

"(c) otherwise discriminate against an individual with respect to promotion, compensation, or terms, conditions, or privileges of employment on the basis of such individual's race, color, religion, sex, national origin, age, or state of physical handicap.".

(2) APPLICATION TO SENATE EMPLOYMENT. -- The rights and protections provided pursuant to this Act, the Civil Rights Act of 1990 (S. 2104, 101st Congress), the Civil Rights Act of 1964, the Age Discrimination in Employment Act of 1967, and the Rehabilitation Act of 1973 shall apply with respect to employment by the United States Senate.

(3) INVESTIGATION AND ADJUDICATION OF CLAIMS. -- All claims raised by any individual with respect to Senate employment, pursuant to the Acts referred to in paragraph (2), shall be investigated and adjudicated by the Select Committee on Ethics, pursuant to S. Res. 338, 88th Congress, as amended, or such other entity as the Senate may designate.

(4) RIGHTS OF EMPLOYEES. -- The Committee on Rules and Administration shall ensure that Senate employees are informed of their rights under the Acts referred to in paragraph (2).

(5) APPLICABLE REMEDIES. -- When assigning remedies to individuals found to have a valid claim under the Acts referred to in paragraph (2), the Select Committee on Ethics, or such other entity as the Senate may designate, should to the extent practicable apply the same remedies applicable to all other employees covered by the Acts referred to in paragraph (2). Such remedies shall apply exclusively.

(6) MATTERS OTHER THAN EMPLOYMENT. --

(A) IN GENERAL. -- The rights and protections under this Act shall, subject to subparagraph (B), apply with respect to the conduct of the Senate regarding matters other than employment.

(B) REMEDIES. -- The Architect of the Capitol shall establish remedies and procedures to be utilized with respect to the rights and protections provided pursuant to subparagraph (A). Such remedies and procedures shall apply exclusively, after approval in accordance with subparagraph (C).

(C) PROPOSED REMEDIES AND PROCEDURES. -- For purposes of subparagraph (B), the Architect of shall submit proposed remedies and procedures to the Senate Committee on Rules and Administration. The remedies and procedures shall be effective upon the approval of the Committee on Rules and Administration.

(7) EXERCISE OF RULEMAKING POWER. -- Notwithstanding any other provision of law, enforcement and adjudication of the rights and protections referred to in paragraph (2) and (6)(A) shall be within the exclusive jurisdiction of the United States Senate. The provisions of paragraph (1), (3), (4), (5), (6)(B), and (6)(C) are enacted by the Senate as an exercise of the rulemaking power of the Senate, with full recognition of the right of the Senate to change its rules, in the same manner, and to the same extent, as in the case of any other rule of the Senate.

(b) COVERAGE OF THE HOUSE OF REPRESENTATIVES. --

(1) IN GENERAL. -- Notwithstanding any other provision of this Act or of law, the purposes of this Act shall, subject to paragraphs (2) and (3), apply in their entirety to the House of Representatives.

(2) EMPLOYMENT IN THE HOUSE. --

(A) APPLICATION. -- The rights and protections under this Act shall, subject to subparagraph (B), apply with respect to any employee in an employment position in the House of Representatives and any employing authority of the House of Representatives.

(B) ADMINISTRATION.

(i) IN GENERAL. -- In the administration of this paragraph, the remedies and procedures made applicable pursuant to the resolution described in clause (ii) shall apply exclusively.

(ii) RESOLUTION. -- The resolution referred to in clause (i) is House Resolution 15 of the One Hundred First Congress, as agreed to January 3, 1989, or any other provision that continues in effect the provisions of, or is a successor to, the Fair Employment Practices Resolution (House Resolution 558 of the One Hundredth Congress, as agreed to October 4, 1988).

(C) EXERCISE OF RULEMAKING POWER. -- The provisions of subparagraph (B) are enacted by the House of Representatives as an exercise of the rulemaking power of the House of Representatives, with full recognition of the right of the House to change its rules, in the same manner, and to the same extent as in the case of any other rule of the House.

(3) MATTERS OTHER THAN EMPLOYMENT. --

(A) IN GENERAL. -- The rights and protections under this Act shall, subject to subparagraph (B), apply with respect to the conduct of the House of Representatives regarding matters other than employment.

(B) REMEDIES. -- The Architect of the Capitol shall establish remedies and procedures to be utilized with respect to the rights and protections provided pursuant to subparagraph (A). Such remedies and procedures shall apply exclusively, after approval in accordance with subparagraph (C).

(C) APPROVAL. -- For purposes of subparagraph (B), the Architect of the Capitol shall submit proposed remedies and procedures to the Speaker of the House of Representatives. The remedies and procedures shall be effective upon the approval of the Speaker, after consultation with the House Office Building Commission.

(c) INSTRUMENTALITIES OF CONGRESS. --

(1) IN GENERAL. -- The rights and protections under this Act shall, subject to paragraph (2), apply with respect to the conduct of each instrumentality of the Congress.

(2) ESTABLISHMENT OF REMEDIES AND PROCEDURES BY INSTRUMENT ALITIES. -- The chief official of each instrumentality of the Congress shall establish remedies and procedures to be utilized with respect to the rights and protections provided pursuant to paragraph (1). Such remedies and procedures shall apply exclusively.

(3) REPORT TO CONGRESS. -- The chief official of each instrumentality of Congress shall, after establish-

ing remedies and procedures for purposes of paragraph (2), submit to the Congress a report describing the remedies and procedures.

(4) DEFINITION OF INSTRUMENTALITIES. -- For purposes of this section, instrumentalities of the Congress include the following: the Architect of the Capitol, the Congressional Budget Office, the General Accounting Office, the Government Printing Office, the Library of Congress, the Office of Technology Assessment, and the United States Botanic Garden.

(5) CONSTRUCTION. -- Nothing in this section shall alter the enforcement procedures for individuals with disabilities provided in the General Accounting Office Personnel Act 1980 and regulations promulgated pursuant to that Act.

SEC. 510. ILLEGAL USE OF DRUGS.

(a) IN GENERAL. -- For purposes of this Act, the term "individual with a disability" does not include an individual who is currently engaging in the illegal use of drugs, when the covered entity acts on the basis of such use.

(b) RULES OF CONSTRUCTION. -- Nothing in subsection (a) shall be construed to exclude as an individual with a disability an individual who --

(1) has successfully completed a supervised drug rehabilitation program and is no longer engaging in the illegal use of drugs, or has otherwise been rehabilitated successfully and is no longer engaging in such use;

(2) is participating in a supervised rehabilitation program and is no longer engaging in such use; or

(3) is erroneously regarded as engaging in such use, but is not engaging in such use; except that it shall not be a violation of this Act for a covered entity to adopt or administer reasonable policies or procedures, including but not limited to drug testing, designed to ensure that an individual described in paragraph (1) or (2) is no longer engaging in the illegal use of drugs; however, nothing in this

section shall be construed to encourage, prohibit, restrict, or authorize the conducting of testing for the illegal use of drugs.

(c) HEALTH AND OTHER SERVICES. -- Notwithstanding subsection (a) and section 511(b)(3), an individual shall not be denied health services, or services provided in connection with drug rehabilitation, on the basis of the current illegal use of drugs if the individual is otherwise entitled to such services.

(d) DEFINITION OF ILLEGAL USE OF DRUGS. --

(1) IN GENERAL. -- The term "illegal use of drugs" means the use of drugs, the possession or distribution of which is unlawful under the Controlled Substances Act (21 U.S.C. 812). Such term does not include the use of a drug taken under supervision by a licensed health care professional, or other uses authorized by the Controlled Substances Act or other provisions of Federal law.

(2) DRUGS. -- The term "drug" means a controlled substance, as defined in schedules I through V of section 202 of the Controlled Substances Act.

SEC. 511. DEFINITIONS.

(a) HOMOSEXUALITY AND BISEXUALITY. -- For purposes of the definition of "disability" in section 3(2), homosexuality and bisexuality are not impairments and as such are not disabilities under this Act.

(b) CERTAIN CONDITIONS. -- Under this Act, the term "disability" shall not include --

(1) transvestism, transsexualism, pedophilia, exhibitionism, voyeurism, gender identity disorders not resulting from physical impairments, or other sexual behavior disorders;

(2) compulsive gambling, kleptomania, or pyromania; or

(3) psychoactive substance use disorders resulting from current illegal use of drugs.

SEC. 512. AMENDMENTS TO THE REHABILITATION ACT.

(a) DEFINITION OF HANDICAPPED INDIVIDUAL. -- Section 7(8) of the Rehabilitation Act of 1973 (29 U.S.C.

706(8)) is amended by redesignating subparagraph (C) as subparagraph (D), and by inserting after subparagraph (B) the following subparagraph:

"(C)(i) For purposes of title V, the term 'individual with handicaps' does not include an individual who is currently engaging in the illegal use of drugs, when a covered entity acts on the basis of such use.

"(ii) Nothing in clause (i) shall be construed to exclude as an individual with handicaps an individual who --

"(I) has successfully completed a supervised drug rehabilitation program and is no longer engaging in the illegal use of drugs, or has otherwise been rehabilitated successfully and is no longer engaging in such use;

"(II) is participating in a supervised rehabilitation program and is no longer engaging in such use; or

"(III) is erroneously regarded as engaging in such use, but is not engaging in such use;
except that it shall not be a violation of this Act for a covered entity to adopt or administer reasonable policies or procedures, including but not limited to drug testing, designed to ensure that an individual described in subclause (I) or (II) is no longer engaging in the illegal use of drugs.

"(iii) Notwithstanding clause (i), for purposes of programs and activities providing health services and services provided under titles I, II and III, an individual shall not be excluded from the benefits of such programs or activities on the basis of his or her current illegal use of drugs if he or she is otherwise entitled to such services.

"(iv) For purposes of programs and activities providing educational services, local educational agencies may take disciplinary action pertaining to the use or possession of illegal drugs or alcohol against any handicapped student who currently is engaging in the illegal use of drugs or in the use of alcohol to the same extent that such disciplinary action is taken against nonhandicapped students. Furthermore, the due process procedures at 34 CFR 104.36 shall not apply to such disciplinary actions.

"(v) For purposes of sections 503 and 504 as such sections relate to employment, the term 'individual with handicaps' does not include any individual who is an alcoholic whose current use of alcohol prevents such individual from performing the duties of the job in question or whose employment, by reason of such current alcohol abuse, would constitute a direct threat to property or the safety of others.".

(b) DEFINITION OF ILLEGAL DRUGS. -- Section 7 of the Rehabilitation Act of 1973 (29 U.S.C. 706) is amended by adding at the end the following new paragraph:

"(22)(A) The term 'drug' means a controlled substance, as defined in schedules I through V of section 202 of the Controlled Substances Act (21 U.S.C. 812).

"(B) The term 'illegal use of drugs' means the use of drugs, the possession or distribution of which is unlawful under the Controlled Substances Act. Such term does not include the use of a drug taken under supervision by a licensed health care professional, or other uses authorized by the Controlled Substances Act or other provisions of Federal law.".

(c) CONFORMING AMENDMENTS. -- Section 7(8)(B) of the Rehabilitation Act of 1973 (29 U.S.C. 706(8)(B)) is amended --

(1) in the first sentence, by striking "Subject to the second sentence of this subparagraph," and inserting "Subject to subparagraphs (C) and (D),";
and   (2) by striking the second sentence.

SEC. 513. ALTERNATIVE MEANS OF DISPUTE RESOLUTION.

Where appropriate and to the extent authorized by law, the use of alternative means of dispute resolution, including settlement negotiations, conciliation, facilitation, mediation, factfinding, minitrials, and arbitration, is encouraged to resolve disputes arising under this Act.

SEC. 514. SEVERABILITY.

Should any provision in this Act be found to be unconstitutional by a court of law, such provision shall be severed from the remainder of the Act, and such action shall not affect the enforceability of the remaining provisions of the Act.

ADA: Implementation Dates

Title	Laws Effective Date	Regulations Due by Federal Agency	Enforcement Jurisdiction
Title I **Employment**	July 26, 1992 for employers with twenty-five (25) or more employees; July 26, 1994 for employers with fifteen (15) or more employees	July 26, 1991 all regulations due from Equal Employment Opportunity Commission (EEOC).	Remedies identical to those under Title VII of the Civil Rights Act of 1964 which are private right of action, injunctive relief (i.e., job reinstatement, back pay, and EEOC enforcement).
Title II **Public Services** All activities of local and state governments	January 26, 1992	July 26, 1991, all regulations due from Attorney General	Remedies identical to those under the Rehabilitation Act of 1973 Section 505 which are private right of action, injunctive relief, and some damages.
(Part I) Public transportation (buses, light and rapid rail including fixed-route systems, paratransit, demand response systems and transportation facilities).	August 26, 1990, all orders for purchases or leases of new vehicles must be for accessible vehicles; one-car-per-train must be accessible as soon as practicable, but no later than July 26, 1995; paratransit services must be provided after January 26, 1992; new stations built after January 26, 1992 must be accessible. Key stations must be retrofitted by July 26, 1993; with some extensions allowed up to July 26, 2020.	July 26, 1991, all regulations due from Secretary of Transportation.	Same as above.
(Part II) Public transportation by intercity Amtrak and commuter rail (including transportation facilities).	By July 26, 2000, Amtrak passenger coaches must have same number of accessible seats as would have been available if every car were built accessible; half of such seats must be available by July 26, 1995. Same one-car-per-train rule and new stations rule as above. All existing Amtrak stations must be retrofitted by July 26, 2010; key commuter stations must be retrofitted by July 26, 1993 with some extensions allowed up to 20 years.	July 26, 1991, all regulations due from Secretary of Transportation.	Same as above.

(Continued on next page)

ADA: Implementation Dates

(Continued)

Title	Laws Effective Date	Regulations Due by Federal Agency	Enforcement Jurisdiction
Title III **Public accommodations operated by private entities** A. Public accommodations (all business and service providers).	January 26, 1992, for businesses with twenty-five (25) or less employees and revenue $1 million or less; January 26, 1993 for businesses with ten (10) or less employees and revenue $500,000 or less.	July 26, 1991, regulations due from Attorney General. Regulations will be based on standards issued by the Architectural and Transportation Barriers Compliance Board (ATBCB). Due April 26, 1991.	For individuals, remedies identical to Title II of the Civil Rights Act of 1964 which are private right of action, injunctive relief: For Attorney General enforcement in pattern or practice cases or cases of general importance with civil penalties and compensatory damages.
B. New construction/alteration to public accommodations and commercial facilities.	January 26, 1992, for alterations. January 26, 1993 for new construction.	Same as above.	Same as above.
C. Public transportation provided by private entities.	In general, January 26, 1992, but by August 26, 1990 all orders for purchases or leases of new vehicles must be for accessible vehicles. Calls for a three (3) year study of over-the-road buses to determine access needs with requirements effective July 26, 1996 to July 26, 1997.	July 26, 1991, regulations due from Secretary of Transportation. Regulations will be based on standards issued by the Architectural and Transportation Barriers Compliance Board (ATBCB). Due April 26, 1991.	Same as above.
Title IV **Telecommunications**	July 26, 1993, telecommunications relay services to operate twenty-four (24) hours per day.	July 26, 1991, all regulations due by the Federal Communications Commission.	Private right of action and Federal Communications Commission.
Title V **Miscellaneous**	Effective dates of Title V are those determined by most of the analogous sections in Titles I through IV.	In general, this title depicts the ADA's relationship to other laws, explains insurance issues, prohibits state immunity, provides congressional inclusion, sets regulations by ATBCB, explains implementation of each title and notes amendments to the Rehabilitation Act of 1973.	

Appendix 4

Equal Employment Opportunity Commission
29 CFR Part 1630
Equal Employment Opportunity for Individuals with Disabilities

Equal Employment Opportunity Commission

29 CFR Part 1630

Equal Employment Opportunity for Individuals with Disabilities

AGENCY: Equal Employment Opportunity Commission

ACTION: Final Rule

SUMMARY: On July 26, 1990, the Americans with Disabilities Act (ADA) was signed into law. Section 106 of the ADA requires that the Equal Employment Opportunity Commission (EEOC) issue substantive regulations implementing title I (Employment) within one year of the date of enactment of the Act. Pursuant to this mandate, the Commission is publishing a new part 1630 to its regulations to implement title I and sections 3(2), 3(3), 501, 503, 506(e), 508, 510, and 511 of the ADA as those sections pertain to employment. New part 1630 prohibits discrimination against qualified individuals with disabilities in all aspects of employment.

EFFECTIVE DATE: July 26, 1992.

FOR FURTHER INFORMATION CONTACT: Elizabeth M. Thornton, Deputy Legal Counsel, (202) 663-4638 (voice), (202) 663-7026 (TDD) or Christopher G. Bell, Acting Associate Legal Counsel for Americans with Disabilities Act Services, (202) 663-4679 (voice), (202) 663-7026.

Copies of this final rule and interpretive appendix may be obtained by calling the Office of Communications and Legislative Affairs at (202) 663-4900. Copies in alternate formats may be obtained from the Office of Equal Employment Opportunity by calling (202) 663-4398 or (202) 663-4395 (voice) or (202) 663-4399 (TDD). The alternate formats available are: large print, braille, electronic file on computer disk, and audiotape.

SUPPLEMENTARY INFORMATION:

Rulemaking History

The Commission actively solicited and considered public comment in the development of part 1630. On August 1, 1990, the Commission published an advance notice of proposed rulemaking (ANPRM), 55 FR 31192, informing the public that the Commission had begun the process of developing substantive regulations pursuant to title I of the ADA and inviting comment from interested groups and individuals. The comment period ended on August 31, 1990. In response to the ANPRM, the Commission received 138 comments from various disability rights organizations, employer groups, and individuals. Comments were also solicited at 62 ADA input meetings conducted by Commission field offices throughout the country. More than 2400 representatives from disability rights organizations and employer groups participated in these meetings.

On February 28, 1991, the Commission published a notice of proposed rulemaking (NPRM), 56 FR 8578, setting forth proposed part 1630 for public comment. The comment period ended April 29, 1991. In response to the NPRM, the Commission received 697 timely comments from interested groups and individuals. In many instances, a comment was submitted on behalf of several parties and represented the views of numerous groups, employers, or individuals with disabilities. The comments have been analyzed and considered in the development of this final rule.

Overview of Regulations

The format of part 1630 reflects congressional intent, as expressed in the legislative history, that the regulations implementing the employment provisions of the ADA be modeled on the regulations implementing Section 504 of the Rehabilitation Act of 1973, as amended, 34 CFR part 104. Accordingly, in developing part 1630, the Commission has been guided by the Section 504 regulations and the case law interpreting those regulations.

It is the intent of Congress that the regulations implementing the ADA be comprehensive and easily understood. Part 1630, therefore, defines terms not previously defined in the regulations implementing Section 504 of the Rehabilitation Act, such as "substantially limits," "essential functions," and "reasonable accommodation." Of necessity, many of the determinations that may be required by this part must be made on a case-by-case basis. Where possible, part 1630 establishes parameters to serve as guidelines in such inquiries.

The Commission is also issuing interpretive guidance concurrently with the issuance of part 1630 in order to ensure that qualified individuals with disabilities understand their rights under this part and to facilitate and encourage compliance by covered entities. Therefore, part 1630 is accompanied by an Appendix. This Appendix represents the Commission's interpretation of the issues discussed, and the Commission will be guided by it when resolving charges of employment discrimination. The Appendix addresses the major provisions of part 1630 and explains the major concepts of disability rights. Further, the Appendix cites to the authority, such as the legislative history of the ADA and case law interpreting Section 504 of the Rehabilitation Act, that provides the basis and purpose of the rule and interpretative guidance.

More detailed guidance on specific issues will be forthcoming in the Commission's Compliance Manual. Several Compliance Manual sections and policy guidances on ADA issues are currently under development and are expected to be issued prior to the effective date of the Act. Among the issues to be addressed in depth are the theories of

discrimination; definitions of disability and of qualified individual with a disability; reasonable accommodation and undue hardship, including the scope of reassignment; and preemployment inquiries.

To assist us in the development of this guidance, the Commission requested comment in the NPRM from disability rights organizations, employers, unions, state agencies concerned with employment or workers compensation practices, and interested individuals on specific questions about insurance, workers' compensation, and collective bargaining agreements. Many commenters responded to these questions, and several commenters addressed other matters pertinent to these areas. The Commission has considered these comments in the development of the final rule and will continue to consider them as it develops further ADA guidance.

In the NPRM, the Commission raised questions about a number of insurance-related matters. Specifically, the Commission asked commenters to discuss risk assessment and classification, the relationship between "risk" and "cost," and whether employers should consider the effects that changes in insurance coverage will have on individuals with disabilities before making those changes. Many commenters provided information about insurance practices and explained some of the considerations that affect insurance decisions. In addition, some commenters discussed their experiences with insurance plans and coverage. The commenters presented a wide range of opinions on insurance-related matters, and the Commission will consider the comments as it continues to analyze these complex matters.

The Commission received a large number of comments concerning inquiries about an individual's workers' compensation history. Many employers asserted that such inquiries are job related and consistent with business necessity. Several individuals with disabilities and disability rights organiza-

tions, however, argued that such inquiries are prohibited preemployment inquiries and are not job related and consistent with business necessity. The Commission has addressed this issue in the interpretive guidance accompanying section 1630.14(a) and will discuss the matter further in future guidance.

There was little controversy about the submission of medical information to workers' compensation offices. A number of employers and employer groups pointed out that the workers' compensation offices of many states request medical information in connection with the administration of second injury funds. Further, they noted that the disclosure of medical information may be necessary to the defense of a workers' compensation claim. The Commission has responded to these comments by amending the interpretive guidance accompanying section 1630.14(b). This amendment, discussed below, notes that the submission of medical information to workers' compensation offices in accordance with state workers' compensation laws is not inconsistent with section 1630.14(b). The Commission will address this area in greater detail and will discuss other issues concerning workers' compensation matters in future guidances, including the policy guidance on preemployment inquiries.

With respect to collective bargaining agreements, the Commission asked commenters to discuss the relationship between collective bargaining agreements and such matters as undue hardship, reassignment to a vacant position, the determination of what constitutes a "vacant" position, and the confidentiality requirements of the ADA. The comments that we received reflected a wide variety of views. For example, some commenters argued that it would always be an undue hardship for an employer to provide a reasonable accommodation that conflicted with the provisions of a collective bargaining agreement. Other commenters, however, argued that an accommodation's effect on an agreement should not be considered when assessing undue hardship. Similarly, some commenters stated that the appropriateness of reassignment to a vacant position should depend upon the provisions of a collective bargaining agreement while others asserted that an agreement cannot limit the right to reassignment. Many commenters discussed the relationship between an agreement's seniority provisions and an employer's reasonable accommodation obligations.

In response to comments, the Commission has amended section 1630.2(n)(3) to include "the terms of a collective bargaining agreement" in the types of evidence relevant to determining the essential functions of a position. The Commission has made a corresponding change to the interpretive guidance on section 1630.2(n)(3). In addition, the Commission has amended the interpretive guidance on section 1630.15(d) to note that the terms of a collective bargaining agreement may be relevant to determining whether an accommodation would pose an undue hardship on the operation of a covered entity's business.

The divergent views expressed in the public comments demonstrate the complexity of employment-related issues concerning insurance, workers' compensation, and collective bargaining agreement matters. These highly complex issues require extensive research and analysis and warrant further consideration. Accordingly, the Commission has decided to address the issues in depth in future Compliance Manual sections and policy guidances. The Commission will consider the public comments that it received in response to the NPRM as it develops further guidance on the application of title I of the ADA to these matters.

The Commission has also decided to address burdens-of-proof issues in future guidance

documents, including the Compliance Manual section on the theories of discrimination. Many commenters discussed the allocation of the various burdens of proof under title I of the ADA and asked the Commission to clarify those burdens. The comments in this area addressed such matters as determining whether a person is a qualified individual with a disability, job relatedness and business necessity, and undue hardship. The Commission will consider these comments as it prepares further guidance in this area.

A discussion of other significant comments and an explanation of the changes made in part 1630 since publication of the NPRM follows.

Section-by-Section Analysis of Comments and Revisions

Section 1630.1 Purpose, Applicability, and Construction

The Commission has made a technical correction to section 1630.1(a) by adding section 506(e) to the list of statutory provisions implemented by this part. Section 506(e) of the ADA provides that the failure to receive technical assistance from the federal agencies that administer the ADA is not a defense to failing to meet the obligations of title I.

Some commenters asked the Commission to note that the ADA does not preempt state claims, such as state tort claims, that confer greater remedies than are available under the ADA. The Commission has added a paragraph to that effect in the Appendix discussion of sections 1630.1(b) and (c). This interpretation is consistent with the legislative history of the Act. *See* H.R. Rep. No. 485 Part 3, 101st Cong., 2d Sess. 69-70 (1990) [hereinafter referred to as House Judiciary Report].

In addition, the Commission has made a technical amendment to the Appendix discussion to note that the ADA does not automatically preempt medical standards or safety requirements established by Federal law or regulations. The Commission has also amended

the discussion to refer to a direct threat that cannot be eliminated "or reduced" through reasonable accommodation. This language is consistent with the regulatory definition of direct threat. (See section 1630.2(r), below.)

Section 1630.2 Definitions

Section 1630.2(h) Physical or Mental Impairment

The Commission has amended the interpretive guidance accompanying section 1630.2(h) to note that the definition of the term "impairment" does not include characteristic predisposition to illness or disease.

In addition, the Commission has specifically noted in the interpretive guidance that pregnancy is not an impairment. This change responds to the numerous questions that the Commission has received concerning whether pregnancy is a disability covered by the ADA. Pregnancy, by itself, is not an impairment and is therefore not a disability.

Section 1630.2(j) Substantially Limits

The Commission has revised the interpretive guidance accompanying section 1630.2(j) to make clear that the determination of whether an impairment substantially limits one or more major life activities is to be made without regard to the availability of medicines, assistive devices, or other mitigating measures. This interpretation is consistent with the legislative history of the ADA. *See* S. Rep. No. 116, 101st Cong., 1st Sess. 23 (1989) [hereinafter referred to as Senate Report]; H.R. Rep. No. 9485 Part 2, 101st Cong., 2d Sess. 52 (1990) [hereinafter referred to as House Labor Report]; House Judiciary Report at 28. The Commission has also revised the examples in the third paragraph of this section's guidance. The examples now focus on the individual's capacity to perform major life activities rather than on the presence or absence of mitigating measures. These revisions respond to comments from disability rights groups, which were concerned that the discussion could be misconstrued to exclude from ADA coverage individuals with disabilities who function well because of assistive devices or other mitigating measures.

In an amendment to the paragraph concerning the factors to consider when determining whether an impairment is substantially limiting, the Commission has provided a second example of an impairment's "impact." This example notes that a traumatic head injury's affect on cognitive functions is the "impact" of that impairment.

Many commenters addressed the provisions concerning the definition of "substantially limits" with respect to the major life activity of working (section 1630.2(j)(3)). Some employers generally supported the definition but argued that it should be applied narrowly. Other employers argued that the definition is too broad. Disability rights groups and individuals with disabilities, on the other hand, argued that the definition is too narrow, unduly limits coverage, and places an onerous burden on individuals seeking to establish that they are covered by the ADA. The Commission has responded to these comments by making a number of clarifications in this area.

The Commission has revised section 1630.2(j)(3)(ii) and the accompanying interpretive guidance to note that the listed factors "may" be considered when determining whether an individual is substantially limited in working. This revision clarifies that the factors are relevant to, but are not required elements of, a showing of a substantial limitation in working.

Disability rights groups asked the Commission to clarify that "substantially limited in working" applies only when an individual is not substantially limited in any other major life activity. In addition, several other commenters indicated confusion about whether and when the ability to work should be considered when assessing if

an individual has a disability. In response to these comments, the Commission has amended the interpretive guidance by adding a new paragraph clarifying the circumstances under which one should determine whether an individual is substantially limited in the major life activity of working. This paragraph makes clear that a determination of whether an individual is substantially limited in the ability to work should be made only when the individual is not disabled in any other major life activity. Thus, individuals need not establish that they are substantially limited in working if they already have established that they are, have a record of, or are regarded as being substantially limited in another major life activity.

The proposed interpretive guidance in this area provided an example concerning a surgeon with a slight hand impairment. Several commenters expressed concern about this example. Many of these comments indicated that the example confused, rather than clarified, the matter. The Commission, therefore, has deleted this example. To explain further the application of the "substantially limited in working" concept, the Commission has provided another example (concerning a commercial airline pilot) in the interpretive guidance.

In addition, the Commission has clarified that the terms "numbers and types of jobs" (see section 1630.2(j)(3)(ii)(B)) and "numbers and types of other jobs" (see section 1630.2(j)(3)(ii)(C)) do not require an onerous evidentiary showing.

In the proposed Appendix, after the interpretive guidance accompanying section 1630.2(l), the Commission included a discussion entitled "Frequently Disabling Impairments." Many commenters expressed concern about this discussion. In response to these comments, and to avoid confusion, the Commission has revised the discussion and has deleted the list of frequently disabling impairments. The revised discussion now appears in the

interpretive guidance accompanying section 1630.2(j).

Section 1630.2(l) Is Regarded as Having Such an Impairment

Section 1630.2(l)(3) has been changed to refer to "a substantially limiting impairment" rather than "such an impairment." This change clarifies that an individual meets the definition of the term "disability" when a covered entity treats the individual as having a substantially limiting impairment. That is, section 1630.2(l)(3) refers to any substantially limiting impairment, rather than just to one of the impairments described in sections 1630.2(l)(1) or (2).

The proposed interpretive guidance on section 1630.2(l) stated that, when determining whether an individual is regarded as substantially limited in working, "it should be assumed that all similar employers would apply the same exclusionary qualification standard that the employer charged with discrimination has used." The Commission specifically requested comment on this proposal, and many commenters addressed this issue. The Commission has decided to eliminate this assumption and to revise the interpretive guidance. The guidance now explains that an individual meets the "regarded as" part of the definition of disability if he or she can show that a covered entity made an employment decision because of a perception of a disability based on "myth, fear, or stereotype." This is consistent with the legislative history of the ADA. *See* House Judiciary Report at 30.

Section 1630.2(m) Qualified Individual with a Disability

Under the proposed part 1630, the first step in determining whether an individual with a disability is a qualified individual with a disability was to determine whether the individual "satisfies the requisite skill, experience and education requirements of the employment position" the individual holds or desires.

Many employers and employer groups asserted that the proposed regulation unduly limited job prerequisites to skill, experience, and education requirements and did not permit employers to consider other job-related qualifications. To clarify that the reference to skill, experience, and education requirements was not intended to be an exhaustive list of permissible qualification requirements, the Commission has revised the phrase to include "skill, experience, education, and other job-related requirements." This revision recognizes that other types of job-related requirements may be relevant to determining whether an individual is qualified for a position.

Many individuals with disabilities and disability rights groups asked the Commission to emphasize that the determination of whether a person is a qualified individual with a disability must be made at the time of the employment action in question and cannot be based on speculation that the individual will become unable to perform the job in the future or may cause increased health insurance or workers' compensation costs. The Commission has amended the interpretive guidance on section 1630.2(m) to reflect this point. This guidance is consistent with the legislative history of the Act. See Senate Report at 26, House Labor Report at 55, 136; House Judiciary Report at 34, 71.

Section 1630.2(n) Essential Functions

Many employers and employer groups objected to the use of the terms "primary" and "intrinsic" in the definition of essential functions. To avoid confusion about the meanings of "primary" and "intrinsic," the Commission has deleted these terms from the definition. The final regulation defines essential functions as "fundamental job duties" and notes that essential functions do not include the marginal functions of a position.

The proposed interpretive guidance accompanying section 1630.2(n)(2)(ii) noted that one of

the factors in determining whether a function is essential is the number of employees available to perform a job function or among whom the performance of that function can be distributed. The proposed guidance explained that "[t]his may be a factor either because the total number of employees is low, or because of the fluctuating demands of the business operations." Some employers and employer groups expressed concern that this language could be interpreted as requiring an assessment of whether a job function could be distributed among all employees in any job at any level. The Commission has amended the interpretive guidance on this factor to clarify that the factor refers only to distribution among "available" employees.

Section 1630.2(n)(3) lists several kinds of evidence that are relevant to determining whether a particular job function is essential. Some employers and unions asked the Commission to recognize that collective bargaining agreements may help to identify a position's essential functions. In response to these comments, the Commission has added "[t]he terms of a collective bargaining agreement" to the list. In addition, the Commission has amended the interpretive guidance to note specifically that this type of evidence is relevant to the determination of essential functions. This addition is consistent with the legislative history of the Act. See Senate Report at 32; House Labor Report at 63.

Proposed section 1630.2(n)(3) referred to the evidence on the list as evidence "that may be considered in determining whether a particular function is essential." The Commission has revised this section to refer to evidence "of" whether a particular function is essential. The Commission made this revision in response to concerns about the meaning of the phrase "may be considered." In that regard, some commenters questioned whether the phrase meant that some of the listed evidence might not be considered when

determining whether a function is essential to a position. This revision clarifies that all of the types of evidence on the list, when available, are relevant to the determination of a position's essential functions. As the final rule and interpretive guidance make clear, the list is not an exhaustive list of all types of relevant evidence. Other types of available evidence may also be relevant to the determination.

The Commission has amended the interpretive guidance concerning section 1630.2(n)(3)(ii) to make clear that covered entities are not required to develop and maintain written job descriptions. Such job descriptions are relevant to a determination of a position's essential functions, but they are not required by part 1630.

Several commenters suggested that the Commission establish a rebuttable presumption in favor of the employer's judgment concerning what functions are essential. The Commission has not done so. On that point, the Commission notes that the House Committee on the Judiciary specifically rejected an amendment that would have created such a presumption. See House Judiciary Report at 3334.

The last paragraph of the interpretive guidance on section 1630.2(n) notes that the inquiry into what constitutes a position's essential functions is not intended to second guess an employer's business judgment regarding production standards, whether qualitative or quantitative. In response to several comments, the Commission has revised this paragraph to incorporate examples of qualitative production standards.

Section 1630.2(o) Reasonable Accommodation

The Commission has deleted the reference to undue hardship from the definition of reasonable accommodation. This is a technical change reflecting that undue hardship is a defense to, rather than an aspect of, reasonable accommodation. As some commenters have noted, a defense to a term should not be part of the term's definition. Accordingly, we have separated the concept of undue hardship from the definition of reasonable accommodation. This change does not affect the obligations of employers or the rights of individuals with disabilities. Accordingly, a covered entity remains obligated to make reasonable accommodation to the known physical or mental limitations of an otherwise qualified individual with a disability unless to do so would impose an undue hardship on the operation of the covered entity's business. *See* section 1630.9.

With respect to section 1630.2(o)(1)(i), some commenters expressed confusion about the use of the phrase "qualified individual with a disability." In that regard, they noted that the phrase has a specific definition under this part (see section 1630.2(m)) and questioned whether an individual must meet that definition to request an accommodation with regard to the application process. The Commission has substituted the phrase "qualified applicant with a disability" for "qualified individual with a disability." This change clarifies that an individual with a disability who requests a reasonable accommodation to participate in the application process must be eligible only with respect to the application process.

The Commission has modified section 1630.2(o)(1)(iii) to state that reasonable accommodation includes modifications or adjustments that enable employees with disabilities to enjoy benefits and privileges that are "equal" to (rather than "the same" as) the benefits and privileges that are enjoyed by other employees. This change clarifies that such modifications or adjustments must ensure that individuals with disabilities receive equal access to the benefits and privileges afforded to other employees but may not be able to ensure that the individuals receive the same results of those benefits and

privileges or precisely the same benefits and privileges.

Many commenters discussed whether the provision of daily attendant care is a form of reasonable accommodation. Employers and employer groups asserted that reasonable accommodation does not include such assistance. Disability rights groups and individuals with disabilities, however, asserted that such assistance is a form of reasonable accommodation but that this part did not make that clear. To clarify the extent of the reasonable accommodation obligation with respect to daily attendant care, the Commission has amended the interpretive guidance on section 1630.2(o) to make clear that it may be a reasonable accommodation to provide personal assistants to help with specified duties related to the job.

The Commission also has amended the interpretive guidance to note that allowing an individual with a disability to provide and use equipment, aids, or services that an employer is not required to provide may also be a form of reasonable accommodation. Some individuals with disabilities and disability rights groups asked the Commission to make this clear.

The interpretive guidance points out that reasonable accommodation may include making non-work areas accessible to individuals with disabilities. Many commenters asked the Commission to include rest rooms in the examples of accessible areas that may be required as reasonable accommodations. In response to those comments, the Commission has added rest rooms to the examples.

In response to other comments, the Commission has added a paragraph to the guidance concerning job restructuring as a form of reasonable accommodation. The new paragraph notes that job restructuring may involve changing when or how an essential function is performed.

Several commenters asked the Commission to provide additional guidance concerning the reasonable accommodation

of reassignment to a vacant position. Specifically, commenters asked the Commission to clarify how long an employer must wait for a vacancy to arise when considering reassignment and to explain whether the employer is required to maintain the salary of an individual who is reassigned from a higher-paying position to a lower-paying one. The Commission has amended the discussion of reassignment to refer to reassignment to a position that is vacant "within a reasonable amount of time ... in light of the totality of the circumstances." In addition, the Commission has noted that an employer is not required to maintain the salaries of reassigned individuals with disabilities if it does not maintain the salaries of individuals who are not disabled.

Section 1630.2(p) Undue Hardship

The Commission has substituted "facility" or "facilities" for "site" or "sites" in section 1630.2(p)(2) and has deleted the definition of the term "site." Many employers and employer groups expressed concern about the use and meaning of the term "site." The final regulation's use of the terms "facility" and "facilities" is consistent with the language of the statute.

The Commission has amended the last paragraph of the interpretive guidance accompanying section 1630.2(p) to note that, when the cost of a requested accommodation would result in an undue hardship and outside funding is not available, an individual with a disability should be given the option of paying the portion of the cost that constitutes an undue hardship. This amendment is consistent with the legislative history of the Act. *See* Senate Report at 36; House Labor Report at 69.

Several employers and employer groups asked the Commission to expand the list of factors to be considered when determining if an accommodation would impose an undue hardship on a covered entity by adding another factor: the relationship of an accommodation's cost to the value of the position at issue, as measured by the compensation paid to the holder of the position. Congress, however, specifically rejected this type of factor. *See* House Judiciary Report at 41 (noting that the House Judiciary Committee rejected an amendment proposing that an accommodation costing more than ten percent of the employee's salary be treated as an undue hardship). The Commission, therefore, has not added this to the list.

Section 1630.2(q) Qualification Standards

The Commission has deleted the reference to direct threat from the definition of qualification standards. This revision is consistent with the revisions the Commission has made to sections 1630.10 and 1630.15(b). (See discussion below).

Section 1630.2(r) Direct Threat

Many disability rights groups and individuals with disabilities asserted that the definition of direct threat should not include a reference to the health or safety of the individual with a disability. They expressed concern that the reference to "risk to self" would result in direct threat determinations that are based on negative stereotypes and paternalistic views about what is best for individuals with disabilities. Alternatively, the commenters asked the Commission to clarify that any assessment of risk must be based on the individual's present condition and not on speculation about the individual's future condition. They also asked the Commission to specify evidence other than medical knowledge that may be relevant to the determination of direct threat.

The final regulation retains the reference to the health or safety of the individual with a disability. As the Appendix notes, this is consistent with the legislative history of the ADA and the case law interpreting

section 504 of the Rehabilitation Act.

To clarify the direct threat standard, the Commission has made four revisions to section 1630.2(r). First, the Commission has amended the first sentence of the definition of direct threat to refer to a significant risk of substantial harm that cannot be eliminated "or reduced" by reasonable accommodation. This amendment clarifies that the risk need not be eliminated entirely to fall below the direct threat definition; instead, the risk need only be reduced to the level at which there no longer exists a significant risk of substantial harm. In addition, the Commission has rephrased the second sentence of section 1630.2(r) to clarify that an employer's direct threat standard must apply to all individuals, not just to individuals with disabilities. Further, the Commission has made clear that a direct threat determination must be based on "an individualized assessment of the individual's present ability to safely perform the essential functions of the job." This clarifies that a determination that employment of an individual would pose a direct threat must involve an individualized inquiry and must be based on the individual's current condition. In addition, the Commission has added "the imminence of the potential harm" to the list of factors to be considered when determining whether employment of an individual would pose a direct threat. This change clarifies that both the probability of harm and the imminence of harm are relevant to direct threat determinations. This definition of direct threat is consistent with the legislative history of the Act. *See* Senate Report at 27, House Labor Report at 5657, 7375, House Judiciary Report at 4546.

Further, the Commission has amended the interpretive guidance on section 1630.2(r) to highlight the individualized nature of the direct threat assessment. In addition, the Commission has cited examples of evidence other than medical knowledge that may be relevant to determining whether

employment of an individual would pose a direct threat.

Section 1630.3 Exceptions to the Definitions of "Disability" and "Qualified Individual with a Disability"

Many commenters asked the Commission to clarify that the term "rehabilitation program" includes self-help groups. In response to these comments, the Commission has amended the interpretive guidance in this area to include a reference to professionally recognized self-help programs.

The Commission has added a paragraph to the guidance on section 1630.3 to note that individuals who are not excluded under this provision from the definitions of the terms "disability" and "qualified individual with a disability" must still establish that they meet those definitions to be protected by part 1630. Several employers and employer groups asked the Commission to clarify that individuals are not automatically covered by the ADA simply because they do not fall into one of the exclusions listed in this section.

The proposed interpretive guidance on section 1630.3 noted that employers are entitled to seek reasonable assurances that an individual is not currently engaging in the illegal use of drugs. In that regard, the guidance stated, "It is essential that the individual offer evidence, such as a drug test, to prove that he or she is not currently engaging" in such use. Many commenters interpreted this guidance to require individuals to come forward with evidence even in the absence of a request by the employer. The Commission has revised the interpretive guidance to clarify that such evidence is required only upon request.

1630.6 Contractual or Other Arrangements

The Commission has added a sentence to the first paragraph of the interpretive guidance on section 1630.6 to clarify that this section has no impact on whether one is a covered entity or employer as defined by section 1630.2.

The proposed interpretive guidance on contractual or other relationships noted that section 1630.6 applied to parties on either side of the relationship. To illustrate this point, the guidance stated that "a copier company would be required to ensure the provision of any reasonable accommodation necessary to enable its copier service representative with a disability to service a client's machine." Several employers objected to this example. In that respect, the commenters argued that the language of the example was too broad and could be interpreted as requiring employers to make all customers' premises accessible. The Commission has revised this example to provide a clearer, more concrete indication of the scope of the reasonable accommodation obligations in this area.

In addition, the Commission has clarified the interpretive guidance by noting that the existence of a contractual relationship adds no new obligations "under this part."

1630.8 Relationship or Association With an Individual With a Disability

The Commission has added the phrase "or otherwise discriminate against" to section 1630.8. This change clarifies that harassment or any other form of discrimination against a qualified individual because of the known disability of a person with whom the individual has a relationship or an association is also a prohibited form of discrimination.

The Commission has revised the first sentence of the interpretive guidance to refer to a person's relationship or association with an individual who has a "known" disability. This revision makes the language of the interpretive guidance consistent with the language of the regulation. In addition, to reflect current, preferred terminology, the Commission has substituted the term "people who have AIDS" for the term "AIDS patients." Finally, the Commission has

added a paragraph to clarify that this provision applies to discrimination in other employment privileges and benefits, such as health insurance benefits.

1630.9 Not Making Reasonable Accommodation

Section 1630.9(c) provides that "[a] covered entity shall not be excused from the requirements of this part because of any failure to receive technical assistance...." Some employers asked the Commission to revise this section and to state that the failure to receive technical assistance is a defense to not providing reasonable accommodation. The Commission has not made the requested revision. Section 1630.9(c) is consistent with section 506(e) of the ADA, which states that the failure to receive technical assistance from the federal agencies that administer the ADA does not excuse a covered entity from compliance with the requirements of the Act.

The first paragraph of the interpretive guidance accompanying section 1630.9 notes that the reasonable accommodation obligation does not require employers to provide adjustments or modifications that are primarily for the personal use of the individual with a disability. The Commission has amended this guidance to clarify that employers may be required to provide items that are customarily personal use items where the items are specifically designed or required to meet job-related needs.

In addition, the Commission has amended the interpretive guidance to clarify that there must be a nexus between an individual's disability and the need for accommodation. Thus, the guidance notes that an individual with a disability is "otherwise qualified" if he or she is qualified for the job except that, "because of the disability," the individual needs reasonable accommodation to perform the essential functions of the job. Similarly, the guidance notes that employers are required to accommodate only the physical or mental limitations "resulting from the

disability" that are known to the employer.

In response to commenters' requests for clarification, the Commission has noted that employers may require individuals with disabilities to provide documentation of the need for reasonable accommodation when the need for a requested accommodation is not obvious.

In addition, the Commission has amended the last paragraph of the interpretive guidance on the "Process of Determining the Appropriate Reasonable Accommodation." This amendment clarifies that an employer must consider allowing an individual with a disability to provide his or her own accommodation if the individual wishes to do so. The employer, however, may not require the individual to provide the accommodation.

1630.10 Qualification Standards, Tests, and Other Selection Criteria

The Commission has added the phrase "on the basis of disability" to section 1630.10(a) to clarify that a selection criterion that is not job related and consistent with business necessity violates this section only when it screens out an individual with a disability (or a class of individuals with disabilities) on the basis of disability. That is, there must be a nexus between the exclusion and the disability. A selection criterion that screens out an individual with a disability for reasons that are not related to the disability does not violate this section. The Commission has made similar changes to the interpretive guidance on this section.

Proposed section 1630.10(b) stated that a covered entity could use as a qualification standard the requirement that an individual not pose a direct threat to the health or safety of the individual or others. Many individuals with disabilities objected to the inclusion of the direct threat reference in this section and asked the Commission to clarify that the direct threat standard must be raised by the covered entity as a defense. In that regard, they specifically asked the Commission to move the direct threat provision from section 1630.10 (qualification standards) to section 1630.15 (defenses). The Commission has deleted the direct threat provision from section 1630.10 and has moved it to section 1630.15. This is consistent with section 103 of the ADA, which refers to defenses and states (in section 103(b)) that the term "qualification standards" may include a requirement that an individual not pose a direct threat.

1630.11 Administration of Tests

The Commission has revised the interpretive guidance concerning section 1630.11 to clarify that a request for an alternative test format or other testing accommodation generally should be made prior to the administration of the test or as soon as the individual with a disability becomes aware of the need for accommodation. In addition, the Commission has amended the last paragraph of the guidance on this section to note that an employer can require a written test of an applicant with dyslexia if the ability to read is "the skill the test is designed to measure." This language is consistent with the regulatory language, which refers to the skills a test purports to measure.

Some commenters noted that certain tests are designed to measure the speed with which an applicant performs a function. In response to these comments, the Commission has amended the interpretive guidance to state that an employer may require an applicant to complete a test within a specified time frame if speed is one of the skills being tested.

In response to comments, the Commission has amended the interpretive guidance accompanying section 1630.14(a) to clarify that employers may invite applicants to request accommodations for taking tests. (See section 1630.14(a), below)

1630.12 Retaliation and Coercion

The Commission has amended section 1630.12 to clarify that this section also prohibits harassment.

1630.13 Prohibited Medical Examinations and Inquiries

In response to the Commission's request for comment on certain workers' compensation matters, many commenters addressed whether a covered entity may ask applicants about their history of workers' compensation claims. Many employers and employer groups argued that an inquiry about an individual's workers' compensation history is job related and consistent with business necessity. Disability rights groups and individuals with disabilities, however, asserted that such an inquiry could disclose the existence of a disability. In response to comments and to clarify this matter, the Commission has amended the interpretive guidance accompanying section 1630.13(a). The amendment states that an employer may not inquire about an individual's workers' compensation history at the preoffer stage.

The Commission has made a technical change to section 1630.13(b) by deleting the phrase "unless the examination or inquiry is shown to be job-related and consistent with business necessity" from the section. This change does not affect the substantive provisions of section 1630.13(b). The Commission has incorporated the job-relatedness and business necessity requirement into a new section 1630.14(c), which clarifies the scope of permissible examinations or inquiries of employees. (See section 1630.14(c), below.)

1630.14 Medical Examinations and Inquiries Specifically Permitted

Section 1630.14(a) Acceptable Pre-employment Inquiry

Proposed section 1630.14(a) stated that a covered entity may make pre-employment inquiries into an applicant's ability to

perform job-related functions. The interpretive guidance accompanying this section noted that an employer may ask an individual whether he or she can perform a job function with or without reasonable accommodation.

Many employers asked the Commission to provide additional guidance in this area. Specifically, the commenters asked whether an employer may ask how an individual will perform a job function when the individual's known disability appears to interfere with or prevent performance of job-related functions. To clarify this matter, the Commission has amended section 1630.14(a) to state that a covered entity "may ask an applicant to describe or to demonstrate how, with or without reasonable accommodation, the applicant will be able to perform job-related functions." The Commission has amended the interpretive guidance accompanying section 1630.14(a) to reflect this change.

Many commenters asked the Commission to state that employers may inquire, before tests are taken, whether candidates will require any reasonable accommodations to take the tests. They asked the Commission to acknowledge that such inquiries constitute permissible pre-employment inquiries. In response to these comments, the Commission has added a new paragraph to the interpretive guidance on section 1630.14(a). This paragraph clarifies that employers may ask candidates to inform them of the need for reasonable accommodation within a reasonable time before the administration of the test and may request documentation verifying the need for accommodation.

The Commission has received many comments from law enforcement and other public safety agencies concerning the administration of physical agility tests. In response to those comments, the Commission has added a new paragraph clarifying that such tests are not medical examinations.

Many employers and employer groups have asked

the Commission to discuss whether employers may invite applicants to self-identify as individuals with disabilities. In that regard, many of the commenters noted that Section 503 of the Rehabilitation Act imposes certain obligations on government contractors. The interpretive guidance accompanying sections 1630.1(b) and (c) notes that "title I of the ADA would not be a defense to failing to collect information required to satisfy the affirmative action requirements of Section 503 of the Rehabilitation Act." To reiterate this point, the Commission has amended the interpretive guidance accompanying section 1630.14(a) to note specifically that this section does not restrict employers from collecting information and inviting individuals to identify themselves as individuals with disabilities as required to satisfy the affirmative action requirements of Section 503 of the Rehabilitation Act.

Section 1630.14(b) Employment Entrance Examinations

Section 1630.14(b) has been amended to include the phrase "(and/or inquiry)" after references to medical examinations. Some commenters were concerned that the regulation as drafted prohibited covered entities from making any medical inquiries or administering questionnaires that did not constitute examinations. This change clarifies that the term "employment entrance examinations" includes medical inquiries as well as medical examinations.

Section 1630.14(b)(2) has been revised to state that the results of employment entrance examinations "shall not be used for any purpose inconsistent with this part." This language is consistent with the language used in section 1630.14(c)(2).

The second paragraph of the proposed interpretive guidance on this section referred to "relevant" physical and psychological criteria. Some commenters questioned the use of the term "relevant" and expressed concern about its meaning. The Commission has

deleted this term from the paragraph.

Many commenters addressed the confidentiality provisions of this section. They noted that it may be necessary to disclose medical information in defense of workers' compensation claims or during the course of other legal proceedings. In addition, they pointed out that the workers' compensation offices of many states request such information for the administration of second-injury funds or for other administrative purposes.

The Commission has revised the last paragraph of the interpretive guidance on section 1630.14(b) to reflect that the information obtained during a permitted employment entrance examination or inquiry may be used only "in a manner not inconsistent with this part." In addition, the Commission has added language clarifying that it is permissible to submit the information to state workers' compensation offices.

Several commenters asked the Commission to clarify whether information obtained from employment entrance examinations and inquiries may be used for insurance purposes. In response to these comments, the Commission has noted in the interpretive guidance that such information may be used for insurance purposes described in section 1630.16(f).

Section 1630.14(c) Examination of Employees

The Commission has added a new section 1630.14(c), Examination of employees, that clarifies the scope of permissible medical examinations and inquiries. Several employers and employer groups expressed concern that the proposed version of part 1630 did not make it clear that covered entities may require employee medical examinations, such as fitness-for-duty examinations, that are job related and consistent with business necessity. New section 1630.14(c) clarifies this by expressly permitting covered entities to require employee medical examinations and inquiries that are job related

and consistent with business necessity. The information obtained from such examinations or inquiries must be treated as a confidential medical record. This section also incorporates the last sentence of proposed section 1630.14(c). The remainder of proposed section 1630.14(c) has become section 1630.14(d).

To comport with this technical change in the regulation, the Commission has made corresponding changes in the interpretive guidance. Thus, the Commission has moved the second paragraph of the proposed guidance on section 1630.13(b) to the guidance on section 1630.14(c). In addition, the Commission has reworded the paragraph to note that this provision permits (rather than does not prohibit) certain medical examinations and inquiries.

Some commenters asked the Commission to clarify whether employers may make inquiries or require medical examinations in connection with the reasonable accommodation process. The Commission has noted in the interpretive guidance that such inquiries and examinations are permissible when they are necessary to the reasonable accommodation process described in this part.

1630.15 Defenses

The Commission has added a sentence to the interpretive guidance on section 1630.15(a) to clarify that the assertion that an insurance plan does not cover an individual's disability or that the disability would cause increased insurance or workers' compensation costs does not constitute a legitimate, nondiscriminatory reason for disparate treatment of an individual with a disability. This clarification, made in response to many comments from individuals with disabilities and disability rights groups, is consistent with the legislative history of the ADA. *See* Senate Report at 85; House Labor Report at 136; House Judiciary Report at 71.

The Commission has amended section 1630.15(b) by stating that the term "qualification standard" may include a requirement that an individual not pose a direct threat. As noted above, this is consistent with section 103 of the ADA and responds to many comments from individuals with disabilities.

The Commission has made a technical correction to section 1630.15(c) by changing the phrase "an individual or class of individuals with disabilities" to "an individual with a disability or a class of individuals with disabilities."

Several employers and employer groups asked the Commission to acknowledge that undue hardship considerations about reasonable accommodations at temporary work sites may be different from the considerations relevant to permanent work sites. In response to these comments, the Commission has amended the interpretive guidance on section 1630.15(d) to note that an accommodation that poses an undue hardship in a particular job setting, such as a temporary construction site, may not pose an undue hardship in another setting. This guidance is consistent with the legislative history of the ADA. *See* House Labor Report at 69-70; House Judiciary Report at 41-42.

The Commission also has amended the interpretive guidance to note that the terms of a collective bargaining agreement may be relevant to the determination of whether a requested accommodation would pose an undue hardship on the operation of a covered entity's business. This amendment, which responds to commenters' requests that the Commission recognize the relevancy of collective bargaining agreements, is consistent with the legislative history of the Act. *See* Senate Report at 32; House Labor Report at 63.

Section 1630.2(p)(2)(v) provides that the impact of an accommodation on the ability of other employees to perform their duties is one of the factors to be considered when determining whether the accommodation would impose an undue hardship on a covered

entity. Many commenters addressed whether an accommodation's impact on the morale of other employees may be relevant to a determination of undue hardship. Some employers and employer groups asserted that a negative impact on employee morale should be considered an undue hardship. Disability rights groups and individuals with disabilities, however, argued that undue hardship determinations must not be based on the morale of other employees. It is the Commission's view that a negative effect on morale, by itself, is not sufficient to meet the undue hardship standard. Accordingly, the Commission has noted in the guidance on section 1630.15(d) that an employer cannot establish undue hardship by showing only that an accommodation would have a negative impact on employee morale.

1630.16 Specific Activities Permitted

The Commission has revised the second sentence of the interpretive guidance on section 1630.16(b) to state that an employer may hold individuals with alcoholism and individuals who engage in the illegal use of drugs to the same performance and conduct standards to which it holds "all of its" other employees. In addition, the Commission has deleted the term "otherwise" from the third sentence of the guidance. These revisions clarify that employers may hold all employees, disabled (including those disabled by alcoholism or drug addiction) and nondisabled, to the same performance and conduct standards.

Many commenters asked the Commission to clarify that the drug testing provisions of section 1630.16(c) pertain only to tests to determine the illegal use of drugs. Accordingly, the Commission has amended section 1630.16(c)(1) to refer to the administration of "such" drug tests and section 1630.16(c)(3) to refer to information obtained from a "test to determine the illegal use of drugs." We have also

made a change in the grammatical structure of the last sentence of section 1630.16(c)(1). We have made similar changes to the corresponding section of the interpretive guidance. In addition, the Commission has amended the interpretive guidance to state that such tests are neither encouraged, "authorized," nor prohibited. This amendment conforms the language of the guidance to the language of section 1630.16(c)(1).

The Commission has revised section 1630.16(e)(1) to refer to communicable diseases that "are" (rather than "may be") transmitted through the handling of food. Several commenters asked the Commission to make this technical change, which adopts the statutory language.

Several commenters also asked the Commission to conform the language of proposed sections 1630.16(f)(1) and (2) to the language of sections 501(c)(1) and (2) of the Act. The Commission has made this change. Thus, sections 1630.16(f)(1) and (2) now refer to risks that are "not inconsistent with State law."

Executive Order 12291 and Regulatory Flexibility Act

The Commission published a Preliminary Regulatory Impact Analysis on February 28, 1991 (56 FR 8578). Based on the Preliminary Regulatory Impact Analysis, the Commission certifies that this final rule will not have a significant economic impact on a substantial number of small business entities. The Commission is issuing this final rule at this time in the absence of a Final Regulatory Impact Analysis in order to meet the statutory deadline. The Commission's Preliminary Regulatory Impact Analysis was based upon existing data on the costs of reasonable accommodation. The Commission received few comments on this aspect of its rulemaking. Because of the complexity inherent in assessing the economic costs and benefits of this rule and the relative paucity of data on this issue, the Commission will further study the economic impact of the regulation and intends to issue a Final Regulatory Impact Analysis prior to January 1, 1992. As indicated above, the Preliminary Regulatory Impact Analysis was published on February 28, 1991 (56 F.R. 8578) for comment. The Commission will also provide a copy to the public upon request by calling the Commission's Office of Communications and Legislative Affairs at (202) 663-4900. Commenters are urged to provide additional information as to the costs and benefits associated with this rule. This will further facilitate the development of a Final Regulatory Impact Analysis. Comments must be received by September 26, 1991. Written comments should be submitted to Frances M. Hart, Executive Officer, Executive Secretariat, Equal Employment Opportunity Commission, 1801 "L" Street, NW, Washington, D.C. 20507.

As a convenience to commenters, the Executive Secretariat will accept public comments transmitted by facsimile ("FAX") machine. The telephone number of the FAX receiver is (202) 663-4114. (This is not a toll-free number). Only public comments of six or fewer pages will be accepted via FAX transmittal. This limitation is necessary in order to assure access to the equipment. Comments sent by FAX in excess of six pages will not be accepted. Receipt of FAX transmittals will not be acknowledged, except that the sender may request confirmation of receipt by calling the Executive Secretariat Staff at (202) 663-4078. (This is not a toll-free number).

Comments received will be available for public inspection in the EEOC Library, room 6502, by appointment only, from 9 a.m. to 5 p.m., Monday through Friday except legal holidays from October 15, 1991, until the Final Regulatory Impact Analysis is published. Persons who need assistance to review the comments will be provided with appropriate aids such as readers or print magnifiers. To schedule an appointment call

(202) 663-4630 (voice), (202) 663-4630 (TDD).

List of Subjects in 29 CFR Part 1630

Equal employment opportunity, Handicapped, Individuals with disabilities.

For the Commission,

Evan J. Kemp, Jr.
Chairman.

Accordingly, 29 CFR Chapter XIV is amended by adding part 1630 to read as follows:

PART 1630 REGULATIONS TO IMPLEMENT THE EQUAL EMPLOYMENT PROVISIONS OF THE AMERICANS WITH DISABILITIES ACT

Sec.

1630.1   Purpose, applicability, and construction.
1630.2   Definitions.
1630.3   Exceptions to the definitions of "Disability" and "Qualified Individual with a Disability."
1630.4   Discrimination prohibited.
1630.5   Limiting, segregating, and classifying.
1630.6   Contractual or other arrangements.
1630.7   Standards, criteria, or methods of administration.
1630.8   Relationship or association with an individual with a disability.
1630.9   Not making reasonable accommodation.
1630.10   Qualification standards, tests, and other selection criteria.
1630.11   Administration of tests.
1630.12   Retaliation and coercion.
1630.13   Prohibited medical examinations and inquiries.
1630.14   Medical examinations and inquiries specifically permitted.
1630.15   Defenses.
1630.16   Specific activities permitted.
Appendix to part 1630   Interpretive Guidance on Title I of the Americans with Disabilities Act.
Authority: 42 U.S.C. 12116.

§ 1630.1 Purpose, applicability, and construction.

(a) *Purpose.* The purpose of this part is to implement title I of the Americans with Disabilities Act (42 U.S.C. 12101, *et seq.*) (ADA), requiring equal employment opportunities for qualified individuals

with disabilities, and sections 3(2), 3(3), 501, 503, 506(e), 508, 510, and 511 of the ADA as those sections pertain to the employment of qualified individuals with disabilities.

(b) *Applicability.* This part applies to "covered entities" as defined at section 1630.2(b).

(c) *Construction.*

(1) *In general.* Except as otherwise provided in this part, this part does not apply a lesser standard than the standards applied under title V of the Rehabilitation Act of 1973 (29 U.S.C. 790 794a), or the regulations issued by Federal agencies pursuant to that title.

(2) *Relationship to other laws.* This part does not invalidate or limit the remedies, rights, and procedures of any Federal law or law of any State or political subdivision of any State or jurisdiction that provides greater or equal protection for the rights of individuals with disabilities than are afforded by this part.

§ 1630.2 Definitions.

(a) *Commission* means the Equal Employment Opportunity Commission established by Section 705 of the Civil Rights Act of 1964 (42 U.S.C. 2000e-4).

(b) *Covered Entity* means an employer, employment agency, labor organization, or joint labor management committee.

(c) *Person, labor organization, employment agency, commerce and industry affecting commerce* shall have the same meaning given those terms in Section 701 of the Civil Rights Act of 1964 (42 U.S.C. 2000e).

(d) *State* means each of the several States, the District of Columbia, the Commonwealth of Puerto Rico, Guam, American Samoa, the Virgin Islands, the Trust Territory of the Pacific Islands, and the Commonwealth of the Northern Mariana Islands.

(e) *Employer.* --

(1) *In general.* The term "employer" means a person engaged in an industry affecting commerce who has 15 or more employees for each working day in each of 20 or more

calendar weeks in the current or preceding calendar year, and any agent of such person, except that, from July 26, 1992 through July 25, 1994, an employer means a person engaged in an industry affecting commerce who has 25 or more employees for each working day in each of 20 or more calendar weeks in the current or preceding year and any agent of such person.

(2) *Exceptions.* The term employer does not include -

(i) the United States, a corporation wholly owned by the government of the United States, or an Indian tribe; or

(ii) a bona fide private membership club (other than a labor organization) that is exempt from taxation under Section 501(c) of the Internal Revenue Code of 1986.

(f) *Employee* means an individual employed by an employer.

(g) *Disability* means, with respect to an individual --

(1) a physical or mental impairment that substantially limits one or more of the major life activities of such individual;

(2) a record of such an impairment; or

(3) being regarded as having such an impairment. (See section 1630.3 for exceptions to this definition).

(h) *Physical or mental impairment* means:

(1) Any physiological disorder, or condition, cosmetic disfigurement, or anatomical loss affecting one or more of the following body systems: neurological, musculoskeletal, special sense organs, respiratory (including speech organs), cardiovascular, reproductive, digestive, genitourinary, hemic and lymphatic, skin, and endocrine; or

(2) Any mental or psychological disorder, such as mental retardation, organic brain syndrome, emotional or mental illness, and specific learning disabilities.

(i) *Major Life Activities* means functions such as caring for oneself, performing manual tasks, walking, seeing, hearing, speaking, breathing, learning, and working.

(j) *Substantially limits.* --

(1) The term *substantially limits* means:

(i) Unable to perform a major life activity that the average person in the general population can perform; or

(ii) Significantly restricted as to the condition, manner or duration under which an individual can perform a particular major life activity as compared to the condition, manner, or duration under which the average person in the general population can perform that same major life activity.

(2) The following factors should be considered in determining whether an individual is substantially limited in a major life activity:

(i) The nature and severity of the impairment;

(ii) The duration or expected duration of the impairment; and

(iii) The permanent or long term impact, or the expected permanent or long term impact of or resulting from the impairment.

(3) With respect to the major life activity of *working* --

(i) The term *substantially limits* means significantly restricted in the ability to perform either a class of jobs or a broad range of jobs in various classes as compared to the average person having comparable training, skills and abilities. The inability to perform a single, particular job does not constitute a substantial limitation in the major life activity of working.

(ii) In addition to the factors listed in paragraph (j)(2) of this section, the following factors may be considered in determining whether an individual is substantially limited in the major life activity of "working":

(A) The geographical area to which the individual has reasonable access;

(B) The job from which the individual has been disqualified because of an impairment, and the number and types of jobs utilizing similar training, knowledge, skills or abilities, within that geographical area, from which the individual is also disqualified because of the impairment (class of jobs); and/or

(C) The job from which the individual has been disqualified because of an impairment, and

the number and types of other jobs not utilizing similar training, knowledge, skills or abilities, within that geographical area, from which the individual is also disqualified because of the impairment (broad range of jobs in various classes).

(k) *Has a record of such impairment* means has a history of, or has been misclassified as having, a mental or physical impairment that substantially limits one or more major life activities.

(l) *Is regarded as having such an impairment* means:

(1) Has a physical or mental impairment that does not substantially limit major life activities but is treated by a covered entity as constituting such limitation;

(2) Has a physical or mental impairment that substantially limits major life activities only as a result of the attitudes of others toward such impairment; or

(3) Has none of the impairments defined in paragraphs (h)(1) or (2) of this section but is treated by a covered entity as having a substantially limiting impairment.

(m) *Qualified individual with a disability* means an individual with a disability who satisfies the requisite skill, experience, education and other job-related requirements of the employment position such individual holds or desires, and who, with or without reasonable accommodation, can perform the essential functions of such position. (See section 1630.3 for exceptions to this definition).

(n) *Essential functions.* --

(1) *In general.* The term *essential functions* means the fundamental job duties of the employment position the individual with a disability holds or desires. The term "essential functions" does not include the marginal functions of the position.

(2) A job function may be considered essential for any of several reasons, including but not limited to the following:

(i) The function may be essential because the reason the position exists is to perform that function;

(ii) The function may be essential because of the limited number of employees available among whom the performance of that job function can be distributed; and/or

(iii) The function may be highly specialized so that the incumbent in the position is hired for his or her expertise or ability to perform the particular function.

(3) Evidence of whether a particular function is essential includes, but is not limited to:

(i) The employer's judgment as to which functions are essential;

(ii) Written job descriptions prepared before advertising or interviewing applicants for the job;

(iii) The amount of time spent on the job performing the function;

(iv) The consequences of not requiring the incumbent to perform the function;

(v) The terms of a collective bargaining agreement;

(vi) The work experience of past incumbents in the job; and/or

(vii) The current work experience of incumbents in similar jobs.

(o) *Reasonable accommodation.* --

(1) The term *reasonable accommodation* means:

(i) Modifications or adjustments to a job application process that enable a qualified applicant with a disability to be considered for the position such qualified applicant desires; or

(ii) Modifications or adjustments to the work environment, or to the manner or circumstances under which the position held or desired is customarily performed, that enable a qualified individual with a disability to perform the essential functions of that position; or

(iii) Modifications or adjustments that enable a covered entity's employee with a disability to enjoy equal benefits and privileges of employment as are enjoyed by its other similarly situated employees without disabilities.

(2) *Reasonable accommodation* may include but is not limited to:

(i) Making existing facilities used by employees readily accessible to and usable by individuals with disabilities; and

(ii) Job restructuring; part-time or modified work schedules; reassignment to a vacant position; acquisition or modifications of equipment or devices; appropriate adjustment or modifications of examinations, training materials, or policies; the provision of qualified readers or interpreters; and other similar accommodations for individuals with disabilities.

(3) To determine the appropriate reasonable accommodation it may be necessary for the covered entity to initiate an informal, interactive process with the qualified individual with a disability in need of the accommodation. This process should identify the precise limitations resulting from the disability and potential reasonable accommodations that could overcome those limitations.

(p) *Undue hardship.* --

(1) *In general.* "Undue hardship" means, with respect to the provision of an accommodation, significant difficulty or expense incurred by a covered entity, when considered in light of the factors set forth in paragraph (p)(2) of this section.

(2) *Factors to be considered.* In determining whether an accommodation would impose an undue hardship on a covered entity, factors to be considered include:

(i) The nature and net cost of the accommodation needed under this part, taking into consideration the availability of tax credits and deductions, and/or outside funding;

(ii) The overall financial resources of the facility or facilities involved in the provision of the reasonable accommodation, the number of persons employed at such facility, and the effect on expenses and resources;

(iii) The overall financial resources of the covered entity, the overall size of the business of the covered entity with respect to the number of its employees, and the number, type and location of its facilities;

(iv) The type of operation or operations of the covered entity, including the composition, structure and functions of the workforce of such entity, and the geographic separateness and administrative or fiscal relationship of the facility or facilities in question to the covered entity; and

(v) The impact of the accommodation upon the operation of the facility, including the impact on the ability of other employees to perform their duties and the impact on the facility's ability to conduct business.

(q) *Qualification standards* means the personal and professional attributes including the skill, experience, education, physical, medical, safety and other requirements established by a covered entity as requirements which an individual must meet in order to be eligible for the position held or desired.

(r) *Direct Threat* means a significant risk of substantial harm to the health or safety of the individual or others that cannot be eliminated or reduced by reasonable accommodation. The determination that an individual poses a "direct threat" shall be based on an individualized assessment of the individual's present ability to safely perform the essential functions of the job. This assessment shall be based on a reasonable medical judgment that relies on the most current medical knowledge and/or on the best available objective evidence. In determining whether an individual would pose a direct threat, the factors to be considered include:

(1) The duration of the risk;

(2) The nature and severity of the potential harm;

(3) The likelihood that the potential harm will occur; and

(4) The imminence of the potential harm.

§ 1630.3 Exceptions to the definitions of "disability" and "qualified individual with a disability."

(a) The terms *disability* and *qualified individual with a disability* do not include individuals currently engaging in the illegal use of drugs, when the covered entity acts on the basis of such use.

(1) *Drug* means a controlled substance, as defined in schedules I through V of Section 202 of the Controlled Substances Act (21 U.S.C 812).

(2) *Illegal use of drugs* means the use of drugs the possession or distribution of which is unlawful under the Controlled Substances Act, as periodically updated by the Food and Drug Administration. This term does not include the use of a drug taken under the supervision of a licensed health care professional, or other uses authorized by the Controlled Substances Act or other provisions of Federal law.

(b) However, the terms *disability* and *qualified* individual with a disability may not exclude an individual who:

(1) Has successfully completed a supervised drug rehabilitation program and is no longer engaging in the illegal use of drugs, or has otherwise been rehabilitated successfully and is no longer engaging in the illegal use of drugs; or

(2) Is participating in a supervised rehabilitation program and is no longer engaging in such use; or

(3) Is erroneously regarded as engaging in such use, but is not engaging in such use.

(c) It shall not be a violation of this part for a covered entity to adopt or administer reasonable policies or procedures, including but not limited to drug testing, designed to ensure that an individual described in paragraph (b)(1) or (2) of this section is no longer engaging in the illegal use of drugs. (See section 1630.16(c) Drug testing).

(d) *Disability* does not include:

(1) Transvestism, transsexualism, pedophilia, exhibitionism, voyeurism, gender identity disorders not resulting from physical impairments, or other sexual behavior disorders;

(2) Compulsive gambling, kleptomania, or pyromania; or

(3) Psychoactive substance use disorders resulting from current illegal use of drugs.

(e) *Homosexuality and bisexuality* are not impairments and so are not disabilities as defined in this part.

§ 1630.4 Discrimination prohibited.

It is unlawful for a covered entity to discriminate on the basis of disability against a qualified individual with a disability in regard to:

(a) Recruitment, advertising, and job application procedures;

(b) Hiring, upgrading, promotion, award of tenure, demotion, transfer, layoff, termination, right of return from layoff, and rehiring;

(c) Rates of pay or any other form of compensation and changes in compensation;

(d) Job assignments, job classifications, organizational structures, position descriptions, lines of progression, and seniority lists;

(e) Leaves of absence, sick leave, or any other leave;

(f) Fringe benefits available by virtue of employment, whether or not administered by the covered entity;

(g) Selection and financial support for training, including: apprenticeships, professional meetings, conferences and other related activities, and selection for leaves of absence to pursue training;

(h) Activities sponsored by a covered entity including social and recreational programs; and

(i) Any other term, condition, or privilege of employment.

The term *discrimination* includes, but is not limited to, the acts described in sections 1630.5 through 1630.13 of this part.

§ 1630.5 Limiting, segregating, and classifying.

It is unlawful for a covered entity to limit, segregate, or classify a job applicant or employee in a way that adversely affects his or her employment opportunities or status on the basis of disability.

§ 1630.6 Contractual or other arrangements.

(a) *In general.* It is unlawful for a covered entity to participate in a contractual or other arrangement or relationship that has the effect of subjecting the covered entity's own qualified applicant or employee with a disability to the discrimination prohibited by this part.

(b) *Contractual or other arrangement defined.* The phrase "contractual or other arrangement or relationship" includes, but is not limited to, a relationship with an employment or referral agency; labor union, including collective bargaining agreements; an organization providing fringe benefits to an employee of the covered entity; or an organization providing training and apprenticeship programs.

(c) *Application.* This section applies to a covered entity, with respect to its own applicants or employees, whether the entity offered the contract or initiated the relationship, or whether the entity accepted the contract or acceded to the relationship. A covered entity is not liable for the actions of the other party or parties to the contract which only affect that other party's employees or applicants.

§ 1630.7 Standards, criteria, or methods of administration.

It is unlawful for a covered entity to use standards, criteria, or methods of administration, which are not job-related and consistent with business necessity, and:

(a) That have the effect of discriminating on the basis of disability; or

(b) That perpetuate the discrimination of others who are subject to common administrative control.

§ 1630.8 Relationship or association with an individual with a disability.

It is unlawful for a covered entity to exclude or deny equal jobs or benefits to, or otherwise discriminate against, a qualified individual because of the known disability of an individual with whom the qualified individual is known to have a family, business, social or other relationship or association.

§ 1630.9 Not making reasonable accommodation.

(a) It is unlawful for a covered entity not to make reasonable accommodation to the known physical or mental limitations of an otherwise qualified applicant or employee with a disability, unless such covered entity can demonstrate that the accommodation would impose an undue hardship on the operation of its business.

(b) It is unlawful for a covered entity to deny employment opportunities to an otherwise qualified job applicant or employee with a disability based on the need of such covered entity to make reasonable accommodation to such individual's physical or mental impairments.

(c) A covered entity shall not be excused from the requirements of this part because of any failure to receive technical assistance authorized by section 506 of the ADA, including any failure in the development or dissemination of any technical assistance manual authorized by that Act.

(d) A qualified individual with a disability is not required to accept an accommodation, aid, service, opportunity or benefit which such qualified individual chooses not to accept. However, if such individual rejects a reasonable accommodation, aid, service, opportunity or benefit that is necessary to enable the individual to perform the essential functions of the position held or desired, and cannot, as a result of that rejection, perform the essential functions of the position, the individual will not be considered a qualified individual with a disability.

§ 1630.10 Qualification standards, tests, and other selection criteria.

It is unlawful for a covered entity to use qualification standards, employment tests or other selection criteria that

screen out or tend to screen out an individual with a disability or a class of individuals with disabilities, on the basis of disability, unless the standard, test or other selection criteria, as used by the covered entity, is shown to be job-related for the position in question and is consistent with business necessity.

§ 1630.11 Administration of tests.

It is unlawful for a covered entity to fail to select and administer tests concerning employment in the most effective manner to ensure that, when a test is administered to a job applicant or employee who has a disability that impairs sensory, manual or speaking skills, the test results accurately reflect the skills, aptitude, or whatever other factor of the applicant or employee that the test purports to measure, rather than reflecting the impaired sensory, manual, or speaking skills of such employee or applicant (except where such skills are the factors that the test purports to measure).

§ 1630.12 Retaliation and coercion.

(a) Retaliation. It is unlawful to discriminate against any individual because that individual has opposed any act or practice made unlawful by this part or because that individual made a charge, testified, assisted, or participated in any manner in an investigation, proceeding, or hearing to enforce any provision contained in this part.

(b) Coercion, interference or intimidation. It is unlawful to coerce, intimidate, threaten, harass or interfere with any individual in the exercise or enjoyment of, or because that individual aided or encouraged any other individual in the exercise of, any right granted or protected by this part.

§ 1630.13 Prohibited medical examinations and inquiries.

(a) Pre-employment examination or inquiry. Except as permitted by section 1630.14, it is unlawful for a covered entity

to conduct a medical examination of an applicant or to make inquiries as to whether an applicant is an individual with a disability or as to the nature or severity of such disability.

(b) Examination or inquiry of employees. Except as permitted by section 1630.14, it is unlawful for a covered entity to require a medical examination of an employee or to make inquiries as to whether an employee is an individual with a disability or as to the nature or severity of such disability.

§ 1630.14 Medical examinations and inquiries specifically permitted.

(a) Acceptable pre-employment inquiry. A covered entity may make pre-employment inquiries into the ability of an applicant to perform job-related functions, and/or may ask an applicant to describe or to demonstrate how, with or without reasonable accommodation, the applicant will be able to perform job-related functions.

(b) Employment entrance examination. A covered entity may require a medical examination (and/or inquiry) after making an offer of employment to a job applicant and before the applicant begins his or her employment duties, and may condition an offer of employment on the results of such examination (and/or inquiry), if all entering employees in the same job category are subjected to such an examination (and/or inquiry) regardless of disability.

(1) Information obtained under paragraph (b) of this section regarding the medical condition or history of the applicant shall be collected and maintained on separate forms and in separate medical files and be treated as a confidential medical record, except that:

(i) Supervisors and managers may be informed regarding necessary restrictions on the work or duties of the employee and necessary accommodations;

(ii) First aid and safety personnel may be informed, when appropriate, if the disability might require emergency treatment; and

(iii) Government officials investigating compliance with this part shall be provided relevant information on request.

(2) The results of such examination shall not be used for any purpose inconsistent with this part.

(3) Medical examinations conducted in accordance with this section do not have to be job-related and consistent with business necessity. However, if certain criteria are used to screen out an employee or employees with disabilities as a result of such an examination or inquiry, the exclusionary criteria must be job-related and consistent with business necessity, and performance of the essential job functions cannot be accomplished with reasonable accommodation as required in this part. (See section 1630.15(b) Defenses to charges of discriminatory application of selection criteria).

(c) *Examination of Employees.* A covered entity may require a medical examination (and/or inquiry) of an employee that is job-related and consistent with business necessity. A covered entity may make inquiries into the ability of an employee to perform job-related functions.

(1) Information obtained under paragraph (c) of this section regarding the medical condition or history of any employee shall be collected and maintained on separate forms and in separate medical files and be treated as a confidential medical record, except that:

(i) Supervisors and managers may be informed regarding necessary restrictions on the work or duties of the employee and necessary accommodations;

(ii) First aid and safety personnel may be informed, when appropriate, if the disability might require emergency treatment; and

(iii) Government officials investigating compliance with this part shall be provided relevant information on request.

(2) Information obtained under paragraph (c) of this section regarding the medical condition or history of any employee shall not be used for

any purpose inconsistent with this part.

(d) *Other Acceptable Examinations and Inquiries.* A covered entity may conduct voluntary medical examinations and activities, including voluntary medical histories, which are part of an employee health program available to employees at the work site.

(1) Information obtained under paragraph (d) of this section regarding the medical condition or history of any employee shall be collected and maintained on separate forms and in separate medical files and be treated as a confidential medical record, except that:

(i) Supervisors and managers may be informed regarding necessary restrictions on the work or duties of the employee and necessary accommodations;

(ii) First aid and safety personnel may be informed, when appropriate, if the disability might require emergency treatment; and

(iii) Government officials investigating compliance with this part shall be provided relevant information on request.

(2) Information obtained under paragraph (d) of this section regarding the medical condition or history of any employee shall not be used for any purpose inconsistent with this part.

§ 1630.15 Defenses.

Defenses to an allegation of discrimination under this part may include, but are not limited to, the following:

(a) *Disparate treatment charges.* It may be a defense to a charge of disparate treatment brought under sections 1630.4 through 1630.8 and 1630.11 through 1630.12 that the challenged action is justified by a legitimate, nondiscriminatory reason.

(b) *Charges of discriminatory application of selection criteria.* --

(1) *In general.* It may be a defense to a charge of discrimination, as described in section 1630.10, that an alleged application of qualification standards, tests, or selection criteria that screens out or tends to screen out or otherwise

denies a job or benefit to an individual with a disability has been shown to be job-related and consistent with business necessity, and such performance cannot be accomplished with reasonable accommodation, as required in this part.

(2) *Direct threat as a qualification standard.* The term "qualification standard" may include a requirement that an individual shall not pose a direct threat to the health or safety of the individual or others in the workplace. (See section 1630.2(r) defining direct threat).

(c) *Other disparate impact charges.* It may be a defense to a charge of discrimination brought under this part that a uniformly applied standard, criterion, or policy has a disparate impact on an individual with a disability or a class of individuals with disabilities that the challenged standard, criterion or policy has been shown to be job-related and consistent with business necessity, and such performance cannot be accomplished with reasonable accommodation, as required in this part.

(d) *Charges of not making reasonable accommodation.* It may be a defense to a charge of discrimination, as described in section 1630.9, that a requested or necessary accommodation would impose an undue hardship on the operation of the covered entity's business.

(e) *Conflict with other federal laws.* It may be a defense to a charge of discrimination under this part that a challenged action is required or necessitated by another Federal law or regulation, or that another Federal law or regulation prohibits an action (including the provision of a particular reasonable accommodation) that would otherwise be required by this part.

(f) *Additional defenses.* It may be a defense to a charge of discrimination under this part that the alleged discriminatory action is specifically permitted by sections 1630.14 or 1630.16.

§ 1630.16 Specific activities permitted.

(a) *Religious entities.* A religious corporation, association, educational institution, or society is permitted to give preference in employment to individuals of a particular religion to perform work connected with the carrying on by that corporation, association, educational institution, or society of its activities. A religious entity may require that all applicants and employees conform to the religious tenets of such organization. However, a religious entity may not discriminate against a qualified individual, who satisfies the permitted religious criteria, because of his or her disability.

(b) *Regulation of alcohol and drugs.* A covered entity:

(1) May prohibit the illegal use of drugs and the use of alcohol at the workplace by all employees;

(2) May require that employees not be under the influence of alcohol or be engaging in the illegal use of drugs at the workplace;

(3) May require that all employees behave in conformance with the requirements established under the Drug-Free Workplace Act of 1988 (41 U.S.C. 701 et seq.);

(4) May hold an employee who engages in the illegal use of drugs or who is an alcoholic to the same qualification standards for employment or job performance and behavior to which the entity holds its other employees, even if any unsatisfactory performance or behavior is related to the employee's drug use or alcoholism;

(5) May require that its employees employed in an industry subject to such regulations comply with the standards established in the regulations (if any) of the Departments of Defense and Transportation, and of the Nuclear Regulatory Commission, regarding alcohol and the illegal use of drugs; and

(6) May require that employees employed in sensitive positions comply with the regulations (if any) of the Departments of Defense and Transportation and of the Nuclear Regulatory Commission that apply to employment in sensitive positions subject to such regulations.

(c) *Drug testing.* --

(1) *General policy.* For purposes of this part, a test to determine the illegal use of drugs is not considered a medical examination. Thus, the administration of such drug tests by a covered entity to its job applicants or employees is not a violation of section 1630.13 of this part. However, this part does not encourage, prohibit, or authorize a covered entity to conduct drug tests of job applicants or employees to determine the illegal use of drugs or to make employment decisions based on such test results.

(2) *Transportation Employees.* This part does not encourage, prohibit, or authorize the otherwise lawful exercise by entities subject to the jurisdiction of the Department of Transportation of authority to:

(i) Test employees of entities in, and applicants for, positions involving safety sensitive duties for the illegal use of drugs or for on duty impairment by alcohol; and

(ii) Remove from safety sensitive positions persons who test positive for illegal use of drugs or on duty impairment by alcohol pursuant to paragraph (c)(2)(i) of this section.

(3) *Confidentiality.* Any information regarding the medical condition or history of any employee or applicant obtained from a test to determine the illegal use of drugs, except information regarding the illegal use of drugs, is subject to the requirements of section 1630.14(b)(2) and (3) of this part.

(d) *Regulation of smoking.* A covered entity may prohibit or impose restrictions on smoking in places of employment. Such restrictions do not violate any provision of this part.

(e) *Infectious and communicable diseases; food handling jobs.*--

(1) *In general.* Under title I of the ADA, section 103(d)(1), the Secretary of Health and Human Services is to prepare a list, to be updated annually, of infectious and communicable diseases which are transmitted through the handling of food. If an individual with a disability is disabled by one of the infectious or communicable diseases included on this list, and if the risk of transmitting the disease associated with the handling of food cannot be eliminated by reasonable accommodation, a covered entity may refuse to assign or continue to assign such individual to a job involving food handling. However, if the individual with a disability is a current employee, the employer must consider whether he or she can be accommodated by reassignment to a vacant position not involving food handling.

(2) *Effect on state or other laws.* This part does not preempt, modify, or amend any State, county, or local law, ordinance or regulation applicable to food handling which:

(i) Is in accordance with the list, referred to in paragraph (e)(1) of this section, of infectious or communicable diseases and the modes of transmissibility published by the Secretary of Health and Human Services; and

(ii) Is designed to protect the public health from individuals who pose a significant risk to the health or safety of others, where that risk cannot be eliminated by reasonable accommodation.

(f) *Health insurance, life insurance, and other benefit plans.*--

(1) An insurer, hospital, or medical service company, health maintenance organization, or any agent or entity that administers benefit plans, or similar organizations may underwrite risks, classify risks, or administer such risks that are based on or not inconsistent with State law.

(2) A covered entity may establish, sponsor, observe or administer the terms of a bona fide benefit plan that are based on underwriting risks, classifying risks, or administering such risks that are based on or not inconsistent with State law.

(3) A covered entity may establish, sponsor, observe, or

administer the terms of a bona fide benefit plan that is not subject to State laws that regulate insurance.

(4) The activities described in paragraphs (f)(1),(2), and (3) of this section are permitted unless these activities are being used as a subterfuge to evade the purposes of this part.

Appendix to Part 1630 - Interpretive Guidance on Title I of the Americans with Disabilities Act

Background

The ADA is a federal antidiscrimination statute designed to remove barriers which prevent qualified individuals with disabilities from enjoying the same employment opportunities that are available to persons without disabilities.

Like the Civil Rights Act of 1964 that prohibits discrimination on the bases of race, color, religion, national origin, and sex, the ADA seeks to ensure access to equal employment opportunities based on merit. It does not guarantee equal results, establish quotas, or require preferences favoring individuals with disabilities over those without disabilities.

However, while the Civil Rights Act of 1964 prohibits any consideration of personal characteristics such as race or national origin, the ADA necessarily takes a different approach. When an individual's disability creates a barrier to employment opportunities, the ADA requires employers to consider whether reasonable accommodation could remove the barrier.

The ADA thus establishes a process in which the employer must assess a disabled individual's ability to perform the essential functions of the specific job held or desired. While the ADA focuses on eradicating barriers, the ADA does not relieve a disabled employee or applicant from the obligation to perform the essential functions of the job. To the contrary, the ADA is intended to enable disabled persons to compete in the workplace based on the same performance standards and requirements that employers expect of persons who are not disabled.

However, where that individual's functional limitation impedes such job performance, an employer must take steps to reasonably accommodate, and thus help overcome the particular impediment, unless to do so would impose an undue hardship. Such accommodations usually take the form of adjustments to the way a job customarily is performed, or to the work environment itself.

This process of identifying whether, and to what extent, a reasonable accommodation is required should be flexible and involve both the employer and the individual with a disability. Of course, the determination of whether an individual is qualified for a particular position must necessarily be made on a case-by-case basis. No specific form of accommodation is guaranteed for all individuals with a particular disability. Rather, an accommodation must be tailored to match the needs of the disabled individual with the needs of the job's essential functions.

This case-by-case approach is essential if qualified individuals of varying abilities are to receive equal opportunities to compete for an infinitely diverse range of jobs. For this reason, neither the ADA nor this regulation can supply the "correct" answer in advance for each employment decision concerning an individual with a disability. Instead, the ADA simply establishes parameters to guide employers in how to consider, and take into account, the disabling condition involved.

Introduction

The Equal Employment Opportunity Commission (the Commission or EEOC) is responsible for enforcement of title I of the Americans with Disabilities Act (ADA), 42 U.S.C. 12101 *et seq.* (1990), which prohibits employment discrimination on the basis of disability. The Commission believes that it is essential to issue interpretive guidance concurrently with the issuance of this part in order to ensure that qualified individuals with disabilities understand their rights under this part and to facilitate and encourage compliance by covered entities. This Appendix represents the Commission's interpretation of the issues discussed, and the Commission will be guided by it when resolving charges of employment discrimination. The Appendix addresses the major provisions of this part and explains the major concepts of disability rights.

The terms "employer" or "employer or other covered entity" are used interchangeably throughout the Appendix to refer to all covered entities subject to the employment provisions of the ADA.

Section 1630.1 Purpose, Applicability and Construction

Section 1630.1(a) Purpose

The Americans with Disabilities Act was signed into law on July 26, 1990. It is an antidiscrimination statute that requires that individuals with disabilities be given the same consideration for employment that individuals without disabilities are given. An individual who is qualified for an employment opportunity cannot be denied that opportunity because of the fact that the individual is disabled. The purpose of title I and this part is to ensure that qualified individuals with disabilities are protected from discrimination on the basis of disability.

The ADA uses the term "disabilities" rather than the term "handicaps" used in the Rehabilitation Act of 1973, 29 U.S.C. 701-796. Substantively, these terms are equivalent. As noted by the House Committee on the Judiciary, "[t]he use of the term 'disabilities' instead of the term 'handicaps' reflects the desire of the Committee to use the most current terminology. It reflects the preference of persons with disabilities to use that term rather than 'handicapped' as used in previous laws, such as the Rehabilitation Act of 1973 ...." H.R. Rep. No.

485 Part 3, 101st Cong., 2d Sess. 26-27 (1990) [hereinafter House Judiciary Report]; *see also* S. Rep. No. 116, 101st Cong., 1st Sess. 21 (1989) [hereinafter Senate Report]; H.R. Rep. No. 485 Part 2, 101st Cong., 2d Sess. 50-51 (1990) [hereinafter House Labor Report].

The use of the term "Americans" in the title of the ADA is not intended to imply that the Act only applies to United States citizens. Rather, the ADA protects all qualified individuals with disabilities, regardless of their citizenship status or nationality.

Section 1630.1(b) and (c) Applicability and Construction

Unless expressly stated otherwise, the standards applied in the ADA are not intended to be lesser than the standards applied under the Rehabilitation Act of 1973.

The ADA does not preempt any Federal law, or any state or local law, that grants to individuals with disabilities protection greater than or equivalent to that provided by the ADA. This means that the existence of a lesser standard of protection to individuals with disabilities under the ADA will not provide a defense to failing to meet a higher standard under another law. Thus, for example, title I of the ADA would not be a defense to failing to collect information required to satisfy the affirmative action requirements of Section 503 of the Rehabilitation Act. On the other hand, the existence of a lesser standard under another law will not provide a defense to failing to meet a higher standard under the ADA. *See* House Labor Report at 135; House Judiciary Report at 69-70.

This also means that an individual with a disability could choose to pursue claims under a state discrimination or tort law that does not confer greater substantive rights, or even confers fewer substantive rights, if the potential available remedies would be greater than those available under the ADA and this part. The ADA does not restrict an individual with a disability from pursuing such

claims in addition to charges brought under this part. House Judiciary at 69-70.

The ADA does not automatically preempt medical standards or safety requirements established by Federal law or regulations. It does not preempt State, county, or local laws, ordinances or regulations that are consistent with this part, and are designed to protect the public health from individuals who pose a direct threat, that cannot be eliminated or reduced by reasonable accommodation, to the health or safety of others. However, the ADA does preempt inconsistent requirements established by state or local law for safety or security sensitive positions. *See* Senate Report at 27; House Labor Report at 57.

An employer allegedly in violation of this part cannot successfully defend its actions by relying on the obligation to comply with the requirements of any state or local law that imposes prohibitions or limitations on the eligibility of qualified individuals with disabilities to practice any occupation or profession. For example, suppose a municipality has an ordinance that prohibits individuals with tuberculosis from teaching school children. If an individual with dormant tuberculosis challenges a private school's refusal to hire him or her because of the tuberculosis, the private school would not be able to rely on the city ordinance as a defense under the ADA.

Sections 1630.2(a)-(f) Commission, Covered Entity, etc.

The definitions section of part 1630 includes several terms that are identical, or almost identical, to the terms found in title VII of the Civil Rights Act of 1964. Among these terms are "Commission," "Person," "State," and "Employer." These terms are to be given the same meaning under the ADA that they are given under title VII.

In general, the term "employee" has the same meaning that it is given under title VII. However, the ADA's definition of "employee" does

not contain an exception, as does title VII, for elected officials and their personal staffs. It should be further noted that all state and local governments are covered by title II of the ADA whether or not they are also covered by this part. Title II, which is enforced by the Department of Justice, becomes effective on January 26, 1992. *See* 28 CFR part 35.

The term "covered entity" is not found in title VII. However, the title VII definitions of the entities included in the term "covered entity" (*e.g.*, employer, employment agency, *etc.*) are applicable to the ADA.

Section 1630.2(g) Disability

In addition to the term "covered entity," there are several other terms that are unique to the ADA. The first of these is the term "disability." Congress adopted the definition of this term from the Rehabilitation Act definition of the term "individual with handicaps." By so doing, Congress intended that the relevant caselaw developed under the Rehabilitation Act be generally applicable to the term "disability" as used in the ADA. Senate Report at 21; House Labor Report at 50; House Judiciary Report at 27.

The definition of the term "disability" is divided into three parts. An individual must satisfy at least one of these parts in order to be considered an individual with a disability for purposes of this part. An individual is considered to have a "disability" if that individual either (1) has a physical or mental impairment which substantially limits one or more of that person's major life activities, (2) has a record of such an impairment, or, (3) is regarded by the covered entity as having such an impairment.

To understand the meaning of the term "disability," it is necessary to understand, as a preliminary matter, what is meant by the terms "physical or mental impairment," "major life activity," and "substantially limits." Each of these terms is discussed below.

Section 1630.2(h) Physical or Mental Impairment

This term adopts the definition of the term "physical or mental impairment" found in the regulations implementing Section 504 of the Rehabilitation Act at 34 CFR part 104. It defines physical or mental impairment as any physiological disorder or condition, cosmetic disfigurement, or anatomical loss affecting one or more of several body systems, or any mental or psychological disorder.

The existence of an impairment is to be determined without regard to mitigating measures such as medicines, or assistive or prosthetic devices. *See* Senate Report at 23, House Labor Report at 52, House Judiciary Report at 28. For example, an individual with epilepsy would be considered to have an impairment even if the symptoms of the disorder were completely controlled by medicine. Similarly, an individual with hearing loss would be considered to have an impairment even if the condition were correctable through the use of a hearing aid.

It is important to distinguish between conditions that are impairments and physical, psychological, environmental, cultural and economic characteristics that are not impairments. The definition of the term "impairment" does not include physical characteristics such as eye color, hair color, left-handedness, or height, weight or muscle tone that are within "normal" range and are not the result of a physiological disorder. The definition, likewise, does not include characteristic predisposition to illness or disease. Other conditions, such as pregnancy, that are not the result of a physiological disorder are also not impairments. Similarly, the definition does not include common personality traits such as poor judgment or a quick temper where these are not symptoms of a mental or psychological disorder. Environmental, cultural, or economic disadvantages such as poverty, lack of education or a prison record are not impair-

ments. Advanced age, in and of itself, is also not an impairment. However, various medical conditions commonly associated with age, such as hearing loss, osteoporosis, or arthritis would constitute impairments within the meaning of this part. *See* Senate Report at 22-23; House Labor Report at 51-52; House Judiciary Report at 28-29.

Section 1630.2(i) Major Life Activities

This term adopts the definition of the term "major life activities" found in the regulations implementing Section 504 of the Rehabilitation Act at 34 CFR part 104. "Major life activities" are those basic activities that the average person in the general population can perform with little or no difficulty. Major life activities include caring for oneself, performing manual tasks, walking, seeing, hearing, speaking, breathing, learning, and working. This list is not exhaustive. For example, other major life activities include, but are not limited to, sitting, standing, lifting, reaching. *See* Senate Report at 22; House Labor Report at 52; House Judiciary Report at 28.

Section 1630.2(j) Substantially Limits

Determining whether a physical or mental impairment exists is only the first step in determining whether or not an individual is disabled. Many impairments do not impact an individual's life to the degree that they constitute disabling impairments. An impairment rises to the level of disability if the impairment substantially limits one or more of the individual's major life activities. Multiple impairments that combine to substantially limit one or more of an individual's major life activities also constitute a disability.

The ADA and this part, like the Rehabilitation Act of 1973, do not attempt a "laundry list" of impairments that are "disabilities." The determination of whether an individual has a disability is not necessarily based on the name or

diagnosis of the impairment the person has, but rather on the effect of that impairment on the life of the individual. Some impairments may be disabling for particular individuals but not for others, depending on the stage of the disease or disorder, the presence of other impairments that combine to make the impairment disabling or any number of other factors.

Other impairments, however, such as HIV infection, are inherently substantially limiting.

On the other hand, temporary, nonchronic impairments of short duration, with little or no long term or permanent impact, are usually not disabilities. Such impairments may include, but are not limited to, broken limbs, sprained joints, concussions, appendicitis, and influenza. Similarly, except in rare circumstances, obesity is not considered a disabling impairment.

An impairment that prevents an individual from performing a major life activity substantially limits that major life activity. For example, an individual whose legs are paralyzed is substantially limited in the major life activity of walking because he or she is unable, due to the impairment, to perform that major life activity.

Alternatively, an impairment is substantially limiting if it significantly restricts the duration, manner or condition under which an individual can perform a particular major life activity as compared to the average person in the general population's ability to perform that same major life activity. Thus, for example, an individual who, because of an impairment, can only walk for very brief periods of time would be substantially limited in the major life activity of walking. An individual who uses artificial legs would likewise be substantially limited in the major life activity of walking because the individual is unable to walk without the aid of prosthetic devices. Similarly, a diabetic who without insulin would lapse into a coma would be substantially limited because the individual cannot perform major life activities without the aid of medication. See Senate Report at 23; House Labor Report at 52. It should be noted that the term "average person" is not intended to imply a precise mathematical "average."

Part 1630 notes several factors that should be considered in making the determination of whether an impairment is substantially limiting. These factors are (1) the nature and severity of the impairment, (2) the duration or expected duration of the impairment, and (3) the permanent or long term impact, or the expected permanent or long term impact of, or resulting from, the impairment. The term "duration," as used in this context, refers to the length of time an impairment persists, while the term "impact" refers to the residual effects of an impairment. Thus, for example, a broken leg that takes eight weeks to heal is an impairment of fairly brief duration. However, if the broken leg heals improperly, the "impact" of the impairment would be the resulting permanent limp. Likewise, the effect on cognitive functions resulting from traumatic head injury would be the "impact" of that impairment.

The determination of whether an individual is substantially limited in a major life activity must be made on a case by case basis, without regard to mitigating measures such as medicines, or assistive or prosthetic devices. An individual is not substantially limited in a major life activity if the limitation, when viewed in light of the factors noted above, does not amount to a significant restriction when compared with the abilities of the average person. For example, an individual who had once been able to walk at an extraordinary speed would not be substantially limited in the major life activity of walking if, as a result of a physical impairment, he or she were only able to walk at an average speed, or even at moderately below average speed.

It is important to remember that the restriction on the performance of the major life activity must be the result of a condition that is an impairment. As noted earlier, advanced age, physical or personality characteristics, and environmental, cultural, and economic disadvantages are not impairments. Consequently, even if such factors substantially limit an individual's ability to perform a major life activity, this limitation will not constitute a disability. For example, an individual who is unable to read because he or she was never taught to read would not be an individual with a disability because lack of education is not an impairment. However, an individual who is unable to read because of dyslexia would be an individual with a disability because dyslexia, a learning disability, is an impairment.

If an individual is not substantially limited with respect to any other major life activity, the individual's ability to perform the major life activity of working should be considered. If an individual is substantially limited in any other major life activity, no determination should be made as to whether the individual is substantially limited in working. For example, if an individual is blind, i.e., substantially limited in the major life activity of seeing, there is no need to determine whether the individual is also substantially limited in the major life activity of working. The determination of whether an individual is substantially limited in working must also be made on a case by case basis.

This part lists specific factors that may be used in making the determination of whether the limitation in working is "substantial." These factors are:

(1) the geographical area to which the individual has reasonable access;

(2) the job from which the individual has been disqualified because of an impairment, and the number and types of jobs utilizing similar training, knowledge, skills or abilities, within that geographical area,

from which the individual is also disqualified because of the impairment (class of jobs); and/or

(3) the job from which the individual has been disqualified because of an impairment, and the number and types of other jobs not utilizing similar training, knowledge, skills or abilities, within that geographical area, from which the individual is also disqualified because of the impairment (broad range of jobs in various classes).

Thus, an individual is not substantially limited in working just because he or she is unable to perform a particular job for one employer, or because he or she is unable to perform a specialized job or profession requiring extraordinary skill, prowess or talent. For example, an individual who cannot be a commercial airline pilot because of a minor vision impairment, but who can be a commercial airline copilot or a pilot for a courier service, would not be substantially limited in the major life activity of working. Nor would a professional baseball pitcher who develops a bad elbow and can no longer throw a baseball be considered substantially limited in the major life activity of working. In both of these examples, the individuals are not substantially limited in the ability to perform any other major life activity and, with regard to the major life activity of working, are only unable to perform either a particular specialized job or a narrow range of jobs. See Forrisi v. Bowen, 794 F.2d 931 (4th Cir. 1986); Jasany v. U.S. Postal Service, 755 F.2d 1244 (6th Cir. 1985); E.E Black, Ltd. v. Marshall, 497 F. Supp. 1088 (D. Hawaii 1980).

On the other hand, an individual does not have to be totally unable to work in order to be considered substantially limited in the major life activity of working. An individual is substantially limited in working if the individual is significantly restricted in the ability to perform a class of jobs or a broad range of jobs in various classes, when compared with the ability of the average person with comparable qualifications to perform those same jobs. For example, an individual who has a back condition that prevents the individual from performing any heavy labor job would be substantially limited in the major life activity of working because the individual's impairment eliminates his or her ability to perform a class of jobs. This would be so even if the individual were able to perform jobs in another class, e.g., the class of semi-skilled jobs. Similarly, suppose an individual has an allergy to a substance found in most high rise office buildings, but seldom found elsewhere, that makes breathing extremely difficult. Since this individual would be substantially limited in the ability to perform the broad range of jobs in various classes that are conducted in high rise office buildings within the geographical area to which he or she has reasonable access, he or she would be substantially limited in working.

The terms "number and types of jobs" and "number and types of other jobs," as used in the factors discussed above, are not intended to require an onerous evidentiary showing. Rather, the terms only require the presentation of evidence of general employment demographics and/or of recognized occupational classifications that indicate the approximate number of jobs (e.g., "few," "many," "most") from which an individual would be excluded because of an impairment.

If an individual has a "mental or physical impairment" that "substantially limits" his or her ability to perform one or more "major life activities," that individual will satisfy the first part of the regulatory definition of "disability" and will be considered an individual with a disability. An individual who satisfies this first part of the definition of the term "disability" is not required to demonstrate that he or she satisfies either of the other parts of the definition. However, if an individual is unable to satisfy this part of the definition, he or

she may be able to satisfy one of the other parts of the definition.

Section 1630.2(k) Record of a Substantially Limiting Condition

The second part of the definition provides that an individual with a record of an impairment that substantially limits a major life activity is an individual with a disability. The intent of this provision, in part, is to ensure that people are not discriminated against because of a history of disability. For example, this provision protects former cancer patients from discrimination based on their prior medical history. This provision also ensures that individuals are not discriminated against because they have been misclassified as disabled. For example, individuals misclassified as learning disabled are protected from discrimination on the basis of that erroneous classification. Senate Report at 23; House Labor Report at 52-53; House Judiciary Report at 29.

This part of the definition is satisfied if a record relied on by an employer indicates that the individual has or has had a substantially limiting impairment. The impairment indicated in the record must be an impairment that would substantially limit one or more of the individual's major life activities. There are many types of records that could potentially contain this information, including but not limited to, education, medical, or employment records.

The fact that an individual has a record of being a disabled veteran, or of disability retirement, or is classified as disabled for other purposes does not guarantee that the individual will satisfy the definition of "disability" under part 1630. Other statutes, regulations and programs may have a definition of "disability" that is not the same as the definition set forth in the ADA and contained in part 1630. Accordingly, in order for an individual who has been classified in a record as "disabled" for some other purpose to be considered disabled for purposes of part

1630, the impairment indicated in the record must be a physical or mental impairment that substantially limits one or more of the individual's major life activities.

Section 1630.2(l) Regarded as Substantially Limited in a Major Life Activity

If an individual cannot satisfy either the first part of the definition of "disability" or the second "record of" part of the definition, he or she may be able to satisfy the third part of the definition. The third part of the definition provides that an individual who is regarded by an employer or other covered entity as having an impairment that substantially limits a major life activity is an individual with a disability.

There are three different ways in which an individual may satisfy the definition of "being regarded as having a disability":

(1) The individual may have an impairment which is not substantially limiting but is perceived by the employer or other covered entity as constituting a substantially limiting impairment;

(2) the individual may have an impairment which is only substantially limiting because of the attitudes of others toward the impairment; or

(3) the individual may have no impairment at all but is regarded by the employer or other covered entity as having a substantially limiting impairment.

Senate Report at 23; House Labor Report at 53; House Judiciary Report at 29.

An individual satisfies the first part of this definition if the individual has an impairment that is not substantially limiting, but the covered entity perceives the impairment as being substantially limiting. For example, suppose an employee has controlled high blood pressure that is not substantially limiting. If an employer reassigns the individual to less strenuous work because of unsubstantiated fears that the individual will suffer a heart attack if he or she continues to perform strenuous work, the employer would be regarding the individual as disabled.

An individual satisfies the second part of the "regarded as" definition if the individual has an impairment that is only substantially limiting because of the attitudes of others toward the condition. For example, an individual may have a prominent facial scar or disfigurement, or may have a condition that periodically causes an involuntary jerk of the head but does not limit the individual's major life activities. If an employer discriminates against such an individual because of the negative reactions of customers, the employer would be regarding the individual as disabled and acting on the basis of that perceived disability. *See* Senate Report at 24; House Labor Report at 53; House Judiciary Report at 30-31.

An individual satisfies the third part of the "regarded as" definition of "disability" if the employer or other covered entity erroneously believes the individual has a substantially limiting impairment that the individual actually does not have. This situation could occur, for example, if an employer discharged an employee in response to a rumor that the employee is infected with Human Immunodeficiency Virus (HIV). Even though the rumor is totally unfounded and the individual has no impairment at all, the individual is considered an individual with a disability because the employer perceived of this individual as being disabled. Thus, in this example, the employer, by discharging this employee, is discriminating on the basis of disability.

The rationale for the "regarded as" part of the definition of disability was articulated by the Supreme Court in the context of the Rehabilitation Act of 1973 in *School Board of Nassau County v. Arline*, 480 U.S. 273 (1987). The Court noted that, although an individual may have an impairment that does not in fact substantially limit a major life activity, the reaction of others may prove just as disabling.

"Such an impairment might not diminish a person's physical or mental capabilities, but could nevertheless substantially limit that person's ability to work as a result of the negative reactions of others to the impairment." 480 U.S. at 283. The Court concluded that by including "regarded as" in the Rehabilitation Act's definition, "Congress acknowledged that society's accumulated myths and fears about disability and diseases are as handicapping as are the physical limitations that flow from actual impairment." 480 U.S. at 284.

An individual rejected from a job because of the "myths, fears and sterotypes" associated with disabilities would be covered under this part of the definition of disability, whether or not the employer's or other covered entity's perception were shared by others in the field and whether or not the individual's actual physical or mental condition would be considered a disability under the first or second part of this definition. As the legislative history notes, sociologists have identified common attitudinal barriers that frequently result in employers excluding individuals with disabilities. These include concerns regarding productivity, safety, insurance, liability, attendance, cost of accommodation and accessibility, workers' compensation costs, and acceptance by coworkers and customers.

Therefore, if an individual can show that an employer or other covered entity made an employment decision because of a perception of disability based on "myth, fear or stereotype," the individual will satisfy the "regarded as" part of the definition of disability. If the employer cannot articulate a non-discriminatory reason for the employment action, an inference that the employer is acting on the basis of "myth, fear or stereotype" can be drawn.

Section 1630.2(m) Qualified Individual With a Disability

The ADA prohibits discrimination on the basis of disability against qualified

individuals with disabilities. The determination of whether an individual with a disability is "qualified" should be made in two steps. The first step is to determine if the individual satisfies the prerequisites for the position, such as possessing the appropriate educational background, employment experience, skills, licenses, etc. For example, the first step in determining whether an accountant who is paraplegic is qualified for a certified public accountant (CPA) position is to examine the individual's credentials to determine whether the individual is a licensed CPA. This is sometimes referred to in the Rehabilitation Act caselaw as determining whether the individual is "otherwise qualified" for the position. *See* Senate Report at 33; House Labor Report at 64-65. (See section 1630.9 Not Making Reasonable Accommodation).

The second step is to determine whether or not the individual can perform the essential functions of the position held or desired, with or without reasonable accommodation. The purpose of this second step is to ensure that individuals with disabilities who can perform the essential functions of the position held or desired are not denied employment opportunities because they are not able to perform marginal functions of the position. House Labor Report at 55.

The determination of whether an individual with a disability is qualified is to be made at the time of the employment decision. This determination should be based on the capabilities of the individual with a disability at the time of the employment decision, and should not be based on speculation that the employee may become unable in the future or may cause increased health insurance premiums or workers' compensation costs.

Section 1630.2(n) Essential Functions

The determination of which functions are essential may be

critical to the determination of whether or not the individual with a disability is qualified. The essential functions are those functions that the individual who holds the position must be able to perform unaided or with the assistance of a reasonable accommodation.

The inquiry into whether a particular function is essential initially focuses on whether the employer actually requires employees in the position to perform the functions that the employer asserts are essential. For example, an employer may state that typing is an essential function of a position. If, in fact, the employer has never required any employee in that particular position to type, this will be evidence that typing is not actually an essential function of the position.

If the individual who holds the position is actually required to perform the function the employer asserts is an essential function, the inquiry will then center around whether removing the function would fundamentally alter that position. This determination of whether or not a particular function is essential will generally include one or more of the following factors listed in part 1630.

The first factor is whether the position exists to perform a particular function. For example, an individual may be hired to proofread documents. The ability to proofread the documents would then be an essential function, since this is the only reason the position exists.

The second factor in determining whether a function is essential is the number of other employees available to perform that job function or among whom the performance of that job function can be distributed. This may be a factor either because the total number of available employees is low, or because of the fluctuating demands of the business operation. For example, if an employer has a relatively small number of available employees for the volume of work to be performed, it may be necessary that each employee perform a multitude of different functions.

Therefore, the performance of those functions by each employee becomes more critical and the options for reorganizing the work become more limited. In such a situation, functions that might not be essential if there were a larger staff may become essential because the staff size is small compared to the volume of work that has to be done. *See Treadwell v. Alexander*, 707 F.2d 473 (11th Cir. 1983).

A similar situation might occur in a larger work force if the workflow follows a cycle of heavy demand for labor intensive work followed by low demand periods. This type of workflow might also make the performance of each function during the peak periods more critical and might limit the employer's flexibility in reorganizing operating procedures. *See Dexler v. Tisch*, 660 F. Supp. 1418 (D. Conn. 1987).

The third factor is the degree of expertise or skill required to perform the function. In certain professions and highly skilled positions the employee is hired for his or her expertise or ability to perform the particular function. In such a situation, the performance of that specialized task would be an essential function.

Whether a particular function is essential is a factual determination that must be made on a case by case basis. In determining whether or not a particular function is essential, all relevant evidence should be considered. Part 1630 lists various types of evidence, such as an established job description, that should be considered in determining whether a particular function is essential. Since the list is not exhaustive, other relevant evidence may also be presented. Greater weight will not be granted to the types of evidence included on the list than to the types of evidence not listed.

Although part 1630 does not require employers to develop or maintain job descriptions, written job descriptions prepared before advertising or interviewing applicants for the job, as well as the employer's judgment as to what functions

are essential are among the relevant evidence to be considered in determining whether a particular function is essential. The terms of a collective bargaining agreement are also relevant to the determination of whether a particular function is essential. The work experience of past employees in the job or of current employees in similar jobs is likewise relevant to the determination of whether a particular function is essential. *See* H.R. Conf. Rep. No. 101-596, 101st Cong., 2d Sess. 58 (1990) [hereinafter Conference Report]; House Judiciary Report at 33-34. *See also Hall v. U.S. Postal Service*, 857 F.2d 1073 (6th Cir. 1988).

The time spent performing the particular function may also be an indicator of whether that function is essential. For example, if an employee spends the vast majority of his or her time working at a cash register, this would be evidence that operating the cash register is an essential function. The consequences of failing to require the employee to perform the function may be another indicator of whether a particular function is essential. For example, although a firefighter may not regularly have to carry an unconscious adult out of a burning building, the consequence of failing to require the firefighter to be able to perform this function would be serious.

It is important to note that the inquiry into essential functions is not intended to second guess an employer's business judgment with regard to production standards, whether qualitative or quantitative, nor to require employers to lower such standards. (See section 1630.10 Qualification Standards, Tests and Other Selection Criteria). If an employer requires its typists to be able to accurately type 75 words per minute, it will not be called upon to explain why an inaccurate work product, or a typing speed of 65 words per minute, would not be adequate. Similarly, if a hotel requires its service workers to thoroughly clean 16 rooms per day, it will not have to explain why it requires thorough cleaning, or why it chose a 16 room rather than a 10 room requirement. However, if an employer does require accurate 75 word per minute typing or the thorough cleaning of 16 rooms, it will have to show that it actually imposes such requirements on its employees in fact, and not simply on paper. It should also be noted that, if it is alleged that the employer intentionally selected the particular level of production to exclude individuals with disabilities, the employer may have to offer a legitimate, nondiscriminatory reason for its selection.

Section 1630.2(o) Reasonable Accommodation

An individual is considered a "qualified individual with a disability" if the individual can perform the essential functions of the position held or desired with or without reasonable accommodation. In general, an accommodation is any change in the work environment or in the way things are customarily done that enables an individual with a disability to enjoy equal employment opportunities. There are three categories of reasonable accommodation. These are (1) accommodations that are required to ensure equal opportunity in the application process; (2) accommodations that enable the employer's employees with disabilities to perform the essential functions of the position held or desired; and (3) accommodations that enable the employer's employees with disabilities to enjoy equal benefits and privileges of employment as are enjoyed by employees without disabilities. It should be noted that nothing in this part prohibits employers or other covered entities from providing accommodations beyond those required by this part.

Part 1630 lists the examples, specified in title I of the ADA, of the most common types of accommodation that an employer or other covered entity may be required to provide. There are any number of other specific accommodations that may be appropriate

for particular situations but are not specifically mentioned in this listing. This listing is not intended to be exhaustive of accommodation possibilities. For example, other accommodations could include permitting the use of accrued paid leave or providing additional unpaid leave for necessary treatment, making employer provided transportation accessible, and providing reserved parking spaces. Providing personal assistants, such as a page turner for an employee with no hands or a travel attendant to act as a sighted guide to assist a blind employee on occasional business trips, may also be a reasonable accommodation. Senate Report at 31; House Labor Report at 62; House Judiciary Report at 39.

It may also be a reasonable accommodation to permit an individual with a disability the opportunity to provide and utilize equipment, aids or services that an employer is not required to provide as a reasonable accommodation. For example, it would be a reasonable accommodation for an employer to permit an individual who is blind to use a guide dog at work, even though the employer would not be required to provide a guide dog for the employee.

The accommodations included on the list of reasonable accommodations are generally self explanatory. However, there are a few that require further explanation. One of these is the accommodation of making existing facilities used by employees readily accessible to, and usable by, individuals with disabilities. This accommodation includes both those areas that must be accessible for the employee to perform essential job functions, as well as nonwork areas used by the employer's employees for other purposes. For example, accessible break rooms, lunch rooms, training rooms, restrooms etc., may be required as reasonable accommodations.

Another of the potential accommodations listed is "job restructuring." An employer or other covered entity may restructure a job by reallocating

or redistributing nonessential, marginal job functions. For example, an employer may have two jobs, each of which entails the performance of a number of marginal functions. The employer hires a qualified individual with a disability who is able to perform some of the marginal functions of each job but not all of the marginal functions of either job. As an accommodation, the employer may redistribute the marginal functions so that all of the marginal functions that the qualified individual with a disability can perform are made a part of the position to be filled by the qualified individual with a disability. The remaining marginal functions that the individual with a disability cannot perform would then be transferred to the other position. See Senate Report at 31; House Labor Report at 62.

An employer or other covered entity is not required to reallocate essential functions. The essential functions are by definition those that the individual who holds the job would have to perform, with or without reasonable accommodation, in order to be considered qualified for the position. For example, suppose a security guard position requires the individual who holds the job to inspect identification cards. An employer would not have to provide an individual who is legally blind with an assistant to look at the identification cards for the legally blind employee. In this situation the assistant would be performing the job for the individual with a disability rather than assisting the individual to perform the job. See Coleman v. Darden, 595 F.2d 533 (10th Cir. 1979).

An employer or other covered entity may also restructure a job by altering when and/or how an essential function is performed. For example, an essential function customarily performed in the early morning hours may be rescheduled until later in the day as a reasonable accommodation to a disability that precludes performance of the function at the customary hour. Likewise, as a reasonable accommodation, an employee with a disability that inhibits the ability to write, may be permitted to computerize records that were customarily maintained manually.

Reassignment to a vacant position is also listed as a potential reasonable accommodation. In general, reassignment should be considered only when accommodation within the individual's current position would pose an undue hardship. Reassignment is not available to applicants. An applicant for a position must be qualified for, and be able to perform the essential functions of, the position sought with or without reasonable accommodation.

Reassignment may not be used to limit, segregate, or otherwise discriminate against employees with disabilities by forcing reassignments to undesirable positions or to designated offices or facilities. Employers should reassign the individual to an equivalent position, in terms of pay, status, etc., if the individual is qualified, and if the position is vacant within a reasonable amount of time. A "reasonable amount of time" should be determined in light of the totality of the circumstances. As an example, suppose there is no vacant position available at the time that an individual with a disability requests reassignment as a reasonable accommodation. The employer, however, knows that an equivalent position for which the individual is qualified, will become vacant next week. Under these circumstances, the employer should reassign the individual to the position when it becomes available.

An employer may reassign an individual to a lower graded position if there are no accommodations that would enable the employee to remain in the current position and there are no vacant equivalent positions for which the individual is qualified with or without reasonable accommodation. An employer, however, is not required to maintain the reassigned individual with a disability at the salary of the higher graded position if it does not so maintain reassigned employees who are not

disabled. It should also be noted that an employer is not required to promote an individual with a disability as an accommodation. See Senate Report at 31-32; House Labor Report at 63.

The determination of which accommodation is appropriate in a particular situation involves a process in which the employer and employee identify the precise limitations imposed by the disability and explore potential accommodations that would overcome those limitations. This process is discussed more fully in section 1630.9 Not Making Reasonable Accommodation.

Section 1630.2(p) Undue Hardship

An employer or other covered entity is not required to provide an accommodation that will impose an undue hardship on the operation of the employer's or other covered entity's business. The term "undue hardship" means significant difficulty or expense in, or resulting from, the provision of the accommodation. The "undue hardship" provision takes into account the financial realities of the particular employer or other covered entity. However, the concept of undue hardship is not limited to financial difficulty. "Undue hardship" refers to any accommodation that would be unduly costly, extensive, substantial, or disruptive, or that would fundamentally alter the nature or operation of the business. See Senate Report at 35; House Labor Report at 67.

For example, suppose an individual with a disabling visual impairment that makes it extremely difficult to see in dim lighting applies for a position as a waiter in a nightclub and requests that the club be brightly lit as a reasonable accommodation. Although the individual may be able to perform the job in bright lighting, the nightclub will probably be able to demonstrate that that particular accommodation, though inexpensive, would impose an undue hardship if the bright lighting would destroy the ambience of the nightclub and/or make it

difficult for the customers to see the stage show. The fact that that particular accommodation poses an undue hardship, however, only means that the employer is not required to provide that accommodation. If there is another accommodation that will not create an undue hardship, the employer would be required to provide the alternative accommodation.

An employer's claim that the cost of a particular accommodation will impose an undue hardship will be analyzed in light of the factors outlined in part 1630. In part, this analysis requires a determination of whose financial resources should be considered in deciding whether the accommodation is unduly costly. In some cases the financial resources of the employer or other covered entity in its entirety should be considered in determining whether the cost of an accommodation poses an undue hardship. In other cases, consideration of the financial resources of the employer or other covered entity as a whole may be inappropriate because it may not give an accurate picture of the financial resources available to the particular facility that will actually be required to provide the accommodation. See House Labor Report at 68-69; House Judiciary Report at 40-41; see also Conference Report at 56-57.

If the employer or other covered entity asserts that only the financial resources of the facility where the individual will be employed should be considered, part 1630 requires a factual determination of the relationship between the employer or other covered entity and the facility that will provide the accommodation. As an example, suppose that an independently owned fast food franchise that receives no money from the franchisor refuses to hire an individual with a hearing impairment because it asserts that it would be an undue hardship to provide an interpreter to enable the individual to participate in monthly staff meetings. Since the financial relationship between the franchisor and the franchise is limited to payment of an annual franchise fee, only the financial resources of the franchise would be considered in determining whether or not providing the accommodation would be an undue hardship. *See* House Labor Report at 68; House Judiciary Report at 40.

If the employer or other covered entity can show that the cost of the accommodation would impose an undue hardship, it would still be required to provide the accommodation if the funding is available from another source, *e.g.*, a State vocational rehabilitation agency, or if Federal, State or local tax deductions or tax credits are available to offset the cost of the accommodation. If the employer or other covered entity receives, or is eligible to receive, monies from an external source that would pay the entire cost of the accommodation, it cannot claim cost as an undue hardship. In the absence of such funding, the individual with a disability requesting the accommodation should be given the option of providing the accommodation or of paying that portion of the cost which constitutes the undue hardship on the operation of the business. To the extent that such monies pay or would pay for only part of the cost of the accommodation, only that portion of the cost of the accommodation that could not be recovered the final net cost to the entity - may be considered in determining undue hardship. (See section 1630.9 Not Making Reasonable Accommodation). *See* Senate Report at 36; House Labor Report at 69.

Section 1630.2(r) Direct Threat

An employer may require, as a qualification standard, that an individual not pose a direct threat to the health or safety of himself/herself or others. Like any other qualification standard, such a standard must apply to all applicants or employees and not just to individuals with disabilities. If, however, an individual poses a direct threat as a result of a disability, the employer must

determine whether a reasonable accommodation would either eliminate the risk or reduce it to an acceptable level. If no accommodation exists that would either eliminate or reduce the risk, the employer may refuse to hire an applicant or may discharge an employee who poses a direct threat.

An employer, however, is not permitted to deny an employment opportunity to an individual with a disability merely because of a slightly increased risk. The risk can only be considered when it poses a significant risk, *i.e.*, high probability, of substantial harm; a speculative or remote risk is insufficient. *See* Senate Report at 27; House Report Labor Report at 56-57; House Judiciary Report at 45.

Determining whether an individual poses a significant risk of substantial harm to others must be made on a case by case basis. The employer should identify the specific risk posed by the individual. For individuals with mental or emotional disabilities, the employer must identify the specific behavior on the part of the individual that would pose the direct threat. For individuals with physical disabilities, the employer must identify the aspect of the disability that would pose the direct threat. The employer should then consider the four factors listed in part 1630:

(1) the duration of the risk;
(2) the nature and severity of the potential harm;
(3) the likelihood that the potential harm will occur; and
(4) the imminence of the potential harm.

Such consideration must rely on objective, factual evidence – not on subjective perceptions, irrational fears, patronizing attitudes, or stereotypes – about the nature or effect of a particular disability, or of disability generally. *See* Senate Report at 27; House Labor Report at 56-57; House Judiciary Report at 45-46. See also *Strathie v. Department of Transportation*, 716 F.2d 227 (3d Cir. 1983). Relevant evidence may include input from the individual with a disability, the experience of the

individual with a disability in previous similar positions, and opinions of medical doctors, rehabilitation counselors, or physical therapists who have expertise in the disability involved and/or direct knowledge of the individual with the disability.

An employer is also permitted to require that an individual not pose a direct threat of harm to his or her own safety or health. If performing the particular functions of a job would result in a high probability of substantial harm to the individual, the employer could reject or discharge the individual unless a reasonable accommodation that would not cause an undue hardship would avert the harm. For example, an employer would not be required to hire an individual, disabled by narcolepsy, who frequently and unexpectedly loses consciousness for a carpentry job the essential functions of which require the use of power saws and other dangerous equipment, where no accommodation exists that will reduce or eliminate the risk.

The assessment that there exists a high probability of substantial harm to the individual, like the assessment that there exists a high probability of substantial harm to others, must be strictly based on valid medical analyses and/or on other objective evidence. This determination must be based on individualized factual data, using the factors discussed above, rather than on stereotypic or patronizing assumptions and must consider potential reasonable accommodations. Generalized fears about risks from the employment environment, such as exacerbation of the disability caused by stress, cannot be used by an employer to disqualify an individual with a disability. For example, a law firm could not reject an applicant with a history of disabling mental illness based on a generalized fear that the stress of trying to make partner might trigger a relapse of the individual's mental illness. Nor can generalized fears about risks to individuals with disabilities in the event of an evacuation or other emergency be used by an employer to disqualify an individual with a disability. *See* Senate Report at 56; House Labor Report at 73-74; House Judiciary Report at 45. See also *Mantolete v. Bolger*, 767 F.2d 1416 (9th Cir. 1985); *Bentivegna v. U.S. Department of Labor*, 694 F.2d 619 (9th Cir. 1982).

Section 1630.3 Exceptions to the Definitions of "Disability" and "Qualified Individual with a Disability"

Section 1630.3 (a) through (c) Illegal Use of Drugs

Part 1630 provides that an individual currently engaging in the illegal use of drugs is not an individual with a disability for purposes of this part when the employer or other covered entity acts on the basis of such use. Illegal use of drugs refers both to the use of unlawful drugs, such as cocaine, and to the unlawful use of prescription drugs.

Employers, for example, may discharge or deny employment to persons who illegally use drugs, on the basis of such use, without fear of being held liable for discrimination. The term "currently engaging" is not intended to be limited to the use of drugs on the day of, or within a matter of days or weeks before, the employment action in question. Rather, the provision is intended to apply to the illegal use of drugs that has occurred recently enough to indicate that the individual is actively engaged in such conduct. See Conference Report at 64.

Individuals who are erroneously perceived as engaging in the illegal use of drugs, but are not in fact illegally using drugs are not excluded from the definitions of the terms "disability" and "qualified individual with a disability." Individuals who are no longer illegally using drugs and who have either been rehabilitated successfully or are in the process of completing a rehabilitation program are, likewise, not excluded from the definitions of those terms. The term "rehabilitation program" refers to both inpatient and outpatient programs, as well as to appropriate employee assistance programs, professionally recognized self-help programs, such as Narcotics Anonymous, or other programs that provide professional (not necessarily medical) assistance and counseling for individuals who illegally use drugs. See Conference Report at 64; *see also* House Labor Report at 77; House Judiciary Report at 47.

It should be noted that this provision simply provides that certain individuals are not excluded from the definitions of "disability" and "qualified individual with a disability." Consequently, such individuals are still required to establish that they satisfy the requirements of these definitions in order to be protected by the ADA and this part. An individual erroneously regarded as illegally using drugs, for example, would have to show that he or she was regarded as a drug addict in order to demonstrate that he or she meets the definition of "disability" as defined in this part.

Employers are entitled to seek reasonable assurances that no illegal use of drugs is occurring or has occurred recently enough so that continuing use is a real and ongoing problem. The reasonable assurances that employers may ask applicants or employees to provide include evidence that the individual is participating in a drug treatment program and/or evidence, such as drug test results, to show that the individual is not currently engaging in the illegal use of drugs. An employer, such as a law enforcement agency, may also be able to impose a qualification standard that excludes individuals with a history of illegal use of drugs if it can show that the standard is job-related and consistent with business necessity. (See section 1630.10 Qualification Standards, Tests and Other Selection Criteria) See Conference Report at 64.

Section 1630.4 Discrimination Prohibited

This provision prohibits discrimination against a qualified individual with a disability in all aspects of the employment relationship. The range of employment decisions covered by this nondiscrimination mandate is to be construed in a manner consistent with the regulations implementing Section 504 of the Rehabilitation Act of 1973.

Part 1630 is not intended to limit the ability of covered entities to choose and maintain a qualified workforce. Employers can continue to use job-related criteria to select qualified employees, and can continue to hire employees who can perform the essential functions of the job.

Section 1630.5 Limiting, Segregating and Classifying

This provision and the several provisions that follow describe various specific forms of discrimination that are included within the general prohibition of section 1630.4. Covered entities are prohibited from restricting the employment opportunities of qualified individuals with disabilities on the basis of stereotypes and myths about the individual's disability. Rather, the capabilities of qualified individuals with disabilities must be determined on an individualized, case by case basis. Covered entities are also prohibited from segregating qualified employees with disabilities into separate work areas or into separate lines of advancement.

Thus, for example, it would be a violation of this part for an employer to limit the duties of an employee with a disability based on a presumption of what is best for an individual with such a disability, or on a presumption about the abilities of an individual with such a disability. It would be a violation of this part for an employer to adopt a separate track of job promotion or progression for employees with disabilities based on a presumption that employees with disabilities are uninterested in, or incapable of, performing particular jobs. Similarly, it would be a violation for an employer to assign or reassign (as a reasonable accommodation) employees with disabilities to one particular office or installation, or to require that employees with disabilities only use particular employer provided non-work facilities such as segregated breakrooms, lunch rooms, or lounges. It would also be a violation of this part to deny employment to an applicant or employee with a disability based on generalized fears about the safety of an individual with such a disability, or based on generalized assumptions about the absenteeism rate of an individual with such a disability.

In addition, it should also be noted that this part is intended to require that employees with disabilities be accorded equal access to whatever health insurance coverage the employer provides to other employees. This part does not, however, affect preexisting condition clauses included in health insurance policies offered by employers. Consequently, employers may continue to offer policies that contain such clauses, even if they adversely affect individuals with disabilities, so long as the clauses are not used as a subterfuge to evade the purposes of this part.

So, for example, it would be permissible for an employer to offer an insurance policy that limits coverage for certain procedures or treatments to a specified number per year. Thus, if a health insurance plan provided coverage for five blood transfusions a year to all covered employees, it would not be discriminatory to offer this plan simply because a hemophiliac employee may require more than five blood transfusions annually. However, it would not be permissible to limit or deny the hemophiliac employee coverage for other procedures, such as heart surgery or the setting of a broken leg, even though the plan would not have to provide coverage for the additional

blood transfusions that may be involved in these procedures. Likewise, limits may be placed on reimbursements for certain procedures or on the types of drugs or procedures covered (e.g. limits on the number of permitted X-rays or non-coverage of experimental drugs or procedures), but that limitation must be applied equally to individuals with and without disabilities. See Senate Report at 28-29; House Labor Report at 58-59; House Judiciary Report at 36.

Leave policies or benefit plans that are uniformly applied do not violate this part simply because they do not address the special needs of every individual with a disability. Thus, for example, an employer that reduces the number of paid sick leave days that it will provide to all employees, or reduces the amount of medical insurance coverage that it will provide to all employees, is not in violation of this part, even if the benefits reduction has an impact on employees with disabilities in need of greater sick leave and medical coverage. Benefits reductions adopted for discriminatory reasons are in violation of this part. See *Alexander v. Choate*, 469 U.S. 287 (1985). See Senate Report at 85; House Labor Report at 137. (See also, the discussion at section 1630.16(f) Health Insurance, Life Insurance, and Other Benefit Plans).

Section 1630.6 Contractual or Other Arrangements

An employer or other covered entity may not do through a contractual or other relationship what it is prohibited from doing directly. This provision does not affect the determination of whether or not one is a "covered entity" or "employer" as defined in section 1630.2.

This provision only applies to situations where an employer or other covered entity has entered into a contractual relationship that has the effect of discriminating against its own employees or applicants with disabilities. Accordingly, it would be a violation for an

employer to participate in a contractual relationship that results in discrimination against the employer's employees with disabilities in hiring, training, promotion, or in any other aspect of the employment relationship. This provision applies whether or not the employer or other covered entity intended for the contractual relationship to have the discriminatory effect.

Part 1630 notes that this provision applies to parties on either side of the contractual or other relationship. This is intended to highlight that an employer whose employees provide services to others, like an employer whose employees receive services, must ensure that those employees are not discriminated against on the basis of disability. For example, a copier company whose service representative is a dwarf could be required to provide a stepstool, as a reasonable accommodation, to enable him to perform the necessary repairs. However, the employer would not be required, as a reasonable accommodation, to make structural changes to its customer's inaccessible premises.

The existence of the contractual relationship adds no new obligations under part 1630. The employer, therefore, is not liable through the contractual arrangement for any discrimination by the contractor against the contractor's own employees or applicants, although the contractor, as an employer, may be liable for such discrimination.

An employer or other covered entity, on the other hand, cannot evade the obligations imposed by this part by engaging in a contractual or other relationship. For example, an employer cannot avoid its responsibility to make reasonable accommodation subject to the undue hardship limitation through a contractual arrangement. See Conference Report at 59; House Labor Report at 59-61; House Judiciary Report at 36-37.

To illustrate, assume that an employer is seeking to contract with a company to provide training for its employees. Any responsibilities of reasonable accommodation applicable to the employer in providing the training remain with that employer even if it contracts with another company for this service. Thus, if the training company were planning to conduct the training at an inaccessible location, thereby making it impossible for an employee who uses a wheelchair to attend, the employer would have a duty to make reasonable accommodation unless to do so would impose an undue hardship. Under these circumstances, appropriate accommodations might include (1) having the training company identify accessible training sites and relocate the training program; (2) having the training company make the training site accessible; (3) directly making the training site accessible or providing the training company with the means by which to make the site accessible; (4) identifying and contracting with another training company that uses accessible sites; or (5) any other accommodation that would result in making the training available to the employee.

As another illustration, assume that instead of contracting with a training company, the employer contracts with a hotel to host a conference for its employees. The employer will have a duty to ascertain and ensure the accessibility of the hotel and its conference facilities. To fulfill this obligation the employer could, for example, inspect the hotel first-hand or ask a local disability group to inspect the hotel. Alternatively, the employer could ensure that the contract with the hotel specifies it will provide accessible guest rooms for those who need them and that all rooms to be used for the conference, including exhibit and meeting rooms, are accessible. If the hotel breaches this accessibility provision, the hotel may be liable to the employer, under a non-ADA breach of contract theory, for the cost of any accommodation needed to provide access to the hotel and conference, and for any other costs accrued by the employer. (In addition, the hotel

may also be independently liable under title III of the ADA. However, this would not relieve the employer of its responsibility under this part nor shield it from charges of discrimination by its own employees. See House Labor Report at 40; House Judiciary Report at 37.

Section 1630.8 Relationship or Association With an Individual With a Disability

This provision is intended to protect any qualified individual, whether or not that individual has a disability, from discrimination because that person is known to have an association or relationship with an individual who has a known disability. This protection is not limited to those who have a familial relationship with an individual with a disability.

To illustrate the scope of this provision, assume that a qualified applicant without a disability applies for a job and discloses to the employer that his or her spouse has a disability. The employer thereupon declines to hire the applicant because the employer believes that the applicant would have to miss work or frequently leave work early in order to care for the spouse. Such a refusal to hire would be prohibited by this provision. Similarly, this provision would prohibit an employer from discharging an employee because the employee does volunteer work with people who have AIDS, and the employer fears that the employee may contract the disease.

This provision also applies to other benefits and privileges of employment. For example, an employer that provides health insurance benefits to its employees for their dependents may not reduce the level of those benefits to an employee simply because that employee has a dependent with a disability. This is true even if the provision of such benefits would result in increased health insurance costs for the employer.

It should be noted, however, that an employer need not

provide the applicant or employee without a disability with a reasonable accommodation because that duty only applies to qualified applicants or employees with disabilities. Thus, for example, an employee would not be entitled to a modified work schedule as an accommodation to enable the employee to care for a spouse with a disability. See Senate Report at 30; House Labor Report at 61-62; House Judiciary Report at 38-39.

Section 1630.9 Not Making Reasonable Accommodation

The obligation to make reasonable accommodation is a form of non-discrimination. It applies to all employment decisions and to the job application process. This obligation does not extend to the provision of adjustments or modifications that are primarily for the personal benefit of the individual with a disability. Thus, if an adjustment or modification is job-related, e.g., specifically assists the individual in performing the duties of a particular job, it will be considered a type of reasonable accommodation. On the other hand, if an adjustment or modification assists the individual throughout his or her daily activities, on and off the job, it will be considered a personal item that the employer is not required to provide. Accordingly, an employer would generally not be required to provide an employee with a disability with a prosthetic limb, wheelchair, or eyeglasses. Nor would an employer have to provide as an accommodation any amenity or convenience that is not job-related, such as a private hot plate, hot pot or refrigerator that is not provided to employees without disabilities. See Senate Report at 31; House Labor Report at 62.

It should be noted, however, that the provision of such items may be required as a reasonable accommodation where such items are specifically designed or required to meet job-related rather than personal needs. An employer, for example, may have to provide an individual with a disabling visual impairment with eyeglasses specifically designed to enable the individual to use the office computer monitors, but that are not otherwise needed by the individual outside of the office.

The term "supported employment," which has been applied to a wide variety of programs to assist individuals with severe disabilities in both competitive and noncompetitive employment, is not synonymous with reasonable accommodation. Examples of supported employment include modified training materials, restructuring essential functions to enable an individual to perform a job, or hiring an outside professional ("job coach") to assist in job training. Whether a particular form of assistance would be required as a reasonable accommodation must be determined on an individualized, case by case basis without regard to whether that assistance is referred to as "supported employment." For example, an employer, under certain circumstances, may be required to provide modified training materials or a temporary "job coach" to assist in the training of a qualified individual with a disability as a reasonable accommodation. However, an employer would not be required to restructure the essential functions of a position to fit the skills of an individual with a disability who is not otherwise qualified to perform the position, as is done in certain supported employment programs. See 34 CFR part 363. It should be noted that it would not be a violation of this part for an employer to provide any of these personal modifications or adjustments, or to engage in supported employment or similar rehabilitative programs.

The obligation to make reasonable accommodation applies to all services and programs provided in connection with employment, and to all nonwork facilities provided or maintained by an employer for use by its employees. Accordingly, the obligation to accommodate is applicable to employer sponsored placement or counseling services, and to employer provided cafeterias,

lounges, gymnasiums, auditoriums, transportation and the like.

The reasonable accommodation requirement is best understood as a means by which barriers to the equal employment opportunity of an individual with a disability are removed or alleviated. These barriers may, for example, be physical or structural obstacles that inhibit or prevent the access of an individual with a disability to job sites, facilities or equipment. Or they may be rigid work schedules that permit no flexibility as to when work is performed or when breaks may be taken, or inflexible job procedures that unduly limit the modes of communication that are used on the job, or the way in which particular tasks are accomplished.

The term "otherwise qualified" is intended to make clear that the obligation to make reasonable accommodation is owed only to an individual with a disability who is qualified within the meaning of section 1630.2(m) in that he or she satisfies all the skill, experience, education and other job-related selection criteria. An individual with a disability is "otherwise qualified," in other words, if he or she is qualified for a job, except that, because of the disability, he or she needs a reasonable accommodation to be able to perform the job's essential functions.

For example, if a law firm requires that all incoming lawyers have graduated from an accredited law school and have passed the bar examination, the law firm need not provide an accommodation to an individual with a visual impairment who has not met these selection criteria. That individual is not entitled to a reasonable accommodation because the individual is not "otherwise qualified" for the position.

On the other hand, if the individual has graduated from an accredited law school and passed the bar examination, the individual would be "otherwise qualified." The law firm would thus be required to provide a reasonable accommodation,

such as a machine that magnifies print, to enable the individual to perform the essential functions of the attorney position, unless the necessary accommodation would impose an undue hardship on the law firm. See Senate Report at 33-34; House Labor Report at 64-65.

The reasonable accommodation that is required by this part should provide the qualified individual with a disability with an equal employment opportunity. Equal employment opportunity means an opportunity to attain the same level of performance, or to enjoy the same level of benefits and privileges of employment as are available to the average similarly situated employee without a disability. Thus, for example, an accommodation made to assist an employee with a disability in the performance of his or her job must be adequate to enable the individual to perform the essential functions of the relevant position. The accommodation, however, does not have to be the "best" accommodation possible, so long as it is sufficient to meet the job-related needs of the individual being accommodated. Accordingly, an employer would not have to provide an employee disabled by a back impairment with a state-of-the art mechanical lifting device if it provided the employee with a less expensive or more readily available device that enabled the employee to perform the essential functions of the job. See Senate Report at 35; House Labor Report at 66; see also Carter v. Bennett, 840 F.2d 63 (D.C. Cir. 1988).

Employers are obligated to make reasonable accommodation only to the physical or mental limitations resulting from the disability of a qualified individual with a disability that are known to the employer. Thus, an employer would not be expected to accommodate disabilities of which it is unaware. If an employee with a known disability is having difficulty performing his or her job, an employer may inquire whether the employee is in need of a reasonable accommodation. In general, however, it is the responsibility of the individual with a disability to inform the employer that an accommodation is needed. When the need for an accommodation is not obvious, an employer, before providing a reasonable accommodation, may require that the individual with a disability provide documentation of the need for accommodation. *See* Senate Report at 34; House Labor Report at 65.

Process of Determining the Appropriate Reasonable Accommodation

Once a qualified individual with a disability has requested provision of a reasonable accommodation, the employer must make a reasonable effort to determine the appropriate accommodation. The appropriate reasonable accommodation is best determined through a flexible, interactive process that involves both the employer and the qualified individual with a disability. Although this process is described below in terms of accommodations that enable the individual with a disability to perform the essential functions of the position held or desired, it is equally applicable to accommodations involving the job application process, and to accommodations that enable the individual with a disability to enjoy equal benefits and privileges of employment. *See* Senate Report at 34-35; House Labor Report at 65-67.

When a qualified individual with a disability has requested a reasonable accommodation to assist in the performance of a job, the employer, using a problem solving approach, should:

(1) analyze the particular job involved and determine its purpose and essential functions;

(2) consult with the individual with a disability to ascertain the precise job-related limitations imposed by the individual's disability and how those limitations could be overcome with a reasonable accommodation;

(3) in consultation with the individual to be accommodated, identify potential accommodations and assess the effectiveness each would have in

enabling the individual to perform the essential functions of the position; and

(4) consider the preference of the individual to be accommodated and select and implement the accommodation that is most appropriate for both the employee and the employer.

In many instances, the appropriate reasonable accommodation may be so obvious to either or both the employer and the qualified individual with a disability that it may not be necessary to proceed in this step-by-step fashion. For example, if an employee who uses a wheelchair requests that his or her desk be placed on blocks to elevate the desktop above the arms of the wheelchair and the employer complies, an appropriate accommodation has been requested, identified, and provided without either the employee or employer being aware of having engaged in any sort of "reasonable accommodation process."

However, in some instances neither the individual requesting the accommodation nor the employer can readily identify the appropriate accommodation. For example, the individual needing the accommodation may not know enough about the equipment used by the employer or the exact nature of the work site to suggest an appropriate accommodation. Likewise, the employer may not know enough about the individual's disability or the limitations that disability would impose on the performance of the job to suggest an appropriate accommodation. Under such circumstances, it may be necessary for the employer to initiate a more defined problem solving process, such as the step-by-step process described above, as part of its reasonable effort to identify the appropriate reasonable accommodation.

This process requires the individual assessment of both the particular job at issue, and the specific physical or mental limitations of the particular individual in need of reasonable accommodation. With regard to assessment of the job, "individual assessment" means

analyzing the actual job duties and determining the true purpose or object of the job. Such an assessment is necessary to ascertain which job functions are the essential functions that an accommodation must enable an individual with a disability to perform.

After assessing the relevant job, the employer, in consultation with the individual requesting the accommodation, should make an assessment of the specific limitations imposed by the disability on the individual's performance of the job's essential functions. This assessment will make it possible to ascertain the precise barrier to the employment opportunity which, in turn, will make it possible to determine the accommodation(s) that could alleviate or remove that barrier.

If consultation with the individual in need of the accommodation still does not reveal potential appropriate accommodations, then the employer, as part of this process, may find that technical assistance is helpful in determining how to accommodate the particular individual in the specific situation. Such assistance could be sought from the Commission, from state or local rehabilitation agencies, or from disability constituent organizations. It should be noted, however, that, as provided in section 1630.9(c) of this part, the failure to obtain or receive technical assistance from the federal agencies that administer the ADA will not excuse the employer from its reasonable accommodation obligation.

Once potential accommodations have been identified, the employer should assess the effectiveness of each potential accommodation in assisting the individual in need of the accommodation in the performance of the essential functions of the position. If more than one of these accommodations will enable the individual to perform the essential functions or if the individual would prefer to provide his or her own accommodation, the preference of the individual with a disability should be given primary consideration. However, the employer providing the accommodation has the ultimate discretion to choose between effective accommodations, and may choose the less expensive accommodation or the accommodation that is easier for it to provide. It should also be noted that the individual's willingness to provide his or her own accommodation does not relieve the employer of the duty to provide the accommodation should the individual for any reason be unable or unwilling to continue to provide the accommodation.

Reasonable Accommodation Process Illustrated

The following example illustrates the informal reasonable accommodation process. Suppose a Sack Handler position requires that the employee pick up fifty pound sacks and carry them from the company loading dock to the storage room, and that a sack handler who is disabled by a back impairment requests a reasonable accommodation. Upon receiving the request, the employer analyzes the Sack Handler job and determines that the essential function and purpose of the job is not the requirement that the job holder physically lift and carry the sacks, but the requirement that the job holder cause the sack to move from the loading dock to the storage room.

The employer then meets with the sack handler to ascertain precisely the barrier posed by the individual's specific disability to the performance of the job's essential function of relocating the sacks. At this meeting the employer learns that the individual can, in fact, lift the sacks to waist level, but is prevented by his or her disability from carrying the sacks from the loading dock to the storage room. The employer and the individual agree that any of a number of potential accommodations, such as the provision of a dolly, hand truck, or cart, could enable the individual to transport the sacks that he or she has lifted.

Upon further consideration, however, it is determined that the provision of a cart is not a feasible effective option. No carts are currently available at the company, and those that can be purchased by the company are the wrong shape to hold many of the bulky and irregularly shaped sacks that must be moved. Both the dolly and the hand truck, on the other hand, appear to be effective options. Both are readily available to the company, and either will enable the individual to relocate the sacks that he or she has lifted. The sack handler indicates his or her preference for the dolly. In consideration of this expressed preference, and because the employer feels that the dolly will allow the individual to move more sacks at a time and so be more efficient than would a hand truck, the employer ultimately provides the sack handler with a dolly in fulfillment of the obligation to make reasonable accommodation.

Section 1630.9(b).

This provision states that an employer or other covered entity cannot prefer or select a qualified individual without a disability over an equally qualified individual with a disability merely because the individual with a disability will require a reasonable accommodation. In other words, an individual's need for an accommodation cannot enter into the employer's or other covered entity's decision regarding hiring, discharge, promotion, or other similar employment decisions, unless the accommodation would impose an undue hardship on the employer. *See* House Labor Report at 70.

Section 1630.9(d).

The purpose of this provision is to clarify that an employer or other covered entity may not compel a qualified individual with a disability to accept an accommodation, where that accommodation is neither requested nor needed by the individual. However, if a necessary

reasonable accommodation is refused, the individual may not be considered qualified. For example, an individual with a visual impairment that restricts his or her field of vision but who is able to read unaided would not be required to accept a reader as an accommodation. However, if the individual were not able to read unaided and reading was an essential function of the job, the individual would not be qualified for the job if he or she refused a reasonable accommodation that would enable him or her to read. *See* Senate Report at 34; House Labor Report at 65; House Judiciary Report at 71-72.

Section 1630.10 Qualification Standards, Tests, and Other Selection Criteria

The purpose of this provision is to ensure that individuals with disabilities are not excluded from job opportunities unless they are actually unable to do the job. It is to ensure that there is a fit between job criteria and an applicant's (or employee's) actual ability to do the job. Accordingly, job criteria that even unintentionally screen out, or tend to screen out, an individual with a disability or a class of individuals with disabilities because of their disability may not be used unless the employer demonstrates that that criteria, as used by the employer, are job-related to the position to which they are being applied and are consistent with business necessity. The concept of "business necessity" has the same meaning as the concept of "business necessity" under Section 504 of the Rehabilitation Act of 1973.

Selection criteria that exclude, or tend to exclude, an individual with a disability or a class of individuals with disabilities because of their disability but do not concern an essential function of the job would not be consistent with business necessity.

The use of selection criteria that are related to an essential function of the job may be consistent with business necessity. However, selection criteria that are related to an essential function of the job may not be used to exclude an individual with a disability if that individual could satisfy the criteria with the provision of a reasonable accommodation. Experience under a similar provision of the regulations implementing Section 504 of the Rehabilitation Act indicates that challenges to selection criteria are, in fact, most often resolved by reasonable accommodation. It is therefore anticipated that challenges to selection criteria brought under this part will generally be resolved in a like manner.

This provision is applicable to all types of selection criteria, including safety requirements, vision or hearing requirements, walking requirements, lifting requirements, and employment tests. *See* Senate Report at 37-39; House Labor Report at 70-72; House Judiciary Report at 42. As previously noted, however, it is not the intent of this part to second guess an employer's business judgment with regard to production standards. (See section 1630.2(n) Essential Functions). Consequently, production standards will generally not be subject to a challenge under this provision.

The Uniform Guidelines on Employee Selection Procedures (UGESP) 29 CFR part 1607 do not apply to the Rehabilitation Act and are similarly inapplicable to this part.

Section 1630.11 Administration of Tests

The intent of this provision is to further emphasize that individuals with disabilities are not to be excluded from jobs that they can actually perform merely because a disability prevents them from taking a test, or negatively influences the results of a test, that is a prerequisite to the job. Read together with the reasonable accommodation requirement of section 1630.9, this provision requires that employment tests be administered to eligible applicants or employees with disabilities that impair sensory, manual, or speaking skills in formats that do not require the use of the impaired skill.

The employer or other covered entity is, generally, only required to provide such reasonable accommodation if it knows, prior to the administration of the test, that the individual is disabled and that the disability impairs sensory, manual or speaking skills. Thus, for example, it would be unlawful to administer a written employment test to an individual who has informed the employer, prior to the administration of the test, that he is disabled with dyslexia and unable to read. In such a case, as a reasonable accommodation and in accordance with this provision, an alternative oral test should be administered to that individual. By the same token, a written test may need to be substituted for an oral test if the applicant taking the test is an individual with a disability that impairs speaking skills or impairs the processing of auditory information.

Occasionally, an individual with a disability may not realize, prior to the administration of a test, that he or she will need an accommodation to take that particular test. In such a situation, the individual with a disability, upon becoming aware of the need for an accommodation, must so inform the employer or other covered entity. For example, suppose an individual with a disabling visual impairment does not request an accommodation for a written examination because he or she is usually able to take written tests with the aid of his or her own specially designed lens. If, when the test is distributed, the individual with a disability discovers that the lens is insufficient to distinguish the words of the test because of the unusually low color contrast between the paper and the ink, the individual would be entitled, at that point, to request an accommodation. The employer or other covered entity would, thereupon, have to provide a test with higher contrast, schedule a retest, or provide any other effective accommodation unless to do so would impose an undue hardship.

Other alternative or accessible test modes or formats

include the administration of tests in large print or braille, or via a reader or sign interpreter. Where it is not possible to test in an alternative format, the employer may be required, as a reasonable accommodation, to evaluate the skill to be tested in another manner (*e.g.*, through an interview, or through education license, or work experience requirements). An employer may also be required, as a reasonable accommodation, to allow more time to complete the test. In addition, the employer's obligation to make reasonable accommodation extends to ensuring that the test site is accessible. (See section 1630.9 Not Making Reasonable Accommodation) *See* Senate Report at 37-38; House Labor Report at 70-72; House Judiciary Report at 42; *see also Stutts v. Freeman,* 694 F.2d 666 (11th Cir. 1983); *Crane v. Dole,* 617 F. Supp. 156 (D.D.C. 1985).

This provision does not require that an employer offer every applicant his or her choice of test format. Rather, this provision only requires that an employer provide, upon advance request, alternative, accessible tests to individuals with disabilities that impair sensory, manual, or speaking skills needed to take the test.

This provision does not apply to employment tests that require the use of sensory, manual, or speaking skills where the tests are intended to measure those skills. Thus, an employer could require that an applicant with dyslexia take a written test for a particular position if the ability to read is the skill the test is designed to measure. Similarly, an employer could require that an applicant complete a test within established time frames if speed were one of the skills for which the applicant was being tested. However, the results of such a test could not be used to exclude an individual with a disability unless the skill was necessary to perform an essential function of the position and no reasonable accommodation was available to enable the individual to perform that function, or the necessary accommodation would impose an undue hardship.

Section 1630.13 Prohibited Medical Examinations and Inquiries

Section 1630.13(a) Pre-employment Examination or Inquiry

This provision makes clear that an employer cannot inquire as to whether an individual has a disability at the preoffer stage of the selection process. Nor can an employer inquire at the preoffer stage about an applicant's workers' compensation history.

Employers may ask questions that relate to the applicant's ability to perform job-related functions. However, these questions should not be phrased in terms of disability. An employer, for example, may ask whether the applicant has a driver's license, if driving is a job function, but may not ask whether the applicant has a visual disability. Employers may ask about an applicant's ability to perform both essential and marginal job functions. Employers, though, may not refuse to hire an applicant with a disability because the applicant's disability prevents him or her from performing marginal functions. *See* Senate Report at 39; House Labor Report at 72-73; House Judiciary Report at 42-43.

Section 1630.13(b) Examination or Inquiry of Employees

The purpose of this provision is to prevent the administration to employees of medical tests or inquiries that do not serve a legitimate business purpose. For example, if an employee suddenly starts to use increased amounts of sick leave or starts to appear sickly, an employer could not require that employee to be tested for AIDS, HIV infection, or cancer unless the employer can demonstrate that such testing is job-related and consistent with business necessity. *See* Senate Report at 39; House Labor Report at 75; House Judiciary Report at 44.

Section 1630.14 Medical Examinations and Inquiries Specifically Permitted

Section 1630.14(a) Pre-employment Inquiry

Employers are permitted to make pre-employment inquiries into the ability of an applicant to perform job-related functions. This inquiry must be narrowly tailored. The employer may describe or demonstrate the job function and inquire whether or not the applicant can perform that function with or without reasonable accommodation. For example, an employer may explain that the job requires assembling small parts and ask if the individual will be able to perform that function, with or without reasonable accommodation. *See* Senate Report at 39; House Labor Report at 73; House Judiciary Report at 43.

An employer may also ask an applicant to describe or to demonstrate how, with or without reasonable accommodation, the applicant will be able to perform job-related functions. Such a request may be made of all applicants in the same job category regardless of disability. Such a request may also be made of an applicant whose known disability may interfere with or prevent the performance of a job-related function, whether or not the employer routinely makes such a request of all applicants in the job category. For example, an employer may ask an individual with one leg who applies for a position as a home washing machine repairman to demonstrate or to explain how, with or without reasonable accommodation, he would be able to transport himself and his tools down basement stairs. However, the employer may not inquire as to the nature or severity of the disability. Therefore, for example, the employer cannot ask how the individual lost the leg or whether the loss of the leg is indicative of an underlying impairment.

On the other hand, if the known disability of an applicant will not interfere with or prevent the performance of a job-related function, the employer may only request a description or demonstration by the applicant if it routinely makes such a request of all applicants in the same job category. So, for example, it would not be permitted for an employer to request that an applicant with one leg demonstrate his ability to assemble small parts while seated at a table, if the employer does not routinely request that all applicants provide such a demonstration.

An employer that requires an applicant with a disability to demonstrate how he or she will perform a job-related function must either provide the reasonable accommodation the applicant needs to perform the function or permit the applicant to explain how, with the accommodation, he or she will perform the function. If the job-related function is not an essential function, the employer may not exclude the applicant with a disability because of the applicant's inability to perform that function. Rather, the employer must, as a reasonable accommodation, either provide an accommodation that will enable the individual to perform the function, transfer the function to another position, or exchange the function for one the applicant is able to perform.

An employer may not use an application form that lists a number of potentially disabling impairments and ask the applicant to check any of the impairments he or she may have. In addition, as noted above, an employer may not ask how a particular individual became disabled or the prognosis of the individual's disability. The employer is also prohibited from asking how often the individual will require leave for treatment or use leave as a result of incapacitation because of the disability. However, the employer may state the attendance requirements of the job and inquire whether the applicant can meet them.

An employer is permitted to ask, on a test announcement or application form, that individuals with disabilities who will require a reasonable accommodation in order to take the test so inform the employer within a reasonable established time period prior to the administration of the test. The employer may also request that documentation of the need for the accommodation accompany the request. Requested accommodations may include accessible testing sites, modified testing conditions and accessible test formats. (See section 1630.11 Administration of Tests).

Physical agility tests are not medical examinations and so may be given at any point in the application or employment process. Such tests must be given to all similarly situated applicants or employees regardless of disability. If such tests screen out or tend to screen out an individual with a disability or a class of individuals with disabilities, the employer would have to demonstrate that the test is job-related and consistent with business necessity and that performance cannot be achieved with reasonable accommodation. (See section 1630.9 Not Making Reasonable Accommodation: Process of Determining the Appropriate Reasonable Accommodation).

As previously noted, collecting information and inviting individuals to identify themselves as individuals with disabilities as required to satisfy the affirmative action requirements of Section 503 of the Rehabilitation Act is not restricted by this part. (See section 1630.1(b) and (c) Applicability and Construction).

Section 1630.14(b) Employment Entrance Examination

An employer is permitted to require post-offer medical examinations before the employee actually starts working. The employer may condition the offer of employment on the results of the examination, provided that all entering employees in the same job category are subjected to such an examination, regardless of disability, and that the confidentiality requirements specified in this part are met.

This provision recognizes that in many industries, such as air transportation or construction, applicants for certain positions are chosen on the basis of many factors including physical and psychological criteria, some of which may be identified as a result of post-offer medical examinations given prior to entry on duty. Only those employees who meet the employer's physical and psychological criteria for the job, with or without reasonable accommodation, will be qualified to receive confirmed offers of employment and begin working.

Medical examinations permitted by this section are not required to be job-related and consistent with business necessity. However, if an employer withdraws an offer of employment because the medical examination reveals that the employee does not satisfy certain employment criteria, either the exclusionary criteria must not screen out or tend to screen out an individual with a disability or a class of individuals with disabilities, or they must be job-related and consistent with business necessity. As part of the showing that an exclusionary criteria is job-related and consistent with business necessity, the employer must also demonstrate that there is no reasonable accommodation that will enable the individual with a disability to perform the essential functions of the job. *See* Conference Report at 59–60; Senate Report at 39; House Labor Report at 73–74; House Judiciary Report at 43.

As an example, suppose an employer makes a conditional offer of employment to an applicant, and it is an essential function of the job that the incumbent be available to work every day for the next three months. An employment entrance examination then reveals that the applicant has a disabling impairment that, according to reasonable medical judgment that relies on the most current medical knowledge, will require treatment that will render the applicant unable to work for a portion of the three month period. Under these

circumstances, the employer would be able to withdraw the employment offer without violating this part.

The information obtained in the course of a permitted entrance examination or inquiry is to be treated as a confidential medical record and may only be used in a manner not inconsistent with this part. State workers' compensation laws are not preempted by the ADA or this part. These laws require the collection of information from individuals for state administrative purposes that do not conflict with the ADA or this part. Consequently, employers or other covered entities may submit information to state workers' compensation offices or second injury funds in accordance with state workers' compensation laws without violating this part.

Consistent with this section and with section 1630.16(f) of this part, information obtained in the course of a permitted entrance examination or inquiry may be used for insurance purposes described in section 1630.16(f).

Section 1630.14(c) Examination of Employees

This provision permits employers to make inquiries or require medical examinations (fitness for duty exams) when there is a need to determine whether an employee is still able to perform the essential functions of his or her job. The provision permits employers or other covered entities to make inquiries or require medical examinations necessary to the reasonable accommodation process described in this part. This provision also permits periodic physicals to determine fitness for duty or other medical monitoring if such physicals or monitoring are required by medical standards or requirements established by Federal, state, or local law that are consistent with the ADA and this part (or in the case of a federal standard, with Section 504 of the Rehabilitation Act) in that they are job-related and consistent with business necessity.

Such standards may include federal safety regulations that regulate bus and truck driver qualifications, as well as laws establishing medical requirements for pilots or other air transportation personnel. These standards also include health standards promulgated pursuant to the Occupational Safety and Health Act of 1970, the Federal Coal Mine Health and Safety Act of 1969, or other similar statutes that require that employees exposed to certain toxic and hazardous substances be medically monitored at specific intervals. *See* House Labor Report at 74-75.

The information obtained in the course of such examination or inquiries is to be treated as a confidential medical record and may only be used in a manner not inconsistent with this part.

Section 1630.14(d) Other Acceptable Examinations and Inquiries

Part 1630 permits voluntary medical examinations, including voluntary medical histories, as part of employee health programs. These programs often include, for example, medical screening for high blood pressure, weight control counseling, and cancer detection. Voluntary activities, such as blood pressure monitoring and the administering of prescription drugs, such as insulin, are also permitted. It should be noted, however, that the medical records developed in the course of such activities must be maintained in the confidential manner required by this part and must not be used for any purpose in violation of this part, such as limiting health insurance eligibility. House Labor Report at 75; House Judiciary Report at 43-44.

Section 1630.15 Defenses

The section on defenses in part 1630 is not intended to be exhaustive. However, it is intended to inform employers of some of the potential defenses available to a charge of discrimination under the ADA and this part.

Section 1630.15(a) Disparate Treatment Defenses

The "traditional" defense to a charge of disparate treatment under title VII, as expressed in *McDonnell Douglas Corp. v. Green*, 411 U.S. 792 (1973), *Texas Department of Community Affairs v. Burdine*, 450 U.S. 248 (1981), and their progeny, may be applicable to charges of disparate treatment brought under the ADA. *See Prewitt v. U.S. Postal Service*, 662 F.2d 292 (5th Cir. 1981). Disparate treatment means, with respect to title I of the ADA, that an individual was treated differently on the basis of his or her disability. For example, disparate treatment has occurred where an employer excludes an employee with a severe facial disfigurement from staff meetings because the employer does not like to look at the employee. The individual is being treated differently because of the employer's attitude towards his or her perceived disability. Disparate treatment has also occurred where an employer has a policy of not hiring individuals with AIDS regardless of the individuals' qualifications.

The crux of the defense to this type of charge is that the individual was treated differently not because of his or her disability but for a legitimate nondiscriminatory reason such as poor performance unrelated to the individual's disability. The fact that the individual's disability is not covered by the employer's current insurance plan or would cause the employer's insurance premiums or workers' compensation costs to increase, would not be a legitimate nondiscriminatory reason justifying disparate treatment of a individual with a disability. Senate Report at 85; House Labor Report at 136 and House Judiciary Report at 70. The defense of a legitimate nondiscriminatory reason is rebutted if the alleged nondiscriminatory reason is shown to be pretextual.

Section 1630.15(b) and (c) Disparate Impact Defenses

Disparate impact means, with respect to title I of the ADA and this part, that uniformly applied criteria have an adverse impact on an individual with a disability or a disproportionately negative impact on a class of individuals with disabilities. Section 1630.15(b) clarifies that an employer may use selection criteria that have such a disparate impact, *i.e.*, that screen out or tend to screen out an individual with a disability or a class of individuals with disabilities only when they are job-related and consistent with business necessity.

For example, an employer interviews two candidates for a position, one of whom is blind. Both are equally qualified. The employer decides that while it is not essential to the job it would be convenient to have an employee who has a driver's license and so could occasionally be asked to run errands by car. The employer hires the individual who is sighted because this individual has a driver's license. This is an example of a uniformly applied criterion, having a driver's permit, that screens out an individual who has a disability that makes it impossible to obtain a driver's permit. The employer would, thus, have to show that this criterion is job-related and consistent with business necessity. *See* House Labor Report at 55.

However, even if the criterion is job-related and consistent with business necessity, an employer could not exclude an individual with a disability if the criterion could be met or job performance accomplished with a reasonable accommodation. For example, suppose an employer requires, as part of its application process, an interview that is job-related and consistent with business necessity. The employer would not be able to refuse to hire a hearing impaired applicant because he or she could not be interviewed. This is so because an interpreter could be provided as a reasonable accommodation that would allow the individual to be interviewed, and thus satisfy the selection criterion.

With regard to safety requirements that screen out or tend to screen out an individual with a disability or a class of individuals with disabilities, an employer must demonstrate that the requirement, as applied to the individual, satisfies the "direct threat" standard in section 1630.2(r) in order to show that the requirement is job related and consistent with business necessity.

Section 1630.15(c) clarifies that there may be uniformly applied standards, criteria and policies not relating to selection that may also screen out or tend to screen out an individual with a disability or a class of individuals with disabilities. Like selection criteria that have a disparate impact, non-selection criteria having such an impact may also have to be job-related and consistent with business necessity, subject to consideration of reasonable accommodation.

It should be noted, however, that some uniformly applied employment policies or practices, such as leave policies, are not subject to challenge under the adverse impact theory. "No-leave" policies (*e.g.*, no leave during the first six months of employment) are likewise not subject to challenge under the adverse impact theory. However, an employer, in spite of its "no-leave" policy, may, in appropriate circumstances, have to consider the provision of leave to an employee with a disability as a reasonable accommodation, unless the provision of leave would impose an undue hardship. See discussion at section 1630.5 Limiting, Segregating and Classifying, and section 1630.10 Qualification Standards, Tests, and Other Selection Criteria.

Section 1630.15(d) Defense to Not Making Reasonable Accommodation

An employer or other covered entity alleged to have discriminated because it did not make a reasonable accommodation, as required by this part,

may offer as a defense that it would have been an undue hardship to make the accommodation.

It should be noted, however, that an employer cannot simply assert that a needed accommodation will cause it undue hardship, as defined in section 1630.2(p), and thereupon be relieved of the duty to provide accommodation. Rather, an employer will have to present evidence and demonstrate that the accommodation will, in fact, cause it undue hardship. Whether a particular accommodation will impose an undue hardship for a particular employer is determined on a case by case basis. Consequently, an accommodation that poses an undue hardship for one employer at a particular time may not pose an undue hardship for another employer, or even for the same employer at another time. Likewise, an accommodation that poses an undue hardship for one employer in a particular job setting, such as a temporary construction worksite, may not pose an undue hardship for another employer, or even for the same employer at a permanent worksite. *See* House Judiciary Report at 42.

The concept of undue hardship that has evolved under Section 504 of the Rehabilitation Act and is embodied in this part is unlike the "undue hardship" defense associated with the provision of religious accommodation under title VII of the Civil Rights Act of 1964. To demonstrate undue hardship pursuant to the ADA and this part, an employer must show substantially more difficulty or expense than would be needed to satisfy the "de minimis" title VII standard of undue hardship. For example, to demonstrate that the cost of an accommodation poses an undue hardship, an employer would have to show that the cost is undue as compared to the employer's budget. Simply comparing the cost of the accommodation to the salary of the individual with a disability in need of the accommodation will not suffice. Moreover, even if it is determined that the cost of an

accommodation would unduly burden an employer, the employer cannot avoid making the accommodation if the individual with a disability can arrange to cover that portion of the cost that rises to the undue hardship level, or can otherwise arrange to provide the accommodation. Under such circumstances, the necessary accommodation would no longer pose an undue hardship. *See* Senate Report at 36; House Labor Report at 68-69; House Judiciary Report at 40-41.

Excessive cost is only one of several possible bases upon which an employer might be able to demonstrate undue hardship. Alternatively, for example, an employer could demonstrate that the provision of a particular accommodation would be unduly disruptive to its other employees or to the functioning of its business. The terms of a collective bargaining agreement may be relevant to this determination. By way of illustration, an employer would likely be able to show undue hardship if the employer could show that the requested accommodation of the upward adjustment of the business' thermostat would result in it becoming unduly hot for its other employees, or for its patrons or customers. The employer would thus not have to provide this accommodation. However, if there were an alternate accommodation that would not result in undue hardship, the employer would have to provide that accommodation.

It should be noted, moreover, that the employer would not be able to show undue hardship if the disruption to its employees were the result of those employees' fears or prejudices toward the individual's disability and not the result of the provision of the accommodation. Nor would the employer be able to demonstrate undue hardship by showing that the provision of the accommodation has a negative impact on the morale of its other employees but not on the ability of these employees to perform their jobs.

Section 1630.15(e) Defense Conflicting Federal Laws and Regulations

There are several Federal laws and regulations that address medical standards and safety requirements. If the alleged discriminatory action was taken in compliance with another Federal law or regulation, the employer may offer its obligation to comply with the conflicting standard as a defense. The employer's defense of a conflicting Federal requirement or regulation may be rebutted by a showing of pretext, or by showing that the Federal standard did not require the discriminatory action, or that there was a non-exclusionary means to comply with the standard that would not conflict with this part. *See* House Labor Report at 74.

Section 1630.16 Specific Activities Permitted

Section 1630.16(a) Religious Entities

Religious organizations are not exempt from title I of the ADA or this part. A religious corporation, association, educational institution, or society may give a preference in employment to individuals of the particular religion, and may require that applicants and employees conform to the religious tenets of the organization. However, a religious organization may not discriminate against an individual who satisfies the permitted religious criteria because that individual is disabled. The religious entity, in other words, is required to consider qualified individuals with disabilities who satisfy the permitted religious criteria on an equal basis with qualified individuals without disabilities who similarly satisfy the religious criteria. *See* Senate Report at 42; House Labor Report at 7677; House Judiciary Report at 46.

Section 1630.16(b) Regulation of Alcohol and Drugs

This provision permits employers to establish or comply with certain standards regulating the use of drugs and alcohol in the workplace. It also allows employers to hold alcoholics and persons who engage in the illegal use of drugs to the same performance and conduct standards to which it holds all of its other employees. Individuals disabled by alcoholism are entitled to the same protections accorded other individuals with disabilities under this part. As noted above, individuals currently engaging in the illegal use of drugs are not individuals with disabilities for purposes of part 1630 when the employer acts on the basis of such use.

Section 1630.16(c) Drug Testing

This provision reflects title I's neutrality toward testing for the illegal use of drugs. Such drug tests are neither encouraged, authorized nor prohibited. The results of such drug tests may be used as a basis for disciplinary action. Tests for the illegal use of drugs are not considered medical examinations for purposes of this part. If the results reveal information about an individual's medical condition beyond whether the individual is currently engaging in the illegal use of drugs, this additional information is to be treated as a confidential medical record. For example, if a test for the illegal use of drugs reveals the presence of a controlled substance that has been lawfully prescribed for a particular medical condition, this information is to be treated as a confidential medical record. *See* House Labor Report at 79; House Judiciary Report at 47.

Section 1630.16(e) Infectious and Communicable Diseases; Food Handling Jobs

This provision addressing food handling jobs applies the "direct threat" analysis to the particular situation of accommodating individuals with infectious or communicable diseases that are transmitted through the handling of food. The Department of Health and Human Services is to prepare a list of infectious and communicable diseases that are transmitted through the handling of food. If an individual with a disability has one of the listed diseases and works in or applies for a position in food handling, the employer must determine whether there is a reasonable accommodation that will eliminate the risk of transmitting the disease through the handling of food. If there is an accommodation that will not pose an undue hardship, and that will prevent the transmission of the disease through the handling of food, the employer must provide the accommodation to the individual. The employer, under these circumstances, would not be permitted to discriminate against the individual because of the need to provide the reasonable accommodation and would be required to maintain the individual in the food handling job.

If no such reasonable accommodation is possible, the employer may refuse to assign, or to continue to assign the individual to a position involving food handling. This means that if such an individual is an applicant for a food handling position the employer is not required to hire the individual. However, if the individual is a current employee, the employer would be required to consider the accommodation of reassignment to a vacant position not involving food handling for which the individual is qualified. Conference Report at 61-63. (See section 1630.2(r) Direct Threat).

Section 1630.16(f) Health Insurance, Life Insurance, and Other Benefit Plans

This provision is a limited exemption that is only applicable to those who establish, sponsor, observe or administer benefit plans, such as health and life insurance plans. It does not apply to those who establish, sponsor, observe or administer plans not involving benefits, such as liability insurance plans.

The purpose of this provision is to permit the development and administration of benefit plans in accordance with accepted principles of risk assessment.

This provision is not intended to disrupt the current regulatory structure for self-insured employers. These employers may establish, sponsor, observe, or administer the terms of a bona fide benefit plan not subject to state laws that regulate insurance. This provision is also not intended to disrupt the current nature of insurance underwriting, or current insurance industry practices in sales, underwriting, pricing, administrative and other services, claims and similar insurance related activities based on classification of risks as regulated by the States.

The activities permitted by this provision do not violate part 1630 even if they result in limitations on individuals with disabilities, provided that these activities are not used as a subterfuge to evade the purposes of this part. Whether or not these activities are being used as a subterfuge is to be determined without regard to the date the insurance plan or employee benefit plan was adopted.

However, an employer or other covered entity cannot deny a qualified individual with a disability equal access to insurance or subject a qualified individual with a disability to different terms or conditions of insurance based on disability alone, if the disability does not pose increased risks. Part 1630 requires that decisions not based on risk classification be made in conformity with nondiscrimination requirements. *See* Senate Report at 84-86; House Labor Report at 136-138; House Judiciary Report at 70-71. See the discussion of section 1630.5 Limiting, Segregating and Classifying.

EQUAL EMPLOYMENT OPPORTUNITY COMMISSION

29 CFR Parts 1602 and 1627

Recordkeeping and Reporting Under Title VII and the ADA

AGENCY: Equal Employment Opportunity Commission (EEOC).

ACTION: Final rule.

SUMMARY: This final rule is based on two separate Notices of Proposed Rulemaking (NPRM) published on February 13, 1989 (54 FR 6551), and March 5, 1991 (56 FR 9185). This final rule amends 29 CFR part 1602, EEOC's regulations on Recordkeeping and Reporting under title VII of the Civil Rights Act of 1964 (title VII), to add recordkeeping requirements under the Americans with Disabilities Act of 1990 (ADA). It increases the records retention period required in part 1602 for title VII and the ADA from 6 months to one year. The Commission also is adding a new subpart R to part 1602, 29 CFR 1602.56, that will clarify that the Commission has the authority to investigate persons to determine whether they comply with the reporting or recordkeeping requirements of part 1602. In addition, the Commission is making several minor changes to §§ 1602.7 and 1602.10.

The Commission also is deleting § 1602.14(b) of its title VII record keeping regulations, which provides that the § 1602 record keeping requirements do not apply to temporary or seasonal positions. Information regarding such employees now must be reported on Standard Form 100 on September 30 of each year, in the same fashion as information regarding permanent employees is reported. Similarly, the Commission is deleting §§ 1627.3(b) and 1627.4(a)(2) of the Age Discrimination in Employment Act record keeping regulations, which

provide for a 90-day retention period for temporary positions, and is clarifying the mandatory nature of such record keeping. The Commission is not issuing a final rule on proposed § 1602.57 at this time.

EFFECTIVE DATE: August 26, 1991.

FOR FURTHER INFORMATION CONTACT: Thomas J. Schlageter, Acting Assistant Legal Counsel, Grace C. Karmiol, General Attorney, or Wendy Adams, General Attorney, at (202) 663-4669 (voice) or (202) 663-4399 (TDD).

SUPPLEMENTARY INFORMATION: The Commission received nine comments in response to the NPRM published in the March 5, 1991 **Federal Register** on Recordkeeping and Reporting under title VII and the ADA. The comments responded to the invitation in the preamble of the NPRM for comment on whether there should be a reporting requirement under the ADA, how the reported information should be used, and how it should be collected. Four comments recommended that there be a reporting requirement although one of them suggested that it be collected by sampling rather than universal reporting. Five comments opposed any new reporting requirements on the grounds of administrative burden. One of these suggested that no reporting requirement be imposed at this time, but that the need for reporting be reassessed at a later date. Another of these argued that if a reporting requirement is necessary, it should be accomplished by using the existing EEO-1 rather than a separate report, should be collected by both employer visual identification and employee self-identification, and should be used to monitor the impact of the ADA and to document utilization of persons with disabilities, not for affirmative action purposes. The Commission is continuing its consideration of possible reporting requirements under the ADA and will confer with the Department of Labor, and any other affected federal agency, to discuss whether a reporting requirement would be appropriate under the ADA. If it concludes that a reporting requirement may be appropriate, it will issue an NPRM.

The Commission received over 20 comments in response to the February 13, 1989 NPRM. While this preamble does not address each individual comment, it addresses the most significant issues raised in the comments. Current § 1602.7 concerns the filing of Standard Form 100, and has been interpreted in conjunction with the instructions accompanying the form. In order to clarify which of the employers that are subject to title VII must file the report, the Commission has incorporated some of the information that is contained in the instructions into § 1602.7.

Current § 1602.14 provides that personnel or employment records made or kept by an employer shall be preserved by the employer for a period of six months from the date of the making of the record or of the personnel action involved, whichever is later. This requirement was promulgated before title VII was amended in 1972 to change the time limit for filing a charge from 90 days to 180 days (or, in some instances, to 300 days). Requiring an employer or labor organization to maintain records for six months when the charge filing limit was 90 days ensured that all applicable records were kept. Due to the lengthening of the filing period, however, it no longer is true that employers or labor organizations necessarily will have retained records until the title VII filing period expires. Under the current regulation, an employer or labor organization may have already lawfully destroyed its employment records before it is notified that a charge has been filed. Moreover, a one year retention period for employers and labor organizations subject to title VII and the ADA will make the records retention period the same as that required by the Commission's regulations under the Age Discrimination in Employment Act, 29 U.S.C. 621 *et seq.* (ADEA), 29

CFR 1627.3(b)(1) and 1627.4(a)(1). This uniform retention period will simplify and clarify record keeping for employers who are also subject to the ADEA.

In order to promote efficiency and to eliminate confusion as to record keeping requirements regarding temporary and seasonal employees, the Commission is deleting § 1602.14(b) which provides that the part 1602 record keeping requirements do not apply to temporary or seasonal positions. Similarly, the Commission is deleting §§ 1627.3(b)(3) and 1627.4(a)(2) of the ADEA recordkeeping regulations, which provide for a 90 day records retention period for temporary positions, and is clarifying the mandatory nature of such record keeping. These changes will require employers to retain records on all employees, permanent and temporary, for a one year period. They will, however, impose a new record keeping requirement only on the relatively few employers who are not subject to the record keeping provisions of the ADEA.

Section 709(c) of title VII, 42 U.S.C. 2000e-8(c), provides, *inter alia*, that any person who fails to maintain information as required by that subsection and by Commission regulations may, upon application of the Commission or the Attorney General in a case involving a government, governmental agency or political subdivision, be ordered to comply by the appropriate United States district court. At present, Commission regulations do not explicitly provide that the Commission may conduct an investigation when it has reason to believe an employer or other entity subject to title VII has failed to comply with the record keeping requirements of part 1602, as when, for example, an employer does not provide the required record keeping information to the Commission. The Commission is adding § 1602.56 to give clear notice of its authority to enforce section 709(c) of title VII. The addition of this section is consistent with the Commission's authority to

issue suitable procedural regulations to carry out the provisions of title VII, 42 U.S.C. 2000e-12(a), and is an appropriate procedural mechanism for investigating apparent violations of those provisions.

The revisions to § 1602.7 change the annual Standard Form 100 reporting date from March 31 to September 30. By changing the reporting date the Commission also is changing the dates for which the information should be reported, i.e., from the three months preceding March 31, to the three months preceding September 30. Any employer that has received permission to use a different period for reporting may continue to use that approved period. The Commission has determined that this change will result in a reporting date that is less affected by the variation in seasonal employment, such as employment in the construction industry, than the present date and will provide employment figures which reflect annual average employment more closely than the present date does. This change will not affect the date by which employers must report VETS information to the United States Department of Labor, as the VETS data and the Standard Form 100 data are processed separately. The revisions also change the address for obtaining necessary reporting supplies from "Jeffersonville, Indiana" to "the Commission or its delegate."

The revision to § 1602.10 deletes the reference to "section 4(c) of the instructions" and substitutes "section 5 of the instructions." The reference to the 100 employee jurisdictional test of section 701(b) of title VII is deleted since the number of employees required for an employer to be subject to title VII now is 15 or more. This change in no way affects the present Standard Form 100 reporting requirement of 100 or more employees that is set out in the instructions accompanying the form and now is made explicit in the regulation.

In order to provide a mechanism for those subject to the reporting requirements to seek a change in the reporting date or the date by which data should be reported, the Commission has revised § 1602.10 to permit employers to seek changes in those requirements. The Commission notes that retention of the records for the period of one year will increase only minimally, if at all, the employer's cost of maintaining the records. Employers already are required to maintain the records for a period of six months. The cost of retaining the records for an additional six months will be minimal. Moreover, most employers subject to Title VII also are subject to the ADEA, which presently requires that these records be retained for a period of one year.

The Commission estimates that the changes to §§ 1602.14 and 1602.28(a) increasing the title VII records retention period from six months to one year will result in an increased recordkeeping burden on employers of approximately 9,000 burden hours annually. The Commission estimates that the changes in the title VII and ADEA recordkeeping require-ments for employers with temporary employees will result in an increased record keeping burden of approxi-mately 20,800 burden hours annually. The Commission believes that this increase in burden hours is *de minimis* and that the modifications will not have a significant impact on a substantial number of small employers. Further, the Commission believes that the above cited benefits of the modifications, by establishing a uniform period of record keeping for full time and part time employees under title VII, ADA and the ADEA, outweigh the minimal increase in record keeping burden hours on employers. For the above reasons, the regulatory change will simplify the record keeping requirements. The Commission also certifies under 5 U.S.C. 605(b), enacted by the Regula-tory Flexibility Act (Pub. L. No. 96-354), that these modifications will not result in a significant economic impact on a substan-tial number of small employers and that a regulatory flexibility

analysis therefore is not required.

List of Subjects in 29 CFR Parts 1602 and 1627

Equal employment opportunity, Reporting and record keeping requirements.

For the Commission,
Evan J. Kemp, Jr.,
Chairman.

Accordingly, 29 CFR parts 1602 and 1627 are amended as follows:

PART 1602--(AMENDED)

1. The heading for part 1602 is revised to read as follows:

PART 1602--RECORD KEEPING AND REPORTING REQUIREMENTS UNDER TITLE VII AND THE ADA

2. The authority citation for part 1602 is revised to read as follows:

Authority: 42 U.S.C. 2000e-8, 2000e-12; 44 U.S.C. 3501 et seq.; 42 U.S.C. 12117.

3. Section 1602.1 is revised to read as follows:

§ 1602.1 Purpose and scope.

Section 709 of title VII (42 U.S.C. 2000e) and section 107 of the Americans with Disabilities Act (ADA) (42 U.S.C. 12117) require the Commission to establish regulations pursuant to which employers, labor organizations, joint labor-management committees, and employment agencies subject to those Acts shall make and preserve certain records and shall furnish specified informa-tion to aid in the administration and enforcement of the Acts.

4. The heading for Subpart A is revised to read as follows:

Subpart A--General

§ 1602.1 [Amended]

5. Section 1602.1 is moved under subpart A.

§§ 1602.2-1602.6 [Removed]

6. Sections 1602.2-1602.6 are removed and reserved.

§ 1602.7 [Amended]

7. Section 1602.7 is amended by revising the first and last sentences to read as follows:

§ 1602.7 Requirement for filing of report.

On or before September 30 of each year, every employer that is subject to title VII of the Civil Rights Act of 1964, as amended, and that has 100 or more employees, shall file with the Commission or its delegate executed copies of Standard Form 100, as revised (otherwise known as "Employer Informa-tion Report EEO-1") in conformity with the directions set forth in the form and accompanying instructions. * * * Appropriate copies of Standard Form 100 in blank will be supplied to every employer known to the Commission to be subject to the reporting requirements, but it is the responsibility of all such employers to obtain necessary supplies of the form from the Commission or its delegate prior to the filing date.

8. Section 1602.10 is revised to read as follows:

§ 1602.10 Employer's exemption from reporting requirements.

If an employer claims that the preparation or filing of the report would create undue hardship, the employer may apply to the Commission for an exemption from the require-ments set forth in this part, according to instruction 5. If an employer is engaged in activities for which the reporting unit criteria described in section 5 of the instructions are not readily adaptable, special reporting procedures may be required. If an employer seeks to change the date for filing its Standard Form 100 or seeks to change the period for which data are reported, an alternative reporting date or period may be permitted. In such instances, the employer

THE AMERICANS WITH DISABILITIES ACT: ACCESS AND ACCOMMODATIONS
THE AMERICANS WITH DISABILITIES ACT: ACCESS AND ACCOMMODATIONS

should so advise the Commis-should so advise the Commission by submitting to the
Commission or its delegate a
specific written proposal for an
alternative reporting system
prior to the date on which the
report is due.

§ 1602.11 [Amended]

9. Section 1602.11 is
amended as follows:
a. In the first sentence, after
"purposes of title VII" insert
"or the ADA".
b. In the second sentence,
after "section 709(c) of title VII"
insert "or section 107 of the
ADA".

§ 1602.12 [Amended]

10. Section 1602.12 is
amended as follows:
a. In the first sentence, after
"purposes of Title VII" insert
"or the ADA".
b. In the second sentence,
after "section 709(c)" insert "of
Title VII, or section 107 of the
ADA".
c. By revising the paren-
thetical at the end of the section
to read as follows:

(Approved by the Office of
Management and Budget under
control number 3046-0040)

§ 1602.14 [Amended]

11. Section 1602.14(a) is
amended as follows:
a. By removing the words
"6 months" wherever they
appear and replacing them with
the words "one year".
b. In the first sentence, after
"not necessarily limited to"
insert "requests for reasonable
accommodation,".
c. In the third sentence, after
"under title VII" insert "or the
ADA".
d. By revising the paren-
thetical at the end of the section
to read as follows:
(Approved by the Office of
Management and Budget under
control number 3046-0040)

§ 1602.14 [Amended]

12. Section 1602.14 is
amended by removing
paragraph (b), by removing the
designation from paragraph (a),
and by revising the parentheti-

cal at the end of the section to
read as follows:

(Approved by the Office of
Management and Budget under
control number 3046-0040)

§ 1602.19 [Amended]

13. Section 1602.19 is
amended as follows:
a. In the first sentence, after
"purpose of Title VII" insert "or
the ADA".
b. In the second sentence,
after "section 709(c) of title VII"
insert "or section 107 of the
ADA".

§ 1602.21 [Amended]

14. Section 1602.21(b) is
amended as follows:
a. In the first sentence, after
"not necessarily limited to"
insert "requests for reasonable
accommodation,".
b. In the second sentence,
after "under Title VII" insert
"or the ADA".

§ 1602.26 [Amended]

15. Section 1602.26 is
amended as follows:
a. In the first sentence, after
"purposes of Title VII" insert
"or the ADA".
b. In the second sentence,
after "section 709(c)" insert "of
Title VII or section 107 of the
ADA".

§ 1602.28 [Amended]

16. Section 1602.28(a) is
amended as follows:
a. By removing the words
"6 months" wherever they
appear and replacing them with
the words "one year".
b. In the third sentence, after
"under title VII" insert "or the
ADA".
c. By revising the paren-
thetical at the end of the section
to read as follows:

(Approved by the Office of
Management and Budget under
control number 3046-0040)

§ 1602.31 [Amended]

17. Section 1602.31 is
amended as follows:
a. By removing paragraph
(b) and the designation from
paragraph (a).

b. In the first sentence, after
"not necessarily limited to"
insert "requests for reasonable
accommodation,".
c. In the third sentence, after
"under title VII" insert "or the
ADA".
d. By revising the paren-
thetical at the end of the section
to read as follows:

(Approved by the Office of
Management and Budget under
control number 3046-0040)

§ 1602.37 [Amended]

18. Section 1602.37 is
amended as follows:
a. In the first sentence, after
"purposes of title VII" insert
"or the ADA".
b. In the second sentence,
after "section 709(c) of title VII"
insert "or section 107 of the
ADA".

§ 1602.40 [Amended]

19. Section 1602.40 is
amended as follows:
a. By removing paragraph
(b) and the designation from
paragraph (a).
b. In the first sentence, after
"not necessarily limited to"
insert "requests for reasonable
accommodation,".
c. By revising the paren-
thetical at the end of the section
to read as follows:

(Approved by the Office of
Management and Budget under
control number 3046-0040)

§ 1602.45 [Amended]

20. Section 1602.45 is
amended as follows:
a. In the first sentence, after
"purposes of title VII" insert
"or the ADA".
b. In the second sentence,
after "section 709(c) of title VII"
insert "or section 107 of the
ADA".

§ 1602.49 [Amended]

21. Section 1602.49 is
amended as follows:
a. By removing paragraph
(b) and redesignating paragraph
(c) as new paragraph (b).
b. In the first sentence of
paragraph (a), after "not
necessarily limited to" insert

"requests for reasonable accommodation,".

c. By revising the parenthetical at the end of the section to read as follows:

(Approved by the Office of Management and Budget under control number 3046-0040)

§ 1602.54 [Amended]

22. Section 1602.54 is amended as follows:

a. In the first sentence, after "purposes of title VII" insert "or the ADA".

b. In the second sentence, after "section 709(c) of title VII" insert "or section 107 of the ADA".

23. A new subpart R consisting of § 1602.56 is added, to read as follows:

Subpart R--Investigation of Reporting or Recordkeeping Violations

§ 1602.56 Investigation of reporting or recordkeeping violations.

When it has received an allegation, or has reason to believe, that a person has not complied with the reporting or recordkeeping requirements of this Part or of Part 1607 of this chapter, the Commission may conduct an investigation of the alleged failure to comply.

Part 1627--(Amended)

24. The authority citation for 29 CFR part 1627 continues to read as follows:

Authority: Sec. 7, 81 Stat. 604; 29 U.S.C. 626; sec. 11, 52 Stat. 1066; 29 U.S.C. 211; sec. 12, 29 U.S.C. 631, Pub. L. No. 99-592, 100 Stat. 3342; sec. 2, Reorg. Plan No. 1 of 1978, 43 FR 19807.

§ 1627.3 [Amended]

25. In § 1627.3, paragraph (b)(3) is removed and paragraph (b)(4) is redesignated as new paragraph (b)(3).

26. Newly designate § 1627.3(b)(3) is amended by removing the word "may" and replacing it with the word "shall" and by revising the words "paragraph (b) (1), (2), or (3)" to read "paragraph (b) (1) or (2)".

§ 1627.4 [Amended]

27. In § 1627.4, paragraph (a)(2) is removed and paragraph (a)(3) is redesignated as new paragraph (a)(2).

28. Newly designated § 1627.4(a)(2) is amended by removing the word "may" and replacing it with the word "shall" and by revising the words "paragraph (a) (1) or (2)" to read "paragraph (a)(1)".

§ 1627.5 [Amended]

29. Section 1627.5(c) is amended by removing the word "may" and replacing it with the word "shall".

[FR Doc. 91-17513 Filed 7-25-91; 8:45 am]

BILLING CODE 6750-06-M

Department of Justice
28 CFR Part 36
Nondiscrimination on the Basis of Disability by Public Accommodations and in Commercial Facilities

DEPARTMENT OF JUSTICE

Office of the Attorney General

28 CFR Part 36

(Order No. 1513-91)

Nondiscrimination on the Basis of Disability by Public Accommodations and in Commercial Facilities

AGENCY: Department of Justice.

ACTION: Final rule.

SUMMARY: This rule implements title III of the Americans with Disabilities Act, Public Law 101-336, which prohibits discrimination on the basis of disability by private entities in places of public accommodation, requires that all new places of public accommodation and commercial facilities be designed and constructed so as to be readily accessible to and usable by persons with disabilities, and requires that examinations or courses related to licensing or certification for professional and trade purposes be accessible to persons with disabilities.

EFFECTIVE DATE: January 26, 1992.

FOR FURTHER INFORMATION CONTACT: Barbara S. Drake, Deputy Assistant Attorney General, Civil Rights Division; Stewart B. Oneglia, Chief, Coordination and Review Section, Civil Rights Division; and John Wodatch, Director, Office on the Americans with Disabilities Act, Civil Rights Division; all of the U.S. Department of Justice, Washington, DC 20530. They may be contacted through the Division's ADA Information Line at (202) 514-0301 (Voice), (202) 514-0381 (TDD), or (202) 514-0383 (TDD). These telephone numbers are not toll-free numbers.

Copies of this rule are available in the following alternate formats: large print, Braille, electronic file on computer disk, and audio-tape. Copies may be obtained from the Office on the Americans with Disabilities Act at (202) 514-0301 (Voice) or (202) 514-0381 (TDD). The rule is also available on electronic bulletin board at (202) 514-6193. These telephone numbers are not toll-free numbers.

SUPPLEMENTARY INFORMATION:

Background

The landmark Americans with Disabilities Act ("ADA" or "the Act"), enacted on July 26, 1990, provides comprehensive civil rights protections to individuals with disabilities in the areas of employment, public accommodations, State and local government services, and telecommunications.

The legislation was originally developed by the National Council on Disability, an independent Federal agency that reviews and makes recommendations concerning Federal laws, programs, and policies affecting individuals with disabilities. In its 1986 study, "Toward Independence," the National Council on Disability recognized the inadequacy of the existing, limited patchwork of protections for individuals with disabilities, and recommended the enactment of a comprehensive civil rights law requiring equal opportunity for individuals with disabilities throughout American life. Although the 100th Congress did not act on the legislation, which was first introduced in 1988, then-Vice-President George Bush endorsed the concept of comprehensive disability rights legislation during his presidential campaign and became a dedicated advocate of the ADA.

The ADA was reintroduced in modified form in May 1989 for consideration by the 101st Congress. In June 1989, Attorney General Dick Thornburgh, in testimony before the Senate Committee on Labor and Human Resources, reiterated the Bush Administration's support for the ADA and suggested changes in the proposed legislation. After extensive negotiations between Senate sponsors and the Administration, the Senate passed an amended version of the ADA on September 7, 1989, by a vote of 76-8.

In the House, jurisdiction over the ADA was divided among four committees, each of which conducted extensive hearings and issued detailed committee reports: the Committee on Education and Labor, the Committee on the Judiciary, the Committee on Public Works and Transportation, and the Committee on Energy and Commerce. On October 12, 1989, the Attorney General testified in favor of the legislation before the Committee on the Judiciary. The Civil Rights Division, on February 22, 1990, provided testimony to the Committee on Small Business, which although technically without jurisdiction over the bill, conducted hearings on the legislation's impact on small business.

After extensive committee consideration and floor debate, the House of Representatives passed an amended version of the Senate bill on May 22, 1990, by a vote of 403-20. After resolving their differences in conference, the Senate and House took final action on the bill--the House passing it by a vote of 377-28 on July 12, 1990, and the Senate, a day later, by a vote of 91-6. The ADA was enacted into law with the President's signature at a White House ceremony on July 26, 1990.

Rulemaking History

On February 22, 1991, the Department of Justice published a notice of proposed rulemaking (NPRM) implementing title III of the ADA in the **Federal Register** (56 FR 7452). On February 28, 1991, the Department published a notice of proposed rulemaking implementing subtitle A of title II of the ADA in the **Federal Register** (56 FR 8538). Each NPRM solicited comments on the definitions, standards, and procedures of the proposed

rules. By the April 29, 1991, close of the comment period of the NPRM for title II, the Department had received 2,718 comments on the two proposed rules. Following the close of the comment period, the Department received an additional 222 comments.

In order to encourage public participation in the development of the Department's rules under the ADA, the Department held four public hearings. Hearings were held in Dallas, Texas on March 4-5, 1991; in Washington, DC on March 13-14-15, 1991; in San Francisco, California on March 18-19, 1991; and in Chicago, Illinois on March 27-28, 1991. At these hearings, 329 persons testified and 1,567 pages of testimony were compiled. Transcripts of the hearings were included in the Department's rulemaking docket.

The comments that the Department received occupy almost six feet of shelf space and contain over 10,000 pages. The Department received comments from individuals from all fifty States and the District of Columbia. Nearly 75% of the comments came from individuals and from organizations representing the interests of persons with disabilities. The Department received 292 comments from entities covered by the ADA and trade associations representing businesses in the private sector, and 67 from government units, such as mayors' offices, public school districts, and various State agencies working with individuals with disabilities.

The Department received one comment from a consortium of 511 organizations representing a broad spectrum of persons with disabilities. In addition, at least another 25 commenters endorsed the position expressed by this consortium or submitted identical comments on one or both proposed regulations.

An organization representing persons with hearing impairments submitted a large number of comments. This organization presented the Department with 479 individual comments, each

providing in chart form a detailed representation of what type of auxiliary aid or service would be useful in the various categories of places of public accommodation.

The Department received a number of comments based on almost ten different form letters. For example, individuals who have a heightened sensitivity to a variety of chemical substances submitted 266 postcards detailing how exposure to various environmental conditions restricts their access to places of public accommodation and to commercial facilities. Another large group of form letters came from groups affiliated with independent living centers.

The vast majority of the comments addressed the Department's proposal implementing title III. Just over 100 comments addressed only issues presented in the proposed title II regulation.

The Department read and analyzed each comment that was submitted in a timely fashion. Transcripts of the four hearings were analyzed along with the written comments. The decisions that the Department has made in response to these comments, however, were not made on the basis of the number of commenters addressing any one point but on a thorough consideration of the merits of the points of view expressed in the comments. Copies of the written comments, including transcripts of the four hearings, will remain available for public inspection in room 854 of the HOLC Building, 320 First Street, NW., Washington, DC from 10 a.m. to 5 p.m., Monday through Friday, except for legal holidays, until August 30, 1991.

The Americans with Disabilities Act gives to individuals with disabilities civil rights protections with respect to discrimination that are parallel to those provided to individuals on the basis of race, color, national origin, sex, and religion. It combines in its own unique formula elements drawn principally from two key civil rights statutes--the Civil Rights Act of 1964 and title V of the Rehabilitation Act of 1973. The

ADA generally employs the framework of titles II (42 U.S.C. 2000a to 2000a-6) and VII (42 U.S.C. 2000e to 2000e-16) of the Civil Rights Act of 1964 for coverage and enforcement and the terms and concepts of section 504 of the Rehabilitation Act of 1973 (29 U.S.C. 794) for what constitutes discrimination.

Other recently enacted legislation will facilitate compliance with the ADA. As amended in 1990, the Internal Revenue Code allows a deduction of up to $15,000 per year for expenses associated with the removal of qualified architectural and transportation barriers. The 1990 amendment also permits eligible small businesses to receive a tax credit for certain costs of compliance with the ADA. An eligible small business is one whose gross receipts do not exceed $1,000,000 or whose workforce does not consist of more than 30 full-time workers. Qualifying businesses may claim a credit of up to 50 percent of eligible access expenditures that exceed $250 but do not exceed $10,250. Examples of eligible access expenditures include the necessary and reasonable costs of removing barriers, providing auxiliary aids, and acquiring or modifying equipment or devices.

In addition, the Communications Act of 1934 has been amended by the Television Decoder Circuitry Act of 1990, Public Law 101-431, to require as of July 1, 1993, that all televisions with screens of 13 inches or wider have built-in decoder circuitry for displaying closed captions. This new law will eventually lessen dependence on the use of portable decoders in achieving compliance with the auxiliary aids and services requirements of the rule.

Overview of the Rule

The final rule establishes standards and procedures for the implementation of title III of the Act, which addresses discrimination by private entities in places of public accommodation, commercial facilities, and certain examina-tions and courses. The careful consideration Congress gave title III is reflected in the detailed statutory provisions and the expansive reports of the Senate Committee on Labor and Human Resources and the House Committees on the Judiciary, and Education and Labor. The final rule follows closely the language of the Act and supplements it, where appropriate, with interpretive material found in the committee reports.

The rule is organized into six subparts. Subpart A, "General," includes the purpose and application sections, describes the relationship of the Act to other laws, and defines key terms used in the regulation.

Subpart B, "General Requirements," contains material derived from what the statute calls the "General Rule," and the "General Prohibition," in sections 302(a) and 302(b)(1), respectively, of the Act. Topics addressed by this subpart include discriminatory denials of access or participation, landlord and tenant obligations, the provision of unequal benefits, indirect discrimination through contracting, the participation of individuals with disabilities in the most integrated setting appropriate to their needs, and discrimination based on association with individuals with disabilities. Subpart B also contains a number of "miscellaneous" provisions derived from title V of the Act that involve issues such as retaliation and coercion for asserting ADA rights, illegal drug use, insurance, and restrictions on smoking in places of public accommodation. Finally, subpart B contains additional general provisions regarding direct threats to health or safety, maintenance of accessible features of facilities and equipment, and the coverage of places of public accommodation located in private residences.

Subpart C, "Specific Requirements," addresses the "Specific Prohibitions" in section 302(b)(2) of the Act. Included in this subpart are topics such as discriminatory eligibility criteria; reasonable modifications in policies, practices or procedures; auxiliary aids and services; the readily achievable removal of barriers and alternatives to barrier removal; the extent to which inventories of accessible or special goods are required; seating in assembly areas; personal devices and services; and transportation provided by public accommodations. Subpart C also incorporates the requirements of section 309 of title III relating to examinations and courses.

Subpart D, "New Construction and Alterations," sets forth the requirements for new construction and alterations based on section 303 of the Act. It addresses such issues as what facilities are covered by the new construction requirements, what an alteration is, the application of the elevator exception, the path of travel obligations resulting from an alteration to a primary function area, requirements for commercial facilities located in private residences, and the application of alterations requirements to historic buildings and facilities.

Subpart E, "Enforcement," describes the Act's title III enforcement procedures, including private actions, as well as investigations and litigation conducted by the Attorney General. These provisions are based on sections 308 and 310(b) of the Act.

Subpart F, "Certification of State Laws or Local Building Codes," establishes procedures for the certification of State or local building accessibility ordinances that meet or exceed the new construction and alterations requirements of the ADA. These provisions are based on section 308(b)(1)(A)(ii) of the Act.

The section-by-section analysis of the rule explains in detail the provisions of each of these subparts.

The Department is also today publishing a final rule for the implementation and enforcement of subtitle A of title II of the Act. This rule prohibits discrimination on the basis of disability against qualified individuals with disabilities in all services, programs, or activities of State and local government.

Regulatory Process Matters

This final rule has been reviewed by the Office of Management and Budget (OMB) under Executive Order 12291. The Department is preparing a regulatory impact analysis (RIA) of this rule, and the Architectural and Transportation Barriers Compliance Board is preparing an RIA for its Americans with Disabilities Act Accessibility Guidelines for Buildings and Facilities (ADAAG) that are incorporated in Appendix A of the Department's final rule. Draft copies of both preliminary RIAs are available for comment; the Department will provide copies of these documents to the public upon request. Commenters are urged to provide additional information as to the costs and benefits associated with this rule. This will facilitate the development of a final RIA by January 1, 1992.

The Department's RIA will evaluate the economic impact of the final rule. Included among those title III provisions that are likely to result in significant economic impact are the requirements for auxiliary aids, barrier removal in existing facilities, and readily accessible new construction and alterations. An analysis of the costs of these provisions will be included in the RIA.

The preliminary RIA prepared for the notice of proposed rulemaking contained all of the available information that would have been included in a preliminary regulatory flexibility analysis, had one been prepared under the Regulatory Flexibility Act, concerning the rule's impact on small entities. The final RIA will contain all of the information that is required in a final regulatory flexibility analysis, and will serve as such an analysis. Moreover, the extensive notice and comment procedure followed by the Department in the promulgation of this rule, which included public hearings, dissemination of materials, and provision of speakers to affected groups,

clearly provided any interested small entities with the notice and opportunity for comment provided for under the Regulatory Flexibility Act procedures.

This final rule will preempt State laws affecting entities subject to the ADA only to the extent that those laws directly conflict with the statutory requirements of the ADA. Therefore, this rule is not subject to Executive Order 12612, and a Federalism Assessment is not required.

The reporting and recordkeeping requirements described in subpart F of the rule are considered to be information collection requirements as that term is defined by the Office of Management and Budget in 5 CFR part 1320. Accordingly, those information collection requirements have been submitted to OMB for review pursuant to the Paperwork Reduction Act.

Section-By-Section Analysis and Response to Comments

Subpart A--General

Section 36.101 Purpose

Section 36.101 states the purpose of the rule, which is to effectuate title III of the Americans with Disabilities Act of 1990. This title prohibits discrimination on the basis of disability by public accommodations, requires places of public accommodation and commercial facilities to be designed, constructed, and altered in compliance with the accessibility standards established by this part, and requires that examinations or courses related to licensing or certification for professional or trade purposes be accessible to persons with disabilities.

Section 36.102 Application

Section 36.102 specifies the range of entities and facilities that have obligations under the final rule. The rule applies to any public accommodation or commercial facility as those terms are defined in § 36.104. It also applies, in accordance with

section 309 of the ADA, to private entities that offer examinations or courses related to applications, licensing, certification, or credentialing for secondary or postsecondary education, professional, or trade purposes. Except as provided in § 36.206, "Retaliation or coercion," this part does not apply to individuals other than public accommodations or to public entities. Coverage of private individuals and public entities is discussed in the preamble to § 36.206.

As defined in § 36.104, a public accommodation is a private entity that owns, leases or leases to, or operates a place of public accommodation. Section 36.102(b)(2) emphasizes that the general and specific public accommodations requirements of subparts B and C obligate a public accommodation only with respect to the operations of a place of public accommodation. This distinction is drawn in recognition of the fact that a private entity that meets the regulatory definition of public accommodation could also own, lease or lease to, or operate facilities that are not places of public accommodation. The rule would exceed the reach of the ADA if it were to apply the public accommodations requirements of subparts B and C to the operations of a private entity that do not involve a place of public accommodation. Similarly, § 36.102(b)(3) provides that the new construction and alterations requirements of subpart D obligate a public accommodation only with respect to facilities used as, or designed or constructed for use as, places of public accommodation or commercial facilities.

On the other hand, as mandated by the ADA and reflected in § 36.102(c), the new construction and alterations requirements of subpart D apply to a commercial facility, whether or not the facility is a place of public accommodation, or is owned, leased, leased to, or operated by a public accommodation.

Section 36.102(e) states that the rule does not apply to any private club, religious entity, or public entity. Each of these terms is defined in § 36.104. The exclusion of private clubs and religious entities is derived from section 307 of the ADA; and the exclusion of public entities is based on the statutory definition of public accommodation in section 301(7) of the ADA, which excludes entities other than private entities from coverage under title III of the ADA.

Section 36.103 Relationship to Other Laws

Section 36.103 is derived from sections 501 (a) and (b) of the ADA. Paragraph (a) provides that, except as otherwise specifically provided by this part, the ADA is not intended to apply lesser standards than are required under title V of the Rehabilitation Act of 1973, as amended (29 U.S.C. 790-794), or the regulations implementing that title. The standards of title V of the Rehabilitation Act apply for purposes of the ADA to the extent that the ADA has not explicitly adopted a different standard from title V. Where the ADA explicitly provides a different standard from section 504, the ADA standard applies to the ADA, but not to section 504. For example, section 504 requires that all federally assisted programs and activities be readily accessible to and usable by individuals with handicaps, even if major structural alterations are necessary to make a program accessible. Title III of the ADA, in contrast, only requires alterations to existing facilities if the modifications are "readily achievable," that is, able to be accomplished easily and without much difficulty or expense. A public accommodation that is covered under both section 504 and the ADA is still required to meet the "program accessibility" standard in order to comply with section 504, but would not be in violation of the ADA unless it failed to make "readily achievable" modifications. On the other hand, an entity covered by the ADA is required to make "readily achievable" modifications, even if the program can be made accessible without any architectural modifications. Thus, an entity covered by both section 504 and title III of the ADA must meet both the "program accessibility" requirement and the "readily achievable" requirement.

Paragraph (b) makes explicit that the rule does not affect the obligation of recipients of Federal financial assistance to comply with the requirements imposed under section 504 of the Rehabilitation Act of 1973.

Paragraph (c) makes clear that Congress did not intend to displace any of the rights or remedies provided by other Federal laws or other State or local laws (including State common law) that provide greater or equal protection to individuals with disabilities. A plaintiff may choose to pursue claims under a State law that does not confer greater substantive rights, or even confers fewer substantive rights, if the alleged violation is protected under the alternative law and the remedies are greater. For example, assume that a person with a physical disability seeks damages under a State law that allows compensatory and punitive damages for discrimination on the basis of physical disability, but does not allow them on the basis of mental disability. In that situation, the State law would provide narrower coverage, by excluding mental disabilities, but broader remedies, and an individual covered by both laws could choose to bring an action under both laws. Moreover, State tort claims confer greater remedies and are not preempted by the ADA. A plaintiff may join a State tort claim to a case brought under the ADA. In such a case, the plaintiff must, of course, prove all the elements of the State tort claim in order to prevail under that cause of action.

A commenter had concerns about privacy requirements for banking transactions using telephone relay services. Title IV of the Act provides adequate protections for ensuring the confidentiality of communications using the relay services. This issue is more appropriately addressed by the Federal Communications Commission in its regulation implementing title IV of the Act.

Section 36.104 Definitions

"Act." The word "Act" is used in the regulation to refer to the Americans with Disabilities Act of 1990, Pub. L. 101-336, which is also referred to as the "ADA."

"Commerce." The definition of "commerce" is identical to the statutory definition provided in section 301(l) of the ADA. It means travel, trade, traffic, commerce, transportation, or communication among the several States, between any foreign country or any territory or possession and any State, or between points in the same State but through another State or foreign country. Commerce is defined in the same manner as in title II of the Civil Rights Act of 1964, which prohibits racial discrimination in public accommodations.

The term "commerce" is used in the definition of "place of public accommodation." According to that definition, one of the criteria that an entity must meet before it can be considered a place of public accommodation is that its operations affect commerce. The term "commerce" is similarly used in the definition of "commercial facility."

The use of the phrase "operations affect commerce" applies the full scope of coverage of the Commerce Clause of the Constitution in enforcing the ADA. The Constitution gives Congress broad authority to regulate interstate commerce, including the activities of local business enterprises (e.g., a physician's office, a neighborhood restaurant, a laundromat, or a bakery) that affect interstate commerce through the purchase or sale of products manufactured in other States, or by providing services to individuals from other States. Because of the integrated nature of the national economy, the ADA and this final rule will have extremely broad application.

"Commercial facilities" are those facilities that are intended for nonresidential use by a private entity and whose operations affect commerce. As explained under § 36.401, "New construction," the new construction and alteration requirements of subpart D of the rule apply to all commercial facilities, whether or not they are places of public accommodation. Those commercial facilities that are not places of public accommodation are not subject to the requirements of subparts B and C (e.g., those requirements concerning auxiliary aids and general nondiscrimination provisions).

Congress recognized that the employees within commercial facilities would generally be protected under title I (employment) of the Act. However, as the House Committee on Education and Labor pointed out, "[t]o the extent that new facilities are built in a manner that make[s] them accessible to all individuals, including potential employees, there will be less of a need for individual employers to engage in reasonable accommodations for particular employees." H.R. Rep. No. 485, 101st Cong., 2d Sess., pt. 2, at 117 (1990) [hereinafter "Education and Labor report"]. While employers of fewer than 15 employees are not covered by title I's employment discrimination provisions, there is no such limitation with respect to new construction covered under title III. Congress chose not to so limit the new construction provisions because of its desire for a uniform requirement of accessibility in new construction, because accessibility can be accomplished easily in the design and construction stage, and because future expansion of a business or sale or lease of the property to a larger employer or to a business that is a place of public accommodation is always a possibility.

The term "commercial facilities" is not intended to be defined by dictionary or common industry definitions. Included in this category are factories, warehouses, office buildings, and other buildings in which employment may occur. The phrase, "whose operations affect commerce," is to be read broadly, to include all types of activities reached under the commerce clause of the Constitution.

Privately operated airports are also included in the category of commercial facilities. They are not, however, places of public accommodation because they are not terminals used for "specified public transportation." (Transportation by aircraft is specifically excluded from the statutory definition of "specified public transportation.") Thus, privately operated airports are subject to the new construction and alteration requirements of this rule (subpart D) but not to subparts B and C. (Airports operated by public entities are covered by title II of the Act.) Places of public accommodation located within airports, such as restaurants, shops, lounges, or conference centers, however, are covered by subparts B and C of this part.

The statute's definition of "commercial facilities" specifically includes only facilities "that are intended for nonresidential use" and specifically exempts those facilities that are covered or expressly exempted from coverage under the Fair Housing Act of 1968, as amended (42 U.S.C. 3601-3631). The interplay between the Fair Housing Act and the ADA with respect to those facilities that are "places of public accommodation" was the subject of many comments and is addressed in the preamble discussion of the definition of "place of public accommodation."

"Current illegal use of drugs." The phrase "current illegal use of drugs" is used in § 36.209. Its meaning is discussed in the preamble for that section.

"Disability." The definition of the term "disability" is comparable to the definition of the term "individual with handicaps" in section 7(8)(B) of the Rehabilitation Act and section 802(h) of the Fair Housing Act. The Education and Labor Committee report makes clear that the analysis of the term "individual with handicaps" by the Department of Health, Education, and Welfare in its regulations implementing section 504 (42 FR 22685 (May 4, 1977)) and the analysis by the Department of Housing and Urban Development in its regulation implementing the Fair Housing Amendments Act of 1988 (54 FR 3232 (Jan. 23, 1989)) should also apply fully to the term "disability" (Education and Labor report at 50).

The use of the term "disability" instead of "handicap" and the term "individual with a disability" instead of "individual with handicaps" represents an effort by the Congress to make use of up-to-date, currently accepted terminology. The terminology applied to individuals with disabilities is a very significant and sensitive issue. As with racial and ethnic terms, the choice of words to describe a person with a disability is overlaid with stereotypes, patronizing attitudes, and other emotional connotations. Many individuals with disabilities, and organizations representing such individuals, object to the use of such terms as "handicapped person" or "the handicapped." In other recent legislation, Congress also recognized this shift in terminology, e.g., by changing the name of the National Council on the Handicapped to the National Council on Disability (Pub. L. 100-630).

In enacting the Americans with Disabilities Act, Congress concluded that it was important for the current legislation to use terminology most in line with the sensibilities of most Americans with disabilities. No change in definition or substance is intended nor should be attributed to this change in phraseology.

The term "disability" means, with respect to an individual--

(A) A physical or mental impairment that substantially limits one or more of the major life activities of such individual;

(B) A record of such an impairment; or

(C) Being regarded as having such an impairment.

If an individual meets any one of these three tests, he or she is considered to be an individual with a disability for purposes of coverage under the Americans with Disabilities Act.

Congress adopted this same basic definition of "disability," first used in the Rehabilitation Act of 1973 and in the Fair Housing Amendments Act of 1988, for a number of reasons. It has worked well since it was adopted in 1974. There is a substantial body of administrative interpretation and judicial precedent on this definition. Finally, it would not be possible to guarantee comprehensiveness by providing a list of specific disabilities, especially because new disorders may be recognized in the future, as they have since the definition was first established in 1974.

Test A--A Physical or Mental Impairment That Substantially Limits One or More of the Major Life Activities of Such Individual

Physical or mental impairment. Under the first test, an individual must have a physical or mental impairment. As explained in paragraph (1) (i) of the definition, "impairment" means any physiological disorder or condition, cosmetic disfigurement, or anatomical loss affecting one or more of the following body systems: Neurological; musculoskeletal; special sense organs (including speech organs that are not respiratory, such as vocal cords, soft palate, and tongue); respiratory, including speech organs; cardiovascular; reproductive; digestive; genitourinary; hemic and lymphatic; skin; and endocrine. It also means any mental or psychological disorder, such as mental retardation, organic brain syndrome, emotional or mental illness, and specific learning disabilities. This list closely tracks the one used in the regulations for section 504 of the Rehabilitation Act of 1973 (see, *e.g.*, 45 CFR 84.3(j)(2)(i)).

Many commenters asked that "traumatic brain injury" be added to the list in paragraph (1)(i). Traumatic brain injury is already included because it is a physiological condition affecting one of the listed body

systems, i.e., "neurological." Therefore, it was unnecessary for the Department to add the term to the regulation.

It is not possible to include a list of all the specific conditions, contagious and noncontagious diseases, or infections that would constitute physical or mental impairments because of the difficulty of ensuring the comprehensiveness of such a list, particularly in light of the fact that other conditions or disorders may be identified in the future. However, the list of examples in paragraph (1)(iii) of the definition includes: Orthopedic, visual, speech and hearing impairments; cerebral palsy; epilepsy, muscular dystrophy, multiple sclerosis, cancer, heart disease, diabetes, mental retardation, emotional illness, specific learning disabilities, HIV disease (symptomatic or asymptomatic), tuberculosis, drug addiction, and alcoholism.

The examples of "physical or mental impairments" in paragraph (1)(iii) are the same as those contained in many section 504 regulations, except for the addition of the phrase "contagious and noncontagious" to describe the types of diseases and conditions included, and the addition of "HIV disease (symptomatic or asymptomatic)" and "tuberculosis" to the list of examples. These additions are based on the ADA committee reports, caselaw, and official legal opinions interpreting section 504. In *School Board of Nassau County v. Arline*, 480 U.S. 273 (1987), a case involving an individual with tuberculosis, the Supreme Court held that people with contagious diseases are entitled to the protections afforded by section 504. Following the *Arline* decision, this Department's Office of Legal Counsel issued a legal opinion that concluded that symptomatic HIV disease is an impairment that substantially limits a major life activity; therefore it has been included in the definition of disability under this part. The opinion also concluded that asymptomatic HIV disease is an impairment that substantially limits a major life activity,

either because of its actual effect on the individual with HIV disease or because the reactions of other people to individuals with HIV disease cause such individuals to be treated as though they are disabled. See Memorandum from Douglas W. Kmiec, Acting Assistant Attorney General, Office of Legal Counsel, Department of Justice, to Arthur B. Culvahouse, Jr., Counsel to the President (Sept. 27, 1988), *reprinted* in Hearings on §. 933, the Americans with Disabilities Act, Before the Subcomm. on the Handicapped of the Senate Comm. on Labor and Human Resources, 101st Cong., 1st Sess. 346 (1989). The phrase "symptomatic or asymptomatic" was inserted in the final rule after "HIV disease" in response to commenters who suggested that the clarification was necessary to give full meaning to the Department's opinion.

Paragraph (1)(iv) of the definition states that the phrase "physical or mental impairment" does not include homosexuality or bisexuality. These conditions were never considered impairments under other Federal disability laws. Section 511(a) of the statute makes clear that they are likewise not to be considered impairments under the Americans with Disabilities Act.

Physical or mental impairment does not include simple physical characteristics, such as blue eyes or black hair. Nor does it include environmental, cultural, economic, or other disadvantages, such as having a prison record, or being poor. Nor is age a disability. Similarly, the definition does not include common personality traits such as poor judgment or a quick temper where these are not symptoms of a mental or psychological disorder. However, a person who has these characteristics and also has a physical or mental impairment may be considered as having a disability for purposes of the Americans with Disabilities Act based on the impairment.

Substantial limitation of a major life activity. Under Test A, the impairment must be one that "substantially limits a major life activity." Major life activities include such things as caring for one's self, performing manual tasks, walking, seeing, hearing, speaking, breathing, learning, and working. For example, a person who is paraplegic is substantially limited in the major life activity of walking, a person who is blind is substantially limited in the major life activity of seeing, and a person who is mentally retarded is substantially limited in the major life activity of learning. A person with traumatic brain injury is substantially limited in the major life activities of caring for one's self, learning, and working because of memory deficit, confusion, contextual difficulties, and inability to reason appropriately.

A person is considered an individual with a disability for purposes of Test A, the first prong of the definition, when the individual's important life activities are restricted as to the conditions, manner, or duration under which they can be performed in comparison to most people. A person with a minor, trivial impairment, such as a simple infected finger, is not impaired in a major life activity. A person who can walk for 10 miles continuously is not substantially limited in walking merely because, on the eleventh mile, he or she begins to experience pain, because most people would not be able to walk eleven miles without experiencing some discomfort.

The Department received many comments on the proposed rule's inclusion of the word "temporary" in the definition of "disability." The preamble indicated that impairments are not necessarily excluded from the definition of "disability" simply because they are temporary, but that the duration, or expected duration, of an impairment is one factor that may properly be considered in determining whether the impairment substantially limits a major life activity. The preamble recognized, however, that temporary impairments, such as a broken leg, are not commonly regarded as

disabilities, and only in rare circumstances would the degree of the limitation and its expected duration be substantial: Nevertheless, many commenters objected to inclusion of the word "temporary" both because it is not in the statute and because it is not contained in the definition of "disability" set forth in the title I regulations of the Equal Employment Opportunity Commission (EEOC). The word "temporary" has been deleted from the final rule to conform with the statutory language. The question of whether a temporary impairment is a disability must be resolved on a case-by-case basis, taking into consideration both the duration (or expected duration) of the impairment and the extent to which it actually limits a major life activity of the affected individual.

The question of whether a person has a disability should be assessed without regard to the availability of mitigating measures, such as reasonable modifications or auxiliary aids and services. For example, a person with hearing loss is substantially limited in the major life activity of hearing, even though the loss may be improved through the use of a hearing aid. Likewise, persons with impairments, such as epilepsy or diabetes, that substantially limit a major life activity, are covered under the first prong of the definition of disability, even if the effects of the impairment are controlled by medication.

Many commenters asked that environmental illness (also known as multiple chemical sensitivity) as well as allergy to cigarette smoke be recognized as disabilities. The Department, however, declines to state categorically that these types of allergies or sensitivities are disabilities, because the determination as to whether an impairment is a disability depends on whether, given the particular circumstances at issue, the impairment substantially limits one or more major life activities (or has a history of, or is regarded as having such an effect).

Sometimes respiratory or neurological functioning is so severely affected that an individual will satisfy the requirements to be considered disabled under the regulation. Such an individual would be entitled to all of the protections afforded by the Act and this part. In other cases, individuals may be sensitive to environmental elements or to smoke but their sensitivity will not rise to the level needed to constitute a disability. For example, their major life activity of breathing may be somewhat, but not substantially, impaired. In such circumstances, the individuals are not disabled and are not entitled to the protections of the statute despite their sensitivity to environmental agents.

In sum, the determination as to whether allergies to cigarette smoke, or allergies or sensitivities characterized by the commenters as environmental illness are disabilities covered by the regulation must be made using the same case-by-case analysis that is applied to all other physical or mental impairments. Moreover, the addition of specific regulatory provisions relating to environmental illness in the final rule would be inappropriate at this time pending future consideration of the issue by the Architectural and Transportation Barriers Compliance Board, the Environmental Protection Agency, and the Occupational Safety and Health Administration of the Department of Labor.

Test B--A Record of Such an Impairment

This test is intended to cover those who have a record of an impairment. As explained in paragraph (3) of the rule's definition of disability, this includes a person who has a history of an impairment that substantially limited a major life activity, such as someone who has recovered from an impairment. It also includes persons who have been misclassified as having an impairment. This provision is included in the definition in part to protect individuals who have recovered from a physical or mental impairment that previously substantially limited them in a major life activity. Discrimination on the basis of such a past impairment is prohibited. Frequently occurring examples of the first group (those who have a history of an impairment) are persons with histories of mental or emotional illness, heart disease, or cancer; examples of the second group (those who have been misclassified as having an impairment) are persons who have been misclassified as having mental retardation or mental illness.

Test C—Being Regarded as Having Such an Impairment

This test, as contained in paragraph (4) of the definition, is intended to cover persons who are treated by a private entity or public accommodation as having a physical or mental impairment that substantially limits a major life activity. It applies when a person is treated as if he or she has an impairment that substantially limits a major life activity, regardless of whether that person has an impairment.

The Americans with Disabilities Act uses the same "regarded as" test set forth in the regulations implementing section 504 of the Rehabilitation Act. See, e.g., 28 CFR 42.540(k)(2)(iv), which provides:

(iv) "Is regarded as having an impairment" means (A) Has a physical or mental impairment that does not substantially limit major life activities but that is treated by a recipient as constituting such a limitation; (B) Has a physical or mental impairment that substantially limits major life activities only as a result of the attitudes of others toward such impairment; or (C) Has none of the impairments defined in paragraph (k)(2)(i) of this section but is treated by a recipient as having such an impairment.

The perception of the private entity or public accommodation is a key element of this test. A person who perceives himself or herself to have an impairment, but does not have an impairment, and is not treated as if he or she has an impairment, is not protected under this test. A person would be covered under this test if a restaurant refused to serve that person because of a fear of "negative reactions" of others to that person. A person would also be covered if a public accommodation refused to serve a patron because it perceived that the patron had an impairment that limited his or her enjoyment of the goods or services being offered.

For example, persons with severe burns often encounter discrimination in community activities, resulting in substantial limitation of major life activities. These persons would be covered under this test based on the attitudes of others towards the impairment, even if they did not view themselves as "impaired."

The rationale for this third test, as used in the Rehabilitation Act of 1973, was articulated by the Supreme Court in *Arline*, 480 U.S. 273 (1987). The Court noted that, although an individual may have an impairment that does not in fact substantially limit a major life activity, the reaction of others may prove just as disabling. "Such an impairment might not diminish a person's physical or mental capabilities, but could nevertheless substantially limit that person's ability to work as a result of the negative reactions of others to the impairment." *Id.* at 283. The Court concluded that, by including this test in the Rehabilitation Act's definition, "Congress acknowledged that society's accumulated myths and fears about disability and disease are as handicapping as are the physical limitations that flow from actual impairment." *Id.* at 284.

Thus, a person who is not allowed into a public accommodation because of the myths, fears, and stereotypes associated with disabilities would be covered under this third test whether or not the person's physical or mental condition would be considered a disability under the first or second test in the definition.

If a person is refused admittance on the basis of an actual or perceived physical or mental condition, and the public accommodation can articulate no legitimate reason for the refusal (such as failure to meet eligibility criteria), a perceived concern about admitting persons with disabilities could be inferred and the individual would qualify for coverage under the "regarded as" test. A person who is covered because of being regarded as having an impairment is not required to show that the public accommodation's perception is inaccurate (e.g., that he will be accepted by others, or that insurance rates will not increase) in order to be admitted to the public accommodation.

Paragraph (5) of the definition lists certain conditions that are not included within the definition of "disability." The excluded conditions are: transvestism, transsexualism, pedophilia, exhibitionism, voyeurism, gender identity disorders not resulting from physical impairments, other sexual behavior disorders, compulsive gambling, kleptomania, pyromania, and psychoactive substance use disorders resulting from current illegal use of drugs. Unlike homosexuality and bisexuality, which are not considered impairments under either the Americans with Disabilities Act (see the definition of "disability," paragraph (1)(iv)) or section 504, the conditions listed in paragraph (5), except for transvestism, are not necessarily excluded as impairments under section 504. (Transvestism was excluded from the definition of disability for section 504 by the Fair Housing Amendments Act of 1988, Pub. L. 100-430, § 6(b).) The phrase "current illegal use of drugs" used in this definition is explained in the preamble to § 36.209.

"Drug." The definition of the term "drug" is taken from section 510(d)(2) of the ADA.

"Facility." "Facility" means all or any portion of buildings, structures, sites, complexes, equipment, rolling stock or other conveyances, roads, walks, passageways, parking lots, or other real or personal property, including the site where the building, property, structure, or equipment is located. Committee reports made clear that the definition of facility was drawn from the definition of facility in current Federal regulations (*see, e.g.,* Education and Labor report at 114). It includes both indoor and outdoor areas where human-constructed improvements, structures, equipment, or property have been added to the natural environment.

The term "rolling stock or other conveyances" was not included in the definition of facility in the proposed rule. However, commenters raised questions about the applicability of this part to places of public accommodation operated in mobile facilities (such as cruise ships, floating restaurants, or mobile health units). Those places of public accommodation are covered under this part, and would be included in the definition of "facility." Thus the requirements of subparts B and C would apply to those places of public accommodation. For example, a covered entity could not discriminate on the basis of disability in the full and equal enjoyment of the facilities § 36.201). Similarly, a cruise line could not apply eligibility criteria to potential passengers in a manner that would screen out individuals with disabilities, unless the criteria are "necessary," as provided in § 36.301.

However, standards for new construction and alterations of such facilities are not yet included in the Americans with Disabilities Act Accessibility Guidelines for Buildings and Facilities (ADAAG) adopted by § 36.406 and incorporated in Appendix A. The Department therefore will not interpret the new construction and alterations provisions of subpart D to apply to the types of facilities discussed here, pending further development of specific requirements.

Requirements pertaining to accessible transportation services provided by public accommodations are included in § 36.310 of this part; standards pertaining to accessible vehicles will be issued by the Secretary of

Transportation pursuant to section 306 of the Act, and will be codified at 49 CFR part 37.

A public accommodation has obligations under this rule with respect to a cruise ship to the extent that its operations are subject to the laws of the United States.

The definition of "facility" only includes the site over which the private entity may exercise control or on which a place of public accommodation or a commercial facility is located. It does not include, for example, adjacent roads or walks controlled by a public entity that is not subject to this part. Public entities are subject to the requirements of title II of the Act. The Department's regulation implementing title II, which will be codified at 28 CFR part 35, addresses the obligations of public entities to ensure accessibility by providing curb ramps at pedestrian walkways.

"Illegal use of drugs." The definition of "illegal use of drugs" is taken from section 510(d)(1) of the Act and clarifies that the term includes the illegal use of one or more drugs.

"Individual with a disability" means a person who has a disability but does not include an individual who is currently illegally using drugs, when the public accommodation acts on the basis of such use. The phrase "current illegal use of drugs" is explained in the preamble to § 36.209.

"Place of public accommodation." The term "place of public accommodation" is an adaptation of the statutory definition of "public accommodation" in section 301(7) of the ADA and appears as an element of the regulatory definition of public accommodation. The final rule defines "place of public accommodation" as a facility, operated by a private entity, whose operations affect commerce and fall within at least one of 12 specified categories. The term "public accommodation," on the other hand, is reserved by the final rule for the private entity that owns, leases (or leases to), or operates a place of public accommodation. It is the public accommodation, and not the

place of public accommodation, that is subject to the regulation's nondiscrimination requirements. Placing the obligation not to discriminate on the public accommodation, as defined in the rule, is consistent with section 302(a) of the ADA, which places the obligation not to discriminate on any person who owns, leases (or leases to), or operates a place of public accommodation.

Facilities operated by government agencies or other public entities as defined in this section do not qualify as places of public accommodation. The actions of public entities are governed by title II of the ADA and will be subject to regulations issued by the Department of Justice under that title. The receipt of government assistance by a private entity does not by itself preclude a facility from being considered as a place of public accommodation.

The definition of place of public accommodation incorporates the 12 categories of facilities represented in the statutory definition of public accommodation in section 301(7) of the ADA:

1. Places of lodging.
2. Establishments serving food or drink.
3. Places of exhibition or entertainment.
4. Places of public gathering.
5. Sales or rental establishments.
6. Service establishments.
7. Stations used for specified public transportation.
8. Places of public display or collection.
9. Places of recreation.
10. Places of education.
11. Social service center establishments.
12. Places of exercise or recreation.

In order to be a place of public accommodation, a facility must be operated by a private entity, its operations must affect commerce, and it must fall within one of these 12 categories. While the list of categories is exhaustive, the representative examples of facilities within each category are not. Within each category only a few examples are given.

The category of social service center establishments would include not only the types of establishments listed, day care centers, senior citizen centers, homeless shelters, food banks, adoption agencies, but also establishments such as substance abuse treatment centers, rape crisis centers, and halfway houses. As another example, the category of sales or rental establishments would include an innumerable array of facilities that would sweep far beyond the few examples given in the regulation. For example, other retail or wholesale establishments selling or renting items, such as bookstores, videotape rental stores, car rental establishment, pet stores, and jewelry stores would also be covered under this category, even though they are not specifically listed.

Several commenters requested clarification as to the coverage of wholesale establishments under the category of "sales or rental establishments." The Department intends for wholesale establishments to be covered under this category as places of public accommodation except in cases where they sell exclusively to other businesses and not to individuals. For example, a company that grows food produce and supplies its crops exclusively to food processing corporations on a wholesale basis does not become a public accommodation because of these transactions. If this company operates a road side stand where its crops are sold to the public, the road side stand would be a sales establishment covered by the ADA. Conversely, a sales establishment that markets its goods as "wholesale to the public" and sells to individuals would not be exempt from ADA coverage despite its use of the word "wholesale" as a marketing technique.

Of course, a company that operates a place of public accommodation is subject to this part only in the operation of that place of public accommodation. In the example given above, the wholesale produce company that operates a road side stand would be a public accommodation only for the purposes of the operation of that stand. The company would be prohibited from discriminating on the basis of disability in the operation of the road side stand, and it would be required to remove barriers to physical access to the extent that it is readily achievable to do so (see § 36.304); however, in the event that it is not readily achievable to remove barriers, for example, by replacing a gravel surface or regrading the area around the stand to permit access by persons with mobility impairments, the company could meet its obligations through alternative methods of making its goods available, such as delivering produce to a customer in his or her car (see § 36.305). The concepts of readily achievable barrier removal and alternatives to barrier removal are discussed further in the preamble discussion of §§ 36.304 and 36.305.

Even if a facility does not fall within one of the 12 categories, and therefore does not qualify as a place of public accommodation, it still may be a commercial facility as defined in § 36.104 and be subject to the new construction and alterations requirements of subpart D.

A number of commenters questioned the treatment of residential hotels and other residential facilities in the Department's proposed rule. These commenters were essentially seeking resolution of the relationship between the Fair Housing Act and the ADA concerning facilities that are both residential in nature and engage in activities that would cause them to be classified as "places of public accommodation" under the ADA. The ADA's express exemption relating to the Fair Housing Act applies only to "commercial facilities" and not to "places of public accommodation."

A facility whose operations affect interstate commerce is a place of public accommodation for purposes of the ADA to the extent that its operations include those types of activities engaged in or services provided by the facilities contained on the list of 12 categories in section 301(7) of the ADA. Thus, a facility that provides social services would be considered a "social service center establishment." Similarly, the category "places of lodging" would exclude solely residential facilities because the nature of a place of lodging contemplates the use of the facility for short-term stays.

Many facilities, however, are mixed use facilities. For example, in a large hotel that has a separate residential apartment wing, the residential wing would not be covered by the ADA because of the nature of the occupancy of that part of the facility. This residential wing would, however, be covered by the Fair Housing Act. The separate nonresidential accommodations in the rest of the hotel would be a place of lodging, and thus a public accommodation subject to the requirements of this final rule. If a hotel allows both residential and short-term stays, but does not allocate space for these different uses in separate, discrete units, both the ADA and the Fair Housing Act may apply to the facility. Such determinations will need to be made on a case-by-case basis. Any place of lodging of the type described in paragraph (1) of the definition of place of public accommodation and that is an establishment located within a building that contains not more than five rooms for rent or hire and is actually occupied by the proprietor of the establishment as his or her residence is not covered by the ADA. (This exclusion from coverage does not apply to other categories of public accommodations, for example, professional offices or homeless shelters, that are located in a building that is also occupied as a private residence.)

A number of commenters noted that the term "residential hotel" may also apply to a type of hotel commonly known as a "single room occupancy hotel." Although such hotels or portions of such hotels may fall under the Fair Housing Act when operated or used as long-term residences, they are also considered "places of lodging" under the ADA when guests of such hotels are free to use them on a short-term basis. In addition, "single room occupancy hotels" may provide social services to their guests, often through the operation of Federal or State grant programs. In such a situation, the facility would be considered a "social service center establishment" and thus covered by the ADA as a place of public accommodation, regardless of the length of stay of the occupants.

A similar analysis would also be applied to other residential facilities that provide social services, including homeless shelters, shelters for people seeking refuge from domestic violence, nursing homes, residential care facilities, and other facilities where persons may reside for varying lengths of time. Such facilities should be analyzed under the Fair Housing Act to determine the application of that statute. The ADA, however, requires a separate and independent analysis. For example, if the facility, or a portion of the facility, is intended for or permits short-term stays, or if it can appropriately be categorized as a service establishment or as a social service establishment, then the facility or that portion of the facility used for the covered purpose is a place of public accommodation under the ADA. For example, a homeless shelter that is intended and used only for long-term residential stays and that does not provide social services to its residents would not be covered as a place of public accommodation. However, if this facility permitted short-term stays or provided social services to its residents, it would be covered under the ADA either as a "place of lodging" or as a "social service center establishment," or as both.

A private home, by itself, does not fall within any of the 12 categories. However, it can be covered as a place of public accommodation to the extent that it is used as a facility that would fall within one of the 12 categories. For example, if a professional office of a dentist, doctor, or psychologist is located in a private home, the portion of the home dedicated to office use (including areas used both for the residence and the office, e.g., the entrance to the home that is also used as the entrance to the professional office) would be considered a place of public accommodation. Places of public accommodation located in residential facilities are specifically addressed in § 36.207.

If a tour of a commercial facility that is not otherwise a place of public accommodation, such as, for example, a factory or a movie studio production set, is open to the general public, the route followed by the tour is a place of public accommodation and the tour must be operated in accordance with the rule's requirements for public accommodations. The place of public accommodation defined by the tour does not include those portions of the commercial facility that are merely viewed from the tour route. Hence, the barrier removal requirements of § 36.304 only apply to the physical route followed by the tour participants and not to work stations or other areas that are merely adjacent to, or within view of, the tour route. If the tour is not open to the general public, but rather is conducted, for example, for selected business colleagues, partners, customers, or consultants, the tour route is not a place of public accommodation and the tour is not subject to the requirements for public accommodations.

Public accommodations that receive Federal financial assistance are subject to the requirements of section 504 of the Rehabilitation Act as well as the requirements of the ADA.

Private schools, including elementary and secondary schools, are covered by the rule as places of public accommodation. The rule itself, however, does not require a private school to provide a free appropriate education or develop an individualized education program in accordance with regulations of the Department of Education implementing section 504 of the Rehabilitation Act of 1973, as amended (34 CFR part 104), and regulations implementing the Individuals with Disabilities Education Act (34 CFR part 300). The receipt of Federal assistance by a private school, however, would trigger application of the Department of Education's regulations to the extent mandated by the particular type of assistance received.

"Private club." The term "private club" is defined in accordance with section 307 of the ADA as a private club or establishment exempted from coverage under title II of the Civil Rights Act of 1964. Title II of the 1964 Act exempts any "private club or other establishment not in fact open to the public, except to the extent that the facilities of such establishment are made available to the customers or patrons of [a place of public accommodation as defined in title II]." The rule, therefore, as reflected in § 36.102(e) of the application section, limits the coverage of private clubs accordingly. The obligations of a private club that rents space to any other private entity for the operation of a place of public accommodation are discussed further in connection with § 36.201.

In determining whether a private entity qualifies as a private club under title II, courts have considered such factors as the degree of member control of club operations, the selectivity of the membership selection process, whether substantial membership fees are charged, whether the entity is operated on a nonprofit basis, the extent to which the facilities are open to the public, the degree of public funding, and whether the club was created specifically to avoid compliance with the Civil Rights Act. See e.g., Tillman v. Wheaton-Haven Recreation Ass'n, 410 U.S. 431 (1973); Daniel v. Paul, 395 U.S. 298 (1969); Olzman v. Lake Hills Swim Club, Inc., 495 F.2d 1333 (2d Cir. 1974); Anderson v. Pass Christian Isles Golf Club, Inc., 488 F.2d 855 (5th Cir. 1974); Smith v. YMCA, 462 F.2d 634 (5th Cir. 1972); Stout v. YMCA, 404 F.2d 687 (5th Cir. 1968); United States v. Richberg, 398 F.2d 523 (5th Cir. 1968); Nesmith v. YMCA, 397 F.2d 96 (4th Cir. 1968);

United States v. Lansdowne Swim Club, 713 F. Supp. 785 (E.D. Pa. 1989); *Durham v. Red Lake Fishing and Hunting Club, Inc.*, 666 F. Supp. 954 (W.D. Tex. 1987); *New York v. Ocean Club, Inc.*, 602 F. Supp. 489 (E.D.N.Y. 1984); *Brown v. Loudoun Golf and Country Club, Inc.*, 573 F. Supp. 399 (E.D. Va. 1983); *United States v. Trustees of Fraternal Order of Eagles*, 472 F. Supp. 1174 (E.D. Wis. 1979); *Cornelius v. Benevolent Protective Order of Elks*, 382 F. Supp. 1182 (D. Conn. 1974).

"Private entity." The term "private entity" is defined as any individual or entity other than a public entity. It is used as part of the definition of "public accommodation" in this section.

The definition adds "individual" to the statutory definition of private entity (see section 301(6) of the ADA). This addition clarifies that an individual may be a private entity and, therefore, may be considered a public accommodation if he or she owns, leases (or leases to), or operates a place of public accommodation. The explicit inclusion of individuals under the definition of private entity is consistent with section 302(a) of the ADA, which broadly prohibits discrimination on the basis of disability by any person who owns, leases (or leases to), or operates a place of public accommodation.

"Public accommodation." The term "public accommodation" means a private entity that owns, leases (or leases to), or operates a place of public accommodation. The regulatory term, "public accommodation," corresponds to the statutory term, "person," in section 302(a) of the ADA. The ADA prohibits discrimination "by any person who owns, leases (or leases to), or operates a place of public accommodation." The text of the regulation consequently places the ADA's nondiscrimination obligations on "public accommodations" rather than on "persons" or on "places of public accommodation."

As stated in § 36.102(b)(2), the requirements of subparts B and C obligate a public accommodation only with respect to the operations of a place of public accommodation. A public accommodation must also meet the requirements of subpart D with respect to facilities used as, or designed or constructed for use as, places of public accommodation or commercial facilities.

"Public entity." The term "public entity" is defined in accordance with section 201(1) of the ADA as any State or local government; any department, agency, special purpose district, or other instrumentality of a State or States or local government; and the National Railroad Passenger Corporation, and any commuter authority (as defined in section 103(8) of the Rail Passenger Service Act). It is used in the definition of "private entity" in § 36.104. Public entities are excluded from the definition of private entity and therefore cannot qualify as public accommodations under this regulation. However, the actions of public entities are covered by title II of the ADA and by the Department's title II regulations codified at 28 CFR part 35.

"Qualified interpreter." The Department received substantial comment regarding the lack of a definition of "qualified interpreter." The proposed rule defined auxiliary aids and services to include the statutory term, "qualified interpreters" (§ 36.303(b)), but did not define that term. Section 36.303 requires the use of a qualified interpreter where necessary to achieve effective communication, unless an undue burden or fundamental alteration would result. Commenters stated that a lack of guidance on what the term means would create confusion among those trying to secure interpreting services and often result in less than effective communication.

Many commenters were concerned that, without clear guidance on the issue of "qualified" interpreter, the rule would be interpreted to mean "available, rather than qualified" interpreters. Some claimed that few public accommodations would understand the difference between a qualified interpreter and a person who simply knows a few signs or how to fingerspell.

In order to clarify what is meant by "qualified interpreter" the Department has added a definition of the term to the final rule. A qualified interpreter means an interpreter who is able to interpret effectively, accurately, and impartially both receptively and expressively, using any necessary specialized vocabulary. This definition focuses on the actual ability of the interpreter in a particular interpreting context to facilitate effective communication between the public accommodation and the individual with disabilities.

Public comment also revealed that public accommodations have at times asked persons who are deaf to provide family members or friends to interpret. In certain circumstances, notwithstanding that the family member or friend is able to interpret or is a certified interpreter, the family member or friend may not be qualified to render the necessary interpretation because of factors such as emotional or personal involvement or considerations of confidentiality that may adversely affect the ability to interpret "effectively, accurately, and impartially."

"Readily achievable." The definition of "readily achievable" follows the statutory definition of that term in section 301(9) of the ADA. Readily achievable means easily accomplishable and able to be carried out without much difficulty or expense. The term is used as a limitation on the obligation to remove barriers under §§ 36.304(a), 36.305(a), 36.308(a), and 36.310(b). Further discussion of the meaning and application of the term "readily achievable" may be found in the preamble section for § 36.304.

The definition lists factors to be considered in determining whether barrier removal is readily achievable in any particular circumstance. A significant number of commenters objected to § 36.306 of the proposed rule, which listed identical factors to be considered for determining "readily achievable" and "undue burden" together in one section. They asserted that providing a consolidated section blurred the distinction between the level of effort required by a public accommodation under the two standards. The readily achievable standard is a "lower" standard than the "undue burden" standard in terms of the level of effort required, but the factors used in determining whether an action is readily achievable or would result in an undue burden are identical (See Education and Labor report at 109). Although the preamble to the proposed rule clearly delineated the relationship between the two standards, to eliminate any confusion the Department has deleted § 36.306 of the proposed rule. That section, in any event, as other commenters noted, had merely repeated the lists of factors contained in the definitions of readily achievable and undue burden.

The list of factors included in the definition is derived from section 301(9) of the ADA. It reflects the congressional intention that a wide range of factors be considered in determining whether an action is readily achievable. It also takes into account that many local facilities are owned or operated by parent corporations or entities that conduct operations at many different sites. This section makes clear that, in some instances, resources beyond those of the local facility where the barrier must be removed may be relevant in determining whether an action is readily achievable. One must also evaluate the degree to which any parent entity has resources that may be allocated to the local facility.

The statutory list of factors in section 301(9) of the Act uses the term "covered entity" to refer to the larger entity of which a particular facility may be a part. "Covered entity" is not a defined term in the ADA and is not used consistently throughout the Act. The definition, therefore, substitutes the term "parent entity" in place of "covered entity" in paragraphs (3), (4), and (5)

when referring to the larger private entity whose overall resources may be taken into account. This usage is consistent with the House Judiciary Committee's use of the term "parent company" to describe the larger entity of which the local facility is a part (H.R. Rep. No. 485, 101st Cong., 2d Sess., pt. 3, at 40-41, 54-55 (1990) (hereinafter "Judiciary report")).

A number of commenters asked for more specific guidance as to when and how the resources of a parent corporation or entity are to be taken into account in determining what is readily achievable. The Department believes that this complex issue is most appropriately resolved on a case-by-case basis. As the comments reflect, there is a wide variety of possible relationships between the site in question and any parent corporation or other entity. It would be unwise to posit legal ramifications under the ADA of even generic relationships (e.g., banks involved in foreclosures or insurance companies operating as trustees or in other similar fiduciary relationships), because any analysis will depend so completely on the detailed fact situations and the exact nature of the legal relationships involved. The final rule does, however, reorder the factors to be considered. This shift and the addition of the phrase "if applicable" make clear that the line of inquiry concerning factors will start at the site involved in the action itself. This change emphasizes that the overall resources, size, and operations of the parent corporation or entity should be considered to the extent appropriate in light of "the geographic separateness, and the administrative or fiscal relationship of the site or sites in question to any parent corporation or entity."

Although some commenters sought more specific numerical guidance on the definition of readily achievable, the Department has declined to establish in the final rule any kind of numerical formula for determining whether an action

is readily achievable. It would be difficult to devise a specific ceiling on compliance costs that would take into account the vast diversity of enterprises covered by the ADA's public accommodations requirements and the economic situation that any particular entity would find itself in at any moment. The final rule, therefore, implements the flexible case-by-case approach chosen by Congress.

A number of commenters requested that security considerations be explicitly recognized as a factor in determining whether a barrier removal action is readily achievable. The Department believes that legitimate safety requirements, including crime prevention measures, may be taken into account so long as they are based on actual risks and are necessary for safe operation of the public accommodation. This point has been included in the definition.

Some commenters urged the Department not to consider acts of barrier removal in complete isolation from each other in determining whether they are readily achievable. The Department believes that it is appropriate to consider the cost of other barrier removal actions as one factor in determining whether a measure is readily achievable.

"Religious entity." The term "religious entity" is defined in accordance with section 307 of the ADA as a religious organization or entity controlled by a religious organization, including a place of worship. Section 36.102(e) of the rule states that the rule does not apply to any religious entity.

The ADA's exemption of religious organizations and religious entities controlled by religious organizations is very broad, encompassing a wide variety of situations. Religious organizations and entities controlled by religious organizations have no obligations under the ADA. Even when a religious organization carries out activities that would otherwise make it a public accommodation, the religious organization is exempt from ADA coverage. Thus, if a church itself operates a day care center, a nursing home, a private school, or a diocesan school system, the operations of the center, home, school, or schools would not be subject to the requirements of the ADA or this part. The religious entity would not lose its exemption merely because the services provided were open to the general public. The test is whether the church or other religious organization operates the public accommodation, not which individuals receive the public accommodation's services.

Religious entities that are controlled by religious organizations are also exempt from the ADA's requirements. Many religious organizations in the United States use lay boards and other secular or corporate mechanisms to operate schools and an array of social services. The use of a lay board or other mechanism does not itself remove the ADA's religious exemption. Thus, a parochial school, having religious doctrine in its curriculum and sponsored by a religious order, could be exempt either as a religious organization or as an entity controlled by a religious organization, even if it has a lay board. The test remains a factual one--whether the church or other religious organization controls the operations of the school or of the service or whether the school or service is itself a religious organization.

Although a religious organization or a religious entity that is controlled by a religious organization has no obligations under the rule, a public accommodation that is not itself a religious organization, but that operates a place of public accommodation in leased space on the property of a religious entity, which is not a place of worship, is subject to the rule's requirements if it is not under control of a religious organization. When a church rents meeting space, which is not a place of worship, to a local community group or to a private, independent day care center, the ADA applies to the activities of the local community group and day care center if a lease exists and consideration is paid.

"Service animal." The term "service animal" encompasses any guide dog, signal dog, or other animal individually trained to provide assistance to an individual with a disability. The term is used in § 36.302(c), which requires public accommodations generally to modify policies, practices, and procedures to accommodate the use of service animals in places of public accommodation.

"Specified public transportation." The definition of "specified public transportation" is identical to the statutory definition in section 301(10) of the ADA. The term means transportation by bus, rail, or any other conveyance (other than by aircraft) that provides the general public with general or special service (including charter service) on a regular and continuing basis. It is used in category (7) of the definition of "place of public accommodation," which includes stations used for specified public transportation.

The effect of this definition, which excludes transportation by aircraft, is that it excludes privately operated airports from coverage as places of public accommodation. However, places of public accommodation located within airports would be covered by this part. Airports that are operated by public entities are covered by title II of the ADA and, if they are operated as part of a program receiving Federal financial assistance, by section 504 of the Rehabilitation Act. Privately operated airports are similarly covered by section 504 if they are operated as part of a program receiving Federal financial assistance. The operations of any portion of any airport that are under the control of an air carrier are covered by the Air Carrier Access Act. In addition, airports are covered as commercial facilities under this rule.

"State." The definition of "State" is identical to the statutory definition in section 3(3) of the ADA. The term is used in the definitions of "commerce" and "public entity" in § 36.104.

"Undue burden." The definition of "undue burden" is analogous to the statutory definition of "undue hardship" in employment under section 101(10) of the ADA. The term undue burden means "significant difficulty or expense" and serves as a limitation on the obligation to provide auxiliary aids and services under § 36.303 and §§ 36.309 (b)(3) and (c)(3). Further discussion of the meaning and application of the term undue burden may be found in the preamble discussion of § 36.303.

The definition lists factors considered in determining whether provision of an auxiliary aid or service in any particular circumstance would result in an undue burden. The factors to be considered in determining whether an action would result in an undue burden are identical to those to be considered in determining whether an action is readily achievable. However, "readily achievable" is a lower standard than "undue burden" in that it requires a lower level of effort on the part of the public accommodation (see Education and Labor report at 109).

Further analysis of the factors to be considered in determining undue burden may be found in the preamble discussion of the definition of the term "readily achievable."

Subpart B--General Requirements

Subpart B includes general prohibitions restricting a public accommodation from discriminating against people with disabilities by denying them the opportunity to benefit from goods or services, by giving them unequal goods or services, or by giving them different or separate goods or services. These general prohibitions are patterned after the basic, general prohibitions that exist in other civil rights laws that prohibit discrimination on the basis of race, sex, color, religion, or national origin.

Section 36.201 General

Section 36.201(a) contains the general rule that prohibits discrimination on the basis of disability in the full and equal enjoyment of goods, services, facilities, privileges, advantages, and accommodations of any place of public accommodation.

Full and equal enjoyment means the right to participate and to have an equal opportunity to obtain the same results as others to the extent possible with such accommodations as may be required by the Act and these regulations. It does not mean that an individual with a disability must achieve an identical result or level of achievement as persons without a disability. For example, an exercise class cannot exclude a person who uses a wheelchair because he or she cannot do all of the exercises and derive the same result from the class as persons without a disability.

Section 302(a) of the ADA states that the prohibition against discrimination applies to "any person who owns, leases (or leases to), or operates a place of public accommodation," and this language is reflected in § 36.201(a). The coverage is quite extensive and would include subleases, management companies, and any other entity that owns, leases, leases to, or operates a place of public accommodation, even if the operation is only for a short time.

The first sentence of paragraph (b) of § 36.201 reiterates the general principle that both the landlord that owns the building that houses the place of public accommodation, as well as the tenant that owns or operates the place of public accommodation, are public accommodations subject to the requirements of this part. Although the statutory language could be interpreted as placing equal responsibility on all private entities, whether lessor, lessee, or operator of a public accommodation, the committee reports suggest that liability may be allocated. Section 36.201(b) of that section of the proposed rule attempted to allocate liability in the regulation itself. Paragraph (b)(2) of that section made a specific allocation of liability for the obligation to take readily achievable measures to remove barriers, and paragraph (b)(3) made a specific allocation for

the obligation to provide auxiliary aids.

Numerous commenters pointed out that these allocations would not apply in all situations. Some asserted that paragraph (b)(2) of the proposed rule only addressed the situation when a lease gave the tenant the right to make alterations with permission of the landlord, but failed to address other types of leases, e.g., those that are silent on the right to make alterations, or those in which the landlord is not permitted to enter a tenant's premises to make alterations. Several commenters noted that many leases contain other clauses more relevant to the ADA than the alterations clause. For example, many leases contain a "compliance clause," a clause which allocates responsibility to a particular party for compliance with all relevant Federal, State, and local laws. Many commenters pointed out various types of relationships that were left unaddressed by the regulation, e.g., sale and lease back arrangements where the landlord is a financial institution with no control or responsibility for the building; franchises; subleases; and management companies which, at least in the hotel industry, often have control over operations but are unable to make modifications to the premises.

Some commenters raised specific questions as to how the barrier removal allocation would work as a practical matter. Paragraph (b)(2) of the proposed rule provided that the burden of making readily achievable modifications within the tenant's place of public accommodation would shift to the landlord when the modifications were not readily achievable for the tenant or when the landlord denied a tenant's request for permission to make such modifications. Commenters noted that the rule did not specify exactly when the burden would actually shift from tenant to landlord and whether the landlord would have to accept a tenant's word that a particular action is not readily achievable. Others

questioned if the tenant should be obligated to use alternative methods of barrier removal before the burden shifts. In light of the fact that readily achievable removal of barriers can include such actions as moving of racks and displays, some commenters doubted the appropriateness of requiring a landlord to become involved in day-to-day operations of its tenants' businesses.

The Department received widely differing comments in response to the preamble question asking whether landlord and tenant obligations should vary depending on the length of time remaining on an existing lease. Many suggested that tenants should have no responsibilities in "shorter leases," which commenters defined as ranging anywhere from 90 days to three years. Other commenters pointed out that the time remaining on the lease should not be a factor in the rule's allocation of responsibilities, but is relevant in determining what is readily achievable for the tenant. The Department agrees with this latter approach and will interpret the rule in that manner.

In recognition of the somewhat limited applicability of the allocation scheme contained in the proposed rule, paragraphs (b)(2) and (b)(3) have been deleted from the final rule. The Department has substituted instead a statement that allocation of responsibility as between the parties for taking readily achievable measures to remove barriers and to provide auxiliary aids and services both in common areas and within places of public accommodation may be determined by the lease or other contractual relationships between the parties. The ADA was not intended to change existing landlord/tenant responsibilities as set forth in the lease. By deleting specific provisions from the rule, the Department gives full recognition to this principle. As between the landlord and tenant, the extent of responsibility for particular obligations may be, and in many cases probably will be, determined by contract.

The suggested allocation of responsibilities contained in the proposed rule may be used if appropriate in a particular situation. Thus, the landlord would generally be held responsible for making readily achievable changes and providing auxiliary aids and services in common areas and for modifying policies, practices, or procedures applicable to all tenants, and the tenant would generally be responsible for readily achievable changes, provision of auxiliary aids, and modification of policies within its own place of public accommodation.

Many commenters objected to the proposed rule's allocation of responsibility for providing auxiliary aids and services solely to the tenant, pointing out that this exclusive allocation may not be appropriate in the case of larger public accommodations that operate their businesses by renting space out to smaller public accommodations. For example, large theaters often rent to smaller traveling companies and hospitals often rely on independent contractors to provide childbirth classes. Groups representing persons with disabilities objected to the proposed rule because, in their view, it permitted the large theater or hospital to evade ADA responsibilities by leasing to independent smaller entities. They suggested that these types of public accommodations are not really landlords because they are in the business of providing a service, rather than renting space, as in the case of a shopping center or office building landlord. These commenters believed that responsibility for providing auxiliary aids should shift to the landlord, if the landlord relies on a smaller public accommodation or independent contractor to provide services closely related to those of the larger public accommodation, and if the needed auxiliary aids prove to be an undue burden for the smaller public accommodation. The final rule no longer lists specific allocations to specific parties but, rather,

leaves allocation of responsibilities to the lease negotiations. Parties are, therefore, free to allocate the responsibility for auxiliary aids.

Section 36.201(b)(4) of the proposed rule, which provided that alterations by a tenant on its own premises do not trigger a path of travel obligation on the landlord, has been moved to § 36.403(d) of the final rule.

An entity that is not in and of itself a public accommodation, such as a trade association or performing artist, may become a public accommodation when it leases space for a conference or performance at a hotel, convention center, or stadium. For an entity to become a public accommodation when it is the lessee of space, however, the Department believes that consideration in some form must be given. Thus, a Boy Scout troop that accepts donated space does not become a public accommodation because the troop has not "leased" space, as required by the ADA.

As a public accommodation, the trade association or performing artist will be responsible for compliance with this part. Specific responsibilities should be allocated by contract, but, generally, the lessee should be responsible for providing auxiliary aids and services (which could include interpreters, Braille programs, etc.) for the participants in its conference or performance as well as for assuring that displays are accessible to individuals with disabilities.

Some commenters suggested that the rule should allocate responsibilities for areas other than removal of barriers and auxiliary aids. The final rule leaves allocation of all areas to the lease negotiations. However, in general landlords should not be given responsibility for policies a tenant applies in operating its business, if such policies are solely those of the tenant. Thus, if a restaurant tenant discriminates by refusing to seat a patron, it would be the tenant, and not the landlord, who would be responsible, because the discriminatory policy is imposed solely by the tenant and not by the landlord.

If, however, a tenant refuses to modify a "no pets" rule to allow service animals in its restaurant because the landlord mandates such a rule, then both the landlord and the tenant would be liable for violation of the ADA when a person with a service dog is refused entrance. The Department wishes to emphasize, however, that the parties are free to allocate responsibilities in any way they choose.

Private clubs are also exempt from the ADA. However, consistent with title II of the Civil Rights Act (42 U.S.C. 2000a(e), a private club is considered a public accommodation to the extent that "the facilities of such establishment are made available to the customers or patrons" of a place of public accommodation. Thus, if a private club runs a day care center that is open exclusively to its own members, the club, like the church in the example above, would have no responsibility for compliance with the ADA. Nor would the day care center have any responsibilities because it is part of the private club exempt from the ADA.

On the other hand, if the private club rents to a day care center that is open to the public, then the private club would have the same obligations as any other public accommodation that functions as a landlord with respect to compliance with title III within the day care center. In such a situation, both the private club that "leases to" a public accommodation and the public accommodation lessee (the day care center) would be subject to the ADA. This same principle would apply if the private club were to rent to, for example, a bar association, which is not generally a public accommodation but which, as explained above, becomes a public accommodation when it leases space for a conference.

Section 36.202 Activities

Section 36.202 sets out the general forms of discrimination prohibited by title III of the ADA. These general prohibitions are further refined by the specific prohibitions in subpart

C. Section 36.213 makes clear that the limitations on the ADA's requirements contained in subpart C, such as "necessity" (§ 36.301(a)) and "safety" (§ 36.301(b)), are applicable to the prohibitions in § 36.202. Thus, it is unnecessary to add these limitations to § 36.202 as has been requested by some commenters. In addition, the language of § 36.202 very closely tracks the language of section 302(b)(1)(A) of the Act, and that statutory provision does not expressly contain these limitations.

Deny participation--Section 36.202(a) provides that it is discriminatory to deny a person with a disability the right to participate in or benefit from the goods, services, facilities, privileges, advantages, or accommodations of a place of public accommodation.

A public accommodation may not exclude persons with disabilities on the basis of disability for reasons other than those specifically set forth in this part. For example, a public accommodation cannot refuse to serve a person with a disability because its insurance company conditions coverage or rates on the absence of persons with disabilities. This is a frequent basis of exclusion from a variety of community activities and is prohibited by this part.

Unequal benefit--Section 36.202(b) prohibits services or accommodations that are not equal to those provided others. For example, persons with disabilities must not be limited to certain performances at a theater.

Separate benefit--Section 36.202(c) permits different or separate benefits or services only when necessary to provide persons with disabilities opportunities as effective as those provided others. This paragraph permitting separate benefits "when necessary" should be read together with § 36.203(a), which requires integration in "the most integrated setting appropriate to the needs of the individual." The preamble to that section provides further guidance on separate programs. Thus, this section would not prohibit the

designation of parking spaces for persons with disabilities.

Each of the three paragraphs (a)-(c) prohibits discrimination against an individual or class of individuals "either directly or through contractual, licensing, or other arrangements." The intent of the contractual prohibitions of these paragraphs is to prohibit a public accommodation from doing indirectly, through a contractual relationship, what it may not do directly. Thus, the "individual or class of individuals" referenced in the three paragraphs is intended to refer to the clients and customers of the public accommodation that entered into a contractual arrangement. It is not intended to encompass the clients or customers of other entities. A public accommodation, therefore, is not liable under this provision for discrimination that may be practiced by those with whom it has a contractual relationship, when that discrimination is not directed against its own clients or customers. For example, if an amusement park contracts with a food service company to operate its restaurants at the park, the amusement park is not responsible for other operations of the food service company that do not involve clients or customers of the amusement park. Section 36.202(d) makes this clear by providing that the term "individual or class of individuals" refers to the clients or customers of the public accommodation that enters into the contractual, licensing, or other arrangement.

Section 36.203 Integrated Settings

Section 36.203 addresses the integration of persons with disabilities. The ADA recognizes that the provision of goods and services in an integrated manner is a fundamental tenet of nondiscrimination on the basis of disability. Providing segregated accommodations and services relegates persons with disabilities to the status of second-class citizens. For example, it would be a violation of this provision to require persons with mental disabilities

to eat in the back room of a restaurant or to refuse to allow a person with a disability the full use of a health spa because of stereotypes about the person's ability to participate. Section 36.203(a) states that a public accommodation shall afford goods, services, facilities, privileges, advantages, and accommodations to an individual with a disability in the most integrated setting appropriate to the needs of the individual. Section 36.203(b) specifies that, notwithstanding the existence of separate or different programs or activities provided in accordance with this section, an individual with a disability shall not be denied the opportunity to participate in such programs or activities that are not separate or different. Section 306.203(c), which is derived from section 501(d) of the Americans with Disabilities Act, states that nothing in this part shall be construed to require an individual with a disability to accept an accommodation, aid, service, opportunity, or benefit that he or she chooses not to accept.

Taken together, these provisions are intended to prohibit exclusion and segregation of individuals with disabilities and the denial of equal opportunities enjoyed by others, based on, among other things, presumptions, patronizing attitudes, fears, and stereotypes about individuals with disabilities. Consistent with these standards, public accommodations are required to make decisions based on facts applicable to individuals and not on the basis of presumptions as to what a class of individuals with disabilities can or cannot do.

Sections 36.203 (b) and (c) make clear that individuals with disabilities cannot be denied the opportunity to participate in programs that are not separate or different. This is an important and overarching principle of the Americans with Disabilities Act. Separate, special, or different programs that are designed to provide a benefit to persons with disabilities cannot be used to restrict the participation of persons with disabilities in general, integrated activities.

For example, a person who is blind may wish to decline participating in a special museum tour that allows persons to touch sculptures in an exhibit and instead tour the exhibit at his or her own pace with the museum's recorded tour. It is not the intent of this section to require the person who is blind to avail himself or herself of the special tour. Modified participation for persons with disabilities must be a choice, not a requirement.

Further, it would not be a violation of this section for an establishment to offer recreational programs specially designed for children with mobility impairments in those limited circumstances. However, it would be a violation of this section if the entity then excluded these children from other recreational services made available to nondisabled children, or required children with disabilities to attend only designated programs.

Many commenters asked that the Department clarify a public accommodation's obligations within the integrated program when it offers a separate program, but an individual with a disability chooses not to participate in the separate program. It is impossible to make a blanket statement as to what level of auxiliary aids or modifications are required in the integrated program. Rather, each situation must be assessed individually. Assuming the integrated program would be appropriate for a particular individual, the extent to which that individual must be provided with modifications will depend not only on what the individual needs but also on the limitations set forth in subpart C. For example, it may constitute an undue burden for a particular public accommodation, which provides a full-time interpreter in its special guided tour for individuals with hearing impairments, to hire an additional interpreter for those individuals who choose to attend the integrated program. The Department cannot identify

categorically the level of assistance or aid required in the integrated program.

The preamble to the proposed rule contained a statement that some interpreted as encouraging the continuation of separate schools, sheltered workshops, special recreational programs, and other similar programs. It is important to emphasize that § 36.202(c) only calls for separate programs when such programs are "necessary" to provide as effective an opportunity to individuals with disabilities as to other individuals. Likewise, § 36.203(a) only permits separate programs when a more integrated setting would not be "appropriate." Separate programs are permitted, then, in only limited circumstances. The sentence at issue has been deleted from the preamble because it was too broadly stated and had been erroneously interpreted as Departmental encouragement of separate programs without qualification.

The proposed rule's reference in § 36.203(b) to separate programs or activities provided in accordance with "this section" has been changed to "this subpart" in recognition of the fact that separate programs or activities may, in some limited circumstances, be permitted not only by § 36.203(a) but also by § 36.202(c).

In addition, some commenters suggested that the individual with the disability is the only one who can decide whether a setting is "appropriate" and what the "needs" are. Others suggested that only the public accommodation can make these determinations. The regulation does not give exclusive responsibility to either party. Rather, the determinations are to be made based on an objective view, presumably one which would take into account views of both parties.

Some commenters expressed concern that § 36.203(c), which states that nothing in the rule requires an individual with a disability to accept special accommodations and services provided under the ADA, could be interpreted to allow

guardians of infants or older people with disabilities to refuse medical treatment for their wards. Section 36.203(c) has been revised to make it clear that paragraph (c) is inapplicable to the concern of the commenters. A new paragraph (c)(2) has been added stating that nothing in the regulation authorizes the representative or guardian of an individual with a disability to decline food, water, medical treatment, or medical services for that individual. New paragraph (c) clarifies that neither the ADA nor the regulation alters current Federal law ensuring the rights of incompetent individuals with disabilities to receive food, water, and medical treatment. See, e.g., Child Abuse Amendments of 1984 (42 U.S.C. 5106a(b)(10), 5106g(10)); Rehabilitation Act of 1973, as amended (29 U.S.C 794); Developmentally Disabled Assistance and Bill of Rights Act (42 U.S.C. 6042).

Sections 36.203(c) (1) and (2) are based on section 501(d) of the ADA. Section § 501(d) was designed to clarify that nothing in the ADA requires individuals with disabilities to accept special accommodations and services for individuals with disabilities that may segregate them:

The Committee added this section (501(d)) to clarify that nothing in the ADA is intended to permit discriminatory treatment on the basis of disability, even when such treatment is rendered under the guise of providing an accommodation, service, aid or benefit to the individual with disability. For example, a blind individual may choose not to avail himself or herself of the right to go to the front of a line, even if a particular public accommodation has chosen to offer such a modification of a policy for blind individuals. Or, a blind individual may choose to decline to participate in a special museum tour that allows persons to touch sculptures in an exhibit and instead tour the exhibits at his or her own pace with the museum's recorded tour.

(Judiciary report at 71-72.) The Act is not to be construed to mean that an individual with disabilities must accept special accommodations and services for individuals with disabilities when that individual chooses to participate in the regular services already offered. Because medical treatment, including treatment for particular conditions, is not a special accommodation or service for individuals with disabilities under section 501(d), neither the Act nor this part provides affirmative authority to suspend such treatment. Section 501(d) is intended to clarify that the Act is not designed to foster discrimination through mandatory acceptance of special services when other alternatives are provided; this concern does not reach to the provision of medical treatment for the disabling condition itself.

Section 36.213 makes clear that the limitations contained in subpart C are to be read into subpart B. Thus, the integration requirement is subject to the various defenses contained in subpart C, such as safety, if eligibility criteria are at issue (§ 36.301(b)), or fundamental alteration and undue burden, if the concern is provision of auxiliary aids (§ 36.303(a)).

Section 36.204 Administrative Methods

Section 36.204 specifies that an individual or entity shall not, directly, or through contractual or other arrangements, utilize standards or criteria or methods of administration that have the effect of discriminating on the basis of disability or that perpetuate the discrimination of others who are subject to common administrative control. The preamble discussion of § 36.301 addresses eligibility criteria in detail.

Section 36.204 is derived from section 302(b)(1)(D) of the Americans with Disabilities Act, and it uses the same language used in the employment section of the ADA (section 102(b)(3)). Both sections incorporate a disparate impact standard to ensure the effectiveness of the legislative mandate to end discrimination. This standard is consistent with the interpretation of section 504

by the U.S. Supreme Court in *Alexander v. Choate*, 469 U.S. 287 (1985). The Court in *Choate* explained that members of Congress made numerous statements during passage of section 504 regarding eliminating architectural barriers, providing access to transportation, and eliminating discriminatory effects of job qualification procedures. The Court then noted: "These statements would ring hollow if the resulting legislation could not rectify the harms resulting from action that discriminated by effect as well as by design." *Id* at 297 (footnote omitted).

Of course, § 36.204 is subject to the various limitations contained in subpart C including, for example, necessity (§ 36.301(a)), safety § 36.301(b)), fundamental alteration (§ 36.302(a)), readily achievable (§ 36.304(a)), and undue burden (§ 36.303(a)).

Section 36.205 Association

Section 36.205 implements section 302(b)(1)(E) of the Act, which provides that a public accommodation shall not exclude or otherwise deny equal goods, services, facilities, privileges, advantages, accommodations, or other opportunities to an individual or entity because of the known disability of an individual with whom the individual or entity is known to have a relationship or association. This section is unchanged from the proposed rule.

The individuals covered under this section include any individuals who are discriminated against because of their known association with an individual with a disability. For example, it would be a violation of this part for a day care center to refuse admission to a child because his or her brother has HIV disease.

This protection is not limited to those who have a familial relationship with the individual who has a disability. If a place of public accommodation refuses admission to a person with cerebral palsy and his or her companions, the companions have an indepen-

dent right of action under the ADA and this section.

During the legislative process, the term "entity" was added to section 302(b)(1)(E) to clarify that the scope of the provision is intended to encompass not only persons who have a known association with a person with a disability, but also entities that provide services to or are otherwise associated with such individuals. This provision was intended to ensure that entities such as health care providers, employees of social service agencies, and others who provide professional services to persons with disabilities are not subjected to discrimination because of their professional association with persons with disabilities. For example, it would be a violation of this section to terminate the lease of a entity operating an independent living center for persons with disabilities, or to seek to evict a health care provider because that individual or entity provides services to persons with mental impairments.

Section 36.206 Retaliation or Coercion

Section 36.206 implements section 503 of the ADA, which prohibits retaliation against any individual who exercises his or her rights under the Act. This section is unchanged from the proposed rule. Paragraph (a) of § 36.206 provides that no private entity or public entity shall discriminate against any individual because that individual has exercised his or her right to oppose any act or practice made unlawful by this part, or because that individual made a charge, testified, assisted, or participated in any manner in an investigation, proceeding, or hearing under the Act or this part.

Paragraph (b) provides that no private entity or public entity shall coerce, intimidate, threaten, or interfere with any individual in the exercise of his or her rights under this part or because that individual aided or encouraged any other individual in the exercise or enjoyment of any right granted or protected by the Act or this part.

Illustrations of practices prohibited by this section are contained in paragraph (c), which is modeled on a similar provision in the regulations issued by the Department of Housing and Urban Development to implement the Fair Housing Act (see 24 CFR 100.400(c)(1)). Prohibited actions may include:

(1) Coercing an individual to deny or limit the benefits, services, or advantages to which he or she is entitled under the Act or this part;

(2) Threatening, intimidating, or interfering with an individual who is seeking to obtain or use the goods, services, facilities, privileges, advantages, or accommodations of a public accommodation;

(3) Intimidating or threatening any person because that person is assisting or encouraging an individual or group entitled to claim the rights granted or protected by the Act or this part to exercise those rights; or

(4) Retaliating against any person because that person has participated in any investigation or action to enforce the Act or this part.

This section protects not only individuals who allege a violation of the Act or this part, but also any individuals who support or assist them. This section applies to all investigations or proceedings initiated under the Act or this part without regard to the ultimate resolution of the underlying allegations. Because this section prohibits any act of retaliation or coercion in response to an individual's effort to exercise rights established by the Act and this part (or to support the efforts of another individual), the section applies not only to public accommodations that are otherwise subject to this part, but also to individuals other than public accommodations or to public entities. For example, it would be a violation of the Act and this part for a private individual, e.g., a restaurant customer, to harass or intimidate an individual with a disability in an effort to prevent that individual from patroniz-

ing the restaurant. It would, likewise, be a violation of the Act and this part for a public entity to take adverse action against an employee who appeared as a witness on behalf of an individual who sought to enforce the Act.

Section 36.207 Places of Public Accommodation Located in Private Residences

A private home used exclusively as a residence is not covered by title III because it is neither a "commercial facility" nor a "place of public accommodation." In some situations, however, a private home is not used exclusively as a residence, but houses a place of public accommodation in all or part of a home (e.g., an accountant who meets with his or her clients at his or her residence). Section 36.207(a) provides that those portions of the private residence used in the operation of the place of public accommodation are covered by this part.

For instance, a home or a portion of a home may be used as a day care center during the day and a residence at night. If all parts of the house are used for the day care center, then the entire residence is a place of public accommodation because no part of the house is used exclusively as a residence. If an accountant uses one room in the house solely as his or her professional office, then a portion of the house is used exclusively as a place of public accommodation and a portion is used exclusively as a residence. Section 36.207 provides that when a portion of a residence is used exclusively as a residence, that portion is not covered by this part. Thus, the portions of the accountant's house, other than the professional office and areas and spaces leading to it, are not covered by this part. All of the requirements of this rule apply to the covered portions, including requirements to make reasonable modifications in policies, eliminate discriminatory eligibility criteria, take readily achievable measures to remove barriers or provide readily achievable alternatives (e.g., making house calls), provide auxiliary aids and

services and undertake only accessible new construction and alterations.

Paragraph (b) was added in response to comments that sought clarification on the extent of coverage of the private residence used as the place of public accommodation. The final rule makes clear that the place of accommodation extends to all areas of the home used by clients and customers of the place of public accommodation. Thus, the ADA would apply to any door or entry way, hallways, a restroom, if used by customers and clients; and any other portion of the residence, interior or exterior, used by customers or clients of the public accommodation. This interpretation is simply an application of the general rule for all public accommodations, which extends statutory requirements to all portions of the facility used by customers and clients, including, if applicable, restrooms, hallways, and approaches to the public accommodation. As with other public accommodations, barriers at the entrance and on the sidewalk leading up to the public accommodation, if the sidewalk is under the control of the public accommodation, must be removed if doing so is readily achievable.

The Department recognizes that many businesses that operate out of personal residences are quite small, often employing only the homeowner and having limited total revenues. In these circumstances the effect of ADA coverage would likely be quite minimal. For example, because the obligation to remove existing architectural barriers is limited to those that are easily accomplishable without much difficulty or expense (see § 36.304), the range of required actions would be quite modest. It might not be readily achievable for such a place of public accommodation to remove any existing barriers. If it is not readily achievable to remove existing architectural barriers, a public accommodation located in a private residence may meet its obligations under the Act and this part by providing its goods or services to clients or customers with disabilities through the use of alternative measures, including delivery of goods or services in the home of the customer or client, to the extent that such alternative measures are readily achievable (*See* § 36.305).

Some commenters asked for clarification as to how the new construction and alteration standards of subpart D will apply to residences. The new construction standards only apply to the extent that the residence or portion of the residence was designed or intended for use as a public accommodation. Thus, for example, if a portion of a home is designed or constructed for use exclusively as a lawyer's office or for use both as a lawyer's office and for residential purposes, then it must be designed in accordance with the new construction standards in the appendix. Likewise, if a homeowner is undertaking alterations to convert all or part of his residence to a place of public accommodation, that work must be done in compliance with the alterations standards in the appendix.

The preamble to the proposed rule addressed the applicable requirements when a commercial facility is located in a private residence. That situation is now addressed in § 36.401(b) of subpart D.

Section 36.208 Direct Threat

Section 36.208(a) implements section 302(b)(3) of the Act by providing that this part does not require a public accommodation to permit an individual to participate in or benefit from the goods, services, facilities, privileges, advantages and accommodations of the public accommodation, if that individual poses a direct threat to the health or safety of others. This section is unchanged from the proposed rule.

The Department received a significant number of comments on this section. Commenters representing individuals with disabilities generally supported this provision, but suggested revisions to further limit its application. Commenters representing public accommodations generally endorsed modifications that would permit a public accommodation to exercise its own judgment in determining whether an individual poses a direct threat.

The inclusion of this provision is not intended to imply that persons with disabilities pose risks to others. It is intended to address concerns that may arise in this area. It establishes a strict standard that must be met before denying service to an individual with a disability or excluding that individual from participation.

Paragraph (b) of this section explains that a "direct threat" is a significant risk to the health or safety of others that cannot be eliminated by a modification of policies, practices, or procedures, or by the provision of auxiliary aids and services. This paragraph codifies the standard first applied by the Supreme Court in *School Board of Nassau County v. Arline*, 480 U.S. 273 (1987), in which the Court held that an individual with a contagious disease may be an "individual with handicaps" under section 504 of the Rehabilitation Act. In *Arline*, the Supreme Court recognized that there is a need to balance the interests of people with disabilities against legitimate concerns for public safety. Although persons with disabilities are generally entitled to the protection of this part, a person who poses a significant risk to others may be excluded if reasonable modifications to the public accommodation's policies, practices, or procedures will not eliminate that risk. The determination that a person poses a direct threat to the health or safety of others may not be based on generalizations or stereotypes about the effects of a particular disability; it must be based on an individual assessment that conforms to the requirements of paragraph (c) of this section.

Paragraph (c) establishes the test to use in determining whether an individual poses a direct threat to the health or safety of others. A public accommodation is required to make an individualized assessment, based on reasonable judgment that relies on current medical evidence or on the best available objective evidence, to determine: The nature, duration, and severity of the risk; the probability that the potential injury will actually occur; and whether reasonable modifications of policies, practices, or procedures will mitigate the risk. This is the test established by the Supreme Court in *Arline*. Such an inquiry is essential if the law is to achieve its goal of protecting disabled individuals from discrimination based on prejudice, stereotypes, or unfounded fear, while giving appropriate weight to legitimate concerns, such as the need to avoid exposing others to significant health and safety risks. Making this assessment will not usually require the services of a physician. Sources for medical knowledge include guidance from public health authorities, such as the U.S. Public Health Service, the Centers for Disease Control, and the National Institutes of Health, including the National Institute of Mental Health.

Many of the commenters sought clarification of the inquiry requirement. Some suggested that public accommodations should be prohibited from making any inquiries to determine if an individual with a disability would pose a direct threat to other persons. The Department believes that to preclude all such inquiries would be inappropriate. Under § 36.301 of this part, a public accommodation is permitted to establish eligibility criteria necessary for the safe operation of the place of public accommodation. Implicit in that right is the right to ask if an individual meets the criteria. However, any eligibility or safety standard established by a public accommodation must be based on actual risk, not on speculation or stereotypes; it must be applied to all clients or customers of the place of public accommodation; and inquiries must be limited to matters necessary to the application of the standard.

Some commenters suggested that the test established in the *Arline* decision, which was developed in the context of an employment case, is too stringent to apply in a public accommodations context where interaction between the public accommodation and its client or customer is often very brief. One suggested alternative was to permit public accommodations to exercise "good faith" judgment in determining whether an individual poses a direct threat, particularly when a public accommodation is dealing with a client or customer engaged in disorderly or disruptive behavior.

The Department believes that the ADA clearly requires that any determination to exclude an individual from participation must be based on an objective standard. A public accommodation may establish neutral eligibility criteria as a condition of receiving its goods or services. As long as these criteria are necessary for the safe provision of the public accommodation's goods and services and applied neutrally to all clients or customers, regardless of whether they are individuals with disabilities, a person who is unable to meet the criteria may be excluded from participation without inquiry into the underlying reason for the inability to comply. In places of public accommodation such as restaurants, theaters, or hotels, where the contact between the public accommodation and its clients is transitory, the uniform application of an eligibility standard precluding violent or disruptive behavior by any client or customer should be sufficient to enable a public accommodation to conduct its business in an orderly manner.

Some other commenters asked for clarification of the application of this provision to persons, particularly children, who have short-term, contagious illnesses, such as fevers, influenza, or the common cold. It is common practice in schools and day care settings to exclude persons with such illnesses until the symptoms subside. The Department believes that these commenters misunderstand the scope of this rule. The ADA only prohibits discrimination against an individual with a disability. Under the ADA and this part, a "disability" is defined as a physical or mental impairment that substantially limits one or more major life activities. Common, short-term illnesses that predictably resolve themselves within a matter of days do not "substantially limit" a major life activity; therefore, it is not a violation of this part to exclude an individual from receiving the services of a public accommodation because of such transitory illness. However, this part does apply to persons who have long-term illnesses. Any determination with respect to a person who has a chronic or long-term illness must be made in compliance with the requirements of this section.

Section 36.209 Illegal Use of Drugs

Section 36.209 effectuates section 510 of the ADA, which clarifies the Act's application to people who use drugs illegally. Paragraph (a) provides that this part does not prohibit discrimination based on an individual's current illegal use of drugs.

The Act and the regulation distinguish between illegal use of drugs and the legal use of substances, whether or not those substances are "controlled substances," as defined in the Controlled Substances Act (21 U.S.C. 812). Some controlled substances are prescription drugs that have legitimate medical uses. Section 36.209 does not affect use of controlled substances pursuant to a valid prescription, under supervision by a licensed health care professional, or other use that is authorized by the Controlled Substances Act or any other provision of Federal law. It does apply to illegal use of those substances, as well as to illegal use of controlled substances that are not prescription drugs. The key question is whether the individual's use of the substance is illegal, not whether the substance has recognized legal uses. Alcohol is not a controlled substance, so use of alcohol is not addressed by

§ 36.209. Alcoholics are individuals with disabilities, subject to the protections of the statute.

A distinction is also made between the use of a substance and the status of being addicted to that substance. Addiction is a disability, and addicts are individuals with disabilities protected by the Act. The protection, however, does not extend to actions based on the illegal use of the substance. In other words, an addict cannot use the fact of his or her addiction as a defense to an action based on illegal use of drugs. This distinction is not artificial. Congress intended to deny protection to people who engage in the illegal use of drugs, whether or not they are addicted, but to provide protection to addicts so long as they are not currently using drugs.

A third distinction is the difficult one between current use and former use. The definition of "current illegal use of drugs" in § 36.104, which is based on the report of the Conference Committee, H.R. Conf. Rep. No. 596, 101st Cong., 2d Sess. 64 (1990), is "illegal use of drugs that occurred recently enough to justify a reasonable belief that a person's drug use is current or that continuing use is a real and ongoing problem."

Paragraph (a)(2)(i) specifies that an individual who has successfully completed a supervised drug rehabilitation program or has otherwise been rehabilitated successfully and who is not engaging in current illegal use of drugs is protected. Paragraph (a)(2)(ii) clarifies that an individual who is currently participating in a supervised rehabilitation program and is not engaging in current illegal use of drugs is protected. Paragraph (a)(2)(iii) provides that a person who is erroneously regarded as engaging in current illegal use of drugs, but who is not engaging in such use, is protected.

Paragraph (b) provides a limited exception to the exclusion of current illegal users of drugs from the protections of the Act. It prohibits denial of health services, or services provided in connection with drug rehabilitation, to an individual on the basis of current illegal use of drugs, if the individual is otherwise entitled to such services. As explained further in the discussion of § 36.302, a health care facility that specializes in a particular type of treatment, such as care of burn victims, is not required to provide drug rehabilitation services, but it cannot refuse to treat an individual's burns on the grounds that the individual is illegally using drugs.

A commenter argued that health care providers should be permitted to use their medical judgment to postpone discretionary medical treatment of individuals under the influence of alcohol or drugs. The regulation permits a medical practitioner to take into account an individual's use of drugs in determining appropriate medical treatment. Section 36.209 provides that the prohibitions on discrimination in this part do not apply when the public accommodation acts on the basis of current illegal use of drugs. Although those prohibitions do apply under paragraph (b), the limitations established under this part also apply. Thus, under § 36.208, a health care provider or other public accommodation covered under § 36.209(b) may exclude an individual whose current illegal use of drugs poses a direct threat to the health or safety of others, and, under § 36.301, a public accommodation may impose or apply eligibility criteria that are necessary for the provision of the services being offered, and may impose legitimate safety requirements that are necessary for safe operation. These same limitations also apply to individuals with disabilities who use alcohol or prescription drugs. The Department believes that these provisions address this commenter's concerns.

Other commenters pointed out that abstention from the use of drugs is an essential condition for participation in some drug rehabilitation programs, and may be a necessary requirement in inpatient or residential settings. The Department believes that this comment is well-founded.

Congress clearly did not intend to exclude from drug treatment programs the very individuals who need such programs because of their use of drugs. In such a situation, however, once an individual has been admitted to a program, abstention may be a necessary and appropriate condition to continued participation. The final rule therefore provides that a drug rehabilitation or treatment program may deny participation to individuals who use drugs while they are in the program.

Paragraph (c) expresses Congress' intention that the Act be neutral with respect to testing for illegal use of drugs. This paragraph implements the provision in section 510(b) of the Act that allows entities "to adopt or administer reasonable policies or procedures, including but not limited to drug testing," that ensure an individual who is participating in a supervised rehabilitation program, or who has completed such a program or otherwise been rehabilitated successfully, is no longer engaging in the illegal use of drugs. Paragraph (c) is not to be construed to encourage, prohibit, restrict, or authorize the conducting of testing for the illegal use of drugs.

Paragraph (c) of § 36.209 clarifies that it is not a violation of this part to adopt or administer reasonable policies or procedures to ensure that an individual who formerly engaged in the illegal use of drugs is not currently engaging in illegal use of drugs. Any such policies or procedures must, of course, be reasonable, and must be designed to identify accurately the illegal use of drugs. This paragraph does not authorize inquiries, tests, or other procedures that would disclose use of substances that are not controlled substances or are taken under supervision by a licensed health care professional, or other uses authorized by the Controlled Substances Act or other provisions of Federal law, because such uses are not included in the definition of "illegal use of drugs."

One commenter argued that the rule should permit testing for lawful use of prescription drugs, but most favored the explanation that tests must be limited to unlawful use in order to avoid revealing the use of prescription medicine used to treat disabilities. Tests revealing legal use of prescription drugs might violate the prohibition in § 36.301 of attempts to unnecessarily identify the existence of a disability.

Section 36.210 Smoking

Section 36.210 restates the clarification in section 501(b) of the Act that the Act does not preclude the prohibition of, or imposition of restrictions on, smoking. Some commenters argued that § 36.210 does not go far enough, and that the regulation should prohibit smoking in all places of public accommodation. The reference to smoking in section 501 merely clarifies that the Act does not require public accommodations to accommodate smokers by permitting them to smoke in places of public accommodations.

Section 36.211 Maintenance of Accessible Features

Section 36.211 provides that a public accommodation shall maintain in operable working condition those features of facilities and equipment that are required to be readily accessible to and usable by persons with disabilities by the Act or this part. The Act requires that, to the maximum extent feasible, facilities must be accessible to, *and usable by*, individuals with disabilities. This section recognizes that it is not sufficient to provide features such as accessible routes, elevators, or ramps, if those features are not maintained in a manner that enables individuals with disabilities to use them. Inoperable elevators, locked accessible doors, or "accessible" routes that are obstructed by furniture, filing cabinets, or potted plants are neither "accessible to" nor "usable by" individuals with disabilities.

Some commenters objected that this section appeared to

establish an absolute requirement and suggested that
language from the preamble be
included in the text of the
regulation. It is, of course,
impossible to guarantee that
mechanical devices will never
fail to operate. Paragraph (b) of
the final regulation provides
that this section does not
prohibit isolated or temporary
interruptions in service or
access due to maintenance or
repairs. This paragraph is
intended to clarify that
temporary obstructions or
isolated instances of mechanical
failure would not be considered
violations of the Act or this part.
However, allowing obstructions
or "out of service" equipment
to persist beyond a reasonable
period of time would violate
this part, as would repeated
mechanical failures due to
improper or inadequate
maintenance. Failure of the
public accommodation to
ensure that accessible routes are
properly maintained and free of
obstructions, or failure to
arrange prompt repair of
inoperable elevators or other
equipment intended to provide
access, would also violate this
part.

Other commenters
requested that this section be
expanded to include specific
requirements for inspection and
maintenance of equipment, for
training staff in the proper
operation of equipment, and for
maintenance of specific items.
The Department believes that
this section properly establishes
the general requirement for
maintaining access and that
further, more detailed requirements are not necessary.

Section 36.212 Insurance

The Department received
numerous comments on
proposed § 36.212. Most
supported the proposed
regulation but felt that it did not
go far enough in protecting
individuals with disabilities
and persons associated with
them from discrimination.
Many commenters argued that
language from the preamble to
the proposed regulation should
be included in the text of the
final regulation. Other
commenters argued that even

that language was not strong
enough, and that more stringent
standards should be established. Only a few commenters
argued that the Act does not
apply to insurance underwriting practices or the terms of
insurance contracts. These
commenters cited language
from the Senate committee
report (S. Rep. No. 116, 101st
Cong., 1st Sess., at 84-86 (1989)
(hereinafter "Senate report")),
indicating that Congress did not
intend to affect existing
insurance practices.

The Department has
decided to adopt the language
of the proposed rule without
change. Sections 36.212 (a) and
(b) restate section 501(c) of the
Act, which provides that the
Act shall not be construed to
restrict certain insurance
practices on the part of
insurance companies and
employers, as long as such
practices are not used to evade
the purposes of the Act. Section
36.212(c) is a specific application of § 36.202(a), which
prohibits denial of participation
on the basis of disability. It
provides that a public accommodation may not refuse to
serve an individual with a
disability because of limitations
on coverage or rates in its
insurance policies (see Judiciary
report at 56).

Many commenters
supported the requirements of
§ 36.212(c) in the proposed rule
because it addressed an
important reason for denial of
services by public accommodations. One commenter argued
that services could be denied if
the insurance coverage required
exclusion of people whose
disabilities were reasonably
related to the risks involved in
that particular place of public
accommodation. Sections 36.208
and 36.301 establish criteria for
denial of participation on the
basis of legitimate safety
concerns. This paragraph does
not prohibit consideration of
such concerns in insurance
policies, but provides that any
exclusion on the basis of
disability must be based on the
permissible criteria, rather than
on the terms of the insurance
contract.

Language in the committee
reports indicates that Congress

intended to reach insurance
practices by prohibiting
differential treatment of
individuals with disabilities in
insurance offered by public
accommodations unless the
differences are justified. "Under
the ADA, a person with a
disability cannot be denied
insurance or be subject to
different terms or conditions of
insurance based on disability
alone, if the disability does not
pose increased risks" (Senate
report at 84; Education and
Labor report at 136). Section
501(c) (1) of the Act was
intended to emphasize that
"insurers may continue to sell
to and underwrite individuals
applying for life, health, or
other insurance on an individually underwritten basis, or to
service such insurance
products, *so long as the standards
used are based on sound actuarial
data and not on speculation"*
(Judiciary report at 70 (emphasis added); see also Senate
report at 85; Education and
Labor report at 137).

The committee reports
indicate that underwriting and
classification of risks must be
"based on sound actuarial
principles or be related to actual
or reasonably anticipated
experience" (see, *e.g.*, Judiciary
report at 71). Moreover, "while
a plan which limits certain
kinds of coverage based on
classification of risk would be
allowed * * *, the plan may not
refuse to insure, or refuse to
continue to insure, or limit the
amount, extent, or kind of
coverage available to an
individual, or charge a different
rate for the same coverage
solely because of a physical or
mental impairment, except
where the refusal, limitation, or
rate differential is based on
sound actuarial principles or is
related to actual or reasonably
anticipated experience" (Senate
report at 85; Education and
Labor report at 136-37; Judiciary
report at 71). The ADA,
therefore, does not prohibit use
of legitimate actuarial considerations to justify differential
treatment of individuals with
disabilities in insurance.

The committee reports
provide some guidance on how
nondiscrimination principles in
the disability rights area relate

to insurance practices. For example, a person who is blind may not be denied coverage based on blindness independent of actuarial risk classification. With respect to group health insurance coverage, an individual with a pre-existing condition may be denied coverage for that condition for the period specified in the policy, but cannot be denied coverage for illness or injuries unrelated to the pre-existing condition. Also, a public accommodation may offer insurance policies that limit coverage for certain procedures or treatments, but may not entirely deny coverage to a person with a disability.

The Department requested comment on the extent to which data that would establish statistically sound correlations are available. Numerous commenters cited pervasive problems in the availability and cost of insurance for individuals with disabilities and parents of children with disabilities. No commenters cited specific data, or sources of data, to support specific exclusionary practices. Several commenters reported that, even when statistics are available, they are often outdated and do not reflect current medical technology and treatment methods. Concern was expressed that adequate efforts are not made to distinguish those individuals who are high users of health care from individuals in the same diagnostic groups who may be low users of health care. One insurer reported that "hard data and actuarial statistics are not available to provide precise numerical justifications for every underwriting determination," but argued that decisions may be based on "logical principles generally accepted by actuarial science and fully consistent with state insurance laws." The commenter urged that the Department recognize the validity of information other than statistical data as a basis for insurance determinations.

The most frequent comment was a recommendation that the final regulation should require the insurance company to provide a copy of the actuarial data on which its actions are based when requested by the applicant. Such a requirement would be beyond anything contemplated by the Act or by Congress and has therefore not been included in the Department's final rule. Because the legislative history of the ADA clarifies that different treatment of individuals with disabilities in insurance may be justified by sound actuarial data, such actuarial data will be critical to any potential litigation on this issue. This information would presumably be obtainable in a court proceeding where the insurer's actuarial data was the basis for different treatment of persons with disabilities. In addition, under some State regulatory schemes, insurers may have to file such actuarial information with the State regulatory agency and this information may be obtainable at the State level.

A few commenters representing the insurance industry conceded that underwriting practices in life and health insurance are clearly covered, but argued that property and casualty insurance are not covered. The Department sees no reason for this distinction. Although life and health insurance are the areas where the regulation will have its greatest application, the Act applies equally to unjustified discrimination in all types of insurance provided by public accommodations. A number of commenters, for example, reported difficulties in obtaining automobile insurance because of their disabilities, despite their having good driving records.

Section 36.213 Relationship of Subpart B to Subparts C and D

This section explains that subpart B sets forth the general principles of nondiscrimination applicable to all entities subject to this regulation, while subparts C and D provide guidance on the application of this part to specific situations. The specific provisions in subparts C and D, including the limitations on those provisions, control over the general provisions in circumstances where both specific and general provisions apply. Resort to the general provisions of subpart B is only appropriate where there are no applicable specific rules of guidance in subparts C or D. This interaction between the specific requirements and the general requirements operates with regard to contractual obligations as well.

One illustration of this principle is its application to the obligation of a public accommodation to provide access to services by removal of architectural barriers or by alternatives to barrier removal. The general requirement, established in subpart B by § 36.203, is that a public accommodation must provide its services to individuals with disabilities in the most integrated setting appropriate. This general requirement would appear to categorically prohibit "segregated" seating for persons in wheelchairs. Section 36.304, however, only requires removal of architectural barriers to the extent that removal is "readily achievable." If providing access to all areas of a restaurant, for example, would not be "readily achievable," a public accommodation may provide access to selected areas only. Also, § 36.305 provides that, where barrier removal is not readily achievable, a public accommodation may use alternative, readily achievable methods of making services available, such as curbside service or home delivery. Thus, in this manner, the specific requirements of §§ 36.304 and 36.305 control over the general requirement of § 36.203.

Subpart C--Specific Requirements

In general, subpart C implements the "specific prohibitions" that comprise section 302(b)(2) of the ADA. It also addresses the requirements of section 309 of the ADA regarding examinations and courses.

Section 36.301 Eligibility Criteria

Section 36.301 of the rule prohibits the imposition or application of eligibility criteria that screen out or tend to screen out an individual with a disability or any class of individuals with disabilities from fully and equally enjoying any goods, services, facilities, privileges, advantages, and accommodations, unless such criteria can be shown to be necessary for the provision of the goods, services, facilities, privileges, advantages, or accommodations being offered. This prohibition is based on section 302(b)(2)(A)(i) of the ADA.

It would violate this section to establish exclusive or segregative eligibility criteria that would bar, for example, all persons who are deaf from playing on a golf course or all individuals with cerebral palsy from attending a movie theater, or limit the seating of individuals with Down's syndrome to only particular areas of a restaurant. The wishes, tastes, or preferences of other customers may not be asserted to justify criteria that would exclude or segregate individuals with disabilities.

Section 36.301 also prohibits attempts by a public accommodation to unnecessarily identify the existence of a disability; for example, it would be a violation of this section for a retail store to require an individual to state on a credit application whether the applicant has epilepsy, mental illness, or any other disability, or to inquire unnecessarily whether an individual has HIV disease.

Section 36.301 also prohibits policies that unnecessarily impose requirements or burdens on individuals with disabilities that are not placed on others. For example, public accommodations may not require that an individual with a disability be accompanied by an attendant. As provided by § 36.306, however, a public accommodation is not required to provide services of a personal nature including assistance in toileting, eating, or dressing.

Paragraph (c) of § 36.301 provides that public accommodations may not place a surcharge on a particular individual with a disability or any group of individuals with disabilities to cover the costs of

measures, such as the provision of auxiliary aids and services, barrier removal, alternatives to barrier removal, and reasonable modifications in policies, practices, and procedures, that are required to provide that individual or group with the nondiscriminatory treatment required by the Act or this part.

A number of commenters inquired as to whether deposits required for the use of auxiliary aids, such as assistive listening devices, are prohibited surcharges. It is the Department's view that reasonable, completely refundable, deposits are not to be considered surcharges prohibited by this section. Requiring deposits is an important means of ensuring the availability of equipment necessary to ensure compliance with the ADA.

Other commenters sought clarification as to whether § 36.301(c) prohibits professionals from charging for the additional time that it may take in certain cases to provide services to an individual with disabilities. The Department does not intend § 36.301(c) to prohibit professionals who bill on the basis of time from charging individuals with disabilities on that basis. However, fees may not be charged for the provision of auxiliary aids and services, barrier removal, alternatives to barrier removal, reasonable modifications in policies, practices, and procedures, or any other measures necessary to ensure compliance with the ADA.

Other commenters inquired as to whether day care centers may charge for extra services provided to individuals with disabilities. As stated above, § 36.302(c) is intended only to prohibit charges for measures necessary to achieve compliance with the ADA.

Another commenter asserted that charges may be assessed for home delivery provided as an alternative to barrier removal under § 36.305, when home delivery is provided to all customers for a fee. Charges for home delivery are permissible if home delivery is not considered an alternative to barrier removal. If the public

accommodation offers an alternative, such as curb, carryout, or sidewalk service for which no surcharge is assessed, then it may charge for home delivery in accordance with its standard pricing for home delivery.

In addition, § 36.301 prohibits the imposition of criteria that "tend to" screen out an individual with a disability. This concept, which is derived from current regulations under section 504 (see, e.g., 45 CFR 84.13), makes it discriminatory to impose policies or criteria that, while not creating a direct bar to individuals with disabilities, indirectly prevent or limit their ability to participate. For example, requiring presentation of a driver's license as the sole means of identification for purposes of paying by check would violate this section in situations where, for example, individuals with severe vision impairments or developmental disabilities or epilepsy are ineligible to receive a driver's license and the use of an alternative means of identification, such as another photo I.D. or credit card, is feasible.

A public accommodation may, however, impose neutral rules and criteria that screen out, or tend to screen out, individuals with disabilities, if the criteria are necessary for the safe operation of the public accommodation. Examples of safety qualifications that would be justifiable in appropriate circumstances would include height requirements for certain amusement park rides or a requirement that all participants in a recreational rafting expedition be able to meet a necessary level of swimming proficiency. Safety requirements must be based on actual risks and not on speculation, stereotypes, or generalizations about individuals with disabilities.

Section 36.302 Modifications in Policies, Practices, or Procedures

Section 36.302 of the rule prohibits the failure to make reasonable modifications in policies, practices, and procedures when such modifications may be necessary to afford any goods, services, facilities, privileges, advantages, or accommodations, unless the entity can demonstrate that making such modifications would fundamentally alter the nature of such goods, services, facilities, privileges, advantages, or accommodations. This prohibition is based on section 302(b)(2)(A)(ii) of the ADA.

For example, a parking facility would be required to modify a rule barring all vans or all vans with raised roofs, if an individual who uses a wheelchair-accessible van wishes to park in that facility, and if overhead structures are high enough to accommodate the height of the van. A department store may need to modify a policy of only permitting one person at a time in a dressing room, if an individual with mental retardation needs and requests assistance in dressing from a companion. Public accommodations may need to revise operational policies to ensure that services are available to individuals with disabilities. For instance, a hotel may need to adopt a policy of keeping an accessible room unoccupied until an individual with a disability arrives at the hotel, assuming the individual has properly reserved the room.

One example of application of this principle is specifically included in a new § 36.302(d) on check-out aisles. That paragraph provides that a store with check-out aisles must ensure that an adequate number of accessible check-out aisles is kept open during store hours, or must otherwise modify its policies and practices, in order to ensure that an equivalent level of convenient service is provided to individuals with disabilities as is provided to others. For example, if only one check-out aisle is accessible, and it is generally used for express service, one way of providing equivalent service is to allow persons with mobility impairments to make all of their purchases at that aisle. This principle also applies with respect to other accessible elements and services. For

example, a particular bank may be in compliance with the accessibility guidelines for new construction incorporated in appendix A with respect to automated teller machines (ATM) at a new branch office by providing one accessible walk-up machine at that location, even though an adjacent walk-up ATM is not accessible and the drive-up ATM is not accessible. However, the bank would be in violation of this section if the accessible ATM was located in a lobby that was locked during evening hours while the drive-up ATM was available to customers without disabilities during those same hours. The bank would need to ensure that the accessible ATM was available to customers during the hours that any of the other ATM's was available.

A number of commenters inquired as to the relationship between this section and § 36.307, "Accessible or special goods." Under § 36.307, a public accommodation is not required to alter its inventory to include accessible or special goods that are designed for, or facilitate use by, individuals with disabilities. The rule enunciated in § 36.307 is consistent with the "fundamental alteration" defense to the reasonable modifications requirement of § 36.302. Therefore, § 36.302 would not require the inventory of goods provided by a public accommodation to be altered to include goods with accessibility features. For example, § 36.302 would not require a bookstore to stock Brailled books or order Brailled books, if it does not do so in the normal course of its business.

The rule does not require modifications to the legitimate areas of specialization of service providers. Section 36.302(b) provides that a public accommodation may refer an individual with a disability to another public accommodation, if that individual is seeking, or requires, treatment or services outside of the referring public accommodation's area of specialization, and if, in the normal course of its operations, the referring public accommodation would make a similar

referral for an individual without a disability who seeks or requires the same treatment or services.

For example, it would not be discriminatory for a physician who specializes only in burn treatment to refer an individual who is deaf to another physician for treatment of an injury other than a burn injury. To require a physician to accept patients outside of his or her specialty would fundamentally alter the nature of the medical practice and, therefore, not be required by this section.

A clinic specializing exclusively in drug rehabilitation could similarly refuse to treat a person who is not a drug addict, but could not refuse to treat a person who is a drug addict simply because the patient tests positive for HIV. Conversely, a clinic that specializes in the treatment of individuals with HIV could refuse to treat an individual that does not have HIV, but could not refuse to treat a person for HIV infection simply because that person is also a drug addict.

Some commenters requested clarification as to how this provision would apply to situations where manifestations of the disability in question, itself, would raise complications requiring the expertise of a different practitioner. It is not the Department's intention in § 36.302(b) to prohibit a physician from referring an individual with a disability to another physician, if the disability itself creates specialized complications for the patient's health that the physician lacks the experience or knowledge to address (see Education and Labor report at 106).

Section 36.302(c)(1) requires that a public accommodation modify its policies, practices, or procedures to permit the use of a service animal by an individual with a disability in any area open to the general public. The term "service animal" is defined in § 36.104 to include guide dogs, signal dogs, or any other animal individually trained to provide assistance to an individual with a disability.

A number of commenters pointed to the difficulty of making the distinction required by the proposed rule between areas open to the general public and those that are not. The ambiguity and uncertainty surrounding these provisions has led the Department to adopt a single standard for all public accommodations.

Section 36.302(c)(1) of the final rule now provides that "[g]enerally, a public accommodation shall modify policies, practices, and procedures to permit the use of a service animal by an individual with a disability." This formulation reflects the general intent of Congress that public accommodations take the necessary steps to accommodate service animals and to ensure that individuals with disabilities are not separated from their service animals. It is intended that the broadest feasible access be provided to service animals in all places of public accommodation, including movie theaters, restaurants, hotels, retail stores, hospitals, and nursing homes (see Education and Labor report at 106; Judiciary report at 59). The section also acknowledges, however, that, in rare circumstances, accommodation of service animals may not be required because a fundamental alteration would result in the nature of the goods, services, facilities, privileges, or accommodations offered or provided, or the safe operation of the public accommodation would be jeopardized.

As specified in § 36.302(c)(2), the rule does not require a public accommodation to supervise or care for any service animal. If a service animal must be separated from an individual with a disability in order to avoid a fundamental alteration or a threat to safety, it is the responsibility of the individual with the disability to arrange for the care and supervision of the animal during the period of separation.

A museum would not be required by § 36.302 to modify a policy barring the touching of delicate works of art in order to enhance the participation of individuals who are blind, if the touching threatened the integrity of the work. Damage to a museum piece would clearly be a fundamental alteration that is not required by this section.

Section 36.303 Auxiliary Aids and Services.

Section 36.303 of the final rule requires a public accommodation to take such steps as may be necessary to ensure that no individual with a disability is excluded, denied services, segregated or otherwise treated differently than other individuals because of the absence of auxiliary aids and services, unless the public accommodation can demonstrate that taking such steps would fundamentally alter the nature of the goods, services, facilities, advantages, or accommodations being offered or would result in an undue burden. This requirement is based on section 302(b)(2)(A)(iii) of the ADA.

Implicit in this duty to provide auxiliary aids and services is the underlying obligation of a public accommodation to communicate effectively with its customers, clients, patients, or participants who have disabilities affecting hearing, vision, or speech. To give emphasis to this underlying obligation, § 36.303(c) of the rule incorporates language derived from section 504 regulations for federally conducted programs (see *e.g.*, 28 CFR 39.160(a)) that requires that appropriate auxiliary aids and services be furnished to ensure that communication with persons with disabilities is as effective as communication with others.

Auxiliary aids and services include a wide range of services and devices for ensuring effective communication. Use of the most advanced technology is not required so long as effective communication is ensured. The Department's proposed § 36.303(b) provided a list of examples of auxiliary aids and services that was taken from the definition of auxiliary aids and services in section 3(1) of the ADA and was supplemented by examples from regulations implementing section 504 in federally conducted programs (see e.g., 28 CFR 39.103). A substantial number of commenters suggested that additional examples be added to this list. The Department has added several items to this list but wishes to clarify that the list is not an all-inclusive or exhaustive catalogue of possible or available auxiliary aids or services. It is not possible to provide an exhaustive list, and such an attempt would omit new devices that will become available with emerging technology.

The Department has added videotext displays, computer-aided transcription services, and open and closed captioning to the list of examples. Videotext displays have become an important means of accessing auditory communications through a public address system. Transcription services are used to relay aurally delivered material almost simultaneously in written form to persons who are deaf or hard of hearing. This technology is often used at conferences, conventions, and hearings. While the proposed rule expressly included television decoder equipment as an auxiliary aid or service, it did not mention captioning itself. The final rule rectifies this omission by mentioning both closed and open captioning.

In this section, the Department has changed the proposed rule's phrase, "orally delivered materials," to the phrase, "aurally delivered materials." This new phrase tracks the language in the definition of "auxiliary aids and services" in section 3 of the ADA and is meant to include nonverbal sounds and alarms and computer-generated speech.

Several persons and organizations requested that the Department replace the term "telecommunications devices for deaf persons" or "TDD's" with the term "text telephone." The Department has declined to do so. The Department is aware that the Architectural and Transportation Barriers Compliance Board has used the phrase "text telephone" in lieu of the statutory term "TDD" in its final accessibility guidelines.

Title IV of the ADA, however, uses the term "Telecommunications Device for the Deaf," and the Department believes it would be inappropriate to abandon this statutory term at this time.

Paragraph (b)(2) lists examples of aids and services for making visually delivered materials accessible to persons with visual impairments. Many commenters proposed additional examples such as signage or mapping, audio description services, secondary auditory programs (SAP), telebraillers, and reading machines. While the Department declines to add these items to the list in the regulation, they may be considered appropriate auxiliary aids and services.

Paragraph (b)(3) refers to the acquisition or modification of equipment or devices. For example, tape players used for an audio-guided tour of a museum exhibit may require the addition of Brailled adhesive labels to the buttons on a reasonable number of the tape players to facilitate their use by individuals who are blind. Similarly, permanent or portable assistive listening systems for persons with hearing impairments may be required at a hotel conference center.

Several commenters suggested the addition of current technological innovations in microelectronics and computerized control systems (e.g., voice recognition systems, automatic dialing telephones, and infrared elevator and light control systems) to the list of auxiliary aids and services. The Department interprets auxiliary aids and services as those aids and services designed to provide effective communications, i. e., making aurally and visually delivered information available to persons with hearing, speech, and vision impairments. Methods of making services, programs, or activities accessible to, or usable by, individuals with mobility or manual dexterity impairments are addressed by other sections of this part, including the requirements for modifications in policies, practices, or procedures (§ 36.302), the elimination of existing architectural barriers (§ 36.304), and the provision of alternatives to barriers removal § 36.305).

Paragraph (b)(4) refers to other similar services and actions. Several commenters asked for clarification that "similar services and actions" include retrieving items from shelves, assistance in reaching a marginally accessible seat, pushing a barrier aside in order to provide an accessible route, or assistance in removing a sweater or coat. While retrieving an item from a shelf might be an "auxiliary aid or service" for a blind person who could not locate the item without assistance, it might be a readily achievable alternative to barrier removal for a person using a wheelchair who could not reach the shelf, or a reasonable modification to a self-service policy for an individual who lacked the ability to grasp the item. (Of course, a store would not be required to provide a personal shopper.) As explained above, auxiliary aids and services are those aids and services required to provide effective communications. Other forms of assistance are more appropriately addressed by other provisions of the final rule.

The auxiliary aid requirement is a flexible one. A public accommodation can choose among various alternatives as long as the result is effective communication. For example, a restaurant would not be required to provide menus in Braille for patrons who are blind, if the waiters in the restaurant are made available to read the menu. Similarly, a clothing boutique would not be required to have Brailled price tags if sales personnel provide price information orally upon request; and a bookstore would not be required to make available a sign language interpreter, because effective communication can be conducted by notepad.

A critical determination is what constitutes an effective auxiliary aid or service. The Department's proposed rule recommended that, in determining what auxiliary aid to use, the public accommodation consult with an individual before providing him or her with a particular auxiliary aid or service. This suggestion sparked a significant volume of public comment. Many persons with disabilities, particularly persons who are deaf or hard of hearing, recommended that the rule should require that public accommodations give "primary consideration" to the "expressed choice" of an individual with a disability. These commenters asserted that the proposed rule was inconsistent with congressional intent of the ADA, with the Department's proposed rule implementing title II of the ADA, and with longstanding interpretations of section 504 of the Rehabilitation Act.

Based upon a careful review of the ADA legislative history, the Department believes that Congress did not intend under title III to impose upon a public accommodation the requirement that it give primary consideration to the request of the individual with a disability. To the contrary, the legislative history demonstrates congressional intent to strongly encourage consulting with persons with disabilities. In its analysis of the ADA's auxiliary aids requirement for public accommodations, the House Education and Labor Committee stated that it "expects" that "public accommodation(s) will consult with the individual with a disability before providing a particular auxiliary aid or service" (Education and Labor report at 107). Some commenters also cited a different committee statement that used mandatory language as evidence of legislative intent to require primary consideration. However, this statement was made in the context of reasonable accommodations required by title I with respect to employment (Education and Labor report at 67). Thus, the Department finds that strongly encouraging consultation with persons with disabilities, in lieu of mandating primary consideration of their expressed choice, is consistent with congressional intent.

The Department wishes to emphasize that public accommodations must take steps necessary to ensure that an individual with a disability will not be excluded, denied services, segregated or otherwise treated differently from other individuals because of the use of inappropriate or ineffective auxiliary aids. In those situations requiring an interpreter, the public accommodations must secure the services of a qualified interpreter, unless an undue burden would result.

In the analysis of § 36.303(c) in the proposed rule, the Department gave as an example the situation where a note pad and written materials were insufficient to permit effective communication in a doctor's office when the matter to be decided was whether major surgery was necessary. Many commenters objected to this statement, asserting that it gave the impression that only decisions about major surgery would merit the provision of a sign language interpreter. The statement would, as the commenters also claimed, convey the impression to other public accommodations that written communications would meet the regulatory requirements in all but the most extreme situations. The Department, when using the example of major surgery, did not intend to limit the provision of interpreter services to the most extreme situations.

Other situations may also require the use of interpreters to ensure effective communication depending on the facts of the particular case. It is not difficult to imagine a wide range of communications involving areas such as health, legal matters, and finances that would be sufficiently lengthy or complex to require an interpreter for effective communication. In some situations, an effective alternative to use of a notepad or an interpreter may be the use of a computer terminal upon which the representative of the public accommodation and the customer or client can exchange typewritten messages.

Section 36.303(d) specifically addresses requirements for TDD's. Partly because of the availability of telecommunications relay services to be established under title IV of the ADA, § 36.303(d)(2) provides that a public accommodation is not required to use a telecommunication device for the deaf (TDD) in receiving or making telephone calls incident to its operations. Several commenters were concerned that relay services would not be sufficient to provide effective access in a number of situations. Commenters argued that relay systems (1) do not provide effective access to the automated systems that require the caller to respond by pushing a button on a touch tone phone, (2) cannot operate fast enough to convey messages on answering machines, or to permit a TDD user to leave a recorded message, and (3) are not appropriate for calling crisis lines relating to such matters as rape, domestic violence, child abuse, and drugs where confidentiality is a concern. The Department believes that it is more appropriate for the Federal Communications Commission to address these issues in its rulemaking under title IV.

A public accommodation is, however, required to make a TDD available to an individual with impaired hearing or speech, if it customarily offers telephone service to its customers, clients, patients, or participants on more than an incidental convenience basis. Where entry to a place of public accommodation requires use of a security entrance telephone, a TDD or other effective means of communication must be provided for use by an individual with impaired hearing or speech.

In other words, individual retail stores, doctors' offices, restaurants, or similar establishments are not required by this section to have TDD's, because TDD users will be able to make inquiries, appointments, or reservations with such establishments through the relay system established under title IV of the ADA. The public accommodation will likewise be able to contact TDD users through the relay system. On the other hand, hotels, hospitals, and other similar establishments that offer nondisabled individuals the opportunity to make outgoing telephone calls on more than an incidental convenience basis must provide a TDD on request.

Section 36.303(e) requires places of lodging that provide televisions in five or more guest rooms and hospitals to provide, upon request, a means for decoding closed captions for use by an individual with impaired hearing. Hotels should also provide a TDD or similar device at the front desk in order to take calls from guests who use TDD's in their rooms. In this way guests with hearing impairments can avail themselves of such hotel services as making inquiries of the front desk and ordering room service. The term "hospital" is used in its general sense and should be interpreted broadly.

Movie theaters are not required by § 36.303 to present open-captioned films. However, other public accommodations that impart verbal information through soundtracks on films, video tapes, or slide shows are required to make such information accessible to persons with hearing impairments. Captioning is one means to make the information accessible to individuals with disabilities.

The rule specifies that auxiliary aids and services include the acquisition or modification of equipment or devices. For example, tape players used for an audio-guided tour of a museum exhibit may require the addition of Brailled adhesive labels to the buttons on a reasonable number of the tape players to facilitate their use by individuals who are blind. Similarly, a hotel conference center may need to provide permanent or portable assistive listening systems for persons with hearing impairments.

As provided in § 36.303(f), a public accommodation is not required to provide any particular aid or service that would result either in a fundamental alteration in the nature of the goods, services, facilities, privileges, advantages, or accommodations offered or in an undue burden. Both of these statutory limitations are derived from existing regulations and caselaw under section 504 and are to be applied on a case-by-case basis (see, e.g., 28 CFR 39.160(d) and *Southeastern Community College v. Davis*, 442 U.S. 397 (1979)). Congress intended that "undue burden" under § 36.303 and "undue hardship," which is used in the employment provisions of title I of the ADA, should be determined on a case-by-case basis under the same standards and in light of the same factors (Judiciary report at 59). The rule, therefore, in accordance with the definition of undue hardship in section 101(10) of the ADA, defines undue burden as "significant difficulty or expense" (see §§ 36.104 and 36.303(a)) and requires that undue burden be determined in light of the factors listed in the definition in 36.104.

Consistent with regulations implementing section 504 in federally conducted programs (see, e.g., 28 CFR 39.160(d)), § 36.303(f) provides that the fact that the provision of a particular auxiliary aid or service would result in an undue burden does not relieve a public accommodation from the duty to furnish an alternative auxiliary aid or service, if available, that would not result in such a burden.

Section 36.303(g) of the proposed rule has been deleted from this section and included in a new § 36.306. That new section continues to make clear that the auxiliary aids requirement does not mandate the provision of individually prescribed devices, such as prescription eyeglasses or hearing aids.

The costs of compliance with the requirements of this section may not be financed by surcharges limited to particular individuals with disabilities or any group of individuals with disabilities (§ 36.301(c)).

Section 36.304 Removal of Barriers

Section 36.304 requires the removal of architectural barriers and communication barriers that are structural in nature in existing facilities, where such removal is readily achievable, i.e., easily accomplishable and able to be carried out without much difficulty or expense. This requirement is based on section 302(b)(2)(A)(iv) of the ADA.

A number of commenters interpreted the phrase "communication barriers that are structural in nature" broadly to encompass the provision of communications devices such as TDD's, telephone handset amplifiers, assistive listening devices, and digital check-out displays. The statute, however, as read by the Department, limits the application of the phrase "communications barriers that are structural in nature" to those barriers that are an integral part of the physical structure of a facility. In addition to the communications barriers posed by permanent signage and alarm systems noted by Congress (see Education and Labor report at 110), the Department would also include among the communications barriers covered by § 36.304 the failure to provide adequate sound buffers, and the presence of physical partitions that hamper the passage of sound waves between employees and customers. Given that § 36.304's proper focus is on the removal of physical barriers, the Department believes that the obligation to provide communications equipment and devices such as TDD's, telephone handset amplifiers, assistive listening devices, and digital check-out displays is more appropriately determined by the requirements for auxiliary aids and services under § 36.303 (see Education and Labor report at 107-108). The obligation to remove communications barriers that are structural in nature under § 36.304, of course, is independent of any obligation to provide auxiliary aids and services under § 36.303.

The statutory provision also requires the readily achievable removal of certain barriers in existing vehicles and rail passenger cars. This transportation requirement is not included in § 36.304, but rather in § 36.310(b) of the rule.

In striking a balance between guaranteeing access to individuals with disabilities and recognizing the legitimate cost concerns of businesses and other private entities, the ADA establishes different standards for existing facilities and new construction. In existing facilities, which are the subject of § 36.304, where retrofitting may prove costly, a less rigorous degree of accessibility is required than in the case of new construction and alterations (see §§ 36.401-36.406) where accessibility can be more conveniently and economically incorporated in the initial stages of design and construction.

For example, a bank with existing automatic teller machines (ATM's) would have to remove barriers to the use of the ATM's, if it is readily achievable to do so. Whether or not it is necessary to take actions such as ramping a few steps or raising or lowering an ATM would be determined by whether the actions can be accomplished easily and without much difficulty or expense.

On the other hand, a newly constructed bank with ATM's would be required by § 36.401 to have an ATM that is "readily accessible to and usable by" persons with disabilities in accordance with accessibility guidelines incorporated under § 36.406.

The requirement to remove architectural barriers includes the removal of physical barriers of any kind. For example, § 36.304 requires the removal, when readily achievable, of barriers caused by the location of temporary or movable structures, such as furniture, equipment, and display racks. In order to provide access to individuals who use wheelchairs, for example, restaurants may need to rearrange tables and chairs, and department stores may need to reconfigure display racks and shelves. As stated in § 36.304(f), such actions are not readily achievable to the extent that they would result in a significant loss of selling or serving space. If the widening of all aisles in selling or serving areas is not readily achievable, then selected widening should be undertaken to maximize the amount of merchandise or the number of tables accessible to individuals who use wheelchairs. Access to goods and services provided in any remaining inaccessible areas must be made available through alternative methods to barrier removal, as required by § 36.305.

Because the purpose of title III of the ADA is to ensure that public accommodations are accessible to their customers, clients, or patrons (as opposed to their employees, who are the focus of title I), the obligation to remove barriers under § 36.304 does not extend to areas of a facility that are used exclusively as employee work areas.

Section 36.304(b) provides a wide-ranging list of the types of modest measures that may be taken to remove barriers and that are likely to be readily achievable. The list includes examples of measures, such as adding raised letter markings on elevator control buttons and installing flashing alarm lights, that would be used to remove communications barriers that are structural in nature. It is not an exhaustive list, but merely an illustrative one. Moreover, the inclusion of a measure on this list does not mean that it is readily achievable in all cases. Whether or not any of these measures is readily achievable is to be determined on a case-by-case basis in light of the particular circumstances presented and the factors listed in the definition of readily achievable (§ 36.104).

A public accommodation generally would not be required to remove a barrier to physical access posed by a flight of steps, if removal would require extensive ramping or an elevator. Ramping a single step, however, will likely be readily achievable, and ramping several steps will in many circumstances also be readily achievable. The readily achievable standard does not

require barrier removal that requires extensive restructuring or burdensome expense. Thus, where it is not readily achievable to do, the ADA would not require a restaurant to provide access to a restroom reachable only by a flight of stairs.

Like § 36.405, this section permits deference to the national interest in preserving significant historic structures. Barrier removal would not be considered "readily achievable" if it would threaten or destroy the historic significance of a building or facility that is eligible for listing in the National Register of Historic Places under the National Historic Preservation Act (16 U.S.C. 470, et seq.), or is designated as historic under State or local law.

The readily achievable defense requires a less demanding level of exertion by a public accommodation than does the undue burden defense to the auxiliary aids requirements of § 36.303. In that sense, it can be characterized as a "lower" standard than the undue burden standard. The readily achievable defense is also less demanding than the undue hardship defense in section 102(b)(5) of the ADA, which limits the obligation to make reasonable accommodation in employment. Barrier removal measures that are not easily accomplishable and are not able to be carried out without much difficulty or expense are not required under the readily achievable standard, even if they do not impose an undue burden or an undue hardship.

Section 36.304(f)(1) of the proposed rule, which stated that "barrier removal is not readily achievable if it would result in significant loss of profit or significant loss of efficiency of operation," has been deleted from the final rule. Many commenters objected to this provision because it impermissibly introduced the notion of profit into a statutory standard that did not include it. Concern was expressed that, in order for an action not to be considered readily achievable, a public accommodation would inappropriately have to show, for example, not only that the

action could not be done without "much difficulty or expense", but that a significant loss of profit would result as well. In addition, some commenters asserted use of the word "significant," which is used in the definition of undue hardship under title I (the standard for interpreting the meaning of undue burden as a defense to title III's auxiliary aids requirements) (see §§ 36.104, 36.303(f)), blurs the fact that the readily achievable standard requires a lower level of effort on the part of a public accommodation than does the undue burden standard.

The obligation to engage in readily achievable barrier removal is a continuing one. Over time, barrier removal that initially was not readily achievable may later be required because of changed circumstances. Many commenters expressed support for the Department's position that the obligation to comply with § 36.304 is continuing in nature. Some urged that the rule require public accommodations to assess their compliance on at least an annual basis in light of changes in resources and other factors that would be relevant to determining what barrier removal measures would be readily achievable.

Although the obligation to engage in readily achievable barrier removal is clearly a continuing duty, the Department has declined to establish any independent requirement for an annual assessment or self-evaluation. It is best left to the public accommodations subject to § 36.304 to establish policies to assess compliance that are appropriate to the particular circumstances faced by the wide range of public accommodations covered by the ADA. However, even in the absence of an explicit regulatory requirement for periodic self-evaluations, the Department still urges public accommodations to establish procedures for an ongoing assessment of their compliance with the ADA's barrier removal requirements. The Department recommends that this process include appropriate consultation with individuals with disabilities or organizations representing them. A serious effort at self-assessment and consultation can diminish the threat of litigation and save resources by identifying the most efficient means of providing required access.

The Department has been asked for guidance on the best means for public accommodations to comply voluntarily with this section. Such information is more appropriately part of the Department's technical assistance effort and will be forthcoming over the next several months. The Department recommends, however, the development of an implementation plan designed to achieve compliance with the ADA's barrier removal requirements before they become effective on January 26, 1992. Such a plan, if appropriately designed and diligently executed, could serve as evidence of a good faith effort to comply with the requirements of § 36.104. In developing an implementation plan for readily achievable barrier removal, a public accommodation should consult with local organizations representing persons with disabilities and solicit their suggestions for cost-effective means of making individual places of public accommodation accessible. Such organizations may also be helpful in allocating scarce resources and establishing priorities. Local associations of businesses may want to encourage this process and serve as the forum for discussions on the local level between disability rights organizations and local businesses.

Section 36.304(c) recommends priorities for public accommodations in removing barriers in existing facilities. Because the resources available for barrier removal may not be adequate to remove all existing barriers at any given time, § 36.304(c) suggests priorities for determining which types of barriers should be mitigated or eliminated first. The purpose of these priorities is to facilitate long-term business planning and to maximize, in light of limited resources, the degree of effective access that will result

from any given level of expenditure.

Although many commenters expressed support for the concept of establishing priorities, a significant number objected to their mandatory nature in the proposed rule. The Department shares the concern of these commenters that mandatory priorities would increase the likelihood of litigation and inappropriately reduce the discretion of public accommodations to determine the most effective mix of barrier removal measures to undertake in particular circumstances. Therefore, in the final rule the priorities are no longer mandatory.

In response to comments that the priorities failed to address communications issues, the Department wishes to emphasize that the priorities encompass the removal of communications barriers that are structural in nature. It would be counter to the ADA's carefully wrought statutory scheme to include in this provision the wide range of communication devices that are required by the ADA's provisions on auxiliary aids and services. The final rule explicitly includes Brailled and raised letter signage and visual alarms among the examples of steps to remove barriers provided in § 36.304(c)(2).

Section 36.304(c)(1) places the highest priority on measures that will enable individuals with disabilities to physically enter a place of public accommodation. This priority on "getting through the door" recognizes that providing actual physical access to a facility from public sidewalks, public transportation, or parking is generally preferable to any alternative arrangements in terms of both business efficiency and the dignity of individuals with disabilities.

The next priority, which is established in § 36.304(c)(2), is for measures that provide access to those areas of a place of public accommodation where goods and services are made available to the public. For example, in a hardware store, to the extent that it is readily achievable to do so, individuals

with disabilities should be given access not only to assistance at the front desk, but also access, like that available to other customers, to the retail display areas of the store.

The Department agrees with those commenters who argued that access to the areas where goods and services are provided is generally more important than the provision of restrooms. Therefore, the final rule reverses priorities two and three of the proposed rule in order to give lower priority to accessible restrooms. Consequently, the third priority in the final rule (§ 36.304(c)(3)) is for measures to provide access to restroom facilities and the last priority is placed on any remaining measures required to remove barriers.

Section 36.304(d) requires that measures taken to remove barriers under § 36.304 be subject to subpart D's requirements for alterations (except for the path of travel requirements in § 36.403). It only permits deviations from the subpart D requirements when compliance with those requirements is not readily achievable. In such cases, § 36.304(d) permits measures to be taken that do not fully comply with the subpart D requirements, so long as the measures do not pose a significant risk to the health or safety of individuals with disabilities or others.

This approach represents a change from the proposed rule which stated that "readily achievable" measures taken solely to remove barriers under § 36.304 are exempt from the alterations requirements of subpart D. The intent of the proposed rule was to maximize the flexibility of public accommodations in undertaking barrier removal by allowing deviations from the technical standards of subpart D. It was thought that allowing slight deviations would provide access and release additional resources for expanding the amount of barrier removal that could be obtained under the readily achievable standard.

Many commenters, however, representing both businesses and individuals with disabilities, questioned this approach because of the likelihood that unsafe or ineffective measures would be taken in the absence of the subpart D standards for alterations as a reference point. Some advocated a rule requiring strict compliance with the subpart D standard.

The Department in the final rule has adopted the view of many commenters that (1) public accommodations should in the first instance be required to comply with the subpart D standards for alterations where it is readily achievable to do so and (2) safe, readily achievable measures must be taken when compliance with the subpart D standards is not readily achievable. Reference to the subpart D standards in this manner will promote certainty and good design at the same time that permitting slight deviations will expand the amount of barrier removal that may be achieved under § 36.304.

Because of the inconvenience to individuals with disabilities and the safety problems involved in the use of portable ramps, § 36.304(e) permits the use of a portable ramp to comply with § 36.304(a) only when installation of a permanent ramp is not readily achievable. In order to promote safety, § 36.304(e) requires that due consideration be given to the incorporation of features such as nonslip surfaces, railings, anchoring, and strength of materials in any portable ramp that is used.

Temporary facilities brought in for use at the site of a natural disaster are subject to the barrier removal requirements of § 36.304.

A number of commenters requested clarification regarding how to determine when a public accommodation has discharged its obligation to remove barriers in existing facilities. For example, is a hotel required by § 36.304 to remove barriers in all of its guest rooms? Or is some lesser percentage adequate? A new paragraph (g) has been added to § 36.304 to address this issue. The Department believes that the degree of barrier removal required under § 36.304 may be

less, but certainly would not be required to exceed, the standards for alterations under the ADA Accessibility Guidelines incorporated by subpart D of this part (ADAAG). The ADA's requirements for readily achievable barrier removal in existing facilities are intended to be substantially less rigorous than those for new construction and alterations. It, therefore, would be obviously inappropriate to require actions under § 36.304 that would exceed the ADAAG requirements. Hotels, then, in order to satisfy the requirements of § 36.304, would not be required to remove barriers in a higher percentage of rooms than required by ADAAG. If relevant standards for alterations are not provided in ADAAG, then reference should be made to the standards for new construction.

Section 36.305 Alternatives to Barrier Removal

Section 36.305 specifies that where a public accommodation can demonstrate that removal of a barrier is not readily achievable, the public accommodation must make its goods, services, facilities, privileges, advantages, or accommodations available through alternative methods, if such methods are readily achievable. This requirement is based on section 302(b)(2)(A)(v) of the ADA.

For example, if it is not readily achievable for a retail store to raise, lower, or remove shelves or to rearrange display racks to provide accessible aisles, the store must, if readily achievable, provide a clerk or take other alternative measures to retrieve inaccessible merchandise. Similarly, if it is not readily achievable to ramp a long flight of stairs leading to the front door of a restaurant or a pharmacy, the restaurant or the pharmacy must take alternative measures, if readily achievable, such as providing curb service or home delivery. If, within a restaurant, it is not readily achievable to remove physical barriers to a certain section of a restaurant, the restaurant must, where it is readily achievable to do so,

offer the same menu in an accessible area of the restaurant.

Where alternative methods are used to provide access, a public accommodation may not charge an individual with a disability for the costs associated with the alternative method (see § 36.301(c)). Further analysis of the issue of charging for alternative measures may be found in the preamble discussion of § 36.301(c).

In some circumstances, because of security considerations, some alternative methods may not be readily achievable. The rule does not require a cashier to leave his or her post to retrieve items for individuals with disabilities, if there are no other employees on duty.

Section 36.305(c) of the proposed rule has been deleted and the requirements have been included in a new § 36.306. That section makes clear that the alternative methods requirement does not mandate the provision of personal devices, such as wheelchairs, or services of a personal nature.

In the final rule, § 36.305(c) provides specific requirements regarding alternatives to barrier removal in multiscreen cinemas. In some situations, it may not be readily achievable to remove enough barriers to provide access to all of the theaters of a multiscreen cinema. If that is the case, § 36.305(c) requires the cinema to establish a film rotation schedule that provides reasonable access for individuals who use wheelchairs to films being presented by the cinema. It further requires that reasonable notice be provided to the public as to the location and time of accessible showings. Methods for providing notice include appropriate use of the international accessibility symbol in a cinema's print advertising and the addition of accessibility information to a cinema's recorded telephone information line.

Section 36.306 Personal Devices and Services

The final rule includes a new § 36.306, entitled "Personal

devices and services." Section 36.306 of the proposed rule, "Readily achievable and undue burden: Factors to be considered," was deleted for the reasons described in the preamble discussion of the definition of the term "readily achievable" in § 36.104. In place of §§ 36.303(g) and 36.305(c) of the proposed rule, which addressed the issue of personal devices and services in the contexts of auxiliary aids and alternatives to barrier removal, § 36.306 provides a general statement that the regulation does not require the provision of personal devices and services. This section states that a public accommodation is not required to provide its customers, clients, or participants with personal devices, such as wheelchairs; individually prescribed devices, such as prescription eyeglasses or hearing aids; or services of a personal nature including assistance in eating, toileting, or dressing.

This statement serves as a limitation on all the requirements of the regulation. The personal devices and services limitation was intended to have general application in the proposed rule in all contexts where it was relevant. The final rule, therefore, clarifies this point by including a general provision that will explicitly apply not just to auxiliary aids and services and alternatives to barrier removal, but across-the-board to include such relevant areas as modifications in policies, practices, and procedures (§ 36.302) and examinations and courses (§ 36.309), as well.

The Department wishes to clarify that measures taken as alternatives to barrier removal, such as retrieving items from shelves or providing curb service or home delivery, are not to be considered personal services. Similarly, minimal actions that may be required as modifications in policies, practices, or procedures under § 36.302, such as a waiter's removing the cover from a customer's straw, a kitchen's cutting up food into smaller pieces, or a bank's filling out a deposit slip, are not services of

a personal nature within the meaning of § 36.306. (Of course, such modifications may be required under § 36.302 only if they are "reasonable.") Similarly, this section does not preclude the short-term loan of personal receivers that are part of an assistive listening system.

Of course, if personal services are customarily provided to the customers or clients of a public accommodation, e.g., in a hospital or senior citizen center, then these personal services should also be provided to persons with disabilities using the public accommodation.

Section 36.307 Accessible or Special Goods.

Section 36.307 establishes that the rule does not require a public accommodation to alter its inventory to include accessible or special goods with accessibility features that are designed for, or facilitate use by, individuals with disabilities. As specified in § 36.307(c), accessible or special goods include such items as Brailled versions of books, books on audio-cassettes, closed captioned video tapes, special sizes or lines of clothing, and special foods to meet particular dietary needs.

The purpose of the ADA's public accommodations requirements is to ensure accessibility to the goods offered by a public accommodation, not to alter the nature or mix of goods that the public accommodation has typically provided. In other words, a bookstore, for example, must make its facilities and sales operations accessible to individuals with disabilities, but is not required to stock Brailled or large print books. Similarly, a video store must make its facilities and rental operations accessible, but is not required to stock closed-captioned video tapes. The Department has been made aware, however, that the most recent titles in video-tape rental establishments are, in fact, closed captioned.

Although a public accommodation is not required by

§ 36.307(a) to modify its inventory, it is required by § 36.307(b), at the request of an individual with disabilities, to order accessible or special goods that it does not customarily maintain in stock if, in the normal course of its operation, it makes special orders for unstocked goods, and if the accessible or special goods can be obtained from a supplier with whom the public accommodation customarily does business. For example, a clothing store would be required to order specially-sized clothing at the request of an individual with a disability, if it customarily makes special orders for clothing that it does not keep in stock, and if the clothing can be obtained from one of the store's customary suppliers.

One commenter asserted that the proposed rule could be interpreted to require a store to special order accessible or special goods of all types, even if only one type is specially ordered in the normal course of its business. The Department, however, intends for § 36.307(b) to require special orders only of those particular types of goods for which a public accommodation normally makes special orders. For example, a book and recording store would not have to specially order Brailled books if, in the normal course of its business, it only specially orders recordings and not books.

Section 36.308 Seating in Assembly Areas.

Section 36.308 establishes specific requirements for removing barriers to physical access in assembly areas, which include such facilities as theaters, concert halls, auditoriums, lecture halls, and conference rooms. This section does not address the provision of auxiliary aids or the removal of communications barriers that are structural in nature. These communications requirements are the focus of other provisions of the regulation (see §§ 36.303-36.304).

Individuals who use wheelchairs historically have been relegated to inferior seating in the back of assembly areas separate from accompanying family members and friends. The provisions of § 36.308 are intended to promote integration and equality in seating.

In some instances it may not be readily achievable for auditoriums or theaters to remove seats to allow individuals with wheelchairs to sit next to accompanying family members or friends. In these situations, the final rule retains the requirement that the public accommodation provide portable chairs or other means to allow the accompanying individuals to sit with the persons in wheelchairs. Persons in wheelchairs should have the same opportunity to enjoy movies, plays, and similar events with their families and friends, just as other patrons do. The final rule specifies that portable chairs or other means to permit family members or companions to sit with individuals who use wheelchairs must be provided only when it is readily achievable to do so.

In order to facilitate seating of wheelchair users who wish to transfer to existing seating, paragraph (a)(1) of the final rule adds a requirement that, to the extent readily achievable, a reasonable number of seats with removable aisle-side armrests must be provided. Many persons in wheelchairs are able to transfer to existing seating with this relatively minor modification. This solution avoids the potential safety hazard created by the use of portable chairs and fosters integration. The final ADA Accessibility Guidelines incorporated by subpart D (ADAAG) also add a requirement regarding aisle seating that was not in the proposed guidelines. In situations when a person in a wheelchair transfers to existing seating, the public accommodation shall provide assistance in handling the wheelchair of the patron with the disability.

Likewise, consistent with ADAAG, the final rule adds in § 36.308(a)(1)(ii)(B) a requirement that, to the extent readily achievable, wheelchair seating provide lines of sight and choice of admission prices comparable

to those for members of the general public.

Finally, because Congress intended that the requirements for barrier removal in existing facilities be substantially less rigorous than those required for new construction and alterations, the final rule clarifies in § 36.308(a)(3) that in no event can the requirements for existing facilities be interpreted to exceed the standards for alterations under ADAAG. For example, § 4.33 of ADAAG only requires wheelchair spaces to be provided in more than one location when the seating capacity of the assembly area exceeds 300. Therefore, paragraph (a) of § 36.308 may not be interpreted to require readily achievable dispersal of wheelchair seating in assembly areas with 300 or fewer seats. Similarly, § 4.1.3(19) of ADAAG requires six accessible wheelchair locations in an assembly area with 301 to 500 seats. The reasonable number of wheelchair locations required by paragraph (a), therefore, may be less than six, but may not be interpreted to exceed six.

Proposed Section 36.309 Purchase of Furniture and Equipment

Section 36.309 of the proposed rule would have required that newly purchased furniture or equipment made available for use at a place of public accommodation be accessible, to the extent such furniture or equipment is available, unless this requirement would fundamentally alter the goods, services, facilities, privileges, advantages, or accommodations offered, or would not be readily achievable. Proposed § 36.309 has been omitted from the final rule because the Department has determined that its requirements are more properly addressed under other sections, and because there are currently no appropriate accessibility standards addressing many types of furniture and equipment.

Some types of equipment will be required to meet the accessibility requirements of subpart D. For example, ADAAG establishes technical

and scoping requirements in new construction and alterations for automated teller machines and telephones. Purchase or modification of equipment is required in certain instances by the provisions in §§ 36.201 and 36.202. For example, an arcade may need to provide accessible video machines in order to ensure full and equal enjoyment of the facilities and to provide an opportunity to participate in the services and facilities it provides. The barrier removal requirements of § 36.304 will apply as well to furniture and equipment (lowering shelves, rearranging furniture, adding Braille labels to a vending machine).

Section 36.309 Examinations and Courses

Section 36.309(a) sets forth the general rule that any private entity that offers examinations or courses related to applications, licensing, certification, or credentialing for secondary or postsecondary education, professional, or trade purposes shall offer such examinations or courses in a place and manner accessible to persons with disabilities or offer alternative accessible arrangements for such individuals.

Paragraph (a) restates section 309 of the Americans with Disabilities Act. Section 309 is intended to fill the gap that is created when licensing, certification, and other testing authorities are not covered by section 504 of the Rehabilitation Act or title II of the ADA. Any such authority that is covered by section 504, because of the receipt of Federal money, or by title II, because it is a function of a State or local government, must make all of its programs accessible to persons with disabilities, which includes physical access as well as modifications in the way the test is administered, e.g., extended time, written instructions, or assistance of a reader.

Many licensing, certification, and testing authorities are not covered by section 504, because no Federal money is received; nor are they covered by title II of the ADA because they are not State or local agencies. However, States often require the licenses provided by such authorities in order for an individual to practice a particular profession or trade. Thus, the provision was included in the ADA in order to assure that persons with disabilities are not foreclosed from educational, professional, or trade opportunities because an examination or course is conducted in an inaccessible site or without needed modifications.

As indicated in the "Application" section of this part (§ 36.102), § 36.309 applies to any private entity that offers the specified types of examinations or courses. This is consistent with section 309 of the Americans with Disabilities Act, which states that the requirements apply to "any person" offering examinations or courses.

The Department received a large number of comments on this section, reflecting the importance of ensuring that the key gateways to education and employment are open to individuals with disabilities. The most frequent comments were objections to the fundamental alteration and undue burden provisions in §§ 36.309 (b)(3) and (c)(3) and to allowing courses and examinations to be provided through alternative accessible arrangements, rather than in an integrated setting.

Although section 309 of the Act does not refer to a fundamental alteration or undue burden limitation, those limitations do appear in section 302(b)(2)(A)(iii) of the Act, which establishes the obligation of public accommodations to provide auxiliary aids and services. The Department, therefore, included it in the paragraphs of § 36.309 requiring the provision of auxiliary aids. One commenter argued that similar limitations should apply to all of the requirements of § 36.309, but the Department did not consider this extension appropriate.

Commenters who objected to permitting "alternative accessible arrangements"

argued that such arrangements allow segregation and should not be permitted, unless they are the least restrictive available alternative, for example, for someone who cannot leave home. Some commenters made a distinction between courses, where interaction is an important part of the educational experience, and examinations, where it may be less important. Because the statute specifically authorizes alternative accessible arrangements as a method of meeting the requirements of section 309, the Department has not adopted this suggestion. The Department notes, however, that, while examinations of the type covered by § 36.309 may not be covered elsewhere in the regulation, courses will generally be offered in a "place of education," which is included in the definition of "place of public accommodation" in § 36.104, and, therefore, will be subject to the integrated setting requirement of § 36.203.

Section 36.309(b) sets forth specific requirements for examinations. Examinations covered by this section would include a bar exam or the Scholastic Aptitude Test prepared by the Educational Testing Service. Paragraph (b)(1) is adopted from the Department of Education's section 504 regulation on admission tests to postsecondary educational programs (34 CFR 104.42(b)(3)). Paragraph (b)(1)(i) requires that a private entity offering an examination covered by the section must assure that the examination is selected and administered so as to best ensure that the examination accurately reflects an individual's aptitude or achievement level or other factor the examination purports to measure, rather than reflecting the individual's impaired sensory, manual, or speaking skills (except where those skills are the factors that the examination purports to measure).

Paragraph (b)(1)(ii) requires that any examination specially designed for individuals with disabilities be offered as often and in as timely a manner as

other examinations. Some commenters noted that persons with disabilities may be required to travel long distances when the locations for examinations for individuals with disabilities are limited, for example, to only one city in a State instead of a variety of cities. The Department has therefore revised this paragraph to add a requirement that such examinations be offered at locations that are as convenient as the location of other examinations.

Commenters representing organizations that administer tests wanted to be able to require individuals with disabilities to provide advance notice and appropriate documentation, at the applicants' expense, of their disabilities and of any modifications or aids that would be required. The Department agrees that such requirements are permissible, provided that they are not unreasonable and that the deadline for such notice is no earlier than the deadline for others applying to take the examination. Requiring individuals with disabilities to file earlier applications would violate the requirement that examinations designed for individuals with disabilities be offered in as timely a manner as other examinations.

Examiners may require evidence that an applicant is entitled to modifications or aids as required by this section, but requests for documentation must be reasonable and must be limited to the need for the modification or aid requested. Appropriate documentation might include a letter from a physician or other professional, or evidence of a prior diagnosis or accommodation, such as eligibility for a special education program. The applicant may be required to bear the cost of providing such documentation, but the entity administering the examination cannot charge the applicant for the cost of any modifications or auxiliary aids, such as interpreters, provided for the examination.

Paragraph (b)(1)(iii) requires that examinations be administered in facilities that are accessible to individuals with disabilities or alternative accessible arrangements are made.

Paragraph (b)(2) gives examples of modifications to examinations that may be necessary in order to comply with this section. These may include providing more time for completion of the examination or a change in the manner of giving the examination, e.g., reading the examination to the individual.

Paragraph (b)(3) requires the provision of auxiliary aids and services, unless the private entity offering the examination can demonstrate that offering a particular auxiliary aid would fundamentally alter the examination or result in an undue burden. Examples of auxiliary aids include taped examinations, interpreters or other effective methods of making aurally delivered materials available to individuals with hearing impairments, readers for individuals with visual impairments or learning disabilities, and other similar services and actions. The suggestion that individuals with learning disabilities may need readers is included, although it does not appear in the Department of Education regulation, because, in fact, some individuals with learning disabilities have visual perception problems and would benefit from a reader.

Many commenters pointed out the importance of ensuring that modifications provide the individual with a disability an equal opportunity to demonstrate his or her knowledge or ability. For example, a reader who is unskilled or lacks knowledge of specific terminology used in the examination may be unable to convey the information in the questions or to follow the applicant's instructions effectively. Commenters pointed out that, for persons with visual impairments who read Braille, Braille provides the closest functional equivalent to a printed test. The Department has, therefore, added Brailled examinations to the examples of auxiliary aids and services that may be required. For similar reasons, the Department also

added to the list of examples of auxiliary aids and services large print examinations and answer sheets; "qualified" readers; and transcribers to write answers.

A commenter suggested that the phrase "fundamentally alter the examination" in this paragraph of the proposed rule be revised to more accurately reflect the function affected. In the final rule the Department has substituted the phrase "fundamentally alter the measurement of the skills or knowledge the examination is intended to test."

Paragraph (b)(4) gives examples of alternative accessible arrangements. For instance, the private entity might be required to provide the examination at an individual's home with a proctor. Alternative arrangements must provide conditions for individuals with disabilities that are comparable to the conditions under which other individuals take the examinations. In other words, an examination cannot be offered to an individual with a disability in a cold, poorly lit basement, if other individuals are given the examination in a warm, well lit classroom.

Some commenters who provide examinations for licensing or certification for particular occupations or professions urged that they be permitted to refuse to provide modifications or aids for persons seeking to take the examinations if those individuals, because of their disabilities, would be unable to perform the essential functions of the profession or occupation for which the examination is given, or unless the disability is reasonably determined in advance as not being an obstacle to certification. The Department has not changed its rule based on this comment. An examination is one stage of a licensing or certification process. An individual should not be barred from attempting to pass that stage of the process merely because he or she might be unable to meet other requirements of the process. If the examination is not the first stage of the qualification process, an applicant may be

required to complete the earlier stages prior to being admitted to the examination. On the other hand, the applicant may not be denied admission to the examination on the basis of doubts about his or her abilities to meet requirements that the examination is not designed to test.

Paragraph (c) sets forth specific requirements for courses. Paragraph (c)(1) contains the general rule that any course covered by this section must be modified to ensure that the place and manner in which the course is given is accessible. Paragraph (c)(2) gives examples of possible modifications that might be required, including extending the time permitted for completion of the course, permitting oral rather than written delivery of an assignment by a person with a visual impairment, or adapting the manner in which the course is conducted (i.e., providing cassettes of class handouts to an individual with a visual impairment). In response to comments, the Department has added to the examples in paragraph (c)(2) specific reference to distribution of course materials. If course materials are published and available from other sources, the entity offering the course may give advance notice of what materials will be used so as to allow an individual to obtain them in Braille or on tape but materials provided by the course offerer must be made available in alternative formats for individuals with disabilities.

In language similar to that of paragraph (b), paragraph (c)(3) requires auxiliary aids and services, unless a fundamental alteration or undue burden would result, and paragraph (c)(4) requires that courses be administered in accessible facilities. Paragraph (c)(5) gives examples of alternative accessible arrangements. These may include provision of the course through videotape, cassettes, or prepared notes. Alternative arrangements must provide comparable conditions to those provided to others, including similar lighting, room temperature, and the like. An entity offering a variety of courses, to fulfill continuing education requirements for a profession, for example, may not limit the selection or choice of courses available to individuals with disabilities.

Section 36.310 Transportation Provided by Public Accommodations

Section 36.310 contains specific provisions relating to public accommodations that provide transportation to their clients or customers. This section has been substantially revised in order to coordinate the requirements of this section with the requirements applicable to these transportation systems that will be contained in the regulations issued by the Secretary of Transportation pursuant to section 306 of the ADA, to be codified at 49 CFR part 37. The Department notes that, although the responsibility for issuing regulations applicable to transportation systems operated by public accommodations is divided between this Department and the Department of Transportation enforcement authority is assigned only to the Department of Justice.

The Department received relatively few comments on this section of the proposed rule. Most of the comments addressed issues that are not specifically addressed in this part, such as the standards for accessible vehicles and the procedure for determining whether equivalent service is provided. Those standards will be contained in the regulation issued by the Department of Transportation. Other commenters raised questions about the types of transportation that will be subject to this section. In response to these inquiries, the Department has revised the list of examples contained in the regulation.

Paragraph (a)(1) states the general rule that covered public accommodations are subject to all of the specific provisions of subparts B, C, and D, except as provided in § 36.310. Examples of operations covered by the requirements are listed in paragraph (a)(2). The stated examples include hotel and motel airport shuttle services, customer shuttle bus services operated by private companies and shopping centers, student transportation, and shuttle operations of recreational facilities such as stadiums, zoos, amusement parks, and ski resorts. This brief list is not exhaustive. The section applies to any fixed route or demand responsive transportation system operated by a public accommodation for the benefit of its clients or customers. The section does not apply to transportation services provided only to employees. Employee transportation will be subject to the regulations issued by the Equal Employment Opportunity Commission to implement title I of the Act. However, if employees and customers or clients are served by the same transportation system, the provisions of this section will apply.

Paragraph (b) specifically provides that a public accommodation shall remove transportation barriers in existing vehicles to the extent that it is readily achievable to do so, but that the installation of hydraulic or other lifts is not required.

Paragraph (c) provides that public accommodations subject to this section shall comply with the requirements for transportation vehicles and systems contained in the regulations issued by the Secretary of Transportation.

Subpart D—New Construction and Alterations

Subpart D implements section 303 of the Act, which requires that newly constructed or altered places of public accommodation or commercial facilities be readily accessible to and usable by individuals with disabilities. This requirement contemplates a high degree of convenient access. It is intended to ensure that patrons and employees of places of public accommodation and employees of commercial facilities are able to get to, enter, and use the facility.

Potential patrons of places of public accommodation, such as retail establishments, should be able to get to a store, get into the store, and get to the areas where goods are being provided. Employees should have the same types of access, although those individuals require access to and around the employment area as well as to the area in which goods and services are provided.

The ADA is geared to the future—its goal being that, over time, access will be the rule, rather than the exception. Thus, the Act only requires modest expenditures, of the type addressed in § 36.304 of this part, to provide access to existing facilities not otherwise being altered, but requires all new construction and alterations to be accessible.

The Act does not require new construction or alterations; it simply requires that, when a public accommodation or other private entity undertakes the construction or alteration of a facility subject to the Act, the newly constructed or altered facility must be made accessible. This subpart establishes the requirements for new construction and alterations.

As explained under the discussion of the definition of "facility," § 36.104, pending development of specific requirements, the Department will not apply this subpart to places of public accommodation located in mobile units, boats, or other conveyances.

Section 36.401 New Construction

General

Section 36.401 implements the new construction requirements of the ADA. Section 303 (a)(1) of the Act provides that discrimination for purposes of section 302(a) of the Act includes a failure to design and construct facilities for first occupancy later than 30 months after the date of enactment (i.e., after January 26, 1993) that are readily accessible to and usable by individuals with disabilities.

Paragraph 36.401(a)(1) restates the general requirement for accessible new construction. The proposed rule stated that "any public accommodation or other private entity responsible for design and construction" must ensure that facilities conform to this requirement. Various commenters suggested that the proposed language was not consistent with the statute because it substituted "private entity responsible for design and construction" for the statutory language; because it did not address liability on the part of architects, contractors, developers, tenants, owners, and other entities; and because it limited the liability of entities responsible for commercial facilities. In response, the Department has revised this paragraph to repeat the language of section 303(a) of the ADA. The Department will interpret this section in a manner consistent with the intent of the statute and with the nature of the responsibilities of the various entities for design, for construction, or for both.

Designed and Constructed for First Occupancy

According to paragraph (a)(2), a facility is subject to the new construction requirements only if a completed application for a building permit or permit extension is filed after January 26, 1992, and the facility is occupied after January 26, 1993.

The proposed rule set forth for comment two alternative ways by which to determine what facilities are subject to the Act and what standards apply. Paragraph (a)(2) of the final rule is a slight variation on Option One in the proposed rule. The reasons for the Department's choice of Option One are discussed later in this section.

Paragraph (a)(2) acknowledges that Congress did not contemplate having actual occupancy be the sole trigger for the accessibility requirements, because the statute prohibits a failure to "design and construct for first occupancy," rather than requiring accessibility in facilities actually occupied after a particular date.

The commenters overwhelmingly agreed with the Department's proposal to use a date certain; many cited the reasons given in the preamble to the proposed rule. First, it is helpful for designers and builders to have a fixed date for accessible design, so that they can determine accessibility requirements early in the planning and design stage. It is difficult to determine accessibility requirements in anticipation of the actual date of first occupancy because of unpredictable and uncontrollable events (e.g., strikes affecting suppliers or labor, or natural disasters) that may delay occupancy. To redesign or reconstruct portions of a facility if it begins to appear that occupancy will be later than anticipated would be quite costly. A fixed date also assists those responsible for enforcing, or monitoring compliance with, the statute, and those protected by it.

The Department considered using as a trigger date for application of the accessibility standards the date on which a permit is granted. The Department chose instead the date on which a complete permit application is certified as received by the appropriate government entity. Almost all commenters agreed with this choice of a trigger date. This decision is based partly on information that several months or even years can pass between application for a permit and receipt of a permit. Design is virtually complete at the time an application is complete (i.e., certified to contain all the information required by the State, county, or local government). After an application is filed, delays may occur before the permit is granted due to numerous factors (not necessarily relating to accessibility): for example, hazardous waste discovered on the property, flood plain requirements, zoning disputes, or opposition to the project from various groups. These factors should not require redesign for accessibility if the application was completed before January 26, 1992. However, if the facility must be redesigned for other reasons, such as a change in density or environmental preservation, and the final permit is based on a new application, the rule would require accessibility if that application was certified complete after January 26, 1992.

The certification of receipt of a complete application for a building permit is an appropriate point in the process because certifications are issued in writing by governmental authorities. In addition, this approach presents a clear and objective standard.

However, a few commenters pointed out that in some jurisdictions it is not possible to receive a "certification" that an application is complete, and suggested that in those cases the fixed date should be the date on which an application for a permit is received by the government agency. The Department has included such a provision in § 36.401(a)(2)(i).

The date of January 26, 1992, is relevant only with respect to the last application for a permit or permit extension for a facility. Thus, if an entity has applied for only a "foundation" permit, the date of that permit application has no effect, because the entity must also apply for and receive a permit at a later date for the actual superstructure. In this case, it is the date of the later application that would control, unless construction is not completed within the time allowed by the permit, in which case a third permit would be issued and the date of the application for that permit would be determinative for purposes of the rule.

Choice of Option One for Defining "Designed and Constructed for First Occupancy"

Under the option the Department has chosen for determining applicability of the new construction standards, a building would be considered to be "for first occupancy" after January 26, 1993, only (1) if the last application for a building permit or permit extension for the facility is certified to be complete (or, in some jurisdictions, received) by a State, county, or local government after January 26, 1992, and (2) if the first certificate of occupancy is issued after January 26, 1993. The Department also asked for comment on an Option Two, which would have imposed new construction requirements if a completed application for a building permit or permit extension was filed after the enactment of the ADA (July 26, 1990), and the facility was occupied after January 26, 1993.

The request for comment on this issue drew a large number of comments expressing a wide range of views. Most business groups and some disability rights groups favored Option One, and some business groups and most disability rights groups favored Option Two. Individuals and government entities were equally divided; several commenters proposed other options.

Those favoring Option One pointed out that it is more reasonable in that it allows time for those subject to the new construction requirements to anticipate those requirements and to receive technical assistance pursuant to the Act. Numerous commenters said that time frames for designing and constructing some types of facilities (for example, health care facilities) can range from two to four years or more. They expressed concerns that Option Two, which would apply to some facilities already under design or construction as of the date the Act was signed, and to some on which construction began shortly after enactment, could result in costly redesign or reconstruction of those facilities. In the same vein, some Option One supporters found Option Two objectionable on due process grounds. In their view, Option Two would mean that in July 1991 (upon issuance of the final DOJ rule) the responsible entities would learn that ADA standards had been in effect since July 26, 1990, and this would amount to retroactive application of standards. Numerous commenters characterized Option Two as having no support in the statute and Option One as being more consistent with congressional intent. Those who favored Option Two pointed out that it would include more facilities within the coverage of the new

construction standards. They argued that because similar accessibility requirements are in effect under State laws, no hardship would be imposed by this option. Numerous commenters said that hardship would also be eliminated in light of their view that the ADA requires compliance with the Uniform Federal Accessibility Standards (UFAS) until issuance of DOJ standards. Those supporting Option Two claimed that it was more consistent with the statute and its legislative history.

The Department has chosen Option One rather than Option Two, primarily on the basis of the language of three relevant sections of the statute. First, section 303(a) requires compliance with accessibility standards set forth, or incorporated by reference in, regulations to be issued by the Department of Justice. Standing alone, this section cannot be read to require compliance with the Department's standards before those standards are issued (through this rulemaking). Second, according to section 310 of the statute, section 303 becomes effective on January 26, 1992. Thus, section 303 cannot impose requirements on the design of buildings before that date. Third, while section 306(d) of the Act requires compliance with UFAS if final regulations have not been issued, that provision cannot reasonably be read to take effect until July 26, 1991, the date by which the Department of Justice must issue final regulations under title III.

Option Two was based on the premise that the interim standards in section 306(d) take effect as of the ADA's enactment (July 26, 1990), rather than on the date by which the Department of Justice regulations are due to be issued (July 26, 1991). The initial clause of section 306(d)(1) itself is silent on this question:

If final regulations have not been issued pursuant to this section, for new construction for which a * * * building permit is obtained prior to the issuance of final regulations * * * (interim standards apply).

The approach in Option Two relies partly on the language of section 310 of the Act, which provides that section 306, the interim standards provision, takes effect on the date of enactment. Under this interpretation the interim standards provision would prevail over the operative provision, section 303, which requires that new construction be accessible and which becomes effective January 26, 1992. This approach would also require construing the language of section 306(d)(1) to take effect before the Department's standards are due to be issued. The preferred reading of section 306 is that it would require that, if the Department's final standards had not been issued by July 26, 1991, UFAS would apply to certain buildings until such time as the Department's standards were issued.

General Substantive Requirements of the New Construction Provisions

The rule requires, as does the statute, that covered newly constructed facilities be readily accessible to and usable by individuals with disabilities. The phrase "readily accessible to and usable by individuals with disabilities" is a term that, in slightly varied formulations, has been used in the Architectural Barriers Act of 1968, the Fair Housing Act, the regulations implementing section 504 of the Rehabilitation Act of 1973, and current accessibility standards. It means, with respect to a facility or a portion of a facility, that it can be approached, entered, and used by individuals with disabilities (including mobility, sensory, and cognitive impairments) easily and conveniently. A facility that is constructed to meet the requirements of the rule's accessibility standards will be considered readily accessible and usable with respect to construction. To the extent that a particular type or element of a facility is not specifically addressed by the standards, the language of this section is the safest guide.

A private entity that renders an "accessible" building inaccessible in its operation, through policies or practices, may be in violation of section 302 of the Act. For example, a private entity can render an entrance to a facility inaccessible by keeping an accessible entrance open only during certain hours (whereas the facility is available to others for a greater length of time). A facility could similarly be rendered inaccessible if a person with disabilities is significantly limited in her or his choice of a range of accommodations.

Ensuring access to a newly constructed facility will include providing access to the facility from the street or parking lot, to the extent the responsible entity has control over the route from those locations. In some cases, the private entity will have no control over access at the point where streets, curbs, or sidewalks already exist, and in those instances the entity is encouraged to request modifications to a sidewalk, including installation of curb cuts, from a public entity responsible for them. However, as some commenters pointed out, there is no obligation for a private entity subject to title III of the ADA to seek or ensure compliance by a public entity with title II. Thus, although a locality may have an obligation under title II of the Act to install curb cuts at a particular location, that responsibility is separate from the private entity's title III obligation, and any involvement by a private entity in seeking cooperation from a public entity is purely voluntary in this context.

Work Areas

Proposed paragraph 36.401(b) addressed access to employment areas, rather than to the areas where goods or services are being provided. The preamble noted that the proposed paragraph provided guidance for new construction and alterations until more specific guidance was issued by the ATBCB and reflected in this Department's regulation. The entire paragraph has been

deleted from this section in the final rule. The concepts of paragraphs (b) (1), (2), and (5) of the proposed rule are included, with modifications and expansion, in ADAAG. Paragraphs (3) and (4) of the proposed rule, concerning fixtures and equipment, are not included in the rule or in ADAAG.

Some commenters asserted that questions relating to new construction and alterations of work areas should be addressed by the EEOC under title I, as employment concerns. However, the legislative history of the statute clearly indicates that the new construction and alterations requirements of title III were intended to ensure accessibility of new facilities to all individuals, including employees. The language of section 303 sweeps broadly in its application to all public accommodations and commercial facilities. EEOC's title I regulations will address accessibility requirements that come into play when "reasonable accommodation" to individual employees or applicants with disabilities is mandated under title I.

The issues dealt with in proposed § 36.401(b) (1) and (2) are now addressed in ADAAG section 4.1.1(3). The Department's proposed paragraphs would have required that areas that will be used only by employees as work stations be constructed so that individuals with disabilities could approach, enter, and exit the areas. They would not have required that all individual work stations be constructed or equipped (for example, with shelves that are accessible or adaptable) to be accessible. This approach was based on the theory that, as long as an employee with disabilities could enter the building and get to and around the employment area, modifications in a particular work station could be instituted as a "reasonable accommodation" to that employee if the modifications were necessary and they did not constitute an undue hardship.

Almost all of the commenters agreed with the proposal to require access to a

work area but not to require accessibility of each individual work station. This principle is included in ADAAG 4.1.1(3). Several of the comments related to the requirements of the proposed ADAAG and have been addressed in the accessibility standards.

Proposed paragraphs (b) (3) and (4) would have required that consideration be given to placing fixtures and equipment at accessible heights in the first instance, and to purchasing new equipment and fixtures that are adjustable. These paragraphs have not been included in the final rule because the rule in most instances does not establish accessibility standards for purchased equipment. (See discussion elsewhere in the preamble of proposed § 36.309.) While the Department encourages entities to consider providing accessible or adjustable fixtures and equipment for employees, this rule does not require them to do so.

Paragraph (b)(5) of proposed § 36.401 clarified that proposed paragraph (b) did not limit the requirement that employee areas other than individual work stations must be accessible. For example, areas that are employee "common use" areas and are not solely used as work stations (e.g., employee lounges, cafeterias, health units, exercise facilities) are treated no differently under this regulation than other parts of a building; they must be constructed or altered in compliance with the accessibility standards. This principle is not stated in § 36.401 but is implicit in the requirements of this section and ADAAG.

Commercial Facilities in Private Residences

Section 36.401(b) of the final rule is a new provision relating to commercial facilities located in private residences. The proposed rule addressed these requirements in the preamble to § 36.207, "Places of public accommodation located in private residences." The preamble stated that the approach for commercial facilities would be the same as that for places of public accommodation, i.e., those portions used exclusively as a commercial facility or used as both a commercial facility and for residential purposes would be covered. Because commercial facilities are only subject to new construction and alterations requirements, however, the covered portions would only be subject to subpart D. This approach is reflected in § 36.401(b)(1).

The Department is aware that the statutory definition of "commercial facility" excludes private residences because they are "expressly exempted from coverage under the Fair Housing Act of 1968, as amended." However, the Department interprets that exemption as applying only to facilities that are exclusively residential. When a facility is used as both a residence and a commercial facility, the exemption does not apply.

Paragraph (b)(2) is similar to the new paragraph (b) under § 36.207, "Places of public accommodation located in private residences." The paragraph clarifies that the covered portion includes not only the space used as a commercial facility, but also the elements used to enter the commercial facility, e.g., the homeowner's front sidewalk, if any; the doorway; the hallways; the restroom, if used by employees or visitors of the commercial facility; and any other portion of the residence, interior or exterior, used by employees or visitors of the commercial facility.

As in the case of public accommodations located in private residences, the new construction standards only apply to the extent that a portion of the residence is designed or intended for use as a commercial facility. Likewise, if a homeowner alters a portion of his home to convert it to a commercial facility, that work must be done in compliance with the alterations standards in appendix A.

Structural Impracticability

Proposed § 36.401(c) is included in the final rule with minor changes. It details a statutory exception to the new construction requirement: the requirement that new construction be accessible does not apply where an entity can demonstrate that it is structurally impracticable to meet the requirements of the regulation. This provision is also included in ADAAG, at section 4.1.1(5)(a).

Consistent with the legislative history of the ADA, this narrow exception will apply only in rare and unusual circumstances where unique characteristics of terrain make accessibility unusually difficult. Such limitations for topographical problems are analogous to an acknowledged limitation in the application of the accessibility requirements of the Fair Housing Amendments Act (FHAA) of 1988.

Almost all commenters supported this interpretation. Two commenters argued that the DOJ requirement is too limiting and would not exempt some buildings that should be exempted because of soil conditions, terrain, and other unusual site conditions. These commenters suggested consistency with HUD's Fair Housing Accessibility Guidelines (56 FR 9472 (1991)), which generally would allow exceptions from accessibility requirements, or allow compliance with less stringent requirements, on sites with slopes exceeding 10%.

The Department is aware of the provisions in HUD's guidelines, which were issued on March 6, 1991, after passage of the ADA and publication of the Department's proposed rule. The approach taken in these guidelines, which apply to different types of construction and implement different statutory requirements for new construction, does not bind this Department in regulating under the ADA. The Department has included in the final rule the substance of the proposed provision, which is faithful to the intent of the statute, as expressed in the legislative

history. (See Senate report at 70-71; Education and Labor report at 120.)

The limited structural impracticability exception means that it is acceptable to deviate from accessibility requirements only where unique characteristics of terrain prevent the incorporation of accessibility features and where providing accessibility would destroy the physical integrity of a facility. A situation in which a building must be built on stilts because of its location in marshlands or over water is an example of one of the few situations in which the exception for structural impracticability would apply.

This exception to accessibility requirements should not be applied to situations in which a facility is located in "hilly" terrain or on a plot of land upon which there are steep grades. In such circumstances, accessibility can be achieved without destroying the physical integrity of a structure, and is required in the construction of new facilities.

Some commenters asked for clarification concerning when and how to apply the ADA rules or the Fair Housing Accessibility Guidelines, especially when a facility may be subject to both because of mixed use. Guidance on this question is provided in the discussion of the definitions of place of public accommodation and commercial facility. With respect to the structural impracticability exception, a mixed-use facility could not take advantage of the Fair Housing exemption, to the extent that it is less stringent than the ADA exemption, except for those portions of the facility that are subject only to the Fair Housing Act.

As explained in the preamble to the proposed rule, in those rare circumstances in which it is structurally impracticable to achieve full compliance with accessibility retirements under the ADA, places of public accommodation and commercial facilities should still be designed and constructed to incorporate accessibility features to the extent that the features are structurally practicable. The accessibility requirements should not be viewed as an all-or-nothing proposition in such circumstances.

If it is structurally impracticable for a facility in its entirety to be readily accessible to and usable by people with disabilities, then those portions that can be made accessible should be made accessible. If a building cannot be constructed in compliance with the full range of accessibility requirements because of structural impracticability, then it should still incorporate those features that are structurally practicable. If it is structurally impracticable to make a particular facility accessible to persons who have particular types of disabilities, it is still appropriate to require it to be made accessible to persons with other types of disabilities. For example, a facility that is of necessity built on stilts and cannot be made accessible to persons who use wheelchairs because it is structurally impracticable to do so, must be made accessible for individuals with vision or hearing impairments or other kinds of disabilities.

Elevator Exemption

Section 36.401(d) implements the "elevator exemption" for new construction in section 303(b) of the ADA. The elevator exemption is an exception to the general requirement that new facilities be readily accessible to and usable by individuals with disabilities. Generally, an elevator is the most common way to provide individuals who use wheelchairs "ready access" to floor levels above or below the ground floor of a multi-story building. Congress, however, chose not to require elevators in new small buildings, that is, those with less than three stories or less than 3,000 square feet per story. In buildings eligible for the exemption, therefore, "ready access" from the building entrance to a floor above or below the ground floor is not required, because the statute does not require that an elevator be installed in such buildings. The elevator exemption does not apply, however, to a facility housing a shopping center, a shopping mall, or the professional office of a health care provider, or other categories of facilities as determined by the Attorney General. For example, a new office building that will have only two stories, with no elevator planned, will not be required to have an elevator, even if each story has 20,000 square feet. In other words, having either less than 3000 square feet per story or less than three stories qualifies a facility for the exemption; it need not qualify for the exemption on both counts. Similarly, a facility that has five stories of 2800 square feet each qualifies for the exemption. If a facility has three or more stories at any point, it is not eligible for the elevator exemption unless all the stories are less than 3000 square feet.

The terms "shopping center or shopping mall" and "professional office of a health care provider" are defined in this section. They are substantively identical to the definitions included in the proposed rule in § 36.104, "Definitions." They have been moved to this section because, as commenters pointed out, they are relevant only for the purposes of the elevator exemption, and inclusion in the general definitions section could give the incorrect impression that an office of a health care provider is not covered as a place of public accommodation under other sections of the rule, unless the office falls within the definition.

For purposes of § 36.401, a "shopping center or shopping mall" is (1) a building housing five or more sales or rental establishments, or (2) a series of buildings on a common site, either under common ownership or common control or developed either as one project or as a series of related projects, housing five or more sales or rental establishments. The term "shopping center or shopping mall" only includes floor levels containing at least one sales or rental establishment, or any floor level that was designed or intended for use by at least one sales or rental establishment.

Any sales or rental establishment of the type that is included in paragraph (5) of the definition of "place of public accommodation" (for example, a bakery, grocery store, clothing store, or hardware store) is considered a sales or rental establishment for purposes of this definition; the other types of public accommodations (e.g., restaurants, laundromats, banks, travel services, health spas) are not.

In the preamble to the proposed rule, the Department sought comment on whether the definition of "shopping center or mall" should be expanded to include any of these other types of public accommodations. The Department also sought comment on whether a series of buildings should fall within the definition only if they are physically connected.

Most of those responding to the first question (overwhelmingly groups representing people with disabilities, or individual commenters) urged that the definition encompass more places of public accommodation, such as restaurants, motion picture houses, laundromats, dry cleaners, and banks. They pointed out that often it is not known what types of establishments will be tenants in a new facility. In addition, they noted that malls are advertised as entities, that their appeal is in the "package" of services offered to the public, and that this package often includes the additional types of establishments mentioned.

Commenters representing business groups sought to exempt banks, travel services, grocery stores, drug stores, and freestanding retail stores from the elevator requirement. They based this request on the desire to continue the practice in some locations of incorporating mezzanines housing administrative offices, raised pharmacist areas, and raised areas in the front of supermarkets that house safes and are used by managers to oversee operations of check-out aisles and other functions. Many of these concerns are adequately addressed by ADAAG. Apart from those addressed by ADAAG, the Department sees no reason to treat a particular type of sales or rental establishment differently from any other. Although banks and travel services are not included as "sales or rental establishments," because they do not fall under paragraph (5) of the definition of place of public accommodation, grocery stores and drug stores are included.

The Department has declined to include places of public accommodation other than sales or rental establishments in the definition. The statutory definition of "public accommodation" (section 301(7)) lists 12 types of establishments that are considered public accommodations. Category (E) includes "a bakery, grocery store, clothing store, hardware store, shopping center, or other sales or rental establishment." This arrangement suggests that it is only these types of establishments that would make up a shopping center for purposes of the statute. To include all types of places of public accommodation, or those from 6 or 7 of the categories, as commenters suggest, would overly limit the elevator exemption; the universe of facilities covered by the definition of "shopping center" could well exceed the number of multitenant facilities *not* covered, which would render the exemption almost meaningless.

For similar reasons, the Department is retaining the requirement that a building or series of buildings must house five or more sales or rental establishments before it falls within the definition of "shopping center." Numerous commenters objected to the number and requested that the number be lowered from five to three or four. Lowering the number in this manner would include an inordinately large number of two-story multitenant buildings within the category of those required to have elevators.

The responses to the question concerning whether a series of buildings should be connected in order to be covered were varied. Generally, disability rights groups and some government agencies said a series of buildings should not have to be connected, and

pointed to a trend in some areas to build shopping centers in a garden or village setting. The Department agrees that this design choice should not negate the elevator requirement for new construction. Some business groups answered the question in the affirmative, and some suggested a different definition of shopping center. For example, one commenter recommended the addition of a requirement that the five or more establishments be physically connected on the non-ground floors by a common pedestrian walkway or pathway, because otherwise a series of stand-alone facilities would have to comply with the elevator requirement, which would be unduly burdensome and perhaps infeasible. Another suggested use of what it characterized as the standard industry definition: "A group of retail stores and related business facilities, the whole planned, developed, operated and managed as a unit." While the rule's definition would reach a series of related projects that are under common control but were not developed as a single project, the Department considers such a facility to be a shopping center within the meaning of the statute. However, in light of the hardship that could confront a series of existing small stand-alone buildings if elevators were required in alterations, the Department has included a common access route in the definition of shopping center or shopping mall for purposes of § 36.404.

Some commenters suggested that access to restrooms and other shared facilities open to the public should be required even if those facilities were not on a shopping floor. Such a provision with respect to toilet or bathing facilities is included in the elevator exception in final ADAAG 4.1.3(5).

For purposes of this subpart, the rule does not distinguish between a "shopping mall" (usually a building with a roofed-over common pedestrian area serving more than one tenant in which a majority of the tenants have a main entrance from the

common pedestrian area) and a "shopping center" (e.g., a "shopping strip"). Any facility housing five or more of the types of sales or rental establishments described, regardless of the number of other types of places of public accommodation housed there (e.g., offices, movie theaters, restaurants), is a shopping center or shopping mall.

For example, a two-story facility built for mixed-use occupancy on both floors (e.g., by sales and rental establishments, a movie theater, restaurants, and general office space) is a shopping center or shopping mall if it houses five or more sales or rental establishments. If none of these establishments is located on the second floor, then only the ground floor, which contains the sales or rental establishments, would be a "shopping center or shopping mall," unless the second floor was designed or intended for use by at least one sales or rental establishment. In determining whether a floor was intended for such use, factors to be considered include the types of establishments that first occupied the floor, the nature of the developer's marketing strategy, i.e., what types of establishments were sought, and inclusion of any design features particular to rental and sales establishments.

A "professional office of a health care provider" is defined as a location where a person or entity regulated by a State to provide professional services related to the physical or mental health of an individual makes such services available to the public. In a two-story development that houses health care providers only on the ground floor, the "professional office of a health care provider" is limited to the ground floor unless the second floor was designed or intended for use by a health care provider. In determining if a floor was intended for such use, factors to be considered include whether the facility was constructed with special plumbing, electrical, or other features needed by health care providers, whether the developer marketed the facility as a medical office center, and whether any of the establishments that first occupied the floor was, in fact, a health care provider.

In addition to requiring that a building that is a shopping center, shopping mall, or the professional office of a health care provider have an elevator regardless of square footage or number of floors, the ADA (section 303(b)) provides that the Attorney General may determine that a particular category of facilities requires the installation of elevators based on the usage of the facilities. The Department, as it proposed to do, has added to the nonexempt categories terminals, depots, or other stations used for specified public transportation, and airport passenger terminals. Numerous commenters in all categories endorsed this proposal; none opposed it. It is not uncommon for an airport passenger terminal or train station, for example, to have only two floors, with gates on both floors. Because of the significance of transportation, because a person with disabilities could be arriving or departing at any gate, and because inaccessible facilities could result in a total denial of transportation services, it is reasonable to require that newly constructed transit facilities be accessible, regardless of square footage or number of floors. One comment suggested an amendment that would treat terminals and stations similarly to shopping centers, by requiring an accessible route only to those areas used for passenger loading and unloading and for other passenger services. Paragraph (d)(2)(ii) has been modified accordingly.

Some commenters suggested that other types of facilities (e.g., educational facilities, libraries, museums, commercial facilities, and social service facilities) should be included in the category of nonexempt facilities. The Department has not found adequate justification for including any other types of facilities in the nonexempt category at this time.

Section 36.401(d)(2) establishes the operative requirements concerning the elevator exemption and its application to shopping centers and malls, professional offices of health care providers, transit stations, and airport passenger terminals. Under the rule's framework, it is necessary first to determine if a new facility (including one or more buildings) houses places of public accommodation or commercial facilities that are in the categories for which elevators are required. If so, and the facility is a shopping center or shopping mall, or a professional office of a health care provider, then any area housing such an office or a sales or rental establishment or the professional office of a health care provider is not entitled to the elevator exemption.

The following examples illustrate the application of these principles:

1. A shopping mall has an upper and a lower level. There are two "anchor stores" (in this case, major department stores at either end of the mall, both with exterior entrances and an entrance on each level from the common area). In addition, there are 30 stores (sales or rental establishments) on the upper level, all of which have entrances from a common central area. There are 30 stores on the lower level, all of which have entrances from a common central area. According to the rule, elevator access must be provided to each store and to each level of the anchor stores. This requirement could be satisfied with respect to the 60 stores through elevators connecting the two pedestrian levels, provided that an individual could travel from the elevator to any other point on that level (i.e., into any store through a common pedestrian area) on an accessible path.

2. A commercial (nonresidential) "townhouse" develop-

ment is composed of 20 two-story attached buildings. The facility is developed as one project, with common ownership, and the space will be leased to retailers. Each building has one accessible entrance from a pedestrian walk to the first floor. From that point, one can enter a store on the first floor, or walk up a flight of stairs to a store on the second floor. All 40 stores must be accessible at ground floor level or by accessible vertical access from that level. This does not mean, however, that 20 elevators must be installed. Access could be provided to the second floor by an elevator from the pedestrian area on the lower level to an upper walkway connecting all the areas on the second floor.

3. In the same type of development, it is planned that retail stores will be housed exclusively on the ground floor, with only office space (not professional offices of health care providers) on the second. Elevator access need not be provided to the second floor because all the sales or rental establishments (the entities that make the facility a shopping center) are located on an accessible ground floor.

4. In the same type of development, the space is designed and marketed as medical or office suites, or as a medical office facility. Accessible vertical access must be provided to all areas, as described in example 2.

Some commenters suggested that building owners who knowingly lease or rent space to nonexempt places of public accommodation would violate § 36.401. However, the Department does not consider leasing or renting inaccessible space in itself to constitute a violation of this part. Nor does a change in use of a facility, with no accompanying alterations (e.g., if a psychiatrist replaces an attorney as a tenant in a second-floor office, but no alterations are made to the office) trigger accessibility requirements.

Entities cannot evade the requirements of this section by constructing facilities in such a way that no story is intended to constitute a "ground floor." For example, if a private entity constructs a building whose main entrance leads only to stairways or escalators that connect with upper or lower floors, the Department would consider at least one level of the facility a ground story.

The rule requires in § 36.401(d)(3), consistent with the proposed rule, that, even if a building falls within the elevator exemption, the floor or floors other than the ground floor must nonetheless be accessible, except for elevator access, to individuals with disabilities, including people who use wheelchairs. This requirement applies to buildings that do not house sales or rental establishments or the professional offices of a health care provider as well as to those in which such establishments or offices are all located on the ground floor. In such a situation, little added cost is entailed in making the second floor accessible, because it is similar in structure and floor plan to the ground floor.

There are several reasons for this provision. First, some individuals who are mobility impaired may work on a building's second floor, which they can reach by stairs and the use of crutches; however, the same individuals, once they reach the second floor, may then use a wheelchair that is kept in the office. Secondly, because the first floor will be accessible, there will be little additional cost entailed in making the second floor, with the same structure and generally the same floor plan, accessible. In addition, the second floor must be accessible to those persons with disabilities who do not need elevators for level changes (for example, persons with sight or hearing impairments and those with certain mobility impairments). Finally, if an elevator is installed in the future for any reason, full access to the floor will be facilitated.

One commenter asserted that this provision goes beyond the Department's authority under the Act, and disagreed with the Department's claim that little additional cost would be entailed in compliance. However, the provision is taken directly from the legislative history (see Education and Labor report at 114).

One commenter said that where an elevator is not required, platform lifts should be required. Two commenters pointed out that the elevator exemption is really an exemption from the requirement for providing an accessible route to a second floor not served by an elevator. The Department agrees with the latter comment. Lifts to provide access between floors are not required in buildings that are not required to have elevators. This point is specifically addressed in the appendix to ADAAG (§4.1.3(5)). ADAAG also addresses in detail the situations in which lifts are permitted or required.

Section 36.402 Alterations

Sections 36.402-36.405 implement section 303(a)(2) of the Act, which requires that alterations to existing facilities be made in a way that ensures that the altered portion is readily accessible to and usable by individuals with disabilities. This part does not require alterations; it simply provides that when alterations are undertaken, they must be made in a manner that provides access.

Section 36.402(a)(1) provides that any alteration to a place of public accommodation or a commercial facility, after January 26, 1992, shall be made so as to ensure that, to the maximum extent feasible, the altered portions of the facility are readily accessible to and usable by individuals with disabilities, including individuals who use wheelchairs.

The proposed rule provided that an alteration would be deemed to be undertaken after January 26, 1992, if the physical alteration of the property is in progress after that date. Commenters pointed out that this provision would, in some

cases, produce an unjust result by requiring the redesign or retrofitting of projects initiated before this part established the ADA accessibility standards. The Department agrees that the proposed rule would, in some instances, unfairly penalize projects that were substantially completed before the effective date. Therefore, paragraph (a)(2) has been revised to specify that an alteration will be deemed to be undertaken after January 26, 1992, if the physical alteration of the property begins after that date. As a matter of interpretation, the Department will construe this provision to apply to alterations that require a permit from a State, County or local government, if physical alterations pursuant to the terms of the permit begin after January 26, 1992. The Department recognizes that this application of the effective date may require redesign of some facilities that were planned prior to the publication of this part, but no retrofitting will be required of facilities on which the physical alterations were initiated prior to the effective date of the Act. Of course, nothing in this section in any way alters the obligation of any facility to remove architectural barriers in existing facilities to the extent that such barrier removal is readily achievable.

Paragraph (b) provides that, for the purposes of this part, an "alteration" is a change to a place of public accommodation or a commercial facility that affects or could affect the usability of the building or facility or any part thereof. One commenter suggested that the concept of usability should apply only to those changes that affect access by persons with disabilities. The Department remains convinced that the Act requires the concept of "usability" to be read broadly to include any change that affects the usability of the facility, not simply changes that relate directly to access by individuals with disabilities.

The Department received a significant number of comments on the examples provided in paragraphs (b)(1) and (b)(2) of the proposed rule. Some commenters urged the

Department to limit the application of this provision to major structural modifications, while others asserted that it should be expanded to include cosmetic changes such as painting and wallpapering. The Department believes that neither approach is consistent with the legislative history, which requires this Department's regulation to be consistent with the accessibility guidelines (ADAAG) developed by the Architectural and Transportation Barriers Compliance Board (ATBCB). Although the legislative history contemplates that, in some instances, the ADA accessibility standards will exceed the current MGRAD requirements, it also clearly indicates the view of the drafters that "minor changes such as painting or papering walls * * * do not affect usability" (Education and Labor report at 111, Judiciary report at 64), and, therefore, are not alterations. The proposed rule was based on the existing MGRAD definition of "alter-ation." The language of the final rule has been revised to be consistent with ADAAG, incorporated as appendix A to this part.

Some commenters sought clarification of the intended scope of this section. The proposed rule contained illustrations of changes that affect usability and those that do not. The intent of the illustrations was to explain the scope of the alterations requirement; the effect was to obscure it. As a result of the illustrations, some commenters concluded that any alteration to a facility, even a minor alteration such as relocating an electrical outlet, would trigger an extensive obligation to provide access throughout an entire facility. That result was never contemplated.

Therefore, in this final rule paragraph (b)(1) has been revised to include the major provisions of paragraphs (b)(1) and (b)(2) of the proposed rule. The examples in the proposed rule have been deleted. Paragraph (b)(1) now provides that alterations include, but are not limited to, remodeling, renovation, rehabilitation,

reconstruction, historic restoration, changes or rearrangement in structural parts or elements, and changes or rearrangement in the plan configuration of walls and full-height partitions. Normal maintenance, reroofing, painting or wallpapering, asbestos removal, or changes to mechanical and electrical systems are not alterations unless they affect the usability of building or facility.

Paragraph (b)(2) of this final rule was added to clarify the scope of the alterations requirement. Paragraph (b)(2) provides that if existing elements, spaces, or common areas are altered, then each such altered element, space, or area shall comply with the appli-cable provisions of appendix A (ADAAG). As provided in § 36.403, if an altered space or area is an area of the facility that contains a primary function, then the requirements of that section apply.

Therefore, when an entity undertakes a minor alteration to a place of public accommoda-tion or commercial facility, such as moving an electrical outlet, the new outlet must be installed in compliance with ADAAG. (Alteration of the elements listed in § 36.403(c)(2) cannot trigger a path of travel obligation.) If the alteration is to an area, such as an employee lounge or locker room, that is not an area of the facility that contains a primary function, that area must comply with ADAAG. It is only when an alteration affects access to or usability of an area containing a primary function, as opposed to other areas or the elements listed in § 36.403(c)(2), that the path of travel to the altered area must be made accessible.

The Department received relatively few comments on paragraph (c), which explains the statutory phrase "to the maximum extent feasible." Some commenters suggested that the regulation should specify that cost is a factor in determining whether it is feasible to make an altered area accessible. The legislative history of the ADA indicates that the concept of feasibility only reaches the question of

whether it is possible to make the alteration accessible in compliance with this part. Costs are to be considered only when an alteration to an area containing a primary function triggers an additional require-ment to make the path of travel to the altered area accessible.

Section 36.402(c) is, therefore, essentially unchanged from the proposed rule. At the recommendation of a commenter, the Department has inserted the word "virtually" to modify "impossible" to conform to the language of the legislative history. It explains that the phrase "to the maximum extent feasible" as used in this section applies to the occasional case where the nature of an existing facility makes it virtually impossible to comply fully with applicable accessibility standards through a planned alteration. In the occasional cases in which full compliance is impossible, alterations shall provide the maximum physical accessibility feasible. Any features of the facility that are being altered shall be made accessible unless it is technically infeasible to do so. If providing accessibility in conformance with this section to individuals with certain disabilities (e.g., those who use wheelchairs) would not be feasible, the facility shall be made accessible to persons with other types of disabilities (e.g., those who use crutches or who have impaired vision or hearing, or those who have other types of impairments).

Section 36.403 Alterations: Path of Travel

Section 36.403 implements the statutory requirement that any alteration that affects or could affect the usability of or access to an area of a facility that contains a primary function shall be made so as to ensure that, to the maximum extent feasible, the path of travel to the altered area, and the restrooms, telephones, and drinking fountains serving the altered area, are readily accessible to and usable by individuals with disabilities, including individu-als who use wheelchairs, unless the cost and scope of such alterations is disproportionate to the cost of the overall alteration. Paragraph (a) restates this statutory requirement.

Paragraph (b) defines a "primary function" as a major activity for which the facility is intended. This paragraph is unchanged from the proposed rule. Areas that contain a primary function include, but are not limited to, the customer services lobby of a bank, the dining area of a cafeteria, the meeting rooms in a conference center, as well as offices and all other work areas in which the activities of the public accommodation or other private entities using the facility are carried out. The concept of "areas containing a primary function" is analogous to the concept of "functional spaces" in § 3.5 of the existing Uniform Federal Accessibility Standards, which defines "functional spaces" as "[t]he rooms and spaces in a building or facility that house the major activities for which the building or facility is intended."

Paragraph (b) provides that areas such as mechanical rooms, boiler rooms, supply storage rooms, employee lounges and locker rooms, janitorial closets, entrances, corridors, and restrooms are not areas containing a primary function. There may be exceptions to this general rule. For example, the availability of public restrooms at a place of public accommodation at a roadside rest stop may be a major factor affecting customers' decisions to patronize the public accommodation. In that case, a restroom would be considered to be an "area containing a primary function" of the facility.

Most of the commenters who addressed this issue supported the approach taken by the Department; but a few commenters suggested that areas not open to the general public or those used exclusively by employees should be excluded from the definition of primary function. The preamble to the proposed rule noted that the Department considered an alternative approach to the definition of "primary function," under which a

primary function of a commercial facility would be defined as a major activity for which the facility was intended, while a primary function of a place of public accommodation would be defined as an activity which involves providing significant goods, services, facilities, privileges, advantages, or accommodations. However, the Department concluded that, although portions of the legislative history of the ADA support this alternative, the better view is that the language now contained in § 36.403(b) most accurately reflects congressional intent. No commenter made a persuasive argument that the Department's interpretation of the legislative history is incorrect.

When the ADA was introduced, the requirement to make alterations accessible was included in section 302 of the Act, which identifies the practices that constitute discrimination by a public accommodation. Because section 302 applies only to the operation of a place of public accommodation, the alterations requirement was intended only to provide access to clients and customers of a public accommodation. It was anticipated that access would be provided to employees with disabilities under the "reasonable accommodation" requirements of title I. However, during its consideration of the ADA, the House Judiciary Committee amended the bill to move the alterations provision from section 302 to section 303, which applies to commercial facilities as well as public accommodations. The Committee report accompanying the bill explains that:

New construction and alterations of both public accommodations and commercial facilities must be made readily accessible to and usable by individuals with disabilities * * *. Essentially, [this requirement] is designed to ensure that patrons and employees of public accommodations and commercial facilities are able to get to, enter and use the facility * * *. The rationale for making new construction accessible applies with equal force to alterations.

Judiciary report at 62-63 (emphasis added).

The ADA, as enacted, contains the language of section 303 as it was reported out of the Judiciary Committee. Therefore, the Department has concluded that the concept of "primary function" should be applied in the same manner to places of public accommodation and to commercial facilities, thereby including employee work areas in places of public accommodation within the scope of this section.

Paragraph (c) provides examples of alterations that affect the usability of or access to an area containing a primary function. The examples include: Remodeling a merchandise display area or employee work areas in a department store; installing a new floor surface to replace an inaccessible surface in the customer service area or employee work areas of a bank; redesigning the assembly line area of a factory; and installing a computer center in an accounting firm. This list is illustrative, not exhaustive. Any change that affects the usability of or access to an area containing a primary function triggers the statutory obligation to make the path of travel to the altered area accessible.

When the proposed rule was drafted, the Department believed that the rule made it clear that the ADA would require alterations to the path of travel only when such alterations are not disproportionate to the alteration to the primary function area. However, the comments that the Department received indicated that many commenters believe that even minor alterations to individual elements would require additional alterations to the path of travel. To address the concern of these commenters, a new paragraph (c)(2) has been added to the final rule to provide that alterations to such elements as windows, hardware, controls (e.g. light switches or thermostats), electrical outlets, or signage will not be deemed to be alterations that affect the usability of or access to an area containing a primary function. Of course, each element that is altered must comply with ADAAG (appendix A). The cost of alterations to individual elements would be included in the overall cost of an alteration for purposes of determining disproportionality and would be counted when determining the aggregate cost of a series of small alterations in accordance with § 36.401(h) if the area is altered in a manner that affects access to or usability of an area containing a primary function.

Paragraph (d) concerns the respective obligations of landlords and tenants in the cases of alterations that trigger the path of travel requirement under § 36.403. This paragraph was contained in the landlord/ tenant section of the proposed rule, § 36.201(b). If a tenant is making alterations upon its premises pursuant to terms of a lease that grant it the authority to do so (even if they constitute alterations that trigger the path of travel requirement), and the landlord is not making alterations to other parts of the facility, then the alterations by the tenant on its own premises do not trigger a path of travel obligation upon the landlord in areas of the facility under the landlord's authority that are not otherwise being altered. The legislative history makes clear that the path of travel require- ment applies only to the entity that is already making the alteration, and thus the Department has not changed the final rule despite numerous comments suggesting that the tenant be required to provide a path of travel.

Paragraph (e) defines a "path of travel" as a continu- ous, unobstructed way of pedestrian passage by means of which an altered area may be approached, entered, and exited; and which connects the altered area with an exterior approach (including sidewalks, streets, and parking areas), an entrance to the facility, and other parts of the facility. This concept of an accessible path of travel is analogous to the concepts of "accessible route" and "circulation path" contained in section 3.5 of the current UFAS. Some commenters suggested that this

paragraph should address emergency egress. The Department disagrees. "Path of travel" as it is used in this section is a term of art under the ADA that relates only to the obligation of the public accommodation or commercial facility to provide additional accessible elements when an area containing a primary function is altered. The Department recognizes that emergency egress is an important issue, but believes that it is appropriately addressed in ADAAG (appen- dix A), not in this paragraph. Furthermore, ADAAG does not require changes to emergency egress areas in alterations.

Paragraph (e)(2) is drawn from section 3.5 of UFAS. It provides that an accessible path of travel may consist of walks and sidewalks, curb ramps and other interior or exterior pedestrian ramps; clear floor paths through lobbies, corridors, rooms, and other improved areas; parking access aisles; elevators and lifts; or a combination of such elements. Paragraph (e)(3) provides that, for the purposes of this part, the term "path of travel" also includes the restrooms, telephones, and drinking fountains serving an altered area.

Although the Act estab- lishes an expectation that an accessible path of travel should generally be included when alterations are made to an area containing a primary function, Congress recognized that, in some circumstances, providing an accessible path of travel to an altered area may be sufficiently burdensome in comparison to the alteration being undertaken to the area containing a primary function as to render this requirement unreasonable. Therefore, Congress provided, in section 303(a)(2) of the Act, that alterations to the path of travel that are disproportionate in cost and scope to the overall alteration are not required.

The Act requires the Attorney General to determine at what point the cost of providing an accessible path of travel becomes disproportion- ate. The proposed rule provided

three options for making this determination.

Two committees of Congress specifically addressed this issue: the House Committee on Education and Labor and the House Committee on the Judiciary. The reports issued by each committee suggested that accessibility alterations to a path of travel might be "disproportionate" if they exceed 30% of the alteration costs (Education and Labor report at 113; Judiciary report at 64). Because the Department believed that smaller percent- age rates might be appropriate, the proposed rule sought comments on three options: 10%, 20%, or 30%.

The Department received a significant number of comments on this section. Commenters representing individuals with disabilities generally supported the use of 30% (or more); commenters representing covered entities supported a figure of 10% (or less). The Department believes that alterations made to provide an accessible path of travel to the altered area should be deemed disproportionate to the overall alteration when the cost exceeds 20% of the cost of the alteration to the primary function area. This approach appropriately reflects the intent of Congress to provide access for individuals with disabilities without causing economic hardship for the covered public accommoda- tions and commercial facilities.

The Department has determined that the basis for this cost calculation shall be the cost of the alterations to the area containing the primary function. This approach will enable the public accommoda- tion or other private entity that is making the alteration to calculate its obligation as a percentage of a clearly ascertainable base cost, rather than as a percentage of the "total" cost, an amount that will change as accessibility alterations to the path of travel are made.

Paragraph (f)(2) (paragraph (e)(2) in the proposed rule) is unchanged. It provides examples of costs that may be counted as expenditures required to provide an accessible path of travel. They include:

* Costs associated with providing an accessible entrance and an accessible route to the altered area, for example, the cost of widening doorways or installing ramps;

* Costs associated with making restrooms accessible, such as installing grab bars, enlarging toilet stalls, insulating pipes, or installing accessible faucet controls;

* Costs associated with providing accessible telephones, such as relocating telephones to an accessible height, installing amplification devices, or installing telecommunications devices for deaf persons (TDD's);

* Costs associated with relocating an inaccessible drinking fountain.

Paragraph (f)(1) of the proposed rule provided that when the cost of alterations necessary to make the path of travel serving an altered area fully accessible is disproportionate to the cost of the overall alteration, the path of travel shall be made accessible to the maximum extent feasible. In response to the suggestion of a commenter, the Department has made an editorial change in the final rule (paragraph (g)(1)) to clarify that if the cost of providing a fully accessible path of travel is disproportionate, the path of travel shall be made accessible "to the extent that it can be made accessible without incurring disproportionate costs."

Paragraph (g)(2) (paragraph (f)(2) in the NPRM) establishes that priority should be given to those elements that will provide the greatest access, in the following order: An accessible entrance; an accessible route to the altered area; at least one accessible restroom for each sex or a single unisex restroom; accessible telephones; accessible drinking fountains; and, whenever possible, additional accessible elements such as parking, storage, and alarms. This paragraph is unchanged from the proposed rule.

Paragraph (h) (paragraph (g) in the proposed rule) provides that the obligation to provide an accessible path of

travel may not be evaded by performing a series of small alterations to the area served by a single path of travel if those alterations could have been performed as a single undertaking. If an area containing a primary function has been altered without providing an accessible path of travel to serve that area, and subsequent alterations of that area, or a different area on the same path of travel, are undertaken within three years of the original alteration, the total cost of alterations to primary function areas on that path of travel during the preceding three year period shall be considered in determining whether the cost of making the path of travel serving that area accessible is disproportionate. Only alterations undertaken after January 26, 1992, shall be considered in determining if the cost of providing accessible features is disproportionate to the overall cost of the alterations.

Section 36.404 Alterations: Elevator Exemption

Section 36.404 implements the elevator exemption in section 303(b) of the Act as it applies to altered facilities. The provisions of section 303(b) are discussed in the preamble to § 36.401(d) above. The statute applies the same exemption to both new construction and alterations. The principal difference between the requirements of § 36.401(d) and § 36.404 is that, in altering an existing facility that is not eligible for the statutory exemption, the public accommodation or other private entity responsible for the alteration is not required to install an elevator if the installation of an elevator would be disproportionate in cost and scope to the cost of the overall alteration as provided in § 36.403(f)(1). In addition, the standards referenced in § 36.406 (ADAAG) provide that installation of an elevator in an altered facility is not required if it is "technically infeasible."

This section has been revised to define the terms "professional office of a health

care provider" and "shopping center or shopping mall" for the purposes of this section. The definition of "professional office of a health care provider" is identical to the definition included in § 36.401(d).

It has been brought to the attention of the Department that there is some misunderstanding about the scope of the elevator exemption as it applies to the professional office of a health care provider. A public accommodation, such as the professional office of a health care provider, is required to remove architectural barriers to its facility to the extent that such barrier removal is readily achievable (see § 36.304), but it is not otherwise required by this part to undertake new construction or alterations. This part does not require that an existing two story building that houses the professional office of a health care provider be altered for the purpose of providing elevator access. If, however, alterations to the area housing the office of the health care provider are undertaken for other purposes, the installation of an elevator might be required, but only if the cost of the elevator is not disproportionate to the cost of the overall alteration. Neither the Act nor this part prohibits a health care provider from locating his or her professional office in an existing facility that does not have an elevator.

Because of the unique challenges presented in altering existing facilities, the Department has adopted a definition of "shopping center or shopping mall" for the purposes of this section that is slightly different from the definition adopted under § 36.401(d). For the purposes of this section, a "shopping center or shopping mall" is (1) a building housing five or more sales or rental establishments, or (2) a series of buildings on a common site, connected by a common pedestrian access route above or below the ground floor, either under common ownership or common control or developed either as one project or as a series of related projects, housing five or more sales or rental establishments. As is the case with new construction, the term "shopping center or shopping mall" only includes floor levels housing at least one sales or rental establishment, or any floor level that was designed or intended for use by at least one sales or rental establishment.

The Department believes that it is appropriate to use a different definition of "shopping center or shopping mall" for this section than for § 36.401, in order to make it clear that a series of existing buildings on a common site that is altered for the use of sales or rental establishments does not become a "shopping center or shopping mall" required to install an elevator, unless there is a common means of pedestrian access above or below the ground floor. Without this exemption, separate, but adjacent, buildings that were initially designed and constructed independently of each other could be required to be retrofitted with elevators, if they were later renovated for a purpose not contemplated at the time of construction.

Like § 36.401(d), § 36.404 provides that the exemptions in this paragraph do not obviate or limit in any way the obligation to comply with the other accessibility requirements established in this subpart. For example, alterations to floors above or below the ground floor must be accessible regardless of whether the altered facility has an elevator. If a facility that is not required to install an elevator nonetheless has an elevator, that elevator shall meet, to the maximum extent feasible, the accessibility requirements of this section.

Section 36.405 Alterations: Historic Preservation

Section 36.405 gives effect to the intent of Congress, expressed in section 504(c) of the Act, that this part recognize the national interest in preserving significant historic structures. Commenters criticized the Department's use of descriptive terms in the proposed rule that are different from those used in the ADA to describe eligible historic

properties. In addition, some commenters criticized the Department's decision to use the concept of "substantially impairing" the historic features of a property, which is a concept employed in regulations implementing section 504 of the Rehabilitation Act of 1973. Those commenters recommended that the Department adopt the criteria of "adverse effect" published by the Advisory Council on Historic Preservation under the National Historic Preservation Act (36 CFR 800.9) as the standard for determining whether an historic property may be altered.

The Department agrees with these comments to the extent that they suggest that the language of the rule should conform to the language employed by Congress in the ADA. Therefore, the language of this section has been revised to make it clear that this provision applies to buildings or facilities that are eligible for listing in the National Register of Historic Places under the National Historic Preservation Act (16 U.S.C. 470 *et seq.*) and to buildings or facilities that are designated as historic under State or local law. The Department believes, however, that the criteria of adverse effect employed under the National Historic Preservation Act are inappropriate for this rule because section 504(c) of the ADA specifies that special alterations provisions shall apply only when an alteration would "threaten or destroy the historic significance of qualified historic buildings and facilities."

The Department intends that the exception created by this section be applied only in those very rare situations in which it is not possible to provide access to an historic property using the special access provisions in ADAAG. Therefore, paragraph (a) of §36.405 has been revised to provide that alterations to historic properties shall comply, to the maximum extent feasible, with section 4.1.7 of ADAAG. Paragraph (b) of this section has been revised to provide that if it has been determined, under the procedures established in

ADAAG, that it is not feasible to provide physical access to an historic property that is a place of public accommodation in a manner that will not threaten or destroy the historic significance of the property, alternative methods of access shall be provided pursuant to the requirements of Subpart C.

Section 36.406 Standards for New Construction and Alterations

Section 36.406 implements the requirements of sections 306(b) and 306(c) of the Act, which require the Attorney General to promulgate standards for accessible design for buildings and facilities subject to the Act and this part that are consistent with the supplemental minimum guidelines and requirements for accessible design published by the Architectural and Transportation Barriers Compliance Board (ATBCB or Board) pursuant to section 504 of the Act. This section of the rule provides that new construction and alterations subject to this part shall comply with the standards for accessible design published as appendix A to this part.

Appendix A contains the Americans with Disabilities Act Accessibility Guidelines for Buildings and Facilities (ADAAG) which is being published by the ATBCB as a final rule elsewhere in this issue of the **Federal Register**. As proposed in this Department's proposed rule, § 36.406(a) adopts ADAAG as the accessibility standard applicable under this rule.

Paragraph (b) was not included in the proposed rule. It provides, in chart form, guidance for using ADAAG together with subparts A through D of this part when determining requirements for a particular facility. This chart is intended solely as guidance for the user; it has no effect for purposes of compliance or enforcement. It does not necessarily provide complete or mandatory information.

Proposed § 36.406(b) is not included in the final rule. That provision, which would have taken effect only if the final rule had followed the proposed Option Two for § 36.401(a), is unnecessary because the Department has chosen Option One, as explained in the preamble for that section.

Section 504(a) of the ADA requires the ATBCB to issue minimum guidelines to supplement the existing Minimum Guidelines and Requirements for Accessible Design (MGRAD) (36 CFR part 1190) for purposes of title III. According to section 504(b) of the Act, the guidelines are to establish additional requirements, consistent with the Act, "to ensure that buildings and facilities are accessible, in terms of architecture and design, . . . and communication, to individuals with disabilities." Section 306(c) of the Act requires that the accessibility standards included in the Department's regulations be consistent with the minimum guidelines, in this case ADAAG.

As explained in the ATBCB's preamble to ADAAG, the substance and form of the guidelines are drawn from several sources. They use as their model the 1984 Uniform Federal Accessibility Standards (UFAS) (41 CFR part 101, subpart 101-19.6, appendix), which are the standards implementing the Architectural Barriers Act. UFAS is based on the Board's 1982 MGRAD. ADAAG follows the numbering system and format of the private sector American National Standard Institute's ANSI A117.1 standards. (American National Specifications for Making Buildings and Facilities Accessible to and Usable by Physically Handicapped People (ANSI A117-1980) and American National Standard for Buildings and Facilities–Providing Accessibility and Usability for Physically Handicapped People (ANSI A117.1-1986).) ADAAG supplements MGRAD. In developing ADAAG, the Board made every effort to be consistent with MGRAD and the current and proposed ANSI Standards, to the extent consistent with the ADA.

ADAAG consists of nine main sections and a separate appendix. Sections 1 through 3

contain general provisions and definitions. Section 4 contains scoping provisions and technical specifications applicable to all covered buildings and facilities. The scoping provisions are listed separately for new construction of sites and exterior facilities; new construction of buildings; additions; alterations; and alterations to historic properties. The technical specifications generally reprint the text and illustrations of the ANSI A117.1 standard, except where differences are noted by italics. Sections 5 through 9 of the guidelines are special application sections and contain additional requirements for restaurants and cafeterias, medical care facilities, business and mercantile facilities, libraries, and transient lodging. The appendix to the guidelines contains additional information to aid in understanding the technical specifications. The section numbers in the appendix correspond to the sections of the guidelines to which they relate. An asterisk after a section number indicates that additional information appears in the appendix.

ADAAG's provisions are further explained under Summary of ADAAG below.

General Comments

One commenter urged the Department to move all or portions of subpart D, New Construction and Alterations, to the appendix (ADAAG) or to duplicate portions of subpart D in the appendix. The commenter correctly pointed out that subpart D is inherently linked to ADAAG, and that a self-contained set of rules would be helpful to users. The Department has attempted to simplify use of the two documents by deleting some paragraphs from subpart D (e.g., those relating to work areas), because they are included in ADAAG. However, the Department has retained in subpart D those sections that are taken directly from the statute or that give meaning to specific statutory concepts (e.g., structural impracticability, path of travel). While some of the subpart D provisions are

duplicated in ADAAG, others are not. For example, issues relating to path of travel and disproportionality in alterations are not addressed in detail in ADAAG. (The structure and contents of the two documents are addressed below under Summary of ADAAG.) While the Department agrees that it would be useful to have one self-contained document, the different focuses of this rule and ADAAG do not permit this result at this time. However, the chart included in § 36.406(b) should assist users in applying the provisions of subparts A through D, and ADAAG together.

Numerous business groups have urged the Department not to adopt the proposed ADAAG as the accessibility standards, because the requirements established are too high, reflect the "state of the art," and are inflexible, rigid, and impractical. Many of these objections have been lodged on the basis that ADAAG exceeds the statutory mandate to establish "minimum" guidelines. In the view of the Department, these commenters have misconstrued the meaning of the term "minimum guidelines." The statute clearly contemplates that the guidelines establish a level of access–a minimum– that the standards must meet or exceed. The guidelines are not to be "minimal" in the sense that they would provide for a low level of access. To the contrary, Congress emphasized that the ADA requires a "high degree of convenient access." Education and Labor report at 117-18. The legislative history explains that the guidelines may not "reduce, weaken, narrow or set less accessibility standards than those included in existing MGRAD" and should provide greater guidance in communication accessibility for individuals with hearing and vision impairments. Id. at 139. Nor did Congress contemplate a set of guidelines less detailed than ADAAG; the statute requires that the ADA guidelines supplement the existing MGRAD. When it established the statutory scheme, Congress was aware of the content and purpose of the 1982 MGRAD; as ADAAG does with respect to ADA, MGRAD establishes a minimum level of access that the Architectural Barriers Act standards (i.e., UFAS) must meet or exceed, and includes a high level of detail.

Many of the same commenters urged the Department to incorporate as its accessibility standards the ANSI standard's technical provisions and to adopt the proposed scoping provisions under development by the Council of American Building Officials' Board for the Coordination of Model Codes (BCMC). They contended that the ANSI standard is familiar to and accepted by professionals, and that both documents are developed through consensus. They suggested that ADAAG will not stay current, because it does not follow an established cyclical review process, and that it is not likely to be adopted by nonfederal jurisdictions in State and local codes. They urged the Department and the Board to coordinate the ADAAG provisions and any substantive changes to them with the ANSI A117 committee in order to maintain a consistent and uniform set of accessibility standards that can be efficiently and effectively implemented at the State and local level through the existing building regulatory processes.

The Department shares the commenters' goal of coordination between the private sector and Federal standards, to the extent that coordination can lead to substantive requirements consistent with the ADA. A single accessibility standard, or consistent accessibility standards, that can be used for ADA purposes and that can be incorporated or referenced by State and local governments, would help to ensure that the ADA requirements are routinely implemented at the design stage. The Department plans to work toward this goal.

The Department, however, must comply with the requirements of the ADA, the Federal Advisory Committee Act (5 U.S.C app. 1 et seq.) and the Administrative Procedure Act (5 U.S.C 551 et seq.). Neither the Department nor the Board can adopt private requirements wholesale. Furthermore, neither the 1991 ANSI A117 Standard revision nor the BCMC process is complete. Although the ANSI and BCMC provisions are not final, the Board has carefully considered both the draft BCMC scoping provisions and draft ANSI technical standards and included their language in ADAAG wherever consistent with the ADA.

Some commenters requested that, if the Department did not adopt ANSI by reference, the Department declare compliance with ANSI/BCMC to constitute equivalency with the ADA standards. The Department has not adopted this recommendation but has instead worked as a member of the ATBCB to ensure that its accessibility standards are practical and usable. In addition, as explained under subpart F, Certification of State Laws or Local Building Codes, the proper forum for further evaluation of this suggested approach would be in conjunction with the certification process.

Some commenters urged the Department to allow an additional comment period after the Board published its guidelines in final form, for purposes of affording the public a further opportunity to evaluate the appropriateness of including them as the Departments accessibility standards. Such an additional comment period is unnecessary and would unduly delay the issuance of final regulations. The Department put the public on notice, through the proposed rule, of its intention to adopt the proposed ADAAG, with any changes made by the Board, as the accessibility standards. As a member of the Board and of its ADA Task Force, the Department participated actively in the public hearings held on the proposed guidelines and in preparation of both the proposed and final versions of ADAAG. Many individuals and groups commented directly to the Department's docket, or at its public hearings, about ADAAG. The comments received on ADAAG, whether by the Board or by this Department, were thoroughly analyzed and considered by the Department in the context of whether the proposed ADAAG was consistent with the ADA and suitable for adoption as both guidelines and standards. The Department is convinced that ADAAG as adopted in its final form is appropriate for these purposes. The final guidelines, adopted here as standards, will ensure the high level of access contemplated by Congress, consistent with the ADA's balance between the interests of people with disabilities and the business community.

A few commenters, citing the Senate report (at 70) and the Education and Labor report (at 119), asked the Department to include in the regulations a provision stating that departures from particular technical and scoping requirements of the accessibility standards will be permitted so long as the alternative methods used will provide substantially equivalent or greater access to and utilization of the facility. Such a provision is found in ADAAG 2.2 and by virtue of that fact is included in these regulations.

Comments on specific provisions of proposed ADAAG

During the course of accepting comments on its proposed rule, the Department received numerous comments on ADAAG. Those areas that elicited the heaviest response included assistive listening systems, automated teller machines, work areas, parking, areas of refuge, telephones (scoping for TDD's and volume controls) and visual alarms. Strenuous objections were raised by some business commenters to the proposed provisions of the guidelines concerning check-out aisles, counters, and scoping for hotels and nursing facilities. All these comments were considered in the same manner as other comments on the Department's proposed rule and, in the Department's view, have been addressed adequately in the final ADAAG.

Largely in response to comments, the Board made numerous changes from its proposal, including the following:

* Generally, at least 50% of public entrances to new buildings must be accessible, rather than all entrances, as would often have resulted from the proposed approach.

* Not all check-out aisles are required to be accessible.

* The final guidelines provide greater flexibility in providing access to sales counters, and no longer require a portion of every counter to be accessible.

* Scoping for TDD's or text telephones was increased. One TDD or text telephone, for speech and hearing impaired persons, must be provided at locations with 4, rather than 6, pay phones, and in hospitals and shopping malls. Use of portable (less expensive) TDD's is allowed.

* Dispersal of wheelchair seating areas in theaters will be required only where there are more than 300 seats, rather than in all cases. Seats with removable armrests (i.e., seats into which persons with mobility impairments can transfer) will also be required.

* Areas of refuge (areas with direct access to a stairway, and where people who cannot use stairs may await assistance during a emergency evacuation) will be required, as proposed, but the final provisions are based on the Uniform Building Code. Such areas are not required in alterations.

* Rather than requiring 5% of new hotel rooms to be accessible to people with mobility impairments, between 2 and 4% accessibility (depending on total number of rooms) is required. In addition, 1% of the rooms must have roll-in showers.

* The proposed rule reserved the provisions on alterations to homeless shelters. The final guidelines apply alterations requirements to homeless shelters, but the requirements are less stringent than those applied to other types of facilities.

* Parking spaces that can be used by people in vans (with

lifts) will be required.

* As mandated by the ADA, the Board has established a procedure to be followed with respect to alterations to historic facilities.

Summary of ADAAG

This section of the preamble summarizes the structure of ADAAG, and highlights the more important portions.

* *Sections 1 Through 3*

Sections 1 through 3 contain general requirements, including definitions.

* *Section 4.1.1, Application*

Section 4 contains scoping requirements. Section 4.1.1, Application, provides that all areas of newly designed or newly constructed buildings and facilities and altered portions of existing buildings and facilities required to be accessible by § 4.1.6 must comply with the guidelines unless otherwise provided in § 4.1.1 or a special application section. It addresses areas used only by employees as work areas, temporary structures, and general exceptions.

Section 4.1.1(3) preserves the basic principle of the proposed rule: Areas that may be used by employees with disabilities shall be designed and constructed so that an individual with a disability can approach, enter, and exit the area. The language has been clarified to provide that it applies to any area used only as a work area (not just to areas "that may be used by employees with disabilities"), and that the guidelines do not require that any area used as an individual work station be designed with maneuvering space or equipped to be accessible. The appendix to ADAAG explains that work areas must meet the guidelines' requirements for doors and accessible routes, and recommends, but does not require, that 5% of individual work stations be designed to permit a person using a wheelchair to maneuver within the space.

Further discussion of work areas is found in the preamble concerning proposed § 36.401(b).

Section 4.1.1(5)(a) includes an exception for structural impracticability that corresponds to the one found in § 36.401(c) and discussed in that portion of the preamble.

* *Section 4.1.2, Accessible Sites and Exterior Facilities: New Construction*

This section addresses exterior features, elements, or spaces such as parking, portable toilets, and exterior signage, in new construction. Interior elements and spaces are covered by § 4.1.3.

The final rule retains the UFAS scoping for parking but also requires that at least one of every eight accessible parking spaces be designed with adequate adjacent space to deploy a lift used with a van. These spaces must have a sign indicating that they are van-accessible, but they are not to be reserved exclusively for van users.

* *Section 4.1.3, Accessible Buildings: New Construction*

This section establishes scoping requirements for new construction of buildings and facilities.

Sections 4.1.3 (1) through (4) cover accessible routes, protruding objects, ground and floor surfaces, and stairs.

Section 4.1.3(5) generally requires elevators to serve each level in a newly constructed building, with four exceptions included in the subsection. Exception 1 is the "elevator exception" established in § 36.401(d), which must be read with this section. Exception 4 allows the use of platform lifts under certain conditions.

Section 4.1.3(6), Windows, is reserved. Section 4.1.3(7) applies to doors.

Under § 4.1.3(8), at least 50% of all public entrances must be accessible. In addition, if a building is designed to provide access to enclosed parking, pedestrian tunnels, or elevated walkways, at least one entrance that serves each such function must be accessible. Each tenancy in a building must be served by an accessible entrance. Where local regulations (e.g., fire codes) require that a minimum number of exits be provided, an equivalent number of accessible entrances must be provided. (The latter provision does not require a greater number of entrances than otherwise planned.)

ADAAG Section 4.1.3(9), with accompanying technical requirements in Section 4.3, requires an area of rescue assistance (i.e., an area with direct access to an exit stairway and where people who are • unable to use stairs may await assistance during an emergency evacuation) to be established on each floor of a multi-story building. This was one of the most controversial provisions in the guidelines. The final ADAAG is based on current Uniform Building Code requirements and retains the requirement that areas of refuge (renamed "areas of rescue assistance") be provided, but specifies that this requirement does not apply to buildings that have a supervised automatic sprinkler system. Areas of refuge are not required in alterations.

The next seven subsections deal with drinking fountains § 4.1.3(10)); toilet facilities § 4.1.3(11)); storage, shelving, and display units (§ 4.1.3(12)), controls and operating mechanisms (§ 4.1.3(13)), emergency warning systems § 4.1.3(14)), detectable warnings (§ 4.1.3(15)), and building signage (§ 4.1.3(16)). Paragraph 11 requires that toilet facilities comply with § 4.22, which requires one accessible toilet stall (60" 60") in each newly constructed restroom. In response to public comments, the final rule requires that a second accessible stall (36" 60") be provided in restrooms that have six or more stalls.

ADAAG Section 4.1.3(17) establishes requirements for accessibility of pay phones to persons with mobility impairments, hearing impairments (requiring some phones with volume controls), and those who cannot use voice telephones. It requires one interior

"text telephone" to be provided at any facility that has a total of four or more public pay phones. (The term "text telephone" has been adopted to reflect current terminology and changes in technology.) In addition, text telephones will be required in specific locations, such as covered shopping malls, hospitals (in emergency rooms, waiting rooms, and recovery areas), and convention centers.

Paragraph 18 of Section 4.1.3 generally requires that at least five percent of fixed or built-in seating or tables be accessible.

Paragraph 19, covering assembly areas, specifies the number of wheelchair seating spaces and types and numbers of assistive listening systems required. It requires dispersal of wheelchair seating locations in facilities where there are more than 300 seats. The guidelines also require that at least one percent of all fixed seats be aisle seats without armrests (or with moveable armrests) on the aisle side to increase accessibility for persons with mobility impairments who prefer to transfer from their wheelchairs to fixed seating. In addition, the final ADAAG requires that fixed seating for a companion be located adjacent to each wheelchair location.

Paragraph 20 requires that where automated teller machines are provided, at least one must comply with section 4.34, which, among other things, requires accessible controls, and instructions and other information that are accessible to persons with sight impairments.

Under paragraph 21, where dressing rooms are provided, five percent or at least one must comply with section 4.35.

* Section 4.1.5, Additions

Each addition to an existing building or facility is regarded as an alteration subject to §§ 36.402 through 36.406 of subpart D, including the date established in § 36.402(a). But additions also have attributes of new construction, and to the extent that a space or element in the addition is newly constructed, each new space or element must comply with the

applicable scoping provisions of sections 4.1.1 to 4.1.3 for new construction, the applicable technical specifications of sections 4.2 through 4.34, and any applicable special provisions in sections 5 through 10. For instance, if a restroom is provided in the addition, it must comply with the requirements for new construction. Construction of an addition does not, however, create an obligation to retrofit the entire existing building or facility to meet requirements for new construction. Rather, the addition is to be regarded as an alteration and to the extent that it affects or could affect the usability of or access to an area containing a primary function, the requirements in section 4.1.6(2) are triggered with respect to providing an accessible path of travel to the altered area and making the restrooms, telephones, and drinking fountains serving the altered area accessible. For example, if a museum adds a new wing that does not have a separate entrance as part of the addition, an accessible path of travel would have to be provided through the existing building or facility unless it is disproportionate to the overall cost and scope of the addition as established in § 36.403(f).

* Section 4.1.6, Alterations

An alteration is a change to a building or facility that affects or could affect the usability of or access to the building or facility or any part thereof. There are three general principles for alterations. First, if any existing element or space is altered, the altered element or space must meet new construction requirements (section 4.1.6(1)(b)). Second, if alterations to the elements in a space when considered together amount to an alteration of the space, the entire space must meet new construction requirements (section 4.1.6(1)(c)). Third, if the alteration affects or could affect the usability of or access to an area containing a primary function, the path of travel to the altered area and the restrooms, drinking fountains, and telephones serving the altered area must be made accessible unless it is disproportionate to the overall alterations in terms of cost and scope as determined under criteria established by the Attorney General (§ 4.1.6(2)).

Section 4.1.6 should be read with §§ 36.402 through 36.405. Requirements concerning alterations to an area serving a primary function are addressed with greater detail in the latter sections than in section 4.1.6(2). Section 4.1.6(1)(j) deals with technical infeasibility. Section 4.1.6(3) contains special technical provisions for alterations to existing buildings and facilities.

* Section 4.1.7, Historic Preservation

This section contains scoping provisions and alternative requirements for alterations to qualified historic buildings and facilities. It clarifies the procedures under the National Historic Preservation Act and their application to alterations covered by the ADA. An individual seeking to alter a facility that is subject to the ADA guidelines and to State or local historic preservation statutes shall consult with the State Historic Preservation Officer to determine if the planned alteration would threaten or destroy the historic significance of the facility.

* Sections 4.2 Through 4.35

Sections 4.2 through 4.35 contain the technical specifications for elements and spaces required to be accessible by the scoping provisions (sections 4.1 through 4.1.7) and special application sections (sections 5 through 10). The technical specifications are the same as the 1980 version of ANSI A117.1 standard, except as noted in the text by italics.

* Sections 5 Through 9

These are special application sections and contain additional requirements for restaurants and cafeterias, medical care facilities, business and mercantile facilities,

libraries, and transient lodging. For example, at least 5 percent, but not less than one, of the fixed tables in a restaurant must be accessible.

In section 7, Business and Mercantile, paragraph 7.2 (Sales and Service Counters, Teller Windows, Information Counters) has been revised to provide greater flexibility in new construction than did the proposed rule. At least one of each type of sales or service counter where a cash register is located shall be made accessible. Accessible counters shall be dispersed throughout the facility. At counters such as bank teller windows or ticketing counters, alternative methods of compliance are permitted. A public accommodation may lower a portion of the counter, provide an auxiliary counter, or provide equivalent facilitation through such means as installing a folding shelf on the front of the counter at an accessible height to provide a work surface for a person using a wheelchair.

Section 7.3., Check-out Aisles, provides that, in new construction, a certain number of each design of check-out aisle, as listed in a chart based on the total number of check-out aisles of each design, shall be accessible. The percentage of check-outs required to be accessible generally ranges from 20% to 40%. In a newly constructed or altered facility with less than 5,000 square feet of selling space, at least one of each type of check-out aisle must be accessible. In altered facilities with 5,000 or more square feet of selling space, at least one of each design of check-out aisle must be made accessible when altered, until the number of accessible aisles of each design equals the number that would be required for new construction.

* Section 9, Accessible Transient Lodging

Section 9 addresses two types of transient lodging: hotels, motels, inns, boarding houses, dormitories, resorts, and other similar places (sections 9.1 through 9.4); and homeless shelters, halfway

houses, transient group homes, and other social service establishments (section 9.5). The interplay of the ADA and Fair Housing Act with respect to such facilities is addressed in the preamble discussion of the definition of "place of public accommodation" in § 36.104.

The final rule establishes scoping requirements for accessibility of newly constructed hotels. Four percent of the first hundred rooms, and roughly two percent of rooms in excess of 100, must meet certain requirements for accessibility to persons with mobility or hearing impairments, and an additional identical percentage must be accessible to persons with hearing impairments. An additional 1% of the available rooms must be equipped with roll-in showers, raising the actual scoping for rooms accessible to persons with mobility impairments to 5% of the first hundred rooms and 3% thereafter. The final ADAAG also provides that when a hotel is being altered, one fully accessible room and one room equipped with visual alarms, notification devices, and amplified telephones shall be provided for each 25 rooms being altered until the number of accessible rooms equals that required under the new construction standard. Accessible rooms must be dispersed in a manner that will provide persons with disabilities with a choice of single or multiple-bed accommodations.

In new construction, homeless shelters and other social service entities must comply with ADAAG; at least one type of amenity in each common area must be accessible. In a facility that is not required to have an elevator, it is not necessary to provide accessible amenities on the inaccessible floors if at least one of each type of amenity is provided in accessible common areas. The percentage of accessible sleeping accommodations required is the same as that required for other places of transient lodging. Requirements for facilities altered for use as a homeless shelter parallel the current MGRAD accessibility requirements for leased buildings. A shelter located in an altered facility must have at least one accessible entrance, accessible sleeping accommodations in a number equivalent to that established for new construction, at least one accessible toilet and bath, at least one accessible common area, and an accessible route connecting all accessible areas. All accessible areas in a homeless shelter in an altered facility may be located on one level.

Section 10, Transportation Facilities

Section 10 of ADAAG is reserved. On March 20, 1991, the ATBCB published a supplemental notice of proposed rulemaking (56 FR 11874) to establish special access requirements for transportation facilities. The Department anticipates that when the ATBCB issues final guidelines for transportation facilities, this part will be amended to include those provisions.

Subpart E—Enforcement

Because the Department of Justice does not have authority to establish procedures for judicial review and enforcement, subpart E generally restates the statutory procedures for enforcement.

Section 36.501 describes the procedures for private suits by individuals and the judicial remedies available. In addition to the language in section 308(a)(1) of the Act, § 36.501(a) of this part includes the language from section 204(a) of the Civil Rights Act of 1964 (42 U.S.C. 2000a-3(a)) which is incorporated by reference in the ADA. A commenter noted that the proposed rule did not include the provision in section 204(a) allowing the court to appoint an attorney for the complainant and authorize the commencement of the civil action without the payment of fees, costs, or security. That provision has been included in the final rule.

Section 308(a)(1) of the ADA permits a private suit by an individual who has

reasonable grounds for believing that he or she is "about to be" subjected to discrimination in violation of section 303 of the Act (subpart D of this part), which requires that new construction and alterations be readily accessible to and usable by individuals with disabilities. Authorizing suits to prevent construction of facilities with architectural barriers will avoid the necessity of costly retrofitting that might be required if suits were not permitted until after the facilities were completed. To avoid unnecessary suits, this section requires that the individual bringing the suit have `reasonable grounds" for believing that a violation is about to occur, but does not require the individual to engage in a futile gesture if he or she has notice that a person or organization covered by title III of the Act does not intend to comply with its provisions.

Section 36.501(b) restates the provisions of section 308(a)(2) of the Act, which states that injunctive relief for the failure to remove architectural barriers in existing facilities or the failure to make new construction and alterations accessible "shall include" an order to alter these facilities to make them readily accessible to and usable by persons with disabilities to the extent required by title III. The Report of the Energy and Commerce Committee notes that "an order to make a facility readily accessible to and usable by individuals with disabilities is mandatory" under this standard. H.R. Rep. No. 485, 101st Cong., 2d Sess, pt 4, at 64 (1990). Also, injunctive relief shall include, where appropriate, requiring the provision of an auxiliary aid or service, modification of a policy, or provision of alternative methods, to the extent required by title III of the Act and this part.

Section 36.502 is based on section 308(b)(1)(A)(i) of the Act, which provides that the Attorney General shall investigate alleged violations of title III and undertake periodic reviews of compliance of covered entities. Although the

Act does not establish a comprehensive administrative enforcement mechanism for investigation and resolution of all complaints received, the legislative history notes that investigation of alleged violations and periodic compliance reviews are essential to effective enforcement of title III, and that the Attorney General is expected to engage in active enforcement and to allocate sufficient resources to carry out this responsibility. Judiciary Report at 67.

Many commenters argued for inclusion of more specific provisions for administrative resolution of disputes arising under the Act and this part in order to promote voluntary compliance and avoid the need for litigation. Administrative resolution is far more efficient and economical than litigation, particularly in the early stages of implementation of complex legislation when the specific requirements of the statute are not widely understood. The Department has added a new paragraph (c) to this section authorizing the Attorney General to initiate a compliance review where he or she has reason to believe there may be a violation of this rule.

Section 36.503 describes the procedures for suits by the Attorney General set out in section 308(b)(1)(B) of the Act. If the Department has reasonable cause to believe that any person or group of persons is engaged in a pattern or practice of resistance to the full enjoyment of any of the rights granted by title III or that any person or group of persons has been denied any of the rights granted by title III and such denial raises an issue of general public importance, the Attorney General may commence a civil action in any appropriate United States district court. The proposed rule provided for suit by the Attorney General "or his or her designee." The reference to a "designee" has been omitted in the final rule because it is unnecessary. The Attorney General has delegated enforcement authority under the ADA to the Assistant Attorney General for Civil

Rights. 55 FR 40653 (October 4, 1990) (to be codified at 28 CFR 0.50(l).)

Section 36.504 describes the relief that may be granted in a suit by the Attorney General under section 308(b)(2) of the Act. In such an action, the court may grant any equitable relief it considers to be appropriate, including granting temporary, preliminary, or permanent relief, providing an auxiliary aid or service, modification of policy or alternative method, or making facilities readily accessible to and usable by individuals with disabilities, to the extent required by title III. In addition, a court may award such other relief as the court considers to be appropriate, including monetary damages to persons aggrieved, when requested by the Attorney General.

Furthermore, the court may vindicate the public interest by assessing a civil penalty against the covered entity in an amount not exceeding $50,000 for a first violation and not exceeding $100,000 for any subsequent violation. Section 36.504(b) of the rule adopts the standard of section 308(b)(3) of the Act. This section makes it clear that, in counting the number of previous determinations of violations for determining whether a "first" or "subsequent" violation has occurred, determinations in the same action that the entity has engaged in more than one discriminatory act are to be counted as a single violation. A "second violation" would not accrue to that entity until the Attorney General brought another suit against the entity and the entity was again held in violation. Again, all of the violations found in the second suit would be cumulatively considered as a "subsequent violation."

Section 36.504(c) clarifies that the terms "monetary damages" and "other relief" do not include punitive damages. They do include, however, all forms of compensatory damages, including out-of-pocket expenses and damages for pain and suffering.

Section 36.504(a)(3) is based on section 308(b)(2)(C) of the Act, which provides that, "to vindicate the public interest," a court may assess a civil penalty against the entity that has been found to be in violation of the Act in suits brought by the Attorney General. In addition, § 36.504(d), which is taken from section 308(b)(5) of the Act, further provides that, in considering what amount of civil penalty, if any, is appropriate, the court shall give consideration to "any good faith effort or attempt to comply with this part." In evaluating such good faith, the court shall consider "among other factors it deems relevant, whether the entity could have reasonably anticipated the need for an appropriate type of auxiliary aid needed to accommodate the unique needs of a particular individual with a disability."

The "good faith" standard referred to in this section is not intended to imply a willful or intentional standard—that is, an entity cannot demonstrate good faith simply by showing that it did not willfully, intentionally, or recklessly disregard the law. At the same time, the absence of such a course of conduct would be a factor a court should weigh in determining the existence of good faith.

Section 36.505 states that courts are authorized to award attorneys fees, including litigation expenses and costs, as provided in section 505 of the Act. Litigation expenses include items such as expert witness fees, travel expenses, etc. The Judiciary Committee Report specifies that such items are included under the rubric of "attorneys fees" and not "costs" so that such expenses will be assessed against a plaintiff only under the standard set forth in *Christiansburg Garment Co. v. Equal Employment Opportunity Commission*, 434 U.S. 412 (1978). (Judiciary report at 73.)

Section 36.506 restates section 513 of the Act, which encourages use of alternative means of dispute resolution. Section 36.507 explains that, as provided in section 506(e) of the Act, a public accommodation or other private entity is not excused from compliance with the requirements of this part because of any failure to receive technical assistance.

Section 36.305 Effective Date

In general, title III is effective 18 months after enactment of the Americans with Disabilities Act, i.e., January 26, 1992. However, there are several exceptions to this general rule contained throughout title III. Section 36.508 sets forth all of these exceptions in one place.

Paragraph (b) contains the rule on civil actions. It states that, except with respect to new construction and alterations, no civil action shall be brought for a violation of this part that occurs before July 26, 1992, against businesses with 25 or fewer employees and gross receipts of $1,000,000 or less; and before January 26, 1993, against businesses with 10 or fewer employees and gross receipts of $500,000 or less. In determining what constitutes gross receipts, it is appropriate to exclude amounts collected for sales taxes.

Paragraph (c) concerns transportation services provided by public accommodations not primarily engaged in the business of transporting people. The 18-month effective date applies to all of the transportation provisions except those requiring newly purchased or leased vehicles to be accessible. Vehicles subject to that requirement must be accessible to and usable by individuals with disabilities if the solicitation for the vehicle is made on or after August 26, 1990.

Subpart F—Certification of State Labs or Local Building Codes

Subpart F establishes procedures to implement section 308(b)(1)(A)(ii) of the Act, which provides that, on the application of a State or local government, the Attorney General may certify that a State law or local building code or similar ordinance meets or exceeds the minimum accessibility requirements of the Act. In enforcement proceedings, this certification will constitute rebuttable evidence that the law or code meets or exceeds the ADA's requirements.

Three significant changes, further explained below, were made from the proposed subpart, in response to comments. First, the State or local jurisdiction is required to hold a public hearing on its proposed request for certification and to submit to the Department, as part of the information and materials in support of a request for certification, a transcript of the hearing. Second, the time allowed for interested persons and organizations to comment on the request filed with the Department (§ 36.605(a)(1)) has been changed from 30 to 60 days. Finally, a new § 36.608, Guidance concerning model codes, has been added.

Section 36.601 establishes the definitions to be used for purposes of this subpart. Two of the definitions have been modified, and a definition of "model code" has been added. First, in response to a comment, a reference to a code "or part thereof" has been added to the definition of "code." The purpose of this addition is to clarify that an entire code need not be submitted if only part of it is relevant to accessibility, or if the jurisdiction seeks certification of only some of the portions that concern accessibility. The Department does not intend to encourage "piece-meal" requests for certification by a single jurisdiction. In fact, the Department expects that in some cases, rather than certifying portions of a particular code and refusing to certify others, it may notify a submitting jurisdiction of deficiencies and encourage a reapplication that cures those deficiencies, so that the entire code can be certified eventually. Second, the definition of "submitting official" has been modified. The proposed rule defined the submitting official to be the State or local official who has principal responsibility for administration of a code. Commenters pointed out that in some cases more than one code within the same jurisdiction is relevant for purposes of certification. It was also suggested that the Department

allow a State to submit a single application on behalf of the State, as well as on behalf of any local jurisdictions required to follow the State accessibility requirements. Consistent with these comments, the Department has added to the definition language clarifying that the official can be one authorized to submit a code on behalf of a jurisdiction.

A definition of "model code" has been added in light of new § 36.608.

Most commenters generally approved of the proposed certification process. Some approved of what they saw as the Department's attempt to bring State and local codes into alignment with the ADA. A State agency said that this section will be the backbone of the intergovernmental cooperation essential if the accessibility provisions of the ADA are to be effective.

Some comments disapproved of the proposed process as time-consuming and laborious for the Department, although some of these comments pointed out that, if the Attorney General certified model codes on which State and local codes are based, many perceived problems would be alleviated. (This point is further addressed by new § 36.608.)

Many of the comments received from business organizations, as well as those from some individuals and disability rights groups, addressed the relationship of the ADA requirements and their enforcement, to existing State and local codes and code enforcement systems. These commenters urged the Department to use existing code-making bodies for interpretations of the ADA, and to actively participate in the integration of the ADA into the text of the national model codes that are adopted by State and local enforcement agencies. These issues are discussed in preamble section 36.406 under General comments.

Many commenters urged the Department to evaluate or certify the entire code enforcement system (including any process for hearing appeals from builders of denials by the

building code official of requests for variances, waivers, or modifications). Some urged that certification not be allowed in jurisdictions where waivers can be granted, unless there is a clearly identified decision-making process, with written rulings and notice to affected parties of any waiver or modification request. One commenter urged establishment of a dispute resolution mechanism, providing for interpretation (usually through a building official) and an administrative appeals mechanism (generally called Boards of Appeal, Boards of Construction Appeals, or Boards of Review), before certification could be granted.

The Department thoroughly considered these proposals but has declined to provide for certification of processes of enforcement or administration of State and local codes. The statute clearly authorizes the Department to certify the codes themselves for equivalency with the statute; it would be ill-advised for the Department at this point to inquire beyond the face of the code and written interpretations of it. It would be inappropriate to require those jurisdictions that grant waivers or modifications to establish certain procedures before they can apply for certification, or to insist that no deviations can be permitted. In fact, the Department expects that many jurisdictions will allow slight variations from a particular code, consistent with ADAAG itself. ADAAG includes in § 2.2 a statement allowing departures from particular requirements where substantially equivalent or greater access and usability is provided. Several sections specifically allow for alternative methods providing equivalent facilitation and, in some cases, provide examples. (See, e.g., section 4.31.9, Text Telephones; section 7.2(2) (iii), Sales and Service Counters.) Section 4.1.6 includes less stringent requirements that are permitted in alterations, in certain circumstances.

However, in an attempt to ensure that it does not certify a code that in practice has been or will be applied in a manner that defeats its equivalency with the ADA, the Department will require that the submitting official include, with the application for certification, any relevant manuals, guides, or any other interpretive information issued that pertain to the code. (§ 36.603(c)(1).) The requirement that this information be provided is in addition to the NPRM's requirement that the official provide any pertinent formal opinions of the State Attorney General or the chief legal officer of the jurisdiction.

The first step in the certification process is a request for certification, filed by a "submitting official" (§ 36.603). The Department will not accept requests for certification until after January 26, 1992, the effective date of this part. The Department received numerous comments from individuals and organizations representing a variety of interests, urging that the hearing required to be held by the Assistant Attorney General in Washington, DC, after a preliminary determination of equivalency (§ 36.605(a)(2)), be held within the State or locality requesting certification, in order to facilitate greater participation by all interested parties. While the Department has not modified the requirement that it hold a hearing in Washington, it has added a new subparagraph 36.603(b)(3) requiring a hearing within the State or locality before a request for certification is filed. The hearing must be held after adequate notice to the public and must be on the record; a transcript must be provided with the request for certification. This procedure will insure input from the public at the State or local level and will also insure a Washington, DC, hearing as mentioned in the legislative history.

The request for certification, along with supporting documents (§ 36.603(c)), must be filed in duplicate with the office of the Assistant Attorney General for Civil Rights. The Assistant Attorney General may request further information. The request and supporting materials will be available for public examination at the office

of the Assistant Attorney General and at the office of the State or local agency charged with administration and enforcement of the code. The submitting official must publish public notice of the request for certification.

Next, under § 36.604, the Assistant Attorney General's office will consult with the ATBCB and make a preliminary determination to either (1) find that the code is equivalent (make a "preliminary determination of equivalency") or (2) deny certification. The next step depends on which of these preliminary determinations is made.

If the preliminary determination is to find equivalency, the Assistant Attorney General, under § 36.605, will inform the submitting official in writing of the preliminary determination and publish a notice in the **Federal Register** informing the public of the preliminary determination and inviting comment for 60 days. (This time period has been increased from 30 days in light of public comment pointing out the need for more time within which to evaluate the code.) After considering the information received in response to the comments, the Department will hold an hearing in Washington. This hearing will not be subject to the formal requirements of the Administrative Procedure Act. In fact, this requirement could be satisfied by a meeting with interested parties. After the hearing, the Assistant Attorney General's office will consult again with the ATBCB and make a final determination of equivalency or a final determination to deny the request for certification, with a notice of the determination published in the Federal Register.

If the preliminary determination is to deny certification, there will be no hearing (§ 36.606). The Department will notify the submitting official of the preliminary determination, and may specify how the code could be modified in order to receive a preliminary determination of equivalency. The Department will allow at least 15 days for the submitting

official to submit relevant material in opposition to the preliminary denial. If none is received, no further action will be taken. If more information is received, the Department will consider it and make either a final decision to deny certification or a preliminary determination of equivalency. If at that stage the Assistant Attorney General makes a preliminary determination of equivalency, the hearing procedures set out in § 36.605 will be followed.

Section 36.607 addresses the effect of certification. First, certification will only be effective concerning those features or elements that are both (1) covered by the certified code and (2) addressed by the regulations against which they are being certified. For example, if children's facilities are not addressed by the Department's standards, and the building in question is a private elementary school, certification will not be effective for those features of the building to be used by children. And if the Department's regulations addressed equipment but the local code did not, a building's equipment would not be covered by the certification.

In addition, certification will be effective only for the particular edition of the code that is certified. Amendments will not automatically be considered certified, and a submitting official will need to reapply for certification of the changed or additional provisions.

Certification will not be effective in those situations where a State or local building code official allows a facility to be constructed or altered in a manner that does not follow the technical or scoping provisions of the certified code. Thus, if an official either waives an accessible element or feature or allows a change that does not provide equivalent facilitation, the fact that the Department has certified the code itself will not stand as evidence that the facility has been constructed or altered in accordance with the minimum accessibility requirements of the ADA. The Department's certification of a code is effective only with respect to the standards in the code; it is not to be interpreted to apply to a State or local government's application of the code. The fact that the Department has certified a code with provisions concerning waivers, variances, or equivalent facilitation shall not be interpreted as an endorsement of actions taken pursuant to those provisions.

The final rule includes a new § 36.608 concerning model codes. It was drafted in response to concerns raised by numerous commenters, many of which have been discussed under General comments (§ 36.406). It is intended to assist in alleviating the difficulties posed by attempting to certify possibly tens of thousands of codes. It is included in recognition of the fact that many codes are based on, or incorporate, model or consensus standards developed by nationally recognized organizations (e.g., the American National Standards Institute (ANSI); Building Officials and Code Administrators (BOCA) International; Council of American Building Officials (CABO) and its Board for the Coordination of Model Codes (BCMC); Southern Building Code Congress International (SBCCI)). While the Department will not certify or "precertify" model codes, as urged by some commenters, it does wish to encourage the continued viability of the consensus and model code process consistent with the purposes of the ADA.

The new section therefore allows an authorized representative of a private entity responsible for developing a model code to apply to the Assistant Attorney General for review of the code. The review process will be informal and will not be subject to the procedures of §§ 36.602 through 36.607. The result of the review will take the form of guidance from the Assistant Attorney General as to whether and in what respects the model code is consistent with the ADA's requirements. The guidance will not be binding on any entity or on the Department; it will assist in evaluations of individual State or local codes and may serve as a basis for establishing priorities for consideration of individual codes. The Department anticipates that this approach will foster further cooperation among various government levels, the private entities developing standards, and individuals with disabilities.

List of Subjects in 28 CFR Part 36

Administrative practice and procedure, Alcoholism, Americans with disabilities, Buildings, Business and industry, Civil rights, Consumer protection, Drug abuse, Handicapped, Historic preservation, Reporting and recordkeeping requirements.

By the authority vested in me as Attorney General by 28 U.S.C. 509, 510, 5 U.S.C. 301, and section 306(b) of the Americans with Disabilities Act, Public Law 101-336, and for the reasons set forth in the preamble, Chapter I of title 28 of the Code of Federal Regulations is amended by adding a new part 36 to read as follows:

PART 36– NONDISCRIMINATION ON THE BASIS OF DISABILITY BY PUBLIC ACCOMMODATIONS AND IN COMMERCIAL FACILITIES

Subpart A–General

Sec.
36.101 Purpose.
36.102 Application.
36.103 Relationship to other laws.
36.104 Definitions.
36.105-36.200 [Reserved]

Subpart B–General Requirements

36.201 General.
36.202 Activities.
36.203 Integrated settings.
36.204 Administrative methods.
36.205 Association.
36.206 Retaliation or coercion.
36.207 Places of public accommodations located in private residences.
36.208 Direct threat.
36.209 Illegal use of drugs.
36.210 Smoking.
36.211 Maintenance of accessible features.
36.212 Insurance.

36.213 Relationship of subpart B to subparts C and D of this part.
36.214-36.300 [Reserved]

Subpart C–Specific Requirements

36.301 Eligibility criteria.
36.302 Modifications in policies, practices, or procedures.
36.303 Auxiliary aids and services.
36.304 Removal of barriers.
36.305 Alternatives to barrier removal.
36.306 Personal devices and services.
36.307 Accessible or special goods.
36.308 Seating in assembly areas.
36.309 Examinations and courses.
36.310 Transportation provided by public accommodations.
36.311-36.400 [Reserved]

Subpart D–New Construction and Alterations

36.401 New construction.
36.402 Alterations.
36.403 Alterations: Path of travel.
36.404 Alterations: Elevator exemption.
36.405 Alterations: Historic preservation.
36.406 Standards for new construction and alterations.
36.407-36.500 [Reserved]

Subpart E–Enforcement

36.501 Private suits.
36.502 Investigations and compliance reviews.
36.503 Suit by the Attorney General.
36.504 Relief.
36.505 Attorneys fees.
36.506 Alternative means of dispute resolution.
36.507 Effect of unavailability of technical assistance.
36.508 Effective date.
36.509-36.600 [Reserved]

Subpart F–Certification of State Laws or Local Building Codes

36.601 Definitions.
36.602 General rule.
36.603 Filing a request for certification.
36.604 Preliminary determination.
36.605 Procedure following preliminary determination of equivalency.
36.606 Procedure following preliminary denial of certification.
36.607 Effect of certification.
36.608 Guidance concerning model codes.
36.609-36.999 [Reserved]

Appendix A to Part 36–Standards for Accessible Design

Appendix B to Part 36–Preamble to Regulation on Nondiscrimination on the Basis of Disability by Public Accommodations and in

Commercial Facilities (Published July 26, 1991)
Authority: 5 U.S.C. 301; 28 U.S.C. 509, 510; Pub. L. 101-336, 42 U.S.C. 12186.

Subpart A—General

§ 36.101 Purpose.

The purpose of this part is to implement title III of the Americans with Disabilities Act of 1990 (42 U.S.C. 12181), which prohibits discrimination on the basis of disability by public accommodations and requires places of public accommodation and commercial facilities to be designed, constructed, and altered in compliance with the accessibility standards established by this part.

§ 36.102 Application.

(a) *General*. This part applies to any—
(1) Public accommodation;
(2) Commercial facility; or
(3) Private entity that offers examinations or courses related to applications, licensing, certification, or credentialing for secondary or postsecondary education, professional, or trade purposes.
(b) *Public accommodations*. (1) The requirements of this part applicable to public accommodations are set forth in subparts B, C, and D of this part.
(2) The requirements of subparts B and C of this part obligate a public accommodation only with respect to the operations of a place of public accommodation.
(3) The requirements of subpart D of this part obligate a public accommodation only with respect to—
(i) A facility used as, or designed or constructed for use as, a place of public accommodation; or
(ii) A facility used as, or designed and constructed for use as, a commercial facility.
(c) *Commercial facilities*. The requirements of this part applicable to commercial facilities are set forth in subpart D of this part.
(d) *Examinations and courses*. The requirements of this part applicable to private entities that offer examinations or

courses asspecified in paragraph (a) of this section are set forth in § 36.309.
(e) *Exemptions and exclusions*. This part does not apply to any private club (except to the extent that the facilities of the private club are made available to customers or patrons of a place of public accommodation), or to any religious entity or public entity.

§ 36.103 Relationship to other laws.

(a) *Rule of interpretation*. Except as otherwise provided in this part, this part shall not be construed to apply a lesser standard than the standards applied under title V of the Rehabilitation Act of 1973 (29 U.S.C. 791) or the regulations issued by Federal agencies pursuant to that title.
(b) *Section 504*. This part does not affect the obligations of a recipient of Federal financial assistance to comply with the requirements of section 504 of the Rehabilitation Act of 1973 (29 U.S.C. 794) and regulations issued by Federal agencies implementing section 504.
(c) *Other laws*. This part does not invalidate or limit the remedies, rights, and procedures of any other Federal laws, or State or local laws (including State common law) that provide greater or equal protection for the rights of individuals with disabilities or individuals associated with them.

§ 36.104 Definitions.

For purposes of this part, the term—

Act means the Americans with Disabilities Act of 1990 (Pub. L. 101-336, 104 Stat. 327, 42 U.S.C. 12101-12213 and 47 U.S.C. 225 and 611).

Commerce means travel, trade, traffic, commerce, transportation, or communication—
(1) Among the several States;
(2) Between any foreign country or any territory or possession and any State; or
(3) Between points in the same State but through another State or foreign country.

Commercial facilities means facilities—
(1) Whose operations will affect commerce;
(2) That are intended for nonresidential use by a private entity; and (3) That are not—
(i) Facilities that are covered or expressly exempted from coverage under the Fair Housing Act of 1968, as amended (42 U.S.C. 3601-3631);
(ii) Aircraft; or
(iii) Railroad locomotives, railroad freight cars, railroad cabooses, commuter or intercity passenger rail cars (including coaches, dining cars, sleeping cars, lounge cars, and food service cars), any other railroad cars described in section 242 of the Act or covered under title II of the Act, or railroad rights-of-way. For purposes of this definition, "rail" and "railroad" have the meaning given the term "railroad" in section 202(e) of the Federal Railroad Safety Act of 1970 (45 U.S.C. 431(e)).

Current illegal use of drugs means illegal use of drugs that occurred recently enough to justify a reasonable belief that a person's drug use is current or that continuing use is a real and ongoing problem.

Disability means, with respect to an individual, a physical or mental impairment that substantially limits one or more of the major life activities of such individual; a record of such an impairment; or being regarded as having such an impairment.
(1) The phrase *physical or mental impairment* means—
(i) Any physiological disorder or condition, cosmetic disfigurement, or anatomical loss affecting one or more of the following body systems: neurological; musculoskeletal; special sense organs; respiratory, including speech organs; cardiovascular; reproductive; digestive; genitourinary; hemic and symphatic; skin; and endocrine;
(ii) Any mental or psychological disorder such as mental retardation, organic brain syndrome, emotional or mental illness, and specific learning disabilities;
(iii) The phrase physical or mental impairment includes,

but is not limited to, such contagious and noncontagious diseases and conditions as orthopedic, visual, speech, and hearing impairments, cerebral palsy, epilepsy, muscular dystrophy, multiple sclerosis, cancer, heart disease, diabetes, mental retardation, emotional illness, specific learning disabilities, HIV disease (whether symptomatic or asymptomatic), tuberculosis, drug addiction, and alcoholism;

(iv) The phrase *physical or mental impairment* does not include homosexuality or bisexuality.

(2) The phrase *major life activities* means functions such as caring for one's self, performing manual tasks, walking, seeing, hearing, speaking, breathing, learning, and working.

(3) The phrase *has a record of such an impairment* means has a history of, or has been misclassified as having, a mental or physical impairment that substantially limits one or more major life activities.

(4) The phrase *is regarded as having an impairment* means—

(i) Has a physical or mental impairment that does not substantially limit major life activities but that is treated by a private entity as constituting such a limitation;

(ii) Has a physical or mental impairment that substantially limits major life activities only as a result of the attitudes of others toward such impairment; or

(iii) Has none of the impairments defined in paragraph (1) of this definition but is treated by a private entity as having such an impairment.

(5) The term *disability* does not include—

(i) Transvestism, transsexualism, pedophilia, exhibitionism, voyeurism, gender identity disorders not resulting from physical impairments, or other sexual behavior disorders;

(ii) Compulsive gambling, kleptomania, or pyromania; or

(iii) Psychoactive substance use disorders resulting from current illegal use of drugs.

Drug means a controlled substance, as defined in schedules I through V of section 202 of the Controlled Substances Act (21 U.S.C. 812).

Facility means all or any portion of buildings, structures, sites, complexes, equipment, rolling stock or other conveyances, roads, walks, passageways, parking lots, or other real or personal property, including the site where the building, property, structure, or equipment is located.

Illegal use of drugs means the use of one or more drugs, the possession or distribution of which is unlawful under the Controlled Substances Act (21 U.S.C. 812). The term "illegal use of drugs" does not include the use of a drug taken under supervision by a licensed health care professional, or other uses authorized by the Controlled Substances Act or other provisions of Federal law.

Individual with a disability means a person who has a disability. The term "individual with a disability" does not include an individual who is currently engaging in the illegal use of drugs, when the private entity acts on the basis of such use.

Place of public accommodation means a facility, operated by a private entity, whose operations affect commerce and fall within at least one of the following categories—

(1) An inn, hotel, motel, or other place of lodging, except for an establishment located within a building that contains not more than five rooms for rent or hire and that is actually occupied by the proprietor of the establishment as the residence of the proprietor;

(2) A restaurant, bar, or other establishment serving food or drink;

(3) A motion picture house, theater, concert hall, stadium, or other place of exhibition or entertainment;

(4) An auditorium, convention center, lecture hall, or other place of public gathering;

(5) A bakery, grocery store, clothing store, hardware store, shopping center, or other sales or rental establishment;

(6) A laundromat, dry-cleaner, bank, barber shop, beauty shop, travel service, shoe repair service, funeral parlor, gas station, office of an accountant or lawyer, pharmacy, insurance office, professional office of a health care provider, hospital, or other service establishment;

(7) A terminal, depot, or other station used for specified public transportation;

(8) A museum, library, gallery, or other place of public display or collection;

(9) A park, zoo, amusement park, or other place of recreation;

(10) A nursery, elementary, secondary, undergraduate, or postgraduate private school, or other place of education;

(11) A day care center, senior citizen center, homeless shelter, food bank, adoption agency, or other social service center establishment; and

(12) A gymnasium, health spa, bowling alley, golf course, or other place of exercise or recreation.

Private club means a private club or establishment exempted from coverage under title II of the Civil Rights Act of 1964 (42 U.S.C. 2000a(e)).

Private entity means a person or entity other than a public entity.

Public accommodation means a private entity that owns, leases (or leases to), or operates a place of public accommodation.

Public entity means—

(1) Any State or local government;

(2) Any department, agency, special purpose district, or other instrumentality of a State or States or local government; and

(3) The National Railroad Passenger Corporation, and any commuter authority (as defined in section 103(8) of the Rail Passenger Service Act). (45 U.S.C. 541)

Qualified interpreter means an interpreter who is able to interpret effectively, accurately and impartially both receptively and expressively, using any necessary specialized vocabulary.

Readily achievable means easily accomplishable and able to be carried out without much difficulty or expense. In determining whether an action is readily achievable factors to be considered include—

(1) The nature and cost of the action needed under this part;

(2) The overall financial resources of the site or sites involved in the action; the number of persons employed at the site; the effect on expenses and resources; legitimate safety requirements that are necessary for safe operation, including crime prevention measures; or the impact otherwise of the action upon the operation of the site;

(3) The geographic separateness, and the administrative or fiscal relationship of the site or sites in question to any parent corporation or entity;

(4) If applicable, the overall financial resources of any parent corporation or entity; the overall size of the parent corporation or entity with respect to the number of its employees; the number, type, and location of its facilities; and

(5) If applicable, the type of operation or operations of any parent corporation or entity, including the composition, structure, and functions of the workforce of the parent corporation or entity.

Religious entity means a religious organization, including a place of worship.

Service animal means any guide dog, signal dog, or other animal individually trained to do work or perform tasks for the benefit of an individual with a disability, including, but not limited to, guiding individuals with impaired vision, alerting individuals with impaired hearing to intruders or sounds, providing minimal protection or rescue work, pulling a wheelchair, or fetching dropped items.

Specified public transportation means transportation by bus, rail, or any other conveyance (other than by aircraft) that provides the general public with general or special service (including charter service) on a regular and continuing basis.

State means each of the several States, the District of Columbia, the Commonwealth of Puerto Rico, Guam, American Samoa, the Virgin Islands, the Trust Territory of the Pacific Islands, and the Commonwealth of the Northern Mariana Islands.

Undue burden means significant difficulty or expense. In determining whether an action would result in an undue burden, factors to be considered include—

(1) The nature and cost of the action needed under this part;

(2) The overall financial resources of the site or sites involved in the action; the number of persons employed at the site; the effect on expenses and resources; legitimate safety requirements that are necessary for safe operation, including crime prevention measures; or the impact otherwise of the action upon the operation of the site;

(3) The geographic separateness, and the administrative or fiscal relationship of the site or sites in question to any parent corporation or entity;

(4) If applicable, the overall financial resources of any parent corporation or entity; the overall size of the parent corporation or entity with respect to the number of its employees; the number, type, and location of its facilities; and

(5) If applicable, the type of operation or operations of any parent corporation or entity, including the composition, structure, and functions of the workforce of the parent corporation or entity.

§§ 36.105-36.200 [Reserved]

Subpart B—General Requirements

§ 36.201 General.

(a) *Prohibition of discrimination.* No individual shall be discriminated against on the basis of disability in the full and equal enjoyment of the goods, services, facilities, privileges, advantages, or accommodations of any place of public accommodation by any private entity who owns, leases (or leases to), or operates a place of public accommodation.

(b) *Landlord and tenant responsibilities.* Both the landlord who owns the building that houses a place of public accommodation and the tenant who owns or operates the place of public accommodation are public accommodations subject to the requirements of this part. As between the parties, allocation of responsibility for complying with the obligations of this part may be determined by lease or other contract.

§ 36.202 Activities.

(a) *Denial of participation.* A public accommodation shall not subject an individual or class of individuals on the basis of a disability or disabilities of such individual or class, directly, or through contractual, licensing, or other arrangements, to a denial of the opportunity of the individual or class to participate in or benefit from the goods, services, facilities, privileges, advantages, or accommodations of a place of public accommodation.

(b) *Participation in unequal benefit.* A public accommodation shall not afford an individual or class of individuals, on the basis of a disability or disabilities of such individual or class, directly, or through contractual, licensing, or other arrangements, with the opportunity to participate in or benefit from a good, service, facility, privilege, advantage, or accommodation that is not equal to that afforded to other individuals.

(c) *Separate benefit.* A public accommodation shall not provide an individual or class of individuals, on the basis of a disability or disabilities of such individual or class, directly, or through contractual, licensing, or other arrangements with a good, service, facility, privilege, advantage, or accommodation that is different or separate from that provided to other individuals, unless such action is necessary to provide the individual or class of individuals with a good, service, facility, privilege, advantage, or accommodation, or other opportunity that is as effective as that provided to others.

(d) *Individual or class of individuals.* For purposes of paragraphs (a) through (c) of this section, the term "individual or class of individuals" refers to the clients or customers of the public accommodation that enters into the contractual, licensing, or other arrangement.

§ 36.203 Integrated settings.

(a) *General.* A public accommodation shall afford goods, services, facilities, privileges, advantages, and accommodations to an individual with a disability in the most integrated setting appropriate to the needs of the individual.

(b) *Opportunity to participate.* Notwithstanding the existence of separate or different programs or activities provided in accordance with this subpart, a public accommodation shall not deny an individual with a disability an opportunity to participate in such programs or activities that are not separate or different.

(c) *Accommodations and services.* (1) Nothing in this part shall be construed to require an individual with a disability to accept an accommodation, aid, service, opportunity, or benefit available under this part that such individual chooses not to accept.

(2) Nothing in the Act or this part authorizes the representative or guardian of an individual with a disability to decline food, water, medical treatment, or medical services for that individual.

§ 36.204 Administrative methods.

A public accommodation shall not, directly or through contractual or other arrangements, utilize standards or criteria or methods of administration that have the effect of discriminating on the basis of disability, or that perpetuate the discrimination of others who are subject to common administrative control.

§ 36.205 Association.

A public accommodation shall not exclude or otherwise deny equal goods, services, facilities, privileges, advantages, accommodations, or other opportunities to an individual or entity because of the known disability of an individual with whom the individual or entity is known to have a relationship or association.

§ 36.206 Retaliation or coercion.

(a) No private or public entity shall discriminate against any individual because that individual has opposed any act or practice made unlawful by this part, or because that individual made a charge, testified, assisted, or participated in any manner in an investigation, proceeding, or hearing under the Act or this part.

(b) No private or public entity shall coerce, intimidate, threaten, or interfere with any individual in the exercise or enjoyment of, or on account of his or her having exercised or enjoyed, or on account of his or her having aided or encouraged any other individual in the exercise or enjoyment of, any right granted or protected by the Act or this part.

(c) Illustrations of conduct prohibited by this section include, but are not limited to:

(1) Coercing an individual to deny or limit the benefits, services, or advantages to which he or she is entitled under the Act or this part;

(2) Threatening, intimidating, or interfering with an individual with a disability who is seeking to obtain or use the goods, services, facilities, privileges, advantages, or accommodations of a public accommodation;

(3) Intimidating or threatening any person because that person is assisting or encouraging an individual or group entitled to claim the rights granted or protected by the Act or this part to exercise those rights; or

(4) Retaliating against any person because that person has participated in any investigation or action to enforce the Act or this part.

§ 36.207 Places of public accommodation located in private residences.

(a) When a place of public accommodation is located in a private residence, the portion of the residence used exclusively as a residence is not covered by this part, but that portion used exclusively in the operation of the place of public accommodation or that portion used both for the place of public accommodation and for residential purposes is covered by this part.

(b) The portion of the residence covered under paragraph (a) of this section extends to those elements used to enter the place of public accommodation, including the homeowner's front sidewalk, if any, the door or entryway, and hallways; and those portions of the residence, interior or exterior, available to or used by customers or clients, including restrooms.

§ 36.208 Direct threat.

(a) This part does not require a public accommodation to permit an individual to participate in or benefit from the goods, services, facilities, privileges, advantages and accommodations of that public accommodation when that individual poses a direct threat to the health or safety of others.

(b) *Direct threat* means a significant risk to the health or safety of others that cannot be eliminated by a modification of policies, practices, or procedures, or by the provision of auxiliary aids or services.

(c) In determining whether an individual poses a direct threat to the health or safety of others, a public accommodation must make an individualized assessment, based on reasonable judgment that relies on current medical knowledge or on the best available objective evidence, to ascertain: the nature, duration, and severity of the risk; the probability that the potential injury will actually occur; and whether reasonable modifications of policies, practices, or procedures will mitigate the risk.

§ 36.209 Illegal use of drugs.

(a) *General.* (1) Except as provided in paragraph (b) of this section, this part does not prohibit discrimination against an individual based on that individual's current illegal use of drugs.

(2) A public accommodation shall not discriminate on the basis of illegal use of drugs against an individual who is not engaging in current illegal use of drugs and who—

(i) Has successfully completed a supervised drug rehabilitation program or has otherwise been rehabilitated successfully;

(ii) Is participating in a supervised rehabilitation program; or (iii) Is erroneously regarded as engaging in such use.

(b) *Health and drug rehabilitation services.* (1) A public accommodation shall not deny health services, or services provided in connection with drug rehabilitation, to an individual on the basis of that individual's current illegal use of drugs, if the individual is otherwise entitled to such services.

(2) A drug rehabilitation or treatment program may deny participation to individuals who engage in illegal use of drugs while they are in the program.

(c) *Drug testing.* (1) This part does not prohibit a public accommodation from adopting or administering reasonable policies or procedures, including but not limited to drug testing, designed to ensure that an individual who formerly engaged in the illegal use of drugs is not now engaging in current illegal use of drugs.

(2) Nothing in this paragraph (c) shall be construed to encourage, prohibit, restrict, or authorize the conducting of testing for the illegal use of drugs.

§ 36.210 Smoking.

This part does not preclude the prohibition of, or the imposition of restrictions on, smoking in places of public accommodation.

§ 36.211 Maintenance of accessible features.

(a) A public accommodation shall maintain in operable working condition those features of facilities and equipment that are required to be readily accessible to and

usable by persons with disabilities by the Act or this part.

(b) This section does not prohibit isolated or temporary interruptions in service or access due to maintenance or repairs.

§ 36.212 Insurance.

(a) This part shall not be construed to prohibit or restrict—

(1) An insurer, hospital or medical service company, health maintenance organization, or any agent, or entity that administers benefit plans, or similar organizations from underwriting risks, classifying risks, or administering such risks that are based on or not inconsistent with State law; or

(2) A person or organization covered by this part from establishing, sponsoring, observing or administering the terms of a bona fide benefit plan that are based on underwriting risks, classifying risks, or administering such risks that are based on or not inconsistent with State law; or

(3) A person or organization covered by this part from establishing, sponsoring, observing or administering the terms of a bona fide benefit plan that is not subject to State laws that regulate insurance.

(b) Paragraphs (a) (1), (2), and (3) of this section shall not be used as a subterfuge to evade the purposes of the Act or this part.

(c) A public accommodation shall not refuse to serve an individual with a disability because its insurance company conditions coverage or rates on the absence of individuals with disabilities.

§ 36.213 Relationship of subpart B to subparts C and D of this part.

Subpart B of this part sets forth the general principles of nondiscrimination applicable to all entities subject to this part. Subparts C and D of this part provide guidance on the application of the statute to specific situations. The specific provisions, including the limitations on those provisions, control over the general

provisions in circumstances where both specific and general provisions apply.

§§ 36.214-36.300 [Reserved]

Subpart C--Specific Requirements

§ 36.301 Eligibility criteria.

(a) *General.* A public accommodation shall not impose or apply eligibility criteria that screen out or tend to screen out an individual with a disability or any class of individuals with disabilities from fully and equally enjoying any goods, services, facilities, privileges, advantages, or accommodations, unless such criteria can be shown to be necessary for the provision of the goods, services, facilities, privileges, advantages, or accommodations being offered.

(b) *Safety.* A public accommodation may impose legitimate safety requirements that are necessary for safe operation. Safety requirements must be based on actual risks and not on mere speculation, stereotypes, or generalizations about individuals with disabilities.

(c) *Charges.* A public accommodation may not impose a surcharge on a particular individual with a disability or any group of individuals with disabilities to cover the costs of measures, such as the provision of auxiliary aids, barrier removal, alternatives to barrier removal, and reasonable modifications in policies, practices, or procedures, that are required to provide that individual or group with the nondiscriminatory treatment required by the Act or this part.

§ 36.302 Modifications in policies, practices, or procedures.

(a) *General.* A public accommodation shall make reasonable modifications in policies, practices, or procedures, when the modifications are necessary to afford goods, services, facilities, privileges, advantages, or accommodations to individuals with disabilities, unless the public accommodation can demonstrate that making the modifications would fundamentally alter the nature of the goods, services, facilities, privileges, advantages, or accommodations.

(b) *Specialties—*(1) *General.* A public accommodation may refer an individual with a disability to another public accommodation, if that individual is seeking, or requires, treatment or services outside of the referring public accommodation's area of specialization, and if, in the normal course of its operations, the referring public accommodation would make a similar referral for an individual without a disability who seeks or requires the same treatment or services.

(2) *Illustration—medical specialties.* A health care provider may refer an individual with a disability to another provider, if that individual is seeking, or requires, treatment or services outside of the referring provider's area of specialization, and if the referring provider would make a similar referral for an individual without a disability who seeks or requires the same treatment or services. A physician who specializes in treating only a particular condition cannot refuse to treat an individual with a disability for that condition, but is not required to treat the individual for a different condition.

(c) *Service animals—*(1) *General.* Generally, a public accommodation shall modify policies, practices, or procedures to permit the use of a service animal by an individual with a disability.

(2) *Care or supervision of service animals.* Nothing in this part requires a public accommodation to supervise or care for a service animal.

(d) *Check-out aisles.* A store with check-out aisles shall ensure that an adequate number of accessible check-out aisles are kept open during store hours, or shall otherwise modify its policies and practices, in order to ensure that an equivalent level of convenient service is provided to individuals with disabilities as

is provided to others. If only one check-out aisle is accessible, and it is generally used for express service, one way of providing equivalent service is to allow persons with mobility impairments to make all their purchases at that aisle.

§ 36.303 Auxiliary aids and services.

(a) *General.* A public accommodation shall take those steps that may be necessary to ensure that no individual with a disability is excluded, denied services, segregated or otherwise treated differently than other individuals because of the absence of auxiliary aids and services, unless the public accommodation can demonstrate that taking those steps would fundamentally alter the nature of the goods, services, facilities, privileges, advantages, or accommodations being offered or would result in an undue burden, i.e., significant difficulty or expense.

(b) *Examples.* The term "auxiliary aids and services" includes—

(1) Qualified interpreters, notetakers, computer-aided transcription services, written materials, telephone handset amplifiers, assistive listening devices, assistive listening systems, telephones compatible with hearing aids, closed caption decoders, open and closed captioning, telecommunications devices for deaf persons (TDD's), videotext displays, or other effective methods of making aurally delivered materials available to individuals with hearing impairments; ·

(2) Qualified readers, taped texts, audio recordings, Brailled materials, large print materials, or other effective methods of making visually delivered materials available to individuals with visual impairments;

(3) Acquisition or modification of equipment or devices; and

(4) Other similar services and actions.

(c) *Effective communication.* A public accommodation shall furnish appropriate auxiliary aids and services where necessary to ensure effective

communication with individuals with disabilities.

(d) *Telecommunication devices for the deaf (TDD's).* (1) A public accommodation that offers a customer, client, patient, or participant the opportunity to make outgoing telephone calls on more than an incidental convenience basis shall make available, upon request, a TDD for the use of an individual who has impaired hearing or a communication disorder.

(2) This part does not require a public accommodation to use a TDD for receiving or making telephone calls incident to its operations.

(e) *Closed caption decoders.* Places of lodging that provide televisions in five or more guest rooms and hospitals that provide televisions for patient use shall provide, upon request, a means for decoding captions for use by an individual with impaired hearing.

(f) *Alternatives.* If provision of a particular auxiliary aid or service by a public accommodation would result in a fundamental alteration in the nature of the goods, services, facilities, privileges, advantages, or accommodations being offered or in an undue burden, i.e., significant difficulty or expense, the public accommodation shall provide an alternative auxiliary aid or service, if one exists, that would not result in an alteration or such burden but would nevertheless ensure that, to the maximum extent possible, individuals with disabilities receive the goods, services, facilities, privileges, advantages, or accommodations offered by the public accommodation.

§ 36.304 Removal of barriers.

(a) *General.* A public accommodation shall remove architectural barriers in existing facilities, including communication barriers that are structural in nature, where such removal is readily achievable, i.e., easily accomplishable and able to be carried out without much difficulty or expense.

(b) *Examples.* Examples of steps to remove barriers include, but are not limited to, the following actions—

(1) Installing ramps;

(2) Making curb cuts in sidewalks and entrances;

(3) Repositioning shelves;

(4) Rearranging tables, chairs, vending machines, display racks, and other furniture;

(5) Repositioning telephones;

(6) Adding raised markings on elevator control buttons;

(7) Installing flashing alarm lights;

(8) Widening doors;

(9) Installing offset hinges to widen doorways;

(10) Eliminating a turnstile or providing an alternative accessible path;

(11) Installing accessible door hardware;

(12) Installing grab bars in toilet stalls;

(13) Rearranging toilet partitions to increase maneuvering space;

(14) Insulating lavatory pipes under sinks to prevent burns;

(15) Installing a raised toilet seat;

(16) Installing a full-length bathroom mirror;

(17) Repositioning the paper towel dispenser in a bathroom;

(18) Creating designated accessible parking spaces;

(19) Installing an accessible paper cup dispenser at an existing inaccessible water fountain;

(20) Removing high pile, low density carpeting; or

(21) Installing vehicle hand controls.

(c) *Priorities.* A public accommodation is urged to take measures to comply with the barrier removal requirements of this section in accordance with the following order of priorities.

(1) First, a public accommodation should take measures to provide access to a place of public accommodation from public sidewalks, parking, or public transportation. These measures include, for example, installing an entrance ramp, widening entrances, and providing accessible parking spaces.

(2) Second, a public accommodation should take measures to provide access to those areas of a place of public accommodation where goods and services are made available to the public. These measures include, for example, adjusting the layout of display racks, rearranging tables, providing Brailled and raised character signage, widening doors, providing visual alarms, and installing ramps.

(3) Third, a public accommodation should take measures to provide access to restroom facilities. These measures include, for example, removal of obstructing furniture or vending machines, widening of doors, installation of ramps, providing accessible signage, widening of toilet stalls, and installation of grab bars.

(4) Fourth, a public accommodation should take any other measures necessary to provide access to the goods, services, facilities, privileges, advantages, or accommodations of a place of public accommodation.

(d) *Relationship to alterations requirements of subpart D of this part.* (1) Except as provided in paragraph (d)(2) of this section, measures taken to comply with the barrier removal requirements of this section shall comply with the applicable requirements for alterations in § 36.402 and §§ 36.404-36.406 of this part for the element being altered. The path of travel requirements of § 36.403 shall not apply to measures taken solely to comply with the barrier removal requirements of this section.

(2) If, as a result of compliance with the alterations requirements specified in paragraph (d)(1) of this section, the measures required to remove a barrier would not be readily achievable, a public accommodation may take other readily achievable measures to remove the barrier that do not fully comply with the specified requirements. Such measures include, for example, providing a ramp with a steeper slope or widening a doorway to a narrower width than that mandated by the alterations requirements. No measure shall be taken, however, that poses a significant risk to the health or safety of individuals with disabilities or others.

(e) *Portable ramps.* Portable ramps should be used to comply with this section only when installation of a permanent ramp is not readily achievable. In order to avoid any significant risk to the health or safety of individuals with disabilities or others in using portable ramps, due consideration shall be given to safety features such as nonslip surfaces, railings, anchoring, and strength of materials.

(f) *Selling or serving space.* The rearrangement of temporary or movable structures, such as furniture, equipment, and display racks is not readily achievable to the extent that it results in a significant loss of selling or serving space.

(g) *Limitation on barrier removal obligations.* (1) The requirements for barrier removal under § 36.304 shall not be interpreted to exceed the standards for alterations in subpart D of this part.

(2) To the extent that relevant standards for alterations are not provided in subpart D of this part, then the requirements of § 36.304 shall not be interpreted to exceed the standards for new construction in subpart D of this part.

(3) This section does not apply to rolling stock and other conveyances to the extent that § 36.310 applies to rolling stock and other conveyances.

§ 36.305 Alternatives to barrier removal.

(a) *General.* Where a public accommodation can demonstrate that barrier removal is not readily achievable, the public accommodation shall not fail to make its goods, services, facilities, privileges, advantages, or accommodations available through alternative methods, if those methods are readily achievable.

(b) *Examples.* Examples of alternatives to barrier removal include, but are not limited to, the following actions—

(1) Providing curb service or home delivery;

(2) Retrieving merchandise from inaccessible shelves or racks;

(3) Relocating activities to accessible locations;

(c) *Multiscreen cinemas*. If it is not readily achievable to remove barriers to provide access by persons with mobility impairments to all of the theaters of a multiscreen cinema, the cinema shall establish a film rotation schedule that provides reasonable access for individuals who use wheelchairs to all films. Reasonable notice shall be provided to the public as to the location and time of accessible showings.

§ 36.306 **Personal devices and services.**

This part does not require a public accommodation to provide its customers, clients, or participants with personal devices, such as wheelchairs; individually prescribed devices, such as prescription eyeglasses or hearing aids; or services of a personal nature including assistance in eating, toileting, or dressing.

§ 36.307 **Accessible or special goods.**

(a) This part does not require a public accommodation to alter its inventory to include accessible or special goods that are designed for, or facilitate use by, individuals with disabilities.

(b) A public accommodation shall order accessible or special goods at the request of an individual with disabilities, if, in the normal course of its operation, it makes special orders on request for unstocked goods, and if the accessible or special goods can be obtained from a supplier with whom the public accommodation customarily does business.

(c) Examples of accessible or special goods include items such as Brailled versions of books, books on audio cassettes, closed-captioned video tapes, special sizes or lines of clothing, and special foods to meet particular dietary needs.

§ 36.308 **Seating in assembly areas.**

(a) *Existing facilities*. (1) To the extent that it is readily achievable, a public accommodation in assembly areas shall—

(i) Provide a reasonable number of wheelchair seating spaces and seats with removable aisle-side arm rests; and

(ii) Locate the wheelchair seating spaces so that they—

(A) Are dispersed throughout the seating area;

(B) Provide lines of sight and choice of admission prices comparable to those for members of the general public;

(C) Adjoin an accessible route that also serves as a means of egress in case of emergency; and

(D) Permit individuals who use wheelchairs to sit with family members or other companions.

(2) If removal of seats is not readily achievable, a public accommodation shall provide, to the extent that it is readily achievable to do so, a portable chair or other means to permit a family member or other companion to sit with an individual who uses a wheelchair.

(3) The requirements of paragraph (a) of this section shall not be interpreted to exceed the standards for alterations in subpart D of this part.

(b) *New construction and alterations*. The provision and location of wheelchair seating spaces in newly constructed or altered assembly areas shall be governed by the standards for new construction and alterations in subpart D of this part.

§ 36.309 **Examinations and courses.**

(a) *General*. Any private entity that offers examinations or courses related to applications, licensing, certification, or credentialing for secondary or postsecondary education, professional, or trade purposes shall offer such examinations or courses in a place and manner accessible to persons with disabilities or offer alternative accessible arrangements for such individuals.

(b) *Examinations*. (1) Any private entity offering an examination covered by this section must assure that—

(i) The examination is selected and administered so as to best ensure that, when the examination is administered to

an individual with a disability that impairs sensory, manual, or speaking skills, the examination results accurately reflect the individual's aptitude or achievement level or whatever other factor the examination purports to measure, rather than reflecting the individual's impaired sensory, manual, or speaking skills (except where those skills are the factors that the examination purports to measure);

(ii) An examination that is designed for individuals with impaired sensory, manual, or speaking skills is offered at equally convenient locations, as often, and in as timely a manner as are other examinations; and

(iii) The examination is administered in facilities that are accessible to individuals with disabilities or alternative accessible arrangements are made.

(2) Required modifications to an examination may include changes in the length of time permitted for completion of the examination and adaptation of the manner in which the examination is given.

(3) A private entity offering an examination covered by this section shall provide appropriate auxiliary aids for persons with impaired sensory, manual, or speaking skills, unless that private entity can demonstrate that offering a particular auxiliary aid would fundamentally alter the measurement of the skills or knowledge the examination is intended to test or would result in an undue burden. Auxiliary aids and services required by this section may include taped examinations, interpreters or other effective methods of making orally delivered materials available to individuals with hearing impairments, Brailled or large print examinations and answer sheets or qualified readers for individuals with visual impairments or learning disabilities, transcribers for individuals with manual impairments, and other similar services and actions.

(4) Alternative accessible arrangements may include, for example, provision of an examination at an individual's home with a proctor if

accessible facilities or equipment are unavailable. Alternative arrangements must provide comparable conditions to those provided for nondisabled individuals.

(c) *Courses.* (1) Any private entity that offers a course covered by this section must make such modifications to that course as are necessary to ensure that the place and manner in which the course is given are accessible to individuals with disabilities.

(2) Required modifications may include changes in the length of time permitted for the completion of the course, substitution of specific requirements, or adaptation of the manner in which the course is conducted or course materials are distributed.

(3) A private entity that offers a course covered by this section shall provide appropriate auxiliary aids and services for persons with impaired sensory, manual, or speaking skills, unless the private entity can demonstrate that offering a particular auxiliary aid or service would fundamentally alter the course or would result in an undue burden. Auxiliary aids and services required by this section may include taped texts, interpreters or other effective methods of making orally delivered materials available to individuals with hearing impairments, Brailled or large print texts or qualified readers for individuals with visual impairments and learning disabilities, classroom equipment adapted for use by individuals with manual impairments, and other similar services and actions.

(4) Courses must be administered in facilities that are accessible to individuals with disabilities or alternative accessible arrangements must be made.

(5) Alternative accessible arrangements may include, for example, provision of the course through videotape, cassettes, or prepared notes. Alternative arrangements must provide comparable conditions to those provided for nondisabled individuals.

§ 36.310 Transportation provided by public accommodations.

(a) *General.* (1) A public accommodation that provides transportation services, but that is not primarily engaged in the business of transporting people, is subject to the general and specific provisions in subparts B, C, and D of this part for its transportation operations, except as provided in this section.

(2) *Examples.* Transportation services subject to this section include, but are not limited to, shuttle services operated between transportation terminals and places of public accommodation, customer shuttle bus services operated by private companies and shopping centers, student transportation systems, and transportation provided within recreational facilities such as stadiums, zoos, amusement parks, and ski resorts.

(b) *Barrier removal.* A public accommodation subject to this section shall remove transportation barriers in existing vehicles and rail passenger cars used for transporting individuals (not including barriers that can only be removed through the retrofitting of vehicles or rail passenger cars by the installation of a hydraulic or other lift) where such removal is readily achievable.

(c) *Requirements for vehicles and systems.* A public accommodation subject to this section shall comply with the requirements pertaining to vehicles and transportation systems in the regulations issued by the Secretary of Transportation pursuant to section 306 of the Act.

§ § 36.311-36.400 [Reserved]

Subpart D--New Construction and Alterations

§ 36.401 New construction.

(a) *General.* (1) Except as provided in paragraphs (b) and (c) of this section, discrimination for purposes of this part includes a failure to design and construct facilities for first occupancy after January 26, 1993, that are readily accessible to and usable by individuals with disabilities.

(2) For purposes of this section, a facility is designed and constructed for first occupancy after January 26, 1993, only—

(i) If the last application for a building permit or permit extension for the facility is certified to be complete, by a State, County, or local government after January 26, 1992 (or, in those jurisdictions where the government does not certify completion of applications, if the last application for a building permit or permit extension for the facility is received by the State, County, or local government after January 26, 1992); and

(ii) If the first certificate of occupancy for the facility is issued after January 26, 1993.

(b) *Commercial facilities located in private residences.* (1) When a commercial facility is located in a private residence, the portion of the residence used exclusively as a residence is not covered by this subpart, but that portion used exclusively in the operation of the commercial facility or that portion used both for the commercial facility and for residential purposes is covered by the new construction and alterations requirements of this subpart.

(2) The portion of the residence covered under paragraph (b)(1) of this section extends to those elements used to enter the commercial facility, including the homeowner's front sidewalk, if any, the door or entryway, and hallways; and those portions of the residence, interior or exterior, available to or used by employees or visitors of the commercial facility, including restrooms.

(c) *Exception for structural impracticability.* (1) Full compliance with the requirements of this section is not required where an entity can demonstrate that it is structurally impracticable to meet the requirements. Full compliance will be considered structurally impracticable only in those rare circumstances when the unique characteristics of terrain prevent the incorporation of accessibility features.

(2) If full compliance with this section would be structurally impracticable, compliance with this section is required to the extent that it is not structurally impracticable. In that case, any portion of the facility that can be made accessible shall be made accessible to the extent that it is not structurally impracticable.

(3) If providing accessibility in conformance with this section to individuals with certain disabilities (e.g., those who use wheelchairs) would be structurally impracticable, accessibility shall nonetheless be ensured to persons with other types of disabilities (e.g., those who use crutches or who have sight, hearing, or mental impairments) in accordance with this section.

(d) *Elevator exemption.* (1) For purposes of this paragraph (d)—

(i) *Professional office of a health care provider* means a location where a person or entity regulated by a State to provide professional services related to the physical or mental health of an individual makes such services available to the public. The facility housing the "professional office of a health care provider" only includes floor levels housing at least one health care provider, or any floor level designed or intended for use by at least one health care provider.

(ii) *Shopping center or shopping mall means*—

(A) A building housing five or more sales or rental establishments; or

(B) A series of buildings on a common site, either under common ownership or common control or developed either as one project or as a series of related projects, housing five or more sales or rental establishments. For purposes of this section, places of public accommodation of the types listed in paragraph (5) of the definition of "place of public accommodation" in section § 36.104 are considered sales or rental establishments. The facility housing a "shopping center or shopping mall" only includes floor levels housing at least one sales or rental establishment, or any floor level

designed or intended for use by at least one sales or rental establishment.

(2) This section does not require the installation of an elevator in a facility that is less than three stories or has less than 3000 square feet per story, except with respect to any facility that houses one or more of the following:

(i) A shopping center or shopping mall, or a professional office of a health care provider.

(ii) A terminal, depot, or other station used for specified public transportation, or an airport passenger terminal. In such a facility, any area housing passenger services, including boarding and debarking, loading and unloading, baggage claim, dining facilities, and other common areas open to the public, must be on an accessible route from an accessible entrance.

(3) The elevator exemption set forth in this paragraph (d) does not obviate or limit, in any way the obligation to comply with the other accessibility requirements established in paragraph (a) of this section. For example, in a facility that houses a shopping center or shopping mall, or a professional office of a health care provider, the floors that are above or below an accessible ground floor and that do not house sales or rental establishments or a professional office of a health care provider, must meet the requirements of this section but for the elevator.

§ 36.402 Alterations.

(a) *General.* (1) Any alteration to a place of public accommodation or a commercial facility, after January 26, 1992, shall be made so as to ensure that, to the maximum extent feasible, the altered portions of the facility are readily accessible to and usable by individuals with disabilities, including individuals who use wheelchairs.

(2) An alteration is deemed to be undertaken after January 26, 1992, if the physical alteration of the property begins after that date.

(b) *Alteration.* For the purposes of this part, an

alteration is a change to a place of public accommodation or a commercial facility that affects or could affect the usability of the building or facility or any part thereof.

(1) Alterations include, but are not limited to, remodeling, renovation, rehabilitation, reconstruction, historic restoration, changes or rearrangement in structural parts or elements, and changes or rearrangement in the plan configuration of walls and full-height partitions. Normal maintenance, reroofing, painting or wallpapering, asbestos removal, or changes to mechanical and electrical systems are not alterations unless they affect the usability of the building or facility.

(2) If existing elements, spaces, or common areas are altered, then each such altered element, space, or area shall comply with the applicable provisions of appendix A to this part.

(c) *To the maximum extent feasible.* The phrase "to the maximum extent feasible," as used in this section, applies to the occasional case where the nature of an existing facility makes it virtually impossible to comply fully with applicable accessibility standards through a planned alteration. In these circumstances, the alteration shall provide the maximum physical accessibility feasible. Any altered features of the facility that can be made accessible shall be made accessible. If providing accessibility in conformance with this section to individuals with certain disabilities (e.g., those who use wheelchairs) would not be feasible, the facility shall be made accessible to persons with other types of disabilities (e.g., those who use crutches, those who have impaired vision or hearing, or those who have other impairments).

§ 36.403 Alterations: Path of travel.

(a) *General.* An alteration that affects or could affect the usability of or access to an area of a facility that contains a primary function shall be made so as to ensure that, to the maximum extent feasible, the path of travel to the altered area and the restrooms, telephones, and drinking fountains serving the altered area, are readily accessible to and usable by individuals with disabilities, including individuals who use wheelchairs, unless the cost and scope of such alterations is disproportionate to the cost of the overall alteration.

(b) *Primary function.* A "primary function" is a major activity for which the facility is intended. Areas that contain a primary function include, but are not limited to, the customer services lobby of a bank, the dining area of a cafeteria, the meeting rooms in a conference center, as well as offices and other work areas in which the activities of the public accommodation or other private entity using the facility are carried out. Mechanical rooms, boiler rooms, supply storage rooms, employee lounges or locker rooms, janitorial closets, entrances, corridors, and restrooms are not areas containing a primary function.

(c) *Alterations to an area containing a primary function.* (1) Alterations that affect the usability of or access to an area containing a primary function include, but are not limited to—

(i) Remodeling merchandise display areas or employee work areas in a department store;

(ii) Replacing an inaccessible floor surface in the customer service or employee work areas of a bank;

(iii) Redesigning the assembly line area of a factory; or

(iv) Installing a computer center in an accounting firm.

(2) For the purposes of this section, alterations to windows, hardware, controls, electrical outlets, and signage shall not be deemed to be alterations that affect the usability of or access to an area containing a primary function.

(d) *Landlord/tenant:* If a tenant is making alterations as defined in § 36.402 that would trigger the requirements of this section, those alterations by the tenant in areas that only the tenant occupies do not trigger a path of travel obligation upon the landlord with respect to

areas of the facility under the landlord's authority, if those areas are not otherwise being altered.

(e) *Path of travel.* (1) A "path of travel" includes a continuous, unobstructed way of pedestrian passage by means of which the altered area may be approached, entered, and exited, and which connects the altered area with an exterior approach (including sidewalks, streets, and parking areas), an entrance to the facility, and other parts of the facility.

(2) An accessible path of travel may consist of walks and sidewalks, curb ramps and other interior or exterior pedestrian ramps; clear floor paths through lobbies, corridors, rooms, and other improved areas; parking access aisles; elevators and lifts; or a combination of these elements.

(3) For the purposes of this part, the term "path of travel" also includes the restrooms, telephones, and drinking fountains serving the altered area.

(f) *Disproportionality.* (1) Alterations made to provide an accessible path of travel to the altered area will be deemed disproportionate to the overall alteration when the cost exceeds 20% of the cost of the alteration to the primary function area.

(2) Costs that may be counted as expenditures required to provide an accessible path of travel may include:

(i) Costs associated with providing an accessible entrance and an accessible route to the altered area, for example, the cost of widening doorways or installing ramps;

(ii) Costs associated with making restrooms accessible, such as installing grab bars, enlarging toilet stalls, insulating pipes, or installing accessible faucet controls;

(iii) Costs associated with providing accessible telephones, such as relocating the telephone to an accessible height, installing amplification devices, or installing a telecommunications device for deaf persons (TDD);

(iv) Costs associated with relocating an inaccessible drinking fountain.

(g) *Duty to provide accessible features in the event of disproportionality.* (1) When the cost of alterations necessary to make the path of travel to the altered area fully accessible is disproportionate to the cost of the overall alteration, the path of travel shall be made accessible to the extent that it can be made accessible without incurring disproportionate costs.

(2) In choosing which accessible elements to provide, priority should be given to those elements that will provide the greatest access, in the following order:

(i) An accessible entrance;

(ii) An accessible route to the altered area;

(iii) At least one accessible restroom for each sex or a single unisex restroom;

(iv) Accessible telephones;

(v) Accessible drinking fountains; and

(vi) When possible, additional accessible elements such as parking, storage, and alarms.

(h) *Series of smaller alterations.* (1) The obligation to provide an accessible path of travel may not be evaded by performing a series of small alterations to the area served by a single path of travel if those alterations could have been performed as a single undertaking.

(2) (i) If an area containing a primary function has been altered without providing an accessible path of travel to that area, and subsequent alterations of that area, or a different area on the same path of travel, are undertaken within three years of the original alteration, the total cost of alterations to the primary function areas on that path of travel during the preceding three year period shall be considered in determining whether the cost of making that path of travel accessible is disproportionate.

(ii) Only alterations undertaken after January 26, 1992, shall be considered in determining if the cost of providing an accessible path of travel is disproportionate to the overall cost of the alterations.

§ 36.404 Alterations: Elevator exemption.

(a) This section does not require the installation of an elevator in an altered facility that is less than three stories or has less than 3,000 square feet per story, except with respect to any facility that houses a shopping center, a shopping mall, the professional office of a health care provider, a terminal, depot, or other station used for specified public transportation, or an airport passenger terminal.

(1) For the purposes of this section, "professional office of a health care provider" means a location where a person or entity regulated by a State to provide professional services related to the physical or mental health of an individual makes such services available to the public. The facility that houses a "professional office of a health care provider" only includes floor levels housing by at least one health care provider, or any floor level designed or intended for use by at least one health care provider.

(2) For the purposes of this section, shopping center or shopping mall means— (i) A building housing five or more sales or rental establishments; or

(ii) A series of buildings on a common site, connected by a common pedestrian access route above or below the ground floor, that is either under common ownership or common control or developed either as one project or as a series of related projects, housing five or more sales or rental establishments. For purposes of this section, places of public accommodation of the types listed in paragraph (5) of the definition of "place of public accommodation" in § 36.104 are considered sales or rental establishments. The facility housing a "shopping center or shopping mall" only includes floor levels housing at least one sales or rental establishment, or any floor level designed or intended for use by at least one sales or rental establishment.

(b) The exemption provided in paragraph (a) of this section does not obviate or limit in any way the obligation to comply with the other accessibility requirements established in this subpart. For example, alterations to floors above or below the accessible ground floor must be accessible regardless of whether the altered facility has an elevator.

§ 36.405 Alterations: Historic preservation.

(a) Alterations to buildings or facilities that are eligible for listing in the National Register of Historic Places under the National Historic Preservation Act (16 U.S.C. 470 et seq.), or are designated as historic under State or local law, shall comply to the maximum extent feasible with section 4.1.7 of appendix A to this part.

(b) If it is determined under the procedures set out in section 4.1.7 of appendix A that it is not feasible to provide physical access to an historic property that is a place of public accommodation in a manner that will not threaten or destroy the historic significance of the building or facility, alternative methods of access shall be provided pursuant to the requirements of subpart C of this part.

§ 36.406 Standards for new construction and alterations.

(a) New construction and alterations subject to this part shall comply with the standards for accessible design published as appendix A to this part (ADAAG).

(b) The chart in the appendix to this section provides guidance to the user in reading appendix A to this part (ADAAG) together with subparts A through D of this part, when determining requirements for a particular facility.

Appendix to § 36.406

This chart has no effect for purposes of compliance or enforcement. It does not necessarily provide complete or mandatory information.

	Subparts A–D	ADAAG
Application, General	36.102(b)(3): public accommodation. 36.102(c): commercial facilities. 36.102(e): public entities. 36.103 (other laws). 36.401 ("for first occupancy"). 36.402(a) (alterations).	1, 2, 3, 4.1.1
Definitions	36.104: commercial facilities facility, place of public accommodation, private club, public accommodation, public entity, religious entity.	3.5 Definitions including: addition, alteration, building, element, facility, space, story.
	36.401(d)(1)(iii), 36.404(a)(2): shopping center or shopping mall.	4.1.6.(j). technical infeasibility.
	36.401(d)(1)(x), 36.404(a)(1): professional office of a health care provider. 36.402: alteration; usability. 36.402(c): to the maximum extent feasible.	
New Construction: General	36.401(a) General	4.1.2.
	36.401(b) Commercial facilities in private residences. 36.207 Places of public accommodation in private residences.	4.1.3.
Work Areas	. . . .	4.1.1(3).
Structural Impracticability.	36.401(c)	4.1.1(5)(a).
Elevator Exemption.	36.401(d).	4.1.3(5).
Other Exemptions.	. . . .	4.1.1(5), 4.1.3(5) and throughout.
Alterations: General.	36.401(b): commercial facilities in private residences.	
	36.402.	4.1.6(1).
Alterations Affecting an Area Containing A Primary Function; Path of Travel; Disproportionality.	36.403.	4.1.6(2).
Alterations: Special Technical Provisions.	. . . .	4/1/6(3).
Additions	36.401 - 36.405	4.1.5.
Historic Preservation.	36.405	4.1.7.
Technical Provisions.	. . . .	4.2 through 4.35

	Subparts A-D	ADAAG
Restaurants and Cafeterias.	. . . .	5.
Medical Care Facilities.	. . . .	6.
Business and Mercantile.	. . . .	7.
Libraries	. . . .	8.
Transient Lodging (Hotels, Homeless Shelters, Etc.).	. . . .	9.
Transportation Facilities.	. . . .	10.

§§ 36.407-36.500 [Reserved]

Subpart E—Enforcement

§36.501 Private suits.

(a) *General.* Any person who is being subjected to discrimination on the basis of disability in violation of the Act or this part or who has reasonable grounds for believing that such person is about to be subjected to discrimination in violation of section 303 of the Act or subpart D of this part may institute a civil action for preventive relief, including an application for a permanent or temporary injunction, restraining order, or other order. Upon timely application, the court may, in its discretion, permit the Attorney General to intervene in the civil action if the Attorney General or his or her designee certifies that the case is of general public importance. Upon application by the complainant and in such circumstances as the court may deem just, the court may appoint an attorney for such complainant and may authorize the commencement of the civil action without the payment of fees, costs, or security. Nothing in this section shall require a person with a disability to engage in a futile gesture if the person has actual notice that a person or organization covered by title III of the Act or this part does not intend to comply with its provisions.

(b) *Injunctive relief.* In the case of violations of § 36.304, § 36.308, § 36.310(b), § 36.401, § 36.402, § 36.403, and § 36.405 of this part, injunctive relief shall include an order to alter facilities to make such facilities

readily accessible to and usable by individuals with disabilities to the extent required by the Act or this part. Where appropriate, injunctive relief shall also include requiring the provision of an auxiliary aid or service, modification of a policy, or provision of alternative methods, to the extent required by the Act or this part.

§ 36.502 Investigations and compliance reviews.

(a) The Attorney General shall investigate alleged violations of the Act or this part.

(b) Any individual who believes that he or she or a specific class of persons has been subjected to discrimination prohibited by the Act or this part may request the Department to institute an investigation.

(c) Where the Attorney General has reason to believe that there may be a violation of this part, he or she may initiate a compliance review.

§ 36.503 Suit by the Attorney General.

Following a compliance review or investigation under § 36.502, or at any other time in his or her discretion, the Attorney General may commence a civil action in any appropriate United States district court if the Attorney General has reasonable cause to believe that—

(a) Any person or group of persons is engaged in a pattern or practice of discrimination in violation of the Act or this part; or

(b) Any person or group of persons has been discriminated against in violation of the Act or this part and the discrimination raises an issue of general public importance.

§ 36.504 Relief.

(a) *Authority of court.* In a civil action under § 36.503, the court—

(1) May grant any equitable relief that such court considers to be appropriate, including, to the extent required by the Act or this part—

(i) Granting temporary, preliminary, or permanent relief;

(ii) Providing an auxiliary aid or service, modification of policy, practice, or procedure, or alternative method; and

(iii) Making facilities readily accessible to and usable by individuals with disabilities;

(2) May award other relief as the court considers to be appropriate, including monetary damages to persons aggrieved when requested by the Attorney General; and

(3) May, to vindicate the public interest, assess a civil penalty against the entity in an amount

(i) Not exceeding $50,000 for a first violation; and

(ii) Not exceeding $100,000 for any subsequent violation.

(b) *Single violation.* For purposes of paragraph (a) (3) of this section, in determining whether a first or subsequent violation has occurred, a determination in a single action, by judgment or settlement, that the covered entity has engaged in more than one discriminatory act shall be counted as a single violation.

(c) *Punitive damages.* For purposes of paragraph (a)(2) of this section, the terms "monetary damages" and "such other relief" do not include punitive damages.

(d) *Judicial consideration.* In a civil action under § 36.503, the court, when considering what amount of civil penalty, if any, is appropriate, shall give consideration to any good faith effort or attempt to comply with this part by the entity. In evaluating good faith, the court shall consider, among other factors it deems relevant, whether the entity could have reasonably anticipated the need for an appropriate type of auxiliary aid needed to accommodate the unique needs of a particular individual with a disability.

§ 36.505 Attorneys fees.

In any action or administrative proceeding commenced pursuant to the Act or this part, the court or agency, in its discretion, may allow the prevailing party, other than the

United States, a reasonable attorney's fee, including litigation expenses, and costs, and the United States shall be liable for the foregoing the same as a private individual.

§ 36.506 Alternative means of dispute resolution.

Where appropriate and to the extent authorized by law, the use of alternative means of dispute resolution, including settlement negotiations, conciliation, facilitation, mediation, factfinding, minitrials, and arbitration, is encouraged to resolve disputes arising under the Act and this part.

§ 36.507 Effect of unavailability of technical assistance.

A public accommodation or other private entity shall not be excused from compliance with the requirements of this part because of any failure to receive technical assistance, including any failure in the development or dissemination of any technical assistance manual authorized by the Act.

§ 36.508 Effective date.

(a) *General.* Except as otherwise provided in this section and in this part, this part shall become effective on January 26, 1992.

(b) *Civil actions.* Except for any civil action brought for a violation of section 303 of the Act, no civil action shall be brought for any act or omission described in section 302 of the Act that occurs—

(1) Before July 26, 1992, against businesses with 25 or fewer employees and gross receipts of $1,000,000 or less.

(2) Before January 26, 1993, against businesses with 10 or fewer employees and gross receipts of $500,000 or less.

(c) *Transportation services provided by public accommodations.* Newly purchased or leased vehicles required to be accessible by § 36.310 must be readily accessible to and usable by individuals with disabilities, including individuals who use wheelchairs, if the solicitation

for the vehicle is made after August 25, 1990.

§§ 36.509-36.600 [Reserved]

Subpart F—Certification of State Laws or Local Building Codes

§ 36.601 Definitions.

Assistant Attorney General means the Assistant Attorney General for Civil Rights or his or her designee.

Certification of equivalency means a final certification that a code meets or exceeds the minimum requirements of title III of the Act for accessibility and usability of facilities covered by that title.

Code means a State law or local building code or similar ordinance, or part thereof, that establishes accessibility requirements.

Model code means a nationally recognized document developed by a private entity for use by State or local jurisdictions in developing codes as defined in this section. A model code is intended for incorporation by reference or adoption in whole or in part, with or without amendment, by State or local jurisdictions.

Preliminary determination of equivalency means a preliminary determination that a code appears to meet or exceed the minimum requirements of title III of the Act for accessibility and usability of facilities covered by that title.

Submitting official means the State or local official who—

(1) Has principal responsibility for administration of a code, or is authorized to submit a code on behalf of a jurisdiction; and

(2) Files a request for certification under this subpart.

§ 36.602 General rule.

On the application of a State or local government, the Assistant Attorney General may certify that a code meets or exceeds the minimum requirements of the Act for the accessibility and usability of places of public accommodation and commercial facilities under this part by issuing a certifica-

tion of equivalency. At any enforcement proceeding under title III of the Act, such certification shall be rebuttable evidence that such State law or local ordinance does meet or exceed the minimum requirements of title III.

§ 36.603 Filing request for certification.

(a) A submitting official may file a request for certification of a code under this subpart. (b) Before filing a request for certification of a code, the submitting official shall ensure that—

(1) Adequate public notice of intention to file a request for certification, notice of a hearing, and notice of the location at which the request and materials can be inspected is published within the relevant jurisdiction;

(2) Copies of the proposed request and supporting materials are made available for public examination and copying at the office of the State or local agency charged with administration and enforcement of the code; and

(3) The local or State jurisdiction holds a public hearing on the record, in the State or locality, at which the public is invited to comment on the proposed request for certification.

(c) The submitting official shall include the following materials and information in support of the request:

(1) The text of the jurisdiction's code; any standard, regulation, code, or other relevant document incorporated by reference or otherwise referenced in the code; the law creating and empowering the agency; any relevant manuals, guides, or any other interpretive information issued that pertain to the code; and any formal opinions of the State Attorney General or the chief legal officer of the jurisdiction that pertain to the code;

(2) Any model code or statute on which the pertinent code is based, and an explanation of any differences between the model and the pertinent code;

(3) A transcript of the public hearing required by paragraph (b)(3) of this section; and

(4) Any additional information that the submitting official may wish to be considered.

(d) The submitting official shall file the original and one copy of the request and of supporting materials with the Assistant Attorney General. The submitting official shall clearly label the request as a "request for certification" of a code. A copy of the request and supporting materials will be available for public examination and copying at the offices of the Assistant Attorney General in Washington, DC. The submitting official shall ensure that copies of the request and supporting materials are available for public examination and copying at the office of the State or local agency charged with administration and enforcement of the code. The submitting official shall ensure that adequate public notice of the request for certification and of the location at which the request and materials can be inspected is published within the relevant jurisdiction.

(e) Upon receipt of a request for certification, the Assistant Attorney General may request further information that he or she considers relevant to the determinations required to be made under this subpart.

§ 36.604 Preliminary determination.

After consultation with the Architectural and Transportation Barriers Compliance Board, the Assistant Attorney General shall make a preliminary determination of equivalency or a preliminary determination to deny certification.

§ 36.605 Procedure following preliminary determination of equivalency.

(a) If the Assistant Attorney General makes a preliminary determination of equivalency under § 36.604, he or she shall inform the submitting official, in writing, of that preliminary

determination. The Assistant Attorney General shall also--

(1) Publish a notice in the **Federal Register** that advises the public of the preliminary determination of equivalency with respect to the particular code, and invite interested persons and organizations, including individuals with disabilities, during a period of at least 60 days following publication of the notice, to file written comments relevant to whether a final certification of equivalency should be issued;

(2) After considering the information received in response to the notice described in paragraph (a) of this section, and after publishing a separate notice in the **Federal Register**, hold an informal hearing in Washington, DC at which interested persons, including individuals with disabilities, are provided an opportunity to express their views with respect to the preliminary determination of equivalency; and

(b) The Assistant Attorney General, after consultation with the Architectural and Transportation Barriers Compliance Board, and consideration of the materials and information submitted pursuant to this section and § 36.603, shall issue either a certification of equivalency or a final determination to deny the request for certification. He or she shall publish notice of the certification of equivalency or denial of certification in the **Federal Register**.

§ 36.606 Procedure following preliminary denial of certification.

(a) If the Assistant Attorney General makes a Preliminary determination to deny certification of a code under § 36.604, he or she shall notify the submitting official of the determination. The notification may include specification of the manner in which the code could be amended in order to qualify for certification.

(b) The Assistant Attorney General shall allow the submitting official not less than 15 days to submit data, views, and arguments in opposition to the preliminary determination to deny certification. If the

submitting official does not submit materials, the Assistant Attorney General shall not be required to take any further action. If the submitting official submits materials, the Assistant Attorney General shall evaluate those materials and any other relevant information. After evaluation of any newly submitted materials, the Assistant Attorney General shall make either a final denial of certification or a preliminary determination of equivalency.

§ 36.607 Effect of certification.

(a)(1) A certification shall be considered a certification of equivalency only with respect to those features or elements that are both covered by the certified code and addressed by the standards against which equivalency is measured.

(2) For example, if certain equipment is not covered by the code, the determination of equivalency cannot be used as evidence with respect to the question of whether equipment in a building built according to the code satisfies the Act's requirements with respect to such equipment. By the same token, certification would not be relevant to construction of a facility for children, if the regulations against which equivalency is measured do not address children's facilities.

(b) A certification of equivalency is effective only with respect to the particular edition of the code for which certification is granted. Any amendments or other changes to the code after the date of the certified edition are not considered part of the certification.

(c) A submitting official may reapply for certification of amendments or other changes to a code that has already received certification.

§ 36.608 Guidance concerning model codes.

Upon application by an authorized representative of a private entity responsible for developing a model code, the Assistant Attorney General may review the relevant model code and issue guidance concerning whether and in what respects the model code is consistent with the minimum requirements of the Act for the accessibility and usability of places of public accommodation and commercial facilities under this part.

§§ 36.609-36.999 [Reserved]

BILLING CODE 4410-01-M

Appendix A to Part 36--Standards for Accessible Design

[GRAPH/ILLUSTRATION #2]

BILLING CODE 4410-01-C

Appendix B to Part 36--Preamble to Regulation on Nondiscrimination on the Basis of Disability by Public Accommodations and in Commercial Facilities (Published July 26, 1991)
Note: For the convenience of the reader, this appendix contains the text of the preamble to the final regulation on nondiscrimination on the basis of disability by public accommodations and in commercial facilities beginning at the heading "Section-by-Section Analysis and Response to Comments" and ending before "List of Subjects in 28 CFR part 36" (56 FR July 26, 1991). Dated: July 17, 1991.

Dick Thornburgh,

Attorney General.

[FR Doc. 91-17482 Filed 7-25-91; 8:45 am]

BILLING CODE 4410-01-M

Americans with Disabilities Act (ADA)

Accessibility Guidelines
for Buildings and Facilities

U.S. Architectural & Transportation Barriers
Compliance Board
1111 18th Street, N.W., Suite 501
Washington, D.C. 20036-3894
(202) 653-7834 v/TDD
(202) 653-7863 FAX

ADA ACCESSIBILITY GUIDELINES FOR BUILDINGS AND FACILITIES

TABLE OF CONTENTS

1. **PURPOSE**

2. **GENERAL**
    2.1   Provisions for Adults
    2.2   Equivalent Facilitation

3. **MISCELLANEOUS INSTRUCTIONS AND DEFINITIONS**
    3.1   Graphic Conventions
    3.2   Dimensional Tolerances
    3.3   Notes
    3.4   General Terminology
    3.5   Definitions

4. **ACCESSIBLE ELEMENTS AND SPACES:**
    SCOPE AND TECHNICAL REQUIREMENTS
    4.1   Minimum Requirements
        4.1.1   Application
        4.1.2   Accessible Sites and Exterior Facilities: New Construction
        4.1.3   Accessible Buildings: New Construction
        4.1.4   (Reserved)
        4.1.5   Accessible Buildings: Additions
        4.1.6   Accessible Buildings: Alterations
        4.1.7   Accessible Buildings: Historic Preservation
    4.2   Space Allowance and Reach Ranges
    4.3   Accessible Route
    4.4   Protruding Objects
    4.5   Ground and Floor Surfaces
    4.6   Parking and Passenger Loading Zones
    4.7   Curb Ramps
    4.8   Ramps
    4.9   Stairs
    4.10   Elevators
    4.11   Platform Lifts (Wheelchair Lifts)
    4.12   Windows
    4.13   Doors
    4.14   Entrances
    4.15   Drinking Fountains and Water Coolers
    4.16   Water Closets
    4.17   Toilet Stalls
    4.18   Urinals
    4.19   Lavatories and Mirrors
    4.20   Bathtubs

4.21 Shower Stalls
4.22 Toilet Rooms
4.23 Bathrooms, Bathing Facilities, and Shower Rooms
4.24 Sinks
4.25 Storage
4.26 Handrails, Grab Bars, and Tub and Shower Seats
4.27 Controls and Operating Mechanisms
4.28 Alarms
4.29 Detectable Warnings
4.30 Signage
4.31 Telephones
4.32 Fixed or Built-in Seating and Tables
4.33 Assembly Areas
4.34 Automated Teller Machines
4.35 Dressing and Fitting Rooms

5. RESTAURANTS AND CAFETERIAS

6. MEDICAL CARE FACILITIES

7. BUSINESS AND MERCANTILE

8. LIBRARIES

9. ACCESSIBLE TRANSIENT LODGING

10. TRANSPORTATION FACILITIES

APPENDIX

1. PURPOSE.

This document sets guidelines for accessibility to buildings and facilities by individuals with disabilities under the Americans with Disabilities Act (ADA) of 1990. These guidelines are to be applied during the design, construction, and alteration of buildings and facilities covered by Titles II and III of the ADA to the extent required by regulations issued by Federal agencies, including the Department of Justice and the Department of Transportation, under the ADA.

The technical specifications 4.2 through 4.35, of these guidelines are the same as those of the American National Standard Institute's document A117.1-1980, except as noted in this text by italics. However, sections 4.1.1 through 4.1.7 and sections 5 through 10 are different from ANSI A117.1 in their entirety and are printed in standard type.

The illustrations and text of ANSI A117.1 are reproduced with permission from the American National Standards Institute. Copies of the standard may be purchased from the American National Standards Institute at 1430 Broadway, New York, New York 10018.

2. GENERAL.

2.1 Provisions for Adults. *The specifications in these guidelines are based upon adult dimensions and anthropometrics.*

2.2* Equivalent Facilitation. *Departures from particular technical and scoping requirements of this guideline by the use of other designs and technologies are permitted where the alternative designs and technologies used will provide substantially equivalent or greater access to and usability of the facility.*

3. MISCELLANEOUS INSTRUCTIONS AND DEFINITIONS.

3.1 Graphic Conventions. Graphic conventions are shown in Table 1. Dimensions that are not marked minimum or maximum are absolute, unless otherwise indicated in the text or captions.

Table 1
Graphic Conventions

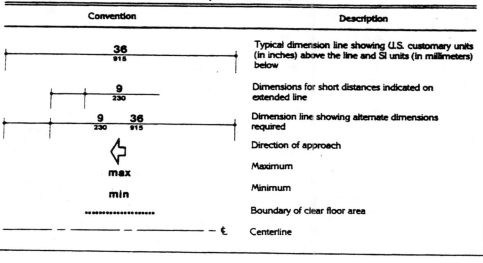

Convention	Description
36 / 915	Typical dimension line showing U.S. customary units (in inches) above the line and SI units (in millimeters) below
9 / 230	Dimensions for short distances indicated on extended line
9 36 / 230 915	Dimension line showing alternate dimensions required
(arrow)	Direction of approach
max	Maximum
min	Minimum
••••••••••••••••••	Boundary of clear floor area
—— – – —— – – —— – ₵	Centerline

3.4 General Terminology

3.2 Dimensional Tolerances. All dimensions are subject to conventional building industry tolerances for field conditions.

3.3 Notes. The text of *these guidelines* does not contain notes or footnotes. Additional information, explanations, and advisory materials are located in the Appendix. Paragraphs marked with an asterisk have related, non-mandatory material in the Appendix. In the Appendix, the corresponding paragraph numbers are preceded by an A.

3.4 General Terminology.

comply with. Meet one or more specifications of *these guidelines*.

if, if ... then. Denotes a specification that applies only when the conditions described are present.

may. Denotes an option or alternative.

shall. Denotes a mandatory specification or requirement.

should. Denotes an advisory specification or recommendation.

3.5 Definitions.

Access Aisle. An accessible pedestrian space between elements, such as parking spaces, seating, and desks, that provides clearances appropriate for use of the elements.

Accessible. Describes a site, building, facility, or portion thereof that complies with *these guidelines*.

Accessible Element. An *element* specified by *these guidelines* (for example, telephone, controls, and the like).

Accessible Route. A continuous unobstructed path connecting all accessible elements and spaces of a building or facility. Interior accessible routes may include corridors, floors, ramps, elevators, lifts, and clear floor space at fixtures. Exterior accessible routes may include parking access aisles, curb ramps, *crosswalks at vehicular ways*, walks, ramps, and lifts.

Accessible Space. *Space that complies with these guidelines.*

Adaptability. The ability of certain building spaces and elements, such as kitchen counters, sinks, and grab bars, to be added or altered so as to accommodate the needs of *individuals with or without disabilities* or to accommodate the needs of persons with different types or degrees of disability.

Addition. *An expansion, extension, or increase in the gross floor area of a building or facility.*

Administrative Authority. *A governmental agency that adopts or enforces regulations and guidelines for the design, construction, or alteration of buildings and facilities.*

Alteration. *An alteration is a change to a building or facility made by, on behalf of, or for the use of a public accommodation or commercial facility, that affects or could affect the usability of the building or facility or part thereof. Alterations include, but are not limited to, remodeling, renovation, rehabilitation, reconstruction, historic restoration, changes or rearrangement of the structural parts or elements, and changes or rearrangement in the plan configuration of walls and full-height partitions. Normal maintenance, reroofing, painting or wallpapering, or changes to mechanical and electrical systems are not alterations unless they affect the usability of the building or facility.*

Area of Rescue Assistance. *An area, which has direct access to an exit, where people who are unable to use stairs may remain temporarily in safety to await further instructions or assistance during emergency evacuation.*

Assembly Area. A room or space accommodating a *group of* individuals for recreational, educational, political, social, or amusement purposes, or for the consumption of food and drink.

Automatic Door. A door equipped with a power-operated mechanism and controls that open and close the door automatically upon receipt of a momentary actuating signal. The switch that begins the automatic cycle may be a photoelectric device, floor mat, or manual switch (see power-assisted door).

Building. Any structure used and intended for supporting or sheltering any use or occupancy.

Circulation Path. An exterior or interior way of passage from one place to another for pedestrians, including, but not limited to, walks, hallways, courtyards, stairways, and stair landings.

Clear. Unobstructed.

Clear Floor Space. *The minimum unobstructed floor or ground space required to accommodate a single, stationary wheelchair and occupant.*

Closed Circuit Telephone. *A telephone with dedicated line(s) such as a house phone, courtesy phone or phone that must be used to gain entrance to a facility.*

Common Use. Refers to those interior and exterior rooms, spaces, or elements that are made available for the use of a restricted group of people (for example, *occupants of a homeless shelter,* the occupants of an office building, or the guests of such occupants).

Cross Slope. The slope that is perpendicular to the direction of travel (see running slope).

Curb Ramp. A short ramp cutting through a curb or built up to it.

Detectable Warning. *A standardized surface feature built in or applied to walking surfaces or other elements to warn visually impaired people of hazards on a circulation path.*

Dwelling Unit. A single unit which provides a kitchen or food preparation area, in addition to rooms and spaces for living, bathing, sleeping, and the like. *Dwelling units include a single family home or a townhouse used as a transient group home; an apartment building used as a shelter; guestrooms in a hotel that provide sleeping accommodations and food preparation areas; and other similar facilities used on a transient basis. For purposes of these guidelines, use of the term "Dwelling Unit" does not imply the unit is used as a residence.*

Egress, Means of. *A continuous and unobstructed way of exit travel from any point in a building or facility to a public way. A means of egress comprises vertical and horizontal travel and may include intervening room spaces, doorways, hallways, corridors, passageways, balconies, ramps, stairs, enclosures, lobbies, horizontal exits, courts and yards. An accessible means of egress is one that complies with these guidelines and does not include stairs, steps, or escalators. Areas of rescue assistance or evacuation elevators may be included as part of accessible means of egress.*

Element. *An architectural or mechanical component of a building, facility, space, or site, e.g., telephone, curb ramp, door, drinking fountain, seating, or water closet.*

Entrance. *Any access point to a building or portion of a building or facility used for the purpose of entering. An entrance includes the approach walk, the vertical access leading to the entrance platform, the entrance platform itself, vestibules if provided, the entry door(s) or gate(s), and the hardware of the entry door(s) or gate(s).*

Facility. *All or any portion of buildings, structures, site improvements, complexes, equipment, roads, walks, passageways, parking lots, or other real or personal property located on a site.*

Ground Floor. *Any occupiable floor less than one story above or below grade with direct access to grade. A building or facility always has at least one ground floor and may have more than one ground floor as where a split level entrance has been provided or where a building is built into a hillside.*

Mezzanine or Mezzanine Floor. *That portion of a story which is an intermediate floor level placed within the story and having occupiable space above and below its floor.*

Marked Crossing. *A crosswalk or other identified path intended for pedestrian use in crossing a vehicular way.*

Multifamily Dwelling. Any building containing more than two dwelling units.

Occupiable. *A room or enclosed space designed for human occupancy in which individuals congregate for amusement, educational or similar purposes, or in which occupants are engaged at labor, and which is equipped with means of egress, light, and ventilation.*

3.5 Definitions

Operable Part. A part of a piece of equipment or appliance used to insert or withdraw objects, or to activate, deactivate, or adjust the equipment or appliance (for example, coin slot, pushbutton, handle).

Path of Travel. (Reserved).

Power-assisted Door. A door used *for human passage* with a mechanism that helps to open the door, or relieves the opening resistance of a door, upon the activation of a switch or a continued force applied to the door itself.

Public Use. Describes interior or exterior rooms or spaces that are made available to the general public. Public use may be provided at a building or facility that is privately or publicly owned.

Ramp. A walking surface which has a running slope greater than 1:20.

Running Slope. The slope that is parallel to the direction of travel (see cross slope).

Service Entrance. An entrance intended primarily for delivery of goods or services.

Signage. *Displayed verbal, symbolic, tactile, and pictorial information.*

Site. A parcel of land bounded by a property line or a designated portion of a public right-of-way.

Site Improvement. Landscaping, paving for pedestrian and vehicular ways, outdoor lighting, recreational facilities, and the like, added to a site.

Sleeping Accommodations. Rooms in which people sleep; for example, dormitory and hotel or motel guest rooms or suites.

Space. *A definable area, e.g., room, toilet room, hall, assembly area, entrance, storage room, alcove, courtyard, or lobby.*

Story. *That portion of a building included between the upper surface of a floor and upper surface of the floor or roof next above. If such* portion of a building does not include occupiable space, it is not considered a story for purposes of these guidelines. There may be more than one floor level within a story as in the case of a mezzanine or mezzanines.

Structural Frame. The structural frame shall be considered to be the columns and the girders, beams, trusses and spandrels having direct connections to the columns and all other members which are essential to the stability of the building as a whole.

Tactile. Describes an object that can be perceived using the sense of touch.

Text Telephone. *Machinery or equipment that employs interactive graphic (i.e., typed) communications through the transmission of coded signals across the standard telephone network. Text telephones can include, for example, devices known as TDD's (telecommunication display devices or telecommunication devices for deaf persons) or computers.*

Transient Lodging. *A building, facility, or portion thereof, excluding inpatient medical care facilities, that contains one or more dwelling units or sleeping accommodations. Transient lodging may include, but is not limited to, resorts, group homes, hotels, motels, and dormitories.*

Vehicular Way. A route intended for vehicular traffic, such as a street, driveway, or parking lot.

Walk. An exterior pathway with a prepared surface intended for pedestrian use, including general pedestrian areas such as plazas and courts.

NOTE: Sections 4.1.1 through 4.1.7 are different from ANSI A117.1 in their entirety and are printed in standard type (ANSI A117.1 does not include scoping provisions).

4.0 Accessible Elements and Spaces: Scope and Technical Requirements

4. ACCESSIBLE ELEMENTS AND SPACES: SCOPE AND TECHNICAL REQUIREMENTS.

4.1 Minimum Requirements

4.1.1° Application.

(1) General. All areas of newly designed or newly constructed buildings and facilities required to be accessible by 4.1.2 and 4.1.3 and altered portions of existing buildings and facilities required to be accessible by 4.1.6 shall comply with these guidelines, 4.1 through 4.35, unless otherwise provided in this section or as modified in a special application section.

(2) Application Based on Building Use. Special application sections 5 through 10 provide additional requirements for restaurants and cafeterias, medical care facilities, business and mercantile, libraries, accessible transient lodging, and transportation facilities. When a building or facility contains more than one use covered by a special application section, each portion shall comply with the requirements for that use.

(3)° Areas Used Only by Employees as Work Areas. Areas that are used only as work areas shall be designed and constructed so that individuals with disabilities can approach, enter, and exit the areas. These guidelines do not require that any areas used only as work areas be constructed to permit maneuvering within the work area or be constructed or equipped (i.e., with racks or shelves) to be accessible.

(4) Temporary Structures. These guidelines cover temporary buildings or facilities as well as permanent facilities. Temporary buildings and facilities are not of permanent construction but are extensively used or are essential for public use for a period of time. Examples of temporary buildings or facilities covered by these guidelines include, but are not limited to: reviewing stands, temporary classrooms, bleacher areas, exhibit areas, temporary banking facilities, temporary health screening services, or temporary safe pedestrian passageways around a construction site. Structures, sites and equipment directly associated with the actual processes of construction, such as scaffolding, bridging, materials hoists, or construction trailers are not included.

(5) General Exceptions.

(a) In new construction, a person or entity is not required to meet fully the requirements of these guidelines where that person or entity can demonstrate that it is structurally impracticable to do so. Full compliance will be considered structurally impracticable only in those rare circumstances when the unique characteristics of terrain prevent the incorporation of accessibility features. If full compliance with the requirements of these guidelines is structurally impracticable, a person or entity shall comply with the requirements to the extent it is not structurally impracticable. Any portion of the building or facility which can be made accessible shall comply to the extent that it is not structurally impracticable.

(b) Accessibility is not required to (i) observation galleries used primarily for security purposes; or (ii) in non-occupiable spaces accessed only by ladders, catwalks, crawl spaces, very narrow passageways, or freight (non-passenger) elevators, and frequented only by service personnel for repair purposes; such spaces include, but are not limited to, elevator pits, elevator penthouses, piping or equipment catwalks.

4.1.2 Accessible Sites and Exterior Facilities: New Construction. An accessible site shall meet the following minimum requirements:

(1) At least one accessible route complying with 4.3 shall be provided within the boundary of the site from public transportation stops, accessible parking spaces, passenger loading zones if provided, and public streets or sidewalks, to an accessible building entrance.

(2) At least one accessible route complying with 4.3 shall connect accessible buildings, accessible facilities, accessible elements, and accessible spaces that are on the same site.

(3) All objects that protrude from surfaces or posts into circulation paths shall comply with 4.4.

4.1.2 Accessible Sites and Exterior Facilities: New Construction

(4) Ground surfaces along accessible routes and in accessible spaces shall comply with 4.5.

(5) (a) If parking spaces are provided for self-parking by employees or visitors, or both, then accessible spaces complying with 4.6 shall be provided in each such parking area in conformance with the table below. Spaces required by the table need not be provided in the particular lot. They may be provided in a different location if equivalent or greater accessibility, in terms of distance from an accessible entrance, cost and convenience is ensured.

Total Parking in Lot	Required Minimum Number of Accessible Spaces
1 to 25	1
26 to 50	2
51 to 75	3
76 to 100	4
101 to 150	5
151 to 200	6
201 to 300	7
301 to 400	8
401 to 500	9
501 to 1000	2 percent of total
1001 and over	20 plus 1 for each 100 over 1000

Except as provided in (b), access aisles adjacent to accessible spaces shall be 60 in (1525 mm) wide minimum.

(b) One in every eight accessible spaces, but not less than one, shall be served by an access aisle 96 in (2440 mm) wide minimum and shall be designated "van accessible" as required by 4.6.4. The vertical clearance at such spaces shall comply with 4.6.5. All such spaces may be grouped on one level of a parking structure.

EXCEPTION: Provision of all required parking spaces in conformance with "Universal Parking Design" (see appendix A4.6.3) is permitted.

(c) If passenger loading zones are provided, then at least one passenger loading zone shall comply with 4.6.6.

(d) At facilities providing medical care and other services for persons with mobility impairments, parking spaces complying with 4.6 shall be provided in accordance with 4.1.2(5)(a) except as follows:

(i) Outpatient units and facilities: 10 percent of the total number of parking spaces provided serving each such outpatient unit or facility;

(ii) Units and facilities that specialize in treatment or services for persons with mobility impairments: 20 percent of the total number of parking spaces provided serving each such unit or facility.

(e) *Valet parking: Valet parking facilities shall provide a passenger loading zone complying with 4.6.6 located on an accessible route to the entrance of the facility. Paragraphs 5(a), 5(b), and 5(d) of this section do not apply to valet parking facilities.

(6) If toilet facilities are provided on a site, then each such public or common use toilet facility shall comply with 4.22. If bathing facilities are provided on a site, then each such public or common use bathing facility shall comply with 4.23.

For single user portable toilet or bathing units clustered at a single location, at least 5% but no less than one toilet unit or bathing unit complying with 4.22 or 4.23 shall be installed at each cluster whenever typical inaccessible units are provided. Accessible units shall be identified by the International Symbol of Accessibility.

EXCEPTION: Portable toilet units at construction sites used exclusively by construction personnel are not required to comply with 4.1.2(6).

(7) Building Signage. Signs which designate permanent rooms and spaces shall comply with 4.30.1, 4.30.4, 4.30.5 and 4.30.6. Other signs which provide direction to, or information about, functional spaces of the building shall comply with 4.30.1, 4.30.2, 4.30.3, and 4.30.5. Elements and spaces of accessible facilities which shall be identified by the International Symbol of Accessibility and which shall comply with 4.30.7 are:

(a) Parking spaces designated as reserved for individuals with disabilities;

(b) Accessible passenger loading zones;

(c) Accessible entrances when not all are accessible (inaccessible entrances shall have directional signage to indicate the route to the nearest accessible entrance);

(d) Accessible toilet and bathing facilities when not all are accessible.

4.1.3 Accessible Buildings: New Construction. Accessible buildings and facilities shall meet the following minimum requirements:

(1) At least one accessible route complying with 4.3 shall connect accessible building or facility entrances with all accessible spaces and elements within the building or facility.

(2) All objects that overhang or protrude into circulation paths shall comply with 4.4.

(3) Ground and floor surfaces along accessible routes and in accessible rooms and spaces shall comply with 4.5.

(4) Interior and exterior stairs connecting levels that are not connected by an elevator, ramp, or other accessible means of vertical access shall comply with 4.9.

(5)* One passenger elevator complying with 4.10 shall serve each level, including mezzanines, in all multi-story buildings and facilities unless exempted below. If more than one elevator is provided, each full passenger elevator shall comply with 4.10.

EXCEPTION 1: Elevators are not required in facilities that are less than three stories or that have less than 3000 square feet per story unless the building is a shopping center, a shopping mall, or the professional office of a health care provider, or another type of facility as determined by the Attorney General. The elevator exemption set forth in this paragraph does not obviate or limit in any way the obligation to comply with the other accessibility requirements established in section 4.1.3. For example, floors above or below the accessible ground floor must meet the requirements of this section except for elevator service. If toilet or bathing facilities are provided on a level not served by an elevator, then toilet or bathing facilities must be provided on the accessible

ground floor. In new construction if a building or facility is eligible for this exemption but a full passenger elevator is nonetheless planned, that elevator shall meet the requirements of 4.10 and shall serve each level in the building. A full passenger elevator that provides service from a garage to only one level of a building or facility is not required to serve other levels.

EXCEPTION 2: Elevator pits, elevator penthouses, mechanical rooms, piping or equipment catwalks are exempted from this requirement.

EXCEPTION 3: Accessible ramps complying with 4.8 may be used in lieu of an elevator.

EXCEPTION 4: Platform lifts (wheelchair lifts) complying with 4.11 of this guideline and applicable state or local codes may be used in lieu of an elevator only under the following conditions:

(a) To provide an accessible route to a performing area in an assembly occupancy.

(b) To comply with the wheelchair viewing position line-of-sight and dispersion requirements of 4.33.3.

(c) To provide access to incidental occupiable spaces and rooms which are not open to the general public and which house no more than five persons, including but not limited to equipment control rooms and projection booths.

(d) To provide access where existing site constraints or other constraints make use of a ramp or an elevator infeasible.

(6) Windows: (Reserved).

(7) Doors:

(a) At each accessible entrance to a building or facility, at least one door shall comply with 4.13.

(b) Within a building or facility, at least one door at each accessible space shall comply with 4.13.

(c) Each door that is an element of an accessible route shall comply with 4.13.

4.1.3 Accessible Buildings: New Construction

(d) Each door required by 4.3.10, Egress, shall comply with 4.13.

(8) In new construction, at a minimum, the requirements in (a) and (b) below shall be satisfied independently:

(a)(i) At least 50% of all public entrances (excluding those in (b) below) must be accessible. At least one must be a ground floor entrance. Public entrances are any entrances that are not loading or service entrances.

(ii) Accessible entrances must be provided in a number at least equivalent to the number of exits required by the applicable building/fire codes. (This paragraph does not require an increase in the total number of entrances planned for a facility.)

(iii) An accessible entrance must be provided to each tenancy in a facility (for example, individual stores in a strip shopping center).

One entrance may be considered as meeting more than one of the requirements in (a). Where feasible, accessible entrances shall be the entrances used by the majority of people visiting or working in the building.

(b)(i) In addition, if direct access is provided for pedestrians from an enclosed parking garage to the building, at least one direct entrance from the garage to the building must be accessible.

(ii) If access is provided for pedestrians from a pedestrian tunnel or elevated walkway, one entrance to the building from each tunnel or walkway must be accessible.

One entrance may be considered as meeting more than one of the requirements in (b).

Because entrances also serve as emergency exits whose proximity to all parts of buildings and facilities is essential, it is preferable that all entrances be accessible.

(c) If the only entrance to a building, or tenancy in a facility, is a service entrance, that entrance shall be accessible.

(d) Entrances which are not accessible shall have directional signage complying with 4.30.1, 4.30.2, 4.30.3, and 4.30.5, which indicates the location of the nearest accessible entrance.

(9)* In buildings or facilities, or portions of buildings or facilities, required to be accessible, accessible means of egress shall be provided in the same number as required for exits by local building/life safety regulations. Where a required exit from an occupiable level above or below a level of accessible exit discharge is not accessible, an area of rescue assistance shall be provided on each such level (in a number equal to that of inaccessible required exits). Areas of rescue assistance shall comply with 4.3.11. A horizontal exit, meeting the requirements of local building/life safety regulations, shall satisfy the requirement for an area of rescue assistance.

EXCEPTION: Areas of rescue assistance are not required in buildings or facilities having a supervised automatic sprinkler system.

(10)* Drinking Fountains:

(a) Where only one drinking fountain is provided on a floor there shall be a drinking fountain which is accessible to individuals who use wheelchairs in accordance with 4.15 and one accessible to those who have difficulty bending or stooping. (This can be accommodated by the use of a "hi-lo" fountain; by providing one fountain accessible to those who use wheelchairs and one fountain at a standard height convenient for those who have difficulty bending; by providing a fountain accessible under 4.15 and a water cooler; or by such other means as would achieve the required accessibility for each group on each floor.)

(b) Where more than one drinking fountain or water cooler is provided on a floor, 50% of those provided shall comply with 4.15 and shall be on an accessible route.

(11) Toilet Facilities: If toilet rooms are provided, then each public and common use toilet room shall comply with 4.22. Other toilet rooms provided for the use of occupants of specific spaces (i.e., a private toilet room for the occupant of a private office) shall be adaptable. If bathing rooms are provided, then each public and common use bathroom shall comply with 4.23. Accessible toilet rooms and bathing facilities shall be on an accessible route.

4.1.3 Accessible Buildings: New Construction

(12) Storage, Shelving and Display Units:

(a) If fixed or built-in storage facilities such as cabinets, shelves, closets, and drawers are provided in accessible spaces, at least one of each type provided shall contain storage space complying with 4.25. Additional storage may be provided outside of the dimensions required by 4.25.

(b) Shelves or display units allowing self-service by customers in mercantile occupancies shall be located on an accessible route complying with 4.3. Requirements for accessible reach range do not apply.

(13) Controls and operating mechanisms in accessible spaces, along accessible routes, or as parts of accessible elements (for example, light switches and dispenser controls) shall comply with 4.27.

(14) If emergency warning systems are provided, then they shall include both audible alarms and visual alarms complying with 4.28. Sleeping accommodations required to comply with 9.3 shall have an alarm system complying with 4.28. Emergency warning systems in medical care facilities may be modified to suit standard health care alarm design practice.

(15) Detectable warnings shall be provided at locations as specified in 4.29.

(16) Building Signage:

(a) Signs which designate permanent rooms and spaces shall comply with 4.30.1, 4.30.4, 4.30.5 and 4.30.6.

(b) Other signs which provide direction to or information about functional spaces of the building shall comply with 4.30.1, 4.30.2, 4.30.3, and 4.30.5.

EXCEPTION: Building directories, menus, and all other signs which are temporary are not required to comply.

(17) Public Telephones:

(a) If public pay telephones, public closed circuit telephones, or other public telephones are provided, then they shall comply with 4.31.2 through 4.31.8 to the extent required by the following table:

Number of each type of telephone provided on each floor	Number of telephones required to comply with 4.31.2 through 4.31.8[1]
1 or more single unit	1 per floor
1 bank[2]	1 per floor
2 or more banks[2]	1 per bank. Accessible unit may be installed as a single unit in proximity (either visible or with signage) to the bank. At least one public telephone per floor shall meet the requirements for a forward reach telephone[3].

[1] Additional public telephones may be installed at any height. Unless otherwise specified, accessible telephones may be either forward or side reach telephones.

[2] A bank consists of two or more adjacent public telephones, often installed as a unit.

[3] EXCEPTION: For exterior installations only, if dial tone first service is available, then a side reach telephone may be installed instead of the required forward reach telephone (i.e., one telephone in proximity to each bank shall comply with 4.31).

(b)* All telephones required to be accessible and complying with 4.31.2 through 4.31.8 shall be equipped with a volume control. In addition, 25 percent, but never less than one, of all other public telephones provided shall be equipped with a volume control and shall be dispersed among all types of public telephones, including closed circuit telephones, throughout the building or facility. Signage complying with applicable provisions of 4.30.7 shall be provided.

(c) The following shall be provided in accordance with 4.31.9:

(i) if a total number of four or more public pay telephones (including both interior and exterior phones) is provided at a site, and at least one is in an interior location, then at least one interior public text telephone shall be provided.

(ii) if an interior public pay telephone is provided in a stadium or arena, in a convention center, in a hotel with a convention center, or

4.1.3 Accessible Buildings: New Construction

in a covered mall, at least one interior public text telephone shall be provided in the facility.

(iii) If a public pay telephone is located in or adjacent to a hospital emergency room, hospital recovery room, or hospital waiting room, one public text telephone shall be provided at each such location.

(d) Where a bank of telephones in the interior of a building consists of three or more public pay telephones, at least one public pay telephone in each such bank shall be equipped with a shelf and outlet in compliance with 4.31.9(2).

(18) If fixed or built-in seating or tables (including, but not limited to, study carrels and student laboratory stations), are provided in accessible public or common use areas, at least five percent (5%), but not less than one, of the fixed or built-in seating areas or tables shall comply with 4.32. An accessible route shall lead to and through such fixed or built-in seating areas, or tables.

(19)° Assembly areas:

(a) In places of assembly with fixed seating accessible wheelchair locations shall comply with 4.33.2, 4.33.3, and 4.33.4 and shall be provided consistent with the following table:

Capacity of Seating in Assembly Areas	Number of Required Wheelchair Locations
4 to 25	1
26 to 50	2
51 to 300	4
301 to 500	6
over 500	6, plus 1 additional space for each total seating capacity increase of 100

In addition, one percent, but not less than one, of all fixed seats shall be aisle seats with no armrests on the aisle side, or removable or folding armrests on the aisle side. Each such seat shall be identified by a sign or marker. Signage notifying patrons of the availability of such seats shall be posted at the ticket office. Aisle seats are not required to comply with 4.33.4.

(b) This paragraph applies to assembly areas where audible communications are integral to the use of the space (e.g., concert and lecture halls, playhouses and movie theaters, meeting rooms, etc.). Such assembly areas, if (1) they accommodate at least 50 persons, or if they have audio-amplification systems, and (2) they have fixed seating, shall have a permanently installed assistive listening system complying with 4.33. For other assembly areas, a permanently installed assistive listening system, or an adequate number of electrical outlets or other supplementary wiring necessary to support a portable assistive listening system shall be provided. The minimum number of receivers to be provided shall be equal to 4 percent of the total number of seats, but in no case less than two. Signage complying with applicable provisions of 4.30 shall be installed to notify patrons of the availability of a listening system.

(20) Where automated teller machines (ATMs) are provided, each ATM shall comply with the requirements of 4.34 except where two or more are provided at a location, then only one must comply.

EXCEPTION: Drive-up-only automated teller machines are not required to comply with 4.27.2, 4.27.3 and 4.34.3.

(21) Where dressing and fitting rooms are provided for use by the general public, patients, customers or employees, 5 percent, but never less than one, of dressing rooms for each type of use in each cluster of dressing rooms shall be accessible and shall comply with 4.35.

Examples of types of dressing rooms are those serving different genders or distinct and different functions as in different treatment or examination facilities.

4.1.4 (Reserved).

4.1.5 Accessible Buildings: Additions.
Each addition to an existing building or facility shall be regarded as an alteration. Each space or element added to the existing building or facility shall comply with the applicable provisions of 4.1.1 to 4.1.3, Minimum Requirements (for New Construction) and the applicable technical specifications of 4.2 through 4.35 and sections 5 through 10. Each addition that

affects or could affect the usability of an area containing a primary function shall comply with 4.1.6(2).

4.1.6 Accessible Buildings: Alterations.

(1) General. Alterations to existing buildings and facilities shall comply with the following:

(a) No alteration shall be undertaken which decreases or has the effect of decreasing accessibility or usability of a building or facility below the requirements for new construction at the time of alteration.

(b) If existing elements, spaces, or common areas are altered, then each such altered element, space, feature, or area shall comply with the applicable provisions of 4.1.1 to 4.1.3 Minimum Requirements (for New Construction). If the applicable provision for new construction requires that an element, space, or common area be on an accessible route, the altered element, space, or common area is not required to be on an accessible route except as provided in 4.1.6(2) (Alterations to an Area Containing a Primary Function.)

(c) If alterations of single elements, when considered together, amount to an alteration of a room or space in a building or facility, the entire space shall be made accessible.

(d) No alteration of an existing element, space, or area of a building or facility shall impose a requirement for greater accessibility than that which would be required for new construction. For example, if the elevators and stairs in a building are being altered and the elevators are, in turn, being made accessible, then no accessibility modifications are required to the stairs connecting levels connected by the elevator. If stair modifications to correct unsafe conditions are required by other codes, the modifications shall be done in compliance with these guidelines unless technically infeasible.

(e) At least one interior public text telephone complying with 4.31.9 shall be provided if:

(i) alterations to existing buildings or facilities with less than four exterior or interior public pay telephones would increase the total number to four or more telephones with at least one in an interior location; or

(ii) alterations to one or more exterior or interior public pay telephones occur in an existing building or facility with four or more public telephones with at least one in an interior location.

(f) If an escalator or stair is planned or installed where none existed previously and major structural modifications are necessary for such installation, then a means of accessible vertical access shall be provided that complies with the applicable provisions of 4.7, 4.8, 4.10, or 4.11.

(g) In alterations, the requirements of 4.1.3(9), 4.3.10 and 4.3.11 do not apply.

(h)*Entrances: If a planned alteration entails alterations to an entrance, and the building has an accessible entrance, the entrance being altered is not required to comply with 4.1.3(8), except to the extent required by 4.1.6(2). If a particular entrance is not made accessible, appropriate accessible signage indicating the location of the nearest accessible entrance(s) shall be installed at or near the inaccessible entrance, such that a person with disabilities will not be required to retrace the approach route from the inaccessible entrance.

(i) If the alteration work is limited solely to the electrical, mechanical, or plumbing system, or to hazardous material abatement, or automatic sprinkler retrofitting, and does not involve the alteration of any elements or spaces required to be accessible under these guidelines, then 4.1.6(2) does not apply.

(j) EXCEPTION: In alteration work, if compliance with 4.1.6 is technically infeasible, the alteration shall provide accessibility to the maximum extent feasible. Any elements or features of the building or facility that are being altered and can be made accessible shall be made accessible within the scope of the alteration.

Technically Infeasible. Means, with respect to an alteration of a building or a facility, that it has little likelihood of being accomplished because existing structural conditions would require removing or altering a load-bearing member which is an essential part of the structural frame; or because other existing physical or site constraints prohibit modification or

4.1.6 Accessible Buildings: Alterations

addition of elements, spaces, or features which are in full and strict compliance with the minimum requirements for new construction and which are necessary to provide accessibility.

(k) EXCEPTION:

(1) These guidelines do not require the installation of an elevator in an altered facility that is less than three stories or has less than 3,000 square feet per story unless the building is a shopping center, a shopping mall, the professional office of a health care provider, or another type of facility as determined by the Attorney General.

(ii) The exemption provided in paragraph (i) does not obviate or limit in any way the obligation to comply with the other accessibility requirements established in these guidelines. For example, alterations to floors above or below the ground floor must be accessible regardless of whether the altered facility has an elevator. If a facility subject to the elevator exemption set forth in paragraph (i) nonetheless has a full passenger elevator, that elevator shall meet, to the maximum extent feasible, the accessibility requirements of these guidelines.

(2) Alterations to an Area Containing a Primary Function: In addition to the requirements of 4.1.6(1), an alteration that affects or could affect the usability of or access to an area containing a primary function shall be made so as to ensure that, to the maximum extent feasible, the path of travel to the altered area and the restrooms, telephones, and drinking fountains serving the altered area, are readily accessible to and usable by individuals with disabilities, unless such alterations are disproportionate to the overall alterations in terms of cost and scope (as determined under criteria established by the Attorney General).

(3) Special Technical Provisions for Alterations to Existing Buildings and Facilities:

(a) Ramps: Curb ramps and interior or exterior ramps to be constructed on sites or in existing buildings or facilities where space limitations prohibit the use of a 1:12 slope or less may have slopes and rises as follows:

(i) A slope between 1:10 and 1:12 is allowed for a maximum rise of 6 inches.

(ii) A slope between 1:8 and 1:10 is allowed for a maximum rise of 3 inches. A slope steeper than 1:8 is not allowed.

(b) Stairs: Full extension of handrails at stairs shall not be required in alterations where such extensions would be hazardous or impossible due to plan configuration.

(c) Elevators:

(i) If safety door edges are provided in existing automatic elevators, automatic door reopening devices may be omitted (see 4.10.6).

(ii) Where existing shaft configuration or technical infeasibility prohibits strict compliance with 4.10.9, the minimum car plan dimensions may be reduced by the minimum amount necessary, but in no case shall the inside car area be smaller than 48 in by 48 in.

(iii) Equivalent facilitation may be provided with an elevator car of different dimensions when usability can be demonstrated and when all other elements required to be accessible comply with the applicable provisions of 4.10. For example, an elevator of 47 in by 69 in (1195 mm by 1755 mm) with a door opening on the narrow dimension, could accommodate the standard wheelchair clearances shown in Figure 4.

(d) Doors:

(i) Where it is technically infeasible to comply with clear opening width requirements of 4.13.5, a projection of 5/8 in maximum will be permitted for the latch side stop.

(ii) If existing thresholds are 3/4 in high or less, and have (or are modified to have) a beveled edge on each side, they may remain.

(e) Toilet Rooms:

(i) Where it is technically infeasible to comply with 4.22 or 4.23, the installation of at least one unisex toilet/bathroom per floor, located in the same area as existing toilet facilities, will be permitted in lieu of modifying existing toilet facilities to be accessible. Each unisex toilet room shall contain one water closet complying with 4.16 and one lavatory complying with 4.19, and the door shall have a privacy latch.

(ii) Where it is technically infeasible to install a required standard stall (Fig. 30(a)), or where other codes prohibit reduction of the fixture count (i.e., removal of a water closet in order to create a double-wide stall), either alternate stall (Fig.30(b)) may be provided in lieu of the standard stall.

(iii) When existing toilet or bathing facilities are being altered and are not made accessible, signage complying with 4.30.1, 4.30.2, 4.30.3, 4.30.5, and 4.30.7 shall be provided indicating the location of the nearest accessible toilet or bathing facility within the facility.

(f) Assembly Areas:

(i) Where it is technically infeasible to disperse accessible seating throughout an altered assembly area, accessible seating areas may be clustered. Each accessible seating area shall have provisions for companion seating and shall be located on an accessible route that also serves as a means of emergency egress.

(ii) Where it is technically infeasible to alter all performing areas to be on an accessible route, at least one of each type of performing area shall be made accessible.

(g) Platform Lifts (Wheelchair Lifts): In alterations, platform lifts (wheelchair lifts) complying with 4.11 and applicable state or local codes may be used as part of an accessible route. The use of lifts is not limited to the four conditions in exception 4 of 4.1.3(5).

(h) Dressing Rooms: In alterations where technical infeasibility can be demonstrated, one dressing room for each sex on each level shall be made accessible. Where only unisex dressing rooms are provided, accessible unisex dressing rooms may be used to fulfill this requirement.

4.1.7 Accessible Buildings: Historic Preservation.

(1) Applicability:

(a) General Rule. Alterations to a qualified historic building or facility shall comply with 4.1.6 Accessible Buildings: Alterations, the applicable technical specifications of 4.2

through 4.35 and the applicable special application sections 5 through 10 unless it is determined in accordance with the procedures in 4.1.7(2) that compliance with the requirements for accessible routes (exterior and interior), ramps, entrances, or toilets would threaten or destroy the historic significance of the building or facility in which case the alternative requirements in 4.1.7(3) may be used for the feature.

EXCEPTION: (Reserved).

(b) Definition. A qualified historic building or facility is a building or facility that is:

(i) Listed in or eligible for listing in the National Register of Historic Places; or

(ii) Designated as historic under an appropriate State or local law.

(2) Procedures:

(a) Alterations to Qualified Historic Buildings and Facilities Subject to Section 106 of the National Historic Preservation Act:

(i) Section 106 Process. Section 106 of the National Historic Preservation Act (16 U.S.C. 470 f) requires that a Federal agency with jurisdiction over a Federal, federally assisted, or federally licensed undertaking consider the effects of the agency's undertaking on buildings and facilities listed in or eligible for listing in the National Register of Historic Places and give the Advisory Council on Historic Preservation a reasonable opportunity to comment on the undertaking prior to approval of the undertaking.

(ii) ADA Application. Where alterations are undertaken to a qualified historic building or facility that is subject to section 106 of the National Historic Preservation Act, the Federal agency with jurisdiction over the undertaking shall follow the section 106 process. If the State Historic Preservation Officer or Advisory Council on Historic Preservation agrees that compliance with the requirements for accessible routes (exterior and interior), ramps, entrances, or toilets would threaten or destroy the historic significance of the building or facility, the alternative requirements in 4.1.7(3) may be used for the feature.

4.2 Space Allowance and Reach Ranges

(b) Alterations to Qualified Historic Buildings and Facilities Not Subject to Section 106 of the National Historic Preservation Act. Where alterations are undertaken to a qualified historic building or facility that is not subject to section 106 of the National Historic Preservation Act, if the entity undertaking the alterations believes that compliance with the requirements for accessible routes (exterior and interior), ramps, entrances, or toilets would threaten or destroy the historic significance of the building or facility and that the alternative requirements in 4.1.7(3) should be used for the feature, the entity should consult with the State Historic Preservation Officer. If the State Historic Preservation Officer agrees that compliance with the accessibility requirements for accessible routes (exterior and interior), ramps, entrances or toilets would threaten or destroy the historical significance of the building or facility, the alternative requirements in 4.1.7(3) may be used.

(c) Consultation With Interested Persons. Interested persons should be invited to participate in the consultation process, including State or local accessibility officials, individuals with disabilities, and organizations representing individuals with disabilities.

(d) Certified Local Government Historic Preservation Programs. Where the State Historic Preservation Officer has delegated the consultation responsibility for purposes of this section to a local government historic preservation program that has been certified in accordance with section 101(c) of the National Historic Preservation Act of 1966 (16 U.S.C. 470a (c)) and implementing regulations (36 CFR 61.5), the responsibility may be carried out by the appropriate local government body or official.

(3) Historic Preservation: Minimum Requirements:

(a) At least one accessible route complying with 4.3 from a site access point to an accessible entrance shall be provided.

EXCEPTION: A ramp with a slope no greater than 1:6 for a run not to exceed 2 ft (610 mm) may be used as part of an accessible route to an entrance.

(b) At least one accessible entrance complying with 4.14 which is used by the public shall be provided.

EXCEPTION: If it is determined that no entrance used by the public can comply with 4.14, then access at any entrance not used by the general public but open (unlocked) with directional signage at the primary entrance may be used. The accessible entrance shall also have a notification system. Where security is a problem, remote monitoring may be used.

(c) If toilets are provided, then at least one toilet facility complying with 4.22 and 4.1.6 shall be provided along an accessible route that complies with 4.3. Such toilet facility may be unisex in design.

(d) Accessible routes from an accessible entrance to all publicly used spaces on at least the level of the accessible entrance shall be provided. Access shall be provided to all levels of a building or facility in compliance with 4.1 whenever practical.

(e) Displays and written information, documents, etc., should be located where they can be seen by a seated person. Exhibits and signage displayed horizontally (e.g., open books), should be no higher than 44 in (1120 mm) above the floor surface.

NOTE: The technical provisions of sections 4.2 through 4.35 are the same as those of the American National Standard Institute's document A117.1-1980, except as noted in the text.

4.2 Space Allowance and Reach Ranges.

4.2.1* Wheelchair Passage Width. The minimum clear width for single wheelchair passage shall be 32 in (815 mm) at a point and 36 in (915 mm) continuously (see Fig. 1 and 24(e)).

4.2.2 Width for Wheelchair Passing. The minimum width for two wheelchairs to pass is 60 in (1525 mm) (see Fig. 2).

4.2.3* Wheelchair Turning Space. The space required for a wheelchair to make a 180-degree turn is a clear space of 60 in (1525 mm)

4.2.4° Clear Floor or Ground Space for Wheelchairs

diameter (see Fig. 3(a)) or a T-shaped space (see Fig. 3(b)).

4.2.4° Clear Floor or Ground Space for Wheelchairs.

4.2.4.1 Size and Approach. The minimum clear floor or ground space required to accommodate a single, stationary wheelchair and occupant is 30 in by 48 in (760 mm by 1220 mm) (see Fig. 4(a)). The minimum clear floor or ground space for wheelchairs may be positioned for forward or parallel approach to an object (see Fig. 4(b) and (c)). Clear floor or ground space for wheelchairs may be part of the knee space required under some objects.

4.2.4.2 Relationship of Maneuvering Clearance to Wheelchair Spaces. One full unobstructed side of the clear floor or ground space for a wheelchair shall adjoin or overlap an accessible route or adjoin another wheelchair clear floor space. If a clear floor space is located in an alcove or otherwise confined on all or part of three sides, additional maneuvering clearances shall be provided as shown in Fig. 4(d) and (e).

4.2.4.3 Surfaces for Wheelchair Spaces. Clear floor or ground spaces for wheelchairs shall comply with 4.5.

4.2.5° Forward Reach. If the clear floor space only allows forward approach to an object, the maximum high forward reach allowed shall be 48 in (1220 mm) (see Fig. 5(a)). *The minimum low forward reach is 15 in (380 mm).* If the high forward reach is over an obstruction, reach and clearances shall be as shown in Fig. 5(b).

4.2.6° Side Reach. If the clear floor space allows parallel approach by a person in a wheelchair, the maximum high side reach allowed shall be 54 in (1370 mm) and the low side reach shall be no less than 9 in (230 mm) above the floor (Fig. 6(a) and (b)). If the side reach is over an obstruction, the reach and clearances shall be as shown in Fig 6(c).

4.3 Accessible Route.

4.3.1° General. All walks, halls, corridors, aisles, *skywalks, tunnels,* and other spaces

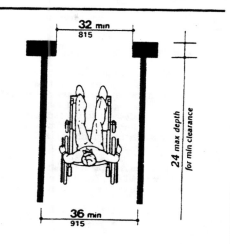

Fig. 1
Minimum Clear Width
for Single Wheelchair

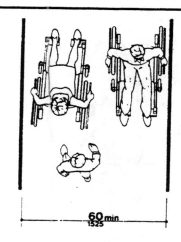

Fig. 2
Minimum Clear Width
for Two Wheelchairs

4.3 Accessible Route

that are part of an accessible route shall comply with 4.3.

4.3.2 Location.

(1) At least one accessible route *within the boundary of the site* shall be provided from public transportation stops, accessible parking, and accessible passenger loading zones, and public streets or sidewalks to the accessible building entrance they serve. *The accessible route shall, to the maximum extent feasible, coincide with the route for the general public.*

(2) At least one accessible route shall connect accessible buildings, facilities, elements, and spaces that are on the same site.

(3) At least one accessible route shall connect accessible building or facility entrances with all accessible spaces and elements and with all accessible dwelling units within the building or facility.

(4) An accessible route shall connect at least one accessible entrance of each accessible

dwelling unit with those exterior and interior spaces and facilities that serve the accessible dwelling unit.

4.3.3 Width.
The minimum clear width of an accessible route shall be 36 in (915 mm) except at doors (see 4.13.5 and 4.13.6). If a person in a wheelchair must make a turn around an obstruction, the minimum clear width of the accessible route shall be as shown in Fig. 7(a) and (b).

4.3.4 Passing Space.
If an accessible route has less than 60 in (1525 mm) clear width, then passing spaces at least 60 in by 60 in (1525 mm by 1525 mm) shall be located at reasonable intervals not to exceed 200 ft (61 m). A T-intersection of two corridors or walks is an acceptable passing place.

4.3.5 Head Room.
Accessible routes shall comply with 4.4.2.

4.3.6 Surface Textures.
The surface of an accessible route shall comply with 4.5.

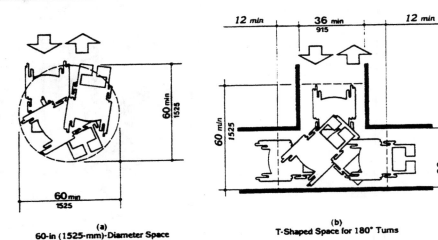

(a)
60-in (1525-mm)-Diameter Space

(b)
T-Shaped Space for 180° Turns

Fig. 3
Wheelchair Turning Space

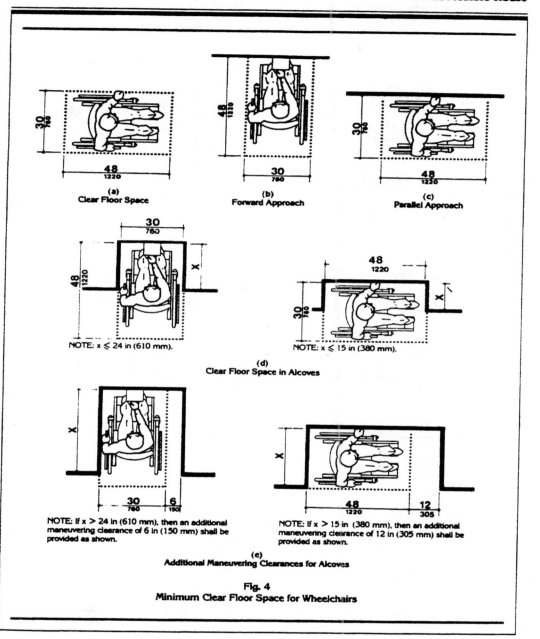

(a)
Clear Floor Space

(b)
Forward Approach

(c)
Parallel Approach

NOTE: x ≤ 24 in (610 mm).

NOTE: x ≤ 15 in (380 mm).

(d)
Clear Floor Space in Alcoves

NOTE: If x > 24 in (610 mm), then an additional maneuvering clearance of 6 in (150 mm) shall be provided as shown.

NOTE: If x > 15 in (380 mm), then an additional maneuvering clearance of 12 in (305 mm) shall be provided as shown.

(e)
Additional Maneuvering Clearances for Alcoves

Fig. 4
Minimum Clear Floor Space for Wheelchairs

4.3 Accessible Route

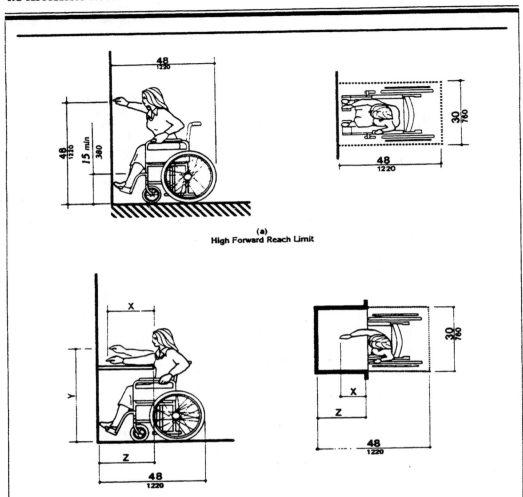

(a)
High Forward Reach Limit

NOTE: x shall be ≤ 25 in (635 mm); z shall be ≥ x. When x < 20 in (510 mm), then y shall be 48 in (1220 mm) maximum. When x is 20 to 25 in (510 to 635 mm), then y shall be 44 in (1120 mm) maximum.

(b)
Maximum Forward Reach over an Obstruction

Fig. 5
Forward Reach

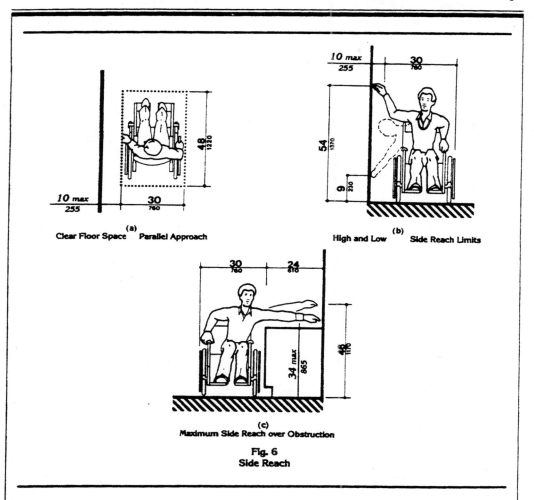

(a)
Clear Floor Space   Parallel Approach

(b)
High and Low   Side Reach Limits

(c)
Maximum Side Reach over Obstruction

Fig. 6
Side Reach

4.3.7 Slope. An accessible route with a running slope greater than 1:20 is a ramp and shall comply with 4.8. Nowhere shall the cross slope of an accessible route exceed 1:50.

4.3.8 Changes in Levels. Changes in levels along an accessible route shall comply with 4.5.2. If an accessible route has changes in level greater than 1/2 in (13 mm), then a curb ramp, ramp, elevator, or platform lift *(as permitted in 4.1.3 and 4.1.6)* shall be provided that complies with 4.7, 4.8, 4.10, or 4.11, respectively. An accessible route does not include stairs, steps, or escalators. See definition of "egress, means of" in 3.5.

4.3.9 Doors. Doors along an accessible route shall comply with 4.13.

4.3.10° Egress

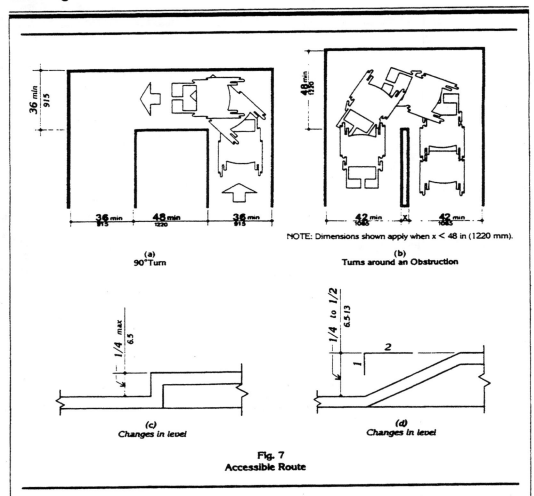

(a)
90°Turn

(b)
Turns around an Obstruction

NOTE: Dimensions shown apply when x < 48 in (1220 mm).

(c)
Changes in level

(d)
Changes in level

Fig. 7
Accessible Route

4.3.10° Egress. Accessible routes serving any accessible space or element shall also serve as a means of egress for emergencies or connect to an accessible area of *rescue assistance.*

4.3.11 *Areas of Rescue Assistance.*

4.3.11.1 Location and Cónstruction. An area *of rescue assistance shall be one of the following:*

(1) A portion of a stairway landing within a smokeproof enclosure (complying with local requirements).

(2) A portion of an exterior exit balcony located immediately adjacent to an exit stairway when the balcony complies with local requirements for exterior exit balconies. Openings to the interior of the building located within 20 feet (6 m) of the

area of rescue assistance shall be protected with fire assemblies having a three-fourths hour fire protection rating.

(3) A portion of a one-hour fire-resistive corridor (complying with local requirements for fire-resistive construction and for openings) located immediately adjacent to an exit enclosure.

(4) A vestibule located immediately adjacent to an exit enclosure and constructed to the same fire-resistive standards as required for corridors and openings.

(5) A portion of a stairway landing within an exit enclosure which is vented to the exterior and is separated from the interior of the building with not less than one-hour fire-resistive doors.

(6) When approved by the appropriate local authority, an area or a room which is separated from other portions of the building by a smoke barrier. Smoke barriers shall have a fire-resistive rating of not less than one hour and shall completely enclose the area or room. Doors in the smoke barrier shall be tight-fitting smoke- and draft-control assemblies having a fire-protection rating of not less than 20 minutes and shall be self-closing or automatic closing. The area or room shall be provided with an exit directly to an exit enclosure. Where the room or area exits into an exit enclosure which is required to be of more than one-hour fire-resistive construction, the room or area shall have the same fire-resistive construction, including the same opening protection, as required for the adjacent exit enclosure.

(7) An elevator lobby when elevator shafts and adjacent lobbies are pressurized as required for smokeproof enclosures by local regulations and when complying with requirements herein for size, communication, and signage. Such pressurization system shall be activated by smoke detectors on each floor located in a manner approved by the appropriate local authority. Pressurization equipment and its duct work within the building shall be separated from other portions of the building by a minimum two-hour fire-resistive construction.

4.3.11.2 Size. Each area of rescue assistance shall provide at least two accessible areas each being not less than 30 inches by 48 inches (760 mm by 1220 mm). The area of rescue

assistance shall not encroach on any required exit width. The total number of such 30-inch by 48-inch (760 mm by 1220 mm) areas per story shall be not less than one for every 200 persons of calculated occupant load served by the area of rescue assistance.

EXCEPTION: The appropriate local authority may reduce the minimum number of 30-inch by 48-inch (760 mm by 1220 mm) areas to one for each area of rescue assistance on floors where the occupant load is less than 200.

4.3.11.3° Stairway Width. Each stairway adjacent to an area of rescue assistance shall have a minimum clear width of 48 inches between handrails.

4.3.11.4° Two-way Communication. A method of two-way communication, with both visible and audible signals, shall be provided between each area of rescue assistance and the primary entry. The fire department or appropriate local authority may approve a location other than the primary entry.

4.3.11.5 Identification. Each area of rescue assistance shall be identified by a sign which states "AREA OF RESCUE ASSISTANCE" and displays the international symbol of accessibility. The sign shall be illuminated when exit sign illumination is required. Signage shall also be installed at all inaccessible exits and where otherwise necessary to clearly indicate the direction to areas of rescue assistance. In each area of rescue assistance, instructions on the use of the area under emergency conditions shall be posted adjoining the two-way communication system.

4.4 Protruding Objects.

4.4.1° General. Objects projecting from walls (for example, telephones) with their leading edges between 27 in and 80 in (685 mm and 2030 mm) above the finished floor shall protrude no more than 4 in (100 mm) into walks, halls, corridors, passageways, or aisles (see Fig. 8(a)). Objects mounted with their leading edges at or below 27 in (685 mm) above the finished floor may protrude any amount (see Fig. 8(a) and (b)). Free-standing objects mounted on posts or pylons may overhang 12 in (305 mm) maximum from 27 in to 80 in (685 mm to 2030 mm) above the ground or

4.4 Protruding Objects

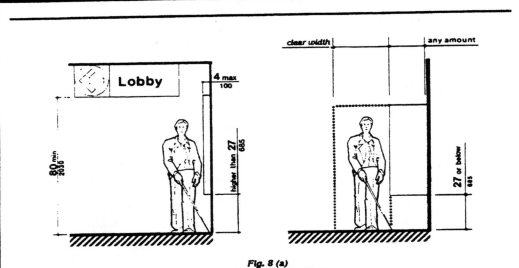

Fig. 8 (a)
Walking Parallel to a Wall

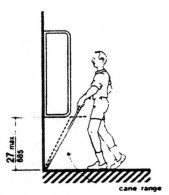

Fig. 8 (b)
Walking Perpendicular to a Wall

Fig. 8
Protruding Objects

finished floor (see Fig. 8(c) and (d)). Protruding objects shall not reduce the clear width of an accessible route or maneuvering space (see Fig. 8(e)).

4.4.2 Head Room. Walks, halls, corridors, passageways, aisles, or other circulation spaces shall have 80 in (2030 mm) minimum clear head room (see Fig. 8(a)). *If vertical clearance of an area adjoining an accessible route is reduced to less than 80 in (nominal dimension), a barrier to warn blind or visually-impaired persons shall be provided (see Fig. 8(c-1)).*

4.5 Ground and Floor Surfaces.

4.5.1° General. Ground and floor surfaces along accessible routes and in accessible rooms and spaces including floors, walks, ramps, stairs, and curb ramps, shall be stable, firm, slip-resistant, and shall comply with 4.5.

4.5.2 Changes in Level. Changes in level up to 1/4 in (6 mm) may be vertical and without edge treatment (*see Fig. 7(c)*). Changes in level between 1/4 in and 1/2 in (6 mm and 13 mm)

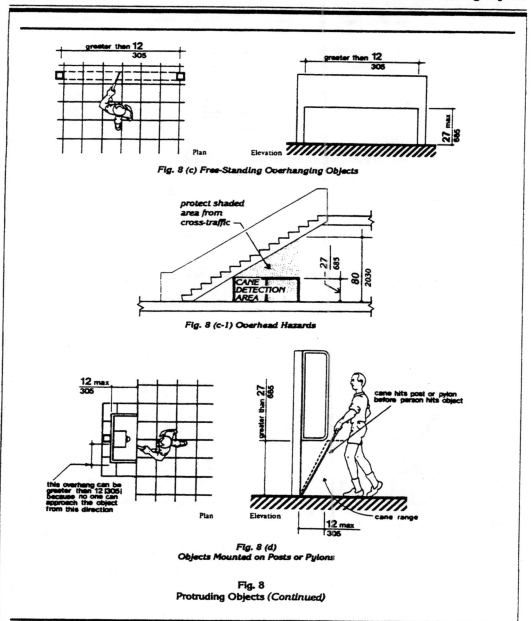

Fig. 8 (c) Free-Standing Overhanging Objects

Fig. 8 (c-1) Overhead Hazards

Fig. 8 (d)
Objects Mounted on Posts or Pylons

Fig. 8
Protruding Objects (Continued)

4.5 Ground and Floor Surfaces

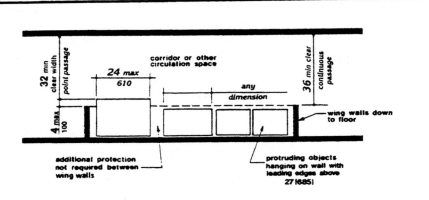

Fig. 8 (e)
Example of Protection around Wall-Mounted Objects and Measurements of Clear Widths

Fig. 8
Protruding Objects *(Continued)*

shall be beveled with a slope no greater than 1:2 *(see Fig. 7(d))*. Changes in level greater than 1/2 in (13 mm) shall be accomplished by means of a ramp that complies with 4.7 or 4.8.

4.5.3° Carpet. If carpet or carpet tile is used on a ground or floor surface, then it shall be securely attached; have a firm cushion, pad, or backing, or no cushion or pad; and have a level loop, textured loop, level cut pile, or level cut/uncut pile texture. The maximum pile *thickness* shall be 1/2 in (13 mm) (see Fig. 8(f)). Exposed edges of carpet shall be fastened to floor surfaces and have trim along the entire length of the exposed edge. Carpet edge trim shall comply with 4.5.2.

4.5.4 Gratings. If gratings are located in walking surfaces, then they shall have spaces no greater than 1/2 in (13 mm) wide in one direction *(see Fig. 8(g))*. If gratings have elongated openings, then they shall be placed so that the long dimension is perpendicular to the dominant direction of travel *(see Fig. 8(h))*.

4.6 Parking and Passenger Loading Zones.

4.6.1 Minimum Number. *Parking spaces required to be accessible by 4.1 shall comply with 4.6.2 through 4.6.5. Passenger loading zones required to be accessible by 4.1 shall comply with 4.6.5 and 4.6.6.*

4.6 Parking and Passenger Loading Zones

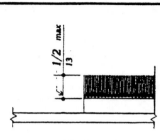

Fig. 8 (f)
Carpet Pile Thickness

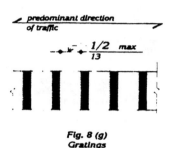

Fig. 8 (g)
Gratings

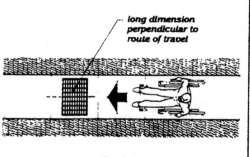

Fig. 8 (h)
Grating Orientation

4.6.2 Location. *Accessible parking spaces serving* a particular building shall be located on the shortest accessible route of travel *from adjacent parking* to an accessible entrance. *In parking facilities that do not serve a particular building, accessible parking* shall be located on the shortest accessible route *of travel* to an accessible pedestrian entrance of the parking facility. *In buildings with multiple accessible entrances with adjacent parking, accessible parking spaces shall be dispersed and located closest to the accessible entrances.*

4.6.3° Parking Spaces. *Accessible* parking spaces shall be at least 96 in (2440 mm) wide. Parking access aisles shall be part of an accessible route to the building or facility entrance and shall comply with 4.3. Two accessible parking spaces may share a common access aisle (see Fig. 9). Parked vehicle overhangs shall not reduce the clear width of an accessible route. *Parking spaces and access aisles shall be level with surface slopes not exceeding 1:50 (2%) in all directions.*

4.6.4° Signage. Accessible parking spaces shall be designated as reserved by a sign showing the symbol of accessibility (see 4.30.7). *Spaces complying with 4.1.2(5)(b) shall have an additional sign "Van-Accessible" mounted below the symbol of accessibility.* Such signs shall be located so they cannot be obscured by a vehicle parked in the space.

4.6.5° Vertical Clearance. *Provide minimum vertical clearance of 114 in (2895 mm) at accessible passenger loading zones and along at least one vehicle access route to such areas from site entrance(s) and exit(s). At parking spaces complying with 4.1.2(5)(b), provide minimum vertical clearance of 98 in (2490 mm) at the parking space and along at least one vehicle access route to such spaces from site entrance(s) and exit(s).*

4.6.6 Passenger Loading Zones. Passenger loading zones shall provide an access aisle at least 60 in (1525 mm) wide and 20 ft (240 in) (6100 mm) long adjacent and parallel to the vehicle pull-up space (see Fig. 10). If there are curbs between the access aisle and the vehicle pull-up space, then a curb ramp complying with 4.7 shall be provided. *Vehicle standing spaces and access aisles shall be level with*

4.7 Curb Ramps

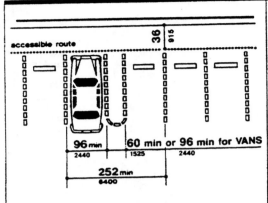

Fig. 9
Dimensions of Parking Spaces

---

surface slopes not exceeding 1:50 (2%) in all directions.

4.7 Curb Ramps.

4.7.1 Location. Curb ramps complying with 4.7 shall be provided wherever an accessible route crosses a curb.

4.7.2 Slope. Slopes of curb ramps shall comply with 4.8.2. The slope shall be measured as shown in Fig. 11. *Transitions from ramps to walks, gutters, or streets shall be flush and free of abrupt changes. Maximum slopes of adjoining gutters, road surface immediately adjacent to the curb ramp, or accessible route shall not exceed 1:20.*

4.7.3 Width. The minimum width of a curb ramp shall be 36 in (915 mm), exclusive of flared sides.

4.7.4 Surface. Surfaces of curb ramps shall comply with 4.5.

4.7.5 Sides of Curb Ramps. If a curb ramp is located where pedestrians must walk across the ramp, *or where it is not protected by hand-rails or guardrails,* it shall have flared sides; the maximum slope of the flare shall be 1:10 (see Fig. 12(a)). Curb ramps with returned curbs

may be used where pedestrians would not normally walk across the ramp (see Fig. 12(b)).

4.7.6 Built-up Curb Ramps. Built-up curb ramps shall be located so that they do not project into vehicular traffic lanes (see Fig. 13).

4.7.7 Detectable Warnings. A curb ramp shall have a *detectable* warning complying with 4.29.2. *The detectable warning shall extend* the full width and depth of the curb ramp.

4.7.8 Obstructions. Curb ramps shall be located or protected to prevent their obstruction by parked vehicles.

4.7.9 Location at Marked Crossings. Curb ramps at marked crossings shall be wholly contained within the markings, excluding any flared sides (see Fig. 15).

4.7.10 Diagonal Curb Ramps. If diagonal (or corner type) curb ramps have returned curbs or other well-defined edges, such edges shall be parallel to the direction of pedestrian flow. The bottom of diagonal curb ramps shall have 48 in (1220 mm) minimum clear space as shown in Fig. 15(c) and (d). If diagonal curb ramps are provided at marked crossings, the 48 in (1220 mm) clear space shall be within the markings (see Fig. 15(c) and (d)). If diagonal curb ramps have flared sides, they shall also have at least a 24 in (610 mm) long segment of straight curb located on each side of the curb ramp and within the marked crossing (see Fig. 15(c)).

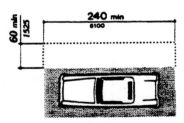

Fig. 10
Access Aisle at Passenger Loading Zones

4.8 Ramps

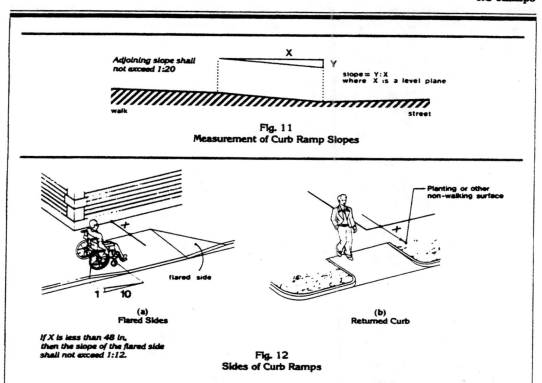

Fig. 11
Measurement of Curb Ramp Slopes

(a)
Flared Sides

(b)
Returned Curb

*If X is less than 48 in,
then the slope of the flared side
shall not exceed 1:12.*

Fig. 12
Sides of Curb Ramps

4.7.11 Islands. Any raised islands in crossings shall be cut through level with the street or have curb ramps at both sides and a level area at least 48 in (1220 mm) long between the curb ramps in the part of the island intersected by the crossings (see Fig. 15(a) and (b)).

4.8 Ramps.

4.8.1° General. Any part of an accessible route with a slope greater than 1:20 shall be considered a ramp and shall comply with 4.8.

4.8.2° Slope and Rise. The least possible slope shall be used for any ramp. The maximum slope of a ramp in new construction shall be 1:12. The maximum rise for any run shall be 30 in (760 mm) (see Fig. 16). Curb ramps

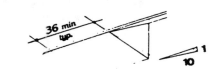

Fig. 13
Built-Up Curb Ramp

and ramps to be constructed on existing sites or in existing buildings or facilities may have slopes and rises as *allowed in 4.1.6(3)(a)* if space limitations prohibit the use of a 1:12 slope or less.

4.8 Ramps

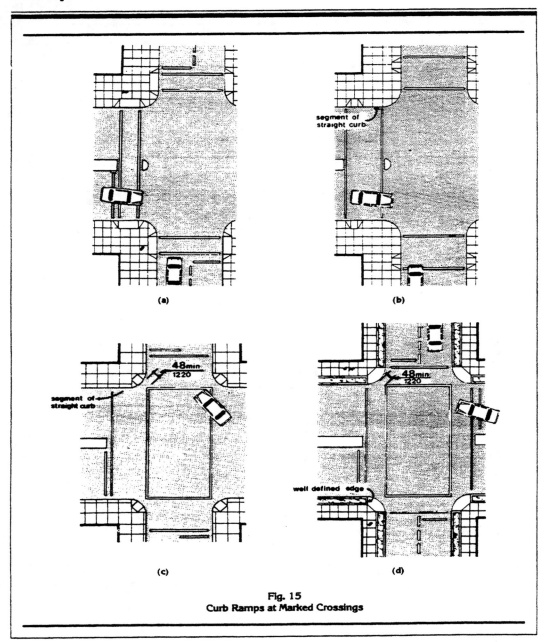

Fig. 15
Curb Ramps at Marked Crossings

4.8 Ramps

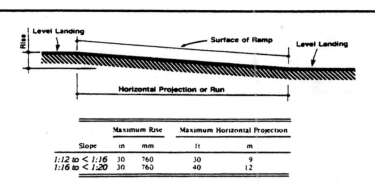

Fig. 16
Components of a Single Ramp Run and Sample Ramp Dimensions

Slope	Maximum Rise		Maximum Horizontal Projection	
	in	mm	ft	m
1:12 to < 1:16	30	760	30	9
1:16 to < 1:20	30	760	40	12

4.8.3 Clear Width. The minimum clear width of a ramp shall be 36 in (915 mm).

4.8.4* Landings. Ramps shall have level landings at bottom and top of *each ramp and each ramp* run. Landings shall have the following features:

(1) The landing shall be at least as wide as the ramp run leading to it.

(2) The landing length shall be a minimum of 60 in (1525 mm) clear.

(3) If ramps change direction at landings, the minimum landing size shall be 60 in by 60 in (1525 mm by 1525 mm).

(4) If a doorway is located at a landing, then the area in front of the doorway shall comply with 4.13.6.

4.8.5* Handrails. If a ramp run has a rise greater than 6 in (150 mm) or a horizontal projection greater than 72 in (1830 mm), then it shall have handrails on both sides. Handrails are not required on curb ramps *or adjacent to seating in assembly areas.* Handrails shall comply with 4.26 and shall have the following features:

(1) Handrails shall be provided along both sides of ramp segments. The inside handrail on switchback or dogleg ramps shall always be continuous.

(2) If handrails are not continuous, they shall extend at least 12 in (305 mm) beyond the top and bottom of the ramp segment and shall be parallel with the floor or ground surface (see Fig. 17).

(3) The clear space between the handrail and the wall shall be 1 - 1/2 in (38 mm).

(4) Gripping surfaces shall be continuous.

(5) *Top of handrail gripping surfaces shall be mounted between 34 in and 38 in (865 mm and 965 mm) above ramp surfaces.*

(6) *Ends of handrails shall be either rounded or returned smoothly to floor, wall, or post.*

(7) *Handrails shall not rotate within their fittings.*

4.8.6 Cross Slope and Surfaces. The cross slope of ramp surfaces shall be no greater than 1:50. Ramp surfaces shall comply with 4.5.

4.8.7 Edge Protection. Ramps and landings with drop-offs shall have curbs, walls, railings, or projecting surfaces that prevent people from slipping off the ramp. Curbs shall be a minimum of 2 in (50 mm) high (see Fig. 17).

4.8.8 Outdoor Conditions. Outdoor ramps and their approaches shall be designed so that water will not accumulate on walking surfaces.

4.9 Stairs.

4.9.1* Minimum Number. *Stairs required to be accessible by 4.1 shall comply with 4.9.*

4.9.2 Treads and Risers. On any given flight of stairs, all steps shall have uniform riser heights and uniform tread widths. Stair treads shall be no less than 11 in (280 mm) wide, measured from riser to riser (see Fig. 18(a)). *Open risers are not permitted.*

4.9.3 Nosings. The undersides of nosings shall not be abrupt. The radius of curvature at the leading edge of the tread shall be no greater than 1/2 in (13 mm). Risers shall be sloped or the underside of the nosing shall have an angle not less than 60 degrees from the horizontal. Nosings shall project no more than 1-1/2 in (38 mm) (see Fig. 18).

4.9.4 Handrails. Stairways shall have handrails at both sides of all stairs. Handrails shall comply with 4.26 and shall have the following features:

(1) Handrails shall be continuous along both sides of stairs. The inside handrail on switchback or dogleg stairs shall always be continuous (see Fig. 19(a) and (b)).

(2) If handrails are not continuous, they shall extend at least 12 in (305 mm) beyond the top riser and at least 12 in (305 mm) plus the width of one tread beyond the bottom riser. At the top, the extension shall be parallel with the floor or ground surface. At the bottom, the handrail shall continue to slope for a distance of the width of one tread from the bottom riser; the remainder of the extension shall be horizontal (see Fig. 19(c) and (d)). Handrail extensions shall comply with 4.4.

(3) The clear space between handrails and wall shall be 1-1/2 in (38 mm).

(4) Gripping surfaces shall be uninterrupted by newel posts, other construction elements, or obstructions.

(5) *Top of handrail gripping surface shall be mounted between 34 in and 38 in (865 mm and 965 mm) above stair nosings.*

(6) *Ends of handrails shall be either rounded or returned smoothly to floor, wall or post.*

(7) *Handrails shall not rotate within their fittings.*

4.9.5 Detectable Warnings at Stairs. *(Reserved).*

4.9.6 Outdoor Conditions. Outdoor stairs and their approaches shall be designed so that water will not accumulate on walking surfaces.

4.10 Elevators.

4.10.1 General. *Accessible* elevators shall be on an accessible route and shall comply with 4.10 and with the *ASME A17.1-1990,* Safety Code for Elevators and Escalators. *Freight elevators shall not be considered as meeting the requirements of this section unless the only elevators provided are used as combination passenger and freight elevators for the public and employees.*

4.10.2 Automatic Operation. Elevator operation shall be automatic. Each car shall be equipped with a self-leveling feature that will automatically bring the car to floor landings within a tolerance of 1/2 in (13 mm) under rated loading to zero loading conditions. This self-leveling feature shall be automatic and independent of the operating device and shall correct the overtravel or undertravel.

4.10.3 Hall Call Buttons. Call buttons in elevator lobbies and halls shall be centered at 42 in (1065 mm) above the floor. Such call buttons shall have visual signals to indicate when each call is registered and when each call is answered. Call buttons shall be a minimum of 3/4 in (19 mm) in the smallest dimension. The button designating the up direction shall be on top. (See Fig. 20.) *Buttons shall be raised or flush. Objects mounted beneath hall call buttons shall not project into the elevator lobby more than 4 in (100 mm).*

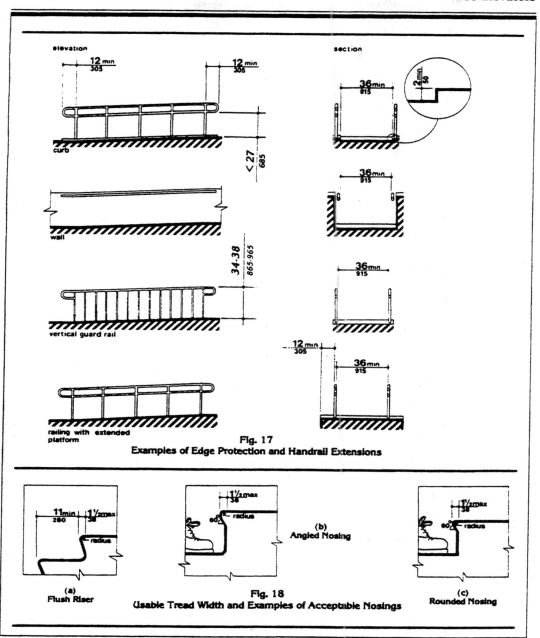

Fig. 17
Examples of Edge Protection and Handrail Extensions

Fig. 18
Usable Tread Width and Examples of Acceptable Nosings

(a)
Flush Riser

(b)
Angled Nosing

(c)
Rounded Nosing

4.10 Elevators

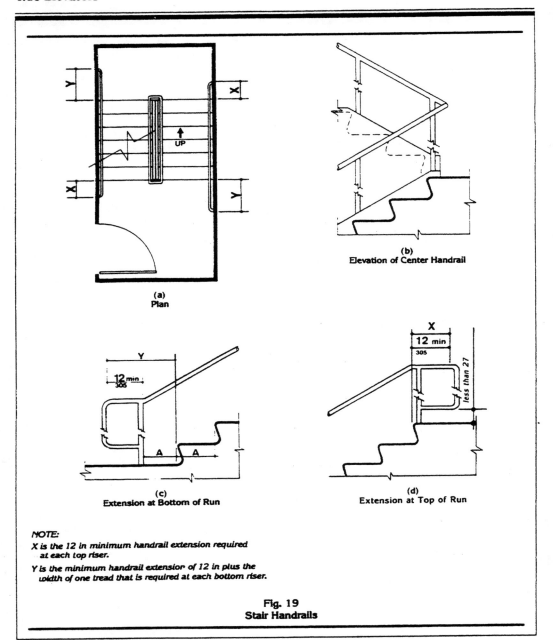

NOTE:

X is the 12 in minimum handrail extension required at each top riser.

Y is the minimum handrail extension of 12 in plus the width of one tread that is required at each bottom riser.

Fig. 19
Stair Handrails

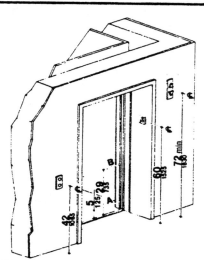

NOTE: The automatic door reopening device is activated if an object passes through either line A or line B. Line A and line B represent the vertical locations of the door reopening device not requiring contact.

Fig. 20
Hoistway and Elevator Entrances

4.10.4 Hall Lanterns. A visible and audible signal shall be provided at each hoistway entrance to indicate which car is answering a call. Audible signals shall sound once for the up direction and twice for the down direction or shall have verbal annunciators that say "up" or "down." Visible signals shall have the following features:

(1) Hall lantern fixtures shall be mounted so that their centerline is at least 72 in (1830 mm) above the lobby floor. (See Fig. 20.)

(2) Visual elements shall be at least 2-1/2 in (64 mm) in the smallest dimension.

(3) Signals shall be visible from the vicinity of the hall call button (see Fig. 20). In-car lanterns located in cars, visible from the vicinity of hall call buttons, and conforming to the above requirements, shall be acceptable.

4.10.5 Raised and Braille Characters on Hoistway Entrances. All elevator hoistway entrances shall have *raised and Braille* floor designations provided on both jambs. The centerline of the characters shall be 60 in (1525 mm) *above finish* floor. Such characters shall be 2 in (50 mm) high and shall comply with 4.30.4. Permanently applied plates are acceptable if they are permanently fixed to the jambs. (See Fig. 20).

4.10.6* Door Protective and Reopening Device. Elevator doors shall open and close automatically. They shall be provided with a reopening device that will stop and reopen a car door and hoistway door automatically if the door becomes obstructed by an object or person. The device shall be capable of completing these operations without requiring contact for an obstruction passing through the opening at heights of 5 in and 29 in (125 mm and 735 mm) above finish floor (see Fig. 20). Door reopening devices shall remain effective for at least 20 seconds. After such an interval, doors may close in accordance with the requirements of *ASME A17.1-1990.*

4.10.7* Door and Signal Timing for Hall Calls. The minimum acceptable time from notification that a car is answering a call until the doors of that car start to close shall be calculated from the following equation:

$$T = D/(1.5 \text{ ft/s}) \text{ or } T = D/(445 \text{ mm/s})$$

where T total time in seconds and D distance (in feet or millimeters) from a point in the lobby or corridor 60 in (1525 mm) directly in front of the farthest call button controlling that car to the centerline of its hoistway door (see Fig. 21). For cars with in-car lanterns, T begins when the lantern is visible from the vicinity of hall call buttons and an audible signal is sounded. *The minimum acceptable notification time shall be 5 seconds.*

4.10.8 Door Delay for Car Calls. The minimum time for elevator doors to remain fully open in response to a car call shall be 3 seconds.

4.10.9 Floor Plan of Elevator Cars. The floor area of elevator cars shall provide space for wheelchair users to enter the car, maneuver

4.10.12 Car Controls

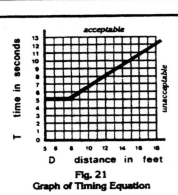

Fig. 21
Graph of Timing Equation

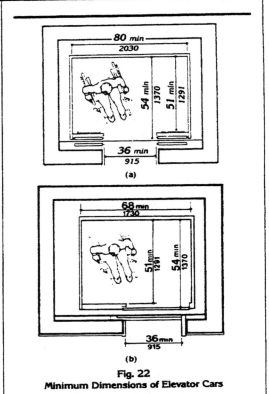

Fig. 22
Minimum Dimensions of Elevator Cars

within reach of controls, and exit from the car. Acceptable door opening and inside dimensions shall be as shown in Fig. 22. The clearance between the car platform sill and the edge of any hoistway landing shall be no greater than 1-1/4 in (32 mm).

4.10.10 Floor Surfaces. Floor surfaces shall comply with 4.5.

4.10.11 Illumination Levels. The level of illumination at the car controls, platform, and car threshold and landing sill shall be at least 5 footcandles (53.8 lux).

4.10.12* Car Controls. Elevator control panels shall have the following features:

(1) Buttons. All control buttons shall be at least 3/4 in (19 mm) in their smallest dimension. They *shall* be *raised* or flush.

(2) Tactile, *Braille*, and Visual Control Indicators. All control buttons shall be designated by *Braille and by raised* standard alphabet characters for letters, arabic characters for numerals, or standard symbols as shown in Fig. 23(a), and as required in *ASME A17.1-1990. Raised and Braille* characters and symbols shall comply with 4.30. The call button for the main entry floor shall be designated by a *raised* star at the left of the floor designation (see Fig. 23(a)). All raised designations for control buttons shall be placed immediately to the left of the button to which they apply. Applied plates.

permanently attached, are an acceptable means to provide raised control designations. Floor buttons shall be provided with visual indicators to show when each call is registered. The visual indicators shall be extinguished when each call is answered.

(3) Height. All floor buttons shall be no higher than 54 in (1370 mm) above the *finish floor for side approach and 48 in (1220 mm) for front approach.* Emergency controls, including the emergency alarm and emergency stop, shall be grouped at the bottom of the panel and shall have their centerlines no less than 35 in (890 mm) above the finish floor (see Fig. 23(a) and (b)).

4.10.13° Car Position Indicators

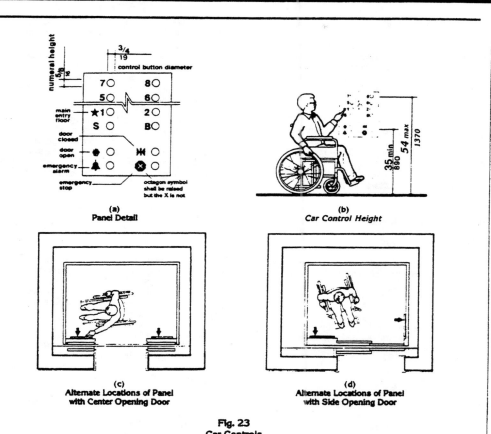

(a)
Panel Detail

(b)
Car Control Height

(c)
**Alternate Locations of Panel
with Center Opening Door**

(d)
**Alternate Locations of Panel
with Side Opening Door**

Fig. 23
Car Controls

(4) Location. Controls shall be located on a front wall if cars have center opening doors, and at the side wall or at the front wall next to the door if cars have side opening doors (see Fig. 23(c) and (d)).

4.10.13° Car Position Indicators. In elevator cars, a visual car position indicator shall be provided above the car control panel or over the door to show the position of the elevator in the hoistway. As the car passes or stops at a floor served by the elevators, the corresponding numerals shall illuminate.

and an audible signal shall sound. Numerals shall be a minimum of 1/2 in (13 mm) high. The audible signal shall be no less than 20 decibels with a frequency no higher than 1500 Hz. An automatic verbal announcement of the floor number at which a car stops or which a car passes may be substituted for the audible signal.

4.10.14° Emergency Communications. If provided, emergency two-way communication systems between the elevator and a point outside the hoistway shall comply with *ASME*

4.11 Platform Lifts (Wheelchair Lifts)

A17.1-1990. The highest operable part of a two-way communication system shall be a maximum of 48 in (1220 mm) from the floor of the car. It shall be identified by a raised symbol and lettering complying with 4.30 and located adjacent to the device. If the system uses a handset then the length of the cord from the panel to the handset shall be at least 29 in (735 mm). *If the system is located in a closed compartment the compartment door hardware shall conform to 4.27, Controls and Operating Mechanisms. The emergency inter-communication system shall not require voice communication.*

4.11 Platform Lifts (Wheelchair Lifts).

4.11.1 Location. *Platform lifts (wheelchair lifts) permitted by 4.1 shall comply with the requirements of 4.11.*

4.11.2° Other Requirements. If platform lifts (wheelchair lifts) are used, they shall comply with 4.2.4, 4.5, 4.27, and *ASME A17.1 Safety Code for Elevators and Escalators, Section XX, 1990.*

4.11.3 Entrance. *If platform lifts are used then they shall facilitate unassisted entry, operation, and exit from the lift in compliance with 4.11.2.*

4.12 Windows.

4.12.1° General. *(Reserved).*

4.12.2° Window Hardware. *(Reserved).*

4.13 Doors.

4.13.1 General. *Doors required to be accessible by 4.1 shall comply with the requirements of 4.13.*

4.13.2 Revolving Doors and Turnstiles. Revolving doors or turnstiles shall not be the only means of passage at an accessible entrance or along an accessible route. *An accessible gate or door shall be provided adjacent to the turnstile or revolving door and shall be so designed as to facilitate the same use pattern.*

4.13.3 Gates. Gates, including ticket gates, shall meet all applicable specifications of 4.13.

4.13.4 Double-Leaf Doorways. If doorways have two *independently operated* door leaves, then at least one leaf shall meet the specifications in 4.13.5 and 4.13.6. That leaf shall be an active leaf.

4.13.5 Clear Width. Doorways shall have a minimum clear opening of 32 in (815 mm) with the door open 90 degrees, measured between the face of the door and the *opposite* stop (see Fig. 24(a), (b), (c), and (d)). Openings more than 24 in (610 mm) in depth shall comply with 4.2.1 and 4.3.3 (see Fig. 24(e)).

EXCEPTION: Doors not requiring full user passage, such as shallow closets, may have the clear opening reduced to 20 in (510 mm) minimum.

4.13.6 Maneuvering Clearances at Doors. Minimum maneuvering clearances at doors that are not automatic or power-assisted shall be as shown in Fig. 25. The floor or ground area within the required clearances shall be level and clear.

EXCEPTION: Entry doors to acute care hospital bedrooms for in-patients shall be exempted from the requirement for space at the latch side of the door (see dimension "x" in Fig. 25) if the door is at least 44 in (1120 mm) wide.

4.13.7 Two Doors in Series. The minimum space between two hinged or pivoted doors in series shall be 48 in (1220 mm) plus the width of any door swinging into the space. Doors in series shall swing either in the same direction or away from the space between the doors (see Fig. 26).

4.13.8° Thresholds at Doorways. Thresholds at doorways shall not exceed 3/4 in (19 mm) in height for exterior sliding doors or 1/2 in (13 mm) for other types of doors. Raised thresholds and floor level changes at accessible doorways shall be beveled with a slope no greater than 1:2 (see 4.5.2).

4.13.9° Door Hardware. Handles, pulls, latches, locks, and other operating devices on accessible doors shall have a shape that is easy

4.13 Doors

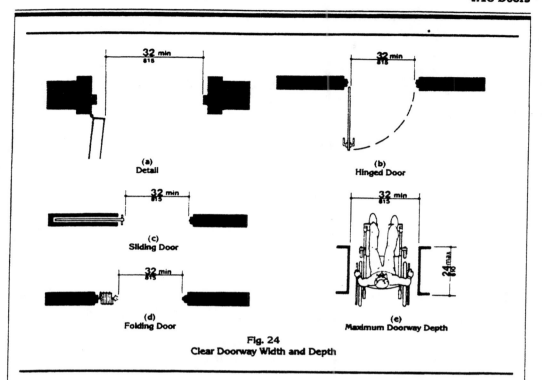

(a)
Detail

(b)
Hinged Door

(c)
Sliding Door

(d)
Folding Door

(e)
Maximum Doorway Depth

Fig. 24
Clear Doorway Width and Depth

to grasp with one hand and does not require tight grasping, tight pinching, or twisting of the wrist to operate. Lever-operated mechanisms, push-type mechanisms, and U-shaped handles are acceptable designs. When sliding doors are fully open, operating hardware shall be exposed and usable from both sides. *Hardware required for accessible door passage shall be mounted no higher than 48 in (1220 mm) above finished floor.*

4.13.10° Door Closers. If a door has a closer, then the sweep period of the closer shall be adjusted so that from an open position of 70 degrees, the door will take at least 3 seconds to move to a point 3 in (75 mm) from the latch, measured to the leading edge of the door.

4.13.11° Door Opening Force. The maximum force for pushing or pulling open a door shall be as follows:

(1) Fire doors shall have the minimum opening force allowable by the appropriate administrative authority.

(2) Other doors.

(a) exterior hinged doors: *(Reserved)*.

(b) interior hinged doors: 5 lbf (22.2N)

(c) sliding or folding doors: 5 lbf (22.2N)

These forces do not apply to the force required to retract latch bolts or disengage other devices that may hold the door in a closed position.

4.13 Doors

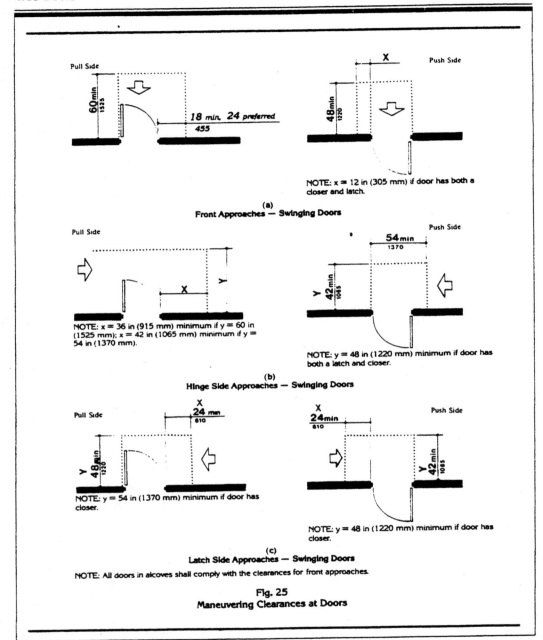

NOTE: x = 12 in (305 mm) if door has both a closer and latch.

(a)
Front Approaches — Swinging Doors

NOTE: x = 36 in (915 mm) minimum if y = 60 in (1525 mm); x = 42 in (1065 mm) minimum if y = 54 in (1370 mm).

NOTE: y = 48 in (1220 mm) minimum if door has both a latch and closer.

(b)
Hinge Side Approaches — Swinging Doors

NOTE: y = 54 in (1370 mm) minimum if door has closer.

NOTE: y = 48 in (1220 mm) minimum if door has closer.

(c)
Latch Side Approaches — Swinging Doors

NOTE: All doors in alcoves shall comply with the clearances for front approaches.

Fig. 25
Maneuvering Clearances at Doors

4.13 Doors

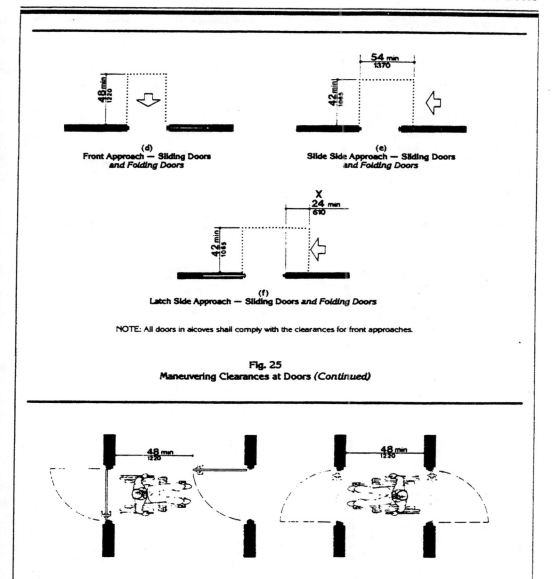

(d)
Front Approach — Sliding Doors
and Folding Doors

(e)
Slide Side Approach — Sliding Doors
and Folding Doors

(f)
Latch Side Approach — Sliding Doors and Folding Doors

NOTE: All doors in alcoves shall comply with the clearances for front approaches.

Fig. 25
Maneuvering Clearances at Doors (Continued)

Fig. 26
Two Hinged Doors in Series

4.13.12° Automatic Doors and Power-Assisted Doors. If an automatic door is used, then it shall comply with *ANSI/BHMA A156.10-1985*. Slowly opening, low-powered, automatic doors shall *comply with ANSI A156.19-1984*. Such doors shall not open to back check faster than 3 seconds and shall require no more than 15 lbf (66.6N) to stop door movement. If a power-assisted door is used, its door-opening force shall comply with 4.13.11 and its closing shall conform to the requirements in *ANSI A156.19-1984*.

4.14 Entrances.

4.14.1 Minimum Number. *Entrances required to be accessible by 4.1* shall be part of an accessible route complying with 4.3. Such entrances shall be connected by an accessible route to public transportation stops, to accessible parking and passenger loading zones, and to public streets or sidewalks if available (see 4.3.2(1)). They shall also be connected by an accessible route to all accessible spaces or elements within the building or facility.

4.14.2 Service Entrances. A service entrance shall not be the sole accessible entrance unless it is the only entrance to a building or facility (for example, in a factory or garage).

4.15 Drinking Fountains and Water Coolers.

4.15.1 Minimum Number. *Drinking fountains or water coolers required to be accessible by 4.1* shall comply with 4.15.

4.15.2° Spout Height. Spouts shall be no higher than 36 in (915 mm), measured from the floor or ground surfaces to the spout outlet (see Fig. 27(a)).

4.15.3 Spout Location. The spouts of drinking fountains and water coolers shall be at the front of the unit and shall direct the water flow in a trajectory that is parallel or nearly parallel to the front of the unit. The spout shall provide a flow of water at least 4 in (100 mm) high so as to allow the insertion of a cup or glass under the flow of water. *On an accessible drinking fountain with a round or*

oval bowl, the spout must be positioned so the flow of water is within 3 in (75 mm) of the front edge of the fountain.

4.15.4 Controls. Controls shall comply with 4.27.4. *Unit controls shall be front mounted or side mounted near the front edge.*

4.15.5 Clearances.

(1) Wall- and post-mounted cantilevered units shall have a clear knee space between the bottom of the apron and the floor or ground at least 27 in (685 mm) high, 30 in (760 mm) wide, and 17 in to 19 in (430 mm to 485 mm) deep (see Fig. 27(a) and (b)). Such units shall also have a minimum clear floor space 30 in by 48 in (760 mm by 1220 mm) to allow a person in a wheelchair to approach the unit facing forward.

(2) Free-standing or built-in units not having a clear space under them shall have a clear floor space at least 30 in by 48 in (760 mm by 1220 mm) that allows a person in a wheelchair to make a parallel approach to the unit (see Fig. 27(c) and (d)). This clear floor space shall comply with 4.2.4.

4.16 Water Closets.

4.16.1 General. Accessible water closets shall comply with 4.16.

4.16.2 Clear Floor Space. Clear floor space for water closets not in stalls shall comply with Fig. 28. Clear floor space may be arranged to allow either a left-handed or right-handed approach.

4.16.3° Height. The height of water closets shall be 17 in to 19 in (430 mm to 485 mm), measured to the top of the toilet seat (see Fig. 29(b)). *Seats shall not be sprung to return to a lifted position.*

4.16.4° Grab Bars. Grab bars for water closets not located in stalls shall comply with 4.26 and Fig. 29. *The grab bar behind the water closet shall be 36 in (915 mm) minimum.*

4.16.5° Flush Controls. Flush controls shall be hand operated or *automatic* and shall comply with 4.27.4. Controls for flush valves shall be mounted on the wide side of toilet areas no more than 44 in (1120 mm) above the floor.

4.16.6 Dispensers. Toilet paper dispensers shall be installed within reach, as shown in Fig. 29(b). *Dispensers that control delivery, or that do not permit continuous paper flow, shall not be used.*

4.17 Toilet Stalls.

4.17.1 Location. Accessible toilet stalls shall be on an accessible route and shall meet the requirements of 4.17.

4.17.2 Water Closets. Water closets in accessible stalls shall comply with 4.16.

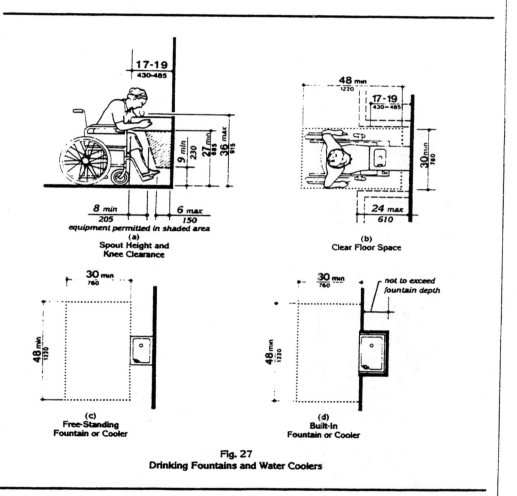

(a)
Spout Height and
Knee Clearance

(b)
Clear Floor Space

(c)
Free-Standing
Fountain or Cooler

(d)
Built-In
Fountain or Cooler

Fig. 27
Drinking Fountains and Water Coolers

4.17 Toilet Stalls

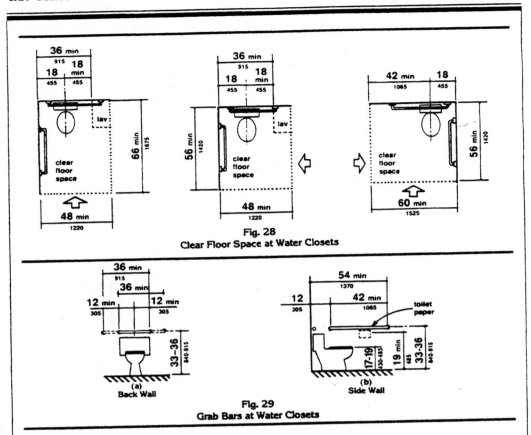

Fig. 28
Clear Floor Space at Water Closets

Fig. 29
Grab Bars at Water Closets

4.17.3° Size and Arrangement. The size and arrangement of the standard toilet stall shall comply with Fig. 30(a), *Standard Stall*. Standard toilet stalls with a minimum depth of 56 in (1420 mm) (see Fig. 30(a)) shall have wall-mounted water closets. If the depth of a standard toilet stall is increased at least 3 in (75 mm), then a floor-mounted water closet may be used. Arrangements shown for standard toilet stalls may be reversed to allow either a left- or right-hand approach. Additional stalls shall be provided in conformance with 4.22.4.

EXCEPTION: In instances of alteration work where provision of a standard stall (Fig. 30(a))

is technically infeasible or where plumbing code requirements prevent combining existing stalls to provide space, either alternate stall (Fig. 30(b)) may be provided in lieu of the standard stall.

4.17.4 Toe Clearances. In standard stalls, the front partition and at least one side partition shall provide a toe clearance of at least 9 in (230 mm) above the floor. If the depth of the stall is greater than 60 in (1525 mm), then the toe clearance is not required.

4.17.5° Doors. Toilet stall doors, *including door hardware*, shall comply with 4.13. *If toilet stall approach is from the latch side of the stall door, clearance between the door side of the*

4.17 Toilet Stalls

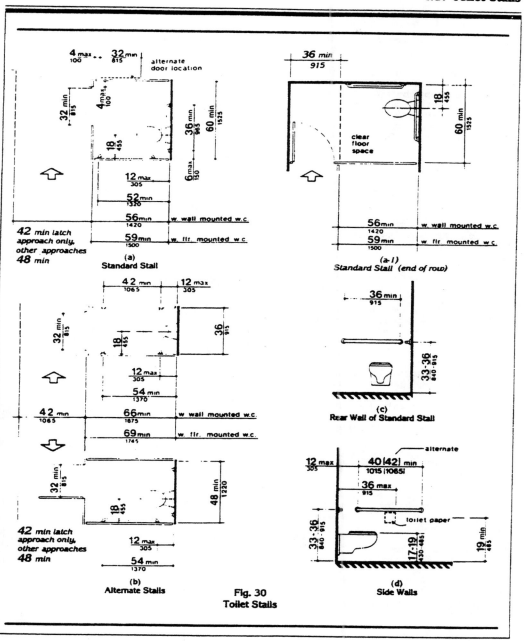

**Fig. 30
Toilet Stalls**

4.19 Lavatories and Mirrors

stall and any obstruction may be reduced to a minimum of 42 in (1065 mm) (Fig. 30).

4.17.6 Grab Bars. Grab bars complying with the length and positioning shown in Fig. 30(a), (b), (c), and (d) shall be provided. Grab bars may be mounted with any desired method as long as they have a gripping surface at the locations shown and do not obstruct the required clear floor area. Grab bars shall comply with 4.26.

4.18 Urinals.

4.18.1 General. Accessible urinals shall comply with 4.18.

4.18.2 Height. Urinals shall be stall-type or wall-hung with an elongated rim at a maximum of 17 in (430 mm) above the finish floor.

4.18.3 Clear Floor Space. A clear floor space 30 in by 48 in (760 mm by 1220 mm) shall be provided in front of urinals to allow forward approach. This clear space shall adjoin or overlap an accessible route and shall comply with 4.2.4. *Urinal shields that do not extend beyond the front edge of the urinal rim may be provided with 29 in (735 mm) clearance between them.*

4.18.4 Flush Controls. Flush controls shall be hand operated or automatic, and shall comply with 4.27.4, and shall be mounted no more than 44 in (1120 mm) above the finish floor.

4.19 Lavatories and Mirrors.

4.19.1 General. The requirements of 4.19 shall apply to lavatory fixtures, vanities, and built-in lavatories.

4.19.2 Height and Clearances. Lavatories shall be mounted with *the rim or counter surface no higher than 34 in (865 mm) above the finish floor.* Provide a clearance of at least 29 in (735 mm) above the finish floor to the bottom of the apron. Knee and toe clearance shall comply with Fig. 31.

4.19.3 Clear Floor Space. A clear floor space 30 in by 48 in (760 mm by 1220 mm) complying with 4.2.4 shall be provided in front of a lavatory to allow forward approach. Such

clear floor space shall adjoin or overlap an accessible route and shall extend a maximum of 19 in (485 mm) underneath the lavatory (see Fig. 32).

4.19.4 Exposed Pipes and Surfaces. Hot water and drain pipes under lavatories shall be insulated or otherwise *configured to protect against contact.* There shall be no sharp or abrasive surfaces under lavatories.

4.19.5 Faucets. Faucets shall comply with 4.27.4. Lever-operated, push-type, and electronically controlled mechanisms are examples of acceptable designs. *If self-closing valves are*

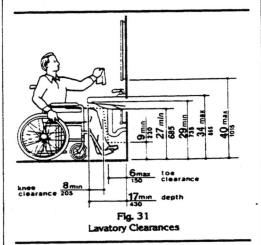

Fig. 31
Lavatory Clearances

Fig. 32
Clear Floor Space at Lavatories

used the faucet *shall remain* open for at least 10 seconds.

4.19.6* Mirrors. Mirrors shall be mounted with the bottom edge *of the reflecting surface* no higher than 40 in (1015 mm) *above the finish* floor (see Fig. 31).

4.20 Bathtubs.

4.20.1 General. Accessible bathtubs shall comply with 4.20.

4.20.2 Floor Space. Clear floor space in front of bathtubs shall be as shown in Fig. 33.

4.20.3 Seat. An in-tub seat or a seat at the head end of the tub shall be provided as shown in Fig. 33 and 34. The structural strength of seats and their attachments shall comply with 4.26.3. Seats shall be mounted securely and shall not slip during use.

4.20.4 Grab Bars. Grab bars complying with 4.26 shall be provided as shown in Fig. 33 and 34.

4.20.5 Controls. Faucets and other controls complying with 4.27.4 shall be located as shown in Fig. 34.

4.20.6 Shower Unit. A shower spray unit with a hose at least 60 in (1525 mm) long that can be used *both* as a fixed shower head *and* as a hand-held shower shall be provided.

4.20.7 Bathtub Enclosures. If provided, enclosures for bathtubs shall not obstruct controls or transfer from wheelchairs onto bathtub seats or into tubs. Enclosures on bathtubs shall not have tracks mounted on their rims.

4.21 Shower Stalls.

4.21.1* General. Accessible shower stalls shall comply with 4.21.

4.21.2 Size and Clearances. Except as specified in 9.1.2, shower stall size and clear floor space shall comply with Fig. 35(a) or (b). The shower stall in Fig. 35(a) shall be 36 in by 36 in (915 mm by 915 mm). Shower stalls required by 9.1.2 shall comply with Fig. 57(a)

or (b). The shower stall in Fig. 35(b) will fit into the space required for a bathtub.

4.21.3 Seat. A seat shall be provided in shower stalls 36 in by 36 in (915 mm by 915 mm) and shall be as shown in Fig. 36. The seat shall be mounted 17 in to 19 in (430 mm to 485 mm) from the bathroom floor and shall extend the full depth of the stall. In a 36 in by 36 in (915 mm by 915 mm) shower stall, the seat shall be on the wall opposite the controls. *Where a fixed seat is provided in a 30 in by 60 in minimum (760 mm by 1525 mm) shower stall, it shall be a folding type and shall be mounted on the wall adjacent to the controls as shown in Fig. 57.* The structural strength of seats and their attachments shall comply with 4.26.3.

4.21.4 Grab Bars. Grab bars complying with 4.26 shall be provided as shown in Fig. 37.

4.21.5 Controls. Faucets and other controls complying with 4.27.4 shall be located as shown in Fig. 37. In shower stalls 36 in by 36 in (915 mm by 915 mm), all controls, faucets, and the shower unit shall be mounted on the side wall opposite the seat.

4.21.6 Shower Unit. A shower spray unit with a hose at least 60 in (1525 mm) long that can be used *both* as a fixed shower head *and* as a hand-held shower shall be provided.

EXCEPTION: In unmonitored facilities where vandalism is a consideration, a fixed shower head mounted at 48 in (1220 mm) above the shower floor may be used in lieu of a hand-held shower head.

4.21.7 Curbs. If provided, curbs in shower stalls 36 in by 36 in (915 mm by 915 mm) shall be no higher than 1/2 in (13 mm). Shower stalls that are 30 in by 60 in (760 mm by 1525 mm) minimum shall not have curbs.

4.21.8 Shower Enclosures. If provided, enclosures for shower stalls shall not obstruct controls or obstruct transfer from wheelchairs onto shower seats.

4.22 Toilet Rooms.

4.22.1 Minimum Number. *Toilet facilities required to be accessible by 4.1 shall comply*

4.21 Shower Stalls

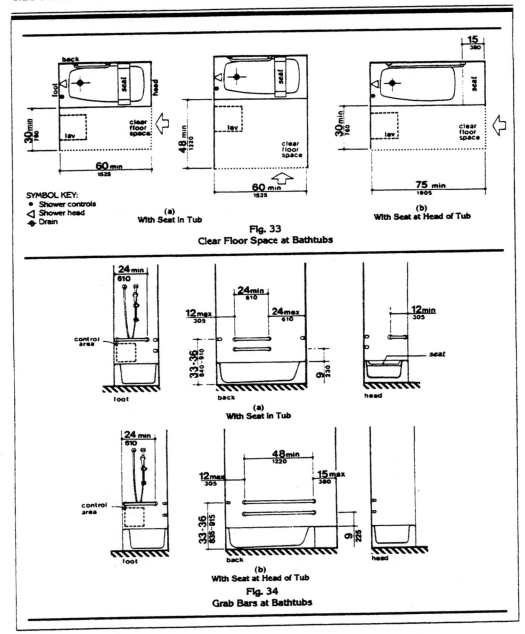

SYMBOL KEY:
● Shower controls
◁ Shower head
◆ Drain

(a)
With Seat in Tub

(b)
With Seat at Head of Tub

Fig. 33
Clear Floor Space at Bathtubs

(a)
With Seat in Tub

(b)
With Seat at Head of Tub

Fig. 34
Grab Bars at Bathtubs

4.22 Toilet Rooms

with 4.22. Accessible toilet rooms shall be on an accessible route.

4.22.2 Doors. All doors to accessible toilet rooms shall comply with 4.13. Doors shall not swing into the clear floor space required for any fixture.

4.22.3* Clear Floor Space. The accessible fixtures and controls required in 4.22.4, 4.22.5, 4.22.6, and 4.22.7 shall be on an accessible route. An unobstructed turning space complying with 4.2.3 shall be provided within an accessible toilet room. The clear floor space at fixtures and controls, the accessible route, and the turning space may overlap.

4.22.4 Water Closets. If toilet stalls are provided, then at least one shall be a standard

toilet stall complying with 4.17; *where 6 or more stalls are provided, in addition to the stall complying with 4.17.3, at least one stall 36 in (915 mm) wide with an outward swinging, self-closing door and parallel grab bars complying with Fig. 30(d) and 4.26 shall be provided.* Water closets in such stalls shall comply with 4.16. If water closets are not in stalls, then at least one shall comply with 4.16.

4.22.5 Urinals. If urinals are provided, *then* at least one shall comply with 4.18.

4.22.6 Lavatories and Mirrors. If lavatories and mirrors are provided, *then* at least one of each shall comply with 4.19.

4.22.7 Controls and Dispensers. If controls, dispensers, receptacles, or other

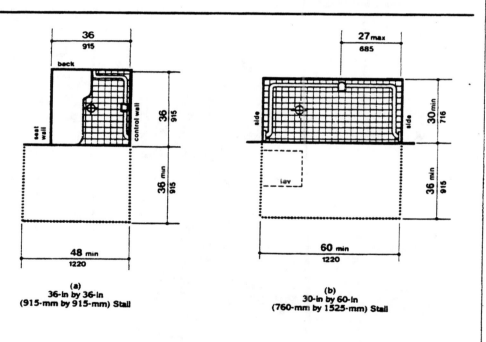

(a)
36-in by 36-in
(915-mm by 915-mm) Stall

(b)
30-in by 60-in
(760-mm by 1525-mm) Stall

Fig. 35
Shower Size and Clearances

4.23 Bathrooms, Bathing Facilities, and Shower Rooms

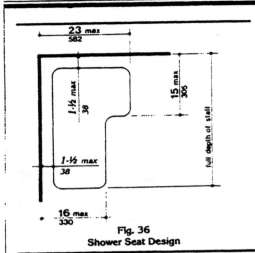

Fig. 36
Shower Seat Design

equipment are provided, *then* at least one of each shall be on an accessible route and shall comply with 4.27.

4.23 Bathrooms, Bathing Facilities, and Shower Rooms.

4.23.1 Minimum Number. Bathrooms, bathing facilities, or shower rooms *required to be accessible by 4.1* shall comply with 4.23 and shall be on an accessible route.

4.23.2 Doors. Doors to accessible bathrooms shall comply with 4.13. Doors shall not swing into the floor space required for any fixture.

4.23.3° Clear Floor Space. The accessible fixtures and controls required in 4.23.4, 4.23.5, 4.23.6, 4.23.7, 4.23.8, and 4.23.9 shall be on an accessible route. An unobstructed turning

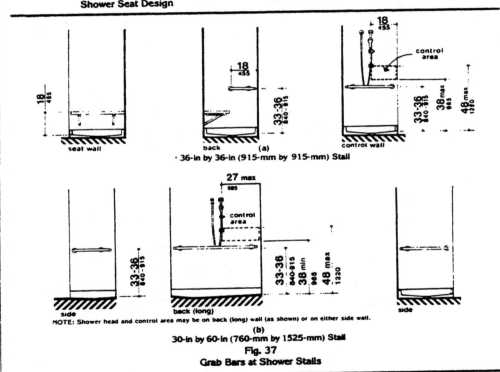

NOTE: Shower head and control area may be on back (long) wall (as shown) or on either side wall.

(b)
30-in by 60-in (760-mm by 1525-mm) Stall
Fig. 37
Grab Bars at Shower Stalls

space complying with 4.2.3 shall be provided within an accessible bathroom. The clear floor spaces at fixtures and controls, the accessible route, and the turning space may overlap.

4.23.4 Water Closets. If toilet stalls are provided, then at least one shall be a standard toilet stall complying with 4.17; *where 6 or more stalls are provided, in addition to the stall complying with 4.17.3, at least one stall 36 in (915 mm) wide with an outward swinging, self-closing door and parallel grab bars complying with Fig. 30(d) and 4.26 shall be provided.* Water closets in such stalls shall comply with 4.16. If water closets are not in stalls, then at least one shall comply with 4.16.

4.23.5 Urinals. If urinals are provided, then at least one shall comply with 4.18.

4.23.6 Lavatories and Mirrors. If lavatories and mirrors are provided, then at least one of each shall comply with 4.19.

4.23.7 Controls and Dispensers. If controls, dispensers, receptacles, or other equipment *are* provided, *then* at least one of each shall be on an accessible route and shall comply with 4.27.

4.23.8 Bathing and Shower Facilities. If tubs or showers are provided, then at least one accessible tub that complies with 4.20 or at least one accessible shower that complies with 4.21 shall be provided.

4.23.9* Medicine Cabinets. If medicine cabinets are provided, at least one shall be located with a usable shelf no higher than 44 in (1120 mm) above the floor space. The floor space shall comply with 4.2.4.

4.24 Sinks.

4.24.1 General. Sinks required to be *accessible by 4.1* shall comply with 4.24.

4.24.2 Height. Sinks shall be mounted with the counter or rim no higher than 34 in (865 mm) *above the finish floor.*

4.24.3 Knee Clearance. Knee clearance that is at least 27 in (685 mm) high, 30 in (760 mm) wide, and 19 in (485 mm) deep shall be pro-

vided underneath sinks.

4.24.4 Depth. Each sink shall be a maximum of 6-1/2 in (165 mm) deep.

4.24.5 Clear Floor Space. A clear floor space at least 30 in by 48 in (760 mm by 1220 mm) complying with 4.2.4 shall be provided in front of a sink to allow forward approach. The clear floor space shall be on an accessible route and shall extend a maximum of 19 in (485 mm) underneath the sink (see Fig. 32).

4.24.6 Exposed Pipes and Surfaces. Hot water and drain pipes exposed under sinks shall be insulated or otherwise *configured so as to protect against contact.* There shall be no sharp or abrasive surfaces under sinks.

4.24.7 Faucets. Faucets shall comply with 4.27.4. Lever-operated, push-type, touch-type, or electronically controlled mechanisms are acceptable designs.

4.25 Storage.

4.25.1 General. *Fixed* storage facilities such as cabinets, shelves, closets, and drawers *required to be accessible by 4.1* shall comply with 4.25.

4.25.2 Clear Floor Space. A clear floor space at least 30 in by 48 in (760 mm by 1220 mm) complying with 4.2.4 that allows either a forward or parallel approach by a person using a wheelchair shall be provided at accessible storage facilities.

4.25.3 Height. Accessible storage spaces shall be within at least one of the reach ranges specified in 4.2.5 and 4.2.6 *(see Fig. 5 and Fig. 6).* Clothes rods or shelves shall be a maximum of 54 in (1370 mm) *above the finish floor for a side approach. Where the distance from the wheelchair to the clothes rod or shelf exceeds 10 in (255 mm) (as in closets without accessible doors) the height and depth to the rod or shelf shall comply with Fig. 38(a) and Fig. 38(b).*

4.25.4 Hardware. Hardware for accessible storage facilities shall comply with 4.27.4. Touch latches and U-shaped pulls are acceptable.

4.26 Handrails, Grab Bars, and Tub and Shower Seats

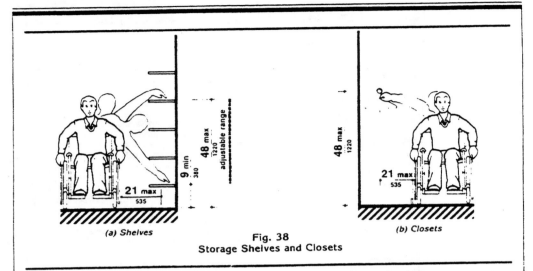

(a) Shelves

(b) Closets

Fig. 38
Storage Shelves and Closets

4.26 Handrails, Grab Bars, and Tub and Shower Seats.

4.26.1* General. All handrails, grab bars, and tub and shower seats *required to be accessible by 4.1, 4.8, 4.9, 4.16, 4.17, 4.20 or 4.21* shall comply with 4.26.

4.26.2* Size and Spacing of Grab Bars and Handrails. The diameter or width of the gripping surfaces of a handrail or grab bar shall be 1-1/4 in to 1-1/2 in (32 mm to 38 mm), or the shape shall provide an equivalent gripping surface. If handrails or grab bars are mounted adjacent to a wall, the space between the wall and the grab bar shall be 1-1/2 in (38 mm) (see Fig. 39(a), (b), (c), and *(e)*). Handrails may be located in a recess if the recess is a maximum of 3 in (75 mm) deep and extends at least 18 in (455 mm) above the top of the rail (see Fig. 39(d)).

4.26.3 Structural Strength. The structural strength of grab bars, tub and shower seats, fasteners, and mounting devices shall meet the following specification:

(1) Bending stress in a grab bar or seat induced by the maximum bending moment from the application of 250 lbf (1112N) shall be less than the allowable stress for the material of the grab bar or seat.

(2) Shear stress induced in a grab bar or seat by the application of 250 lbf (1112N) shall be less than the allowable shear stress for the material of the grab bar or seat. If the connection between the grab bar or seat and its mounting bracket or other support is considered to be fully restrained, then direct and torsional shear stresses shall be totaled for the combined shear stress, which shall not exceed the allowable shear stress.

(3) Shear force induced in a fastener or mounting device from the application of 250 lbf (1112N) shall be less than the allowable lateral load of either the fastener or mounting device or the supporting structure, whichever is the smaller allowable load.

(4) Tensile force induced in a fastener by a direct tension force of 250 lbf (1112N) plus the maximum moment from the application of 250 lbf (1112N) shall be less than the allowable withdrawal load between the fastener and the supporting structure.

(5) Grab bars shall not rotate within their fittings.

4.26 Handrails, Grab Bars, and Tub and Shower Seats

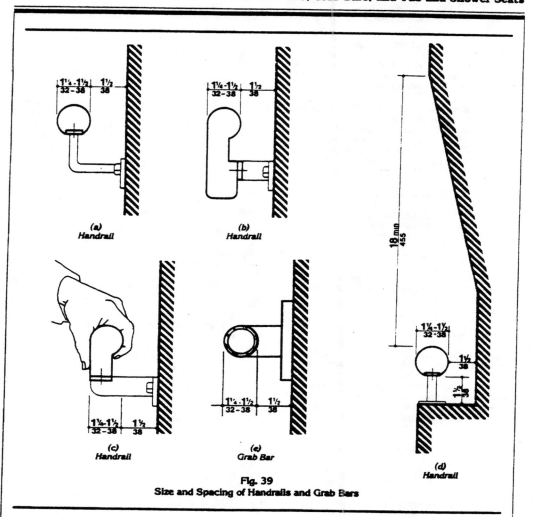

(a)
Handrail

(b)
Handrail

(c)
Handrail

(e)
Grab Bar

(d)
Handrail

Fig. 39
Size and Spacing of Handrails and Grab Bars

4.26.4 Eliminating Hazards. A handrail or grab bar and any wall or other surface adjacent to it shall be free of any sharp or abrasive elements. Edges shall have a minimum radius of 1/8 in (3.2 mm).

4.27 Controls and Operating Mechanisms.

4.27.1 General. Controls and operating mechanisms required to be accessible by 4.1 shall comply with 4.27.

4.28 Alarms

4.27.2 Clear Floor Space. Clear floor space complying with 4.2.4 that allows a forward or a parallel approach by a person using a wheelchair shall be provided at controls, dispensers, receptacles, and other operable equipment.

4.27.3° Height. The highest operable part of controls, dispensers, receptacles, and other operable equipment shall be placed within at least one of the reach ranges specified in 4.2.5 and 4.2.6. Electrical and communications system receptacles on walls shall be mounted no less than 15 in (380 mm) above the floor.

EXCEPTION: These requirements do not apply where the use of special equipment dictates otherwise or where electrical and communications systems receptacles are not normally intended for use by building occupants.

4.27.4 Operation. Controls and operating mechanisms shall be operable with one hand and shall not require tight grasping, pinching, or twisting of the wrist. The force required to activate controls shall be no greater than 5 lbf (22.2 N).

4.28 Alarms.

4.28.1 General. *Alarm systems required to be accessible by 4.1 shall comply with 4.28. At a minimum, visual signal appliances shall be provided in buildings and facilities in each of the following areas: restrooms and any other general usage areas (e.g., meeting rooms), hallways, lobbies, and any other area for common use.*

4.28.2° Audible Alarms. If provided, audible emergency alarms shall produce a sound that exceeds the prevailing equivalent sound level in the room or space by at least 15 dbA or exceeds any maximum sound level with a duration of 60 seconds by 5 dbA, whichever is louder. Sound levels for alarm signals shall not exceed 120 dbA.

4.28.3° Visual Alarms. *Visual alarm signal appliances shall be integrated into the building or facility alarm system. If single station audible alarms are provided then single station visual alarm signals shall be provided. Visual alarm signals shall have the following minimum photometric and location features:*

(1) The lamp shall be a xenon strobe type or equivalent.

(2) The color shall be clear or nominal white (i.e., unfiltered or clear filtered white light).

(3) The maximum pulse duration shall be two-tenths of one second (0.2 sec) with a maximum duty cycle of 40 percent. The pulse duration is defined as the time interval between initial and final points of 10 percent of maximum signal.

(4) The intensity shall be a minimum of 75 candela.

(5) The flash rate shall be a minimum of 1 Hz and a maximum of 3 Hz.

(6) The appliance shall be placed 80 in (2030 mm) above the highest floor level within the space or 6 in (152 mm) below the ceiling, whichever is lower.

(7) In general, no place in any room or space required to have a visual signal appliance shall be more than 50 ft (15 m) from the signal (in the horizontal plane). In large rooms and spaces exceeding 100 ft (30 m) across, without obstructions 6 ft (2 m) above the finish floor, such as auditoriums, devices may be placed around the perimeter, spaced a maximum 100 ft (30 m) apart, in lieu of suspending appliances from the ceiling.

(8) No place in common corridors or hallways in which visual alarm signalling appliances are required shall be more than 50 ft (15 m) from the signal.

4.28.4° Auxiliary Alarms. Units and sleeping accommodations shall have a visual alarm connected to the building emergency alarm system or shall have a standard 110-volt electrical receptacle into which such an alarm can be connected and a means by which a signal *from the building emergency alarm system can trigger such an auxiliary alarm. When visual alarms are in place the signal shall be visible in all areas of the unit or room. Instructions for use of the auxiliary alarm or receptacle shall be provided.*

4.29 Detectable Warnings.

4.29.1 General. *Detectable warnings required by 4.1 and 4.7 shall comply with 4.29.*

4.29.2* Detectable Warnings on Walking Surfaces. *Detectable warnings shall consist of raised truncated domes with a diameter of nominal 0.9 in (23 mm), a height of nominal 0.2 in (5 mm) and a center-to-center spacing of nominal 2.35 in (60 mm) and shall contrast visually with adjoining surfaces, either light-on-dark, or dark-on-light.*

The material used to provide contrast shall be an integral part of the walking surface. Detectable warnings used on interior surfaces shall differ from adjoining walking surfaces in resiliency or sound-on-cane contact.

4.29.3 Detectable Warnings on Doors To Hazardous Areas. *(Reserved).*

4.29.4 Detectable Warnings at Stairs. *(Reserved).*

4.29.5 Detectable Warnings at Hazardous Vehicular Areas. *If a walk crosses or adjoins a vehicular way, and the walking surfaces are not separated by curbs, railings, or other elements between the pedestrian areas and vehicular areas, the boundary between the areas shall be defined by a continuous detectable warning which is 36 in (915 mm) wide, complying with 4.29.2.*

4.29.6 Detectable Warnings at Reflecting Pools. *The edges of reflecting pools shall be protected by railings, walls, curbs, or detectable warnings complying with 4.29.2.*

4.29.7 Standardization. *(Reserved).*

4.30 Signage.

4.30.1* General. *Signage required to be accessible by 4.1 shall comply with the applicable provisions of 4.30.*

4.30.2* Character Proportion. Letters and numbers on signs shall have a width-to-height ratio between 3:5 and 1:1 and a stroke-width-to-height ratio between 1:5 and 1:10.

4.30.3 Character Height. *Characters and numbers on signs shall be sized according to the viewing distance from which they are to be read. The minimum height is measured using an upper case X. Lower case characters are permitted.*

Height Above Finished Floor	Minimum Character Height
Suspended or Projected Overhead in compliance with 4.4.2	3 in. (75 mm) minimum

4.30.4* Raised and Brailled Characters and Pictorial Symbol Signs (Pictograms). Letters and numerals shall be raised 1/32 in. upper case, sans serif or simple serif type and shall be accompanied with Grade 2 Braille. Raised characters shall be at least 5/8 in (16 mm) high, but no higher than 2 in (50 mm). Pictograms shall be accompanied by the equivalent verbal description placed directly below the pictogram. The border dimension of the pictogram shall be 6 in (152 mm) minimum in height.

4.30.5* Finish and Contrast. The characters and background of signs shall be eggshell, matte, or other non-glare finish. Characters and symbols shall contrast with their background — either light characters on a dark background or dark characters on a light background.

4.30.6 Mounting Location and Height. *Where permanent identification is provided for rooms and spaces, signs shall be installed on the wall adjacent to the latch side of the door. Where there is no wall space to the latch side of the door, including at double leaf doors, signs shall be placed on the nearest adjacent wall. Mounting height shall be 60 in (1525 mm) above the finish floor to the centerline of the sign. Mounting location for such signage shall be so that a person may approach within 3 in (76 mm) of signage without encountering protruding objects or standing within the swing of a door.*

4.30.7* Symbols of Accessibility.

(1) *Facilities and elements required to be identified as accessible by 4.1 shall use the international symbol of accessibility. The*

4.30 Signage

(a)
Proportions
International Symbol of Accessibility

(b)
Display Conditions
International Symbol of Accessibility

(c)
International TDD Symbol

(d)
International Symbol of Access for Hearing Loss

Fig. 43
International Symbols

symbol shall be displayed as shown in Fig. 43(a) and (b).

(2) *Volume Control Telephones. Telephones required to have a volume control by 4.1.3(17)(b) shall be identified by a sign containing a depiction of a telephone handset with radiating sound waves.*

(3) *Text Telephones. Text telephones required by 4.1.3 (17)(c) shall be identified by the international TDD symbol (Fig 43(c)). In addition, if a facility has a public text telephone, directional signage indicating the location of the nearest text telephone shall be placed adjacent to all banks of telephones which do not contain a text telephone. Such directional signage shall include the international TDD symbol. If a facility has no banks of telephones, the directional signage shall be provided at the entrance (e.g., in a building directory).*

(4) *Assistive Listening Systems. In assembly areas where permanently installed assistive listening systems are required by 4.1.3(19)(b) the availability of such systems shall be identified with signage that includes the international symbol of access for hearing loss (Fig 43(d)).*

4.30.8° Illumination Levels. (Reserved).

4.31 Telephones.

4.31.1 General. Public telephones *required to be accessible by 4.1* shall comply with 4.31.

4.31.2 Clear Floor or Ground Space. A clear floor or ground space at least 30 in by 48 in (760 mm by 1220 mm) that allows either a forward or parallel approach by a person using a wheelchair shall be provided at telephones (see Fig. 44). The clear floor or ground space shall comply with 4.2.4. Bases, enclosures, and fixed seats shall not impede approaches to telephones by people who use wheelchairs.

4.31.3° Mounting Height. The highest operable part of the telephone shall be within the reach ranges specified in 4.2.5 or 4.2.6.

4.31.4 Protruding Objects. *Telephones shall comply with 4.4.*

4.31 Telephones

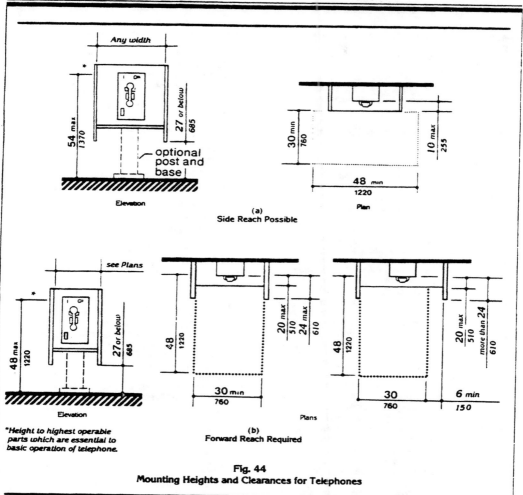

Fig. 44
Mounting Heights and Clearances for Telephones

4.31.5 Hearing Aid Compatible and Volume Control Telephones Required by 4.1.

(1) Telephones shall be hearing aid compatible.

(2) Volume controls, *capable of a minimum of 12 dbA and a maximum of 18 dbA above*

normal, shall be provided in accordance with 4.1.3. If an automatic reset is provided then 18 dbA may be exceeded.

4.31.6 Controls. Telephones shall have pushbutton controls where service for such equipment is available.

4.32 Fixed or Built-in Seating and Tables

4.31.7 Telephone Books. Telephone books, if provided, shall be located *in a position that complies with the reach ranges specified in 4.2.5 and 4.2.6.*

4.31.8 Cord Length. The cord from the telephone to the handset shall be at least 29 in (735 mm) long.

4.31.9* Text Telephones Required by 4.1.

(1) Text telephones used with a pay telephone shall be permanently affixed within, or adjacent to, the telephone enclosure. If an acoustic coupler is used, the telephone cord shall be sufficiently long to allow connection of the text telephone and the telephone receiver.

(2) Pay telephones designed to accommodate a portable text telephone shall be equipped with a shelf and an electrical outlet within or adjacent to the telephone enclosure. The telephone handset shall be capable of being placed flush on the surface of the shelf. The shelf shall be capable of accommodating a text telephone and shall have 6 in (152 mm) minimum vertical clearance in the area where the text telephone is to be placed.

(3) Equivalent facilitation may be provided. For example, a portable text telephone may be made available in a hotel at the registration desk if it is available on a 24-hour basis for use with nearby public pay telephones. In this instance, at least one pay telephone shall comply with paragraph 2 of this section. In addition, if an acoustic coupler is used, the telephone handset cord shall be sufficiently long so as to allow connection of the text telephone and the telephone receiver. Directional signage shall be provided and shall comply with 4.30.7.

4.32 Fixed or Built-in Seating and Tables.

4.32.1 Minimum Number. Fixed or built-in seating or tables *required to be accessible by 4.1* shall comply with 4.32.

4.32.2 Seating. If seating spaces for people in wheelchairs are provided at *fixed* tables or counters, clear floor space complying with 4.2.4 shall be provided. Such clear floor space shall not overlap knee space by more than 19 in (485 mm) (see Fig. 45).

4.32.3 Knee Clearances. If seating for people in wheelchairs is provided at tables *or* counters, knee spaces at least 27 in (685 mm) high, 30 in (760 mm) wide, and 19 in (485 mm) deep shall be provided (see Fig. 45).

4.32.4* Height of Tables or Counters. The tops of *accessible* tables and *counters* shall be from 28 in to 34 in (710 mm to 865 mm) *above the finish* floor or ground.

4.33 Assembly Areas.

4.33.1 Minimum Number. Assembly *and associated areas required to be accessible by 4.1 shall comply with 4.33.*

4.33.2* Size of Wheelchair Locations. Each wheelchair location shall provide minimum clear ground or floor spaces as shown in Fig. 46.

4.33.3* Placement of Wheelchair Locations. Wheelchair areas shall be an integral part of any fixed seating plan and shall be *provided so as to provide people with physical disabilities a choice of admission prices and lines of sight comparable to those for members of the general public. They shall adjoin an accessible route that also serves as a means of egress in case of emergency. At least one companion fixed seat shall be provided next to each wheelchair seating area. When the seating capacity exceeds 300, wheelchair spaces shall be provided in more than one location. Readily removable seats may be installed in wheelchair spaces when the spaces are not required to accommodate wheelchair users.*

EXCEPTION: Accessible viewing positions may be clustered for bleachers, balconies, and other areas having sight lines that require slopes of greater than 5 percent. Equivalent accessible viewing positions may be located on levels having accessible egress.

4.33.4 Surfaces. The ground or floor at wheelchair locations shall be level and shall comply with 4.5.

4.33 Assembly Areas

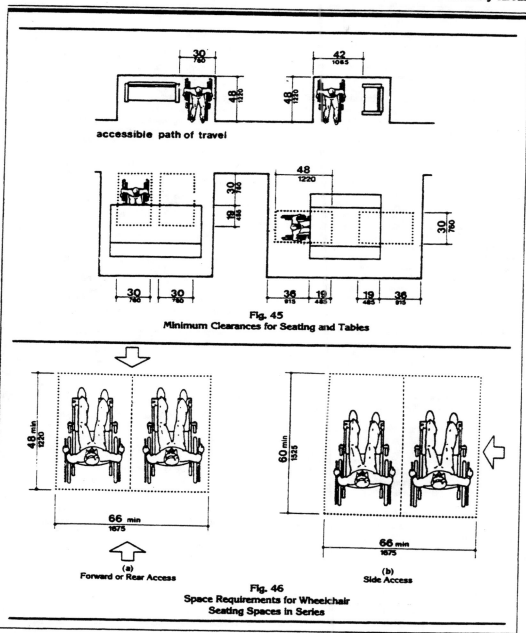

accessible path of travel

Fig. 45
Minimum Clearances for Seating and Tables

(a)
Forward or Rear Access

(b)
Side Access

Fig. 46
Space Requirements for Wheelchair
Seating Spaces in Series

4.34 Automated Teller Machines

4.33.5 Access to Performing Areas.
An accessible route shall connect wheelchair seating locations with performing areas, including stages, arena floors, dressing rooms, locker rooms, and other spaces used by performers.

4.33.6* Placement of Listening Systems.
If the listening system provided serves individual fixed seats, then such seats shall be located within a 50 ft (15 m) viewing distance of the stage or playing area and shall have a complete view of the stage or playing area.

4.33.7* Types of Listening Systems.
Assistive listening systems (ALS) are intended to augment standard public address and audio systems by providing signals which can be received directly by persons with special receivers or their own hearing aids and which eliminate or filter background noise. The type of assistive listening system appropriate for a particular application depends on the characteristics of the setting, the nature of the program, and the intended audience. Magnetic induction loops, infra-red and radio frequency systems are types of listening systems which are appropriate for various applications.

4.34 Automated Teller Machines.

4.34.1 General. *Each machine required to be accessible by 4.1.3 shall be on an accessible route and shall comply with 4.34.*

4.34.2 Controls. *Controls for user activation shall comply with the requirements of 4.27.*

4.34.3 Clearances and Reach Range. *Free standing or built-in units not having a clear space under them shall comply with 4.27.2 and 4.27.3 and provide for a parallel approach and both a forward and side reach to the unit allowing a person in a wheelchair to access the controls and dispensers.*

4.34.4 Equipment for Persons with Vision Impairments. *Instructions and all information for use shall be made accessible to and independently usable by persons with vision impairments.*

4.35 Dressing and Fitting Rooms.

4.35.1 General. *Dressing and fitting rooms required to be accessible by 4.1 shall comply with 4.35 and shall be on an accessible route.*

4.35.2 Clear Floor Space. *A clear floor space allowing a person using a wheelchair to make a 180-degree turn shall be provided in every accessible dressing room entered through a swinging or sliding door. No door shall swing into any part of the turning space. Turning space shall not be required in a private dressing room entered through a curtained opening at least 32 in (815 mm) wide if clear floor space complying with section 4.2 renders the dressing room usable by a person using a wheelchair.*

4.35.3 Doors. *All doors to accessible dressing rooms shall be in compliance with section 4.13.*

4.35.4 Bench. *Every accessible dressing room shall have a 24 in by 48 in (610 mm by 1220 mm) bench fixed to the wall along the longer dimension. The bench shall be mounted 17 in to 19 in (430 mm to 485 mm) above the finish floor. Clear floor space shall be provided alongside the bench to allow a person using a wheelchair to make a parallel transfer onto the bench. The structural strength of the bench and attachments shall comply with 4.26.3. Where installed in conjunction with showers, swimming pools, or other wet locations, water shall not accumulate upon the surface of the bench and the bench shall have a slip-resistant surface.*

4.35.5 Mirror. *Where mirrors are provided in dressing rooms of the same use, then in an accessible dressing room, a full-length mirror, measuring at least 18 in wide by 54 in high (460 mm by 1370 mm), shall be mounted in a position affording a view to a person on the bench as well as to a person in a standing position.*

NOTE: Sections 4.1.1 through 4.1.7 and sections 5 through 10 are different from ANSI A117.1 in their entirety and are printed in standard type.

5. RESTAURANTS AND CAFETERIAS.

5.1° General. Except as specified or modified in this section, restaurants and cafeterias shall comply with the requirements of 4.1 to 4.35. Where fixed tables (or dining counters where food is consumed but there is no service) are provided, at least 5 percent, but not less than one, of the fixed tables (or a portion of the dining counter) shall be accessible and shall comply with 4.32 as required in 4.1.3(18). In establishments where separate areas are designated for smoking and non-smoking patrons, the required number of accessible fixed tables (or counters) shall be proportionally distributed between the smoking and non-smoking areas. In new construction, and where practicable in alterations, accessible fixed tables (or counters) shall be distributed throughout the space or facility.

5.2 Counters and Bars. Where food or drink is served at counters exceeding 34 in (865 mm) in height for consumption by customers seated on stools or standing at the counter, a portion of the main counter which is 60 in (1525 mm) in length minimum shall be provided in compliance with 4.32 or service shall be available at accessible tables within the same area.

5.3 Access Aisles. All accessible fixed tables shall be accessible by means of an access aisle at least 36 in (915 mm) clear between parallel edges of tables or between a wall and the table edges.

5.4 Dining Areas. In new construction, all dining areas, including raised or sunken dining areas, loggias, and outdoor seating areas, shall be accessible. In non-elevator buildings, an accessible means of vertical access to the mezzanine is not required under the following conditions: 1) the area of mezzanine seating measures no more than 33 percent of the area of the total accessible seating area; 2) the same services and decor are provided in an accessible space usable by the general public; and, 3) the accessible areas are not restricted to use by people with disabilities. In alterations, accessibility to raised or sunken dining areas, or to all parts of outdoor seating areas is not required provided that the same services and decor are provided in an accessible space usable by the general public and are not restricted to use by people with disabilities.

5.5 Food Service Lines. Food service lines shall have a minimum clear width of 36 in (915 mm), with a preferred clear width of 42 in (1065 mm) to allow passage around a person using a wheelchair. Tray slides shall be mounted no higher than 34 in (865 mm) above the floor (see Fig. 53). If self-service shelves

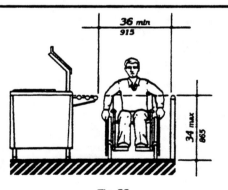

Fig. 53
Food Service Lines

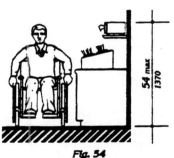

Fig. 54
Tableware Areas

6.0 Medical Care Facilities

are provided, at least 50 percent of each type must be within reach ranges specified in 4.2.5 and 4.2.6.

5.6 Tableware and Condiment Areas. Self-service shelves and dispensing devices for tableware, dishware, condiments, food and beverages shall be installed to comply with 4.2 (see Fig. 54).

5.7 Raised Platforms. In banquet rooms or spaces where a head table or speaker's lectern is located on a raised platform, the platform shall be accessible in compliance with 4.8 or 4.11. Open edges of a raised platform shall be protected by placement of tables or by a curb.

5.8 Vending Machines and Other Equipment. Spaces for vending machines and other equipment shall comply with 4.2 and shall be located on an accessible route.

5.9 Quiet Areas. (Reserved).

6. | MEDICAL CARE FACILITIES.

6.1 General. Medical care facilities included in this section are those in which people receive physical or medical treatment or care and where persons may need assistance in responding to an emergency and where the period of stay may exceed twenty-four hours. In addition to the requirements of 4.1 through 4.35, medical care facilities and buildings shall comply with 6.

(1) Hospitals - general purpose hospitals, psychiatric facilities, detoxification facilities — At least 10 percent of patient bedrooms and toilets, and all public use and common use areas are required to be designed and constructed to be accessible.

(2) Hospitals and rehabilitation facilities that specialize in treating conditions that affect mobility, or units within either that specialize in treating conditions that affect mobility — All patient bedrooms and toilets, and all public use and common use areas are required to be designed and constructed to be accessible.

(3) Long term care facilities, nursing homes — At least 50 percent of patient bedrooms and toilets, and all public use and common use areas are required to be designed and constructed to be accessible.

(4) Alterations to patient bedrooms.

(a) When patient bedrooms are being added or altered as part of a planned renovation of an entire wing, a department, or other discrete area of an existing medical facility, a percentage of the patient bedrooms that are being added or altered shall comply with 6.3. The percentage of accessible rooms provided shall be consistent with the percentage of rooms required to be accessible by the applicable requirements of 6.1(1), 6.1(2), or 6.1(3), until the number of accessible patient bedrooms in the facility equals the overall number that would be required if the facility were newly constructed. (For example, if 20 patient bedrooms are being altered in the obstetrics department of a hospital, 2 of the altered rooms must be made accessible. If, within the same hospital, 20 patient bedrooms are being altered in a unit that specializes in treating mobility impairments, all of the altered rooms must be made accessible.) Where toilet/bath rooms are part of patient bedrooms which are added or altered and required to be accessible, each such patient toilet/bathroom shall comply with 6.4.

(b) When patient bedrooms are being added or altered individually, and not as part of an alteration of the entire area, the altered patient bedrooms shall comply with 6.3, unless either: a) the number of accessible rooms provided in the department or area containing the altered patient bedroom equals the number of accessible patient bedrooms that would be required if the percentage requirements of 6.1(1), 6.1(2), or 6.1(3) were applied to that department or area; or b) the number of accessible patient bedrooms in the facility equals the overall number that would be required if the facility were newly constructed. Where toilet/bathrooms are part of patient bedrooms which are added or altered and required to be accessible, each such toilet/bathroom shall comply with 6.4.

6.2 Entrances. At least one accessible entrance that complies with 4.14 shall be protected from the weather by canopy or roof overhang. Such entrances shall incorporate a passenger loading zone that complies with 4.6.6.

6.3 Patient Bedrooms. Provide accessible patient bedrooms in compliance with 4.1 through 4.35. Accessible patient bedrooms shall comply with the following:

(1) Each bedroom shall have a door that complies with 4.13.

EXCEPTION: Entry doors to acute care hospital bedrooms for in-patients shall be exempted from the requirement in 4.13.6 for maneuvering space at the latch side of the door if the door is at least 44 in (1120 mm) wide.

(2) Each bedroom shall have adequate space to provide a maneuvering space that complies with 4.2.3. In rooms with 2 beds, it is preferable that this space be located between beds.

(3) Each bedroom shall have adequate space to provide a minimum clear floor space of 36 in (915 mm) along each side of the bed and to provide an accessible route complying with 4.3.3 to each side of each bed.

6.4 Patient Toilet Rooms. Where toilet/bath rooms are provided as a part of a patient bedroom, each patient bedroom that is required to be accessible shall have an accessible toilet/bath room that complies with 4.22 or 4.23 and shall be on an accessible route.

7. BUSINESS AND MERCANTILE.

7.1 General. In addition to the requirements of 4.1 to 4.35, the design of all areas used for business transactions with the public shall comply with 7.

7.2 Sales and Service Counters, Teller Windows, Information Counters.

(1) In department stores and miscellaneous retail stores where counters have cash registers and are provided for sales or distribution of goods or services to the public, at least one of each type shall have a portion of the counter which is at least 36 in (915 mm) in length with a maximum height of 36 in (915 mm) above the finish floor. It shall be on an accessible route complying with 4.3. The accessible counters must be dispersed throughout the building or facility. In alterations where it is technically infeasible to provide an accessible counter, an auxiliary counter meeting these requirements may be provided.

(2) At ticketing counters, teller stations in a bank, registration counters in hotels and motels, box office ticket counters, and other counters that may not have a cash register but at which goods or services are sold or distributed, either:

(i) a portion of the main counter which is a minimum of 36 in (915 mm) in length shall be provided with a maximum height of 36 in (915 mm); or

(ii) an auxiliary counter with a maximum height of 36 in (915 mm) in close proximity to the main counter shall be provided; or

(iii) equivalent facilitation shall be provided (e.g., at a hotel registration counter, equivalent facilitation might consist of: (1) provision of a folding shelf attached to the main counter on which an individual with disabilities can write, and (2) use of the space on the side of the counter or at the concierge desk, for handing materials back and forth).

All accessible sales and service counters shall be on an accessible route complying with 4.3.

(3)* Assistive Listening Devices. (Reserved)

8.0 Libraries

7.3* Check-out Aisles.

(1) In new construction, accessible check-out aisles shall be provided in conformance with the table below:

Total Check-out Aisles of Each Design	Minimum Number of Accessible Check-out Aisles (of each design)
1 – 4	1
5 – 8	2
8 – 15	3
over 15	3, plus 20% of additional aisles

EXCEPTION: In new construction, where the selling space is under 5000 square feet, only one check-out aisle is required to be accessible.

EXCEPTION: In alterations, at least one check-out aisle shall be accessible in facilities under 5000 square feet of selling space. In facilities of 5000 or more square feet of selling space, at least one of each design of check-out aisle shall be made accessible when altered until the number of accessible check-out aisles of each design equals the number required in new construction.

Examples of check-out aisles of different "design" include those which are specifically designed to serve different functions. Different "design" includes but is not limited to the following features - length of belt or no belt; or permanent signage designating the aisle as an express lane.

(2) Clear aisle width for accessible check-out aisles shall comply with 4.2.1 and maximum adjoining counter height shall not exceed 38 in (965 mm) above the finish floor. The top of the lip shall not exceed 40 in (1015 mm) above the finish floor.

(3) Signage identifying accessible check-out aisles shall comply with 4.30.7 and shall be mounted above the check-out aisle in the same location where the check-out number or type of check-out is displayed.

7.4 Security Bollards. Any device used
to prevent the removal of shopping carts from store premises shall not prevent access or egress to people in wheelchairs. An alternate entry that is equally convenient to that provided for the ambulatory population is acceptable.

8. | LIBRARIES.

8.1 General. In addition to the requirements of 4.1 to 4.35, the design of all public areas of a library shall comply with 8, including reading and study areas, stacks, reference rooms, reserve areas, and special facilities or collections.

8.2 Reading and Study Areas. At least 5 percent or a minimum of one of each element of fixed seating, tables, or study carrels shall comply with 4.2 and 4.32. Clearances between fixed accessible tables and between study carrels shall comply with 4.3.

8.3 Check-Out Areas. At least one lane at each check-out area shall comply with 7.2(1). Any traffic control or book security gates or turnstiles shall comply with 4.13.

8.4 Card Catalogs and Magazine Displays. Minimum clear aisle space at card catalogs and magazine displays shall comply with Fig. 55. Maximum reach height shall comply with 4.2, with a height of 48 in (1220 mm) preferred irrespective of approach allowed.

8.5 Stacks. Minimum clear aisle width between stacks shall comply with 4.3, with a minimum clear aisle width of 42 in (1065 mm) preferred where possible. Shelf height in stack areas is unrestricted (see Fig. 56).

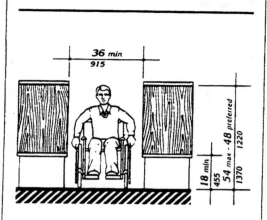

Fig. 55
Card Catalog

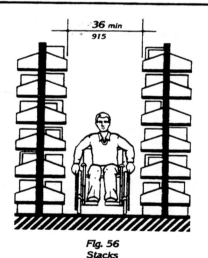

Fig. 56
Stacks

9. ACCESSIBLE TRANSIENT LODGING.

(1) Except as specified in the special technical provisions of this section, accessible transient lodging shall comply with the applicable requirements of 4.1 through 4.35. Transient lodging includes facilities or portions thereof used for sleeping accommodations, when not classed as a medical care facility.

9.1 Hotels, Motels, Inns, Boarding Houses, Dormitories, Resorts and Other Similar Places of Transient Lodging.

9.1.1 General. All public use and common use areas are required to be designed and constructed to comply with section 4 (Accessible Elements and Spaces: Scope and Technical Requirements).

EXCEPTION: Sections 9.1 through 9.4 do not apply to an establishment located within a building that contains not more than five rooms for rent or hire and that is actually occupied by the proprietor of such establishment as the residence of such proprietor.

9.1.2 Accessible Units, Sleeping Rooms, and Suites. Accessible sleeping rooms or suites that comply with the requirements of 9.2 (Requirements for Accessible Units, Sleeping Rooms, and Suites) shall be provided in conformance with the table below. In addition, in hotels, of 50 or more sleeping rooms or suites, additional accessible sleeping rooms or suites that include a roll-in shower shall also be provided in conformance with the table below. Such accommodations shall comply with the requirements of 9.2, 4.21, and Figure 57(a) or (b).

9.1.3 Sleeping Accommodations for Persons with Hearing Impairments

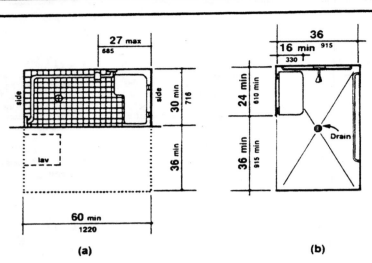

(a)   **(b)**

Fig. 57
Roll-in Shower with Folding Seat

Number of Rooms	Accessible Rooms	Rooms with Roll-in Showers
1 to 25	1	
26 to 50	2	
51 to 75	3	1
76 to 100	4	1
101 to 150	5	2
151 to 200	6	2
201 to 300	7	3
301 to 400	8	4
401 to 500	9	4 plus one for each additional 100 over 400
501 to 1000	2% of total	
1001 and over	20 plus 1 for each 100 over 1000	

and suites that comply with 9.3 (Visual Alarms, Notification Devices, and Telephones) shall be provided in conformance with the following table:

Number of Elements	Accessible Elements
1 to 25	1
26 to 50	2
51 to 75	3
76 to 100	4
101 to 150	5
151 to 200	6
201 to 300	7
301 to 400	8
401 to 500	9
501 to 1000	2% of total
1001 and over	20 plus 1 for each 100 over 1000

9.1.3 Sleeping Accommodations for Persons with Hearing Impairments.
In addition to those accessible sleeping rooms and suites required by 9.1.2, sleeping rooms

9.2 Requirements for Accessible Units, Sleeping Rooms and Suites

9.1.4 Classes of Sleeping Accommodations.

(1) In order to provide persons with disabilities a range of options equivalent to those available to other persons served by the facility, sleeping rooms and suites required to be accessible by 9.1.2 shall be dispersed among the various classes of sleeping accommodations available to patrons of the place of transient lodging. Factors to be considered include room size, cost, amenities provided, and the number of beds provided.

(2) Equivalent Facilitation. For purposes of this section, it shall be deemed equivalent facilitation if the operator of a facility elects to limit construction of accessible rooms to those intended for multiple occupancy, provided that such rooms are made available at the cost of a single-occupancy room to an individual with disabilities who requests a single-occupancy room.

9.1.5. Alterations to Accessible Units, Sleeping Rooms, and Suites. When sleeping rooms are being altered in an existing facility, or portion thereof, subject to the requirements of this section, at least one sleeping room or suite that complies with the requirements of 9.2 (Requirements for Accessible Units, Sleeping Rooms, and Suites) shall be provided for each 25 sleeping rooms, or fraction thereof, of rooms being altered until the number of such rooms provided equals the number required to be accessible with 9.1.2. In addition, at least one sleeping room or suite that complies with the requirements of 9.3 (Visual Alarms, Notification Devices, and Telephones) shall be provided for each 25 sleeping rooms, or fraction thereof, of rooms being altered until the number of such rooms equals the number required to be accessible by 9.1.3.

9.2 Requirements for Accessible Units, Sleeping Rooms and Suites.

9.2.1 General. Units, sleeping rooms, and suites required to be accessible by 9.1 shall comply with 9.2.

9.2.2 Minimum Requirements. An accessible unit, sleeping room or suite shall be on an accessible route complying with 4.3 and have the following accessible elements and spaces.

(1) Accessible sleeping rooms shall have a 36 in (915 mm) clear width maneuvering space located along both sides of a bed, except that where two beds are provided, this requirement can be met by providing a 36 in (915 mm) wide maneuvering space located between the two beds.

(2) An accessible route complying with 4.3 shall connect all accessible spaces and elements, including telephones, within the unit, sleeping room, or suite. This is not intended to require an elevator in multi-story units as long as the spaces identified in 9.2.2(6) and (7) are on accessible levels and the accessible sleeping area is suitable for dual occupancy.

(3) Doors and doorways designed to allow passage into and within all sleeping rooms, suites or other covered units shall comply with 4.13.

(4) If fixed or built-in storage facilities such as cabinets, shelves, closets, and drawers are provided in accessible spaces, at least one of each type provided shall contain storage space complying with 4.25. Additional storage may be provided outside of the dimensions required by 4.25.

(5) All controls in accessible units, sleeping rooms, and suites shall comply with 4.27.

(6) Where provided as part of an accessible unit, sleeping room, or suite, the following spaces shall be accessible and shall be on an accessible route:

(a) the living area.

(b) the dining area.

(c) at least one sleeping area.

(d) patios, terraces, or balconies.

EXCEPTION: The requirements of 4.13.8 and 4.3.8 do not apply where it is necessary to utilize a higher door threshold or a change in level to protect the integrity of the unit from wind/water damage. Where this exception results in patios, terraces or balconies that are not at an accessible level, equivalent facilitation

9.3 Visual Alarms, Notification Devices and Telephones

shall be provided. (E.g., equivalent facilitation at a hotel patio or balcony might consist of providing raised decking or a ramp to provide accessibility.)

(e) at least one full bathroom (i.e., one with a water closet, a lavatory, and a bathtub or shower).

(f) if only half baths are provided, at least one half bath.

(g) carports, garages or parking spaces.

(7) Kitchens, Kitchenettes, or Wet Bars. When provided as accessory to a sleeping room or suite, kitchens, kitchenettes, wet bars, or similar amenities shall be accessible. Clear floor space for a front or parallel approach to cabinets, counters, sinks, and appliances shall be provided to comply with 4.2.4. Countertops and sinks shall be mounted at a maximum height of 34 in (865 mm) above the floor. At least fifty percent of shelf space in cabinets or refrigerator/freezers shall be within the reach ranges of 4.2.5 or 4.2.6 and space shall be designed to allow for the operation of cabinet and/or appliance doors so that all cabinets and appliances are accessible and usable. Controls and operating mechanisms shall comply with 4.27.

(8) Sleeping room accommodations for persons with hearing impairments required by 9.1 and complying with 9.3 shall be provided in the accessible sleeping room or suite.

9.3 Visual Alarms, Notification Devices and Telephones.

9.3.1 General. In sleeping rooms required to comply with this section, auxiliary visual alarms shall be provided and shall comply with 4.28.4. Visual notification devices shall be provided in units, sleeping rooms and suites to alert room occupants of incoming telephone calls and a door knock or bell. Notification devices shall not be connected to auxiliary visual alarm signal appliances. Permanently installed telephones shall have volume controls complying with 4.31.5; an accessible electrical outlet within 4 ft (1220 mm) of a telephone connection shall be provided to facilitate the use of a text telephone.

9.3.2 Equivalent Facilitation. For purposes of this section, equivalent facilitation shall include the installation of electrical outlets (including outlets connected to a facility's central alarm system) and telephone wiring in sleeping rooms and suites to enable persons with hearing impairments to utilize portable visual alarms and communication devices provided by the operator of the facility.

9.4 Other Sleeping Rooms and Suites. Doors and doorways designed to allow passage into and within all sleeping units or other covered units shall comply with 4.13.5.

9.5 Transient Lodging in Homeless Shelters, Halfway Houses, Transient Group Homes, and Other Social Service Establishments.

9.5.1 New Construction. In new construction all public use and common use areas are required to be designed and constructed to comply with section 4. At least one of each type of amenity (such as washers, dryers and similar equipment installed for the use of occupants) in each common area shall be accessible and shall be located on an accessible route to any accessible unit or sleeping accommodation.

EXCEPTION: Where elevators are not provided as allowed in 4.1.3(5), accessible amenities are not required on inaccessible floors as long as one of each type is provided in common areas on accessible floors.

9.5.2 Alterations.

(1) Social service establishments which are not homeless shelters:

(a) The provisions of 9.5.3 and 9.1.5 shall apply to sleeping rooms and beds.

(b) Alteration of other areas shall be consistent with the new construction provisions of 9.5.1.

(2) Homeless shelters. If the following elements are altered, the following requirements apply:

(a) at least one public entrance shall allow a person with mobility impairments to approach, enter and exit including a minimum clear door width of 32 in (815 mm).

(b) sleeping space for homeless persons as provided in the scoping provisions of 9.1.2 shall include doors to the sleeping area with a minimum clear width of 32 in (815 mm) and maneuvering space around the beds for persons with mobility impairments complying with 9.2.2(1).

(c) at least one toilet room for each gender or one unisex toilet room shall have a minimum clear door width of 32 in (815 mm), minimum turning space complying with 4.2.3, one water closet complying with 4.16, one lavatory complying with 4.19 and the door shall have a privacy latch; and, if provided, at least one tub or shower shall comply with 4.20 or 4.21, respectively.

(d) at least one common area which a person with mobility impairments can approach, enter and exit including a minimum clear door width of 32 in (815 mm).

(e) at least one route connecting elements (a), (b), (c) and (d) which a person with mobility impairments can use including minimum clear width of 36 in (915 mm), passing space complying with 4.3.4, turning space complying with 4.2.3 and changes in levels complying with 4.3.8.

(f) homeless shelters can comply with the provisions of (a)-(e) by providing the above elements on one accessible floor.

9.5.3. Accessible Sleeping Accommodations in New Construction.

Accessible sleeping rooms shall be provided in conformance with the table in 9.1.2 and shall comply with 9.2 Accessible Units, Sleeping Rooms and Suites (where the items are provided). Additional sleeping rooms that comply with 9.3 Sleeping Accommodations for Persons with Hearing Impairments shall be provided in conformance with the table provided in 9.1.3.

In facilities with multi-bed rooms or spaces, a percentage of the beds equal to the table provided in 9.1.2 shall comply with 9.2.2(1).

10. TRANSPORTATION FACILITIES.

10.1 General. Every station, bus stop, bus stop pad, terminal, building or other transportation facility, shall comply with the applicable provisions of 4.1 through 4.35, sections 5 through 9, and the applicable provisions of this section. The exceptions for elevators in 4.1.3(5), exception 1 and 4.1.6(1)(k) do not apply to a terminal, depot, or other station used for specified public transportation, or an airport passenger terminal, or facilities subject to Title II.

10.2 Bus Stops and Terminals.

10.2.1 New Construction.

(1) Where new bus stop pads are constructed at bus stops, bays or other areas where a lift or ramp is to be deployed, they shall have a firm, stable surface; a minimum clear length of 96 inches (measured from the curb or vehicle roadway edge) and a minimum clear width of 60 inches (measured parallel to the vehicle roadway) to the maximum extent allowed by legal or site constraints; and shall be connected to streets, sidewalks or pedestrian paths by an accessible route complying with 4.3 and 4.4. The slope of the pad parallel to the roadway shall, to the extent practicable, be the same as the roadway. For water drainage, a maximum slope of 1:50 (2%) perpendicular to the roadway is allowed.

(2) Where provided, new or replaced bus shelters shall be installed or positioned so as to permit a wheelchair or mobility aid user to enter from the public way and to reach a location, having a minimum clear floor area of 30 inches by 48 inches, entirely within the perimeter of the shelter. Such shelters shall be connected by an accessible route to the boarding area provided under paragraph (1) of this section.

(3) Where provided, all new bus route identification signs shall comply with 4.30.5. In addition, to the maximum extent practicable, all new bus route identification signs shall comply with 4.30.2 and 4.30.3. Signs

10.3 Fixed Facilities and Stations

that are sized to the maximum dimensions permitted under legitimate local, state or federal regulations or ordinances shall be considered in compliance with 4.30.2 and 4.30.3 for purposes of this section.

EXCEPTION: Bus schedules, timetables, or maps that are posted at the bus stop or bus bay are not required to comply with this provision.

10.2.2 Bus Stop Siting and Alterations.

(1) Bus stop sites shall be chosen such that, to the maximum extent practicable, the areas where lifts or ramps are to be deployed comply with section 10.2.1(1) and (2).

(2) When new bus route identification signs are installed or old signs are replaced, they shall comply with the requirements of 10.2.1(3).

10.3 Fixed Facilities and Stations.

10.3.1 New Construction. New stations in rapid rail, light rail, commuter rail, intercity bus, intercity rail, high speed rail, and other fixed guideway systems (e.g., automated guideway transit, monorails, etc.) shall comply with the following provisions, as applicable:

(1) Elements such as ramps, elevators or other circulation devices, fare vending or other ticketing areas, and fare collection areas shall be placed to minimize the distance which wheelchair users and other persons who cannot negotiate steps may have to travel compared to the general public. The circulation path, including an accessible entrance and an accessible route, for persons with disabilities shall, to the maximum extent practicable, coincide with the circulation path for the general public. Where the circulation path is different, signage complying with 4.30.1, 4.30.2, 4.30.3, 4.30.5, and 4.30.7(1) shall be provided to indicate direction to and identify the accessible entrance and accessible route.

(2) In lieu of compliance with 4.1.3(8), at least one entrance to each station shall comply with 4.14, Entrances. If different entrances to a station serve different transportation fixed routes or groups of fixed routes, at least one entrance serving each group or route shall

comply with 4.14, Entrances. All accessible entrances shall, to the maximum extent practicable, coincide with those used by the majority of the general public.

(3) Direct connections to commercial, retail, or residential facilities shall have an accessible route complying with 4.3 from the point of connection to boarding platforms and all transportation system elements used by the public. Any elements provided to facilitate future direct connections shall be on an accessible route connecting boarding platforms and all transportation system elements used by the public.

(4) Where signs are provided at entrances to stations identifying the station or the entrance, or both, at least one sign at each entrance shall comply with 4.30.4 and 4.30.6. Such signs shall be placed in uniform locations at entrances within the transit system to the maximum extent practicable.

EXCEPTION: Where the station has no defined entrance, but signage is provided, then the accessible signage shall be placed in a central location.

(5) Stations covered by this section shall have identification signs complying with 4.30.1, 4.30.2, 4.30.3, and 4.30.5. Signs shall be placed at frequent intervals and shall be clearly visible from within the vehicle on both sides when not obstructed by another train. When station identification signs are placed close to vehicle windows (i.e., on the side opposite from boarding) each shall have the top of the highest letter or symbol below the top of the vehicle window and the bottom of the lowest letter or symbol above the horizontal mid-line of the vehicle window.

(6) Lists of stations, routes, or destinations served by the station and located on boarding areas, platforms, or mezzanines shall comply with 4.30.1, 4.30.2, 4.30.3, and 4.30.5. A minimum of one sign identifying the specific station and complying with 4.30.4 and 4.30.6 shall be provided on each platform or boarding area. All signs referenced in this paragraph shall, to the maximum extent practicable, be placed in uniform locations within the transit system.

10.3 Fixed Facilities and Stations

(7)* Automatic fare vending, collection and adjustment (e.g., add-fare) systems shall comply with 4.34.2, 4.34.3, and 4.34.4. At each accessible entrance such devices shall be located on an accessible route. If self-service fare collection devices are provided for the use of the general public, at least one accessible device for entering, and at least one for exiting, unless one device serves both functions, shall be provided at each accessible point of entry or exit. Accessible fare collection devices shall have a minimum clear opening width of 32 inches; shall permit passage of a wheelchair; and, where provided, coin or card slots and controls necessary for operation shall comply with 4.27. Gates which must be pushed open by wheelchair or mobility aid users shall have a smooth continuous surface extending from 2 inches above the floor to 27 inches above the floor and shall comply with 4.13. Where the circulation path does not coincide with that used by the general public, accessible fare collection systems shall be located at or adjacent to the accessible point of entry or exit.

(8) Platform edges bordering a drop-off and not protected by platform screens or guard rails shall have a detectable warning. Such detectable warnings shall comply with 4.29.2 and shall be 24 inches wide running the full length of the platform drop-off.

(9) In stations covered by this section, rail-to-platform height in new stations shall be coordinated with the floor height of new vehicles so that the vertical difference, measured when the vehicle is at rest, is within plus or minus 5/8 inch under normal passenger load conditions. For rapid rail, light rail, commuter rail, high speed rail, and intercity rail systems in new stations, the horizontal gap, measured when the new vehicle is at rest, shall be no greater than 3 inches. For slow moving automated guideway "people mover" transit systems, the horizontal gap in new stations shall be no greater than 1 inch.

EXCEPTION 1: Existing vehicles operating in new stations may have a vertical difference with respect to the new platform within plus or minus 1-1/2 inches.

EXCEPTION 2: In light rail, commuter rail and intercity rail systems where it is not operation-ally or structurally feasible to meet the horizontal gap or vertical difference requirements, mini-high platforms, car-borne or platform-mounted lifts, ramps or bridge plates, or similar manually deployed devices, meeting the applicable requirements of 36 CFR part 1192, or 49 CFR part 38 shall suffice.

(10) Stations shall not be designed or constructed so as to require persons with disabilities to board or alight from a vehicle at a location other than one used by the general public.

(11) Illumination levels in the areas where signage is located shall be uniform and shall minimize glare on signs. Lighting along circulation routes shall be of a type and configuration to provide uniform illumination.

(12) Text Telephones: The following shall be provided in accordance with 4.31.9:

(a) If an interior public pay telephone is provided in a transit facility (as defined by the Department of Transportation) at least one interior public text telephone shall be provided in the station.

(b) Where four or more public pay telephones serve a particular entrance to a rail station and at least one is in an interior location, at least one interior public text telephone shall be provided to serve that entrance. Compliance with this section constitutes compliance with section 4.1.3(17)(c).

(13) Where it is necessary to cross tracks to reach boarding platforms, the route surface shall be level and flush with the rail top at the outer edge and between the rails, except for a maximum 2-1/2 inch gap on the inner edge of each rail to permit passage of wheel flanges. Such crossings shall comply with 4.29.5. Where gap reduction is not practicable, an above-grade or below-grade accessible route shall be provided.

(14) Where public address systems are provided to convey information to the public in terminals, stations, or other fixed facilities, a means of conveying the same or equivalent information to persons with hearing loss or who are deaf shall be provided.

10.3.2 Existing Facilities: Key Stations.

(15) Where clocks are provided for use by the general public, the clock face shall be uncluttered so that its elements are clearly visible. Hands, numerals, and/or digits shall contrast with the background either light-on-dark or dark-on-light. Where clocks are mounted overhead, numerals and/or digits shall comply with 4.30.3. Clocks shall be placed in uniform locations throughout the facility and system to the maximum extent practicable.

(16) Where provided in below grade stations, escalators shall have a minimum clear width of 32 inches. At the top and bottom of each escalator run, at least two contiguous treads shall be level beyond the comb plate before the risers begin to form. All escalator treads shall be marked by a strip of clearly contrasting color, 2 inches in width, placed parallel to and on the nose of each step. The strip shall be of a material that is at least as slip resistant as the remainder of the tread. The edge of the tread shall be apparent from both ascending and descending directions.

(17) Where provided, elevators shall be glazed or have transparent panels to allow an unobstructed view both in to and out of the car. Elevators shall comply with 4.10.

EXCEPTION: Elevator cars with a clear floor area in which a 60 inch diameter circle can be inscribed may be substituted for the minimum car dimensions of 4.10, Fig. 22.

(18) Where provided, ticketing areas shall permit persons with disabilities to obtain a ticket and check baggage and shall comply with 7.2.

(19) Where provided, baggage check-in and retrieval systems shall be on an accessible route complying with 4.3, and shall have space immediately adjacent complying with 4.2. If unattended security barriers are provided, at least one gate shall comply with 4.13. Gates which must be pushed open by wheelchair or mobility aid users shall have a smooth continuous surface extending from 2 inches above the floor to 27 inches above the floor.

10.3.2 Existing Facilities: Key Stations.

(1) Rapid, light and commuter rail key stations, as defined under criteria established by the Department of Transportation in subpart C of 49 CFR part 37 and existing intercity rail stations shall provide at least one accessible route from an accessible entrance to those areas necessary for use of the transportation system.

(2) The accessible route required by 10.3.2(1) shall include the features specified in 10.3.1 (1), (4)-(9), (11)-(15), and (17)-(19).

(3) Where technical infeasibility in existing stations requires the accessible route to lead from the public way to a paid area of the transit system, an accessible fare collection system, complying with 10.3.1(7), shall be provided along such accessible route.

(4) In light rail, rapid rail and commuter rail key stations, the platform or a portion thereof and the vehicle floor shall be coordinated so that the vertical difference, measured when the vehicle is at rest, within plus or minus 1-1/2 inches under all normal passenger load conditions, and the horizontal gap, measured when the vehicle is at rest, is no greater than 3 inches for at least one door of each vehicle or car required to be accessible by 49 CFR part 37.

EXCEPTION 1: Existing vehicles retrofitted to meet the requirements of 49 CFR 37.93 (one-car-per-train rule) shall be coordinated with the platform such that, for at least one door, the vertical difference between the vehicle floor and the platform, measured when the vehicle is at rest with 50% normal passenger capacity, is within plus or minus 2 inches and the horizontal gap is no greater than 4 inches.

EXCEPTION 2: Where it is not structurally or operationally feasible to meet the horizontal gap or vertical difference requirements, mini-high platforms, car-borne or platform mounted lifts, ramps or bridge plates, or similar manually deployed devices, meeting the applicable requirements of 36 CFR Part 1192 shall suffice.

(5) New direct connections to commercial, retail, or residential facilities shall, to the maximum extent feasible, have an accessible route complying with 4.3 from the point of connection to boarding platforms and all transportation system elements used by the public. Any elements provided to facilitate future direct connections shall be on an accessible route connecting boarding platforms and all transportation system elements used by the public.

10.3.3 Existing Facilities: Alterations.

(1) For the purpose of complying with 4.1.6(2) Alterations to an Area Containing a Primary Function, an area of primary function shall be as defined by applicable provisions of 49 CFR 37.43(c) (Department of Transportation's ADA Rule) or 28 CFR 36.403 (Department of Justice's ADA Rule).

10.4. Airports.

10.4.1 New Construction.

(1) Elements such as ramps, elevators or other vertical circulation devices, ticketing areas, security checkpoints, or passenger waiting areas shall be placed to minimize the distance which wheelchair users and other persons who cannot negotiate steps may have to travel compared to the general public.

(2) The circulation path, including an accessible entrance and an accessible route, for persons with disabilities shall, to the maximum extent practicable, coincide with the circulation path for the general public. Where the circulation path is different, directional signage complying with 4.30.1, 4.30.2, 4.30.3 and 4.30.5 shall be provided which indicates the location of the nearest accessible entrance and its accessible route.

(3) Ticketing areas shall permit persons with disabilities to obtain a ticket and check baggage and shall comply with 7.2.

(4) Where public pay telephones are provided, and at least one is at an interior location, a public text telephone shall be provided in compliance with 4.31.9. Additionally, if four or more public pay telephones are located

in any of the following locations, at least one public text telephone shall also be provided in that location:

(a) a main terminal outside the security areas;
(b) a concourse within the security areas; or
(c) a baggage claim area in a terminal.

Compliance with this section constitutes compliance with section 4.1.3(17)(c).

(5) Baggage check-in and retrieval systems shall be on an accessible route complying with 4.3, and shall have space immediately adjacent complying with 4.2.4. If unattended security barriers are provided, at least one gate shall comply with 4.13. Gates which must be pushed open by wheelchair or mobility aid users shall have a smooth continuous surface extending from 2 inches above the floor to 27 inches above the floor.

(6) Terminal information systems which broadcast information to the general public through a public address system shall provide a means to provide the same or equivalent information to persons with a hearing loss or who are deaf. Such methods may include, but are not limited to, visual paging systems using video monitors and computer technology. For persons with certain types of hearing loss such methods may include, but are not limited to, an assistive listening system complying with 4.33.7.

(7) Where clocks are provided for use by the general public the clock face shall be uncluttered so that its elements are clearly visible. Hands, numerals, and/or digits shall contrast with their background either light-on-dark or dark-on-light. Where clocks are mounted overhead, numerals and/or digits shall comply with 4.30.3. Clocks shall be placed in uniform locations throughout the facility to the maximum extent practicable.

(8) Security Systems. [Reserved]

10.5 Boat and Ferry Docks.
[Reserved]

APPENDIX

This appendix contains *materials of an advisory nature* and provides additional information that should help the reader to understand the minimum requirements of the *guidelines* or to design buildings or facilities for greater accessibility. The paragraph numbers correspond to the sections or paragraphs of the *guideline* to which the material relates and are therefore not consecutive (for example, A4.2.1 contains additional information relevant to 4.2.1). Sections *of the guidelines* for which additional material appears in this appendix have been indicated by an asterisk. *Nothing in this appendix shall in any way obviate any obligation to comply with the requirements of the guidelines itself.*

A2.2 Equivalent Facilitation. *Specific examples of equivalent facilitation are found in the following sections:*

4.1.6(3)(c)	*Elevators in Alterations*
4.31.9	*Text Telephones*
7.2	*Sales and Service Counters, Teller Windows, Information Counters*
9.1.4	*Classes of Sleeping Accommodations*
9.2.2(6)(d)	*Requirements for Accessible Units, Sleeping Rooms, and Suites*

A4.1.1 Application.

A4.1.1(3) Areas Used Only by Employees as Work Areas. *Where there are a series of individual work stations of the same type (e.g., laboratories, service counters, ticket booths), 5%, but not less than one, of each type of work station should be constructed so that an individual with disabilities can maneuver within the work stations. Rooms housing individual offices in a typical office building must meet the requirements of the guidelines concerning doors, accessible routes, etc. but do not need to allow for maneuvering space around individual desks. Modifications required to permit maneuvering within the work area may be accomplished as a reasonable accommodation to individual employees with disabilities under Title I of the ADA. Consideration should also be given to placing shelves in employee work areas at a* convenient height for accessibility or installing commercially available shelving that is adjustable so that reasonable accommodations can be made in the future.

If work stations are made accessible they should comply with the applicable provisions of 4.2 through 4.35.

A4.1.2 Accessible Sites and Exterior Facilities: New Construction.

A4.1.2(5)(e) Valet Parking. *Valet parking is not always usable by individuals with disabilities. For instance, an individual may use a type of vehicle controls that render the regular controls inoperable or the driver's seat in a van may be removed. In these situations, another person cannot park the vehicle. It is recommended that some self-parking spaces be provided at valet parking facilities for individuals whose vehicles cannot be parked by another person and that such spaces be located on an accessible route to the entrance of the facility.*

A4.1.3 Accessible Buildings: New Construction.

A4.1.3(5) *Only full passenger elevators are covered by the accessibility provisions of 4.10. Materials and equipment hoists, freight elevators not intended for passenger use, dumbwaiters, and construction elevators are not covered by these guidelines. If a building is exempt from the elevator requirement, it is not necessary to provide a platform lift or other means of vertical access in lieu of an elevator.*

Under Exception 4, platform lifts are allowed where existing conditions make it impractical to install a ramp or elevator. Such conditions generally occur where it is essential to provide access to small raised or lowered areas where space may not be available for a ramp. Examples include, but are not limited to, raised pharmacy platforms, commercial offices raised above a sales floor, or radio and news booths.

A4.1.3(9) *Supervised automatic sprinkler systems have built in signals for monitoring features of the system such as the opening and closing of water control valves, the power supplies for needed pumps, water tank levels, and for indicating conditions that will impair the satisfactory operation of the sprinkler system.*

A4.2 Space Allowances and Reach Ranges

Because of these monitoring features, super-vised automatic sprinkler systems have a high level of satisfactory performance and response to fire conditions.

A4.1.3(10) *If an odd number of drinking fountains is provided on a floor, the requirement in 4.1.3(10)(b) may be met by rounding down the odd number to an even number and calculating 50% of the even number. When more than one drinking fountain on a floor is required to comply with 4.15, those fountains should be dispersed to allow wheelchair users convenient access. For example, in a large facility such as a convention center that has water fountains at several locations on a floor, the accessible water fountains should be located so that wheelchair users do not have to travel a greater distance than other people to use a drinking fountain.*

A4.1.3(17)(b) *In addition to the requirements of section 4.1.3(17)(b), the installation of additional volume controls is encouraged. Volume controls may be installed on any telephone.*

A4.1.3(19)(a) *Readily removable or folding seating units may be installed in lieu of providing an open space for wheelchair users. Folding seating units are usually two fixed seats that can be easily folded into a fixed center bar to allow for one or two open spaces for wheelchair users when necessary. These units are more easily adapted than removable seats which generally require the seat to be removed in advance by the facility management.*

Either a sign or a marker placed on seating with removable or folding arm rests is required by this section. Consideration should be given for ensuring identification of such seats in a darkened theater. For example, a marker which contrasts (light on dark or dark on light) and which also reflects light could be placed on the side of such seating so as to be visible in a lighted auditorium and also to reflect light from a flashlight.

A4.1.6 Accessible Buildings: Alterations.

A4.1.6(1)(h) *When an entrance is being altered, it is preferable that those entrances being altered be made accessible to the extent feasible.*

A4.2 Space Allowances and Reach Ranges.

A4.2.1 Wheelchair Passage Width.

(1) Space Requirements for Wheelchairs. Many persons who use wheelchairs need a 30 in (760 mm) clear opening width for doorways, gates, and the like, when the latter are entered head-on. If the person is unfamiliar with a building, if competing traffic is heavy, if sudden or frequent movements are needed, or if the wheelchair must be turned at an opening, then greater clear widths are needed. For most situations, the addition of an inch of leeway on either side is sufficient. Thus, a minimum clear width of 32 in (815 mm) will provide adequate clearance. However, when an opening or a restriction in a passageway is more than 24 in (610 mm) long, it is essentially a passageway and must be at least 36 in (915 mm) wide.

(2) Space Requirements for Use of Walking Aids. Although people who use walking aids can maneuver through clear width openings of 32 in (815 mm), they need 36 in (915 mm) wide passageways and walks for comfortable gaits. Crutch tips, often extending down at a wide angle, are a hazard in narrow passageways where they might not be seen by other pedestrians. Thus, the 36 in (915 mm) width provides a safety allowance both for the person *with a disability* and for others.

(3) Space Requirements for Passing. Able-bodied *persons* in winter clothing, walking

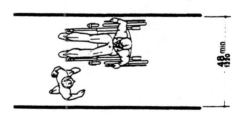

Fig. A1
Minimum Passage Width for One Wheelchair
and One Ambulatory Person

A4.2 Space Allowances and Reach Ranges

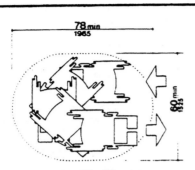

Fig. A2
Space Needed for Smooth U-Turn in a Wheelchair

straight ahead with arms swinging, need 32 in (815 mm) of width, which includes 2 in (50 mm) on either side for sway, and another 1 in (25 mm) tolerance on either side for clearing nearby objects or other pedestrians. Almost all wheelchair users and those who use walking aids can also manage within this 32 in (815 mm) width for short distances. Thus, two streams of traffic can pass in 64 in (1625 mm) in a comfortable flow. Sixty inches (1525 mm) provides a minimum width for a somewhat more restricted flow. If the clear width is less than 60 in (1525 mm), two wheelchair users will not be able to pass but will have to seek a wider place for passing. Forty-eight inches (1220 mm) is the minimum width needed for an ambulatory person to pass a nonambulatory or semi-ambulatory person. Within this 48 in (1220 mm) width, the ambulatory person will have to twist to pass a wheelchair user, a person with a *service animal*, or a

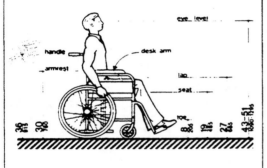

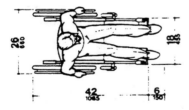

NOTE: Footrests may extend further for tall people

Fig. A3
Dimensions of Adult-Sized Wheelchairs

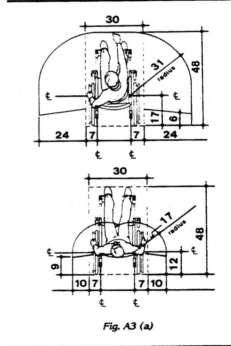

Fig. A3 (a)

A4.3 Accessible Route

semi-ambulatory person. There will be little leeway for swaying or missteps (see Fig. A1).

A4.2.3 Wheelchair Turning Space.
These guidelines specify a minimum space of 60 in (1525 mm) diameter or a 60 in by 60 in (1525 mm by 1525 mm) T-shaped space for a pivoting 180-degree turn of a wheelchair. This space is usually satisfactory for turning around, but many people will not be able to turn without repeated tries and bumping into surrounding objects. The space shown in Fig. A2 will allow most wheelchair users to complete U-turns without difficulty.

A4.2.4 Clear Floor or Ground Space for Wheelchairs.
The wheelchair and user shown in Fig. A3 represent typical dimensions for a large adult male. The space requirements in this *guideline* are based upon maneuvering clearances that will accommodate most wheelchairs. Fig. A3 provides a uniform reference for design not covered by this *guideline*.

A4.2.5 & A4.2.6 Reach.
Reach ranges for persons seated in wheelchairs may be further clarified by Fig. A3(a). These drawings approximate in the plan view the information shown in Fig. 4, 5, and 6.

A4.3 Accessible Route.

A4.3.1 General.

(1) Travel Distances. Many people with mobility impairments can move at only very slow speeds; for many, traveling 200 ft (61 m) could take about 2 minutes. This assumes a rate of about 1.5 ft/s (455 mm/s) on level ground. It also assumes that the traveler would move continuously. However, on trips over 100 ft (30 m), disabled people are apt to rest frequently, which substantially increases their trip times. Resting periods of 2 minutes for every 100 ft (30 m) can be used to estimate travel times for people with severely limited stamina. In inclement weather, slow progress and resting can greatly increase a disabled person's exposure to the elements.

(2) Sites. Level, indirect routes or those with running slopes lower than 1:20 can sometimes provide more convenience than direct routes with maximum allowable slopes or with ramps.

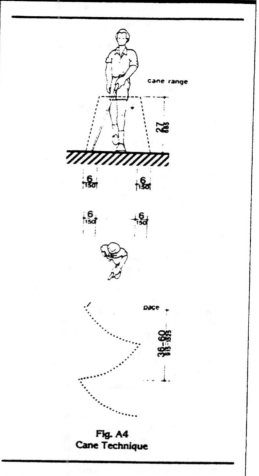

**Fig. A4
Cane Technique**

A4.3.10 Egress. Because people with disabilities may visit, be employed or be a resident in any building, emergency management plans with specific provisions to ensure their safe evacuation also play an essential role in fire safety and life safety.

A4.3.11.3 Stairway Width. *A 48 inch (1220 mm) wide exit stairway is needed to allow assisted evacuation (e.g., carrying a person in a wheelchair) without encroaching on the exit path for ambulatory persons.*

A4.3.11.4 Two-way Communication. *It is essential that emergency communication not be dependent on voice communications alone because the safety of people with hearing or speech impairments could be jeopardized. The visible signal requirement could be satisfied with something as simple as a button in the area of rescue assistance that lights, indicating that help is on the way, when the message is answered at the point of entry.*

A4.4 Protruding Objects.

A4.4.1 General. Service animals are trained to recognize and avoid hazards. However, most people with severe impairments of vision use the long cane as an aid to mobility. The two principal cane techniques are the touch technique, where the cane arcs from side to side and touches points outside both shoulders; and the diagonal technique, where the cane is held in a stationary position diagonally across the body with the cane tip touching or just above the ground at a point outside one shoulder and the handle or grip extending to a point outside the other shoulder. The touch technique is used primarily in uncontrolled areas, while the diagonal technique is used primarily in certain limited, controlled, and familiar environments. Cane users are often trained to use both techniques.

Potential hazardous objects are noticed only if they fall within the detection range of canes (see Fig. A4). Visually impaired people walking toward an object can detect an overhang if its lowest surface is not higher than 27 in (685 mm). When walking alongside *protruding* objects, they cannot detect overhangs. Since proper cane and *service animal* techniques keep people away from the edge of a path or from walls, a slight overhang of no more than 4 in (100 mm) is not hazardous.

A4.5 Ground and Floor Surfaces.

A4.5.1 General. People who have difficulty *walking or* maintaining balance *or who use crutches, canes, or walkers,* and those with restricted gaits are particularly sensitive to slipping and tripping hazards. For such people, a stable and regular surface is necessary for safe walking, particularly on stairs. Wheelchairs can be propelled most easily on surfaces that are hard, stable, and regular. Soft loose surfaces such as shag carpet, loose sand or gravel, wet clay, and irregular surfaces such as cobblestones can significantly impede wheelchair movement.

Slip resistance is based on the frictional force necessary to keep a shoe heel or crutch tip from slipping on a walking surface under conditions likely to be found on the surface. *While the dynamic coefficient of friction during walking varies in a complex and non-uniform way, the static coefficient of friction, which can be measured in several ways, provides a close approximation of the slip resistance of a surface. Contrary to popular belief, some slippage is necessary to walking, especially for persons with restricted gaits; a truly "non-slip" surface could not be negotiated.*

The Occupational Safety and Health Administration recommends that walking surfaces have a static coefficient of friction of 0.5. A research project sponsored by the Architectural and Transportation Barriers Compliance Board (Access Board) conducted tests with persons with disabilities and concluded that a higher coefficient of friction was needed by such persons. A static coefficient of friction of 0.6 is recommended for accessible routes and 0.8 for ramps.

It is recognized that the coefficient of friction varies considerably due to the presence of contaminants, water, floor finishes, and other factors not under the control of the designer or builder and not subject to design and construction guidelines and that compliance would be difficult to measure on the building site. Nevertheless, many common building materials suitable for flooring are now labeled with information on the static coefficient of friction. While it may not be possible to compare one product directly with another, or to guarantee a constant measure, builders and designers are encouraged to specify materials with appropriate values. As more products include information on slip resistance, improved uniformity in measurement and specification is likely. The Access Board's advisory guidelines on Slip Resistant Surfaces provides additional information on this subject.

Cross slopes on walks and ground or floor surfaces can cause considerable difficulty in propelling a wheelchair in a straight line.

A4.6 Parking and Passenger Loading Zones

A4.5.3 Carpet. Much more needs to be done in developing both quantitative and qualitative criteria for carpeting *(i.e., problems associated with texture and weave need to be studied).* However, certain functional characteristics are well established. When both carpet and padding are used, it is desirable to have minimum movement (preferably none) between the floor and the pad and the pad and the carpet which would allow the carpet to hump or warp. In heavily trafficked areas, a thick, soft (plush) pad or cushion, particularly in combination with long carpet pile, makes it difficult for individuals in wheelchairs and those with other ambulatory disabilities to get about. Firm carpeting can be achieved through proper selection and combination of pad and carpet, sometimes with the elimination of the pad or cushion, and with proper installation. *Carpeting designed with a weave that causes a zig-zag effect when wheeled across is strongly discouraged.*

A4.6 Parking and Passenger Loading Zones.

A4.6.3 Parking Spaces. *The increasing use of vans with side-mounted lifts or ramps by persons with disabilities has necessitated some revisions in specifications for parking spaces and adjacent access aisles. The typical accessible parking space is 96 in (2440 mm) wide with an adjacent 60 in (1525 mm) access aisle. However, this aisle does not permit lifts or ramps to be deployed and still leave room for a person using a wheelchair or other mobility aid to exit the lift platform or ramp. In tests conducted with actual lift/van/wheelchair combinations, (under a Board-sponsored Accessible Parking and Loading Zones Project) researchers found that a space and aisle totaling almost 204 in (5180 mm) wide was needed to deploy a lift and exit conveniently. The "van accessible" parking space required by these guidelines provides a 96 in (2440 mm) wide space with a 96 in (2440 mm) adjacent access aisle which is just wide enough to maneuver and exit from a side mounted lift. If a 96 in (2440 mm) access aisle is placed between two spaces, two "van accessible" spaces are created. Alternatively, if the wide access aisle is provided at the end of a row (an area often unused), it may be possible to provide the wide access aisle without additional space (see Fig. A5(a)).*

A sign is needed to alert van users to the presence of the wider aisle, but the space is not intended to be restricted only to vans.

"Universal" Parking Space Design. An alternative to the provision of a percentage of spaces with a wide aisle, and the associated need to include additional signage, is the use of what has been called the "universal" parking space design. Under this design, all accessible spaces are 132 in (3350 mm) wide with a 60 in (1525 mm) access aisle (see Fig. A5(b)). One

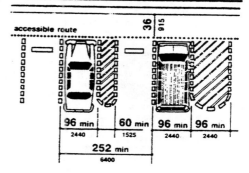

96 min 2440 | 60 min 1525 | 96 min 2440 | 96 min 2440

252 min
6400

(a)
Van Accessible Space at End Row

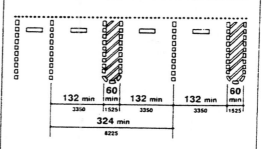

132 min 3350 | 60 min 1525 | 132 min 3350 | 132 min 3350 | 60 min 1525

324 min
8225

(b)
Universal Parking Space Design

Fig. A5
Parking Space Alternatives

advantage to this design is that no additional signage is needed because all spaces can accommodate a van with a side-mounted lift or ramp. Also, there is no competition between cars and vans for spaces since all spaces can accommodate either. Furthermore, the wider space permits vehicles to park to one side or the other within the 132 in (3350 mm) space to allow persons to exit and enter the vehicle on either the driver or passenger side, although, in some cases, this would require exiting or entering without a marked access aisle.

An essential consideration for any design is having the access aisle level with the parking space. Since a person with a disability, using a lift or ramp, must maneuver within the access aisle, the aisle cannot include a ramp or sloped area. The access aisle must be connected to an accessible route to the appropriate accessible entrance of a building or facility. The parking access aisle must either blend with the accessible route or have a curb ramp complying with 4.7. Such a curb ramp opening must be located within the access aisle boundaries, not within the parking space boundaries. Unfortunately, many facilities are designed with a ramp that is blocked when any vehicle parks in the accessible space. Also, the required dimensions of the access aisle cannot be restricted by planters, curbs or wheel stops.

A4.6.4 Signage. Signs designating parking places for disabled people can be seen from a driver's seat if the signs are mounted high enough above the ground and located at the front of a parking space.

A4.6.5 Vertical Clearance. High-top vans, which disabled people or transportation services often use, require higher clearances in parking garages than automobiles.

A4.8 Ramps.

A4.8.1 General. Ramps are essential for wheelchair users if elevators or lifts are not available to connect different levels. However, some people who use walking aids have difficulty with ramps and prefer stairs.

A4.8.2 Slope and Rise. Ramp slopes between 1:16 and 1:20 are preferred. The ability to manage an incline is related to both its slope and its length. Wheelchair users with

disabilities affecting their arms or with low stamina have serious difficulty using inclines. Most ambulatory people and most people who use wheelchairs can manage a slope of 1:16. Many people cannot manage a slope of 1:12 for 30 ft (9 m).

A4.8.4 Landings. Level landings are essential toward maintaining an aggregate slope that complies with these guidelines. A ramp landing that is not level causes individuals using wheelchairs to tip backward or bottom out when the ramp is approached.

A4.8.5 Handrails. The requirements for stair and ramp handrails in this guideline are for adults. When children are principal users in a building or facility, a second set of handrails at an appropriate height can assist them and aid in preventing accidents.

A4.9 Stairs.

A4.9.1 Minimum Number. Only interior and exterior stairs connecting levels that are not connected by an elevator, ramp, or other accessible means of vertical access have to comply with 4.9.

A4.10 Elevators.

A4.10.6 Door Protective and Reopening Device. The required door reopening device would hold the door open for 20 seconds if the doorway remains obstructed. After 20 seconds, the door may begin to close. However, if designed in accordance with ASME A17.1-1990, the door closing movement could still be stopped if a person or object exerts sufficient force at any point on the door edge.

A4.10.7 Door and Signal Timing for Hall Calls. This paragraph allows variation in the location of call buttons, advance time for warning signals, and the door-holding period used to meet the time requirement.

A4.10.12 Car Controls. Industry-wide standardization of elevator control panel design would make all elevators significantly more convenient for use by people with severe visual impairments. In many cases, it will be possible to locate the highest control on elevator panels within 48 in (1220 mm) from the floor.

A4.11 Platform Lifts (Wheelchair Lifts)

A4.10.13 Car Position Indicators. A special button may be provided that would activate the audible signal within the given elevator only for the desired trip, rather than maintaining the audible signal in constant operation.

A4.10.14 Emergency Communications. A device that requires no handset is easier to use by people who have difficulty reaching. Also, *small handles on handset compartment doors are not usable by people who have difficulty grasping.*

Ideally, emergency two-way communication systems should provide both voice and visual display intercommunication so that persons with hearing impairments and persons with vision impairments can receive information regarding the status of a rescue. A voice intercommunication system cannot be the only means of communication because it is not accessible to people with speech and hearing impairments. While a voice intercommunication system is not required, at a minimum, the system should provide both an audio and visual indication that a rescue is on the way.

A4.11 Platform Lifts (Wheelchair Lifts).

A4.11.2 Other Requirements. *Inclined stairway chairlifts, and inclined and vertical platform lifts (wheelchair lifts) are available* for short-distance, vertical transportation of people with disabilities. Care should be taken in selecting lifts *as some lifts are not equally suitable for use by both wheelchair users and semi-ambulatory individuals.*

A4.12 Windows.

A4.12.1 General. *Windows intended to be operated by occupants in accessible spaces should comply with 4.12.*

A4.12.2 Window Hardware. *Windows requiring pushing, pulling, or lifting to open (for example, double-hung, sliding, or casement and awning units without cranks) should require no more than 5 lbf (22.2 N) to open or close. Locks, cranks, and other window hardware should comply with 4.27.*

A4.13 Doors.

A4.13.8 Thresholds at Doorways. Thresholds and surface height changes in doorways are particularly inconvenient for wheelchair users who also have low stamina or restrictions in arm movement because complex maneuvering is required to get over the level change while operating the door.

A4.13.9 Door Hardware. Some disabled persons must push against a door with their chair or walker to open it. Applied kickplates on doors with closers can reduce required maintenance by withstanding abuse from wheelchairs and canes. To be effective, they should cover the door width, less approximately 2 in (51 mm), up to a height of 16 in (405 mm) from its bottom edge and be centered across the *width of the door.*

A4.13.10 Door Closers. Closers with delayed action features give a person more time to maneuver through doorways. They are particularly useful on frequently used interior doors such as entrances to toilet rooms.

A4.13.11 Door Opening Force. Although most people with disabilities can exert at least 5 lbf (22.2N), both pushing and pulling from a stationary position, a few people with severe disabilities cannot exert 3 lbf (13.13N). Although some people cannot manage the allowable forces in this guideline and many others have difficulty, door closers must have certain minimum closing forces to close doors satisfactorily. Forces for pushing or pulling doors open are measured with a push-pull scale under the following conditions:

(1) Hinged doors: Force applied perpendicular to the door at the door opener or 30 in (760 mm) from the hinged side, whichever is farther from the hinge.

(2) Sliding or folding doors: Force applied parallel to the door at the door pull or latch.

(3) Application of force: Apply force gradually so that the applied force does not exceed the resistance of the door. In high-rise buildings, air-pressure differentials may require a modification of this specification in order to meet the functional intent.

A4.13.12 Automatic Doors and Power-Assisted Doors. Sliding automatic doors do not need guard rails and are more convenient for wheelchair users and visually impaired people to use. If slowly opening automatic doors can be reactivated before their closing cycle is completed, they will be more convenient in busy doorways.

A4.15 Drinking Fountains and Water Coolers.

A4.15.2 Spout Height. Two drinking fountains, mounted side by side or on a single post, are usable by people with disabilities and people who find it difficult to bend over.

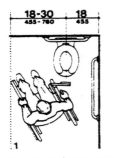

1
Takes transfer position, swings footrest out of the way, sets brakes.

2
Removes armrest, transfers.

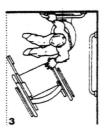

3
Moves wheelchair out of the way, changes position (some people fold chair or pivot it 90° to the toilet).

4
Positions on toilet, releases brake.

(a)
Diagonal Approach

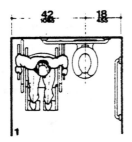

1
Takes transfer position, removes armrest, sets brakes.

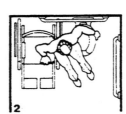

2
Transfers.

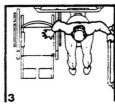

3
Positions on toilet.

(b)
Side Approach

Fig. A6
Wheelchair Transfers

A4.16 Water Closets

A4.16 Water Closets.

A4.16.3 Height. Height preferences for toilet seats vary considerably among disabled people. Higher seat heights may be an advantage to some ambulatory disabled people, but are often a disadvantage for wheelchair users and others. Toilet seats 18 in (455 mm) high seem to be a reasonable compromise. Thick seats and filler rings are available to adapt standard fixtures to these requirements.

A4.16.4 Grab Bars. Fig. A6(a) and (b) show the diagonal and side approaches most commonly used to transfer from a wheelchair to a water closet. Some wheelchair users can transfer from the front of the toilet while others use a 90-degree approach. Most people who use the two additional approaches can also use either the diagonal approach or the side approach.

A4.16.5 Flush Controls. Flush valves and related plumbing can be located behind walls or to the side of the toilet, or a toilet seat lid can be provided if plumbing fittings are directly behind the toilet seat. Such designs reduce the chance of injury and imbalance caused by leaning back against the fittings. Flush controls for tank-type toilets have a standardized mounting location on the left side of the tank (facing the tank). Tanks can be obtained by special order with controls mounted on the right side. If administrative authorities require flush controls for flush valves to be located in a position that conflicts with the location of the rear grab bar, then that bar may be split or shifted toward the wide side of the toilet area.

A4.17 Toilet Stalls.

A4.17.3 Size and Arrangement. This section requires use of the 60 in (1525 mm) standard stall (Figure 30(a)) and permits the 36 in (915 mm) or 48 in (1220 mm) wide alternate stall (Figure 30(b)) only in alterations where provision of the standard stall is technically infeasible or where local plumbing codes prohibit reduction in the number of fixtures. A standard stall provides a clear space on one side of the water closet to enable persons who use wheelchairs to perform a side or diagonal transfer from the wheelchair to the water closet. However, some persons with disabilities who use mobility aids such as walkers, canes or crutches

are better able to use the two parallel grab bars in the 36 in (915 mm) wide alternate stall to achieve a standing position.

In large toilet rooms, where six or more toilet stalls are provided, it is therefore required that a 36 in (915 mm) wide stall with parallel grab bars be provided in addition to the standard stall required in new construction. The 36 in (915 mm) width is necessary to achieve proper use of the grab bars; wider stalls would position the grab bars too far apart to be easily used and narrower stalls would position the grab bars too close to the water closet. Since the stall is primarily intended for use by persons using canes, crutches and walkers, rather than wheelchairs, the length of the stall could be conventional. The door, however, must swing outward to ensure a usable space for people who use crutches or walkers.

A4.17.5 Doors. To make it easier for wheelchair users to close toilet stall doors, doors can be provided with closers, spring hinges, or a pull bar mounted on the inside surface of the door near the hinge side.

A4.19 Lavatories and Mirrors.

A4.19.6 Mirrors. If mirrors are to be used by both ambulatory people and wheelchair users, then they must be at least 74 in (1880 mm) high at their topmost edge. A single full length mirror can accommodate all people, including children.

A4.21 Shower Stalls.

A4.21.1 General. Shower stalls that are 36 in by 36 in (915 mm by 915 mm) wide provide additional safety to people who have difficulty maintaining balance because all grab bars and walls are within easy reach. Seated people use the walls of 36 in by 36 in (915 mm by 915 mm) showers for back support. Shower stalls that are 60 in (1525 mm) wide and have no curb may increase usability of a bathroom by wheelchair users because the shower area provides additional maneuvering space.

A4.22 Toilet Rooms.

A4.22.3 Clear Floor Space. In many small facilities, single-user restrooms may be the only

A4.22 Toilet Rooms

facilities provided for all building users. In addition, the guidelines allow the use of "unisex" or "family" accessible toilet rooms in alterations when technical infeasibility can be demonstrated. Experience has shown that the provision of accessible "unisex" or single-user restrooms is a reasonable way to provide access for wheelchair users and any attendants, especially when attendants are of the opposite sex. Since these facilities have proven so useful, it is often considered advantageous to install a "unisex" toilet room in new facilities in addition to making the multi-stall restrooms accessible, especially in shopping malls, large auditoriums, and convention centers.

Figure 28 (section 4.16) provides minimum clear floor space dimensions for toilets in accessible "unisex" toilet rooms. The dotted lines designate the minimum clear floor space, depending on the direction of approach, required for wheelchair users to transfer onto the water closet. The dimensions of 48 in (1220 mm) and 60 in (1525 mm), respectively, correspond to the space required for the two common transfer approaches utilized by wheelchair users (see Fig. A6). It is important to keep in mind that the placement of the lavatory on the immediate side of the water closet will preclude the side approach transfer illustrated in Figure A6(b).

To accommodate the side transfer, the space adjacent to the water closet must remain clear of obstruction for 42 in (1065 mm) from the centerline of the toilet (Figure 28) and the lavatory must not be located within this clear space. A turning circle or T-turn, the clear floor space at the lavatory, and maneuvering space at the door must be considered when determining the possible wall locations. A privacy latch or other accessible means of ensuring privacy during use should be provided at the door.

RECOMMENDATIONS:

1. In new construction, accessible single-user restrooms may be desirable in some situations because they can accommodate a wide variety of building users. However, they cannot be used in lieu of making the multi-stall toilet rooms accessible as required.

2. Where strict compliance to the guidelines for accessible toilet facilities is technically infeasible in the alteration of existing facilities, accessible "unisex" toilets are a reasonable alternative.

3. In designing accessible single-user restrooms, the provisions of adequate space to allow a side transfer will provide accommodation to the largest number of wheelchair users.

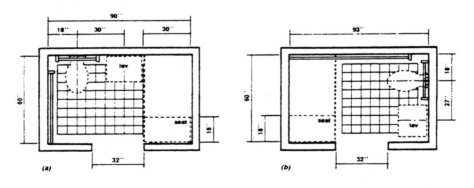

(a)   (b)

Fig. A7

A4.23 Bathrooms, Bathing Facilities, and Shower Rooms

A4.23 Bathrooms, Bathing Facilities, and Shower Rooms.

A4.23.3 Clear Floor Space. *Figure A7 shows two possible configurations of a toilet room with a roll-in shower. The specific shower shown is designed to fit exactly within the dimensions of a standard bathtub. Since the shower does not have a lip, the floor space can be used for required maneuvering space. This would permit a toilet room to be smaller than would be permitted with a bathtub and still provide enough floor space to be considered accessible. This design can provide accessibility in facilities where space is at a premium (i.e., hotels and medical care facilities). The alternate roll-in shower (Fig. 57b) also provides sufficient room for the "T-turn" and does not require plumbing to be on more than one wall.*

A4.23.9 Medicine Cabinets. Other alternatives for storing medical and personal care items are very useful to disabled people. Shelves, drawers, and floor-mounted cabinets can be provided within the reach ranges of disabled people.

A4.26 Handrails, Grab Bars, and Tub and Shower Seats.

A4.26.1 General. Many disabled people rely heavily upon grab bars and handrails to maintain balance and prevent serious falls. Many people brace their forearms between supports and walls to give them more leverage and stability in maintaining balance or for lifting. The grab bar clearance of 1-1/2 in (38 mm) required in this guideline is a safety clearance to prevent injuries resulting from arms slipping through the openings. It also provides adequate gripping room.

A4.26.2 Size and Spacing of Grab Bars and Handrails. This specification allows for alternate shapes of handrails as long as they allow an opposing grip similar to that provided by a circular section of 1-1/4 in to 1-1/2 in (32 mm to 38 mm).

A4.27 Controls and Operating Mechanisms.

A4.27.3 Height. *Fig. A8 further illustrates*

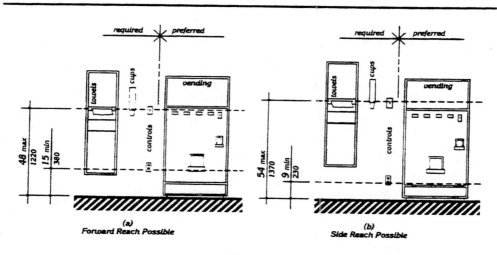

(a)
Forward Reach Possible

(b)
Side Reach Possible

Fig. A8
Control Reach Limitations

mandatory and advisory control mounting height provisions for typical equipment.

Electrical receptacles installed to serve individual appliances and not intended for regular or frequent use by building occupants are not required to be mounted within the specified reach ranges. Examples would be receptacles installed specifically for wall-mounted clocks, refrigerators, and microwave ovens.

A4.28 Alarms.

A4.28.2 Audible Alarms. Audible emergency signals must have an intensity and frequency that can attract the attention of individuals who have partial hearing loss. People over 60 years of age generally have difficulty perceiving frequencies higher than 10,000 Hz. An alarm signal which has a periodic element to its signal, such as single stroke bells (clang-pause-clang-pause), hi-low (up-down-up-down) and fast whoop (on-off-on-off) are best. Avoid continuous or reverberating tones. Select a signal which has a sound characterized by three or four clear tones without a great deal of "noise" in between.

A4.28.3 Visual Alarms. The specifications in this section do not preclude the use of zoned or coded alarm systems.

A4.28.4 Auxiliary Alarms. Locating visual emergency alarms in rooms where persons who are deaf may work or reside alone can ensure that they will always be warned when an emergency alarm is activated. To be effective, such devices must be located and oriented so that they will spread signals and reflections throughout a space or raise the overall light level sharply. However, visual alarms alone are not necessarily the best means to alert sleepers. A study conducted by Underwriters Laboratory (UL) concluded that a flashing light more than seven times brighter was required (110 candela v. 15 candela, at the same distance) to awaken sleepers as was needed to alert awake subjects in a normal daytime illuminated room.

For hotel and other rooms where people are likely to be asleep, a signal-activated vibrator placed between mattress and box spring or under a pillow was found by UL to be much more effective in alerting sleepers. Many readily available devices are sound-activated so that they could respond to an alarm clock, clock

radio, wake-up telephone call or room smoke detector. Activation by a building alarm system can either be accomplished by a separate circuit activating an auditory alarm which would, in turn, trigger the vibrator or by a signal transmitted through the ordinary 110-volt outlet. Transmission of signals through the power line is relatively simple and is the basis of common, inexpensive remote light control systems sold in many department and electronic stores for home use. So-called "wireless" intercoms operate on the same principal.

A4.29 Detectable Warnings.

A4.29.2 Detectable Warnings on Walking Surfaces. The material used to provide contrast should contrast by at least 70%. Contrast in percent is determined by:

$$Contrast = [(B_1 - B_2)/B_1] \times 100$$

where B_1 = light reflectance value (LRV) of the lighter area
and B_2 = light reflectance value (LRV) of the darker area.

Note that in any application both white and black are never absolute; thus, B_1 never equals 100 and B_2 is always greater than 0.

A4.30 Signage.

A4.30.1 General. In building complexes where finding locations independently on a routine basis may be a necessity (for example, college campuses), tactile maps or prerecorded instructions can be very helpful to visually impaired people. Several maps and auditory instructions have been developed and tested for specific applications. The type of map or instructions used must be based on the information to be communicated, which depends highly on the type of buildings or users.

Landmarks that can easily be distinguished by visually impaired individuals are useful as orientation cues. Such cues include changes in illumination level, bright colors, unique patterns, wall murals, location of special equipment or other architectural features.

Many people with disabilities have limitations in movement of their heads and reduced peripheral vision. Thus, signage positioned

A4.30 Signage

perpendicular to the path of travel is easiest for them to notice. People can generally distinguish signage within an angle of 30 degrees to either side of the centerlines of their faces without moving their heads.

A4.30.2 Character Proportion. The legibility of printed characters is a function of the viewing distance, character height, the ratio of the stroke width to the height of the character, the contrast of color between character and background, and print font. The size of characters must be based upon the intended viewing distance. A severely nearsighted person may have to be much closer to recognize a character of a given size than a person with normal visual acuity.

A4.30.4 Raised and Brailled Characters and Pictorial Symbol Signs (Pictograms). *The standard dimensions for literary Braille are as follows:*

Dot diameter	.059 in.
Inter-dot spacing	.090 in.
Horizontal separation between cells	.241 in.
Vertical separation between cells	.395 in.

Raised borders around signs containing raised characters may make them confusing to read unless the border is set far away from the characters. *Accessible signage with descriptive materials about public buildings, monuments, and objects of cultural interest may not provide sufficiently detailed and meaningful information. Interpretive guides, audio tape devices, or other methods may be more effective in presenting such information.*

A4.30.5 Finish and Contrast. *An eggshell finish (11 to 19 degree gloss on 60 degree glossmeter) is recommended. Research indicates that signs are more legible for persons with low vision when characters contrast with their background by at least 70 percent. Contrast in percent shall be determined by:*

$$Contrast = [(B_1 - B_2)/B_1] \times 100$$

where B_1 = light reflectance value (LRV) of the lighter area
and B_2 = light reflectance value (LRV) of the darker area.

Note that in any application both white and black are never absolute; thus, B_1 never equals 100 and B_2 is always greater than 0.

The greatest readability is usually achieved through the use of light-colored characters or symbols on a dark background.

A4.30.7 Symbols of Accessibility for Different Types of Listening Systems. *Paragraph 4 of this section requires signage indicating the availability of an assistive listening system. An appropriate message should be displayed with the international symbol of access for hearing loss since this symbol conveys general accessibility for people with hearing loss. Some suggestions are:*

INFRARED
ASSISTIVE LISTENING SYSTEM
AVAILABLE
——PLEASE ASK——

AUDIO LOOP IN USE
TURN T-SWITCH FOR
BETTER HEARING
——OR ASK FOR HELP——

FM
ASSISTIVE LISTENING
SYSTEM AVAILABLE
——PLEASE ASK——

The symbol may be used to notify persons of the availability of other auxiliary aids and services such as: real time captioning, captioned note taking, sign language interpreters, and oral interpreters.

A4.30.8 Illumination Levels. *Illumination levels on the sign surface shall be in the 100 to 300 lux range (10 to 30 footcandles) and shall be uniform over the sign surface. Signs shall be located such that the illumination level on the surface of the sign is not significantly exceeded by the ambient light or visible bright lighting source behind or in front of the sign.*

A4.31 Telephones.

A4.31.3 Mounting Height. In localities where the dial-tone first system is in operation, calls can be placed at a coin telephone through the operator without inserting coins. The operator button is located at a height of 46 in (1170 mm) if the coin slot of the telephone is at 54 in (1370 mm). A generally available public telephone with a coin slot mounted lower on the equipment would allow universal installation of telephones at a height of 48 in (1220 mm) or less to all operable parts.

A4.31.9 Text Telephones. *A public text telephone may be an integrated text telephone pay phone unit or a conventional portable text telephone that is permanently affixed within, or adjacent to, the telephone enclosure. In order to be usable with a pay phone, a text telephone which is not a single integrated text telephone pay phone unit will require a shelf large enough (10 in (255mm) wide by 10 in (255 mm) deep with a 6 in (150 mm) vertical clearance minimum) to accommodate the device, an electrical outlet, and a power cord. Movable or portable text telephones may be used to provide equivalent facilitation. A text telephone should be readily available so that a person using it may access the text telephone easily and conveniently. As currently designed pocket-type text telephones for personal use do not accommodate a wide range of users. Such devices would not be considered substantially equivalent to conventional text telephones. However, in the future as technology develops this could change.*

A4.32 Fixed or Built-in Seating and Tables.

A4.32.4 Height of Tables or Counters. Different types of work require different *table or counter* heights for comfort and optimal performance. Light detailed work such as writing requires a *table or counter* close to elbow height for a standing person. Heavy manual work such as rolling dough requires *a counter or table* height about 10 in (255 mm) below elbow height for a standing person. This principle of *high/low table or counter heights* also applies for seated persons; however, the limiting condition for seated manual work is clearance under the *table or counter.*

Table A1 shows convenient *counter heights* for seated persons. The great variety of heights for comfort and optimal performance indicates a need for alternatives or a compromise in height if people who stand and people who sit will be using the same counter area.

Table A1
Convenient Heights of Tables and Counters for Seated People[1]

Conditions of Use	Short Women in	mm	Tall Men in	mm
Seated in a wheelchair:				
Manual work–				
Desk or removeable armrests	26	660	30	760
Fixed, full-size armrests[2]	32[3]	815	32[3]	815
Light detailed work:				
Desk or removable armrests	29	735	34	865
Fixed, full-size armrests[2]	32[3]	815	34	865
Seated in a 16-in. (405-mm)				
High chair:				
Manual work	26	660	27	685
Light detailed work	28	710	31	785

[1] All dimensions are based on a work-surface thickness of 1 1/2 in (38 mm) and a clearance of 1 1/2 in (38 mm) between legs and the underside of a work surface.

[2] This type of wheelchair arm does not interfere with the positioning of a wheelchair under a work surface.

[3] This dimension is limited by the height of the armrests: a lower height would be preferable. Some people in this group prefer lower work surfaces, which require positioning the wheelchair back from the edge of the counter.

A4.33 Assembly Areas.

A4.33.2 Size of Wheelchair Locations. Spaces large enough for two wheelchairs allow people who are coming to a performance together to sit together.

A4.33.3 Placement of Wheelchair Locations. The location of wheelchair areas can be planned so that a variety of positions

Table A2. Summary of Assistive Listening Devices

within the seating area are provided. This will allow choice in viewing and price categories.

Building/life safety codes set minimum distances between rows of fixed seats with consideration of the number of seats in a row, the exit aisle width and arrangement, and the location of exit doors. "Continental" seating, with a greater number of seats per row and a

commensurate increase in row spacing and exit doors, facilitates emergency egress for all people and increases ease of access to mid-row seats especially for people who walk with difficulty. Consideration of this positive attribute of "continental" seating should be included along with all other factors in the design of fixed seating areas.

Table A2. Summary of Assistive Listening Devices

System	Advantages	Disadvantages	Typical Applications
Induction Loop Transmitter: Transducer wired to induction loop around listening area. Receiver: Self-contained induction receiver or personal hearing aid with telecoil.	Cost-Effective Low Maintenance Easy to use Unobtrusive May be possible to integrate into existing public address system. Some hearing aids can function as receivers.	Signal spills over to adjacent rooms. Susceptible to electrical interference. Limited portability Inconsistent signal strength. Head position affects signal strength. Lack of standards for induction coil performance.	Meeting areas Theaters Churches and Temples Conference rooms Classrooms TV viewing
FM Transmitter: Flashlight-sized worn by speaker. Receiver: With personal hearing aid via DAI or induction neck-loop and telecoil; or self-contained with earphone(s).	Highly portable Different channels allow use by different groups within the same room. High user mobility Variable for large range of hearing losses.	High cost of receivers Equipment fragile Equipment obtrusive High maintenance Expensive to maintain Custom fitting to individual user may be required.	Classrooms Tour groups Meeting areas Outdoor events One-on-one
Infrared Transmitter: Emitter in line-of-sight with receiver. Receiver: Self-contained. Or with personal hearing aid via DAI or induction neckloop and telecoil.	Easy to use Insures privacy or confidentiality Moderate cost Can often be integrated into existing public address system.	Line-of-sight required between emitter and receiver. Ineffective outdoors Limited portability Requires installation	Theaters Churches and Temples Auditoriums Meetings requiring confidentiality TV viewing

Source: Rehab Brief, National Institute on Disability and Rehabilitation Research, Washington, DC, Vol. XII, No. 10, (1990).

A4.33.6 Placement of Listening Systems.
A distance of 50 ft (15 m) allows a person to distinguish performers' facial expressions.

A4.33.7 Types of Listening Systems.
An assistive listening system appropriate for an assembly area for a group of persons or where the specific individuals are not known in advance, such as a playhouse, lecture hall or movie theater, may be different from the system appropriate for a particular individual provided as an auxiliary aid or as part of a reasonable accommodation. The appropriate device for an individual is the type that individual can use, whereas the appropriate system for an assembly area will necessarily be geared toward the "average" or aggregate needs of various individuals. A listening system that can be used from any seat in a seating area is the most flexible way to meet this specification. Earphone jacks with variable volume controls can benefit only people who have slight hearing loss and do not help people who use hearing aids. At the present time, magnetic induction loops are the most feasible type of listening system for people who use hearing aids equipped with "T-coils," but people without hearing aids or those with hearing aids not equipped with inductive pick-ups cannot use them without special receivers. Radio frequency systems can be extremely effective and inexpensive. People without hearing aids can use them, but people with hearing aids need a special receiver to use them as they are presently designed. If hearing aids had a jack to allow a by-pass of microphones, then radio frequency systems would be suitable for people with and without hearing aids. Some listening systems may be subject to interference from other equipment and feedback from hearing aids of people who are using the systems. Such interference can be controlled by careful engineering design that anticipates feedback sources in the surrounding area.

Table A2, reprinted from a National Institute of Disability and Rehabilitation Research "Rehab Brief," shows some of the advantages and disadvantages of different types of assistive listening systems. In addition, the Architectural and Transportation Barriers Compliance Board (Access Board) has published a pamphlet on Assistive Listening Systems which lists demonstration centers across the country where technical assistance can be obtained in selecting and installing appropriate systems. The state of New York has also adopted a detailed technical specification which may be useful.

A5.0 Restaurants and Cafeterias.

A5.1 General. *Dining counters (where there is no service) are typically found in small carry-out restaurants, bakeries, or coffee shops and may only be a narrow eating surface attached to a wall. This section requires that where such a dining counter is provided, a portion of the counter shall be at the required accessible height.*

A7.0 Business and Mercantile.

A7.2(3) Assistive Listening Devices. *At all sales and service counters, teller windows, box offices, and information kiosks where a physical barrier separates service personnel and customers, it is recommended that at least one permanently installed assistive listening device complying with 4.33 be provided at each location or series. Where assistive listening devices are installed, signage should be provided identifying those stations which are so equipped.*

A7.3 Check-out Aisles. *Section 7.2 refers to counters without aisles; section 7.3 concerns check-out aisles. A counter without an aisle (7.2) can be approached from more than one direction such as in a convenience store. In order to use a check-out aisle (7.3), customers must enter a defined area (an aisle) at a particular point, pay for goods, and exit at a particular point.*

A10.3 Fixed Facilities and Stations.

A10.3.1(7) Route Signs. *One means of making control buttons on fare vending machines usable by persons with vision impairments is to raise them above the surrounding surface. Those activated by a mechanical motion are likely to be more detectable. If farecard vending, collection, and adjustment devices are designed to accommodate farecards having one tactually distinctive corner, then a person who has a vision impairment will insert the card with greater ease. Token collection devices that are designed to accommodate tokens which are perforated can allow a person to distinguish more readily between tokens and common coins. Thoughtful placement of accessible gates and fare vending machines in relation to inaccessible devices will make their use and detection easier for all persons with disabilities.*

Department of Justice
28 CFR Part 35
Nondiscrimination on the Basis of Disability in State and Local Government Services

DEPARTMENT OF JUSTICE

28 CFR Part 35

(Order No. 1512-91)

Nondiscrimination on the Basis of Disability in State and Local Government Services

AGENCY: Department of Justice.

ACTION: Final rule.

SUMMARY: This rule implements subtitle A of title II of the Americans with Disabilities Act, Public Law 101-336, which prohibits discrimination on the basis of disability by public entities. Subtitle A protects qualified individuals with disabilities from discrimination on the basis of disability in the services, programs, or activities of all State and local governments. It extends the prohibition of discrimination in federally assisted programs established by section 504 of the Rehabilitation Act of 1973 to all activities of State and local governments, including those that do not receive Federal financial assistance, and incorporates specific prohibitions of discrimination on the basis of disability from titles I, III, and V of the Americans with Disabilities Act. This rule, therefore, adopts the general prohibitions of discrimination

established under section 504, as well as the requirements for making programs accessible to individuals with disabilities and for providing equally effective communications. It also sets forth standards for what constitutes discrimination on the basis of mental or physical disability, provides a definition of disability and qualified individual with a disability, and establishes a complaint mechanism for resolving allegations of discrimination.

EFFECIVE DATE: January 26, 1992.

FOR FURTHER INFORMATION CONTACT: Barbara S. Drake, Deputy Assistant Attorney General, Civil Rights Division; Stewart B. Oneglia, Chief, Coordination and Review Section, Civil Rights Division; John L. Wodatch, Director, Office on the Americans with Disabilities Act, Civil Rights Division; all of the U.S. Department of Justice, Washington, DC 20530. These individuals may be contacted through the Division's ADA Information Line at (202) 514-0301 (Voice), (202) 514-0381 (TDD), or (202) 514-0383 (TDD). These telephone numbers are not toll-free numbers.

SUPPLEMENTARY INFORMATION:

Background

The landmark Americans with Disabilities Act ("ADA" or "the Act"), enacted on July 26, 1990, provides comprehensive civil rights protections to individuals with disabilities in the areas of employment, public accommodations, State and local government services, and telecommunications.

This regulation implements subtitle A of title II of the ADA, which applies to State and local governments. Most programs and activities of State and local governments are recipients of Federal financial assistance from one or more Federal funding agencies and, therefore, are already covered by section 504 of the Rehabilitation Act of 1973, as amended (29 U.S.C. 794) ("section 504"), which prohibits discrimination on the basis of handicap in federally assisted programs and activities. Because title II of the ADA essentially extends the nondiscrimination mandate of section 504 to those State and local governments that do not receive Federal financial assistance, this rule hews closely to the provisions of existing section 504 regulations. This approach is also based on section 204 of the ADA, which provides that the regulations issued by the Attorney General to implement title II shall be consistent with the ADA and with the Department of Health, Education, and Welfare's coordination regulation, now codified at 28 CFR part 41, and, with respect to "program accessibility, existing facilities," and "communications," with the Department of Justice's regulation for its federally conducted programs and activities, codified at 28 CFR part 39.

The first regulation implementing section 504 was issued in 1977 by the Department of Health, Education, and Welfare (HEW) for the programs and activities to which it provided Federal financial assistance. The following year, pursuant to Executive Order 11914, HEW issued its coordination regulation for federally assisted programs, which served as the model for regulations issued by the other Federal agencies that administer grant programs. HEW's coordination authority, and the coordination regulation issued under that authority, were transferred to the Department of Justice by Executive Order 12250 in 1980.

In 1978, Congress extended application of section 504 to programs and activities conducted by Federal Executive agencies and the United States Postal Service. Pursuant to Executive Order 12250, the Department of Justice developed a prototype regulation to implement the 1978 amendment for federally conducted programs and activities. More than 80 Federal agencies have now issued final regulations based on that prototype, prohibiting discrimination based on handicap in the programs and activities they conduct. Despite the large number of regulations implementing section 504 for federally assisted and federally conducted programs and activities, there is very little variation in their substantive requirements, or even in their language. Major portions of this regulation, therefore, are taken directly from the existing regulations.

In addition, section 204(b) of the ADA requires that the Department's regulation implementing subtitle A of title II be consistent with the ADA. Thus, the Department's final regulation includes provisions and concepts from titles I and III of the ADA.

Rulemaking History

On February 22, 1991, the Department of Justice published a notice of proposed rulemaking (NPRM) implementing title III of the ADA in the **Federal Register**. 56 FR 7452. On February 28, 1991, the Department published a notice of proposed rulemaking implementing subtitle A of title II of the ADA in the **Federal Register**. 56 FR 8538. Each NPRM solicited comments on the definitions, standards, and procedures of the proposed rules. By the April 29, 1991, close of the comment period of the NPRM for title II, the Department had received 2,718 comments. Following the close of the comment period, the Department received an additional 222 comments.

In order to encourage public participation in the development of the Department's rules under the ADA, the Department held four public hearings. Hearings were held in Dallas, Texas on March 4-5, 1991, in Washington, DC on March 13-15, 1991, in San Francisco, California on March 18-19, 1991, and in Chicago, Illinois on March 27-28, 1991. At these hearings, 329 persons testified and 1,567 pages of testimony were compiled. Transcripts of the hearings were included in the Department's rulemaking docket.

The comments that the Department received occupy almost six feet of shelf space and contain over 10,000 pages. The Department received comments from individuals from all fifty States and the District of Columbia. Nearly 75% of the comments that the Department received came from individuals and from organizations representing the interests of persons with disabilities. The Department received 292 comments from entities covered by the ADA and trade associations representing businesses in the private sector, and 67 from government units, such as mayors' offices, public school districts, and various State agencies working with individuals with disabilities.

The Department received one comment from a consortium of 540 organizations representing a broad spectrum of persons with disabilities. In addition, at least another 25 commenters endorsed the position expressed by this consortium, or submitted identical comments on one or both proposed regulations.

An organization representing persons with hearing impairments submitted a large number of comments. This organization presented the Department with 479 individual comments, each providing in chart form a detailed representation of what type of auxiliary aid or service would be useful in the various categories of places of public accommodation.

The Department received a number of comments based on almost ten different form letters. For example, individuals who have a heightened sensitivity to a variety of chemical substances submitted 266 post cards detailing how exposure to various environmental conditions restricts their access to public and commercial buildings. Another large group of form letters came from groups affiliated with independent living centers.

The vast majority of the comments addressed the Department's proposal implementing title III. Slightly more than 100 comments addressed only issues presented in the proposed title II regulation.

The Department read and analyzed each comment that was submitted in a timely fashion. Transcripts of the four hearings were analyzed along with the written comments. The decisions that the Department has made in response to these comments, however, were not made on the basis of the number of commenters addressing any one point but on a thorough consideration of the merits of the points of view expressed in the comments.

Copies of the written comments, including transcripts of the four hearings, will remain available for public inspection in room 854 of the HOLC Building, 320 First Street, NW., Washington, DC from 10 a.m. to 5 p.m., Monday through Friday, except for legal holidays, until August 30, 1991.

Overview of the Rule

The rule is organized into seven subparts. Subpart A, "General," includes the purpose and application sections, describes the relationship of the Act to other laws, and defines key terms used in the regulation. It also includes administrative requirements adapted from section 504 regulations for self-evaluations, notices, designation of responsible employees, and adoption of grievance procedures by public entities.

Subpart B, "General Requirements," contains the general prohibitions of discrimination based on the Act and the section 504 regulations. It also contains certain "miscellaneous" provisions derived from title V of the Act that involve issues such as retaliation and coercion against those asserting ADA rights, illegal use of drugs, and restrictions on smoking. These provisions are also included in the Department's proposed title III regulation, as is the general provision on maintenance of accessible features.

Subpart C addresses employment by public entities, which is also covered by title I of the Act. Subpart D, which is also based on the section 504 regulations, sets out the requirements for program accessibility in existing facilities and for new construction and alterations. Subpart E contains specific requirements relating to communications. Subpart F establishes administrative procedures for enforcement of title II. As provided by section 203 of the Act, these are based on the procedures for enforcement of section 504, which, in turn, are based on the enforcement procedures for title VI of the Civil Rights Act of 1964 (42 U.S.C. 2000d to 2000d-4a). Subpart F also restates the

provisions of title V of the ADA on attorneys fees, alternative means of dispute resolution, the effect of unavailability of technical assistance, and State immunity.

Subpart G designates the Federal agencies responsible for investigation of complaints under this part. It assigns enforcement responsibility for particular public entities, on the basis of their major functions, to eight Federal agencies that currently have substantial responsibilities for enforcing section 504. It provides that the Department of Justice would have enforcement responsibility for all State and local government entities not specifically assigned to other designated agencies, but that the Department may further assign specific functions to other agencies. The part would not, however, displace the existing enforcement authorities of the Federal funding agencies under section 504.

Regulatory Process Matters

This final rule has been reviewed by the Office of Management and Budget under Executive Order 12291. The Department is preparing a final regulatory impact analysis (RIA) of this rule and the Architectural and Transportation Barriers Compliance Board is preparing an RIA for its Americans with Disabilities Act Accessibility Guidelines for Buildings and Facilities (ADAAG) that are incorporated in appendix A of the Department's final rule implementing title III of the ADA. Draft copies of both preliminary RIAs are available for comment; the Department will provide copies of these documents to the public upon request. Commenters are urged to provide additional information as to the costs and benefits associated with this rule. This will facilitate the development of a final RIA by January 1, 1992.

The Department's RIA will evaluate the economic impact of the final rule. Included among those title II provisions that are likely to result in significant economic impact are the

requirements for auxiliary aids, barrier removal in existing facilities, and readily accessible new construction and alterations. An analysis of these costs will be included in the RIA.

The Preliminary RIA prepared for the notice of proposed rulemaking contained all of the available information that would have been included in a preliminary regulatory flexibility analysis, had one been prepared under the Regulatory Flexibility Act, concerning the rule's impact on small entities. The final RIA will contain all of the information that is required in a final regulatory flexibility analysis and will serve as such an analysis. Moreover, the extensive notice and comment procedure followed by the Department in the promulgation of this rule, which included public hearings, dissemination of materials, and provision of speakers to affected groups, clearly provided any interested small entities with the notice and opportunity for comment provided for under the Regulatory Flexibility Act procedures.

The Department is preparing a statement of the federalism impact of the rule under Executive Order 12612 and will provide copies of this statement on request.

The reporting and recordkeeping requirements described in the rule are considered to be information collection requirements as that term is defined by the Office of Management and Budget in 5 CFR part 1320. Accordingly, those information collection requirements have been submitted to OMB for review pursuant to the Paperwork Reduction Act.

Section-by-Section Analysis

Subpart A--General

Section 35.101 Purpose

Section 35.101 states the purpose of the rule, which is to effectuate subtitle A of title II of the Americans with Disabilities Act of 1990 (the Act), which prohibits discrimination on the basis of disability by public entities. This part does not, however, apply to matters within the scope of the authority of the Secretary of Transportation under subtitle B of title II of the Act.

Section 35.102 Application

This provision specifies that, except as provided in paragraph (b), the regulation applies to all services, programs, and activities provided or made available by public entities, as that term is defined in § 35.104. Section 504 of the Rehabilitation Act of 1973 (29 U.S.C. 794), which prohibits discrimination on the basis of handicap in federally assisted programs and activities, already covers those programs and activities of public entities that receive Federal financial assistance. Title II of the ADA extends this prohibition of discrimination to include all services, programs, and activities provided or made available by State and local governments or any of their instrumentalities or agencies, regardless of the receipt of Federal financial assistance. Except as provided in § 35.134, this part does not apply to private entities.

The scope of title II's coverage of public entities is comparable to the coverage of Federal Executive agencies under the 1978 amendment to section 504, which extended section 504's application to all programs and activities "conducted by" Federal Executive agencies, in that title II applies to anything a public entity does. Title II coverage, however, is not limited to "Executive" agencies, but includes activities of the legislative and judicial branches of State and local governments. All governmental activities of public entities are covered, even if they are carried out by contractors. For example, a State is obligated by title II to ensure that the services, programs, and activities of a State park inn operated under contract by a private entity are in compliance with title II's requirements. The private entity operating the inn would also be subject to the obligations of public accommodations under title III of the Act and the Department's title III regulations at 28 CFR part 36.

Aside from employment, which is also covered by title I of the Act, there are two major categories of programs or activities covered by this regulation: those involving general public contact as part of ongoing operations of the entity and those directly administered by the entities for program beneficiaries and participants. Activities in the first category include communication with the public (telephone contacts, office walk-ins, or interviews) and the public's use of the entity's facilities. Activities in the second category include programs that provide State or local government services or benefits.

Paragraph (b) of § 35.102 explains that to the extent that the public transportation services, programs, and activities of public entities are covered by subtitle B of title II of the Act, they are subject to the regulation of the Department of Transportation (DOT) at 49 CFR part 37, and are not covered by this part. The Department of Transportation's ADA regulation establishes specific requirements for construction of transportation facilities and acquisition of vehicles. Matters not covered by subtitle B, such as the provision of auxiliary aids, are covered by this rule. For example, activities that are covered by the Department of Transportation's regulation implementing subtitle B are not required to be included in the self-evaluation required by § 35.105. In addition, activities not specifically addressed by DOT's ADA regulation may be covered by DOT's regulation implementing section 504 for its federally assisted programs and activities at 49 CFR part 27. Like other programs of public entities that are also recipients of Federal financial assistance, those programs would be covered by both the section 504 regulation and this part. Although airports operated by public entities are not subject to DOT's ADA regulation, they are subject to subpart A of title II and to this rule.

Some commenters asked for clarification about the responsibilities of public school systems under section 504 and the ADA with respect to programs, services, and activities that are not covered by the Individuals with Disabilities Education Act (IDEA), including, for example, programs open to parents or to the public, graduation ceremonies, parent-teacher organization meetings, plays and other events open to the public, and adult education classes. Public school systems must comply with the ADA in all of their services, programs, or activities, including those that are open to parents or to the public. For instance, public school systems must provide program accessibility to parents and guardians with disabilities to these programs, activities, or services, and appropriate auxiliary aids and services whenever necessary to ensure effective communication, as long as the provision of the auxiliary aids results neither in an undue burden or in a fundamental alteration of the program.

Section 35.103 Relationship to Other Laws

Section 35.103 is derived from sections 501 (a) and (b) of the ADA. Paragraph (a) of this section provides that, except as otherwise specifically provided by this part, title II of the ADA is not intended to apply lesser standards than are required under title V of the Rehabilitation Act of 1973, as amended (29 U.S.C. 790-94), or the regulations implementing that title. The standards of title V of the Rehabilitation Act apply for purposes of the ADA to the extent that the ADA has not explicitly adopted a different standard than title V. Because title II of the ADA essentially extends the antidiscrimination prohibition embodied in section 504 to all actions of State and local governments, the standards adopted in this part are generally the same as those required under section 504 for federally assisted programs. Title II, however, also incorporates those provisions of titles I and III of the ADA that are not inconsistent with the regulations implementing section 504. Judiciary Committee report, H.R. Rep. No. 485, 101st Cong., 2d Sess., pt. 3, at 51 (1990) (hereinafter "Judiciary report"); Education and Labor Committee report, H.R. Rep. No. 485, 101st Cong., 2d Sess., pt. 2, at 84 (1990) (hereinafter "Education and Labor report"). Therefore, this part also includes appropriate provisions derived from the regulations implementing those titles. The inclusion of specific language in this part, however, should not be interpreted as an indication that a requirement is not included under a regulation implementing section 504.

Paragraph (b) makes clear that Congress did not intend to displace any of the rights or remedies provided by other Federal laws (including section 504) or other State laws (including State common law) that provide greater or equal protection to individuals with disabilities. As discussed above, the standards adopted by title II of the ADA for State and local government services are generally the same as those required under section 504 for federally assisted programs and activities. Subpart F of the regulation establishes compliance procedures for processing complaints covered by both this part and section 504.

With respect to State law, a plaintiff may choose to pursue claims under a State law that does not confer greater substantive rights, or even confers fewer substantive rights, if the alleged violation is protected under the alternative law and the remedies are greater. For example, a person with a physical disability could seek damages under a State law that allows compensatory and punitive damages for discrimination on the basis of physical disability, but not on the basis of mental disability. In that situation, the State law would provide narrower coverage, by excluding mental disabilities, but broader remedies, and an individual covered by both laws could choose to bring an action under both laws. Moreover, State tort claims confer greater

remedies and are not pre-empted by the ADA. A plaintiff may join a State tort claim to a case brought under the ADA. In such a case, the plaintiff must, of course, prove all the elements of the State tort claim in order to prevail under that cause of action.

Section 35.104 Definitions

"Act." The word "Act" is used in this part to refer to the Americans with Disabilities Act of 1990, Public Law 101-336, which is also referred to as the "ADA."

"Assistant Attorney General." The term "Assistant Attorney General" refers to the Assistant Attorney General of the Civil Rights Division of the Department of Justice.

"Auxiliary aids and services." Auxiliary aids and services include a wide range of services and devices for ensuring effective communication. The proposed definition in § 35.104 provided a list of examples of auxiliary aids and services that were taken from the definition of auxiliary aids and services in section 3(1) of the ADA and were supplemented by examples from regulations implementing section 504 in federally conducted programs (see 28 CFR 39.103).

A substantial number of commenters suggested that additional examples be added to this list. The Department has added several items to this list but wishes to clarify that the list is not an all-inclusive or exhaustive catalogue of possible or available auxiliary aids or services. It is not possible to provide an exhaustive list, and an attempt to do so would omit the new devices that will become available with emerging technology.

Subparagraph (1) lists several examples, which would be considered auxiliary aids and services to make aurally delivered materials available to individuals with hearing impairments. The Department has changed the phrase used in the proposed rules, "orally delivered materials," to the statutory phrase, "aurally delivered materials," to track

section 3 of the ADA and to include non-verbal sounds and alarms, and computer generated speech.

The Department has added videotext displays, transcription services, and closed and open captioning to the list of examples. Videotext displays have become an important means of accessing auditory communications through a public address system. Transcription services are used to relay aurally delivered material almost simultaneously in written form to persons who are deaf or hearing-impaired. This technology is often used at conferences, conventions, and hearings. While the proposed rule expressly included television decoder equipment as an auxiliary aid or service, it did not mention captioning itself. The final rule rectifies this omission by mentioning both closed and open captioning.

Several persons and organizations requested that the Department replace the term "telecommunications devices for deaf persons" or "TDD's" with the term "text telephone." The Department has declined to do so. The Department is aware that the Architectural and Transportation Barriers Compliance Board (ATBCB) has used the phrase "text telephone" in lieu of the statutory term "TDD" in its final accessibility guidelines. Title IV of the ADA, however, uses the term "Telecommunications Device for the Deaf" and the Department believes it would be inappropriate to abandon this statutory term at this time.

Several commenters urged the Department to include in the definition of "auxiliary aids and services" devices that are now available or that may become available with emerging technology. The Department declines to do so in the rule. The Department, however, emphasizes that, although the definition would include "state of the art" devices, public entities are not required to use the newest or most advanced technologies as long as the auxiliary aid or service that is selected affords effective communication.

Subparagraph (2) lists examples of aids and services for making visually delivered materials accessible to persons with visual impairments. Many commenters proposed additional examples, such as signage or mapping, audio description services, secondary auditory programs, telebraillers, and reading machines. While the Department declines to add these items to the list, they are auxiliary aids and services and may be appropriate depending on the circumstances.

Subparagraph (3) refers to acquisition or modification of equipment or devices. Several commenters suggested the addition of current technological innovations in microelectronics and computerized control systems (e.g., voice recognition systems, automatic dialing telephones, and infrared elevator and light control systems) to the list of auxiliary aids. The Department interprets auxiliary aids and services as those aids and services designed to provide effective communications, i.e., making aurally and visually delivered information available to persons with hearing, speech, and vision impairments. Methods of making services, programs, or activities accessible to, or usable by, individuals with mobility or manual dexterity impairments are addressed by other sections of this part, including the provision for modifications in policies, practices, or procedures (§ 35.130 (b)(7)).

Paragraph (b)(4) deals with other similar services and actions. Several commenters asked for clarification that "similar services and actions" include retrieving items from shelves, assistance in reaching a marginally accessible seat, pushing a barrier aside in order to provide an accessible route, or assistance in removing a sweater or coat. While retrieving an item from a shelf might be an "auxiliary aid or service" for a blind person who could not locate the item without assistance, it might be a method of providing program access for a person using a wheelchair who could not reach the shelf, or a reasonable modification to a self-service policy for an individual who lacked the ability to grasp the item. As explained above, auxiliary aids and services are those aids and services required to provide effective communications. Other forms of assistance are more appropriately addressed by other provisions of the final rule.

"Complete complaint." "Complete complaint" is defined to include all the information necessary to enable the Federal agency designated under subpart G as responsible for investigation of a complaint to initiate its investigation.

"Current illegal use of drugs." The phrase "current illegal use of drugs" is used in § 35.131. Its meaning is discussed in the preamble for that section.

"Designated agency." The term "designated agency" is used to refer to the Federal agency designated under subpart G of this rule as responsible for carrying out the administrative enforcement responsibilities established by subpart F of the rule.

"Disability." The definition of the term "disability" is the same as the definition in the title III regulation codified at 28 CFR part 36. It is comparable to the definition of the term "individual with handicaps" in section 7(8) of the Rehabilitation Act and section 802(h) of the Fair Housing Act. The Education and Labor Committee report makes clear that the analysis of the term "individual with handicaps" by the Department of Health, Education, and Welfare (HEW) in its regulations implementing section 504 (42 FR 22685 (May 4, 1977)) and the analysis by the Department of Housing and Urban Development in its regulation implementing the Fair Housing Amendments Act of 1988 (54 FR 3232 (Jan. 23, 1989)) should also apply fully to the term "disability" (Education and Labor report at 50).

The use of the term "disability" instead of "handicap" and the term "individual with a disability" instead of "individual with handicaps" represents an effort by Congress to make use of up-to-date, currently accepted terminology. As with racial and ethnic epithets, the choice of terms to apply to a person with a disability is overlaid with stereotypes, patronizing attitudes, and other emotional connotations. Many individuals with disabilities, and organizations representing such individuals, object to the use of such terms as "handicapped person" or "the handicapped." In other recent legislation, Congress also recognized this shift in terminology, e.g., by changing the name of the National Council on the Handicapped to the National Council on Disability (Pub. L. 100-630).

In enacting the Americans with Disabilities Act, Congress concluded that it was important for the current legislation to use terminology most in line with the sensibilities of most Americans with disabilities. No change in definition or substance is intended nor should one be attributed to this change in phraseology.

The term "disability" means, with respect to an individual—

(A) A physical or mental impairment that substantially limits one or more of the major life activities of such individual;

(B) A record of such an impairment; or

(C) Being regarded as having such an impairment. If an individual meets any one of these three tests, he or she is considered to be an individual with a disability for purposes of coverage under the Americans with Disabilities Act.

Congress adopted this same basic definition of "disability," first used in the Rehabilitation Act of 1973 and in the Fair Housing Amendments Act of 1988, for a number of reasons. First, it has worked well since it was adopted in 1974. Second, it would not be possible to guarantee comprehensiveness by providing a list of specific disabilities, especially because new disorders may be recognized in the future, as they have since the definition was first established in 1974.

Test A—A physical or mental impairment that substantially limits one or more of the major life activities of such individual

Physical or mental impairment. Under the first test, an individual must have a physical or mental impairment. As explained in paragraph (1)(i) of the definition, "impairment" means any physiological disorder or condition, cosmetic disfigurement, or anatomical loss affecting one or more of the following body systems: neurological; musculoskeletal; special sense organs (which would include speech organs that are not respiratory such as vocal cords, soft palate, tongue, etc.); respiratory, including speech organs; cardiovascular; reproductive; digestive; genitourinary; hemic and lymphatic; skin; and endocrine. It also means any mental or psychological disorder, such as mental retardation, organic brain syndrome, emotional or mental illness, and specific learning disabilities. This list closely tracks the one used in the regulations for section 504 of the Rehabilitation Act of 1973 (see, e.g., 45 CFR 84.3(j)(2)(i)).

Many commenters asked that "traumatic brain injury" be added to the list in paragraph (1)(i). Traumatic brain injury is already included because it is a physiological condition affecting one of the listed body systems, i.e., "neurological." Therefore, it was unnecessary to add the term to the regulation, which only provides representative examples of physiological disorders.

It is not possible to include a list of all the specific conditions, contagious and noncontagious diseases, or infections that would constitute physical or mental impairments because of the difficulty of ensuring the comprehensiveness of such a list, particularly in light of the fact that other conditions or disorders may be identified in the future. However, the list of examples in paragraph (1)(ii) of the definition includes: orthopedic, visual, speech and hearing impairments, cerebral palsy, epilepsy, muscular dystrophy, multiple sclerosis, cancer, heart disease, diabetes,

mental retardation, emotional illness, specific learning disabilities, HIV disease (symptomatic or asymptomatic), tuberculosis, drug addiction, and alcoholism. The phrase "symptomatic or asymptomatic" was inserted in the final rule after "HIV disease" in response to commenters who suggested the clarification was necessary.

The examples of "physical or mental impairments" in paragraph (1)(ii) are the same as those contained in many section 504 regulations, except for the addition of the phrase "contagious and noncontagious" to describe the types of diseases and conditions included, and the addition of "HIV disease (symptomatic or asymptomatic)" and "tuberculosis" to the list of examples. These additions are based on the committee reports, caselaw, and official legal opinions interpreting section 504. In *School Board of Nassau County v. Arline*, 480 U.S. 273 (1987), a case involving an individual with tuberculosis, the Supreme Court held that people with contagious diseases are entitled to the protections afforded by section 504. Following the *Arline* decision, this Department's Office of Legal Counsel issued a legal opinion that concluded that symptomatic HIV disease is an impairment that substantially limits a major life activity; therefore it has been included in the definition of disability under this part. The opinion also concluded that asymptomatic HIV disease is an impairment that substantially limits a major life activity, either because of its actual effect on the individual with HIV disease or because the reactions of other people to individuals with HIV disease cause such individuals to be treated as though they are disabled. See Memorandum from Douglas W. Kmiec, Acting Assistant Attorney General, Office of Legal Counsel, Department of Justice, to Arthur B. Culvahouse, Jr., Counsel to the President (Sept. 27, 1988), reprinted in Hearings on S. 933, the Americans with Disabilities Act, Before the Subcomm. on the Handicapped of the Senate

Comm. on Labor and Human Resources, 101st. Cong., 1st Sess. 346 (1989).

Paragraph (1)(iii) states that the phrase "physical or mental impairment" does not include homosexuality or bisexuality. These conditions were never considered impairments under other Federal disability laws. Section 511(a) of the statute makes clear that they are likewise not to be considered impairments under the Americans with Disabilities Act.

Physical or mental impairment does not include simple physical characteristics, such as blue eyes or black hair. Nor does it include environmental, cultural, economic, or other disadvantages, such as having a prison record, or being poor. Nor is age a disability. Similarly, the definition does not include common personality traits such as poor judgment or a quick temper where these are not symptoms of a mental or psychological disorder. However, a person who has these characteristics and also has a physical or mental impairment may be considered as having a disability for purposes of the Americans with Disabilities Act based on the impairment.

Substantial Limitation of a Major Life Activity. Under Test A, the impairment must be one that "substantially limits a major life activity." Major life activities include such things as caring for one's self, performing manual tasks, walking, seeing, hearing, speaking, breathing, learning, and working.

For example, a person who is paraplegic is substantially limited in the major life activity of walking, a person who is blind is substantially limited in the major life activity of seeing, and a person who is mentally retarded is substantially limited in the major life activity of learning. A person with traumatic brain injury is substantially limited in the major life activities of caring for one's self, learning, and working because of memory deficit, confusion, contextual difficulties, and inability to reason appropriately.

A person is considered an individual with a disability for purposes of Test A, the first prong of the definition, when the individual's important life activities are restricted as to the conditions, manner, or duration under which they can be performed in comparison to most people. A person with a minor, trivial impairment, such as a simple infected finger, is not impaired in a major life activity. A person who can walk for 10 miles continuously is not substantially limited in walking merely because, on the eleventh mile, he or she begins to experience pain, because most people would not be able to walk eleven miles without experiencing some discomfort.

The Department received many comments on the proposed rule's inclusion of the word "temporary" in the definition of "disability." The preamble indicated that impairments are not necessarily excluded from the definition of "disability" simply because they are temporary, but that the duration, or expected duration, of an impairment is one factor that may properly be considered in determining whether the impairment substantially limits a major life activity. The preamble recognized, however, that temporary impairments, such as a broken leg, are not commonly regarded as disabilities, and only in rare circumstances would the degree of the limitation and its expected duration be substantial. Nevertheless, many commenters objected to inclusion of the word "temporary" both because it is not in the statute and because it is not contained in the definition of "disability" set forth in the title I regulations of the Equal Employment Opportunity Commission (EEOC). The word "temporary" has been deleted from the final rule to conform with the statutory language.

The question of whether a temporary impairment is a disability must be resolved on a case-by-case basis, taking into consideration both the duration (or expected duration) of the impairment and the extent to which it actually limits a major

life activity of the affected individual.

The question of whether a person has a disability should be assessed without regard to the availability of mitigating measures, such as reasonable modification or auxiliary aids and services. For example, a person with hearing loss is substantially limited in the major life activity of hearing, even though the loss may be improved through the use of a hearing aid. Likewise, persons with impairments, such as epilepsy or diabetes, that substantially limit a major life activity, are covered under the first prong of the definition of disability, even if the effects of the impairment are controlled by medication. Many commenters asked that environmental illness (also known as multiple chemical sensitivity) as well as allergy to cigarette smoke be recognized as disabilities. The Department, however, declines to state categorically that these types of allergies or sensitivities are disabilities, because the determination as to whether an impairment is a disability depends on whether, given the particular circumstances at issue, the impairment substantially limits one or more major life activities (or has a history of, or is regarded as having such an effect).

Sometimes respiratory or neurological functioning is so severely affected that an individual will satisfy the requirements to be considered disabled under the regulation. Such an individual would be entitled to all of the protections afforded by the Act and this part. In other cases, individuals may be sensitive to environmental elements or to smoke but their sensitivity will not rise to the level needed to constitute a disability. For example, their major life activity of breathing may be somewhat, but not substantially, impaired. In such circumstances, the individuals are not disabled and are not entitled to the protections of the statute despite their sensitivity to environmental agents.

In sum, the determination as to whether allergies to cigarette smoke, or allergies or

sensitivities characterized by the commenters as environmental illness are disabilities covered by the regulation must be made using the same case-by-case analysis that is applied to all other physical or mental impairments. Moreover, the addition of specific regulatory provisions relating to environmental illness in the final rule would be inappropriate at this time pending future consideration of the issue by the Architectural and Transportation Barriers Compliance Board, the Environmental Protection Agency, and the Occupational Safety and Health Administration of the Department of Labor.

Test B—A record of such an impairment

This test is intended to cover those who have a record of an impairment. As explained in paragraph (3) of the rule's definition of disability, this includes a person who has a history of an impairment that substantially limited a major life activity, such as someone who has recovered from an impairment. It also includes persons who have been misclassified as having an impairment.

This provision is included in the definition in part to protect individuals who have recovered from a physical or mental impairment that previously substantially limited them in a major life activity. Discrimination on the basis of such a past impairment is prohibited. Frequently occurring examples of the first group (those who have a history of an impairment) are persons with histories of mental or emotional illness, heart disease, or cancer; examples of the second group (those who have been misclassified as having an impairment) are persons who have been misclassified as having mental retardation or mental illness.

Test C—Being regarded as having such an impairment

This test, as contained in paragraph (4) of the definition, is intended to cover persons who are treated by a public entity as having a physical or mental impairment that substantially limits a major life activity. It applies when a person is treated as if he or she has an impairment that substantially limits a major life activity, regardless of whether that person has an impairment.

The Americans with Disabilities Act uses the same "regarded as" test set forth in the regulations implementing section 504 of the Rehabilitation Act. See, e.g., 28 CFR 42.540(k)(2)(iv), which provides:

(iv) "Is regarded as having an impairment" means (A) Has a physical or mental impairment that does not substantially limit major life activities but that is treated by a recipient as constituting such a limitation; (B) Has a physical or mental impairment that substantially limits major life activities only as a result of the attitudes of others toward such impairment; or (C) Has none of the impairments defined in paragraph (k)(2)(i) of this section but is treated by a recipient as having such an impairment.

The perception of the covered entity is a key element of this test. A person who perceives himself or herself to have an impairment, but does not have an impairment, and is not treated as if he or she has an impairment, is not protected under this test.

A person would be covered under this test if a public entity refused to serve the person because it perceived that the person had an impairment that limited his or her enjoyment of the goods or services being offered.

For example, persons with severe burns often encounter discrimination in community activities, resulting in substantial limitation of major life activities. These persons would be covered under this test based on the attitudes of others towards the impairment, even if they did not view themselves as "impaired."

The rationale for this third test, as used in the Rehabilitation Act of 1973, was articulated by the Supreme Court in *Arline*, 480 U.S. 273 (1987). The Court noted that although an individual may have an

impairment that does not in fact substantially limit a major life activity, the reaction of others may prove just as disabling. "Such an impairment might not diminish a person's physical or mental capabilities, but could nevertheless substantially limit that person's ability to work as a result of the negative reactions of others to the impairment." *Id.* at 283. The Court concluded that, by including this test in the Rehabilitation Act's definition, "Congress acknowledged that society's accumulated myths and fears about disability and diseases are as handicapping as are the physical limitations that flow from actual impairment." *Id.* at 284.

Thus, a person who is denied services or benefits by a public entity because of myths, fears, and stereotypes associated with disabilities would be covered under this third test whether or not the person's physical or mental condition would be considered a disability under the first or second test in the definition.

If a person is refused admittance on the basis of an actual or perceived physical or mental condition, and the public entity can articulate no legitimate reason for the refusal (such as failure to meet eligibility criteria), a perceived concern about admitting persons with disabilities could be inferred and the individual would qualify for coverage under the "regarded as" test. A person who is covered because of being regarded as having an impairment is not required to show that the public entity's perception is inaccurate (e.g., that he will be accepted by others) in order to receive benefits from the public entity.

Paragraph (5) of the definition lists certain conditions that are not included within the definition of "disability." The excluded conditions are: Transvestism, transsexualism, pedophilia, exhibitionism, voyeurism, gender identity disorders not resulting from physical impairments, other sexual behavior disorders, compulsive gambling, kleptomania, pyromania, and psychoactive substance use disorders

resulting from current illegal use of drugs. Unlike homosexuality and bisexuality, which are not considered impairments under either section 504 or the Americans with Disabilities Act (see the definition of "disability," paragraph (1)(iv)), the conditions listed in paragraph (5), except for transvestism, are not necessarily excluded as impairments under section 504. (Transvestism was excluded from the definition of disability for section 504 by the Fair Housing Amendments Act of 1988, Pub. L. 100-430, section 6(b)).

"Drug." The definition of the term "drug" is taken from section 510(d)(2) of the ADA.

"Facility." "Facility" means all or any portion of buildings, structures, sites, complexes, equipment, rolling stock or other conveyances, roads, walks, passageways, parking lots, or other real or personal property, including the site where the building, property, structure, or equipment is located. It includes both indoor and outdoor areas where human-constructed improvements, structures, equipment, or property have been added to the natural environment.

Commenters raised questions about the applicability of this part to activities operated in mobile facilities, such as bookmobiles or mobile health screening units. Such activities would be covered by the requirement for program accessibility in § 35.150, and would be included in the definition of "facility" as "other real or personal property," although standards for new construction and alterations of such facilities are not yet included in the accessibility standards adopted by § 35.151. Sections 35.150 and 35.151 specifically address the obligations of public entities to ensure accessibility by providing curb ramps at pedestrian walkways.

"Historic preservation programs" and "Historic properties" are defined in order to aid in the interpretation of §§ 35.150 (a)(2) and (b)(2), which relate to accessibility of historic preservation programs, and § 35.151(d), which relates to the alteration of historic properties.

"Illegal use of drugs." The definition of "illegal use of drugs" is taken from section 510(d)(1) of the Act and clarifies that the term includes the illegal use of one or more drugs.

"Individual with a disability" means a person who has a disability but does not include an individual who is currently illegally using drugs, when the public entity acts on the basis of such use. The phrase "current illegal use of drugs" is explained in § 35.131.

"Public entity." The term "public entity" is defined in accordance with section 201(1) of the ADA as any State or local government; any department, agency, special purpose district, or other instrumentality of a State or States or local government; or the National Railroad Passenger Corporation, and any commuter authority (as defined in section 103(8) of the Rail Passenger Service Act).

"Qualified individual with a disability." The definition of "qualified individual with a disability" is taken from section 201(2) of the Act, which is derived from the definition of "qualified handicapped person" in the Department of Health and Human Services' regulation implementing section 504 (45 CFR § 84.3(k)). It combines the definition at 45 CFR 84.3(k)(1) for employment ("a handicapped person who, with reasonable accommodation, can perform the essential functions of the job in question") with the definition for other services at 45 CFR 84.3(k)(4) ("a handicapped person who meets the essential eligibility requirements for the receipt of such services").

Some commenters requested clarification of the term "essential eligibility requirements." Because of the variety of situations in which an individual's qualifications will be at issue, it is not possible to include more specific criteria in the definition. The "essential eligibility requirements" for participation in some activities covered under this part may be minimal. For example, most public entities provide information about their operations as a public service to anyone who requests it. In such situations, the only "eligibility requirement" for receipt of such information would be the request for it. Where such information is provided by telephone, even the ability to use a voice telephone is not an "essential eligibility requirement," because § 35.161 requires a public entity to provide equally effective telecommunication systems for individuals with impaired hearing or speech.

For other activities, identification of the "essential eligibility requirements" may be more complex. Where questions of safety are involved, the principles established in § 36.208 of the Department's regulation implementing title III of the ADA, to be codified at 28 CFR, part 36, will be applicable. That section implements section 302(b)(3) of the Act, which provides that a public accommodation is not required to permit an individual to participate in or benefit from the goods, services, facilities, privileges, advantages and accommodations of the public accommodation, if that individual poses a direct threat to the health or safety of others.

A "direct threat" is a significant risk to the health or safety of others that cannot be eliminated by a modification of policies, practices, or procedures, or by the provision of auxiliary aids or services. In *School Board of Nassau County v. Arline*, 480 U.S. 273 (1987), the Supreme Court recognized that there is a need to balance the interests of people with disabilities against legitimate concerns for public safety. Although persons with disabilities are generally entitled to the protection of this part, a person who poses a significant risk to others will not be "qualified," if reasonable modifications to the public entity's policies, practices, or procedures will not eliminate that risk.

The determination that a person poses a direct threat to the health or safety of others may not be based on generalizations or stereotypes about the effects of a particular disability. It must be based on an individualized assessment, based on reasonable judgment that relies on current medical evidence or on the best available objective evidence, to determine: the nature, duration, and severity of the risk; the probability that the potential injury will actually occur; and whether reasonable modifications of policies, practices, or procedures will mitigate the risk. This is the test established by the Supreme Court in *Arline*. Such an inquiry is essential if the law is to achieve its goal of protecting disabled individuals from discrimination based on prejudice, stereotypes, or unfounded fear, while giving appropriate weight to legitimate concerns, such as the need to avoid exposing others to significant health and safety risks. Making this assessment will not usually require the services of a physician. Sources for medical knowledge include guidance from public health authorities, such as the U.S. Public Health Service, the Centers for Disease Control, and the National Institutes of Health, including the National Institute of Mental Health.

"Qualified interpreter." The Department received substantial comment regarding the lack of a definition of "qualified interpreter." The proposed rule defined auxiliary aids and services to include the statutory term, "qualified interpreters" (§ 35.104), but did not define it. Section 35.160 requires the use of auxiliary aids including qualified interpreters and commenters stated that a lack of guidance on what the term means would create confusion among those trying to secure interpreting services and often result in less than effective communication.

Many commenters were concerned that, without clear guidance on the issue of "qualified" interpreter, the rule would be interpreted to mean "available, rather than qualified" interpreters. Some claimed that few public entities would understand the difference between a qualified interpreter and a person who simply knows a few signs or how to fingerspell.

In order to clarify what is meant by "qualified interpreter" the Department has added a definition of the term to the final rule. A qualified interpreter means an interpreter who is able to interpret effectively, accurately, and impartially both receptively and expressively, using any necessary specialized vocabulary. This definition focuses on the actual ability of the interpreter in a particular interpreting context to facilitate effective communication between the public entity and the individual with disabilities.

Public comment also revealed that public entities have at times asked persons who are deaf to provide family members or friends to interpret. In certain circumstances, notwithstanding that the family member of friend is able to interpret or is a certified interpreter, the family member or friend may not be qualified to render the necessary interpretation because of factors such as emotional or personal involvement or considerations of confidentiality that may adversely affect the ability to interpret "effectively, accurately, and impartially."

The definition of "qualified interpreter" in this rule does not invalidate or limit standards for interpreting services of any State or local law that are equal to or more stringent than those imposed by this definition. For instance, the definition would not supersede any requirement of State law for use of a certified interpreter in court proceedings.

"Section 504." The Department added a definition of "section 504" because the term is used extensively in subpart F of this part.

"State." The definition of "State" is identical to the statutory definition in section 3(3) of the ADA.

Section 35.105 Self-evaluation

Section 35.105 establishes a requirement, based on the section 504 regulations for federally assisted and federally conducted programs, that a public entity evaluate its current policies and practices to identify and correct any that are not consistent with the requirements of this part. As noted in the discussion of § 35.102, activities covered by the Department of Transportation's regulation implementing subtitle B of title II are not required to be included in the self-evaluation required by this section.

Experience has demonstrated the self-evaluation process to be a valuable means of establishing a working relationship with individuals with disabilities, which has promoted both effective and efficient implementation of section 504. The Department expects that it will likewise be useful to public entities newly covered by the ADA.

All public entities are required to do a self-evaluation. However, only those that employ 50 or more persons are required to maintain the self-evaluation on file and make it available for public inspection for three years. The number 50 was derived from the Department of Justice's section 504 regulations for federally assisted programs, 28 CFR 42.505(c). The Department received comments critical of this limitation, some suggesting the requirement apply to all public entities and others suggesting that the number be changed from 50 to 15. The final rule has not been changed. Although many regulations implementing section 504 for federally assisted programs do use 15 employees as the cut-off for this record-keeping requirement, the Department believes that it would be inappropriate to extend it to those smaller public entities covered by this regulation that do not receive Federal financial assistance. This approach has the benefit of minimizing paperwork burdens on small entities.

Paragraph (d) provides that the self-evaluation required by this section shall apply only to programs not subject to section 504 or those policies and practices, such as those involving communications access, that have not already been included in a self-evaluation required under an existing regulation implement-ing section 504. Because most self-evaluations were done from five to twelve years ago, however, the Department expects that a great many public entities will be reexamining all of their policies and programs. Programs and functions may have changed, and actions that were supposed to have been taken to comply with section 504 may not have been fully implemented or may no longer be effective. In addition, there have been statutory amendments to section 504 which have changed the coverage of section 504, particularly the Civil Rights Restoration Act of 1987, Public Law No. 100-259, 102 Stat. 28 (1988), which broadened the definition of a covered "program or activity."

Several commenters suggested that the Department clarify public entities' liability during the one-year period for compliance with the self-evaluation requirement. The self-evaluation requirement does not stay the effective date of the statute nor of this part. Public entities are, therefore, not shielded from discrimination claims during that time.

Other commenters suggested that the rule require that every self-evaluation include an examination of training efforts to assure that individuals with disabilities are not subjected to discrimination because of insensitivity, particularly in the law enforcement area. Although the Department has not added such a specific requirement to the rule, it would be appropriate for public entities to evaluate training efforts because, in many cases, lack of training leads to discriminatory practices, even when the policies in place are nondiscriminatory.

Section 35.106 Notice

Section 35.106 requires a public entity to disseminate sufficient information to applicants, participants, beneficiaries, and other interested persons to inform them of the rights and protections afforded by the ADA and this regulation. Methods of providing this information include, for example, the publication of information in handbooks, manuals, and pamphlets that are distributed to the public to describe a public entity's programs and activities; the display of informative posters in service centers and other public places; or the broadcast of information by television or radio. In providing the notice, a public entity must comply with the requirements for effective communication in § 35.160. The preamble to that section gives guidance on how to effectively communicate with individuals with disabilities.

Section 35.107 Designation of Responsible Employee and Adoption of Grievance Procedures

Consistent with § 35.105, self-evaluation, the final rule requires that public entities with 50 or more employees designate a responsible employee and adopt grievance procedures. Most of the commenters who suggested that the requirement that self-evaluation be maintained on file for three years not be limited to those employing 50 or more persons made a similar suggestion concerning § 35.107. Commenters recommended either that all public entities be subject to § 35.107, or that "50 or more persons" be changed to "15 or more persons." As explained in the discussion of § 35.105, the Department has not adopted this suggestion.

The requirement for designation of an employee responsible for coordination of efforts to carry out responsibilities under this part is derived from the HEW regulation implementing section 504 in federally assisted programs. The requirement for designation of a particular employee and dissemination of information about how to locate that employee helps to ensure that individuals dealing with large agencies are able to easily find a responsible person who is familiar with the requirements of the Act and this part and can communicate those requirements to other individuals in the agency who may be unaware of their responsibili-

ties. This paragraph in no way limits a public entity's obligation to ensure that all of its employees comply with the requirements of this part, but it ensures that any failure by individual employees can be promptly corrected by the designated employee.

Section 35.107(b) requires public entities with 50 or more employees to establish grievance procedures for resolving complaints of violations of this part. Similar requirements are found in the section 504 regulations for federally assisted programs (see, e.g., 45 CFR 84.7(b)). The rule, like the regulations for federally assisted programs, provides for investigation and resolution of complaints by a Federal enforcement agency. It is the view of the Department that public entities subject to this part should be required to establish a mechanism for resolution of complaints at the local level without requiring the complainant to resort to the Federal complaint procedures established under subpart F. Complainants would not, however, be required to exhaust the public entity's grievance procedures before filing a complaint under subpart F. Delay in filing the complaint at the Federal level caused by pursuit of the remedies available under the grievance procedure would generally be considered good cause for extending the time allowed for filing under § 35.170(b).

Subpart B--General Requirements

Section 35.130 General Prohibitions Against Discrimination

The general prohibitions against discrimination in the rule are generally based on the prohibitions in existing regulations implementing section 504 and, therefore, are already familiar to State and local entities covered by section 504. In addition, § 35.130 includes a number of provisions derived from title III of the Act that are implicit to a certain degree in the requirements of regulations implementing section 504.

Several commenters suggested that this part should include the section of the proposed title III regulation that implemented section 309 of the Act, which requires that courses and examinations related to applications, licensing, certification, or credentialing be provided in an accessible place and manner or that alternative accessible arrangements be made. The Department has not adopted this suggestion. The requirements of this part, including the general prohibitions of discrimination in this section, the program access requirements of subpart D, and the communications requirements of subpart E, apply to courses and examinations provided by public entities. The Department considers these requirements to be sufficient to ensure that courses and examinations administered by public entities meet the requirements of section 309. For example, a public entity offering an examination must ensure that modifications of policies, practices, or procedures or the provision of auxiliary aids and services furnish the individual with a disability an equal opportunity to demonstrate his or her knowledge or ability. Also, any examination specially designed for individuals with disabilities must be offered as often and in as timely a manner as are other examinations. Further, under this part, courses and examinations must be offered in the most integrated setting appropriate. The analysis of § 35.130(d) is relevant to this determination.

A number of commenters asked that the regulation be amended to require training of law enforcement personnel to recognize the difference between criminal activity and the effects of seizures or other disabilities such as mental retardation, cerebral palsy, traumatic brain injury, mental illness, or deafness. Several disabled commenters gave personal statements about the abuse they had received at the hands of law enforcement personnel. Two organizations that commented cited the Judiciary report at 50 as authority to require law enforcement training.

The Department has not added such a training requirement to the regulation. Discriminatory arrests and brutal treatment are already unlawful police activities. The general regulatory obligation to modify policies, practices, or procedures requires law enforcement to make changes in policies that result in discriminatory arrests or abuse of individuals with disabilities. Under this section law enforcement personnel would be required to make appropriate efforts to determine whether perceived strange or disruptive behavior or unconsciousness is the result of a disability. The Department notes that a number of States have attempted to address the problem of arresting disabled persons for noncriminal conduct resulting from their disability through adoption of the Uniform Duties to Disabled Persons Act, and encourages other jurisdictions to consider that approach.

Paragraph (a) restates the nondiscrimination mandate of section 202 of the ADA. The remaining paragraphs in § 35.130 establish the general principles for analyzing whether any particular action of the public entity violates this mandate.

Paragraph (b) prohibits overt denials of equal treatment of individuals with disabilities. A public entity may not refuse to provide an individual with a disability with an equal opportunity to participate in or benefit from its program simply because the person has a disability.

Paragraph (b)(1)(i) provides that it is discriminatory to deny a person with a disability the right to participate in or benefit from the aid, benefit, or service provided by a public entity. Paragraph (b)(1)(ii) provides that the aids, benefits, and services provided to persons with disabilities must be equal to those provided to others, and paragraph (b)(1)(iii) requires that the aids, benefits, or services provided to individuals with disabilities must be as effective in affording equal

opportunity to obtain the same result, to gain the same benefit, or to reach the same level of achievement as those provided to others. These paragraphs are taken from the regulations implementing section 504 and simply restate principles long established under section 504.

Paragraph (b)(1)(iv) permits the public entity to develop separate or different aids, benefits, or services when necessary to provide individuals with disabilities with an equal opportunity to participate in or benefit from the public entity's programs or activities, but only when necessary to ensure that the aids, benefits, or services are as effective as those provided to others. Paragraph (b)(1)(iv) must be read in conjunction with paragraphs (b)(2), (d), and (e). Even when separate or different aids, benefits, or services would be more effective, paragraph (b)(2) provides that a qualified individual with a disability still has the right to choose to participate in the program that is not designed to accommodate individuals with disabilities. Paragraph (d) requires that a public entity administer services, programs, and activities in the most integrated setting appropriate to the needs of qualified individuals with disabilities.

Paragraph (b)(2) specifies that, notwithstanding the existence of separate or different programs or activities provided in accordance with this section, an individual with a disability shall not be denied the opportunity to participate in such programs or activities that are not separate or different. Paragraph (e), which is derived from section 501(d) of the Americans with Disabilities Act, states that nothing in this part shall be construed to require an individual with a disability to accept an accommodation, aid, service, opportunity, or benefit that he or she chooses not to accept.

Taken together, these provisions are intended to prohibit exclusion and segregation of individuals with disabilities and the denial of equal opportunities enjoyed by others, based on, among other

things, presumptions, patronizing attitudes, fears, and stereotypes about individuals with disabilities. Consistent with these standards, public entities are required to ensure that their actions are based on facts applicable to individuals and not on presumptions as to what a class of individuals with disabilities can or cannot do.

Integration is fundamental to the purposes of the Americans with Disabilities Act. Provision of segregated accommodations and services relegates persons with disabilities to second-class status. For example, it would be a violation of this provision to require persons with disabilities to eat in the back room of a government cafeteria or to refuse to allow a person with a disability the full use of recreation or exercise facilities because of stereotypes about the person's ability to participate.

Many commenters objected to proposed paragraphs (b)(1)(iv) and (d) as allowing continued segregation of individuals with disabilities. The Department recognizes that promoting integration of individuals with disabilities into the mainstream of society is an important objective of the ADA and agrees that, in most instances, separate programs for individuals with disabilities will not be permitted. Nevertheless, section 504 does permit separate programs in limited circumstances, and Congress clearly intended the regulations issued under title II to adopt the standards of section 504. Furthermore, Congress included authority for separate programs in the specific requirements of title III of the Act. Section 302(b)(1)(A)(iii) of the Act provides for separate benefits in language similar to that in § 35.130(b)(1)(iv), and section 302(b)(1)(B) includes the same requirement for "the most integrated setting appropriate" as in § 35.130(d).

Even when separate programs are permitted, individuals with disabilities cannot be denied the opportunity to participate in programs that are not separate or different. This is an important and overarching principle of the

Americans with Disabilities Act. Separate, special, or different programs that are designed to provide a benefit to persons with disabilities cannot be used to restrict the participation of persons with disabilities in general, integrated activities.

For example, a person who is blind may wish to decline participating in a special museum tour that allows persons to touch sculptures in an exhibit and instead tour the exhibit at his or her own pace with the museum's recorded tour. It is not the intent of this section to require the person who is blind to avail himself or herself of the special tour. Modified participation for persons with disabilities must be a choice, not a requirement.

In addition, it would not be a violation of this section for a public entity to offer recreational programs specially designed for children with mobility impairments. However, it would be a violation of this section if the entity then excluded these children from other recreational services for which they are qualified to participate when these services are made available to nondisabled children, or if the entity required children with disabilities to attend only designated programs.

Many commenters asked that the Department clarify a public entity's obligations within the integrated program when it offers a separate program but an individual with a disability chooses not to participate in the separate program. It is impossible to make a blanket statement as to what level of auxiliary aids or modifications would be required in the integrated program. Rather, each situation must be assessed individually. The starting point is to question whether the separate program is in fact necessary or appropriate for the individual. Assuming the separate program would be appropriate for a particular individual, the extent to which that individual must be provided with modifications in the integrated program will depend not only on what the individual needs but also on the

limitations and defenses of this part. For example, it may constitute an undue burden for a public accommodation, which provides a full-time interpreter in its special guided tour for individuals with hearing impairments, to hire an additional interpreter for those individuals who choose to attend the integrated program. The Department cannot identify categorically the level of assistance or aid required in the integrated program.

Paragraph (b)(1)(v) provides that a public entity may not aid or perpetuate discrimination against a qualified individual with a disability by providing significant assistance to an agency, organization, or person that discriminates on the basis of disability in providing any aid, benefit, or service to beneficiaries of the public entity's program. This paragraph is taken from the regulations implementing section 504 for federally assisted programs.

Paragraph (b)(1)(vi) prohibits the public entity from denying a qualified individual with a disability the opportunity to participate as a member of a planning or advisory board.

Paragraph (b)(1)(vii) prohibits the public entity from limiting a qualified individual with a disability in the enjoyment of any right, privilege, advantage, or opportunity enjoyed by others receiving any aid, benefit, or service.

Paragraph (b)(3) prohibits the public entity from utilizing criteria or methods of administration that deny individuals with disabilities access to the public entity's services, programs, and activities or that perpetuate the discrimination of another public entity, if both public entities are subject to common administrative control or are agencies of the same State. The phrase "criteria or methods of administration" refers to official written policies of the public entity and to the actual practices of the public entity. This paragraph prohibits both blatantly exclusionary policies or practices and nonessential policies and

practices that are neutral on their face, but deny individuals with disabilities an effective opportunity to participate. This standard is consistent with the interpretation of section 504 by the U.S. Supreme Court in *Alexander v. Choate*, 469 U.S. 287 (1985). The Court in *Choate* explained that members of Congress made numerous statements during passage of section 504 regarding eliminating architectural barriers, providing access to transportation, and eliminating discriminatory effects of job qualification procedures. The Court then noted: "These statements would ring hollow if the resulting legislation could not rectify the harms resulting from action that discriminated by effect as well as by design." *Id.* at 297 (footnote omitted).

Paragraph (b)(4) specifically applies the prohibition enunciated in § 35.130(b)(3) to the process of selecting sites for construction of new facilities or selecting existing facilities to be used by the public entity. Paragraph (b)(4) does not apply to construction of additional buildings at an existing site.

Paragraph (b)(5) prohibits the public entity, in the selection of procurement contractors, from using criteria that subject qualified individuals with disabilities to discrimination on the basis of disability.

Paragraph (b)(6) prohibits the public entity from discriminating against qualified individuals with disabilities on the basis of disability in the granting of licenses or certification. A person is a "qualified individual with a disability" with respect to licensing or certification if he or she can meet the essential eligibility requirements for receiving the license or certification (see § 35.104).

A number of commenters were troubled by the phrase "essential eligibility requirements" as applied to State licensing requirements, especially those for health care professions. Because of the variety of types of programs to which the definition of "qualified individual with a disability" applies, it is not possible to use more specific language in the definition. The phrase "essential eligibility requirements," however, is taken from the definitions in the regulations implementing section 504, so caselaw under section 504 will be applicable to its interpretation. In *Southeastern Community College v. Davis*, 442 U.S. 397, for example, the Supreme Court held that section 504 does not require an institution to "lower or effect substantial modifications of standards to accommodate a handicapped person," 442 U.S. at 413, and that the school had established that the plaintiff was not "qualified" because she was not able to "serve the nursing profession in all customary ways," *id.* Whether a particular requirement is "essential" will, of course, depend on the facts of the particular case.

In addition, the public entity may not establish requirements for the programs or activities of licensees or certified entities that subject qualified individuals with disabilities to discrimination on the basis of disability. For example, the public entity must comply with this requirement when establishing safety standards for the operations of licensees. In that case the public entity must ensure that standards that it promulgates do not discriminate against the employment of qualified individuals with disabilities in an impermissible manner.

Paragraph (b)(6) does not extend the requirements of the Act or this part directly to the programs or activities of licensees or certified entities themselves. The programs or activities of licensees or certified entities are not themselves programs or activities of the public entity merely by virtue of the license or certificate.

Paragraph (b)(7) is a specific application of the requirement under the general prohibitions of discrimination that public entities make reasonable modifications in policies, practices, or procedures where necessary to avoid discrimination on the basis of disability. Section 302(b)(2)(A)(ii) of the ADA sets out this requirement

specifically for public accommodations covered by title III of the Act, and the House Judiciary Committee Report directs the Attorney General to include those specific requirements in the title II regulation to the extent that they do not conflict with the regulations implementing section 504. Judiciary report at 52.

Paragraph (b)(8), a new paragraph not contained in the proposed rule, prohibits the imposition or application of eligibility criteria that screen out or tend to screen out an individual with a disability or any class of individuals with disabilities from fully and equally enjoying any service, program, or activity, unless such criteria can be shown to be necessary for the provision of the service, program, or activity being offered. This prohibition is also a specific application of the general prohibitions of discrimination and is based on section 302(b)(2)(A)(i) of the ADA. It prohibits overt denials of equal treatment of individuals with disabilities, or establishment of exclusive or segregative criteria that would bar individuals with disabilities from participation in services, benefits, or activities.

Paragraph (b)(8) also prohibits policies that unnecessarily impose requirements or burdens on individuals with disabilities that are not placed on others. For example, public entities may not require that a qualified individual with a disability be accompanied by an attendant. A public entity is not, however, required to provide attendant care, or assistance in toileting, eating, or dressing to individuals with disabilities, except in special circumstances, such as where the individual is an inmate of a custodial or correctional institution.

In addition, paragraph (b)(8) prohibits the imposition of criteria that "tend to" screen out an individual with a disability. This concept, which is derived from current regulations under section 504 (*see, e.g.*, 45 CFR 84.13), makes it discriminatory to impose policies or criteria that, while not creating a direct bar to individuals with disabilities,

indirectly prevent or limit their ability to participate. For example, requiring presentation of a driver's license as the sole means of identification for purposes of paying by check would violate this section in situations where, for example, individuals with severe vision impairments or developmental disabilities or epilepsy are ineligible to receive a driver's license and the use of an alternative means of identification, such as another photo I.D. or credit card, is feasible.

A public entity may, however, impose neutral rules and criteria that screen out, or tend to screen out, individuals with disabilities if the criteria are necessary for the safe operation of the program in question. Examples of safety qualifications that would be justifiable in appropriate circumstances would include eligibility requirements for drivers' licenses, or a requirement that all participants in a recreational rafting expedition be able to meet a necessary level of swimming proficiency. Safety requirements must be based on actual risks and not on speculation, stereotypes, or generalizations about individuals with disabilities.

Paragraph (c) provides that nothing in this part prohibits a public entity from providing benefits, services, or advantages to individuals with disabilities, or to a particular class of individuals with disabilities, beyond those required by this part. It is derived from a provision in the section 504 regulations that permits programs conducted pursuant to Federal statute or Executive order that are designed to benefit only individuals with disabilities or a given class of individuals with disabilities to be limited to those individuals with disabilities. Section 504 ensures that federally assisted programs are made available to all individuals, without regard to disabilities, unless the Federal program under which the assistance is provided is specifically limited to individuals with disabilities or a particular class of individuals with disabilities. Because coverage under this part is not limited to federally assisted programs, paragraph (c) has been revised to clarify that State and local governments may provide special benefits, beyond those required by the nondiscrimination requirements of this part, that are limited to individuals with disabilities or a particular class of individuals with disabilities, without thereby incurring additional obligations to persons without disabilities or to other classes of individuals with disabilities.

Paragraphs (d) and (e), previously referred to in the discussion of paragraph (b)(1)(iv), provide that the public entity must administer services, programs, and activities in the most integrated setting appropriate to the needs of qualified individuals with disabilities, i.e., in a setting that enables individuals with disabilities to interact with nondisabled persons to the fullest extent possible, and that persons with disabilities must be provided the option of declining to accept a particular accommodation.

Some commenters expressed concern that § 35.130(e), which states that nothing in the rule requires an individual with a disability to accept special accommodations and services provided under the ADA, could be interpreted to allow guardians of infants or older people with disabilities to refuse medical treatment for their wards. Section 35.130(e) has been revised to make it clear that paragraph (e) is inapplicable to the concern of the commenters. A new paragraph (e)(2) has been added stating that nothing in the regulation authorizes the representative or guardian of an individual with a disability to decline food, water, medical treatment, or medical services for that individual. New paragraph (e) clarifies that neither the ADA nor the regulation alters current Federal law ensuring the rights of incompetent individuals with disabilities to receive food, water, and medical treatment. See, e.g., Child Abuse Amendments of 1984 (42 U.S.C. 5106a(b)(10), 5106g(10)); Rehabilitation Act of 1973, as

amended (29 U.S.C. 794); the Developmentally Disabled Assistance and Bill of Rights Act (42 U.S.C. 6042).

Sections 35.130(e) (1) and (2) are based on section 501(d) of the ADA. Section 501(d) was designed to clarify that nothing in the ADA requires individuals with disabilities to accept special accommodations and services for individuals with disabilities that may segregate them:

The Committee added this section [501(d)] to clarify that nothing in the ADA is intended to permit discriminatory treatment on the basis of disability, even when such treatment is rendered under the guise of providing an accommodation, service, aid or benefit to the individual with disability. For example, a blind individual may choose not to avail himself or herself of the right to go to the front of a line, even if a particular public accommodation has chosen to offer such a modification of a policy for blind individuals. Or, a blind individual may choose to decline to participate in a special museum tour that allows persons to touch sculptures in an exhibit and instead tour the exhibits at his or her own pace with the museum's recorded tour.

Judiciary report at 71–72. The Act is not to be construed to mean that an individual with disabilities must accept special accommodations and services for individuals with disabilities when that individual can participate in the regular services already offered. Because medical treatment, including treatment for particular conditions, is not a special accommodation or service for individuals with disabilities under section 501(d), neither the Act nor this part provides affirmative authority to suspend such treatment. Section 501(d) is intended to clarify that the Act is not designed to foster discrimination through mandatory acceptance of special services when other alternatives are provided; this concern does not reach to the provision of medical treatment for the disabling condition itself.

Paragraph (f) provides that a public entity may not place a

surcharge on a particular individual with a disability, or any group of individuals with disabilities, to cover any costs of measures required to provide that individual or group with the nondiscriminatory treatment required by the Act or this part. Such measures may include the provision of auxiliary aids or of modifications required to provide program accessibility.

Several commenters asked for clarification that the costs of interpreter services may not be assessed as an element of "court costs." The Department has already recognized that imposition of the cost of courtroom interpreter services is impermissible under section 504. The preamble to the Department's section 504 regulation for its federally assisted programs states that where a court system has an obligation to provide qualified interpreters, "it has the corresponding responsibility to pay for the services of the interpreters." (45 FR 37630 (June 3, 1980)). Accordingly, recouping the costs of interpreter services by assessing them as part of court costs would also be prohibited.

Paragraph (g), which prohibits discrimination on the basis of an individual's or entity's known relationship or association with an individual with a disability, is based on sections 102(b)(4) and 302(b)(1)(E) of the ADA. This paragraph was not contained in the proposed rule. The individuals covered under this paragraph are any individuals who are discriminated against because of their known association with an individual with a disability. For example, it would be a violation of this paragraph for a local government to refuse to allow a theater company to use a school auditorium on the grounds that the company had recently performed for an audience of individuals with HIV disease.

This protection is not limited to those who have a familial relationship with the individual who has a disability. Congress considered, and rejected, amendments that would have limited the scope of this provision to specific associations and relationships. Therefore, if a public entity refuses admission to a person with cerebral palsy and his or her companions, the companions have an independent right of action under the ADA and this section.

During the legislative process, the term "entity" was added to section 302(b)(1)(E) to clarify that the scope of the provision is intended to encompass not only persons who have a known association with a person with a disability, but also entities that provide services to or are otherwise associated with such individuals. This provision was intended to ensure that entities such as health care providers, employees of social service agencies, and others who provide professional services to persons with disabilities are not subjected to discrimination because of their professional association with persons with disabilities.

Section 35.131 Illegal Use of Drugs

Section 35.131 effectuates section 510 of the ADA, which clarifies the Act's application to people who use drugs illegally. Paragraph (a) provides that this part does not prohibit discrimination based on an individual's current illegal use of drugs.

The Act and the regulation distinguish between illegal use of drugs and the legal use of substances, whether or not those substances are "controlled substances," as defined in the Controlled Substances Act (21 U.S.C. 812). Some controlled substances are prescription drugs that have legitimate medical uses. Section 35.131 does not affect use of controlled substances pursuant to a valid prescription under supervision by a licensed health care professional, or other use that is authorized by the Controlled Substances Act or any other provision of Federal law. It does apply to illegal use of those substances, as well as to illegal use of controlled substances that are not prescription drugs. The key question is whether the individual's use of the

substance is illegal, not whether the substance has recognized legal uses. Alcohol is not a controlled substance, so use of alcohol is not addressed by § 35.131 (although alcoholics are individuals with disabilities, subject to the protections of the statute).

A distinction is also made between the use of a substance and the status of being addicted to that substance. Addiction is a disability, and addicts are individuals with disabilities protected by the Act. The protection, however, does not extend to actions based on the illegal use of the substance. In other words, an addict cannot use the fact of his or her addiction as a defense to an action based on illegal use of drugs. This distinction is not artificial. Congress intended to deny protection to people who engage in the illegal use of drugs, whether or not they are addicted, but to provide protection to addicts so long as they are not currently using drugs.

A third distinction is the difficult one between current use and former use. The definition of "current illegal use of drugs" in § 35.104, which is based on the report of the Conference Committee, H.R. Conf. Rep. No. 596, 101st Cong., 2d Sess. 64 (1990) (hereinafter "Conference report"), is "illegal use of drugs that occurred recently enough to justify a reasonable belief that a person's drug use is current or that continuing use is a real and ongoing problem."

Paragraph (a)(2)(i) specifies that an individual who has successfully completed a supervised drug rehabilitation program or has otherwise been rehabilitated successfully and who is not engaging in current illegal use of drugs is protected. Paragraph (a)(2)(ii) clarifies that an individual who is currently participating in a supervised rehabilitation program and is not engaging in current illegal use of drugs is protected. Paragraph (a)(2)(iii) provides that a person who is erroneously regarded as engaging in current illegal use of drugs, but who is not engaging in such use, is protected.

Paragraph (b) provides a limited exception to the exclusion of current illegal users of drugs from the protections of the Act. It prohibits denial of health services, or services provided in connection with drug rehabilitation to an individual on the basis of current illegal use of drugs, if the individual is otherwise entitled to such services. A health care facility, such as a hospital or clinic, may not refuse treatment to an individual in need of the services it provides on the grounds that the individual is illegally using drugs, but it is not required by this section to provide services that it does not ordinarily provide. For example, a health care facility that specializes in a particular type of treatment, such as care of burn victims, is not required to provide drug rehabilitation services, but it cannot refuse to treat a individual's burns on the grounds that the individual is illegally using drugs.

Some commenters pointed out that abstention from the use of drugs is an essential condition of participation in some drug rehabilitation programs, and may be a necessary requirement in inpatient or residential settings. The Department believes that this comment is well-founded. Congress clearly intended to prohibit exclusion from drug treatment programs of the very individuals who need such programs because of their use of drugs, but, once an individual has been admitted to a program, abstention may be a necessary and appropriate condition to continued participation. The final rule therefore provides that a drug rehabilitation or treatment program may prohibit illegal use of drugs by individuals while they are participating in the program.

Paragraph (c) expresses Congress' intention that the Act be neutral with respect to testing for illegal use of drugs. This paragraph implements the provision in section 510(b) of the Act that allows entities "to adopt or administer reasonable policies or procedures, including but not limited to drug testing," that ensure that an individual who is participating in a supervised rehabilitation program, or who has completed such a program or otherwise been rehabilitated successfully is no longer engaging in the illegal use of drugs. The section is not to be "construed to encourage, prohibit, restrict, or authorize the conducting of testing for the illegal use of drugs."

Paragraph 35.131(c) clarifies that it is not a violation of this part to adopt or administer reasonable policies or procedures to ensure that an individual who formerly engaged in the illegal use of drugs is not currently engaging in illegal use of drugs. Any such policies or procedures must, of course, be reasonable, and must be designed to identify accurately the illegal use of drugs. This paragraph does not authorize inquiries, tests, or other procedures that would disclose use of substances that are not controlled substances or are taken under supervision by a licensed health care professional, or other uses authorized by the Controlled Substances Act or other provisions of Federal law, because such uses are not included in the definition of "illegal use of drugs." A commenter argued that the rule should permit testing for lawful use of prescription drugs, but most commenters preferred that tests must be limited to unlawful use in order to avoid revealing the lawful use of prescription medicine used to treat disabilities.

Section 35.132 Smoking

Section 35.132 restates the clarification in section 501(b) of the Act that the Act does not preclude the prohibition of, or imposition of restrictions on, smoking in transportation covered by title II. Some commenters argued that this section is too limited in scope, and that the regulation should prohibit smoking in all facilities used by public entities. The reference to smoking in section 501, however, merely clarifies that the Act does not require public entities to accommodate smokers by permitting them to smoke in transportation facilities.

Section 35.133 Maintenance of Accessible Features

Section 35.133 provides that a public entity shall maintain in operable working condition those features of facilities and equipment that are required to be readily accessible to and usable by persons with disabilities by the Act or this part. The Act requires that, to the maximum extent feasible, facilities must be accessible to, and usable by, individuals with disabilities. This section recognizes that it is not sufficient to provide features such as accessible routes, elevators, or ramps, if those features are not maintained in a manner that enables individuals with disabilities to use them. Inoperable elevators, locked accessible doors, or "accessible" routes that are obstructed by furniture, filing cabinets, or potted plants are neither "accessible to" nor "usable by" individuals with disabilities.

Some commenters objected that this section appeared to establish an absolute requirement and suggested that language from the preamble be included in the text of the regulation. It is, of course, impossible to guarantee that mechanical devices will never fail to operate. Paragraph (b) of the final regulation provides that this section does not prohibit isolated or temporary interruptions in service or access due to maintenance or repairs. This paragraph is intended to clarify that temporary obstructions or isolated instances of mechanical failure would not be considered violations of the Act or this part. However, allowing obstructions or "out of service" equipment to persist beyond a reasonable period of time would violate this part, as would repeated mechanical failures due to improper or inadequate maintenance. Failure of the public entity to ensure that accessible routes are properly maintained and free of obstructions, or failure to arrange prompt repair of inoperable elevators or other equipment intended to provide access would also violate this part.

Other commenters requested that this section be expanded to include specific requirements for inspection and maintenance of equipment, for training staff in the proper operation of equipment, and for maintenance of specific items. The Department believes that this section properly establishes the general requirement for maintaining access and that further details are not necessary.

Section 35.134 Retaliation or Coercion

35.134 implements section 503 of the ADA, which prohibits retaliation against any individual who exercises his or her rights under the Act. This section is unchanged from the proposed rule. Paragraph (a) of § 35.134 provides that no private or public entity shall discriminate against any individual because that individual has exercised his or her right to oppose any act or practice made unlawful by this part, or because that individual made a charge, testified, assisted, or participated in any manner in an investigation, proceeding, or hearing under the Act or this part.

Paragraph (b) provides that no private or public entity shall coerce, intimidate, threaten, or interfere with any individual in the exercise of his or her rights under this part or because that individual aided or encouraged any other individual in the exercise or enjoyment of any right granted or protected by the Act or this part.

This section protects not only individuals who allege a violation of the Act or this part but also any individuals who support or assist them. This section applies to all investigations or proceedings initiated under the Act or this part without regard to the ultimate resolution of the underlying allegations. Because this section prohibits any act of retaliation or coercion in response to an individual's effort to exercise rights established by the Act and this part (or to support the efforts of another individual), the section applies not only to public entities subject to this part, but also to persons acting in an individual capacity or to private entities. For example, it would be a violation of the Act and this part for a private individual to harass or intimidate an individual with a disability in an effort to prevent that individual from attending a concert in a State-owned park. It would, likewise, be a violation of the Act and this part for a private entity to take adverse action against an employee who appeared as a witness on behalf of an individual who sought to enforce the Act.

Section 35.135 Personal Devices and Services

The final rule includes a new § 35.135, entitles "Personal devices and services," which states that the provision of personal devices and services is not required by title II. This new section, which serves as a limitation on all of the requirements of the regulation, replaces § 35.160(b)(2) of the proposed rule, which addressed the issue of personal devices and services explicitly only.in the context of communications. The personal devices and services limitation was intended to have general application in the proposed rule in all contexts where it was relevant. The final rule, therefore, clarifies this point by including a general provision that will explicitly apply not only to auxiliary aids and services but across-the-board to include other relevant areas such as, for example, modifications in policies, practices, and procedures (§ 35.130(b)(7)). The language of § 35.135 parallels an analogous provision in the Department's title III regulations (28 CFR36.306) but preserves the explicit reference to "readers for personal use or study" in § 35.160(b)(2) of the proposed rule. This section does not preclude the short-term loan of personal receivers that are part of an assistive listening system.

Subpart C—Employment

Section 35.140 Employment Discrimination Prohibited

Title II of the ADA applies to all activities of public entities, including their employment practices. The proposed rule cross-referenced the definitions, requirements, and procedures of title I of the ADA, as established by the Equal Employment Opportunity Commission in 29 CFR part 1630. This proposal would have resulted in use, under § 35.140, of the title I definition of "employer," so that a public entity with 25 or more employees would have become subject to the requirements of § 35.140 on July 26, 1992, one with 15 to 24 employees on July 26, 1994, and one with fewer than 15 employees would have been excluded completely.

The Department received comments objecting to this approach. The commenters asserted that Congress intended to establish nondiscrimination requirements for employment by all public entities, including those that employ fewer than 15 employees; and that Congress intended the employment requirements of title II to become effective at the same time that the other requirements of this regulation become effective, January 26, 1992. The Department has reexamined the statutory language and legislative history of the ADA on this issue and has concluded that Congress intended to cover the employment practices of all public entities and that the applicable effective date is that of title II.

The statutory language of section 204(b) of the ADA requires the Department to issue a regulation that is consistent with the ADA and the Department's coordination regulation under section 504, 28 CFR part 41. The coordination regulation specifically requires nondiscrimination in employment, 28 CFR 41.52-41.55, and does not limit coverage based on size of employer. Moreover, under all section 504 implementing regulations issued in accordance with the Department's coordination

regulation, employment coverage under section 504 extends to all employers with federally assisted programs or activities, regardless of size, and the effective date for those employment requirements has always been the same as the effective date for nonemployment requirements established in the same regulations. The Department therefore concludes tha § 35.140 must apply to all public entities upon the effective date of this regulation.

In the proposed regulation the Department cross-referenced the regulations implementing title I of the ADA, issued by the Equal Employment Opportunity Commission at 29 CFR part 1630, as a compliance standard for § 35.140 because, as proposed, the scope of coverage and effective date of coverage under title II would have been coextensive with title I. In the final regulation this language is modified slightly. Subparagraph (1) of new paragraph (b) makes it clear that the standards established by the Equal Employment Opportunity Commission in 29 CFR part 1630 will be the applicable compliance standards if the public entity is subject to title I. If the public entity is not covered by title I, or until it is covered by title I, subparagraph (b)(2) cross-references section 504 standards for what constitutes employment discrimination, as established by the Department of Justice in 28 CFR part 41. Standards for title I of the ADA and section 504 of the Rehabilitation Act are for the most part identical because title I of the ADA was based on requirements set forth in regulations implementing section 504.

The Department, together with the other Federal agencies responsible for the enforcement of Federal laws prohibiting employment discrimination on the basis of disability, recognizes the potential for jurisdictional overlap that exists with respect to coverage of public entities and the need to avoid problems related to overlapping coverage. The other Federal agencies include the Equal

Employment Opportunity Commission, which is the agency primarily responsible for enforcement of title I of the ADA, the Department of Labor, which is the agency responsible for enforcement of section 503 of the Rehabilitation Act of 1973, and 26 Federal agencies with programs of Federal financial assistance, which are responsible for enforcing section 504 in those programs. Section 107 of the ADA requires that coordination mechanisms be developed in connection with the administrative enforcement of complaints alleging discrimination under title I and complaints alleging discrimination in employment in violation of the Rehabilitation Act. Although the ADA does not specifically require inclusion of employment complaints under title II in the coordinating mechanisms required by title I, Federal investigations of title II employment complaints will be coordinated on a government-wide basis also. The Department is currently working with the EEOC and other affected Federal agencies to develop effective coordinating mechanisms, and final regulations on this issue will be issued on or before January 26, 1992.

Subpart D--Program Accessibility

Section 35.149 Discrimination Prohibited

Section 35.149 states the general nondiscrimination principle underlying the program accessibility requirements of §§ 35.150 and 35.151.

Section 35.150 Existing Facilities

Consistent with section 204(b) of the Act, this regulation adopts the program accessibility concept found in the section 504 regulations for federally conducted programs or activities (e.g., 28 CFR part 39). The concept of "program accessibility" was first used in the section 504 regulation adopted by the Department of Health, Education, and Welfare for its federally assisted programs and activities in 1977. It allowed recipients to make

their federally assisted programs and activities available to individuals with disabilities without extensive retrofitting of their existing buildings and facilities, by offering those programs through alternative methods. Program accessibility has proven to be a useful approach and was adopted in the regulations issued for programs and activities conducted by Federal Executive agencies. The Act provides that the concept of program access will continue to apply with respect to facilities now in existence, because the cost of retrofitting existing facilities is often prohibitive.

Section 35.150 requires that each service, program, or activity conducted by a public entity, when viewed in its entirety, be readily accessible to and usable by individuals with disabilities. The regulation makes clear, however, that a public entity is not required to make each of its existing facilities accessible (§ 35.150(a)(1)). Unlike title III of the Act, which requires public accommodations to remove architectural barriers where such removal is "readily achievable," or to provide goods and services through alternative methods, where those methods are "readily achievable," title II requires a public entity to make its programs accessible in all cases, except where to do so would result in a fundamental alteration in the nature of the program or in undue financial and administrative burdens. Congress intended the "undue burden" standard in title II to be significantly higher than the "readily achievable" standard in title III. Thus, although title II may not require removal of barriers in some cases where removal would be required under title III, the program access requirement of title II should enable individuals with disabilities to participate in and benefit from the services, programs, or activities of public entities in all but the most unusual cases.

Paragraph (a)(2), which establishes a special limitation on the obligation to ensure program accessibility in historic

preservation programs, is discussed below in connection with paragraph (b).

Paragraph (a)(3), which is taken from the section 504 regulations for federally conducted programs, generally codifies case law that defines the scope of the public entity's obligation to ensure program accessibility. This paragraph provides that, in meeting the program accessibility requirement, a public entity is not required to take any action that would result in a fundamental alteration in the nature of its service, program, or activity or in undue financial and administrative burdens. A similar limitation is provided in § 35.164.

This paragraph does not establish an absolute defense; it does not relieve a public entity of all obligations to individuals with disabilities. Although a public entity is not required to take actions that would result in a fundamental alteration in the nature of a service, program, or activity or in undue financial and administrative burdens, it nevertheless must take any other steps necessary to ensure that individuals with disabilities receive the benefits or services provided by the public entity.

It is the Department's view that compliance with § 35.150(a), like compliance with the corresponding provisions of the section 504 regulations for federally conducted programs, would in most cases not result in undue financial and administrative burdens on a public entity. In determining whether financial and administrative burdens are undue, all public entity resources available for use in the funding and operation of the service, program, or activity should be considered. The burden of proving that compliance with paragraph (a) of § 35.150 would fundamentally alter the nature of a service, program, or activity or would result in undue financial and administrative burdens rests with the public entity.

The decision that compliance would result in such alteration or burdens must be made by the head of the public entity or his or her designee and must be accompanied by a written statement of the reasons for reaching that conclusion. The Department recognizes the difficulty of identifying the official responsible for this determination, given the variety of organizational forms that may be taken by public entities and their components. The intention of this paragraph is that the determination must be made by a high level official, no lower than a Department head, having budgetary authority and responsibility for making spending decisions.

Any person who believes that he or she or any specific class of persons has been injured by the public entity head's decision or failure to make a decision may file a complaint under the compliance procedures established in subpart F.

Paragraph (b)(1) sets forth a number of means by which program accessibility may be achieved, including redesign of equipment, reassignment of services to accessible buildings, and provision of aides.

The Department wishes to clarify that, consistent with longstanding interpretation of section 504, carrying an individual with a disability is considered an ineffective and therefore an unacceptable method for achieving program accessibility. Department of Health, Education, and Welfare, Office of Civil Rights, Policy Interpretation No. 4, 43 FR 36035 (August 14, 1978). Carrying will be permitted only in manifestly exceptional cases, and only if all personnel who are permitted to participate in carrying an individual with a disability are formally instructed on the safest and least humiliating means of carrying. "Manifestly exceptional" cases in which carrying would be permitted might include, for example, programs conducted in unique facilities, such as an oceanographic vessel, for which structural changes and devices necessary to adapt the facility for use by individuals with mobility impairments are unavailable or prohibitively expensive. Carrying is not permitted as an alternative to structural modifications such as installation of a ramp or a chairlift.

In choosing among methods, the public entity shall give priority consideration to those that will be consistent with provision of services in the most integrated setting appropriate to the needs of individuals with disabilities. Structural changes in existing facilities are required only when there is no other feasible way to make the public entity's program accessible. (It should be noted that "structural changes" include all physical changes to a facility; the term does not refer only to changes to structural features, such as removal of or alteration to a load-bearing structural member.) The requirements of § 35.151 for alterations apply to structural changes undertaken to comply with this section. The public entity may comply with the program accessibility requirement by delivering services at alternate accessible sites or making home visits as appropriate.

Historic Preservation Programs

In order to avoid possible conflict between the congressional mandates to preserve historic properties, on the one hand, and to eliminate discrimination against individuals with disabilities on the other, paragraph (a)(2) provides that a public entity is not required to take any action that would threaten or destroy the historic significance of an historic property. The special limitation on program accessibility set forth in paragraph (a)(2) is applicable only to historic preservation programs, as defined in § 35.104, that is, programs that have preservation of historic properties as a primary purpose. Narrow application of the special limitation is justified because of the inherent flexibility of the program accessibility requirement. Where historic preservation is not a primary purpose of the program, the public entity is not required to use a particular facility. It can relocate all or part of its program to an accessible facility, make home visits, or use other standard methods of achieving program accessibility without making structural alterations that might threaten or destroy significant historic features of the historic property. Thus, government programs located in historic properties, such as an historic State capitol, are not excused from the requirement for program access.

Paragraph (a)(2), therefore, will apply only to those programs that uniquely concern the preservation and experience of the historic property itself. Because the primary benefit of an historic preservation program is the experience of the historic property, paragraph (b)(2) requires the public entity to give priority to methods of providing program accessibility that permit individuals with disabilities to have physical access to the historic property. This priority on physical access may also be viewed as a specific application of the general requirement that the public entity administer programs in the most integrated setting appropriate to the needs of qualified individuals with disabilities (§ 35.130(d)). Only when providing physical access would threaten or destroy the historic significance of an historic property, or would result in a fundamental alteration in the nature of the program or in undue financial and administrative burdens, may the public entity adopt alternative methods for providing program accessibility that do not ensure physical access. Examples of some alternative methods are provided in paragraph (b)(2).

Time Periods

Paragraphs (c) and (d) establish time periods for complying with the program accessibility requirement. Like the regulations for federally assisted programs (e.g., 28 CFR 41.57(b)), paragraph (c) requires the public entity to make any necessary structural changes in facilities as soon as practicable, but in no event later than three years after the effective date of this regulation.

The proposed rule provided that, aside from structural changes, all other necessary steps to achieve compliance with this part must be taken within sixty days. The sixty day period was taken from regulations implementing section 504, which generally were effective no more than thirty days after publication. Because this regulation will not be effective until January 26, 1992, the Department has concluded that no additional transition period for non-structural changes is necessary, so the sixty day period has been omitted in the final rule. Of course, this section does not reduce or eliminate any obligations that are already applicable to a public entity under section 504.

Where structural modifications are required, paragraph (d) requires that a transition plan be developed by an entity that employs 50 or more persons, within six months of the effective date of this regulation. The legislative history of title II of the ADA makes it clear that, under title II, "local and state governments are required to provide curb cuts on public streets." Education and Labor report at 84. As the rationale for the provision of curb cuts, the House report explains, "The employment, transportation, and public accommodation sections of (the ADA) would be meaningless if people who use wheelchairs were not afforded the opportunity to travel on and between the streets." Id. Section 35.151(e), which establishes accessibility requirements for new construction and alterations, requires that all newly constructed or altered streets, roads, or highways must contain curb ramps or other sloped areas at any intersection having curbs or other barriers to entry from a street level pedestrian walkway, and all newly constructed or altered street level pedestrian walkways must have curb ramps or other sloped areas at intersections to streets, roads, or highways. A new paragraph (d)(2) has been added to the final rule to clarify the application of the general

requirement for program accessibility to the provision of curb cuts at existing crosswalks. This paragraph requires that the transition plan include a schedule for providing curb ramps or other sloped areas at existing pedestrian walkways, giving priority to walkways serving entities covered by the Act, including State and local government offices and facilities, transportation, public accommodations, and employers, followed by walkways serving other areas. Pedestrian "walkways" include locations where access is required for use of public transportation, such as bus stops that are not located at intersections or crosswalks.

Similarly, a public entity should provide an adequate number of accessible parking spaces in existing parking lots or garages over which it has jurisdiction.

Paragraph (d)(3) provides that, if a public entity has already completed a transition plan required by a regulation implementing section 504, the transition plan required by this part will apply only to those policies and practices that were not covered by the previous transition plan. Some commenters suggested that the transition plan should include all aspects of the public entity's operations, including those that may have been covered by a previous transition plan under section 504. The Department believes that such a duplicative requirement would be inappropriate. Many public entities may find, however, that it will be simpler to include all of their operations in the transition plan than to attempt to identify and exclude specifically those that were addressed in a previous plan. Of course, entities covered under section 504 are not shielded from their obligations under that statute merely because they are included under the transition plan developed under this section.

Section 35.151 New Construction and Alterations

Section 35.151 provides that those buildings that are constructed or altered by, on

behalf of, or for the use of a public entity shall be designed, constructed, or altered to be readily accessible to and usable by individuals with disabilities if the construction was commenced after the effective date of this part. Facilities under design on that date will be governed by this section if the date that bids were invited falls after the effective date. This interpretation is consistent with Federal practice under section 504.

Section 35.151(c) establishes two standards for accessible new construction and alteration. Under paragraph (c), design, construction, or alteration of facilities in conformance with the Uniform Federal Accessibility Standards (UFAS) or with the Americans with Disabilities Act Accessibility Guidelines for Buildings and Facilities (hereinafter ADAAG) shall be deemed to comply with the requirements of this section with respect to those facilities except that, if ADAAG is chosen, the elevator exemption contained at §§ 36.401(d) and 36.404 does not apply. ADAAG is the standard for private buildings and was issued as guidelines by the Architectural and Transportation Barriers Compliance Board (ATBCB) under title III of the ADA. It has been adopted by the Department of Justice and is published as appendix A to the Department's title III rule in today's **Federal Register**. Departures from particular requirements of these standards by the use of other methods shall be permitted when it is clearly evident that equivalent access to the facility or part of the facility is thereby provided. Use of two standards is a departure from the proposed rule.

The proposed rule adopted UFAS as the only interim accessibility standard because that standard was referenced by the regulations implementing section 504 of the Rehabilitation Act promulgated by most Federal funding agencies. It is, therefore, familiar to many State and local government entities subject to this rule. The Department, however, received many comments objecting to the adoption of UFAS. Commenters pointed out that, except for the elevator exemption, UFAS is not as stringent as ADAAG. Others suggested that the standard should be the same to lessen confusion.

Section 204(b) of the Act states that title II regulations must be consistent not only with section 504 regulations but also with "this Act." Based on this provision, the Department has determined that a public entity should be entitled to choose to comply either with ADAAG or UFAS.

Public entities who choose to follow ADAAG, however, are not entitled to the elevator exemption contained in title III of the Act and implemented in the title III regulation at § 36.401(d) for new construction and § 36.404 for alterations. Section 303(b) of title III states that, with some exceptions, elevators are not required in facilities that are less than three stories or have less than 3000 square feet per story. The section 504 standard, UFAS, contains no such exemption. Section 501 of the ADA makes clear that nothing in the Act may be construed to apply a lesser standard to public entities than the standards applied under section 504. Because permitting the elevator exemption would clearly result in application of a lesser standard than that applied under section 504, paragraph (c) states that the elevator exemption does not apply when public entities choose to follow ADAAG. Thus, a two-story courthouse, whether built according to UFAS or ADAAG, must be constructed with an elevator. It should be noted that Congress did not include an elevator exemption for public transit facilities covered by subtitle B of title II, which covers public transportation provided by public entities, providing further evidence that Congress intended that public buildings have elevators.

Section 504 of the ADA requires the ATBCB to issue supplemental Minimum Guidelines and Requirements for Accessible Design of buildings and facilities subject to the Act, including title II.

Section 204(c) of the ADA provides that the Attorney General shall promulgate regulations implementing title II that are consistent with the ATBCB's ADA guidelines. The ATBCB has announced its intention to issue title II guidelines in the future. The Department anticipates that, after the ATBCB's title II guidelines have been published, this rule will be amended to adopt new accessibility standards consistent with the ATBCB's rulemaking. Until that time, however, public entities will have a choice of following UFAS or ADAAG, without the elevator exemption.

Existing buildings leased by the public entity after the effective date of this part are not required by the regulation to meet accessibility standards simply by virtue of being leased. They are subject, however, to the program accessibility standard for existing facilities in § 35.150. To the extent the buildings are newly constructed or altered, they must also meet the new construction and alteration requirements of § 35.151.

The Department received many comments urging that the Department require that public entities lease only accessible buildings. Federal practice under section 504 has always treated newly leased buildings as subject to the existing facility program accessibility standard. Section 204(b) of the Act states that, in the area of "program accessibility, existing facilities," the title II regulations must be consistent with section 504 regulations. Thus, the Department has adopted the section 504 principles for these types of leased buildings. Unlike the construction of new buildings where architectural barriers can be avoided at little or no cost, the application of new construction standards to an existing building being leased raises the same prospect of retrofitting buildings as the use of an existing Federal facility, and the same program accessibility standard should apply to both owned and leased existing buildings. Similarly, requiring that public entities only lease accessible space

would significantly restrict the options of State and local governments in seeking leased space, which would be particularly burdensome in rural or sparsely populated areas.

On the other hand, the more accessible the leased space is, the fewer structural modifications will be required in the future for particular employees whose disabilities may necessitate barrier removal as a reasonable accommodation. Pursuant to the requirements for leased buildings contained in the Minimum Guidelines and Requirements for Accessible Design published under the Architectural Barriers Act by the ATBCB, 36 CFR 1190.34, the Federal Government may not lease a building unless it contains (1) One accessible route from an accessible entrance to those areas in which the principal activities for which the building is leased are conducted, (2) accessible toilet facilities, and (3) accessible parking facilities, if a parking area is included within the lease (36 CFR 1190.34). Although these requirements are not applicable to buildings leased by public entities covered by this regulation, such entities are encouraged to look for the most accessible space available to lease and to attempt to find space complying at least with these minimum Federal requirements.

Section 35.151(d) gives effect to the intent of Congress, expressed in section 504(c) of the Act, that this part recognize the national interest in preserving significant historic structures. Commenters criticized the Department's use of descriptive terms in the proposed rule that are different from those used in the ADA to describe eligible historic properties. In addition, some commenters criticized the Department's decision to use the concept of "substantially impairing" the historic features of a property, which is a concept employed in regulations implementing section 504 of the Rehabilitation Act of 1973. Those commenters recommended that the Department adopt the criteria of "adverse effect" published by the Advisory Council on Historic Preservation under the National Historic Preservation Act, 36 CFR 800.9, as the standard for determining whether an historic property may be altered.

The Department agrees with these comments to the extent that they suggest that the language of the rule should conform to the language employed by Congress in the ADA. A definition of "historic property," drawn from section 504 of the ADA, has been added to § 35.104 to clarify that the term applies to those properties listed or eligible for listing in the National Register of Historic Places, or properties designated as historic under State or local law.

The Department intends that the exception created by this section be applied only in those very rare situations in which it is not possible to provide access to an historic property using the special access provisions established by UFAS and ADAAG. Therefore, paragraph (d)(1) of § 35.151 has been revised to clearly state that alterations to historic properties shall comply, to the maximum extent feasible, with section 4.1.7 of UFAS or section 4.1.7 of ADAAG. Paragraph (d)(2) has been revised to provide that, if it has been determined under the procedures established in UFAS and ADAAG that it is not feasible to provide physical access to an historic property in a manner that will not threaten or destroy the historic significance of the property, alternative methods of access shall be provided pursuant to the requirements of § 35.150.

In response to comments, the Department has added to the final rule a new paragraph (e) setting out the requirements of § 36.151 as applied to curb ramps. Paragraph (e) is taken from the statement contained in the preamble to the proposed rule that all newly constructed or altered streets, roads, and highways must contain curb ramps at any intersection having curbs or other barriers to entry from a street level pedestrian walkway, and that all newly constructed or altered

street level pedestrian walkways must have curb ramps at intersections to streets, roads, or highways.

Subpart E—Communications

Section 35.160 General

Section 35.160 requires the public entity to take such steps as may be necessary to ensure that communications with applicants, participants, and members of the public with disabilities are as effective as communications with others.

Paragraph (b)(1) requires the public entity to furnish appropriate auxiliary aids and services when necessary to afford an individual with a disability an equal opportunity to participate in, and enjoy the benefits of, the public entity's service, program, or activity. The public entity must provide an opportunity for individuals with disabilities to request the auxiliary aids and services of their choice. This expressed choice shall be given primary consideration by the public entity (§ 35.160(b)(2)). The public entity shall honor the choice unless it can demonstrate that another effective means of communication exists or that use of the means chosen would not be required under § 35.164.

Deference to the request of the individual with a disability is desirable because of the range of disabilities, the variety of auxiliary aids and services, and different circumstances requiring effective communication. For instance, some courtrooms are now equipped for "computer-assisted transcripts," which allow virtually instantaneous transcripts of courtroom argument and testimony to appear on displays. Such a system might be an effective auxiliary aid or service for a person who is deaf or has a hearing loss who uses speech to communicate, but may be useless for someone who uses sign language.

Although in some circumstances a notepad and written materials may be sufficient to permit effective communication, in other circumstances they may not be sufficient. For

example, a qualified interpreter may be necessary when the information being communicated is complex, or is exchanged for a lengthy period of time. Generally, factors to be considered in determining whether an interpreter is required include the context in which the communication is taking place, the number of people involved, and the importance of the communication.

Several commenters asked that the rule clarify that the provision of readers is sometimes necessary to ensure access to a public entity's services, programs or activities. Reading devices or readers should be provided when necessary for equal participation and opportunity to benefit from any governmental service, program, or activity, such as reviewing public documents, examining demonstrative evidence, and filling out voter registration forms or forms needed to receive public benefits. The importance of providing qualified readers for examinations administered by public entities is discussed under § 35.130. Reading devices and readers are appropriate auxiliary aids and services where necessary to permit an individual with a disability to participate in or benefit from a service, program, or activity.

Section 35.160(b)(2) of the proposed rule, which provided that a public entity need not furnish individually prescribed devices, readers for personal use or study, or other devices of a personal nature, has been deleted in favor of a new section in the final rule on personal devices and services (see § 35.135).

In response to comments, the term "auxiliary aids and services" is used in place of "auxiliary aids" in the final rule. This phrase better reflects the range of aids and services that may be required under this section.

A number of comments raised questions about the extent of a public entity's obligation to provide access to television programming for persons with hearing impairments. Television and videotape programming produced by public entities are covered by this section. Access to audio portions of such programming may be provided by closed captioning.

Section 35.161 Telecommunication Devices for the Deaf (TDD's)

Section 35.161 requires that, where a public entity communicates with applicants and beneficiaries by telephone, TDD's or equally effective telecommunication systems be used to communicate with individuals with impaired speech or hearing.

Problems arise when a public entity which does not have a TDD needs to communicate with an individual who uses a TDD or vice versa. Title IV of the ADA addresses this problem by requiring establishment of telephone relay services to permit communications between individuals who communicate by TDD and individuals who communicate by the telephone alone. The relay services required by title IV would involve a relay operator using both a standard telephone and a TDD to type the voice messages to the TDD user and read the TDD messages to the standard telephone user.

Section 204(b) of the ADA requires that the regulation implementing title II with respect to communications be consistent with the Department's regulation implementing section 504 for its federally conducted programs and activities at 28 CFR part 39. Section 35.161, which is taken from § 39.160(a)(2) of that regulation, requires the use of TDD's or equally effective telecommunication systems for communication with people who use TDD's. Of course, where relay services, such as those required by title IV of the ADA are available, a public entity may use those services to meet the requirements of this section.

Many commenters were concerned that public entities should not rely heavily on the establishment of relay services. The commenters explained that while relay services would be of

vast benefit to both public entities and individuals who use TDD's, the services are not sufficient to provide access to all telephone services. First, relay systems do not provide effective access to the increasingly popular automated systems that require the caller to respond by pushing a button on a touch tone phone. Second, relay systems cannot operate fast enough to convey messages on answering machines, or to permit a TDD user to leave a recorded message. Third, communication through relay systems may not be appropriate in cases of crisis lines pertaining to rape, domestic violence, child abuse, and drugs. The Department believes that it is more appropriate for the Federal Communications Commission to address these issues in its rulemaking under title IV.

Some commenters requested that those entities with frequent contacts with clients who use TDD's have on-site TDD's to provide for direct communication between the entity and the individual. The Department encourages those entities that have extensive telephone contact with the public such as city halls, public libraries, and public aid offices, to have TDD's to insure more immediate access. Where the provision of telephone service is a major function of the entity, TDD's should be available.

Section 35.162 Telephone Emergency Services

Many public entities provide telephone emergency services by which individuals can seek immediate assistance from police, fire, ambulance, and other emergency services. These telephone emergency services—including "911" services—are clearly an important public service whose reliability can be a matter of life or death. The legislative history of title II specifically reflects congressional intent that public entities must ensure that telephone emergency services, including 911 services, be accessible to persons with impaired hearing and speech through telecommunication technology (Conference report

at 67; Education and Labor report at 84-85).

Proposed § 35.162 mandated that public entities provide emergency telephone services to persons with disabilities that are "functionally equivalent" to voice services provided to others. Many commenters urged the Department to revise the section to make clear that direct access to telephone emergency services is required by title II of the ADA as indicated by the legislative history (Conference report at 67-68; Education and Labor report at 85). In response, the final rule mandates "direct access," instead of "access that is functionally equivalent" to that provided to all other telephone users. Telephone emergency access through a third party or through a relay service would not satisfy the requirement for direct access.

Several commenters asked about a separate seven-digit emergency call number for the 911 services. The requirement for direct access disallows the use of a separate seven-digit number where 911 service is available. Separate seven-digit emergency call numbers would be unfamiliar to many individuals and also more burdensome to use. A standard emergency 911 number is easier to remember and would save valuable time spent in searching in telephone books for a local seven-digit emergency number.

Many commenters requested the establishment of minimum standards of service (e.g., the quantity and location of TDD's and computer modems needed in a given emergency center). Instead of establishing these scoping requirements, the Department has established a performance standard through the mandate for direct access.

Section 35.162 requires public entities to take appropriate steps, including equipping their emergency systems with modern technology, as may be necessary to promptly receive and respond to a call from users of TDD's and computer modems. Entities are allowed the flexibility to determine what is the appropriate technology for their particular needs. In order to avoid mandating use of particular technologies that may become outdated, the Department has eliminated the references to the Baudot and ASCII formats in the proposed rule.

Some commenters requested that the section require the installation of a voice amplification device on the handset of the dispatcher's telephone to amplify the dispatcher's voice. In an emergency, a person who has a hearing loss may be using a telephone that does not have an amplification device. Installation of speech amplification devices on the handsets of the dispatchers' telephones would respond to that situation. The Department encourages their use.

Several commenters emphasized the need for proper maintenance of TDD's used in telephone emergency services. Section 35.133, which mandates maintenance of accessible features, requires public entities to maintain in operable working condition TDD's and other devices that provide direct access to the emergency system.

Section 35.163 Information and Signage

Section 35.163(a) requires the public entity to provide information to individuals with disabilities concerning accessible services, activities, and facilities. Paragraph (b) requires the public entity to provide signage at all inaccessible entrances to each of its facilities that directs users to an accessible entrance or to a location with information about accessible facilities.

Several commenters requested that, where TDD-equipped pay phones or portable TDD's exist, clear signage should be posted indicating the location of the TDD. The Department believes that this is required by paragraph (a). In addition, the Department recommends that, in large buildings that house TDD's, directional signage indicating the location of available TDD's should be placed adjacent to banks of

telephones that do not contain a TDD.

Section 35.164 Duties

Section 35.164, like paragraph (a)(3) of § 35.150, is taken from the section 504 regulations for federally conducted programs. Like paragraph (a)(3), it limits the obligation of the public entity to ensure effective communication in accordance with Davis and the circuit court opinions interpreting it. It also includes specific requirements for determining the existence of undue financial and administrative burdens. The preamble discussion of § 35.150(a) regarding that determination is applicable to this section and further explains the public entity's obligation to comply with §§ 35.160-35.164. Because of the essential nature of the services provided by telephone emergency systems, the Department assumes that § 35.164 will rarely be applied to § 35.162.

Subpart F—Compliance Procedures

Subpart F sets out the procedures for administrative enforcement of this part. Section 203 of the Act provides that the remedies, procedures, and rights set forth in section 505 of the Rehabilitation Act of 1973 (29 U.S.C. 794a) for enforcement of section 504 of the Rehabilitation Act, which prohibits discrimination on the basis of handicap in programs and activities that receive Federal financial assistance, shall be the remedies, procedures, and rights for enforcement of title II. Section 505, in turn, incorporates by reference the remedies, procedures, and rights set forth in title VI of the Civil Rights Act of 1964 (42 U.S.C. 2000d to 2000d-4a). Title VI, which prohibits discrimination on the basis of race, color, or national origin in federally assisted programs, is enforced by the Federal agencies that provide the Federal financial assistance to the covered programs and activities in question. If voluntary compliance cannot be achieved, Federal agencies enforce title VI either by the

termination of Federal funds to a program that is found to discriminate, following an administrative hearing, or by a referral to this Department for judicial enforcement.

Title II of the ADA extended the requirements of section 504 to all services, programs, and activities of State and local governments, not only those that receive Federal financial assistance. The House Committee on Education and Labor explained the enforcement provisions as follows:

It is the Committee's intent that administrative enforcement of section 202 of the legislation should closely parallel the Federal government's experience with section 504 of the Rehabilitation Act of 1973. The Attorney General should use section 504 enforcement procedures and the Department's coordination role under Executive Order 12250 as models for regulation in this area.

The Committee envisions that the Department of Justice will identify appropriate Federal agencies to oversee compliance activities for State and local governments. As with section 504, these Federal agencies, including the Department of Justice, will receive, investigate, and where possible, resolve complaints of discrimination. If a Federal agency is unable to resolve a complaint by voluntary means, * * * the major enforcement sanction for the Federal government will be referral of cases by these Federal agencies to the Department of Justice.

The Department of Justice may then proceed to file suits in Federal district court. As with section 504, there is also a private right of action for persons with disabilities, which includes the full panoply of remedies. Again, consistent with section 504, it is not the Committee's intent that persons with disabilities need to exhaust Federal administrative remedies before exercising their private right of action.

Education & Labor report at 98. See also S. Rep. No. 116, 101st Cong., 1st Sess., at 57-58 (1989).

Subpart F effectuates the congressional intent by deferring to section 504 procedures where those procedures are applicable, that is, where a Federal agency has jurisdiction under section 504 by virtue of its provision of Federal financial assistance to the program or activity in which the discrimination is alleged to have occurred. Deferral to the 504 procedures also makes the sanction of fund termination available where necessary to achieve compliance. Because the Civil Rights Restoration Act (Pub. L. 100-259) extended the application of section 504 to all of the operations of the public entity receiving the Federal financial assistance, many activities of State and local governments are already covered by section 504. The procedures in subpart F apply to complaints concerning services, programs, and activities of public entities that are covered by the ADA.

Subpart G designates the Federal agencies responsible for enforcing the ADA with respect to specific components of State and local government. It does not, however, displace existing jurisdiction under section 504 of the various funding agencies. Individuals may still file discrimination complaints against recipients of Federal financial assistance with the agencies that provide that assistance, and the funding agencies will continue to process those complaints under their existing procedures for enforcing section 504. The substantive standards adopted in this part for title II of the ADA are generally the same as those required under section 504 for federally assisted programs, and public entities covered by the ADA are also covered by the requirements of section 504 to the extent that they receive Federal financial assistance. To the extent that title II provides greater protection to the rights of individuals with disabilities, however, the funding agencies will also apply the substantive requirements established under title II and this part in processing complaints covered by both this part and section 504, except that fund termination procedures may be used only for violations of section 504.

Subpart F establishes the procedures to be followed by the agencies designated in subpart G for processing complaints against State and local government entities when the designated agency does not have jurisdiction under section 504.

Section 35.170 Complaints

Section 35.170 provides that any individual who believes that he or she or a specific class of individuals has been subjected to discrimination on the basis of disability by a public entity may, by himself or herself or by an authorized representative, file a complaint under this part within 180 days of the date of the alleged discrimination, unless the time for filing is extended by the agency for good cause. Although § 35.107 requires public entities that employ 50 or more persons to establish grievance procedures for resolution of complaints, exhaustion of those procedures is not a prerequisite to filing a complaint under this section. If a complainant chooses to follow the public entity's grievance procedures, however, any resulting delay may be considered good cause for extending the time allowed for filing a complaint under this part.

Filing the complaint with any Federal agency will satisfy the requirement for timely filing. As explained below, a complaint filed with an agency that has jurisdiction under section 504 will be processed under the agency's procedures for enforcing section 504.

Some commenters objected to the complexity of allowing complaints to be filed with different agencies. The multiplicity of enforcement jurisdiction is the result of following the statutorily mandated enforcement scheme. The Department has, however, attempted to simplify procedures for complainants by making the Federal agency that receives the complaint responsible for referring it to an appropriate agency.

The Department has also added a new paragraph (c) to this section providing that a complaint may be filed with any agency designated under subpart G of this part, or with any agency that provides funding to the public entity that is the subject of the complaint, or with the Department of Justice. Under § 35.171(a)(2), the Department of Justice will refer complaints for which it does not have jurisdiction under section 504 to an agency that does have jurisdiction under section 504, or to the agency designated under subpart G as responsible for complaints filed against the public entity that is the subject of the complaint or in the case of an employment complaint that is also subject to title I of the Act, to the Equal Employment Opportunity Commission. Complaints filed with the Department of Justice may be sent to the Coordination and Review Section, P.O. Box 66118, Civil Rights Division, U.S. Department of Justice, Washington, DC 20035-6118.

Section 35.171 Acceptance of Complaints

Section 35.171 establishes procedures for determining jurisdiction and responsibility for processing complaints against public entities. The final rule provides complainants an opportunity to file with the Federal funding agency of their choice. If that agency does not have jurisdiction under section 504, however, and is not the agency designated under subpart G as responsible for that public entity, the agency must refer the complaint to the Department of Justice, which will be responsible for referring it either to an agency that does have jurisdiction under section 504 or to the appropriate designated agency, or in the case of an employment complaint that is also subject to title I of the Act, to the Equal Employment Opportunity Commission.

Whenever an agency receives a complaint over which it has jurisdiction under section 504, it will process the complaint under its section 504 procedures. When the agency designated under subpart G receives a complaint for which it does not have jurisdiction under section 504, it will treat the complaint as an ADA complaint under the procedures established in this subpart.

Section 35.171 also describes agency responsibilities for the processing of employment complaints. As described in connection with § 35.140, additional procedures regarding the coordination of employment complaints will be established in a coordination regulation issued by DOJ and EEOC. Agencies with jurisdiction under section 504 for complaints alleging employment discrimination also covered by title I will follow the procedures established by the coordination regulation for those complaints. Complaints covered by title I but not section 504 will be referred to the EEOC, and complaints covered by this part but not title I will be processed under the procedures in this part.

Section 35.172 Resolution of Complaints

Section 35.172 requires the designated agency to either resolve the complaint or issue to the complainant and the public entity a Letter of Findings containing findings of fact and conclusions of law and a description of a remedy for each violation found.

The Act requires the Department of Justice to establish administrative procedures for resolution of complaints, but does not require complainants to exhaust these administrative remedies. The Committee Reports make clear that Congress intended to provide a private right of action with the full panoply of remedies for individual victims of discrimination. Because the Act does not require exhaustion of administrative remedies, the complainant may elect to proceed with a private suit at any time.

Section 35.173 Voluntary Compliance Agreements

Section 35.173 requires the agency to attempt to resolve all complaints in which it finds noncompliance through voluntary compliance agreements enforceable by the Attorney General.

Section 35.174 Referral

Section 35.174 provides for referral of the matter to the Department of Justice if the agency is unable to obtain voluntary compliance.

Section 35.175 Attorney's Fees

Section 35.175 states that courts are authorized to award attorneys fees, including litigation expenses and costs, as provided in section 505 of the Act. Litigation expenses include items such as expert witness fees, travel expenses, etc. The Judiciary Committee Report specifies that such items are included under the rubric of "attorneys fees" and not "costs" so that such expenses will be assessed against a plaintiff only under the standard set forth in *Christiansburg Garment Co. v. Equal Employment Opportunity Commission*, 434 U.S. 412 (1978). (Judiciary report at 73.)

Section 35.176 Alternative Means of Dispute Resolution

Section 35.176 restates section 513 of the Act, which encourages use of alternative means of dispute resolution.

Section 35.177 Effect of Unavailability of Technical Assistance

Section 35.177 explains that, as provided in section 506(e) of the Act, a public entity is not excused from compliance with the requirements of this part because of any failure to receive technical assistance.

Section 35.178 State Immunity

Section 35.178 restates the provision of section 502 of the Act that a State is not immune under the eleventh amendment to the Constitution of the United States from an action in Federal or State court for violations of the Act, and that the same remedies are available for any such violations as are available in an action against an entity other than a State.

Subpart G—Designated Agencies

Section 35.190 Designated Agencies

Subpart G designates the Federal agencies responsible for investigating complaints under this part. At least 26 agencies currently administer programs of Federal financial assistance that are subject to the nondiscrimination requirements of section 504 as well as other civil rights statutes. A majority of these agencies administer modest programs of Federal financial assistance and/or devote minimal resources exclusively to "external" civil rights enforcement activities. Under Executive Order 12250, the Department of Justice has encouraged the use of delegation agreements under which certain civil rights compliance responsibilities for a class of recipients funded by more than one agency are delegated by an agency or agencies to a "lead" agency. For example, many agencies that fund institutions of higher education have signed agreements that designate the Department of Education as the "lead" agency for this class of recipients.

The use of delegation agreements reduces overlap and duplication of effort, and thereby strengthens overall civil rights enforcement. However, the use of these agreements to date generally has been limited to education and health care recipients. These classes of recipients are funded by numerous agencies and the logical connection to a lead agency is clear (e.g., the Department of Education for colleges and universities, and the Department of Health and Human Services for hospitals).

The ADA's expanded coverage of State and local government operations further complicates the process of establishing Federal agency jurisdiction for the purpose of investigating complaints of discrimination on the basis of disability. Because all operations of public entities now are covered irrespective of the presence or absence of Federal financial assistance, many additional State and local government functions and organizations now are subject to Federal jurisdiction. In some cases, there is no historical or single clear-cut subject matter relationship with a Federal agency as was the case in the education example described above. Further, the 33,000 governmental jurisdictions subject to the ADA differ greatly in their organization, making a detailed and workable division of Federal agency jurisdiction by individual State, county, or municipal entity unrealistic.

This regulation applies the delegation concept to the investigation of complaints of discrimination on the basis of disability by public entities under the ADA. It designates eight agencies, rather than all agencies currently administering programs of Federal financial assistance, as responsible for investigating complaints under this part. These "designated agencies" generally have the largest civil rights compliance staffs, the most experience in complaint investigations and disability issues, and broad yet clear subject area responsibilities. This division of responsibilities is made functionally rather than by public entity type or name designation. For example, all entities (regardless of their title) that exercise responsibilities, regulate, or administer services or programs relating to lands and natural resources fall within the jurisdiction of the Department of Interior.

Complaints under this part will be investigated by the designated agency most closely related to the functions exercised by the governmental component against which the complaint is lodged. For example, a complaint against a State medical board, where such a board is a recognizable entity, will be investigated by the Department of Health and Human Services (the designated agency for regulatory activities relating to the provision of health care), even if the board is part of a general umbrella department of planning and regulation (for which the Department of Justice is the designated agency). If two or

more agencies have apparent responsibility over a complaint, § 35.190(c) provides that the Assistant Attorney General shall determine which one of the agencies shall be the designated agency for purposes of that complaint.

Thirteen commenters, including four proposed designated agencies, addressed the Department of Justice's identification in the proposed regulation of nine "designated agencies" to investigate complaints under this part. Most comments addressed the proposed specific delegations to the various individual agencies. The Department of Justice agrees with several commenters who pointed out that responsibility for "historic and cultural preservation" functions appropriately belongs with the Department of Interior rather than the Department of Education. The Department of Justice also agrees with the Department of Education that "museums" more appropriately should be delegated to the Department of Interior, and that "preschool and daycare programs" more appropriately should be assigned to the Department of Health and Human Services, rather than to the Department of Education. The final rule reflects these decisions.

The Department of Commerce opposed its listing as the designated agency for "commerce and industry, including general economic development, banking and finance, consumer protection, insurance, and small business". The Department of Commerce cited its lack of a substantial existing section 504 enforcement program and experience with many of the specific functions to be delegated. The Department of Justice accedes to the Department of Commerce's position, and has assigned itself as the designated agency for these functions.

In response to a comment from the Department of Health and Human Services, the regulation's category of "medical and nursing schools" has been clarified to read "schools of medicine, dentistry, nursing, and other health-

related fields". Also in response to a comment from the Department of Health and Human Services, "correctional institutions" have been specifically added to the public safety and administration of justice functions assigned to the Department of Justice.

The regulation also assigns the Department of Justice as the designated agency responsible for all State and local government functions not assigned to other designated agencies. The Department of Justice, under an agreement with the Department of the Treasury, continues to receive and coordinate the investigation of complaints filed under the Revenue Sharing Act. This entitlement program, which was terminated in 1986, provided civil rights compliance jurisdiction for a wide variety of complaints regarding the use of Federal funds to support various general activities of local governments. In the absence of any similar program of Federal financial assistance administered by another Federal agency, placement of designated agency responsibilities for miscellaneous and otherwise undesignated functions with the Department of Justice is an appropriate continuation of current practice.

The Department of Education objected to the proposed rule's inclusion of the functional area of "arts and humanities" within its responsibilities, and the Department of Housing and Urban Development objected to its proposed designation as responsible for activities relating to rent control, the real estate industry, and housing code enforcement. The Department has deleted these areas from the lists assigned to the Departments of Education and Housing and Urban Development, respectively, and has added a new paragraph (c) to § 35.190, which provides that the Department of Justice may assign responsibility for components of State or local governments that exercise responsibilities, regulate, or administer services, programs, or activities relating to functions not assigned to specific designated agencies by paragraph (b) of this section to other appropriate agencies. The Department believes that this approach will provide more flexibility in determining the appropriate agency for investigation of complaints involving those components of State and local governments not specifically addressed by the listings in paragraph (b). As provided in §§ 35.170 and 35.171, complaints filed with the Department of Justice will be referred to the appropriate agency.

Several commenters proposed a stronger role for the Department of Justice, especially with respect to the receipt and assignment of complaints, and the overall monitoring of the effectiveness of the enforcement activities of Federal agencies. As discussed above, §§ 35.170 and 35.171 have been revised to provide for referral of complaints by the Department of Justice to appropriate enforcement agencies. Also, language has been added to § 35.190(a) of the final regulation stating that the Assistant Attorney General shall provide policy guidance and interpretations to designated agencies to ensure the consistent and effective implementation of this part.

List of Subjects in 28 CFR Part 35

Administrative practice and procedure, Alcoholism, Americans with disabilities, Buildings, Civil rights, Drug abuse, Handicapped, Historic preservation, Intergovernmental relations, Reporting and recordkeeping requirements.

By the authority vested in me as Attorney General by 28 U.S.C. 509, 510, 5 U.S.C. 301, and section 204 of the Americans with Disabilities Act, and for the reasons set forth in the preamble, chapter I of title 28 of the Code of Federal Regulations is amended by adding a new part 35 to read as follows:

PART 35-- NONDISCRIMINATION ON THE BASIS OF DISABILITY IN STATE AND LOCAL GOVERNMENT SERVICES

Subpart A--General

Sec.
35.101 Purpose.
35.102 Application.
35.103 Relationship to other laws.
35.104 Definitions.
35.105 Self-evaluation.
35.106 Notice.
35.107 Designation of responsible employee and adoption of grievance procedures.
35.108-35.129 [Reserved]

Subpart B--General Requirements

35.130 General prohibitions against discrimination.
35.131 Illegal use of drugs.
35.132 Smoking.
35.133 Maintenance of accessible features.
35.134 Retaliation or coercion.
35.135 Personal devices and services.
35.136-35.139 [Reserved]

Subpart C--Employment

35.140 Employment discrimination prohibited.
35.141-35.148 [Reserved]

Subpart D--Program Accessibility

35.149 Discrimination prohibited.
35.150 Existing facilities.
35.151 New construction and alterations.
35.152-35.159 [Reserved]

Subpart E--Communications

35.160 General.
35.161 Telecommunication devices for the deaf (TDD's).
35.162 Telephone emergency services.
35.163 Information and signage.
35.164 Duties.
35.165-35.169 [Reserved]

Subpart F--Compliance Procedures

35.170 Complaints.
35.171 Acceptance of complaints.
35.172 Resolution of complaints.
35.173 Voluntary compliance agreements.
35.174 Referral.
35.175 Attorney's fees.
35.176 Alternative means of dispute resolution.
35.177 Effect of unavailability of technical assistance.
35.178 State immunity.
35.179-35.189 [Reserved]

Subpart G--Designated Agencies

5.190 Designated agencies.
35.191-35.999 [Reserved]

Appendix A to Part 35--Preamble to Regulation on Nondiscrimination on the Basis of Disability in State and Local Government Services (Published July 26, 1991)
Authority: 5 U.S.C. 301; 28 U.S.C. 509, 510; Title II, Pub. L. 101-336 (42 U.S.C. 12134).

Subpart A--General

35.101 Purpose.

The purpose of this part is to effectuate subtitle A of title II of the Americans with Disabilities Act of 1990 (42 U.S.C. 12131), which prohibits discrimination on the basis of disability by public entities.

§ 35.102 Application.

(a) Except as provided in paragraph (b) of this section, this part applies to all services, programs, and activities provided or made available by public entities.

(b) To the extent that public transportation services, programs, and activities of public entities are covered by subtitle B of title II of the ADA (42 U.S.C. 12141), they are not subject to the requirements of this part.

§ 35.103 Relationship to other laws.

(a) *Rule of interpretation.* Except as otherwise provided in this part, this part shall not be construed to apply a lesser standard than the standards applied under title V of the Rehabilitation Act of 1973 (29 U.S.C. 791) or the regulations issued by Federal agencies pursuant to that title.

(b) *Other laws.* This part does not invalidate or limit the remedies, rights, and procedures of any other Federal laws, or State or local laws (including State common law) that provide greater or equal protection for the rights of individuals with disabilities or individuals associated with them.

§ 35.104 Definitions.

For purposes of this part, the term—*Act* means the Americans with Disabilities Act (Pub. L. 101-336, 104 Stat. 327, 42 U.S.C. 12101-12213 and 47 U.S.C. 225 and 611).

Assistant Attorney General means the Assistant Attorney General, Civil Rights Division, United States Department of Justice.

Auxiliary aids and services includes—

(1) Qualified interpreters, notetakers, transcription services, written materials, telephone handset amplifiers, assistive listening devices, assistive listening systems, telephones compatible with hearing aids, closed caption decoders, open and closed captioning, telecommunications devices for deaf persons (TDD's), videotext displays, or other effective methods of making aurally delivered materials available to individuals with hearing impairments;

(2) Qualified readers, taped texts, audio recordings, Brailled materials, large print materials, or other effective methods of making visually delivered materials available to individuals with visual impairments;

(3) Acquisition or modification of equipment or devices; and

(4) Other similar services and actions.

Complete complaint means a written statement that contains the complainant's name and address and describes the public entity's alleged discriminatory action in sufficient detail to inform the agency of the nature and date of the alleged violation of this part. It shall be signed by the complainant or by someone authorized to do so on his or her behalf. Complaints filed on behalf of classes or third parties shall describe or identify (by name, if possible) the alleged victims of discrimination.

Current illegal use of drugs means illegal use of drugs that occurred recently enough to justify a reasonable belief that a person's drug use is current or that continuing use is a real and ongoing problem.

Designated agency means the Federal agency designated under subpart G of this part to oversee compliance activities under this part for particular components of State and local governments.

Disability means, with respect to an individual, a physical or mental impairment that substantially limits one or more of the major life activities of such individual; a record of such an impairment; or being regarded as having such an impairment.

(1)(i) The phrase *physical or mental impairment* means—

(A) Any physiological disorder or condition, cosmetic disfigurement, or anatomical loss affecting one or more of the following body systems: Neurological, musculoskeletal, special sense organs, respiratory (including speech organs), cardiovascular, reproductive, digestive, genitourinary, hemic and lymphatic, skin, and endocrine;

(B) Any mental or psychological disorder such as mental retardation, organic brain syndrome, emotional or mental illness, and specific learning disabilities.

(ii) The phrase *physical or mental impairment* includes, but is not limited to, such contagious and noncontagious diseases and conditions as orthopedic, visual, speech and hearing impairments, cerebral palsy, epilepsy, muscular dystrophy, multiple sclerosis, cancer, heart disease, diabetes, mental retardation, emotional illness, specific learning disabilities, HIV disease (whether symptomatic or asymptomatic), tuberculosis, drug addiction, and alcoholism.

(iii) The phrase *physical or mental impairment* does not include homosexuality or bisexuality.

(2) The phrase *major life activities* means functions such as caring for one's self, performing manual tasks, walking, seeing, hearing, speaking, breathing, learning, and working.

(3) The phrase *has a record of such an impairment* means has a history of, or has been misclassified as having, a mental or physical impairment that substantially limits one or more major life activities.

(4) The phrase *is regarded as having an impairment* means—

(i) Has a physical or mental impairment that does not substantially limit major life activities but that is treated by a public entity as constituting such a limitation;

(ii) Has a physical or mental impairment that substantially limits major life activities only as a result of the attitudes of others toward such impairment; or

(iii) Has none of the impairments defined in paragraph (1) of this definition but is treated by a public entity as having such an impairment.

(5) The term *disability* does not include—

(i) Transvestism, transsexualism, pedophilia, exhibitionism, voyeurism, gender identity disorders not resulting from physical impairments, or other sexual behavior disorders;

(ii) Compulsive gambling, kleptomania, or pyromania; or

(iii) Psychoactive substance use disorders resulting from current illegal use of drugs.

Drug means a controlled substance, as defined in schedules I through V of section 202 of the Controlled Substances Act (21 U.S.C. 812).

Facility means all or any portion of buildings, structures, sites, complexes, equipment, rolling stock or other conveyances, roads, walks, passageways, parking lots, or other real or personal property, including the site where the building, property, structure, or equipment is located.

Historic preservation programs means programs conducted by a public entity that have preservation of historic properties as a primary purpose.

Historic Properties means those properties that are listed or eligible for listing in the National Register of Historic Places or properties designated as historic under State or local law.

Illegal use of drugs means the use of one or more drugs, the possession or distribution of which is unlawful under the Controlled Substances Act (21

U.S.C. 812). The term *illegal use of drugs* does not include the use of a drug taken under supervision by a licensed health care professional, or other uses authorized by the Controlled Substances Act or other provisions of Federal law.

Individual with a disability means a person who has a disability. The term *individual with a disability* does not include an individual who is currently engaging in the illegal use of drugs, when the public entity acts on the basis of such use.

Public entity means—

(1) Any State or local government;

(2) Any department, agency, special purpose district, or other instrumentality of a State or States or local government; and

(3) The National Railroad Passenger Corporation, and any commuter authority (as defined in section 103(8) of the Rail Passenger Service Act).

Qualified individual with a disability means an individual with a disability who, with or without reasonable modifications to rules, policies, or practices, the removal of architectural, communication, or transportation barriers, or the provision of auxiliary aids and services, meets the essential eligibility requirements for the receipt of services or the participation in programs or activities provided by a public entity.

Qualified interpreter means an interpreter who is able to interpret effectively, accurately, and impartially both receptively and expressively, using any necessary specialized vocabulary.

Section 504 means section 504 of the Rehabilitation Act of 1973 (Pub. L. 93-112, 87 Stat. 394 (29 U.S.C. 794)), as amended.

State means each of the several States, the District of Columbia, the Commonwealth of Puerto Rico, Guam, American Samoa, the Virgin Islands, the Trust Territory of the Pacific Islands, and the Commonwealth of the Northern Mariana Islands.

§ 35.105 Self-evaluation.

(a) A public entity shall, within one year of the effective date of this part, evaluate its current services, policies, and practices, and the effects thereof, that do not or may not meet the requirements of this part and, to the extent modification of any such services, policies, and practices is required, the public entity shall proceed to make the necessary modifications.

(b) A public entity shall provide an opportunity to interested persons, including individuals with disabilities or organizations representing individuals with disabilities, to participate in the self-evaluation process by submitting comments.

(c) A public entity that employs 50 or more persons shall, for at least three years following completion of the self-evaluation, maintain on file and make available for public inspection:

(1) A list of the interested persons consulted;

(2) A description of areas examined and any problems identified; and

(3) A description of any modifications made.

(d) If a public entity has already complied with the self-evaluation requirement of a regulation implementing section 504 of the Rehabilitation Act of 1973, then the requirements of this section shall apply only to those policies and practices that were not included in the previous self-evaluation.

§ 35.106 Notice.

A public entity shall make available to applicants, participants, beneficiaries, and other interested persons information regarding the provisions of this part and its applicability to the services, programs, or activities of the public entity, and make such information available to them in such manner as the head of the entity finds necessary to apprise such persons of the protections against discrimination assured them by the Act and this part.

§ 35.107 Designation of responsible employee and adoption of grievance procedures.

(a) *Designation of responsible employee.* A public entity that employs 50 or more persons shall designate at least one employee to coordinate its efforts to comply with and carry out its responsibilities under this part, including any investigation of any complaint communicated to it alleging its noncompliance with this part or alleging any actions that would be prohibited by this part. The public entity shall make available to all interested individuals the name, office address, and telephone number of the employee or employees designated pursuant to this paragraph.

(b) *Complaint procedure.* A public entity that employs 50 or more persons shall adopt and publish grievance procedures providing for prompt and equitable resolution of complaints alleging any action that would be prohibited by this part.

§§ 35.108-35.129 [Reserved]

Subpart B—General Requirements

§ 35.130 General prohibitions against discrimination.

(a) No qualified individual with a disability shall, on the basis of disability, be excluded from participation in or be denied the benefits of the services, programs, or activities of a public entity, or be subjected to discrimination by any public entity.

(b) (1) A public entity, in providing any aid, benefit, or service, may not, directly or through contractual, licensing, or other arrangements, on the basis of disability—

(i) Deny a qualified individual with a disability the opportunity to participate in or benefit from the aid, benefit, or service;

(ii) Afford a qualified individual with a disability an opportunity to participate in or benefit from the aid, benefit, or service that is not equal to that afforded others;

(iii) Provide a qualified individual with a disability with an aid, benefit, or service that is not as effective in affording equal opportunity to obtain the same result, to gain the same benefit, or to reach the same level of achievement as that provided to others;

(iv) Provide different or separate aids, benefits, or services to individuals with disabilities or to any class of individuals with disabilities than is provided to others unless such action is necessary to provide qualified individuals with disabilities with aids, benefits, or services that are as effective as those provided to others;

(v) Aid or perpetuate discrimination against a qualified individual with a disability by providing significant assistance to an agency, organization, or person that discriminates on the basis of disability in providing any aid, benefit, or service to beneficiaries of the public entity's program;

(vi) Deny a qualified individual with a disability the opportunity to participate as a member of planning or advisory boards;

(vii) Otherwise limit a qualified individual with a disability in the enjoyment of any right, privilege, advantage, or opportunity enjoyed by others receiving the aid, benefit, or service.

(2) A public entity may not deny a qualified individual with a disability the opportunity to participate in services, programs, or activities that are not separate or different, despite the existence of permissibly separate or different programs or activities.

(3) A public entity may not, directly or through contractual or other arrangements, utilize criteria or methods of administration:

(i) That have the effect of subjecting qualified individuals with disabilities to discrimination on the basis of disability;

(ii) That have the purpose or effect of defeating or substantially impairing accomplishment of the objectives of the public entity's program with respect to individuals with disabilities; or

(iii) That perpetuate the discrimination of another public entity if both public entities are subject to common administrative control or are agencies of the same State.

(4) A public entity may not, in determining the site or location of a facility, make selections—

(i) That have the effect of excluding individuals with disabilities from, denying them the benefits of, or otherwise subjecting them to discrimination; or

(ii) That have the purpose or effect of defeating or substantially impairing the accomplishment of the objectives of the service, program, or activity with respect to individuals with disabilities.

(5) A public entity, in the selection of procurement contractors, may not use criteria that subject qualified individuals with disabilities to discrimination on the basis of disability.

(6) A public entity may not administer a licensing or certification program in a manner that subjects qualified individuals with disabilities to discrimination on the basis of disability, nor may a public entity establish requirements for the programs or activities of licensees or certified entities that subject qualified individuals with disabilities to discrimination on the basis of disability. The programs or activities of entities that are licensed or certified by a public entity are not, themselves, covered by this part.

(7) A public entity shall make reasonable modifications in policies, practices, or procedures when the modifications are necessary to avoid discrimination on the basis of disability, unless the public entity can demonstrate that making the modifications would fundamentally alter the nature of the service, program, or activity.

(8) A public entity shall not impose or apply eligibility criteria that screen out or tend to screen out an individual with a disability or any class of individuals with disabilities from fully and equally enjoying any service, program, or activity, unless such criteria can be shown to be necessary for the provision of the service, program, or activity being offered.

(c) Nothing in this part prohibits a public entity from providing benefits, services, or advantages to individuals with disabilities, or to a particular class of individuals with disabilities beyond those required by this part.

(d) A public entity shall administer services, programs, and activities in the most integrated setting appropriate to the needs of qualified individuals with disabilities.

(e)(1) Nothing in this part shall be construed to require an individual with a disability to accept an accommodation, aid, service, opportunity, or benefit provided under the ADA or this part which such individual chooses not to accept.

(2) Nothing in the Act or this part authorizes the representative or guardian of an individual with a disability to decline food, water, medical treatment, or medical services for that individual.

(f) A public entity may not place a surcharge on a particular individual with a disability or any group of individuals with disabilities to cover the costs of measures, such as the provision of auxiliary aids or program accessibility, that are required to provide that individual or group with the nondiscriminatory treatment required by the Act or this part.

(g) A public entity shall not exclude or otherwise deny equal services, programs, or activities to an individual or entity because of the known disability of an individual with whom the individual or entity is known to have a relationship or association.

§ 35.131 Illegal use of drugs.

(a) *General.* (1) Except as provided in paragraph (b) of this section, this part does not prohibit discrimination against an individual based on that individual's current illegal use of drugs.

(2) A public entity shall not discriminate on the basis of illegal use of drugs against an individual who is not engaging in current illegal use of drugs and who—

(i) Has successfully completed a supervised drug rehabilitation program or has otherwise been rehabilitated successfully;

(ii) Is participating in a supervised rehabilitation program; or

(iii) Is erroneously regarded as engaging in such use.

(b) *Health and drug rehabilitation services.* (1) A public entity shall not deny health services, or services provided in connection with drug rehabilitation, to an individual on the basis of that individual's current illegal use of drugs, if the individual is otherwise entitled to such services.

(2) A drug rehabilitation or treatment program may deny participation to individuals who engage in illegal use of drugs while they are in the program.

(c) *Drug testing.* (1) This part does not prohibit a public entity from adopting or administering reasonable policies or procedures, including but not limited to drug testing, designed to ensure that an individual who formerly engaged in the illegal use of drugs is not now engaging in current illegal use of drugs.

(2) Nothing in paragraph (c) of this section shall be construed to encourage, prohibit, restrict, or authorize the conduct of testing for the illegal use of drugs.

§ 35.132 Smoking.

This part does not preclude the prohibition of, or the imposition of restrictions on, smoking in transportation covered by this part.

§ 35.133 Maintenance of accessible features.

(a) A public accommodation shall maintain in operable working condition those features of facilities and equipment that are required to be readily accessible to and

usable by persons with disabilities by the Act or this part.

(b) This section does not prohibit isolated or temporary interruptions in service or access due to maintenance or repairs.

§ 35.134 Retaliation or coercion.

(a) No private or public entity shall discriminate against any individual because that individual has opposed any act or practice made unlawful by this part, or because that individual made a charge, testified, assisted, or participated in any manner in an investigation, proceeding, or hearing under the Act or this part.

(b) No private or public entity shall coerce, intimidate, threaten, or interfere with any individual in the exercise or enjoyment of, or on account of his or her having exercised or enjoyed, or on account of his or her having aided or encouraged any other individual in the exercise or enjoyment of, any right granted or protected by the Act or this part.

§ 35.135 Personal devices and services.

This part does not require a public entity to provide to individuals with disabilities personal devices, such as wheelchairs; individually prescribed devices, such as prescription eyeglasses or hearing aids; readers for personal use or study; or services of a personal nature including assistance in eating, toileting, or dressing.

§§ 35.136-35.139 [Reserved]

Subpart C—Employment

§ 35.140 Employment discrimination prohibited.

(a) No qualified individual with a disability shall, on the basis of disability, be subjected to discrimination in employment under any service, program, or activity conducted by a public entity.

(b)(1) For purposes of this part, the requirements of title I

of the Act, as established by the regulations of the Equal Employment Opportunity Commission in 29 CFR part 1630, apply to employment in any service, program, or activity conducted by a public entity if that public entity is also subject to the jurisdiction of title I.

(2) For the purposes of this part, the requirements of section 504 of the Rehabilitation Act of 1973, as established by the regulations of the Department of Justice in 28 CFR part 41, as those requirements pertain to employment, apply to employment in any service, program, or activity conducted by a public entity if that public entity is not also subject to the jurisdiction of title I.

§§ 35.141-35.148 [Reserved]

Subpart D—Program Accessibility

§ 35.149 Discrimination prohibited.

Except as otherwise provided in § 35.150, no qualified individual with a disability shall, because a public entity's facilities are inaccessible to or unusable by individuals with disabilities, be excluded from participation in, or be denied the benefits of the services, programs, or activities of a public entity, or be subjected to discrimination by any public entity.

§ 35.150 Existing facilities.

(a) *General.* A public entity shall operate each service, program, or activity so that the service, program, or activity, when viewed in its entirety, is readily accessible to and usable by individuals with disabilities. This paragraph does not—

(1) Necessarily require a public entity to make each of its existing facilities accessible to and usable by individuals with disabilities;

(2) Require a public entity to take any action that would threaten or destroy the historic significance of an historic property; or

(3) Require a public entity to take any action that it can demonstrate would result in a fundamental alteration in the

nature of a service, program, or activity or in undue financial and administrative burdens. In those circumstances where personnel of the public entity believe that the proposed action would fundamentally alter the service, program, or activity or would result in undue financial and administrative burdens, a public entity has the burden of proving that compliance with § 35.150(a) of this part would result in such alteration or burdens. The decision that compliance would result in such alteration or burdens must be made by the head of a public entity or his or her designee after considering all resources available for use in the funding and operation of the service, program, or activity, and must be accompanied by a written statement of the reasons for reaching that conclusion. If an action would result in such an alteration or such burdens, a public entity shall take any other action that would not result in such an alteration or such burdens but would nevertheless ensure that individuals with disabilities receive the benefits or services provided by the public entity.

(b) *Methods*—(1) *General.* A public entity may comply with the requirements of this section through such means as redesign of equipment, reassignment of services to accessible buildings, assignment of aides to beneficiaries, home visits, delivery of services at alternate accessible sites, alteration of existing facilities and construction of new facilities, use of accessible rolling stock or other conveyances, or any other methods that result in making its services, programs, or activities readily accessible to and usable by individuals with disabilities. A public entity is not required to make structural changes in existing facilities where other methods are effective in achieving compliance with this section. A public entity, in making alterations to existing buildings, shall meet the accessibility requirements of § 35.151. In choosing among available methods for meeting the requirements of this section, a public entity shall give priority to those methods that

offer services, programs, and activities to qualified individuals with disabilities in the most integrated setting appropriate.

(2) *Historic preservation programs.* In meeting the requirements of § 35.150(a) in historic preservation programs, a public entity shall give priority to methods that provide physical access to individuals with disabilities. In cases where a physical alteration to an historic property is not required because of paragraph (a)(2) or (a)(3) of this section, alternative methods of achieving program accessibility include—

(i) Using audio-visual materials and devices to depict those portions of an historic property that cannot otherwise be made accessible;

(ii) Assigning persons to guide individuals with handicaps into or through portions of historic properties that cannot otherwise be made accessible; or

(iii) Adopting other innovative methods.

(c) *Time period for compliance.* Where structural changes in facilities are undertaken to comply with the obligations established under this section, such changes shall be made within three years of January 26, 1992, but in any event as expeditiously as possible.

(d) *Transition plan.* (1) In the event that structural changes to facilities will be undertaken to achieve program accessibility, a public entity that employs 50 or more persons shall develop, within six months of January 26, 1992, a transition plan setting forth the steps necessary to complete such changes. A public entity shall provide an opportunity to interested persons, including individuals with disabilities or organizations representing individuals with disabilities, to participate in the development of the transition plan by submitting comments. A copy of the transition plan shall be made available for public inspection.

(2) If a public entity has responsibility or authority over streets, roads, or walkways, its transition plan shall include a schedule for providing curb ramps or other sloped areas where pedestrian walks cross

curbs, giving priority to walkways serving entities covered by the Act, including State and local government offices and facilities, transportation, places of public accommodation, and employers, followed by walkways serving other areas.

(3) The plan shall, at a minimum—

(i) Identify physical obstacles in the public entity's facilities that limit the accessibility of its programs or activities to individuals with disabilities;

(ii) Describe in detail the methods that will be used to make the facilities accessible;

(iii) Specify the schedule for taking the steps necessary to achieve compliance with this section and, if the time period of the transition plan is longer than one year, identify steps that will be taken during each year of the transition period; and

(iv) Indicate the official responsible for implementation of the plan.

(4) If a public entity has already complied with the transition plan requirement of a Federal agency regulation implementing section 504 of the Rehabilitation Act of 1973, then the requirements of this paragraph (d) shall apply only to those policies and practices that were not included in the previous transition plan.

§ 35.151 New construction and alterations.

(a) *Design and construction.* Each facility or part of a facility constructed by, on behalf of, or for the use of a public entity shall be designed and constructed in such manner that the facility or part of the facility is readily accessible to and usable by individuals with disabilities, if the construction was commenced after January 26, 1992.

(b) *Alteration.* Each facility or part of a facility altered by, on behalf of, or for the use of a public entity in a manner that affects or could affect the usability of the facility or part of the facility shall, to the maximum extent feasible, be altered in such manner that the altered portion of the facility is readily accessible to and usable by individuals with disabilities, if the alteration was commenced after January 26, 1992.

(c) *Accessibility standards.* Design, construction, or alteration of facilities in conformance with the Uniform Federal Accessibility Standards (UFAS) (Appendix A to 41 CFR part 101-19.6) or with the Americans with Disabilities Act Accessibility Guidelines for Buildings and Facilities (ADAAG) (Appendix A to 28 CFR part 36) shall be deemed to comply with the requirements of this section with respect to those facilities, except that the elevator exemption contained at section 4.1.3(5) and section 4.1.6(1)(j) of ADAAG shall not apply. Departures from particular requirements of either standard by the use of other methods shall be permitted when it is clearly evident that equivalent access to the facility or part of the facility is thereby provided.

(d) *Alterations: Historic properties.* (1) Alterations to historic properties shall comply, to the maximum extent feasible, with section 4.1.7 of UFAS or section 4.1.7 of ADAAG.

(2) If it is not feasible to provide physical access to an historic property in a manner that will not threaten or destroy the historic significance of the building or facility, alternative methods of access shall be provided pursuant to the requirements of § 35.150.

(e) *Curb ramps.* (1) Newly constructed or altered streets, roads, and highways must contain curb ramps or other sloped areas at any intersection having curbs or other barriers to entry from a street level pedestrian walkway.

(2) Newly constructed or altered street level pedestrian walkways must contain curb ramps or other sloped areas at intersections to streets, roads, or highways.

§§ 35.152-35.159 [Reserved]

Subpart E—Communications

§ 35.160 General.

(a) A public entity shall take appropriate steps to ensure that communications with applicants, participants, and members of the public with disabilities are as effective as communications with others.

(b)(1) A public entity shall furnish appropriate auxiliary aids and services where necessary to afford an individual with a disability an equal opportunity to participate in, and enjoy the benefits of, a service, program, or activity conducted by a public entity.

(2) In determining what type of auxiliary aid and service is necessary, a public entity shall give primary consideration to the requests of the individual with disabilities.

§ 35.161 Telecommunication devices for the deaf (TDD's).

Where a public entity communicates by telephone with applicants and beneficiaries, TDD's or equally effective telecommunication systems shall be used to communicate with individuals with impaired hearing or speech.

§ 35.162 Telephone emergency services.

Telephone emergency services, including 911 services, shall provide direct access to individuals who use TDD's and computer modems.

§ 35.163 Information and signage.

(a) A public entity shall ensure that interested persons, including persons with impaired vision or hearing, can obtain information as to the existence and location of accessible services, activities, and facilities.

(b) A public entity shall provide signage at all inaccessible entrances to each of its facilities, directing users to an accessible entrance or to a location at which they can obtain information about accessible facilities. The international symbol for accessibility shall be used at each accessible entrance of a facility.

§ 35.164 Duties.

This subpart does not require a public entity to take any action that it can demonstrate would result in a fundamental alteration in the nature of a service, program, or activity or in undue financial and administrative burdens. In those circumstances where personnel of the public entity believe that the proposed action would fundamentally alter the service, program, or activity or would result in undue financial and administrative burdens, a public entity has the burden of proving that compliance with this subpart would result in such alteration or burdens. The decision that compliance would result in such alteration or burdens must be made by the head of the public entity or his or her designee after considering all resources available for use in the funding and operation of the service, program, or activity and must be accompanied by a written statement of the reasons for reaching that conclusion. If an action required to comply with this subpart would result in such an alteration or such burdens, a public entity shall take any other action that would not result in such an alteration or such burdens but would nevertheless ensure that, to the maximum extent possible, individuals with disabilities receive the benefits or services provided by the public entity.

§§ 35.165-35.169 [Reserved]

Subpart F—Compliance Procedures

§ 35.170 Complaints.

(a) *Who may file.* An individual who believes that he or she or a specific class of individuals has been subjected to discrimination on the basis of disability by a public entity may, by himself or herself or by an authorized representative, file a complaint under this part.

(b) *Time for filing.* A complaint must be filed not later than 180 days from the date of the alleged discrimination, unless the time for filing is extended by the designated agency for good cause shown. A complaint is deemed to be filed under this section on the date it is first filed with any Federal agency.

(c) *Where to file.* An individual may file a complaint with any agency that he or she believes to be the appropriate agency designated under subpart G of this part, or with any agency that provides funding to the public entity that is the subject of the complaint, or with the Department of Justice for referral as provided in § 35.171(a)(2).

§ 35. 171 Acceptance of complaints.

(a) *Receipt of complaints.* (1)(i) Any Federal agency that receives a complaint of discrimination on the basis of disability by a public entity shall promptly review the complaint to determine whether it has jurisdiction over the complaint under section 504.

(ii) If the agency does not have section 504 jurisdiction, it shall promptly determine whether it is the designated agency under subpart G of this part responsible for complaints filed against that public entity.

(2)(i) If an agency other than the Department of Justice determines that it does not have section 504 jurisdiction and is not the designated agency, it shall promptly refer the complaint, and notify the complainant that it is referring the complaint to the Department of Justice.

(ii) When the Department of Justice receives a complaint for which it does not have jurisdiction under section 504 and is not the designated agency, it shall refer the complaint to an agency that does have jurisdiction under section 504 or to the appropriate agency designated in subpart G of this part or, in the case of an employment complaint that is also subject to title I of the Act, to the Equal Employment Opportunity Commission.

(3)(i) If the agency that receives a complaint has section 504 jurisdiction, it shall process the complaint according to its procedures for enforcing section 504.

(ii) If the agency that receives a complaint does not have section 504 jurisdiction, but is the designated agency, it shall process the complaint according to the procedures established by this subpart.

(b) *Employment complaints.* (1) If a complaint alleges employment discrimination subject to title I of the Act, and the agency has section 504 jurisdiction, the agency shall follow the procedures issued by the Department of Justice and the Equal Employment Opportunity Commission under section 107(b) of the Act.

(2) If a complaint alleges employment discrimination subject to title I of the Act, and the designated agency does not have section 504 jurisdiction, the agency shall refer the complaint to the Equal Employment Opportunity Commission for processing under title I of the Act.

(3) Complaints alleging employment discrimination subject to this part, but not to title I of the Act shall be processed in accordance with the procedures established by this subpart.

(c) *Complete complaints.* (1) A designated agency shall accept all complete complaints under this section and shall promptly notify the complainant and the public entity of the receipt and acceptance of the complaint.

(2) If the designated agency receives a complaint that is not complete, it shall notify the complainant and specify the additional information that is needed to make the complaint a complete complaint. If the complainant fails to complete the complaint, the designated agency shall close the complaint without prejudice.

§ 35.172 Resolution of complaints.

(a) The designated agency shall investigate each complete complaint, attempt informal resolution, and, if resolution is not achieved, issue to the complainant and the public entity a Letter of Findings that shall include–

(1) Findings of fact and conclusions of law;

(2) A description of a remedy for each violation found; and

(3) Notice of the rights available under paragraph (b) of this section.

(b) If the designated agency finds noncompliance, the procedures in §§ 35.173 and 35.174 shall be followed. At any time, the complainant may file a private suit pursuant to section 203 of the Act, whether or not the designated agency finds a violation.

§ 35.173 Voluntary compliance agreements.

(a) When the designated agency issues a noncompliance Letter of Findings, the designated agency shall–

(1) Notify the Assistant Attorney General by forwarding a copy of the Letter of Findings to the Assistant Attorney General; and

(2) Initiate negotiations with the public entity to secure compliance by voluntary means.

(b) Where the designated agency is able to secure voluntary compliance, the voluntary compliance agreement shall–

(1) Be in writing and signed by the parties;

(2) Address each cited violation;

(3) Specify the corrective or remedial action to be taken, within a stated period of time, to come into compliance;

(4) Provide assurance that discrimination will not recur; and

(5) Provide for enforcement by the Attorney General.

§ 35.174 Referral.

If the public entity declines to enter into voluntary compliance negotiations or if negotiations are unsuccessful, the designated agency shall refer the matter to the Attorney General with a recommendation for appropriate action.

§ 35.175 Attorney's fees.

In any action or administrative proceeding commenced pursuant to the Act or this part, the court or agency, in its discretion, may allow the prevailing party, other than the United States, a reasonable attorney's fee, including litigation expenses, and costs, and the United States shall be liable for the foregoing the same as a private individual.

§ 35.176 Alternative means of dispute resolution.

Where appropriate and to the extent authorized by law, the use of alternative means of dispute resolution, including settlement negotiations, conciliation, facilitation, mediation, factfinding, minitrials, and arbitration, is encouraged to resolve disputes arising under the Act and this part.

§ 35.177 Effect of unavailability of technical assistance.

A public entity shall not be excused from compliance with the requirements of this part because of any failure to receive technical assistance, including any failure in the development or dissemination of any technical assistance manual authorized by the Act.

§ 35.178 State immunity.

A State shall not be immune under the eleventh amendment to the Constitution of the United States from an action in Federal or State court of competent jurisdiction for a violation of this Act. In any action against a State for a violation of the requirements of this Act, remedies (including remedies both at law and in equity) are available for such a violation to the same extent as such remedies are available for such a violation in an action against any public or private entity other than a State.

§§ 35.179-35.189 [Reserved]

Subpart G—Designated Agencies

§ 35.190 Designated agencies.

(a) The Assistant Attorney General shall coordinate the compliance activities of Federal agencies with respect to State

and local government components, and shall provide policy guidance and interpretations to designated agencies to ensure the consistent and effective implementation of the requirements of this part.

(b) The Federal agencies listed in paragraph (b) (1) through (8) of this section shall have responsibility for the implementation of subpart F of this part for components of State and local governments that exercise responsibilities, regulate, or administer services, programs, or activities in the following functional areas.

(1) *Department of Agriculture*: All programs, services, and regulatory activities relating to farming and the raising of livestock, including extension services.

(2) *Department of Education*: All programs, services, and regulatory activities relating to the operation of elementary and secondary education systems and institutions, institutions of higher education and vocational education (other than schools of medicine, dentistry, nursing, and other health-related schools), and libraries.

(3) *Department of Health and Human Services*: All programs, services, and regulatory activities relating to the provision of health care and social services, including schools of medicine, dentistry, nursing, and other health-related schools, the operation of health care and social service providers and institutions, including "grass-roots" and community services organizations and programs, and preschool and daycare programs.

(4) *Department of Housing and Urban Development*: All programs, services, and regulatory activities relating to state and local public housing, and housing assistance and referral.

(5) *Department of Interior*: All programs, services, and regulatory activities relating to lands and natural resources, including parks and recreation, water and waste management, environmental protection, energy, historic and cultural preservation, and museums.

(6) *Department of Justice*: All programs, services, and regulatory activities relating to law enforcement, public safety, and the administration of justice, including courts and correctional institutions; commerce and industry, including general economic development, banking and finance, consumer protection, insurance, and small business; planning, development, and regulation (unless assigned to other designated agencies); state and local government support services (e.g., audit, personnel, comptroller, administrative services); all other government functions not assigned to other designated agencies.

(7) *Department of Labor*: All programs, services, and regulatory activities relating to labor and the work force.

(8) *Department of Transportation*: All programs, services, and regulatory activities relating to transportation, including highways, public transportation, traffic management (non-law enforcement), automobile licensing and inspection, and driver licensing.

(c) Responsibility for the implementation of subpart F of this part for components of State or local governments that exercise responsibilities, regulate, or administer services, programs, or activities relating to functions not assigned to specific designated agencies by paragraph (b) of this section may be assigned to other specific agencies by the Department of Justice.

(d) If two or more agencies have apparent responsibility over a complaint, the Assistant Attorney General shall determine which one of the agencies shall be the designated agency for purposes of that complaint.

§§ 35.191-35.999 [Reserved]

Appendix A to Part 35—Preamble to Regulation on Nondiscrimination on the Basis of Disability in State and Local Government Services (Published July 26, 1991)

Note: For the convenience of the reader, this appendix contains the text of the preamble to the final regulation on nondiscrimination on the basis of disability in State and

local government services beginning
at the heading "Section-by-Section
Analysis" and ending before "List of
Subjects in 28 CFR Part 35" (56 FR
(INSERT FR PAGE CITATIONS);
July 26, 1991).
Dated: July 17, 1991.
Dick Thornburgh,
Attorney General.
[FR Doc. 91-17368 Filed 7-25-91; 8:45
am]
BILLING CODE 4410-01-M

Architectural and Transportation Barriers Compliance Board
36 CFR Part 1191
Americans With Disabilities Act (ADA) Accessibility Guidelines for Buildings and Facilities

ARCHITECTURAL AND TRANSPORTATION BARRIERS COMPLIANCE BOARD

36 CFR Part 1191

(Docket No. 90-2)

RIN 3014-AA09

Americans With Disabilities Act (ADA) Accessibility Guidelines for Buildings and Facilities

AGENCY: Architectural and Transportation Barriers Compliance Board.

ACTION: Final guidelines.

SUMMARY: The Architectural and Transportation Barriers Compliance Board is issuing final guidelines to assist the Department of Justice to establish accessibility standards for new construction and alterations in places of public accommodation and commercial facilities, as required by title III the Americans with Disabilities Act (ADA) of 1990. The guidelines will ensure that newly constructed and altered portions of buildings and facilities covered by title III of the ADA are readily accessible to and usable by individuals with disabilities in terms of architecture and design, and communication. The Depart-

ment of Justice has proposed to adopt the guidelines as the accessibility standards for new construction and alterations in places of public accommodation and commercial facilities for purposes of title III of the ADA.

EFFECTIVE DATE: July 26, 1991.

FOR FURTHER INFORMATION CONTACT: James Raggio, Office of the General Counsel, Architectural and Transportation Barriers Compliance Board, 1111-18th Street, NW., Suite 501, Washington, DC 20036. Telephone (202) 653-7834 (Voice/TDD). This is not a toll-free number. This document is available in accessible formats (cassette tape, braille, large print, or computer disc) upon request.

SUPPLEMENTARY INFORMATION:

Statutory Background

The Americans with Disabilities Act (ADA) of 1990 extends to individuals with disabilities comprehensive civil rights protections similar to those provided to persons on the basis of race, sex, national origin, and religion under the Civil Rights Act of 1964. Title III of the ADA, which becomes effective on January 26, 1992, prohibits discrimination on the basis of disability in places of public accommodation by any person who owns, leases or

leases to, or operates a place of public accommodation. As discussed below, title III establishes accessibility requirements for new construction and alterations in places of public accommodation and commercial facilities.

"Public accommodation" is defined by section 301(7) of the ADA as including the following twelve categories of private entities if their operations affect commerce:

(1) An inn, hotel, motel, or other place of lodging, except for an establishment located within a building that contains not more than five rooms for rent or hire and that is actually occupied by the proprietor of such establishment as the residence of such proprietor;

(2) A restaurant, bar, or other establishment serving food or drink;

(3) A motion picture house, theater, concert hall, stadium, or other place of exhibition or entertainment;

(4) An auditorium, convention center, lecture hall, or other place of public gathering;

(5) A bakery, grocery store, clothing store, hardware store, shopping center, or other sales or rental establishment;

(6) A laundromat, dry-cleaner, bank, barber shop, beauty shop, travel service, shoe repair service, funeral parlor, gas station, office of an accountant or lawyer, pharmacy, insurance office, professional office of a health care provider, hospital, or other service establishment;

(7) A terminal, depot, or other station used for specified public transportation;

(8) A museum, library, gallery, or other place of public display or collection;

(9) A park, zoo, amusement park, or other place of recreation;

(10) A nursery, elementary, secondary, undergraduate, or postgraduate private school, or other place of education;

(11) A day care center, senior citizen center, homeless shelter, food bank, adoption agency, or other social service center establishment; and

(12) A gymnasium health spa, bowling alley, golf course, or other place of exercise or recreation.

The legislative history states that these twelve categories "should be construed liberally consistent with the intent of the legislation that people with disabilities should have equal access to the array of establishments that are available to others who do not currently have disabilities." H. Rept. 101-485, pt. 2, at 100.

"Commercial facilities" are defined by section 301(1) of the ADA as facilities that are intended for nonresidential use and whose operations will affect commerce. The legislative history states that the term is to be interpreted broadly to cover commercial establishments that are not included within the specific definition of "public accommodation" such as office buildings, factories, and other places in which employment will occur. H. Rept. 101-485, pt. 2, at 116-17.

Section 303 of the ADA establishes accessibility requirements for new construction and alterations in places of public accommodation and commercial facilities. With respect to new construction, section 303(a)1) requires that places of public accommodation and commercial facilities designed or constructed for first occupancy after January 26, 1993, must be readily accessible to and usable by individuals with disabilities, except where an entity can demonstrate that it is structurally impracticable. When alterations are made that affect or could affect usability of or access to a place of public accommodation or commercial facility, section 303(a)(2) requires that the alterations be made in such a manner that, to the maximum extent feasible,

the altered portions of the facility are readily accessible to and usable by individuals with disabilities. In addition, where alterations affect or could affect usability of or access to an area of the facility containing a primary function, section 303(a)(2) requires that the alterations be made in such a manner that, to the maximum extent feasible, the path of travel to the altered area, and the restrooms, telephones, and drinking fountains serving the altered area are readily accessible to and usable by individuals with disabilities unless it is disproportionate to the overall alterations in terms of cost and scope, as determined under criteria established by the Attorney General.

Section 303(b) of the ADA contains an exception which specifies that the installation of an elevator is not required for newly constructed or altered facilities that are less than three stories or have less than 3,000 square feet per story unless the building is a shopping center, shopping mall, the professional office of a health care provider, or another type of facility determined by the Attorney General to require the installation of an elevator based on the usage of the facility.

According to the legislative history, the term "readily accessible to and usable by" is intended to provide "a high degree of convenient accessibility" and "enable people with disabilities (including mobility, sensory, and cognitive impairments) to get to, enter and use a facility." H. Rept. 101-485, pt. 2, at 117-18. The term includes "accessibility of parking areas, accessible routes to and from the facility, accessible entrances, usable bathrooms and water fountains, accessibility of public and common use areas, and access to the goods, services, programs, facilities, accommodations and work areas available at the facility.' Id. The legislative history further explains that when identical features will generally serve the same function, only a reasonable number must be accessible depending on such factors as their use, location, and number;

however, when identical features will generally be used in different ways, each one must be accessible in most situations. H. Rept. 101-485, pt. 2, at 118; H. Rept. 101-485, pt. 3, at 61. For example, only a reasonable number of spaces in a parking lot or stalls within a restroom would have to be accessible, but all meeting rooms at a conference center would have to be accessible because each one may be used for different purposes at any given time. Id.

Under section 504 of the ADA, the Architectural and Transportation Barriers Compliance Board is required to issue guidelines to assist the Department of Justice to establish accessibility standards for new construction and alterations in places of public accommodation and commercial facilities covered by title III.[1] Section 504 requires that the guidelines supplement the existing Minimum Guidelines and Requirements for Accessible Design (MGRAD) and "establish additional requirements, consistent with this Act, to ensure that buildings (and) facilities * * * are accessible in terms of architecture and design * * * and communication, to individuals with disabilities.[2] Section 504 also requires that the guidelines include provisions for alterations to qualified historic properties.

The Department of Justice is responsible for issuing final regulations to implement the provisions of title III of the ADA except for transportation vehicles. Section 306(c) of the ADA requires that the Department of Justice's final regulations include accessibility standards for new construction and alterations of buildings and facilities covered by title III of the ADA that are consistent with the Board's guidelines. On February 22, 1991, the Department of Justice proposed to adopt the Board's proposed guidelines with any changes made by the Board as the accessibility standards for purposes of title III of the ADA. See Department of Justice's proposed regulations, 28 CFR 34.406(a) and Appendix A to part 36—Standards for Accessible Design at 56 FR 7478, 7492, 7494 (February 22, 1991).

Proposed Guidelines

On January 22, 1991, the Board published a notice of proposed rulemaking (NPRM) in the **Federal Register** which contained the proposed Americans With Disabilities Act (ADA) Accessibility Guidelines For Buildings and Facilities (56 FR 2296). The proposed guidelines were modeled on the Uniform Federal Accessibility Standards (UFAS) which are generally consistent with MGRAD and use the same format and numbering system as the American National Standard Specifications for Making Buildings and Facilities Accessible to and Usable by Physically Handicapped People (ANSI A117.1-1980).[3] Where the ADA establishes requirements that differ from MGRAD or UFAS, the ADA requirements were followed.

The proposed guidelines contained:

* General provisions (sections 1 through 3) which include the purpose section, general information about the guidelines, miscellaneous instructions, and definitions.

* Scoping provisions (sections 4.1.1 through 4.1.7) which include the application section and scoping requirements for new construction of sites and exterior facilities, new construction of buildings and facilities, additions, alterations, and alterations to qualified historic properties.

* Technical specifications (sections 4.2 through 4.34) which reprint the test and illustrations of the ANSI A117.1-1980 standard with differences in the text noted by italics.

* Special application sections (sections 5 through 10) which include additional requirements for restaurants and cafeterias, medical care facilities, business and mercantile facilities, libraries, transient lodging, and transportation facilities.[4]

* An appendix which contains additional information to aid in understanding the guidelines, and designing buildings and facilities for greater accessibility.

The NPRM also asked questions and sought information on a number of specific issues related to the proposed guidelines.

Public Hearings and Comments

The Board held 14 public hearings around the country on the proposed guidelines between February 11, 1991 and March 7, 1991. A total of 450 people presented testimony on the proposed guidelines at the hearings. In addition, 1,585 written comments were submitted to the Board by the end of the comment period on March 25, 1991. Another 280 comments were received between March 26, 1991 and April 3, 1991. Although those comments were not timely, they were analyzed along with the comments received by March 25, 1991. The Board did not find it practical to consider comments received after April 3, 1991. In all, the Board received over 12,000 pages of comments and testimony on the proposed guidelines.

The Board received comments and testimony from a broad range of interested individuals and groups. Ten categories were identified and approximately the following numbers submitted timely comments or testimony for each category:

1270	Individuals who identified themselves as having a disability or who voiced a "consumer" perspective, and organizations representing these persons. For purposes of convenience, this category is referred to as "individuals with disabilities and their organizations" in the section-by-section analysis.
100	Government agencies involved with disability issues.
60	Building code officials and State agencies responsible for accessiblity.
80	Architects, designers, engineers, and organizations representing these persons.
320	Businesses and organizations representing businesses.
60	Manufacturers.
20	Transit agencies.
50	Building owners and managers, and organizations representing these persons.
50	Other government agencies
20	Other persons or organizations not in the above categories.

The comments and testimony were sorted by section and analyzed. For some sections, the comments were grouped around certain issues or questions identified in the NPRM. For other sections, the comments were scattered. A large number of commenters, especially individuals with disabilities and their organizations, expressed support for the guidelines, as proposed. Some commenters requested that sections be clarified or made recommendations for changes, including deletion of sections. Further, it was evident from some comments that a few of the proposed provisions in the NPRM were unclear and needed to be revised. With respect to those commenters who recommended changes, a few submitted data or studies in support of their recommendations; however, most recommendations were based on individual opinions or preferences. Where data or studies were not submitted in support of a recommended change, the Board was inclined to retain the provisions taken from the MGRAD, UFAS, and the ANSI A117.1 standard, especially with respect to the technical specifications in 4.2 through 4.34, unless more than a few commenters or an organization representing the interests of a large group believed that the provision was inadequate or otherwise in need of change. The Board considered each of those recommended changes on its merits. In some sections, commenters pointed out a need for new or additional requirements but further research or study is necessary for the Board to develop guidelines in the area. Some commenters asked questions regarding application of the guidelines to specific situations.

Due to the large number of comments received and the deadline for issuing the final guidelines, it is not possible for the Board to respond to each comment in this preamble. The Board has made every effort within the time available to respond to significant comments in the section-by-section analysis. As discussed under specific sections, the Board has reserved action in some areas pending further study or research. The Board has an on-going research and technical assistance program and plans to periodically review and up-date the guidelines to ensure that they remain consistent with technological developments and changes in model codes and national standards, and meet the needs of individuals with disabilities.

General Issues

Coordination of Board and ANSI Processes

Many commenters generally supported using the ANSI A117.1–1980 standard as the basis for the technical specifications of the guidelines since that standard or its 1986 update is incorporated or reference in many State and local building codes and is generally accepted and understood by the building industry. The Council of American Building Officials (CABO), National Conference of States on Building Codes and Standards (NCSBCS), American Institute of Architects (AIA), and other commenters recommended that the Board coordinate any substantive changes to the ANSI A117.1 standard with the ANSI A117 Committee in order to maintain a consistent and uniform set of accessibility standards which can be efficiently and effectively implemented at the State and local level through established building regulatory processes.[5]

The Board is a member of the ANSI A117 Committee and is committed to working cooperatively with the Committee. The ANSI A117 Committee solicited proposals for changes to the ANSI A117.1 standard in July 1989, a full year before the ADA was enacted.

When the ADA was enacted in July 1990, the Board was charged with the responsibility of issuing final guidelines in nine months. In order to meet this responsibility, the Board issued the NPRM on January 22, 1991. The ANSI A117 Committee published draft revisions to the ANSI A117.1 standard on February 22, 1991. The timing of these events did not permit the Board and the ANSI A117 Committee to fully coordinate their processes.[6]

Members of the ANSI A117 Committee have objected to various changes proposed in the February 1991 draft revisions to the ANSI A117.1 standard and the group is scheduled to meet in July 1991 to review the objections. In voting on the draft revisions to the ANSI A117.1 standard, the Board recommended that the ANSI A117 Committee consider the final ADA guidelines with the goal of establishing a single accessibility standard that meets the requirements of the ADA and that can be incorporated or referenced by the Federal government, model codes, and State and local building codes.

A single accessibility standard would greatly facilitate the certification of State and local codes by the Department of Justice.[7] Establishing a single accessibility standard that meets the requirements of the ADA and that can be incorporated or referenced by all levels of government will also ensure that the ADA requirements are routinely implemented at the design stage when building plans are reviewed and permits issued by state and local building officials and that non-compliance can be discovered and corrected through the building inspection process before buildings are occupied.

Several commenters also recommended that the Board adopt the draft scoping provisions developed by the CABO Board for the Coordination of the Model Codes (BCMC). The draft BCMC scoping provisions were developed before the ADA was enacted and do not meet all the requirements of the ADA.

Further, the draft BCMC scoping provisions were not developed in accordance with the same due process and consensus procedures followed by the ANSI A117 Committee.[8] Nonetheless, as discussed under specific provisions, the Board has considered the draft BCMC scoping provisions where they are consistent with the requirements of the ADA.

Minimum Guidelines

Several commenters remarked that section 504 of the ADA provides that the guidelines issued by the Board are to be "minimum guide-lines" and that the NPRM exceeded the Board's statutory authority. Specifically, some of the commenters noted that the provisions in the NPRM for areas of refuge [areas of rescue assistance in the final guide-lines], visual alarms, detectable warnings, and signage go beyond existing codes and standards.

As discussed under the statutory background, section 504(a) of the ADA requires the Board to "issue minimum guidelines that shall supple-ment the existing Minimum Guidelines and Requirements for Accessible Design (MGRAD) * * *." The Board was autho-rized to develop MGRAD by the 1978 amendments to the Rehabilitation Act of 1973 which required the Board to "establish minimum guidelines and requirements for the standards issued pursuant to * * * the Architectural Barriers Act of 1968." 29 U.S.C. 502(b)(7).[9] As originally promulgated by the Board, MGRAD contained detailed technical specifications which described how to make entrances, telephones, drinking fountains, toilet rooms, and other elements and spaces of a building or facility accessible; and scoping provisions which specified the extent to which the technical specifications must be followed, including which and how many elements and spaces are to be made accessible within a building or facility. The scoping provisions and technical specifications in MGRAD are considered to be "minimum guidelines" in that the four standard setting agencies under the Architectural Barriers Act of 1968 may exceed MGRAD's requirements and establish standard that provide a greater level of accessibility. The Department of Justice and other standard setting agencies under the ADA can also exceed the Board's "minimum guidelines" and establish standards that provide greater accessibility.

Congress specifically required in section 504 of the ADA that the Board "supplement the existing [MGRAD]" for purposes of title III of the ADA and further required that the "supplemental guidelines * * * establish additional requirements, consistent with this Act, to ensure that buildings (and) facilities * * * are accessible in terms of architecture and design, * * * and communication, to individuals with disabilities." The legislative history further explains the Board's responsibilities as follows:

In issuing the supplemental minimum guidelines and requirements called for under this legislation, the Board should consider whether other revisions or improvements of the existing MGRAD (including scoping provisions) are called for to achieve consistency with the intent and the requirements of this legislation. Particular attention should be paid to providing greater guidance regarding communication accessibility.

In no event shall the minimum guidelines issued under this legislation reduce, weaken, narrow, or set less accessibility standards than those included in existing MGRAD. H. Rept. 101-485, pt. 2, at 139.

Further, Congress was clear that it intended "a high degree of convenient accessibility" and that minimum guidelines do not mean "minimal accessibility." H. Rept. 101-485, pt. 2, at 118. Thus, Congress authorized the Board to revise MGRAD and to establish new requirements where appropriate to ensure that newly constructed and altered buildings and facilities covered by title III of the ADA

provide a high degree of convenient accessibility to individuals with disabilities.

In carrying out its responsibilities, the Board considered research and studies which have been conducted since MGRAD was last revised; the work of the ANSI A117 Committee in updating the ANSI A117.1 standard; and developments in the model codes. As directed by Congress, the Board paid particular attention to those areas relating to communication accessibility, including public telephones equipped with volume controls, public text telephones, assistive listening systems for assembly areas, visual alarms, detectable warnings, and signage. Where possible and consistent with the ADA, the Board attempted to make provisions in the NPRM consistent with the planned revisions to the ANSI A117.1 standard. This was done for visual alarms, detectable warnings, and signage. In developing provisions for areas of rescue assistance, as further explained in the NPRM the Board looked to the proposed BCMC scoping provisions for the ANSI A117.1 standard and the 1991 Uniform Building Code. See 56 FR 2296, at 2304 and 2309 (January 22, 1991).

The Board received many comments on the new provisions proposed in the NPRM. As further discussed under the section-by-section analysis, the Board has carefully considered all the comments and many of the new provisions have been revised or clarified based on the comments. The Board believes that it has acted consistent with the statute in supplementing MGRAD and establishing new requirements where appropriate to ensure that buildings and facilities covered by title III of the ADA provide a high degree of convenient accessibility to individuals with disabilities.

"User Friendly" Guidelines

Several commenters recommended editorial changes to the guidelines. Some of these commenters noted that editorial changes have been proposed to the ANSI A117.1 standard and requested that the Board

incorporate the proposed changes in the guidelines.

The Board has attempted to make the guidelines as "user friendly" as possible, including using the ANSI format and numbering system and providing additional explanatory information in the appendix to the guidelines. The Board also intends to make available manuals explaining the guidelines and to provide training and technical assistance. With respect to the proposed editorial changes to the ANSI A117.1 standard, the Board will consider all editorial changes to that standard after they have been approved by the ANSI A117 Committee.

Relationship to Other Regulations and Laws

A number of commenters requested clarification of the relationship between the Board's guidelines and section 302(b)(2)(A)(iv) of the ADA which requires the removal of architectural barriers, and communication barriers that are structural in nature, in existing facilities, where such removal is readily achievable.

The Board's guidelines are to be applied to the design, construction, and alteration of buildings and facilities to the extent required by regulations issued by other Federal agencies, including the Department of Justice, under the ADA. The Department of Justice's final regulations will address whether the Board's guidelines are applicable to removal of barriers in existing facilities where measures are taken solely to comply with section 302(b)(2)(A)(iv) of the ADA.

Several commenters also requested the Board to clarify the relationship between its guidelines and areas used only by employees as work areas. As further discussed under the section-by-section analysis, the provision in 4.1.1(3) has been revised to clarify that such areas must be designed and constructed so that individuals with disabilities can approach, enter and exit the areas. Modifications to particular work areas to meet the needs of an individual employee or applicant with a disability would be addressed by title I of the ADA which prohibits discrimination in employment on the basis of disability and which requires reasonable accommodation. This issue is within the jurisdiction of the Equal Employment Opportunity Commission.

Some commenters requested clarification regarding what requirements apply if an entity is covered by both the ADA and other Federal laws or regulations which require accessibility in new construction and alterations such as the Architectural Barriers Act of 1968 or section 504 of the Rehabilitation Act of 1973. UFAS is the applicable standard for purposes of the Architectural Barriers Act of 1968 and is also referenced as the accessibility standard in many regulations issued by other Federal agencies under section 504 of the Rehabilitation Act of 1973. In some areas, the ADA guidelines provide for greater accessibility than UFAS (e.g., provisions relating to communication access); and in other areas, UFAS provides for greater accessibility than the ADA guidelines (e.g., no elevator exception for facilities that are less than three stories or that have less than 3,000 square feet per story). An entity that is covered by both the ADA and another Federal law or regulation which requires compliance with accessibility standards must comply with the specific provisions that provide for greater accessibility.

State and Local Government Buildings

The Board is also required by section 504 of the ADA to issue accessibility guidelines for newly constructed and altered State and local government buildings which are covered by title II of the ADA. The requirements in title II of the ADA for State and local government buildings differ in some aspects from those in title III for places of public accommodation and commercial facilities. For example, the title III structural impracticability

exception in new construction and the elevator exception for newly constructed or altered facilities that are less than three stories or have less than 3,000 square feet per story do not apply to State and local government buildings. The NPRM requested information on several issues relating to State and local government buildings for purposes of developing accessibility guidelines for those facilities, including providing access to various areas in courthouses (e.g., jury boxes, witness standards, and judge's benches); experience of detention and correctional facilities in complying with the UFAS scoping provisions under current regulations issued under section 504 of the Rehabilitation Act of 1973; and whether the requirements for alterations to State and local government buildings should be the same as for places of public accommodation and commercial facilities. The Board received many comments on these issues. The Board intends to further analyze those comments and to issue proposed guidelines for State and local government buildings for public comment after these final guidelines and the final guidelines for transportation vehicles and facilities are published.

The Department of Justice's final regulations will include requirements for new construction and alterations of State and local government buildings and further address the applicable accessibility standards.

Children's Environments and Recreational Facilities

The NPRM also requested information relevant to establishing accessibility guidelines for children's environments and recreational facilities. The Board received comments in each of these areas. The Board has undertaken several activities in preparation for developing accessibility guidelines in these areas. The Board is sponsoring a research project on "Accessibility Standards for Children's Environments". The Board is

also working with the U.S. Forest Service, National Park Service, and other Federal agencies with recreation responsibilities in the development of comprehensive accessibility guidelines for outdoor recreational facilities, including boating access, water access at beaches, fishing piers, and horse back riding. It is anticipated that these projects will be completed in the Fall of 1991 and the Board intends to initiate rulemaking activity in the areas of children's environments and recreational facilities at that time.

Although the final guidelines do not include accessibility guidelines for children's environments and recreational facilities at this time, newly constructed or altered children's facilities and recreational facilities subject to title III of the ADA must comply with these guidelines where applicable. For example, an accessible route must be provided to a swimming pool deck area even though the guidelines do not presently include specific requirements for providing access to the pool itself. Technical assistance is available from the Board in this area.

Chemical and Environmental Sensitivities

The Board received over 400 comments from individuals who identified themselves as chemically sensitive. Many of the comments were sent in on preprinted postcards distributed by the National Center for Environmental Health Strategies (NCEHS). The commenters described the health problems that they have experienced due to exposure to chemical substances and indoor contaminants in buildings, including certain building materials, furnishings, cleaning products and fragrances, and tobacco smoke. They requested that the Board address their need for access to place of public accommodation and commercial facilities. Action on Smoking and Health (ASH) also requested the Board to address tobacco smoke in buildings. NCEHS and the Environmental

Health Network provided additional background materials on chemical sensitivities. Among the suggestions made to lessen exposure to chemical substances and indoor contaminants in buildings were providing windows that open; improving the design and requirements for heating, cooling, and ventilation systems; and selecting building materials and furnishings that do not contain certain chemical substances.

Chemical and environmental sensitivities present some complex issues which require coordination and cooperation with other Federal agencies and private standard setting agencies. Pending further study of these issues, the Board does not believe it is appropriate to address them at this time.

Section-by-Section Analysis

This section of the preamble contains a concise summary of the significant comments received on the NPRM, the Board's response to those comments, and any changes made to the guidelines.

1. Purpose

The purpose section has been clarified to state that the guidelines are to be applied during the design, construction, and alteration of places of public accommodation and commercial facilities to the extent required by regulations issued by Federal agencies, including the Department of Justice, under the ADA. The Department of Justice's final regulations will address the extent to which the guidelines are applicable to places of public accommodation and commercial facilities under new construction and alteration sections, including alterations to an area containing a primary function and cost disproportionality. The Department of Justice's final regulations will also address whether the guidelines are applicable to the removal of architectural barriers, and communications barriers that are structural in nature, in existing buildings and facilities where such removal is

readily achievable. The Equal Employment Opportunity Commission's final regulations will address whether the guidelines are applicable for purposes of reasonable accommodation under title I of the ADA.

2. General

2.1 Provisions for Adults

There were no comments on this section. As discussed under the general issues, the Board will develop guidelines for children's environments.

2.2 Equivalent Facilitation

Comment. Commenters generally supported the equivalent facilitation provision which permits departures from the guidelines where substantially equivalent or greater access to or usability of a building or facility is provided. Some commenters requested that the guidelines include examples of alternatives that would provide equivalent facilitation. Other commenters expressed concerns about enforcement and a few recommended that a process be established for reviewing whether equivalent facilitation is provided.

Response. The equivalent facilitation provision has been clarified by substituting the words "designs and technologies" for "methods." The purpose of the provision is to allow for flexibility to design for unique and special circumstances and to facilitate the application of new technologies. The accessibility and usability of design solutions developed for unique and special circumstances must be evaluated on a case by case basis. In the case of new technologies which provide equivalent facilitation, as those technologies become more common, the Board will consider incorporating them in the guidelines.

The final guidelines in corporate specific provisions for equivalent facilitation in five sections. In 4.1.6(3)(c), in the case of alterations to an existing facility the guidelines permit an

elevator car to have different dimensions when usability can be demonstrated and all other elements required to be accessible comply with the applicable provisions of 4.10 (e.g., a 49 inch by 69 inch elevator car with a door opening on the narrow dimension could accommodate the standard wheelchair clearances shown in figure 4). In 4.31.9, the guidelines permit the use of a portable text telephone if it is readily available for use with a nearby public pay telephone that is equipped with a shelf; an electrical outlet within, or adjacent to, the telephone enclosure; and a long enough telephone handset cord to allow connection of the text telephone and the telephone receiver if an acoustic coupler is used. In 7.2, the guidelines provide for equivalent facilitation at counters that may not have a cash register but at which goods or services are distributed (e.g., teller stations in banks, registration counters in hotels and motels) by permitting use of a folding shelf attached to the main counter on which an individual with a disability can write, and use of the space on the side of the counter or at the concierge desk for handling materials back and forth. In 9.1.4, the guidelines deem it equivalent facilitation if the operator of a hotel or similar place of transient lodging elects to limit construction of accessible rooms to those intended for multiple occupancy provided that such rooms are made available to an individual with a disability who requests a single-occupancy room. In 9.2.2(b)(d), hotels and other similar places of transient lodging are permitted to utilize a higher door threshold or a change in level at patios, terraces and balconies where necessary to protect the integrity of the unit from wind and water damage but equivalent facilitation is required where it results in patios, terraces, or balconies that are not on an accessible level (e.g., raised decking or a ramp must be provided to permit access to the patio, terrace or balcony).

Equivalent facilitation is appropriate and applies to the entire guidelines and not only those sections mentioned above. For example, other areas where equivalent facilitation may be appropriate include the use of automatic door openers for double leaf doors, and provision of audible signage for individuals with vision impairments. The use of a portable ramp, however, is not considered equivalent facilitation.

The ADA does not require any process to be established for reviewing whether equivalent facilitation is provided.

3. Miscellaneous Instructions and Definitions

3.1 Graphic Conventions

3.2 Dimensional Tolerances

3.3 Notes

3.4 General Terminology

Few comments were receive on these sections and they did not warrant any changes.

3.5 Definitions

Comment. Several commenters recommended that the term "individual with a disability" should be defined the same as in the ADA.

Response. The definition of the term "individual with a disability" has been deleted from the guidelines as unnecessary since the guidelines will be incorporated in the Department of Justice's regulations implementing title III of the ADA which will include a definition of the term. The NPRM defined "accessible" in terms of being used "by individuals with disabilities, including those affecting mobility, sensory, or cognitive functions." The definition of the term "accessible" has been revised in the final guidelines to mean a site, building, facility, or portion thereof that complies with the guidelines. In other words, buildings and facilities that meet the requirements of the guidelines are by definition accessible to individuals with disabilities.

Comment. Commenters made several recommendations for changes in the definition of the term "technically infeasible."

Response. The Definition of the term "technically infeasible" has been revised and moved to the scoping provisions for alterations at 4.1.6(1)(j). Changes to that definition are discussed under that section. A new term "structural frame" has been added to 3.5 in connection with the revised definition of "technically infeasible" which is also discussed under the scoping provision for alterations.

Comment. A commenter requested that the term "text telephone" be used in place of "telecommunication display device or telecommunication device for the deaf (TDD)."

Response. The term "text telephone" is used in the final guidelines. The term "TDD" is often understood to include devices which use only the Baudot code. Many newer models are also capable of transmitting in the ASCII code and this appears to be the trend. Other systems of communication based on computer hardware and software are also being used for communication by individuals with disabilities and their rapid proliferation suggests that they may become the dominant modes of communication in the future. The Board is concerned that the term "TDD" will become outmoded, and that entities will assume that they have satisfied their responsibilities by providing access only in an obsolete format that may be incompatible with many devices. By using the more inclusive term "text telephone," the Board intends that, as technology develops in this rapidly changing area, entities will be able to choose from a broader range of appropriate devices and formats.

Further, although the term TDD refers to a "telecommunication device for the deaf," TDDs are not used only by individuals who are deaf. Nor do all individuals who are deaf use TDDs to communicate over the telephone. The legislative history recognizes that many individuals who are deaf, hard of hearing, and speech impaired use other kinds of non-voice terminal devices. The term "text telephone" would encompass the various types of telecommunication devices. This term is currently used in Europe to describe telephones with keyboards and visual screens, and it is generally understood to mean TDDs, computer hardware and software, and other non-voice terminal devices. "Text telephones" do not include facsimile (fax) equipment.

4. Accessible Elements and Spaces: Scope and Technical Requirements

4.1 Minimum Requirements

The scoping provisions are contained in 4.1.1 through 4.1.7 and are discussed below.

4.1.1 Application

This section describes the application of the guidelines.

General (4.1.1 (1))

Comment. Several commenters requested that the application of the guidelines be clarified with respect to existing buildings.

Response. The general provision in 4.1.1(1) has been revised to clarify that all areas of newly designed or constructed buildings and facilities, and altered portions of existing buildings and facilities required to be accessible by 4.1.6, must comply with the guidelines unless otherwise provided in 4.1.1 or a special application section. The specific requirements for alterations to existing buildings are discussed under 4.1.6.

Application Based on Building Use (4.1.1(2))

Comment. Several commenters requested that application of the guidelines be clarified with respect to transportation facilities.

Response. The special application sections 5 through 10 provide additional requirements for restaurants and cafeterias, medical care facilities, business and mercantile facilities, libraries, transient lodging, and transportation facilities. Section 10 on transportation facilities was reserved in the NPRM. The Board issued a supplemental notice of proposed rulemaking (SNPRM) on March 20, 1991 in connection with its proposed guidelines on transportation vehicles containing proposed additional requirements for transportation facilities (56 FR 11874).[10] A final section 10 on transportation facilities will be issued at the same time as the final guidelines for transportation vehicles. Although the final guidelines do not contain any additional requirements for transportation facilities at this time, newly constructed or altered transportation facilities subject to tile III of the ADA must comply with these guidelines where applicable. For example, the restrooms in a newly constructed transportation facility such as a bus depot must comply with the requirements for accessible toilet facilities.

Areas Used Only By Employees As Work Areas (4.1.1(3))

Comment. A number of commenters requested that the application of the guidelines to areas used only by employees as work areas be clarified. Some commenters wanted employee work areas to be adaptable with adjustable elements and to comply with requirements for clear floor space, reach ranges and visual alarms.
Response. The legislative history explains that areas used only by employees as work areas are covered by the guidelines but individual work stations are not required to be constructed in a fully accessible manner. H. Rept. 101-485, pt. 3, at 63. Modifications to an individual workstation would be covered by reasonable accommodation under title I of the ADA which prohibits discrimination in employment on the basis of disability. The Equal Employment Opportunity Commission is responsible for issuing regulations to implement title I of the ADA.

The provision in 4.1.1(3) has been revised to clarify that areas that are used only by employees as work areas shall be designed and constructed so that individuals with disabilities can approach, enter, and exit the areas. For instance, individual office rooms in a typical office building must be on an accessible route and the doors to the rooms must comply with the technical specifications in 4.13.

The guidelines do not require that any work areas be constructed to permit maneuvering within the work area (e.g., maneuvering spaces around a desk) or that fixed or built-in equipment be accessible (e.g., counters or shelves). However, modifications may be required to a particular work area for an individual employee or applicant with a disability as a reasonable accommodation under title I of the ADA.

The appendix includes advisory guidance on individual work stations at A4.1.1(3). Where there are a series of built-in or fixed individual work stations of the same type (e.g., laboratories, service counters, ticket booths), in order to facilitate reasonable accommodation at a future date, it is recommended that 5% or at least one of each type of work station should be constructed so that an individual with disabilities can maneuver within the work station. Consideration should also be given to placing shelves in an employee work area at a convenient height for accessibility or installing commercially available shelving that is adjustable so that reasonable accommodations can be made in the future.
Comment. The NPRM requested information on fixed or built-in equipment in physician's offices that is used by patients and should be addressed by the guidelines. Commenters recommended that examining tables, diagnostic machinery, and dental chairs should be accessible or adaptable. However, anecdotal information suggests that most of the equipment is not fixed or built-in the structure of the building. No information was

submitted on technical specifications for such equipment.
Response. These guidelines are intended to address only that equipment that is fixed or built into the structure of the building. The Board believes that this issue requires further study before it can be addressed in the guidelines. The Board may provide technical assistance in this area.

Temporary Structures (4.1.1(4))

Comment. The NPRM asked whether trailers at construction sites should be included in the list of temporary structures in 4.1.1(4) covered by the guidelines. Most of the commenters from each category who responded to the question stated that such structures should not be required to comply with the guidelines. The Associated General Contractors of America pointed out that the legislative history specifically states that construction sites are not to be considered a public accommodation. See H. Rept. 101-485, pt. 1, at 36.
Response. Based on legislative history, the list of temporary structures in 4.1.1(4) has been revised to state that construction trailers are not included.

General Exceptions (4.1.1(5))

Comment. With respect to the exception in 4.1.1(5)(a) for structural impracticability in new construction, some commenters questioned whether such an exception is necessary in new construction. Other commenters requested that the term be further defined. A few commenters suggested that the exception implied that the entire building or facility was exempt from the guidelines.
Response. The exception in 4.1.1(5)(a) is based on section 303(a)(1) of the ADA. The legislative history explains that the exception is a narrow one and applies only in rare circumstances where unique characteristics of terrain prevent the incorporation of accessibility features. H. Rept. 101-485, pt. 2, at 120. The

legislative history further explains that the exception is not to be viewed as totally exempting the entire building or facility for the guidelines. id. The exception has been revised to clarify that if full compliance with the guidelines is structurally impracticable in new construction, the entity must comply with the guidelines to the extent that it is not structurally impracticable. Any portion of the building or facility which can be made accessible and is required by the guidelines to be accessible must comply with the guidelines.

Comment. The NPRM asked whether other spaces should be included in the list in 4.1.1(5)(b) of spaces exempt from complying with the guidelines and whether functional criteria should be developed for identifying such spaces. Most of the commenters who responded to the question favored the functional criteria approach. Commenters also recommended specific spaces to be included in the exception.

Response. The exception in 4.1.1(5)(b) has been revised to include functional criteria and exempts non-occupiable spaces that are: (a) Accessed only by ladders, catwalks, crawl spaces, very narrow passageways, or freight or non-passenger elevators; and (b) frequented only by service personnel for repair purposes. Such spaces include but are not limited to elevator pits, elevator penthouses, and piping or equipment catwalks. Some of the spaces recommended by commenters such as cooling towers and utility tunnels would be covered by the functional criteria. Other spaces suggested by commenters such as mechanical rooms or closets that are not accessed by ladders or very narrow passageways are considered employee work areas and are covered under 4.1.1(3) which only requires that individuals with disabilities be able to approach, enter, and exit the area but does not require maneuvering space to be provided in the area.

Observation galleries that are raised to look out over an area below and are used primarily for security purposes

have also been included in the spaces exempt from the guidelines. This exemption prevails over the requirement in 4.1.1(3) that employee work areas be designed and constructed so that individuals with disabilities can approach, enter, and exit the area. Under the exemption, a vertical means of accessibility is not required to such galleries. However, modifications to such galleries to provide a vertical means of access to an employee with a disability may be required as a reasonable accommodation under title I of the ADA.

4.1.2 Accessible Sites and Exterior Facilities

This section contains scoping provisions for accessible sites and exterior facilities.

Accessible Route (4.1.2(1) and (2))

Protruding Objects (4.1.2(3))

Ground Surfaces (4.1.2(4))

Few comments were received on these scoping provisions and they did not warrant any changes.

Parking (4.1.2(5))

Comment. A number of commenters from each category stated that the number of accessible parking spaces specified in the table in 4.1.2.(5)(a) is adequate. Some commenters stated that the number should be increased, and other commenters stated that the number should be reduced. One commenter submitted a report prepared for the institute of Traffic Engineers (ITE) which was based on a survey of 198 sites taken between 1986 and 1987. The ITE report recommended that the number of accessible spaces be based on occupancy type and gross floor area of the building or facility. The National Parking Association (NPA) and some members of its Parking Consultants Council (PCC) submitted recommended standards based on the ITE report. The NPA/PCC

standards recommend that three categories be established for accessible parking spaces: High use, moderate use, and low use. The high use category would provide a number of accessible parking spaces similar to that contained in the table in 4.1.2(5)(a) and apply to occupancy types where an above average number of individuals with disabilities might reasonably be anticipated. The NPA/PCC suggested that high use occupancy types would include hospitals, nursing homes, medical office buildings, and social service agencies. The low use category would provide for approximately one-half the number of accessible spaces as the high use category and apply to occupancy types which generate primarily regular, long-term parking (3 hours or more in duration) such as airports, schools, universities, office buildings (except medical), warehousing, manufacturing, and industries. The medium use category would provide for a number of accessible parking spaces between the high use and low use categories and apply to any occupancy type that does not clearly qualify as either high or low use. The NPA submitted a revised set of recommendations after the close of the comment period based on a recent survey by its members. In place of the high, medium, and low use categories, the NPA recommended three classes of occupancy types. Class I would consist of medical facilities and have a slightly higher number of accessible parking spaces then contained in the table in 4.1.2(5)(a). Class II would consist of public accommodations except those specifically included in Classes I or III and provide for a number of accessible parking spaces similar to that contained in the table in 4.1.2(5)(a). According to the NPA, the recent survey data showed the number of parking spaces specified in the table in 4.1.2(5)(a) "appears to reasonably fit the Class II uses [public accommodations] and the requirements of smaller facilities are not unreasonable." Class III would consist of commercial uses, mixed uses in which the majority of parkers are generated by a commercial use, public parking facilities in central business districts, and universities and provide for about one-half the number of accessible parking spaces specified in the table in 4.1.2(5)(a).

Response. The number of parking spaces required for specific occupancy uses is usually established by State and local zoning and land use codes. The guidelines require that a percentage of the parking spaces required under State and local codes be accessible. As noted above, the recent NPA survey supports the adequacy of the table contained in 4.1.2(5)(a) for most public accommodations. A recent study conducted for the Board on accessible parking spaces and loading zones also concluded that the table in 4.1.2(5)(a) was adequate and recommended that surveys be taken every two to three years to evaluate its continuing adequacy. No changes have been made in the table contained in 4.1.2(5)(a) because the comments and two surveys support the table.

A sentence has been added to 4.1.2(5)(a) to clarify that spaces required by the table need not be provided in the particular lot. They may be provided in a different location if equivalent or greater accessibility in terms of distance from an accessible entrance, cost, and convenience is ensured.

The NPRM proposed to add a provision to 4.1.5(a) requiring accessible parking spaces to be located as close as practical to an accessible entrance. In the final guidelines, requirements regarding the location of accessible parking spaces have been consolidated in the technical specifications for parking at 4.6.2 and are further discussed there.

Facilities that provide medical care and other services for persons with mobility impairments are discussed under a separate comment below. As for so called "low use" of "Class III" occupancy types, the ITE and NPA surveys

apparently did not consider the level of accessibility provided at the buildings and facilities which would affect usage by individuals with disabilities. The Board finds no basis for concluding that individuals with disabilities have less need for using buildings and facilities included in the so called "low use" or "Class III" occupancy types, including airports, schools, universities, office buildings, and public parking facilities in central business districts. The passage and implementation of the ADA will enable and encourage many more individuals with disabilities to use these buildings and facilities and, therefore, the Board rejects establishing a separate table with a lower number of accessible parking spaces for so called "low use" or "Class III" occupancy types.

Comment. The NPRM asked whether accessible parking spaces should be required for vans and, if so, whether such spaces should be in addition to the number of accessible parking spaces specified in the table in 4.1.2(5)(a) or a percentage of those spaces. Most of the persons in each category who responded to the question were in favor of requiring accessible parking spaces for vans and recommended that those spaces should be a percentage of the spaces specified in the table in 4.1.2(5)(a). Specific recommendations ranged from 0.5% to 75%. Commenters also submitted various recommendations for the minimum width of accessible parking spaces needed to accommodate vans which ranged from 13 feet to 18 feet, including an adjacent access aisle. Recommendations for vertical clearance needed for vans ranged from 96 inches to 144 inches. Several commenters recommended that all accessible parking spaces should be the same size and be capable of accommodating vans. Some commenters recommended adoption of the universal parking design guidelines developed by the City of Phoenix Fire Department which provides for all accessible parking spaces to be at least 11

feet wide and to have an adjacent access aisle at least 5 feet wide.

Response. The technical specification in 4.6.3 for accessible parking spaces require such spaces to be 8 feet (96 inches) wide minimum and to have an adjacent access aisle 5 feet (60 inches) wide minimum. Two accessible parking spaces may share a common access aisle. An access aisle that is 60 inches wide does not provide sufficient space to permit a lift to be deployed from the side of a van and still leave room for a person using a wheelchair or other mobility aid to exit from the lift platform. A recent Board sponsored study on accessible parking and loading zones conducted tests with various van, lift, and wheelchair combinations and found that a parking space and access aisle almost 17 feet wide is needed to deploy a lift and exit conveniently.

Requirements have been added to the scoping provisions in 4.1.2(5)(b) requiring that one in every eight accessible parking spaces, but not less than one, be served by an access aisle 96 inches (8 feet) wide minimum and be designated "van accessible." For instance, if there are 16 accessible parking spaces, at least two wider access aisles must be provided. If a wider access aisle is placed between two accessible parking spaces, then both parking spaces can accommodate vans.

Requirements have also been added to the technical specifications in 4.6.5 regarding the vertical clearance to be provided at van accessible parking spaces. The NPRM proposed that the minimum vertical clearances should be 114 inches. This figure was taken from MGRAD and UFAS which was based on a survey of paratransit vehicles for purposes of establishing the vertical clearance needed at passenger loading zones. The survey found that the highest paratransit vehicle had a height of 120 inches but that a vertical clearance of 114 inches would accommodate most paratransit vehicles. MGRAD and UFAS used the same figure for accessible parking spaces for vans; however, such spaces were not mandatory. Personal vans are usually not as tall as paratransit vehicles. This is especially true with growing use of accessible mini-vans. California requires a minimum vertical clearance of 98 inches which accommodates most vans without seriously affecting multi-level parking structures. Based on the experience with the California standard, the technical specifications in 4.6.5 adopt a minimum vertical clearance of 98 inches for van accessible parking spaces. The vertical clearance must be provided along at least one vehicle access route from the site entrance(s) and exit(s) to the van accessible parking space. The technical specifications in 4.6.5 permit the van accessible parking spaces to be grouped on one level of a parking structure.

An exception has also been added to 4.1.2(5)(a) permitting all required accessible parking spaces to conform to the universal parking design guidelines developed by the City of Phoenix Fire Department. As discussed above, those guidelines provide for accessible parking spaces to be at least 11 feet wide and to have an adjacent access aisle at least 5 feet wide. Additional information on the universal parking design guidelines is provided in the appendix at A4.6.3

Comment. A number of commenters recommended that the scoping provision for accessible parking spaces at transient lodging (4.1.2(5)(d) in the NPRM) be revised. The provision would require that where parking is provided for all occupants, one accessible parking space be provided for each accessible unit or sleeping room; and where parking is provided for visitors, 2% of the spaces or a least one be accessible. Some commenters pointed out that the provision was not workable because many places of transient lodging, such as hotels, do not provide parking spaces for each room.

Response. The provision was based on similar requirement in MGRAD and UFAS which was

intended for accessible housing. The provision may not be applicable to all places of transient lodging and has been deleted from the final guidelines. Instead, places of transient lodging must provide the number of accessible parking spaces specified in the table in 4.1.2(5)(a).

Comment. The NPRM asked whether the scoping provision in 4.1.2(5)(d) (4.1.2(5)(e) in the NPRM) should require nonmedical facilities that specialize in providing services for persons with mobility impairments such as vocational rehabilitation facilities to provide a higher number of accessible parking spaces. Most of the commenters who responded to the question favored requiring such facilities to provide a higher number of accessible parking spaces. Some commenters recommended that the percentage be greater than that proposed in the NPRM.

Response. The scoping provision in 4.1.2(5)(d) (4.1.2(5)(e) in the NPRM) has been revised and clarified. The provision has been clarified as applying to facilities that provide medical care and other services for persons with mobility impairments and units of such facilities. Generally, facilities that provide medical care and other services for persons with mobility impairments are required to provide the number of accessible parking spaces specified in the table in 4.1.2(5)(a) except in two cases. The first case applies to outpatient units and facilities where 10% of the total number of parking spaces serving each such unit or facility must be accessible. The second case applies to units and facilities that specialize in treatment or services for persons with mobility impairments where 20% of the total number of parking spaces serving each such unit or facility must be accessible. The latter case would include vocational rehabilitation facilities.

Comment. The National Parking Association (NPA) requested that valet parking facilities not be required to comply with the guidelines.

Response. Valet parking facilities are different from self-parking facilities. In valet parking facilities, the driver and passenger usually leave the vehicle at the entrance of the facility and another person parks the vehicle. The final guidelines require in 4.1.2(5)(e) that valet parking facilities provide an accessible passenger loading zone located on an accessible route to the entrance of the facility. Additional advisory material on valet parking is included in the appendix at A4.1.2(5)(e).

Portable Toilet and Bathing Units (4.1.2(6))

Comment. The NPRM asked whether the scoping provision of accessible portable toilets and bathing units should be advisory or mandatory. Most persons who responded to the question favored making the provision mandatory. As for how many accessible units should be required when single user units are clustered at a single location, the recommendations ranged from at least one unit to 100%.

Response. The provision has been revised to require that where single user portable toilet or bathing units are clustered at a single location, at least 5% but no less than one of the units at each cluster must be accessible.

Comment. Several commenters recommended that portable toilet units at construction sites should not be required to be accessible.

Response. An exception has been added for portable toilet units at construction sites used exclusively by construction personnel.

Exterior Signage (4.1.2(7))

Comment. Based on the comments received from graphic designers and sign manufacturers, the Board concluded that the scoping provisions and technical specifications for signage were unclear and needed to be revised. Many interpreted the NPRM as requiring all signs to have raised and brailled characters and all upper case letters.

Response. The scoping provisions for exterior and interior signage and the accompanying technical specifications have been clarified and revised in response to the comments. See 4.1.3(16) for scoping provisions for interior signage; and 4.30 for technical specifications for signage. Exterior signs which designate permanent rooms and spaces must comply with the technical specifications in 4.30.1 and 4.30.4 through 4.30.6 for raised and brailled characters, finish and contrast, and mounting location and height. For instance, signs on toilet facilities at a zoo must have raised and brailled characters designating the men's and women's toilet facilities, and also meet the finish and contrast, and mounting location and height requirements. Exterior signs which provide directions to or information about functional spaces of a building or facility must comply with the technical specifications in 4.30.1, 4.30.2 and 4.30.5 for character proportion, and finish and contrast. The technical specifications in 4.30.3 for character height must also be complied with if the signage is suspended or projected overhead in compliance with the technical specifications in 4.4.2 for head room for protruding objects. For instance, a sign adjacent to a pedestrian walkway directing the public to an accessible entrance to a building or facility must meet the character proportion and finish and contrast requirements, as well as the character height requirements if suspended or projected above the walkway in compliance with 4.4.2.

4.1.3 Accessible Buildings: New Construction

This section contains scoping provisions for new construction of accessible buildings and facilities.

Accessible Route (4.1.3(1))

Protruding Objects (4.1.3(2))

Ground and Floor Surfaces (4.1.3(3))

Few comments were received on these scoping provisions and they did not warrant any changes.

Stairs (4.1.3(4))

Comment. Several commenters requested clarification regarding whether 4.1.3(4) applies to exterior stairs, as well as interior stairs.

Response. The provision has been clarified that interior and exterior stairs must comply with the technical specifications in 4.9 for stairs when they connect levels that are not connected by an elevator or other accessible means of vertical access (e.g., ramp or lift). In other words, for example, if an elevator serves as a means of going from one floor to another, the stairs connecting the two floors are not required to comply with 4.9.

Comment. The NPRM asked whether in new construction stairs connecting levels that are also served by an elevator should be required to comply with the technical specifications in 4.9 for stairs especially since stairs must be used in emergency evacuations. Most persons who responded to the question favored such a requirement. Several commenters recommended that the provision should apply only to stairs required by State and local building codes for egress. Other commenters noted that the model codes are incorporating more safety features for stairs and that it is unnecessary to address the same features in accessibility standards.

Response. The technical specifications in 4.9 regarding stair treads and risers, nosings, and handrails are safety features which affect all members of the public. As the model codes are updated, more general safety features which also provide greater accessibility are being incorporated in those codes. The problem identified in the NPRM may be addressed through the model codes. The Board plans to monitor the development of the model codes and has not made

any changes to the scoping provision for stairs other than to clarify that the provisions applies to exterior stairs, as well as interior stairs.

Elevators (4.1.3(5))

Elevator Exemption (4.1.3(5) Exception 1).

Comment. A number of commenters objected to exempting buildings and facilities that are less than three stories or have less than 3,000 square feet per story from the elevator requirement unless the building or facility is a shopping center, a shopping mall, the professional office of a health care provider, or another type of facility that has been determined by the Attorney General to require an elevator.

Response. The elevator exemption is based on section 303(b) of the ADA. The Department of Justice is responsible for implementing this section of the ADA and that agency's final regulations will address definitions and application of the section.

A statement has been added to the appendix at 4.1.3(8) explaining that if a building or facility is exempt from the elevator requirement, it is not necessary to provide another accessible means of vertical access (e.g., ramps, platform lifts or wheelchair lifts) between each level of the building or facility.

Comment. Some commenters requested that basements, attics, and mezzanines be counted for purposes of determining whether a building or facility is less than three stories. Other commenters requested that basements, attics, and mezzanines not be counted.

Response. A "story" is defined in 3.5 as including "occupiable" space which in turn is defined as space that is: (a) Designed for human occupancy in which individuals congregate for amusement, educational or similar purposes, or in which occupants are engaged at labor; and (b) equipped with means of egress, light, and ventilation. If a basement or attic is designed or intended to be used as occupiable space or is later altered to be occupiable, it is counted for purposes of determining whether a building or facility is less than three stories.

As for mezzanines, the model codes do not consider mezzanines to be a story. Where possible, the Board defines terms in the guidelines to be consistent with the model codes when they are also consistent with the ADA and, therefore, mezzanines are not counted for purposes of determining whether a building or facility is less than three stories. However, as further discussed below, if a building or facility is exempt from the elevator requirement, but nonetheless has a full passenger elevator, that elevator must serve each level, including the mezzanine.

Comment. Several commenters questioned why buildings and facilities that are exempt from the elevator requirement must comply with other requirements in 4.1.3 on floors above or below the accessible ground floor.

Response. This provision is based on the legislative history which states that "the exception regarding elevators does not obviate or limit in any way the obligation to comply with the other accessibility requirements established by this legislation, including requirements applicable to floors which, pursuant to the exception, are not served by an elevator." H. Rept. 101-485, pt 2, at 114. There are several reasons for this provision. Some individuals who are mobility impaired may work on a building's second floor, which they can reach by stairs and the use of crutches; however, the same individuals, once they reach the second floor, may then use a wheelchair that is kept in the office. Further, an elevator may be installed at a future date, or an addition to the building or a second building which is later connected may include an elevator. The second floor must also be accessible to individuals with visual or hearing impairments.

Comment. With respect to a new building or facility that is exempt from the elevator

requirement but an elevator is nonetheless planned, the NPRM asked whether it was appropriate to require the elevator in such a building or facility to meet the technical specifications in 4.10 for elevators and to serve each level in the building or facility. Most persons who responded to the question favored the requirement. Some commenters recommended that the provision be limited to full passenger elevators and not freight elevators.

Response. This provision is also based on the legislative history. See H. Rept. 101-485, pt. 2, at 114. The Board agrees that the provision should apply only to full passenger elevators and has added appropriate language to the elevator exemption. A sentence has also been added to the provision that if a full passenger elevator provides service from a garage to only one level of a building or facility, it is not required to serve the other levels of the building or facility.

Platform Lifts/Wheelchair Lifts (4.1.3(5) Exception 4)

Comment. The NPRM noted that some building codes and the proposed BCMC scoping provisions prohibit the installation of platform lifts or wheelchair lifts as part of a required accessible route in new construction and asked a series of questions regarding their use. Individuals with disabilities and their organizations who responded to the questions viewed platform lifts or wheelchair lifts as inferior to ramps, not independently operated, poorly maintained, dangerous, and undignified. However, some of these commenters acknowledged that in some alteration projects, and in limited areas in new construction, a platform lift or wheelchair lift may be the only viable option for accessibility. Lift manufacturers and vendors acknowledged that there have been significant problems in the past but believed that improvements have been made, and gave examples where a platform lift or wheelchair lift provided a better design solution than a ramp. Several

architects and other commenters recommended that the Board specify conditions for the use of platform lifts or wheelchair lifts.

Response. Rather than prohibit platform lifts or wheelchair lifts in new construction, the Board believes that the better approach is to specify the conditions where their use is allowed. The applicable exception under 4.1.3(5) has been revised to permit the use of platform lifts or wheelchair lifts complying with 4.11 and applicable State or local codes in new construction under the following conditions:

(a) To provide an accessible route to performing area in an assembly occupancy;

(b) To comply with the wheelchair viewing position line-of-sight and dispersion requirements of 4.33.3 (e.g., to provide access to seating areas located above a cross aisle or to box seats);

(c) To provide access to incidental occupant spaces and rooms which are not open to the general public and which house no more than five persons (e.g., equipment control rooms, projection booths, radio and news booths, raised pharmacy platforms, manager's stations in food stores); and

(d) To provide access when existing site constraints or other constraints make use of a ramp or an elevator infeasible.

The last condition allows the use of platform lifts or wheelchair lifts only in very limited circumstances where use of a ramp or an elevator is infeasible due to existing site constraints or other constraints. For example, if a new infill building is being constructed incorporating a historic facade which must be maintained, thereby effectively predetermining the entry floor level, and space for a ramp to the entry floor level was not available, a platform lift or wheelchair lift would be permitted. Windows (4.1.3(6)) The NPRM proposed to require that operable windows comply with the technical specifications in 4.12 for windows. For reasons explained under 4.12, the Board has decided to reserve the technical specifications for windows in the final guidelines and, therefore, the scoping provision is also reserved.

Doors (4.1.3(7))

Comment. Several commenters requested that a requirement be added for at least one automated door at a principal entrance, or at each entrance, or at certain rooms (e.g., restrooms, meeting rooms).

Response. The force required to open a door can affect usability of a building or facility by individuals with disabilities. This is especially true for exterior doors where a variety of factors can affect closing force (e.g., wind pressure, weight of door, heating and ventilation systems, positive or negative pressure within a building). Neither UFAS nor these guidelines specify an opening force for exterior doors because of these variable factors. Requiring an automated door in certain occupancies or large buildings could provide a solution to the problem. The Board plans to study this issue to determine where and in what types of buildings and facilities automated doors may be practical or necessary and cost feasible for future revision of the guidelines.

Entrances (4.1.3(8))

Comment. The NPRM asked two questions regarding entrances in new construction. First, in the case of buildings that have more than one ground floor level (e.g., buildings with a split level entrance leading only to stairs or escalators which connect with upper and lower levels less than one story above or below grade, and buildings built on hillsides with more than one floor having direct access to grade), should each ground floor level have an accessible entrance?[11] Second, should all entrances to every building be accessible? Businesses generally favored providing an accessible entrance at only one ground floor level in response to the first question and making some but not all entrances accessible

in response to the second question. Individuals with disabilities and their organizations, and commenters from other categories, generally favored providing an accessible entrance at each ground floor level in response to the first question and making all entrances accessible in response to the second question.

Response. The NPRM proposed to follow UFAS which establishes two requirements for entrances. First, at least one principal entrance at each ground floor would be required to be accessible.[12] Second, when a building or facility has entrances which normally serve transportation facilities, passenger loading zones, accessible parking facilities, public streets and sidewalks, or accessible interior vertical access, at least one of the entrances serving each function would have to be accessible.

Depending on the interpretation of what it means for an entrance to "normally serve" a function, the NPRM could result in all the entrances to a building being accessible as illustrated by the following example. A building has four entrances: One on each side. Two of the entrances lead directly to parking lots of equal size on opposite sides of the building. People who use the building usually arrive by car and enter through the two parking lot entrances making them principal entrances. Each parking lot has accessible parking spaces and the two parking lot entrances are accessible and connected by an accessible route to the accessible parking spaces. The third entrance leads directly to a driveway with a bus stop and the fourth entrance leads directly to a public sidewalk. Even if the bus stop and the public sidewalk are connected by an accessible route to the two parking lot entrances, the third and fourth entrances could nonetheless be required to be accessible under the NPRM if an entrance which "normally serves" a function means the nearest entrance which directly leads to the function.

The legislative history makes clear that not every

feature of every building needs to be accessible but rather a high level of convenient access is contemplated. The legislative history further states that "(a)ccessibility requirements shall not be evaded by constructing facilities in such a way that no story constitutes a `ground floor,' for example, by constructing a building whose main entrance leads to stairways or escalators that connect with upper or lower floors; at least one accessible ground story must be provided." H. Rept. 101-596, at 77. Thus, each newly constructed building or facility must have at least one ground story entrance and at least one accessible entrance. The legislative history does not state that all or even most entrances must be accessible.

The Board wants to ensure a high level of access to all new buildings consistent with the statute. The Board has sought to require accessible entrances in a number that is easily definable and reasonable. The Board also wants to ensure that the requirements can be and will be met in all instances, except in those rare cases where the structural impracticability exception applies. In some urban and suburban areas, much new construction is "infill" between existing facilities and is constricted by slope and other site considerations, such as existing sidewalks and nearby property lines. In some areas there are land use plans and other restrictions that, in effect, limit development to sites where slopes are between 10% and 25%. For example, Maryland is considering imposing a land use plan on its localities which would preserve "agricultural" land (generally less than 10% slope) and steeply sloped land (more than 25% slope) and thus focus new development in areas with slopes between 10% and 25%. The Board understands that other States are considering similar proposals. Structural impracticability is a very narrow exception and, as explained in the legislative history, does not apply to situations where a building is constructed on "hilly" terrain or on a plot of land with steep slopes. H. Rept. 101-485, pt. 2, at 120. The Board believes it would be unreasonable to require all entrances to be accessible in these cases.

There is very little data available concerning the impact of site considerations on entrance accessibility. The Department of Housing and Urban Development's analysis of its Fair Housing Accessibility (FHA) Guidelines estimated the cost of providing 27 accessible entrances in new constructions at three different apartment complexes at sites having slopes of less than 10%, as ranging from an additional $240 to $1636 per entrance. The average cost was $836 per entrance. This data is not easily transferable to commercial construction because of the differences between residential and commercial construction and the differences in the FHA guidelines and the ADA guidelines. The Board's draft final regulatory impact analysis estimates the cost of an accessible building entrance ramp with a 1:12 slope for a 5-feet rise and railings extensions to be $6460 for offices and hotels. This cost does not take grading or retaining walls into account.

Thus, the Board is not at this time mandating 100% accessible entrances in new construction. At the same time, the Board recognizes that providing only one accessible entrance to a building with multiple public entrances will not always achieve the high level of convenient access contemplated by the ADA. In light of all these concerns, the Board has established two independent requirements for entrances in 4.1.3(8) (a) and (b). First, 4.1.3(8)(a)(i) requires that at least 50% of all public entrances be accessible. One of these must be a ground floor entrance. In addition, 4.1.3(8)(a)(ii) requires that accessible entrances must be provided in a number at least equivalent to the number of exits required by the applicable State or local building or life safety code. This provision acknowledges the importance of life safety issues in access to, use of, and egress from a

building. Model building and life safety codes are generally consistent in their method of determining the number of exits required, the exit width necessary, and the separation of exits needed to ensure safe egress during an emergency. Since not all exits are required to serve as entrances, if only one building entrance is planned, and a building or life safety code requires two fire exits, 4.1.3(8)(ii) would not require the provision of more than the one planned entrance. Furthermore, 4.1.8(a)(iii) requires accessible entrances be provided to each tenancy in a facility. One entrance may be considered as meeting more than one of the requirements in 4.1.3(8)(a) (i) through (iii). Where feasible, the accessible entrances must be the entrances used by the majority of people visiting or working in the building.

Second, 4.1.3(8)(b) (i) and (ii) require that accessible entrances be provided from any indoor garages, pedestrian tunnels, or elevated walkways that have entrances to the facility. One entrance may be considered as meeting more than one of the requirements in 4.1.3(8)(b) (i) and (ii).

The Board believes that these provisions, combined with the other requirements described above, will ensure access at least equivalent to that required by MGRAD and UFAS and intended by Congress.

The NPRM included a requirement in the technical specifications for signage at 4.30.1 that entrances which are not accessible to have directional signage complying with 4.30 indicating the location of the nearest accessible entrance. This requirement has been placed in the scoping provisions for entrances in the final guidelines.

Comment. Several commenters recommended including sections from the proposed BCMC scoping provisions in the guidelines requiring an accessible entrance to be provided to each tenancy within a building (e.g., retail stores in a strip shopping center), and all entrances having walkways with a change

in elevation of 6 inches or less at the entrance to be accessible.

Response. Multi-tenant facilities such as a strip shopping center are generally viewed as one building. To ensure that each retail store and other places of public accommodation within such facilities are accessible, a requirement has been added to 4.1.3(8)(a)(iii) for an accessible entrance to be provided to each tenancy within a building. As for entrances having walkways with a change in elevation of 6 inches or less at the entrance, the provision is not necessary in light of 4.1.3(8) in its entirety. Further, the proposed BCMC scoping provision does not address the fact that site preparation can usually be made to ensure an elevation change of more than 6 inches, thereby circumventing the intent of the requirement.

Egress and Areas of Rescue Assistance (4.1.3(9))

Comment. The NPRM proposed to require "areas of refuge" in newly constructed buildings and facilities which were defined as areas, which have direct access to an exit stairway, where people who are unable to use stairs may remain safely to await further instructions or assistance during emergency evacuation. Building owners and managers and businesses objected to the concept of "area of refuge." Many of these commenters, including the Building Owners and Managers Association (BOMA), expressed concern that such areas would result in restricting evacuation of individuals with disabilities during an emergency. Evacuation plans were recommended instead. Individuals with disabilities and their organizations who commented on the provision supported it.

Response. The Board wishes to emphasize that the purpose of areas of refuge is to facilitate and not restrict the evacuation of wheelchair users and other individuals with mobility impairments during an emergency. MGRAD, UFAS, and the ANSI A117.1 standard, all require that accessible routes connect to an accessible place of refuge in the event of an emergency. Since elevators are generally not available for egress during a fire, a safe area is needed where wheelchair users and other individuals with mobility impairments who cannot exit by stairways can temporarily await further instructions or evacuation assistance. To clarify this point, the area has been renamed "areas of rescue assistance" in the final guidelines. The appendix to the guidelines recognizes in A4.3.10 that an emergency management plan for the evacuation of people with disabilities is essential in providing for fire safety in buildings and facilities. However, an evacuation plan alone is not sufficient to ensure the safety of individuals with mobility impairments during an emergency since individuals may not be able to transfer to an evacuation device or may require assistance from trained personnel.

The final guidelines incorporate modified scoping provisions and technical specifications from chapter 31, section 3104 of the 1991 Uniform Building Code. In buildings and facilities, or portions of buildings and facilities, required to be accessible under the ADA, accessible means of egress must be provided in the same number as required for exits by State or local building and life safety codes. Where a required exit from an occupiable level above or below a level of accessible exit discharge is not accessible, areas of rescue assistance must be provided on each level in a number equal to that of inaccessible required exits. A horizontal exit which meets the requirements of state or local building or life safety codes may also be used for an area of rescue assistance.

The scoping provisions in 4.1.3(9) for areas of rescue assistance do not apply to exterior facilities covered by 4.1.2. For example, parking lots and open parking garages are covered only by 4.1.2 and are not required to comply with the scoping provisions in 4.1.3(9) for areas of rescue assistance.

The technical specifications for areas of rescue assistance are discussed under 4.3.11 and provide several alternatives for design of such areas. The draft final regulatory impact estimates the additional direct costs for creation of an area of rescue assistance in a portion of a stairway landing in a new building to be $624. Although there are less expensive alternatives, this option was analyzed in the draft final regulatory impact analysis because it is commonly used at the current time in buildings that provide area of rescue assistance and because it represents the highest range of cost that will be incurred. Based on this estimate, the additional direct costs for providing areas of rescue assistance in stairway landings in a new low-rise office building 6 stories and 40,000 square feet per story would be $6,240 or $.03 per square foot of building area; and in a high-rise office building with 25 stories 30,000 square feet per story would be $29,952 or $.04 per square foot of building area. In many cases the cost of providing areas of rescue assistance will be much lower because such areas can be provided in elevator lobbies, office rooms, and similar space used for other purposes. No costs will be incurred in alterations or in new buildings with supervised automatic sprinkler systems because of exceptions which are included in the final guidelines as explained below. The Board believes these costs to be reasonable in light of this important life safety issue.

Comment. Several commenters requested that buildings and facilities equipped with a supervised automatic sprinkler system be exempted from the requirements for areas of rescue assistance.

Response. An exception has been added exempting buildings and facilities having a supervised automatic sprinkler from the requirements for areas of rescue assistance. Supervised automatic sprinkler systems have built in signals for monitoring features of the system such as the opening and

closing of water control valves, the power supplies for needed pumps, and water tank levels, and for indicating conditions that will impair the satisfactory operation of the sprinkler system. Because of these monitoring features, supervised automatic sprinkler systems have a high level of satisfactory performance and response to fire conditions and the Board does not believe that additional measures are needed in buildings and facilities with such systems.

Comment. The American Hotel and Motel Association requested that in the case of hotels and motels on floors used exclusively for guest rooms, such rooms be permitted to serve as areas of rescue assistance because State and local building and life safety codes require them to be fire-resistive.

Response. The organization responsible for development of the Uniform Building Code rejected this proposal on the grounds that it is inappropriate to designate a room or space that is not available to the public as an area of rescue assistance. The Board declines to accept the proposal for the same reason. In addition, there are some inconsistencies among State and local building and life safety codes regarding requirements for fire-resistive construction.

Comment. Several commenters raised questions regarding the application of the requirements for areas of rescue of assistance to alterations of existing facilities.

Response. The guidelines require areas of rescue assistance only in new construction. For the reasons discussed under 4.1.6(1)(g), a paragraph has been added to the scoping provisions for alterations to clarify that the requirements for areas of rescue assistance do not apply to alterations of existing facilities.

Drinking Fountains (4.1.3(10))

Comment. The NPRM asked whether a specific percentage of accessible drinking fountains should be required and, if so, whether at least 50% would be an appropriate number. Most persons who commented on the question stated that at least 50% was an appropriate number. Several commenters requested that the provisions address the distance between accessible drinking fountains.

Response. The Board wants to ensure that drinking fountains are accessible to wheelchair users and individuals who have difficulty bending or stooping. The final guidelines provide that where there is only one drinking fountain on a floor, there must be a drinking fountain that is accessible to wheelchair users in accordance with 4.15 and individuals who have difficulty bending or stooping. This can be accomplished by use of a "hi-lo" drinking fountain; by providing one drinking fountain accessible to wheelchair users and one drinking fountain at a standard height convenient for those who have difficulty bending or stooping; by providing a drinking fountain accessible under 4.15 and a water cooler; or by such other means as would achieve the required accessibility for each group on each floor. Where more than one drinking fountain or water cooler is provided on a floor, 50% of those provided must comply with 4.15 and be on an accessible route. In the event an odd number of drinking fountains are provided on a floor, the requirement can be met by rounding down the odd number to an even number and calculating 50% of the even number. Additional advisory material on drinking fountains is included in the appendix at A4.1.3(10).

Toilet Rooms (4.1.3(11))

Comment. Some commenters were opposed to the scoping provision in 4.1.3(11) requiring that each public and common use toilet room be accessible.

Response. Although each common and public use toilet room must be accessible, if more than one toilet stall, lavatory, or other feature is provided in such a toilet room, generally only one of each feature is required to be accessible. See 4.22.4 through

4.22.7. Toilet rooms serving specific sleeping accommodations in dormitories, hotels, and other similar places of transient lodging are not public or common use toilet rooms.

Comment. A few commenters objected to requiring other toilet rooms to be adaptable.

Response. The scoping provision in 4.1.3(11) has been clarified that the adaptability requirement applies to toilet rooms that are designed or intended for the use of the occupant of a specific space such as a private toilet room which is part of an executive's office. Exempting such toilet rooms in new construction from the adaptability requirement would make reasonable accommodation in the future impossible in many cases.

Comment. Several commenters requested clarification whether every toilet room provided as part of a sleeping accommodation in medical care facilities and transient lodging must be accessible or adaptable.

Response. As stated in 4.1.1(1), in new construction all areas of buildings and facilities must comply with 4.1 through 4.35, unless otherwise provided in the general application section or a special application section. Medical care facilities and transient lodging are covered by special application sections 6 and 9 respectively which require that a specific percentage of sleeping accommodations, including toilet rooms, be accessible. The guidelines do not require toilet rooms in other sleeping accommodations to be accessible except that, in the case of hotels, motels and other similar places of transient lodging, doors and doorways must be designed to allow passage into the toilet room.

Comment. A few commenters recommended that an accessible unisex toilet room should be required either in addition to or in place of separate toilet rooms for men and women.

Response. Unisex toilet rooms are discussed in the technical specifications for toilet rooms in 4.22.

Storage, Shelving and Display Units (4.1.3(12))

Comment. Several commenters requested clarification regarding whether all storage, shelving and display units must be within the forward and side reach ranges for wheelchair users.

Response. The scoping provision in 4.1.3(12)(a) applies only to fixed cabinets, shelves, closets, and drawers and expressly states that additional storage space may be provided outside the forward and side reach ranges for wheelchair users. The technical specifications for reach ranges for storage spaces have also been clarified. See 4.25.3; and figures 38a and 38b.

The scoping provision in 4.1.3(12)(b) applies to fixed shelves or display units allowing self-service by customers and requires such shelves and display units be located on an accessible route. A sentence has been added to the provision to clarify that compliance with the forward and side reach ranges for wheelchair users is not required.

Comment. Businesses requested that shelves in employee work areas (e.g., stockrooms, baggage rooms, maids closets) be exempt from the scoping provision in 4.1.3(12)(a).

Response. As stated in 4.1.1(1), in new construction all areas of buildings and facilities must comply with 4.1 through 4.35, unless otherwise provided in the general application section or a special application section. Areas used only by employees as work areas are covered by 4.1.1(3) which requires that such areas be designed and constructed so that individuals with disabilities can approach, enter, and exit the areas. This provision expressly states that employee work areas are not required to be equipped with accessible shelves. The appendix includes advisory guidance at A4.1.1(3) that consideration should be given to placing shelves in employee work areas at a convenient height for accessibility or installing commercially available shelving that is adjustable so that reasonable accommodation can be made in the future.

Controls and Operating Maintenance (4.1.3(13))

Comment. Several commenters requested clarification whether controls not intended for public use must be within the forward or side reach ranges for wheelchair users.

Response. An exception has been added to the technical specifications in 4.27.3 stating that the forward and side reach range requirements do not apply where the use of special equipment dictates otherwise or where electrical and communications systems receptacles are not normally intended for use by building occupants.

Audible and Visual Alarms (4.1.3(14))

Comment. Commenters generally supported the inclusion of visual alarms in the guidelines. Some businesses considered requiring visual alarms in new buildings and facilities to be excessive and recommended that such alarms should be provided only in areas where an individual with a hearing impairment was an occupant or that portable or personal alarm devices should be permitted. A few commenters requested that buildings with automatic sprinkler systems be exempt from the requirement for visual alarms.

Response. Builders and designers cannot know in advance whether a space will be occupied by a person with a hearing impairment. If visual alarms are not included in the design of new buildings and facilities but instead are required only where an individual with a hearing impairment was an occupant, buildings and facilities would have to be retrofitted at potentially greater cost.

Further, visual alarms are intended to alert visitors, and not just regular tenants, to emergencies. Portable or personal alarm devices are carried by an individual and are triggered by a signal from the building emergency alarm system. Provision of these devices is not an acceptable alternative, especially in places of public accommodation such as retail stores, assembly areas, and transportation facilities where the number of visitors and temporary users greatly exceeds the number of tenants. They have been demonstrably ineffective in both drill and emergency situations in such places and have resulted in visitors being left unaware of the need for evacuation. The only situation where portable or personal alarm devices are permitted under the guidelines is in sleeping accommodations in hotels and other similar places of transient lodging where guests are assigned temporarily to a specific room and can be provided appropriate devices when registering for the room. See 9.3.2. Even then, hallways, lobbies and other common areas in hotels and other similar places of transient lodging must have permanently installed visual alarms.

As for buildings with automatic sprinkler systems, visual alarms are generally required only where audible alarms are required or provided. Since buildings with automatic sprinkler systems are required to provide audible alarms, the Board believes that persons with hearing impairments are entitled to access the same emergency warning system.

The draft final regulatory impact analysis estimates the direct additional cost per visual alarm device in new construction, including installation, to be $169. A high-rise office building with 25 stores and 30,000 square feet per story is estimated to require 160 devices for a total cost of $27,040 or $.04 per square foot of building area. The Board believes that this cost is reasonable in light of the importance of this life safety issue.

Detectable Warnings (4.1.3(15))

A large number of comments was received in support of and in opposition to detectable warnings in general and at specific locations. As further discussed under 4.29, the requirements for detectable warnings have been revised and some sections have been reserved pending further study and research for future revisions to the guidelines. An editorial change has been made to 4.1.3(15) stating that detectable warnings shall be provided at locations specified in 4.29.

Interior Signage (4.1.3(16))

Comment. As discussed under 4.1.2(7), the Board has concluded based on review of the comments that the scoping provisions and technical specifications for signage were unclear and needed to be revised.

Response. The scoping provisions for interior and exterior signage and the accompanying technical specifications have been clarified and revised in response to the comments. See 4.1.2(7) for scoping provisions for exterior signage; and 4.30 for technical specifications for signage. Interior signs which designate permanent rooms and spaces must comply with the technical specifications in 4.30.1 and 4.30.4 through 4.30.6 for raised and brailled characters, finish and contrast, and mounting locations and height. For instance, numbers on hotel guest rooms, patient rooms in hospitals, office suites, and signs designating men's and women's toilet facilities must have raised and brailled characters, and also must meet the finish and contrast, and mounting height requirements. Interior signs which provide direction to or information about functional spaces of a building or facility must comply with the technical specifications in 4.30.1, 4.30.2 and 4.30.5 for character proportion and finish and contrast. The technical specifications in 4.30.3 for character height must also be complied with if the signage is suspended or projected overhead in compliance with the technical specifications in 4.4.2 for head room for protruding objects.

An exception has also been added to 4.1.3(16) to clarify that building directories, menus, and other signs which provide temporary information about rooms and spaces such as the current occupant's name do not have to comply with the requirements for signage.

Comment. The NPRM asked whether additional types of signage such as informational and directional signage about functional spaces, rules of conduct, or hazards should be tactile (i.e., comply with technical specifications in 4.30.4 and 4.30.6 for raised and braille characters and mounting location and height). The NPRM also requested information on available technologies such as audible signs for overhead and remote signage. Comments from individuals with disabilities and their organizations regarding additional types of signage that should be tactile were scattered with no clear consensus of opinion that would be useful for purposes of establishing guidelines. Technical information was submitted by Love Electronics regarding infrared signage.

Response. Although technology is available for making overhead and remote signage accessible, the Board plans to further study this issue to determine where and in what types of buildings and facilities such technology may be necessary for future revision of the guidelines.

Accessible Public Telephones (4.1.17(a))

Comment. Individuals with disabilities and their organizations requested that more accessible telephones be required. One commenter recommended that a maximum distance of 300 feet be established between accessible public telephones in large buildings and facilities. A telephone company objected to requiring at least one public telephone per floor to meet the technical specifications in 4.31.2 for forward reach by wheelchair users when two or more banks of telephones are provided on each floor. One commenter recommended that the

exception under 4.1.3(17)(a) for exterior public telephones should permit a side reach telephone instead of a forward reach telephone if dial tone first service is available.

Response. The exception under 4.1.3(17)(a) has been revised as recommended. It has also been clarified that accessible public telephones required by 4.1.3(17)(a) do not include text telephones which are covered by 4.1.3(17)(c).

Public Telephones Equipped With Volume Controls (4.1.3(17)(b))

Comment. Most individuals with disabilities and their organizations supported the NPRM proposal to require 25% of public telephones in newly constructed buildings and facilities to be equipped with a volume control in addition to the requirement in 4.1.3(17)(a) for accessible public telephones. A few requested that the number be increased. Some recommended that scoping be based on occupancy. Telephone companies responded that they have adopted voluntary programs to install public telephones equipped with volume controls and recommended that the Board defer to a Federal Communication Commission (FCC) proceeding which declined to require 25% of all public telephones to be equipped with volume controls. See Order Completing Inquiry and Providing Further Notice of Proposed Rulemaking, CC Docket No. 87-124 (July 27, 1989).

Response. The FCC declined to require 25% of all public telephones to be equipped with volume controls based on cost estimates provided by telephone companies for retrofitting all existing public telephones with a volume control. The NPRM proposal was more modest and only required 25% of public telephones installed in newly constructed buildings and facilities to be accessible. The American Telephone and Telegraph Company reported that its newly designed public telephones incorporate volume controls as a standard feature.

Southwestern Bell Telephone Company also reported that it installs volume controls in its public telephones free upon the request of its customers. Cost data provided by other telephone companies for equipping public telephones with volume controls ranged from $10 to $80. Since the additional direct cost of requiring 25% of public telephones in newly constructed buildings and facilities is nothing to minimal depending on the telephone manufacturer or company, the requirement has been retained in the final guidelines.

Comment. The American Public Communication Council requested that the requirement be postponed for one year to permit suppliers to test and evaluate equipment.

Response. The American Telephone and Telegraph Company and other telephone companies currently offer public telephones equipped with volume controls as a standard feature or upon request. In addition, many telephone companies incorporate the volume control feature into the base of the telephone rather than the handset which has virtually eliminated concerns about vandalism. The Board does not believe that any delay is warranted beyond the January 26, 1992 effective date for title III of the ADA.

Public Text Telephones (4.1.3(17)(c)-(d))

Comment. The NPRM asked whether the scoping provision for public text telephones should be based on the total number of public pay telephones in a building or facility and whether six public pay telephones should be the trigger point. As an alternative, the NPRM asked whether the scoping provision should be based on occupancy type as is done in Michigan. The NPRM also asked for information about the need for public text telephones in general and at specific types of facilities. Most individuals with disabilities and their organizations and other commenters who responded to the questions recommended basing the scoping provision on occupancy type in addition to the total number of public pay telephones in a building or facility and generally supported the need for public text telephones in the same occupancy types as required in Michigan (e.g., transportation facilities, hospitals, shopping malls, convention centers, hotels with a convention center). Many of these commenters expressed concern that smaller or rural communities may have buildings and facilities where there is a need for public text telephones regardless of the number of public pay telephones. As for the trigger point for a scoping provision based on total number of public pay telephones, many individuals with disabilities and their organizations and other commenters recommended that the trigger point be less than six public pay telephones and offered a variety of percentage, bank, and cluster options. Businesses and telephone companies were generally opposed to public text telephones and expressed concerns about cost, utilization, and maintenance. One telephone company stated that the presence of six public telephones would indicate a high volume of traffic and suggests a potential for cost recovery. Other telephone companies referred to a Federal Communications Commission proceeding to gather information concerning the telecommunication needs of individuals with hearing impairments which concluded that "requiring that pay telephones be designed to accommodate portable TDDs, however, should be less costly, and may well provide benefits that outweigh the costs." Order Completing Inquiry and Providing Further Notice of Proposed Rulemaking, CC Docket No. 87-124 (July 27, 1989) at paragraph 110.

Response. A number of changes have been made to the scoping provision for public text telephones in response to the comments. The final guidelines include requirements based on (1) the total number of interior and exterior public pay telephones provided at a site and (2) certain occupancy types, regardless of the number or public pay telephones provided at the site. The trigger point has been set at four or more interior and exterior public pay telephones at a site where at least one is in an interior location. For instance, if a building or facility has two exterior and two interior public pay telephones on the site, the scoping provisions for a public text telephone is triggered. On the other hand, if all public pay telephones are located outdoors, a public text telephone is not required because text telephones do not currently work well outdoors and the use of portable text telephones at such locations is impractical.

The final guidelines further provide that if an interior public pay telephone is provided in a stadium or arena, a convention center, a hotel with a convention center, or a covered mall, at least one interior public text telephone must be provided in the facility. In the case of hospitals, if a public pay telephone is located in or adjacent to an emergency room, recovery room, or waiting room, one public text telephone must be provided at each such location.

The scoping provision for public text telephones in transportation facilities will be included in section 10 of the final guidelines. The Board will also incorporate a scoping provision for public text telephones in State and local government buildings when the guidelines are supplemented for purposes of title II of the ADA.

The final guidelines also include new technical specifications for public text telephones at 4.31.9 and additional explanatory information in the appendix at A4.31.9. The technical specifications permit the use of either an integrated text telephone and pay telephone unit, or a conventional text telephone that is permanently affixed within, or adjacent to, the telephone enclosure. In addition, the technical specifications permit the use of portable text telephones as equivalent

facilitation under certain conditions. At the present time, pocket-type text telephones do not accommodate a wide range of individuals with disabilities and are not considered appropriate for purposes of equivalent facilitation. As technology develops, this may change. To be considered equivalent facilitation, the portable text telephone must be readily available for use with nearby public pay telephones. For example, if a hotel has portable text telephones available at the registration desk on a 24 hour basis for use with nearby public pay telephones, substantially equivalent access to and usability of the public pay telephone would be provided. On the other hand, if the portable text telephone is kept at a remote location from the public pay telephones or is stored in a space near the public pay telephones but the user must search for personnel not regularly stationed near the public pay telephones, substantially equivalent access to and use of the public pay telephone would not be provided. If a portable text telephone is provided as equivalent facilitation, at least one nearby public pay telephone must be equipped with a shelf and an electrical outlet to accommodate the portable text telephone. The technical specifications for the shelf are in 4.31.9(2). If an acoustic coupler is used, the telephone handset cord must be long enough to connect the public pay phone with the text telephone. Regardless of whether the public text telephone is portable or permanently affixed, the technical specifications for signage in 4.30.7(3) require that directional signage indicating the location of the nearest public text telephone must be provided near all banks of telephones which do not contain a text telephone. If a building or facility has no banks of telephones, the directional signage must be provided at the entrance (e.g., in a building directory).

Comment. Several commenters recommended that,

in addition to requiring at least one public text telephone in certain buildings and facilities, public pay telephones should be designed to accommodate portable text telephones so that individuals who carry their own devices can use public pay telephones, especially in larger facilities where one may have to walk a considerable distance to find a public text telephone.

Response. A new scoping provision has been added at 4.1.3(17)(d) requiring at least one public pay telephone in each bank of three or more interior public pay telephones to be designed to accommodate a portable text telephone. The public pay telephone must comply with the technical specifications in 4.31.9(2), and be equipped with a shelf on which to place a portable text telephone, an electrical outlet, and a telephone handset cord long enough to reach the shelf for acoustical coupling. Some telephone enclosure companies currently have several models on the market which comply with these requirements.

Fixed Seating and Tables (4.1.3(18))

Comment. The NPRM asked whether the five percent scoping provision for fixed seating and tables was adequate. Many commenters interpreted the provision as applying to seating in assembly areas or restaurants and stated that the number was too low. Some commenters stated that similar scoping provisions in their states were adequate.

Response. Wheelchair seating spaces in assembly areas and restaurants are addressed in separate provisions. See 4.1.3(19)(a) for assembly areas; and 5.1 for restaurants. The five percent figure has not been changed. Several editorial changes have been made to the provision to be consistent with 4.1.1(3) regarding areas used only by employees as work areas. The term "accessible public or common use areas" has been substituted for "accessible spaces" and the reference to "work surfaces" has been deleted. As clarified, the provision applies to fixed

seating and tables in accessible public and common use areas such as study carrels or laboratory stations in a classroom.

Wheelchair Seating Spaces in Assembly Areas (4.1.3(19)(a))

Comment. Individuals with disabilities and their organizations and other commenters recommended that the scoping provisions for wheelchair seating spaces in assembly areas include such spaces for areas with less than 50 seats and generally favored an increase in the number of wheelchair seating spaces. Several commenters, including theater owners, believed that the requirements for wheelchair seating spaces in assembly areas were excessive.

Response. The table in 4.1.3(19)(a) specifying the number of wheelchair seating spaces in assembly areas has been revised in response to the comments. The new scoping provision is generally taken from the California building code. In smaller assembly areas, one wheelchair seating space is required in areas having a seating capacity of 4 to 25, and two wheelchair seating spaces are required in areas having a seating capacity of 26 to 50. The NPRM required no accessible seating in assembly areas with fewer than 50 seats. Unlike the NPRM, the new scoping provision also requires that one percent, but not less than one, of all fixed seats be aisle seats that have either no armrests, or removable or folding armrests on the aisle side of the seat to increase accessibility for wheelchair users who wish to transfer to a fixed seat and individuals with other mobility impairments for whom armrests present an obstacle. These seats must be identified by a sign or marker and a sign must be posted in the ticket office notifying patrons of their availability.

The total number of seating spaces for individuals with mobility impairments is generally the same under the NPRM and the final guidelines. For instance, in an assembly area with a seating capacity of

200, the NPRM required 6 wheelchair seating spaces; and the final guidelines require 4 wheelchair seating spaces and 2 accessible aisle seats. In an assembly area with a seating capacity of 1,000, the NPRM required 20 wheelchair seating spaces; and the final guidelines require 11 wheelchair seating spaces and 10 accessible aisle seats. To address the concerns regarding the number of wheelchair seating spaces required in larger facilities, a paragraph has been added to the appendix explaining that readily removable or folding seating units may be installed in wheelchair seating spaces which may be used by other persons when not needed for wheelchair users or individuals with other mobility impairments. Folding seating units usually consists of two fixed seats that can be easily folded into a fixed center bar to allow for open spaces for wheelchair users when needed.

Assistive Listening Systems (4.1.3(19)(b))

Comment. The NPRM asked whether certain assembly areas with fixed seating should be required to have permanently installed assistive listening systems, and whether other areas should be permitted to have an adequate number of electrical outlets or other supplementary wiring to accommodate portable assistive listening systems. Most commenters who responded to the question favored requiring permanently installed assistive listening systems in assembly areas with fixed seating and permitting the use of portable systems in other areas. For instance, hotels pointed out that larger meeting rooms are frequently subdivided into smaller meeting rooms and a permanently installed assistive listening system may not be usable in such spaces. Some commenters recommended that all assistive listening systems should be portable.

Response. The scoping provision for assistive listening systems has been revised. The provision applies to concert and lecture halls, playhouses and movie theaters, meeting rooms, and other assembly areas where audible communication is integral to use of the space. If such an assembly area (a) accommodates at least 50 persons or has an audio-amplification system and (b) has fixed seating, a permanently installed assistive listening system is required. Other assembly areas are permitted to have an adequate number of electrical outlets or other supplementary wiring to accommodate portable assistive listening systems. The requirement assures that individuals with hearing impairments can attend functions in assembly areas with fixed seating without having to give advance notice or disrupt the event to have a portable assistive listening system set up. The requirement also provides for flexibility for smaller assembly areas and rooms and spaces with changeable seating arrangements.

The provision in the NPRM which would have required assistive listening systems to be installed in rooms if they are used regularly as meeting or conference rooms was deleted because it would have covered individual offices which are used for meetings which was not intended.

Comment. Several commenters requested that the scoping provision not be limited to indoor assembly areas and include such facilities as baseball stadiums.

Response. The baseball stadium in Boston has a permanently installed assistive listening system. Since the technology currently exists for providing communication access to such facilities, the scoping provision is not limited to indoor assembly areas.

Comment. Most commenters supported requiring that the minimum number of receivers be equal to four percent of the total number of seats but not less than two. Some commenters believed that the number was excessive and other commenters wanted the number to be increased.

Response. The four percent figure is based on a Bureau of the Census estimate of the

number of persons aged 15 and over who have difficulty hearing what is said in a normal conversation with another person, excluding those who cannot hear at all. See Bureau of Census, Disability Functional Limitation and Insurance Coverage, 1984-85. There are other studies which indicate that the numbers may be as high as eight to ten percent. As assistive listening systems become more readily available, it is expected that their usage will increase. The Board intends to monitor this issue and if a need for an increase in the number of receivers is demonstrated, the scoping provision will be revised.

Comment. The NPRM requested information regarding which types of assistive listening systems (induction loop, FM, and infra red) work best in particular environments. Each of the three types of systems received some support for all applications. Many commenters described their personal experiences with particular types of systems. Those who provided extensive information on the advantages and disadvantages of the various systems recommended that a specific type should be selected only after consultation with experts in the field.

Response. The appendix in A4.33.6 has been expanded to provide additional information on the various types of assistive listening systems. The appendix includes a table reprinted from a National Institute of Disability and Rehabilitation Research "Rehab Brief" which shows some of the advantages and disadvantages of each system and typical applications. New York has also adopted technical specifications which may be useful. A pamphlet is available from the Board which lists demonstration centers across the country where technical assistance can be obtained in selecting and installing appropriate systems.

Comment. The NPRM also requested information regarding the need for an assistive listening device at sales and service counters, teller windows, box offices, and information kiosks where a

physical barrier separates service personnel and customers. Most commenters favored the provision of an assistive listening device at these places. Those who were opposed to this provision recommended alternative means to address the problem such as training personnel how to communicate effectively with individuals who have hearing impairments.

Response. A provision has been added to the appendix at A7.2(3) recommending that at least one permanently installed assistive listening system be installed at sales and service counters, teller windows, box offices, and information kiosks where a physical barrier separates service personnel and customers.

Automated Teller Machines (4.1.3 (20))

The legislative history of the ADA specifically mentions automatic teller machines (ATMs) as covered by the accessibility requirements. The NPRM included proposed scoping provisions and technical specifications for ATMs. The scoping provisions in the final guidelines have been revised and require that where ATMs are provided, each machine shall comply with 4.34 except where two or more machines are provided at one location, then only one machine shall comply with 4.34. For example, if a large shopping mall has an ATM located at each end of the mall, then each ATM must be accessible. On the other hand, if the ATMs are located adjacent to each other, then only one ATM must be accessible. Comments regarding ATMs and the requirements of the final guidelines are discussed under the technical specifications at 4.34.

Dressing and Fitting Rooms (4.1.3(21))

Comment. The NPRM asked whether the guidelines should include requirements for accessible dressing and fitting rooms. Individuals with disabilities and their organizations supported such requirements. Businesses expressed concern about having sufficient space for accessible dressing and fitting rooms, especially in existing buildings and facilities.

Response. A new scoping provision has been added at 4.1.3(21) for new construction requiring that where dressing and fitting rooms are provided for use by the public or employees, 5 percent, but not less than one, of such rooms for each type of use in each cluster of dressing rooms must be accessible. For instance, in a hospital where dressing rooms are provided for specific treatment or examination rooms, 5 percent, but not less than one, of the dressing rooms provided for each type of treatment or examination rooms must be accessible.

The Board recognizes that in some cases it may be technically infeasible to comply with the scoping provisions for new construction when altering dressing rooms in existing facilities due to space limitations and has included a provision in 4.1.6(3)(h) that requires only one dressing room for each sex on each level to be accessible in alterations where technical infeasibility can be demonstrated. Accessible unisex dressing rooms may be used to meet the requirement in 4.1.6(3)(h) where only unisex dressing rooms are provided.

Technical specifications for accessible dressing rooms are provided in 4.35.

4.1.5 Accessible Buildings: Additions

This section contains the scoping provisions for additions to existing buildings and facilities.

Comment. Several commenters raised questions regarding whether an addition to an existing building is to be treated as new construction or an alteration.

Response. Additions to existing buildings have attributes of both new construction and an alteration. To the extent that a space or element in the addition is newly constructed, each new space or element must comply with the applicable scoping provisions of 4.1.1 to 4.1.3 for new construc-

tion, the applicable technical specifications of 4.2 through 4.35, and the applicable special application sections 5 through 10. For instance, if a restroom is provided in the addition, it must comply with the requirements for new construction. Construction of an addition does not, however, create an obligation to retrofit the entire existing building or facility to meet requirements for new construction. Rather, the addition is to be regarded as an alteration and to the extent that it affects or could affect the usability of or access to an area containing a primary function, the requirements in 4.1.6(2) are triggered with respect to providing an accessible path of travel to the altered area and making the restrooms, telephones, and drinking fountains serving the altered area accessible. For example, if a museum adds a new wing that does not have a separate entrance as part of the addition, an accessible path of travel would have to be provided through the existing building or facility unless it is disproportionate to the overall cost and scope of the addition as determined under criteria established by the Attorney General. The scoping provision in 4.1.5 has been clarified to reflect these requirements.

4.1.6 Accessible Buildings: Alterations

This section contains scoping provisions for alterations.

General (4.1.6(1))

Comment. Some commenters pointed out that the provision in 4.1.6(1)(a) prohibiting any decrease in accessibility when an alteration is undertaken was inconsistent with the provision in 4.1.6(1)(d) [4.1.6(1)(e) in the NPRM] which does not impose any greater requirements in alterations than in new construction.

Response. The provision has been revised to state that no alteration shall be undertaken which decreases or has the affect of decreasing accessibility or usability of a building or

facility below the requirements for new construction at the time of the alteration.

Comment. Several businesses expressed concern about minor alterations triggering extensive retrofitting of existing buildings and facilities to meet the requirements for new construction.

Response. The Board wishes to make it clear that minor alterations do not trigger extensive retrofitting of existing buildings. There are three general principles for alterations. First, if any existing element, space, or common area is altered, the altered element, space, or common area must meet new construction requirements. 4.1.6(1)(b). Second, if alterations to the elements in a space when considered together amount to an alteration of the space, the entire space must meet new construction requirements. 4.1.6(1)(c). Third, if the alteration affects or could affect the usability of or access to an area containing a primary function, the path of travel to the altered area and the restrooms, drinking fountains, and telephones serving the altered area must be made accessible unless it is disproportionate to the overall alterations in terms of cost and scope as determined under criteria established by the Attorney General. 4.1.6(2). This last requirement will be addressed in greater detail in the Department of Justice's final regulations.

There are two general exceptions that apply to alterations. First, compliance with a specific scoping provision or technical specification is not required if it is technically infeasible. 4.1.6(1)(j). As further discussed below, the definition of the term "technically infeasible" has been revised and does not require compliance with new construction requirements where existing structural conditions would require removing or altering a load-bearing member which is an essential part of the structural frame or where existing physical or site constraints prohibit full and strict compliance. Second, the installation of an elevator is not required in an altered building or facility that is less than three stories or has less than 3,000 square feet per story unless the building is a shopping center, a shopping mall, the professional office of a health care provider, or another type of facility determined by the Attorney General. 4.1.6(1)(k). The elevator exception is established by section 303(b) of the ADA and is the same as that contained in the scoping provisions for new construction. As discussed above, if a building or facility is not exempt from the elevator requirement and the requirement for an accessible path of travel is triggered under 4.1.6(2), the installation of an elevator is subject to the disproportionality limitation. However, if an escalator or stair is planned or installed where none existed previously and major structural modifications are necessary for such installation, then an elevator or other vertical means of access must be provided. 4.1.6(1)(f).

The following examples illustrate the application of these principles and exceptions:

1. If a door handle is replaced, the new door handle must comply with 4.13.9 which states that door hardware shall have a shape that is easy to grasp and does not require tight grasping, tight pinching, or turning of the wrist (e.g., lever handles, U-shaped handles). Replacing the door handle does not trigger any other accessibility requirements for the door.

2. A common practice when replacing doors is to install a complete door assembly consisting of the frame and a pre-hung door. In interior light-frame construction (e.g., wood or metal studs), a wider door assembly can be installed without altering a load-bearing structural member which is an essential part of the structural frame. If a complete door assembly is installed in interior light-frame construction and space is available to comply with the clear width and maneuvering clearances specified in 4.13.5 and 4.13.6, those requirements must be met. However, if space is

restricted, as in the case of some hotel guest rooms where narrow doorways are defined by bathroom and closet walls, it may be technically infeasible to comply with the clear width or maneuvering clearances specified in 4.13.5 and 4.13.6 due to existing physical constraints.

3. If a parking lot is resurfaced and does not have the number of accessible parking spaces required by 4.1.2(5) or the parking spaces do not comply with 4.6.3, those requirements must be met unless it is technically infeasible. If the resurfacing does not include regrading, it may be technically infeasible to comply with the requirement in 4.6.3 that accessible parking spaces and access aisles be level with surface slopes not exceeding 1:50 (2%) in all directions due to existing site constraints. If a local zoning or land use code requires the parking lot to have a certain number of parking spaces and providing the number of accessible parking spaces in 4.1.2(5) would result in reducing the total number of parking spaces below that required by the local code, it would be technically infeasible to fully comply with the scoping provision due to site constraints resulting from legitimate requirements of the local code.

For instance, if 4.1.2(5) requires five accessible parking spaces to be provided, but the parking lot can only accommodate four accessible parking spaces and still meet the local code requirement for total number of parking spaces, then four accessible parking spaces must be provided.

4. If the water closets, toilet stalls, lavatories and mirrors in a toilet room are all replaced, the new fixtures must comply with the technical specifications in 4.16, 4.17, and 4.19 for those elements. Since replacing the water closets, toilet stalls, lavatories and mirrors also amounts to an alteration of the toilet room, the entire toilet room must comply with the technical specifications in 4.22 for toilet rooms which include a requirement for the doors to the toilet room to comply with 4.13.

The Board has added provisions to the final guidelines to clarify when accessible routes and accessible entrances are required in alterations to existing buildings and facilities. A provision has been added at 4.1.6(1)(b) that, if the requirements for new construction provide for an element, space, or common area to be on an accessible route, alteration of the element, space, or common area does not trigger the requirement for an accessible route unless the alteration affects the usability of or access to an area containing a primary function in which case an accessible path of travel is required by 4.1.6(2) subject to the disproportionality limitation. For instance, in new construction the scoping provision in 4.1.3(10) requires that drinking fountains be on an accessible route. If a drinking fountain is replaced on the third story of a building that does not have an elevator, installation of a new accessible drinking fountain does not trigger the installation of an elevator.

A provision has also been added to the final guidelines at 4.1.6(1)(h) that, if a planned alteration entails alterations to an entrance, and the building has an accessible entrance, the entrance being altered is not required to comply with the new construction requirements unless the alteration affects the usability of or access to an area containing a primary function in which case an accessible path of travel is required by 4.1.6(2) subject to the disproportionality limitation. If an entrance is altered and is not made accessible, appropriate signage must be provided indicating the location of the nearest accessible entrance. Additional advisory material on alterations to entrances is included in the appendix at A4.1.6(2)(h).

Comment. A few commenters requested that a waiver process be established.

Response. The ADA does not provide for a waiver process. The technical infeasibility and elevator exceptions in 4.1.6(1) (i) and (j) are similar to a waiver in that compliance with specific scoping provisions and technical specifications is not required if certain conditions are met. Special scoping provisions and technical specifications are provided for in the case of some elements and spaces where technical infeasibility exists. See 4.1.6(3). However, the exceptions differ from a waiver in that to obtain a waiver an entity must usually submit documentation to a reviewing authority showing that conditions exist to warrant not complying with a specific scoping provision or technical specification and the reviewing authority must decide whether to grant or deny the waiver. The ADA only provides for review after the fact if a complaint is filed with the Department of Justice or a court. Entities should maintain documentation of conditions warranting an exemption in the event of such review.

Comment. Several commenters questioned why altered elements and spaces must be made accessible if the rest of the building or facility is inaccessible.

Response. Congress recognized that it would be costly to retrofit entire buildings and facilities to be accessible and that it would be more cost effective to incorporate accessibility gradually as elements and spaces are altered. See H. Rept. 101-485, pt. 3, at 60. The scoping provisions are based on the statute and ensure that individuals with disabilities will have access to the goods, services, and employment available in the altered parts of buildings and facilities.

Comment. Several commenters requested that the guidelines specifically address when public text telephones are required in existing buildings and facilities.

If alterations to existing buildings or facilities with less than four interior or exterior public pay telephones would increase the number to four or more public pay telephones with at least one in an interior location, then at least one interior public text telephone must be provided. For instance, if an existing building or facility has one interior and one exterior public pay telephone and two more are added, then

at least one interior public text telephone would be required. If one or more interior or exterior public pay telephones in an existing facility with four or more public pay telephones with at least one in an interior location is altered, then at least one interior public text telephone must be provided. For instance, if an existing building or facility has two interior and two exterior public pay telephones and one or more of them is replaced, then at least one interior public text telephone would be required.

Comment. Several commenters requested that areas of rescue assistance not be required in existing buildings and facilities because it would require costly and extensive renovations.

Response. The Board recognizes that providing areas of rescue assistance in existing buildings may require costly and extensive renovations. Pending further study, a provision has been added in 4.1.6(1)(g) stating that the requirements in 4.1.6(9), 4.3.10, and 4.3.11 regarding areas of rescue assistance do not apply to alterations of existing buildings.

Comment. Several commenters requested that hazardous materials abatement and automatic sprinkling retrofitting be added to the list of alterations in 4.1.6(1)(i) (4.1.6(1)(f) in the NPRM) exempt from guidelines.

Response. Alterations which are limited solely to hazardous materials abatement and automatic sprinkling retrofitting and which do not involve changes to any elements or spaces required to be accessible by the guidelines have been added to the list of alterations in 4.1.6(1)(i) exempt from the guidelines.

Comment. A number of commenters requested changes in the definition of the term "technically infeasible." Some commenters requested that in the case of alterations that would require removing or altering a load-bearing member, a distinction should be made between: (a) wood and metal studs or joists used in light-frame construction of interior

walls and floors; and (b) concrete, masonry, heavy timber or steel columns, beams, girders and structural slabs. Other commenters requested that a cost factor be included in the definition of "technically infeasible."

Response. The definition of "technically infeasible" has been moved from the definitions in 3.5 to 4.1.6(1)(i). With respect to alterations that would require removing or altering a load-bearing member, the definition has been revised to apply to a load-bearing member which is an essential part of the structural frame. The structural frame is defined in 3.5 as consisting of the columns and the girders, beams, trusses and spandrels having direct connections to the columns, and all other members which are essential to the stability of the building as a whole. This definition would not include wood or metal studs or joists used in light-frame construction of interior walls and floors. With respect to existing physical or site constraints prohibiting full and strict compliance, such constraints can result from legitimate legal requirements (e.g., a right of way agreement preventing construction of a ramp in front of a building).

As for costs, that factor has been taken into account in several places in the scoping provisions for alterations. First, as further discussed above where requirements for an accessible path of travel, including vertical access by means of an elevator, ramp, or platform lift or wheelchair lift, are triggered by an alteration that affects access to or usability of an area containing a primary function, there is a disproportionality limitation which will be addressed in the Department of Justice's final regulations. See 4.1.6(2). Second, the technical infeasibility exception is designed to limit costs by not requiring the removal or alteration of a load-bearing member which is an essential part of the structural frame and not requiring compliance with new construction requirements where there are existing physical or site constraints. Third, where commenters have pointed out specific new construction requirements which would require costly and extensive renovations to existing buildings and facilities such as those for areas of rescue assistance, the Board has not required them. See 4.1.6(1)(g). Fourth, the installation of elevators is not required in alterations of existing buildings and facilities which are less than three stories or have less than 3,000 square feet per story except for certain types of facilities. See 4.1.6(1)(k).

4.1.6(2) Alterations To An Area Containing A Primary Function

Comment. A number of commenters requested that the terms "an area containing a primary function;" "path of travel;" and "disproportionate" be defined.

Response. The Department of Justice's final regulations will define and apply these terms.

4.1.6(3) Special Technical Provisions For Alterations

Comment. A few commenters requested that the application of the special provisions in 4.1.6(3) be clarified. Some commenters objected to allowing a short ramp to be steeper and elevators to have a 48 inch by 48 inch inside car dimension. Other commenters made recommendations for elevator car sizes and alternative provisions that require further study or will be discussed in the technical assistance manual.

Response. The special provisions in 4.1.6(3) contain requirements for ramps, stairs, elevators, doors, toilet facilities, assembly areas, and dressing and fitting rooms that may be used in alterations to existing buildings and facilities when it is technically infeasible to comply with new construction requirements or other specified conditions exist. The Board recognizes that the special provisions for ramps and elevators do not accommodate as many individuals with disabilities as do the technical specifications in 4.7.2, 4.8.2, and

4.10.9. However, faced with the choice between providing no access or a lesser degree of access to existing buildings and facilities that are altered, the Board has opted for the latter. As noted above, other recommendations have been made for elevator car sizes and alternative provisions that will be studied for future revision of the guidelines or will be discussed in the technical assistance manual.

A new provision has been added at 4.1.6(3)(g) that platform lifts or wheelchair lifts complying with 4.11 and applicable State and local codes are allowed as part of an accessible route in alterations and that the use of lifts is not limited to the conditions specified in the scoping provisions for new construction.

4.1.7 Accessible Buildings: Historic Preservation

This section contains scoping provisions and alternative requirements for alterations to qualified historic buildings and facilities.

Comment: A number of commenters requested that the Board clarify the application of 4.1.7(1) and the procedures under section 106 of the National Historic Preservation Act.

Response: The provision has been revised to clarify that alterations to a qualified historic building or facility shall comply with the scoping provisions for alterations (4.1.6), the applicable technical specifications (4.2 through 4.35), and the applicable special application sections (5 through 10) unless it is determined in accordance with the procedures discussed below that compliance with the requirements for accessible routes (exterior and interior), ramps, entrances, or toilets would threaten or destroy the historic significance of the building or facility in which case the alternative requirements in 4.1.7(3) (4.1.7(2) in the NPRM) may be used. The alternative requirements allow for flexibility to accommodate the national interest in historic preservation.

The definition of a "qualified historic building or facility" has been moved to 4.1.7(1)(b) and retains the UFAS definition as required by section 504(c)(1) of the ADA.

New paragraphs have been added at 4.1.7(2)(a)(i) and (ii) to clarify the procedures under section 106 of the National Historic Preservation Act (16 U.S.C. 470f) and their application to alterations covered by the ADA. Section 106 requires that a Federal agency with jurisdiction over a Federal, federally assisted, or federally licensed undertaking consider the effects of the agency's undertaking on buildings and facilities listed in or eligible for listing in the National Register of Historic Places and give the Advisory Council on Historic Preservation a reasonable opportunity to comment on the undertaking prior to approval of the undertaking. The Advisory Council on Historic Preservation has established a process to implement section 106. See 36 CFR part 800. The section 106 process provides for the Federal agency to consult with the State Historic Preservation Officer established under section 101(b) of the National Historic Preservation Act (16 U.S.C. 470a(b)) whose responsibilities include cooperating with Federal and State agencies, local governments, and organizations and individuals to ensure that historic properties are taken into consideration at all levels of planning and development. The section 106 process encourages the Federal agency and State Historic Preservation Officer to agree on alternatives to avoid or minimize adverse effects on buildings and facilities listed in or eligible for listing in the National Register of Historic Places. The section 106 process does not apply to buildings and facilities that are designated as historic under an appropriate State or local law but are not listed in or eligible for listing in the National Register of Historic Places. For example, the section 106 process applies if the National Park Service leases a federally owned building listed in the National Register of Historic Places to a private entity with permission to renovate the building for use as a bed and breakfast inn or if the Small Business Administration loans funds to a private entity to renovate a building eligible for listing in the National Register of Historic Places for use as a restaurant. Where alterations are undertaken to a qualified historic building or facility that is subject to section 106 of the National Historic Preservation Act, the Federal agency with jurisdiction over the undertaking is responsible for following the section 106 process. If the State Historic Preservation Officer or Advisory Council on Historic Preservation agrees that compliance with the requirements for accessible routes (exterior and interior), ramps, entrances, or toilets would threaten or destroy the historic significance of the building or facility, the alternative requirements may be used.

Comment: Section 504(c)(3) of the ADA requires the Board to establish procedures for determining whether the alternative requirements may be used for qualified historic buildings and facilities that are not subject to section 106 of the National Historic Preservation Act. The NPRM requested information on what procedures should be followed. The National Park Service, Advisory Council on Historic Preservation, National Conference of State Historic Preservation Officers, and other commenters responsible for historic preservation programs recommended that an entity undertaking alterations to a qualified historic building or facility should consult with the State Historic Preservation Officer whenever the entity believes that compliance with the accessibility requirements would threaten or destroy the historical significance of the building or facility and that the alternative requirements should be used. Individuals with disabilities and their organizations requested that criteria be established for determining whether compliance with the accessibility requirements would threaten or destroy the

historical significance of a building or facility and that State and local accessibility officials and organizations representing individuals with disabilities should be involved in the consultation process.

Response: The State Historic Preservation Officer is a key public official in the Federal-State partnership envisioned under the National Historic Preservation Act. Every State currently has a State Historic Preservation Officer approved by the Secretary of the Interior whose responsibilities include advising and assisting Federal and State agencies and local governments in carrying out their historic preservation responsibilities; cooperating with organizations and individuals to ensure that historic properties are taken into consideration at all levels of planning and development; and providing technical assistance relating to Federal and State historic preservation programs. See 16 U.S.C. 470a(b)(3)(E) through (F). The State Historic Preservation Officer is required to have a full-time professional staff in each of the following disciplines: history, archeology, and architectural history. See 36 CFR 61.4(d).

The Board believes that it is consistent with the State Historic Preservation Officer's existing responsibilities under the National Historic Preservation Act to provide for that official to be consulted with whenever an entity undertakes alterations to a qualified historic building or facility that is not subject to the section 106 process and the entity believes that compliance with the accessibility requirements would threaten or destroy the historical significance of the building or facility and that the alternative requirements should be used. An entity may not unilaterally decide to use the alternative requirements. Rather, if an entity wants to use the alternative requirements, the entity must consult with the State Historic Preservation Officer and if that official agrees that compliance with the accessibility requirements would threaten or destroy the

historic significance of the building or facility, then the alternative requirements may be used. A new paragraph has been added at 4.1.7(2)(b) for this purpose.

The Board wishes to emphasize that when applying this provision, the inquiry should focus on whether compliance with the accessibility requirements would threaten or destroy the characteristics of a building or facility that make it eligible for listing in the National Register of Historic Places or designation as historic under an appropriate State or local law. The National Park Service and Advisory Council on Historic Preservation have had considerable experience with making accessible alterations to qualified historic buildings and facilities and have expressed interest in working with the Board to develop technical guidance and procedures to assist State Historic Preservation Officers in carrying out their consultation responsibilities and to ensure consistent and uniform application of the provision at the State and local level.

The National Conference of State Historic Preservation Officers reported that some State historic preservation programs have established good working relationships with their State and local accessibility officials and that the guidelines should encourage these relationships. The section 106 process also provides for involving other interested parties in the consultation process. See 36 CFR 800.5(e)(1). A new paragraph has been added at 4.1.7(2)(c) recommending that State and local accessibility officials, and individuals with disabilities and their organizations be involved in the consultation process.

Section 101(c)(1) of the National Historic Preservation Act (16 U.S.C. 407a(c)(1)) allows for responsibilities to be delegated to a local government historic preservation program certified by the State Historic Preservation Officer and the Secretary of the Interior. To be certified, a local government must meet certain minimum requirements, including professional expertise in architectural history. See 36 CFR 61.5. There are about 600 certified local governments. A new paragraph has been added at 4.1.7(2)(d) to allow the State Historic Preservation Officer to delegate consultation responsibilities for purposes of this section to a certified local government.

Comment: Commenters generally expressed support for using the alternative requirements in 4.1.7(3) (4.1.7(2) in the NPRM) in those cases were accessibility cannot be achieved without threatening or destroying the historical significance of a building or facility. The National Park Service noted that based on its experience accessibility can be achieved in most cases with some alteration of non-significant features. The National Park Service, Advisory Council on Historic Preservation, National Trust for Historic Preservation, and other commenters with historic preservation responsibilities expressed a need for greater flexibility in providing accessibility to qualified historic buildings and facilities. These commenters expressed concern that it may be technically infeasible to comply with specific accessibility requirements in the case of some buildings and facilities. These commenters also recommended that an exception be established for a small group of buildings and facilities such as a historic house museum that has only one entrance and where modifying the doorway or cutting out a window to create an accessible entrance would destroy the characteristics that make the building eligible for listing on the National Register of Historic Places.

Response: As stated in 4.1.7(1)(a), the provisions of 4.1.6 relating to alterations apply to qualified historic buildings and facilities. If it is technically infeasible to comply with a specific accessibility requirement, the other elements and features of the building or facility that are being altered and can be made accessible

must be made accessible within the scope of the alteration. See 4.1.6(1)(g). Flexibility is also allowed under 2.2 which permits alternative designs and technologies to be used on a case-by-case basis where they will provide substantially equivalent or greater access to and usability of a building or facility. As for those buildings and facilities where it may not be possible to achieve compliance with the alternative requirements without destroying the historic significance of the building, the Board plans to consult with the National Park Service and Advisory Council on Historic Preservation about this issue and propose an exception in the next phase of rulemaking. An exception is reserved under 4.1.7(1)(a) for this purpose.

Comment: With respect to the exception in 4.1.7(3)(b) (4.1.7(2)(b) in the NPRM) which permits access by means of an entrance not generally used by the public if a public entrance cannot be made accessible provided that the alternative entrance is unlocked and directional signage is provided, the NPRM asked how security concerns can be addressed and convenient and independent access facilitated at the same time. Most persons who responded to the question favored retaining the requirement that the alternative entrance be unlocked and independently operable, and recommended that a notification system also be provided.

Response: The requirement for the alternative entrance to be unlocked has been retained and a new requirement has been added for a notification system to be provided. A provision has also been added permitting use of a remote monitoring system where security is a concern. If a remote monitoring system is used, the alternative entrance must remain unlocked.

4.2 through 4.35 Technical Specifications

Sections 4.2 through 4.35 contain the technical specifications for elements and spaces required to be accessible by the

scoping provisions (4.1 through 4.1.7) and special application sections (5 through 10). The technical specifications are the same as the 1980 version of ANSI A117.1 standard, except as noted in the text of italics.[13]

4.2 Space Allowances and Reach Ranges

Comment. Several commenters recommended that the technical specifications for clear floor turning, and maneuvering spaces should be increased for individuals who use power wheelchairs and three wheeled scooters. A few commenters also recommended changes to the side reach ranges.

Response. Additional research is needed regarding space allowances and reach ranges for individuals who use power wheelchairs or three wheeled scooters. No change has been made in the guidelines.

4.3 Accessible Route

Comment. A number of commenters recommended that skywalks and tunnels be specifically included as part of accessible routes.

Response. Since skywalks and tunnels can be part of an accessible route, they have been specifically included in 4.3.1.

Comment. The NPRM requested comments on various options for language to include in 4.3.2 regarding travel distances between points on an accessible route. Most commenters from each category who responded to the question favored stating that the accessible route shall, to the maximum extent feasible, coincide with the route for the general public.

Response. A requirement has been added to 4.3.2 that the accessible route shall, to the maximum extent feasible, coincide with the route for the general public. Since the route provided for the general public is usually the shortest and most direct route, the requirement will result in that route being made accessible in most cases.

Comment. Several commenters stated that the

minimum widths for accessible routes and passing space requirements were not adequate and should be increased. No research or supportive data was provided.

Response. No changes have been made.

4.3.11 Areas of Rescue Assistance

Comment. Many commenters favored including technical specifications for areas of rescue assistance in the guidelines. Commenters, including the National Fire Protection Association (NFPA), submitted various recommendations for changes to the technical specifications, including permitting the use of exit stairway landings with a standpipe and areas having direct access to elevators specifically designed for emergency evacuation purposes. Several commenters recommended that the 1991 Uniform Building Code provisions for areas of rescue assistance be adopted.

Response. The 1991 Uniform Building Code provisions for areas of rescue assistance have been modified and incorporated in 4.3.11 since they represent the most current and comprehensive provisions on the subject. See 1991 Uniform Building Code, chapter 31, section 3104(b). The final guidelines permit seven different areas meeting certain conditions to be used as areas of rescue assistance. The final guidelines do not restrict the use of exit stairway landings with standpipes because the first duty of firefighters is to assist in the evacuation of individuals from the building or facility before undertaking the protection of property. The final guidelines also permit use of elevator lobbies with direct access to an emergency evacuation elevator when elevator shafts and adjacent lobbies are pressurized as required for smokeproof enclosures by local regulations and when complying with certain other requirements. The Uniform Building Code provisions for size, stairway width, two-way communication

and signage have also been adopted with a clarification that the communication system must include both visual and audible signals.

4.4 Protruding Objects

Comment. The NPRM asked questions regarding the adequacy of the technical specifications for protruding objects. About one-fourth of the commenters believed that they were adequate. The other commenters made over 30 different suggestions for changes.

Response. No changes have been made. The comments suggest that additional research is needed in this area.

4.5 Ground and Floor Surfaces

Comment. The NPRM asked whether a quantitative value should be assigned for slip resistance of ground and floor surfaces. Although there was general support for the concept, commenters presented information on a variety of issues, including the variability of measurement techniques and the likelihood of obtaining different values; lack of consensus regarding appropriate testing methods; and manufacturers certification of products.

Response. Recommended values for slip resistant surfaces on accessible routes and ramps have been included in the appendix at A 4.5.1. Many common building materials suitable for flooring are now labelled with information on the static coefficient of friction. Although it may not be possible to compare one product directly with another, or to guarantee a constant measure, builders and designers are encouraged to specify materials with appropriate values. As more products include information on slip resistance, improved uniformity in measurement and specification is likely.

Comment. The greenhouse industry raised questions about the coverage of gravel pathways in greenhouses.

Response. If a greenhouse is used only as an employee work area, the guidelines only require

that the work area be designed and constructed so that individuals with disabilities can approach, enter, and exit the area. See 4.1.1(3) Thus, ground and floor surfaces within the greenhouse are not required to comply with 4.5 where the facility is used only as an employee work area. On the other hand, if the greenhouse is also used for retail sales purposes, the facility must be designed and constructed to be accessible, including having an accessible route which has a ground or floor surface that complies with 4.5. Gravel is generally used for drainage under plant beds and walkways can be made of asphalt or concrete. Even where walkway drainage is needed, there are a variety of methods for providing firm, stable, and slip resistant surfaces.

Comment. A number of comments were received on the technical specifications for carpets in 4.5.3. Some commenters expressed concern about the 1/2 inch maximum pile height and recommended that it should not apply to carpeting off an accessible route. Other commenters recommended that performance requirements should be developed for carpets with pile height higher than 1/2 inch.

Response. The technical specifications for carpets in 4.5.3 are taken directly from the ANSI A117.1 standard. The requirements only apply to ground and floor surfaces along accessible routes and in accessible rooms and spaces, including public use and common use areas. If an area is used only as an employee work area, the ground and floor surfaces within the work area are not required to comply with 4.5, consistent with the provision in 4.1.1(3) that requires the work area to be designed and constructed so that individuals with disabilities can approach, enter, and exit the area. Additional advisory material on carpets is included in the appendix at A4.5.3.

4.6 Parking and Passenger Loading Zones[14]

Comment. Several commenters requested that the requirements regarding the location of accessible parking spaces be clarified. Some commenters recommended that a maximum distance such as 200 feet be specified between accessible parking spaces and accessible entrances.

Response. The technical specifications in 4.6.2 have been revised based on the proposed BCMC scoping provisions and provide that accessible parking spaces serving a particular building must be located on the shortest accessible route of travel from adjacent parking to an accessible entrance. In parking facilities that do not serve a particular building, the accessible parking spaces must be located on the shortest accessible route of travel to an accessible pedestrian entrance of the parking facility. In buildings with multiple accessible entrances with adjacent parking, accessible parking spaces must be dispersed and located closest to the accessible entrances. For instance, at a shopping mall with several accessible entrances or a strip shopping center where each separate tenancy is required to have an accessible entrance, the accessible parking spaces would be dispersed and located closest to the accessible entrances.

A maximum distance has not been included in the guidelines because the requirement that accessible parking spaces be located on the shortest accessible route of travel to an accessible entrance will in most cases result in the spaces being located as close as practical to the nearest accessible entrance. Specifying a maximum distance such as 200 feet could result in the provision being misinterpreted as requiring that the spaces be within 200 feet but not necessarily located closest to an accessible entrance.

Comment. Several commenters from the parking industry questioned the requirement in 4.6.3 that accessible parking spaces and adjacent access aisles must be level with surface slopes not exceeding 1:50 (2%) in all directions. For instance, the National Parking Association (NPA) noted that paved surfaces must have a designed slope of at least 1:100 (1%) to provide drainage and that structural systems frequently used in parking structures have cambered elements where the member must be sloped more than 2% to get a 1% actual slope at the high end of element.

Response. The requirement in 4.6.3 for a level surface with slopes not exceeding 1:50 (2%) applies only to accessible parking spaces and adjacent access aisles and not to the entire floor area of the parking facility. A level surface is necessary at accessible parking spaces and adjacent access aisles to enable individuals who use wheelchairs to safely transfer to and from a vehicle and to permit the deployment of lifts from vans. As the NPA's comment recognizes, it is possible to achieve an actual 1% slope at parts of the floor area of the parking facility. When planned for in the early design phase, it is possible to achieve a level surface with a slope not exceeding 1:50 (2%) at the accessible spaces and adjacent access aisles.

Comment. Several commenters recommended additional requirements for access aisles, including location of curb ramps and striping or otherwise designating access aisles.

Response. Figure 9 shows that the access aisle must be demarcated (a wide parking space alone is not in compliance) and that the connection to the accessible route is at the front of the aisle. Additional information has been included in the appendix on access aisles. The access aisle must be connected to an accessible route to the appropriate accessible entrance of a building a facility. The access aisle must either blend with the accessible route or have a curb ramp complying with 4.7. The curb ramp opening must be located within the boundaries of the access aisle, and not the parking space, and the curb ramp cannot project into the aisle. The required dimensions of the access aisle cannot be restricted by planters, curbs, or wheel stops.

4.7 Curb Ramps

Few comments were received on the technical specifications for curb ramps in 4.7 and they did not warrant any changes. Some comments concerned wayfinding for persons with visual impairments and detectable warnings at curb ramps which are addressed under 4.29.

4.8 Ramps

Comment. The NPRM asked whether the technical specification in 4.8.2 requiring a maximum 1:12 slope for ramps in new construction should be changed. Most persons in each category who responded to the question favored retaining the maximum 1:12 ramp slope. Those commenters who recommended a change preferred ramp slopes between 1:16 and 1:20.

Response. The technical specification in 4.8.2 has not been changed. However, information has been added to the appendix at A4.8.2 explaining that the ability to manage an incline is related to both its slope and its length. Wheelchair users with disabilities affecting their arms or with low stamina have serious difficulty using inclines. Many wheelchair users, for instance, cannot manage a slope of 1:12 for 30 feet. Most wheelchair users and people with mobility impairments who are ambulatory can manage a slope of 1:16. For these reasons, ramp slopes between 1:16 and 1:20 are preferred. The technical specifications in 4.8.4 have also been revised to clarify that a level landing is required at the top of each ramp and each ramp run. A statement has been added to the appendix at A4.8.4 explaining that level landings are essential toward maintaining an aggregate slope that complies with the guidelines. A ramp landing that is not level can cause individuals using wheelchairs to tip backward or bottom out when the ramp is approached.

Comment. Several commenters recommended changes to the technical specifications for handrails in 4.8.5, including making the height ranges consistent with the model codes and not requiring handrails on ramps adjacent to seating in assembly areas.

Response. The height ranges for handrails in 4.8.5(5) has been changed from "between 30 inches and 34 inches" to "between 34 inches and 38 inches" to be consistent with the model codes. A similar change has been made to the technical specifications for handrails on stairs in 4.9.4. A provision has also been added to 4.8.5 clarifying that handrails are not required on ramps adjacent to seating in assembly areas.

Comment. A number of commenters recommended that additional railings or higher edge protection be provided for persons with visual impairments.

Response. These recommendations will be studied for future revisions of the guidelines.

4.9 Stairs

Comment. Several commenters recommended that open risers should be permitted on stairs under certain conditions such as where ventilation is critical or on monumental and decorative stairs.

Response. The prohibition against open risers in 4.9.2 applies only to stairs covered by the scoping provision in 4.1.3(4). That provision requires that interior and exterior stairs connecting levels that are not connected by an elevator must comply with 4.9. Thus, open risers may be used on stairs which connect levels also served by an elevator or other accessible means of vertical access.

Comment. Several commenters recommended that steps should have contrasting nosings or tread markings. Some commenters also

recommend that the nosing projection should be reduced from 1 1/2 inches to 1/2 inch maximum.

Response. The Board is not aware of any research that supports these recommendations. There is some controversy over whether each step should have the contrast nosing or only the top and bottom step of each stair. The Board is aware that the February 1991 draft revisions to the ANSI A117.1 standard proposed to add a technical specification for tread markings on stairs. Pending further research or action by the ANSI A117 Committee, the Board is not inclined to include this provision in the guidelines.

Comment. Commenters made several recommendations for changes to the technical specifications for handrails in 4.9.4, including making the height ranges consistent with the model codes; permitting the 1 1/2 inch clearance between handrails and the wall to be a minimum; and adopting a provision from the California code on handrail extensions. Some commenters also presented detailed comments regarding wayfinding problems when persons who are visually impaired encounter diagonal or circular stairs.

Response. The height range for handrails in 4.9.4(5) has been changed from "between 30 inches and 34 inches" to "between 34 inches and 38 inches" to be consistent with the model codes. A similar change has been made to the technical specifications for handrails on ramps in 4.8.5. The Board has retained the 1 1/2 inch clearance between the handrails and the wall as an absolute. As explained in the appendix at A4.26.1, many people brace their forearms between supports and walls to give them more leverage and stability in maintaining balance. The 1 1/2 inch clearance is a safety clearance to prevent injuries from arms slipping through the openings. It also provides adequate gripping room. The other recommendations require further study.

Comment. A number of comments were received raising safety concerns about the use of

the raised truncated domes as detectable warnings at stairs. These comments are further discussed under 4.29.

Response. For the reasons explained under 4.29, the requirement in 4.9.5 for detectable warnings at stairs has been reserved until further research is conducted regarding the use of raised truncated domes as a detectable warning at stairs.

4.10 Elevators

Comment. Several commenters recommended that the February 1991 draft revisions to the ANSI A117.1 standard be adopted. Some commenters also recommended that references to the elevator safety code be updated.

Response. The February 1991 draft revisions to the ANSI A117.1 standard proposed to establish separate technical specifications for new and existing elevators. The Board believes that it is best to await further action by the ANSI A117 Committee in this area. In the meantime, the references to the elevator safety code in 4.10.1, 4.10.6, and 4.10.14 have been updated to the current code, ASME A17.1-1990. The reference to platform lifts or wheelchair lifts has also been deleted from 4.10.1 in light of the revised scoping provisions for those devices in 4.1.3(5) and 4.1.6(3)(g).

Comment. Commenters generally supported the requirement for braille characters on hoistway entrances, control panels, and emergency communication systems. Several commenters requested that the technical specifications in 4.10.5, 4.10.12, and 4.10.14 be clarified to specify that raised characters must be accompanied by braille. Some commenters requested that the reference to the use of recessed letters or symbols in 4.10.14 for identifying emergency communication systems be deleted. A number of commenters recommended that automatic verbal announcements of floor stops be required in place of audible signals.

Response. The NPRM provided in 4.10.5, 4.10.12, and

4.10.14 that hoistway entrances, control panels, and emergency communication systems have raised characters complying with 4.30.4. That provision provided for raised characters to be accompanied by braille. The final guidelines have been clarified by including the requirement for brailled characters in 4.10.5, 4.10.12, and 4.10.14. The technical specifications in 4.30.4 do not permit the use of recessed letters. To be consistent with that provision, the reference to recessed letters or symbols in 4.10.14 for identifying emergency communication systems has been deleted.

The Board recognizes that automatic verbal announcements of floor stops is preferred by individuals with visual impairments. The technical specifications in 4.10.13 permit their use in place of audible signals.

Comment. A number of commenters recommended that the ANSI A117.1–1986 standard for control panel height should be adopted in place of the NPRM.

Response. The NPRM provided in 4.10.12(3) that all floor buttons on elevator control panels be no higher than 48 inches, unless there is a substantial increase in cost, in which case the maximum mounting height may be increased to 54 inches. Commenters questioned what constitutes a "substantial increase in cost" and pointed out that the ANSI A117.1-1986 standard provides for greater flexibility by requiring all floor buttons to be no higher than 54 inches above the floor for side approach and 48 inches for front approach. The final guidelines adopt the ANSI A117.1-1986 standard for control panel height in 4.10.12(3).

Comment. A number of commenters requested additional guidance on the technical specification in 4.10.14 for an emergency two-way communication system.

Response. Additional information has been included in the appendix at A4.10.14 on emergency two-way communication systems. Such systems

should ideally provide both voice and visual display intercommunication so that persons with visual impairments and persons with speech and hearing impairments can receive information regarding the status of a rescue. A voice intercommunication system cannot be the only means of communication because it is not accessible to persons with speech and hearing impairments. While a voice intercommunication system is not required, at a minimum, the system must provide both an audio and visual indication, such as a recorded message and flashing light, to announce that a rescue is on the way.

4.11 Platform Lifts/Wheelchair Lifts

Comment. Most of the comments received on platform lifts or wheelchair lifts were in response to questions in the NPRM regarding scoping provisions which are discussed under 4.1.3(5). Commenters from the lift industry recommended that the technical specifications should reference current safety standards. Individuals with disabilities and their organizations recommended that the technical specifications should specifically provide for independent operation.

Response. The technical specifications in 4.11.2 have been revised to reference the current safety standard, ASME A17.1-1990, part XX. The scoping provisions in 4.1.3(5) Exception 4 also require that platform lifts or wheelchair lifts comply with applicable state or local codes. The technical specification in 4.11.3 has also been revised in response to comments regarding independent operation to specifically require the platform lifts or wheelchair lifts provide for unassisted operation. This requirement does not preclude the use of a key to operate a lift as long as the key is readily available and allows for unassisted operation. The appendix in A4.11 has also been revised to provide more up-to-date information on platform lifts or wheelchair lifts.

Comment. Commenters from the lift industry requested that an exception be established to permit the use of inclined lifts with a 30 inch by 40 inch platform size in stairwells with space limitations.

Response. Inclined lifts are required to comply with the technical specifications in 4.2.4 for clear floor space which provides for a minimum clear space of 30 inches by 48 inches to accommodate a wheelchair user. The Board is aware that this space will not accommodate some powered wheelchairs or three wheeled scooters which are increasing in popularity, especially among older people. The Board does not believe that any exceptions should be established permitting the use of shorter platform lifts or wheelchair lifts.

4.12 Windows

Comment. The NPRM proposed to adopt the ANSI A117.1 standard for windows which provides for a maximum 5 pounds of force (lbf.) to open operable windows and for locks, cranks, and other hardware to comply with the technical specifications for controls and operating mechanisms, including reach ranges for forward or side approaches. A number of commenters expressed concern that the 5 lbf. maximum force requirement is not currently achievable.

Response. The technical specifications for windows have been reserved in the final guidelines and information has been placed in the appendix at A4.12.1 and A4.12.2. When the Board issued MGRAD in 1982, it reserved the technical specifications for windows pending further study or experience with the ANSI A117.1 standard. See 47 FR 33862. (August 4, 1982). The Board subsequently sponsored a research project on hand anthropometrics which studied the capabilities of selected individuals with disabilities to operate mechanisms and building components. The findings from the research project suggested design criteria for window opening hardware and indicated appropriate operable forces based on specific types of hardware that were compatible with the ANSI A117.1 standard. Based on the results of the research project, Board adopted the ANSI A117.1 standard when it revised MGRAD in 1989. See 36 CFR 1190.31(j), 54 FR 5434 (February 3, 1989). Information obtained during the current rulemaking revealed that the existing industry standards for operable windows are 25 lbf. for sliding windows and 45 lbf. for double hung windows and that windows meeting the ANSI A117.1 standard are not commonly available for use in heavy construction. The Board needs additional information about existing products and technologies before it can adopt final technical specifications for windows.

4.13 Doors

Comment. Commenters made individual recommendations for changes or clarifications to the technical specifications for doors in 4.13 and the accompanying figures. For instance, clarification was requested regarding whether all or part of the clear space on the latch side of the door in figure 25(a) can be provided by other accessible space such as an open space for hanging clothes in a hotel guestroom.

Response. Two minor changes have been included in the technical specifications for door hardware in 4.13.9. First, the sentence in the NPRM referring to doors in dwelling units has been deleted since it was not consistent with the requirements for doors in accessible units in transient lodging in 9.2.2(3) which requires all doors designed to allow passage into and within all accessible sleeping rooms and units to comply with 4.13. Second, the sentence in the NPRM referring to doors to hazardous areas has been deleted because the technical specifications in 4.29.3 for detectable warnings on doors to hazardous areas has been reserved. An additional change has been made to 4.13.6 to label

the exemption in the last sentence of that technical specification as an "exception."

With regard to figure 25(a), the guidelines do not preclude other accessible space from being used to provide the required clearance on the latch side of the door as long as the specified dimensions are met and other uses of the space do not interfere with or intrude upon the clearance required by a wheelchair user or crutch user to reach and open the door or present other barriers not allowed in the guidelines. For example, an open rack mounted on the wall in such a way so as to provide clearance for a wheelchair user or crutch user could be a protruding object. An enclosed closet area would not likely permit adequate maneuvering space.

4.14 Entrances

All the comments on entrances concerned the scoping provision and are discussed under 4.1.3(8). No changes have been made to the technical specifications.

4.15 Drinking Fountains and Water Coolers

Comment. Commenters made individual recommendations for changes or clarifications to the technical specifications for drinking fountains and water coolers in 4.15. For instance, clarification was requested regarding the spout location on a drinking fountain with a round or oval bowl.

Response. A sentence has been added to the technical specification for spout location in 4.15.3 to clarify that on a drinking fountain with a round or oval bowl, the spout must be positioned so the flow of water is within 3 inches of the front edge of the fountain. The sentence in appendix at A4.15.2 has also been clarified that two drinking fountains, mounted side by side or on a single post, are usable by individuals with disabilities and people who find it difficult to bend over.

4.16 Water Closets

Comment. Commenters made individual recommendations for changes or clarifications to the technical specifications for water closets in 4.16 and accompanying figures. For instance, clarification was requested regarding the dimensions of the grab bar behind the water closet in figure 29(a) and the location of the lavatory in figure 28.

Response. A sentence has been added to the technical specifications in 4.16.4 to clarify that the grab bar behind the water closet must be 36 inches minimum. The grab bar dimensions have also been clarified in figure 29(a). Additional information has been provided in the appendix at A4.22 regarding figure 28 and the placement of the lavatory. The dotted lines in figure 28 designate the minimum clear floor space, depending on the direction of approach, required for wheelchair users to transfer onto the water closet. The dimensions of 48 inches and 60 inches, respectively, correspond to the space required for wheelchair users to perform a diagonal approach transfer and side approach transfer. See Fig. A6 (a) and (b). Placement of the lavatory to the immediate side of the water closet will preclude use of the side approach transfer. To accommodate the side approach transfer, the space adjacent to the water closet must remain clear of obstruction for 42 inches from the center line of the toilet and the lavatory must not be located within this space. A turning circle or T-turn, the clear floor space of the lavatory, and maneuvering space at the door must be considered when determining the possible wall location. See Fig. 3, 25 and 32.

4.17 Toilet Stalls

Comment. The NPRM presented two approaches for accommodating the needs of persons with mobility impairments who are ambulatory with respect to use of toilet stalls: (a) provide for moveable grab bar in the 60 inch wide standard stall; or (b) provide for a 36 inch wide alternate stall or a conventional, non-accessible stall equipped with dual parallel grab bars in addition to the 60 inch standard stall. Most persons in each category who commented on the two approaches opposed the use of moveable grab bars and supported the provisions of a 36 inch wide alternate stall with dual grab bars in addition to the 60 inch wide standard stall. Some commenters questioned why the 36 inch or 48 inch alternate stalls are only permitted in alterations where the provision of a 60 inch wide standard stall is technically infeasible.

Response. The guidelines require use of the 60 inch wide standard stall unless it is technically infeasible in alterations because that stall provides clear floor space and grab bars to enable wheelchair users to perform a side approach transfer or diagonal approach transfer from a wheelchair to the toilet. See Fig. A6 (a) and (b). Although many wheelchair users are unable to use either alternate stall, persons with mobility impairments who are ambulatory can use them. Many of those persons find it more convenient to use the two parallel grab bars in the 36 inch wide alternate stall. Based on the comments, a provision has been added to the technical specifications for toilet rooms in 4.22.4 requiring that a 36 inch wide alternate stall with parallel grab bars be provided in addition to the 60 inch wide standard stall where six or more toilet stalls are provided. Since the stall is primarily intended for use by persons with mobility impairments who are ambulatory rather than wheelchair users, the length of the stall could be conventional. The door, however, must swing outward to ensure a usable space by persons with mobility impairments who are ambulatory.

Comment. Several commenters recommended that the width dimensions in figure 30 (a) and (b) should be labeled as minimum. A number of commenters requested that the requirements for hardware on toilet stall doors be clarified.

Response. The width dimensions in figure 30 (a) and (b) have been labeled as minimum. The technical specification in 4.19.5 has been clarified that toilet stall doors including hardware, must comply with 4.13. That provision requires in relevant part at 4.13.9 that handles, pulls, latches, locks, and other operating devices on accessible doors must have a shape that is easy to grasp with one hand and does not require tight grasping, tight pinching, or twisting of the wrist to operate.

4.18 Urinals

Few comments were received on the technical specifications for urinals in 4.18 and they did not warrant any changes.

4.19 Lavatories and Mirrors

Comment. Commenters made individual recommendations for changes or clarifications to the technical specification for lavatories and mirrors in 4.19. For instance, it was pointed out that hot water and drain pipes under lavatories can be configured near the back wall so as to prevent contact but the technical specifications only allowed insulation for protection.

Response. The technical specifications for exposed pipes and surfaces in 4.19.4 have been revised to require that hot water and drain pipes under lavatories be insulated or otherwise configured to protect against contact.

4.20 Bathtubs

Comment. Commenters made individual recommendations for changes or clarifications to the technical specifications for bathtubs in 4.20. For instance, clarification was requested that the lavatory in figure 33 must provide clear space under it to reach the bathtub control area and that the shower spray unit required by 4.20.6 can be used both as a fixed shower head and as a hand-held shower.

Response. The technical specifications for lavatories in 4.19.2 and 4.19.3 require that a clearance of at least 29 inches be provided from the floor to the bottom of the apron of the lavatory and that a clear floor space of 30 inches by 48 inches be provided in front of the lavatory. The technical specifications in 4.20.6 has been clarified to provide that the shower spray unit can be used both as a fixed shower head and as a hand-held shower.

Comment. The NPRM asked whether a vertical grab bar should be provided in addition to the dual horizontal grab bars required by 4.20.4. Most persons in each category who responded to the question favored the provision of a vertical grab bar. However, the commenters made differing recommendations regarding the location and size of the vertical grab bar.

Response. The location and size of the vertical grab bar requires further study before it can be specified.

4.21 Shower Stalls

Comment. As further discussed under 9.1.2, the final guidelines require that hotels with 50 or more sleeping rooms or suites must provide a certain number of sleeping rooms or suites that include a 30 inch by 60 inch or 36 inch by 60 inch roll-in shower as illustrated in figure 57 (a) and (b). The NPRM asked several questions regarding the design of the roll-in shower. Most persons from each category who responded to the question favored: (a) including a fold-up seat in the shower; (b) requiring the seat to be slip-resistant; (c) allowing the shower head and controls to be located in the center of the long wall of the shower; and (d) providing two mounting hooks for the shower spray unit.

Response. The technical specifications for seats in 4.21.3 have been revised to add a provision for a fold-up seat in the 30 inch by 60 inch roll-in shower required for hotels. The seat must be mounted on the wall adjacent to the controls or shower as shown in figure 57. A requirement has not been included for the seat to be slip-resistant pending further study. A note has been added to figure

37(b) allowing the shower head to be located on the long wall or on either side wall. A requirement has not been included for two mounting hooks pending further study of mounting heights. However, the technical specification in 4.20.6 has been clarified to provide that the shower spray unit must be useable both as a fixed shower head and as a hand-held shower.

Comment. One commenter pointed out that the American Society of Testing and Materials (ASTM) and the Consumer Product Safety Commission have developed slip resistant standards for shower stalls. Another commenter submitted data showing that shower stall drains should be located in a corner to avoid the potential hazards of slipping on a sloping surface and to provide an even surface for portable shower seats.

Response. These matters will be further studied for future revisions of the guidelines.

4.22 Toilet Rooms

Comment. As further discussed under 4.17, most persons who responded to questions in the NPRM regarding accommodating the needs of persons with mobility impairments who are ambulatory with respect to use of toilet stalls favored the provision of a 36 inch wide alternate stall with dual grab bars in addition to the 60 inch wide standard stall.

Response. A provision has been added to the technical specifications for toilet rooms in 4.22.4 requiring that a 36 inch wide alternate stall with parallel grab bars be provided in addition to the 60 inch wide standard stall where six or more toilet stalls are provided. Additional information on the design of this stall is provided in the appendix at A4.17.3 and is discussed under 4.17.

Comment. Some commenters recommended that accessible "unisex" toilet rooms be provided.

Response. Accessible "unisex" toilet rooms are preferred by some wheelchair users, especially those who may be assisted by another person.

Information on the design of accessible "unisex" toilet rooms has been included in the appendix at A4.22.3. The appendix recommends that consideration be given to providing accessible "unisex" toilet rooms in new construction, in addition to providing the required accessible toilet stalls in other rest rooms. The appendix also points out that accessible "unisex" toilet rooms are permitted in alterations where it is technically infeasible to make existing toilet rooms accessible.

4.23 Bathrooms, Bathing Facilities, and Shower Rooms

Comment. Commenters made individual recommendations for changes to the technical specifications for bathrooms, bathing facilities, and shower rooms. For instance, it was recommended that group showers in locker rooms be addressed.

Response. Group showers will be more fully addressed in future revisions of the guidelines. The technical specifications for the placement of controls and the shower head in roll-in showers can be used in a corner of a group shower to provide access.

4.24 Sinks

Few comments were received on the technical specifications for sinks in 4.24 and they did not warrant any changes. To be consistent with the change made to technical specifications for lavatories in 4.19, 4.24.6 has been revised to require that hot water and drain pipes under sinks be insulated or otherwise configured to protect against contact.

4.25 Storage

Comment. Commenters made individual recommendations for changes or clarifications to the technical specifications for storage in 4.25. For instance, it was requested that the height and depth for closet rods and shelves be clarified.

Response. The technical specifications in 4.25.3 for the height and depth of closet rods

and shelves have been clarified. Accessible storage must be within the reach ranges in 4.2.5 or 4.2.6 for a forward approach (Fig. 5) or a side approach (Fig. 6). For a side approach where the distance from the wheelchair to the clothes rod or shelves does not exceed 10 inches, the height of the clothes rod cannot exceed 54 inches and shelves must be provided between 9 inches and 54 inches. In reach-in closets without accessible doors where the distance from the wheelchair to the clothes rod or shelves exceeds 10 inches, but is less than 21 inches, the height of the clothes rod cannot exceed 48 inches and shelves must be provided between 9 inches and 48 inches. These dimensions are shown in figures 38 (a) and (b). An additional closet rod or shelves may be provided outside the specified dimensions.

4.26 Handrails, Grab Bars, and Tub and Shower Seats

Few comments were received on the technical specifications for handrails and grab bars in 4.26 and they did not warrant any changes.

4.27 Controls and Operating Mechanisms

Comment. Several commenters asked whether controls and operating mechanisms that are not normally intended for public use must comply with the technical specifications in 4.27.

Response. An exception has been added to the technical specifications at 4.27.3 which provides that the requirements do not apply where the use of special equipment dictates otherwise or where electrical and communications systems receptacles are not normally intended for use by building occupants. For instance, electrical receptacles installed specifically for wall-mounted clocks and refrigerators or microwave ovens in transient lodging or lunch rooms in an office building are not required to be placed within the specified reach ranges if the receptacles are not intended for regular or frequent use by building occupants.

Comment. The American Hotel and Motel Association (AHMA) stated, without any explanation, that thermostats must be mounted at 60 inches and cannot be placed at an accessible height. A few commenters also expressed concern that State and local codes require electrical outlets be placed lower than 15 inches above the floor.

Response. The technical specifications in 4.27.3 require that the highest operable part of controls, dispensers, receptacles, and other operable equipment be placed within the forward reach range in 4.2.5 (maximum high forward reach is 48 inches and minimum low forward reach is 15 inches, where there is no obstruction) or the side reach range in 4.2.6 (maximum high side reach is 54 inches and minimum low side reach is 9 inches, where there is no obstruction). Thermostats and electrical outlets that are intended for use by building occupants are controls subject to 4.27. The technical specifications in 4.27.3 regarding the location of such controls are taken directly from the ANSI A117.1 standard. AHMA did not cite to any State or local code provision that requires thermostats to be mounted at 60 inches and the Board is not aware of any. State and local building codes allow the lower placement of electrical outlets but do not preclude what is required in 4.27.3. The Fair Housing Accessibility Guidelines also provide for thermostats and electrical outlets to be placed within similar heights. Therefore, there is no basis for establishing different requirements for thermostats or electrical outlets.

4.28 Alarms

Comment. The NPRM asked whether requirements should be established for the standardization of audible alarms to distinguish them from other sounds. The commenters were divided on the issue. The National Fire Protection Association (NFPA) and several other commenters recom-

mended that the technical specifications for audible alarms in 4.28.2 should be consistent with the NFPA 72A Standard for Protective Signalling Systems. NFPA 72A recommends that the duration of a sound which an alarm should exceed by 5 decibels should be 60 seconds rather than 30 seconds. NFPA 72A also recommends a 130 decibel maximum sound level. NFPA further recommended that the requirements should be stated in terms of the "A" weighted scale.

Response. The technical specifications for audible alarms in 4.28.2 have been revised to conform to NFPA 72A, except that the maximum sound level of 120 decibels has not been changed. The Board understands that the 120 decibel level is commonly known as the "threshold of pain." The 130 decibel level recommended in NFPA 72A was primarily intended for industrial application where noise is a problem and may be appropriate only for industrial occupancies. The 120 decibel level limit has been retained pending further information. The comments did not otherwise present any information beyond that obtained through the Board's research project which concluded that there was not enough known about the problem to develop specific requirements for the standardization of audible alarms. Instead, additional information developed by the Board's research project has been included in the appendix to assist builders and designers in selecting appropriate systems.

Comment. NFPA and several other commenters recommended that the technical specifications for visual alarms in 4.28.3 should be consistent with NFPA 72G Guide for Installation, Maintenance, and Use of Notification Appliances for Protective Signalling Systems. A few commenters recommended that the Board reserve establishing any requirements for visual alarms until it evaluated a recent study by the Underwriters Laboratory (UL) on such alarms. Some building owners and managers

requested that the requirements should be more performance oriented. For example, a system was suggested in which some or all of the building lights would flash in some fashion. Several commenters stated that the requirements should address ambient light levels due to concern that the intensity of the visual signal might temporarily blind people in areas with low light. A few commenters were also concerned about the effect of strobe lights in inducing seizures in certain individuals.

Response. The technical specifications for visual alarms in 4.28.3 have been revised as follows to be consistent with NFPA 72G:

(a) A new paragraph has been added at 4.28.3(3) to provide for a maximum pulse duration of 0.2 sec. with a maximum duty cycle of 40%.

(b) The maximum 120 candela intensity has been deleted from 4.28.3(4) (4.28.3(3) in the NPRM). NFPA 72G permits intensities up to 1000 candela and the UL study found no evidence that such bright devices caused any eye damage in view of the shortness of the flash pulse.

(c) The height requirement for placement of visual signal devices in 4.28.3(6) (4.28.3(5) in the NPRM) has been amended to specify that the devices be at least 6 inches below the ceiling to reduce the potential concealment by smoke.

The requirements in 4.28.3 (7) and (8) (4.28.3 (6) and (7) in the NPRM) have been revised to clarify that the spacing distance applies only in rooms or spaces which are required to have visual signal appliances. The requirement that no place be more than 50 feet from the signal means that the signaling devices would be spaced 100 feet apart as recommended in NFPA 72G. A sentence has also been added to address the spacing of signaling devices in large rooms and spaces such as auditoriums that are more than 100 feet across and are not divided by walls or partitions above 6 feet. In such rooms and spaces, the signaling devices may be placed 100 feet apart around the perimeter of the room or space instead of suspending the devices from the ceiling.

The Board has reviewed the UL study and it generally supports the technical specifications in 4.28.3. The Board notes that NFPA 72G is scheduled to be revised in 1993 and that the UL is planning to develop standards for visual signal devices. The Board intends to monitor these standards and update the guidelines, as appropriate.

The Board has not opted for more performance oriented requirements because the lack of specificity in the current UFAS and ANSI A117.1 standards have resulted in the provision of some ineffective visual alarm systems. As new systems and technologies are developed and tested, the equivalent facilitation provision in 2.2 provides sufficient flexibility for builders and designers to use them. The Board will also consider new systems and technologies when it periodically updates the guidelines.

NFPA 72G and the UL study indicate that the 75 candela minimum signal intensity specified in 4.28.3(4) is not harmful at different lighting levels. The ambient lighting level of typical offices, classrooms, and hotel rooms as tested by UL ranges from 20 to 75 lumens per square foot. NFPA 72G recommends a signal intensity of 100 to 1000 candela for that lighting level. The UL study tested strobe lights with intensity levels equivalent to those required by 4.28.3(4), including tests conducted in a totally dark room where the strobe flash provided the only light. Not only were the subjects not blinded, but they were able to move about the room and find specific objects on a table. As for the possible effect of strobe lights in inducing seizures in certain individuals, the Board's research project and other available information indicate that the problem does not occur if the flash rate is less than 5 HZ. The Board has set the maximum rate at 3 HZ for additional safety.

Comment. Several commenters pointed out that if portable visual alarms are permitted in dwelling units and sleeping rooms, they should be triggered by the emergency alarm system for the building. A few commenters recommended that portable vibrating alarms should also be required to awaken sleepers. Some commenters noted that the requirement that the signal be visible in all areas of the dwelling unit or sleeping room would be difficult in some unusually shaped rooms and spaces.

Response. The intent of the technical specifications for auxiliary alarms in 4.28.4 is that the portable devices will be equivalent to a permanently installed visual alarm that is connected to the building emergency alarm system. The requirement has been clarified by specifying that a means must be provided by which a signal from the building emergency alarm system can trigger the auxiliary alarm. This can be accomplished by providing a separate circuit or transmitting a signal through the normal wiring system to trigger the portable device.

The UL study found that it required a signal of 110 candela to wake a sleeping person compared to a 15 candela signal to alert people in normal work situations. The UL study also found that vibrating alarms were more effective than visual signals for waking sleeping persons. This information has been included in the appendix at A4.28.4.

The requirement that the signal be visible in all areas of the dwelling unit or sleeping room is reasonable since the purpose of the alarm is to alert persons to emergencies. NFPA 72G states that the signal should be visible "regardless of the orientation" of the individual. The signal can reflect off the walls and be visible in various areas of the room. Some unusually shaped rooms and spaces may require more than one visual alarm device. Builders and designers should take this into consideration when designing and building new facilities.

4.29 Detectable Warnings

Comment. The NPRM proposed to include new provisions for detectable warnings based on research and planned revisions to the ANSI A117.1 standard. A detectable warning is a standardized surface feature built in or applied to walking surfaces or other elements to warn individuals with visual impairments of hazards on a circulation path. The detectable warning should consist of raised truncated domes. Comments were received in support of and in opposition to including detectable warnings in the guidelines. Commenters who opposed detectable warnings gave a variety of reasons. Some individuals with visual impairments stated that with proper training and use of mobility aids they can avoid dangers in the physical environment. These commenters believed that detectable warnings are unnecessary and the people with visual impairments may tend to rely on detectable warnings rather than learn adequate mobility skills. They also expressed concern that detectable warnings might cause hazards for people with visual impairments because the warnings are distracting and can cause people to lose their balance. They noted that detectable warnings may also be hazardous for people with mobility impairments who are ambulatory especially in outdoor conditions where ice and snow removal may be adversely affected by the raised truncated domes. Other commenters stated that detectable warnings create and perpetuate misconceptions and attitudinal barriers about people who have visual impairments. They expressed concern that detectable warnings would negatively affect the employment of people with visual impairments because employers might mistakenly perceive that such individuals cannot function in an environment that is not specially equipped. In their view, detectable warnings could result in "unintended discriminatory effects." A few commenters questioned the adequacy of the research; the long term durability of raised truncated domes; the ability of the construction industry to comply with the requirement; and the aesthetics of detectable warnings.

Commenters who supported detectable warnings also gave a variety of reasons. They pointed out that there is a significant number of people with visual impairments who are not able to fully master mobility skills due to a range of factors, including age of onset, type of disability, and innate abilities. They further pointed out that necessary cues such as traffic sounds are not always distinguishable due to various circumstances which are beyond the control of the individual. These commenters were concerned about the safety of persons who cannot depend on using mobility skills to detect hazardous conditions. They believed that detectable warnings can prevent unnecessary accidents and deaths and do not stigmatize people who have visual impairments because the warnings are helpful to all people. They noted that detectable warnings are frequently used in industrial settings to warn workers whose vision may be temporarily obscured of hazards in the workplace and have been proven effective in preventing accidents and injuries.

Some commenters generally supported the concept of detectable warnings but suggested that the guidelines should allow for a variety of surface treatments in order to accommodate variations in walking surfaces and design techniques.

Response. Accessibility includes ensuring that individuals with disabilities can safely use the built environment. Some of the requirements in the guidelines such as those for areas of rescue assistance and visual alarms are based primarily on concern for the safety of individuals with disabilities. The purpose of detectable warnings is to alert individuals with visual impairments of hazards on a circulation path that might otherwise go unnoticed and result in serious injury. Although mobility

training is essential, as some of the commenters pointed out, a significant number of people with visual impairments are not able to fully master mobility skills. Further, mobility training is not always readily available.

The Board's goal is to provide appropriate cues in the built environment to facilitate the use of mobility skills. The Board does not believe that detectable warnings are any more stigmatizing than ramps. Like other accessibility features, detectable warnings benefit all people.

As discussed in the NPRM, studies have demonstrated the raised truncated dome pattern to be an effective detectable warning. See Tactile Warnings to Promote Safety in the Vicinity of Transit Platform Edges, Urban Mass Transportation Administration (1987); Pathfinder Tactile Tile Demonstration Test Project, Metro-Dade Transit Agency (1988). The domes can be constructed using a variety of methods including concrete stamping or the application of a prefabricated surface treatment. Although there are other common surface treatments that are detectable, the concept of a detectable warning is to provide consistent and uniform surface treatment that is distinctive from other materials and consistently recognized as a warning in order to alert pedestrians that they are approaching a potentially dangerous area.

The final guidelines retain the requirements in 4.29.2 for detectable warnings to consist of raised truncated domes. The requirement for detectable warnings used on interior surfaces to differ from adjoining walking surfaces in resiliency or sound on cane contract has also been retained. However, for the reasons discussed under the comments below, the Board has limited the application of detectable warnings to hazardous vehicular ways, reflecting pools that are not otherwise protected, and curb ramps. The provisions for detectable warnings at stairs and on doors to hazardous areas have been reserved pending further study.

Comment. The NPRM provided in 4.29.2 for detectable warnings to contrast visually with adjoining surfaces and proposed to specify a 70% contrast ratio. The NPRM asked several questions regarding the proposed contrast ratio, including whether it was too difficult to achieve and whether a one inch black band between the detectable warning and adjoining surfaces would provide sufficient contrast for persons with low vision. Most of the persons who responded to the question objected to the contrast ratio. Several commenters stated that it could not be measured or enforced under field conditions. Some commenters noted that materials with demonstrated low maintenance and durability characteristics often have low reflective values and would not meet the criteria. Many commenters also opposed the use of a black band. Several commenters recommended that detectable warnings should be a yellow color.

Response. The final guidelines provide in 4.29.2 that detectable warnings must contrast visually with adjoining surfaces, either light-on-dark or dark-on-light. The 70% contrast ratio has been placed in the appendix at A4.29.2 and is advisory only.

Comment. A number of commenters opposed the requirements in 4.9.5 and 4.29.4 for detectable warnings at stairs primarily based on concern that the raised truncated domes will create a tripping hazard. Several commenters, including industries which use detectable warnings to alert workers of hazards such as loading docks, requested that the depth of the warning be decreased from 36 inches to 24 inches.

Response. Although detectable warnings have been successfully used at such locations at transit platform edges and loading dock edges, there is no data available regarding this application at stairs. People may use a different gait when they approach stairs compared to other walking surfaces. The requirement in 4.9.5 and 4.29.4 for detectable warnings at stairs have been reserved pending further study regarding possible tripping hazards. The requirements in 4.29.3 and 4.29.7 for detectable warnings on doors to hazardous areas and for standardization of such warnings within a building, facility or site have also been reserved pending further study.

Comment. A number of commenters requested that detectable warnings also be required at uncurbed and unprotected drop off areas where a fall may be extremely hazardous or life threatening such as transit platforms and loading docks. Some commenters were opposed to detectable warnings at those locations. Several commenters recommended that detectable warnings should be required where the drop-off separating the pedestrian and vehicular way is more than curb height.

Response. The requirement in 4.29.5 has been clarified that a detectable warning is required when a walk crosses or adjoins a vehicular way, and the walking surfaces are not separated by curbs, railings, or other elements between the pedestrian areas and vehicular areas. For instance, some hotels have driveways that adjoin walkways at entrances. If there is no curb separating the pedestrian and vehicular area, a detectable warning would have to be provided. Detectable warnings for transportation facilities will be addressed in section 10 of the final guidelines which will be published separately in the Federal Register. Detectable warnings have not been required at loading docks and loading ramps because those areas are generally not open to the public. If an individual employee with a visual impairment works in an area with hazardous drop-offs, detectable warnings would be covered by reasonable accommodation under title I of the ADA.

Comment. Some commenters questioned the requirement in 4.7.7 for detectable warnings at curb ramps. A few commenters expressed concerns about maintenance, including snow and ice removal. Other commenters suggested changes

to the requirement that the detectable warnings extend the full width and depth of the curb ramp.

Response. Properly designed curb ramps have gentle slopes which may not be easily detectable by some persons with visual impairments. Furthermore, changes in slope along pedestrian ways are commonplace and persons with visual impairments cannot predictably know when a change in slope indicates the presence of a curb ramp. The Board is concerned about the safety of persons with visual impairments who may unknowingly enter a vehicular way due to the lack of any cue or warnings at curb ramps to prevent serious injuries and deaths. The requirement in 4.7.7 for detectable warnings at curb ramps has therefore been retained.

4.30 Signage

Comment. A number of commenters, including graphic designers and sign manufacturers, objected to the technical specifications for character height and letter spacing in 4.30.3. Their primary concern was the impact of the requirements on the size of the sign. For instance, the NPRM proposed that letters on building directories by 5/8-inch minimum. One commenter pointed out that the current industry standard for film negative directories is 3/16-inch which is roughly 1/4 the size proposed in the NPRM. Building directories would need to be 16 times their current size (4 times as high and 4 times as wide) to meet the 5/8-inch minimum. The commenter noted that larger office buildings have difficulty just accommodating a directory large enough to list their occupants in 3/16-inch type. Several individuals with disabilities and other commenters objected to wide letter spacing because they believed it would make it more difficult to read by word shape or "footprint."

Response. The minimum height requirements for building directories and wall

mounted signs and the provision for wide letter spacing have been deleted from the technical specifications in 4.30.3. Signs that are suspended or projected overhead in compliance with the technical specifications for protruding objects in 4.4.2 (i.e., more than 80 inches above the floor or ground) are required to have a character height of 3 inches minimum. A sentence has also been added to 4.30.3 to clarify that lower case letters are permitted.

Comment. Individuals with disabilities and government agencies involved with disability issues supported the technical specifications for raised and brailled characters in 4.30.4. Many of the commenters who opposed the technical specifications, including graphic designers and sign manufacturers, interpreted the NPRM as requiring all signs to have raised and brailled characters and all upper case letters and apparently objected to the scoping provisions and technical specifications on that basis. A few commenters also expressed concern that raised and braille characters may be more prone to vandalism.

Response. As discussed earlier, the scoping provisions for exterior and interior signage have been clarified in response to the comments. See 4.1.2(7) and 4.1.3(16). Only those signs which designate permanent rooms and spaces must comply with the technical specifications in 4.30.4 through 4.30.6 for raised and brailled characters, finish and contrast, and mounting location and height. No changes have been made to the technical specifications for raised and brailled characters in 4.30.4. Raised and brailled characters can be designed to be as vandal resistant as other signage.

Comment. Several graphic designers and sign manufacturers objected to eggshell finish being specified in the technical specifications for finish and contrast in 4.30.5. They felt that it unnecessarily restricts the industry. A number of commenters also objected to the 70% contrast ratio proposed in the NPRM because they believed that it could not be measured or enforced in the field.

Response. The Board sponsored research project on which the technical specifications for finish and contrast in 4.30.5 are based found that eggshell and matte finishes are equally readable by persons with low vision. The NPRM proposed to require only eggshell because of its relative resistance to soiling compared to matte. The final guidelines provide for eggshell, matte, or other non-glare finish. The 70% contrast formula has been placed in the appendix at A4.30.5 and is advisory only. The appendix also recommends an eggshell finish and light characters on a dark background.

Comment. The NPRM proposed in 4.30.6 that signs providing permanent identification of rooms and spaces be mounted on the wall adjacent to the latch side of the door at a height between 54 and 66 inches. These signs are required to include raised and brailled characters. A number of commenters recommended different mounting heights. Some pointed out that the 66 inch height was not within the reach range for wheelchair users. Other commenters pointed out that a more uniform and consistent mounting height would make it easier for persons with visual impairments to locate the signage.

Response. The technical specifications in 4.30.6 have been revised to require that signs providing permanent identification of rooms and spaces be mounted 60 inches above the finish floor to the center of the sign. The 60 inch mounting height was recommended in the original research for the ANSI A117.1–1980 standard. See Accessible Buildings for People with Severe Visual Impairments, Steinfeld (1978). Lowering the maximum height also reduces the viewing distance for persons with low vision and places the sign at a more comfortable reading height for users of braille and raised characters. A sentence has also been added to 4.30.6 clarifying

that where there is no wall space to the latch side of the door, including at double leaf doors, signs are to be placed on the nearest adjacent wall.

Comment. A number of commenters recommended that the international symbol of access for hearing loss be used to identify the availability of permanently installed assistive listening systems in assembly areas required to have such systems by 4.1.3(19)(b).

Response. A requirement has been added to the technical specifications for symbols of accessibility in 4.30.7 that assistive listening systems be identified by signage that includes the international symbol of access for hearing loss. See Fig. 43(d). Additional information is provided in the appendix at A4.30.7 regarding appropriate messages to include with the symbol (e.g., infrared Assistive Listening System Available—Please Ask).

Comment. The NPRM proposed in 4.30.8 that illumination levels on the sign surface be in the 200 to 300 lux range (10 to 30 footcandles) and that the illumination level on the surface of the sign not be significantly exceeded by the ambient light or visible bright lighting source behind or in front of the sign. A number of commenters objected to this provision as unenforceable. Other commenters noted that the proposed levels were generally met or exceeded in indoor lighted areas.

Response. The technical specifications for illumination levels in 4.30.8 has been reserved pending further study. The NPRM provision has been included in the appendix at A4.30.8 and is advisory only.

4.31 Telephones

Comment. The NPRM asked what decibel range should be specified for volume control telephones. Persons who responded to the question generally favored a range of 12 decibels to 18 decibels. Some commenters requested higher levels, stating that those with lower levels were not helpful. Although most telephone companies who responded to

the question indicated that their equipment would fall within this range, they were opposed to specifying any decibel level.

Response. The final guidelines provide in 4.31.5(2) that public telephones required to be equipped with volume controls by 4.1.3(17)(b) must be capable of a minimum of 12 decibels and a maximum of 18 decibels above normal because higher levels can damage the ear. If an automatic reset button is provided, the 18 decibel level may be exceeded.

Comment. A number of commenters recommended that the requirement in 4.31.5 for a magnetic field in the area of the receiver cup should be changed to require hearing aid compatible telephones.

Response. The technical specifications in 4.31.5(1) have been revised to require that public telephones required to be equipped with volume controls by 4.1.3(17)(b) must be hearing aid compatible. The Hearing Aid Compatibility Act of 1988 requires that nearly all telephones be hearing aid compatible.

4.32 Fixed or Built-In Seating and Tables

Comment. Commenters made individual recommendations for changes and clarifications to the technical specifications for fixed or built-in seating and tables in 4.32. For instance, it was recommended that the depth requirement under tables be increased to accommodate guide dogs.

Response. The reference to "work surfaces" have been deleted from the technical specifications in 4.32 since those features are not required to be accessible by 4.1.1(3). The appendix recommends at A4.1.1(3) that if individual work stations are made accessible, they should comply with the applicable technical specifications. As for change to the depth requirements under tables, further study is needed.

4.33 Assembly Areas

Comment. Individuals with disabilities and their organizations supported the requirements in 4.33.3 for wheelchair seating spaces to be dispersed throughout the seating area. Several commenters requested that companion seating also be provided next to wheelchair seating spaces. Commenters from the theater industry expressed concern about the loss of seats if wheelchair seating spaces are placed mid-row. Motion picture theater owners pointed out that new movie theaters are typically a multiplex of small auditoriums each of which seats between 150 and 300 people and that each seat is situated to provide a clear line of sight to the screen. They requested that such small auditoriums be exempt from the dispersal requirement. A few commenters recommended that ramped aisles which are part of an accessible route to wheel-chair seating spaces should be permitted to have steeper slopes if necessary to provide adequate sightlines.

Response. The requirements in 4.33.3 for dispersal of wheelchair seating spaces have been modified. Wheelchair seating spaces must be an integral part of any fixed seating plan and be situated so as to provide wheelchair users a choice of admission prices and lines of sight comparable to those available to the rest of the public. A provision has been added for at least one companion fixed seat to be provided next to each wheelchair seating space. The final guidelines require that when the seating capacity exceeds 300, wheel-chair seating spaces must be provided in more than one location. This provision is based on the California code and balances considerations of cost and lost of other seating spaces with the need for access. It should be noted, however, that the guidelines do not require wheelchair seating spaces to be placed mid-row. No significant loss of seats is anticipated. As discussed under the scoping provisions in 4.1.3(19)(a), to address concerns regarding the number of wheelchair seating spaces required in large facilities, a provision has also been added to 4.33.3 permitting readily removable seats to be installed in wheelchair seating

spaces which may be used by other persons when these spaces are not needed by wheelchair users or other individuals with mobility impairments. As explained in the appendix at 4.33.3, folding seating units usually consist of two fixed seats that can be easily folded into a fixed center bar to allow for open spaces for wheelchair users when needed.

As for ramped aisles which are part of an accessible route to wheelchair seating spaces, the Board is not convinced that slopes steeper than the maximum 1:12 permitted in 4.8.2 are necessary to provide adequate sightlines. Sightlines and visibility are affected by several factors, including the slope of the floor; the height of the screen; the distance between rows; and the staggering of seats. The Board understands that there are theaters designed with ramp aisles that comply with the maximum 1:12 slope and provide adequate sightlines.

Comment. The NPRM asked questions regarding row spacing and lines of sight over standing spectators in sports arenas and other similar assembly areas. Many of the persons who responded to the question stated that they have difficulty accessing mid-row seats in an assembly area. Many commenters also recommended that lines of sight should be provided over standing spectators.

Response. Building and life safety codes set minimum distances between rows of fixed seats with consideration of the number of seats in a row, the exit aisle width and arrange-ment, and the location of exit doors. Because row spacing is related to these other factors, the Board does not believe that it is appropriate for the guidelines to set requirements in this area. However, informa-tion has been included in the appendix at A4.33.3 on "continental" seating which allows a greater number of seats per row with a commensurate increase in row spacing and exit doors. This alternative increases ease of access to mid-row seats for people who walk with difficulty and facilitates

emergency egress for all people. Builders and designers are encouraged to consider "continental" seating along with other factors when planning seating in assembly areas.

The issue of lines of sight over standing spectators will be addressed in guidelines for recreational facilities.

Comment. As discussed under the scoping provision in 4.1.3(19)(b) for assistive listening systems in assembly areas, the NPRM requested information regarding which types of assistive listening systems (magnetic induction loops, FM, and infra-red) work best in particular environments. Many comments described their personal experiences with particular types of systems. Those who provide extensive information on the various systems recommended that a specific type should be selected only after consultation with experts in the field.

Response. Additional information on assistive listening systems is provided in the technical specifications in 4.33.6 and in the appendix at A4.33.6. The type of assistive listening system appropriate for a particular application depends on the characteristics of the setting, the nature of the program, and the intended audience. The appendix includes a table reprinted from a National Institute of Disability and Rehabilitation Research "Rehab Brief" which shows some of the advantages and disadvantages of each system and typical applications. New York has also adopted technical specifications which may be useful. A pamphlet is available from the Board which lists demonstration centers across the country where technical assistance can be obtained in selecting and installing appropriate systems.

4.34 Automated Teller Machines

Comment. The NPRM contained an exception in 4.1.3(20) for drive-up-only ATMs, which provided that drive-up ATMs are not required to comply with the requirements in 4.34.2 and 4.34.3 for controls and clearances and reach ranges because they are designed to be used from motor vehicles. The NPRM requested information on reach range requirements from standard size motor vehicles. The American Bankers Association (ABA) stated:

A number of uncontrollable variables are inherent in designing drive-up ATMs, e.g., the size of the driver; car dimensions; the skill of the driver in stopping the car close to the ATM. * * * However, given the number of uncontrollable variables, it is inevitable that certain drivers will be unable to use comfortably the drive-up ATM or will have to exit the car in order to complete a transaction.

Response. Because of the uncontrollable variables involved in utilizing drive-up ATMs, the Board, in the NPRM, provided an exception in the scoping provisions in 4.1.3(20) for drive-up ATMs. The drive-up ATMs do not have to comply with 4.34.2 (Controls) (which refers to 4.27) and 4.34.3 (Clearances and Reach Range) because they are designed to be used from motor vehicles. The Board maintained that exception with a minor change in referencing the provisions. The current provision states that the drive-up ATMs are not required to comply with 4.27.2, 4.27.3 and 4.34.3.

Comment. The ABA took the position that drive-up ATMs should be exempt from requirements that they be accessible to persons with visual impairments. The basis for their position was that drive-up ATMs are supposed to be used by the driver of the car who must have sufficient vision to drive legally. Should a passenger wish to use the ATM, stated the ABA, the driver could assist. Another commenter supported this position stating that a person who is visually impaired cannot use the drive-up ATM from the rear seat because most newer cars do not have fully openable windows.

Response. While the Board understands that the driver must have sufficient vision to operate the automobile, a passenger riding in either the front or back seat of the automobile may be visually impaired. Although the ABA cites the availability of the driver for assistance, this method would not allow the individual to use the ATM independently. In responding to the issue of drive-up ATMs in general, the ABA stated that given the number of uncontrollable variables, it is inevitable that some drivers will have to exit the car in order to complete a transaction. Thus it is entirely conceivable and not unexpected that a passenger may exit the automobile to use the drive-up ATM and this passenger may be an individual who is visually impaired. Furthermore, while some cars do not have fully operable rear windows, many cars do and, as with the front seat passenger, the individual in the rear seat may exit the car to utilize the ATM.

Consistent with the scoping provisions in 4.1.3(20) where a drive-up ATM is located adjacent to a walk-up ATM, only one ATM would have to be accessible to persons with visual impairments. Operational issues regarding the availability of accessible ATM services (e.g., accessible ATM being open same hours as non-accessible ATM) would be covered by the Department of Justice's regulations.

Comment. Section 4.34.4 provides that instructions and all information for use of ATMs shall be made accessible to and independently usable by persons with vision impairments. In the NPRM, the Board sought additional information on equipment presently in use or available technologies for making instructions and other information relating to the use of ATMs accessible to persons with vision impairments. There were over 50 different suggestions for making ATMs accessible to persons with vision impairments including (1) The installation of a handset voice output telephone device; (2) using large print and braille; (3) a "talking machine"; (4) using phone type receivers behind locked doors; (5) cassette instructions; (6) braille instructions; and (7) using a consumer electronics bus or

universal interface bus for output accessibility.

The ABA took the position that while some technology does exist to assist many visually impaired persons, there does not appear to be technology to ensure in every case ATM accessibility to all visually impaired persons. The ABA stated that current technology supplied to assist visually impaired persons includes raised key identification overlay; high quality contrast screens; character font design selections to ensure easiest reading; and character enlargement. The ABA suggested that educational audio tapes and braille manuals offer at least one source of immediate accommodation for persons with vision impairments.

The ABA further recommended that the regulations concerning ATMs be "flexible and fluid." The ABA stated that "(i)t would be unfortunate if the initial or later regulations locked in specifications and standards in a manner which discourages future innovations and improvements" and that "(a)s technology develops and improves and as disabled persons determine and convey their suggestions, the facilities should evolve to provide better accessibility to disabled persons." The ABA was of the opinion that flexibility is particularly crucial with regard to providing ATM access to persons with vision impairments.

Response. While not stated specifically in the rule, braille and large print instructions (as proposed in the planned revisions to the ANSI A117.1 standard), when used in conjunction with tactually marked keys or other means of identification, do serve as one source of accommodation for persons with vision impairments. In an article recently published in the ABA Banking Journal, it was noted that at least one manufacturer provides ATMs with brailled keys as a standard feature. The manufacturer also provides training kits for bank customers with vision impairments that include a braille workbook on how to use the machine. *Access Comes to ATMs*, ABA Banking Journal (November 1990).

In light of the evolving technology in this area and to allow flexibility in design, the Board has stated the requirement for accessibility for persons with vision impairments in general performance terms. No changes were made to this section from the proposed rule which provides that instructions and all information for use of ATMs shall be made accessible to and independently usable by persons with vision impairments. While the planned revisions to the ANSI A117.1 standard may contain more specific provisions with respect to equipping ATMs for use by persons with vision impairments, the Board has chosen to maintain its position of flexibility in this area.

Comment. The Board sought comment on whether or not visual displays should be required to maintain accessibility for persons with hearing impairments where telephone handsets are used to convey printed and displayed information to persons with vision impairments. The Board queried whether there was a possibility that handsets would entirely replace video display screens. The overwhelming majority of comments from individuals with disabilities and their organizations indicated that where telephone handsets are used, visual displays should also be provided. The ABA took the position that it is inconceivable at this time that telephone handsets would ever replace a visual display. The American Council of the Blind was in agreement with this position stating that whatever accommodations that are made for persons with visual impairments should not preclude use by persons with other disabilities. One commenter indicated that visual displays must be maintained for people with limited use of arms or hands and another commenter stated that many persons with hearing loss are not able to use instructions via telephones or intercoms.

Response. The Board is also of the opinion that if telephone handsets or similar devices are provided, these will be in addition to and not preclude video display screens. Although it is unlikely that this should ever occur, the Board may address this issue in the future.

Comment. The Board also sought information concerning vandalism and the use of telephone handsets. The ABA took the position that telephone handsets furnished with ATMs are more susceptible to vandalism than telephone handsets currently used for public telephones, citing the reason that ATM telephone handsets are often vandalized for reasons which do not apply to telephone handsets. As an example, the ABA cited the instance where people who try to access someone else's account using a debit card which does not belong to them could become angry enough to vandalize an ATM when they are denied access to the ATM. The Wells Fargo Bank, the Service Centers Corporation and other commenters also expressed concern that telephone handsets are subject to vandalism.

Response. The Board is not requiring telephone handsets. Telephone handsets were suggested because they are one way that some banks have chosen to address the need for accommodation for persons with visual impairments. As cited in the ABA article, other means are available for providing information for use of ATMs by persons with vision impairments. These other means are not precluded should the banks prefer to use them. (The handset alternative was chosen to cost out in the regulatory impact analysis because of its high initial cost.)

Comment. The Board sought comment on whether information provided on video display screens (such as "deposit or withdrawal" and "checking or savings") can also be provided in braille when the user presses various keys. Additionally, the Board inquired whether receipts can be made accessible by braille or voice synthesis if a telephone handset or other

listening device is used. Since many ATMs are located in an outdoor environment, the Board requested comment on how screen illumination and contrast can be provided in an outdoor environment where glare may be a problem.

The ABA stated that they are not aware of the availability of video display screens which are capable of displaying information in braille. Braille printers for receipts are available; however, the ABA took the position that such printers cannot be integrated with ATMs as a practical matter.

Further, according to the ABA, ATM manufacturers have researched in depth how to minimize glare through screen illumination and contrast. The ABA further stated that as new materials and techniques are developed, the effects of glare will be reduced and readability improved. They took the position that the Board should not enumerate specific contrast and color requirements as competition alone will ensure that the most readable combinations are marketed and used.

Response. Given the lack of technology which allows for the practical integration of braille printers in ATMs, the Board has not required braille printers at this time.

The Board believes that technology in the industry must improve before specific contrast and color requirements can be included in the guidelines. The Board believes that this area needs further research.

Comment. The Board invited comments on how privacy needs can be met in the context of accessible ATMs. Comments received in response to this section were primarily based on individual concerns and no research or supportive documentation was included. The ABA took the position that given the unavailability of voice synthesis, the use of a speaker is a viable option at this point which will not threaten the privacy of the user. Another commenter suggested using a system of beeps to confirm the transaction, while other commenters noted that audio output could result in a loss of privacy and security. Other suggestions for increased privacy included (1) installation of a "next in line" area behind which the visual display is unreadable; (2) making the display of information optional; (3) having a screen with a narrow viewing range or one which is not readable from all directions and angles; (4) enclosing ATMs in a booth; and (5) modifying the video display or viewing slot so it can be angled down farther or turned to the left or right, both manually and automatically, for individuals who use wheelchairs and others.

An issue which is interrelated with privacy matters is the concern for security. The Board sought comments concerning what security issues, if any, should be considered relative to an individual with a disability and whether or not there were considerations with respect to the environment around ATMs that may cause difficulty complying with the provisions of this section. The majority of the comments received addressed the need for security at ATMs based on use by the general public and not just by those individuals with disabilities. A limited number of commenters took the position that individuals with disabilities are "easier prey" and that use by visually impaired persons may increase the opportunity for criminal activity. One commenter stated that complex or costly security measures may be unreasonable in relation to the actual use by disabled people. Many commenters stressed the need for proper lighting at ATMs. Several other commenters took the position that security must not be compromised for access, and another comment asked that flexibility be allowed because the location and security considerations at ATMs vary widely. Suggestions to improve security included (1) using a telephone handset (audio output through speakers is undesirable since it can be overheard by others) or shaded screen and keeping the handset in a closed compartment accessible by card users only to

prevent vandalism; (2) providing both 1/8 and 1/4 inch jacks so personal headphones can be plugged into an ATM (the jacks can be protected from tampering or vandalism by a sliding cover until the ATM is activated by logging in a correct user identification); and (3) video monitoring around ATMs, as is done in convenience stores.

Response. Based on the response that the Board received concerning these areas, it is apparent that security and privacy are issues of general concern which apply to all ATM users and not just to individuals with disabilities and are issues which the industry must address. Until such time as additional research can be conducted into the issues of security and privacy at ATMs, the Board does not propose to include requirements for such measures.

Comment. The Board sought comment on whether other point of sale machines, such as machines selling insurance at airports or machines used for overnight delivery of letters and packages, should be covered by these guidelines and, if so, what requirements would be appropriate. Many persons who responded to the question favored providing access to the machines. A few commenters questioned whether the machines were fixed or built-in parts of a building or facility. Some commenters recommended that the machines should be addressed on a case-by-case basis as the services develop because blanket coverage in the early development stage could significantly lessen their distribution and the variety and quality of services provided.

Response. The Board believes this issue needs further study. However, the Board tends to agree with comments saying that a majority of the machines are equipment and therefore not within the Board's purview.

4.35 Dressing and Fitting Rooms

As discussed in the scoping provisions at 4.1.3(21), requirements have been added to the final guidelines for

accessible dressing and fitting rooms. Technical specifications are provided for clear floor space, doors, a bench, and mirrors where provided.

5. Restaurants and Cafeterias

5.1 General

Section 5 contains specific requirements for restaurants and cafeterias, in addition to those contained in 4.1 through 4.35 and provides that where fixed tables are provided (or dining counters where food is consumed but there is no service) at least 5 percent, but not less than one, of the fixed tables (or a portion of the dining counter) shall be accessible and comply with 4.32 as required in 4.1.3(18).

Comment. The NPRM did not contain a specific reference to "counters" and a number of the commenters questioned whether restaurants that provide only high counters along the wall are covered.

Response. Such counters are covered by the guidelines and the Board has clarified this coverage by specifically referencing "counters" in this section. The board further clarified the language to reflect that the 5% requirement of fixed or built-in seating or tables is not in addition to section 4.1.3(18). To avoid confusion with section 5.2 (Counters and Bars), the Board inserted language to clarify that this section refers to dining counters where food is consumed but is not served at the counter as opposed to section 5.2 which addresses counters where food or drink is served at the counter for consumption. Where counters are provided solely for the sale of food and drink and not consumption then those counters must comply with 7.2 Sales and Service Counters.

Comment. The Board invited comment on whether requiring that at least 5%, but not less than one, of the fixed tables be accessible and comply with 4.32 (Seating Tables, and Work Surfaces) was adequate or whether a higher or lower percent should be specified. The Board sought comment on the impact of the different percentages on space layouts and revenues.

Response. While a slight majority of the commenters favored a higher percentage, little supporting information was provided to assess the impact of the higher (or lower) percentage on space layouts and revenues. The requirement of 5% accessibility of fixed tables is based on current building codes. The Board retained the 5% provision with no further changes to this paragraph.

5.2 Counters and Bars

This section requires that where food or drink is served at counters exceeding 34 inches in height to customers seated on stools or standing at the counter, a portion of the main counter which is 60 inches in length minimum shall be provided in compliance with 4.32 (Fixed or Built-in Seating and Tables) or service shall be available at accessible tables within the same area.

Comment. The NPRM did not explain the term "portion" and at least half of those responding to this section urged the Board to clarify the reference to a "portion".

Response. The Board provided language to reflect that a "portion of the counter" refers to a portion of the main counter which is 60 inches in length minimum. The 60 inches space provides for two wheelchairs or one wheelchair and one seat or chair.

5.3 Access Aisles

This section contains technical specifications for access aisles to accessible fixed tables. No changes were made to this paragraph.

5.4 Dining Areas

Section 5.4 requires that, in newly constructed restaurants and cafeterias, raised or sunken dining areas, loggias, and outdoor seating areas must be accessible. In alterations, accessibility to raised or sunken dining areas, or to all parts of outdoors seating areas is not required provided that the same

services and decor are provided in an accessible space usable by the general public and not restricted to use by people with disabilities.

In non-elevator buildings, an accessible means of vertical access to the mezzanine is not required provided the area of mezzanine seating measures no more than 33 percent of the area of the accessible seating area and the same services and decor are provided in an accessible space usable by the general public and are not restricted to use by persons with disabilities. This exception does not apply to buildings required to have an elevator.

Comment. Several commenters indicated that clarification was needed regarding the requirement that dining rooms be accessible. Based on the language of the NPRM, it was unclear whether all dining rooms or just those which are raised or sunken are required to be accessible.

Response. The Board clarified its intent that all dining areas are to be accessible in new construction.

5.5 Food Service Lines

Section 5.5 is taken from UFAS and provides technical specification for accessible food service lines. Instead of requiring a "reasonable portion" of self-service shelves to be within forward and side reach ranges (4.2.5 and 4.2.6), the guidelines require at least 50% of each type of self-service shelves to be within the required reach ranges. No changes were made to this paragraph.

5.6 Tableware and Condiment Areas

This section requires that self-service shelves and dispensing devices for tableware, dishware, condiments, food and beverages be installed to comply with 4.2 (Space Allowance and Reach Ranges). No changes were made to this section.

5.7 Raised Platforms

Section 5.7 requires that a raised platform used for the head table or speaker's lectern in banquet rooms or spaces shall be accessible by means of a ramp or platform lift complying with 4.8 or 4.11, respectively. Open edges of a raised platform must be protected by the placement of tables or by a curb. No changes were made to this section.

5.8 Vending Machines and Other Equipment

This section requires that spaces for vending machines and other equipment shall comply with 4.2 and shall be located on an accessible route. The NPRM also provided that the equipment comply with 4.27 (Controls and Operating Mechanisms). This latter provision was deleted as it relates to equipment not under the jurisdiction of these guidelines.

5.9 Quiet Areas (Reserved)

Comment. A significant number of responses raised the issue of the need for "Quiet Areas" in restaurants. According to these commenters, extraneous noise and dim lights make it difficult for persons with hearing impairments to communicate when dining out.

Response. The Board has reserved this section until such time as research can be conducted on appropriate requirements which address the need for a quiet area in restaurants.

6. *Medical Care Facilities*

These sections establish specific requirements for medical care facilities, in addition to those contained in 4.1 through 4.35. The sections apply to medical care facilities such as hospitals where persons may need assistance in responding to an emergency and where the period of stay may exceed twenty-four hours. Doctors' and dentists' offices are not included in this section but are subject to the requirements of section 4.

6.1 General

Comment. Regarding the scoping provision for hospitals specifically approximately half of the commenters proposed increasing the percentage while the other half suggested that it be reduced. In addition to those comments, there were other commenters who favored increasing the percentage for medical facilities in general. Those arguing for a reduced figure in hospitals, did so based on the impact on cost and space. Humana Inc. expressed concern that the requirements of the guidelines for accessible bed and toilet rooms could result in a loss of 10% of beds in alterations. They further expressed concern about the requirement that all employee work areas be accessible. The American Hospital Association estimated cost increases of 20% for new construction and 40% to 60% for alterations.

Response. The scoping requirement of 10% is based on the current MGRAD. The draft final regulatory impact analysis shows that the cost per square foot increase is $1.00 per square foot for an overall percentage increase in new construction costs of 1.02%. The draft final regulatory analysis further shows that the cost increase per bed in a 100 bed hospital is $879.50. Over the 40 year useful life of the facility this cost amounts to $21.99 per bed per year. These figures support the requirement for 10% accessibility.

A portion of the commenters' anticipated cost was attributable to the health care industry's concern over the perceived 100% accessibility required in employee areas. To avoid any misunderstanding that the Board is requiring 100% accessibility for all rooms as a result of the reference to "employee use areas," the Board has deleted that reference. Provisions concerning areas used only by employees as work areas and individual work stations are covered under section 4.1.1(3). That section requires access to employee work areas to the extent that individuals with disabilities can approach, enter, and exit the areas.

Furthermore, retrofitting existing facilities solely for accessibility reasons is not required by the guidelines. Additionally, the distribution of accessible beds in a hospital can vary based on the anticipated need in different specialized units. For example, more than 10% may be needed in a general surgical unit and less than 10% in obstetrics and pediatrics.

The loss of beds referenced in the comments could result only from alteration of existing units and would be unlikely in most situations. A new section 6.1(4) has been added to address concerns about the impact of the alterations requirements. Section 6.1(4)(a) provides that when patient bedrooms (and toilet/bath rooms that are part of the patient bedroom) are being added or altered as part of a planned renovation to a discrete department of an existing medical facility, accessible patient bedrooms shall be provided in a percentage consistent with the percentage of rooms required to be accessible by the applicable requirements of 6.1(1), 6.1(2), or 6.1(3), until the number of accessible patient bedrooms in the facility equals the overall number of accessible patient bedrooms that would be required if the facility were newly constructed. For example, if 20 patient bedrooms are being altered in the obstetrics department of a hospital, 2 of the altered rooms must be made accessible. If 20 patient bedrooms are being altered in a unit within the same hospital that specializes in treating mobility impairments, all of the altered rooms must be made accessible.

Section 6.1(4)(b) addresses alterations within departments that are not undergoing a complete renovation. Under section 6.1(4)(b), when patient bedrooms are being added or altered individually, and not as part of an alteration of the entire area, the altered patient bedrooms shall comply with 6.3, unless either (1) the number of accessible rooms provided in the department or area containing the altered patient bedroom equals the number of

accessible patient bedrooms that would be required if the percentage requirements of 6.1(1), 6.1(2), or 6.1(3) were applied to that department or area or (2) the number of accessible patient bedrooms in the facility equals the overall number that would be required if the facility were newly constructed. For example, if a patient bedroom in a rehabilitation unit in a general hospital is altered, it must be made accessible because 6.1(2) requires all rehabilitation unit beds to be accessible. A patient bedroom in the obstetrics ward of a general hospital which is altered must be made accessible unless 10% of the beds in that ward are currently accessible or unless the facility as a whole already meets the new construction accessibility requirements. Where toilet or bath rooms are part of patient bedrooms which are added or altered and are required to be accessible, each such patient toilet or bathroom shall comply with 6.4. These provisions will enable a medical care facility to ensure that accessible rooms are distributed appropriately among the various units within the facility.

Comment. Many of the comments received on this section addressed the issue of scoping requirements for nursing homes. The majority of the comments received from nursing homes felt that the requirement for 50% of the patient bedrooms and toilets, all public use, common use and employee use areas was too excessive and suggested a figure of 5%. The justification given for the reduction was the substantial impact this requirement would have on cost and space. Many of those comments estimated that the cost increase per bed would be $8,000.

Response. The scoping requirement of 50% is based on the current MGRAD. The draft final regulatory impact analysis shows that the cost per square foot increase is $1.70 per square foot for an overall percentage increase in new construction costs of 1.74%. The draft final regulatory impact analysis further shows that the cost increase per bed in a 76 bed nursing home is $1553. Over the 40 year useful life of the facility this cost amounts to $38.83 per year. These figures support the requirement for 50% accessibility.

Comment. The majority of the comments received from the nursing homes took the position that, "residential care facilities" should be exempt from the guidelines. The basis for their position was that, by definition, those facilities are not medical care facilities since they are primarily residential in nature and are not providing medical care.

Response. The Board considered the issue of residential care facilities. It is the understanding of the Board that clarification of the applicability of these guidelines to "residential care facilities" will be addressed in the rules to be issued by the Department of Justice. To avoid any misunderstanding, the term "period of residence" used in this section was revised to read "period of stay".

Comment. The responses from the nursing homes took exception to requiring that "employee work areas" be accessible. Those commenters reasoned that since nursing facility residents are dependent upon staff to assist them in the event of a fire or life-threatening emergency, staff must be physically capable of providing assistance as a requirement of employment. The provision for employee access to all patient rooms was characterized as a needless expense.

Response. The Board is of the opinion that not all nursing home staff are expected to be physically capable of providing assistance in emergency situations (e.g. clinicians, administrative personnel). As indicated above, to avoid any misunderstanding that the Board is requiring 100% accessibility for all rooms as a result of the reference to "employee use areas," the Board has deleted that reference.

Comment. The Board sought comment on whether other types of facilities should be listed in the scoping table. A majority of the responses

supported the provision as proposed in the NPRM. Approximately 25% of the responses recommended adding clinics. Other facilities which were recommended for inclusion were outpatient/ ambulatory care facilities, medical professional buildings, and dentist offices. Also suggested were hospices, assisted living and congregate care facilities and rehabilitation facilities.

Response. Clinics can vary considerably in the type of services provided, and many do not provide patient bedrooms or provide overnight accommodation. If the clinics do provide patient bedrooms or overnight accommodation, they are covered under the provisions of this section of the guidelines, otherwise, they would be subject only to the requirements of section 4. The medical care facilities listed are meant to be illustrative. If a specific medical care facility is not mentioned, it is required to meet the requirements for the type of facility that it most closely resembles. For instance, an orthopedic hospital would be considered a rehabilitation facility. The Board considered outpatient care facilities, medical professional buildings and dentists offices, but did not consider these to be medical care facilities under this section as the period of stay does not exceed 24 hours.

The Board considered and included rehabilitation facilities in the guidelines based on the reason that those facilities would also specialize in treating conditions that affect mobility.

Additionally, the Board revised the language to reflect that if a hospital or a rehabilitation facility has a "unit" within the facility that specializes in treating conditions that affect mobility, then that unit, not the entire facility must meet the higher level of requirements for accessibility.

6.2 Entrances

This section contains technical specifications for entrances. No changes were made to this paragraph.

6.3 Patient Bedrooms

Section 6.3 provides that accessible patient bedrooms shall be provided in compliance with 4.1 through 4.35. Each accessible bedroom shall have a door that complies with 4.13, except that entry doors to acute care hospital bedrooms for in-patients shall be exempted from the requirement in 4.13.6 for maneuvering space at the latch side of the door if the door is at least 44 inches wide. Each accessible bedroom shall also have adequate space to provide a maneuvering space that complies with 4.2.3. In rooms with 2 beds, it is preferable that this space be located between beds. Furthermore, each accessible bedroom shall have adequate space to provide a minimum clear floor space of 36 inches along each side of the bed and to provide an accessible route complying with 4.3.3 to each side of each bed.

Comment. The NPRM provided that each bedroom would have a turning space preferably located near the entrance and a minimum clear floor space of 36 inches along each side of the bed. Approximately one-third of the comments received which addressed this section considered the space requirements at entrances to patient bedrooms and along side beds to be too restrictive or excessive and would have a substantial impact on costs and availability of space. The American Association of Homes for the Aging (AAHA) recommended that the guidelines only require a minimum amount of square footage per room and leave the configuration of the room to the discretion of facility operators. The AAHA argued that existing requirements such as those issued by the Health Care Finance Administration (HCFA) on environmental quality already address the needs of patients including those who are disabled.

Response. The HCFA requirements cannot be regarded as an effective alternative to these guidelines as they address environmental quality and are not designed to address accessibility.

The NPRM recommended that a turning space in compliance with 4.2.3 be located near the entrance. As the provisions in 4.13 for doors addresses the issue of maneuvering space at doors, this was deleted.

In the NPRM, the Board distinguished between requirements for two-bed rooms and four-bed rooms. With the exception of stating that in rooms with two beds, it is preferable that the maneuvering space be located between the beds, the Board has revised the language to provide that each bedroom shall have adequate space to provide a minimum clear floor space of 36 inches along each side of the bed and to provide an accessible route complying with 4.3.3 to each side of the bed. The Board determined that the additional requirements for space between the foot of the bed and the wall or the foot of the opposing bed of 42 and 48 inches was excessive and not consistent with other accessibility requirements in the guidelines. Accordingly, the Board revised the guidelines to provide that only a provision of 36 inches along all sides of the bed is required.

For purposes of clarity, the Board restated the exception to 4.13 that entry doors to acute care hospital bedrooms for in-patients shall be exempted from the requirement in 4.13.6 for maneuvering space at the latch side of the door if the door is at least 44 inches wide.

6.4 Patient Toilet Rooms

This section was revised to clarify that where private toilet/bath rooms are provided as part of an accessible patient bedroom, the toilet/bath room must comply with 4.22 or 4.23 and be on an accessible route.

7. Business and Mercantile

7.1 General

These sections contain specific requirements for all areas used for business transactions with the public, and are in addition to those in 4.1 through 4.35.

The comments received on this section generally involved operational issues which, pursuant to the ADA, are under the jurisdiction of the Department of Justice and not these guidelines. With the exception of providing that the provisions of this section are in addition to those in 4.1 through 4.35 (as opposed to 4.34 in the NPRM), no changes were made to this paragraph.

7.2 Sales and Service Counters, Teller Windows, Information Counters

Section 7.2 requires that where counters with cash registers are provided in department stores and miscellaneous retail stores for sales or distribution of goods or services to the public, at least one of each type shall have a portion of the counter which is at least 36 inches in length with a maximum height of 36 inches above the finish floor. It shall be on an accessible route complying with 4.3. The accessible counters must be dispersed throughout the building or facility. In alterations where it is technically infeasible to provide an accessible counter, an auxiliary counter meeting these requirements may be provided. Where counters without cash registers are provided and at which goods or services are sold or distributed, this section provides for three options: (1) A portion of the main counter which is a minimum of 36 inches in length shall be provided with a maximum height of 36 inches in; (or) (2) an auxiliary counter with a maximum height of 36 inches in close proximity to the main counter shall be provided; or (3) equivalent facilitation shall be provided. All accessible sales and service counters shall be on an accessible route complying with 4.3.

Comment. The NPRM did not explain the term "portion" and the Board was urged to clarify the reference to "portion".

Response. The Board provided language to reflect that a "portion of the counter" refers to a portion of the counter which is at least 36 inches in

length with a maximum height of 36 inches above the finish floor.

Comment. The Board sought comments on whether a portion of each teller station or ticketing area should be accessible or whether a percentage of the stations should be accessible where services are available at several points. Approximately 25% of the commenters to this section supported the requirement that a percentage should comply. Only a third of those responses recommended a specific percentage which ranged from 5% to 100%, but not less than one. Almost 50% of the responses preferred that a portion of each counter/station comply. The latter group of commenters argued that a portion of each is better because (1) it is difficult to ensure that the accessible counter will be staffed at all times; (2) it eliminates the stigma of a "handicap counter"; (3) counter functions may change throughout the day; (4) often there is only one queuing line rather than a separate line for each station which lessens the chance of getting the "accessible station"; and (5) equipment may break down rendering the accessible counter unusable.

Comments from banking institutions raised the concern that lower counters are a security risk for their tellers, banks, employees and customers. The hotel/motel industry was equally concerned over the security risks for their employees and also raised the issue that a higher counter is more ergonomically efficient for standing work areas. Supermarkets were concerned with how to make the refrigerated display cases in the meat, deli, and seafood accessible. They proposed serving disabled customers at the end of the counter. Retailers were concerned over the showcase islands which they use, as well as security and the loss of storage and display areas if they have to have a lower counter at every island.

Response. The Board amended the language of this section to take into consideration the different types of businesses and the varying uses of counters.

Counters with cash registers: In a department store or other retail store where counters with cash registers are provided, there must be at least one of each type which shall have a portion of the counter which is at least 36 inches with a maximum height of 36 inches above the finish floor. It shall be on an accessible route complying with 4.3. Accordingly, if the retailer chooses to have an express cash lane and one which takes only charges, one of each must be accessible.

Counters without cash registers, but where goods or services are sold or distributed: Where there are no cash registers at the counter, the Board provided for three options: (1) A portion of the main counter that is 36 inches in width minimum shall be provided with a maximum height of 36 inches; or (2) an auxiliary counter with a height of 36 inches in close proximity to the main counter shall be provided; or (3) equivalent facilitation shall be provided.

The NPRM provided that where counters exceeding 36 inches in height are provided, a portion of the main counter shall be provided with a maximum height of between 28 inches to 34 inches above the floor. To address the concerns of safety raised by the commenters in response to the Board's question, the Board changed the scoping from "a portion of the main counter" to "at least one of each type" and raised the height requirement to a maximum of 36 inches above the finish floor. Additionally, where there is a cash register, only a portion of the counter need comply and that portion would not have to contain the cash register. Furthermore, for counters where there is no cash register, equivalent facilitation such as providing an auxiliary counter in close proximity to the main counter can be provided and may accommodate security concerns.

The Board has also added a provision in the appendix which recommends that an assistive listening device which complies with 4.33 be perma-

nently installed at each location or series.

7.3 Check-out Aisles

Section 7.2 refers to counters without aisles whereas this section concerns counters with aisles which are identified here as check out aisles. A counter without an aisle can be approached in more than one direction such as in a convenience store, whereas a counter with an aisle has a circulation route having one approach and one exit and is therefore only approachable in one direction.

Comment. Of the comments received on this section, there was strong support from individuals with disabilities and their organizations for requiring that all check-out aisles be accessible. The response from the business community was strong in its opposition to requiring 100% accessibility. In support of their position, the business industry cited security risks, expense and difficult employee working conditions. The businesses provided statistics to support their concern for the costs involved. In connection with the cost impact of lost space, the International Mass Retail Association advised that sales per square foot equalled $185 in the last year and on the average it was $224.

Response. In the NPRM, the Board pointed out options which are available that can be designed and constructed to be accessible with only minor variations from what is considered the "typical" design and little or no increase in overall square footage. The Board cited examples such as cashiers' stations that can be staggered front-to-back, or two narrow check-out aisles can be combined into a double-wide aisle served by cashiers on both the right and left sides of the aisle. The Board sought comments relating to the experience of stores which have utilized these designs to provide wider check-out aisles and whether the designs presented security considerations or required additional space. The comments received from the business industry

reflected a concern over the loss of store space that would result with each accessible aisle and security problems. The Board has addressed these concerns by changing the requirement for 100% accessibility to a requirement that the number of accessible aisles be provided in accordance with a sliding scale which is based on the number of each "design" of check-out aisles. Check-out aisles of different design include those which are specifically designed to serve different functions and includes the following features: length of belt or no belt; or permanent signage designating the aisle as an express lane. Signage identifying accessible check-out aisles shall comply with 4.30.7 and shall be mounted above the check-out aisle in the same location where the check-out number or type of check-out is displayed. For small businesses, where the selling space is under 5000 square feet, only one check-out aisle is required to be accessible.

In alterations, at least one check-out aisle shall be accessible in facilities under 5000 square feet of selling space. In facilities over 5000 square feet of selling space, at least one of each design of check-out aisle shall be made accessible when altered until the number of accessible check-out aisles of each design equals the number required in new construction.

7.4 Security Bollards

No changes were made to this paragraph.

8. Libraries

These sections are taken from UFAS without change and provide specific requirements for the design of all public areas of libraries, including reading and study areas, stacks, reference rooms, reserve areas, and special facilities and collections. They are in addition to the requirements contained in 4.1 through 4.35.

Comment. The majority of the comments received regarding this section were from individuals with disabilities and their organizations and included changes related primarily to individual concerns or preferences. Except for one commenter who stated that the North Carolina Building Code requires all fixed tables, stacks and carrels to be accessible, no research or supporting data was cited in the recommended changes.

Several commenters did raise concerns over the lack of requirements for braille/voice input/output terminals for book catalogs and existing electronic catalogs.

Response. The issue of braille/voice input/output terminals is an operational matter and is under the purview of the Department of Justice and is not addressed in the guidelines.

The Board retained the language of this section with only two minor changes. In section 8.3, the reference for the check out area was changed to reference 7.2(1) to be consistent with the requirements under sales and service counters. In section 8.4 (Card Catalogs and Magazine Displays), the term "reference stacks" was deleted to avoid confusion with section 8.5 which places no limit on the height of "stacks".

9. Accessible Transient Lodging

Section 9 contains specific requirements for transient lodging which are in addition to those contained in section 4.1 through 4.35.

Comment. Many of the comments on this particular section came from the hotel industry, the majority of which recommended that the cross-reference to sections 5 and 7 should be deleted as it is redundant.

Response. Since 4.1.1(2) identifies the requirements for buildings with multiple functions, the cross-reference to sections 5 and 7 has been deleted.

Comment. The response from individuals with disabilities and their organizations generally recommended additional provisions for signage for persons who are visually impaired, such as requirements for tactile characters on doors, braille

instructions on the use of phones, television, appliances, environmental controls, and other necessities and amenities which are provided by the hotel, as well as directional signage.

Response. No changes were made to this section regarding signage since section 4.30 addresses this issue and is applicable to transient lodging. In particular, sections 4.30.4 through 4.30.6 provide for permanent identification of rooms and spaces. Requiring brailled instructions for the use of phones, televisions and other portable items as suggested by commenters, is an operational issue which falls under the jurisdiction of the Department of Justice and is not addressed in these guidelines.

Comment. One commenter noted that requiring all rooms to be on an accessible route would require the installation of elevators in two story hotels previously excluded in 4.1.3(5).

Response. In lieu of installing an elevator, the accessible rooms may be located on a ground floor which is accessible and thus elevators are not mandatory in two story hotels.

Section 9.1 Hotels, Motels, Inns, Boarding Houses, Dormitories, Resorts and other Similar Places of Transient Lodging

The proposed guidelines provided that all public use and common use areas and five percent, but never fewer than one, of each class of sleeping rooms or suites are required to be designed and constructed to comply with section 4 and sections 9.2 through 9.3. The proposed guidelines further provided that in addition to the 5% accessible room requirement, another 5% must comply with 9.3 (sleeping accommodations for persons with hearing impairments) for a total of 10% of each class.

These requirements were enumerated in paragraph 9.1 of the proposed guidelines. The final guidelines address these areas in individually numbered sub-paragraphs in 9.1. They are discussed below in the order they appear under the new numbering system.

9.1.2 Accessible Units, Sleeping Rooms, and Suites

Comment—Number of accessible rooms. The majority of the comments from individuals with disabilities and their organizations supported the provision of a minimum of 5% accessible rooms. A small number of commenters suggested that the percentage of accessible rooms should equal the percentage of persons with disabilities; that at least 8% of the rooms should be accessible; that the 5% figure should increase to 10% in new construction; the exemption for facilities with fewer than 5 units should be deleted or that long term lodging (i.e. dormitories) should have additional rooms if the demand exceeds the supply.

Comments received from the business and industry groups strongly argued against the 5% figure stating that there was no foundation to support that requirement. Several commenters suggested a 2 to 4% figure. The American Hotel and Motel Association (AHMA) argued for a lower figure citing (1) the Department of Justice Preliminary Regulatory Impact Analysis which states that according to a 1984 study by Mathematica Policy Research, 645,000 persons use wheelchairs; and (2) the US Travel Data Center statistics which found that 65% of all US residents take one or more trips for business or pleasure at least 100 miles away from home each year. Using these statistics, the AHMA found that a goal of achieving an equivalent amount of travel for disabled people would result in 419,000 travelers who use wheelchairs in the United States which equates to less than 0.3% of all travelers. Using the Board's statistics, of 1,341,000 people who use a wheelchair and/or a walker (National Health Institute Services, Home Care Supplement: 1980) and assuming 65% traveling, the AHMA found this to result in slightly more than 0.5%. The AHMA also cited the 1990 California Hotel and Motel Association survey of its members which indicated that the "incidence of demand as demonstrated by reservations for wheelchair accessible rooms was less than 0.1%." Based on that survey, the AHMA proposed that only 1% of the rooms should be required to be accessible.

Comment. Roll-in showers. The Board invited comments relative to a requirement for the larger roll-in showers in transient lodging. The majority of the responses received were strongly in favor of the larger stalls but varied on the number which should be required. Some of the issues raised in the responses included (1) requiring roll-in showers for people with disabilities who are unable to transfer into a bathtub or onto a shower seat; (2) requiring 5 feet by 5 feet showers; (3) providing fold down bench seats in all shower stalls; (4) placing shower controls along the side wall adjacent to the bathroom; (5) requiring both bath tubs and showers in accessible units; and (6) providing accessible shower chairs.

Response. The Board based the requirement for 5% accessible rooms on Board sponsored research which provided that 1,341,000 individuals are reported to use a wheelchair and/or walker (National Health Institute Services, Home Care Supplement: 1980); and 5,191,000 individuals have other mobility impairments (Bureau of Census, Disability Functional Limitation and Insurance coverage: 1984-85). While the statistics provided by AHMA and others in the lodging industry would suggest a much lower percentage of 1%, the comments received from individuals with disabilities and their organizations were overwhelmingly in favor of a higher percentage citing instances where no rooms or an insufficient number of rooms were available, thus making travel difficult or impossible for individuals with disabilities. The Board took note of a voluntary standard approved by the AHMA Executive Engineers Committee and published by both AHMA and the Paralyzed Veterans of America. The standard proposed a 2% to 4% criteria for the number of accessible guest

rooms in newly constructed hotels and motels (An Interpretation of ANSI A117.1 (1986) The American National Standard for Buildings and Facilities—Providing Accessibility and Usability for Physically Handicapped People as applicable to New Hotels and Motels).

Taking into consideration the additional statistics provided by AHMA regarding the percentage of people who travel as well the response from individuals with disabilities and their organizations regarding the difficulty experienced in traveling and the overwhelmingly favorable response to requiring a roll-in shower, the Board revised this section to provide that accessible sleeping rooms and roll-in showers in compliance with 9.2, 4.21 and Figure 57 shall be provided on a sliding scale in accordance with the table in 9.1.2. The table provides for 4% of the first 100 rooms to be accessible, decreasing to 20 accessible rooms in a facility with 1000 rooms, plus 1% for each 100 over that 1000. The table also provides that in facilities with over 50 rooms, 1% of the rooms shall have roll-in showers.

9.1.3 Sleeping Accommodations for Persons with Hearing Impairments

Comment. A number of commenters misunderstood the provisions relating to the number of rooms which must comply with section 9.3 (Visual Alarms, Notification Devices, and Telephones). Many did not understand that the requirement that a number of rooms must comply with 9.3 was in addition to those required to comply with 9.2.

Response. The Board has revised the language to clearly reflect that the provision for sleeping accommodations for persons with hearing impairments is in addition to the accessible room requirements for section 9.2.

Comment. As with 9.1.2, there was strong support from individuals with disabilities and their organizations in support of accessible rooms for

people with hearing impairments, and strong objections from the business community over the basis for requiring 5%. The lodging industry based its objections on statistics cited by the Board in its preamble which provide that 1,741,000 individuals are deaf in both ears (National Institute on Disability and Rehabilitation Research, Data on Disability from the National Health Interview Survey: 1983) and the US Travel Data Center statistics which found that 65% of all US residents take one or more trips for business or pleasure at least 100 miles away from home each year. Using these statistics, the result would be .7% travelers. The lodging industry suggested that 1% would be a more appropriate requirement.

Response. In the preamble to the proposed guidelines, the Board also cited the Bureau of Census statistics which stated that 7,694,000 individuals have difficulty hearing what is said in a normal conversation with another person, including those who cannot hear at all (Bureau of Census, Disability Functional Limitation and Insurance Coverage: 1984-85). The Board further pointed out that an analysis of demographic date reveals there are at least as many persons with hearing impairments as there are persons with mobility impairments. Other studies indicate that a greater percentage of individuals have a hearing impairment (i.e., the National Center for Health Statistics found a 7.9 percent rate, National Health Interview Survey, 1979-80). Based on that data and the ADA's mandate that the Board provide greater guidance with respect to communication accessibility, the proposed guidelines required compliance with section 9.3 for an additional number of rooms equal to that required to comply with section 9.2. Taking into consideration the statistical data provided by the AHMA regarding the percentage of travelers as discussed in 9.1.2 above, the Board has revised this section to provide that in addition to those accessible sleeping rooms and suites required by 9.1.2, sleeping rooms which comply with 9.3 shall be provided in conformance with the table in 9.1.3. That table provides for 4% of the first 100 rooms to comply with 9.3, decreasing to 20 accessible rooms in a facility with 1000 rooms, plus 1% for each 100 over that 1000.

9.1.4 Classes of Sleeping Accommodations

Comment. The majority of the comments received from individuals with disabilities and their organizations suggested that "class" should take into consideration price, the size of the room (i.e. number of beds) and the various amenities and features provided. Two commenters from the building code group/state access agency category suggested that in lieu of using the term "class" it would be preferable to require that the rooms be dispersed throughout the facility to ensure that a person with a disability the fullest range of room reservations available to the general public.

The lodging industry urged the use of the "standard industry classification" to define "class": (a) Standard rooms; (b) premium rooms (where a distinctly different level of service is provided); (c) suites (all types). Use of this classification would take into consideration the size of the room, amenities and features and, indirectly, price.

Response. In order to provide persons with disabilities with a range of options which are available to others, the Board has revised this section to provide that the rooms will be dispersed among the various classes of sleeping accommodations available. Factors to be considered in determining the various classes include room size, cost, amenities provided, and the number of beds provided.

The Board added a provision for equivalent facilitation to this section which allows the operator of a facility to limit construction of accessible rooms to those intended for multiple occupancy, provided that such

rooms are made available to those who request a single occupancy room at the cost of a single occupancy room. This provision allows for more flexibility in the distribution of accessible rooms for the operator of a facility and provides accessible rooms for those who request a single occupancy room and rate.

9.1.5 Alterations to Accessible Units, Sleeping Rooms, and Suites

The Board took the position that a section on alterations specifically for transient lodging was appropriate for the reason that there are a number of problems peculiar to hotels, which regularly implement a seven or eight year cycle of alterations. For instance, if a percentage of rooms is required to be accessible and the hotel later alters a non-accessible room, a question is raised as to whether to make that room an accessible room or that element an accessible element, and as to how this would apply to wings of hotels. Accordingly, the Board has added a paragraph to section 9 which provides requirements for accessibility when sleeping rooms or a portion of the rooms are altered in an existing facility. The guidelines provide that where alterations occur, at least one sleeping room or suite that complies with the requirement of 9.2 (Requirements for Accessible Units, Sleeping Rooms, and Suites) shall be provided for each 25 sleeping rooms, or fraction thereof, of rooms being altered until the number of such rooms provided equals the number required to be accessible by 9.1.2. For each 25 sleeping rooms, or fraction, of rooms being altered, at least one sleeping room or suite that complies with the requirement of 9.3 (Visual Alarms, Notification Devices, and telephones) shall be provided until the number of such rooms equals the number required to be accessible by 9.1.3. For further discussion regarding alteration requirements which directly affect transient lodging, see 4.1.6 (Accessible Buildings: Alterations).

9.2 Requirements for Accessible Units, Sleeping Rooms and Suites

9.2.1 General

This section provides that units, sleeping rooms and suites required to be accessible by 9.1 shall comply with 9.2.

No comments were received for this section and the Board has not made any changes.

9.2.2 Minimum Requirements

This section provides the minimum requirements for accessible units, sleeping rooms and suites.

Maneuvering Space (9.2.2(1))

This section requires a maneuvering space of 36 inches clear width located along both sides of a bed, except that where two beds are provided, this requirement can be met by providing a 36 inches wide maneuvering space located between the two beds.

Comment. The Board sought comments on whether maneuvering space should be required along both sides of a bed to accommodate individuals who use wheelchairs and can transfer from a wheelchair to a bed from only one side. The results were divided among individuals with disabilities and their organizations and the business organizations. Individuals with disabilities and their organizations, government agencies involved with disability issues and other government agencies overwhelmingly supported the provision of maneuvering space on both sides of a bed. The lodging industry however, overwhelmingly took the opposite position based on the reasoning that the maneuvering clearances required by section 9.2.2(1) allow forward or reverse approach, thus permitting side access from either the right or the left.

Response. Because an individual can transfer from the left or the right as a result of the ability to go forward or reverse, does not mean that the individual can also turn themselves around 180 degrees to be at one end of the bed or the other. Thus, such an individual would not be able to utilize amenities provided such as television or necessities such as telephones. For this reason, the forward and reverse argument of the lodging industry was not acceptable.

The Board took the position that a maneuvering space should be required on both sides of a bed and that a 36 inches clear width maneuvering space was appropriate. Where two beds are provided, the requirement is met by providing the maneuvering space between the two beds.

Accessible Route (9.2.2.(2))

This section requires that an accessible route complying with 4.3 connect all accessible spaces and elements including telephones within the unit. This does not require an elevator in multi-story units as long as the spaces identified in 9.2.2 (6) and (7) are on accessible levels and the accessible sleeping area is suitable for dual occupancy.

Comment. One commenter suggested that the route should be required into and through the unit. This latter was reference to HUD's guidelines which provides in 24 CFR 100.205(c)(3)(ii) that there shall be an accessible route into and through the covered dwelling.

The lodging industry noted that there are a number of transient lodging facilities that have types of sleeping accommodations or dwelling units that are multi-story or split level. They took the position that vertical access should not be required to each story or level as long as all primary functions are available on accessible levels.

Response. To require an accessible route into and through each multi-story unit would be cost prohibitive unless the occupant exited their living space into a common area, used public use elevator, and reentered the unit from a different level at great inconvenience to the occupant.

The final guidelines address the concerns of the lodging industry and clarify that it is not

the Board's intent to require vertical access to each story or level. However, this is provided that the spaces identified in 9.2.2 (6) and (7) are on accessible levels and are suitable for dual occupancy.

Doors (9.2.2(3))

This section requires that doors and doorways designed to allow passage into and within all sleeping rooms, suites or other covered units shall comply with 4.13.

Comment. The AHMA and other members of the lodging industry took the position that the Board should not require doors to non-usable space to be accessible.

Response. The response from individuals with disabilities and their organizations was overwhelmingly in favor of this requirement. Many individuals with disabilities stated that rooms not required to be fully accessible would still be usable by some if they were able to enter the doorways. For instance, if the doorways are accessible, individuals with varying mobility impairments may be able to use a room that does not have grab bars or a room that does not have maneuvering space.

The legislative history of the ADA states that, with respect to hotels, accessibility includes "requiring all doors and doorways designed to allow passage into and within all hotel rooms and bathrooms to be sufficiently wide to allow passage by individuals who use wheelchairs." H. Rept. 101-485, pt. 2, at 118. The Board retained this provision with no changes.

Storage (9.2.2(4))

This section requires that if fixed or built-in storage facilities such as cabinets, shelves, closets, and drawers are provided in accessible spaces, at least one of each type provided shall contain storage space complying with 4.25. Additional storage may be provided outside those dimensions.

Comment. The majority of the comments on this section were from the lodging industry,

who suggested that the accessible rooms should also be usable by other than disabled guests. This could be accomplished they suggested, by such practices as installing two door viewers, two clothes closet rods—one at an "accessible" height and one at a standard height.

Response. The Board has addressed the concerns of the lodging industry by clarifying that as long as the minimum requirements are met, additional storage may be provided outside the dimensions required in 4.25.

Controls (9.2.2(5))

This section provides that all controls shall comply with 4.27. No changes were made to this section.

Accessible Areas (9.2.2(6))

This section requires that where provided the following shall be accessible and on an accessible route:
(a) The living area; (b) the dining area; (c) at least one sleeping area; (d) patios, terraces or balconies; (e) at least one full bathroom; (f) if only half baths are provided, at least one half bath, and (g) carports, garages or parking spaces.

Of the comments received on transient lodging, the majority concerned this section. The comments mainly focused on two areas—(d) patios and terraces; and (e) the bathroom area. Those areas are addressed below.

Patios, Terraces and Balconies (9.2.2(6)(d))

Comment. One commenter objected to this provision as it placed an unreasonable restraint on exterior architecture and window/door systems. The AHMA and others in the lodging industry however, were almost unanimous in their opposition to this requirement due to weather protection needs at ocean side resort property and other areas subject to high wind and water damage from hurricanes and storms which result in door sills higher than 1/2 inch.

Response. The Board understands the need to protect the integrity of the unit from water and weather damage and that many local building codes require higher door thresholds or a change in the level of the balcony to prevent structural damage from water. The Board also recognizes that to provide for higher thresholds or a change in level would, in all probability, eliminate the use of a balcony or deck area by individuals with disabilities. The final guidelines therefore provide that the requirements of 4.13.8 (Thresholds at Doorways) and 4.3.8 (Changes in Level) do no apply where it is necessary to utilize a higher door threshold or a change in level to protect the integrity of the unit from wind and water damage. The final guidelines also provide that where the exception to 4.13.8 and 4.3.8 would result in an inaccessible route to patios, terraces or balconies, that equivalent facilitation shall be provided. Equivalent facilitation at a hotel patio or balcony might consist of providing raised decking or a ramp to achieve accessibility.

Bathrooms (9.2.2(6)(e))

Comment. The responses to this paragraph were primarily from the disability community and focused on the need for accessible showers.

Response. The Board has responded to the issue of a roll-in shower under section 9.1.2 (Accessible Units, Sleeping Rooms, and Suites) and has included a requirement for a roll-in shower based on a sliding scale.

Kitchens, Kitchenettes, or Wet Bars (9.2.2(7))

This section provides for minimum requirements when kitchens, kitchenettes or wet bars are provided as accessory to a sleeping room or suite.

Comment. The AHMA and other commenters from the lodging industry urged the Board to reduce the requirement that 50% of the shelf space shall be accessible to 20% due to conventional design and cabinet fabrication practices.

Response. The Board considered the position of the lodging industry, however no further data was submitted in support of this position. The Board is of the opinion that current conventional design and fabrication practices are available which allow for the provision of 50% accessibility.

Comment. The AHMA and others in the lodging industry also expressed concern that many appliances are not manufactured with controls which are accessible according to 4.27 (such as coffee makers, toasters, microwave ovens, and other appliances).

Response. Under the ADA, the Board has jurisdiction to provide guidelines for built in appliances -- not items such as toasters and coffee makers. Those items are therefore not addressed in the guidelines. Although portable devices are allowed under equivalent facilitation, the guidelines do not prescribe the features or controls of such devices. The Board does propose to address the issue of such appliances in the ADA manual.

9.3 Sleeping Room Accommodations for Persons with Hearing Impairments

9.3.1 General.

These requirements were enumerated in paragraph 9.3 of the proposed guidelines. The final guidelines address this area in 9.3.1. This section specifies the features which must be provided in units, sleeping rooms, or suites required to accommodate persons with hearing impairments. Visual alarms which comply with 4.28.4 must be provided. Visual notification devices which alert room occupants of incoming telephone calls and a door knock or bell must also be provided. The visual notification device may not be connected to visual alarm signal appliances. If a permanently installed telephone is provided, it shall have a volume control. An accessible electrical outlet within 4 feet of a telephone connection shall be provided to facilitate the use of a text telephone.

Comment. The disability groups generally supported the requirements of this provision. The comments suggested additional considerations which primarily involved the provision of portable devices. Members of the lodging industry took the position that guests could provide their own notification devices and that only electrical outlets should be required.

In the PRM, the Board noted the availability of both portable and built-in visual alarms and visual notification devices. The Board sought information on the effectiveness and usability of portable devices as compared to built-in devices.

Generally, individuals with disabilities and their organizations were divided on which was preferable. In all, 25% of the comments (the majority of which were from the disability community) preferred built-in devices while 23% of the comments (the majority of which were from the disability community) preferred portable devices; 12% of the comments stated that portable devices were acceptable; 2% of the comments supported the use of portable devices when built-in devices are not available; 5% of the comments opposed the use of portable devices; and 18% of the comments supported the use of both.

The lodging industry took the position that if it was the intent of the guidelines to use portable devices only when they can be activated by a building alarm system then permanent devices will be required due to the lack of availability of such a portable system. The lodging industry stated that permanent devices will result in excessive costs and less flexibility in room selections.

Response. The guidelines require that auxiliary visual alarms shall be provided and comply with 4.28.4. Visual notification devices shall also be provided to alert room occupants of incoming telephone calls and a door knock or bell. The guidelines do allow for equivalent facilitation which requires the installation of electrical outlets and telephone wiring in order to enable the use of portable visual alarms and communications devices provided by the operator of the facility.

9.4 Other Sleeping Rooms and Suites

This section provides that doors and doorways designed to allow passage into and within all sleeping units or other covered units shall comply with 4.13.5.

Comment. The responses from individuals with disabilities and their organizations were overwhelmingly in favor of the accessibility of all doors and doorways. Responses from the lodging industry however, were overwhelmingly against this provision arguing that accessible doors should not be required to non-usable units as it is an undue burden without proven demand. Comments from the lodging industry cite the incurring of extraordinary costs by necessitating greater square footage in guest rooms and bathrooms to accommodate door swings and clearance. As for existing buildings which are altered, the industry commenters argued that it would be prohibitively expensive and architecturally or structurally impractical. The industry further took the position that the 32-inch minimum clearance should apply only to the guestroom entrance doors and only in new construction.

Response. Comments from individuals with disabilities however, frequently identified situations where a standard room could be used if it has an accessible entrance and bathroom doors.

The legislative history of the ADA states that, with respect to hotels, accessibility includes "requiring all doors and doorways designed to allow passage into and within all hotel rooms and bathrooms to be sufficiently wide to allow passage by individuals who use wheelchairs." H. Rept. 101-485, pt. 2, at 118.

The Board retained this provision with no changes.

9.5 Transient Lodging in Homeless Shelters, Halfway Houses, Transient Group Homes, and other Social Services Establishments

The Board received few comments specifically from organizations who were advocates for the homeless, however overall the comments received on this section from individuals with disabilities, disability groups and the business community generally expressed a sensitivity to the issues of cost and availability and the needs of those who are homeless.

9.5.1 New Construction

This section provides that in new construction all public use and common use areas are required to comply with section 4. At least one of each type of amenity in each common area shall be accessible and shall be located on an accessible route to any accessible unit or sleeping accommodation.

Comment. The Board sought comment on whether it is necessary or appropriate to require at least one of every amenity to be accessible in each of the common areas. The majority of the responses were from individuals with disabilities and their organizations. The responses were split on whether or not the Board should amend the proposed language to provide that at least one of each type of amenity be available in an accessible common area.

Response. The Board has retained the language of this provision without change but has added a provision to acknowledge the elevator exception provided in section 4.1.3(5). Where elevators are not provided, as allowed in 4.1.3(5), accessible amenities are not required on inaccessible floors as long as one of each type is provided in common areas on accessible floors.

9.5.2 Alterations

This section was previously reserved in the NPRM. The Board recognized that unique problems may arise when homeless shelters and similar

establishments are placed in existing facilities originally designed for different purposes. The Board sought comments on what scoping provisions should apply to homeless shelters. Factors to be considered are the needs of the population to be served, service availability, and the significant demand for these important and scarce facilities.

Comment. Approximately 25% of the commenters took the position that the scoping should be the same as in other transient lodging. Just over 10% suggested that the scoping should be less than that in transient lodging. Some commenters responded by urging the Board to consider the cost vs. usage issue and to be sensitive to the realization that the number of shelters may be limited by the standards. A few commenters suggested a proportion (5% to 10%) of the shelter space should be accessible.

Response. The Board is mindful of the considerations in assessing the appropriate scoping requirements for alterations in homeless shelters and sought comments concerning this issue. The responses, however did not provide sufficient information regarding the need and the impact of applying the guidelines developed for other transient lodging, such as hotel and motels, to homeless shelters.

The Board is concerned that without homeless shelters, the most vulnerable members of society, including those homeless people who are disabled, will be without shelter. The Board wishes to avoid guidelines which result in a shelter not opening or expanding or result in the closing of shelters which are out of compliance.

The Board intends to conduct further study of this issue. Until such research is completed and guidelines are adopted, the Board has provided interim minimum guidelines.

The guidelines provide the provisions of 9.5.3 (Accessible Sleeping Accommodations in New Construction) and 9.1.5 (Alterations to Accessible Units, Sleeping Rooms, and Suites) shall apply to sleeping rooms and beds in social service establishments which are not homeless shelters and the alterations of other areas in such establishments shall be consistent with the new construction provisions of 9.5.1 (New Construction).

In homeless shelters, where the following elements are altered, the following require- ments apply: (a) at least one public entrance shall allow a person with mobility impair- ments to approach, enter and exit including a minimum clear door width of 32 inches; (b) sleeping space for homeless persons as provided in the scoping provision of 9.1.2 (Accessible Units, Sleeping Rooms, and Suites in Transient Lodging) shall include doors to the sleeping area with a minimum clear width of 32 inches and maneuvering space around the beds for persons with mobility impairments complying with 9.2.2(1); (c) at least one toilet room for each gender or one unisex toilet room shall have a minimum clear door width of 32 inches, minimum turning space complying with 4.2.3 (Wheel- chair Turning Space), one water closet complying with 4.16 (Water Closets), one lavatory complying with 4.19 (Lavatories and Mirrors), and the door shall have a privacy latch and, if provided, at least one tub or shower shall comply with 4.20 (Bathtubs) or 4.21 (Shower Stalls) respectively; (d) at least one common area which a person with mobility impair- ments can approach, enter and exit including a minimum clear door width of 32 inches; (e) at least one route connecting elements (a), (b), (c) and (d) which a person with mobility impairments can use including minimum clear width of 36 inches, passing space comply- ing with 4.3.4 (Passing Space) turning space complying with 4.2.3 (Wheelchair Turning Space) and changes in levels complying with 4.3.8 (Changes in Levels); and (f) homeless shelters can comply with the provisions of (a)-(e) by providing the above elements on one floor.

9.5.3 Accessible Sleeping Accommodations in New Construction

The Board previously reserved this section in the NPRM and sought comments on whether the Board should require 5% of sleeping accommodations to be fully accessible, with an additional 2% for people with hearing impairments.

Comment. With respect to accessible sleeping rooms, approximately 50% of the responses supported requiring 5% of the sleeping rooms to be fully accessible.

Response. The Board is mindful of the desire to balance the need for accessibility in homeless shelters versus the impact of additional construc- tion requirements. In the section on transient lodging for establishments such as hotels and motels, the Board adopted a sliding scale and it is the position of the Board that homeless shelters should not be held to more stringent scoping provisions. Accordingly, the scoping provisions for homeless shelters in new construction provide for accessible sleeping rooms in accordance with the table in 9.1.2 (Accessible Units, Sleeping Rooms, and Suites) and shall comply with 9.2 (Accessible Units, Sleeping Rooms and Suites) where such items are provided.

The Board recognizes that in some homeless shelters, the room or rooms contain a number of beds. In those instances, a percentage of the beds equal to the table provided in 9.1.2 shall comply with 9.2.2(1).

Comment. With respect to sleeping accommodations for persons with hearing impair- ments, approximately 25% of the responses favored requiring an additional 2% of the rooms to accommodate persons with hearing impairments. Approxi- mately 50% of the commenters took the position that the 2% was too low. A number of commenters suggested that 9.5.3 should be consistent with the requirements for hotels, motels and other similar establishments.

Response. As in the requirements for accessible sleeping rooms in homeless shelters, the Board took the position that scoping provisions equal to those applicable to hotels, motels and similar establishments were appropri- ate. The guidelines provide that in addition to the rooms required to comply with the table in 9.1.2 (Accessible Units, Sleeping Rooms, and Suites), sleeping rooms that comply with 9.3 (Visual Alarms, Notification Devices and Telephones) shall be provided in accordance with the table in 9.1.3 (Sleeping Accommoda- tions for Persons with Hearing Impairments).

10. Transportation Facilities (Reserved)

Regulatory Process Matters

The guidelines are issued to assist the Department of Justice to establish accessibility standards for new construction and alterations in places of public accommodation and commercial facilities as required by title III of the ADA. The Department of Justice has proposed to incorporate the guidelines in its final regula- tions as the accessibility standards for purposes of title III of the ADA. The guidelines thus meet the criteria for a major rule under Executive Order 12291 and have been reviewed by the Office of Management and Budget.

The Board has prepared a draft final regulatory impact analysis (RIA) of the guidelines. The draft final RIA is available for public comment. The Board will provide copies of the document to the public upon request. The public is encour- aged to provide additional information as to the costs and benefits associated with the guidelines. Comments on costs and benefits that are received within 60 days of publication of these guidelines will be analyzed in the final RIA which will be completed by January 1, 1992.

Accessibility does not generally add features to a building or facility but rather simply requires that features commonly provided have certain characteristics. Several studies discussed in the draft final RIA have shown that designing buildings and facilities to be accessible, from the conceptual phase onward, adds less than 1% to the total construction costs. The draft final RIA analyzes the cost impact of accessibility elements which have the potential of adding to the cost of a building or facility. Included in the analysis are: Areas of rescue assistance; parking (signage); curb ramps (detectable warnings); ramps (handrail extensions and edge protection); stairs (handrail extensions); elevators (raised characters on hoistway entrances, reopening devices, tactile and braille control indicators, and audible signage for car position); entrances (ramps); water closets and toilet stalls (grab bars); lavatories and sinks (insulation of hot water and drain pipes); bath tubs and shower stalls (seat, grab bars, and hand-held showers); alarms (visual systems); signage (tactile and braille characters); telephones (volume controls, text telephones, and signage); assembly areas (assistive listening systems); automated teller machines (equipment for persons with visual impairments); dressing and fitting rooms (curtained opening and swinging door); and roll-in showers and visual notification devices for accessible sleeping accommodations.

The draft final RIA also assesses the cost of space increases in certain building and facility types which are caused when accessible elements are repeated (e.g., accessible parking spaces in a parking lot and a parking garage; accessible patient bedrooms in a hospital and a nursing home). The element related costs are aggregated to estimate the costs for certain building types, including high-rise and low-rise office buildings, high-rise and low-rise hotels, auditoriums and movie theaters, parking lots and parking garages, and hospitals and nursing homes. For parking lots and parking garages, and hospitals and nursing homes,

the aggregate costs also include the cost of space increases. The draft final RIA also discusses the indirect costs of the accessibility elements such as maintenance, operation and opportunity costs. Space allocation and re-allocation issues are analyzed with respect to maneuvering space in corridors; the standard toilet stall versus the alternate toilet stall; check-out aisles; and areas of rescue assistance.

As for regulatory alternatives, section 504 of the ADA specifically requires that the guidelines "supplement the existing (MGRAD)" on which the current UFAS is based and "establish additional requirements, consistent with this Act, to ensure that buildings (and) facilities * * * are accessible, in terms of architecture and design, * * * and communication, to individuals with disabilities." The legislative history states that the guidelines may not "reduce, weaken, narrow, or set less accessibility standards than those included in existing MGRAD" and should provide greater guidance in the area of communication accessibility for individuals with hearing and visual impairments. As mandated by the statute, the final guidelines use MGRAD and UFAS as their base or floor. The draft final RIA discusses regulatory alternatives considered for major provisions which go beyond MGRAD and UFAS. These include provisions for accessible parking; areas of rescue assistance; volume controls for public telephones; text telephones; detectable warnings; assistive listening systems; signage; and automated teller machines.

The draft final RIA also contains information that would be included in a final regulatory flexibility analysis under the Regulatory Flexibility Act and the final RIA will serve as the final regulatory flexibility analysis. The extensive notice and public comment procedure followed by the Board in the promulgation of these guidelines, which included public hearings, dissemination of materials, and provision of speakers to affected groups,

clearly provided any interested small entities with the notice and opportunity for comment provided under the Regulatory Flexibility Act procedures.

The Board wishes to point out that Congress amended the Internal Revenue Code in 1990 to facilitate compliance by small entities with the ADA. Under section 44 of the Internal Revenue Code, as amended, eligible small businesses can receive a tax credit for certain costs of compliance with the ADA. An eligible small business is one whose gross receipts do not exceed $1,000,000 or whose workforce does not consist of more than 30 full-time workers. Qualifying businesses may claim a credit of up to 50 percent of eligible access expenditures that exceed $250 but do not exceed $10,250. Examples of eligible access expenditures include the necessary and reasonable costs of removing barriers, providing auxiliary aids, and acquiring or modifying equipment or devices. Section 190 of the Internal Revenue Code, as amended, also provides for a deduction of up to $15,000 per year for expenses associated with the removal of qualified architectural and transportation barriers for any entity, regardless of size.

The guidelines do not preempt State and local regulation of the construction and alteration of places of public accommodation and commercial facilities. Section 308(b)(1)(A)(ii) of the ADA permits State and local governments to apply to the Attorney General for certification that a State or local code meets or exceeds the accessibility requirements of the ADA. Therefore, a Federalism assessment has not been prepared under Executive Order 12612.

The guidelines are effective immediately so that they can be incorporated in the Department of Justice's final regulations. The Department of Justice's final regulations will establish the effective date for the accessibility standards.

List of Subjects in 36 CFR Part 1191

Buildings, Civil rights, Handicapped, Individuals with disabilities.

Authorized by vote of the Board on July 1 and 12, 1991.

William H. McCabe,

Chairman, Architectural and Transportation Barriers Compliance Board.

For the reasons set forth in the preamble, the Board adds part 1191 to title 36 of the Code of Federal Regulations to read as follows:

PART 1191--AMERICANS WITH DISABILITIES ACT (ADA) ACCESSIBILITY GUIDELINES FOR BUILDINGS AND FACILITIES

Sec. 1191.1 Accessibility guidelines.

Appendix to part 1191–Americans With Disabilities Act (ADA) Accessibility Guidelines for Buildings and Facilities.

Authority: Americans With Disabilities Act of 1990, Pub. L. 101-336, 42 U.S.C. 12204.

§ 1191.1 Accessibility guidelines.

The accessibility guidelines for buildings and facilities for purposes of the Americans With Disabilities Act are found in the appendix to this part. The guidelines are issued to assist the Department of Justice to establish accessibility standards to implement the legislation.

BILLING CODE 8150-01-M

[GRAPH/ILLUSTRATION #1]

[FR Doc. 91-17481 Filed 7-25-91; 8:45 am]

BILLING CODE 8150-01-C

FOOTNOTES

[1] The Board is an independent Federal agency established pursuant to section 502 of the Rehabilitation Act of 1973 to ensure that the requirements of the Architectural Barriers Act of 1968 are met and to propose alternative solutions to architectural, transportation, communication, and attitudinal barriers faced by individuals with disabilities. The Board consists of 12 members appointed by the President from among the general public, at least six of whom are required to be individuals with disabilities, and the heads of 11 Federal agencies or their designees whose positions are Executive Level IV or above. The Federal agencies are: The Departments of Health and Human Services, Education, Transportation, Housing and Urban Development, Labor, Interior, Defense, Justice, and Veterans Affairs; General Services Administration; and United States Postal Service.

[2] The Board developed MGRAD to assist the General Services Administration, Department of Defense, Department of Housing and Urban Development, and United States Postal Service to establish accessibility standards for those federally owned, leased, or financed buildings covered by the Architectural Barriers Act of 1968. See 36 CFR part 1190. The standards established by those agencies are known as the Uniform Federal Accessibility Standards (UFAS) and are generally consistent with MGRAD.

[3] The ANSI A117.1 standard was revised in 1986 after UFAS was adopted. The 1980 and 1986 versions of the ANSI A117.1 standard are very similar and both are currently in use. As discussed under the general issues, the ANSI A117.1 standard is in the process of being revised again and the Board intends to coordinate its work with the ANSI A117 Committee.

[4] The NPRM reserved section 10 for transportation facilities. The Board issued a supplemental notice of proposed rulemaking

(SNPRM) in the Federal Register on March 20, 1990 which proposed additional requirements for transportation facilities that would make the guidelines also applicable to transportation facilities constructed or altered by public entities covered by title II of the ADA (56 FR 11874). The Department of Transportation has also proposed to adopt the Board's guidelines as the accessibility standards for transportation facilities for purposes of title II of the ADA. See Department of Transportation's proposed regulations, 49 CFR 37.13(b) and Appendix B to Part 37-Standards for Accessible Transportation Facilities at 56 FR 13861, 13881, and 13907 (April 4, 1991).

[5] The ANSI A117 Committee is responsible for periodically reviewing and up-dating the ANSI A117.1 standard. The Committee consists of 42 organizations representing individuals with disabilities, architects and designers, building owners and managers, building product manufacturers, model code groups, building code officials, and government agencies. The Committee operates under due process and consensus procedures established by the American National Standards Institute. See American National Standards Institute, Procedures for the Development and Coordination of American National Standards, approved by ANSI Board of Directors September 9, 1987.

[6] In an effort to make the guidelines generally consistent with the planned revisions to the ANSI A117.1 standard, the Board based some sections of the NPRM (e.g., alarms, detectable warnings, signage) on proposed changes considered by the ANSI A117 Committee.

[7] Section 308(b)(1)(A)(ii) of the ADA provides that, on the application of a state or local government, the Attorney General may, in consultation with the Board, and after prior notice and a public hearing, certify that a state or local code meets or exceeds the accessibility requirements of the ADA.

[8] The February 22, 1991 draft revisions to the ANSI A117.1 standard reprinted the draft BCMC scoping provisions with modifications as an appendix to the standard. However, the draft BCMC scoping provisions are not part of the ANSI A117.1 standard and are not approved by the American National Standards Institute.

[9] The Architectural Barriers Act of 1968 requires that certain federally owned, leased, or financed buildings be accessible to individuals with disabilities. The General Services Administration, Department of Defense, Department of Housing and Urban Development, and United States Postal Service are responsible for establishing accessibility standards for those buildings covered by the Architectural Barriers Act of 1968.

[10] The SNPRM also proposed to amend the guidelines to make them applicable to transportation facilities constructed or altered by public entities covered by title II of the ADA. Until final notice of the amended guidelines is published in the Federal Register, the guidelines do not apply to transportation facilities constructed or altered by public entities covered by title II of the ADA.

[11] This question was suggested by the legislative history which stated that: "[a]ccessibility requirements shall not be evaded by constructing facilities in such a way that no story constitutes a `ground floor,' for example, by constructing a building whose main entrance leads only to stairways or escalators that connect with upper or lower floors; at least one accessible ground story must be provided," H. Rept. 101-596, at 77.

[12] UFAS defines a "principal entrance" as "the main door through which most people enter." The NPRM defined a "principal entrance" as "one through which a significant number of people enter" in recognition of the fact that buildings, especially larger ones, typically have several principal entrances.

[13] The ANSI A117.1 standard is reprinted with permission from the American National Standards Institute. Copies of the ANSI A117.1 standard may be purchased from the American National Standards Institute at 1430 Broadway, New York, NY 10016.

[14] As discussed under the scoping provisions for parking in 4.1.2(5), the final guidelines include requirements for van accessible parking spaces and the technical specifications in 4.6.4 and 4.6.5 relating to vans have been modified.

The material in Appendices 5 and 6 was compiled by the following:

> Linda R. Shaw
> Ginny C. Linder
> The Chicago Bar Association Young
>   Lawyers Section Committee on
>   Delivery of Legal Services to
>   Persons with Disabilities

It is reprinted here by permission. If you would like a copy of the complete pamphlet, please write to:

Chicago Bar Association
Young Lawyers Division
321 South Plymouth Court
Chicago, Illinois 60604

Appendix 5

COMPENDIUM OF LEGAL RESOURCES

A.D.A.P.T. (Americans Disabled for Accessible Public Transportation)

P. O. Box 146491
Chicago, IL 60614-6491
Telephone—
        Voice: TDD:
   Grassroots organization for persons with disabilities which advocates for quality attendant services and public way transportation access, by using the legal and political process and social demonstration.

AIDS Legal Council of Chicago

220 S. State St.
Chicago, IL 60604
Telephone—
        Voice: (312) 427-8990   TDD:
   Legal advice and services for persons who are HIV positive or have AIDS, and their companions, families, etc.

American Bar Association/Young Lawyers Division

750 N. Lake Shore Dr.
Chicago, IL 60611
Telephone—
        Voice: (312) 988-5608 or (312) 988-5671   TDD: (312) 988-5168
        Fax: (312) 988-6281
   Offers two publications: *Layperson's Guide to Federal Laws Affecting Persons with Disabilities* and *Lawyer's Guide to Communicating with Deaf and Hearing-Impaired Clients*. Single copies are free; write for information about bulk orders.

Architectural and Transportation Barriers Compliance Board

1111 Eighteenth St., N.W., Suite 501
Washington, DC 20036-3894
Telephone—
        Voice: (202) 653-7834
    The ATBCB is responsible for drafting accessibility guidelines for buildings and facilities in the Federal Register (56 FR 2296). These cover new construction and alterations to public and commercial facilities. These guidelines can help employers and public facility-owners understand and comply with legal mandates about accommodation accessibility.

Other publications include:
About Barriers
Access America–The Architectural Barriers Act and You
Access America–Newsletter
Accessible Design Bulletin No. 1
ADA Fact Sheet
ADA in Brief
Air Carrier Policies on Transport of Battery-Powered Wheelchairs
Airport TDD Access: Two Case Studies
Annual Report
Assistive Listening Devices
Laws Concerning the ATBCB
Lifts and Wheelchair Securement
Publications Checklist
Resource Guide to Literature on a Barrier-Free Environment
Securement of Wheelchairs and other Mobility Aids
Slip Resistant Surfaces
Technical Paper on Accessibility
Toward an Accessible Environment
Transit Facility Design
UFAS Accessibility Checklist
UFAS Standards
Visual Alarms

Committee on Patients' Rights and Education (COPE)

7742 Golf Dr.
Palos Heights, IL 60463
Telephone—
        Voice: (708) 448-2349   TDD:
    Advocacy, education, information, and publications concerning patient's rights when dealing with the medical community.

Council for Disability Rights

208 S. LaSalle St., Room 1330
Chicago, IL 60604
Telephone—
    Voice: (312) 444-9484   TDD: (312) 444-9484
    Promotes human rights of persons with disabilities and their families. Offers
a job preparation for placement service.

Disability Rights Center

1346 Connecticut Ave., N.W.
Washington, DC 20036
Telephone—
    Voice: (202) 223-3304   TDD:

Disability Rights Education & Defense Fund, Inc.

2032 San Pablo Ave.
Berkeley, CA 94702
Telephone—
    Voice: (415) 644-2555   TDD:

Disabled Americans Rally for Equality (DARE)

4752 S. Kilpatrick
Chicago, IL 60632
Telephone—
    Voice: (312) 582-5930   TDD:
    Promotes awareness and lobbies.

Equal Employment Advisory Council (EEAC)

1015 15th St., N.W.
Suite 1200
Washington, DC 20005
Telephone—
    Voice: (202) 789-8650
    The EEAC is a nonprofit association organized in 1976 initially for the purpose
of monitoring federal equal employment litigation and filing amicus curiae briefs
in precedent-setting cases. They now also file comments on equal opportunity
employment and affirmative action regulatory proposals, analyze legislation, and
monitor judicial and legislative developments at the state and local level.

Federal Communications Commission (FCC)

1919 M St., N.W.
Washington, DC 20554
Telephone—
          Voice: (202) 632-7000   TDD:
     The FCC has responsibility for Title IV of the Americans with Disabilities Act. It will enforce compliance with requirements for relay services and other means by which speech- and hearing-impaired persons may communicate via the telephone and other services.

Guardianship and Advocacy Commission

1735 West Taylor St.
Chicago, IL 60612
Telephone—
          Voice: (312) 996-1650   TDD:
     Advocacy, counseling, information and referral, and legal aid, especially regarding rights violations by service providers and other agencies.

Guardianship Service Associates

41 A South Blvd.
Oak Park, IL 60302
Telephone—
          Voice: (708) 386-5398   TDD:
     Information and counseling on guardianship issues; limited provisions of guardianship.

Hands Organization

2501 West 103rd St.
Chicago, IL 60655
Telephone—
          Voice: (312) 239-6632   TDD: (312) 239-6662
     Advocacy for the deaf and hearing impaired; information and referrals; social and educational events; sign-language summer youth camp; and a monthly newsletter.

Illinois Guardianship and Advocacy Commission

Executive offices: 527 S. Wells St., Suite 300
Chicago, IL 60607
Other office: 1735 W. Taylor
Chicago, IL 60612
Telephone—
          Voice: (312) 996-1650   TDD:
   Guardianship, legal assistance, and human rights violation investigations for
mentally and physically handicapped persons.

Law Lab, Inc.

707 Skokie Blvd.
Northbrook, IL 60062
Telephone—
          Voice: (312) 236-5920   TDD:

Lawyers' Committee for Civil Rights Under Law

220 S. State St., Room 300
Chicago, IL 60604
Telephone—
          Voice: (312) 939-5797   TDD:
   Legal aid, including class action suits and impact cases concerning the rights
of persons with disabilities and their families.

Legal Center for the Elderly and Disabled

1722 J St., Suite 19
Sacramento, CA 95814
Telephone—
          Voice: (916) 446-4851   TDD:

Legal Clinic for the Disabled, Inc.

448 E. Ontario St., Sixth Floor
Chicago, IL 60611
Telephone—
          Voice: (312) 908-4463   TDD: (312) 908-8705

Pro bono legal services for low income, physically disabled, visually impaired, and hearing impaired residents of Cook County; sign language interpreter available. Model for other legal clinics nationwide.

National Organization of Social Security
Claimants Representatives

19 E. Central Ave.
Pearl River, NY 10965
Telephone—
          Voice: (800) 431-2804   TDD:

National Center on Law and the Deaf

Gaullaudet University
800 Florida Ave., N.E.
Washington, DC 20002
Telephone—
          Voice: (202) 651-5051   TDD: (202) 651-5052

National Multiple Sclerosis Society

205 East 42nd St.
New York, NY 10017
Telephone—
          Voice: (212) 986-3240   TDD:
     Services include advocacy.

National Senior Citizens Law Center

1636 West 8th St., Suite 201
Los Angeles, CA 90017
Telephone—
          Voice: (213) 388-1381   TDD:

Nursing Home Information and Abuse Report

Telephone—
          Voice: (800) 252-4343   TDD:

Paralyzed Veterans of America

National office: 801 18th St., N.W.
Washington, DC 20006
Telephone–
      Voice: (202) USA-1300   TDD:
   National Advocacy Program, National Legislation Program, and publications such as Design Guidelines Qualifying for the Tax Advantages of Section 190, a free publication which assists in meeting federal requirements.

The President's Committee on Employment of People with Disabilities

1111 20th St., N.W.
Washington, DC 20036
Telephone–
      Voice: (202) 653-3044   TDD: (202) 653-5050
      Fax: (202) 653-7386
   The committee makes information available about technical aids and job accommodation methods. A database has been developed along with the 38-page publication *Ready, Willing, and Able - A Business Guide for Hiring People with Disabilities.*

Protection & Advocacy, Inc.

Northeast: 11 E. Adams St., Suite 1200
Chicago, IL 60603
   (312) 341-0022 (voice/TDD)

Northwest: 1612 Second Ave.
P. O. Box 3753
Rock Island, IL 61204
   (309) 786-6868 (voice/TDD)

West Central: 427 E. Monroe
Springfield, IL 62705
   (217) 544-0464 (voice/TDD)

East Central: 115 N. Neil
Champaign, IL 61820
   (217) 351-1446 (voice/TDD)

Southern: 103 S. Washington, #200
Carbondale, IL 62901
   (618) 457-3304

By state statute, the designated protection and advocacy agency in Illinois for persons with developmental disabilities and/or mental illness. Promotes the legal and human rights of these persons, while assisting them in understanding and using those rights, and improving the laws, policies, and programs which affect them. Publishes *Equalizer,* a free, quarterly, informational newsletter and other self-advocacy publications.

REACH (Rehabilitation/Education/Advocacy for Citizens with Handicaps)

617 Seventh Ave.
Fort Worth, TX 76104
Telephone—
        Voice: (817) 870-9082   TDD: (817) 870-9086
    Offers training in computer use to persons with disabilities; also offers clearinghouse of computer information.

Rehabilitation Services Administration (RSA)
Offices of Vocational Rehabilitation (VR)

Regional RSA offices have federal jurisdiction over state vocational rehabilitation programs. Local VR offices are excellent resources for information on many topics relating to disability and employment; the regional RSA office can provide you with the address and telephone number of your VR.

Region I: (617) 223-4083 CT, ME, NH, RI, VT, MA
Region II: (212) 264-4016 NJ, PR, VI, NY
Region III: (215) 596-0317 DC, DE, MD, VA, WV, PA
Region IV: (404) 331-2352 AL, FL, KY, NC, SC, TN, GA, MS
Region V: (312) 886-5372 IL, IN, MI, MN, OH, WI
Region VI: (214) 767-2961 AR, LA, NM, OK, TX
Region VII: (816) 891-8015 IA, KS, NE, MO
Region VIII: (303) 844-2135 MT, ND, SD, UT, WY, CO
Region IX: (415) 556-7333 AZ, CA, HI, NV
Region X: (206) 553-5331 AK, ID, OR, WA

Social Security Administration

Telephone –
        Voice: (800) 772-1213   TDD: (800) 325-0778

U.S. Department of Education

Office of Civil Rights
Washington, DC
Telephone–
            Voice: (202) 708-5366   TDD:
    Publishes the *Directory of National Information Sources on Handicapping Conditions and Related Services,* which is available through the U.S. Government Printing Office and U.S. Government Bookstores, and the *OCR Handbook for the Implementation of Section 504 of the Rehabilitation Act of 1973.*

U.S. Department of Health and Human Services Office for Civil Rights

105 W. Adams St., 16th Floor
Chicago, IL 60603
Telephone–
            Voice: (312) 886-5077 or (312) 886-2359   TDD: (312) 353-5693
            Fax: (312) 886-1807
    Enforces section 504 of the Rehabilitation Act of 1973, which prohibits discrimination against handicapped persons by recipients of federal funding; complaints must be filed within 180 days after incident. Enforces the community services provision of the Hill-Burton Act, which prohibits discrimination against any person on any ground unrelated to their need for service.

U.S. Department of Labor

200 Constitution Ave., N.W.
Washington, DC 20210
Telephone–
            Voice: (202) 523-6666   TDD: (202) 523-7090
    Offers publications to assist employers in determining and achieving workplace accessibility, including *A Guide to Job Analysis* (1982) and *A Handbook for Job Restructuring* (1970).

U.S. Department of Labor Office of Federal Contract Compliance Programs (OFCCP)

Regional office: 230 S. Dearborn, Room 570
Chicago, IL 60604

North Cook County (north of 75th St.):
411 S. Wells, Second Floor
Chicago, IL 60607

South Cook County (south of 75th St.):
230 S. Dearborn, Room 406
Chicago, IL 60604
(also NW Indiana)
Telephone—
    Voice: (312) 353-6603   TDD:
    Investigates complaints brought under section 504 of the Rehabilitation Act of 1973 against federal contractors. Published *A Study of Accommodations Provided to Handicapped Employees by Federal Contractors: Final Report* (1982).

U.S. Equal Employment Opportunity Commission

(Chicago Division)
536 S. Clark St., 9th Floor
Chicago, IL 60605
Telephone—
    Voice: (312) 353-8906   TDD: (312) 353-2401
    Conducts hearings on discrimination complaints of current and former federal employees or applicants for federal employment. Complaints must fall under section 504 of the Rehabilitation Act of 1973, the Age Discrimination in Employment Act of 1967, or Title VII of the Civil Rights Act of 1964.

U. S. Equal Employment Opportunity Commission

1801 L Street, N.W.
Washington, DC 20507
Telephone—
    Voice: (202) 663-4903   TDD:
    This agency within the Department of Justice is responsible for drafting and implementing the regulations of Title I of the ADA. It hears complaints of discrimination and noncompliance with the ADA and can provide brochures and speaker to inform the public about aspects of the ADA.

Western Law Center for the Handicapped

849 S. Broadway, Suite M-22
Los Angeles, CA 90014
Telephone
    Voice: (213) 972-0061   TDD:

Appendix 6

COMPENDIUM OF TECHNICAL ASSISTANCE RESOURCES

Abledata

426 W. Jefferson
Springfield, IL 62702
Telephone—
      Voice: (800) 447-4221   TDD: (217) 523-2587
   Computerized national data base for rehabilitation products.

AbleData (Newington Children's Hospital)

181 E. Cedar St.
Newington, CT 06111
Telephone—
      Voice: (800) 344-5405 or (203) 667-5405 or (202) 635-5826
      TDD:
   Database of over 15,000 entries regarding adaptive devices for persons with all types of disability.

Accent on Living

P.O. Box 700
Bloomington, IL 61702
Telephone—
      Voice: TDD:
   Offers a database of rehabilitation products for independent living, and a quarterly newsletter of independence-enhancing solutions for persons with disabilities.

ACCENT Special Publications

Box 700
Bloomington, IL 61702
Telephone—
          Voice: (309) 378-2961   TDD:
     Publishes *Accent on Living*, a quarterly publication containing a variety of information for persons with physical disabilities. Subscriptions are $8.00 for one year; $14.00 for two years; or $20.00 for three years.

Access Living

301 S. Peoria, Suite 201
Chicago, IL 60602
Telephone—
          Voice: (312) 226-5900   TDD: (312) 226-1687
     Offers services designed to enhance and expand the options available to persons with disabilities so they may choose and maintain individualized and satisfying lifestyles. Accepts housing discrimination complaints.

Access Publishers

1078 E. Otero Ave.
Littleton, CO 80122
Telephone—
          Voice: (303) 797-2821   TDD:
     Offers books on computer disks.

Access Travel

U.S. General Service Administration
Washington, DC 20405
Telephone—
          Voice: (202) 708-5082   TDD:
     A guide to accessibility of airport terminals.

Action

1100 Vermont Ave., N.W.
Washington, DC 20525
Telephone—   Voice: (202) 634-9108   TDD:
     National agency which emphasizes the abilities of persons with disabilities. Call for address and telephone number of local office.

Ada S. McKinley Community Services, Inc.

6033 S. Wentworth Ave.
Chicago, IL 60621
Telephone—
   Voice: (312) 955-2900   TDD:
 Vocational services for persons over age 16 who are mentally retarded, emotionally disturbed, physically disabled, behavior disordered, or multiply disabled. These services include vocational evaluation, developmental training, work adjustment, work intensive training and counseling, job placement, work services, academic and supportive services, and supported employment.

Adamlab

33500 Van Bord Rd.
Wayne, MI 48184
Telephone—
   Voice: (313) 467-1415   TDD:
 Information, training, and referrals for persons with all types of disabilities; special expertise with mental and speech-related disabilities.

A.D.A.P.T. (Americans Disabled for Accessible Public Transportation)

P.O. Box 146491
Chicago, IL 60614-6491
Telephone—
   Voice: (312) 281-5599   TDD:
 Grassroots organization for persons with disabilities which advocates for quality attendant services and public way transportation access, by using the legal and political process and social demonstration.

Adaptive Device Locator System

331 W. Second St.
Lexington, KY 40507
Telephone—
   Voice: (606) 233-2332   TDD:
 Computer resource for assistive technology for elderly persons and persons with disabilities.

Adaptive Environments Center

Contact: Elaine Ostroff
374 Congress St., Suite 301
Boston, MA 02210
Telephone—
        Voice: (617) 695-1225   TDD:
    Services to assist with accessibility needs and issues.

Adaptive Products, Inc.

645 S. Addison Rd.
Addison, IL 60101
Telephone—
        Voice: (312) 832-0203   TDD:
    Evaluation, modification, and custom conversion for persons with disabilities, both personal and commercial vehicles. REHAB+PLUS offers consultation and management services for persons with long- or short-term handicaps.

Adult Community Outreach Network (ACORN)

909 Foster
Evanston, IL 60201
Telephone—
        Voice: (708) 475-7873   TDD:
    "Drop In" center to support and assist adults coping with social, emotional, and economic difficulties. Housing referral and assistance program; employment training program.

Advanced Rehabilitation Technology Network (ARTN)

25825 Eshelman Ave.
Lomita, CA 90717
Telephone—
        Voice: (213) 325-3058   TDD:
    Database of information pertinent to rehabilitation and employment.

Albany House

901 Maple Ave.
Evanston, IL 60202
Telephone—
        Voice: (708) 475-4000   TDD:
    Intermediate nursing care facility. Special program for persons with chronic mental illness.

Alexander Graham Bell Association for the Deaf

3417 Volta Pl., N.W.
Washington, DC 20007
Telephone–
        Voice: (202) 337-5220
Chicago Chapter:
2325 W. Greenleaf
Chicago, IL 60645
Telephone–
        Voice: (312) 262-1128   TDD: (312)
    Organization for parents of deaf children. Offers support groups and
information.

Alliance for the Mentally Ill

833 N. Orleans
Chicago, IL 60610
Telephone–
        Voice: (312) 642-3338   TDD:
    Support services for families with a mentally ill member.

Alzheimer's & Related Disorders Center

Telephone–
        Voice: (800) 621-0379 (outside Illinois) (800) 572-6037 (in Illinois) or
(217) 782-8249
        TDD:
    People can receive a variety of information on Alzheimer's disease and referral
to one of 210 chapters nationwide which facilitate more than 1,600 support groups.

Alzheimer's Disease and Related Disorders Association

National Office:
70 E. Lake St., Suite 600
Chicago, IL 60601-5997
Telephone–
        Voice: (312) 853-3060 or (800) 572-6037 (outside Chicago)
        TDD:

Chicago Area Chapter:
845 Chicago Ave.
Evanston, IL 60201
Telephone–
        Voice: (312) 864-0045
    Provide support and assistance to patients with Alzheimer's disease and their
families.

AMC Cancer Research Center

Telephone—
          Voice: (800) 525-3777   TDD:
    Provides trained counsellors who provide understanding and support for cancer patients; information on the causes and prevention of cancer, methods of detection and diagnosis, treatment and treatment facilities, rehabilitation and counseling. Sponsors annual colo-rectal screening program using stool sample kits distributed in cooperation with the Medicine Shoppes Pharmacies. Provides publications on cancer and referral to local resources.

American Association for the Advancement of Science

1333 H Street, N.W., 10th Floor
Washington, DC 20005
Telephone—
          Voice: (202) 326-6671   TDD:
    Scientists with disabilities offer information and encouragement to other persons with disabilities who are interested in science and engineering.

American Association of Kidney Patients

One Davis Blvd., Suite LL-1
Tampa, FL 33606
Telephone—
          Voice: (813) 251-0725   TDD:
    Support and information for persons undergoing dialysis treatments. Publishes pamphlet for travellers entitled *Dialysis Worldwide for the Travelling Patient.*

American Association for Retarded Citizens

Telephone—
          Voice: (800) 433-5255   TDD:
    Referral to state or local chapters for services within the area, depending upon the needs and resources available.

American Bar Association–Young Lawyers Division

750 N. Lake Shore Dr.
Chicago, IL 60611
Telephone–
      Voice: (312) 988-5608 or (312) 988-5671   TDD: (312) 988-5168
      Fax: (312) 988-6281
    Offers two publications: *Laypersons's Guide to Federal Laws Affecting Persons with Disabilities* and *Lawyer's Guide to Communicating with Deaf and Hearing-Impaired Clients.* Single copies are free; write for information about bulk orders.

American Blind Skiing Foundation

610 S. Williams
Mt. Prospect, IL 60056
Executive Director: Sam Schobel
Telephone–
      Voice: (312) 255-1739   TDD:
President: Michael Hise
Telephone–
      Voice: (708) 386-6211 or (708) 574-6343   TDD:
    Instructs and promotes skiing for blind individuals.

American Cancer Society

77 E. Monroe St.
Chicago, IL 60603
      Voice: (312) 372-0471   TDD:
    Aims to prevent cancer and eradicate its effects through education and research.

American Council of the Blind

1155 15th St., N.W., Suite 720
Washington, DC 20005
Telephone–
      Voice: (800) 424-8666 or (202) 467-5081   TDD:
    Clearinghouse on blindness, available 3:00 p.m. to 5:30 p.m. (EST). Membership organization comprised of blind persons throughout the U.S. dealing with legislative issues. Provides information on vision loss and technology as related to blind and vision-impaired persons. Offers free national magazine in braille, cassette tapes, and large-print formats. Organizations in virtually every state in U.S.

American Diabetes Association

National Service Center
1660 Duke St.
Alexandria, VA 22314
Telephone—
          Voice: (800) 232-3472
          Education, equipment, information, and referrals.

American Foundation for the Blind, Inc.

15 W. 16th St.
New York, NY 10011
Telephone—
          Voice: (800) 232-5463 or (212) 620-2032   TDD: (212) 620-2158
          Consumer products for blind and visually impaired persons; publications; social and technological research; and referral services. Offers a national technology database of resources for visually impaired persons. Offers various publications for employers, blind persons, and others, as well as bibliographies on orientation and mobility through the M. C. Migel Memorial Library.

American Foundation for Technology Assistance (AFTA)

Route 14, Box 230
Morgantown, NC 28655
Telephone—
          Voice: (704) 438-9697   TDD:
          Offers information, technology assistance, and funding to persons with disabilities.

American Handicapped Association

476 Main St., Suite One
West Chicago, IL 60185
Telephone—
          Voice: 1-800-627-2AHA (312) 231-0220   TDD: (312) 231-0220
          Information and service about converting vans for personal transportation. Has a store called "Handicrafts" which sells goods made by persons with disabilities and elder persons on a consignment basis.

American Hearing Impaired Hockey Association, Inc.

1141 W. Lake St.
Chicago, IL 60607
Telephone—
  Voice: (312) 829-2250   TDD: (312)
  Sports activities for hearing-impaired youth.

American Heart Association

7320 Greenville Ave.
Dallas, TX 75231
Telephone—
  Voice: (214) 706-1179   TDD:
  Information about heart disease and prevention strategies; screenings.

American Lung Association

1740 Broadway
New York, NY 10019
Telephone—
  Voice: (212) 315-8700   TDD:

American National Standards Institute (ANSI)

1430 Broadway
New York, NY 10018
Telephone—
  Voice: (212) 354-3300   TDD:
  Private National Group that publishes standards, developed with input from consumers and professionals, such as the *ANSI Specifications for Making Buildings and Facilities Accessible to and Usable by Physically Handicapped People* (1986 ed.).

American Paralysis Association

2201 Argonne Dr.
Baltimore, MD 21218
Telephone—
  Voice: (800) 225-0292 or (800) 526-3456   TDD:

American Parkinson's Disease Association

115 John St.
New York, NY 10038
Telephone—
        Voice: (800) 223-APDA   TDD:

American Society for Deaf Children

814 Thayer Ave.
Silver Springs, MD 20910
Telephone—
        Voice: (301) 585-5400   TDD:
    Advocacy, counseling, and education.

American Speech-Language-Hearing Association

10801 Rockville Pike
Rockville, MD 20852
Telephone—
        Voice: (301) 897-5700 or (800) 638-8255
        TDD: (301) 897-0157 or (800) 638-8255
    Information and referral about child and adult communication disorders.

Amputee's Service Association (A.S.A.)

P. O. Box A8319
Chicago, IL 60690
or:
3949 W. Irving Park
Chicago, IL 60618
Telephone—
        Voice: (312) 583-3949   TDD:
    Support group for new amputees, outreach and visitation; publishes a newsletter. Information, education, and recreation services to speed amputees' integration into the community.

Amyotrophic Lateral Sclerosis (ALS) Association

21021 Ventura Blvd., Suite 321
Woodland Hills, CA 91364
Telephone—
        Voice: (800) 782-4747 or (818) 340-7500   TDD:
    Research and information regarding ALS (Lou Gerhig's Disease).

Apple Office of Special Education

Corporate Headquarters
20525 Mariani Ave.
Cupertino, CA 95014
Telephone–
           Voice: (800) 732-3131, ext. 274   TDD:
   Information and support for purchasing computers and software for use by
persons with various disabilities.

Architectural & Transportation Barriers Compliance Board (ATBCB)

1111 Eighteenth St., N.W., Suite 501
Washington, DC 20036-3894
Telephone–
           Voice: (202) 653-7834   TDD:
   In addition to drafting accessibility guidelines for commercial and other public
facilities, the ATBCB publishes numerous booklets, including *About Barriers;
Access America: The Architectural Barriers Act and You; ADA Fact Sheet; ADA
in Brief; Air Carrier Policies on Transport of Battery-Powered Wheelchairs;
Airport TDD Access: Two Case Studies; Assistive Listening Devices; Resource
Guide to Literature on a Barrier-Free Environment; Toward an Accessible
Environment*; and *Visual Alarms*. Write for the publication checklist.

The ARK

6450 N. California
Chicago, IL 60645
Telephone–
           Voice: (312) 973-1000   TDD:
   Crisis intervention service. Telecare program for homebound people. Project
Tzemach: rehabilitation program for adults with a chronic mental illness. Legal
clinic staffed by volunteer attorneys. Medical clinic staffed by volunteer health
professionals. Supportive living program. Project Chizuk offers outpatient mental
health services staffed by volunteer practitioners.

Arthritis Foundation

79 W. Monroe St., Suite 510
Chicago, IL 60603
Telephone–
           Voice: (312) 782-1367   TDD:

Arts Unlimited

55 E. Washington St.
Chicago, IL 60602
Telephone—
      Voice: (312) 332-0093   TDD:
  Arts, programs, and workshops for the elderly and mentally retarded.

Aspen Publishers, Inc.

200 Orchard Ridge Dr.
Gaithersburg, MD 20878
Telephone—
      Voice: (800) 638-8437 or (301) 417-7500   TDD:
      Fax: (301) 417-7550
  Publishes a variety of titles on topics including special education, physical and occupational therapy, speech and hearing, and gerontology.

Assist Therapeutic Systems, Inc.

7710 Reading Rd., Suite 110
Cincinnati, OH 45237
Telephone—
      Voice: (513) 761-2868   TDD:
  Uses team approach to assist persons who need adaptive equipment.

Assistive Device Center

Cal State University-Sacramento
6000 J Street
Sacramento, CA 95819-2694
Telephone—
      Voice: TDD:

Assistive Device Database System (ADDS)

650 University Ave., Suite 1018
Sacramento, CA 95825
Telephone—
      Voice: (916) 924-0280   TDD:
  Information about assistive technology and aids.

Association for Information and Referral for the Blind

3032 North Albany Ave.
Chicago, IL 60618
Telephone—
        Voice: (312) 267-1123

Association for Late-Deafened Adults

1027 Oakton
Evanston, IL 60202
Telephone—
        Voice: (708) 245-2836   TDD: (708) 604-4192 or (708) 524-0144
    Self-help services for people who have become deafened as adults. Recreational/
social activities.

The Association for Persons with Severe Handicaps (TASH)

7010 Roosevelt Way, N.E.
Seattle, WA 98115
Telephone—
        Voice: (206) 523-8446   TDD: (206) 524-6198
        Fax: (206) 523-9495
    Information and support for families of persons with severe and/or multiple
disabilities, including about placement and federal programs.

Association for Retarded Citizens (ARC)–National Office

1522 K Street, N.W., Suite 516
Washington, DC 20005
Telephone—
        Voice: (202) 529-5020   TDD:
    Information, referrals, and support to persons with developmental disabilities
and their families of all types. Local chapters; publications. Advocacy, information, and referral for individuals and groups.

Association for the Retarded Citizens of the U.S.

2501 Avenue J
Arlington, TX 76006
Telephone—
        Voice: (800) 433-5255 or (817) 640-0204   TDD:
    Offers a database about assistive technology, the *Developmental Disabilities
Technology Library*.

Asthma and Allergy Foundation

1717 Massachusetts Ave., N.E., Suite 305
Washington, DC 20036
Telephone—
        Voice: (202) 265-0265   TDD:

AT&T Special Needs Center

2001 Route 46, Suite 310
Parsippany, NJ 07054-1315
Telephone—
        Voice: (800) 233-1222   TDD: (800) 833-3232
    Telephone equipment for hearing-, speech-, vision-, and motion-impaired persons; offers consultations to answer questions about installation and use of equipment in home, work, and other settings.

ATP Testing Program/The College Board

CN 6226
Princeton, NJ 08541-6226
Telephone—
        Voice: (609) 771-7617   (609) 771-7137 (registration/testing)
        TDD:
    College testing program for students with special needs. High school equivalency exams.

Attorney General's Disabled Advocacy Division

State of Illinois Building, 12th Floor
100 West Randolph St.
Chicago, IL 60601
Telephone—
        Voice: (312) 814-7123   TDD: (312) 814-7123
    Information about Illinois' Comprehensive Health Insurance Plan (CHIP), architectural accessibility, and other subjects, as well as referrals. Investigates reports of inaccessibility to buildings and housing.

Augustana Center for Children and Adults with Developmental Disabilities

7464 N. Sheridan Rd.
Chicago, IL 60626
Telephone–
        Voice: (312) 973-5200   TDD:
   Offers opportunities for children and adults with developmental disabilities and administers three group homes and nine programs, including custom care, day school, developmental training, foster parent training, home infant stimulation, residential skilled nursing care, and respite care. Part of Lutheran Social Services.

Barrier Free Environments

P. O. Box 30634
Raleigh, NC 27622
Contact: Ron Mace, President
Telephone–
        Voice: (919) 782-7823   TDD:

Better Hearing Institute

P. O. Box 1840
Washington, DC 20013
Telephone–
        Voice: TDD:
   Provides information on hearing loss and hearing devices. Publishes *The Communicators*.

Blackhawk Club of the Deaf

104 Chestnut
Rockford, IL 61101
Telephone–
        Voice: (815)   TDD: (815) 968-7467
   Social and athletic club.

Blind Service Association, Inc.

22 W. Monroe St.
Chicago, IL 60603
Telephone—
        Voice: (312) 236-0808   TDD:
    Reading services: tape recording, one-to-one.

Blinded Veterans Association

477 H Street, N.W.
Washington, DC 20001
Telephone—
        Voice: (202) 371-8880   TDD:

B'nai B'rith Foundation–Echad Program

9933 Lawler, Suite 100
Skokie, IL 60077
Telephone—
        Voice: (708) 674-5542   TDD:
    Recreation and social programs for Jewish adults age 25 years and older. Target population is adults with developmental disabilities, but they accept all adults with disabilities.

Boy Scouts of America–Chicago Area Council Scouting for People with Disabilities

730 W. Lake St.
Chicago, IL 60606
Telephone—
        Voice: (312) 559-0990   TDD:
    Many special activities for Scouts with physical and developmental disabilities, including two special Skills Days and Nature Hikes each year. Has a full-service overnight camp that offers boating, a swimming pool, and all camp activities to Scouts with and without disabilities. Volunteers to work with the Scouts are always welcome.

Brace-Park Press

P. O. Box 526
Lake Forest, IL 60045
Telephone—
          Voice: (708) 433-0434   TDD:
     Publishes *Managing and Employing the Handicapped: The Untapped Potential* (G. C. Pati, J. I. Adkins, and G. Morrison, 1981).

Builders of Skills

9021 N. Clifton
Niles, IL 60648
Telephone—
          Voice: (708) 296-6783   TDD:
     Residential setting for hearing-impaired, developmentally disabled adults who are assisted with daily living skills. Social services available.

Cancer Information Hotline (Community Oncology Programs)

Telephone
          Voice: (800) 4-CANCER   TDD:
     Provides information regarding cancer treatment options as well as physician referral services. Se habla español.

Canine Helpers for the Disabled

5699-5705 Ridge Rd., (Route 104)
Lockport, NY 14094
Telephone—
          Voice: (716) 433-4035   TDD:
     Trains dogs to assist persons with disabilities, such as those with paraplegia and quadriplegia.

Carroll Center for the Blind

770 Centre St.
Newton, MA 02158-2597
Telephone—
          Voice: (800) 852-3131 or (617) 969-6200   TDD:

Catholic Office of the Deaf

155 E. Superior St.
Chicago, IL 60611
Telephone—
Voice: (312) 751-8370   TDD: (312) 751-8368

Serves deaf and hearing-impaired persons and their families in Cook and Lake counties. Provides information and referral services, Catholic religious services, Catholic religious education, counseling, and advocacy.

Center for Disabled Student Services–Chicago City-Wide College

226 W. Jackson Blvd.
Chicago, IL 60606
Telephone—
Voice: (312) 368-8814   TDD: (312) 443-5229

Admissions, specialized educational programs, vocational training, student support and tutoring, supported employment, and a job club offered to residents of the City of Chicago who are 18 years or older.

Center on Evaluation of Assistive Technology

102 Irving St, N.W.
Washington, DC 20010-2949
Telephone—
Voice: (202) 877-1932   TDD: (202) 726-3996

Offers information about assistive technology to those selecting it and using it.

Centers for Independent Living

Access Living (AL)
310 S. Peoria, Suite 201
Chicago, IL 60602
Telephone—
Voice: (312) 226-5900   TDD: (312) 226-1687

Central Illinois CIL (CICIL)
222 North Western Ave.
Peoria, IL 61604
Telephone—
Voice: (309) 676-0192   TDD:

Champaign-Urbana CIL (CUCIL)
County Bank Building Plaza, Suite 302
102 E. Main
Urbana, IL 61801
Telephone–
         Voice: (217) 344-5433   TDD:

Fox River Valley CIL (FRVCIL)
730 B W. Chicago St.
Elgin, IL 60120
Telephone–
         Voice: (708) 695-5818   TDD:

Illinois Independent Living Center
710 E. Ogden, Suite 207
Naperville, IL 60540
Telephone–
         Voice: (708) 357-0077   TDD:

IMPACT Center for Independent Living
2735 East Broadway
P. O. Box 338
Alton, IL 62002
Telephone–
         Voice: (618) 462-1411   TDD:

Living Independence for Everyone (LIFE)
1544 E. College Ave.
Normal, IL 61761
Telephone–
         Voice: (309) 452-5433   TDD:

Northwestern Illinois CIL (NICIL)
205 Second Ave.
Sterling, IL 61081
Telephone–
         Voice: (815) 625-7860   TDD: (815) 625-6863

Rockford Access and Mobilization Project (RAMP)
104 Chestnut St.
Rockford, IL 61106
Telephone—
            Voice: (815) 968-7467   TDD: (815) 968-7467

Southern Illinois CIL (SICIL)
780 East Grand Ave.
Carbondale, IL 62901
Telephone—
            Voice: (618) 457-3318   TDD:

Springfield Center for Independent Living (SCIL)
426 W. Jefferson St.
Springfield, IL 62702
Telephone—
            Voice: (217) 523-2587   TDD:

Center for Rehabilitation Engineering and Appropriate Technology Education (CREATE)

1600 Holloway Ave.
San Francisco State University
San Francisco, CA 94132
Telephone—
            Voice: (415) 338-1333   TDD:
    Offers federally funded education programs leading to a master's degree in several areas.

Center for Rehabilitation & Training of Persons with Disabilities

2032 N. Clybourn
Chicago, IL 60614
Telephone—
            Voice: (312) 929-8200   TDD: (312) 929-8210
    Vocational evaluation and training; personal adjustment training; independent living training; supported and transitional employment programs; placement services; and other programs for physically and developmentally handicapped persons. Includes behavioral education and a Communications Disorders Rehabilitation Center. Trains developmentally, mentally, and physically disabled persons for jobs in maintenance, word processing, and other areas. Publishes

Options, a free quarterly newsletter aimed at Chicago-area employers. The Placement Office is located at:
   2011 N. Clybourn, Suite 202
   Chicago, IL 60614
      Voice: (312) 248-6500   TDD: (312) 248-6941

Center for Rehabilitation & Training of Persons with Disabilities
Substance Abuse Program for the Hearing-Impaired

108 N. Sangamon
Chicago, IL 60607
Telephone–
      Voice: (312) 243-7696   TDD: (312) 243-7698
   Offers a special 90-day inpatient substance abuse treatment program tailored to the needs of patients who are hearing-impaired or deaf. Participants must be Illinois residents, but ability to pay is not a criterion for receiving treatment.

Center for Rehabilitation Technology

1410-C Boston Ave.
West Columbia, SC 29171
Telephone–
      Voice: (803) 739-5362   TDD:
   A rehabilitation engineering center offering consultation and training to those undergoing rehabilitation.

Center for Learning

National-Louis University
2840 Sheridan Rd.
Evanston, IL 60201
Telephone–
      Voice: (708) 256-5150   TDD:
   Psychoeducational evaluations for children, adolescents, and adults. Individualized remedial academic programs; individual counseling.

Center for Special Education Technology

Council for Exceptional Children
1920 Association Dr.
Reston, VA 22091
Telephone—
        Voice: (800) 873-8255 or (703) 620-3660   TDD:
    Offers information about the use of technology in special education,
nationwide.

Center on Deafness

10100 Dee Road
Des Plaines, IL 60016
Telephone—
        Voice: (708) 297-1022   TDD: (708) 297-1022
    School for adolescents with hearing impairments and emotional problems,
residential programs, job and residential placement for adults, social/leisure
activities, bookstore, hospitalization placements. Diagnostic clinic tests and
produces psychoeducational evaluations for hearing-impaired children and adults.

Center on Evaluation of Assistive Technology

102 Irving St., N.W.
Washington, DC 20010-2949
Telephone—
        Voice: (202) 877-1932   TDD: (202) 726-3996
    Distributes information about assistive technology to those using and selecting it.

The Cheney Company

3186 MacArthur Blvd.
Northbrook, IL 60062
Telephone—
        Voice: (800) 678-5678   TDD:
    Sells and installs chair lifts and wheelchair lifts for residential and commercial
buildings.

Chicago Hearing Society

332 S. Michigan Ave., Suite 714
Chicago, IL 60604
Telephone—
        Voice: (312) 939-6888   TDD: (312) 427-2166
    Advocacy for hearing-impaired Chicago residents; American Sign Language interpreters; information and referral services; workshops on topics of interest to the hearing-impaired; crisis intervention; and community education. Services at no charge. Also offers sign language classes at a nominal cost at various sites throughout Chicago.

Chicago Lighthouse for the Blind

1850 W. Roosevelt Rd.
Chicago, IL 60608
Telephone—
        Voice: (312) 666-1331   TDD:
    Employment and vocational services; job placement and training; advocacy; information and referrals.

Chicago Park District

Judd Goldman Adaptive Sailing Access Program
Burnham Harbor
1300 Lynn White Dr.
Chicago, IL 60605
Telephone—
        Voice: (312) 294-2399   TDD:
    Individual sailing lessons for persons with disabilities aged 10 years and older, in adapted sailboats.

Chicago Public Library - Illinois Regional Library for the Blind and Physically Handicapped

1055 W. Roosevelt Rd.
Chicago, IL 60608
Telephone—
    Voice: (312) 738-9210   TDD:

Chicago Public Library - Deaf Services Project

Conrad Sulzer Library
4455 N. Lincoln Ave.
Chicago, IL 60625
Telephone—
     Voice: (312) 728-8652   TDD: (312) 728-2062
   Captioned videocassettes for children and adults; special loan program for Telecaption II Adapters; recreational/arts programs.

Chicago-Read Mental Health Center
Mentally Ill Hearing-Impaired Program (MI-HIP)

4201 N. Oak Park Ave.
Chicago, IL 60634
Telephone—
     Voice: (312) 794-5560   TDD: (312)
   Inpatient intermediate care unit for mentally or emotionally ill persons who are hearing-impaired. Offers psychiatric evaluations, psycho-social rehabilitation, testing, therapy, and nursing care.

Chicagoland Advocates for Signed Theater (CAST)

67 E. Madison St., Room 2115
Chicago, IL 60603
Telephone—
     Voice: (312) 346-5588   TDD: (312) 346-5589
   Assists professional theaters to interpret plays in American Sign Language.

Chicagoland Project with Industry, Inc.

122 S. Michigan Ave., Suite 1960
Chicago, IL 60603
Telephone—
     Voice: (312) 427-1374   TDD: (312) 427-1378
   Business-initiated effort to develop job placement opportunities for qualified applicants with handicaps. Maintains a pool of persons at various skill levels, such as professional, clerical, data processing, technical, production, and service.

Chicagoland Radio Information Service, Inc. (CRIS)

400 N. Franklin St.
Chicago, IL 60610
Telephone—
        Voice: (312) 645-9800   TDD:
    For the blind and print handicapped - news and other information.

Children of Deaf Adults (CODA)

P. O. Box 41043
Chicago, IL 60641
Telephone—
        Voice: (312) 745-2919   TDD:
    Support group for hearing children of deaf adults.

Children's Memorial Hospital

2300 Children's Plaza
Chicago, IL 60614
Telephone—
        Voice: (312) 880-4649   TDD:
    Counseling, emergency services, information and referrals. Medical and nursing services for children up to age 16.

Chrysler Corporation

Physically Challenged Assistance Program (P-CAP Resource Center)
Telephone—
        Voice: (800) 255-9877   TDD:
    Provides resource information about driver education. Per-state listing of conversion companies. Consultations on physical needs (especially first-time physically challenged persons). Database list of manufacturers in U.S. and Canada. Rebate program with purchase of qualified Chrysler vehicle and qualified installation; adaptation must be medically required and on new Chrysler automobile (current or immediately past model year). Rebate of up to $500 on cost of item.

City of Chicago - Chicago Fire Department

Public Education
1010 S. Clinton
Chicago, IL 60607
Telephone—
          Voice: (312) 744-6691   TDD: (312) 744-5047
     Offers lectures on fire safety for persons with disabilities, and a registration
program.

Clearbook Center

2800 W. Central Rd.
Rolling Meadows, IL 60008
Telephone—
          Voice: (708) 632-0700   TDD:
     Offers educational, vocational, and residential services to the developmentally
disabled. Other facilities include:

Special Needs and Pre-Vocational:
          3201 W. Campbell Rd.
          Rolling Meadows, IL 60008
          Voice: (708) 255-0120
          TDD:

Residential (Community and Sheltered Sites):
     1.   3201 W. Campbell Rd.
            Rolling Meadows, IL 60008
            Voice: (708) 255-0120
            TDD:
     2.   3802 Old Wilke Rd.
            Rolling Meadows, IL 60008
            Voice: (708) 870-0745
            TDD:
     3.   420 S. Walnut
            Arlington Heights, IL 60005
            Voice: (708) 259-6820
            TDD:

Clearinghouse on the Handicapped

330 C Street, S.W.
Washington, DC 20202
Telephone—
          Voice: (202) 732-1250   TDD:
     Offers information on a variety of disabling conditions.

Closing the Gap

P. O. Box 68
Henderson, MN 56044
Telephone—
          Voice: (612) 248-3294   TDD:
  Offers resources, publications, and workshops on technological solutions to disabilities. Publishes a bi-monthly newsletter outlining the use of computer technology to enhance the advancement of persons with disabilities.

College Hill Press

34 Beacon St.
Boston, MA 02108
Telephone—
          Voice: (617) 227-0730   TDD:
  Publishes texts on disability- and technology-related topics.

Committee on Patients' Rights and Education (COPE)

7742 Golf Dr.
Palos Heights, IL 60463
Telephone—
          Voice: (708) 448-2349   TDD:
  Advocacy, education, information, and publications concerning patient's rights when dealing with the medical community.

Communication Assistance Resource Service

3101 Marshall Rd.
Dayton, OH 45429
Telephone—
          Voice: (513) 294-8086   TDD:
  Demonstrations of PhoneCommunicator, SpeechViewer, and Screen Reader.

Communicative Disorders Rehabilitation Center

2032 N. Clybourn
Chicago, IL 60614
Telephone—
          Voice: (312) 929-8200, ext. 210
          TDD: (312) 929-8210   (312) 929-0020
  Diagnostic and therapeutic services for children and adults with communications disorders.

Compuserve - Handicapped Users' Database

5000 Arlington Centre Blvd.
Columbus, OH 43220
Telephone—
          Voice: (800) 818-8199 or (800) 848-8990   TDD:
     National resource for issues regarding disability and technology information.
Referral and information about a variety of disabilities.

ComputAbility

40000 Grand River, Suite 109
Novi, MI 48050
Telephone—
          Voice: (313) 477-6720   TDD:
     Offers own products and IBM Independence Series products; write for catalog.

Compute Able Network

P. O. Box 1706
Portland, OR 97207
Telephone—
          Voice: (503) 645-0009   TDD: Fax: (503) 645-2049
     Adaptive computer technology and equipment.

Computer Retrieval: Information on Scientific Projects (CRISP)

5333 Westbard Ave., Room 148
Bethesda, MD 20205
Telephone—
          Voice: (301) 496-7543   TDD:
     Database of up-to-date information on health- and science-related topics.

Congregation Bene Shalom

(Hebrew Association for the Deaf)
4435 Oakton Blvd.
Skokie, IL 60076
Telephone—
          Voice: (708) 677-3330   TDD: (708) 674-0327
     Synagogue for deaf and hearing-impaired Jews.

Congress of Organizations - Physically Handicapped

P. O. Box 7701
Chicago, IL 60660-7701
Telephone—
  Voice: (312) 421-3373 (TAAD Center) (708) 389-9361 (Sandra Kosch)
  (708) 866-8195 (CPCH)   TDD:
 Consumer advocacy with a special emphasis on applying computer technology to the needs of persons with disabilities. Operates the TAAD Center with computer equipment for persons with disabilities and the Committee of Personal Computers and the Handicapped (CPCH).

Conquerors Gym and Swim Program

c/o Leaning Tower YMCA
600 West Touhy
Niles, IL 60648
Telephone—
  Voice: (708) 647-8222   TDD:

Coordinating Council for Handicapped Children

20 E. Jackson Blvd., Room 900
Chicago, IL 60604
Telephone—
  Voice: (312) 939-3513   TDD: (312) 939-3519
 Referrals, parental support, and training on a child's rights to special education.

Council for Disability Rights

208 S. LaSalle St., Room 1330
Chicago, IL 60604
Telephone—
  Voice: (312) 444-9484   TDD: (312) 444-9484
 Promotes human rights of persons with disabilities and their families. Offers a job preparation for placement service.

Council for Exceptional Children

1920 Association Dr.
Reston, VA 22091
Telephone—
  Voice: (703) 620-3660   TDD:
 Information, referrals, and support to families with exceptional children of all types. Local groups; publications.

Council of Rehabilitation Affiliates

8 S. Michigan Ave.
Chicago, IL 60604
Telephone—
         Voice: (312) 782-0918   TDD:

Cove School, Inc.

520 Glendale Ave.
Winnetka, IL 60093
Telephone—
         Voice: (708) 441-9300   TDD:
   Educational services for learning disabled children aged 5-18 years (day program).

Dayspring Associates, Inc.

2111 Foley Rd.
Havre de Grace, MD 21078
Telephone—
         Voice: (301) 939-5900   TDD:
   Publishes a directory of over 1,000 rehabilitation aids.

DeafTek, USA

International Deaf/Tek, Inc.
P. O. Box 2431
Framingham, MA 01701-0404
Telephone—
         Voice: (508) 620-1777   TDD: (508) 879-0410

Deicke Center of Marklund Children's Home, Inc.

27 W. 751 Shady Way
Winfield, IL 60190
Telephone—
         Voice: (708) 653-8090   TDD:
   Care, education, and rehabilitation for developmentally disabled persons aged 22 years and older.

Department of Agricultural Engineering

Purdue University
West Lafayette, IN 47907
Telephone—
         Voice: (317) 494-1167   TDD:
   Publishes *Agricultural Tools, Equipment, Machinery & Buildings for Farmers
& Ranchers with Physical Handicaps* (Vol. 1) (William Field and Terry Willkomm),
which discusses using technology to assist farmers and ranchers who have
disabilities.

Design for Independent Living, Inc.

7360 N. Damen
Chicago, IL 60645
Telephone—
         Voice: (312) 973-4776   TDD:
   The Adaptable Home is a factory-built home designed for the handicapped, with
modules and materials designed and chosen to meet the needs of physically
handicapped persons. The Home Modifications Program assists persons in adapting their current dwelling for special needs, whether temporary or permanent.

Design Without Limits

Simplicity Pattern Co.
Department 0693
Box 4000
Niles, MI 49120-4000
Telephone—
         Voice: (616) 683-4100
   Publication which addresses special clothing needs of persons in wheelchairs
or with limited mobility, including home sewing tips and advice on adapting ready-
to-wear clothing. Cost is $11.95 plus $2.75 for first-class postage and handling
($14.70 total), plus tax if sent to California, Michigan, or New York. It is also
available through *Nancy's Notions, Ltd.*, 333 Beichl Ave., P. O. Box 683, Beaver
Dam, Wisconsin 53916-0683—cost is $12.95 plus $3.00 postage and handling
($15.95 total), ask for Item # DWL-100.

Developmental Disabilities Technology Library

Association for Retarded Citizens of the U. S.
2501 Avenue J
Arlington, TX 76006
Telephone—
   Voice: (817) 640-0204   TDD:
   Offers substantial information about assistive technology.

Diabetic Traveller

P. O. Box 8223 RW
Stamford, CT 06905
   Newsletter published quarterly; cost is $19.95 per year. Gives detailed advice to travellers with diabetes and their families.

Dial-a-Hearing Screening Test

P.O. Box 1880
Media, PA 19063
Telephone—
         Voice: (800) 222-EARS
   Hearing help information center. Provides local phone number for Dial-a-Hearing Screening Test and hearing information.

Dialogue Publications, Inc.

3100 S. Oak Park
Berwyn, IL 60402
Telephone—
   Voice: (708) 749-1908   TDD:
   Counseling, information, vocational assistance, referrals, and publications for adults with hearing and visual impairments.

Direct Link for the Disabled

P. O. Box 1036
Solvang, CA 93464
Telephone—
         Voice: (805) 688-1603   TDD:
   Has database of over 10,000 community resources; refers persons to appropriate resources.

Disability Access Network

P. O. Box 6541
San Rafael, CA 94903-0541
Telephone—
         Voice: (415) 499-3877   TDD:
   Database of disability-related information.

Disability Bookshop

P. O. Box 129
Vancouver, WA 98666
Telephone–
      Voice: (206) 694-2462   TDD:
  Provides many texts for persons with disabilities and their families, including the *Directory of Travel Agencies for the Disabled* ($14.95, including shipping).

Disability Information & Referral Services

3805 Marshall St.
Wheat Ridge, CO 80033
Telephone–
      Voice: (303) 420-2942   TDD: (800) 255-3477
  Referrals from its computerized database for persons with disabilities, their families, caregivers, and support groups.

Disabled American Veterans

V.A. Regional Office
941 N. Capital St., N.E.
Washington, DC 20421
Telephone–
      Voice: (202) 872-1151   TDD:
  Assists veterans with disabilities to maximize independence.

Disabled Americans Rally for Equality (DARE)

2752 S. Kilpatrick
Chicago, IL 60632
Telephone–
      Voice: (312) 582-5930   TDD:
  Promotes awareness and lobbies.

Disabled Outdoors Foundation

20 Lake St.
Oak Park, IL 60302
Telephone–
      Voice: (312) 284-2206   TDD:
  Outdoor activities for persons with disabilities. Publishes *Disabled Outdoors Magazine* ($8 per year) with information on boating, camping, fishing, hunting, skydiving, scuba-diving, mountain climbing, and other outdoor activities.

Dystonia Medical Research Foundation - Chicago Chapter

17 Lakeside Place
Highland Park, IL 60035
Telephone—
      Voice: TDD:
    Counseling, education, information, and referrals.

E. I. DuPont De Nemours & Co.

Human Resources Department
1007 Market St.
Wilmington, DE 19898
Telephone—
      Voice: (800) 441-7515   TDD:
    In addition to corporate philosophy of employing persons with disabilities, offers publication entitled *Equal to the Task* (1982).

Easter Seal Rehabilitation Center

1230 N. Highland Ave.
Aurora, IL 60506
Telephone—
      Voice: (708) 896-1961   TDD:
    Physical, occupational, and speech therapy for children and adults; infant program; summer camp; and equipment loan.

Easter Seal Society

National Headquarters
5120 S. Hyde Park Blvd., Suite 100
Chicago, IL 60615
Telephone—
    Voice: (312) 667-8400   TDD:
    In addition to other services, has joined IBM to offer discounted personal computers to persons with disabilities.

Eastern Paralyzed Veterans Association

435 Park Ave. South
New York, NY 10016
Telephone—
      Voice: (212) 686-6700   TDD:
    Publishes *Building Design Requirements for the Handicapped*.

Educational Tape-Recording for the Blind

3915 West 103rd St.
Chicago, IL 60655
Telephone—
        Voice: (312) 445-3533   TDD:
    Educational tape recordings for students with visual, physical, or mental impairments.

ELDERLINK

Nationwide Link to Aging Services
Telephone—
        Voice: (800) 252-8966   TDD:

Electronic Industries Foundation

1901 Pennsylvania Ave., N.W., Suite 700
Washington, DC 20006
Telephone—
        Voice: (202) 955-5816   TDD:
    Assists persons with disabilities to find employment; offers scholarships for study in technical fields. Sponsors the "Projects with Industry" series.

Mark A. Elmore - Architect

7707 Northwest Highway
Crystal Lake, IL 60014
Telephone—
        Voice: (815) 455-7260   TDD:
    Architectural designs for accessible residential and commercial buildings.

Epilepsy Foundation of America

351 Garden City Dr., Suite 406
Landover, MD 20785
Telephone—
        Voice: (800) EFA-1000 or (301) 459-3700   TDD:
    Offers information and referral services; phone counseling. Information about epilepsy and coping with a seizure; support to epileptics, including vocational assistance and information about obtaining insurance.

Equal Employment Advisory Council

1015 Fifteenth St., N.W., Suite 1200
Washington, DC 20005
Telephone—
      Voice: (202) 789-8650   TDD: Fax: (202) 789-1708
      Founded by a group of large corporations to assist in the progress of equalizing employment opportunities.

Equal Employment Opportunity Commission

536 South Clark St. - 9th Floor
Chicago, IL 60605
Telephone—
      Voice: (312) 353-8906   TDD: (312) 353-2401
      Conducts hearings on discrimination complaints of current and former federal employees or applicants for federal employment. Complaints must fall under Section 504 of the Rehabilitation Act of 1973, the Age Discrimination in Employment Act of 1967, or Title VII of the Civil Rights Act of 1964.

Federal Communications Commission (FCC)

1919 M Street, N.W.
Washington, DC 20554
Telephone—
      Voice: (202) 632-7000   TDD:
      The FCC has responsibility for Title IV of the Americans with Disabilities Act. It will enforce compliance with requirements for relay services and other means by which speech- and hearing-impaired persons may communicate via the telephone and other services.

Feingold Path of Illinois

1804 N. Summit
Wheaton, IL 60187
Telephone—
      Voice: (312) 832-8724   TDD:
      Support group for followers of the Feingold theory of diet management as treatment for hyperactive, learning disabled, and/or behaviorally disabled children and adults.

Field Museum of Natural History

South Lake Shore Dr. at Roosevelt Rd.
Chicago, IL 60605
Telephone—
    Voice: (312) 922-9410   TDD:
    "Place for Wonder" is a Braille-equipped hands-on mini-museum. Museum is open daily 9:00 a.m. - 5:00 p.m., cost is $2.00 (no fee on Thursdays).

Florida Development Disabilities Planning Council

1317 Winewood Blvd.
Building 5–Room 210
Tallahassee, FL 32301
Telephone—
        Voice: (904) 488-3673   TDD:
    Published the *Technological Aids & Information Resource Guide* (Rick Lupcchino, ed.).

Foundation for Science and the Handicapped, Inc.

154 Julian Court
Clarendon Hills, IL 60514
Telephone—
    Voice: (708) 323-4181   TDD:
    Advocacy and education.

Free Hearing Test

Telephone—
    Voice: (312) 427-4327   TDD:
    Simple hearing test performed over the telephone 24 hours per day, seven days per week.

Freedom Driving Aids, Inc.

901 Salzburg Ave.
Bay City, MI 48706
Telephone—
    Voice: (517) 895-9733   TDD:
    Converts vans with wheelchair lifts and hand controls; new and used vans for sale.

Friends of Handicapped Riders

203 N. Wabash Ave., Room 1614
Chicago, IL 60601
Telephone
          Voice: (312) 782-9375   TDD:
     Therapeutic horseback riding for emotionally, mentally, and physically handicapped persons.

Glaucoma Foundation

310 East 14th St.
New York, NY 10003
Telephone–
          Voice: (800) 832-3826 or (212) 260-1000   TDD:

Goodwill Industries

601 W. Polk St.
Chicago, IL 60607
Telephone–
          Voice: (312) 939-0040   TDD: (312) 939-5759
     Evaluation, case management, job training, and placement for disabled persons.

Greg Trobaugh

39-44 24th St. - #3B
Long Island City, NY 11101
Telephone–
          Voice: (718) 482-0088   TDD:
     Computerized service focusing on the incorporation of computers into jobs and the rehabilitation of persons with disabilities.

Guardianship and Advocacy Commission

1735 W. Taylor St.
Chicago, IL 60612
Telephone–
          Voice: (312) 996-1650   TDD:
     Advocacy, counseling, information and referral, and legal aid, especially regarding rights violations by service providers and other agencies.

Guide Dog Foundation for the Blind Training Center

371 E. Jericho
Smithtown, NY 11787-2976
Telephone–
        Voice: (516) 265-2121 or (800) 548-4337   TDD:
    Trains guide dogs to assist blind persons. Will send copious amounts of literature to your house - free.

The Guided Tour

555 Ashbourne Rd.
Elkins Park, PA 19117
Telephone–
        Voice: (215) 782-1370   TDD:
    Travel program for mildly retarded adults.

Guild for the Blind

180 N. Michigan Ave., Suite 170
Chicago, IL 60601
Telephone–
        Voice: (312) 236-8569   TDD:
    Produces material in Braille and on tape; training in computer Braille and use of a cane.

Hadley School for the Blind

700 Elm St.
Winnetka, IL 60093
Telephone–
    Voice: (800) 323-4238 or (708) 446-8111   TDD:
    Offers free home-study courses in Braille or large print, or on cassette.

Hanson Center

5 W 431 59th St.
Burr Ridge, IL 60521
Telephone–
    Voice: (708) 325-3857   TDD:
    Gateway Recreational Center offers persons with disabilities classes in the arts, physical fitness, and horseback riding at a 12-acre facility. Bonaparte School offers after-school group respite.

Hanson Construction

410 Lake Ave.
Woodstock, IL 60098
Telephone—
        Voice: (815) 338-1505   TDD:
    New constructions and modifications to make homes accessible to the handicapped. All work is customized for individual needs and personal taste. Estimates given without charge.

H.B.S. News Co.

P.O. Box 173
Lyons, IL 60534
Telephone—
        Voice: (708) 839-0505   TDD:
    Publishes *Frontiers - Recreational News for Wheelriders* (six times per year, 75¢ per issue or by subscription: $3.00 for one year, $5.50 for two years, $8.00 for three years). Offers consulting and support services to handicapped persons, including seminars, clinics, and overnight or weekend camping trips.

Health Care Hotline

Telephone—
        Voice: (800) 325-9564   TDD:

Hearing Aids: Consumer Protection Program

Telephone—
        Voice: (800) 572-3270   TDD:

Hearing Aid Help Line

2036 Middlebelt Rd.
Livonia, MI 48152
Telephone—
        Voice: (800) 521-5247   TDD:

Helen Keller National Center for Deaf-Blind Youth and Adults

35 E. Wacker Dr., Suite 618
Chicago, IL 60601
Telephone–
    Voice: (312) 726-2090   TDD: (312) 726-2090
    Regional office for Illinois, Indiana, Michigan, Minnesota, and Wisconsin. Provides consultation with agencies serving the deaf/blind and consultation with deaf/blind adults age 16 or older.

Hemophilia Foundation of Illinois

410 S. Michigan Ave., Room 208
Chicago, IL 60605
Telephone–
       Voice: (312) 427-1495   TDD:
    Advocacy, education, information, referrals, and educational services.

Higher Education and Adult Training for Persons with Handicaps (HEATH) Resource Center

American Council on Education
One DuPont Circle, N.W., Suite 800
Washington, DC 20036-1193
Telephone–
       Voice: 1-800-544-3284 or 1-800-54-HEATH   TDD: (202) 939-9320
    Offers free publications on a wide variety of topics regarding post-secondary education for persons with all types of disabilities. Provides information about and reasonable accommodations for persons with disabilities, and student responsibilities and rights. A clearinghouse relating to post-secondary education for persons with disabilities.

HiTec Group International, Inc.

8205 S. Cass Ave., Suite 109
Darien, IL 60559
Telephone–
       Voice: (708) 963-5588   TDD: (708) 963-5588
    Distributes free TDDs through ITAC program. Sells devices for hearing-impaired persons, including clocks, phones, amplifiers, lights, and telecaption decoders.

Horizons for the Blind

7001 N. Clark St.
Chicago, IL 60626
Telephone—
        Voice: (312) 973-7600   TDD:
    Braille and large-print books offered at museums, zoos, and theaters; also provides tactile pictures. Goal is to increase accessibility to culture, education, recreation, and consumer information via broadcasts, newsletters, and brochures as well as assisting cultural and governmental organizations to make their programs accessible.

Human Factors Society

P. O. Box 1369
Santa Monica, CA 90406
Telephone—
        Voice: (213) 394-1811   TDD: Fax: (213) 394-2410
    Focuses on interactions of humans and environments, with emphases on engineering, safety, and function.

Human Resources Center

I. U. Willets Rd.
Albertson, NY 11507
Telephone—
        Voice: (516) 747-5400   TDD:
    Publishes various Human Resources Center publications.

Human Resources Development Institute, Inc.

c/o Illinois Guardianship & Advocacy Commission
1735 W. Taylor
Chicago, IL 60612
Telephone—
        Voice: (312) 996-1650   TDD:
    Treatment services, education, training, and housing for the mentally disabled.

Huntington's Disease Society of America

140 West 22nd St.
New York, NY 10011-2420
Telephone—
        Voice: (800) 345-HDSA or (212) 242-1968   TDD:

IBM Corporation

Neighborhood Rd.
Kingston, NY 12401
Telephone—
        Voice: (800) 426-3333   TDD:
    Publishes the *Directory of Services and Specialized Equipment for the Physically Impaired* (1982).

IBM National Support Center for Persons with Disabilities

P. O. Box 2150
Atlanta, Georgia 30310-2150
Telephone—
        Voice: (800) 426-2133   TDD: (800) 284-9482
    Clearinghouse for products of IBM and other vendors to help persons with disabilities use computers. Offers information about support organizations and program-related services for persons with disabilities, including *Guide to Resources for Persons with Disabilities* (1987).

Illinois Affirmative Recruitment Program

100 W. Randolph St.
Chicago, IL 60601
Telephone—
        Voice: (312) 917-6888   TDD:
    Vocational services for persons with disabilities who seek employment with the State of Illinois.

Illinois Assistive Technology Project (IATP)

411 E. Adams St.
Springfield, IL 62701
Telephone—
        Voice: (800) 524-1030 or (217) 522-7985
        Information/Referrals: (800) 852-5110
        TDD: (800) 524-1030 or (217) 522-7985
        Information/Referrals: (800) 852-5110
        Fax: (217) 522-8067
    Consumer-responsive statewide program to promote assistive technology devices and services for persons of all ages with all disabilities. Information and referral service provides information about devices, where to obtain them, and the cost. IATP also offers five demonstration and loan centers where devices may be viewed, tried, and/or borrowed; three service delivery models (including one in the Chicago Public Schools); a mobile unit for demonstrations and service delivery in other areas; a bi-monthly newsletter; public presentations on assistive technology; and assistance to employers for job accommodations.

Illinois Department of Rehabilitation Services

100 W. Randolph St., Suite 8-100
Chicago, IL 60601
Telephone—
        Voice: (312) 814-2934   TDD: (312) 814-3040
    There are numerous DORS offices throughout Illinois, all with both voice and
TDD telephone lines; call 1-800-233-DIAL for the office nearest you. DORS offers
the following services:
    (1) Vocational Rehabilitation Program and Employment Initiatives program
assists handicapped persons in gaining employment, and may include educational
assistance, vocational training, and help in acquiring accessible housing and
transportation.
    (2) Home Services Program enables persons with severe disabilities to live at
home instead of a nursing home when the cost of home care is the same as or less
than the cost of institutional care.
    (3) DORS publishes a quarterly newsletter, DORS Openers, and other free
publications such as of *State Services for People with Disabilities, Illinois Laws
Concerning Persons with Disabilities, Illinois' Human Rights Act and You,
Learning Disabilities: The Hidden Handicap, Schools for Children with Disabilities,* and *What Do You Say After You See They're Disabled?*

Illinois Foundation of Dentistry for the Handicapped

211 E. Chicago Ave., Suite 820
Chicago, IL 60611
Telephone—
        Voice: (312) 440-8976   TDD:
    Dental services provided to the homebound.

Illinois Head Injury Association, Inc.

507 S. Gilbert, Suite 205C
LaGrange, IL 60525
Telephone—
        Voice: (800) 284-4442 or (708) 352-3383   TDD:
    Offers advocacy and support to survivors of head injury and their families.
Educational programs to increase awareness of head injury causes and preven-
tion; information and resource center; offers newsletters and special events.
Membership on a sliding scale according to ability to pay.

Illinois Hearing Aid Consumer Protection Act

Telephone–
      Voice: (800) 572-3270   TDD: (800) 572-3270
    Toll-free action line for consumers and hearing aid dispensers the organization licenses. Answers inquiries, receives consumer complaints regarding dispensers, offers financial aid, publications, and answers questions regarding the Illinois Aid Consumer Protection Act itself.

Illinois Parents of the Hearing Impaired

8702 N. Osceola
Niles, IL 60648
Telephone–
      Voice: (708) 966-7187   TDD: (708) 948-5415
    Advocacy, education, information and referrals for parents and families of persons with hearing impairments.

Illinois Regional Library for the Blind and Physically Handicapped

1055 W. Roosevelt Rd.
Chicago, IL 60608
Telephone–
      Voice: (312) 738-9210   TDD:
    Tapes, books, and records for the blind.

Illinois Relay Center

Telephone–
      Voice: 1 (800) 526-0857   TDD: 1 (800) 526-0844
    Allows hearing-impaired persons with a TDD to contact persons without a TDD, and vice-versa, at no cost. Operates 24 hours a day, seven days a week.

Illinois School for the Deaf

125 Webster
Jacksonville, IL 62650
Telephone–
      Voice: (217) 245-5141   TDD: same
    Educational services for persons up to age 21 with severe hearing impairments; free to Illinois residents.

Illinois Secretary of State's Office - Senior Citizens and Human Resources, and Veterans Department

Centennial Building, Room 450
Springfield, IL 62756
Telephone—
          Voice: (800) 252-2904 or (217) 782-8893   TDD: (800) 252-2904
     Booklets on *Law Enforcement and the Disabled, Your Encounter with the Disabled, A Guide to Services for Persons with Disabilities,* and *Parent to Parent* (sources of support, education, and advocacy for parents of special-needs children), *Pedestrian Safety Training Curriculum for Persons with Developmental Disabilities,* and *Handicap Parking Booklet.* Conducts disability awareness training workshops. Reduced-fee license plates for elder and handicapped persons, and special license plates and parking cards for handicapped persons. Offers a special Illinois Disabled Persons Identification Card to be used as proof of disability and enables bearer to receive special benefits from the Illinois Department of Conservation, Illinois Department of Labor, Illinois Department of Public Aid, Illinois Department of Revenue, Illinois State Board of Elections, and Illinois Secretary of State Vehicle Services Department Non-Standard Plate Section.

Illinois Society for the Prevention of Blindness

407 S. Dearborn, Suite 1000
Chicago, IL 60605
Telephone—
          Voice: (312) 922-8710   TDD:
     Many support services and publications, including a listing of eye clinics in the metropolitan Chicago area. Educational material and programs.

Illinois Telecommunications Access Corp. (ITAC)

P. O. Box 64509
Chicago, IL 60664
Telephone—
          Voice: (312) 419-4200   TDD: (312) 419-4211
     Directs an Illinois statewide TDD distribution program for deaf, hearing-impaired, speech-impaired, and blind persons. Also responsible for the Illinois Relay Service (see listing, above), which enables persons without TDDs to communicate with persons with TDDs. For TDD Distribution: (800) 844-0048

Illinois Visually Handicapped Institute (IVHI)

1151 S. Wood St.
Chicago, IL 60612
Telephone–
          Voice: (312) 996-1508   TDD:
    Residential rehabilitation center for adults who are blind or visually impaired. Full adjustment program, with educational and social services based on each client's individual needs.

ILR Press

Cornell University
Ithaca, NY 14850
Telephone–
          Voice: (607) 255-3061   TDD: Fax: (607) 255-2763
    Publishes *Disability and the Labor Market: The Role of Reasonable Accommodation in Employing Disabled Persons in Private Industry* (F. Collgnon, 1986).

Independent Living Aids, Inc.

1500 New Horizons Blvd.
Amityville, NY 11701
Telephone -   Voice: (800) 262-7827
TDD:
    Equipment for persons with disabilities; free catalog available.

Independent Mobility Systems™

3900 Bloomfield Highway
Farmington, NM 87401
Telephone–
          Voice: (800) 622-0623   TDD:
    Adaptive vans for personal transportation.

Information Center for Individuals with Disabilities

20 Park Plaza, Room 330
Boston, MA 02116
Telephone–
          Voice: (617) 727-5540
    Special emphasis on computer solutions for persons with disabilities in employment placement.

Innovators

Holy Cross Hospital
2701 West 68th St.
Chicago, IL 60629
Telephone—
          Voice: (312) 471-5652   TDD:
     Self-help group for physically handicapped persons.

Institute for Human Resources Development

78 Eastern Blvd.
Glastonbury, CT 06033
Telephone—
          Voice: (203) 659-1166   TDD:
     Offers information about the Americans with Disabilities Act, including a two-page brochure which briefly describes the major provisions of the ADA.

Institute for Therapy Through the Arts

300 Green Bay Rd.
Winnetka, IL 60093
Telephone—
          Voice: (708) 446-3822   TDD:
     Registered arts therapists provide therapy for emotionally, mentally, and physically handicapped persons.

International Association of Machinists

3830 S. Meridian
Wichita, KS 67217
Telephone—
          Voice: (316) 522-1591   TDD:
     Offers a placement program for persons with disabilities.

International Center for the Disabled

340 East 24th St.
New York, NY 10010
Telephone—
          Voice: (212) 679-0100   TDD:
     Trains persons with disabilities for jobs and offers placement service; special focus on use of computers.

International Hearing Dog, Inc.

5901 East 89th Ave.
Henderson, CO 80640
Telephone—
          Voice: (303) 287-3277   TDD: (303) 287-3277
     Trains dogs to "hear for" deaf persons—telephones, doorbells, babies, etc.

In Touch Networks, Inc.

322 West 48th St.
New York, NY 10036
Telephone—
          Voice: (212) 769-6270   TDD:
     Offers *The Assertive Job Seeker*, a three-cassette series containing "Technology in the Workplace," "Employer Attitudes," and "The Civil Rights of Disabled Employees."

JBI Talking Books

Jewish Braille Institute of America, Inc.
110 East 30th St.
New York, NY 10016
Telephone—
          Voice: (212) 889-2525 or (800) 424-8567   TDD:
     Lending library of books of Jewish content, including books on tape, in Braille, or in large print.

Jewish Council for Youth Services

Camp Red Leaf
25 E. Washington St., Suite 1615
Chicago, IL 60602
Telephone—
          Voice: (312) 726-8891   TDD:
     Residential camping services for mentally retarded children aged 10-21 and mentally retarded adults aged 18-65.

Jewish Vocational Service

One S. Franklin St.
Chicago, IL 60606
Telephone—
          Voice: (312) 346-6700   TDD: (312) 444-2877
     Occupational training and job placement for handicapped persons of all
religions.

Job Accommodation Network

P. O. Box 6122
West Virginia University, 809 Allen Hall
Morgantown, WV 26506
Telephone—
          Voice: (800) 526-7234 or (304) 293-7186   TDD:
     Centralized source for job accommodations for employers nationwide, to assist
in their efforts to recruit and employ persons with disabilities. Has information
database of over 5,000 successful accommodations.

Job Development Laboratory

George Washington University
Rehabilitation Research and Training Center
2300 I Street
Washington, DC 20037
Telephone—
          Voice: (202) 994-1000   TDD:
     Performs research on job accommodation and modification and the assessment
of functional limitations. Publications include *Designing for Functional Limitations* (J. Mueller, 1979).

Job Opportunities for the Blind
(National Federation of the Blind)

1800 Johnson St.
Baltimore, MD 21230
Telephone—
          Voice: (800) 638-7518   TDD:

Job Resources for the Disabled
(Family Friends)

540 W. Briar Place
Chicago, IL 60657
Telephone—
      Voice: (312) 868-0222 or (312) 868-0333   TDD:
    Intake, job development and coaching, placement, follow-up, and support services for disabled and disadvantaged Chicago residents. They also provide help to the disabled person's family and friends, and will send information to your house.

Johanna Bureau for the Blind & Visually Handicapped

8 S. Michigan Ave., Suite 300
Chicago, IL 60603
Telephone—
      Voice: (312) 332-6076   TDD:
   Material in Braille and tape.

Kennedy Job Training Center

123rd and Wolfe Rd.
Palos Park, IL 60464
Telephone—
      Voice: (708) 448-4818   TDD: (708) 448-4818
    Offers vocational evaluation, work adjustment training, training programs, counseling, communication therapy, independent living skill training, and job placement services for developmentally disabled and hearing-impaired persons.

Keshet (Jewish Parents of Children with Special Needs)

3525 W. Peterson, Suite T17
Chicago, IL 60659
Telephone—
      Voice: (312) 588-0551   TDD:
    Support group with monthly meetings for parents of children with special needs; all disabilities and chronic illnesses included. Camp Keshet retreats are family camping experiences sponsored in conjunction with the Olin-Sang-Ruby Institute of the Union of American Hebrew Congregations. Summer day camp program for children with disabilities and their siblings.

Kurzwell Computer Products

185 Albany St.
Cambridge, MA 02139
Telephone—
      Voice: (617) 864-4700   TDD:

The Lambs, Inc. and Lambs Vocational Work Center

Box 520
Libertyville, IL 60048
Telephone—
      Voice: (708) 362-4636   TDD:
  Residential, vocational, and social services for retarded persons 18 years and older.

LaRabida Children's Hospital and Research Center

East 65th and Lake Michigan
Chicago, IL 60649
Telephone—
      Voice: (312) 363-6700   TDD:
  Counseling, educational services, medical, and nursing services for children through age 18.

Leader Dogs for the Blind

1039 S. Rochester Rd.
Rochester, MI 48307
Telephone—
      Voice: (313) 651-9011   TDD:
  Provides guide dogs for the blind.

Learning Disabilities Association

4156 Library Rd.
Pittsburgh, PA 15234
Telephone—
      Voice: (412) 341-1515   TDD:

Learning Initiatives International

One Park Place, Suite 835
Atlanta, GA 30303
Telephone—
         Voice: (800) 233-9233   TDD:
   A resource for educational technology using IBM computers.

Library of Congress Handicapped Hotline

Library Service for the Blind & Physically Handicapped
Washington, DC 20542
Telephone—
         Voice: (800) 424-8567   TDD:

Lifeboat

Telephone—
         Voice: (818) 981-1373   TDD:
   Publishes *The International Directory of Job-Oriented Assistive Devices.*

LIFT, Inc.

17 Windemere Lane
Barrington, IL 60010
Telephone—
         Voice: (708) 202-0346   TDD:
   Places severely physically disabled and visually impaired/blind high school and
college graduates as computer programmers.

Lighthouse Low Vision Products

36-02 Northern Blvd.
Long Island City, NY 11101
Telephone—
         Voice: (718) 937-6959   TDD:
   Offers vision-related products, books, etc.

LINC Resources, Inc.

4820 Indianola Ave.
Columbus, OH 43214
Telephone—
     Voice: (800) 772-7372 or (614) 885-5599   TDD:
  Will perform free searches of data regarding instruction, testing, and administration.

Lions Clubs International

300 West 22nd
Oak Brook, IL 60521-8842
Telephone—
     Voice: (708) 571-5466   TDD: (708) 571-6533
  Many services for the blind and visually impaired.

Little City Foundation

4801 W. Peterson Ave.
Chicago, IL 60646
Telephone—
     Voice: (312) 282-2207   TDD:
  Provides a variety of residential services, including group homes in Palatine, and independent living arrangements around the Chicago area. Offers employment programs, social services, medical and dental services, educational opportunities, and recreation. Families One program provides support, therapy, and training for families with a developmentally disabled child.

Palatine campus:
  1760 W. Algonquin Rd.
  Palatine, IL 60067-4799
  (708) 358-5510

Resale shop:
  5317 N. Clark St.
  Chicago, IL 60640
  (312) 728-6166

Low-Incidence Cooperative Agreement

8257 Harrison
Niles, IL 60648
Telephone—
     Voice: (708) 679-7950   TDD:
  Educational, diagnostic, medical, and nursing services for persons with hearing and/or vision impairments.

Lung Line

Telephone—
>   Voice: (800) 222-LUNG   TDD:
> For persons with respiratory disorders.

Mainstream, Inc.

1030 15th St., N.W., Suite 1010
Washington, DC 20005
Telephone—
>   Voice: (202) 898-1400   TDD:
> Focuses on employment of persons with disabilities; offers national conference and bimonthly newsletter. Other publications include: *ADA Management Kit*; *The Federal Contractor's Guide to Job Accommodations*; *Planning Reasonable Accommodations*; and *Making the Workplace Accessible*.

March of Dimes Birth Defects Foundation
Greater Chicago Area Chapter

One N. Dearborn St.
Chicago, IL 60602
Telephone—
>   Voice: (312) 407-4007   TDD:
> Information and education aimed at the prevention of birth defects.

Marianjoy Rehabilitation Center

26 W. 171 Roosevelt Rd.
P. O. Box 795
Wheaton, IL 60189
Telephone—
>   Voice: (708) 462-4000   TDD:
> Inpatient and outpatient treatment programs include brain injury, pediatric, physical therapy, spinal cord injury, stroke, and cardiac rehabilitation. Publishes booklet giving information on access to DuPage County public buildings and recreational facilities; cost is $2.75. Sponsors a speakers bureau on over 65 topics, ranging from Amputee Rehabilitation and Self-Care Adaptations for the Physically Disabled to Travel for the Physically Disabled and Psychological Reactions to Disability. Also has a toy lending library for special-needs children.

Marklund Children's Home, Inc.

164 S. Prairie Ave.
Bloomingdale, IL 60108
Telephone—
    Voice: (708) 529-2871   TDD:
    Residential nursing care, education, and rehabilitation for developmentally
disabled persons from birth to 22 years. Adult services are offered at the Deilcke
Center (see listing above).

Material Development Center

Stout Vocational Rehabilitation Institute
University of Wisconsin - Stout
Menomonie, WI 54751
Telephone—
    Voice: (715) 232-1342   TDD:
    Offers many printed and audiovisual resources about vocational and rehabili-
tation services, including *A Guide to Job Site Evaluation* (K.F. Botterbusch, 1978),
Rehabilitation Engineering: A Counselor's Guide (Report on the Sixth Institute on
Rehabilitation Issues, 1979), and *Rehabilitation Technology* (Report on the 13th
Institute on Rehabilitation Issues, 1987).

Medic-Alert Foundation International

P. O. Box 1009
Turlock, CA 95381-1009
Telephone—
    Voice: (800) 344-3226
    Emergency equipment; medallions and bracelets containing emergency medi-
cal information and 24-hour emergency information telephone service.

Midwest Association for Sickle-Cell Anemia (MASCA)

36 S. Wabash Ave., Suite 1113
Chicago, IL 60603
Telephone—
    Voice: (312) 663-5700   TDD:
    Services for persons with sickle cell disease, including advocacy, counseling,
educational, financial assistance, information, referrals, recreation, and transportation.

Misericordia, Heart of Mercy Center

6300 N. Ridge
Chicago, IL 60660
Telephone—
      Voice: (312) 973-6300   TDD:
  Residential care and development programs for ambulatory, nonambulatory, and cerebral palsied children, teens, and young adults.

Misericordia South

2916 West 47th St.
Chicago, IL 60632
Telephone—
      Voice: (312) 254-9595   TDD:
  Residential home offering skilled nursing care for infants and children up to age 21 years who are nonambulatory and nonmobile, with severe to profound disabilities. Only children aged 3 years or under are accepted as new admittees.

Multiple Sclerosis Neurological Consultants

1725 W. Harrison
Chicago, IL 60612
Telephone—
      Voice: (312) 942-8011   TDD:
  Clinic within Rush-Presbyterian-St. Luke's Medical Center which includes three neurologists specializing in MS, a nurse specialist, a psychologist, and occupational and physical therapists.

Multiple Sclerosis Society

600 S. Federal, Suite 204
Chicago, IL 60605
Telephone—
      Voice: (312) 922-8000 or (800) 922-0484   TDD:
  Supports research into the cause and cure and prevention of the disease. Offers client programs in five areas: core services for persons with MS and their families (counseling, support, medical, and transportation services); family programs; educational programs; therapeutic programs; and employment programs.

Multiple Sclerosis 24-hour Information Line

Telephone—
          Voice: (800) 624-8236   TDD:

Muscular Dystrophy Association

National Office:
810 Seventh Ave.
New York, NY 10019
Telephone—
          Voice: (212) 586-0808   TDD:
   Offers patient services and clinical care; combats 40 neuromuscular diseases;
worldwide research program.

Myasthenia Gravis Foundation

211 E. Lake St.
Addison, IL 60101
Telephone—
          Voice: (708) 833-4011   TDD:
   Services and information for persons with myasthenia gravis.

National Adoption Center for Special Needs and Physically Disabled Children

Telephone—
          Voice: (800) TO-ADOPT   TDD:

National Amputation Foundation

12-45 150th St.
Whitestone, NY 11357
Telephone—
          Voice: (718) 767-0596   TDD:

National Association of the Deaf (NAD)

814 Thayer Ave.
Silver Spring, MD 20910
Telephone—
      Voice: (301) 587-1788   TDD: (301) 587-1788
  Publications and advocacy on behalf of deaf persons.

National Association for Down Syndrome

P. O. Box 4542
Oak Brook, IL 60522-4542
Telephone—
      Voice: (708) 325-9112   TDD
  Parent support program, community parent groups, information on educational programs for children; newsletter, seminars, and promotion of public awareness; research.

National Braille Press

88th St. & Stephen St.
Boston, MA 02115
Telephone—
      Voice: (617) 266-6160   TDD:

National Cancer Institute

Telephone—
      Voice: (800) 638-6694   TDD:

National Center for a Barrier-Free Environment

Informational Service
1015 15th St., N.W.
Washington, DC 20005
Telephone—
      Voice: (202) 466-6896   TDD:
  Published the *Reasonable Accommodation Handbook* (Frank Bowe, 1983).

National Center for Hearing and Speech Action

Telephone—
          Voice: (800) 638-TALK   TDD:

National Center on Law & the Deaf

Gallaudet University
800 Florida Ave., N.E.
Washington, DC 20002
Telephone—
          Voice: (202) 651-5051   TDD: (202) 651-5052

National Clearinghouse on Technology and Aging

55 Lake Ave., North
Worcester, MA 01655
Telephone—
          Voice: (800) 433-2306 or (508) 865-3662   TDD:
     Clearinghouse for persons with disabilities, especially those with sensory
impairments.

National Council on Disability

800 Independence Ave., S.W., Suite 814
Washington, DC 20591
Telephone—
          Voice: (202) 267-3846   TDD: (202) 267-3232   Fax: (202) 453-4240
     Publishes the free newsletter FOCUS. Also heads the "ADA Watch," a project
to monitor and evaluate implementation of the Americans with Disabilities Act of
1990.

National Deafness Information Center

Telephone—
          Voice: (800) 672-6720   TDD:

National Down Syndrome Congress

Telephone—
          Voice: (800) 232-NDSC or (312) 823-7550   TDD:

National Easter Seal Society

70 E. Lake St.
Chicago, IL 60601
Telephone—
        Voice: (312) 726-6200 or (800) 221-6827   TDD: (312) 726-4258
    Direct therapy and support programs for persons with disabilities. Publishes the *Computer Disability News*, a newsletter which emphasizes computer resources.

National Eye Care Project

Telephone—
        Voice: (800) 222-EYES   TDD:

National Federation of the Blind of Illinois

3032 N. Albany Ave.
Chicago, IL 60618
Telephone—
        Voice: (312) 267-1123   TDD
    Advocacy, education, information, and referral services.

National Fraternal Society of the Deaf

1300 W. Northwest Highway
Mt. Prospect, IL 60056
Telephone—
        Voice: (708) 392-9282   TDD: (708) 392-1409
    Sells quality life insurance at low cost to hearing-impaired individuals. Provides services to hearing-impaired community including advocacy, information, referral, fraternal activities, philanthropic support, scholarships, school awards, camp program, and other services.

National Handicapped Housing Institute, Inc.

12 S. 6th St., Suite 1216
Minneapolis, MN 55402
Telephone—
        Voice: (612) 535-9771   TDD:
    Published the *Product Inventory of Hardware, Equipment, and Appliances for Barrier-Free Design* (2nd ed., 1981).

National Head Injury Foundation

As of September 1992
1776 Massachusetts Ave., N.W., Suite 100
Washington, DC 20036
Telephone—
        Voice: (800) 444-NHIF   TDD:
   Information and referrals; public awareness and prevention activities; support for head injury professionals.

National Health Information Center

Telephone—
        Voice: (800) 336-4797   TDD:

National Hearing Aid Society

Telephone—
        Voice: (800) 521-5247   TDD:

National Hearing Association

721 Enterprise Dr.
Oak Brook, IL 60521
Telephone—
        Voice: (708) 323-7200   TDD:

National Hydrocephalus Foundation

Route 1 - River Rd.
Box 210A
Joliet, IL 60436
Telephone—
        Voice: (815) 467-6543
   Information and support for families of children with hydrocephaly.

National Information Center on Deafness

Gallaudet University
800 Florida Ave., N.E.
Washington, DC 20002
Telephone–
　　　　Voice: (202) 651-5051　　　　TDD: (202) 651-5052

National Information Center for Orphan Drugs & Rare Diseases

P. O. Box 1133
Washington, DC 20013-1133
Telephone–
　　　　Voice: (800) 456-3505　　　　TDD:

National Institute on Aging

Federal Building - Room 6 C 12
9000 Rock
Bethesda, MD 20820
Telephone–
　　　　Voice: (301) 496-1752　　　　TDD:
　　Publications on issues relating to aging; research on the aging process and associated illnesses.

National Institute on Disability and Rehabilitation Research

Office of Special Education & Rehabilitative Services
U.S. Department of Education
4000 Maryland Ave., S.W. - Room 3060 MES
Washington, DC 20202-2572
Telephone–
　　　　Voice: (202) 732-1134　　　　TDD: (202) 732-5079
　　Provides funds for grants, programs, and research for disability-related projects.

National Lekotek Center

2100 Ridge Ave.
Evanston, IL 60201
Telephone
　　　　Voice: (708) 328-0001　　　　TDD:
　　Toy library for children with special needs; branches all over Illinois. Also provides parents/families with support and materials, such as publications and videotapes, and publishes *Lekotek Plan Book of Adaptive Toys*, Volumes I & II & III ($15.00 each or $12.50 each for set of three).

National Multiple Sclerosis Society

205 E. 42nd St.
New York, NY 10017
Telephone
        Voice: (212) 986-3240   TDD:
    Services include advocacy, publications, educational programs, equipment loans, peer support, counseling, recreational activities, the Job Raising program, and MS research and support centers. Gives grants for research.

National Neurofibromatosis Foundation

1403 South St.
Geneva, IL 60134
Telephone—
        Voice: (708) 232-8415   TDD:

National Odd Shoe Exchange

R.R. #4
Indianola, IA 50125
Telephone
        Voice: (515) 961-5125   TDD:
    Arranges shoe exchanges among individuals with similar shoe sizes who wear different sizes on each foot.

National Organization of Social Security Claimants Representatives

19 E. Central Ave.
Pearl River, NY 10965
Telephone—
        Voice: (800) 431-2804   TDD:

National Organization on Disability

2100 Pennsylvania Ave., N.W., Suite 232
Washington, DC 20037
Telephone
        Voice: (800) 248-ABLE or (202) 293-5960   TDD:
    Call for address and telephone number of local office.

National Rehabilitation Association

633 S. Washington St.
Alexandria, VA 22314
Telephone–
        Voice: (703) 836-0850   TDD: (703) 836-0852
    Professional and consumer organization which emphasizes use of multiple resources to maximize quality of life. Publications include *The Revised Manual on Accessibility*, designed originally to provide guidance in selecting accessible meeting sites.

National Rehabilitation Information Center (NARIC)

8455 Colesville Rd., Suite 935
Silver Spring, MD 20910
Telephone–
        Voice: (800) 34-NARIC or (301) 588-9284   TDD:
    Offers information on disability-related topics. Publications include: *ABLEDATA Thesaurus* (updated quarterly); *Adapting Work Sites for People with Disabilities* (published by the Swedish Institute for the Handicapped); *Applications of Telecommunications Technology to Services for Individuals with Disabilities* (Susan Bruyere); *Community Integration of Disabled People*; *Attitudinal and Behavioral Reactions of the Nondisabled* (Carol K. Sigelman); *Computers in Vocational Rehabilitation: Current Trends and Future Applications* (Bruce Growick); *Low Cost Approaches to Technology and Disability* (Gregory L. Dixon and Alexandra Enders); *Use of Computers in Expanding the Employment Opportunities of Persons with Disabilities* (William Crimando and Susan Harrington Godbey); and *Rehabdata Thesaurus*.

National Society for Children & Adults with Autism

419 7th St., N.W., Suite 300
Washington, DC 20004
Telephone–
        Voice: (202) 783-0125   TDD:

National Spinal Cord Injury Association

149 California St.
Newton, MA 02158
Telephone–
        Voice: (800) 962-9629 or (617) 964-0521   TDD:

National Spinal Cord Injury Hotline

Telephone—
          (800) 526-3456   TDD:

National Stroke Association

300 E. Hampden Ave., Suite 240
Englewood, CO 80110-2622
Telephone—
          Voice: (303) 762-9922   TDD:
     Education and referrals for stroke survivors, families, and health care profes-
sionals, including support groups, newsletter, and advocacy.

National Tay Sachs & Allied Diseases

3040 Fresno Ln.
Homewood, IL 60430
Telephone—
          Voice: (708) 748-9101   TDD:
     Conducts research, education, and prevention programs, including mass
screenings. Assists the families of afflicted children through the availability of a
parent peer network, genetic counseling, and a repository of specialized
knowledge.

National Technical Information Service

5285 Port Royal Rd.
Springfield, VA 22161
Telephone—
          Voice: (703) 487-4650   TDD:
     Offers assistance and information regarding assistive devices. Publications
include *Guidelines for Aircraft Boarding Chairs* and *Technical Paper on Mobility
Aids Storage.*

National Technical Institute for the Deaf

One Lomb Memorial Rd.
P. O. Box 9887
Rochester, NY 14623-0887
Telephone—
          Voice: (716) 475-6400   TDD: (716) 475-2181

National Technology Database

American Foundation for the Blind
15 West 16th St.
New York, NY 10011
Telephone—
      Voice: TDD:
  Resources for visually impaired persons.

National Tuberous Sclerosis Association

Telephone—
      Voice: (800) CAL-NTSA   TDD:

National Veterans Training Institute

University of Colorado at Denver
1250 14th St., Suite 650
Denver, CO 80202
Telephone—
      Voice: (800) 331-0562 or (303) 892-1712   TDD:
  Training for specialists who serve veterans with disabilities.

New Ability, Inc.

Six N. Ninth Ave.
Melrose Park, IL 60160
Telephone—
      Voice: (708) 345-3939   TDD:
  Adaptive products for the handicapped driver and installation in vehicles.

Northern Cartographic

P.O. Box 133
Burlington, VT 05402
Telephone—
      Voice: (802) 860-2886   TDD:
  Publishes *Access America*, a guide to wheelchair-accessible facilities and programs at 37 national parks, with charts, maps, photographs, and large-type text; includes information about special programs for persons with hearing or visual impairments. Cost is $89.95, shipping included, with a 50% discount to individuals and not-for-profit organizations. An excerpted guide to Yosemite National Park is available for $7.95 plus $2.00 for shipping.

Nursing Home Information and Abuse Report

Telephone—
 Voice: (800) 252-4343   TDD:

Oak Forest Hospital

15900 S. Cicero Ave.
Oak Forest, IL 60452
Telephone—
 Voice: (312) 928-4200 (Chicago) (708) 687-7200 (suburbs)
 TDD:
 Rehabilitation programs, including physical and occupational therapy; speech, language, and audiology; vocational rehabilitation; and therapeutic recreation. Offers six levels of care, from acute to ambulatory, and a full complement of therapeutic and diagnostic programs and services.

ODPHP National Health Information Center

P. O. Box 1133
Washington, DC 20013-1133
Telephone—
 Voice: (800) 336-4797   TDD:
 Offers resources regarding health information.

Okada Hearing Ear Guide

Route #1 - Box 640F
Fontana, WI 53215
Telephone—
 Voice: (414) 275-5226   TDD: (414) 275-5226
 Trains dogs to aid hearing-impaired persons.

One-on-One Computer Training

2055 Army Trail Rd., Suite 100
Addison, IL 60101
Telephone—
 Voice: (800) 222-3547 or (708) 790-1117   TDD:
 Offers home study computer software, including audio tapes suitable for use by persons with visual impairments.

Opportunity, Inc.

1200 Old Skokie Rd.
Highland Park, IL 60035
Telephone–
      Voice: (708) 831-9400   TDD:
  Assists handicapped adults reach full potential via employment.

Orchard Association for the Retarded

7670 Marmora Manor
Skokie, IL 60077
Telephone–
      Voice: (708) 967-1800   TDD:
  Vocational programs and counselling, respite services, and community living facility for the retarded.

Orchard Village

7670 Marmora Manor
Skokie, IL 60077
Telephone–
      Voice: (708) 967-1800   TDD:
  Provides residential facilities and vocational training for developmentally disabled and mentally retarded adults. Offers respite care.

Orton Dyslexia Society

724 York Rd.
Baltimore, MD 21204
Telephone–
      Voice: (800) 222-3123 or (301) 296-0232   TDD:

PACT, Inc.

6 N. Michigan Ave., Suite 1706
Chicago, IL 60602
Telephone–
      Voice: (312) 853-0226   TDD:

Paralyzed Veterans of America

National Office:
801 18th St., N.W.
Washington, DC 20006
Telephone—
      Voice: (202) USA-1300   TDD:
   Barrier Free Design Program promotes accessibility to buildings, facilities, housing, and employment. Spinal Cord Research Foundation funds research related to spinal cord injury and spinal cord diseases. National Sports Program sponsors and promotes wheelchair sports. Employment program with the Illinois State Lottery. Veteran's benefits. Other programs include National Advocacy Program, National Legislation Program, and publications such as *Paraplegia News* and *Sports 'N Spokes*, and general information brochures. Publishes *Design Guidelines Qualifying for the Tax Advantages of Section 190*, a free publication which assists in meeting federal requirements.

Paraplegia News

5201 N. 19th Ave., Suite 111
Phoenix, AZ 85015
Telephone—
      Voice: (602) 246-9426   TDD:
   Publication focussing upon spinal cord injury and treatment, rehabilitation, accessibility, laws, and products.

Parkinson's Disease Information

Telephone—
      Voice: (800) 223-2732   TDD:

Parkinson's Educational Program

1800 Park Newport - #302
Newport Beach, CA 92660
Telephone—
      Voice: (800) 344-7872   TDD:
   Educational programs for patients and their caregivers, including exercise books, newsletters, video tapes, and information on support groups.

Pass Word

11400 Bacon Rd.
Plainwell, MI 49080
Telephone–
    Voice: (616) 664-5282   TDD:
  Assists persons with disabilities who have need for computer equipment, software, etc.

Paul H. Brookes Publishing Co.

P. O. Box 10624
Baltimore, MD 21285
Telephone–
    Voice: (800) 638-3775 or (301) 337-9580   TDD:
  Offers a variety of rehabilitation-related books.

Paul M. Deutsch Press, Inc.

2211 Hillcrest St.
Orlando, FL 32803
Telephone–
    Voice: (800) 999-8773 or (407) 895-3600   TDD:
    Fax: (407) 895-3610
  Publishes a wide range of disability-related and rehabilitation-related books and periodicals, including *Work Worth Doing: Advances in Brain Injury Rehabilitation* (Brian T. McMahon and Linda R. Shaw, 1991) and *The Americans with Disabilities Act: Access and Accommodations* (Nancy Hablutzel and Brian T. McMahon, 1992).

Philip H. Cohen Institute for the Visually Handicapped

5200 Hyde Park Blvd.
Chicago, IL 60615
Telephone–
    Voice: (312) 643-9857   TDD:
  Braille and large-print books and taped transcriptions for the Jewish Braille Institute of America. Service provided at no cost.

Phoenix Karate Academy

Sokol Hall - Jim Garrett
3909 Prairie Ave.
Brookfield, IL 60513
Telephone—
          Voice: (708) 450-9306   TDD:
     Karate and Tae-kwon-do instruction to handicapped and nonhandicapped
persons.

Post-Polio Support Group

Hinsdale Hospital
120 N. Oak St.
Hinsdale, IL 60521
Telephone—
          Voice: (708) 887-2740   TDD:
     Information and support for polio patients and their families; meets the fourth
Wednesday of each month.

President's Committee on Employment of People with Disabilities

1111 20th St., N.W.
Washington, DC 20036
Telephone—
          Voice: (202) 653-3044   TDD: (202) 653-5050   Fax: (202) 653-7386
     Committee offers information about technical aids and job accommodations,
including its booklet *Ready, Willing and Able: A Business Guide for Hiring People
with Disabilities*. Also publishes a magazine, *WORKLIFE*.

Project REAP

Chicago Public Schools Bureau of Physically Handicapped Children
1819 W. Pershing Rd.
Chicago, IL 60609
Telephone—
          Voice: (312) 535-8356   TDD:
     Arts programming for disabled students.

Rami Rabbi

136 E. 55th St., Suite 8E
New York, NY 10022
Telephone—
        Voice: (212) 371-7766   TDD:
    Published (in 1989) *Employing the Disabled: What are Self-Help Groups and What Assistance Can They Offer the Employer?*

Ray Graham Association for People with Disabilities

340 W. Butterfield Rd., Suite 3C
Elmhurst, IL 60126
Telephone—
        Voice: (708) 530-4554   TDD: (708) 543-2440 ext. 301
    Various programs at various locations, including workshops, early intervention special education, foster care, residential care, respite care, job placement, and evaluation and testing in Addison, Illinois, and Fairwood School, 543 E. Taylor Rd., Lombard, IL 60148 - (708) 495-4670.

REACH (Rehabilitation/Education/Advocacy for Citizens with Handicaps)

617 Seventh Ave.
Fort Worth, TX 76104
Telephone—
        Voice: (817) 870-9082   TDD: (817) 870-9086
    Offers training in computer use to persons with disabilities; also offers clearinghouse of computer information.

REACH Rehabilitation of Manor Health Care Corp.

9401 S. Kostner Ave.
Oak Lawn, IL 60453
Telephone—
        Voice: (708) 423-1440   TDD:
    Provides subacute rehabilitation for persons with head injuries, strokes, spinal cord injuries, amputations, orthopedic and neurologic impairment, arthritis, and other traumas and diseases.

Recording for the Blind

36 S. Wabash Ave., Room 1107
Chicago, IL 60603
Telephone—
      Voice: (312) 236-8715   TDD:
or:
20 Roszel Rd.
Princeton, NJ 08540
      Voice: (800) 221-4792 or (609) 452-0606   TDD:
  Tape-recorded textbooks for sight impaired/blind and physically disabled students.

Red Acre Farm Hearing Dog Center

P. O. Box 278
Stow, MA 01755
Telephone—
      Voice: (617) 897-8343   TDD: (617) 897-8343
  Trains dogs to aid hearing-impaired persons.

Rehabilitation Institute of Chicago

345 E. Superior St.
Chicago, IL 60611
Telephone—
      Voice: (312) 908-6000 or (312) 988-6066   TDD:
  Provides rehabilitative therapy, prosthetics, and other services (both inpatient and outpatient) to persons with amputation, arthritis, brain trauma, burns, cerebral palsy, chronic pain, congenital disabilities, geriatric rehabilitation, multiple sclerosis, neuromuscular disorders, post-polio syndrome, spinal cord injury, sports rehabilitation, stroke, and other disabling conditions. Special programs include the Alan J. Brown Center for Alternate Communication and Environmental Control; the Virginia Wadsworth Wirtz Wheelchair Sports Program; Medical Program for Performing Artists; driver education; vocational evaluation, counseling, and placement; rehabilitation engineering; and recreational activities.

Rehabilitation Services Administration (RSA)
Offices of Vocational Rehabilitation (VR)

  Regional RSA offices have federal jurisdiction over state vocational rehabilitation programs. Local VR offices are excellent resources for information on many topics relating to disability and employment; the regional RSA office can provide you with the address and telephone number of your VR.

Region I: (617) 223-4083 CT, ME, NH, RI, VT, MA
Region II: (212) 264-4016 NJ, PR, VI, NY
Region III: (215) 596-0317 DC, DE, MD, VA, WV, PA
Region IV: (404) 331-2352 AL, FL, KY, NC, SC, TN, GA, MS
Region V: (312) 886-5372 IL, IN, MI, MN, OH, WI
Region VI: (214) 767-2961 AR, LA, NM, OK, TX
Region VII: (816) 891-8015 IA, KS, NE, MO
Region VIII: (303) 844-2135 MT, ND, SD, UT, WY, CO
Region IX: (415) 556-7333 AZ, CA, HI, NV
Region X: (206) 553-5331 AK, ID, OR, WA

Research Grant Guides

P. O. Box 4970
Margate, FL 33063
Telephone–
        Voice: (305) 753-1754   TDD:
   Maintains a *Handicapped Funding Directory*, listing companies that grant
funds for persons with disabilities.

RESNA

1101 Connecticut Ave., N.W., Suite 700
Washington, DC 20036
Telephone–
        Voice: (202) 857-1199   TDD:
   Rehabilitation engineering organization supporting research and technology
development to improve opportunities for persons with disabilities, their families,
caregivers, and employers. Publishes *Rehabilitation Technology Service &
Delivery Programs* (1987).

Resources for Rehabilitation

33 Bedford St., Suite 19A
Lexington, MA 02173
Telephone–
        Voice: (617) 862-6455   TDD:
   Offers information and training to persons with disabilities.

Retinitis Pigmentosa Foundation

Telephone—
      Voice: (800) 638-2300   TDD:

Retinitis Pigmentosa Foundation - Chicago Chapter

1011 S. Waiola
LaGrange, IL 60525
Telephone—
      Voice: (708) 354-8108   TDD: (708) 831-3058
      Information and referrals.

RPM Press, Inc.

Vernandale, MN 56481
Telephone—
      Voice: (612) 886-1990   TDD:
    Publishes *The Job Accommodation Handbook* (Paul M. McCray, 1987), which offers a thorough discussion of various accommodations and includes charts and worksheets, and *The Source*, a biannual directory of accessibility products from over 2,000 manufacturers.

Schwab Rehabilitation Center

1401 S. California Blvd.
Chicago, IL 60608
Telephone—
      Voice: (312) 522-2010   TDD: (312) 522-2032
    Rehabilitation and training of persons with all disabilities. Special programs include the Technical Aids Center, the Computer Assisted Therapy Center, the Driving Center, four-phase head trauma and stroke programs, pediatric rehabilitation, STEPS Industrial Rehabilitation program, the professional voice/foreign accent modification program, and art and recreational therapy.

Self-Sufficiency Trust

340 W. Butterfield Rd., Suite 3C
Elmhurst, IL 60126
Telephone—
      Voice: (708) 941-3498   TDD:
    Lifecare and estate planning; mechanism for families with a disabled member.

Sertoma Career Center

4343 123rd St.
Alsip, IL 60658
Telephone—
        Voice: (708) 371-9700   TDD: (708) 371-9790
    Vocational training and ancillary services for persons with mental and/or physical disabilities. Also provides foster care for developmentally disabled children and adults whose families cannot care for them. Publishes *Network*, an informational newsletter about the Center.

Short Stature Foundation

P. O. Box 5356
Huntington Beach, CA 92165-5356
Telephone—
        Voice: (714) 474-4554 or (714) 558-2405

Shriner's Hospital for Crippled Children

2211 N. Oak Park Ave.
Chicago, IL 60635
Telephone—
        Voice: (312) 622-5400   TDD:
    Medical and rehabilitative services to children with disabilities, often given free of charge or at a reduced charge.

(David T.) Siegel Institute for Communicative Disorders - Michael Reese Hospital

31st St. and Lake Shore Dr.
Chicago, IL 60616
Telephone—
        Voice: (312) 791-2900   TDD: (312) 791-3449
    Programs for hearing-impaired adults, and for hearing-impaired children and their families. Hearing aid dispensary. Multidisciplinary evaluation.

Silent Cooperative

2500 W. Belmont
Chicago, IL 60618
Telephone—
        Voice: (312) 935-0640   TDD: (312) 935-0641
    Residential apartments with special amenities for deaf and physically disabled adults.

Silent Sounds, Inc.

1528 W. Adams St.
Chicago, IL 60607
Telephone—
          Voice: (312) 829-7631   TDD: (312) 274-9803
    Brings the arts to all through sign language.

Skokie Accessible Library Services

Skokie Public Library
5215 Oakton St.
Skokie, IL 60077
Telephone—
          Voice: (708) 673-7774   TDD: (708) 673-7774
    Library services for persons with disabilities, including electronic aids, materials in special formats, programs and special services, and access to the North Suburban Library System. Program is open to all, not just Skokie citizens. Books and other materials can be reserved by voice telephone or TDD.

Smith Kettlewell Rehabilitation Engineering Center

Smith Kettlewell Institute
San Francisco, CA
Telephone—
          Voice: (415) 561-1620   TDD:
    Published *Vocational and Educational Aids* (1982).

Social Security Administration

Telephone—
          Voice: (800) 772-1213   TDD: (800) 325-0778

The Source
Roadrunner Publishing, Inc.

P. O. Box 9134
Crystal Lake, IL 60014
Telephone—
          Voice: (815) 363-0900   TDD: (815) 363-0922
    Newspaper for People with Disabilities.™ A consumer-oriented publication, with regular columns and features covering a broad range of topics dealing with everyday life for persons with disabilities. Topics include employment,

transportation, housing, travel, legislative/legal issues, finance, education, sports, health care, and more. Published monthly except for a combined July/August issue; subscriptions are $10.00 per year.

Special Olympics (Chicago Area)

Chicago Park District
425 E. McFetridge
Chicago, IL 60605
Telephone—
      Voice: (312) 294-2329   TDD:
   Various sports programs at numerous special recreation centers throughout the City of Chicago.

Spina Bifida Association

Telephone—
      Voice: (800) 621-3141   TDD:

Statewide Library of Information for Caregivers of the Disabled

800 Governors Highway
P. O. Box 460
Flossmoor, IL 60422
Telephone—
      Voice: (708) 957-7100 ext. 282 or (708) 957-7130 (after 4:00 pm)
      TDD: Fax: (708) 957-5641
   Statewide reference service with special library collections for all Illinois public libraries and their patrons needing information about disabilities.

Talkline/Kidsline, Inc.

P. O. Box 1321
Elk Grove Village, IL 60007
Telephone—

      Voice: (708) 228-6400 or (708) 228-KIDS   TDD:
   Counseling, emergency information and referrals.

TechLine (Center for Special Education Technology)

1920 Association Dr.
Reston, VA 22091
Telephone—
            Voice: (800) 873-8255   TDD:
      Database of information on use of technology in special education settings.

Technical Aids and Assistance for the Disabled (TAAD Center)

1950 W. Roosevelt Rd.
Chicago, IL 60608
Telephone—
            Voice: (800) 346-2939 or (312) 421-3373   TDD: available
      Assists handicapped persons in selecting and designing computer systems for
personal use; provides technical assistance and literature. Offers access to
AppleNet, SpecialNet, and the national COPH-2 Computer Bulletin Board:
(312) 286-0608.

Tele-Consumer Hotline

1910 K Street, N.W., Suite 610
Washington, DC 20006
·Telephone—
            Voice: (800) 332-1124 or (202) 223-4371   TDD:
      Free service offering information about telephone shopping to persons with
disabilities.

Telesensory Systems, Inc.

455 N. Bernardo Ave.
P. O. Box 7455
Mountain View, CA 94043
Telephone—
            Voice: (415) 960-0920   TDD:

Thompson Publishing Group

1725 K Street, N.W., Suite 200
Washington, DC 20006
Telephone—
            Voice: (800) 424-2959   TDD:
      Publishes *The Americans with Disabilities Act Compliance Guide*, a 400-page
guide with yearly updates discussing the Americans with Disabilities Act and its
requirements.

Tikvah Institute for Childhood Learning Disabilities

1212 S. Michigan Ave.
Chicago, IL 60605
or:
59 E. Van Buren, Suite 1610
Chicago, IL 60605
Telephone—
        Voice: (312) 939-2393   TDD:
    Camp experiences (Camp Ramah in Wisconsin) for learning-disabled Jewish
adolescents aged 13-17.

Time Out to Enjoy

P. O. Box 1084
Evanston, IL 60204
Telephone—
        Voice: (708) 940-9633   TDD:
    Program run by and for learning disabled or minimally brain dysfunctional
adults.

Tourette's Syndrome Association, Inc.

5102 Oakton St., Suite 115
Skokie, IL 60077
Telephone—
        Voice: (708) 675-2121   TDD:
    Information about and support for persons with Tourette's Syndrome. Open
Mondays, Wednesdays, and Fridays only.

Trace Research and Development Center

University of Wisconsin - Madison
Room S-151 - Waisman Center
1500 Highland Ave.
Madison, WI 53705-2208
Telephone—
        Voice: (608) 262-6966   TDD:
    Offers information about accommodations and assistance for persons with
severe communications-related disabilities, with special emphasis on computer
technology. Publishes the *TRACE Resource Book.*

Traveling Healthy

108-48 70th Rd.
Forest Hills, NY 11375
Telephone—
        Voice: TDD:
  Bimonthly newsletter of information for travelers with disabilities. Subscriptions are $24.00 for one year and $40.00 for two years, with back issues available for $4.00 each.

Trilogy

7510 N. Ashland Ave.
Chicago, IL 60626
Telephone—
        Voice: (312) 262-4811 (intake)   TDD:
  General vocational and socialization services for mentally ill adults. Supported living program.

Trio Publications, Inc.

497 Cameron Way
Buffalo Grove, IL 60089
Telephone—
        Voice: (708) 253-9426   TDD:
  Publishes *The Illustrated Guide to Handicapped Products.*

U.S. Department of Education

Office of Civil Rights
Washington, DC
Telephone—
        Voice: (202) 708-5366   TDD:
  Publishes the *Directory of National Information Sources on Handicapping Conditions and Related Services*, which is available through the U.S. Government Printing Office and U.S. Government Bookstores, and the *OCR Handbook for the Implementation of Section 504 of the Rehabilitation Act of 1973.*

U.S. Department of Health and Human Services

Office for Civil Rights
105 W. Adams St., 16th Floor
Chicago, IL 60603
Telephone—
   Voice: (312) 886-2359 or (312) 886-5077   TDD: (312) 353-5693
   Fax: (312) 886-1807
  Enforces section 504 of the Rehabilitation Act of 1973, which prohibits discrimination against handicapped persons by recipients of federal funding; complaints must be filed within 180 days after incident. Enforces the community services provision of the Hill-Burton Act, which prohibits discrimination against any person on any ground unrelated to their need for service.

U.S. Department of Labor

Washington, DC
Telephone—
   Voice: (202) 523-6666   TDD:
  Offers publications to assist employers in determining and achieving workplace accessibility, including A Guide to Job Analysis (1982) and A Handbook for Job Restructuring (1970).

U.S. Department of Labor

Office of Federal Contract Compliance Programs (OFCCP)
Regional Office:
 230 S. Dearborn, Room 570
 Chicago, IL 60604
North Cook County (north of 75th St.):
 411 S. Wells, Second Floor
 Chicago, IL 60607
South Cook County (south of 75th St.):
 230 S. Dearborn, Room 406
 Chicago, IL 60604
 (also NW Indiana)
Telephone—
   Voice: (312) 353-6603   TDD:
  Investigates complaints brought under section 504 of the Rehabilitation Act of 1973 against federal contractors. Published A Study of Accommodations Provided to Handicapped Employees by Federal Contractors: Final Report (1982).

U.S. Equal Employment Opportunity Commission

1801 L Street, N.W.
Washington, DC 20507
Telephone–
          Voice: (202) 663-4903   TDD:

536 S. Clark St., 9th Floor
Chicago, IL 60605
Telephone–
          Voice: (312) 353-8906   TDD: (312) 353-2401
   Conducts hearings on discrimination complaints of current and former federal employees or applicants for federal employment. Complaints must fall under section 504 of the Rehabilitation Act of 1973, the Age Discrimination in Employment Act of 1967, or Title VII of the Civil Rights Act of 1964.

U.S. Office of Consumer Affairs

Consumer Information Center
Pueblo, CO 81009
Telephone–
          Voice: (719) 948-3334   TDD:
   Numerous publications for consumers; request free catalog. Publications include the *U. S. Government TDD Numbers* (#573X - $1.00) and the *Pocket Guide to Federal Help for Individuals with Disabilities* (#111X - $1.00). Checks and money orders should be made payable to **The Superintendent of Documents**.

U.S. Office of Personnel Management

Washington, DC
Telephone–
          Voice: (202) 606-2424   TDD:
   Publishes the *Handbook of Job Analysis for Reasonable Accommodation* and *Reasonable Accommodation for Deaf Employees in White Collar Jobs*.

United Cerebral Palsy Association - National Office

1522 K Street, N.W., Suite 1122
Washington, DC 20055
Telephone–
          Voice: (800) 872-5827 or (202) 842-1266 or (New York) (212) 481-6300
          TDD:
   Provides a wide range of services to persons with cerebral palsy and other developmental disabilities. Serves persons from birth through adulthood. Among the services provided are early intervention program, school program, adult training, supported employment, social services counseling, recreation and community-integrated living facility (CILA).

United Parkinson's Foundation

360 W. Superior St.
Chicago, IL 60610
Telephone—
      Voice: (312) 664-2344   TDD:
  Educational programs for patients and their caregivers, including exercise books, newsletters, video tapes, and information on support groups.

United Post-Polio Survivors, Inc.

P. O. Box 273
Itasca, IL 60143-0273
Telephone—
      Voice: TDD:
  Collects and disseminates information to polio survivors and the general community about the late and residual affects of polio; advocates for the rights of polio survivors; provides reassurance and emotional support to polio survivors and their families.

United Publications, Inc.

645 Stewart Ave.
Garden City, NY 11530
Telephone—
      Voice: (516) 222-2500   TDD:
  Publishes *Electronic Engineers Master Catalog*.

United Way/Crusade of Mercy

560 W. Lake St.
Chicago, IL 60606
Telephone—
      Voice: (312) 876-0010 or (312) 876-1808   TDD
  Community information and referral services.

University of Wisconsin - Madison

School of Education
Vocational Studies Center
Madison, WI 53705-2208
Telephone—
          Voice: (608) 263-2422   TDD:
     Publishes *Tools, Equipment, and Machinery Adapted for the Vocation, Education, and Employment of Handicapped People* (John J. Gugerty and Lloyd W. Tindall, 1983).

Veterans Administration

Washington, DC
Telephone—
          Voice: (202) 233-4000   TDD:
     The V.A. can provide information or funds to enhance the employability of qualified persons with disabilities. Local offices in all states and most larger cities.

Veterans Administration Blind Rehabilitation Center

Memorial Dr.
Waco, TX 76711
Telephone—
          Voice: (817) 752-6581   TDD:

Veterans Administration Information Technology Center

810 Vermont Ave.
Washington, DC 20420
Telephone—
          Voice: (202) 389-5571   TDD:
     Offers computer training to federal employees with disabilities.

Victor C. Neumann Association

2354 N. Milwaukee Ave.
Chicago, IL 60647
Telephone—
          Voice: (312) 278-1124   TDD:
     Developmental training and supported employment opportunities for developmentally disabled persons over the age of 16 years; residential services; educational services for persons aged 6 to 21 years; and numerous other services. Its Microfilm Services division offers a full range of high quality microfilming services to the business community, employing mentally handicapped adults.

Villa Olivia Ski Area

Bartlett, IL 60103
Telephone—
          Voice: (708) 289-5200   TDD:
   Recreational services for persons who are blind or have visual impairments or
physical disabilities.

Virginia Wadsworth Wirtz Wheelchair Sports Program

Rehabilitation Institute of Chicago
345 E. Superior St.
Chicago, IL 60611
Telephone—
          Voice: (312) 908-4292   TDD: (312) 908-4292
   Chicago-area program of sports for adults and children with physical disabilities. Program includes strength and conditioning, power-lifting, track and field,
tennis, wheelchair softball, wheelchair basketball, swimming, snow skiing, winter
sports. Also starting programs in volleyball and team handball. A referral source
for information on other sports and recreational activities.

Visually Impaired Athletic Association

4317 N. Whipple
Chicago, IL 60618
Telephone—
          Voice: (312) 539-0950   TDD:

Visually Impaired Support Association

593A Edinburgh Ln.
Prospect Heights, IL 60070
Telephone—
          Voice: (708) 259-5352   TDD:
   Monthly support group meetings for persons with recent sight loss (partial or
total).

Visutek International, Inc.

100 W. Erie St.
Chicago, IL 60610
Telephone—
        Voice: (312) 943-8737   TDD:

Vocational Services Program

c/o Christ Hospital
4440 W. 95th St.
Oak Lawn, IL 60453
Telephone—
        Voice: (708) 857-1330   TDD: (708) 857-5402
    Vocational evaluation; work adjustment training (on-site work tryouts); job readiness training and job placement services for physically and psychiatrically disabled persons. Traumatic brain injuries, spinal cord injuries, other physical disabilities (back, stroke, arthritis, fractures), psychiatric disability, and substance abuse.

Voice

11931 N. Central Expressway, Suite 11
Dallas, TX 75243
Telephone—
        Voice: (214) 490-0860   TDD:
    A publication about technological assistance for persons with hearing impairments.

Wheelchair Industries. Inc.

527 Fullerton Ave.
Addison, IL 60101
Telephone—
        Voice: (708) 627-3737   TDD:
    Wheelchair and commercial van conversions and custom vehicle design.

Wiley & Sons

One Wiley Drive
Somerset, NJ 08875
Telephone—
        Voice: (800) 225-5945   TDD:
    Publishes *The Americans with Disabilities Act Handbook* (Henry H. Perritt,
1990); *The Biomechanical Basis of Ergonomics* (E. R. Tichauer, 1978); *Ergonomics
at Work* (D. J. Osborne, 1987); *Guide to Basic Information Sources in Engineering*
(Ellis Mount, 1976); *Handbook of Human Factors* (G. Salvendy, ed., 1987); and
Human Factors: Understanding People Systems Relationships (Kantowitz &
Sorkin, 1983).

Windy City Disabled Outdoors Club

c/o Judy Benson
    2757 N. Pinegrove, #1105
    Chicago, IL 60614
    (312) 525-8638
c/o Nick Coletta
    5110 N. St. Louis
    Chicago, IL 60625
    (312) 539-0869
Telephone—
        Voice: (312) 744-7229   TDD:
    Outdoor recreation and activities for the physically disabled; both disabled and
nondisabled persons welcome to join. Monthly meetings held on the first Saturday
of the month at 10:30 a.m. in the Central/West Center, 2102 W. Ogden, Chicago.

Yachad Program - National Conference of Synagogue Youth

5875 N. Lincoln Ave., Suite 128
Chicago, IL 60659
Telephone—
        Voice: (312) 769-NCSY   TDD:
    Youth group for Jewish teens and young adults with developmental disabilities.

Y-ME Breast Cancer Support Program

Telephone—
        Voice: (800) 221-2141   TDD:
24-Hour Hotline: (708) 799-8228
    The toll-free hotline is open 9:00 a.m. to 5:00 p.m. on weekdays to answer
questions from women who have or suspect they have breast cancer.

Appendix 7, *The Technical Assistance Manual on the Employment Provisions (Title I) of the ADA*, was supplied by the Equal Employment Opportunity Commission (EEOC) and is reprinted here, with permission, in its entirety.

Appendix 7

*A TECHNICAL ASSISTANCE MANUAL
ON THE EMPLOYMENT PROVISIONS
(TITLE I) OF THE*

AMERICANS
WITH
DISABILITIES
ACT

EQUAL EMPLOYMENT OPPORTUNITY COMMISSION

January 1992

EEOC-M-1A

TABLE OF CONTENTS

MANUAL

Introduction

How to Use this Manual

I. Title I: An Overview of Legal Requirements

II. Who is Protected by the ADA?

- Individual With a Disability

- Qualified Individual With a Disability

III. The Reasonable Accommodation Obligation

IV. Establishing Nondiscriminatory Qualification Standards and Selection Criteria

V. Nondiscrimination in the Hiring Process: Recruitment; Applications; Pre-Employment Inquiries; Testing

VI. Medical Examinations and Inquiries

VII. Nondiscrimination in Other Employment Practices

VIII. Drug and Alcohol Abuse

IX. Workers' Compensation and Work-Related Injury

X. Enforcement Provisions

APPENDICES

A.   Titles I and V of the ADA

B.   EEOC Title I Regulations and Interpretive Appendix

C.   Diseases Transmitted Through the Food Supply (issued by Centers for Disease Control, Public Health Service, pursuant to Section 103 (d) of the ADA)

D.   Form and Instructions for ADA-Related Small Business Tax Credit (Section 44 of the Internal Revenue Code)

RESOURCE DIRECTORY

Introduction

How to Use the Directory

PART ONE: **FEDERAL AGENCY RESOURCES**

I.   Federal Agencies that Enforce ADA Requirements

II.   Other Federal and Federally Funded ADA Technical Assistance

III.   Other Federal Agency Programs Related to Disability and Employment

IV.   Federal Agencies that Enforce Other Laws Prohibiting Discrimination on the Basis of Disability

PART TWO: **NATIONAL NON-GOVERNMENTAL TECHNICAL ASSISTANCE RESOURCES**

V.   Organizations that Provide Services Related to Employment of People with Disabilities

VI.   Other Organizations with Expertise in Specific Disabilities

VII.   Alternative Dispute Resolution Resources

PART THREE: REGIONAL AND STATE LOCATIONS OF FEDERAL PROGRAMS

VIII.   Equal Employment Opportunity Commission District Offices

IX.   Regional Offices of Agencies that Enforce Other Laws Prohibiiting Employment Discrimination on the Basis of Disability

X.   State Listings of Other Federal Programs Related to Disability and Employment

XI.   State Listings of Centers for Independent Living

XII.   State Technology-Related Assistance Programs

XIII.   State Programs of Education and Assistance for Farmers and Ranchers with Disabilities

TELECOMMUNICATIONS RELAY SERVICES

INDEX

INTRODUCTION

The Equal Employment Opportunity Commission (EEOC) is issuing this Technical Assistance Manual as part of an active technical assistance program to help employers, other covered entities, and persons with disabilities learn about their obligations and rights under the employment provisions of the Americans with Disabilities Act (Title I of the ADA). ADA requirements for nondiscrimination in employment become effective for employers with 25 or more employees and other covered entities on July 26, 1992, and for employers with 15 to 24 employees on July 26, 1994.

The Manual provides guidance on the practical application of legal requirements established in the statute and EEOC regulations. It also provides a directory of resources to aid in compliance. The Manual is designed to be updated periodically with supplements as the Commission develops further policy guidance and identifies additional resources.

Part One of the Manual explains key legal requirements in practical terms, including:

- who is protected by, and who must comply with, the ADA;

- what the law permits and prohibits with respect to establishing qualification standards, assessing the qualifications and capabilities of people with disabilities to perform specific jobs, and requiring medical examinations and other inquiries;

- the nature of the obligation to make a reasonable accommodation;

- how the law's nondiscrimination requirements apply to aspects of the employment process such as promotion, transfer, termination, compensation, leave, fringe benefits and contractual arrangements;

- how ADA provisions regarding drug and alcohol use affect other legal obligations and employer policies concerning drugs and alcohol; and

- how ADA requirements affect workers' compensation policies and practices.

The manual explains many employment provisions through the use of examples. These examples are used only to illustrate the particular point or principle to which they relate in the text and should not be taken out of context as statements of EEOC policy that would apply in different circumstances.

Part Two of the Manual is a <u>Resource Directory</u> listing public and private agencies and organizations that provide information, expertise, and technical assistance on many aspects of employing people with disabilities, including reasonable accommodation.

EEOC has published informational booklets on the ADA for employers and for people with disabilities, and will provide other written and audiovisual educational materials; it will provide ADA training for people with disabilities, for employers and other covered entities, and will participate in meetings and training programs of various organizations. EEOC also has established a free "800" number "Helpline" to respond to individual requests for information and assistance.

The Commission's technical assistance program will be separate and distinct from its enforcement responsibilities. Employers who seek information or assistance from EEOC will not be subject to any enforcement action because of such inquiries. The Commission believes that the majority of employers wish to comply voluntarily with the ADA, and will do so if guidance and technical assistance are provided.

To obtain additional single copies of this Manual or other ADA informational materials, call EEOC at 1-800-669-EEOC (voice) or 1-800-800-3302 (TDD) or write to EEOC Office of Communications and Legislative Affairs, 1801 L Street N.W., Washington, D.C. 20507. Copies of these materials also are available in braille, large print, audiotape, and electronic file on computer disk. To obtain copies in an accessible format, call the EEOC Office of Equal Employment Opportunity at (202) 663-4395 or (202) 663-4398 (voice); (202) 663-4399 (TDD) or write this office at the address above.

HOW TO USE THIS MANUAL

The information in this Manual is presented in an order designed to explain the ADA's basic employment nondiscrimination requirements. The first three chapters provide an overview of Title I legal requirements and discuss in detail the basic requirement not to discriminate against a "qualified individual with a disability," including the requirement for reasonable accommodation. The following chapters apply these legal requirements to specific employment practices and activities. Readers familiar with Title I legal requirements may wish to go directly to chapters that address specific practices. However, in many cases, these chapters refer back to the earlier sections to fully explain the requirements that apply.

The following summary of Manual chapters may be helpful in locating specific types of information.

Chapter I.   Provides a summary of Title I legal requirements with cross-references to the chapters where these requirements are discussed.

Chapter II.   Looks at the definitions of "an individual with a disability" and a "qualified individual with a disability," drawing upon guidance set out in EEOC's Title I regulation and interpretive appendix. These definitions are important, because an individual is only protected by the ADA if s/he meets both definitions. In addition, the second definition incorporates the ADA's basic employment nondiscrimination requirement, by defining a "qualified" individual as a person who can "perform the essential functions of a job . . . with or without reasonable accommodation." Chapter II also provides practical guidance on identifying "essential" job functions.

Chapter III.   Provides guidance on the obligation to make a "reasonable accommodation," including why reasonable accommodation is necessary for nondiscrimination and what is required. This chapter also provides many examples of reasonable accommodations for people with different types of disabilities in different jobs. The following chapters provide further guidance on making reasonable accommodations in the employment practices described in those chapters.

iii

Chapter IV. Explains how to establish qualification standards and selection criteria that do not discriminate under the ADA, including standards necessary to assure health and safety in the workplace.

Chapter V. Provides guidance on nondiscrimination in recruitment and selection, including important ADA requirements regarding pre-employment inquiries. Among other issues, this chapter discusses nondiscrimination in advertising, recruiting, application forms, and the overall application process, including interviews and testing.

Chapter VI. Discusses ADA requirements applicable to medical examinations and medical inquiries, including the different requirements that apply before making a job offer, after making a conditional job offer, and after an individual is employed.

Chapter VII. Discusses and illustrates the obligation to apply ADA nondiscrimination requirements to all other employment practices and activities, and to all terms, conditions, and benefits of employment. In particular, the chapter looks at the application of ADA requirements to promotion and advancement opportunities, training, evaluation, and employee benefits such as insurance. The chapter also discusses the ADA's prohibition of discrimination on the basis of a "relationship or association with a person with a disability."

Chapter VII. Discusses ADA requirements related to employment policies regarding drug and alcohol abuse.

Chapter IX. Provides further guidance on ADA requirements as they relate to workers' compensation practices.

Chapter X. Describes the enforcement provisions of the ADA and how they will be applied by EEOC.

I. TITLE I: AN OVERVIEW OF LEGAL REQUIREMENTS

This chapter of the manual provides a brief overview of the basic requirements of Title I of the ADA. Following chapters look at these and other requirements in more detail and illustrate how they apply to specific employment practices.

Who Must Comply with Title I of the ADA?

Private employers, state and local governments, employment agencies, labor unions, and joint labor-management committees must comply with Title I of the ADA. The ADA calls these 'covered entities." For simplicity, this manual generally refers to all covered entities as "employers," except where there is a specific reason to emphasize the responsibilities of a particular type of entity.

An employer cannot discriminate against qualified applicants and employees on the basis of disability. The ADA's requirements ultimately will apply to employers with 15 or more employees. To give smaller employers more time to prepare for compliance, coverage is phased in two steps as follows:

Number of employees	Coverage begins
25 or more	July 26, 1992
15 or more	July 26, 1994

Covered employers are those who have 25 or more employees (1992) or 15 or more employees (1994), including part-time employees, working for them for 20 or more calendar weeks in the current or preceding calendar year. The ADA's definition of "employee" includes U.S. citizens who work for American companies, their subsidiaries, or firms controlled by Americans outside the USA. However, the Act provides an exemption from coverage for any action in compliance with the ADA which would violate the law of the foreign country in which a workplace is located.

(Note that state and local governments, regardless of size, are covered by employment nondiscrimination requirements under Title II of the ADA as of January 26, 1992. See Coordination of Overlapping Federal Requirements below.)

The definition of "employer" includes persons who are "agents" of the employer, such as managers, supervisors, foremen, or others who act for the employer, such as agencies used to conduct background checks on candidates. Therefore, the employer is responsible for actions of such persons that may violate the law. These coverage requirements are similar to those of Title VII of the Civil Rights Act of 1964.

Special Situations

Religious organizations are covered by the ADA, but they may give employment preference to people of their own religion or religious organization.

> For example: A church organization could require that its employees b members of its religion. However, it could not discriminate in employment on the basis of disability against members of its religion.

The legislative branch of the U.S. Government is covered by the ADA, but i governed by different enforcement procedures established by the Congress for its employees.

Certain individuals appointed by elected officials of state and local governments also are covered by the special enforcement procedures established for Congressional employees.

Who Is Exempt?

Executive agencies of the U.S. Government are exempt from the ADA, but these agencies are covered by similar nondiscrimination requirements and additional affirmative employment requirements under Section 501 of the Rehabilitation Act of 1973. Also exempted from the ADA (as they are from Title VII of the Civil Rights Act) are corporations fully owned by the U.S. Government, Indian tribes, and bona fide private membership clubs that are not labor organizations and that are exempt from taxation under the Internal Revenue Code.

Who Is Protected by Title I?

The ADA prohibits employment discrimination against "qualified individuals with disabilities." A qualified individual with a disability is:

> an individual with a disability who meets the skill, experience, education, and other job-related requirements of a position held or desired, and who, with or without reasonable accommodation, can perform the essential functions of a job.

To understand who is and who is not protected by the ADA, it is first necessary to understand the Act's definition of an "individual with a disability" and then determine if the individual meets the Act's definition of a "qualified individual with a disability."

The ADA definition of individual with a disability is very specific. A person with a "disability" is an individual who:

- has a physical or mental impairment that substantially limits one or more of his/her major life activities;

- has a record of such an impairment; or

- is regarded as having such an impairment.

(See Chapter II.)

Individuals Specifically not Protected by the ADA

The ADA specifically states that certain individuals are not protected by its provisions:

Persons who currently use drugs illegally

Individuals who currently use drugs illegally are not individuals with disabilities protected under the Act when an employer takes action because of their continued use of drugs. This includes people who use prescription drugs illegally as well as those who use illegal drugs.

However, people who have been rehabilitated and do not currently use drugs illegally, or who are in the process of completing a rehabilitation program may be protected by the ADA. (See Chapter VIII.)

Other specific exclusions

The Act states that homosexuality and bisexuality are not impairments and therefore are not disabilities under the ADA. In addition, the Act specifically excludes a number of behavior disorders from the definition of "individual with a disability." (See Chapter II.)

Employment Practices Regulated by Title I of the ADA

Employers cannot discriminate against people with disabilities in regard to any employment practices or terms, conditions, and privileges of employment. This prohibition covers all aspects of the employment process, including:

- application
- testing
- hiring
- assignments
- evaluation
- disciplinary actions
- training

- promotion
- medical examinations
- layoff/recall
- termination
- compensation
- leave
- benefits

Actions which Constitute Discrimination

The ADA specifies types of actions that may constitute discrimination. These actions are discussed more fully in the following chapters, as indicated:

1) Limiting, segregating, or classifying a job applicant or employee in a way that adversely affects employment opportunities for the applicant or employee because of his or her disability. (See Chapter VII.)

2) Participating in a contractual or other arrangement or relationship that subjects an employer's qualified applicant or employee with a disability to discrimination. (See Chapter VII.)

3) Denying employment opportunities to a qualified individual because s/he has a relationship or association with a person with a disability. (See Chapter VII.)

4) Refusing to make reasonable accommodation to the known physical or mental limitations of a qualified applicant or employee with a disability, unless the accommodation would pose an undue hardship on the business. (See Chapters III. and VII.)

5) Using qualification standards, employment tests, or other selection criteria that screen out or tend to screen out an individual with a disability unless they are job-related and necessary for the business. (See Chapter IV.)

6)   Failing to use employment tests in the most effective manner to measure actual abilities. Tests must accurately reflect the skills, aptitude, or other factors being measured, and not the impaired sensory, manual, or speaking skills of an employee or applicant with a disability (unless those are the skills the test is designed to measure). (See Chapter V.)

7)   Denying an employment opportunity to a qualified individual because s/he has a relationship or association with an individual with a disability. (See Chapter VII.)

8)   Discriminating against an individual because s/he has opposed an employment practice of the employer or filed a complaint, testified, assisted, or participated in an investigation, proceeding, or hearing to enforce provisions of the Act. (See Chapter X.)

Reasonable Accommodation and the Undue Hardship Limitation

Reasonable accommodation

Reasonable accommodation is a critical component of the ADA's assurance of nondiscrimination. Reasonable accommodation is any change in the work environment or in the way things are usually done that results in equal employment opportunity for an individual with a disability.

An employer must make a reasonable accommodation to the known physical or mental limitations of a qualified applicant or employee with a disability unless it can show that the accommodation would cause an undue hardship on the operation of its business.

Some examples of reasonable accommodation include:

- making existing facilities used by employees readily accessible to, and usable by, an individual with a disability;

- job restructuring;

- modifying work schedules;

- reassignment to a vacant position;

- acquiring or modifying equipment or devices;

- adjusting or modifying examinations, training materials, or policies;

- providing qualified readers or interpreters.

An employer is not required to lower quality or quantity standards to make an accommodation. Nor is an employer obligated to provide personal use items, such as glasses or hearing aids, as accommodations.

Undue hardship

An employer is not required to provide an accommodation if it will impose an undue hardship on the operation of its business. **Undue hardship** is defined by the ADA as an action that is:

> **"excessively costly, extensive, substantial, or disruptive, or that would fundamentally alter the nature or operation of the business."**

In determining undue hardship, factors to be considered include the nature and cost of the accommodation in relation to the size, the financial resources, the nature and structure of the employer's operation, as well as the impact of the accommodation on the specific facility providing the accommodation. (See Chapter III.)

Health or Safety Defense

An employer may require that an individual not pose a "direct threat" to the health or safety of himself/herself or others. A health or safety risk can only be considered if it is "a significant risk of substantial harm." Employers cannot deny an employment opportunity merely because of a slightly increased risk. An assessment of "direct threat" must be strictly based on valid medical analyses and/or other objective evidence, and not on speculation. Like any qualification standard, this requirement must apply to all applicants and employees, not just to people with disabilities.

If an individual appears to pose a direct threat because of a disability, the employer must first try to eliminate or reduce the risk to an acceptable level with reasonable accommodation. If an effective accommodation cannot be found, the employer may refuse to hire an applicant or discharge an employee who poses a direct threat. (See Chapter IV.)

Pre-employment Inquiries and Medical Examinations

An employer may not ask a job applicant about the existence, nature, or severity of a disability. Applicants may be asked about their ability to perform specific job functions. An employer may not make medical inquiries or conduct a medical examination until after a job offer has been made. A job offer may be conditioned on the results of a medical examination or inquiry,

I-6

but only if this is required for all entering employees in similar jobs. Medical examinations of **employees** must be job-related and consistent with the employer's business needs. (See Chapters V. and VI.)

Drug and Alcohol Use

It is not a violation of the ADA for employers to use drug tests to find out if applicants or employees are currently illegally using drugs. Tests for illegal use of drugs are not subject to the ADA's restrictions on medical examinations. Employers may hold illegal users of drugs and alcoholics to the same performance and conduct standards as other employees. (See Chapter VIII.)

Enforcement and Remedies

The U.S. Equal Employment Opportunity Commission (EEOC) has responsibility for enforcing compliance with Title I of the ADA. An individual with a disability who believes that (s)he has been discriminated against in employment can file a charge with EEOC. The procedures for processing charges of discrimination under the ADA are the same as those under Title VII of the Civil Rights Act of 1964. (See Chapter X.)

Remedies that may be required of an employer who is found to have discriminated against an applicant or employee with a disability include compensatory and punitive damages, back pay, front pay, restored benefits, attorney's fees, reasonable accommodation, reinstatement, and job offers. (See Chapter X.)

Posting Notices

An employer must post notices concerning the provisions of the ADA. The notices must be accessible, as needed, to persons with visual or other reading disabilities. A new equal employment opportunity (EEO) poster, containing ADA provisions and other federal employment nondiscrimination provisions may be obtained by writing EEOC at 1801 L Street N.W., Washington, D.C., 20507, or calling 1-800-669-EEOC or 1-800-800-3302 (TDD).

I-7

Coordination of Overlapping Federal Requirements

Employers covered by Title I of the ADA also may be covered by other federal requirements that prohibit discrimination on the basis of disability. The ADA directs the agencies with enforcement authority for these legal requirements to coordinate their activities to prevent duplication and avoid conflicting standards. Overlapping requirements exist for both public and private employers.

Title II of the ADA, enforced by the U.S. Department of Justice, prohibits discrimination in all **state and local government programs and activities**, including employment, after January 26, 1992.

The Department of Justice regulations implementing Title II provide that EEOC's Title I regulations will constitute the employment nondiscrimination requirements for those state and local governments covered by Title I (governments with 25 or more employees after July 26, 1992; governments with 15 or more employees after July 26, 1994). If a government is not covered by Title I, or until it is covered, the Title II employment nondiscrimination requirements will be those in the Department of Justice coordination regulations applicable to federally assisted programs under Section 504 of the Rehabilitation Act of 1973, which prohibits discrimination on the basis of disability by recipients of federal financial assistance.

Section 504 employment requirements in most respects are the same as those of Title I, because the ADA was based on the Section 504 regulatory requirements. (Note that governments receiving federal financial assistance, as well as federally funded private entities, will continue to be covered by Section 504.)

In addition, some **private employers** are covered by Section 503 of the Rehabilitation Act. Section 503 requires nondiscrimination and affirmative action by federal contractors and subcontractors to employ and advance individuals with disabilities, and is enforced by the Office of Federal Contract Compliance Programs (OFCCP) in the U.S. Department of Labor.

The EEOC, the Department of Labor, the Department of Justice and the other agencies that enforce Section 504 (i.e., Federal agencies with programs of financial assistance) will coordinate their enforcement efforts under the ADA and the Rehabilitation Act, to assure consistent standards and to eliminate unnecessary duplication. (See Chapter X. For further information see Resource Directory: "Federal Agencies that Enforce Other Laws Prohibiting Discrimination on the Basis of Disability.")

I-8

II. WHO IS PROTECTED BY THE ADA?

INDIVIDUAL WITH A DISABILITY
QUALIFIED INDIVIDUAL WITH A DISABILITY

2.1 Introduction

The ADA protects qualified individuals with disabilities from employment discrimination. Under other laws that prohibit employment discrimination, it usually is a simple matter to know whether an individual is covered because of his or her race, color, sex, national origin or age. But to know whether a person is covered by the employment provisions of the ADA can be more complicated. It is first necessary to understand the Act's very specific definitions of "disability" and "qualified individual with a disability." Like other determinations under the ADA, deciding who is a "qualified" individual is a case-by case process, depending on the circumstances of the particular employment situation.

2.2 Individual With a Disability

The ADA has a three-part definition of "disability." This definition, based on the definition under the Rehabilitation Act, reflects the specific types of discrimination experienced by people with disabilities. Accordingly, it is not the same as the definition of disability in other laws, such as state workers' compensation laws or other federal or state laws that provide benefits for people with disabilities and disabled veterans.

Under the ADA, an <u>individual with a disability</u> is a person who has:

- a physical or mental **impairment** that **substantially limits** one or more **major life activities**;

- a **record** of such an impairment; or

- is **regarded as** having such an impairment.

2.1(a) An Impairment that Substantially Limits Major Life Activities

The first part of this definition has three major subparts that further define who is and who is not protected by the ADA.

(i)   **A Physical or Mental Impairment**

A physical impairment is defined by the ADA as:

> "[a]ny physiological disorder, or condition, cosmetic
> disfigurement, or anatomical loss affecting one or more of
> the following body systems: neurological, musculoskeletal,
> special sense organs, respiratory (including speech organs),
> cardiovascular, reproductive, digestive, genito-urinary,
> hemic and lymphatic, skin, and endocrine."

A mental impairment is defined by the ADA as:

> "[a]ny mental or psychological disorder, such as mental
> retardation, organic brain syndrome, emotional or mental
> illness, and specific learning disabilities."

Neither the statute nor EEOC regulations list all diseases or
conditions that make up "physical or mental impairments,"
because it would be impossible to provide a comprehensive list,
given the variety of possible impairments.

A person's impairment is determined without regard to any
medication or assistive device that s/he may use.

> **For example**: A person who has epilepsy and uses
> medication to control seizures, or a person who walks with
> an artificial leg would be considered to have an
> impairment, even if the medicine or prosthesis reduces the
> impact of that impairment.

An impairment under the ADA is a physiological or mental
disorder; simple physical characteristics, therefore, such as eye
or hair color, lefthandedness, or height or weight within a
normal range, are not impairments. A physical condition that
is not the result of a physiological disorder, such as pregnancy,
or a predisposition to a certain disease would not be an
impairment. Similarly, personality traits such as poor
judgment, quick temper or irresponsible behavior, are not
themselves impairments. Environmental, cultural, or economic
disadvantages, such as lack of education or a prison record also
are not impairments.

> **For example**: A person who cannot read due to dyslexia
> is an individual with a disability because dyslexia, which
> is a learning disability, is an impairment. But a person
> who cannot read because she dropped out of school is not

II-2

an individual with a disability, because lack of education is not an impairment.

"Stress" and "depression" are conditions that may or may not be considered impairments, depending on whether these conditions result from a documented physiological or mental disorder.

> **For example**: A person suffering from general "stress" because of job or personal life pressures would not be considered to have an impairment. However, if this person is diagnosed by a psychiatrist as having an identifiable stress disorder, s/he would have an impairment that may be a disability.

A person who has a contagious disease has an impairment. For example, infection with the Human Immunodeficiency Virus (HIV) is an impairment. The Supreme Court has ruled that an individual with tuberculosis which affected her respiratory system had an impairment under Section 504 of the Rehabilitation Act*. However, although a person who has a contagious disease may be covered by the ADA, an employer would not have to hire or retain a person whose contagious disease posed a direct threat to health or safety, if no reasonable accommodation could reduce or eliminate this threat. (See <u>Health and Safety Standards</u>, Chapter IV.)

(ii)   Major Life Activities

To be a disability covered by the ADA, an impairment must substantially limit one or more **major life activities**. These are activities that an average person can perform with little or no difficulty. Examples are:

• **walking**	• **seeing**
• **speaking**	• **hearing**
• **breathing**	• **learning**
• **performing manual tasks**	• **caring for oneself**
	• **working**

These are examples only. Other activities such as sitting, standing, lifting, or reading are also major life activities.

<u>School Board of Nassau Cty. v. Arline</u>, 480 U.S. 273 (1987).

II-3

(iii) Substantially Limits

An impairment is only a "disability" under the ADA if it
substantially limits one or more major life activities. An
individual must be unable to perform, or be significantly limited
in the ability to perform, an activity compared to an average
person in the general population.

The regulations provide three factors to consider in determining
whether a person's impairment substantially limits a major life
activity.

- **its nature and severity;**

- **how long it will last or is expected to last;**

- **its permanent or long term impact, or expected
  impact.**

These factors must be considered because, generally, it is not
the name of an impairment or a condition that determines
whether a person is protected by the ADA, but rather the
effect of an impairment or condition on the life of a particular
person. Some impairments, such as blindness, deafness, HIV
infection or AIDS, are by their nature substantially limiting,
but many other impairments may be disabling for some
individuals but not for others, depending on the impact on their
activities.

> **For example:** Although cerebral palsy frequently
> significantly restricts major life activities such as speaking,
> walking and performing manual tasks, an individual with
> very mild cerebral palsy that only slightly interferes with
> his ability to speak and has no significant impact on other
> major life activities is not an individual with a disability
> under this part of the definition.

The determination as to whether an individual is substantially
limited must always be based on the effect of an impairment on
that individual's life activities.

> **For example:** An individual who had been employed as a
> receptionist-clerk sustained a back injury that resulted in
> considerable pain. The pain permanently restricted her
> ability to walk, sit, stand, drive, care for her home, and
> engage in recreational activities. Another individual who
> had been employed as a general laborer had sustained a

back injury, but was able to continue an active life, including recreational sports, and had obtained a new position as a security guard. The first individual was found by a court to be an individual with a disability; the second individual was found not significantly restricted in any major life activity, and therefore not an individual with a disability.

Sometimes, an individual may have two or more impairments, neither of which by itself substantially limits a major life activity, but that together have this effect. In such a situation, the individual has a disability.

> **For example**: A person has a mild form of arthritis in her wrists and hands and a mild form of osteoporosis. Neither impairment by itself substantially limits a major life activity. Together, however, these impairments significantly restrict her ability to lift and perform manual tasks. She has a disability under the ADA.

Temporary Impairments

Employers frequently ask whether "temporary disabilities" are covered by the ADA. How long an impairment lasts is a factor to be considered, but does not by itself determine whether a person has a disability under the ADA. The basic question is whether an impairment "substantially limits" one or more major life activities. This question is answered by looking at the extent, duration, and impact of the impairment. Temporary, non-chronic impairments that do not last for a long time and that have little or no long term impact usually are not disabilities.

> **For example**: Broken limbs, sprains, concussions, appendicitis, common colds, or influenza generally would not be disabilities. A broken leg that heals normally within a few months, for example, would not be a disability under the ADA. However, if a broken leg took significantly longer than the normal healing period to heal, and during this period the individual could not walk, s/he would be considered to have a disability. Or, if the leg did not heal properly, and resulted in a permanent impairment that significantly restricted walking or other major life activities, s/he would be considered to have a disability.

Substantially Limited in Working

It is not necessary to consider if a person is substantially limited in the major life activity of "working" if the person is substantially limited in any other major life activity.

> **For example**: If a person is substantially limited in seeing, hearing, or walking, there is no need to consider whether the person is also substantially limited in working.

In general, a person will not be considered to be substantially limited in working if s/he is substantially limited in performing only a **particular** job for one employer, or unable to perform a very specialized job in a particular field.

> **For example**: A person who cannot qualify as a commercial airline pilot because of a minor vision impairment, but who could qualify as a co-pilot or a pilot for a courier service, would not be considered substantially limited in working just because he could not perform a particular job. Similarly, a baseball pitcher who develops a bad elbow and can no longer pitch would not be substantially limited in working because he could no longer perform the specialized job of pitching in baseball.

But a person need not be totally unable to work in order to be considered substantially limited in working. The person must be significantly restricted in the ability to perform either a class of jobs or a broad range of jobs in various classes, compared to an average person with similar training, skills, and abilities.

The regulations provide factors to help determine whether a person is substantially limited in working. These include:

• the **type of job** from which the individual has been disqualified because of the impairment;

• the **geographical area** in which the person may reasonably expect to find a job;

• the **number and types of jobs using similar training, knowledge, skill, or abilities** from which the individual is disqualified within the geographical area, and/or

II-6

- the **number and types of other jobs in the area that do not involve similar training, knowledge, skill, or abilities** from which the individual also is disqualified because of the impairment.

> **For example**: A person would be considered significantly restricted in a "class of jobs" if a back condition prevents him from working in any heavy labor job. A person would be considered significantly limited in the ability to perform "a broad range of jobs in various classes" if she has an allergy to a substance found in most high-rise office buildings in the geographic area in which she could reasonably seek work, and the allergy caused extreme difficulty in breathing. In this case, she would be substantially limited in the ability to perform the many different kinds of jobs that are performed in high-rise buildings. By contrast, a person who has a severe allergy to a substance in the particular office in which she works, but who is able to work in many other offices that do not contain this substance, would not be significantly restricted in working.

> **For example**: A computer programmer develops a vision impairment that does not substantially limit her ability to see, but because of poor contrast is unable to distinguish print on computer screens. Her impairment prevents her from working as a computer operator, programmer, instructor, or systems analyst. She is substantially limited in working, because her impairment prevents her from working in the class of jobs requiring use of a computer.

In assessing the "number" of jobs from which a person might be excluded by an impairment, the regulations make clear that it is only necessary to indicate an approximate number of jobs from which an individual would be excluded (such as "few," "many," "most"), compared to an average person with similar training, skills and abilities, to show that the individual would be significantly limited in working.

Specific Exclusions

A person **who currently illegally uses drugs is not protected by the ADA**, as an "individual with a disability", when an employer acts on the basis of such use. However, former drug addicts who have been successfully rehabilitated may be protected by the Act. (See Chapter VIII). (See also

II-7

discussion below of a person "regarded as" a drug addict.)

Homosexuality and **bisexuality** are not impairments and therefore are not disabilities covered by the ADA. The Act also states that the term "disability" does not include the following sexual and behavioral disorders:

- transvestism, transsexualism, pedophilia, exhibitionism, voyeurism, gender identity disorders not resulting from physical impairments, or other sexual behavior disorders;

- compulsive gambling, kleptomania, or pyromania; or

- psychoactive substance use disorders resulting from current illegal use of drugs.

The discussion so far has focused on the first part of the definition of an "individual with a disability," which protects people who currently <u>have</u> an impairment that substantially limits a major life activity. The second and third parts of the definition protect people who may or may not actually have such an impairment, but who may be subject to discrimination because they <u>have a record of</u> or are <u>regarded as</u> having such an impairment.

2.2(b)   Record of a Substantially Limiting Condition

This part of the definition protects people who have a history of a disability from discrimination, whether or not they currently are substantially limited in a major life activity.

> **For example**: It protects people with a history of cancer, heart disease, or other debilitating illness, whose illnesses are either cured, controlled or in remission. It also protects people with a history of mental illness.

This part of the definition also protects people who may have been <u>misclassified</u> or <u>misdiagnosed</u> as having a disability.

> **For example**: It protects a person who may at one time have been erroneously classified as having mental retardation or having a learning disability. These people have a record of disability. (If an employer relies on any record [such as an educational, medical or employment record] containing such information to make an adverse employment decision about a person who currently is qualified to perform a job, the action is

subject to challenge as a discriminatory practice.)

Other examples of individuals who have a record of disability, and of potential violations of the ADA if an employer relies on such a record to make an adverse employment decision:

- A job applicant formerly was a patient at a state institution. When very young she was misdiagnosed as being psychopathic and this misdiagnosis was never removed from her records. If this person is otherwise qualified for a job, and an employer does not hire her based on this record, the employer has violated the ADA.

- A person who has a learning disability applies for a job as secretary/receptionist. The employer reviews records from a previous employer indicating that he was labeled as "mentally retarded." Even though the person's resume shows that he meets all requirements for the job, the employer does not interview him because he doesn't want to hire a person who has mental retardation. This employer has violated the ADA.

- A job applicant was hospitalized for treatment for cocaine addiction several years ago. He has been successfully rehabilitated and has not engaged in the illegal use of drugs since receiving treatment. This applicant has a record of an impairment that substantially limited his major life activities. If he is qualified to perform a job, it would be discriminatory to reject him based on the record of his former addiction.

In the last example above, the individual was protected by the ADA because his drug **addiction** was an impairment that substantially limited his major life activities. However, if an individual had a record of casual drug use, s/he would not be protected by the ADA, because casual drug use, as opposed to addiction, does not substantially limit a major life activity.

To be protected by the ADA under this part of the definition, a person must have a record of a physical or mental impairment that substantially limits one or more major life activities. A person would not be protected, for example, merely because s/he has a record of being a "disabled veteran," or a record of "disability" under another Federal statute or program unless this person also met the ADA definition of an individual with a record of a disability.

II-9

2.2(c)   Regarded as Substantially Limited

This part of the definition protects people who are <u>not</u> substantially limited in a major life activity from discriminatory actions taken because they are perceived to have such a limitation. Such protection is necessary, because, as the Supreme Court has stated and the Congress has reiterated, "society's myths and fears about disability and disease are as handicapping as are the physical limitations that flow from actual impairments."

The legislative history of the ADA indicates that Congress intended this part of the definition to protect people from a range of discriminatory actions based on "myths, fears and stereotypes" about disability, which occur even when a person does not have a substantially limiting impairment.

An individual may be protected under this part of the definition in three circumstances:

1. The individual may have an impairment which is not substantially limiting, but is <u>treated by</u> the employer <u>as having such an impairment</u>.

    For example: An employee has controlled high blood pressure which does not substantially limit his work activities. If an employer reassigns the individual to a less strenuous job because of unsubstantiated fear that the person would suffer a heart attack if he continues in the present job, the employer has "regarded" this person as disabled.

2. The individual has an impairment that is substantially limiting because of <u>attitudes</u> of others toward the condition.

    For example: An experienced assistant manager of a convenience store who had a prominent facial scar was passed over for promotion to store manager. The owner promoted a less experienced part-time clerk, because he believed that customers and vendors would not want to look at this person. The employer discriminated against her on the basis of disability, because he perceived and treated her as a person with a substantial limitation.

3. The individual may have <u>no</u> impairment at all, but is <u>regarded</u> by an employer as <u>having</u> a <u>substantially limiting impairment</u>.

For example: An employer discharged an employee based on a rumor that the individual had HIV disease. This person did not have any impairment, but was treated as though she had a substantially limiting impairment.

This part of the definition protects people who are "perceived" as having disabilities from employment decisions based on stereotypes, fears, or misconceptions about disability. It applies to decisions based on unsubstantiated concerns about **productivity, safety, insurance, liability, attendance, costs of accommodation, accessibility, workers' compensation costs or acceptance by co-workers and customers.**

Accordingly, if an employer makes an adverse employment decision based on unsubstantiated beliefs or fears that a person's perceived disability will cause problems in areas such as those listed above, and cannot show a legitimate, nondiscriminatory reason for the action, that action would be discriminatory under this part of the definition.

2.3 Qualified Individual with a Disability

To be protected by the ADA, a person must not only be an individual with a disability, but must be qualified. An employer is not required to hire or retain an individual who is not qualified to perform a job. The regulations define a qualified individual with a disability as a person with a disability who:

"satisfies the requisite skill, experience, education and other job-related requirements of the employment position such individual holds or desires, and who, with or without reasonable accommodation, can perform the essential functions of such position."

There are two basic steps in determining whether an individual is "qualified" under the ADA:

(1) Determine if the individual meets necessary prerequisites for the job, such as:

- education;

- work experience;

- training;

II-11

- skills;

- licenses;

- certificates;

- other job-related requirements, such as good judgment or ability to work with other people.

> **For example**: The first step in determining whether an accountant who has cerebral palsy is qualified for a certified public accountant job is to determine if the person is a licensed CPA. If not, s/he is not qualified. Or, if it is a company's policy that all its managers have at least three years' experience working with the company, an individual with a disability who has worked for two years for the company would not be qualified for a managerial position.

This first step is sometimes referred to as determining if an individual with a disability is "otherwise qualified." Note, however, that if an individual meets all job prerequisites except those that s/he cannot meet because of a disability, and alleges discrimination because s/he is "otherwise qualified" for a job, the employer would have to show that the requirement that screened out this person is "job related and consistent with business necessity." (See Chapter IV)

If the individual with a disability meets the necessary job prerequisites:

(2) Determine if the individual can perform the <u>essential functions</u> of the job, <u>with or without reasonable accommodation</u>.

This second step, a key aspect of nondiscrimination under the ADA, has two parts:

- Identifying <u>"essential functions of the job"</u>; and

- Considering whether the person with a disability can perform these functions, unaided or with a "reasonable accommodation."

The ADA requires an employer to focus on the essential functions of a job to determine whether a person with a disability is qualified. This is an important nondiscrimination requirement. Many people with disabilities who can perform essential job functions are denied employment because they cannot do things that are only marginal to the job.

For example: A file clerk position description may state that the person holding the job answers the telephone, but if in fact the basic functions of the job are to file and retrieve written materials, and telephones actually or usually are handled by other employees, a person whose hearing impairment prevents use of a telephone and who is qualified to do the basic file clerk functions should not be considered unqualified for this position.

2.3(a)   Identifying the Essential Functions of a Job

Sometimes it is necessary to identify the essential functions of a job in order to know whether an individual with a disability is "qualified" to do the job. The regulations provide guidance on identifying the essential functions of the job. The first consideration is **whether employees in the position actually are required to perform the function.**

> **For example**: A job announcement or job description for a secretary or receptionist may state that typing is a function of the job. If, in fact, the employer has never or seldom required an employee in that position to type, this could not be considered an essential function.

If a person holding a job does perform a function, the next consideration is **whether removing that function would fundamentally change the job.**

The regulations list several reasons why a function could be considered essential:

1. **The position exists to perform the function.**

   For example:

   - A person is hired to proofread documents. The ability to proofread accurately is an essential function, because this is the reason that this position exists.

   - A company advertises a position for a "floating" supervisor to substitute when regular supervisors on the day, night, and graveyard shifts are absent. The only reason this position exists is to have someone who can work on any of the three shifts in place of an absent supervisor. Therefore, the ability to work at any time of day is an essential function of the job.

II-13

2. **There are a limited number of other employees available to perform the function, or among whom the function can be distributed.**

   This may be a factor because there are only a few other employees, or because of fluctuating demands of a business operation.

   > **For example**: It may be an essential function for a file clerk to answer the telephone if there are only three employees in a very busy office and each employee has to perform many different tasks. Or, a company with a large workforce may have periods of very heavy labor-intensive activity alternating with less active periods. The heavy work flow during peak periods may make performance of each function essential, and limit an employer's flexibility to reassign a particular function.

3. **A function is highly specialized, and the person in the position is hired for special expertise or ability to perform it.**

   > **For example**, A company wishes to expand its business with Japan. For a new sales position, in addition to sales experience, it requires a person who can communicate fluently in the Japanese language. Fluent communication in the Japanese language is an essential function of the job.

The regulation also lists several types of **evidence** to be considered in determining whether a function is essential. This list is not all-inclusive, and factors not on the list may be equally important as evidence. Evidence to be considered includes:

a. The employer's judgment

An employer's judgment as to which functions are essential is important evidence. However, the legislative history of the ADA indicates that Congress did not intend that this should be the only evidence, or that it should be the prevailing evidence. Rather, the employer's judgment is a factor to be considered along with other relevant evidence.

However, the consideration of various kinds of evidence to determine which functions are essential does not mean that an employer will be second-guessed on production standards, setting the quality or quantity of work that must be performed by a person holding a job, or be required to set lower standards for the job.

> **For example**: If an employer requires its typists to be able to accurately type 75 words per minute, the employer is not required to show that such speed and accuracy are "essential" to a job or that less accuracy or speed would not be adequate. Similarly, if a hotel requires its housekeepers to thoroughly clean 16 rooms per day, it does not have to justify this standard as "essential." However, in each case, if a person with a disability is disqualified by such a standard, the employer should be prepared to show that it does in fact require employees to perform at this level, that these are not merely paper requirements and that the standard was not established for a discriminatory reason.

b. A written job description prepared before advertising or interviewing applicants for a job

The ADA does not require an employer to develop or maintain job descriptions. A written job description that is prepared before advertising or interviewing applicants for a job will be considered as evidence along with other relevant factors. However, the job description will not be given greater weight than other relevant evidence.

A written job description may state that an employee performs a certain essential function. The job description will be evidence that the function is essential, but if individuals currently performing the job do not in fact perform this function, or perform it very infrequently, a review of the actual work performed will be more relevant evidence than the job description.

If an employer uses written job descriptions, the ADA does not require that they be limited to a description of essential functions or that "essential functions" be identified. However, if an employer wishes to use a job description as evidence of essential functions, it should in some way identify those functions that the employer believes to be important in accomplishing the purpose of the job.

If an employer uses written job descriptions, they should be reviewed to be sure that they accurately reflect the actual functions of the current job. Job descriptions written years ago frequently are inaccurate.

> **For example**: A written job description may state that an employee reads temperature and pressure gauges and adjusts machine controls to reflect these readings. The job description will be evidence that these functions are essential. However, if this job description is not up-to-date, and in fact temperature and pressure are now determined automatically, the machine is controlled by a computer and the current employee does not perform the stated functions or does so very infrequently, a review of actual work performed will be more relevant evidence of what the job requires.

In identifying an essential function to determine if an individual with a disability is qualified, the employer should focus on the purpose of the function and the result to be accomplished, rather than the manner in which the function presently is performed. An individual with a disability may be qualified to perform the function if an accommodation would enable this person to perform the job in a different way, and the accommodation does not impose an undue hardship. Although it may be essential that a function be performed, frequently it is not essential that it be performed in a particular way.

> **For example**: In a job requiring use of a computer, the essential function is the **ability to access, input, and retrieve information from the computer.** It is not "essential" that a person in this job enter information manually, or visually read the information on the computer screen. Adaptive devices or computer software can enable a person without arms or a person with impaired vision to perform the essential functions of the job.

Similarly, an essential function of a job on a loading dock may be to move heavy packages from the dock to a storage room, rather than to lift and carry packages from the dock to the storage room.

(See also discussion of Job Analysis and Essential Functions of a Job, below).

If the employer intends to use a job description as evidence of essential functions, the job description must be prepared before advertising or interviewing for a job; a job description prepared after an alleged discriminatory action will not be considered as evidence.

c. **The amount of time spent performing the function**

> **For example**: If an employee spends most of the time or a majority of the time operating one machine, this would be evidence that operating this machine was an essential function.

d. **The consequences of not requiring a person in this job to perform a function**

Sometimes a function that is performed infrequently may be essential because there will be serious consequences if it is not performed.

> **For example**:

> - An airline pilot spends only a few minutes of a flight landing a plane, but landing the plane is an essential function because of the very serious consequences if the pilot could not perform this function.

> - A firefighter may only occasionally have to carry a heavy person from a burning building, but being able to perform this function would be essential to the firefighter's job.

> - A clerical worker may spend only a few minutes a day answering the telephones, but this could be an essential function if no one else is available to answer the phones at that time, and business calls would go unanswered.

e. **The terms of a collective bargaining agreement**

Where a collective bargaining agreement lists duties to be performed in particular jobs, the terms of the agreement may provide evidence of essential functions. However, like a position description, the agreement would be considered along with other evidence, such as the actual duties performed by people in these jobs.

f. **Work experience of people who have performed a job in the past and work experience of people who currently perform similar jobs**

The work experience of previous employees in a job and the experience of current employees in similar jobs provide pragmatic evidence of actual duties performed. The employer should consult such employees and observe their work operations to identify

II-17

essential job functions, since the tasks actually performed provide significant evidence of these functions.

g. Other relevant factors

The <u>nature of the work operation</u> and the employer's <u>organizational structure</u> may be factors in determining whether a function is essential.

> **For example**:
>
> - A particular manufacturing facility receives large orders for its product intermittently. These orders must be filled under very tight deadlines. To meet these deadlines, it is necessary that each production worker be able to perform a variety of different tasks with different requirements. All of these tasks are essential functions for a production worker at that facility. However, another facility that receives orders on a continuous basis finds it most efficient to organize an assembly line process, in which each production worker repeatedly performs one major task. At this facility, this single task may be the only essential function of the production worker's job.
>
> - An employer may structure production operations to be carried out by a "team" of workers. Each worker performs a different function, but every worker is required, on a rotating basis, to perform each different function. In this situation, all the functions may be considered to be essential for the job, rather than the function that any one worker performs at a particular time.

Changing Essential Job Functions

The ADA does not limit an employer's ability to establish or change the content, nature, or functions of a job. It is the employer's province to establish what a job is and what functions are required to perform it. The ADA simply requires that an individual with a disability's qualifications for a job are evaluated in relation to its essential functions.

> **For example**: A grocery store may have two different jobs at the checkout stand, one titled, "checkout clerk" and the other "bagger." The essential functions of the checkout clerk are entering the price for each item into a cash register, receiving money, making change, and passing items to the bagger. The essential functions of the bagging job are putting items into bags, giving the bags to the

customer directly or placing them in grocery carts.

For legitimate business reasons, the store management decides to combine the two jobs in a new job called "checker-bagger." In the new job, each employee will have to perform the essential functions of both former jobs. Each employee now must enter prices in a new, faster computer-scanner, put the items in bags, give the bags to the customer or place them in carts. The employee holding this job would have to perform all of these functions. There may be some aspects of each function, however, that are not "essential" to the job, or some possible modification in the way these functions are performed, that would enable a person employed as a "checker" whose disability prevented performance of all the bagging operations to do the new job.

For example: If the checker's disability made it impossible to lift any item over one pound, s/he might not be qualified to perform the essential bagging functions of the new job. But if the disability only precluded lifting items of more than 20 pounds, it might be possible for this person to perform the bagging functions, except for the relatively few instances when items or loaded bags weigh more than 20 pounds. If other employees are available who could help this individual with the few heavy items, perhaps in exchange for some incidental functions that they perform, or if this employee could keep filled bags loads under 20 pounds, then bagging loads over 20 pounds would not be an essential function of the new job.

2.3(b)   Job Analysis and the "Essential Functions" of a Job

The ADA does not require that an employer conduct a job analysis or any particular form of job analysis to identify the essential functions of a job. The information provided by a job analysis may or may not be helpful in properly identifying essential job functions, depending on how it is conducted.

The term "job analysis" generally is used to describe a formal process in which information about a specific job or occupation is collected and analyzed. Formal job analysis may be conducted by a number of different methods. These methods obtain different kinds of information that is used for different purposes. Some of these methods will not provide information sufficient to determine if an individual with a disability is qualified to perform "essential" job functions.

For example: One kind of formal job analysis looks at specific job tasks and classifies jobs according to how these tasks deal with data, people, and objects. This type of job analysis is used to set wage rates for various jobs; however, it may not be adequate to identify the essential functions of a particular job, as required by the ADA. Another kind of job analysis looks at the kinds of knowledge, skills, and abilities that are necessary to perform a job. This type of job analysis is used to develop selection criteria for various jobs. The information from this type of analysis sometimes helps to measure the importance of certain skills, knowledge and abilities, but it does not take into account the fact that people with disabilities often can perform essential functions using other skills and abilities.

Some job analysis methods ask current employees and their supervisors to rate the importance of general characteristics necessary to perform a job, such as "strength," "endurance," or "intelligence," without linking these characteristics to specific job functions or specific tasks that are part of a function. Such general information may not identify, for example, whether upper body or lower body "strength" is required, or whether muscular endurance or cardiovascular "endurance" is needed to perform a particular job function. Such information, by itself, would not be sufficient to determine whether an individual who has particular limitations can perform an essential function with or without an accommodation.

As already stated, the ADA does not require a formal job analysis or any particular method of analysis to identify the essential functions of a job. A small employer may wish to conduct an informal analysis by observing and consulting with people who perform the job or have previously performed it and their supervisors. If possible, it is advisable to observe and consult with several workers under a range of conditions, to get a better idea of all job functions and the different ways they may be performed. Production records and workloads also may be relevant factors to consider.

To identify essential job functions under the ADA, a job analysis should focus on the purpose of the job and the importance of actual job functions in achieving this purpose. Evaluating "importance" may include consideration of the frequency with which a function is performed, the amount of time spent on the function, and the consequences if the function is not performed. The analysis may include information on the work environment (such as unusual heat, cold, humidity, dust, toxic substances or stress factors). The job analysis may contain information on the manner in which a job currently is performed, but should not conclude that ability to

perform the job **in that manner** is an essential function, unless
there is no other way to perform the function without causing undue
hardship. A job analysis will be most helpful for purposes of the
ADA if it focuses on the **results** or **outcome** of a function, not
solely on the way it customarily is performed.

<u>**For example**</u>:

- An essential function of a computer programmer job might be
  described as "ability to develop programs that accomplish
  necessary objectives," rather than "ability to manually write
  programs." Although a person currently performing the job
  may write these programs by hand, that is not the essential
  function, because programs can be developed directly on the
  computer.

- If a job requires mastery of information contained in
  technical manuals, this essential function would be "ability to
  learn technical material," rather than "ability to read
  technical manuals." People with visual and other reading
  impairments could perform this function using other means,
  such as audiotapes.

- A job that requires objects to be moved from one place to
  another should state this essential function. The analysis
  may note that the person in the job "lifts 50 pound cartons
  to a height of 3 or 4 feet and loads them into truck-trailers
  5 hours daily," but should not identify the "ability to
  <u>manually</u> lift and load 50 pound cartons" as an essential
  function unless this is the only method by which the function
  can be performed without causing an undue hardship.

A job analysis that is focused on outcomes or results also will be
helpful in establishing appropriate qualification standards, developing
job descriptions, conducting interviews, and selecting people in
accordance with ADA requirements. It will be particularly useful in
helping to identify accommodations that will enable an individual
with specific functional abilities and limitations to perform the job.
(See Chapter III.)

**.3(c) Perform Essential Functions "With or Without Reasonable
Accommodation"**

Many individuals with disabilities are qualified to perform the
essential functions of jobs without need of any accommodation.
However, if an individual with a disability who is otherwise qualified

II-21

cannot perform one or more essential job functions because of his or her disability, the employer, in assessing whether the person is qualified to do the job, must consider whether there are modifications or adjustments that would enable the person to perform these functions. Such modifications or adjustments are called "**reasonable accommodations.**"

Reasonable accommodation is a key nondiscrimination requirement under the ADA. An employer must first consider reasonable accommodation in determining whether an individual with a disability is qualified; reasonable accommodation also must be considered when making many other employment decisions regarding people with disabilities. The following chapter discusses the employer's obligation to provide reasonable accommodation and the limits to that obligation. The chapter also provides examples of reasonable accommodations.

III. THE REASONABLE ACCOMMODATION OBLIGATION

3.1 Overview of Legal Obligations

- An employer must provide a reasonable accommodation to the known physical or mental limitations of a qualified applicant or employee with a disability unless it can show that the accommodation would impose an undue hardship on the business.

- Reasonable accommodation is any modification or adjustment to a job, an employment practice, or the work environment that makes it possible for an individual with a disability to enjoy an equal employment opportunity.

- The obligation to provide a reasonable accommodation applies to all aspects of employment. This duty is ongoing and may arise any time that a person's disability or job changes.

- An employer cannot deny an employment opportunity to a qualified applicant or employee because of the need to provide reasonable accommodation, unless it would cause an undue hardship.

- An employer does not have to make an accommodation for an individual who is not otherwise qualified for a position.

- Generally, it is the obligation of an individual with a disability to request a reasonable accommodation.

- A qualified individual with a disability has the right to refuse an accommodation. However, if the individual cannot perform the essential functions of the job without the accommodation, s/he may not be qualified for the job.

- If the cost of an accommodation would impose an undue hardship on the employer, the individual with a disability should be given the option of providing the accommodation or paying that portion of the cost which would constitute an undue hardship.

3.2 Why Is a Reasonable Accommodation Necessary?

Reasonable accommodation is a key nondiscrimination requirement of the ADA because of the special nature of discrimination faced by people with disabilities. Many people with disabilities can perform jobs without any need for accommodations. But many others are excluded from jobs that they are qualified to perform because of unnecessary barriers in the workplace and the work environment. The ADA recognizes that such barriers may discriminate against qualified people with disabilities just as much as overt exclusionary practices. For this reason, the ADA requires **reasonable accommodation** as a means of overcoming unnecessary barriers that prevent or restrict employment opportunities for otherwise qualified individuals with disabilities.

People with disabilities are restricted in employment opportunities by many different kinds of barriers. Some face physical barriers that make it difficult to get into and around a work site or to use necessary work equipment. Some are excluded or limited by the way people communicate with each other. Others are excluded because of rigid work schedules that allow no flexibility for people with special needs caused by disability. Many are excluded only by barriers in other people's minds; these include unfounded fears, stereotypes, presumptions, and misconceptions about job performance, safety, absenteeism, costs, or acceptance by co-workers and customers.

Under the ADA, when an individual with a disability is qualified to perform the essential functions of a job except for functions that cannot be performed because of related limitations and existing job barriers, an employer must try to find a reasonable accommodation that would enable this person to perform these functions. The reasonable accommodation should reduce or eliminate unnecessary barriers between the individual's abilities and the requirements for performing the essential job functions.

3.3   What Is a Reasonable Accommodation?

Reasonable accommodation is a modification or adjustment to a job, the work environment, or the way things usually are done that enables a qualified individual with a disability to enjoy an equal employment opportunity. An equal employment opportunity means an opportunity to attain the same level of performance or to enjoy equal benefits and privileges of employment as are available to a similarly-situated employee without a disability. The ADA requires reasonable accommodation in three aspects of employment:

- **to ensure equal opportunity in the application process;**

- **to enable a qualified individual with a disability to perform the essential functions of a job; and**

- **to enable an employee with a disability to enjoy equal benefits and privileges of employment.**

Reasonable Accommodation in the Application Process

Reasonable accommodation must be provided in the job application process to enable a qualified applicant to have an equal opportunity to be considered for a job.

> **For example**: A person who uses a wheelchair may need an accommodation if an employment office or interview site is not accessible. A person with a visual disability or a person who lacks manual dexterity may need assistance in filling out an application form. Without such accommodations, these individuals may have no opportunity to be considered for a job.
>
> (See Chapter V. for further discussion of accommodations in the application process).

Accommodations to Perform the Essential Functions of a Job

Reasonable accommodation must be provided to enable a qualified applicant to perform the essential functions of the job s/he is seeking, and to enable a qualified employee with a disability to perform the essential functions of a job currently held. Modifications or adjustments may be required in the work environment, in the manner or circumstances in which the job customarily is performed, or in employment policies. Many accommodations of this nature are discussed later in this chapter.

Accommodations to Ensure Equal Benefits of Employment

Reasonable accommodations must be provided to enable an employee with a disability to enjoy benefits and privileges of employment equal to those enjoyed by similarly situated nondisabled employees.

> **For example**: Employees with disabilities must have equal access to lunchrooms, employee lounges, rest rooms, meeting rooms, and other employer-provided or sponsored services such as health programs, transportation, and social events.
> (See Chapter VII for further discussion of this requirement).

3.4   Some Basic Principles of Reasonable Accommodation

A reasonable accommodation must be an effective accommodation. It must provide an opportunity for a person with a disability to achieve the

III-3

same level of performance or to enjoy benefits or privileges equal to those of a similarly-situated nondisabled person. However, the accommodation does not have to ensure equal results or provide exactly the same benefits or privileges.

> **For example**: An employer provides an employee lunchroom with food and beverages on the second floor of a building that has no elevator. If it would be an undue hardship to install an elevator for an employee who uses a wheelchair, the employer must provide a comparable facility on the first floor. The facility does not have to be exactly the same as that on the second floor, but must provide food, beverages and space for the disabled employee to eat with co-workers. It would not be a reasonable accommodation merely to provide a place for this employee to eat by himself. Nor would it be a reasonable accommodation to provide a separate facility for the employee if access to the common facility could be provided without undue hardship. For example, if the lunchroom was only several steps up, a portable ramp could provide access.

The reasonable accommodation obligation applies only to accommodations that reduce barriers to employment related to a person's disability; it does not apply to accommodations that a disabled person may request for some other reason.

> **For example**: Reassignment is one type of accommodation that may be required under the ADA. If an employee whose job requires driving loses her sight, reassignment to a vacant position that does not require driving would be a reasonable accommodation, if the employee is qualified for that position with or without an accommodation. However, if a blind computer operator working at an employer's Michigan facility requested reassignment to a facility in Florida because he prefers to work in a warmer climate, this would not be a reasonable accommodation required by the ADA. In the second case, the accommodation is not needed **because of** the employee's disability.

A reasonable accommodation need not be the best accommodation available, as long as it is effective for the purpose; that is, it gives the person with a disability an equal opportunity to be considered for a job, to perform the essential functions of the job, or to enjoy equal benefits and privileges of the job.

> **For example**: An employer would not have to hire a full-time reader for a blind employee if a co-worker is available as a part-time reader when needed, and this will enable the blind employee to perform his job duties effectively.

III-4

An employer is not required to provide an accommodation that is primarily for personal use. Reasonable accommodation applies to modifications that specifically assist an individual in performing the duties of a particular job. Equipment or devices that assist a person in daily activities on and off the job are considered personal items that an employer is not required to provide. However, in some cases, equipment that otherwise would be considered "personal" may be required as an accommodation if it is specifically designed or required to meet job-related rather than personal needs.

> **For example**: An employer generally would not be required to provide personal items such as eyeglasses, a wheelchair, or an artificial limb. However, the employer might be required to provide a person who has a visual impairment with glasses that are specifically needed to use a computer monitor. Or, if deep pile carpeting in a work area makes it impossible for an individual to use a manual wheelchair, the employer may need to replace the carpet, place a usable surface over the carpet in areas used by the employee, or provide a motorized wheelchair.

The ADA's requirements for certain types of adjustments and modifications to meet the reasonable accommodation obligation do not prevent an employer from providing accommodations beyond those required by the ADA.

> **For example**: "Supported employment" programs may provide free job coaches and other assistance to enable certain individuals with severe disabilities to learn and/or to progress in jobs. These programs typically require a range of modifications and adjustments to customary employment practices. Some of these modifications may also be required by the ADA as reasonable accommodations. However, supported employment programs may require modifications beyond those **required** under the ADA, such as restructuring of essential job functions. Many employers have found that supported employment programs are an excellent source of reliable productive new employees. Participation in these programs advances the underlying goal of the ADA - - to increase employment opportunities for people with disabilities. Making modifications for supported employment beyond those required by the ADA in no way violates the ADA.

Some Examples of Reasonable Accommodation

The statute and EEOC's regulations provide examples of common types of reasonable accommodation that an employer may be required to provide, but many other accommodations may be appropriate for particular situations. Accommodations may include:

- making facilities readily accessible to and usable by an individual with a disability;

- restructuring a job by reallocating or redistributing marginal job functions;

- altering when or how an essential job function is performed;

- part-time or modified work schedules;

- obtaining or modifying equipment or devices;

- modifying examinations, training materials or policies;

- providing qualified readers and interpreters;

- reassignment to a vacant position;

- permitting use of accrued paid leave or unpaid leave for necessary treatment;

- providing reserved parking for a person with a mobility impairment;

- allowing an employee to provide equipment or devices that an employer is not required to provide.

These and other types of reasonable accommodation are discussed in the pages that follow. However, the examples in this Manual cannot cover the range of potential accommodations, because every reasonable accommodation must be determined on an individual basis. A reasonable accommodation always must take into consideration two unique factors:

- the specific abilities and functional limitations of a particular applicant or employee with a disability; and

- the specific functional requirements of a particular job.

III-6

In considering an accommodation, the focus should be on the abilities and limitations of the **individual**, not on the name of a disability or a particular physical or mental condition. This is necessary because people who have any particular disability may have very different abilities and limitations. Conversely, people with different kinds of disabilities may have similar functional limitations.

> **For example**: If it is an essential function of a job to press a foot pedal a certain number of times a minute and an individual with a disability applying for the job has some limitation that makes this difficult or impossible, the accommodation process should focus on ways that <u>this person</u> might be able to do the job function, not on the nature of her disability or on how persons with this kind of disability generally might be able to perform the job.

3.6 Who Is Entitled to a Reasonable Accommodation?

As detailed in Chapter II, an individual is entitled to a reasonable accommodation if s/he:

> **meets the ADA definition of "a qualified individual with a disability" (meets all prerequisites for performing the essential functions of a job [being considered for a job or enjoying equal benefits and privileges of a job] except any that cannot be met because of a disability).**

If there is a reasonable accommodation that will enable this person to perform the essential functions of a job (be considered, or receive equal benefits, etc.), the employer is obligated to provide it, unless it would impose an undue hardship on the operation of the business.

When is an Employer Obligated to Make a Reasonable Accommodation?

An employer is obligated to make an accommodation only to the <u>known</u> limitations of an otherwise qualified individual with a disability. In general, it is the responsibility of the applicant or employee with a disability to inform the employer that an accommodation is needed to participate in the application process, to perform essential job functions or to receive equal benefits and privileges of employment. An employer is not required to provide an accommodation if unaware of the need.

However, the employer is responsible for **notifying** job applicants and employees of its obligation to provide accommodations for otherwise qualified individuals with disabilities.

The ADA requires an employer to **post notices** containing the provisions of the ADA, including the reasonable accommodation obligation, in conspicuous places on its premises. Such notices should be posted in employment offices and other places where applicants and employees can readily see them. EEOC provides posters for this purpose. (See Chapter I for additional information on the required notice.)

Information about the reasonable accommodation obligation also can be included in job application forms, job vacancy notices, and in personnel manuals, and may be communicated orally.

An applicant or employee does not have to specifically request a "reasonable accommodation," but must only let the employer know that some adjustment or change is needed to do a job because of the limitations caused by a disability.

If a job applicant or employee has a "hidden" disability - - one that is not obvious - - it is up to that individual to make the need for an accommodation known. If an applicant has a known disability, such as a visible disability, that appears to limit, interfere with, or prevent the individual from performing job-related functions, the employer may ask the applicant to describe or demonstrate how s/he would perform the function with or without a reasonable accommodation. Chapter V provides guidance on how to make such an inquiry without violating the ADA prohibition against pre-employment inquiries in the application and interview process.

If an employee with a known disability is not performing well or is having difficulty in performing a job, the employer should assess whether this is due to a disability. The employer may inquire at any time whether the employee needs an accommodation.

Documentation of Need for Accommodation

If an applicant or employee requests an accommodation and the need for the accommodation is not obvious, or if the employer does not believe that the accommodation is needed, the employer may request documentation of the individual's functional limitations to support the request.

> **For example**: An employer may ask for written documentation from a doctor, psychologist, rehabilitation counselor, occupational or physical therapist, independent living specialist, or other professional with knowledge of the person's functional limitations. Such documentation might indicate, for example, that this person cannot lift more than 15 pounds without assistance.

III-8

3.7 How Does an Employer Determine What Is a Reasonable Accommodation?

When a qualified individual with a disability requests an accommodation, the employer must make a reasonable effort to provide an accommodation that is <u>effective for the individual</u> (gives the individual an equally effective opportunity to apply for a job, perform essential job functions, or enjoy equal benefits and privileges).

In many cases, an appropriate accommodation will be obvious and can be made without difficulty and at little or no cost. Frequently, the individual with a disability can suggest a simple change or adjustment, based on his or her life or work experience.

An employer should always consult the person with the disability as the first step in considering an accommodation. Often this person can suggest much simpler and less costly accommodations than the employer might have believed necessary.

> **For example**: A small employer believed it necessary to install a special lower drinking fountain for an employee using a wheelchair, but the employee indicated that he could use the existing fountain if paper cups were provided in a holder next to the fountain.

However, in some cases, the appropriate accommodation may not be so easy to identify. The individual requesting the accommodation may not know enough about the equipment being used or the exact nature of the worksite to suggest an accommodation, or the employer may not know enough about the individual's functional limitations in relation to specific job tasks.

In such cases, the employer and the individual with a disability should work together to identify the appropriate accommodation. EEOC regulations require, when necessary, an informal, interactive process to find an effective accommodation. The process is described below in relation to an accommodation that will enable an individual with a disability to perform the essential functions of a job. However, the same approach can be used to identify accommodations for job applicants and accommodations to provide equal benefits and privileges of employment.

3.8 A process for identifying a reasonable accommodation

1.   **Look at the particular job involved. Determine its purpose and its essential functions.**

Chapter II recommended that the essential functions of the job be identified before advertising or interviewing for a job. However, it is useful to reexamine the specific job at this point to determine or confirm its essential functions and requirements.

2. **Consult with the individual with a disability to find out his or her specific physical or mental abilities and limitations** as they relate to the essential job functions. Identify the barriers to job performance and assess how these barriers could be overcome with an accommodation.

3. **In consultation with the individual, identify potential accommodations and assess how effective each would be in** enabling the individual to perform essential job functions. If this consultation does not identify an appropriate accommodation, technical assistance is available from a number of sources, many without cost. There are also financial resources to help with accommodation costs. (See Financial and Technical Assistance for Accommodations, 4.1 below).

4. If there are several effective accommodations that would provide an equal employment opportunity, **consider the preference of the individual** with a disability and **select the accommodation** that **best serves the needs of the individual and the employer**.

   If more than one accommodation would be effective for the individual with a disability, or if the individual would prefer to provide his or her own accommodation, the individual's preference should be given first consideration. However, the employer is free to choose among effective accommodations, and may choose one that is less expensive or easier to provide.

   The fact that an individual is willing to provide his or her own accommodation does not relieve the employer of the duty to provide this or another reasonable accommodation should this individual for any reason be unable or unwilling to continue to provide the accommodation.

Examples of the Reasonable Accommodation Process:

- A "sack-handler" position requires that the employee in this job pick up 50 pound sacks from a loading dock and carry them to the storage room. An employee who is disabled by a back impairment requests an accommodation. The employer analyzes the job and finds that its real purpose and essential function is to move the sacks from the loading dock to the store room. The person in the job does not necessarily have to lift and carry the sacks. The employer consults with the employee to determine his exact physical abilities and limitations. With medical documentation, it is determined that this person can lift 50 pound sacks to waist level, but cannot carry them to the storage room. A number of potential accommodations are identified: use of a dolly, a hand-truck or a cart. The employee prefers the dolly. After considering the relative cost, efficiency, and availability of the alternative accommodations, and after considering the preference of the employee, the employer provides the dolly as an accommodation. In this case, the employer found the dolly to be the most cost-effective accommodation, as well as the one preferred by the employee. If the employer had found a hand-truck to be as efficient, it could have provided the hand-truck as a reasonable accommodation.

• A company has an opening for a warehouse foreman. Among other functions, the job requires checking stock for inventory, completing bills of lading and other reports, and using numbers. To perform these functions, the foreman must have good math skills. An individual with diabetes who has good experience performing similar warehouse supervisory functions applies for the job. Part of the application process is a computerized test for math skills, but the job itself does not require use of a computer. The applicant tells the employer that although he has no problem reading print, his disability causes some visual impairment which makes it difficult to read a computer screen. He says he can take the test if it is printed out by the computer. However, this accommodation won't work, because the computer test is interactive, and the questions change based on the applicant's replies to each previous question. Instead, the employer offers a reader as an accommodation; this provides an effective equivalent method to test the applicant's math skills.

An individual with a disability is not required to accept an accommodation if the individual has not requested an accommodation and does not believe that one is needed. However, if the individual refuses an accommodation necessary to perform essential job functions, and as a result cannot perform those functions, the individual may not be considered qualified.

For example: An individual with a visual impairment that restricts her field of vision but who is able to read would not be required to accept a reader as an accommodation. However, if this person could not read accurately unaided, and reading is an essential function of the job, she would not be qualified for the job

III-11

if she refused an accommodation that would enable her to read accurately.

3.9   The Undue Hardship Limitation

An employer is not required to make a reasonable accommodation if it would impose an undue hardship on the operation of the business. However, if a particular accommodation would impose an undue hardship, the employer must consider whether there are alternative accommodations that would not impose such hardship.

An undue hardship is an action that requires "significant difficulty or expense" in relation to the size of the employer, the resources available, and the nature of the operation.

Accordingly, whether a particular accommodation will impose an undue hardship must always be determined on a case-by-case basis. An accommodation that poses an undue hardship for one employer at a particular time may not pose an undue hardship for another employer, o even for the same employer at another time. In general, a larger employer would be expected to make accommodations requiring greater effort or expense than would be required of a smaller employer. The concept of undue hardship includes any action that is:

- **unduly costly;**

- **extensive;**

- **substantial;**

- **disruptive; or**

- **that would fundamentally alter the nature or operation of the business.**

The statute and regulations provide **factors to be considered** in determining whether an accommodation would impose an undue hardsh on a particular business:

1. **The nature and net cost of the accommodation needed.** The cost of an accommodation that is considered in determining undue hardship will be the actual cost to the employer. Specific Federal tax credits and tax deductions are available to employers for making accommodations required by the ADA, and there are also sources of funding to help pay for some accommodations. If an employer can receive tax credits or tax deductions or partial

funding for an accommodation, only the <u>net</u> cost to the employer will be considered in a determination of undue hardship. (See <u>Financial and Technical Assistance for Accommodations</u>, 4.1 below);

2. **The financial resources of the facility making the accommodation, the number of employees at this facility, and the effect on expenses and resources of the facility.**

If an employer has only one facility, the cost and impact of the accommodation will be considered in relation to the effect on expenses and resources of that facility. However, if the facility is part of a larger entity that is covered by the ADA, factors 3. and 4. below also will be considered in determinations of undue hardship.

3. **The overall financial resources, size, number of employees, and type and location of facilities of the entity covered by the ADA (if the facility involved in the accommodation is part of a larger entity).**

4. **The type of operation of the covered entity, including the structure and functions of the workforce, the geographic separateness, and the administrative or fiscal relationship of the facility involved in making the accommodation to the larger entity.**

Factor 4. may include consideration of special types of employment operations, on a case-by-case basis, where providing a particular accommodation might be an undue hardship.

> **For example:** It might "fundamentally alter" the nature of a temporary construction site or be unduly costly to make it physically accessible to an employee using a wheelchair, if the terrain and structures are constantly changing as construction progresses.

Factor 4. will be considered, along with factors 2. and 3., where a covered entity operates more than one facility, in order to assess the financial resources actually available to the facility making the accommodation, in light of the interrelationship between the facility and the covered entity. In some cases, consideration of the resources of the larger covered entity may not be justified, because the particular facility making the accommodation may not have access to those resources.

For example: A local, independently owned fast food franchise of a national company that receives no funding from that company may assert that it would be an undue hardship to provide an interpreter to enable a deaf applicant for store manager to participate in weekly staff meetings, because its own resources are inadequate and it has no access to resources of the national company. If the financial relationship between the national company and the local company is limited to payment of an annual franchise fee, only the resources of the local franchise would be considered in determining whether this accommodation would be an undue hardship. However, if the facility was part of a national company with financial and administrative control over all of its facilities, the resources of the company as a whole would be considered in making this determination.

5. **The impact of the accommodation on the operation of the facility that is making the accommodation.**

This may include the impact on the ability of other employees to perform their duties and the impact on the facility's ability to conduct business.

An employer may be able to show that providing a particular accommodation would be unduly disruptive to its other employees or to its ability to conduct business.

For example: If an employee with a disability requested that the thermostat in the workplace be raised to a certain level to accommodate her disability, and this level would make it uncomfortably hot for other employees or customers, the employer would not have to provide this accommodation. However, if there was an alternative accommodation that would not be an undue hardship, such as providing a space heater or placing the employee in a room with a separate thermostat, the employer would have to provide that accommodation.

For example: A person with a visual impairment who requires bright light to see well applies for a waitress position at an expensive nightclub. The club maintains dim lighting to create an intimate setting, and lowers its lights further during the floor show. If the job applicant requested bright lighting as an accommodation so that she could see to take orders, the employer could assert that this would be an undue hardship, because it would seriously affect the nature of its operation.

In determining whether an accommodation would cause an undue hardship, an employer may consider the impact of an accommodation on the ability of other employees to do their jobs. However, an employer may not claim undue hardship solely because providing an accommodation has a negative impact on the morale of other employees. Nor can an employer claim undue hardship because of "disruption" due to employees' fears about, or prejudices toward, a person's disability.

> **For example**: If restructuring a job to accommodate an individual with a disability creates a heavier workload for other employees, this may constitute an undue hardship. But if other employees complain because an individual with a disability is allowed to take additional unpaid leave or to have a special flexible work schedule as a reasonable accommodation, such complaints or other negative reactions would not constitute an undue hardship.

> **For example**: If an employee objects to working with an individual who has a disability because the employee feels uncomfortable or dislikes being near this person, this would not constitute an undue hardship. In this case, the problem is caused by the employee's fear or prejudice toward the individual's disability, not by an accommodation.

Problems of employee morale and employee negative attitudes should be addressed by the employer through appropriate consultations with supervisors and, where relevant, with union representatives. Employers also may wish to provide supervisors, managers and employees with "awareness" training, to help overcome fears and misconceptions about disabilities, and to inform them of the employer's obligations under the ADA.

Other Cost Issues

An employer may not claim undue hardship simply because the cost of an accommodation is high in relation to an employee's wage or salary. When enacting the ADA "factors" for determining undue hardship, Congress rejected a proposed amendment that would have established an undue hardship if an accommodation exceeded 10% of an individual's salary. This approach was rejected because it would unjustifiably harm lower-paid workers who need accommodations. Instead, Congress clearly established that the focus for determining undue hardship should be the resources available to the employer.

If an employer finds that the cost of an accommodation would impose an undue hardship and no funding is available from another source, an applicant or employee with a disability should be offered the option of paying for the portion of the cost that constitutes an undue hardship, or of providing the accommodation.

> **For example**: If the cost of an assistive device is $2000, and an employer believes that it can demonstrate that spending more than $1500 would be an undue hardship, the individual with a disability should be offered the option of paying the additional $500. Or, if it would be an undue hardship for an employer to purchase brailling equipment for a blind applicant, the applicant should be offered the option of providing his own equipment (if there is no other effective accommodation that would not impose an undue hardship).

The terms of a collective bargaining agreement may be relevant in determining whether an accommodation would impose an undue hardship.

> **For example**: A worker who has a deteriorated disc condition and cannot perform the heavy labor functions of a machinist job, requests reassignment to a vacant clerk's job as a reasonable accommodation. If the collective bargaining agreement has specific seniority lists and requirements governing each craft, it might be an undue hardship to reassign this person if others had seniority for the clerk's job.

> However, since both the employer and the union are covered by the ADA's requirements, including the duty to provide a reasonable accommodation, the employer should consult with the union and try to work out an acceptable accommodation.

To avoid continuing conflicts between a collective bargaining agreement and the duty to provide reasonable accommodation, employers may find it helpful to seek a provision in agreements negotiated after the effective date of the ADA permitting the employer to take all actions necessary to comply with this law. (See Chapter VII.)

3.10 Examples of Reasonable Accommodations

1.   Making Facilities Accessible and Usable

The ADA establishes different requirements for accessibility under different sections of the Act. A **private employer's** obligation to make its facilities accessible to its job applicants and employees under Title I of the ADA differs from the obligation of a place of **public accommodation** to provide access in existing facilities to its customers and clients, and from the obligations of public accommodations and **commercial facilities** to provide accessibility in renovated or newly constructed buildings under Title III of the Act. The obligation of a **state and local government** to provide access for applicants and employees under Title I also differs from its obligation to provide accessibility under Title II of the ADA.

The employer's obligation under Title I is to provide access for an _individual_ applicant to participate in the job application process, and for an _individual_ employee with a disability to perform the essential functions of his/her job, including access to a building, to the work site, to needed equipment, and to all facilities used by employees. The employer must provide such access unless it would cause an undue hardship.

Under Title I, an employer is not required to make its existing facilities accessible until a particular applicant or employee with a particular disability needs an accommodation, and then the modifications should meet that individual's work needs. The employer does not have to make changes to provide access in places or facilities that will not be used by that individual for employment related activities or benefits.

In contrast, Title III of the ADA requires that places of public accommodation (such as banks, retail stores, theaters, hotels and restaurants) make their goods and services accessible generally, to all people with disabilities. Under Title III, existing buildings and facilities of a public accommodation must be made accessible by removing architectural barriers or communications barriers that are structural in nature, if this is "readily achievable." If this is not "readily achievable," services must be provided to people with disabilities in some alternative manner if this is "readily achievable."

The obligation for state and local governments to provide "program accessibility" in existing facilities under Title II also differs from their obligation to provide access as employers under Title I. Title II requires that these governments operate each service, program or activity in existing facilities so that, when viewed in its entirety, it is readily accessible to and useable by persons with disabilities, unless this would cause a "fundamental alteration" in the nature of the program or service, or would result in "undue financial and administrative burdens."

III-17

In addition, private employers that occupy commercial facilities or operate places of public accommodation and state and local governments must conform to more extensive accessibility requirements under Title III and Title II when making alterations to existing facilities or undertaking new construction. (see Requirements for Renovation and New Construction below.)

The accessibility requirements under Title II and III are established in Department of Justice regulations. Employers may contact the Justice Department's **Office on the Americans with Disabilities Act** for information on these requirements and for copies of the regulations with applicable accessibility guidelines (see Resource Directory).

When making changes to meet an individual's needs under Title I, an employer will find it helpful to consult the applicable Department of Justice accessibility guidelines as a starting point. It is advisable to make changes that conform to these guidelines, if they meet the individual's needs and do not impose an undue hardship, since such changes will be useful in the future for accommodating others. However, even if a modification meets the standards required under Title II or III, further adaptations may be needed to meet the needs of a particular individual.

> **For example**: A restroom may be modified to meet standard accessibility requirements (including wider door and stalls, and grab bars in specified locations) but it may be necessary to install a lower grab bar for a very short person in a wheelchair so that this person can transfer from the chair to the toilet.

Although the requirement for accessibility in employment is triggered by the needs of a particular individual, employers should consider initiating changes that will provide general accessibility, particularly for job applicants, since it is likely that people with disabilities will apply for jobs in the future.

> **For example**: Employment offices and interview facilities should be accessible to people using wheelchairs and others with mobility impairments. Plans also should be in place for making job information accessible and for communicating with people who have visual or hearing impairments. (See Chapter V. for additional guidance on accommodation in the application process.)

Accessibility to Perform the Essential Functions of the Job

The obligation to provide accessibility for a qualified individual with a disability includes accessibility of the job site itself and all work-related facilities.

Examples of accommodations that may be needed to make facilities accessible and usable include:

- installing a ramp at the entrance to a building;

- removing raised thresholds;

- reserving parking spaces close to the work site that are wide enough to allow people using wheelchairs to get in and out of vehicles;

- making restrooms accessible, including toilet stalls, sinks, soap, and towels;

- rearranging office furniture and equipment;

- making a drinking fountain accessible (for example, by installing a paper cup dispenser);

- making accessible, and providing an accessible "path of travel" to, equipment and facilities used by an employee, such as copying machines, meeting and training rooms, lunchrooms and lounges;

- removing obstacles that might be potential hazards in the path of people without vision;

- adding flashing lights when alarm bells are normally used, to alert an employee with a hearing impairment to emergencies.

Requirements for Renovation or New Construction

While an employer's requirements for accessibility under Title I relate to accommodation of an individual, as described above, employers will have more extensive accessibility requirements under Title II or III of the ADA if they make renovations to their facilities or undertake new construction.

Title III of the ADA requires that any alterations to, or new construction of "commercial facilities," as well as places of public accommodation, made after January 26, 1992, must conform to the "ADA Accessibility Guidelines" (incorporated in Department of Justice Title III regulations). "Commercial facilities" are defined as any nonresidential facility whose operations affect commerce, including office buildings, factories and warehouses; therefore, the facilities of most employers will be subject to this requirement. An alteration is any change that affects the "usability" of a facility; it does not include normal maintenance, such as painting, roofing or changes to mechanical or electrical systems, unless the changes affect the "usability" of the facility.

> **For example**: If, during remodeling or renovation, a doorway is relocated, the new doorway must be wide enough to meet the requirements of the ADA Accessibility Guidelines.

Under Title III, all newly constructed public accommodations and commercial facilities for which the last building permit is certified after January 26, 1992, and which are occupied after January 26, 1993, must be accessible in accordance with the standards of the ADA Accessibility Guidelines. However, Title III does not require elevators in facilities under 3 stories or with less than 3000 square feet per floor, unless the building is a shopping center, mall, professional office of a health provider, or public transportation station.

Under Title II, any alterations to, or new construction of, State or local government facilities made after January 26, 1992, must conform either with the ADA Accessibility Guidelines (however, the exception regarding elevators does not apply to State or local governments) or with the Uniform Federal Accessibility Standards. Facilities under design on January 26, 1992 must comply with this requirement if bids were invited after that date.

Providing accessibility in remodeled and new buildings usually can be accomplished at minimal additional cost. Over time, fully accessible new and remodeled buildings will reduce the need for many types of individualized reasonable accommodations. Employers planning alterations to their facilities or new construction should contact the **Office on the Americans with Disabilities Act in the U.S. Department of Justice** for information on accessibility requirements, including the ADA Accessibility Guidelines and the Uniform Federal Accessibility Guidelines. Employers may get specific technical information and guidance on accessibility by calling, toll-free, the Architectural and

III-20

Transportation Barriers Compliance Board, at 1-800-USA-ABLE. (See <u>Resource Directory</u>.)

2.   Job Restructuring

Job restructuring or job modification is a form of reasonable accommodation which enables many qualified individuals with disabilities to perform jobs effectively. Job restructuring as a reasonable accommodation may involve reallocating or redistributing the marginal functions of a job. However, an employer is not required to reallocate essential functions of a job as a reasonable accommodation. Essential functions, by definition, are those that a qualified individual must perform, with or without an accommodation.

> **For example**: Inspection of identification cards is generally an essential function of the job of a security job. If a person with a visual impairment could not verify the identification of an individual using the photo and other information on the card, the employer would not be required to transfer this function to another employee.

Job restructuring frequently is accomplished by exchanging marginal functions of a job that cannot be performed by a person with a disability for marginal job functions performed by one or more other employees.

> **For example**: An employer may have two jobs, each containing essential functions and a number of marginal functions. The employer may hire an individual with a disability who can perform the essential functions of one job and some, but not all, of the marginal functions of both jobs. As an accommodation, the employer may redistribute the marginal functions so that all of the functions that can be performed by the person with a disability are in this person's job and the remaining marginal functions are transferred to the other job.

Although an employer is not required to reallocate essential job functions, it may be a reasonable accommodation to modify the essential functions of a job by changing **when** or **how** they are done.

III-21

For example:

- An essential function that is usually performed in the early morning might be rescheduled to be performed later in the day, if an individual has a disability that makes it impossible to perform this function in the morning, and this would not cause an undue hardship.

- A person who has a disability that makes it difficult to write might be allowed to computerize records that have been maintained manually.

- A person with mental retardation who can perform job tasks but has difficulty remembering the order in which to do the tasks might be provided with a list to check off each task; the checklist could be reviewed by a supervisor at the end of the day.

Technical assistance in restructuring or modifying jobs for individuals with specific limitations can be obtained from state vocational rehabilitation agencies and other organizations with expertise in job analysis and job restructuring for people with various disabilities. (See Job Restructuring and Job Modification in Resource Directory Index.)

3. Modified Work Schedules

An employer should consider modification of a regular work schedule as a reasonable accommodation unless this would cause an undue hardship. Modified work schedules may include flexibility in work hours or the work week, or part-time work, where this will not be an undue hardship.

Many people with disabilities are fully qualified to perform jobs with the accommodation of a modified work schedule. Some people are unable to work a standard 9-5 work day, or a standard Monday to Friday work week; others need some adjustment to regular schedules.

Some examples of modified work schedules as a reasonable accommodation:

- An accountant with a mental disability required two hours off, twice weekly, for sessions with a psychiatrist. He was permitted to take longer lunch breaks and to make up the time by working later on those days.

- A machinist has diabetes and must follow a strict schedule to keep blood sugar levels stable. She must eat on a regular schedule and take insulin at set times each day. This means that she cannot work the normal shift rotations for machinists. As an accommodation, she is assigned to one shift on a permanent basis.

- An employee who needs kidney dialysis treatment is unable to work on two days because his treatment is only available during work hours on weekdays. Depending on the nature of his work and the nature of the employer's operation, it may be possible, without causing an undue hardship, for him to work Saturday and Sunday in place of the two weekdays, to perform work assignments at home on the weekend, or to work three days a week as part-time employee.

People whose disabilities may need modified work schedules include those who require special medical treatment for their disability (such as cancer patients, people who have AIDS, or people with mental illness); people who need rest periods (including some people who have multiple sclerosis, cancer, diabetes, respiratory conditions, or mental illness); people whose disabilities (such as diabetes) are affected by eating or sleeping schedules; and people with mobility and other impairments who find it difficult to use public transportation during peak hours, or who must depend upon special para-transit schedules.

4. Flexible Leave Policies

Flexible leave policies should be considered as a reasonable accommodation when people with disabilities require time off from work because of their disability. An employer is not required to provide additional paid leave as an accommodation, but should consider allowing use of accrued leave, advanced leave, or leave without pay, where this will not cause an undue hardship.

People with disabilities may require special leave for a number of reasons related to their disability, such as:

- medical treatment related to the disability;

- repair of a prosthesis or equipment;

III-23

- temporary adverse conditions in the work environment (for example, an air-conditioning breakdown causing temperature above 85 degrees could seriously harm the condition of a person with multiple sclerosis);

- training in the use of an assistive device or a dog guide. (However, if an assistive device is used at work and provided as a reasonable accommodation, and if other employees receive training during work hours, the disabled employee should receive training on this device during work hours, without need to take leave.)

5.   Reassignment to a Vacant Position

In general, the accommodation of reassignment should be considered only when an accommodation is not possible in an employee's present job, or when an accommodation in the employee's present job would cause an undue hardship. Reassignment also may be a reasonable accommodation if both employer and employee agree that this is more appropriate than accommodation in the present job.

Consideration of reassignment is only required for **employees**. An employer is not required to consider a different position for a job applicant if s/he is not able to perform the essential functions of the position s/he is applying for, with or without reasonable accommodation.

Reassignment may be an appropriate accommodation when an employee becomes disabled, when a disability becomes more severe, or when changes or technological developments in equipment affect the job performance of an employee with a disability. If there is no accommodation that will enable the person to perform the present job, or if it would be an undue hardship for the employer to provide such accommodation, reassignment should be considered.

Reassignment may not be used to limit, segregate, or otherwise discriminate against an employee with a disability. An employer may not reassign people with disabilities only to certain undesirable positions, or only to certain offices or facilities.

Reassignment should be made to a position equivalent to the one presently held in terms of pay and other job status, if the individual is qualified for the position and if such a position is vacant or will be vacant within a reasonable amount of time. A "reasonable amount of time" should be determined on a case-by-case basis, considering relevant factors such as the types of jobs for which the employee with a disability would be qualified; the frequency with which such jobs become available; the employer's general policies regarding reassignments of employees; and any specific policies regarding sick or injured employees.

> **For example**: If there is no vacant position available at the time that an individual with a disability requires a reassignment, but the employer knows that an equivalent position for which this person is qualified will become vacant within one or two weeks, the employer should reassign the individual to the position when it becomes available.

An employer may reassign an individual to a lower graded position if there are no accommodations that would enable the employee to remain in the current position and there are no positions vacant or soon to be vacant for which the employee is qualified (with or without an accommodation). In such a situation, the employer does not have to maintain the individual's salary at the level of the higher graded position, unless it does so for other employees who are reassigned to lower graded positions.

An employer is not required to create a new job or to bump another employee from a job in order to provide reassignment as a reasonable accommodation. Nor is an employer required to promote an individual with a disability to make such an accommodation.

6. Acquisition or Modification of Equipment and Devices

Purchase of equipment or modifications to existing equipment may be effective accommodations for people with many types of disabilities.

There are many devices that make it possible for people to overcome existing barriers to performing functions of a job. These devices range from very simple solutions, such as an elastic band that can enable a person with cerebral palsy to hold a pencil and write, to "high-tech" electronic equipment that can be operated with eye or head movements by people who cannot use their hands.

There are also many ways to modify standard equipment so as to enable people with different functional limitations to perform jobs effectively and safely.

Many of these assistive devices and modifications are inexpensive. Frequently, applicants and employees with disabilities can suggest effective low cost devices or equipment. They have had a great deal of experience in accommodating their disabilities, and many are informed about new and available equipment. Where the job requires special adaptations of equipment, the employer and the applicant or employee should use the process described earlier (see 3.8) to identify the exact functional abilities and limitations of the individual in relation to functional job needs, and to determine what type of assistance may be needed.

There are many sources of technical assistance to help identify and locate devices and equipment for specific job applications. An employer may be able to get information needed simply by telephoning the <u>Job Accommodation Network</u>, a free consulting service on accommodations, or other sources listed under "Accommodations" in the <u>Resource Directory</u>. Employers who need further assistance may use resources such as vocational rehabilitation specialists, occupational therapists and Independent Living Centers who will come on site to conduct a job analysis and recommend appropriate equipment or job modifications.

As indicated above (see 3.4), an employer is only obligated to provide equipment that is needed to perform a **job**; there is no obligation to provide equipment that the individual uses regularly in daily life, such as glasses, a hearing aid or a wheelchair. However, as previously stated, the employer may be obligated to provide items of this nature if special adaptations are required to perform a job.

> **For example**: It may be a reasonable accommodation to provide an employee with a motorized wheelchair if her job requires movement between buildings that are widely separated, and her disability prevents her operation of a wheelchair manually for that distance, or if heavy, deep-pile carpeting prevents operation of a manual wheelchair.

In some cases, it may be a reasonable accommodation to allow an applicant or employee to provide and use equipment that an employer would not be obligated to provide.

> **For example**: It would be a reasonable accommodation to allow an individual with a visual disability to provide his own guide dog.

Some examples of equipment and devices that may be reasonable accommodations:

- TDDs (Telecommunication Devices for the Deaf) make it possible for people with hearing and/or speech impairments to communicate over the telephone;

- telephone amplifiers are useful for people with hearing impairments;

- special software for standard computers and other equipment can enlarge print or convert print documents to spoken words for people with vision and/or reading disabilities;

- tactile markings on equipment in brailled or raised print are helpful to people with visual impairments;

- telephone headsets and adaptive light switches can be used by people with cerebral palsy or other manual disabilities;

- talking calculators can be used by people with visual or reading disabilities;

- speaker phones may be effective for people who are amputees or have other mobility impairments.

Some examples of effective low cost assistive devices as reported by the Job Accommodation Network and other sources:

- a timer with an indicator light allowed a medical technician who was deaf to perform laboratory tests. Cost $27.00;

- a clerk with limited use of her hands was provided a "lazy susan" file holder that enabled her to reach all materials needed for her job. Cost $85.00;

- A groundskeeper who had limited use of one arm was provided a detachable extension arm for a rake. This enabled him to grasp the handle on the extension with the impaired hand and control the rake with the functional arm. Cost $20.00;

- A desk layout was changed from the right to left side to enable a data entry operator who is visually impaired to perform her job. Cost $0;

III-27

- A telephone amplifier designed to work with a hearing aid allowed a plant worker to retain his job and avoid transfer to a lower paid job. Cost $24.00;

- A blind receptionist was provided a light probe which allowed her to determine which lines on the switchboard were ringing, on hold, or in use. (A light-probe gives an audible signal when held over an illuminated source.) Cost $50.00 to $100.00;

- A person who had use of only one hand, working in a food service position could perform all tasks except opening cans. She was provided with a one-handed can opener. Cost $35.00;

- Purchase of a light weight mop and a smaller broom enabled an employee with Downs syndrome and congenital heart problems to do his job with minimal strain. Cost under $40;

- A truck driver had carpal tunnel syndrome which limited his wrist movement and caused extreme discomfort in cold weather. A special wrist splint used with a glove designed for skin divers made it possible for him to drive even in extreme weather conditions. Cost $55.00;

- A phone headset allowed an insurance salesman with cerebral palsy to write while talking to clients. Rental cost $6.00 per month;

- A simple cardboard form, called a "jig" made it possible for a person with mental retardation to properly fold jeans as a stock clerk in a retail store. Cost $0.

Many recent technological innovations make it possible for people with severe disabilities to be very productive employees. Although some of this equipment is expensive, Federal tax credits, tax deductions, and other sources of financing are available to help pay for higher cost equipment.

For example: A company hired a person who was legally blind as a computer operator. The State Commission for the Blind paid half of the cost of a braille terminal. Since all programmers were provided with computers, the cost of the accommodation to this employer was only one-half of the difference in cost between the braille terminal and a regular computer. A smaller company also would be eligible for a

III-28

tax credit for such cost. (See <u>Tax Credit for Small Business</u>, 4.1a below)

For sources of information and technical assistance to help employers develop or locate "assistive devices and equipment," see this listing in the Index to the <u>Resource Directory</u>.

7. Adjusting and Modifying Examinations, Training Materials, and Policies

An employer may be required to modify, adjust, or make other reasonable accommodations in the ways that tests and training are administered in order to provide equal employment opportunities for qualified individuals with disabilities. Revisions to other employment policies and practices also may be required as reasonable accommodations.

a. Tests and Examinations

Accommodations may be needed to assure that tests or examinations measure the actual ability of an individual to perform job functions, rather than reflecting limitations caused by the disability. The ADA requires that tests be given to people who have sensory, speaking, or manual impairments in a format that does not require the use of the impaired skill, unless that is the job-related skill the test is designed to measure.

> **For example**: An applicant who has dyslexia, which causes difficulty in reading, should be given an oral rather than a written test, unless reading is an essential function of the job. Or, an individual with a visual disability or a learning disability might be allowed more time to take a test, unless the test is designed to measure speed required on a job.

The employer is only required to provide a reasonable accommodation for a test if the individual with a disability requests such an accommodation. But the employer has an obligation to inform job applicants in advance that a test will be given, so that an individual who needs an accommodation can make such a request. (See Chapter V. for further guidance on accommodations in testing.)

b. <u>Training</u>

Reasonable accommodation should be provided, when needed, to give employees with disabilities equal opportunity for training to perform their jobs effectively and to progress in employment. Needed accommodations may include:

- providing accessible training sites;

- providing training materials in alternate formats to accommodate a disability.

  For example: An individual with a visual disability may need training materials on tape, in large print, or on a computer diskette. A person with mental retardation may need materials in simplified language or may need help in understanding test instructions;

- modifying the manner in which training is provided.

  For example: It may be a reasonable accommodation to allow more time for training or to provide extra assistance to people with learning disabilities or people with mental impairments.

Additional guidance on accommodations in training is provided in Chapter VII.

c. <u>Other Policies</u>

Adjustments to various existing policies may be necessary to provide reasonable accommodation. As discussed above (see 3.10.3 and 3.10.4), modifications to existing leave policies and regular work hours may be required as accommodations. Or, for example, a company may need to modify a policy prohibiting animals in the work place, so that a visually impaired person can use a guide dog. Policies on providing information to employees may need adjustment to assure that all information is available in accessible formats for employees with disabilities. Policies on emergency evacuations should be adjusted to provide effective accommodations for people with different disabilities. (See Chapter VII).

8.   **Providing Qualified Readers**

It may be a reasonable accommodation to provide a reader for a qualified individual with a disability, if this would not impose an undue hardship.

> **For example**: A court has held under the Rehabilitation Act that it was not an undue hardship for a large state agency to provide full-time readers for three blind employees, in view of its very substantial budget. However, it may be an undue hardship for a smaller agency or business to provide such an accommodation.

In some job situations a reader may be the most effective and efficient accommodation, but in other situations alternative accommodations may enable an individual with a visual disability to perform job tasks just as effectively.

When an applicant or employee has a visual disability, the employer and the individual should use the "process" outlined in 3.8 above to identify specific limitations of the individual in relation to specific needs of the job and to assess possible accommodations.

> **For example**: People with visual impairments perform many jobs that do not require reading. Where reading is an essential job function, depending on the nature of a visual impairment and the nature of job tasks, print magnification equipment or a talking computer may be more effective for the individual and less costly for an employer than providing another employee as a reader. Where an individual has to read lengthy documents, a reader who transcribes documents onto tapes may be a more effective accommodation.

Providing a reader does not mean that it is necessary to hire a full-time employee for this service. Few jobs require an individual to spend all day reading. A reader may be a part-time employee or full-time employee who performs other duties. However, the person who reads to a visually impaired employee must read well enough to enable the individual to perform his or her job effectively. It would not be a reasonable accommodation to provide a reader whose poor skills hinder the job performance of the individual with a disability.

III-31

9.   **Providing Qualified Interpreters**

Providing an interpreter on an "as-needed" basis may be a reasonable accommodation for a person who is deaf in some employment situations, if this does not impose an undue hardship.

If an individual with a disability is otherwise qualified to perform essential job functions, the employer's basic obligation is to provide an accommodation that will enable this person to perform the job effectively. A person who is deaf or hearing-impaired should be able to communicate effectively with others as required by the duties of the job. Identifying the needs of the individual in relation to specific job tasks will determine whether or when an interpreter may be needed. The resources available to the employer would be considered in determining whether it would be an undue hardship to provide such an accommodation.

> **For example:** It may be necessary to obtain a qualified interpreter for a job interview, because for many jobs the applicant and interviewer must communicate fully and effectively to evaluate whether the applicant is qualified to do the job. Once hired, however, if the individual is doing clerical work, research, computer applications, or other job tasks that do not require much verbal communication, an interpreter may only be needed occasionally. Interpretation may be necessary for training situations, staff meetings or an employee party, so that this person can fully participate in these functions. Communication on the job may be handled through different means, depending on the situation, such as written notes, "signing" by other employees who have received basic sign language training, or by typing on a computer or typewriter.

People with hearing impairments have different communication needs and use different modes of communication. Some use signing in American Sign Language, but others use sign language that has different manual codes. Some people rely on an oral interpreter who silently mouths words spoken by others to make them easier to lip read. Many hearing-impaired people use their voices to communicate, and some combine talking and signing. The individual should be consulted to determine the most effective means of communication.

Communication between a person who is deaf and others through a supervisor and/or co-worker with basic sign language training may be sufficient in many job situations. However, where extensive discussions or complex subject matter is involved, a trained interpreter may be needed to provide effective communication. Experienced interpreters usually have received special training and may be certified by a professional interpreting organization or state or local Commission serving people who are deaf. (See Resource Directory Index listing of "Interpreters" for information about interpreters and how to obtain them).

10. Other Accommodations

There are many other accommodations that may be effective for people with different disabilities in different jobs. The examples of accommodations in EEOC regulations and the examples in this Manual are not the only types of accommodations that may be required. Some other accommodations that may be appropriate include:

*   making transportation provided by the employer accessible;

*   providing a personal assistant for certain job-related functions, such as a page turner for a person who has no hands, or a travel attendant to act as a sighted guide to assist a blind employee on occasional business trips.

*   use of a job coach for people with mental retardation and other disabilities who benefit from individualized on-the job training and services provided at no cost by vocational rehabilitation agencies in "supported employment" programs. (See Resource Directory Index for "Supported Employment.")

3.11 Financial and Technical Assistance for Accommodations

a. Financial Assistance

There are several sources of financial assistance to help employers make accommodations and comply with ADA requirements.

1.   **Tax Credit for Small Business** (Section 44 of the Internal Revenue Code)

     In 1990, Congress established a special tax credit to help smaller employers make accommodations required by the ADA. An eligible small business may take a tax credit of up to $5000 per year for accommodations made to comply with the ADA. The credit is available for one-half the cost of "eligible access expenditures" that are more than $250 but less than $10,250.

     > **For example**: If an accommodation cost $10,250, an employer could get a tax credit of $5000 ($10,250 minus $250, divided by 2). If the accommodation cost $7000, a tax credit of $3375 would be available.

     An **eligible small business** is one with gross receipts of $1 million or less for the taxable year, **or** 30 or fewer full time employees.

     "**Eligible access expenditures**" for which the tax credit may be taken include the types of accommodations required under Title I of the ADA as well as accessibility requirements for commercial facilities and places of public accommodation under Title III. "Eligible access expenditures" include:

     - removal of architectural, communication, physical, or transportation barriers to make the business accessible to, or usable by, people with disabilities.

     - providing qualified interpreters or other methods to make communication accessible to people with hearing disabilities;

     - providing qualified readers, taped texts, or other methods to make information accessible to people with visual disabilities; and/or

- acquiring or modifying equipment or devices for people with disabilities.

To be eligible for the tax credit, changes made to remove barriers or to provide services, materials or equipment must meet technical standards of the ADA Accessibility Guidelines, where applicable. (See p.   above.)

2. **Tax Deduction for Architectural and Transportation Barrier Removal** (Section 190 of the Internal Revenue Code)

Any business may take a full tax deduction, up to $15,000 per year, for expenses of removing specified architectural or transportation barriers. Expenses covered include costs of removing barriers created by steps, narrow doors, inaccessible parking spaces, toilet facilities, and transportation vehicles. **Both** the tax credit and the tax deduction are available to eligible small businesses.

> **For example**: If a small business makes a qualified expenditure of $24,000, it may take the $5000 tax **credit** for the initial $10,250 and, if the remaining $13,750 qualifies under Section 190, may **deduct** that amount from its taxable income. However, a business may not receive a double benefit for the same expense: for example, it may not take both the tax credit and the tax deduction for $10,000 spent to renovate bathrooms.

Information on the Section 44 tax credit and the Section 190 tax deduction can be obtained from a local IRS office, or by contacting the Office of Chief Counsel, Internal Revenue Service. (See Resource Directory.)

3. **Targeted Jobs Tax Credit**

Tax credits also are available under the Targeted Jobs Tax Credit Program (TJTCP) for employers who hire individuals with disabilities referred by state or local vocational rehabilitation agencies, State Commissions on the Blind and the U.S. Department of Veterans Affairs and certified by a State Employment Service. This program promotes hiring of several "disadvantaged" groups, including people with disabilities.

Under the TJTCP, a tax credit may be taken for 40% of the first $6000 of an employee's first-year salary. This program must be reauthorized each year by Congress, and currently has been extended through June 30, 1992. Information about this program can be obtained from the State Employment Services or from State Governor's Committees on the Employment of People with Disabilities. (See State listings in Resource Directory.)

4.   Other Funding Sources

State or local vocational rehabilitation agencies and State Commissions for the Blind can provide financial assistance for equipment and accommodations for their clients. The U.S. Department of Veterans Affairs also provides financial assistance to disabled veterans for equipment needed to help perform jobs. Some organizations that serve people with particular types of disabilities also provide financial assistance for needed accommodations. Other types of assistance may be available in the community. For example, some Independent Living Centers provide transportation service to the workplace for people with disabilities. For further information, see "Financial Assistance for Accommodations" in Resource Directory Index.

b.   Technical Assistance

There are many sources of technical assistance to help employers make effective accommodations for people with different disabilities in various job situations. Many of these resources are available without cost. Major resources for information, assistance, and referral to local specialized resources are 10 new **ADA Regional Business and Disability Technical Assistance Centers** that have been funded by Congress specifically to help implement the ADA. These Centers have been established to provide information, training and technical assistance to employers and all other entities covered by the ADA and to people with disabilities. The Centers also can refer employers to local technical assistance sources. (See ADA Regional Business and Disability Technical Assistance Centers in Resource Directory.) Other resources include:

- **State and local vocational rehabilitation agencies**

- **Independent Living Centers** in some 400 communities around the country provide technical assistance to employers and people with disabilities on accessibility and other accommodations and make referrals to specialized sources of assistance.

- **The Job Accommodation Network** (JAN) a free national consultant service, available through a toll-free number, helps employers make individualized accommodations.

- **ABLEDATA**, a computerized database of disability-related products and services, conducts customized information searches on worksite modifications, assistive devices and other accommodations.

- **The President's Committee on Employment of People with Disabilities** provides technical information, including publications with practical guidance on job analysis and accommodations.

- **Governors' Committees on Employment of People with Disabilities** in each State, allied with the President's Committee, are local resources of information and technical assistance.

These and many other sources of specialized technical assistance are listed in the Resource Directory. The Index to the Directory will be helpful in locating specific types of assistance.

IV. ESTABLISHING NONDISCRIMINATORY QUALIFICATION STANDARDS AND SELECTION CRITERIA

4.1 Introduction

The ADA does not prohibit an employer from establishing job-related qualification standards, including education, skills, work experience, and physical and mental standards necessary for job performance, health and safety.

The Act does not interfere with an employer's authority to establish appropriate job qualifications to hire people who can perform jobs effectively and safely, and to hire the best qualified person for a job. ADA requirements are designed to assure that people with disabilities are not excluded from jobs that they can perform.

ADA requirements apply to all selection standards and procedures, including, but not limited to:

- **education and work experience requirements;**

- **physical and mental requirements;**

- **safety requirements;**

- **paper and pencil tests;**

- **physical or psychological tests;**

- **interview questions; and**

- **rating systems;**

4.2 Overview of Legal Obligations

- Qualification standards or selection criteria that screen out or tend to screen out an individual with a disability on the basis of disability must be **job-related and consistent with business necessity.**

- Even if a standard is job-related and consistent with business necessity, if it screens out an individual with a disability on the basis of disability, the employer **must consider** if the individual could meet the standard with a **reasonable accommodation.**

- An employer is not required to lower existing production standards applicable to the quality or quantity of work for a given job in considering qualifications of an individual with a disability, if these standards are uniformly applied to all applicants and employees in that job.

- If an individual with a disability cannot perform a marginal function of a job because of a disability, an employer may base a hiring decision only on the individual's ability to perform the <u>essential</u> functions of the job, with or without a reasonable accommodation.

4.3   <u>What is Meant by "Job-Related" and "Consistent with Business Necessity"?</u>

1.   Job-Related

If a qualification standard, test or other selection criterion operates to screen out an individual with a disability, or a class of such individuals on the basis of disability, it must be a legitimate measure or qualification for the <u>specific</u> job it is being used for. It is not enough that it measures qualifications for a general class of jobs.

> **For example**: A qualification standard for a secretarial job of "ability to take shorthand dictation" is not job-related if the person in the particular secretarial job actually transcribes taped dictation.

The ADA does not require that a qualification standard or selection criterion apply only to the "essential functions" of a job. A "job-related" standard or selection criterion may evaluate or measure all functions of a job and employers may continue to select and hire people who can perform all of these functions. It is only when an individual's disability prevents or impedes performance of marginal job functions that the ADA requires the employer to evaluate this individual's qualifications solely on his/her ability to perform the essential functions of the job, with or without an accommodation.

For example: An employer has a job opening for an administrative assistant. The essential functions of the job are administrative and organizational. Some occasional typing has been part of the job, but other clerical staff are available who can perform this marginal job function. There are two job applicants. One has a disability that makes typing very difficult, the other has no disability and can type. The employer may not refuse to hire the first applicant because of her inability to type, but must base a job decision on the relative ability of each applicant to perform the essential administrative and organizational job functions, with or without accommodation. The employer may not screen out the applicant with a disability because of the need to make an accommodation to perform the essential job functions. However, if the first applicant could not type for a reason <u>not</u> related to her disability (for example, if she had never learned to type) the employer would be free to select the applicant who could best perform all of the job functions.

2. Business Necessity

"Business necessity" will be interpreted under the ADA as it has been interpreted by the courts under Section 504 of the Rehabilitation Act.

Under the ADA, as under the Rehabilitation Act:

> **If a test or other selection criterion excludes an individual with a disability <u>because of</u> the disability and does not relate to the <u>essential functions of a job</u>, it is not consistent with business necessity.**

This standard is similar to the legal standard under Title VII of the Civil Rights Act which provides that a selection procedure which screens out a disproportionate number of persons of a particular race, sex or national origin "class" must be justified as a "business necessity." However, under the ADA the standard may be applied to an <u>individual</u> who is screened out by a selection procedure because of disability, as well as to a class of persons. It is not necessary to make statistical comparisons between a group of people with disabilities and people who are not disabled to show that a person with a disability is screened out by a selection standard.

Disabilities vary so much that it is difficult, if not impossible, to make general determinations about the effect of various standards, criteria and procedures on "people with disabilities." Often, there may be little or no statistical data to measure the impact of a procedure on any "class" of people with a particular disability compared to people without disabilities. As with other determinations under the ADA, the exclusionary effect of a selection procedure usually must be looked at in relation to a particular individual who has particular limitations caused by a disability.

Because of these differences, the federal Uniform Guidelines on Employee Selection Procedures that apply to selection procedures on the basis of race, sex, and national origin under Title VII of the Civil Rights Act and other Federal authorities do not apply under the ADA to selection procedures affecting people with disabilities.

A standard may be job-related but not justified by business necessity, because it does not concern an essential function of a job.

> For example: An employer may ask candidates for a clerical job if they have a driver's license, because it would be desirable to have a person in the job who could occasionally run errands or take packages to the post office in an emergency. This requirement is "job-related," but it relates to an incidental, not an essential, job function. If it disqualifies a person who could not obtain a driver's license because of a disability, it would not be justified as a "business necessity" for purposes of the ADA.

Further, the ADA requires that even if a qualification standard or selection criterion is job-related and consistent with business necessity, it may not be used to exclude an individual with a disability if this individual could satisfy the legitimate standard or selection criterion with a reasonable accommodation.

> For example: It may be job-related and necessary for a business to require that a secretary produce letters and other documents on a word processor. But it would be discriminatory to reject a person whose disability prevented manual keyboard operation, but who could meet the qualification standard using a computer assistive device, if providing this device would not impose an undue hardship.

4.4 Establishing Job-Related Qualification Standards

The ADA does not restrict an employer's authority to establish needed job qualifications, including requirements related to:

- education;

- skills;

- work experience;

- licenses or certification;

- physical and mental abilities;

- health and safety; or

- other job-related requirements, such as judgment, ability to work under pressure or interpersonal skills.

Physical and Mental Qualification Standards

An employer may establish physical or mental qualifications that are necessary to perform specific jobs (for example, jobs in the transportation and construction industries; police and fire fighter jobs; security guard jobs) or to protect health and safety.

However, as with other job qualification standards, if a physical or mental qualification standard screens out an individual with a disability or a class of individuals with disabilities, the employer must be prepared to show that the standard is:

- **job-related and**
- **consistent with business necessity.**

Even if a physical or mental qualification standard is job-related and necessary for a business, if it is applied to exclude an otherwise qualified individual with a disability, the employer must consider whether there is a reasonable accommodation that would enable this person to meet the standard. The employer does not have to consider such accommodations in establishing a standard, but only when an otherwise qualified person with a disability requests an accommodation.

> **For example:** An employer has a forklift operator job. The essential function of the job is mechanical operation of the forklift machinery. The job has a physical requirement of ability to lift a

70 pound weight, because the operator must be able to remove and replace the 70 pound battery which powers the forklift. This standard is job-related. However, it would be a reasonable accommodation to eliminate this standard for an otherwise qualified forklift operator who could not lift a 70 pound weight because of a disability, if other operators or employees are available to help this person remove and replace the battery.

Evaluating Physical and Mental Qualification Standards Under the ADA

Employers generally have two kinds of physical or mental standards:

1.   Standards that may exclude an entire class of individuals with disabilities.

    For example: No person who has epilepsy, diabetes, or a heart or back condition is eligible for a job.

2.   Standards that measure a physical or mental ability needed to perform a job.

    For example: The person in the job must be able to lift x pounds for x hours daily, or run x miles in x minutes.

Standards that exclude an entire class of individuals with disabilities

"Blanket" exclusions of this kind usually have been established because employers believed them to be necessary for health or safety reasons. Such standards also may be used to screen out people who an employer fears, or assumes, may cause higher medical insurance or workers' compensation costs, or may have a higher rate of absenteeism.

Employers who have such standards should review them carefully. In most cases, they will not meet ADA requirements.

The ADA recognizes legitimate employer concerns and the requirements of other laws for health and safety in the workplace. An employer is not required to hire or retain an individual who would pose a "direct threat" to health or safety (see below). But the ADA requires an objective assessment of a particular individual's current ability to perform a job safely and effectively. Generalized "blanket" exclusions of an entire group of people with a certain disability prevent such an individual consideration. Such class-wide exclusions that do not reflect up-to-date medical knowledge and technology, or that are based on fears about future medical or workers' compensation costs, are unlikely to survive a legal challenge under the ADA. (However, the ADA recognizes employers' obligations to comply with Federal laws that mandate such exclusions in certain occupations. [See Health and Safety Requirements of Other Federal or State Laws below.])

The ADA requires that:

- any determination of a direct threat to health or safety must be based on an individualized assessment of objective and specific evidence about a particular individual's present ability to perform essential job functions, not on general assumptions or speculations about a disability. (See Standards Necessary for Health and Safety: A "Direct Threat" below).

> **For example**: An employer who excludes all persons who have epilepsy from jobs that require use of dangerous machinery will be required to look at the life experience and work history of an individual who has epilepsy. The individual evaluation should take into account the type of job, the degree of seizure control, the type(s) of seizures (if any), whether the person has an "aura" (warning of seizure), the person's reliability in taking prescribed anti-convulsant medication, and any side effects of such medication. Individuals who have no seizures because they regularly take prescribed medication, or who have sufficient advance warning of a seizure so that they can stop hazardous activity, would not pose a "direct threat" to safety.

Standards that measure needed physical or mental ability to perform a job

Specific physical or mental abilities may be needed to perform certain types of jobs.

> **For example**: Candidates for jobs such as airline pilots, policemen and firefighters may be required to meet certain physical and psychological qualifications.

In establishing physical or mental standards for such jobs, an employer does not have to show that these standards are "job related," justified by "business necessity" or that they relate only to "essential" functions of the job. However, if such a standard screens out an otherwise qualified individual with a disability, the employer must be prepared to show that the standard, as applied, is job-related and consistent with business necessity under the ADA. And, even if this can be shown, the employer must consider whether this individual could meet the standard with a **reasonable accommodation**.

> **For example**: A police department that requires all its officers to be able to make forcible arrests and to perform all job functions in the department might be able to justify stringent physical requirements for all officers, if in fact they are all required to be available for any duty in an emergency.

> However, if a position in a mailroom required as a qualification standard that the person in the job be able to reach high enough to place and retrieve packages from 6-foot high shelves, an employer would have to consider whether there was an accommodation that would enable a person with a disability that prevented reaching that high to perform these essential functions. Possible accommodations might include lowering the shelf-height, providing a step stool or other assistive device.

Physical agility tests

An employer may give a physical agility test to determine physical qualifications necessary for certain jobs prior to making a job offer if it is simply an agility test and not a medical examination. Such a test would not be subject to the prohibition against pre-employment medical examinations if given to all similarly situated applicants or employees, regardless of disability. However, if an agility test screens out or tends to screen out an individual with a disability or a class of such individuals because of disability, the employer must be prepared to show that the test is job-related and consistent with business necessity and that the test or the job cannot be performed with a reasonable accommodation.

It is important to understand the distinction between physical agility tests and prohibited pre-employment medical inquiries and examinations. One difference is that agility tests do not involve medical examinations or diagnoses by a physician, while medical examinations may involve a doctor.

> **For example**: At the pre-offer stage, a police department may conduct an agility test to measure a candidate's ability to walk, run, jump, or lift in relation to specific job duties, but it cannot require the applicant to have a medical screening before taking the agility test. Nor can it administer a medical examination before making a conditional job offer to this person.

Some employers currently may require a medical screening before administering a physical agility test to assure that the test will not harm the applicant. There are two ways that an employer can handle this problem under the ADA:

- the employer can request the applicant's physician to respond to a very restricted inquiry which describes the specific agility test and asks: "Can this person safely perform this test?"

- the employer may administer the physical agility test _after_ making a conditional job offer, and in this way may obtain any necessary medical information, as permitted under the ADA. (See Chapter VI.) The employer may find it more cost-efficient to administer such tests only to those candidates who have met other job qualifications.

5 <u>Standards Necessary for Health and Safety: A "Direct Threat"</u>

An employer may require as a qualification standard that an individual not pose a "direct threat" to the health or safety of the individual or others, if this standard is applied to all applicants for a particular job. However, an employer must meet very specific and stringent requirements under the ADA to establish that such a "direct threat" exists.

The employer must be prepared to show that there is:

- <u>significant</u> risk of substantial harm;

- the <u>specific</u> risk must be identified;

- it must be a <u>current</u> risk, not one that is speculative or remote;

- the assessment of risk must be based on objective medical or other factual evidence regarding a particular individual; and

- even if a genuine significant risk of substantial harm exists, the employer must consider whether the risk can be eliminated or reduced below the level of a "direct threat" by <u>reasonable accommodation.</u>

Looking at each of these requirements more closely:

1.   <u>**Significant risk of substantial harm**</u>

An employer cannot deny an employment opportunity to an individual with a disability merely because of a slightly increased risk. The employer must be prepared to show that there is a **significant risk**, that is, **a high probability of substantial harm**, if the person were employed.

The assessment of risk <u>cannot be based on mere speculation</u> unrelated to the individual in question.

> **For example**: An employer cannot assume that a person with cerebral palsy who has restricted manual dexterity cannot work in a laboratory because s/he will pose a risk of breaking vessels with dangerous contents. The abilities or limitations of a particular individual with cerebral palsy must be evaluated.

2.   <u>**The specific risk must be identified**</u>

If an individual has a disability, the employer must identify the aspect of the disability that would pose a direct threat, considering the following factors:

- the **duration** of the risk.

> **For example**: An elementary school teacher who has tuberculosis may pose a risk to the health of children in her classroom. However, with proper medication, this person's disease would be contagious for only a two-week period. With an accommodation of two-weeks absence from the classroom, this teacher would not pose a "direct threat."

- the **nature and severity** of the potential harm.

> **For example**: A person with epilepsy, who has lost consciousness during seizures within the past year, might seriously endanger her own life and the lives of others if employed as a bus driver. But this person would not pose a severe threat of harm if employed in a clerical job.

- the **likelihood** that the potential harm will occur.

> **For example**: An employer may believe that there is a risk of employing an individual with HIV disease as a teacher. However, it is medically established that this disease can only be transmitted through sexual contact, use of infected needles, or other entry into a person's blood stream. There is little or no likelihood that employing this person as a teacher would pose a risk of transmitting this disease.

and

- the **imminence** of the potential harm.

> **For example**: A physician's evaluation of an applicant for a heavy labor job that indicated the individual had a disc condition that might worsen in 8 or 10 years would not be sufficient indication of imminent potential harm.

If the perceived risk to health or safety arises from the behavior of an individual with a mental or emotional disability, the employer must identify the specific behavior that would pose the "direct threat".

3. **The risk must be current, not one that is speculative or remote**

The employer must show that there is a <u>current</u> risk -- "a high probability of substantial harm" -- to health or safety based on the individual's present ability to perform the essential functions of the job. A determination that an individual would pose a "direct threat" cannot be based on speculation about <u>future</u> risk. This includes speculation that an individual's disability may become more severe. An assessment of risk cannot be based on speculation that the individual will become unable to perform a job in the future, or that this individual may cause increased health insurance or workers compensation costs, or will have excessive absenteeism. (See <u>Insurance</u>, Chapter VII., and Workers' Compensation, Chapter IX.)

4. **The assessment of risk must be based on objective medical or other evidence related to a particular individual**

The determination that an individual applicant or employee with a disability poses a "direct threat" to health or safety must be based

IV-11

on objective, factual evidence related to <u>that individual's</u> present ability to safely perform the essential functions of a job. It cannot be based on unfounded assumptions, fears, or stereotypes about the nature or effect of a disability or of disability generally. Nor can such a determination be based on patronizing assumptions that an individual with a disability may endanger himself or herself by performing a particular job.

> <u>For example</u>: An employer may not exclude a person with a vision impairment from a job that requires a great deal of reading because of concern that the strain of heavy reading may further impair her sight.

The determination of a "direct threat" to health or safety must be based on a reasonable medical judgement that relies on the most current medical knowledge and/or the best available objective evidence. This may include:

- **input from the individual with a disability;**

- **the experience of this individual in previous jobs;**

- **documentation from medical doctors, psychologists, rehabilitation counselors, physical or occupational therapists, or others who have expertise in the disability involved and/or direct knowledge of the individual with a disability.**

Where the psychological behavior of an employee suggests a threat to safety, **factual evidence** of this behavior also may constitute evidence of a "direct threat." An employee's violent, aggressive, destructive or threatening behavior may provide such evidence.

Employers should be careful to assure that assessments of "direct threat" to health or safety are based on current medical knowledge and other kinds of evidence listed above, rather than relying on generalized and frequently out-of- date assumptions about risk associated with certain disabilities. They should be aware that Federal contractors who have had similar disability nondiscrimination requirements under the Rehabilitation Act have had to make substantial backpay and other financial payments because they excluded individuals with disabilities who were qualified to perform their jobs, based on generalized assumptions that were not supported by evidence about the individual concerned.

Examples of Contractor Cases:

- A highly qualified experienced worker was rejected for a sheet metal job because of a company's general medical policy excluding anyone with epilepsy from this job. The company asserted that this person posed a danger to himself and to others because of the possibility that he might have a seizure on the job. However, this individual had been seizure-free for 6 years and co-workers on a previous job testified that he carefully followed his prescribed medication schedule. The company was found to have discriminated against this individual and was required to hire him, incurring large back pay and other costs.

- An applicant who was deaf in one ear was rejected for an aircraft mechanic job because the company feared that his impairment might cause a future workers' compensation claim. His previous work record gave ample evidence of his ability to perform the aircraft mechanic job. The company was found to have discriminated because it provided no evidence that this person would have been a danger to himself or to others on the job.

- An experienced carpenter was not hired because a blood pressure reading by the company doctor at the end of a physical exam was above the company's general medical standard. However, his own doctor provided evidence of much lower readings, based on measurements of his blood pressure at several times during a physical exam. This doctor testified that the individual could safely perform the carpenter's job because he had only mild hypertension. Other expert medical evidence confirmed that a single blood pressure reading was not sufficient to determine if a person has hypertension, that such a reading clearly was not sufficient to determine if a person could perform a particular job, and that hypertension has very different effects on different people. In this case, it was found that there was merely a slightly elevated risk, and that a remote possibility of future injury was not sufficient to disqualify an otherwise qualified person. (Note that while it is possible that a person with mild hypertension does not have an impairment that "substantially limits a major life activity," in this case the person was excluded because he was "regarded as" having such an impairment. The employer was still required to show that this person posed a "direct threat" to safety.)

IV-13

"Direct Threat" to Self

An employer may require that an individual not pose a direct
threat of harm to his or her own safety or health, as well as to
the health or safety of others. However, as emphasized above,
such determinations must be strictly based on valid medical
analyses or other objective evidence related to this individual, using
the factors set out above. A determination that a person might
cause harm to himself or herself <u>cannot</u> be based on stereotypes,
patronizing assumptions about a person with a disability, or
generalized fears about risks that might occur if an individual with
a disability is placed in a certain job. Any such determination
must be based on evidence of specific risk to a particular
individual.

> **For example**: An employer would not be required to hire
> an individual disabled by narcolepsy who frequently and
> unexpectedly loses consciousness to operate a power saw or
> other dangerous equipment, if there is no accommodation
> that would reduce or eliminate the risk of harm. But an
> advertising agency could not reject an applicant for a
> copywriter job who has a history of mental illness, based on
> a generalized fear that working in this high stress job
> might trigger a relapse of the individual's mental illness.
> Nor could an employer reject an applicant with a visual or
> mobility disability because of a generalized fear of risks to
> this person in the event of a fire or other emergency.

5.   <u>If there is a significant risk, reasonable accommodation
     must be considered</u>

Where there is a significant risk of substantial harm to health
or safety, an employer still must consider whether there is a
reasonable accommodation that would eliminate this risk or
reduce the risk so that it is below the level of a "direct threat."

> **For example**: A deaf bus mechanic was denied
> employment because the transit authority feared that he
> had a high probability of being injured by buses moving in
> and out of the garage. It was not clear that there was, in
> fact, a "high probability" of harm in this case, but the
> mechanic suggested an effective accommodation that
> enabled him to perform his job with little or no risk. He
> worked in a corner of the garage, facing outward, so that
> he could see moving buses. A co-worker was designated to

alert him with a tap on the shoulder if any dangerous situation should arise.

"Direct Threat" and Accommodation in Food Handling Jobs

The ADA includes a specific application of the "direct threat" standard and the obligation for reasonable accommodation in regard to individuals who have infectious or communicable diseases that may be transmitted through the handling of food.

The law provides that the U.S. Department of Health and Human Services (HHS) must prepare and update annually a list of contagious diseases that are transmitted through the handling of food and the methods by which these diseases are transmitted.

When an individual who has one of the listed diseases applies for work or works in a job involving food handling, the employer must consider whether there is a reasonable accommodation that will eliminate the risk of transmitting the disease through handling of food. If there is such an accommodation, and it would not impose an undue hardship, the employer must provide the accommodation.

An employer would not be required to hire a job **applicant** in such a situation if no reasonable accommodation is possible. However, an employer would be required to consider accommodating an **employee** by reassignment to a position that does not require handling of food, if such a position is available, the employee is qualified for it, and it would not pose an undue hardship.

In August 1991, the Centers for Disease Control (CDC) of the Public Health Service in HHS issued a list of infectious and communicable diseases that are transmitted through handling of food, together with information about how these diseases are transmitted. The list of diseases is brief. In conformance with established medical opinion, it does not include AIDS or the HIV virus. In issuing the list, the CDC emphasized that the greatest danger of food-transmitted illness comes from contamination of infected food-producing animals and contamination in food processing, rather than from handling of food by persons with infectious or communicable diseases. The CDC also emphasized that proper personal hygiene and sanitation in food-handling jobs were the most important measures to prevent transmission of disease.

The CDC list of diseases that are transmitted through food handling and recommendations for preventing such transmission appears in Appendix C.

IV-15

4.6   Health and Safety Requirements of Other Federal or State Laws

The ADA recognizes employers' obligations to comply with requirements of other laws that establish health and safety standards. However, the Act gives greater weight to Federal than to state or local law.

1.   Federal Laws and Regulations

The ADA does not override health and safety requirements established under other Federal laws. If a standard is required by another Federal law, an employer must comply with it and does not have to show that the standard is job related and consistent with business necessity.

> **For example**: An employee who is being hired to drive a vehicle in interstate commerce must meet safety requirements established by the U.S. Department of Transportation. Employers also must conform to health and safety requirements of the U.S. Occupational Safety and Health Administration (OSHA).

However, an employer still has the obligation under the ADA to consider whether there is a reasonable accommodation, consistent with the standards of other Federal laws, that will prevent exclusion of qualified individuals with disabilities who can perform jobs without violating the standards of those laws.

> **For example**: In hiring a person to drive a vehicle in interstate commerce, an employer must conform to existing Department of Transportation regulations that exclude any person with epilepsy, diabetes, and certain other conditions from such a job.

> But, for example, if DOT regulations require that a truck have 3 grab bars in specified places, and an otherwise qualified individual with a disability could perform essential job functions with the assistance of 2 additional grab bars, would be a reasonable accommodation to add these bars, unless this would be an undue hardship.

The Department of Transportation, as directed by Congress, currently is reviewing several motor vehicle standards that require "blanket" exclusions of individuals with diabetes, epilepsy and certain other disabilities.

2. State and Local Laws

The ADA does not override state or local laws designed to protect public health and safety, except where such laws conflict with ADA requirements. This means that if there is a state or local law that would exclude an individual with a disability for a particular job or profession because of a health or safety risk, the employer still must assess whether a particular individual would pose a "direct threat" to health or safety under the ADA standard. If there is such a "direct threat," the employer also must consider whether it could be eliminated or reduced below the level of a "direct threat" by reasonable accommodation. An employer may not rely on the existence of a state or local law that conflicts with ADA requirements as a defense to a charge of discrimination.

> **For example**: A state law that required a schoolbus driver to have a high level of hearing in both ears without use of a hearing aid was found by a court to violate Section 504 of the Rehabilitation Act, and would violate the ADA. The court found that the driver could perform his job with a hearing aid without a risk to safety.

(See further guidance on Medical Examinations and Inquiries in Chapter VI.)

V. NONDISCRIMINATION IN THE HIRING PROCESS:

RECRUITMENT; APPLICATIONS; PRE-EMPLOYMENT INQUIRIES; TESTING

This chapter discusses nondiscrimination requirements that apply to recruitment and the job application process, including pre-employment inquiries. Chapter VI. discusses these requirements more specifically in relation to medical inquiries and examinations.

5.1 Overview of Legal Obligations

- An employer must provide an equal opportunity for an individual with a disability to participate in the job application process and to be considered for a job.

- An employer may not make any **pre-employment** inquiries regarding disability, but may ask questions about the ability to perform specific job functions and may, with certain limitations, ask an individual with a disability to describe or demonstrate how s/he would perform these functions.

- An employer may not require pre-employment medical examinations or medical histories, but may condition a job offer on the results of a post-offer medical examination, if all entering employees in the same job category are required to take this examination.

- Tests for illegal drugs are not medical examinations under the ADA and may be given at any time.

- A test that screens out or tends to screen out a person with a disability on the basis of disability must be job-related and consistent with business necessity.

- Tests must reflect the skills and aptitudes of an individual rather than impaired sensory, manual, or speaking skills, unless those are job-related skills the test is designed to measure.

A careful review of all procedures used in recruiting and selecting employees is advisable to assure nondiscrimination in the hiring process. Reasonable accommodation must be provided as needed, to assure that individuals with disabilities have equal opportunities to participate in this process.

5.2   Job Advertisements and Notices

It is advisable that job announcements, advertisements, and other recruitment notices include information on the essential functions of the job. Specific information about essential functions will attract applicants including individuals with disabilities, who have appropriate qualifications.

Employers may wish to indicate in job advertisements and notices that they do not discriminate on the basis of disability or other legally prohibited bases. An employer may wish to include a statement such as "We are an Equal Opportunity Employer. We do not discriminate on the basis of race, religion, color, sex, age, national origin or disability."

Accessibility of Job Information

Information about job openings should be accessible to people with different disabilities. An employer is not obligated to provide written information in various formats in advance, but should make it available in an accessible format on request.

> **For example**: Job information should be available in a location that is accessible to people with mobility impairments. If a job advertisement provides only a telephone number to call for information, a TDD (telecommunication device for the deaf) number should be included, unless a telephone relay service has been established[1]. Printed job information in an employment office or employee bulletin boards should be made available, as needed, to persons with visual or other reading impairments. Preparing information in large print will help make it available to some people with visual impairments. Information can be recorded on cassette or read to applicants with more severe vision impairments and those who have other disabilities which limit reading ability.

---

[1] Title IV of the ADA requires all telephone carriers to establish relay services by July 1993, that will enable people who use TDDs to speak directly to anyone through use of a relay operator. Many states already have such services. See Resource Directory for Telecommunications Relay Services.

5.3 Employment Agencies

Employment agencies are "covered entities" under the ADA, and must comply with all ADA requirements that are applicable to their activities.

The definition of an "employment agency" under the ADA is the same as that under Title VII of the Civil Rights Act. It includes private and public employment agencies and other organizations, such as college placement services, that regularly procure employees for an employer.

When an employer uses an employment agency to recruit, screen, and refer potential employees, both the employer and the employment agency may be liable if there is any violation of ADA requirements.

> **For example**: An employer uses an employment agency to recruit and the agency places a newspaper advertisement with a telephone number that all interested persons must call, because no address is given. However, there is no TDD number. If there is no telephone relay service, and a deaf person is unable to obtain information about a job for which she is qualified and files a discrimination charge, both the employer and the agency may be liable.

An employer should inform an employment agency used to recruit or screen applicants of the mutual obligation to comply with ADA requirements. In particular, these agencies should be informed about requirements regarding qualification standards, pre-employment inquiries, and reasonable accommodation.

If an employer has a contract with an employment agency, the employer may wish to include a provision stating that the agency will conduct its activities in compliance with ADA and other legal nondiscrimination requirements.

5.4 Recruitment

The ADA is a nondiscrimination law. It does not require employers to undertake special activities to recruit people with disabilities. However, it is consistent with the purpose of the ADA for employers to expand their "outreach" to sources of qualified candidates with disabilities. (See **Locating Qualified Individuals with Disabilities** below).

Recruitment activities that have the effect of screening out potential applicants with disabilities may violate the ADA.

V-3

For example: If an employer conducts recruitment activity at a college campus, job fair, or other location that is physically inaccessible, or does not make its recruitment activity accessible at such locations to people with visual, hearing or other disabilities, it may be liable if a charge of discrimination is filed.

Locating Qualified Individuals with Disabilities

There are many resources for locating individuals with disabilities who are qualified for different types of jobs. People with disabilities represent a large, underutilized human resource pool. Employers who have actively recruited and hired people with disabilities have found valuable sources of employees for jobs of every kind.

Many of the organizations listed in the Resource Directory are excellent sources for recruiting qualified individuals with disabilities as well as sources of technical assistance for any accommodations needed. For example, many colleges and universities have coordinators of services for students with disabilities who can be helpful in recruitment and in making accommodations. The Association on Handicapped Student Service Programs in Postsecondary Education can provide information on these resources. Local Independent Living Centers, state and local vocational rehabilitation agencies, organizations such as Goodwill Industries, and many organizations representing people who have specific disabilities are among other recruitment sources. (See "Recruitment Sources" in Resource Directory Index).

5.5   Pre-Employment Inquiries

The ADA Prohibits Any Pre-Employment Inquiries About a Disability.

This prohibition is necessary to assure that qualified candidates are not screened out because of their disability before their actual ability to do job is evaluated. Such protection is particularly important for people with hidden disabilities who frequently are excluded, with no real opportunity to present their qualifications, because of information requested in application forms, medical history forms, job interviews, and pre-employment medical examinations.

The prohibition on pre-employment inquiries about disability does not prevent an employer from obtaining necessary information regarding an applicant's qualifications, including medical information necessary to assess qualifications and assure health and safety on the job.

The ADA requires only that such inquiries be made in two separate stages of the hiring process.

1.   **Before making a job offer**.

At this stage, an employer:

- _may_ ask questions about an applicant's ability to perform specific job functions;

- _may_ _not_ make an inquiry about a disability;

- _may_ make a job offer that is conditioned on satisfactory results of a _post-offer_ medical examination or inquiry.

2.   **After making a conditional job offer and before an individual starts work**

At this stage, an employer may conduct a medical examination or ask health-related questions, providing that all candidates who receive a conditional job offer in the same job category are required to take the same examination and/or respond to the same inquiries.

Inquiries that may and may not be made at the **pre-offer** stage are discussed in the section that follows. Guidance on obtaining and using information from **post-offer** medical and inquiries and examinations is provided in Chapter VI.

5.5(a)   Basic Requirements Regarding Pre-Offer Inquiries

- An employer may not make any pre-employment inquiry about a disability, or about the nature or severity of a disability:

  -    on application forms

  -    in job interviews

  -    in background or reference checks.

- An employer may not make any medical inquiry or conduct any medical examination prior to making a conditional offer of employment.

- An employer may ask a job applicant questions about ability to perform specific job functions, tasks, or duties, as long as these questions are not phrased in terms of a disability. Questions need not be limited to the "essential" functions of the job.

- An employer may ask all applicants to describe or demonstrate how they will perform a job, with or without an accommodation.

- If an individual has a <u>known</u> disability that might interfere with or prevent performance of job functions, s/he may be asked to describe or demonstrate how these functions will be performed, with or without an accommodation, even if other applicants are not asked to do so; **however,**

- If a known disability would <u>not</u> interfere with performance of job functions, an individual may only be required to describe or demonstrate how s/he will perform a job if this is required of all applicants for the position.

- An employer may condition a job offer on the results of a medical examination or on the responses to medical inquiries if such an examination or inquiry is required of all entering employees in the same job category, regardless of disability; information obtained from such inquiries or examinations must be handled according to the strict confidentiality requirements of the ADA. (See Chapter VI.)

5.5(b)   The Job Application Form

A review of job application forms should be a priority before the ADA's effective date, to eliminate any questions related to disability.

<u>Some Examples of Questions that May Not be Asked on Application Forms or in Job Interviews:</u>

- Have you ever had or been treated for any of the following conditions or diseases? (Followed by a checklist of various conditions and diseases.)

- Please list any conditions or diseases for which you have been treated in the past 3 years.

- Have you ever been hospitalized? If so, for what condition?

- Have you ever been treated by a psychiatrist or psychologist? If so, for what condition?

- Have you ever been treated for any mental condition?

- Is there any health-related reason you may not be able to perform the job for which you are applying?

- Have you had a major illness in the last 5 years?

- How many days were you absent from work because of illness last year?

  (Pre-employment questions about illness may not be asked, because they may reveal the existence of a disability. However, an employer may provide information on its attendance requirements and ask if an applicant will be able to meet these requirements. [See also **The Job Interview** below.])

- Do you have any physical defects which preclude you from performing certain kinds of work? If yes, describe such defects and specific work limitations.

- Do you have any disabilities or impairments which may affect your performance in the position for which you are applying?

  (This question should not be asked even if the applicant is requested in a follow-up question to identify accommodations that would enable job performance. Inquiries should not focus on an applicant's disabilities. The applicant may be asked about ability to perform specific job functions, with or without a reasonable accommodation. [See **Information That May be Asked**, below.])

- Are you taking any prescribed drugs?

  (Questions about use of prescription drugs are not permitted before a conditional job offer, because the answers to such questions might reveal the existence of certain disabilities which require prescribed medication.)

V-7

- Have you ever been treated for drug addiction or alcoholism?

  (Information may not be requested regarding treatment for drug or alcohol addiction, because the ADA protects people addicted to drugs who have been successfully rehabilitated, or who are undergoing rehabilitation, from discrimination based on drug addiction. [See Chapter VI. for discussion of post-offer inquiries and Chapter VIII. for drug and alcohol issues.])

- Have you ever filed for workers' compensation insurance?

  (An employer may _not_ ask about an applicant's workers' compensation history at the pre-offer stage, but may obtain such information after making a conditional job offer. Such questions are prohibited because they are likely to reveal the existence of a disability. In addition, it is discriminatory under the ADA not to hire an individual with a disability because of speculation that the individual will cause increased workers' compensation costs. (See Chapter IV, 4.5(3), and Chapter IX.)

Information about an applicant's ability to perform job tasks, with or without accommodation, can be obtained through the application form and job interview, as explained below. Other needed information may be obtained through medical inquiries or examinations conducted _after_ a conditional offer of employment, as described in Chapter VI.

5.5(c) Exception for Federal Contractors Covered by Section 503 of the Rehabilitation Act and Other Federal Programs Requiring Identification of Disability.

Federal contractors and subcontractors who are covered by the affirmative action requirements of Section 503 of the Rehabilitation Act may invite individuals with disabilities to identify themselves on a job application form or by other pre-employment inquiry, to satisfy the affirmative action requirements of Section 503 of the Rehabilitation Act. Employers who request such information must observe Section 503 requirements regarding the manner in which such information is requested and used, and the procedures for maintaining such information as a separate, confidential record, apart from regular personnel records. (For further information, see **Office of Federal Contract Compliance Programs** listing in <u>Resource Directory</u>.)

A pre-employment inquiry about a disability also is permissible if it is required or necessitated by another Federal law or regulation. **For example**, a number of programs administered or funded by the U.S. Department of Labor target benefits to individuals with disabilities, such as, disabled veterans, veterans of the Vietnam era, individuals eligible for Targeted Job Tax Credits, and individuals eligible for Job Training Partnership Act assistance. Pre-employment inquiries about disabilities may be necessary under these laws to identify disabled applicants or clients in order to provide the required special services for such persons. These inquiries would not violate the ADA.

5.5(d) Information that May Be Requested on Application Forms or in Interviews.

An employer may ask questions to determine whether an applicant can perform specific job functions. The questions should focus on the applicant's <u>ability</u> to perform the job, not on a disability.

> <u>For example</u>: An employer could attach a job description to the application form with information about specific job functions. Or the employer may describe the functions. This will make it possible to ask whether the applicant can perform these functions. It also will give an applicant with a disability needed information to request any accommodation required to perform a task. The applicant could be asked:
>
> - **Are you able to perform these tasks with or without an accommodation?**
>
>   If the applicant indicates that s/he can perform the tasks with an accommodation, s/he may be asked:
>
> - **How would you perform the tasks, and with what accommodation(s)?**

However, the employer must keep in mind that it cannot refuse to hire a qualified individual with a disability because of this person's need for an accommodation that would be required by the ADA.

An employer may inform applicants on an application form that they may request any needed accommodation to participate in the application process. **For example**: accommodation for a test, a job interview, or a job demonstration.

The employer may wish to provide information on the application form and in the employment office about specific aspects of the job application process, so that applicants may request any needed accommodation. The employer is not required to provide such information, but without it the applicant may have no advance notice of the need to request an accommodation. Since the individual with a disability has the responsibility to request an accommodation and the employer has the responsibility to provide the accommodation (unless it would cause an undue hardship), providing advance information on various application procedures may help avoid last minute problems in making necessary accommodations. This information can be communicated orally or on tape for people who are visually impaired. (See also <u>Testing</u>, **5.6** below)

5.5(e) Making Job Applications Accessible

Employers have an obligation to make reasonable accommodations to enable an applicant with a disability to apply for a job. Some of the kinds of accommodations that may be needed have been suggested in the section on <u>Accessibility of Job Information</u>, **5.2** above. Individuals with visual or learning disabilities or other mental disabilities also may require assistance in filling out application forms.

5.5(f) The Job Interview

The basic requirements regarding pre-employment inquiries and the types of questions that are prohibited on job application forms **apply to the job interview as well.** (See 5.5(a) and (b) above.) An interviewer may not ask questions about a disability, but may obtain more specific information about the ability to perform job tasks and about any needed accommodation, as set out below.

To assure that an interview is conducted in a nondiscriminatory manner, interviewers should be well-informed about the ADA's requirements. The employer may wish to provide written guidelines to people who conduct job interviews.

Most employment discrimination against people with disabilities is not intentional. Discrimination most frequently occurs because interviewers and others involved in hiring lack knowledge about the differing capabilities of individuals with disabilities and make decisions based on stereotypes, misconceptions, or unfounded fears. To avoid discrimination in the hiring process, employers may wish to provide "awareness" training for interviewers and others involved in the hiring process. Such training provides factual information about disability and the qualifications of people with disabilities, emphasizes the importance of individualized assessments, and helps interviewers feel more at ease in talking with people who have different disabilities.

Sources that provide "awareness training," some at little or no cost, may be found under this heading in the Resource Directory Index.

The job interview should focus on the ability of an applicant to perform the job, not on disability.

> **For example:** If a person has only one arm and an essential function of a job is to drive a car, the interviewer should not ask if or how the disability would affect this person's driving. The person may be asked if s/he has a valid driver's license, and whether s/he can perform any special aspect of driving that is required, such as frequent long-distance trips, with or without an accommodation.

> The interviewer also could obtain needed information about an applicant's ability and experience in relation to specific job requirements through statements and questions such as: "Eighty-percent of the time of this sales job must be spent on the road covering a three-state territory. What is your outside selling experience? Do you have a valid driver's license? What is your accident record?"

Where an applicant has a visible disability (for example, uses a wheelchair or a guide dog, or has a missing limb) or has volunteered information about a disability, the interviewer may not ask questions about:

V-11

- the nature of the disability;

- the severity of the disability;

- the condition causing the disability;

- any prognosis or expectation regarding the condition or disability; or

- whether the individual will need treatment or special leave because of the disability.

The interviewer may describe or demonstrate the specific functions and tasks of the job and ask whether an applicant can perform these functions with or without a reasonable accommodation.

> **For example**: An interviewer could say: "The person in this mailroom clerk position is responsible for receiving incoming mail and packages, sorting the mail, and taking it in a cart to many offices in two buildings, one block apart. The mailclerk also must receive incoming boxes of supplies up to 50 pounds in weight, and place them on storage shelves up to 6 feet in height. Can you perform these tasks? Can you perform them with or without a reasonable accommodation?"

As suggested above, (see **5.5(d)**), the interviewer also may give the applicant a copy of a detailed position description and ask whether s/he can perform the functions described in the position, with or without a reasonable accommodation.

Questions may be asked regarding ability to perform <u>all</u> job functions, not merely those that are essential to the job.

> **For example**: A secretarial job may involve the following functions:

> 1. transcribing dictation and written drafts from the supervisor and other staff into final written documents;

> 2. proof-reading documents for accuracy;

> 3. developing and maintaining files;

> 4. scheduling and making arrangements for meetings and conferences;

5.   logging documents and correspondence in and out;

6.   placing, answering, and referring telephone calls;

7.   distributing documents to appropriate staff members;

8.   reproducing documents on copying machines; and

9.   occasional travel to perform clerical tasks at out of town conferences.

Taking into account the specific activities of the particular office in which this secretary will work, and availability of other staff, the employer has identified functions 1-6 as essential, and functions 7-9 as marginal to this secretary's job. The interviewer may ask questions related to all 9 functions; however, an applicant with limited mobility should not be screened out because of inability to perform the last 3 functions due to her disability. S/he should be evaluated on ability to perform the first 6 functions, with or without accommodation.

Inquiries Related to Ability to Perform Job Functions and Accommodations

An interviewer may obtain information about an applicant's ability to perform essential job functions and about any need for accommodation in several ways, depending on the particular job applicant and the requirements of a particular job:

- The applicant may be asked to describe or demonstrate how s/he will perform specific job functions, **if this is required of everyone applying for a job in this job category, regardless of disability.**

    For example: An employer might require all applicants for a telemarketing job to demonstrate selling ability by taking a simulated telephone sales test, but could not require that a person using a wheelchair take this test if other applicants are not required to take it.

V-13

- If an applicant has a **known** disability that would appear to interfere with or prevent performance of a job-related function, s/he may be asked to describe or demonstrate how this function would be performed, even if other applicants do not have to do so.

  > **For example**: If an applicant has one arm and the job requires placing bulky items on shelves up to six feet high, the interviewer could ask the applicant to demonstrate how s/he would perform this function, with or without an accommodation. If the applicant states that s/he can perform this function with a reasonable accommodation, for example, with a step stool fitted with a device to assist lifting, the employer either must provide this accommodation so that the applicant can show that s/he can shelve the items, or let the applicant describe how s/he would do this task.

- However, if an applicant has a known disability that would **not** interfere with or prevent performance of a job related function, the employer can only ask the applicant to demonstrate how s/he would perform the function if <u>all</u> applicants in the job category are required to do so, regardless of disability.

  > **For example**: If an applicant with one leg applies for a job that involves sorting small parts while seated, s/he may not be required to demonstrate the ability to do this job unless all applicants are required to do so.

If an applicant indicates that s/he cannot perform an essential job function even with an accommodation, the applicant would not be qualified for the job in question.

Inquiries About Attendance

An interviewer may not ask whether an applicant will need or request leave for medical treatment or for other reasons related to a disability.

The interviewer may provide information on the employer's regular work hours, leave policies, and any special attendance needs of the job, and ask if the applicant can meet these requirements (provided that the requirements actually are applied to employees in a particular job).

For example: "Our regular work hours are 9 to 5, five days weekly, but we expect employees in this job to work overtime, evenings, and weekends for 6 weeks during the Christmas season and on certain other holidays. New employees get 1 week of vacation, 7 sick leave days and may take no more than 5 days of unpaid leave per year. Can you meet these requirements?"

Information about previous work attendance records may be obtained on the application form, in the interview or in reference checks, but the questions should not refer to illness or disability.

If an applicant has had a poor attendance record on a previous job, s/he may wish to provide an explanation that includes information related to a disability, but the employer should not ask whether a poor attendance record was due to illness, accident or disability. For example, an applicant might wish to disclose voluntarily that the previous absence record was due to surgery for a medical condition that is now corrected, treatment for cancer that is now in remission or to adjust medication for epilepsy, but that s/he is now fully able to meet all job requirements.

Accommodations for Interviews

The employer must provide an accommodation, if needed, to enable an applicant to have equal opportunity in the interview process. As suggested earlier, the employer may find it helpful to state in an initial job notice, and/or on the job application form, that applicants who need accommodation for an interview should request this in advance.

Needed accommodations for interviews may include:

* an accessible location for people with mobility impairments;

* a sign interpreter for a deaf person;

* a reader for a blind person.

V-15

Conducting an Interview

The purpose of a job interview is to obtain appropriate information about the background qualifications and other personal qualities of an applicant in relation to the requirements of a specific job.

This chapter has discussed ways to obtain this information by focusing on the abilities rather than the disability of a disabled applicant. However, there are other aspects of an interview that may create barriers to an accurate and objective assessment of an applicant's job qualifications. The interviewer may not know how to communicate effectively with people who have particular disabilities, or may make negative, incorrect assumptions about the abilities of a person with a disability because s/he misinterprets some external manifestation of the disability.

> **For example.** An interviewer may assume that a person who displays certain characteristics of cerebral palsy, such as indistinct speech, lisping, and involuntary or halting movements, is limited in intelligence. In fact, cerebral palsy does not affect intelligence at all.

If an applicant who is known to have a disability was referred by a rehabilitation agency or other source familiar with the person, it may be helpful to contact the agency to learn more about this individual's ability to perform specific job functions; however, questions should not be asked about the nature or extent of the person's disability. General information on different disabilities may be obtained from many organizations listed in the Resource Directory. See Index under the specific disability.

5.5(g)   Background and Reference Checks

Before making a conditional job offer, an employer may not request any information about a job applicant from a previous employer, family member, or other source that it may not itself request of the job applicant.

If an employer uses an outside firm to conduct background checks, the employer should assure that this firm complies with the ADA's prohibitions on pre-employment inquiries. Such a firm is an agent of the employer. The employer is responsible for actions of its agents and may not do anything through a contractual relationship that it may not itself do directly.

Before making a conditional offer of employment, an employer may not ask previous employers or other sources about an applicant's:

- disability;

- illness;

- workers' compensation history;

- or any other questions that the employer itself may not ask of the applicant.

A previous employer may be asked about:

- job functions and tasks performed by the applicant;

- the quality and quantity of work performed;

- how job functions were performed;

- attendance record;

- other job-related issues that do not relate to disability.

If an applicant has a known disability and has indicated that s/he could perform a job with a reasonable accommodation, a previous employer may be asked about accommodations made by that employer.

5   Testing

Employers may use any kind of test to determine job qualifications. The ADA has two major requirements in relation to tests:

1.   **If a test screens out or tends to screen out an individual with a disability or a class of such individuals on the basis of disability, it must be job-related and consistent with business necessity.**

- This requirement applies to all kinds of tests, including, but not limited to: aptitude tests, tests of knowledge and skill, intelligence tests, agility tests, and job demonstrations.

A test will most likely be an accurate predictor of the job performance of a person with a disability when it most directly or closely measures actual skills and ability needed to do a job. **For example**: a typing test, a sales demonstration test, or other job performance test would indicate what the individual actually could do in performing a job, whereas a test that measured general qualities believed to be desirable in a job may screen out people on the basis of disability who could do the job. **For example**, a standardized test used for a job as a heavy equipment operator might screen out a person with dyslexia or other learning disability who was able to perform all functions of the job itself.

An employer is only required to show that a test is job-related and consistent with business necessity if it screens out a person with a disability <u>because of</u> the disability. If a person was screened out for a reason unrelated to disability, ADA requirements do not apply.

> **For example**: If a person with paraplegia who uses a wheelchair is screened out because s/he does not have sufficient speed or accuracy on a typing test, this person probably was not screened out <u>because of</u> his or her disability. The employer has no obligation to consider this person for a job which requires fast, accurate typing.

Even if a test is job-related and justified by business necessity, the employer has an obligation to provide a specific reasonable accommodation, if needed. For example, upon request, test sites must be accessible to people who have mobility disabilities. The ADA also has a very specific requirement for accommodation in testing, described below.

2.   Accommodation in testing

The ADA requires that tests be given to people who have impaired sensory, speaking or manual skills in a format and manner that does not require use of the impaired skill, unless the test is designed to measure that skill. (Sensory skills include the abilities to hear, see and to process information.)

The purpose of this requirement is to assure that tests <u>accurately</u> reflect a person's job skills, aptitudes, or whatever else the test is supposed to measure, rather than the person's impaired skills.

This requirement applies the reasonable accommodation obligation to testing. It protects people with disabilities from being excluded from jobs that they actually can do because a disability prevents them from taking a test or negatively influences a test result. However, an employer does not have to provide an alternative test format for a person with an impaired skill if the purpose of the test is to measure that skill.

For example:

- A person with dyslexia should be given an opportunity to take a written test orally, if the dyslexia seriously impairs the individual's ability to read. But if ability to read is a job-related function that the test is designed to measure, the employer could require that a person with dyslexia take the written test. However, even in this situation, reasonable accommodation should be considered. The person with dyslexia might be accommodated with a reader, unless the ability to read unaided is an essential job function, unless such an accommodation would not be possible on the job for which s/he is being tested, or would be an undue hardship. For example, the ability to read without help would be essential for a proofreader's job. Or, a dyslexic firefighter applicant might be disqualified if he could not quickly read necessary instructions for dealing with specific toxic substances at the site of a fire when no reader would be available.

- Providing extra time to take a test may be a reasonable accommodation for people with certain disabilities, such as visual impairments, learning disabilities, or mental retardation. On the other hand, an employer could require that an applicant complete a test within an established time frame if speed is one of the skills that the test is designed to measure. However, the results of a timed test should not be used to exclude a person with a disability, unless the test measures a particular speed necessary to perform an essential function of the job, and there is no reasonable accommodation that would enable this person to perform that function within prescribed time frames, or the accommodation would cause an undue hardship.

Generally, an employer is only required to provide such an accommodation if it knows, before administering a test, that an accommodation will be needed. Usually, it is the responsibility of the individual with a disability to request any required accommodation for a test. It has been suggested that the employer inform applicants, in advance, of any tests that will be administered as part of the application process so that they may request an accommodation, if needed. (See 5.5(d) above.) The employer may require that an individual with a disability request an accommodation within a specific time period before administration of the test. The employer also may require that documentation of the need for accommodation accompany such a request.

Occasionally, however, an individual with a disability may not realize in advance that s/he will need an accommodation to take a particular test.

> **For example**: A person with a visual impairment who knows that there will be a written test may not request an accommodation because she has her own specially designed lens that usually is effective for reading printed material. However, when the test is distributed, she finds that her lens is not sufficient, because of unusually low color contrast between the paper and the ink. Under these circumstances, she might request an accommodation and the employer would be obligated to provide one. The employer might provide the test in a higher contrast format at that time, reschedule the test, or make any other effective accommodation that would not impose an undue hardship.

An employer is not required to offer an applicant the specific accommodation requested. This request should be given primary consideration, but the employer is only obligated to provide an effective accommodation. (See Chapter III.) The employer is only required to provide, upon request, an "accessible" test format for individuals whose disabilities impair sensory, manual, or speaking skills needed to take the test, unless the test is designed to measure these skills.

Some Examples of Alternative Test Formats and Accommodations:

- Substituting a written test for an oral test (or written instructions for oral instructions) for people with impaired speaking or hearing skills;

- Administering a test in large print, in Braille, by a reader, or on a computer for people with visual or other reading disabilities;

- Allowing people with visual or learning disabilities or who have limited use of their hands to record test answers by tape recorder, dictation or computer;

- Providing extra time to complete a test for people with certain learning disabilities or impaired writing skills;

- Simplifying test language for people who have limited language skills because of a disability;

- Scheduling rest breaks for people with mental and other disabilities that require such relief;

- Assuring that a test site is accessible to a person with a mobility disability;

- Allowing a person with a mental disability who cannot perform well if there are distractions to take a test in a separate room, if a group test setting is not relevant to the job itself;

- Where it is not possible to test an individual with a disability in an alternative format, an employer may be required, as a reasonable accommodation, to evaluate the skill or ability being tested through some other means, such as an interview, education, work experience, licenses or certification, or a job demonstration for a trial period.

There are a number of technical assistance resources for effective alternative methods of testing people with different disabilities. (See "Alternative Testing Formats" in Resource Directory Index).

VI. MEDICAL EXAMINATIONS AND INQUIRIES

6.1 Overview of Legal Obligations

Pre-Employment, Pre-Offer

- An employer may not require a job applicant to take a medical examination, to respond to medical inquiries or to provide information about workers' compensation claims before the employer makes a job offer.

Pre-Employment, Post-Offer

- An employer may condition a job offer on the satisfactory result of a post-offer medical examination or medical inquiry if this is required of all entering employees in the same job category. A post-offer examination or inquiry does not have to be "job-related" and "consistent with business necessity." Questions also may be asked about previous injuries and workers' compensation claims.

- If an individual is not hired because a post-offer medical examination or inquiry reveals a disability, the reason(s) for not hiring must be job-related and necessary for the business. The employer also must show that no reasonable accommodation was available that would enable this individual to perform the essential job functions, or that accommodation would impose an undue hardship.

- A post-offer medical examination may disqualify an individual who would pose a "direct threat" to health or safety. Such a disqualification is job-related and consistent with business necessity.

- A post-offer medical examination may not disqualify an individual with a disability who is currently able to perform essential job functions because of speculation that the disability may cause a risk of future injury.

Employee Medical Examinations and Inquiries

- After a person starts work, a medical examination or inquiry of an employee must be job related and necessary for the business.

- Employers may conduct employee medical examinations where there is evidence of a job performance or safety problem, examinations required by other Federal laws, examinations to determine current "fitness" to perform a particular job and voluntary examinations that are part of employee health programs.

Confidentiality

- Information from all medical examinations and inquiries must be kept apart from general personnel files as a separate, confidential medical record, available only under limited conditions specified in the ADA. (See **6.5** below.)

Drug Testing

- Tests for illegal use of drugs are not medical examinations under the ADA and are not subject to the restrictions on such examinations. (See Chapter VIII.)

6.2 Basic Requirements

The ADA does not prevent employers from obtaining medical and related information necessary to evaluate the ability of applicants and employees to perform essential job functions, or to promote health and safety on the job. However, to protect individuals with disabilities from actions based on such information that are not job-related and consistent with business necessity, including protection of health and safety, the ADA imposes specific and differing obligations on the employer at three stages of the employment process:

1. **Before making a job offer,** an employer may not make any medical inquiry or conduct any medical examination.

2. **After making a conditional job offer,** before a person starts work, an employer may make unrestricted medical inquiries, but may not refuse to hire an individual with a disability based on results of such inquiries, unless the reason for rejection is job-related and justified by business necessity.

3. **After employment,** any medical examination or inquiry required of an employee must be job-related and justified by business necessity. Exceptions are voluntary examinations conducted as part of employee health programs and examinations required by other federal laws.

Under the ADA, "medical" documentation concerning the qualifications of an individual with a disability, or whether this individual constitutes a "direct threat" to health and safety, does not mean only information from medical doctors. It may be necessary to obtain information from other sources, such as rehabilitation experts, occupational or physical therapists, psychologists, and others knowledgeable about the individual and the disability concerned. It also may be more relevant to look at the individual's previous work history in making such determinations than to rely on an examination or tests by a physician.

The basic requirements regarding actions based on medical information and inquiries have been set out in Chapter IV. As emphasized there, such actions taken because of a disability **must be job-related** and **consistent with business necessity.** When an individual is rejected as a "direct threat" to health and safety:

- **the employer must be prepared to show a significant current risk of substantial harm (not a speculative or remote risk);**

- **the specific risk must be identified;**

- **the risk must be documented by objective medical or other factual evidence regarding the particular individual;**

- **even if a genuine significant risk of substantial harm exists, the employer must consider whether it can be eliminated or reduced below the level of a "direct threat" by reasonable accommodation.**

This chapter discusses in more detail the content and manner of medical examinations and inquiries that may be made, and the documentation that may be required (1) before employment and (2) after employment.

6.3   Examinations and Inquiries Before Employment

No Pre-Offer Medical Examination or Inquiry

The ADA prohibits medical inquiries or medical examinations before making a conditional job offer to an applicant. This prohibition is necessary because the results of such inquiries and examinations frequently are used to exclude people with disabilities from jobs they are able to perform.

Some employers have medical policies or rely on doctors' medical assessments that overestimate the impact of a particular condition on a particular individual, and/or underestimate the ability of an individual to cope with his or her condition. Medical policies that focus on **disability**, rather than the **ability** of a particular person, frequently will be discriminatory under the ADA.

> **For example**: A policy that prohibits employment of <u>any</u> individual who has epilepsy, diabetes or a heart condition from a certain type of job, and which does not consider the ability of a <u>particular</u> individual, in most cases would violate the ADA. (See Chapter IV.)

Many employers currently use a pre-employment medical questionnaire, a medical history, or a pre-employment medical examination as one step in a several-step selection process. Where this is so, an individual who has a "hidden" disability such as diabetes, epilepsy, heart disease, cancer, or mental illness, and who is rejected for a job, frequently does not know whether the reason for rejection was information revealed by the medical exam or inquiry (which may not have any relation to this person's ability to do the job), or whether the rejection was based on some other aspect of the selection process.

A history of such rejections has discouraged many people with disabilities from applying for jobs, because of fear that they will automatically be rejected when their disability is revealed by a medical examination. The ADA is designed to remove this barrier to employment.

6.4   Post-Offer Examinations and Inquiries Permitted

The ADA recognizes that employers may need to conduct medical examinations to determine if an applicant can perform certain jobs effectively and safely. The ADA requires only that such examinations be conducted as a separate, second step of the selection process, after an individual has met all other job pre-requisites. The employer may make a job offer to such an individual, conditioned on the satisfactory outcome of a medical examination or inquiry, providing that the employer requires such examination or inquiry for all entering employees in a particular job category, not merely individuals with known disabilities, or those whom the employer believes may have a disability.

A <u>post-offer</u> medical examination does not have to be given to all entering employees in all jobs, only to those in the same job category.

For example: An examination might be given to all entering employees in physical labor jobs, but not to employees entering clerical jobs.

The ADA does not require an employer to justify its requirement of a post-offer medical examination. An employer may wish to conduct a post-offer medical exam or make post-offer medical inquiries for purposes such as:

To determine if an individual currently has the physical or mental qualifications necessary to perform certain jobs:

For example: If a job requires continuous heavy physical exertion, a medical examination may be useful to determine whether an applicant's physical condition will permit him/her to perform the job.

To determine that a person can perform a job without posing a "direct threat" to the health or safety of self or others.

For example:

- A medical examination and evaluation might be required to ensure that prospective construction crane operators do not have disabilities such as uncontrolled seizures that would pose a significant risk to other workers.

- Workers in certain health care jobs may need to be examined to assure that they do not have a current contagious disease or infection that would pose a significant risk of transmission to others, and that could not be accommodated (for example, by giving the individual a delayed starting date until the period of contagion is over).

Compliance with medical requirements of other Federal laws

Employers may comply with medical and safety requirements established under other Federal laws without violating the ADA.

For example: Federal Highway Administration regulations require medical examinations and evaluations of interstate truck drivers, and the Federal Aviation Administration

VI-5

requires examinations for pilots and air controllers.

However, an employer still has an obligation to consider whether there is a reasonable accommodation, consistent with the requirements of other Federal laws, that would not exclude individuals who can perform jobs safely.

Employers also may conduct post-offer medical examinations that are required by state laws, but, as explained in Chapter IV, may not take actions based on such examinations if the state law is inconsistent with ADA requirements. (See Health and Safety Requirements of Other Federal or State Laws, 4.6.)

Information That May Be Requested in Post-Offer Examinations or Inquiries

After making a conditional job offer, an employer may make inquiries or conduct examinations to get any information that it believes to be relevant to a person's ability to perform a job. **For example**, the employer may require a full physical examination. An employer may ask questions that are prohibited as pre-employment inquiries about previou illnesses, diseases or medications. (See Chapter V.)

If a post-offer medical examination is given, it must be administered to all persons entering a job category. If a response to an initial medical inquiry (such as a medical history questionnaire) reveals that an applicant has had a previous injury, illness, or medical condition, the employer cannot require the applicant to undergo a medical examination unless all applicants in the job category are required to have such examination. However, the ADA does not require that the scope of medical examinations must be identical. An employer may give follow-up tests or examinations where an examination indicates that further information is needed.

> **For example**: All potential employees in a job category must be given a blood test, but if a person's initial test indicates a problem that may affect job performance, further tests may be given to that person only, in order to get necessary information.

A **post-offer** medical examination or inquiry, made before an individual starts work, need not focus on ability to perform job functions. Such inquiries and examinations themselves, unlike examinations/inquiries of **employees,** do not have to be "job related" and "consistent with business necessity." However, if a conditional job offer is withdrawn because of the results of such examination or inquiry, an employer must be able to show that:

- the reasons for the exclusion are job-related and consistent with business necessity, or the person is being excluded to avoid a "direct threat" to health or safety; and that

- no reasonable accommodation was available that would enable this person to perform the essential job functions without a significant risk to health or safety, or that such an accommodation would cause undue hardship.

> **Some examples** of post-offer decisions that might be job-related and justified by business necessity, and/or where no reasonable accommodation was possible:

>> - a medical history reveals that the individual has suffered serious multiple re-injuries to his back doing similar work, which have progressively worsened the back condition. Employing this person in this job would incur significant risk that he would further re-injure himself.

>> - a workers' compensation history indicates multiple claims in recent years which have been denied. An employer might have a legitimate business reason to believe that the person has submitted fraudulent claims. Withdrawing a job offer for this reason would not violate the ADA, because the decision is not based on disability.

>> - a medical examination reveals an impairment that would require the individual's frequent lengthy absence from work for medical treatment, and the job requires daily availability for the next 3 months. In this situation, the individual is not available to perform the essential functions of the job, and no accommodation is possible.

> **Examples** of discriminatory use of examination results that are **not** job related and justified by business necessity:

>> - A landscape firm sent an applicant for a laborer's job (who had been doing this kind of work for 20 years) for a physical exam. An x-ray showed that he had a curvature of the spine. The doctor advised the firm not to hire him because there was a risk that he might injure his back at some time in the future. The doctor provided no specific medical documentation that this would happen or was likely to happen. The

VI-7

company provided no description of the job to the doctor. The job actually involved riding a mechanical mower. This unlawful exclusion was based on speculation about future risk of injury, and was not job-related.

- An individual is rejected from a job because he cannot lift more than 50 pounds. The job requires lifting such a weight only occasionally. The employer has not considered possible accommodations, such as sharing the occasional heavy weight lifting with another employee or providing a device to assist lifting.

Risk Cannot be Speculative or Remote

The results of a medical examination may not disqualify persons currently able to perform essential job functions because of unsubstantiated speculation about future risk.

The results of a medical inquiry or examination may not be used to disqualify persons who are currently able to perform the essential functions of a job, either with or without an accommodation, because of **fear or speculation** that a disability may indicate a greater risk of future injury, or absenteeism, or may cause future workers' compensation or insurance costs. An employer may use such information to exclude an individual with a disability where there is specific medical documentation, reflecting current medical knowledge, that this individual would pose a significant, current risk of substantial harm to health or safety. (See Standards for Health and Safety: "Direct Threat" Chapter IV.)

For example:

- An individual who has an abnormal back X-ray may not be disqualified from a job that requires heavy lifting because of fear that she will be more likely to injure her back or cause higher workers' compensation or health insurance costs. However, where there is documentation that this individual has injured and re-injured her back in similar jobs, and the back condition has been aggravated further by injury, and if there is no reasonable accommodation that would eliminate the risk of reinjury or reduce it to an acceptable level, an employer would be justified in rejecting her for this position.

- If a medical examination reveals that an individual has epilepsy and is seizure-free or has adequate warning of a seizure, it would be unlawful to disqualify this person from a job operating a machine because of fear or speculation that he might pose a risk to himself or others. But if the examination and other medical inquiries reveal that an individual with epilepsy has seizures resulting in loss of consciousness, there could be evidence of significant risk in employing this person as a machine operator. However, even where the person might endanger himself by operating a machine, an accommodation, such as placing a shield over the machine to protect him, should be considered.

The Doctor's Role

A doctor who conducts medical examinations for an employer should not be responsible for making employment decisions or deciding whether or not it is possible to make a reasonable accommodation for a person with a disability. That responsibility lies with the employer.

The doctor's role should be limited to advising the employer about an individual's functional abilities and limitations in relation to job functions, and about whether the individual meets the employer's health and safety requirements.

Accordingly, employers should provide doctors who conduct such examinations with **specific** information about the job, including the type of information indicated in the discussions of "job descriptions" and "job analysis" in Chapter II. (See 2.3.)

Often, particularly when an employer uses an outside doctor who is not familiar with actual demands of the job, a doctor may make incorrect assumptions about the nature of the job functions and specific tasks, or about the ability of an individual with a disability to perform these tasks with a reasonable accommodation. It may be useful for the doctor to visit the job site to see how the job is done.

The employer should inform the doctor that any recommendations or conclusions related to hiring or placement of an individual should focus on only two concerns:

1.   **Whether this person currently is able to perform this specific job, with or without an accommodation.**

     This evaluation should look at the individual's specific abilities and limitations in regard to specific job demands.

> **For example**: The evaluation may indicate that a person can lift up to 30 pounds and can reach only 2 feet above the shoulder; the job as usually performed (without accommodation) requires lifting 50 pound crates to shelves that are 6 feet high.

2. **Whether this person can perform this job without posing a "direct threat" to the health or safety of the person or others.**

The doctor should be informed that the employer must be able to show that an exclusion of an individual with a disability because of a risk to health or safety meets the "direct threat" standard of the ADA, based on "the most current medical knowledge and/or the best available objective evidence about this individual." (See Chapter IV., Standards Necessary for Health and Safety, and 6.2 above.)

> **For example**: If a post-offer medical questionnaire indicates that a person has a history of repetitive motion injuries but has had successful surgery with no further problems indicated, and a doctor recommends that the employer reject this candidate because this medical history indicates that she would pose a higher risk of future injury, the employer would violate the ADA if it acted on the doctor's recommendation based only on the history of injuries. In this case, the doctor would not have considered this person's actual current condition as a result of surgery.

A doctor's evaluation of any future risk must be supported by valid medical analyses indicating a high probability of substantial harm if **this individual** performed the particular functions of the particular job in question. Conclusions of general medical studies about work restrictions for people with certain disabilities will not be sufficient evidence, because they do not relate to a particular individual and do not consider reasonable accommodation.

The employer should not rely only on a doctor's opinion, but on the **best available objective evidence**. This may include the experience of the individual with a disability in previous similar jobs, occupations, or non-work activities, the opinions of other doctors with expertise on the particular disability, and the advice of rehabilitation counselors, occupational or physical therapists, and others with direct knowledge of the disability and/or the individual concerned. Organizations such as Independent Living Centers, public and private rehabilitation agencies, and organizations serving people with specific disabilities such as the Epilepsy Foundation, United Cerebral Palsy Associations, National Head Injury Foundation, and many others can provide such assistance. (See <u>Resource Directory</u>.)

Where the doctor's report indicates that an individual has a disability that may prevent performance of essential job functions, or that may pose a "direct threat" to health or safety, the employer also may seek his/her advice on possible accommodations that would overcome these disqualifications.

6.5   <u>Confidentiality and Limitations on Use of Medical Information</u>

Although the ADA does not limit the nature or extent of post-offer medical examinations and inquiries, it imposes very **strict limitations on the use of information** obtained from such examinations and inquiries. These limitations also apply to information obtained from examinations or inquiries of employees.

- All information obtained from post-offer medical examinations and inquiries must be collected and maintained on separate forms, in separate medical files and must be treated as a **confidential medical record.** Therefore, an employer should not place any medical-related material in an employee's personnel file. The employer should take steps to guarantee the security of the employee's medical information, including:

    - keeping the information in a medical file in a separate, locked cabinet, apart from the location of personnel files; and

    - designating a specific person or persons to have access to the medical file.

- All medical-related information must be kept confidential, with the following exceptions:

    - Supervisors and managers may be informed about necessary restrictions on the work or duties of an employee and necessary accommodations;

    - First aid and safety personnel may be informed, when appropriate, if the disability might require emergency treatment or if any specific procedures are needed in the case of fire or other evacuations.

- Government officials investigating compliance with the ADA and other Federal and state laws prohibiting discrimination on the basis of disability or handicap should be provided relevant information on request. (Other Federal laws and regulations also may require disclosure of relevant medical information.)

- Relevant information may be provided to state workers' compensation offices or "second injury" funds, in accordance with state workers' compensation laws. (See Chapter IX., Workers' Compensation and Work-Related Injury.)

- Relevant information may be provided to insurance companies where the company requires a medical examination to provide health or life insurance for employees. (See Health Insurance and Other Benefit Plans Chapter VII.)

6.6 Employee Medical Examinations and Inquiries

The ADA's requirements concerning medical examinations and inquiries of employees are more stringent than those affecting applicants who a being evaluated for employment after a conditional job offer. In order a medical examination or inquiry to be made of an employee, it must b job related and consistent with business necessity. The need for the examination may be triggered by some evidence of problems related to job performance or safety, or an examination may be necessary to determine whether individuals in physically demanding jobs continue to be fit for duty. In either case, the scope of the examination also must job-related.

For example:

- An attorney could not be required to submit to a medical examination or inquiry just because her leg had been amputated. The essential functions of an attorney's job do not require use of both legs; therefore such an inquiry wou not be job related.

- An employer may require a warehouse laborer, whose back impairment affects the ability to lift, to be examined by an orthopedist, but may not require this employee to submit t an HIV test where the test is not related to either the essential functions of his job or to his impairment.

Medical examinations or inquiries may be job related and necessary under several circumstances:

- **When an employee is having difficulty performing his or her job effectively.** In such cases, a medical examination may be necessary to determine if s/he can perform essential job functions with or without an accommodation.

    For example: If an employee falls asleep on the job, has excessive absenteeism, or exhibits other performance problems, an examination may be needed to determine if the problem is caused by an underlying medical condition, and whether medical treatment is needed. If the examination reveals an impairment that is a disability under the ADA, the employer must consider possible reasonable accommodations. If the impairment is not a disability, the employer is not required to make an accommodation.

    For example: An employee may complain of headaches caused by noise at the worksite. A medical examination may indicate that there is no medically discernible mental or physiological disorder causing the headaches. This employee would not be "an individual with a disability" under the ADA, and the employer would have no obligation to provide an accommodation. The employer may voluntarily take steps to improve the noise situation, particularly if other employees also suffer from noise, but would have no obligation to do so under the ADA.

- **When An Employee Becomes Disabled**

    An employee who is injured on or off the job, who becomes ill, or suffers any other condition that meets the ADA definition of "disability," is protected by the Act if s/he can perform the essential functions of the job with or without reasonable accommodation.

    Employers are accustomed to dealing with injured workers through the workers' compensation process and disability management programs, but they have different, although not necessarily conflicting obligations under the ADA. The relationship between ADA, workers' compensation requirements and medical examinations and inquiries is discussed in Chapter IX.

    Under the ADA, medical information or medical examinations may be required when an employee suffers an injury on the job. Such an examination or inquiry also may be required when an employee wishes to return to work after an injury or illness, if it is job-related and consistent with business necessity:

- to determine if the individual meets the ADA definition of "individual with a disability," if an accommodation has been requested.

- to determine if the person can perform essential functions of the job currently held, (or held before the injury or illness), with or without reasonable accommodation, and without posing a "direct threat" to health or safety that cannot be reduced or eliminated by reasonable accommodation.

- to identify an effective accommodation that would enable the person to perform essential job functions in the current (previous) job, or in a vacant job for which the person is qualified (with or without accommodation). (See Chapter IX.)

- **Examination Necessary for Reasonable Accommodation**

A medical examination may be required if an employee requests an accommodation on the basis of disability. An accommodation may be needed in an employee's existing job, or if the employee is being transferred or promoted to a different job. Medical information may be needed to determine if the employee has a disability covered by the ADA and is entitled to an accommodation, and if so, to help identify an effective accommodation.

Medical inquiries related to an employee's disability and functional limitations may include consultations with knowledgeable professional sources, such as occupational and physical therapists, rehabilitation specialists, and organizations with expertise in adaptations for specific disabilities.

- **Medical examinations, screening and monitoring required by other laws.**

Employers may conduct periodic examinations and other medical screening and monitoring required by federal, state or local laws. As indicated in Chapter IV, the ADA recognizes that an action taken to comply with another Federal law is job-related and consistent with business necessity; however, requirements of state and local laws do not necessarily meet this standard unless they are consistent with the ADA.

> **For example**: Employers may conduct medical examinations and medical monitoring required by:

- The U.S. Department of Transportation for interstate bus and truck drivers, railroad engineers, airline pilots and air controllers;

- The Occupational Safety and Health Act:

- The Federal Mine Health and Safety Act;

- Other statutes that require employees exposed to toxic or hazardous substances to be medically monitored at specific intervals.

However, if a state or local law required that employees in a particular job be periodically tested for AIDS or the HIV virus, the ADA would prohibit such an examination unless an employer can show that it is job-related and consistent with business necessity, or required to avoid a direct threat to health or safety. (See Chapter IV.)

- **Voluntary "Wellness" and Health Screening Programs**

An employer may conduct voluntary medical examinations and inquiries as part of an employee health program (such as medical screening for high blood pressure, weight control, and cancer detection), providing that:

- participation in the program is voluntary;

- information obtained is maintained according to the confidentiality requirements of the ADA (See 6.5); and

- this information is not used to discriminate against an employee.

Information from Medical Inquiries May Not be Used to Discriminate

An employer may not use information obtained from an employee medical examination or inquiry to discriminate against the employee in any employment practice. (See Chapter VII.)

Confidentiality

All information obtained from employee medical examinations and inquiries must be maintained and used in accordance with ADA confidentiality requirements. (See **6.5** above.)

VII. NONDISCRIMINATION IN OTHER EMPLOYMENT PRACTICES

7.1 Introduction

The nondiscrimination requirements of the ADA apply to all employment practices and activities. The preceding chapters have explained these requirements as they apply to job qualification and selection standards, the hiring process, and medical examinations and inquiries. This chapter discusses the application of nondiscrimination requirements to other employment practices and activities.

In most cases, an employer need only apply the basic nondiscrimination principles already emphasized; however, there are also some special requirements applicable to certain employment activities. This chapter discusses:

- the ADA's prohibition of discrimination on the basis of a **relationship or association with** an individual with a disability;

- nondiscrimination requirements affecting:

   - **promotion, assignment, training, evaluation, discipline, advancement opportunity and discharge;**

   - **compensation, insurance, leave, and other benefits and privileges of employment; and**

   - **contractual relationships.**

7.2 Overview of Legal Obligations

- An employer may not discriminate against a qualified individual with a disability because of the disability, in any employment practice, or any term, condition or benefit of employment.

- An employer may not deny an employment opportunity because an individual, with or without a disability, has a **relationship or association with** an individual who has a disability.

- An employer may not participate in a contractual or other arrangement that subjects the employer's qualified applicant or employee with a disability to discrimination.

- An employer may not discriminate or retaliate against any individual, whether or not the individual is disabled, because the individual has opposed a discriminatory practice, filed a discrimination charge, or participated in any way in enforcing the ADA.

7.3 Nondiscrimination in all Employment Practices

The ADA prohibits discrimination against a qualified individual with a disability on the basis of disability in the following employment practice

- Recruitment, advertising, and job application procedures;

- Hiring, upgrading, promotion, award of tenure, demotion, transfer layoff, termination, right of return from layoff, and rehiring;

- Rates of pay or any other form of compensation, and changes in compensation;

- Job assignments, job classifications, organizational structures, position descriptions, lines of progression, and seniority lists;

- Leaves of absence, sick leave, or any other leave;

- Fringe benefits available by virtue of employment, whether or no administered by the covered entity;

- Selection and financial support for training, including: apprenticeships, professional meetings, conferences, and other related activities, and selection for leaves of absence to pursue training;

- Activities sponsored by a covered entity including social and recreational programs; and

- Any other term, condition, or privilege of employment.

Nondiscrimination, as applied to all employment practices, means that:

- an individual with a disability should have equal access to any employment opportunity available to a similarly situated individu who is not disabled;

VII-2

- employment decisions concerning an employee or applicant should be based on objective factual evidence about the particular individual, not on assumptions or stereotypes about the individual's disability;

- the qualifications of an individual with a disability may be evaluated on ability to perform all job-related functions, with or without reasonable accommodation. However, an individual may not be excluded from a job because a disability prevents performance of marginal job functions;

- an employer must provide a reasonable accommodation that will enable an individual with a disability to have an equal opportunity in every aspect of employment, unless a particular accommodation would impose an undue hardship;

- an employer may not use an employment practice or policy that screens out or tends to screen out an individual with a disability or a class of individuals with disabilities, unless the practice or policy is job related and consistent with business necessity and the individual cannot be accommodated without undue hardship;

- an employer may not limit, segregate, or classify an individual with a disability in any way that negatively affects the individual in terms of job opportunity and advancement;

- an individual with a disability should not because of a disability be treated differently than a similarly situated individual in any aspect of employment, except when a reasonable accommodation is needed to provide an equal employment opportunity, or when another Federal law or regulation requires different treatment.

These requirements are discussed in this chapter as they apply to various employment practices. The prohibition against retaliation is discussed in Chapter X.

7.4   Nondiscrimination and Relationship or Association with an Individual with a Disability

The ADA specifically provides that an employer or other covered entity may not deny an employment opportunity or benefit to an individual, whether or not that individual is disabled, because that individual has a **known relationship or association** with an individual who has a disability. Nor may an employer discriminate in any other way against an individual, whether or not disabled, because that individual has such a relationship or association.

VII-3

The term "relationship or association" refers to family relationships and any other social or business relationship or association. Therefore, this provision of the law prohibits employers from making employment decisions based on concerns about the disability of a family member of an applicant or employee, or anyone else with whom this person has a relationship or association.

> **For example**: An employer may not:
>
> - refuse to hire or fire an individual because the individual has a spouse, child, or other dependent who has a disability. The employer may not assume that the individual will be unreliable, have to use leave time, or be away from work in order to care for the family member with a disability;
>
> - refuse to hire or fire an individual because s/he has a spouse, child or other dependent who has a disability that is either not covered by the employer's current health insurance plan or that may cause future increased health care costs;
>
> - refuse to insure, or subject an individual to different terms or conditions of insurance, solely because the individual has a spouse, child, or other dependent who has a disability;
>
> - refuse to hire or fire an individual because the individual has a relationship or association with a person or persons who have disabilities.
>
> **For example**: an employer cannot fire an employee because s/he does volunteer work with people who have AIDS.

This provision of the law prohibits discrimination in employment decisions concerning an individual, whether the individual is or is not disabled, because of a known relationship or association with an individual with a disability. However, an employer is not obligated to provide a reasonable accommodation to a **nondisabled** individual, because this person has a relationship or association with a disabled individual. The obligation to make a reasonable accommodation applies only to qualified individuals with disabilities.

> **For example**: The ADA does not require that an employer provide an employee who is not disabled with a modified work schedule as an accommodation, to enable the employee to care for a spouse or child with a disability.

7.5   Nondiscrimination and Opportunity for Advancement

The nondiscrimination requirements that apply to initial selection apply to all aspects of employment, including opportunities for advancement. For example, an employer may not discriminate in promotion, job classification, evaluation, disciplinary action, opportunities for training, or participation in meetings and conferences. In particular, an employer:

- should not assume that an individual is not interested in, or not qualified for, advancement because of disability;

- should not deny a promotion because of the need to make an accommodation, unless the accommodation would cause an undue hardship;

- should not place individuals with disabilities in separate lines of progression or in segregated units or locations that limit opportunity for advancement;

- should assure that supervisors and managers who make decisions regarding promotion and advancement are aware of ADA nondiscrimination requirements.

7.6   Training

Employees with disabilities must be provided equal opportunities to participate in training to improve job performance and provide opportunity for advancement. Training opportunities cannot be denied because of the need to make a reasonable accommodation, unless the accommodation would be an undue hardship. Accommodations that may be necessary, depending on the needs of particular individuals, may include:

- accessible locations and facilities for people with mobility disabilities;

- interpreters and note-takers for employees who are deaf;

- materials in accessible formats and/or readers for people who are visually impaired, for people with learning disabilities, and for people with mental retardation;

- if audiovisual materials are used, captions for people who are deaf, and voice-overs for people who are visually impaired;

VII-5

- good lighting on an interpreter, and good general illumination for people with visual impairments and other disabilities;

- clarification of concepts presented in training for people who have reading or other disabilities;

- individualized instruction for people with mental retardation and certain other disabilities.

If an employer contracts for training with a training company, or contracts for training facilities such as hotels or conference centers, the employer is responsible for assuring accessibility and other needed accommodations.

It is advisable that any contract with a company or facility used for training include a provision requiring the other party to provide needed accommodations. However, if the contractor does not do so, the employer remains responsible for providing the accommodation, unless it would cause an undue hardship.

> **For example**: Suppose a company with which an employer has contracted proposes to conduct training at an inaccessible location. The employer is responsible for providing an accommodation that would enable an employee who uses a wheelchair to obtain this training. The employer might do this by: requiring the training company to relocate the program to an accessible site; requiring the company to make the site (including all facilities used by trainees) accessible; making the site accessible or providing resources that enable the training company to do so; contracting with another training company that uses accessible sites; or providing any other accommodation (such as temporary ramps) that would not impose an undue hardship. If it is impossible to make an accommodation because the need is only discovered when an employee arrives at the training site, the employer may have to provide accessible training at a later date.

> **Or, for example**: An employer contracts with a hotel to hold a conference for its employees. The employer must assure physical and communications accessibility for employees with disabilities, including accessibility of guest rooms and all meeting and other rooms used by attendees. The employer may assure accessibility by inspecting the site, or may ask a local disability group with accessibility expertise (such as an Independent Living Center) to do so. The employer remains responsible for assuring accessibility. However, if the hotel breaches a contract provision requiring accessibility, the hotel may be liable to the employer under regular (non-ADA) breach of contract law. The hotel also may be liable

VII-6

under Title III of the ADA, which requires accessibility in public accommodations.

7.7   Evaluations, Discipline and Discharge

- An employer can hold employees with disabilities to the same standards of production/performance as other similarly situated employees without disabilities for performing essential job functions (with or without reasonable accommodation).

- An employer also can hold employees with disabilities to the same standards of production/performance as other employees regarding marginal job functions, unless the disability affects the ability to perform these marginal functions. If the ability to perform marginal functions is affected by the disability, the employer must provide some type of reasonable accommodation such as job restructuring (unless to do so would be an undue hardship).

- A disabled employee who needs an accommodation (that is not an undue hardship for an employer) in order to perform a job function should not be evaluated on his/her ability to perform the function without the accommodation, and should not be downgraded because such an accommodation is needed to perform the function.

- An employer should not give employees with disabilities "special treatment." They should not be evaluated on a lower standard or disciplined less severely than any other employee. This is not equal employment opportunity.

- An employer must provide an employee with a disability with reasonable accommodation necessary to enable the employee to participate in the evaluation process (for example, counseling or an interpreter).

- If an employee with a disability is not performing well, an employer may require medical and other professional inquiries that are job-related and consistent with business necessity to discover whether the disability is causing the poor performance, and whether any reasonable accommodation or additional accommodation is needed. (See Chapter VI.)

- An employer may take the same disciplinary action against employees with disabilities as it takes against other similarly situated employees, if the illegal use of drugs or alcohol use affects job performance and/or attendance. (See Chapter VIII.)

- An employer may not discipline or terminate an employee with a disability if the employer has refused to provide a requested reasonable accommodation that did not constitute an undue hardship, and the reason for unsatisfactory performance was the lack of accommodation.

7.8   Compensation

- An employer cannot reduce pay to an employee with a disability because of the elimination of a marginal job function or because has provided a reasonable accommodation, such as specialized or modified equipment. The employer can give the employee with a disability other marginal functions that s/he can perform.

- An employee who is reassigned to a lower paying job or provided part-time job as an accommodation may be paid the lower amoun that would apply to such positions, consistent with the employer' regular compensation practices.

7.9   Health Insurance and Other Employee Benefit Plans

As discussed above, an employer or other covered entity may not limit, segregate or classify an individual with a disability, on the basis of disability, in a manner that adversely affects the individual's employment. This prohibition applies to the provision and administrat of health insurance and other benefit plans, such as life insurance and pension plans.

This means that:

- If an employer provides insurance or other benefit plans to its employees, it must provide the same coverage to its employees w disabilities. Employees with disabilities must be given equal acc to whatever insurance or benefit plans the employer provides.

- An employer cannot deny insurance to an individual with a disability or subject an individual with a disability to different terms or conditions of insurance, based on disability alone, if the disability does not pose increased insurance risks. Nor may the employer enter into any contract or agreement with an insuranc company or other entity that has such effect.

- An employer cannot fire or refuse to hire an individual with a disability because the employer's current health insurance plan does not cover the individual's disability, or because the individual may increase the employer's future health care costs.

- An employer cannot fire or refuse to hire an individual (whether or not that individual has a disability) because the individual has a family member or dependent with a disability that is not covered by the employer's current health insurance plan, or that may increase the employer's future health care costs.

While establishing these protections for employees with disabilities, the ADA permits employers to provide insurance plans that comply with existing Federal and state insurance requirements, even if provisions of these plans have an adverse affect on people with disabilities, provided that the provisions are not used as a subterfuge to evade the purpose of the ADA.

Specifically, the ADA provides that:

- Where an employer provides health insurance through an insurance carrier that is regulated by state law, it may provide coverage in accordance with accepted principles of risk assessment and/or risk classification, as required or permitted by such law, even if this causes limitations in coverage for individuals with disabilities.

- Similarly, self-insured plans which are not subject to state law may provide coverage in a manner that is consistent with basic accepted principles of insurance risk classification, even if this results in limitations in coverage to individuals with disabilities.

In each case, such activity is permitted only if it is not being used as a subterfuge to evade the intent of the ADA. Whether or not an activity is being used as a subterfuge will be determined regardless of the date that the insurance plan or employee benefit plan was adopted.

This means that:

- An employer may continue to offer health insurance plans that contain pre-existing condition exclusions, even if this adversely affects individuals with disabilities, unless these exclusions are being used as a subterfuge to evade the purpose of the ADA.

- An employer may continue to offer health insurance plans that limit coverage for certain <u>procedures</u>, and/or limit particular <u>treatments</u> to a specified number per year, even if these restrictions adversely affect individuals with disabilities, as long as

VII-9

the restrictions are uniformly applied to all insured individuals, regardless of the disability.

> **For example**, an employer can offer a health insurance plan that limits coverage of blood transfusions to five transfusions per year for all employees, even though an employee with hemophilia may require more than five transfusions per year. However, the employer could not deny this employee coverage for another, otherwise covered procedure, because the plan will not pay for the additional blood transfusions that the procedure would require.

- An employer may continue to offer health insurance plans that limit reimbursements for certain types of drugs or procedures, even if these restrictions adversely affect individuals with disabilities, as long as the restrictions are uniformly applied without regard to disability.

> **For example**, an employer can offer a health insurance plan that does not cover experimental drugs or procedures, as long as this restriction is applied to all insured individuals.

7.10 Leave

- An employer may establish attendance and leave policies that are uniformly applied to all employees, regardless of disability, but may not refuse leave needed by an employee with a disability if other employees get such leave.

- An employer may be required to make adjustments in leave policy as a reasonable accommodation. The employer is not obligated to provide additional paid leave, but accommodations may include leave flexibility and unpaid leave. (See Chapter III.)

- A uniformly applied leave policy does not violate the ADA because it has a more severe effect on an individual because of his/her disability. However, if an individual with a disability requests a modification of such a policy as a reasonable accommodation, an employer may be required to provide it, unless it would impose an undue hardship.

> **For example**: If an employer has a policy providing 2 weeks paid leave for all employees, with no other provision for sick leave and a "no leave" policy for the first 6 months of employment, an employee with a disability who cannot get leave for needed medical treatment could not successfully

charge that the employer's policy is discriminatory on its face. However, this individual could request leave without pay or advance leave as a reasonable accommodation. Such leave should be provided, unless the employer can show undue hardship: For example, an employer might be able to show that it is necessary for the operation of the business that this employee be available for the time period when leave is requested.

- An employer is not required to give leave as a reasonable accommodation to an employee who has a relationship with an individual with a disability to enable the employee to care for that individual. (See p. 8 above.)

7.11 Contractual or Other Relationships

An employer may not do anything through a contractual relationship that it cannot do directly. This applies to any contracts, including contracts with:

- training organizations (see above);

- insurers (see above);

- employment agencies and agencies used for background checks (see Chapter V);

- labor unions (see below).

7.11(a)   Collective Bargaining Agreements

Labor unions are covered by the ADA and have the same obligation as the employer to comply with its requirements. An employer also is prohibited by the ADA from taking any action through a labor union contract that it may not take itself.

For example: If a union contract contained physical requirements for a particular job that screened out people with disabilities who were qualified to perform the job, and these requirements are not job-related and consistent with business necessity, they could be challenged as discriminatory by a qualified individual with a disability.

The terms of a collective bargaining agreement may be relevant in determining whether a particular accommodation would cause an employer undue hardship.

> **For example**: If the collective bargaining agreement reserves certain jobs for employees with a given amount of seniority, this may be considered as a factor in determining whether it would be an undue hardship to reassign an individual with a disability who does not have seniority to a vacant job.

Where a collective bargaining agreement identifies functions that must be performed in a particular job, the agreement, like a job description, may be considered as evidence of what the employer and union consider to be a job's essential functions. However, just because a function is listed in a union agreement does not mean that it is an essential function. The agreement, like the job description, will be considered along with other types of evidence. (See Chapter II.)

The Congressional Committee Reports accompanying the ADA advised employers and unions that they could carry out their responsibilities under the Act, and avoid conflicts between the bargaining agreement and the employer's duty to provide reasonable accommodation, by adding a provision to agreements negotiated after the effective date of the ADA, permitting the employer to take all actions necessary to comply with the Act.

7.12 Nondiscrimination in Other Benefits and Privileges of Employment

Nondiscrimination requirements, including the obligation to make reasonable accommodation, apply to all social or recreational activities provided or conducted by an employer, to any transportation provided by an employer for its employees or applicants, and to all other benefits and privileges of employment.

This means that:

- Employees with disabilities must have an equal opportunity to attend and participate in any social functions conducted or sponsored by an employer. Functions such as parties, picnics, shows, and award ceremonies should be held in accessible locations, and interpreters or other accommodation should be provided when necessary.

- Employees with disabilities must have equal access to break rooms, lounges, cafeterias, and any other non-work facilities that are provided by an employer for use by its employees.

- Employees with disabilities must have equal access to an exercise room, gymnasium, or health club provided by an employer for use by its employees. However, an employer would not have to eliminate facilities provided for employees because a disabled employee cannot use certain equipment or amenities because of his/her disability. **For example**, an employer would not have to remove certain exercise machines simply because an employee who is a paraplegic could not use them.

- Employees with disabilities must be given an equal opportunity to participate in employer-sponsored sports teams, leagues, or recreational activities such as hiking or biking clubs. However, the employer does not have to discontinue such activities because a disabled employee cannot fully participate due to his/her disability. **For example**, an employer would not have to discontinue the company biking club simply because a blind employee is unable to ride a bicycle.

- Any transportation provided by an employer for use by its employees must be accessible to employees with a disability. This includes transportation between employer facilities, transportation to or from mass transit and transportation provided on a occasional basis to employer-sponsored events.

VIII. DRUG AND ALCOHOL ABUSE

8.1   Introduction

The ADA specifically permits employers to ensure that the workplace is free from the illegal use of drugs and the use of alcohol, and to comply with other Federal laws and regulations regarding alcohol and drug use. At the same time, the ADA provides limited protection from discrimination for recovering drug addicts and for alcoholics.

8.2   Overview of Legal Obligations

- An individual who is currently engaging in the illegal use of drugs is not an "individual with a disability" when the employer acts on the basis of such use.

- An employer may prohibit the illegal use of drugs and the use of alcohol at the workplace.

- It is not a violation of the ADA for an employer to give tests for the illegal use of drugs.

- An employer may discharge or deny employment to persons who currently engage in the illegal use of drugs.

- An employer may not discriminate against a drug addict who is not currently using drugs and who has been rehabilitated, because of a history of drug addiction.

- A person who is an alcoholic is an "individual with a disability" under the ADA.

- An employer may discipline, discharge or deny employment to an alcoholic whose use of alcohol impairs job performance or conduct to the extent that s/he is not a "qualified individual with a disability."

- Employees who use drugs or alcohol may be required to meet the same standards of performance and conduct that are set for other employees.

- Employees may be required to follow the Drug-Free Workplace Act of 1988 and rules set by Federal agencies pertaining to drug and alcohol use in the workplace.

8.3   Illegal Use of Drugs

An employer may discharge or deny employment to current illegal users of drugs, on the basis of such drug use, without fear of being held liable for disability discrimination. Current illegal users of drugs are not "individuals with disabilities" under the ADA.

The illegal use of drugs includes the use, possession, or distribution of drugs which are unlawful under the Controlled Substances Act. It includes the use of illegal drugs and the illegal use of prescription drugs that are "controlled substances".

> **For example**: Amphetamines can be legally prescribed drugs. However, amphetamines, by law, are "controlled substances" because of their abuse and potential for abuse. If a person takes amphetamines without a prescription, that person is using drugs illegally, even though they could be prescribed by a physician.

The illegal use of drugs does not include drugs taken under supervision of a licensed health care professional, including experimental drugs for people with AIDS, epilepsy, or mental illness.

> **For example**: A person who takes morphine for the control of pain caused by cancer is not using a drug illegally if it is taken under the supervision of a licensed physician. Similarly, a participant in a methadone maintenance treatment program cann be discriminated against by an employer based upon the individual's lawful use of methadone.

An individual who illegally uses drugs but also has a disability, such a epilepsy, is only protected by the ADA from discrimination on the basis of the disability (epilepsy). An employer can discharge or deny employment to such an individual on the basis of his/her illegal use of drugs.

What does "current" drug use mean?

If an individual tests positive on a test for the illegal use of drugs, the individual will be considered a current drug user under the ADA wher the test correctly indicates that the individual is engaging in the illega use of a controlled substance.

"Current" drug use means that the illegal use of drugs occurred recent enough to justify an employer's reasonable belief that involvement wit! drugs is an on-going problem. It is not limited to the day of use, or recent weeks or days, in terms of an employment action. It is determined on a case-by-case basis.

> **For example**: An applicant or employee who tests positive for an illegal drug cannot immediately enter a drug rehabilitation program and seek to avoid the possibility of discipline or termination by claiming that s/he now is in rehabilitation and is no longer using drugs illegally. A person who tests positive for illegal use of drugs is not entitled to the protection that may be available to former users who have been or are in rehabilitation (see below).

8.4 Alcoholism

While a current illegal user of drugs has no protection under the ADA if the employer acts on the basis of such use, a person who currently uses alcohol is not automatically denied protection simply because of the alcohol use. An alcoholic is a person with a disability under the ADA and may be entitled to consideration of accommodation, if s/he is qualified to perform the essential functions of a job. However, an employer may discipline, discharge or deny employment to an alcoholic whose use of alcohol adversely affects job performance or conduct to the extent that s/he is not "qualified."

> **For example**: If an individual who has alcoholism often is late to work or is unable to perform the responsibilities of his/her job, an employer can take disciplinary action on the basis of the poor job performance and conduct. However, an employer may not discipline an alcoholic employee more severely than it does other employees for the same performance or conduct.

8.5 Recovering Drug Addicts

Persons addicted to drugs, but who are no longer using drugs illegally and are receiving treatment for drug addiction or who have been rehabilitated successfully, are protected by the ADA from discrimination on the basis of **past** drug addiction.

> **For example**: An addict who is currently in a drug rehabilitation program and has not used drugs illegally for some time is not excluded from the protection of the ADA. This person will be protected by the ADA because s/he has a history of addiction, or if s/he is "regarded as" being addicted. Similarly, an addict who is rehabilitated or who has successfully completed a supervised rehabilitation program and is no longer illegally using drugs is not excluded from the ADA.

However, a person who casually used drugs illegally in the past, but did not become addicted is not an individual with a disability based on the past drug use. In order for a person to be "substantially limited" because of drug use, s/he must be addicted to the drug.

To ensure that drug use is not recurring, an employer may request evidence that an individual is participating in a drug rehabilitation program or may request the results of a drug test (see below).

A "rehabilitation program" may include in-patient, out-patient, or employee assistance programs, or recognized self-help programs such as Narcotics Anonymous.

8.6   Persons "Regarded As" Addicts and Illegal Drug Users

Individuals who are not illegally using drugs, but who are erroneously perceived as being addicts and as currently using drugs illegally, are protected by the ADA.

> **For example**: If an employer perceived someone to be addicted to illegal drugs based upon rumor and the groggy appearance of the individual, but the rumor was false and the appearance was a side-effect of a lawfully prescribed medication, this individual would be "regarded as" an individual with a disability (a drug addict) and would be protected from discrimination based upon that false assumption. If an employer did not regard the individual as an addict, but simply as a social user of illegal drugs, the individual would not be "regarded as" an individual with a disability and would not be protected by the ADA.

As with other disabilities, an individual who claims that s/he was discriminated against because of past or perceived illegal drug addiction, may be asked to prove that s/he has a record of, or is regarded as having, an addiction to drugs.

8.7   Efforts to Prohibit Drug and Alcohol Use in the Workplace

The ADA does not prevent efforts to combat the use of drugs and alcohol in the workplace

The ADA does not interfere with employers' programs to combat the use of drugs and alcohol in the workplace. The Act specifically provides that an employer may:

- prohibit the use of drugs and alcohol in the workplace.

- require that employees not be under the influence of alcohol or drugs in the workplace.

> **For example**: An employer can require that employees not come to work or return from lunch under the influence of alcohol, or drugs used illegally.

- Require that employees who illegally use drugs or alcohol meet the same qualification and performance standards applied to other employees. Unsatisfactory behavior such as absenteeism, tardiness, poor job performance, or accidents caused by alcohol or illegal drug use need not be accepted nor accommodated.

> **For example**: If an employee is often late or does not show up for work because of alcoholism, an employer can take direct action based on the conduct. However, an employer would violate the ADA if it imposed greater sanctions on such an alcoholic employee than it did on other employees for the same misconduct.

While the ADA permits an employer to discipline or discharge an employee for illegal use of drugs or where alcoholism results in poor performance or misconduct, the Act does not require this. Many employers have established employee assistance programs for employees who abuse drugs or alcohol that are helpful to both employee and employer. However, the ADA does not **require** an employer to provide an opportunity for rehabilitation in place of discipline or discharge to such employees. The ADA may, however, require consideration of reasonable accommodation for a drug addict who is rehabilitated and not using drugs or an alcoholic who remains a "qualified individual with a disability." For example, a modified work schedule, to permit the individual to attend an ongoing self-help program, might be a reasonable accommodation for such an employee.

An employer can fire or refuse to hire a person with a past history of illegal drug use, even if the person no longer uses drugs, in specific occupations, such as law enforcement, when an employer can show that this policy is job-related and consistent with business necessity.

> **For example**: A law enforcement agency might be able to show that excluding an individual with a history of illegal drug use from a police officer position was necessary, because such illegal conduct would undermine the credibility of the officer as a witness for the prosecution in a criminal case.

However, even in this case, exclusion of a person with a history of illegal drug use might not be justified automatically as a business necessity, if an applicant with such a history could demonstrate an extensive period of successful performance as a police officer since the time of drug use.

An employer also may fire or refuse to hire an individual with a history of alcoholism or illegal drug use if it can demonstrate that the individual poses a "direct threat" to health or safety because of the high probability that s/he would return to the illegal drug use or alcohol abuse. The employer must be able to demonstrate that such use would result in a high probability of substantial harm to the individual or others which could not be reduced or eliminated with a reasonable accommodation. Examples of accommodations in such cases might be to require periodic drug or alcohol tests, to modify job duties or to provide increased supervision.

An employer cannot prove a "high probability" of substantial harm simply by referring to statistics indicating the likelihood that addicts or alcoholics in general have a specific probability of suffering a relapse. A showing of "significant risk of substantial harm" must be based upon an assessment of the particular individual and his/her history of substance abuse and the specific nature of the job to be performed.

> **For example**: An employer could justify excluding an individual who is an alcoholic with a history of returning to alcohol abuse from a job as a ship captain.

8.8   Pre-Employment Inquiries About Drug and Alcohol Use

An employer may make certain pre-employment, pre-offer inquiries regarding use of alcohol or the illegal use of drugs. An employer may ask whether an applicant drinks alcohol or whether he or she is currently using drugs illegally. However, an employer may not ask whether an applicant is a drug addict or alcoholic, nor inquire whether s/he has ever been in a drug or alcohol rehabilitation program. (See also Pre-Employment Inquiries, Chapter V.)

After a conditional offer of employment, an employer may ask any questions concerning past or present drug or alcohol use. However, the employer may not use such information to exclude an individual with a disability, on the basis of a disability, unless it can show that the reason for exclusion is job-related and consistent with business necessity, and that legitimate job criteria cannot be met with a reasonable accommodation. (For more information on pre-employment medical inquiries, see Chapter VI.)

8.9 Drug Testing

An employer may conduct tests to detect illegal use of drugs. The ADA does not prohibit, require, or encourage drug tests. Drug tests are not considered medical examinations, and an applicant can be required to take a drug test before a conditional offer of employment has been made. An employee also can be required to take a drug test, whether or not such a test is job-related and necessary for the business. (On the other hand, a test to determine an individual's blood alcohol level would be a "medical examination" and only could be required by an employer in conformity with the ADA.)

An employer may refuse to hire an applicant or discharge or discipline an employee based upon a test result that indicates the illegal use of drugs. The employer may take these actions even if an applicant or employee claims that s/he recently stopped illegally using drugs.

Employers may comply with applicable Federal, State, or local laws regulating when and how drug tests may be used, what drug tests may be used, and confidentiality. Drug tests must be conducted to detect **illegal use** of drugs. However, tests for illegal use of drugs also may reveal the presence of lawfully-used drugs. If a person is excluded from a job because the employer erroneously "regarded" him/her to be an addict currently using drugs illegally when a drug test revealed the presence of a lawfully prescribed drug, the employer would be liable under the ADA. To avoid such potential liability, the employer would have to determine whether the individual was using a legally prescribed drug. Because the employer may not ask what prescription drugs an individual is taking before making a conditional job offer, one way to avoid liability is to conduct drug tests after making an offer, even though such tests may be given at anytime under the ADA. Since applicants who test positive for illegal drugs are not covered by the ADA, an employer can withdraw an offer of employment on the basis of illegal drug use.

If the results of a drug test indicate the presence of a lawfully prescribed drug, such information must be kept confidential, in the same way as any medical record. If the results reveal information about a disability in addition to information about drug use, the disability-related information is to be treated as a confidential medical record. (See confidentiality requirements regarding medical inquiries and examinations in Chapter VI.)

For example: If drug test results indicate that an individual is HIV positive, or that a person has epilepsy or diabetes because use of a related prescribed medicine is revealed, this information must remain confidential.

8.10 Laws and Regulations Concerning Drugs and Alcohol

An employer may comply with other Federal laws and regulations concerning the use of drugs and alcohol, including the Drug-Free Workplace Act of 1988; regulations applicable to particular types of employment, such as law enforcement positions; regulations of the Department of Transportation for airline employees, interstate motor carrier drivers and railroad engineers; and regulations for safety sensitive positions established by the Department of Defense and the Nuclear Regulatory Commission. Employers may continue to require that their applicants and employees comply with such Federal laws and regulations.

For example: A trucking company can take appropriate action if an applicant or employee tests positive on a drug test required by Department of Transportation regulations or refuses to take such a drug test.

IX. WORKERS' COMPENSATION AND WORK-RELATED INJURY

9.1 Overview of Legal Obligations

- An employer may not inquire into an applicant's workers' compensation history before making a conditional offer of employment.

- After making a conditional job offer, an employer may ask about a person's workers' compensation history in a medical inquiry or examination that is required of all applicants in the same job category.

- An employer may not base an employment decision on the speculation that an applicant may cause increased workers' compensation costs in the future. However, an employer may refuse to hire, or may discharge an individual who is not currently able to perform a job without posing a significant risk of substantial harm to the health or safety of the individual or others, if the risk cannot be eliminated or reduced by reasonable accommodation. (See Standards Necessary for Health and Safety: A "Direct Threat", Chapter IV.)

- An employer may submit medical information and records concerning employees and applicants (obtained after a conditional job offer) to state workers' compensation offices and "second injury" funds without violating ADA confidentiality requirements.

- Only injured workers who meet the ADA's definition of an "individual with a disability" will be considered disabled under the ADA, regardless of whether they satisfy criteria for receiving benefits under workers' compensation or other disability laws. A worker also must be "qualified" (with or without reasonable accommodation) to be protected by the ADA.

9.2 Is a Worker Injured on the Job Protected by the ADA?

Whether an injured worker is protected by the ADA will depend on whether or not the person meets the ADA definitions of an "individual with a disability" and "qualified individual with a disability." (See Chapter II.) The person must have an impairment that "substantially limits a major life activity," have a "record of" or be "regarded as" having such an impairment. S/he also must be able to perform the essential functions of a job currently held or desired, with or without an accommodation.

Clearly, not every employee injured on the job will meet the ADA definition. Work-related injuries do not always cause physical or mental impairments severe enough to "substantially limit" a major life activity. Also, many on-the-job injuries cause non-chronic impairments which heal within a short period of time with little or no long-term or permanent impact. Such injuries, in most circumstances, are not considered disabilities under the ADA.

The fact that an employee is awarded workers' compensation benefits, or is assigned a high workers' compensation disability rating, does not automatically establish that this person is protected by the ADA. In most cases, the definition of disability under state workers' compensation laws differs from that under the ADA, because the state laws serve a different purpose. Workers' compensation laws are designed to provide needed assistance to workers who suffer many kinds of injuries, whereas the ADA's purpose is to protect people from discrimination on the basis of disability.

Thus, many injured workers who qualify for benefits under workers' compensation or other disability benefits laws may not be protected by the ADA. An employer must consider work-related injuries on a case-by-case basis to know if a worker is protected by the ADA. Many job injuries are not "disabling" under the ADA, but it also is possible that an impairment which is not "substantially limiting" in one circumstance could result in, or lead to, disability in other circumstances.

> **For example**: Suppose a construction worker falls from a ladder and breaks a leg and the leg heals normally within a few months. Although this worker may be awarded workers' compensation benefits for the injury, he would not be considered a person with a disability under the ADA. The impairment suffered from the injury did not "substantially limit" a major life activity, since the injury healed within a short period and had little or no long-term impact. However, if the worker's leg took significantly longer to heal than the usual healing period for this type of injury, and during this period the worker could not walk, s/he would be considered to have a disability. Or, if the injury caused a permanent limp, the worker might be considered disabled under the ADA if the limp substantially limited his walking, as compared to the average person in the general population.

An employee who was seriously injured while working for a former employer, and was unable to work for a year because of the injury, would have a "**record of**" a substantially limiting impairment. If an employer refused to hire or promote this person on the basis of that record, even if s/he had recovered in whole or in part from the injury, this would be a violation of the ADA.

If an impairment or condition caused by an on-the-job injury does not substantially limit an employee's ability to work, but the employer regards the individual as having an impairment that makes him/her unable to perform a class of jobs, such as "heavy labor," this individual would be "**regarded**" by the employer as having a disability. An employer who refused to hire or discharged an individual because of this perception would violate the ADA.

Of course, in each of the examples above, the employer would only be liable for discrimination if the individual was qualified for the position held or desired, with or without an accommodation.

9.3 What Can an Employer Do to Avoid Increased Workers' Compensation Costs and Comply With the ADA?

The ADA allows an employer to take reasonable steps to avoid increased workers' compensation liability while protecting persons with disabilities against exclusion from jobs they can safely perform.

Steps the Employer May Take

After making a conditional job offer, an employer may inquire about a person's workers' compensation history in a medical inquiry or examination that is required of all applicants in the same job category. However, an employer may not require an applicant to have a medical examination because a response to a medical inquiry (as opposed to results from a medical examination) discloses a previous on-the-job injury, unless all applicants in the same job category are required to have the examination. (See Chapter V.)

The employer may use information from medical inquiries and examinations for various purposes, such as:

- to verify employment history;

- to screen out applicants with a history of fraudulent workers' compensation claims;

- to provide information to state officials as required by state laws regulating workers' compensation and "second injury" funds;

- to screen out individuals who would pose a "direct threat" to health or safety of themselves or others, which could not be reduced to an acceptable level or eliminated by a reasonable accommodation. (See Chapter IV.)

9.4   What Can an Employer Do When a Worker is Injured on the Job?

Medical Examinations

An employer may only make medical examinations or inquiries of an employee regarding disability if such examinations are job-related and consistent with business necessity. If a worker has an on-the-job injury which appears to affect his/her ability to do essential job functions, a medical examination or inquiry is job-related and consistent with business necessity. A medical examination or inquiry also may be necessary to provide reasonable accommodation. (See Chapter VI.)

When a worker wishes to return to work after absence due to accident or illness, s/he can only be required to have a "job-related" medical examination, not a full physical exam, as a condition of returning to work.

The ADA prohibits an employer from discriminating against a person with a disability who is "qualified" for a desired job. The employer cannot refuse to let an individual with a disability return to work because the worker is not fully recovered from injury, unless s/he: (1) cannot perform the essential functions of the job s/he holds or desires with or without an accommodation; or (2) would pose a significant risk of substantial harm that could not be reduced to an acceptable level with reasonable accommodation. (See Chapter IV.) Since reasonable accommodation may include reassignment to a vacant position, an employer may be required to consider an employee's qualifications to perform other vacant jobs for which s/he is qualified, as well as the job held when injured.

"Light Duty" Jobs

Many employers have established "light duty" positions to respond to medical restrictions on workers recovering from job-related injuries, in order to reduce workers' compensation liability. Such positions usually place few physical demands on an employee and may include tasks such as answering the telephone and simple administrative work. An employee's placement in such a position is often limited by the employer to a specific period of time.

The ADA does not require an employer to create a "light duty" position unless the "heavy duty" tasks an injured worker can no longer perform are **marginal** job functions which may be reallocated to co-workers as part of the reasonable accommodation of job-restructuring. In most cases however, "light duty" positions involve a totally different job from the job that a worker performed before the injury. Creating such positions by job restructuring is not required by the ADA. However, if an employer already has a vacant light duty position for which an injured worker is qualified, it might be a reasonable accommodation to reassign the worker to that position. If the position was created as a temporary job, a reassignment to that position need only be for a temporary period.

When an employer places an injured worker in a temporary "light duty" position, that worker is "otherwise qualified" for that position for the term of that position; a worker's qualifications must be gauged in relation to the position occupied, not in relation to the job held prior to the injury. It may be necessary to provide additional reasonable accommodation to enable an injured worker in a light duty position to perform the essential functions of that position.

> **For example**: Suppose a telephone line repair worker broke both legs and fractured her knee joints in a fall. The treating physician states that the worker will not be able to walk, even with crutches, for at least nine months. She therefore has a "disability." Currently using a wheelchair, and unable to do her previous job, she is placed in a "light duty" position to process paperwork associated with line repairs. However, the office to which she is assigned is not wheelchair accessible. It would be a reasonable accommodation to place the employee in an office that is accessible. Or, the office could be made accessible by widening the office door, if this would not be an undue hardship. The employer also might have to modify the employee's work schedule so that she could attend weekly physical therapy sessions.

Medical information may be very useful to an employer who must decide whether an injured worker can come back to work, in what job, and, if necessary, with what accommodations. A physician may provide an employer with relevant information about an employee's functional abilities, limitations, and work restrictions. This information will be useful in determining how to return the employee to productive work, but the employer bears the ultimate responsibility for deciding whether the individual is qualified, with or without a reasonable accommodation. Therefore, an employer cannot avoid liability if it relies on a physician's advice which is not consistent with ADA requirements.

9.5 Do the ADA's Pre-Employment Inquiry and Confidentiality Restrictions Prevent an Employer from Filing Second Injury Fund Claims?

Most states have established "second injury" funds designed to remove financial disincentives in hiring employees with a disability. Without a second injury fund, if a worker suffered increased disability from a work-related injury because of a pre-existing condition, the employer would have to pay the full cost. The second injury fund provisions limit the amount the employer must pay in these circumstances, and provide for the balance to be paid out of a common fund.

Many second injury funds require an employer to certify that it knew at the time of hire that the employee had a pre-existing injury. The ADA does not prohibit employers from obtaining information about pre-existing injuries and providing needed information to second injury funds. As discussed in Chapter VI., an employer may make such medical inquiries and require a medical examination <u>after a conditional offer of employment</u>, and before a person starts work, so long as the examination or inquiry is made of all applicants in the same job category. Although the ADA generally requires that medical information obtained from such examinations or inquiries be kept confidential, information may be submitted to second injury funds or state workers' compensation authorities as required by state workers' compensation laws.

9.6 Compliance with State and Federal Workers' Compensation Laws

a. Federal Laws

It may be a defense to a charge of discrimination under the ADA that a challenged action is required by another Federal law or regulation, or that another Federal law prohibits an action that otherwise would be required by the ADA. This defense is not valid, however, if the Federal standard does not require the discriminatory action, or if there is a way that an employer can comply with both legal requirements.

b. State Laws

ADA requirements supersede any **conflicting** state workers' compensation laws.

For example: Some state workers' compensation statutes make an employer liable for paying additional benefits if an injury occurs because the employer assigned a person to a position likely to jeopardize the person's health or safety, or exacerbate an earlier workers' compensation injury. Some of these laws may permit or require an employer to exclude a disabled individual from employment in cases where the ADA would not permit such exclusion. In these cases, the ADA takes precedence over the state law. An employer could not assert, as a valid defense to a charge of discrimination, that it failed to hire or return to work an individual with a disability because doing so would violate a state workers' compensation law that required exclusion of this individual.

9.7 Does Filing a Workers' Compensation Claim Prevent an Injured Worker from Filing a Charge Under the ADA?

Filing a workers' compensation claim does not prevent an injured worker from filing a charge under the ADA. "Exclusivity" clauses in state workers' compensation laws bar all other civil remedies related to an injury that has been compensated by a workers' compensation system. However, these clauses do not prohibit a qualified individual with a disability from filing a discrimination charge with EEOC, or filing a suit under the ADA, if issued a "right to sue" letter by EEOC. (See Chapter X.)

9.8 What if an Employee Provides False Information About his/her Health or Physical Condition?

An employer may refuse to hire or may fire a person who knowingly provides a false answer to a lawful post-offer inquiry about his/her condition or workers' compensation history.

Some state workers' compensation laws release an employer from its obligation to pay benefits if a worker falsely represents his/her health or physical condition at the time of hire and is later injured as a result. The ADA does not prevent use of this defense to a workers' compensation claim. The ADA requires only that information requests about health or workers compensation history are made as part of a post-offer medical examination or inquiry. (See Chapter VI.)

X. ENFORCEMENT PROVISIONS

10.1 Introduction

Title I of the ADA is enforced by the Equal Employment Opportunity Commission (EEOC) under the same procedures used to enforce Title VII of the Civil Rights Acts of 1964. The Commission receives and investigates charges of discrimination and seeks through conciliation to resolve any discrimination found and obtain full relief for the affected individual. If conciliation is not successful, the EEOC may file a suit or issue a "right to sue" letter to the person who filed the charge. Throughout the enforcement process, EEOC makes every effort to resolve issues through conciliation and to avoid litigation.

The Commission also recognizes that differences and disputes about the ADA requirements may arise between employers and people with disabilities as a result of misunderstandings. Such disputes frequently can be resolved more effectively through informal negotiation or mediation procedures, rather than through the formal enforcement process of the ADA. Accordingly, EEOC will encourage efforts to settle such differences through alternative dispute resolution, provided that such efforts do not deprive any individual of legal rights granted by the statute. (See "Alternative Dispute Resolution" in Resource Directory Index.)

10.2 Overview of Enforcement Provisions

- A job applicant or employee who believes s/he has been discriminated against on the basis of disability in employment by a private, state, or local government employer, labor union, employment agency, or joint labor management committee can file a charge with EEOC.

- An individual, whether disabled or not, also may file a charge if s/he believes that s/he has been discriminated against because of an association with a person with a known disability, or believes that s/he has suffered retaliation because of filing a charge or assisting in opposing a discriminatory practice. (See Retaliation below.) Another person or organization also may file a charge on behalf of such applicant or employee.

- The entity charged with violating the ADA should receive written notification of the charge within 10 days after it is filed.

- EEOC will investigate charges of discrimination. If EEOC believes that discrimination occurred, it will attempt to resolve the charge through conciliation and obtain full relief for the aggrieved individual consistent with EEOC's standards for remedies.

- If conciliation fails, EEOC will file suit or issue a "right to sue" letter to the person who filed the charge. (If the charge involves a state or local government agency, EEOC will refer the case to the Department of Justice for consideration of litigation or issuance of a "right to sue" letter.)

- Remedies for violations of Title I of the ADA include hiring, reinstatement, promotion, back pay, front pay, restored benefits, reasonable accommodation, attorneys' fees, expert witness fees, and court costs. Compensatory and punitive damages also may be available in cases of intentional discrimination or where an employer fails to make a good faith effort to provide a reasonable accommodation.

- Employers may not retaliate against any applicant or employee who files a charge, participates in an EEOC investigation or opposes an unlawful employment practice.

10.3 Questions and Answers on the ADA Enforcement Process

When do the ADA's employment enforcement provisions become effective?

Charges of discrimination can be filed against employers with 25 or more employees and other covered entities beginning July 26, 1992. The alleged discriminatory act(s) must have occurred on or after July 26, 1992.

Charges can be filed against employers with 15 or more employees beginning July 26, 1994. The alleged discriminatory act(s) must have occurred on or after July 26, 1994, if the charge is against an employer with 15 to 24 employees.

Who can file charges of discrimination?

An applicant or employee who feels that s/he has been discriminated against in employment on the basis of disability can file a charge with EEOC. An individual, group or organization also can file a charge on behalf of another person. An individual, group or organization that files a charge is called the "charging party."

How are charges of discrimination filed?

A person who feels s/he has been discriminated against, or other potential "charging party" should contact the nearest EEOC office. (See Resource Directory listing.) If there is no EEOC office nearby, call, toll free 1-800-669-4000 (voice) or 1-800-800-3302 (TDD).

What are the time limits for filing charges of discrimination?

A charge of discrimination on the basis of disability must be filed with EEOC within 180 days of the alleged discriminatory act.

If there is a state or local fair employment practices agency that enforces a law prohibiting the same alleged discriminatory practice, it is possible that charges may be filed with EEOC up to 300 days after the alleged discriminatory act. However, to protect legal rights, it is recommended that EEOC be contacted promptly when discrimination is believed to have occurred.

How is a charge of discrimination filed?

A charge can be filed in person, by telephone, or by mail. If an individual does not live near an EEOC office, the charge can be filed by telephone and verified by mail. The type of information that will be requested from a charging party may include:

- the charging party's name, address, and telephone number (if a charge is filed on behalf of another individual, his/her identity may be kept confidential, unless required for a court action);

- the employer's name, address, telephone number, and number of employees;

- the basis or bases of the discrimination claimed by the individual (e.g., disability, race, color, religion, sex, national origin, age, retaliation);

- the issue or issues involved in the alleged discriminatory act(s) (e.g., hiring, promotion, wages, terms and conditions of employment, discharge);

- identification of the charging party's alleged disability (e.g., the physical or mental impairment and how it affects major life activities, the record of disability the employer relied upon, or how the employer regarded the individual as disabled);

- the date of the alleged discriminatory act(s);

- details of what allegedly happened; and

- identity of witnesses who have knowledge of the alleged discriminatory act(s).

Charging parties also may submit additional oral or written evidence on their behalf.

EEOC has work-sharing agreements with many state and local fair employment agencies. Depending on the agreement, some charges may be sent to a state or local agency for investigation; others may be investigated directly by EEOC. (See also Coordination Procedures to Avoid Duplicate Complaint Processing under the ADA and the Rehabilitation Act, below.)

Can a charging party file a charge on more than one basis?

EEOC also enforces other laws that bar employment discrimination based on race, color, religion, sex, national origin, and age (persons 40 years of age and older). An individual with a disability can file a charge of discrimination on more than one basis.

> For example: A cashier who is a paraplegic may claim that she was discriminated against by an employer based on both her sex and her disability. She can file a single charge claiming both disability and sex discrimination.

Can an individual file a lawsuit against an employer?

An individual can file a lawsuit against an employer, but s/he must first file the charge with EEOC. The charging party can request a "right to sue" letter from the EEOC 180 days after the charge was first filed with the Commission. A charging party will then have 90 days to file suit after receiving the notice of right to sue. If the charging party files suit, EEOC will ordinarily dismiss the original charges filed with the Commission. "Right to sue" letters also are issued when EEOC does not believe discrimination occurred or when conciliation attempts fail and EEOC decides not to sue on the charging party's behalf (see below).

Are charging parties protected from retaliation?

It is unlawful for an employer or other covered entity to retaliate against someone who files a charge of discrimination, participates in an investigation, or opposes discriminatory practices. Individuals who believe that they have been retaliated against should contact EEOC immediately. Even if an individual has already filed a charge of discrimination, s/he can file a new charge based on retaliation.

How does EEOC process charges of discrimination?

- A charge of employment discrimination may be filed with EEOC against a private employer, state or local government, employment agency, labor union or joint labor management committee. When a charge has been filed, EEOC calls these covered entities "respondents."

- Within 10 days after receipt of a charge, EEOC sends written notification of receipt to the respondent and the charging party.

- EEOC begins its investigation by reviewing information received from the charging party and requesting information from the respondent. Information requested from the respondent initially, and in the course of the investigation, may include:

  - specific information on the issues raised in the charge;

  - the identity of witnesses who can provide evidence about issues in the charge;

X-5

- information about the business operation, employment process, and workplace; and

- personnel and payroll records.

  (Note: All or part of the data-gathering portion of an investigation may be conducted on-site, depending on the circumstances.)

• A respondent also may submit additional oral or written evidence on its own behalf.

• EEOC also will interview witnesses who have knowledge of the alleged discriminatory act(s).

• EEOC may dismiss a charge during the course of the investigation for various reasons. For example, it may find that the respondent is not covered by the ADA, or that the charge is not timely filed.

• EEOC may request additional information from the respondent and the charging party. They may be asked to participate in a fact-finding conference to review the allegations, obtain additional evidence, and, if appropriate, seek to resolve the charge through a negotiated settlement.

• The charging party and respondent will be informed of the preliminary findings of the investigation -- that is, whether there is cause to believe that discrimination has occurred and the type of relief that may be necessary. Both parties will be provided opportunity to submit further information.

• After reviewing all information, the Commission sends an official "Letter of Determination" to the charging party and the respondent, stating whether it has or has not found "reasonable cause" to believe that discrimination occurred.

What if the EEOC concludes that no discrimination occurred?

If the investigation finds no cause to believe discrimination occurred, EEOC will take no further action. EEOC will issue a "right to sue" letter to the charging party, who may initiate a private suit.

What if the EEOC concludes that discrimination occurred?

If the investigation shows that there is reasonable cause to believe that discrimination occurred, EEOC will attempt to resolve the issue through conciliation and to obtain full relief consistent with EEOC's standards for remedies for the charging party. (See Relief Available to Charging Party, below.) EEOC also can request an employer to post a notice in the workplace stating that the discrimination has been corrected and that it has stopped the discriminatory practice.

What happens if conciliation fails?

At all stages of the enforcement process, EEOC will try to resolve a charge without a costly lawsuit.

If EEOC has found cause to believe that discrimination occurred, but cannot resolve the issue through conciliation, the case will be considered for litigation. If EEOC decides to litigate, a lawsuit will be filed in federal district court. If the Commission decides not to litigate, it will send the charging party a "right-to-sue" letter. The charging party may then initiate a private civil suit within 90 days, if desired. If conciliation fails on a charge against a state or local government, EEOC will refer the case to the Department of Justice for consideration of litigation or issuance of a "right to sue" letter.

10.4 Coordination Procedures to Avoid Duplicative Complaint Processing Under the ADA and the Rehabilitation Act.

The ADA requires EEOC and the federal agencies responsible for Section 503 and Section 504 of the Rehabilitation Act of 1973 to establish coordination procedures to avoid duplication and to assure consistent standards in processing complaints that fall within the overlapping jurisdiction of both laws. EEOC and the Office of Federal Contract Compliance in the Department of Labor (OFCCP) have issued a joint regulation establishing such procedures for complaints against employers covered by the ADA who are also federal contractors or subcontractors. (Published in the Federal Register of January 24, 1992.) EEOC and the Department of Justice also will issue a joint regulation establishing procedures for complaints against employers covered by the ADA who are recipients of federal financial assistance.

The joint EEOC-OFCCP rule provides that a complaint of discrimination on the basis of disability filed with OFCCP under Section 503 will be considered a charge filed simultaneously under the ADA if the complaint

X-7

falls within the ADA's jurisdiction. This will ensure that an individual's ADA rights are preserved. OFCCP will process such complaints/charges for EEOC, with certain exceptions specified in the regulation, where OFCCP will refer the charge to EEOC. OFCCP also will refer to EEOC for litigation review any complaint/charge where a violation has been found, conciliation fails, and OFCCP decides not to pursue administrative enforcement.

EEOC will refer to OFCCP ADA charges that fall under Section 503 jurisdiction when the Commission finds cause to believe that discrimination has occurred but decides not to litigate, for any administrative action that OFCCP finds appropriate. Where a charge involves both allegations of discrimination and violation of OFCCP's affirmative action requirements, EEOC generally will refer the charge to OFCCP for processing and resolution.

(Note: Procedures established in an EEOC-Department of Justice joint rule on processing complaints that are within ADA and Section 504 jurisdiction will be summarized in a future supplement to this Manual, when a final regulation has been issued.)

10.5 Remedies

The "relief" or remedies available for employment discrimination, whether caused by intentional acts or by practices that have a discriminatory effect, may include hiring, reinstatement, promotion, back pay, front pay, reasonable accommodation, or other actions that will make an individual "whole" (in the condition s/he would have been but for the discrimination). Remedies also may include payment of attorneys' fees, expert witness fees and court costs.

Compensatory and punitive damages also may be available where intentional discrimination is found. Damages may be available to compensate for actual monetary losses, for future monetary losses, for mental anguish and inconvenience. Punitive damages also may be available if an employer acted with malice or reckless indifference. The total amount of punitive damages and compensatory damages for future monetary loss and emotional injury for each individual is limited, based upon the size of the employer, using the following schedule:

Number of employees	Damages will not exceed
15-100	$ 50,000
101-200	100,000
201-500	200,000
500 and more	300,000

X-8

Punitive damages are not available against state or local governments.

In cases concerning reasonable accommodation, compensatory or punitive damages may not be awarded to the charging party if an employer can demonstrate that "good faith" efforts were made to provide reasonable accommodation.

What are EEOC's obligations to make the charge process accessible to and usable by individuals with disabilities?

EEOC is required by Section 504 of the Rehabilitation Act of 1973, as amended, to make all of its programs and activities accessible to and usable by individuals with disabilities. EEOC has an obligation to provide services or devices necessary to enable an individual with a disability to participate in the charge filing process. For example, upon request, EEOC will provide an interpreter when necessary for a charging party who is hearing impaired. People with visual or manual disabilities can request on-site assistance in filling out a "charge of discrimination" form and affidavits. EEOC will provide access to the charge process as needed by each individual with a disability, on a case-by-case basis.

Appendix 8

EEAC ADA IMPLEMENTATION PLANNING CHECKLIST

by Lorence L. Kessler

Equal Employoment Advisory Council

Copyright © 1992 Equal Employment Advisory Council, Washington, DC. All rights reserved. No part of this *EEAC ADA Implementation Planning Checklist* may be duplicated without written permission from the EEAC. Copies of this Checklist may be ordered from the EEAC. Discounts are available for bulk orders.

Equal Employment Advisory Council

The Equal Employment Advisory Council is a nonprofit association organized in 1976 initially for the purpose of monitoring federal equal employment litigation and filing amicus curiae briefs in precedent-setting cases. Over the past 16 years the Council has expanded its activities into other areas including filing comments on significant equal employment opportunity and affirmative action regulatory proposals, analyzing legislation, and monitoring judicial and legislative developments at the state and local level.

EEAC's membership, which is limited to private corporations, now includes more than 250 major U.S. employers. In addition to its regular membership meetings, EEAC sponsors a wide variety of educational programs during the course of the year, including comprehensive training programs on basic EEO law and a series of advanced level training seminars on preparing affirmative action plans, managing OFCCP compliance reviews, EEO charge processing, compliance with the ADA, and the use of statistics in affirmative action planning and equal employment litigation. These programs frequently are customized for in-house training seminars for individual EEAC member companies.

For further information about the Council, please write EEAC's membership coordinator at 1015 15th St., N.W., Suite 1200, Washington, DC 20005, or call (202) 789-8650.

EEAC ADA Implementation Planning Checklist ▬▬

This checklist has been prepared by the Equal Employment Advisory Council for the use of member companies planning implementation of the Americans with Disabilities Act. The checklist contains a series of items for you to consider as you plan for implementation of the Americans with Disabilities Act. As indicated, some of the items reflect specific ADA requirements while other items represent suggestions made by the ADA enforcement agencies.

In implementing the employment provisions of the ADA, there are several primary sources of guidance you should review. Have you reviewed the EEOC's regulation including the Interpretive Guidance Appendix? Have you reviewed the *EEOC's Technical Assistance Manual*? A copy of the *EEOC Technical Assistance Manual* may be ordered by calling the Commission at 1-800-669-EEOC (A copy is also provided as an Appendix in this book).

A. JOB APPLICATIONS AND INTERVIEWS

1. Have you reviewed the questions on all application forms?

2   Have you added a tagline to job advertisements indicating the company does not discriminate on the basis of disability?

3. Have you posted notices containing the provisions of the ADA in conspicuous places? (EEOC promises its posters will be available in 1992). Have you considered the EEOC's suggestion that the employer can include information about the reasonable accommodation obligation on job application forms and job vacancy notices? (See *EEOC Technical Assistance Manual*, III-8).

4. Have all of those who do interviewing for the company been briefed on the ADA's prohibitions on pre-employment inquiries about disabilities? Have you prepared written guidelines for these interviewers as suggested by EEOC? (See *EEOC Technical Assistance Manual*, V-11).

5. Have all of those who do interviewing for the company been briefed on approaches that may reduce any anxiety or discomfort they may feel when interviewing individuals with disabilities? Have you conducted awareness training for your interviewers as suggested by EEOC? (See *EEOC Technical Assistance Manual*, V-11).

6. Have you considered similar briefings and awareness training for managers?

7. Have you communicated the ADA's requirements to all agencies you use to recruit or screen applicants? Have you considered the EEOC's suggestion that your written agreement with the employment agency contain a provision stating that the agency will conduct its activities in accordance with the ADA? (See *EEOC Technical Assistance Manual*, V-3).

8. Have company recruiters been briefed on their responsibility to assure that interviews at job fairs and on campuses are conducted in accessible locations? (See *EEOC Technical Assistance Manual*, V-4).

9. Have those persons or firms who do reference checks on job applicants been briefed on the EEOC's restrictions on the types of questions asked? (See *EEOC Technical Assistance Manual*, V-16).

10. Do you provide job applicants with a description of the employment process, as suggested by EEOC, to permit individuals to request accommodations that may be needed at some point in the process? (See *EEOC Technical Assistance Manual*, V-10).

B. JOB FUNCTIONS

1. How will you take advantage of the provisions in Section 101(8) of the ADA with respect to:

   ___ the employer's judgement about which job functions are essential?

   ___ the use of written job descriptions (prepared before advertising or inter-viewing applicants for a job) as evidence of essential job functions?

2. Have you taken steps to assure that these same provisions are not used against the company because of written job descriptions which are incomplete or outdated?

3. With respect to each of the job functions you consider essential:

   ___ Does that function appear in the written job description?

   ___ Can that function be justified as being essential under one or more of the factors listed by the Commission in Section 1630.2(n)?

4. Do your job descriptions reflect the job analysis techniques discussed by the EEOC in the *Technical Assistance Manual* (II-19, 20)?

5. Do your written job descriptions indicate, where appropriate, the fact that certain jobs or functions must be performed alone or in a setting where others will not be available to perform the function? Do they indicate, where appropriate, the consequences of a failure to perform the function? (See *EEOC Technical Assistance Manual*, Chapter II-17).

6. Have you considered providing a written description of the job to applicants during the interview, as suggested by the *EEOC Technical Assistance Manual* (Chapter V-9)?

7. If you do not have written job descriptions, how will you demonstrate to a court or enforcement agency what the essential job functions are?

8. Does your current procedure give the interviewers (and, if necessary, the medical staff) enough information about the job functions to allow them to do their jobs in accordance with the ADA?

C. MEDICAL EXAMINATIONS

1. Are any changes in procedure necessary to comply with the ADA prohibition on medical examinations prior to making a conditional offer of employment?

2. Are any changes in the procedure for collecting medical histories necessary to comply with the ADA prohibition on medical inquiries prior to a conditional offer of employment?

3. If you use outside medical doctors, what steps have you taken to assure that these doctors are familiar with job functions and tasks? Have you considered the EEOC suggestion that it can be useful for such doctors to visit the job site (*EEOC Technical Assistance Manual*, VI-9)? As an alternative, have you considered providing such medical professionals with a videotape showing how the job typically is done?

4. Has your medical staff been briefed on the use of the factors outlined in the EEOC regulations regarding medical opinions on whether an individual is a direct threat to health or safety? (See EEOC Section 1630.2(r); *EEOC Technical Assistance Manual*, Chapters IV and VI). Have relevant forms been revised to reflect the use of these factors? Do your practices and policies reflect the ADA's insistence on individualized assessment?

5. Have medical staff members been briefed on the necessity of a reasonable accommodation determination *after* the medical determination has been made? Do medical forms indicate that following the doctor's final assessment, there will be an assessment of whether a reasonable accommodation can be made? (See discussion of "The Doctor's Role" in *EEOC Technical Assistance Manual*, VI-9).

6. Are any changes in recordkeeping procedures needed to comply with the ADA provisions on the confidentiality of medical files and records?

D. EMPLOYMENT TESTING

1. Have you assessed your use of employment tests in light of the following:

   ___ What skill is the test supposed to measure?

   ___ Do the test results accurately reflect what the test is supposed to measure?

   ___ Do the test results reflect an individual's impaired sensory, manual or speaking skills, even though the test is not intended to measure those skills? If so, is there an alternative that would be a reasonable accommodation?

2. Do candidates who are to be tested receive advance notice of the company's willingness to consider accommodations where appropriate if the company is advised of the need for such accommodations prior to the test?

3. Have your test administrators been briefed on the obligation to provide an accessible testing site?

4. Have your test administrators been briefed on how to respond to someone who requests an accommodation on the day of the test or during the test?

E. REASONABLE ACCOMMODATION PROCESS

1. Do you have a process for dealing with accommodation requests that is similar to the process outlined in Section 1630.9 of the EEOC Interpretive Guidance? (See also *EEOC Technical Assistance Manual*, III-9, 10).

2. Have you developed a form or procedure for keeping a record of requests for accommodation? How long will these records be kept? (EEOC regulations require written requests for accommodation to be maintained for one year).

3. Who has authority to decide to provide an accommodation? Does that person have access to resources that keep him/her apprised of the types of accommodations available and the types of accommodations that have proven successful in the company in the past?

4. Who has authority to deny an accommodation? Is there a form that can be used to record the reasons for the denial? Have the persons who will complete that form been briefed on how to apply the factors in the ADA's undue hardship standard? (See EEOC Section 1630.2(p)).

5. Have you developed an approach to undue hardship factor #3 (the overall resources of the covered entity) and #4 (the type of operation of the covered entity) that will keep that factor from automatically being considered an unlimited source of funds for accommodations?

6. Is it necessary to revise or clarify any existing policies that may be related to particular types of accommodations, such as leave requirements or return to work following a disability? Are such policies applied with the necessary consistency?

7. Have you considered the accommodations necessary to assure employees with disabilities access to all the privileges and benefits of employment, including services and information routinely available to other employees?

8. Is employer-provided transportation accessible to employees with disabilities?

9. Are you aware of external resources that may be useful in making accommodations? Have you reviewed the EEOC's *Resource Directory*? Are you familiar with the types of activities and services offered by the organizations listed for your geographic area?

F. COLLECTIVE BARGAINING

1. Have you reviewed existing collective bargaining agreements in light of ADA requirements? Have you reviewed provisions in collective bargaining agreements that describe job functions?

2. Have you considered the suggestion by Congress and the EEOC that all collective bargaining agreements negotiated after the effective date of the ADA contain a provision permitting the employer to take all actions necessary to comply with the law? (See Report of House Committee on Education and Labor, 101-485, part 2, page 63, May 15, 1990. See also *EEOC Technical Assistance Manual*, III-16).

G. FACILITIES

1. Are all areas of the workplace frequented by employees (such as cafeteria break areas, training rooms, restrooms) accessible to employees with disabilities?

2. Have various company personnel who schedule activities off premises–such as for training, recruiting, public relations, marketing, etc.–been briefed on the extent of the company's obligation to assure accessibility at such activities and any obligation to provide auxiliary aids and services for individuals with disabilities? Have you considered including appropriate language about these obligations in contracts with hotels, etc.?

3. Have all leases been reviewed in light of the obligations imposed by the ADA? Have those who will be negotiating new leases been briefed on the possibility of including language spelling out obligations in light of the ADA? (See *DOJ Title III Technical Assistance Manual*, III-1.2000).

4. Have company facilities professionals reviewed the Title III regulations issued by the Department of Justice and the ADA Accessibility Guidelines (ADAAG)? Have they also reviewed the *Department of Justice Title III Technical Assistance Manual*?

5. Have all building managers been briefed on the new ADA accessibility requirements, including the requirements with respect to alterations begun after January 26, 1992, and the accessible path of travel requirements and priorities? (See *DOJ Title III Technical Assistance Manual*, III-6.0000).

6. Has a process been established to promote communication between human resources managers and facility managers to assure that resources for accessible features are expended in the most efficient manner possible?

7. Have all those company personnel who deal directly with the public been briefed on the company's obligations under the ADA, including the need to make accommodations to potential employees and the requirement to remove barriers (or to provide auxiliary aids or services or alternative methods of service) where appropriate?

8. Have you checked with the local telephone company to determine when TDD relay services will become available in your area? If such services are not yet available, have you considered obtaining a TDD for receiving incoming business (and/or employment) calls? The Department of Justice says that such action is not required, but notes that a business may choose to do so. (See *DOJ Title III Technical Assistance Manual*, Section III-4.3300. But see *EEOC Technical Assistance Manual*, V-3).

9. Have you initiated a self-audit procedure to assist in setting priorities for barrier removal, as suggested by the Department of Justice? Does the self-audit procedure include individuals familiar with disability issues and accessibility features?

10. Have you prepared an implementation plan as suggested by the Department of Justice? (See *DOJ Title III Technical Assistance Manual*, Section III-4.4500).

11. If your business operates a place of public accommodation and incidentally provides transportation services (such as a shuttle bus) in conjunction with that business, have you reviewed the transportation and new vehicle acquisition requirements of Title III? (See *DOJ Title III Technical Assistance Manual*, III-4.4700).

12. Have you adopted procedures to assure regular maintenance and, when necessary, prompt repairs to equipment (such as elevators, automatic doors, etc.) that is necessary to assure the accessibility of the facility? (See *DOJ Title III Technical Assistance Manual*, III-3.7000).

Lorence L. Kessler

Mr. Kessler is a partner in the law firm of McGuiness & Williams in Washington, DC, specializing in the practice of labor and employment law. He has represented employers before courts and agencies in a variety of matters involving labor-management relations and equal employment opportunity. He also advises employers on the development of employment policies and procedures and the preparation of affirmative action plans. He served as one of the representatives of the business community during the negotiations on the Americans with Disabilities Act.

For the past nine years, Mr. Kessler has served as counsel to the Affirmative Action Practices Committee of the Equal Employment Advisory Council, an organization of more than 200 large private employers committed to the principles of equal employment opportunity and nondiscrimination. He also has written and lectured on numerous topics related to the implementation of sound EEO practices and programs. Mr. Kessler is the author of *Managing Diversity in an Equal Opportunity Workplace: A Primer for Today's Manager*, published in 1990.

Mr. Kessler has been in private practice in Washington, DC, since 1979. He formerly served as law clerk to Chief Judge Rabe F. Marsh in the United States District Court, Western District of Pennsylvania.

Index ——————————————

A

Ability management programs, 146
Absenteeism, 106
Access
  public transportation, 219-221, 237-241
  telecommunications, 243-251
Accommodations
  incentives by firm size, 278
  types provided, 277
  verification of need for, 83
ADA
  complete text of law, *See* Appendix 3
  costs of job accommodation, 275-277
  costs of implementation, 204-205, 275
  enforcement of, 52-53, 233, 241
  development of, 3-10
  implementation dates, 331-332
  implementation planning checklist, *See* Appendix 8
  regulations, *See* Appendix 4
ADA Opportunity Task Force, 209-211
Agility tests, 130
Administration of employment tests, 79-80
AIDS (Acquired Immune Deficiency Syndrome), 8, 30, 42, 169-198
  diseases associated with, 172
  guidelines, 190-191
  policies, 189-190
  psychological impact, 176-177
  resources, 193
  services provided, 175
  social impact, 173-175
  sociological impact, 178-181
  symptoms, 171-173
  ten principles for the workplace, 184
  transmission, 171
AIDS-Related Complex (ARC), 181
AIDS Service Organizations (ASOs), 175-176, 187, *See also* Appendix 6
Air Carrier Access Act of 1986 (ACAA), 6, 42-44, 50
Alcohol abuse, 36-37, 39
Alcohol testing, 155-167
Alterations, 218-219
Alternative Dispute Resolution (ADR), 149-151
American Coalition of Citizens with Disabilities, 8
Applications, employment, 71-72

Architectural and Transportation Barriers Compliance Board, 13, 256
Architectural Barriers Act of 1968, 13, 223, *See also* Appendix 4
Assessment of individuals with disabilities, 109-115
Association with individuals with disability, 206
Attitudes
  disabling, 11-33
  of employers, 28-31, 276
Attitudinal barriers to ADA, 143, 202-203, 274
Auxiliary aids and services, 48, 185, 216

B

Barrier removal, 215-223, 229
  tax deduction, 223, 256-257
Behavior description interviews, 115
Benefits eligibility, 97
Birth defect, 22, *See also* Appendix 1
Blind, 22, *See also* Appendix 1
Bush, President George, 5, *See also* Appendix 2

C

Candidiasis, 172
Choosing the words you use, 293-294
Cigarette smoke, unusual sensitivity, 39
Classification of employees, 102-104
COBRA, 97-98
Coelho, Tony, Representative, 6
Commerce, 50
Commercial facilities, 50, 227
Common carrier, 52
Common testing requirements and procedures (alcohol and drugs), 161-164
Communication barriers, 231
Commuter rail transportation, 240
Compensation, 90, 115-116
  -related policies, 108
Comprehensive structured interviews, 115
Compulsive gambling, 36
Confirmation bias, 114
Contrast effects, 113

Costs
of ADA implementation, 204-205, 275
of job accommodation, 275-277
of disability, 142-145
Covered entities, 56, 141-142
Cryptococcosis, 172
Cryptoporidiosis, 172
Customer bill of rights, 262-265
Customer satisfaction, 258-272
Customer service policy, 262-265
Cytomegalovirus, 172

D

Dart, Justin W., Jr., 3-5, 7-9
Deaf, 22. See also Telecommunications, TDDs,
    Title IV, TRS, TTs, TTYs, Appendix 1
Deaf-mute, 23, See also Appendix 1
Deformed, 23, See also Appendix 1
Demand responsive system, 50
Department of Defense Interim Rule, 157
Department of Health and Human Services,
    158
Department of Transportation and Related
    Agencies Appropriations Act, 1992,
    157, 158
Determining disability, 37-38
Deviant, 23, See also Appendix 1
Differently abled, 24, See also Appendix 1
Direct threat, 48, 230
Disability, 35, 44, 80, 225
cost of, 142
definition, 39-40, 293
guidelines for testing and evaluating persons
    with, 80-88
individuals with, 35
known, 80
myth, equals illness, 21
National Council on, 3, 5, 6, 273
qualified person with, 51, 81, 88, 129, 141,
    160
statistics on, 12, 225-226
Disability management, 143-144, 145-146
Disability management, employer-based
    strategies, 139-154
Disabled, 24, See also Appendix 1
layoff of employee, 96-97, 110
marketing to, 265-266
promoting, 91-92, 95-96, 110
transfer of employee, 96-97
Disabled access credit, 254-255
Disciplinary policies, 103-105, 106
Discipline (of employee), 103-105, 106
Discrimination, 229-230
Dispute resolution model, 149-151
Downsizing, 96-97, 99
Drugs, 48
Drug
abuse, 36-37, 39, 155, 160-161
testing, 76, 155-167

Drug-Free Work Force Rule (Also known as
    DOD Rule), 155, 157, 161
Drug-Free Workplace Act of 1988, 36, 155, 156
    157, 158, 161
Dukakis, Michael, 5
Dumb, 23, See also Appendix 1
Durenberger, David, Senator, 6

E

EEAC ADA Implementation Planning Check
    list, See Appendix 8
EEOC, Technical Assistance Manual, See
    Appendix 7
Early retirement, 97-98
Effective dates, 55, 221-222, 331-332
Effective listening, 261
Elevators, 232-233
Employee, 45
absenteeism of, 106
assistance programs, 157, 187
discipline of, 103-106
evaluation, 73-77, 80-88, 110
excused paid time off, 107
human resources support for, 89-100
layoff of, 96-97
promotion of disabled, 91-92
recruitment and selection, 63-78, 102-109
retention of disabled, 92-94
salary administration, 106-108, 115-116
selection interview, 113
termination of, 96-97
transfer of, 96-97
unexcused paid time off, 107
Employer, 45, 56
attitudes, 28-31
-based disability management strategies,
    139-154
perceptions of job accommodations, 275-279
responses to ADA, 201-202
Employment, 45
agencies, 67
-at-will, 104
enforcement of Title I, 52
equal rights to, 44-45
recruitment, 63-78, 102-103, 104, 205
supported, 206-208
testing, 69, 73-77, 79-88, 111-113, 206-207,
    209
Enforcement
of ADA, 52-53, 233, 241
of Title I, 222
Entitlements, 97
Environmental barriers, 225-235
Enzyme Multiple Immunoassay Technique
    (EMIT), 163
Equal Employment Opportunity Commission
    (EEOC), regulations, 55, 57, 71, 73, 76,
    140-141, 160-161, See also Appendix 7
Equal pay, 94-95

Ergonomics, 148
ERISA, 104
Essential functions of the job, 70-71, 81, 91, 114
    115, 117, 120, 124, 129, 133, 135, 142
Exclusions, 228
Excused paid time off, 107
Excused unpaid time off, 107
Executive Order 12564, 155-158
Exhibitionism, 36

F

Fair Housing Amendments Act of 1988, 5, 42,
    44, 222
Failure to meet performance standards, 106
Federal Aviation Authority (FAA) regulations,
    42-44, 50
Federal Communications Commission (FCC),
    53, 245-250
Financial concerns about ADA. 204-205
Financial incentives for access. 223. See also tax
    credits
Fish, Hamilton, Representative, 6
Fit, 23
Fit-for-duty examinations, 130
Fixed route system, 220, 237-238
Focus groups, 260-261, 271
Food handling, 36
For-profit employment agencies, 67
Functional limitation, 14-15

G

Gambling, compulsive, 36
Gas Chromatography/Mass Spectrometry (GC
    MS), 163
Gender identity disorders, 36
Guidelines
    AIDS, 190-191
    for reviewing test administration, 112
    for testing and evaluating persons with
        disabilities, 80-5

H

Halo effects, 113
Handicapped, 24. See also Disabled, disability
    individual, 37
    otherwise qualified person, 42
    severe handicap, 39
Harkin, Thomas, Senator, 6, 169, 185, 186
Health insurance, 97
Hearing carry-over (HCO), 248
Hoyer, Steny, Representative, 6

HIV (Human Immunodeficiency Virus), 8, 169-
    198. See also AIDS
    antibody test, 171
    disease-specific policies, 191-193
    physiological aspects, 171-173
    policies, 191-193
    prejudice, 179-181
    psychological impact, 176-177
    social impact, 173-176, 178-181
    ten principles for the workplace, 184
    transmission, 171
Human needs, 259-262, 265-267, 270
Human resources
    policies, 102
    practices, 101-127
    review process, 107-109
    support of employees, 89-100
    training, 124

I

Idiot, 23, See also Appendix 1
Imbecile, 23, See also Appendix 1
Impaired, 24, See also Appendix 1
Impairment
    definition and examples under reasonable
        accommodation in employment, 46-48
Implementation dates, ADA, 331-332
Independent living centers, 65-66
Individual accommodation discussion (IAD),
    82-85
Individuals with disabilities, 35, See also
        Appendix 1
Insurance, health, 97
Intercity rail transit, 51, 240
Interpretive guidance, Title I, 71, 79, 101, 206
Interviewing
    employment, 74-77, 113-115
Intracity bus and rail, 50

J

Job Accommodation Network (JAN), 29
Job accommodation
    employer perceptions, 275-279
    resources, 273-290
    verification of need for, 83
    analysis, 129-138
    approaches, 117-122
    checklist, 136
    appraisal criteria, 122-124
    descriptions, 108, 116
    dimension-related approach, 119-121
    essential functions of, 70-71, 81
    evaluation factors, 116, 121-122
    value, 108
Joint labor-management committee, 148-149
Journal of American Insurance (JAI), 29

K

Kaposi's Sarcoma (KS), 172
Kennedy, Ted, Senator, 6
Kleptomania, 36
Known disability, 80

L

Labor-management committee, 148-149
Language, usage, 19-24, *See also* Appendix 1
Layoff of disabled employee, 96-97, 110
Legal resources, *See* Appendix 5
Litigation, 233-234
Long-term disability, 98

M

Management by consent, 144
Marketing to the disabled, 265-266
Medical examination, 209
    employment, 74-77
Mental impairment, 35, *See also* Appendix 1
Mentally challenged, 24, *See also* Appendix 1
Mentally deficient/defective, 23, *See also*
    Appendix 1
Monetary damages, 234
Mongoloid (ism), 23, *See also* Appendix 1
Moron, 23, *See also* Appendix 1
Mute, 23, *See also* Appendix 1
Mycobacteriosioses, 172
Myth, "disability-equals-illness," 21

N

National Council on Disability, 3, 5, 6, 273
    See also National Council on the
    Handicapped
Noncompliance penalties (Title III), 233, *See*
    also Appendix 4
Nonprimary providers, 220
Nonprofit rehabilitation programs, 65
Normal, 23, *See also* Appendix 1

O

Obesity, 39
Occupational bonding principle, 147
Office of Federal Contract Compliance
    Programs (U.S. Department of Labor), 56

Omnibus Transportation Employee Testing Act
    of 1991 (OTETA), 157, 161
One-car-per-train rule, 240
Opportunity Task Force, 209-211
Orientation to workplace, 105
Otherwise qualified handicapped person, 42

P

Pedophilia, 36
Penalties, 52-53, 233-234
Pencil-and-paper measures, 70, 110, 111-115
Pension liability, 97-98
Performance evaluation, 108, 110
    appraisal, 122-124, 125
    criteria, 116
    paper-and-pencil measures, 110, 111-115
Personnel files, access, 105
Physical impairment, 35
Physically challenged, 24, *See also* Appendix 1
Physiological aspects of HIV, 171-173
Placement services, 68-69
Pneumocystis carnii Pneumonia (PCP), 172
Post-test interviews, 86
Posting and notice requirements, 54-57
    penalties, 54
Pre-employment screening, 69-70, 73-77, 79-88
Prejudice
    HIV, 179-181
Presumption of qualification, 42
Principle of occupational bonding, 147
Private entity, 49, 51, 53
    barrier removal by, 215-233
Private providers (transportation), 220-221,
    238-240
Process of Determining Appropriate Reasonable
    Accommodation, 129
Programmatic access (Title III), 221
Progressive discipline, 106
Promoting disabled employees, 91-92, 95-96,
    110
Public
    accommodations and transportation. *See also*
    Title III, 49-51, 53, 218, 227, Appendix 4
    entity, 51-52, 237-238
    school transportation, 237
    services, 51. *See also* Title II
    transportation, access, 237-241
Punitive damages, 234
Pyromania, 36

Q

Qualified person with a disability, 51, 81, 88,
    129, 141, 160
Qualification standards, 79, 206

R

Readily achievable, 50, 228-229
Reasonable accommodation
    process of determining, 50, 129
    in employment, 45-48, 69-70, 81, 105, 124, 140, 205
Reasonable modification of policies, 216
Recruitment, 63-78
Regulations, ADA, See Appendix 4
Rehabilitation Act of 1973, 3-4, 13, 19, 37, 222, 275
Rehabilitation consultant, considerations for, 199-213
Related services, 40
Relay service, 52, 244-251
Resources
    legal, See Appendix 5
    technical assistance, See Appendix 6
    vocational rehabilitation agencies, 64-65
Retention of workers, 92-94
Retirement, 97-98
Ritualistic response, 16

S

Salary administration, 106-108, 115-116
School-based placement services, 68-69
Screening, See pre-employment screening.
Selection interview, 113-115
Severe handicap, 39
Sick days, 107
Situation interview, 115
Social
    impact of HIV, 173-176, 178-181
    -psychological theory of victimization, 17-19
    roles, 15-17
Social Security Act (and regulations), 40, 44
Social Security Disability Evaluation, 40-41
Spastic, 23, See also Appendix 1
Special, 24
Spread. See also Wright concept, 16-17
SSDI, 98-99
State
    employment agencies, 67
    rehabilitation programs, 64-65
Structural access, 218-219
Structured interview, 124
Sullivan, Louis, Secretary, U.S. Department of Health and Human Services, 8
Supported employment, 207-208

T

Tardiness, 106
Task Force on the Right and Empowerment of American with Disabilities, 3

Task-oriented job analysis, 118
Tax credits, 45, 223, 234-235, 253-257, 278-279
Taxoplasmosis, 172
Technical Assistance Manual, Employment Provision (Title I), See Appendix 7
Technical assistance resources, See Appendix 6
Telecommunication relay services (TRS), 52, 244-251
Telecommunications, 51-52, See also Title IV
Telecommunications Device for the Deaf (TDDs), 7, 45, 51-52, 243-250, 270
Teletypewriters (TTYs), 204, 243-244
Ten principles for the workplace. See also AIDS, HIV, 184
Termination, 96-97
Testing accommodation plan (TAP), 85-88
Testing,
    administration of, 112-113
    employment, 69, 73-77, 79-88, 111-113, 209
    post-test interviews, 86
Text telephones (TTs), 243-244
Time off, 102, 105-106, 107
Title I, 7, 8, 44-48, 52, 71, 74, 79, 80, 101, 110, 129, 139, 141, 142, 199, 205, 206, 226, 253, See also Appendices 3 and 4
Title II, 6, 8, 50-53, 204, 226, See also Appendices 3 and 4
Title III, 6, 49-51, 53, 204, 215-221, 226-235, 253, See also Appendices 3 and 4
    noncompliance, penalties, 233
    tax incentives, 234-235, 253-257
Title IV, 1, 8, 51-52, 53, 227, 243-250, See also Appendices 3 and 4
Transfer of disabled employee, 96-97
Transitional work, 147
Transmission of HIV, 171
Transportation, 49-51, 239-240
    access, 219-221, See also Appendices 3 and 4
Transsexualism, 36, 39
Transvestism, 36

U

Undue hardship, 45, 82, 204, 229, 231, 275
United States Department of Labor (USDOL), 130

V

Vacation time, 107
Varicose veins, 39
Verification of need for accommodation, 83
Vocational rehabilitation agencies, 64-65
Voice carry-over (VCO), 248
Voyeurism, 36

W

Wechsler scales, 113
Workplace policies, 160-161
Work return transition programs, 139-154
Worker-oriented job analysis, 119
Worker traits, 131-132
Workers' compensation, 142-143
Workplace, ten principles for the (AIDS, HIV),
     184
Wright concept, 16-17. *See also* spread